Second Edition

Goldmine's

Rock'n Roll 45RPM Record Price Guide

BY
NEAL UMPHRED

Published by
Krause Publications, Inc.
700 E. State St.
Iola, WI 54990
Telephone: 715/445-2214

INTERNATIONAL STANDARD BOOK NUMBER: 0-87341-202-8
LIBRARY OF CONGRESS CATALOG NUMBER: 90-60578

Printed in the United States of America

—Dedication—

This book is dedicated to the memory of Mark Edmund, who bought and sold rhythm 'n blues and rock 'n roll records in the spirit in which the best of them were recorded. For those who knew him as Mark's One-Stop in the pages of Goldmine, or as Baytown Records, in Albany, CA, Mark passed away in 1991.

My fondest memory of Mark Edmund is taking him down to an LA swap for the first time. As a neo-socialist quite comfortable in the Bay area, Mark's making the seven hour drive to the dreaded City of Angels was a concession of sorts, but once there, the enthusiasm of the customers worked wonders. On the way back we discussed politics, economics and Elvis, with Mark arguing the merits of "Do The Clam." After listening to me moan about my cowboy boot encased feet for a couple of days he just looked at me and, with no self-deprecation, said "Why don't you get some reasonable shoes..."

Mark, I've been wearing reasonable shoes ever since.

—Acknowledgements—

Without the help and cooperation of the following, this book would not have been possible...

Frankie Avalon
Los Angeles, CA

Dale Blount
Owasso, OK

Stephen Braitman
San Francisco, CA

Lees F. Browne, Jr.
Denver, CO

Chris Chatman
Beyond Records
Los Angeles, CA

Hubert-Michel Chene
Ste-foy, P. Quebec, Canada

John Christenson
Renton, WA

John Pumilia
Collect A Hit Records
Grant's Pass, OR

Perry Cox
Phoenix, AZ

John DeBlaiso
Renton, WA

Dennis Detorie
Baltimore, MD

Eric Engelke
Portland, OR

Charles Gorman
Raymond, Maine

Thomas Grosh
Very English & Rolling Stone
Lancaster, PA

Gary Johnson
Rockaway Records
Los Angeles, CA

Rich Kohler
Strabane, PA

Jeff Logue
Everett, WA

Bob Lucieer
The Gary Lewis Fan Club
Rochester, NY

Brad Olson
Vancouver, BC, Canada

Tony Powell
Cantonment, FL

Rich Rockford
Vancouver, BC, Canada

David Schecter
Sherman Oaks, CA

Ron Tastula
Brockton, MA

John Tefteller
Grant's Pass, OR

Barry Wickham
Terra Linda, CA

George Yakicic III
Summerhill, PA

An Introduction to the 2nd Edition

By Neal Umphred

Well, the field of collecting records is moving forward (assuming the continued escalation of prices can be considered progression) as more and more buyers are realizing the actual rarity of the truly collectible pieces. Just a few years ago a sale of over $1,000 for a rare rockabilly or group vocal record was a bit of a deal. In 1992 there are collectors *pleading* to spend their hard-earned on some desirable single... In the first edition of this book I listed Chess 1662, Billy Barrix's "Cool Off, Baby," with an estimated *near mint* value of $2,000-4,000. In 1991, John Tefteller auctioned a VG + copy in the pages of *Goldmine* for $3,600 to an English collector. The second high bid—in excess of $3,000—was from an American collector.

Which brings us to another dilemma: These record prices are being set during a period of economic malaise in this country. Mr. Tefteller notes that five of his regular customers assured him that they would have all been active in the bidding—and would have gladly *topped* the winning bid—had their fortunes not been drained by the lasting effects of Reaganomics. The continued slump in America's ability to cope with honest competition (versus the collusion of the domestic market in general) may have glutted the coffers of the multi-national corporations that bend our elected officials' ears, but it has also led to a weakened dollar and, thus, the ability of the European and/or Japanese collector to outbid the American collector.

To ignore these events would be both futile and counter-productive. Thus, an item that goes for a bigger dollar overseas but for which the overseas' collectors purchase only a fraction of the copies put up for sale/auction is not unduly affected in this book. But... a record that turns up infrequently (only a few times a year), and invariably leaves the country to an overseas collector who bid two or three times what American collectors believe the record is "really" worth, then those prices *do* determine the value of those records. I would, in effect, be doing you, the reader and user of this book, a disservice were I to choose any other option. *The average American collector needs to know what he or she should expect to have to bid to win a truly rare and desirable record in an open auction on the open market.*

While this book tries to maintain the integrity of the artist credited on the label, there have been a few minor changes in this edition: "Solo" singles by artists from groups who are, in fact, releasing group singles with a solo credit are listed in the group's session. So this didn't get out of hand, I kept it to those artists who took one or two chances and then called it quits, at least temporarily. For instance, Dave Davies' two Reprise singles are simply The Kinks performing Dave's songs instead of brother Ray's. It makes more sense discographically to list these two with The Kinks. Similarly, Brian Wilson's first solo single, "Caroline, No," while intended to launch a solo career for the head Beach Boy, instead wound up as the ultimate track on the group's *Pet Sounds* album; the B-side was an instrumental from the group's previous studio album. Thus, Capitol 5610 is listed under The Beach Boys. Years later, each of these artists signed with different labels and launched careers independent of their respective groups; those records are listed under their name as solo artists.

Conversely, Johnny Maestro twice attempted to issue solo singles during his group career: five on Cameo with The Crests and, later, three on Buddah with The Brooklyn Bridge. But, since his solo career was maintained (another seven sandwiched in between) those singles are listed under his name. I attempted to follow this (possibly confusing) pattern throughout the book.

Now, I'd like to tell you what this book is not... This book is not the bible for record collectors; it is not the blue book of vinyl junkies. And it is certainly not the "Official" price guide for anything. Nor does this book reflect *my opinions* of what *your records* are worth. The prices quoted here are an attempt to reflect the broad differences in markets from region to region, state to state and city to city. The prices here are an attempt *to document what collectible records are worth on the open collectors' market.* While attention was given to the foreign market, this is an *American price guide* that will be purchased *mostly* by American collectors.

Please note that the prices quoted reflect the market during the period in which this book was assembled; *I cannot guarantee that they will remain the same for any length of time following the publication of this book.* In fact, price guides tend to have a direct—and often immediate—effect on the very market they attempt to chronicle. That is, the release of the new information from such a book into the general market can influence what collectors collect and, consequently, what prices are paid. Prices listed here may be made obsolete *by their very listing,* especially when the listing offers new information or information that contradicts previously published (erroneous) information...

For those readers who expect values to rise automatically, the collectibles market is not all that different from the commodities market or the stock market and *everyone* knows the wild fluctuations that occur there. So, while most prices do remain stable, or rise gradually, some rise dramatically while others actually go down in value. Value is established almost solely by supply and demand. Prices go up when the current demand is greater than the available supply; prices go down when the available supply is greater than the current demand.

Any number of factors can cause prices to rise or decline, many of them tied in with an artist's status from year to year. The most dramatic leveller is probably the warehouse find, where boxes of a supposedly rare record turn up in sufficient quantities to meet the immediate demand, driving its value down for the near future. On the most mundane of levels, the value of a fairly common, out-of-print record can decline when that record is released on a compact disc, although the drop is usually temporary, with the record slowly returning to its earlier value when the supply dropped on the market in the wake of its digitalized debut is exhausted.

—What's here and what's not—

This book makes no attempt at completeness; rather, the reader will find approximately 30,000 listings that cover, more or less: 1) the most collectible records in the business; 2) those records that exchange hands the most often; and 3) those records most in need of attention at this point in time. There *are* going to be instances where the information here is incomplete or wrong; it is almost unimaginable for any book listing this many records not to make some errors. These may range in nature from common typographical errors, from pressing the wrong character on the keyboard to transferring erroneous data from an error filled source, to incomplete research (missing catalog numbers or incorrect values assigned to records).

Regarding erroneous listings: Misinformation in this field abounds. Erroneous entries in data bases, discographies, listings and articles—from the fanzine to the professional —occur with regularity and are repeated as each source is used as reference material for another project. For instance, in the first edition, I listed a single by Vince Furnier's (a.k.a. Alice Cooper) mid-'60s group, The Spiders, as Nascot 112. This information has appeared in several publications, including at least two other price guides. The data for Cooper was supplied to me by a member of Cooper's management organization *and he also listed the record as Nascot.* Well, the correct label is Mascot... Should the reader be aware of listed misinformation, please contact me and it will be corrected in succeeding editions.

The listings for Elvis Presley and the Beatles are the lengthiest in this book yet only scratch the surface. There are thousands of label and cover variations for these artists, many more than could be squeezed in. While the listings here are more than adequate for most dealers and collectors to assess their acquisitions, they are less than so for the completist. Recommended is the third edition of *The Beatles Price Guide For American Records* by Perry Cox and Joe Lindsay. 8 1/2" x 11" and 240 pages, this is available for $23.95 (includes postage and handling) from: Perry Cox Ent., P.O. Box 82278, Phoenix, AZ 85071.

An oft repeated complaint is the sometimes incomplete discographies of artists. The reader will find many examples in this edition where an artist or group's listings have been fleshed out (although not necessarily completed) from the first edition. Instances where this was not attempted (nor, given the nature of this particular book, desirable) are rhythm 'n blues and country 'n western artists. So, for the sake of defining the scope of this book, I have differentiated white rock & roll from black rhythm 'n blues, soul music and most country.

For the sake of *balance,* certain black artists whose work is either closely associated with rock & roll (Chuck Berry, Little Richard, Jimi Hendrix) or whose work influenced many white rockers (Ray Charles, Bo Diddley and even Chubby Checker, without whom all of the dance music of the '60s, white or black, would make no conceptual sense) are included. Since the influence of Sun records is so great and since there are many collectors of the entire label, all of that label's 45 releases are included here. Similarly, due to the collectibility of Phil Spector's productions, the Philles' label roster is included here. And Prince, who is both the most innovative mainstream pop musician of his time and the most collectible single artist of the past decade or more.

A book dealing with R&B artists of the '50s is near completion and scheduled for 1992 release. This book will compile the work of male and female vocalists, instrumentals and vocal groups with a working title of *Good Rocking Tonight: A Discography & Price Guide To Rhythm & Blues Records Of The '50s.* Compiled and edited by me, the book contains 500 pages of approximately 25,000 listings of 45s, EPs and LPs.

After Elvis' early success, a number of otherwise straight country artists attempted to cut some rockabilly. When known, those titles are included in this book but the artist's country sides are not. For the rockabilly collector, or the dealer who caters to such collectors' needs, later this year will see *Tear It Up: A Discography & Price Guide To Rockabilly Records Of The '50s* with 300 pages containing 5,000 listings covering singles, EPs and LPs. For the true Elvis collector, or the dealer who caters to such collectors' needs, I recommend my own *A Touch Of Gold.* This book is 8 1/2" x 11" with 350 pages containing nearly 5,000 listings covering singles, EPs, LPs, tapes, compact discs, sheet music and RCA released memorabilia.

For information on *A Touch Of Gold, Tear It Up,* and *Good Rockin' Tonight,* send a stamped, self-addressed envelope to White Dragon Press, 33309 Santiago Rd., Suite 16, Acton, CA 93510.

—*Page Breakdown*—

The records are listed chronologically by label. I have used fairly standard alphabetization throughout; there should be no surprises for anyone familiar with an encyclopedia. Using Frankie Avalon as an example:

AVALON, FRANKIE
The former trumpet whiz kid (the "X" sides below) also recorded with Annette.

"X" 0006	**Trumpet Sorrento / The Book**	*1954*	8.00	40.00
"X" 0026	**Trumpet Tarantella / Dormi Dormi**	*1954*	8.00	40.00
Chancellor 1004	**Cupid / Jivin' With The Saints**	*1957*	3.00	15.00
Chancellor 1006	**Teacher's Pet / Shy Guy**	*1957*	3.00	15.00
Chancellor 1011	**Dede Dinah / Ooh La La**	*1958*	3.00	15.00
Chancellor 1016	**You Excite Me / Darlin'**	*1958*	3.00	15.00
Chancellor 1021	**Gingerbread / Blue Betty**	*1958*	3.00	15.00
Chancellor 1021 *(PS)*	**Gingerbread / Blue Betty**	*1958*	5.00	25.00
Chancellor 1026	**I'll Wait For You / What Little Girl?**	*1958*	3.00	15.00
Chancellor 1026 *(PS)*	**I'll Wait For You / What Little Girl?**	*1958*	5.00	25.00
Chancellor 1031	**Venus / I'm Broke**	*1959*	3.00	15.00
Chancellor 1031	**Venus / I'm Broke** *(Pink label with two horizontal lines)*	*1959*	4.00	20.00
Chancellor 1031 *(PS)*	**Venus / I'm Broke**	*1959*	3.00	15.00
Chancellor 1036	**Bobby Sox To Stockings / A Boy Without A Girl**	*1959*	3.00	15.00
Chancellor 1036 *(PS)*	**Bobby Sox To Stockings / A Boy Without A Girl**	*1959*	4.00	20.00

—Original Chancellor singles above have pink labels.—

In this instance, "(PS)" indicates that the listing and the price is for a picture sleeve only; to arrive at the value of the record with (or in) the sleeve, add the values of the sleeve with the single above it! A "(DJ)" means that the record is promotional. A "(33)" indicates a compact-33 single or EP. This was a format used in the '60s as a way to broaden the market; the records were typical 7" discs with a small, LP spindle hole. By the end of the decade, when stereo jukeboxes were common, the companies were issuing selections from popular albums as stereo, compact-33 "mini-LPs," which are listed here in the appropriate EP sections of each artist. Finally, an "(S)" indicates the single is in stereo, also an attempt in the late '50s and early '60s to broaden the market. These stereo singles are far more difficult to find than their mono counterparts.

The record's title is the middle column; specific notes short enough to place on the same line follow. *All records are on black vinyl unless otherwise noted.* This is followed by the year of release; dating the records was often problematic. The final two columns, the prices, are for two conditions, very-good (VG) and near-mint (NM) and are dealt with at length below.

For those artists who achieved a long lasting popularity that saw their recordings repeatedly re-issued I have attempted to list brief notations about particular records. *Notes indented beneath a single and enclosed in parentheses refer only to the title under which it is listed.* These may refer to that record's particular label or any other aspect that requires attention. *Notes that are centered and open (i.e., lacking parentheses) refer to two or more titles and are almost exclusively dealing with label specifications.* In this case, the note tells the reader the color of the label on first pressings of Frankie's early Chancellor releases.

Artists are listed in bold capital letters. When an artist has recorded under two names that are similar enough to list together, the more common name is listed first followed by the alternate name in brackets: **"CHICAGO [CHICAGO TRANSIT AUTHORITY]."** When a single artist is backed by a not-so-prominent group (i.e., the group itself is not collectible per se), the listing will include the name of the group in parenthesis after the artist: **"KNOX, BUDDY (& THE RHYTHM ORCHIDS)."** Such a listing indicates that some of the sides will credit Knox with the group, but these records were not worth separating from the main body of Buddy's discography. Similarly, when an artist's name is followed by parenthesis and the notation "With the," it indicates that the artist is backed by a vocal group who is uncredited on the label but who affects the value of the record.

For the sake of usefulness, certain artists who started out as members of a group and who then rose to dominate the group have all of the recordings listed under the individual artist's usually better known name. Because this is a price guide, cross-sectioned references are kept to a minimum, as are explanatory notes. Were I to pay this aspect of the book the attention it deserves, we would have a whole other volume in front of us.

—*Promotional Records*—

The term "promo" generally refers to the special pressing of a single issued primarily to radio stations for air play. These are often manufactured before the first commercial pressings are made, thus they predate the first (sic) pressings? As they are generally manufactured in small batches (several hundred to a few thousand), they are often jobbed out by the large label, who are not set up to press so small a run. Thus, aside from being rarer—usually—promos are often of superior quality to the best commercial (or "stock") pressings. In fact, promos were almost always pressed on quality vinyl, unlike their stock counterparts, some of which were pressed on infinitely inferior polystyrene in lieu of the more expensive vinyl, and not only by cost-conscious indies...

The most common method of printing promotional records has been to press them on white labels with plain black print, hence the term "white label promo." As these white labels are obvious manifestations of the label's special attention, they are the most popular with collectors. Some labels used their regular label, or a slightly modified version, and had such mottos as "Audition Copy" or "Promotional Copy" incorporated into the label's typesetting; *labels with such notices stamped on after the fact are not the same!* Needless to say, they are quite collectible and generally command a premium above the normal value of the record, although the premium may be minimal.

The reader familiar with the first edition will find that many promos previously listed have been jettisoned, making the discographies smoother and easier to read. Assuming that a promo variation exists for the overwhelming majority of singles listed herein, the reader should assume that, unless otherwise noted, a promo version of a commercially issued single is worth no less than the value of the commercial single and no more than twice the listed value. This is a rule of thumb; promos may be worth slightly less than the stock or slightly more than twice as much. Those promos worth considerably less or dramatically more than the stock *are* listed (when known).

In response to a number of suggestions, in this edition the reader will find that special promotional records have been moved to their own section at the end of large discographies under "Special/Promotional Releases." That is, while promotional variations of a commercially issued—or stock—title remain in the main body of an artist's listings, records released expressly for promotional use with no corresponding stock copy can now be found at the end of the regular listings. Artists with only one or two such items in their catalog remain unaffected by this change; collectors of such artists as the Beach Boys, the Beatles, the Kingston Trio, Elvis Presley and the Rolling Stones will notice the change. This allows the majority of readers who focus the bulk of their interest on an artist's regular releases to move through each discography more easily.

On a minor note, while most labels differentiated their singles from their EPs by a different catalog numbering, at least one major company, Capitol, released several EPs with single catalog numbers, obviously with intent of garnering singles attention from distributors and, hopefully, singles sales. These few EPs have been listed in their correct chronological order with the singles and are noted with an "(EP)" preceding the title. As most of these were issued with paper picture sleeves rather than the more common cardboard covers, the sleeves are listed and priced separately. Again, this affects only a handful of artists.

—Reissues & Second Pressings—

In this case, reissues refer to the labels' attempt to market previous hits as "golden oldies"; this does not include rereleases of previous tracks on new labels attempting to sell the record to the market as a "new" side. Many labels have their own special designation for reissues of particularly popular singles, whether it is a different catalog numbering system or a special title, such as RCA Victor's "Gold Standard" series, Columbia's "Hall of Fame" or the more common "back-to-back" hits type setup, where a label combines the A-sides of two hits. In most cases, these have little real value to collectors and are therefore not listed. Exceptions exist when a reissue is worth as much or more than the original (many of Elvis' hits on the Gold Standard Series are considerably rarer and more valuable than the originals; both the Beach Boys and the Beatles reissues on Capitol's Starline Series are gaining in value ...)

The term "second pressing" has two contradictory meanings among record collectors: The first and legitimate use refers to any pressing of a record by the original record company that is noticeably different from the original pressing. And this is the term that will suffice for our purposes in this book.

Now, for the confusing aspect: Records that have gone out of print but are still sought after by a small audience are often "reissued" without the consent of the legitimate copyright holders (that is, they are counterfeits). These pressings are also referred to as "second pressings." In an equally confusing manner they are also referred to as bootlegs. In this book they will be referred to as reproductions.

The business of counterfeits is not confined to vinyl: There has been a proliferation of bogus acetates and some picture sleeves (all of the Capitol Beatles' sleeves) on the market in recent years. Thus the active buyer should always be alert for "original pressings" that just don't look quite original enough, or, to borrow a time honored phrase, "Let the buyer beware."

These are far more common than one might expect, ranging from the not-so-professional to the perfect. At the time of their "release" they were almost always sold on the collectors' market as second pressings or bootlegs. Unfortunately, years after the fact, they are readily confused for the originals by novice collectors. Most dealers who carry repros sell them as that; those who attempt to pawn them off as originals are usually novices who are ignorant of the field of repros. (This is not to say that dishonest dealers do not exist; to assume otherwise is naive.)

On the opposite end of the scale, many are of such professional duplication that it is damn near impossible to tell the real from the unreal without being made aware of the differences and having one of each in your hands to compare! There are even duplications of test pressings, acetates and Gold and Platinum Record Awards.

—Chart Hits & Party Records—

One of the fastest growing areas of collecting is the field of chart hits, (many of which end up on collectors' jukeboxe). Traditionally, the big hits have been valued less than non-charting records, which makes sense (i.e., there would be considerably more copies available of the hit). Not so anymore. The demand for chart hits has put the million seller's value alongside the flop. Thus the reader will find that many records in this edition that he or she might think of as "common" have more than doubled in value since the last edition. For instance, two stalwarts of the British Invasion, the Dave Clark Five and the Kinks, have had the bulk of their listed catalog increased from the 1990 value of $4 each to this edition's $10. Should this sound high, consider the likelihood of finding an original pressing of "Bits And Pieces" or "All Day And All Of The Night" in truly Near Mint condition. Well-played copies are a dime a dozen (well, maybe not that low!) with VG copies 50¢ to $1 just about everywhere and VG+ copies selling for a couple bucks, but Near Mint...

Another criteria considered in pricing is what I call the "party record." These are records that may not have sold umpteen bejillion copies but were purchased widely and played to death, often at "teen dance parties." For instance, Elvis' version of "Blue Suede Shoes," while a reasonable hit in 1956, was nowhere near the sales of his smashes (all of Elvis' hits sold millions of copies; "Shoes" probably sold a quarter of a million during the decade). But, everyone who bought that record loved it and played the grooves off of it. Consequently, "Blue Suede Shoes" is probably Elvis' single rarest commercially issued RCA Victor single of the '50s and Near Mint copies can fetch an easy $100 from a serious collector! So, there will be instances in this book where a rather popular title will have a disconcertingly high price; it may be a "party record."

—And Then There Are Producers—

Unbeknownst to many a star-struck fan is the fact that the record that catches their attention—and their disposable cash—is often more the product of the technical people behind the scenes than the actual artists lip-syncing their way to fame and glory on MTV. Without a competent team of technicians, few records can make it through the rigors of selection that place records on top radio play-lists. While a good engineer is one of these people—a must, in fact—of more importance on the creative (sic) level is the role of the producer who, more often than not, decides exactly how the final record will appear to the public, from the final sound to the actual selection of the tracks... including who writes what and who does or does not play on the record!

While the role of the producer and their efforts throughout the history of recorded music can fill an entire book with explanations and anecdotes, this brief chapter will merely point out that many of the classic records of the rock 'n' roll era were created almost entirely by the production team. In fact, there are many "artists" who do not exist, but are merely a nom de plume—a front, if you will—for the otherwise nameless people who do this sort of thing for a living.

Most producers functioned solely at the board, such as the well-known work of George Martin, who, aside from the Beatles, produced many of the best records of the Mersey Sound. Some producers were also recording artists, such as Jan Berry, Steve Barri and Phil Sloan, Ron Dante, Brian Wilson, and Frank Zappa, each of whom has references in their section for artists they produced. For this second edition, two producers have been selected and their work focused on: the late Gary Usher, responsible for some of the best records from the early '60s California sound, and the grandaddy of 'em all, Uncle Phil Spector, best known as the creator of the "wall of sound" production technique that led to such classic singles as "Da Doo Ron Ron" and "Then He Kissed Me" for The Crystals; "Be My Baby" and "Walking In The Rain" for The Ronettes; "You've Lost That Loving Feeling" and "Just Once In My Life" for The Righteous Brothers; and Tina Turner's "River Deep-Mountain High."

Gary Usher's reputation is not quite so grandiose as Spector's (although Japanese collectors have long revered him alongside Brian Wilson). Gary's work as writer (he was involved in many of the early Beach Boys' car songs with Brian), arranger, producer, singer and instrumentalist has produced an enormous body of work, most of which currently languishes in the vaults of major record companies and the hoary recesses of collectors' memories. Gary's work during this period include singles by The Competitors, The

Ghouls, The Hondells, Bruce Johnston, The Kickstands, The Knights, Mr. Gasser & The Weird-Ohs, The Revells, The Road Runners, The Silly Surfers, The Super Stocks, The Surfaris, and The Weird-Ohs, all of which are listed in these pages.

—*Pricing the Records*—

If you will pardon my redundancy: This book is not the work of one person; it does not reflect my opinions of what your records are worth. Instead, I solicited the assistance of collectors and dealers whom I had known for several years, both personally and professionally. Each dealer and collector was requested to provide *current values based on recent sales or purchases,* not transactions from years ago. The records listed here are taken from a variety of printed sources plus the input of the contributors. This input and a constant scrutiny of the set-sale and auctions placed in the pages of *Goldmine* also played a part in the make-up of this book.

I strived for a sense of internal consistency with the pricing. That is, I did not attach East Coast prices to oldies, Northwest prices to garage, Midwest prices to Motown, L.A. prices to surf, etc., but rather sought a balance between them all so that the book as a whole works as a guideline for each region of the country to use as on outline for their own market. *Every item in this book has been scrutinized by several contributors.* The values that were decided upon represent a ball park value that takes into account each of the prices submitted.

It should always be borne in mind that the price that anyone will buy (or sell) an item for is often linked closely with the geographic/economic environment he or she is living in. A collector in Los Angeles, CA, *should expect to pay more*—sometimes considerably more —for a given item than a collector from Tempe, AZ. After all, the California collector pays more for rent, for a restaurant dinner, for tickets to the theater, because a Los Angeles resident will be paid commensurately more for his job (i.e., a waiter in a moderately successful L.A. restaurant will make more than double the tips that a waiter in many of AZ's finest restaurants would make). Similarly, just as a dealer takes for granted that he or she will pay less for records when stocking his or her shop in Denver (a buyer's market), they should also expect to sell them for less *in the same market.*

My own opinion as both a participant and observer varies greatly with some of the values listed here, just as you, the reader, will—*and should*—disagree with some of the prices! Because of this, I have a bit of advice for any *serious* collector: *"When you are offered a record for which you have been actively searching for over five years, do not argue with the price, pay it."* The corollary to this little bit of wisdom would be: *"If you don't, you may not see it again for another five years—and it will cost even more."*

Some records simply could not be accurately priced, due to their scarcity and the lack of documented transactions in recent years. These records are listed with no value in the pricing columns but with a parenthetical note explaining that the record is rare with an "estimated Near Mint value" and a price spread. The spread is based as much as possible on either monies offered to reputable dealers from collectors (should a copy turn up) or from sales of the record in less than VG condition. For example: JeWel 101, "Ooby Dooby" by Roy Orbison's Teen Kings, is listed with a Near Mint spread of $1,000-2,000 due to the fact that the most recent—and only known sale—was a VG + copy *with a crack through the vinyl* that sold at a show last year for $500!

Essentially, what this spread of $1,000 to $2,000 means is that a seller with a Near Mint copy should expect to get at least $1,000 for this record in an open auction. While a buyer might win this record for as little as $1,000, he should not be surprised to find the bidding escalate to the $2,000 range. Similarly, records in lesser condition should cut the estimated range appropriately: a VG + copy would have a range of approximately $500-1,000; a VG copy, $250-500.

If a price on a record *with which you are familiar* seems ludicrously wrong, don't feel obliged to accept it. If other dealers and collectors are puzzled by the same discrepancy, it may be just that—an error of mine. But, at the same time, the *average* dealer or collector is often years (at least months) behind the reality of the market when it comes to the specialized knowledge of truly rare records, mainly because they are so rare that few, if anyone, ever sees them for sale at any price. For example, the prices that are quoted for many obscure British Invasion singles or Prince 12" promos may appear preposterous to a '50s specialist, but the collector of these artists knows that certain titles are difficult to find at any price! And that exists for a good many artists. *The more knowledgeable that you, the reader, are, the more useful and informative this book will be,* if only to be better able to assimilate the information and make use of it on a day to day basis.

So, there are two prices listed for each record: the last and most important is the "Near Mint" price. I use a scale (illustrated below) that evaluates the Very Good condition record as a sliding percentage of the NM value. VG + prices are, for easy reference, approximately one-half (50%) of the listed NM value.

Near Mint Value	VG Value (%)
Less than $250	20%
$300-600	25%
$750-1,500	33%
$2,000 and up	40%

Always keep in mind that the accuracy of these prices are meaningless without a corresponding accuracy in the grading of records. Finally, the prices in this book are for VG + and Near Mint copies without cut-out or drill holes. The presence of such a flaw drastically affects the pricing and, when advertising, such a hole or mark should be noted.

—Grading the Records—

Records are graded by visual standards, not aural; the reason being that when purchasing a record at a show or through the mail the buyer does not get to listen to it. The biggest complaints against the visual method are 1) the subjectivity of the grader's eyes or viewpoint, and 2) the fact that records do not always play as good—or bad—as they look. Both of these are justifiable arguments and, of course, it is the first point that causes the need for articles such as this: *records always look better when selling than when buying.* The arguments against play-grading are similar: the subjectivity of the listener is also a factor, a factor that is multiplied by the type of equipment the grader is playing the record on to form his or her judgement. So, for the sake of convenience and necessity, visual grading is the standard by which almost all dealers and collectors work.

When grading a disc, *grade the overall wear of the vinyl.* A record advertised as "NM" or "VG" should tell the prospective buyer the shape of the playable vinyl (although common sense should be used: unplayed records that are warped cannot be Mint). Such defects as name stickers on the label, tape on the jacket, etc., should be addressed separately with abbreviated notations. A reliable set of these notations have been developed over the years covering virtually every type of defect that can occur to a record or its cover; a list of most of the more common abbreviations and their meanings follow the grading definitions below. When defining the grades, it is difficult to describe several without discussing certain defects and/or the way the disc plays; these are included to help define the grade, not to cause confusion.

Visual grading is most important in mail-order transactions where a buyer doesn't see his purchase until his check has cleared the bank. Grading needs to be as strict, as accurate as possible. Put simply, the aim of grading is to make the buyer visualize the record he or she is purchasing through an advertisement and not be disappointed when that record arrives! A record that is accurately graded will play the same (or better) than the grading! In-person deals do not require a grade of any sort; if you are holding a record that has obviously been played a hundred times, you don't need a grade to determine whether or not you are going to purchase that disc.

Always grade records under a good, steady light. A 100-watt light bulb in a common desk lamp will do an adequate job; most major defects will jump out at you and allow you to make an accurate assessment of the vinyl. Grading a record using light from the ceiling or from deflected sunlight entering the window will often "hide" paper scuffs, discoloration, groove wear and even some fingerprints. Everyone makes mistakes in grading. This is a problem all dealers and collectors are prone to make and must be aware of. Do not condemn a dealer for one mistake; but, when the mistake is the norm, find someone else to buy your records from. Think of these definitions as guidelines around which your experience will build a better understanding of conditions.

Mint. A Mint ("M") record should appear to have just left the manufacturers without any handling; that is, it should appear perfect! No scuffs or scratches, blotches or stains, labels or writing, tears or splits; nothing. *Perfect.* And age has nothing to do with it; *the same standards for Mint apply to a rare rockabilly single from 1954 as they do to a common top 40 record from 1984!* There are no sliding values for Mint.

A Mint record cover should appear to have never have had a record in it; no ring-wear, dog-eared corners, writing, seam-splits. I define ring-wear as any imprint on the cover from the record that it formerly held. *Any* imprint. To many dealers and collectors the ink has to be worn off for them to recognize ring-wear and grade a cover down. Uh-uh. Mint means perfect and nothing else.

Near Mint. A record that is otherwise Mint but has one or two tiny, inconsequential flaws that do not affect the play is Near Mint ("NM") and should command 85-95% of the Mint price. For many, Near Mint and Mint-Minus mean the same thing; for the sake of this article, they are interchangeable. When dealing with a seller that discriminates between the two grades, inquire as to what the dealer means when he calls one record M- and another NM. Many dealers and collectors take the position that any used (opened) record cannot be verified as Mint so they use M- to describe what appears to be a perfect record that has been opened. Covers should still be close to perfect with minor signs of wear or age just becoming evident: slight ring-wear, minor denting to a corner, or writing on the cover should all be noted properly.

Many records *are available* in Near Mint/Mint condition, although these are generally more recent and the prices are nominal. That is, most dealers set a minimum price on the records they sell in their store, usually dollars ($3.99-4.99), just for normal, everyday, all-too-readily-available records. Whether they are unplayed or "merely" Near Mint the price will be the same: it wouldn't be worth the dealer's time to stock the single unless that minimum price was met.

Sometimes referred to as "Excellent," a **Very Good Plus** ("VG+") record has been handled and played either infrequently or very carefully. That is, an item obviously not perfect, but not too far from it. On a disc, this could mean that there are light paper scuffs from sliding in and out of a sleeve; the vinyl may have lost some—*not all*—of its original luster. A slight scratch that did not affect the play in an otherwise Nearly Mint disc would be acceptably VG+ for most collectors; a scratch of any sort that audibly clicked throughout at a level greater than or equal to the music would not be acceptable. Always list the flaws in a VG+ record or cover.

As a rule of thumb, a VG+ item is worth 50%, or one-half, of the Near Mint value, although this ratio varies with the rarity of the item. That is, a record that is fairly common in NM/M condition has little real value in VG+ to most collectors; consequently 25-35% may be more appropriate. On the other hand, truly rare records will fetch 75% in VG+. (By rare, I am referring to items in which the supply is merely a fraction of the demand and the record sells for hundreds of dollars ...) On covers, some wear from storage is acceptable, especially light wear that does not affect the beauty of the artwork. Again, listing the flaws when selling is safest.

Very Good ("VG") records will display visible signs of handling and playing, such as loss of vinyl luster, light surface scratches, groove wear, and spindle trails from countless spins on the turntable. A VG record looks like it will have some audible surface noise when it is played, although any such noise should not overwhelm the music or ruin the listening experience. VG records should appear to have been well-played although well-loved by a responsible owner. Gouges, rips in the label, cracks and maple syrup in the grooves are all unacceptable.

As more and more collectors spend more and more money on their acquisitions, the lower limits of acceptability for an item to be admitted into their collection rises. That is, to many collectors, a record in VG condition is not acceptable unless the item is truly rare and virtually unavailable in any other condition! And then, only if the price is scaled appropriately to match the condition. Used but not abused might sum up this grade. A VG record should command approximately 20-30% of the Near Mint price.

This is a difficult grade when discussing paper goods. Like a disc, usually a cover is VG when a variety of problems are evident: ring wear, seam splits, bent corners, loss of gloss on the photo, stains, etc. An aggravated combination of two of these problems—never all of them—would likely cause a sleeve to be graded VG.

Good ("G") in record collecting parlance all too often means a beat, trashed, take-it-to-the-flea-market frisbee. Good should mean that the record is well-played with any number of defects that collectors normally shy away from, such as an almost complete loss of surface sheen, aggravating surface noise, etc. Still, the purchaser, knowing full well that he or she is buying a Good record, should be able to take it home, slap it onto the turntable and have a good time listening to it. Records that do not provide this most fundamental requirement are just no good. A Good record should command 10-15% of the Near Mint price.

A Good cover has seen considerable handling over the course of the years and displays the obvious physical signs: ring-wear on the front and back; some seam-splitting, particularly along the bottom, which would receive the brunt of the record's sliding in and out; corners may be dog-eared to a light degree; an infatuated owner may have written his or her name somewhere; etc. If a record or cover is beneath your contempt, it is not in "G" condition; look below for the appropriate grade.

Any record or cover that does not qualify for the above "Good" grading should be seen as *Poor.* A "P" record should command 0-5% of the Mint price. Make a friend and give any "P" record away as a freebee to anyone who expresses interest in it...

Finally, it should always be borne in mind that visual evidence can be deceiving: the quality of the vinyl and the plating make all the difference in the world. A record properly manufactured with a high quality plating may look VG + and play Near Mint; this is particularly true of records from the '50s through the mid-'60s, when print runs were dramatically smaller, vinyl was fresher and more care was paid to the entire procedure. Records from this period are a better investment in VG + condition than the more recent American product. In fact, many 45s from the '50s can be purchased in VG condition at reasonable prices and will play far better than the price paid would indicate. A record manufactured from recycled vinyl with poor plating (too many from the past 15 years) may look Mint and play VG. Still, most dealers do not have the time to listen to each item in their inventory, so visual standards remain.

The following books were a source of information for the first edition of this price guide. Additions to this second edition were either submitted by individual contributors or taken from articles and discographies appearing in *Goldmine Magazine.*

Felix Aeppli
Heart of Stone: The Definitive Rolling Stones
Discography, 1962-83
Pierian Press, 1985

John Beecher & Malcolm Jones
The Buddy Holly Story:
A Pictorial Account Of His Life And Music
MCA, 1979

John Blair
The Illustrated Discography of Surf Music 1961-65
Pierian Press, 1985

Benjamin Blake, Jack Rubeck & Allan Shaw
The Kingston Trio On Record
Kingston Korner, 1986

Chuck Brigermann
Record Collector's Fact Book, Vol. 1
Disc Publishing, 1982

Fred Bronson
The Billboard Book Of #1 Hits
Billboard, 1988

Jim Cates
The Official Picture Sleeve Price Guide
Educational Concepts, 1986

Ken Clee
Stack-O-Wax
Self published

Perry Cox & Michael Miller
The Beatles Price & Reference Guide
For American Records, 2nd Edition
Cox-Miller, 1986

Robert Dalley
Surfin' Guitars:
Instrumental Surf Bands Of The Sixties
Robert Dalley, 1988

Howard DeWitt
Chuck Berry: Rock 'N' Roll Music, 2nd Edition
Pierian Press, 1985

Howard DeWitt
Van Morrison: The Mystic's Music
Horizon Books, 1983

L.R. Docks
American Premium Record Guide, 3rd Edition
Books Americana, 1986

Brad Elliott
Surf's Up! The Beach Boys On Record, 1961-1981
Pierian Press, 1982

Fred Heggeness
Rarest of The Rare, 3rd Edition
FH Publishing, 1989

Tom Hibbert
Rare Records & Vinyl Treasures
Proteus Books, 1982

Thomas Hudgeons III
The Official Price Guide To Records, 7th Edition
House of Collectibles, 1985

Patrick Humphries & Chris Hunt
Blinded By The Light
Owl/Henry Holt, 1985

Thomas Kamp
David Bowie 1964-1984
O'Sullivan Woodside, 1985

Don Kirsch
Rock & Roll Obscurities
Self published

Jeff Kreiter
Group Collector's Price Guide, 2nd Edition
Boyd Press, 1988

Albert Leichter
A Discography Of Rhythm & Blues
And Rock & Roll Circa 1946-1964
Albert Leichter, 1975

Jeff Levy
Apple-Log
Monhunprod, 1984

Jerry Osborne & Bruce Hamilton
Rock/Rock & Roll 45s, 4th Edition
O'Sullivan Woodside, 1983

Jon Pareles & Patricia Romanowski
Encyclopedia Of Rock & Roll
Rolling Stone/Summit, 1983

Domenic Priore
The Dumb Angel Gazette #3
Surfin Colours, 1989

Steve Propes
Those Oldies But Goodies:
A Guide To 50's Record Collecting
Collier Books, 1973

Steve Propes
Golden Oldies: A Guide To 60's Record Collecting
Chilton Books, 1974

Don Rogers
Dance Halls & Teenage Armories
Music Archives Press, 1988

Jon Savage
The Kinks: The Official Biography
Faber & Faber, 1984

Joel Whitburn
Top Pop 1955-1982
Record Research, 1983

What is an acetate and why do they cost so much?

By Christopher Chatman

Many times I have been asked the question "What is an acetate?" followed closely by "Why do acetates cost so much money?" Record collectors are continually in search of the "rarest records," the "best pressings." This has much to do with the demand for promotional records: they are usually much rarer than the stock copies and, because of their limited press runs, better sounding. However, promotional copies and even test pressings pale in comparison to acetates, both in terms of sound quality and particularly in rarity.

Acetates, also known as masters or reference discs, are usually black and 7" to 12" in diameter. However, while most records are made of vinyl, acetates are made out of aluminum coated with cellulose acetate; thus, while they look like records, they weigh approximately five times as much. The cellulose acetate for these lacquers is made at a very high level of quality control. Acetates are very expensive to manufacture, therefore record companies normally make only five copies of any one record. Recently, with the sharp reduction of vinyl records, the number of acetates made has dropped dramatically.

An uncut acetate, or "blank," is sent to the mastering lab where it is placed on the turntable of an electronic lathe system. The master tape, after editing and equalization, is played through the lathe system and electronically transmitted to the cutting needle so that the music is literally "cuts" microscopic wiggles (analogous to the sound waves that they represent) directly into the acetate coating. Because of this direct cutting from the master tape and the high quality of the cellulose, the sound is substantially better than a record.

Acetates are made for two reasons, the most obvious being that they are the first in the transfer of music from an electronic signal to the actual pressed record. The second reason for acetates is to allow the musicians and producers to hear what the finished record will sound like without going through the time and expense of the plating and pressing. After all, they may decide that they don't like a particular version of a song and change it or not release it at all. These acetates are called reference disks.

An acetate which has received approval is called a master lacquer. After a lacquer has been cut it is sent to a factory to be electroplated with nickel. This plating is then peeled away, which results in a negative metal print of the lacquer commonly referred to as a "mother." The first pressings to be run off the mother are test pressings; these may have special labels or they may be blank. Test pressings are then checked for sound quality and technical defects; if they are satisfactory, then promotional copies are pressed, generally for radio station distribution. Finally, the commercial, or stock, copies are pressed for sale in your favorite endangered record store.

After cutting, a label from either the mastering lab or the record company is usually glued to the disc; reference disks may have no label at all and master lacquers rarely do. Although acetates are normally packaged in plain paper sleeves, in recent years many are shipped in special boxes with covers; this extra packaging tends to enhance the desirability of the acetate. After the music on a reference disk has been reviewed and the record pressed, the acetate is then discarded, having served its purpose.

Acetates should be treated even more carefully than records. Due to the brittleness of the cellulose, the action of playing an acetate with a phonograph needle is actually deleterious to the playing surface. After five plays, the needle begins to cut away at the finer microscopic grooves which produce the high frequencies. It is therefore advisable to play an acetate *once*, record it on tape, and then carefully store it away. And try not to drop that puppy either, the cellulose surface can chip!

A recent variation to the usual type of acetate is the direct metal master or DMM acetate. Instead of being made of aluminum coated with cellulose acetate, they are made of stainless steel coated with polished copper. The signal from the master tape is cut directly into the copper. This technology designed to improve the sound quality of records was developed just as the dominance of the compact disk was forcing phonograph records into relative obscurity. This combined with the fact that DMM technology is very expensive to convert has resulted in few mastering labs investing in this new method of making records. Therefore, DMM acetates are very rare and because of their beauty, highly prized by collectors.

Since the value of an acetate depends primarily on the collectibility of the artist, they range in value from a few dollars to thousands for a major star. Acetates of released material is lowest on the value pyramid. Next would be released takes before any sweetening (strings, horns, background singers, etc) was added. Above that would be alternate takes of released material; unreleased live recordings would probably settle in between this level and the previous. The most valuable acetates would obviously be those of unreleased material, regardless of said material's aesthetic qualities.

Acetates of 45s by Elvis Presley and The Beatles regularly sell for $500; those by artists who are not quite as collectible have still sold for comparable prices. Hot new artists such as Depeche Mode and the Smiths are attracting serious bids when offered for sale. It is for this reason that some acetates have been bootlegged; be sure to check the reputation of the seller before spending heavy money on an acetate. It is important to note that the value increases dramatically when the material on the acetate is different from the released version of the record. However, whether or not the material is different, acetates are extremely rare and highly prized by collectors interested in owning the supposedly unattainable...

Christopher Chatman, proprietor of Beyond Records, Los Angeles, CA, is a collector and dealer specializing in rare records, acetates, RIAA Gold and Platinum Record awards and rock 'n roll memorabilia. He is a regular advertiser in Goldmine magazine.

How To Realistically Sell Your Records

By Perry Cox

Collectors and dealers keep a watchful eye on current market trends to see how their investments are doing, as well as what they can expect to pay for items that remain on their want lists. The burning questions, then, are: "How does one realistically go about selling their records? Sure, the guide says it's worth X dollar amount, but how do I market my item(s) anywhere near its value estimate?" There are several answers, all of which depend on the seller's situation and needs.

Selling your records to personal contacts is probably the only way to achieve near, at, or above market value in a relatively short period of time; the sale may take no longer than a couple of phone calls to complete. Of course, this method involves plenty of prior invested time and interaction with others. By acquiring a current list of items your friends and colleagues are looking for, you will be better able to determine what you can sell and for how much.

It is important to formulate your selling prices *before* you contact prospective buyers. It is not wise to gauge your pricing on the customers level of desire or by pitting one customer against another. If you agree to a set price, do not raise that price if you later realize another party expresses interest in it. (As well, if you agree to buy an item for a certain price, nit picking at very minor, insignificant flaws in hopes of getting a discount is not wise.)

Set sale through trade publications is the best way to reach the largest market. The *actual* level of exposure depends on what publications you choose. This method is a bit more time consuming: ad preparation, distribution of the publication, and mail transactions involve time. Preparing your ad needs special planning and considerations; you will need to figure the total number of lines each typewritten page gives you (normally between 50 and 60), the cost per ad, then the cost per line. Keep in mind that a full page ad in these types of publications usually will run about $300. Smaller space ads are considerably cheaper. The "Showcase" ad section in the back of *Goldmine* is very effective in presenting select items; the inexpensive rates include typesetting and placement among other eye appealing ads. This is often the first section viewed by readers.

When dealing with mail-order, the buyers may notify you of their intent to reserve any particular item(s) they are interested in. Normally this is done by telephone (many buyers prefer to talk to the people they are dealing with, since it gives an added sense of security and provides an immediate response as to the availability of the item) or mail.

If one has the time, auctioning has the potential of being the most rewarding in terms of highest yield plus it is a good way to learn just how much customers are willing to spend at any given time on any given item. With the mail-order auction, the seller sets a bid deadline; normally an auction runs for one month from the beginning of the issue's publication date. At the deadline all bids are evaluated and the highest bidders then notified.

In some cases, auctions have yielded sales substantially over the going set value; in other cases the results can be most disappointing. The factors involved in determining the final results are far too numerous to detail but the general spending mood of the public is probably the most important factor.

Finally, when selling through the mail, you must be prepared to pack your items well with proper, snug packing and padding (2-3" of padding around the item is a good minimum). Always insure the items you are mailing; it is well worth the extra expense.

Reputable auction establishments such as Sothebys, Christies and Phillips are alternative auction methods. They can, however, take the longest time in that they only hold their auctions a few times a year. Exposure to collectors is also limited but the spending frenzy sometimes associated with these houses can often play a favorable role for the seller. One thing is certain: auctions do take the longest period of time on average to sell your items. From start to completion, a mail-order auction consumes an average of two months.

The quickest manner to sell your items once you have exhausted retail sales to personal contacts is to sell them wholesale to a dealer. If you need cash and you need it right away, selling this way can be quite convenient. One must keep in mind that a dealer is not in a

position to pay top market dollar for your items. Like any commodity, the record dealer has to buy at a modest percentage of full value in order to make enough profit to stay in business.

As a rule, it is safe to say that the more significantly rare and valuable your item is, the more the dealer will probably be willing to pay, especially if they have a ready buyer. Although the dealer takes into consideration many factors when evaluating, the bottom line is usually this: "How long will one have to keep his money tied up before one actually sells the goods and recovers his money?" Some very rare and valuable items have been known to fetch as much as 60-65% of market retail. A good average for slow movers is about 30-40% of the dealer's opinion of the market value. If the period is lengthy or if the dealer has several copies of the item you are trying to sell, he'll be less generous in his offer or may not express any interest at all!

If you intend to solicit offers from various dealers, please advise each dealer of this prior to negotiations. This eliminates the impression the dealer may have in thinking he has an exclusive on your items. *(Editor's note: Similarly, never take the first offer without getting offers from at least two other dealers!)*

Some dealers will agree to place items obtained from the owner on consignment. The retail value is mutually agreed upon, while the dealer assumes responsibility for the custody and sale of the item. The final say in retail value usually goes to the dealer who knows his area and market potential best. The average consignment fee is anywhere from 15% to 30% to the dealer, certainly better than the 40-50% usually obtained in a straight sale to the dealer.

Compared with some of the others, this selling method can be quite time consuming without guaranteed sales, a factor that must be considered before locking your item(s) in a consignment agreement (which is, in effect, a contract).

Common Record Collecting Abbreviations Used For Singles In Advertising

COH	cut-out hole	RPM	revolutions per minute
C-33	compact 33⅓ rpm single or EP	2ND PR	second pressing
CVR	cover	SLT WRP	slight warp
DJ	disc jockey or promotional copy	SLV	sleeve
EP	45 rpm extended play album	SM SPLT	seam split
FLEXI	flexible plastic disc	SOL	sticker on the label
IMP	import	SR	slight ring-wear on the front cover
LBL	label	ST	stereo
NAP	(does) not affect play	STKR	sticker
OL	on label	TOC	tape on the cover
ORG	original	TOL	tape on the label
PLN CVR	plain paper jacket (no picture or titles)	TS	taped seams
PROMO	promotional copy	WLP	white label promo
PS	picture sleeve	WOL	writing on the label
RE	reissue	XOL	an "x" is written on the label
REPRO	reproduction or counterfeit		

A-JACKS, THE

Valiant 6048		Knight Ride / Fury	1964	2.00	10.00

ABBA

Abba is Benny Anderson, Agnetha Flatskog, Anni-frid Lingstad and Bjorn Ulvaeus. Refer to Bjorn & Benny; Frida; The Northern Lights; the Various Artists EP section.

Atlantic 3035	(DJ)	Waterloo / Waterloo	1974	1.00	5.00
Atlantic 3035	(PS)	Waterloo / Waterloo	1974	3.00	15.00
Atlantic 3035		Waterloo / Watch Out	1974	.60	3.00
Atlantic 3209		Honey Honey / Dance While The Music Still Goes On	1975	.60	3.00
Atlantic 3240		Ring Ring / Hasta Manana	1975	.80	4.00
Atlantic 3265		SOS / Man In The Middle	1975	.60	3.00
Atlantic 3310		I Do, I Do, I Do, I Do, I Do / Bang A Boomerang	1976	.60	3.00
Atlantic 3315		Mama Mia / Tropical Loveland	1976	.40	2.00
Atlantic 3346		Fernando / Rock Me	1976	.40	2.00
Atlantic 3372		Dancing Queen / That's Me	1976	.40	2.00
Atlantic 3387		Knowing Me, Knowing You / Happy Hawaii	1977	.40	2.00
Atlantic 3387	(PS)	Knowing Me, Knowing You / Happy Hawaii	1977	.40	2.00
Atlantic 3434		Money, Money, Money / Crazy World	1977	.40	2.00
Atlantic 3434	(PS)	Money, Money, Money / Crazy World	1977	.40	2.00
Atlantic 3449		The Name Of The Game / I Wonder (live)	1977	.40	2.00
Atlantic 3457		Take A Chance On Me / I'm A Marionette	1978	.40	2.00
Atlantic 3457	(PS)	Take A Chance On Me / I'm A Marionette	1978	.40	2.00
Atlantic 3574		Does Your Mother Know? / Kisses Of Fire	1979	.40	2.00
Atlantic 3574	(PS)	Does Your Mother Know? / Kisses Of Fire	1979	.40	2.00
Atlantic 3609		Voulez-Vous / Angeleyes	1979	.40	2.00
Atlantic 3609	(PS)	Voulez-Vous / Angeleyes	1979	.40	2.00
Atlantic 3629		Chiquitita / Lovelight	1979	.40	2.00
Atlantic 3629		Chiquitita (Spanish) / I Have A Dream	1979	.60	3.00
Atlantic 3652		Gimme! Gimme! Gimme! / The King Has Lost His Crown	1980	.40	2.00
Atlantic 3776		The Winner Takes It All / Elaine	1980	.40	2.00
Atlantic 380	(DJ)	Happy New Year / Happy New Year	1980	2.00	10.00
Atlantic 390	(DJ)	Happy New Year (One sided)	1980	2.00	10.00
Atlantic 3806		Super Trouper / The Piper	1981	.40	2.00
Atlantic 3806	(PS)	Super Trouper / The Piper	1981	.40	2.00
Atlantic 3826		On And On And On / Lay All Your Love On Me	1981		
Atlantic 3889		When All Is Said And Done / Should I Laugh Or Cry?	1982	.40	2.00
Atlantic 3889	(PS)	When All Is Said And Done / Should I Laugh Or Cry?	1982	.40	2.00
Atlantic 4031		The Visitors / Head Over Heels	1982	.40	2.00
Atlantic 4031	(PS)	The Visitors / Head Over Heels	1982	.40	2.00
Atlantic 89948		The Day Before You Came / Cassandra	1982	.40	2.00
Atlantic 89881		One Of Us / Should I Laugh Or Cry?	1982	.40	2.00
Atlantic 89881	(PS)	One Of Us / Should I Laugh Or Cry?	1982	.40	2.00

—12" Singles—

Atlantic DSKO-81		Dancing Queen / Dancing Queen	1976	2.00	10.00
Atlantic DSKO-202		Voulez-Vous / Voulez-Vous (Extended remix)	1979	3.00	15.00
Atlantic DMD-259		Lay All Your Love On Me / On And On And On	1980	2.00	10.00

ABBOTT SISTERS, THE

Fabor 4003		We're Gonna Bop / My Heart Has A Conscience	1959	3.00	15.00

ABSTRACT SOUND, THE

S.O.S. 1002		I'm Trying / Blacked Out Mind	1976	8.00	40.00
Gray Sounds		I'm Trying / Blacked Out Mind	1976	8.00	40.00

AC-DC

Atco 7068		It's A Long Way To The Top (If You Want To Rock And Roll) / High Voltage	1977	1.00	5.00
Atco 7086		Problem Child / Let There Be Rock	1977	1.00	5.00
Atlantic 3499		Rock 'N' Roll Damnation / Kicked In The Teeth	1978	.60	3.00
Atlantic 3553		Whole Lotta Rosie / Hell Ain't A Bad Place To Be	1979	.60	3.00
Atlantic 3617		Highway To Hell / Night Prowler	1979	.60	3.00
Atlantic 3644		Touch Too Much / Walk All Over You	1980	.60	3.00
Atlantic 3761		You Shook Me All Night Long / Have A Drink On Me	1980	.40	2.00
Atlantic 3787		Back In Black / What Do You Do For Money, Honey?	1980	.40	2.00
Atlantic 3894		Let's Get It Up / Snowballed	1982	.40	2.00
Atlantic 3894	(PS)	Let's Get It Up / Snowballed	1982	.40	2.00
Atlantic 4029		For Those About To Rock (We Salute You) / T.N.T.	1982	.40	2.00
Atlantic 4029	(PS)	For Those About To Rock (We Salute You) / T.N.T.	1982	.40	2.00
Atlantic 89774		Guns For Hire (Live) / Landslide	1983	.40	2.00
Atlantic 89774	(PS)	Guns For Hire (Live) / Landslide	1983	.40	2.00

Label & Catalog #		A-Side/B-Side	Year	VG	NM
Atlantic 89722		Flick Of The Switch / Badlands	1983	.40	2.00
Atlantic 89722	(PS)	Flick Of The Switch / Badlands	1983	.40	2.00
Atlantic 89614		Jailbreak / Show Business	1984	.40	2.00
Atlantic 89614	(PS)	Jailbreak / Show Business	1984	.40	2.00
Atlantic 89532		Danger / Back In Business	1985	.40	2.00
Atlantic 89532	(PS)	Danger / Back In Business	1985	.40	2.00
Atlantic 89525		Shake Your Foundations / Send For The Man	1985	.40	2.00
Atlantic 89425		Who Made You? / Guns For Hire	1986	.40	2.00
Atlantic 89425	(PS)	Who Made You? / Guns For Hire	1986	.40	2.00
Atlantic 89377		You Shook Me All Night Long / She's Got Balls	1986	.40	2.00
Atlantic 89136		Heatseeker / Go Zone	1988	.40	2.00
Atlantic 89136	(PS)	Heatseeker / Go Zone	1988	.40	2.00
Atlantic 89098		That's The Way I Wanna Rock 'N' Roll / Kissin' Dynamite	1988	.40	2.00
Atlantic 89098	(PS)	That's The Way I Wanna Rock 'N' Roll / Kissin' Dynamite	1988	.40	2.00
Atco 98881		Moneytalks / Borrowed Times	1990	.40	2.00

ACADEMICS, THE

Ancho 100		Darla, My Darling / At My Front Door	195?	8.00	40.00
Ancho 101		Heavenly Love / Too Good To Be True	195?	10.00	50.00
Elmont 1001/2		Drive-In Movie / Something Cool	1958	6.00	30.00

ACCENTS, THE [SANDI & THE ACCENTS]

Charter 1017		I've Got Better Things To Do / Then He Starts To Cry	1964	2.00	10.00
Commerce 5012		Tell Me / Better Watch Out Boy	1964	3.00	15.00
Challenge 59254		Tell Me / Better Watch Out Boy	1964	2.00	10.00
Challenge 59294		Tell Me / Sweet Talk	1965	2.00	10.00
Gazzari 90391		Friendly Stranger / People Are Funny	196?	2.00	10.00

ACCENTS, THE

The Accents also recorded with Ron Peterson.

Panorama 10		All Of Your Life / I Want Your Love	1965	1.20	6.00

ACCENTS, THE

Karate 529		He's The One / On The Run	196?	2.00	10.00

ACCENTS, THE

Twin Town 711		Someone To Love / Muffin Man	1966	4.00	20.00

ACCENTS, THE: *Refer to* SCOTT ENGLISH & THE ACCENTS

ACCIDENTALS, THE

Beau Monde 1933		Twangin' Machine / No Reason	1962	2.00	10.00

ACORNS, THE

Unart 2006		Angel / I'm Going To Stick To You	1958	3.00	15.00
Unart 2006		Your Name And Mine / Please Come Back	1958	4.00	20.00

ACTION, THE

Capitol 5949	(DJ)	Never Ending / 24th Hour	1967	3.00	15.00
Capitol 5949		Never Ending / 24th Hour	1967	5.00	25.00

AD-LIBS, THE

Blue Cat 102		The Boy From New York City / Kicked Around	1965	2.00	10.00
Blue Cat 114		He Ain't No Angel / Ask Anybody	1965	1.60	8.00
Blue Cat 119		On The Corner / Oo-Wee, Oh Me, Oh My	1965	1.60	8.00
Blue Cat 123		Johnny, My Boy / Just A Down Home Girl	1965	1.60	8.00
A.G.P. 100		Human / New York In The Dark	1966	1.20	6.00
Interphon 7717		Lovely Ladies / Neighbor, Neighbor	1966	1.20	6.00
Philips 40461		Don't Ever Leave Me / You're In Love	1967	.80	4.00
Share 104		Giving Up / Appreciation	1969	.80	4.00
Share 106		The Boy From New York City / Nothing Worse Than Being Alone	1969	.80	4.00

ADAMS, BILLY (& THE ROCK-A-TEERS)

Dot 15689		You Heard Me Knockin' / True Love Will Come Your Way	1958	5.00	25.00
Decca 30724		Baby, I'm Bugged / Short Hair And A Turtle Neck Sweater	1958	5.00	25.00
Nau Voo 802		You Gotta Have A Duck Tail / Walking Star	1958	20.00	100.00
Nau Voo 805		Return Of The All American Boy / That's My Baby	1959	8.00	40.00
Nau Voo 808		Blue Eyed Ella / Fun House	1959	7.00	35.00
Quincy 932		Rock Pretty Mama /	1959	40.00	200.00
Capitol 4308		Count Every Star / Peggy's Party	1959	3.00	15.00
Capitol 4373		Can't Get Enough / The Gods Were Angry With Me	1960	3.00	15.00
Fern 807		Darling, Take My Hand / Tender Years	1960	3.00	15.00
Fern 808		Tattle Tale / Born To Be A Loser	1961	3.00	15.00
Sun 389		Betty And Dupree / Got My Mojo Workin'	1964	2.00	10.00
Sun 391		Trouble In Mind / Lookin' For Mary Ann	1964	2.00	10.00
Sun 394		Reconsider Baby / Ruby Jane	1964	2.00	10.00
Sun 401		Rock Me, Baby / Open The Door, Richard	1965	2.00	10.00

Label & Catalog #	A-Side/B-Side	Year	VG	NM
ADAMS, CHARLIE				
Columbia 21355	Cat'n Around / Man Was The Cause Of It All	1955	4.00	20.00
Columbia 21443	Pistol Packin' Mama / They Can't Make A Devil	1955	3.00	15.00
Columbia 21524	Sugar Diet / Black Land Blues	1956	3.00	15.00
ADAMS, LINK				
A-OKay 111	Angel Or Not / Lonely Teen	195?	5.00	25.00
ADAMS, RICHIE				
Richie Adams also recorded with The Fireflies.				
Ribbon 6910	Lonely One / Tell Me, Baby, Did You Wait?	1960	2.00	10.00
Ribbon 6913	Back To School / Don't Go My Love, Don't Go	1960	2.00	10.00
Beltone 1011	What Took You So Long? / Two Initials	1961	2.00	10.00
Imperial 5806	I Got Eyes / Something Inside Me Died	1962	2.00	10.00
MGM 13629	You Were Mine / Better Off Without You	196?	2.00	10.00
Congress 232	What Am I (Without You)? / Slippin' Away	1965	1.20	6.00
Congress 248	I Ain't Gonna Make It Without You / Every Window In The City	1965	1.20	6.00
ADDEO, NICKY, & THE DARCHAES				
Nicky Addeo later recorded with The Central Nervous System. Refer to The Darchaes.				
Savoy 200	Gloria / Bring Back Your Heart	195?	10.00	50.00
Savoy 200	Gloria / Bring Back Your Heart *(Green vinyl)*	195?	25.00	125.00
Savoy 200	Gloria / Bring Back Your Heart *(Red vinyl)*	195?	40.00	200.00
Earls 1533	Gloria / Bring Back Your Heart	195?	2.00	10.00
Melody 1417	Where There Is Love / You Can Depend On Me	195?	3.00	15.00
ADDEO, NICKY, & THE UNIQUES				
Selsom 104	Over The Rainbow / Fool #2	196?	6.00	30.00
ADDRISI, DICK				
Valiant 742	Excuse Me / You're Bad	1965	2.00	10.00
ADDRISI BROTHERS, THE				
The brothers Addrisi are Dick and Don, who also recorded as Dick & Don.				
Brad 003	I'll Be True / Everybody Happy	1958	3.00	15.00
Del-Fi 4116	Cherrystone / Lillies Grow High	1959	3.00	15.00
Del-Fi 4120	Saving My Kisses / Un Jarro	1959	3.00	15.00
Del-Fi 4125	It's Love / Old Salt Mine	1959	3.00	15.00
— Original Del-Fi singles above have grey & black labels with circles. —				
Del-Fi 4130	Gonna See My Baby / Ven Ami	1959	4.00	20.00
Imperial 5715	Four Little Girls / What A Night For Love	1960	3.00	15.00
Pom Pom 4160	The Dance Is Over / Socialite	1962	3.00	20.00
Warner Bros. 5268	The Dance Is Over / Sleeping Beauty	1962	1.60	8.00
Valiant 6047	The Way You Look At Him / Love Me, Baby	1964	1.00	6.00
Valiant 6058	Little Miss Sad / C'mon Home, Baby	1964	2.20	10.00
Valiant 720	Side By Side / Mr. Love	1965	2.00	10.00
Warner Bros. 7249	Time To Love / Good News	1968	.80	4.00
Columbia 45521	We've Got To Get It On Again / You Make It All Worthwhile	1972	.40	2.00
Columbia 45610	One Last Time / I Can Feel You	1972	.40	2.00
Columbia 45705	I Can Count On You / Lifetime	1972	.40	2.00
Buddah 566	Slow Dancin' Don't Turn Me On / Slow Dancin' Don't Turn Me On	1977	.40	2.00
Buddah 579	Does She Do It Like She Dances? / Baby, Love Is A Two Way Street	1977	.40	2.00
Buddah 587	Never My Love / Emergency	1977	.40	2.00
ADELPHIS, THE				
Rim 2020/1	Kathleen / Darlin,' It's You	1958	8.00	40.00
Rim 2020X	Kathleen / Darlin,' It's You	1958	4.00	20.00
Rim 2022	The Sun Will Shine Again / Kiss-A-Kiss	1958	8.00	40.00
Rim 2022	Shine Again / Kiss-A-Kiss	1958	4.00	20.00
ADMIRATIONS, THE				
Atomic 12871	Dear Lady / Memories Are Here To Stay	195?	40.00	200.00
ADMIRATIONS, THE				
Mercury 71521	The Bells Of Rosa Rita / Little Bo-Peep	1959	5.00	25.00
Mercury 71883	To The Aisle / Hey, Senorita	1961	25.00	125.00
ADMIRATIONS, THE				
Kellway 108	Over The Rainbow / In My Younger Days	196?	2.00	10.00
ADRIAN & THE SUNSETS				
Adrian Lloyd also recorded with The Rumblers.				
Sunset 602	Breakthrough / Cherry Pie	1963	40.00	20.00
Sunset 602 *(PS)*	Breakthrough / Cherry Pie	1963	12.00	60.00

Label & Catalog #	A-Side/B-Side	Year	VG	NM
ADVENTURERS, THE				
Mecca A-11	2 O' Clock Express / Shaggin'	1960	3.00	15.00
Miracle 1	2 O' Clock Express / October Days	1960	2.00	10.00
Jerden 105	Excelsior / Little Genie	1960	1.60	8.00
ADVENTURERS, THE				
Ran-Dee 106	It's Alright / I Don't Mind	196?	3.00	15.00
Reading 602	Baby, Baby, My Heart / Lover Doll	1966	5.00	25.00
AEROSMITH				
Columbia 45894	Dream On / Somebody	1973	.80	4.00
Columbia 46029	Same Old Song And Dance / Pandora's Box	1974	.80	4.00
Columbia 10034	Train Kept A Rollin' / Spaced	1974	.80	4.00
Columbia 10105	S.O.S. / Lord Of The Thighs	1974	.60	3.00
Columbia 10155	Sweet Emotion / Uncle Salty	1975	.60	3.00
Columbia 10206	Walk This Way / Round And Round	1975	.60	3.00
Columbia 10253	Toys In The Attic / You See Me Crying	1975	.60	3.00
Columbia 10278	Dream On / Somebody	1975	.60	3.00
Columbia 10359	Last Child / Combination	1976	.60	3.00
Columbia 10407	Home Tonight / Pandora's Box	1976	.60	3.00
Columbia 10449	Walk This Way / Uncle Salty	1976	.60	3.00
Columbia 10516	Back In The Saddle / Nobody's Fault	1977	.60	3.00
Columbia 10637	Draw The Line / Bright, Light, Fright	1977	.60	3.00
Columbia 10699	Critical Mass / Kings And Queens	1978	.60	3.00
Columbia 10727	Get It Up / Milk Cow Blues	1978	.60	3.00
Columbia 10802	Come Together / Kings And Queens	1978	.60	3.00
Columbia 10880	Chip Away The Stone / Chip Away The Stone	1979	.60	3.00
Columbia 11181	Remember (Walking In The Sand) /			
	Bone To Bone (Coney Island White Fish Fox)	1979	.80	4.00
AESOP & THE FABLES				
Panorama 29	Grass / You'll Be My Pride	1966	1.20	6.00
AKI: *Refer to* **AKI ALEONG**				
AKINS, JIM				
Marlo 1517	One Little Girl And One Little Boy / Floating On A Cloud	196?	2.40	12.00
AL-NETTIE				
Gendinson's 6159	Now You Know / San Francisco Twist	1962	1.60	8.00
Art Tone 829	Now You Know / Now You Know, Part 2	1962	1.60	8.00
ALADDIN & THE GENIES				
Drummond 5001	Amazon / Moon Beams	1961	7.00	35.00
ALADDIN, JOHNNY, & THE PASSIONS				
Chip 1001	Why Did You Go? / Happy Together	195?	6.00	30.00
ALADDINS, THE				
Frankie 6	Dot, My Love / My Charlene	1961	100.00	400.00
ALAIMO, STEVE (& THE REDCOATS)				
Steve Alaimo also recorded with The Unknowns.				
Dade 1800	Home By Eleven /	195?	10.00	50.00
Marlin 6064	I Want You To Love Me / Blue Skies	1959	4.00	20.00
Marlin 6067	She's My Baby / Should I Care?	1959	4.00	20.00
Dickson 6445	My Heart Never Said Goodbye / Blue Fire	1960	4.00	20.00
Imperial 5699	I Want You To Love Me / Blue Fire	1960	3.00	15.00
Imperial 5717	It Happens Ev'ry Time / Unchained Melody	1960	3.00	15.00
Checker 981	I Cried All The Way Home / Big Bad Beulah	1961	1.20	6.00
Checker 989	All Night Long / I'm Thankful	1961	1.20	6.00
Checker 1006	Mashed Potatoes / Mashed Potatoes, Part 2	1962	1.20	6.00
Checker 1018	My Friends / Goin' Back To Mary	1962	1.20	6.00
Checker 1024	Cry Myself To Sleep / One Good Reason	1962	1.20	6.00
Checker 1032	Every Day I Have To Cry / Little Girl	1963	2.00	10.00
Checker 1042	It's A Long Way To Happiness / Lifetime Of Loneliness	1963	1.20	6.00
Checker 1047	Don't Let The Sun Catch You Crying / I Told You So	1963	1.20	6.00
Checker 1054	Michael / Michael, Part 2	1963	1.20	6.00
Imperial 66003	Gotta Lotta Love / Happy Pappy	1963	1.20	6.00
ABC-Paramount 10553	Fade Out, Fade In / Love Is A Many Splendored Thing	1964	1.00	5.00
ABC-Paramount 10580	I Don't Know / That's What Love Will Do	1964	1.00	5.00
ABC-Paramount 10605	Everybody Knows But Her / Happy	1964	1.00	5.00
ABC-Paramount 10620	Real Live Girl / Need You	1965	1.20	6.00
ABC-Paramount 10680	Cast Your Fate To The Wind / Mais Oui	1965	1.00	5.00
ABC-Paramount 10712	Lady Of The House / Blowin' In The Wind	1965	1.00	5.00
ABC-Paramount 10805	So Much Love / Truer Than True	1966	1.00	5.00
ABC-Paramount 10833	On The Beach / Happy	1966	1.00	5.00
ABC-Paramount 10873	Pardon Me (It's My First Day Alone) / Savin' All My Love	1966	1.00	5.00

Label & Catalog #	A-Side / B-Side	Year	VG	NM
Atco 6512	New Orleans / Ooh Ooo Pah Doo	1967	1.00	5.00
Atco 6560	Cuando Yo Vuelvo Ami Tierra / Todavia	1968	1.60	8.00
Atco 6561	I Do / Denver	1968	1.00	5.00
Atco 6589	1 x 1 Ain't 2 / My Friend	1969	1.00	5.00
Atco 6620	Thank You For The Sunshine Days / Watching The Trains Go By	1969	1.00	5.00
Atco 6659	I'm Thankful / After The Smoke Is Gone	1969	1.00	5.00
Atco 6710	One Woman / And Then I Tripped Over Your Goodbye	1969	1.00	5.00
Atco 6732	Melissa / Smilin' In My Sleep	1970	1.00	5.00
Atco 6797	(On The) Wild Side Of Life / Can't You See	1970	1.00	5.00
Entrance 7501	When My Little Girl Is Smiling / Gemini	1971	.60	3.00
Entrance 7503	Thorn In Our Roses / Nobody's Fool	1971	.60	3.00
Entrance 7507	Amerikan Music / Nobody's Fool	1972	.60	3.00
	— Extended Play Albums —			
Checker 5135	Everyday I Have To Cry	1963	10.00	50.00

ALAN, LEE

Lee Alan	A Trip To Miami *(Alan's experience with The Fab Four)*	1964	10.00	50.00

ALBANO, LOU: *Refer to NRBQ*

ALDA, ALEX
Alex Alda is a pseudonym for Nick Massi of The Four Seasons.

Topix 6007	Little Pony *(One sided)*	196?	15.00	75.00

ALEONG, AKI (& THE NOBLES)

Reprise 20006	Fall In Love With Me / Voodoo Drums	1961	1.20	6.00
Reprise 20021	Trade Winds, Trade Winds / Without Your Love	1961	1.20	6.00
Reprise 20042	Moon River Twist / Tonight Twist	1962	1.20	6.00
Reprise 20050	Magic Lover Man / How Long?	1962	1.20	6.00
Vee Jay 520	Body Surf / Mary Ann	1963	2.40	12.00
Vee Jay 527	Giving Up On Love / Love Is Funny	1963	1.20	6.00

ALEXANDER, MAX

Caprock 116	Rock, Rock, Rock Everybody / Little Rome	1959	35.00	175.00

ALEXANDER & THE GREATS

Limelight 3040	Hot Dang Mustang / Do The Mustang	1964	4.00	20.00

ALEXANDER & THE HAMILTONS

Warner Bros. 5844	I Don't Need You / Over The Rainbow	1966	3.00	15.00

ALEXANDER QUARTET, JEFF

Aardell 001	Dr. Geek / I'll Pay As I Go	196?	4.00	20.00

ALEXANDER'S TIMELESS BLOOZ BAND

Matamat 101	Love So Strong / Horn Song	196?	2.00	10.00
Kapp 967	Power Of Your Love / Maybe Baby	196?	1.60	8.00

ALEXYS, THE

Dot 16796	Freedom's Child / Evolution of Alexys	1965	1.20	6.00

ALFI & HARRY
Alfi & Harry features David Seville a.k.a. Ross Bagdasarian.

Liberty 55008	The Trouble With Harry / Little Beauty	1955	2.00	10.00
Liberty 55016	Persian On Excursion / Word Game Song	1956	2.00	10.00
Liberty 55066	Safari / Closing Theme	1957	2.00	10.00

ALICIA & THE ROCKAWAYS

Epic 9191	Why Can't I Be Loved? / Never Coming Back	1956	3.00	15.00

ALLAN, CHAD, & THE REFLECTIONS
Chad Allan was originally a member of The Guess Who.

Canadian American 802	Back And Forth / Tribute To Buddy Holly	1964	6.00	30.00
Canadian American 802	Back And Forth / I Just Didn't Have The Heart	1964	2.00	10.00

ALLAN, CHAD

Mala 12033	Through The Looking Glass / Ramona's Hourglass	1970	.80	4.00

ALLAN, DAVIE, & THE ARROWS
Aside from The Arrows (below), Davie also recorded with Annette; Jim Pewter; The Sinners; The Sounds Of Harley; The Starlets; The Streamers; and The 13th Committee. Under Allan, The Arrows also recorded as The Band Without A Name and Max Frost & The Troopers. Note: Some of the singles below may be credited to solely Allan or The Arrows.

Cude 101		War Path / Beyond The Blue	1963	10.00	50.00
Marc 3223		War Path / Beyond The Blue	1963	7.00	35.00
		(The Cude and Marc sides are solely Davie's pre-Arrows.)			
Sidewalk 1	(DJ)	Apache '65 / Blue Guitar	1965	3.00	15.00
Sidewalk 1		Apache '65 / Blue Guitar	1965	6.00	30.00

Label & Catalog #	A-Side / B-Side	Year	VG	NM
Tower 116	Apache '65 / Blue Guitar	1965	2.00	10.00
Tower 133	Moon Dawg '65 / Dance The Freddie	1965	1.60	8.00
Tower 142	Baby Ruth / I'm Looking Over A Four Leaf Clover	1965	1.20	6.00
Tower 158	Space Hop / Granny Goose	1966	2.00	10.00
Tower 267	Theme From The Wild Angels / U.F.O.	1967	1.60	8.00
Tower 295	Blue's Theme / Bongo Party	1967	1.60	8.00
Tower 341	Devil's Angel / Cody's Theme	1967	1.60	8.00
Tower 381	Cycle-Delic / Blue Rides Again	1968	1.60	8.00
Tower 446	Shape Of Things / Wild In The Street	1968	1.60	8.00
MGM 14229	Little Things You Do / You And Me	1971	1.20	6.00
MGM 14374	Head Over Heels / Here It Comes	1972	1.20	6.00
MGM 14432	Dawn Of The 7th Cavalry / Little Big Horn	1972	2.50	12.00
MGM 14432	Dawn At Wounded Knee / Little Big Horn	1972	2.50	12.00
MGM 14560	Pleasure Girl / And Evil Did, Too	1973	1.20	6.00
MGM 14650	Apache '73 / Run Of The Arrow	1973	1.20	6.00
AOA 1134	White Man Beware / Where Do We Go?	1976	1.00	5.00
MRC 0901	Stoked On Surf / Flashback	1984	1.00	5.00

— 12" Singles —

What 601	Stoked On Surf / Outer Surf	1982	1.60	8.00

ALLAN, JOHNNY

MGM 12799	Lonely Days, Lonely Nights / My Baby Is Gone	1959	3.00	15.00

ALLAN & THE FLAMES

Campbell 225-1	Till The End Of Time / Winter Wonderland	1960	8.00	40.00
Colonial 7006	Till The End Of Time / Winter Wonderland	1960	8.00	40.00

ALLEN, ADRIAN, & THE FIVE DISCS

Yale 240	When Love Comes Knocking / Go-Go	1961	25.00	125.00

ALLEN, BARRY

Kapp 806	Sad Souvenirs / (B-side by Wes Dakus)	1967	2.00	10.00

ALLEN, BEAU

L.F.A 1013	Pusher Man / Fallen Angel	196?	2.00	10.00
L.F.A 1013 (PS)	Pusher Man / Fallen Angel	196?	2.00	10.00
L.F.A 1016	Give Me Your Love / What A Love Can Do	196?	2.00	10.00
L.F.A 101?	Georgia Ground / Fallen Angel	196?	2.00	10.00

ALLEN, BILL

Imperial 5500 (DJ)	Please Give Me Something / Since I Have You	195?	15.00	75.00
Imperial 5500	Please Give Me Something / Since I Have You	195?	20.00	100.00

ALLEN, BLINKY

Personality 3502	The Battle Of Beatnik Bay / Make Me Your Leader	1961	2.00	10.00

ALLEN, CHAD

Lama 779	Little Lonely / Domino	1961	3.00	1500
Smash 1720	Little Lonely / Domino	1961	2.00	10.00
Radiant 1508	Come On, Linda / Who Invented The Twist?	1962	2.00	10.00

ALLEN, DEAN

Argo 5272	Rock Me To Sleep / Oooh Oooh Baby Baby	1957	3.00	15.00

ALLEN, DUANE

Keynote 25	Surf Around The World / The World Stands Still	1963	6.00	30.00

ALLEN, IRA (& THE RENEGADES)

Mav-Rick 105	Nursery Rock / Just To Be With You	195?	40.00	200.00
GRC 109	Renegade / The Ballad Of Jack And Joe	196?	2.00	10.00

ALLEN, JIMMY

Al-Brite 1300	When Santa Comes Over The Brooklyn Bridge / What Would You Like To Have For Christmas?	1959	3.00	15.00
Al-Brite 1300 (PS)	When Santa Comes Over The Brooklyn Bridge / What Would You Like To Have For Christmas?	1959	5.00	25.00
Al-Brite 1200	Forgive Me, My Darling / My Girl Is A Pearl	1960	25.00	125.00

(Although uncredited, "Forgive Me, My Darling" features The Two Jays.)

ALLEN, MILTON

RCA Victor 47-6994	Love A, Love A Lover / Just Look, Don't Touch, She's Mine	1957	3.00	15.00
RCA Victor 47-7116	Don't Bug Me, Baby / Jamboree	1958	7.00	35.00

ALLEN, RAY, & THE UPBEATS

Blast 204	Peggy Sue / La Bamba	1962	5.00	25.00
Sinclair 1004	Let Them Talk / Sweet Lorraine	196?	2.00	10.00

Label & Catalog #		A-Side/B-Side	Year	VG	NM
ALLEN, RICHIE					
Era 3058		Goochy Bamba / Blue Holiday	1961	3.00	15.00
Imperial 5683		Stranger From Durango / Redskin	1960	3.00	15.00
Imperial 5720		Haunted Guitar / In A Persian World	1961	3.00	15.00
Imperial 5846		Comin' Back To You / Mr. Hobbs' Theme	1962	2.00	10.00
Imperial 5865		A Touch Of Blue / Not So Quiet	1962	2.00	10.00
Imperial 5872		Caveman / Room 305	1962	3.00	15.00
Imperial 5885		Undercurrent / Kick Off	1962	3.00	15.00
Imperial 5917		Butterscotch / Sunday Picnic	1963	2.00	10.00
Imperial 5929		Foot Stomp U.S.A. / Skeg Along Pete	1963	3.00	15.00
Imperial 5941		Surf Beater / Rising Surf	1963	2.00	10.00
Imperial 5984		Ballad Of The Surf / The Quiet Side	1963	2.00	10.00
ALLEN, RONNIE					
San 208		Juvenile Delinquent / River Of Love	1959	8.00	40.00
ALLEN, RONNIE					
Dapt 205		Flip You Over / Ronnie's Swanee	1961	6.00	30.00
		(First pressings mis-title the a-side.)			
Dapt 205		Flip Over You / Ronnie's Swanee	1961	3.00	15.00
ALLENS, ARVIE					
Arvie Allens is a pseudonym for Ritchie Valens.					
Del Fi 4111		Fast Freight / Big Baby Blues (Circles label)	1958	5.00	25.00
ALLEY CATS, THE					
Philles 108		Puddin' 'N' Tain / Feel So Good	1962	3.00	15.00
		(Produced by Phil Spector.)			
Epic 9778		Lily Of The West / I Should Have Stayed At Home Tonight	1965	1.00	5.00
ALLEYNE, GLORIA					
Josie 767		I Can't Rock It / When I Say My Prayer	195?	4.00	20.00
ALLIE OOP'S GROUP					
Caprice 102		Bloop, Bloop / Dinosaur	1960	3.00	15.00
ALLISON, KEITH ["GUITAR" KEITH ALLISON]					
Keith Allison also recorded with Paul Revere & The Raiders; The Unknowns.					
Warner Bros. 5681		Sweet Little Rock 'N Roller / The Girl Can't Help It	1965	1.60	8.00
Warner Bros. 5681	(PS)	Sweet Little Rock 'N Roller / The Girl Can't Help It	1965	4.00	20.00
Columbia 43619		Look At Me / I Ain't Blaming You	1966	.80	4.00
Columbia 43619	(PS)	Look At Me / I Ain't Blaming You	1966	3.00	15.00
Columbia 44028		Freeborn Man / Louise	1967	1.60	8.00
Columbia 44028	(PS)	Freeborn Man / Louise	1967	3.00	15.00
		(Produced by Gary Usher.)			
Amy 11024		Who Do You Love? / I Don't Want Nobody But You	1969	1.20	6.00
Columbia 44853		Birds Of A Feather / To Know Her Is To Love Her	1969	.80	4.00
Columbia 45115		Everybody / Wednesday's Child	1970	.80	4.00
ALLISONS, THE					
Smash 1849		Lessons In Love / Oh, My Love	1962	2.00	10.00
ALLISONS, THE					
Tip 1011		Surfer Street / Money	1963	3.00	15.00
ALLMAN, DUANE & GREGG					
Bold 200	(DJ)	Morning Dew / Morning Dew (Red vinyl)	1972	5.00	25.00
Bold 200		Morning Dew / Morning Dew	1972	1.60	8.00
ALLMAN, GREGG, & HOUR GLASS					
Liberty 56091		I've Been Trying / Silently	1967	2.00	10.00
ALLMAN, GREGG [THE GREGG ALLMAN BAND]					
Capricorn 0035		Multi-Colored Lady / Midnight Rider	1973	.60	3.00
Capricorn 0042		Please Call Home / Don't Mess Up A Good Thing	1973	.60	3.00
Capricorn 0053		Midnight Rider / Don't Mess Up A Good Thing	1974	.40	2.00
Capricorn 0279		Cryin' Shame / One More Try	1977	.60	3.00
		—Extended Play Albums—			
Capricorn 0116	(33)	Laid Back (Jukebox EP)	1973	3.00	15.00
ALLMAN & WOMAN					
Gregg Allman & Cher.					
Warner Bros. 8504		Love Me / Move Me	197?	.50	2.50
ALLMAN BROTHERS (BAND), THE					
The Allman Brothers feature Duane and Gregg Allman. Refer to Derek & The Dominos; The Hour Glass.					
Capricorn 8803		Black Hearted Woman / Every Hungry Woman	1970	1.00	5.00
Capricorn 8011		Revival (Love Is Everywhere) / Leave My Blues At Home	1971	.80	4.00

Label & Catalog #		A-Side/B-Side	Year	VG	NM
Capricorn 8014		Whipping Post / Midnight Rider	1971	.80	4.00
Capricorn 0003		Ain't Wastin' Time No More / Melissa	1972	.60	3.00
Capricorn 0007		Blue Sky / Melissa	1972	.60	3.00
Capricorn 0014		Stand Back / One Way Out	1972	.60	3.00
Capricorn 0027		Ramblin' Man / Pony Boy	1973	.60	3.00
Capricorn 0036		Jessica / Come And Go Blues	1973	.60	3.00
Capricorn 0050		Ain't Wastin' Time No More / Blue Sky	1975	.60	3.00
Capricorn 0051		Ramblin' Man / Melissa	1975	.60	3.00
Capricorn 0246		Nevertheless / Louisiana Lou And Three Card Monty John	1975	.60	3.00
Capricorn 0320		Crazy Love / Just Ain't Easy	1979	.60	3.00
Capricorn 0326		Can't Take It With You / Sail Away	1979	.60	3.00
		— Extended Play Albums—			
Capricorn 0111	(33)	Brothers And Sisters (Jukebox EP)	1973	3.00	15.00
Atlantic 805	(33)	Beginnings (Jukebox EP)	1973	3.00	15.00

ALLMAN JOYS, THE
The Allman Joys feature Duane and Gregg Allman.

Dial 4046	Spoonful / You Deserve Each Other	1966	4.00	20.00

ALMOND, HERSCHEL

Ace 558	The Great Tragedy / Let's Get It On	1959	4.00	20.00
Challenge 59054	You Are The One / Don't Leave Me	1959	4.00	20.00

ALPINES, THE

Challenge 59230	Shush-Boomer / Skier's Melody	1964	3.00	15.00

ALTAR, ROSALIE

Harmon 1006	The Heartaches Are Here To Stay / Be True	196?	2.00	10.00

ALTECS, THE

Cloister 6201	Yok Yok Yok / Tweeda	196?	2.00	10.00
Felsted 8618	Easy / Recess	1960	2.00	10.00

ALTON & JIMMY

Sun 323	Have Faith In My Love / No More Crying The Blues	1959	3.00	15.00

ALVANS, THE

May 102	Love Is A Game / What Can It Be?	1961	8.00	40.00

AMATO, LARRY

RCA Victor 47-7411	We're Gonna Have A Party / He Made A Miracle	1958	3.00	15.00

AMATO, TONY

Peddy 1003	Brenda (Is Her Name) / I Could Love You So	196?	3.00	15.00

AMBASSADORS, THE
The Ambassadors is a pseudonym for the British group The Saints.

Dot 16528	Big Breaker / Surfin' John Brown	1963	7.00	35.00

AMBASSADORS, THE

Time 1007	Can't Believe Ya / El Grippo	196?	2.00	10.00
Arctic 156	Can't Take My Eyes Off You / A. W. O. L.	1969	2.00	10.00

AMBER, JAN

Clef-Tone 157	Little Martian Man / Waiting	1959	3.00	15.00

AMBERS, THE

Greezie 501	Loving Tree / Listen To Your Heart, Caroline	196?	5.00	25.00

AMBERS, THE

Smash 2111	Another Love / Potion Of Love	1967	2.00	10.00
New Art 104	Blue Birds / Baby (I Need You)	1973	2.00	10.00

AMBERTONES, THE

GNP/Crescendo 329	Charlena / Bandido	1964	3.00	15.00
Dottie 1129	One Summer Night / Chocolate Covered Ants	1965	5.00	25.00
Dottie 1130	I Need Someone / If I Do	1965	5.00	25.00
Treasure Chest 001	I Can Only Give You Everything / I Only Have Eyes For You	1966	5.00	25.00

AMBOY DUKES, THE
The Amboy Dukes feature Ted Nugent.

Mainstream 676	Baby, Please Don't Go / Psalms Of Aftermath	1967	2.00	10.00
Mainstream 684	Journey To The Center Of The Mind / Mississippi Murderer	1968	2.00	10.00
Mainstream 693	You Talk Sunshine, I Breathe Fire / Scottish Tea	1968	2.00	10.00
Mainstream 703	For His Namesake / Loaded For Bear	1969	2.00	10.00
DiscReet 1199	Ain't It The Truth / Sweet Revenge	1974	1.00	5.00

Label & Catalog #		A-Side/B-Side	Year	VG	NM
AMBURGY, REX					
Moonees 1006		Let The Four Winds Blow / Where Will It Stop?	196?	2.00	10.00
AMEN CORNER					
Deram 5013		High In The Sky / Run Run Run	1967	1.00	5.00
Immediate 5013		Hey Hey Girl / Half As Nice	1969	.80	4.00
AMERICA					
American Inter. 5001		Don't Make Me Over / Don't Forget About Me	1970	2.00	10.00
AMERICAN BEETLES, THE					
BYP 1001		She's Mine / Theme Of The American Beetles	1964	3.00	15.00
BYP 101		It's My Last Night In Town / You're Getting To Me	1964	3.00	15.00
Roulette 4550		Don't Be Unkind / You Did It To Me	1964	2.00	10.00
Roulette 4559		Hey Hey Girl / School Days	1964	2.00	10.00
AMERICAN BLUES					
American Blues features Frank Beard and Dusty Hill, future members of ZZ Top.					
Karma 101		If I Were A Carpenter / All I Saw Was You	1967	3.00	15.00
AMERICAN BREED, THE					
The American Breed originally recorded as Gary & The Nite Lites.					
Acta 802		Give Two Young Lovers A Chance / I Don't Think You Know Me	1967	.80	4.00
Acta 804		Step Out Of Your Mind / Same Old Thing	1967	.80	4.00
Acta 808		Don't Forget About Me / Short Skirts	1967	.80	4.00
Acta 811		Bend Me, Shape Me / Mindrocker	1967	1.00	5.00
Acta 821		Green Light / Don't It Make You Cry?	1968	1.00	5.00
Acta 821	(PS)	Green Light / Don't It Make You Cry?	1968	1.00	5.00
Acta 824		Ready, Willing And Able / Take Me If You Want Me	1968	.60	3.00
Acta 827		Anyway That You Want Me / Master Of My Fate	1968	.60	3.00
Acta 830		Keep The Faith / Private Zoo	1968	.60	3.00
Acta 833		Hunky Funky / Enter Her Majesty	1968	.60	3.00
Acta 836		Room At The Top / Walls	1968	.60	3.00
Acta 837		Cool It (We're Not Alone) / The Brain	1969	.60	3.00
Paramount 0040		Can't Make It Without You / When I'm With You	1971	.60	3.00
AMERICAN CHEESE					
Seawest 101		When The Morning Comes / Hey, Good Lookin'	1970	1.00	5.00
AMERICAN FOUR, THE					
The American Four features Arthur Lee, later of Love.					
Selma 2001		Luci Baines / Soul Food	1964	5.00	25.00
AMERICAN REBELS, THE					
Super 106		Rebel Song / Rebel Theme	196?	2.00	10.00
AMERICAN ROCK REVIVAL, THE					
Bell 788		Oh Happy Day / Stompin'	1969	.80	4.00
AMERICAN SPRING: *Refer to* **SPRING**					
AMERICAN ZOO, THE					
Reena 1030		What I Am / Back Street Thoughts	196?	2.00	10.00
AMES, STACEY					
Random 604		Calendar Boy / Look Out	1961	2.00	10.00
ANDERS, PETE					
Corvair 903		Remember Me? / I'm Your Slave	196?	1.20	6.00
Buddah 3		Sunrise Highway / Baby Baby	1967	1.00	5.00
Kama Sutra 240		Virgin Of The Night / So It Goes	1967	1.00	5.00
ANDERS, PETE, & TREASURES					
Shirley 500	(DJ)	Hold Me Tight / Pete Meets Vinnie	1964	3.00	15.00
Shirley 500		Hold Me Tight / Pete Meets Vinnie	1964	5.00	25.00
ANDERS & PONCIA					
Pete Anders and Vinnie Poncia also recorded as The Innocence; The Mulberry Fruit Band; The Penny Arcade; Pete & Vinnie; The Tradewinds; The Treasures; and The Videls.					
Warner Bros. 7294		Make A Change (To Something Better) / Lucky	1969	.80	4.00
ANDERSON, BROTHER JAMES					
Sun 406		I'm Gonna Move In The Room With The Lord / My Soul Needs Resting	1967	5.00	25.00

Label & Catalog #	A-Side/B-Side	Year	VG	NM
ANDERSON, ELIJAH "KID"				
Bolo 732	Days Are Lonely / Tell Like It Is	196?	2.00	10.00
ANDERSON, ERNESTINE				
Mercury 71772	A Lover's Question / That's All I Want From You	1961	2.00	10.00
ANDREWS, GENE				
Rust 5054	Linda, Linda / Lonely Room	1963	1.00	5.00
ANDY & THE LIVE WIRES				
Applause 1249	Maggie / You've Done It Again	1960	5.00	25.00
Liberty 55321	Maggie / You've Done It Again	1960	2.00	10.00
ANDY & THE MARGLOWS				
Liberty 55570	Symphony / Just One Look	1963	2.00	10.00
Liberty 55623	Superman Lover / I'll Get By	1963	2.00	10.00
ANDY & ROCKETS				
Viking 1000	Genevieve / If You Really Care	196?	2.00	10.00
ANGEL, BOBBY, & THE HILLSIDERS				
Rhum 101	Baby-O / That's The Way I Want To Go	1961	2.00	10.00
Astra 300	Heartbreak Hotel / Submarine Races	1962	2.00	10.00
ANGEL, JOHNNY				
Power 250	Starlight / The Story Of Love	196?	10.00	50.00
Vin 1004	Teenage Wedding / Baby, It's Love	195?	3.00	15.00
Imperial 5673	Doubt / Falling Teardrops	1960	4.00	20.00
Gardena 117	Baby, You Got Soul / All Night Party	1961	3.00	15.00
JAF 2024	Lonely Nights / Seven Words	1961	2.00	10.00
Felsted 8646	Mashed Potato Stomp / One More Tomorrow	1962	2.00	10.00
Parliament 778	The Fever / A Day Late And A Dollar Short	196?	1.20	6.00
Markie 113	Johnny Angel / Ooh Ooh La La	196?	1.20	6.00
ANGEL, JOHNNY, & THE CREATIONS				
Refer to The Creations.				
Jamie 1134	Where's My Love? / We're Old Enough	1959	2.00	10.00
ANGEL, JOHNNY, & THE HALOS				
Felsted 8633	Without Her Heart / Lady Of Spain	1961	2.00	10.00
Felsted 8659	Looking For A Fool / Rollaree Motion	1962	2.00	10.00
ANGEL, JOHNNY T.				
Yorksville 45090	The Way I Feel Tonight / Tell Laura I Love Her	197?	1.20	6.00
Bell 472	The Way I Feel Tonight / Tell Laura I Love Her	1974	.80	4.00
ANGEL, RONNIE				
Rita 1011	That's Alright / Angel Tears	1960	3.00	15.00
ANGELO & THE INITIALS				
Congress 229	Someday She'll Love Me / I Should Have Listened	1964	2.00	10.00
ANGELO'S ANGELS				
Tabb 3230	Mach 9 / Dirty Shirt	1963	1.20	6.00
Ermine 55	Spring Cleaning / Tomorrow	1964	1.20	6.00
Ermine 59	I Don't Believe / Shimmy Jimmy	1964	1.20	6.00
ANGELOS, THE				
Cameo 250	You Turn Me On / Raining Teardrops	1963	3.00	15.00
Vee Jay 531	Just Like Takin' Candy From A Baby / Lonely Hours	1963	1.60	8.00
Tollie 9003	Bad Motorcycle / Backfield In Motion	1964	1.60	8.00
ANGELS, THE				
The Angels later recorded as The Safaris.				
Tawny 101	A Lover's Poem (To Her) / A Lover's Poem (To Him)	1959	8.00	40.00
ANGELS, THE				
The Angels are Barbara and Phyllis Allbut with Linda Jansen, who was replaced by Peggy Santiglia after "Cry, Baby, Cry."				
Refer to The Beach Nuts; Dusk; and The Starlets				
Caprice 107	'Til / A Moment Ago	1961	3.00	15.00
Caprice 112	Cry, Baby, Cry / That's All I Ask Of You	1962	2.00	10.00
Caprice 116	Everybody Loves A Lover / Blow, Joe	1962	2.00	10.00
Caprice 118	I'd Be Good For You / You Should Have Told Me	1962	2.00	10.00
Caprice 121	A Moment Ago / Cotton Fields	1962	2.00	10.00
Ascot 2139	Irresistible / Cotton Fields	1963	2.00	10.00
Smash 1834	My Boyfriend's Back / (Love Me) Now	1963	2.00	10.00
Smash 1854	I Adore Him / Thank You And Goodnight	1963	2.00	10.00
Smash 1854 (PS)	I Adore Him / Thank You And Goodnight	1963	4.00	20.00

Label & Catalog #		A-Side/B-Side	Year	VG	NM
Smash 1870		Wow Wow Wee (He's The Boy For Me) /			
		Snowflakes And Teardrops	1963	3.00	15.00
Smash 1885		Little Beatle Boy / Java	1964	3.00	15.00
Smash 1915		Dream Boy / Jamaica Joe	1964	2.00	10.00
Smash 1915	(PS)	Dream Boy / Jamaica Joe	1964	4.00	20.00
Smash 1931		The Boy From 'Cross Town / A World Without Love	1964	2.00	10.00
Smash 1931	(PS)	The Boy From 'Cross Town / A World Without Love	1964	5.00	25.00
RCA Victor 47-9129		What To Do / I Had A Dream I Lost You	1967	1.00	5.00
RCA Victor 47-9246		You'll Never Get To Heaven / Go Out And Play	1967	1.00	5.00
RCA Victor 47-9494		With Love / You're The Cause Of It	1967	1.00	5.00
RCA Victor 47-9541		If I Didn't Love You / Moments To Remember Medley	1968	1.00	5.00
RCA Victor 47-9612		The Boy With The Green Eyes / But For Love	1968	1.00	5.00
RCA Victor 47-9681		Merry Go Round / So Nice	1968	1.00	5.00

ANGIE

Stiff/Epic 50793	(DJ)	Peppermint Lump / Peppermint Lump	1979	2.00	10.00
Stiff/Epic 50793	(PS)	Peppermint Lump / Peppermint Lump	1979	3.00	15.00
		("Peppermint Lump" features Pete Townshend.)			
Stiff/Epic 50793		Peppermint Lump / Breakfast In Naples	1979	1.00	5.00
Stiff/Epic 50793	(PS)	Peppermint Lump / Breakfast In Naples	1979	1.00	5.00

ANGIE & THE CHICKLETTES

Apt 25080		Treat Him Tender, Maureen			
		(Now That Ringo Belongs To You) / Tommy	1965	6.00	30.00

ANGIE & THE CITATIONS

Angela 598		I Wanna Dance / Salt And Pepper	196?	2.00	10.00

ANGLOS, THE

Orbit 201		Incense / Stepping Stone	1965	2.00	10.00

ANGLOS, THE

Scepter 12204		Small Town Boy / Since You've Been Gone	1968	1.20	6.00

ANIMALS, THE

The original group consisted of Eric Burdon, Chas Chandler, Alan Price, John Steel and Hilton Valentine. By the end of '66, only Burdon was left and continued to record with new musicians as Eric Burdon & The Animals.

MGM 13242		Baby, Let Me Take You Home /			
		Gonna Send You Back To Walker	1964	3.00	15.00
MGM 13264		House Of The Rising Sun / Talking 'Bout You	1964	1.60	8.00
MGM 13264	(PS)	House Of The Rising Sun / Talking 'Bout You	1964	3.00	15.00
MGM 13274		I'm Crying / Take It Easy, Baby	1964	1.60	8.00
MGM 13274	(PS)	I'm Crying / Take It Easy, Baby	1964	2.40	12.00
MGM 13298		Boom Boom / Blue Feeling	1964	1.60	8.00
MGM 13298	(PS)	Boom Boom / Blue Feeling	1964	3.00	15.00
MGM 13311		Don't Let Me Be Misunderstood / Club A Go Go	1965	1.60	8.00
MGM 13339		Bring It On Home / For Miss Caulker	1965	1.60	8.00
MGM 13339	(PS)	Bring It On Home / For Miss Caulker	1965	3.00	15.00
MGM 13382		We Gotta Get Out Of This Place / I Can't Believe It	1965	1.60	8.00
MGM 13414		It's My Life / I'm Going To Change The World	1965	1.60	8.00
MGM 13468		Inside Looking Out / You're On My Mind	1966	1.60	8.00
MGM 13514		Don't Bring Me Down / Cheating	1966	1.60	8.00

ANKA, PAUL

R.P.M. 472		I Confess / Blau-Wile Deveest Fontaine	1956	10.00	50.00
ABC-Paramount 9831		Diana / Don't Gamble With Love	1957	3.00	15.00
ABC-Paramount 9855		I Love You, Baby / Tell Me That You Love Me	1957	1.50	10.00
ABC-Paramount 9880		You Are My Destiny / When I Stop Loving You	1958	3.00	15.00
ABC-Paramount 9907		Crazy Love / Let The Bells Keep Ringing	1958	2.00	10.00
ABC-Paramount 9937		Midnight / Verboten	1958	2.00	10.00
ABC-Paramount 9956		Just Young / So It's Goodbye	1958	2.00	10.00
ABC-Paramount 9956	(PS)	Just Young / So It's Goodbye	1958	3.00	15.00
ABC-Paramount 9987		My Heart Sings / That's Love	1958	2.00	10.00
ABC-Paramount 9987	(S)	My Heart Sings / That's Love	1958	5.00	25.00
ABC-Paramount 10011		I Miss You / Late Last Night	1959	2.00	10.00
ABC-Paramount 10011	(PS)	I Miss You / Late Last Night	1959	3.00	15.00
ABC-Paramount 10011	(S)	I Miss You / Late Last Night	1959	5.00	25.00
ABC-Paramount 10022		Lonely Boy / Your Way	1959	2.00	10.00
ABC-Paramount 10022	(S)	Lonely Boy / Your Way	1959	5.00	25.00
ABC-Paramount 10040		Put Your Head On My Shoulder / Don't Ever Leave Me	1959	1.60	8.00
ABC-Paramount 10040	(PS)	Put Your Head On My Shoulder / Don't Ever Leave Me	1959	2.50	12.00
ABC-Paramount 10040	(S)	Put Your Head On My Shoulder / Don't Ever Leave Me	1959	5.00	25.00
ABC-Paramount 10064		It's Time To Cry / Something Has Changed Me	1959	1.60	8.00
ABC-Paramount 10064	(PS)	It's Time To Cry / Something Has Changed Me	1959	2.00	10.00
ABC-Paramount 10064	(S)	It's Time To Cry / Something Has Changed Me	1959	5.00	25.00
ABC-Paramount 10082		Puppy Love / Adam And Eve	1960	1.60	8.00
ABC-Paramount 10082	(PS)	Puppy Love / Adam And Eve	1960	3.00	15.00
ABC-Paramount 10082	(S)	Puppy Love / Adam And Eve	1960	5.00	25.00

Label & Catalog #		A-Side / B-Side	Year	VG	NM
ABC-Paramount 10106		My Home Town / Something Happened	1960	1.60	8.00
ABC-Paramount 10106	(PS)	My Home Town / Something Happened	1960	2.00	10.00
ABC-Paramount 10132		Hello, Young Lovers / I Love You In The Same Old Way	1960	1.60	8.00
ABC-Paramount 10132	(PS)	Hello, Young Lovers / I Love You In The Same Old Way	1960	3.00	15.00
ABC-Paramount 10132	(S)	Hello, Young Lovers / I Love You In The Same Old Way	1960	5.00	25.00
ABC-Paramount 10147		Summer's Gone / I'd Have To Share	1960	1.60	8.00
ABC-Paramount 10147	(PS)	Summer's Gone / I'd Have To Share	1960	2.00	10.00
ABC-Paramount 10147	(S)	Summer's Gone / I'd Have To Share	1960	5.00	25.00
ABC-Paramount 10163		I Saw Mommy Kissing Santa Claus / Rudolph The Red-Nosed Reindeer	1960	1.60	8.00
ABC-Paramount 10168		The Story Of My Love / Don't Say You're Sorry	1961	2.00	10.00
ABC-Paramount 10168	(PS)	The Story Of My Love / Don't Say You're Sorry	1961	2.00	10.00
ABC-Paramount 10168	(S)	The Story Of My Love / Don't Say You're Sorry	1961	5.00	25.00
ABC-Paramount 10169		It's Christmas Everywhere / Rudolph The Red-Nosed Reindeer	1960	1.60	8.00
ABC-Paramount 10169	(PS)	It's Christmas Everywhere / Rudolph The Red-Nosed Reindeer	1960	5.00	25.00
ABC-Paramount 10194		Tonight, My Love, Tonight / I'm Just Your Fool Anyway	1961	1.60	8.00
ABC-Paramount 10194	(PS)	Tonight, My Love, Tonight / I'm Just Your Fool Anyway	1961	2.00	10.00
ABC-Paramount 10220		Dance On, Little Girl / I Talk To You	1961	1.60	8.00
ABC-Paramount 10220	(PS)	Dance On, Little Girl / I Talk To You	1961	3.00	15.00
ABC-Paramount 10239		Cinderella / Kissin' On The Phone	1961	1.60	8.00
ABC-Paramount 10239	(PS)	Cinderella / Kissin' On The Phone	1961	2.00	10.00
ABC-Paramount 10279		Loveland / The Bells At My Wedding	1962	1.00	5.00
ABC-Paramount 10282		The Fool's Hall Of Fame / From The Lights Of Town	1962	1.00	5.00
ABC-Paramount 10311		I'd Never Find Another You / Uh Huh	1962	1.00	5.00
ABC-Paramount 10338		I'm Coming Home / Cry	1962	1.00	5.00
ABC-Paramount 104	(DJ)	(You Can) Share Your Love /	196?	5.00	25.00
RCA Victor 47-7977		Love Me Warm And Tender / I'd Like To Know	1962	1.00	5.00
RCA Victor 47-7977	(PS)	Love Me Warm And Tender / I'd Like To Know	1962	1.00	5.00
RCA Victor 47-8030		A Steel Guitar And A Glass Of Wine / I Never Knew Your Name	1962	1.00	5.00
RCA Victor 47-8030	(PS)	A Steel Guitar And A Glass Of Wine / I Never Knew Your Name	1962	1.00	5.00
RCA Victor 47-8068		Every Night / There You Go	1962	1.00	5.00
RCA Victor 47-8068	(PS)	Every Night / There You Go	1962	1.00	5.00
RCA Victor 47-8097		Give Me Back My Heart / Eso Beso	1962	1.00	5.00
RCA Victor 47-8097	(PS)	Give Me Back My Heart / Eso Beso	1962	1.00	5.00
RCA Victor 47-8115		Love (Makes The World Go Round) / Crying In The Wind	1963	1.00	5.00
RCA Victor 47-8115	(PS)	Love (Makes The World Go Round) / Crying In The Wind	1963	1.00	5.00
RCA Victor 47-8170		Remember Diana / At Night	1963	1.00	5.00
RCA Victor 47-8170	(PS)	Remember Diana / At Night	1963	1.00	5.00
RCA Victor 47-8195		You've Got The Nerve To Call This Love / Hello, Jim	1963	1.00	5.00
RCA Victor 47-8195	(PS)	You've Got The Nerve To Call This Love / Hello, Jim	1963	1.00	5.00
RCA Victor 47-8237		Wondrous Are The Ways Of Love / Hurry Up And Tell Me	1963	1.00	5.00
RCA Victor 47-8237	(PS)	Wondrous Are The Ways Of Love / Hurry Up And Tell Me	1963	1.00	5.00
RCA Victor 47-8272		Did You Have A Happy Birthday? / For No Good Reason At All	1963	1.00	5.00
RCA Victor 47-8272	(PS)	Did You Have A Happy Birthday? / For No Good Reason At All	1963	1.00	5.00
RCA Victor 47-8311		From Rocking Horse To Rocking Chair / Cheer Up	1964	.80	4.00
RCA Victor 47-8311	(PS)	From Rocking Horse To Rocking Chair / Cheer Up	1964	.80	4.00
RCA Victor 47-8349		Baby's Coming Home / No, No	1964	.80	4.00
RCA Victor 47-8349	(PS)	Baby's Coming Home / No, No	1964	.80	4.00
RCA Victor 47-8396		It's Easy To Say / In My Imagination	1964	.80	4.00
RCA Victor 47-8396	(PS)	It's Easy To Say / In My Imagination	1964	.80	4.00
RCA Victor 47-8441		Cindy, Go Home / Ogni Volta	1965	.80	4.00
RCA Victor 47-8441	(PS)	Cindy, Go Home / Ogni Volta	1965	.80	4.00
RCA Victor 47-8493		Behind My Smile / Sylvia	1965	.80	4.00
RCA Victor 47-8595		The Loneliest Boy In The World / Dream Me Happy	1965	.80	4.00
RCA Victor 47-8595	(PS)	The Loneliest Boy In The World / Dream Me Happy	1965	.80	4.00
RCA Victor 47-8662		As If There Were No Tomorrow / Every Day A Heart Is Broken	1965	.80	4.00
RCA Victor 47-8662	(PS)	As If There Were No Tomorrow / Every Day A Heart Is Broken	1965	.80	4.00
RCA Victor 47-8764		Oh, Such A Stranger / Truly Yours	1966	.80	4.00
RCA Victor 47-8839		I Went To Your Wedding / I Wish	1966	.80	4.00
RCA Victor 47-8893		Can't Get Along Very Well Without Her / I Can't Help Loving You	1966	.80	4.00
RCA Victor 47-9032		Poor Old Fool / I'd Rather Be A Stranger	1967	.80	4.00
RCA Victor 47-9128		Until It's Time For You To Go / Would You Still Be My Baby	1967	.80	4.00
RCA Victor 47-9228		That's How Love Is / A Woman Is A Sentimental Thing	1967	.80	4.00
RCA Victor 47-9457		When We Get There / Can't get You Out Of My Mind	1968	.80	4.00
RCA Victor 47-9648		Goodnight, My Love / This Crazy World	1969	.80	4.00
RCA Victor 47-9767		Happy / Can't Get You Out Of My Mind	1969	.80	4.00
RCA Victor 47-9846		Midnight Mistress / Before It's Too Late	1969	.80	4.00
RCA Victor 74-0126		In The Still Of The Night / Pickin' Up The Pieces	1969	.80	4.00
RCA Victor 74-0164		Sincerely / Next Year	1969	.80	4.00

Label & Catalog #		A-Side/B-Side	Year	VG	NM
Barnaby 227		Why Are You Leaning On Me, Sir? /			
		You're Some Kind Of Friend	1970	.60	3.00
Buddah 252		Do I Love You? / So Long City	1971	.60	3.00
Buddah 294		Jubilation / Everything's Been Changed	1972	.60	3.00
Buddah 337		While We're Still Young / This Is Your Song	1972	.60	3.00
Buddah 349		Hey Girl / You And Me Today	1972	.60	3.00
Fame 345		Let Me Get To Know You / Flashback	1974	.60	3.00
United Artists 454		(You're) Having My Baby / Papa	1974	.60	3.00
United Artists 569		One Man Woman-One Woman Man /			
		Let Me Get To Know You	1974	.40	2.00
United Artists 615		I Don't Like To Sleep Alone /			
		How Can Anything Be Beautiful After You?	1975	.40	2.00
United Artists 615	(PS)	I Don't Like To Sleep Alone /			
		How Can Anything Be Beautiful After You?	1975	.40	2.00
United Artists 685		(I Believe) There's Nothing Stronger Than Our Love /			
		Today I Became A Fool	1975	.40	2.00
United Artists 737		Times Of Your Life / Water Runs Deep	1975	.40	2.00
United Artists 737	(PS)	Times Of Your Life / Water Runs Deep	1975	.40	2.00
United Artists 789		Something About You / Anytime (I'll Be There)	1976	.40	2.00
United Artists 911		Happier / Closing Doors	1976	.40	2.00
United Artists 945		Never Gonna Fall In Love Again Like I Fell			
		In Love With You / I'll Help You	1977	.40	2.00
United Artists 972		Never Gonna Fall In Love Again Like I Fell			
		In Love With You / My Best Friend's Wife	1977	.40	2.00
United Artists 1018		Everybody Ought To Be In Love / Tonight	1977	.40	2.00
RCA Victor PB-11351		Brought Up In New York (Brought Down In L.A.) /			
		Love Me, Lady	1978	.40	2.00
RCA Victor PB-11351	(PS)	Brought Up In New York (Brought Down In L.A.) /			
		Love Me, Lady	1978	.40	2.00
RCA Victor PB-11395		This Is Love / I'm By Myself Again	1978	.40	2.00
RCA Victor PB-11662		As Long As We Keep Believing / Headlines	1979	.40	2.00
RCA Victor PB-12225		I've Been Waiting For You All My Life /			
		Think I'm In Love Again	1981	.40	2.00
		—Extended Play Albums—			
ABC-Paramount 296-1		(All Of A Sudden) My Heart Sings	1959	10.00	50.00
ABC-Paramount 296-2		(All Of A Sudden) My Heart Sings	1959	10.00	50.00
ABC-Paramount 296-3		(All Of A Sudden) My Heart Sings	1959	10.00	50.00
RCA Victor 2575	(33)	Let's Sit This One Out (Jukebox EP)	1962	4.00	20.00
RCA Victor 2614	(33)	Our Man Around The World (Jukebox EP)	1963	4.00	20.00
ABC 3704	(33)	Paul Anka Gold (Jukebox EP)	196?	2.00	10.00
Sire LLP-273	(33)	Paul Anka Gold (Jukebox EP)	1974	2.00	10.00

ANKA, PAUL; JOHNNY NASH; & GEORGE HAMILTON IV

Label & Catalog #	A-Side/B-Side	Year	VG	NM
ABC-Paramount 9974	The Teen Commandments / If You Learn To Pray	1958	2.00	10.00

ANN, CHERYL

Label & Catalog #	A-Side/B-Side	Year	VG	NM
Patty 52	I Can't Let Him / Goodbye, Baby	196?	3.00	15.00

ANN MARIE

Label & Catalog #	A-Side/B-Side	Year	VG	NM
Epic 9465	(I Know That) Your Heart's Not Made Of Wood / Dear Teddy	1961	2.00	10.00
Jubilee 5490	Runaround / There Must Be A Reason	1964	2.00	10.00

ANN-MICHAEL

Label & Catalog #	A-Side/B-Side	Year	VG	NM
Kip 0067	Teenage Cleopatra / Nine Out Of Ten	1963	2.00	10.00

ANNETTE (& THE AFTERBEATS)

Annette Funicello. Disneyland 118, Buena Vista 349 and 363 credit Annette & The Afterbeats.

Label & Catalog #		A-Side/B-Side	Year	VG	NM
Disneyland 722		I Can't Do The Sum / Just A Whisper Away	1957	3.00	15.00
Disneyland 758		How Will I Know My Love? / Annette	1957	3.00	15.00
Disneyland 758	(PS)	How Will I Know My Love? / Annette	1957	7.00	35.00
		(B-side by Jimmy Dodd)			
Disneyland 786		Happy Glow / That Crazy Place From Outer Space	1957	3.00	15.00
Disneyland 102		How Will I Know My Love? / Don't Jump To Conclusions	1958	3.00	15.00
Disneyland 102	(PS)	How Will I Know My Love? / Don't Jump To Conclusions	1958	7.00	35.00
Disneyland 105		Meetin' At The Malt Shop /	1958	6.00	30.00
Disneyland 105	(PS)	Meetin' At The Malt Shop /	1958	15.00	75.00
Disneyland 114		Gold Dubloons And Pieces Of Eight /			
		That Crazy Place From Outer Space	1958	6.00	30.00
Disneyland 118		Tall Paul / Ma, He's Making Eyes At Me	1958	3.00	15.00
Buena Vista 336		Jo-Jo The Dog-Faced Boy / Love Me Forever	1959	2.00	10.00
Buena Vista 336		Jo-Jo The Dog-Faced Boy / Lonely Guitar	1959	2.00	10.00
Buena Vista 339		Wild Willie / Lonely Guitar	1959	2.00	10.00
Buena Vista 339	(PS)	Wild Willie / Lonely Guitar	1959	5.00	25.00
Buena Vista 344		Especially For You / My Heart Became Of Age	1959	2.00	10.00
Buena Vista 349		First Name Initial / My Heart Became Of Age	1959	2.00	10.00
Buena Vista 349	(PS)	First Name Initial / My Heart Became Of Age	1959	5.00	25.00
Buena Vista 354		O Dio Mio / It Took Dreams	1960	2.00	10.00
Buena Vista 354	(PS)	O Dio Mio / It Took Dreams	1960	5.00	25.00

Annette Funicello was the main heartthrob for millions of American boys throughout the '50s and early '60s, primarily due to her exposure as a budding Mouseketeer on the original *Mickey Mouse Club* television series and as the star of seemingly countless beach movies. Her career as a recording artist was much less eventful, with only a handful of sides actually making the top 40. These facts tend to make her appeal a bit baffling to younger collectors.

Label & Catalog #		A-Side / B-Side	Year	VG	NM
Buena Vista 359		Train Of Love / Tell Me Who's The Girl?	1960	1.60	8.00
Buena Vista 359	(PS)	Train Of Love / Tell Me Who's The Girl?	1960	8.00	40.00
Buena Vista 362		Pineapple Princess / Luau Cha Cha Cha	1960	1.60	8.00
Buena Vista 362	(PS)	Pineapple Princess / Luau Cha Cha Cha	1960	5.00	25.00
Buena Vista 369		Talk To Me, Baby / I Love You, Baby	1960	1.60	8.00
Buena Vista 369	(PS)	Talk To Me, Baby / I Love You, Baby	1960	5.00	25.00
Buena Vista 374		Dream Boy / Please, Please, Signore	1961	1.60	8.00
Buena Vista 374	(PS)	Dream Boy / Please, Please, Signore	1961	5.00	25.00
Buena Vista 375		Indian Giver / Mama, Mama Rosa	1961	1.60	8.00
Buena Vista 375	(PS)	Indian Giver / Mama, Mama Rosa	1961	6.00	30.00
Buena Vista 384		Hawaiian Love Talk / Blue Muu Muu	1961	1.60	8.00
Buena Vista 384	(PS)	Hawaiian Love Talk / Blue Muu Muu	1961	6.00	30.00
Buena Vista 388		Dreamin' About You / The Strummin' Song	1961	1.60	8.00
Buena Vista 388	(PS)	Dreamin' About You / The Strummin' Song	1961	6.00	30.00
Buena Vista 392		Seven Moons / That Crazy Place From Outer Space	1962	1.60	8.00
Buena Vista 392	(PS)	Seven Moons / That Crazy Place From Outer Space	1962	6.00	30.00
Buena Vista 394		The Truth About Youth / I Can't Do The Swim	1962	1.50	8.00
Buena Vista 394	(PS)	The Truth About Youth / I Can't Do The Swim	1962	7.00	35.00
Buena Vista 400		My Little Grass Shack / Hukilau Song	1962	1.60	8.00
Buena Vista 405		He's My Ideal / Mr. Piano Man	1962	1.60	8.00
Buena Vista 405	(PS)	He's My Ideal / Mr. Piano Man	1962	5.00	25.00
Buena Vista 407		Bella Bella Florence / Canzone D' Amore	1962	1.60	8.00
Buena Vista 407	(PS)	Bella Bella Florence / Canzone D' Amore	1962	20.00	100.00
Buena Vista 414		Teenage Wedding / Walking And Talking	1963	1.60	8.00
Buena Vista 414	(PS)	Teenage Wedding / Walking And Talking	1963	75.00	300.00
Buena Vista 427		Treat Him Nicely / Promise Me Anything	1963	1.60	8.00
Buena Vista 427	(PS)	Treat Him Nicely / Promise Me Anything	1963	8.00	40.00
Buena Vista 431		Merlin Jones / The Scrambled Egghead	1963	1.60	8.00
Buena Vista 431	(PS)	Merlin Jones / The Scrambled Egghead	1963	7.00	35.00
Buena Vista 432		Custom City / Rebel Rider	1963	2.40	12.00
Buena Vista 432	(PS)	Custom City / Rebel Rider	1963	8.00	40.00
Buena Vista 433		Muscle Beach Party / I Dream About Frankie	1964	4.00	20.00
Buena Vista 433	(PS)	Muscle Beach Party / I Dream About Frankie	1964	5.00	25.00
		("Muscle Beach Party" features The Honeys.)			
Buena Vista 436		Bikini Beach Party / The Clyde	1964	4.00	20.00
Buena Vista 436	(PS)	Bikini Beach Party / The Clyde	1964	6.00	30.00
Buena Vista 437		The Wah Watusi / The Clyde	1964	2.00	10.00
Buena Vista 438		Something Borrowed, Something Blue / How Will I Know My Love?	1964	2.50	12.00
Buena Vista 438	(PS)	Something Borrowed, Something Blue / How Will I Know My Love?	1964	16.00	80.00
Buena Vista 440		The Monkey's Uncle / How Will I Know My Love?	1965	2.00	10.00
Buena Vista 440	(PS)	The Monkey's Uncle / How Will I Know My Love?	1965	4.00	20.00
		("The Monkey's Uncle" features The Beach Boys)			
Buena Vista 442		Boy To Love / No One Could Be Prouder	1965	3.00	15.00
Buena Vista 450		No Way To Go But Up / Crystal Ball	1966	3.00	15.00
Buena Vista 475		Merlin Jones / The Computer Wore Tennis Shoes	1966	3.00	15.00
Epic 9828		Baby Needs Me Now / Moment Of Silence	1965	4.00	20.00
Tower 326		What's A Girl To Do? / When You Get What You Want	1967	5.00	25.00
		("What's A Girl To Do" features Davie Allan on guitar.)			
		— Extended Play Albums—			
Disneyland 04		Tall Paul	1959	30.00	150.00
Disneyland 69		Mickey Mouse Club	1959	30.00	150.00
Buena Vista 3301		Annette	1959	30.00	150.00
Famous Stars 378	(DJ)	The Monkey's Uncle (Open-end interview)	1965	30.00	150.00

ANNETTE & TOMMY SANDS

Buena Vista 802		Let's Get Together / The Parent Trap	1961	3.00	15.00
Buena Vista 802	(PS)	Let's Get Together / The Parent Trap	1961	7.00	35.00

ANNETTE & FRANKIE AVALON
Annette and Frankie are backed by The Ventures.

Pacific Star 569		Together We Can Make A Merry Christmas / The Night Before Christmas (Red vinyl)	198?	1.00	5.00
Pacific Star 569	(PS)	Together We Can Make A Merry Christmas / The Night Before Christmas	198?	1.00	5.00

ANNIE & THE ORPHANS

Capitol 5144		My Girl's Been Bitten By The Beatle Bug / A Place Called Happiness	1964	3.00	15.00

ANSWERS, THE

White Whale 225		I'll Be In / Why You Smile	1966	4.00	20.00

ANTELL, PETE

Cameo 234		Night Time / Something About You	1962	1.60	8.00
Cameo 264		Keep It Up / You In Disguise	1963	1.20	6.00
Bounty 101		Land Of Love / ?	1965	1.20	6.00

Label & Catalog #	A-Side/B-Side	Year	VG	NM
Bounty 103	The Times They Are A-Changing /			
	Yesterday And Tomorrow	1965	2.00	10.00

ANTHONY, FRANKIE

Joey 101	Goin' To The River / Brenda	1962	3.00	15.00
Paradise 1003	Goin' To The River / Brenda	1963	2.00	10.00
DRA 329	Little Girls Have Big Ears / I'm A New Personality	1963	2.00	10.00

ANTHONY, MARK

Porter 1005	Wolf Call /	196?	7.00	35.00
LaBelle 779	Mama's Twistin' With Santa / Music From Studio "D"	1961	1.20	6.00

ANTHONY, PAUL

Firefly	Bop Bop Bop / My Promise To You	1958	15.00	75.00
Roulette 4099	Bop Bop Bop / My Promise To You	1958	4.00	20.00
Metro Inter. 1003	Step Up / Look At Me Now	195?	10.00	50.00
Gambit 1103	Angel Face / Hello Teardrops, Goodbye Love	195?	10.00	50.00

ANTHONY, RAYBURN (RAY B. ANTHONY)

Sun 333	Alice Blue Gown / St. Louis Blues	1960	2.00	10.00
Sun 339	There's No Tomorrow /			
	Who's Gonna Shine Your Pretty Little Feet?	1960	2.00	10.00
Sun 373	How Well I Know / Big Dream	1962	2.00	10.00

ANTHONY & THE SOPHOMORES
Anthony & The Sophomores also recorded as Tony Maresca & The Dynamics.

Grand 163	Embraceable You / Beautiful Dreamer	196?	10.00	50.00
Mercury 72103	Play Those Oldies, Mr. DJ / Clap Your Hands	1963	15.00	75.00
Mercury 72168	Better Late Than Never / Swingin' A Chariot	1963	5.00	25.00
Jamie 1330	Serenade / Workout	1965	4.00	20.00
Jamie 1340	One Summer Night / Workout	1965	3.00	15.00
ABC-Paramount 10737	Gee (But I'd Give The World) / It Depends On You	1965	3.00	15.00
ABC-Paramount 10770	Wild For Her / Get Back To You	1966	4.00	20.00
ABC-Paramount 10844	I'll Go Through Life Loving You / Heartbreak	1966	3.00	15.00

ANTOINETTE, MARIE

Providence 405	He's My Dream Boy / Quiet Guy	1963	4.00	20.00

ANUNSON, BRYCE

Nolta 346	Daffodil Lane / I Can't Believe It's True	196?	2.00	10.00

APES, THE

Mercury 72219	Don't Monkey With The Pony / Tarzan's Monkey	1964	1.20	6.00

APOSTLES, THE

A-Square 401	Stranded In The Jungle / Tired Of Waiting	196?	3.00	15.00
Kapp 2011	Six Pack / Soul Fiesta	196?	1.00	5.00

APPALACHIANS, THE

ABC-Paramount 10331	Cleopatra, Queen Of The Nile / All My Trials, Lord	1962	2.00	10.00
ABC-Paramount 10419	It Takes A Man / Bony Moronie	1963	2.00	10.00
ABC-Paramount 10464	Big Betty / Hill-Billy-Ding-Dong-Choo-Choo	1963	2.00	10.00
ABC-Paramount 10498	Lawdy Miss Clawdy / Over Yonder	1963	2.00	10.00

APPARITIONS, THE

Caped Crusader 71	She's So Satisfyin' / Midnight Hour *(White vinyl)*	1966	.80	4.00
Caped Crusader 71 (PS)	She's So Satisfyin' / Midnight Hour	1966	.80	4.00

APPLE, THE

Smash 2143	Thank U Very Much /			
	Your Heart Is Free Just Like The Wind	1968	2.00	10.00

APPLEJACKS, THE

Decca 29218	My Heart Will Wait For You / Smarter	1954	2.00	10.00
Decca 29330	Sweet Patootie / Reunion	1954	2.00	10.00
Tone Craft 200	Honey Bunch / Okey Dokey	1955	2.00	10.00
President 1005	Ring Around My Baby / Love Express	1956	2.00	10.00
President 1006	Teenage Meeting / Ooh Baby, Ooh	1956	2.00	10.00
President 1011	The Rock And Roll Story / Rainbow Of Love	1956	2.00	10.00
Cameo 110	Love In The Jungle / Chitter Chatter Baby	1957	2.00	10.00
Cameo 132	Dinner With Drac / No Name Theme	1958	3.00	15.00
	("Dinner With Drac" features the same backing track as the hit by Zacherle.)			
Cameo 138	Moonlight Serenade / Walk On	1958	2.00	10.00
Cameo 149	Mexican Hat Rock / Sophisticated Swing	1958	2.00	10.00
Cameo 149	Mexican Hat Rock / Stop! Red Light	1958	2.00	10.00
Cameo 155	Rocka Conga / Am I Blue?	1958	2.00	10.00
Cameo 155	Rocka Tonga / Am I Blue?	1958	2.00	10.00
Cameo 158	Bunny Hop / Night Train Stroll	1959	2.00	10.00

Label & Catalog #	A-Side/B-Side	Year	VG	NM
Cameo 170	Love Scene / Circle Dance	1959	2.00	10.00
Cameo 177	The Untouchables / Memories	1960	2.00	10.00
Cameo 184	Theme From "The Young Ones" / September Song	1960	2.00	10.00
Cameo 203	Mexican Hat Twist / Cherry Valley	1961	1.60	8.00
Cameo 222	Struttin' In The Summertime / Anytime	1962	1.60	8.00
Cameo 248	Back In Sixty Seconds / Hippies Waltz	1963	1.60	8.00
Cameo 321	She Loves You / Bongo Beach	1964	2.00	10.00
London 9658	Tell Me / Baby Jane	1964	1.00	5.00
London 9681	Like Dreamers Do / Everybody Fall Down	1964	1.00	5.00
London 9709	You're The One / Send Me Love	1964	1.00	5.00
London 9709	Three Little Words / You're The One	1964	1.00	5.00

APPLETREE THEATRE, THE

Verve 5082	Lotus Flower / What A Way To Go	1967	1.20	6.00

AQUANAUTS, THE

Safari 1005	Rumble On The Docks / Bamboora	1963	8.00	40.00

AQUANAUTS, THE

Sande 104	Swim All Day / Highdivin'	1964	3.00	15.00

AQUATONES, THE

Fargo 1001	You / She's The One For Me	1958	3.00	15.00
Fargo 1002	Say You'll Be Mine / So Fine	1958	3.00	15.00
Fargo 1003	Our First Kiss / The Drive-In	1958	3.00	15.00
Fargo 1005	My One Desire / My Treasure	1959	3.00	15.00
Fargo 1015	Everytime / There's A Long, Long Trail	1959	3.00	15.00
Fargo 1016	Crazy For You / Wanted	1960	4.00	20.00
Fargo 1022	My Treasure / Say You'll Be Mine	1960	3.00	15.00
Fargo 1111	My Darling / For You, For You	1961	3.00	15.00

ARBOGAST & ROSS

Liberty 55197	Chaos / Chaos, Part 2	1959	3.00	15.00

ARCADES, THE

Triad 502	The Soul P.W. / There's Got To Be A Loser	196?	3.00	15.00

ARCHERS, THE

Summer 502	Motorcycle Michael / Golden Girl	196?	6.00	30.00

ARCHIES, THE

The Archies are a studio creation under the direction of Ron Dante.

Calendar 1006		Bang Shang A Lang / Truck Driver	1968	1.00	5.00
Calendar 1006	(PS)	Bang Shang A Lang / Truck Driver	1968	2.00	10.00
Calendar 1007		Feelin' So Good / Love Light	1968	1.00	5.00
Calendar 1007	(PS)	Feelin' So Good / Love Light	1968	2.00	10.00
Calendar 1008		Sugar Sugar / Melody Hill	1969	1.00	5.00
Kirshner 1009		Sunshine / Over And Over	1969	.80	4.00
Post Cereal		Post Cereal Picture Discs	1969	3.00	15.00
		(These are a series of one-sided cardboard, cartoon picture discs from Post Cereal boxes. The price is for any one record still on the cereal box panel.)			
Post Cereal		Post Cereal Picture Discs	1969	1.00	5.00
		(The price is for any of the records cut and trimmed from the box.)			
Kirshner 5002		Jingle Jangle / Justine	1969	1.00	5.00
Kirshner 5003		Who's Your Baby? / Senorita Rita	1970	.60	3.00
Kirshner 5009		Together, We Two / Everything's Alright	1970	.60	3.00
Kirshner 5011		This Is Love / Throw A Little Love My Way	1970	.60	3.00
Kirshner 5014		Maybe I'm Wrong / A Summer Prayer For Peace	1971	.60	3.00
Kirshner 5014	(PS)	Maybe I'm Wrong / A Summer Prayer For Peace	1971	2.00	10.00
Kirshner 5018		Love Is Living In You / Hold On To Lovin'	1971	1.00	5.00
Kirshner 5021		Plumb Crazy / Strangers In The Morning	1972	1.00	5.00

ARDELLS, THE

Marco 102	Every Day Of The Week / Roll On	1961	3.00	15.00
Selma 4001	Seven Lonely Nights / You Can Fall In Love	1963	3.00	15.00
Epic 9621	Effenanny / Lonely Valley	1963	2.00	10.00

ARDEN, BOB

Rich Tone 18361	Giovanni / Party Girl	196?	3.00	15.00

ARGYLES, THE: *Refer to* THE HOLLYWOOD ARGYLES

ARIEL

Brent 7060	It Feels Like I'm Crying / I Love You	196?	2.00	10.00

ARK

MGM 13789	Poverty Train / Daily Reminder	1967	4.00	20.00

Label & Catalog #	A-Side/B-Side	Year	VG	NM
ARLIN, BOB				
Olympia 500	**707 / 708**	*196?*	3.00	15.00
Olympia	**East L.A. /**	*196?*	3.00	15.00
ARMAGEDDON				
Armageddon features Keith Relf, formerly of The Yardbirds.				
Capitol 3142	**Get Yourself Together / Get Yourself Together, Part 2**	1972	1.00	5.00
ARMSTRONG, JIMMY				
Zell's 1009	**Rise Sally, Come To Me /**	1963	2.00	10.00
ARNE, SKIP, & THE DUKES				
Dot 16627	**Sunshine And Rain / Angel**	1964	1.60	8.00
ARNGRIM, STEPHAN				
Jerden 915	**You Got Style / Cloudy Day**	1967	2.00	10.00
Jerden 916	**Where Has Christmas Gone? / Cooper's Lagoon**	1969	2.00	10.00
ACA 102	**The Subliminal Kid /**	1975	1.00	5.00
ARNO, AUDREY				
Decca 31238	**La Pachanga / Believe**	1961	1.20	6.00
ARNOLD, JERRY				
Security 106	**Race For Time / Let's Take A Ride**	1958	25.00	125.00
Cameo 120	**Race For Time / Let's Take A Ride**	1958	10.00	50.00
ARNOLD, P. P.				
Immediate 1901	**First Cut Is The Deepest / Speak To Me**	1967	2.00	10.00
Immediate 5006	**Though It Hurts Me Badly / (If You Think You're) Groovy**	1968	2.00	10.00
ARNOLD, VANCE, & THE AVENGERS				
Vance Arnold is a pseudonym for Joe Cocker.				
Philips 40255	**I'll Cry Instead / Those Precious Words**	1964	6.00	30.00
ARROGANTS, THE				
Big A 12184	**Make Up Your Mind / Tomboy**	1959	4.00	20.00
Lute 6226	**Canadian Sunset / Mirror Mirror**	1962	5.00	25.00
Vaness 200	**Take Life Easy / Stone Broke**	*196?*	4.00	20.00
ARROWS, THE				
Cupid 105	**Run Like The Wind / When You Were Sweet Little Sixteen**	*196?*	2.00	10.00
ARROWS, THE: *Refer to* DAVIE ALLAN & THE ARROWS				
ARTHUR, JAY				
Smash 1805	**Lonely Girl On Sweetheart Mountain / Psychology**	1963	1.20	6.00
ARTIE & LINDA (WITH THE PREMIERS)				
Chancellor 1147	**Laughing On The Outside / Blueberry Hill**	1963	2.00	10.00
ARTIS, RAY				
"A" 111	**Art Of Love / That's All I Want From You**	1961	5.00	25.00
Bundy 222	**Dear Liz / Wella Wella**	1961	6.00	30.00
ASCOTS, THE				
Dual-Tone 1120	**Acapulco Run / The Gladiator**	*196?*	8.00	40.00
ASCOTS, THE				
Super 102	**Monkey See-Monkey Do / You Can't Do That**	*196?*	1.60	8.00
Super 103	**Midnight Hour / Midnight Hour, Part 2**	*196?*	1.60	8.00
Super 104	**Put Your Arms Around Me / Sookie Sookie**	*196?*	1.60	8.00
ASHBY, IRVING				
Imperial 5426	**Loco-Motion / Night Winds**	1957	2.00	10.00
ASHLY, JOHN				
Silver 1002	**Seriously In Love / I Want To Hear It From You**	1958	5.00	25.00
Silver 1005	**Cry Of The Wild Goose / One Love**	1959	3.00	15.00
ASHES, THE				
Vault 924	**Is There Anything I Can Do? / Every Little Prayer**	1964	2.00	10.00
Vault 936	**Dark On You Now / Rosie's Gone**	1964	2.00	10.00
Vault 972	**Homeward Bound / Sleeping Serenade**	1965	2.00	10.00
ASHLEY, DEL				
Del Ashley is a pseudonym for David Gates.				
Planetary 103	**Little Miss Stuck-Up / The Brighter Side**	1965	3.00	15.00
Manchester 101	**She Don't Cry /**	*196?*	4.00	20.00

Label & Catalog #		A-Side/B-Side	Year	VG	NM
ASSOCIATION, THE					
Association members include Jules Alexander, Ted Buechel, Brian Cole, Russ Giguere, Terry Kirkman and Jim Yester,					
who were later joined by Larry Ramos and Richard Thompson.					
Jubilee 5505		Babe, I'm Gonna Leave You /			
		Babe, Can't You Hear Me Call Your Name?	1965	5.00	25.00
Valiant 730		One Too Many Mornings / Forty Times	1966	2.00	10.00
Valiant 741		Along Comes Mary / Your Own Love	1966	2.00	10.00
		(First pressings of Valiant 741 have a wavy black line on the bottom of the label.)			
Valiant 741		Along Comes Mary / Your Own Love	1966	1.00	5.00
Valiant 747		Cherish / Don't Blame It On Me	1966	1.00	5.00
Valiant 755		Pandora's Golden Heebie Jeebies / Standing Still	1966	1.00	5.00
Valiant 755	(PS)	Pandora's Golden Heebie Jeebies / Standing Still	1966	2.00	10.00
Valiant 758		No Fair At All / Looking Glass	1966	1.00	5.00
Warner Bros. 7040		Pandora's Golden Heebie Jeebies / Standing Still	1967	.80	4.00
Warner Bros. 7041		Windy / Sometime	1967	.80	4.00
Warner Bros. 7074		Never My Love / Requiem For The Masses	1967	.80	4.00
Warner Bros. 7163		Everything That Touches You / We Love Us	1968	.80	4.00
		— Warner Bros. singles above have orange labels.—			
Warner Bros. 7195		Time For Livin' / Birthday Morning	1968	.60	3.00
Warner Bros. 7229		Six Man Band / Like Always	1968	.60	3.00
Warner Bros. 7267		Goodbye Columbus / The Time It Is Today	1969	.60	3.00
Warner Bros. 7277		Under Branches / Hear In Here	1969	.60	3.00
Warner Bros. 7305		Yes, I Will / I Am Up For Europe	1970	.60	3.00
Warner Bros. 7349		Are You Ready? / Dubuque Blues	1970	.60	3.00
Warner Bros. 7372		Just About The Same / Look At Me, Look At You	1970	.60	3.00
Warner Bros. 7429		Along The Way / Traveler's Guide	1970	.60	3.00
Warner Bros. 7471		P. F. Sloan / Traveler's Guide	1971	1.00	5.00
Warner Bros. 7515		Bring Yourself Home / It's Gotta Be Real	1971	.60	3.00
Warner Bros. 7524		Makes Me Cry / That's Racin'	1971	.60	3.00
Columbia 45602		Darling, Be Home Soon / Indian Wells Woman	1972	.60	3.00
Columbia 45654		Come The Fall / Kicking The Gong Around	1972	.60	3.00
Mums 6016		Names, Tags, Numbers And Labels / Rainbows Bent	1973	.60	3.00
RCA Victor PB-10217		Life Is A Carnival / One Sunday Morning	1975	.40	2.00
MCA 10217		One Sunday Morning / Life Is A Carnival	1975	.40	2.00
Elektra 47094		Dreamer / You Turn The Light On	1981	.40	2.00
Elektra 47146		Small Town Lovers / Across The Persian Gulf	1982	.40	2.00
		— Extended Play Albums—			
Warner Bros. 1767	(33)	The Association's Greatest Hits	1968	4.00	20.00
ASTRA-LITES, THE					
Tribute 101		It Was A Bomb / Lonely	1962	2.00	10.00
ASTRO JETS, THE					
Imperial 5760		Boom A Lay / Hide And Seek	1961	3.00	15.00
ASTRONAUTS, THE					
Trial 3521		Farewell / Chili Charlene	196?	35.00	175.00
ASTRONAUTS, THE					
Jan Ell 459		Geneva Twist / Take 17	1962	7.00	35.00
Luney 100		Ridge Route / Blast Off	1962	7.00	35.00
Vanrus 1000		Ski Lift / Blues Beat	1962	7.00	35.00
ASTRONAUTS, THE					
The Astronauts also recorded as The Sunshineward.					
Palladium 610		Come Along Baby / Trying To Get To You	1962	20.00	100.00
RCA Victor 47-8194		Baja / Kuk	1963	3.00	15.00
RCA Victor 47-8224		Hot Doggin' / Everyone But Me	1963	3.00	15.00
RCA Victor 47-8224	(PS)	Hot Doggin' / Everyone But Me	1963	6.00	30.00
RCA Victor 47-8298		Surf Party / Competition Coupe	1964	3.00	15.00
RCA Victor 47-8364		Swim, Little Mermaid / Go Fight For Her	1964	2.00	10.00
RCA Victor 47-8419		Ride The Wild Surf / Around And Around	1964	3.00	15.00
RCA Victor 47-8463		I'm A Fool / Can't You See I Do?	1964	2.00	10.00
RCA Victor 47-8499		Almost Grown / My Sin Is Pride	1965	2.00	10.00
RCA Victor 47-8545		Tomorrow's Gonna Be Another Day / Razzamatazz	1965	2.00	10.00
RCA Victor 47-8628		It Doesn't Matter Anymore / The La La Song	1965	2.00	10.00
RCA Victor 47-8885		Main Street / In My Car	1966	2.00	10.00
RCA Victor 47-9109		I Know You, Rider / Better Things	1967	3.00	15.00
		— Extended Play Albums—			
RCA Victor WLP-5-100		The Astronauts	1964	3.00	15.00
RCA Victor WLP-9-100		The Astronauts	1964	3.00	15.00
RCA Victor WLP-10-100		The Astronauts	1964	3.00	15.00
		(WLP 5, 9 and 10 were issued without covers as part of a ten EP jukebox set,			
		"Wurlitzer Discoteque Music," that has little value aside from these three.)			
ASTRONOTES, THE					
Dot 16621		Monkey Workout / Teenage Blues	1964	1.60	8.00

Label & Catalog #	A-Side/B-Side	Year	VG	NM
ASYLUM CHOIR, THE				
The Asylum Choir is Marc Benno and Leon Russell.				
Shelter 7313	Tryin' To Stay / Straight Brother	1971	.60	3.00
ATCHER, RANDY				
MGM	Indian Rock /	195?	2.00	10.00
ATKINS, DAVE, & HIS OFFBEATS				
Viv 106	Shake-Kum-Down /	1963	5.00	25.00
Back-Beat	Shake-Kum-Down /	196?	2.00	10.00
ATLANTICS, THE				
Columbia 42877	Bombora / Greensleeves	1963	4.00	20.00
Columbia 43023	War Of The Worlds / The Bow Man	1963	4.00	20.00
Rampart 643	Beaver Shot / Fine Fine Fine	1965	2.00	10.00
Rampart 647	Sonny And Cher / Sloop Dance	1965	2.00	10.00
ATTIC SOUNDS, THE				
Mike 4007	Shadows / Let Us Be Young	196?	3.00	15.00
ATTILA & THE HUNS				
Sara 65111	Cheryl / Lonely Huns	1966	1.60	8.00
ATTITUDES, THE				
Times Square 110	That Old Black Magic / Mama's Doin' The Jerk	1967	3.00	15.00
ATTITUDES, THE				
Dark Horse 10004	Ain't Love Enough? / The Whole World's Crazy	1975	.40	2.00
Dark Horse 10008	Lend A Hand / Honey, Don't Leave L.A.	1976	.40	2.00
Dark Horse 10011	Sweet Summer Music / If We Want To	1976	.40	2.00
Dark Horse 8404	Sweet Summer Music /	1977	.40	2.00
Dark Horse 8452	In A Stranger's Arms / Good News	1977	.40	2.00
AU GO-GO'S, THE				
Jest 1	Waited For You / All Over Town	196?	2.00	10.00
AUDIO, VI, & THE PULSATIONS				
Bolo 727	How Could I Tell You / Image Of A Boy	196?	2.00	10.00
AUDREY				
Plus 104	Dear Elvis / Dear Elvis, Part 2	1956	10.00	50.00
AUGUST, JUNE				
Groovie 101	Hip Kitty To The Bopper /	195?	6.00	30.00
AUM				
Fillmore 7000	Resurrection / Bye Bye, Baby	1969	1.00	5.00
Fillmore 7001	Little Brown Hen / Aum	1969	1.00	5.00
AUTOGRAPHS, THE				
Joker 715	Do The Duck / Do The Duck	196?	1.60	8.00
AUTUMNS, THE				
Amber 856	Never / Exodus	196?	2.00	10.00
Medieval 208	Dearest Little Angel / Maureen	196?	2.00	10.00
AVALANCHES, THE				
Warner Bros. 5407	Avalanche / Baby, It's Cold Outside	1964	2.00	10.00
AVALON, FRANKIE				
The former trumpet whiz kid (the "X" sides below) also recorded with Annette.				
"X" 0006	Trumpet Sorrento / The Book	1954	8.00	40.00
"X" 0026	Trumpet Tarantella / Dormi Dormi	1954	8.00	40.00
Chancellor 1004	Cupid / Jivin' With The Saints	1957	3.00	15.00
Chancellor 1006	Teacher's Pet / Shy Guy	1957	3.00	15.00
Chancellor 1011	Dede Dinah / Ooh La La	1958	3.00	15.00
Chancellor 1016	You Excite Me / Darlin'	1958	3.00	15.00
Chancellor 1021	Gingerbread / Blue Betty	1958	3.00	15.00
Chancellor 1021 (PS)	Gingerbread / Blue Betty	1958	5.00	25.00
Chancellor 1026	I'll Wait For You / What Little Girl?	1958	3.00	15.00
Chancellor 1026 (PS)	I'll Wait For You / What Little Girl?	1958	5.00	25.00
Chancellor 1031	Venus / I'm Broke	1959	3.00	15.00
Chancellor 1031	Venus / I'm Broke *(Pink label with two horizontal lines)*	1959	4.00	20.00
Chancellor 1031 (PS)	Venus / I'm Broke	1959	3.00	15.00
Chancellor 1036	Bobby Sox To Stockings / A Boy Without A Girl	1959	3.00	15.00
Chancellor 1036 (PS)	Bobby Sox To Stockings / A Boy Without A Girl	1959	4.00	20.00
	—*Original Chancellor singles above have pink labels.*—			

Label & Catalog #		A-Side/B-Side	Year	VG	NM
Chancellor 1004		Cupid / Jivin' With The Saints	1959	2.00	10.00
Chancellor 1006		Teacher's Pet / Shy Guy	1959	2.00	10.00
Chancellor 1011		Dede Dinah / Ooh La La	1959	2.00	10.00
Chancellor 1016		You Excite Me / Darlin'	1959	2.00	10.00
Chancellor 1021		Gingerbread / Blue Betty	1959	2.00	10.00
Chancellor 1026		I'll Wait For You / What Little Girl?	1959	2.00	10.00
Chancellor 1031		Venus / I'm Broke	1959	2.00	10.00
Chancellor 1031	(S)	Venus / I'm Broke	1960	8.00	40.00
Chancellor 1036		Bobby Sox To Stockings / A Boy Without A Girl	1959	2.00	10.00
Chancellor 1036	(S)	Bobby Sox To Stockings / A Boy Without A Girl	1960	6.00	30.00
Chancellor 1040		Just Ask Your Heart / Two Fools	1959	2.00	10.00
Chancellor 1040	(PS)	Just Ask Your Heart / Two Fools	1959	4.00	20.00
Chancellor 1040	(S)	Just Ask Your Heart / Two Fools	1960	6.00	30.00
Chancellor 1045		Why? / Swingin' On A Rainbow	1959	2.00	10.00
Chancellor 1045	(PS)	Why? / Swingin' On A Rainbow	1959	3.00	15.00
Chancellor 1045	(S)	Why? / Swingin' On A Rainbow	1960	6.00	30.00
Chancellor 1048		Don't Throw Away All Those Teardrops / Talk Talk Talk	1960	2.00	10.00
Chancellor 1048	(PS)	Don't Throw Away All Those Teardrops / Talk Talk Talk	1960	4.00	20.00
Chancellor 1052		Where Are You? / Tuxedo Junction	1960	2.00	10.00
Chancellor 1052	(PS)	Where Are You? / Tuxedo Junction	1960	3.00	15.00
Chancellor 1052	(S)	Where Are You? / Tuxedo Junction	1960	5.00	25.00
Chancellor 1056		Togetherness / Don't Let Love Pass By	1960	2.00	10.00
Chancellor 1056	(PS)	Togetherness / Don't Let Love Pass By	1960	3.00	15.00
Chancellor 1056	(S)	Togetherness / Don't Let Love Pass By	1960	5.00	25.00
Chancellor 1065		A Perfect Love / The Puppet Song	1960	2.00	10.00
Chancellor 1065	(PS)	A Perfect Love / The Puppet Song	1960	3.00	15.00
Chancellor 1071		All Of Everything / Call Me Anytime	1961	2.00	10.00
Chancellor 1071	(PS)	All Of Everything / Call Me Anytime	1961	3.00	15.00
Chancellor 5022	(DJ)	Frankie Avalon	196?	20.00	100.00
		(Set of five stereo, compact-33 jukebox singles. The price is for the set of five in a brown paper pack with insert. The five singles are listed and priced separately below.)			
Chancellor 5022-1	(DJ)	Lotta Livin' To Do / I Wish You Love	196?	3.00	15.00
Chancellor 5022-2	(DJ)	Sail A Crooked Ship / It Started All Over Again	196?	3.00	15.00
Chancellor 5022-3	(DJ)	The Music Stopped / Our Love Is Here To Stay	196?	3.00	15.00
Chancellor 5022-4	(DJ)	The Lonely Bit / Can't You Just See Yourself	196?	3.00	15.00
Chancellor 5022-5	(DJ)	What Is This Thing Called Love? / Opposites Attract	196?	3.00	15.00
Chancellor 1077		Gotta Get A Girl / Who Else But You?	1961	1.60	8.00
Chancellor 1081		The Summer Of '61 / Voyage To The Bottom Of The Sea	1961	1.60	8.00
Chancellor 1081	(PS)	The Summer Of '61 / Voyage To The Bottom Of The Sea	1961	2.00	10.00
Chancellor 1087		True, True Love / Married	1961	1.60	8.00
Chancellor 1087	(PS)	True, True Love / Married	1961	3.00	15.00
Chancellor 1095		Sleeping Beauty / The Lonely Bit	1961	1.60	8.00
Chancellor 1095	(PS)	Sleeping Beauty / The Lonely Bit	1961	3.00	15.00
Chancellor 1101		After You've Gone / If You Don't Think I'm Leaving	1961	1.60	8.00
Chancellor 1101	(PS)	After You've Gone / If You Don't Think I'm Leaving	1961	3.00	15.00
Chancellor 1107		You Are Mine / Ponchinella	1962	1.60	8.00
Chancellor 1107	(PS)	You Are Mine / Ponchinella	1962	2.50	12.00
Chancellor 1114		Venus / I'm Broke	1962	1.60	8.00
Chancellor 1115		A Miracle / Don't Let Me Stand In Your Way	1962	1.60	8.00
Chancellor 1115	(PS)	A Miracle / Don't Let Me Stand In Your Way	1962	2.50	12.00
Chancellor 1125		Welcome Back / Dance Bossa Nova	1963	1.60	8.00
Chancellor 1125	(PS)	Welcome Back / Dance Bossa Nova	1963	2.50	12.00
Chancellor 1131		My Ex-Best Friend / First Love Never Dies	1963	1.00	5.00
Chancellor 1134		Come Fly With Me / Girl Back Home	1963	1.00	5.00
Chancellor 1135		Cleopatra / Heartbeats	1963	1.00	5.00
Chancellor 1139		Beach Party / Don't Stop Now	1964	2.00	10.00
Chancellor 11FX-1		Christmas Holiday / Dear Gesu Bambino	196?	2.00	10.00
		—*Chancellor singles above have black labels.*—			
United Artists 728		Again / Don't Make Fun Of Me	1964	.80	4.00
United Artists 748		My Love Is Here To Stay / New Fangled, Jingle Jangle Swimming Suit From Paris	1964	.80	4.00
United Artists 748	(PS)	My Love Is Here To Stay / New Fangled, Jingle Jangle Swimming Suit From Paris	1964	2.00	10.00
United Artists 800		Moon River / Every Girl Should Get Married	1965	.80	4.00
United Artists 895		I'll Take Sweden / There'll Be Rainbows Again	1965	.80	4.00
Reprise 0697		But I Do / Dancing On The Stars	1968	.80	4.00
Reprise 0796		Don't You Do It / It's Over	1968	.80	4.00
Reprise 0826		For You, Love / Why Don't You Understand?	1969	.80	4.00
Amos 127		Woman Crying / The Star	1969	.90	4.00
Metromedia 181		Come On Back To Me, Baby / Empty	1970	.80	4.00
Metromedia 192		I Want You Near Me / Heart Of Everything	1970	.80	4.00
Regalia 5508		I'm In The Mood For Love / It's The Same Old Dream	197?	.60	3.00
De-Lite 1578		Venus *(Disco version)* / Venus	1976	.40	2.00
De-Lite 1582		Thank You For That Extra Sunrise / It's His Game	1976	.40	2.00
De-Lite 1584		It's Never Too Late / Where I Leave Off (And You Begin)	1976	.40	2.00
De-Lite 1589		Does She Wonder Where I Am / Midnight Lady	1977	.40	2.00
De-Lite 1591		Splish Splash / When I Said I Love You	1977	.40	2.00

Label & Catalog #		A-Side/B-Side	Year	VG	NM
De-Lite 1595		Roses Grow Beyond The Walls / Midnight Lady	1978	.40	2.00
De-Lite 907		Beauty School Dropout / Midnight Lady	1978	.40	2.00
De-Lite 907	(PS)	Beauty School Dropout / Midnight Lady	1978	.40	2.00
		—Extended Play Albums—			
"X" EXA-20		A Very Young Man With A Horn	1955	25.00	125.00
Chancellor A-5001		Frankie Avalon	1958	10.00	50.00
Chancellor B-5001		Frankie Avalon	1958	10.00	50.00
Chancellor C-5001		Frankie Avalon	1958	10.00	50.00
Chancellor A-5002		The Young Frankie Avalon	1959	10.00	50.00
Chancellor B-5002		The Young Frankie Avalon	1959	10.00	50.00
Chancellor C-5002		The Young Frankie Avalon	1959	10.00	50.00
Chancellor A-5004		Swingin' On A Rainbow	1959	10.00	50.00
Chancellor B-5004		Swingin' On A Rainbow	1959	10.00	50.00
Chancellor C-5004		Swingin' On A Rainbow	1959	10.00	50.00
Chancellor A-5011		Summer Scene	1960	8.00	40.00
Chancellor B-5011		Summer Scene	1960	8.00	40.00
Chancellor C-5011		Summer Scene	1960	8.00	40.00
Chancellor A-5012		The Good Old Summertime	1960	8.00	40.00
Chancellor B-5012		The Good Old Summertime	1960	8.00	40.00
Chancellor C-5012		The Good Old Summertime	1960	8.00	40.00
Chancellor 300		Sincerely, Frankie Avalon	1960	8.00	40.00
Chancellor 302		Guns Of The Timberland	1960	8.00	40.00
Chancellor 303		Ballad Of The Alamo	1960	8.00	40.00

AVANT-GARDE, THE

Columbia 44388	Yellow Beads / Honey And Gall	1967	1.00	5.00
Columbia 44590	Naturally Stoned / Honey And Gall	1968	1.00	5.00
Columbia 44701	Fly With Me / Revelation's Revolutions	1968	1.00	5.00

AVANTIS, THE

Argo 5436	Keep On Dancing / I Wanna Dance	1963	3.00	15.00

AVANTIS, THE

Chancellor 1144	Wax 'Em Down / Gypsy Surfer	1963	3.00	15.00
Ikon 115	Too Much / Mid-Night Blues	196?	3.00	15.00
Regency 108	Do The Surfin' Granny / Surfin' Granny	1964	5.00	25.00
Regency 110	Phantom Surfer / Lucille	1964	5.00	25.00

AVANTIS, THE

Pepper 435	You Got A Funny Way / One Man's Poison	196?	2.00	10.00

AVENGERS, THE

MGM 13465	Batman Theme / Back Side Blues	1966	2.00	10.00

AVENGERS VI, THE

Mark 56 202	Time Bomb / Slaughter On 10th Avenue	1966	10.00	50.00

AVENGERS, THE

F-G 104	When It's Over / You Can't Hurt Me Anymore	1966	5.00	25.00

AVERONES, THE: *Refer to* BOB & THE AVERONES

AVERSA, MICKEY, & THE INVADERS

LAP 108	Blast Off! / Land Of Broken Dreams	1965	7.00	35.00

AZALEAS, THE

Romulus 3001	One Drummer Can't Keep Time / Hands Off	1963	2.00	10.00

AZTECS, THE

Julian 110	World Of Woe /	196?	2.00	10.00

AZTECS, THE

World Artists 1029	Da Doo Ron Ron / Hi-Heel Sneekers	1964	2.00	10.00
Card 901	Teenage Hall Of Fame / Traffic Jam	196?	2.00	10.00

AZTECS, THE
The Aztecs also recorded with Billy Thorpe.

GNP/Crescendo 346	Summertime Blues / What'cha Gonna Do 'Bout It?	1965	2.00	10.00

B.

B. BUMBLE & THE STINGERS

Wax 13	Slumber Party /	196?	2.00	10.00
Wax 16	Poly Wog / Dolly's House	196?	2.00	10.00
Rendezvous 140	Bumble Boogie / School Day	1961	1.60	8.00
Rendezvous 151	Boogie Woogie / Near You	1961	1.60	8.00
Rendezvous 160	Bee Hive / Caravan	1962	1.60	8.00
Rendezvous 166	Nut Rocker / Nautilus	1962	1.60	8.00
Rendezvous 174	Rockin' On 'N Off / Mashed #5	1962	1.60	8.00
Rendezvous 179	Apple Knocker / The Moon And The Sea	1962	1.60	8.00
Rendezvous 182	Dawn Cracker / Scales	1963	1.60	8.00
Rendezvous 192	Baby Mash / Night Time Madness	1963	1.60	8.00
Mercury 72614	The Green Hornet Theme / Flight Of The Hornet	1966	1.60	8.00

B.R.A.T.T.S., THE
The Brotherhood for the Re-establishment of American Top-Ten Supremacy.

Tollie 9024	Secret Weapon (The British Are Coming) / Jealous Kind Of Woman	1964	3.00	15.00

BABY BUGS, THE

Vee Jay 594		Bingo / Bingo's Bongo Bingo Party	1964	3.00	15.00
Vee Jay 594	(PS)	Bingo / Bingo's Bongo Bingo Party	1964	10.00	50.00

BABY RAY & THE FERNS

Donna 1378	How's Your Bird? / The World's Greatest Sinner	1963	40.00	200.00
	(Both sides written by Frank Zappa.)			

BACHELORS, THE

National 104	From Your Heart / Million Teardrops	1957	8.00	20.00
National 115	Today, Tomorrow, Forever / I Want A Girl	1957	8.00	20.00

BACHELORS, THE

Palace 123	Denied / Since I'm A Lovin,' I'm A Livin'	196?	2.00	10.00

BACK-BEAT PHILHARMONIC, THE

Laurie 3092	Rock And Roll Symphony / Rock And Roll Symphony, Part 2	1961	2.00	10.00

BACK PORCH MAJORITY, THE
The Back Porch Majority features Randy Sparks, formerly of The New Christy Minstrels.

Epic 9689	Friends / Hand-Me-Down Things	1964	.80	4.00
Epic 9754	Ol' Dan Tucker / Hey Nellie, Nellie	1965	.80	4.00
Epic 9769	Jack O' Diamonds / Smash Flops	1964	.80	4.00
Epic 9809	Ramblin' Man / Good-Time Joe	1965	.80	4.00
Epic 9850	Mighty Mississippi / Song Of Hope	1965	.80	4.00
Epic 9879	That's The Way It's Gonna Be / Second Hand Man	1966	.80	4.00
Epic 10036	Honey And Wine / Brother John	1966	.80	4.00
Epic 10079	Once Again / Slippery Sal And Dirty Dan, The Oyster Man	1966	.80	4.00
Epic 10129	Southtown U.S.A. / This Little Light	1967	.80	4.00
Epic	Back Porch Majority Picture Sleeve	196?	.80	4.00
	(Non-titled, omnibus sleeve for use with any of the Epic singles.)			

BAD BOYS, THE

Warner Bros. 5605	The Owl And The Pussycat / That's What I'll Do	1965	2.00	10.00

BAD BOYS, THE

Paula 254	Love / Black Olives	1967	2.00	10.00

BAD COMPANY

Swan Song 70015		Can't Get Enough / Little Miss Fortune	1974	.60	3.00
Swan Song 70100		Gone Gone Gone / Take The Time	1975	.60	3.00
Swan Song 70100	(PS)	Gone Gone Gone / Take The Time	1975	.80	4.00
Swan Song 70101		Movin' On / Easy On My Soul	1975	.60	3.00
Swan Song 70103		Feel Like Makin' Love / Wild Fire Woman	1975	.60	3.00
Swan Song 70108		Youngblood / Do Right By Your Woman	1976	.60	3.00
Swan Song 70109		Honey Child / Fade Away	1976	.60	3.00
Swan Song 70112		Burnin' Sky / Everything I Need	1977	.60	3.00
Swan Song 70119		Rock 'N' Roll Fantasy / Crazy Circles	1979	.60	3.00
Swan Song 70119	(PS)	Rock 'N' Roll Fantasy / Crazy Circles	1979	.60	3.00
Swan Song 71000		Gone, Gone, Gone / Take The Time	1979	.60	3.00

Label & Catalog #	A-Side/B-Side	Year	VG	NM
BAD SEEDS, THE				
J-Beck 1005	All Night Long / Sick And Tired	196?	3.00	15.00
C.O.L.	King Of The Soap Box /	196?	3.00	15.00

BADFINGER
Badfinger was Tom Evans, Mike Gibbins, Pete Ham, and Joey Molland, who originally recorded as The Iveys. Ham and Molland left in 1975, replaced by Peter Clarke and Tony Kaye.

Apple P-1815	*(DJ)* Come And Get It / Rock Of All Ages	1970	8.00	40.00
Apple 1815	Come And Get It / Rock Of All Ages	1970	2.00	10.00
Apple P-1822	*(DJ)* No Matter What / Carry On Till Tomorrow	1970	8.00	40.00
Apple 1822	No Matter What / Carry On Till Tomorrow	1970	2.00	10.00
Apple 1841	*(DJ)* Day After Day / Money *(White label)*	1971	15.00	75.00
Apple 1841	Day After Day / Money	1971	2.00	10.00
Apple 1844	*(DJ)* Baby Blue / Flying *(White label)*	1972	12.00	60.00
Apple 1844	Baby Blue / Flying	1972	2.00	10.00
Apple 1844	*(PS)* Baby Blue / Flying	1972	3.00	15.00
Apple P-1864	*(DJ)* Apple Of My Eye / Blind Owl	1973	800	40.00
Apple 1864	Apple Of My Eye / Blind Owl	1973	2.00	10.00
Warner Bros. 7801	I Miss You / Shine On	1974	1.25	6.00
Elektra 46025	Love Is Gonna Come At Last / Sail Away	1979	1.00	5.00
Elektra 46022	Lost Inside Your Love / Come Down Hard	1979	1.00	5.00
Radio 3793	Hold On / Passin' Time	1981	1.00	5.00
Radio 3815	I Got You / Rock 'N' Roll Contract	1981	1.00	5.00
Radio 3833	Because I Love You / Too Hung Up On You	1981	1.00	5.00

BADMAN, HICKEY
Hickey Badman is a pseudonym for Dickie Goodman.

Nixxon 1976	Revolution '76 / Convention '76	1976	1.00	5.00

BAG

Decca 32409	Up In The Morning / Down And Out	1969	1.00	5.00
Decca 32463	Red, Purple And Blue / I Want You By My Side	1969	1.00	5.00

BAG, THE

Jerden 769	Incubatin' Middle Of The Night Gyratin' Blues / Face It	1965	2.00	10.00

BAGDASARIAN, ROSS
Ross Bagdasarian also recorded as David Seville; Alfi & Harry; The Bedbugs; and The Chipmunks.

Coral 60544	Come On-A-My House / Oh, Beauty	1953	4.00	20.00
Mercury 70254	Lazy Lovers / One Finger Waltz	1954	3.00	15.00
Liberty 55013	The Bold And The Brave / See A Teardrop Fall	1956	2.50	12.00
Liberty 55275	Lazy Lovers / One Finger Waltz	1960	2.00	10.00
Liberty 55557	Cecile / Gotta Get To Your House	1963	2.00	10.00
Liberty 55619	Lucy, Lucy / Scallywags	1963	2.00	10.00
Liberty 55837	Come On-A-My House / Gotta Get To Your House	1965	2.00	10.00
Liberty 56004	Walking Birds Of Carnaby / Red Wine	1967	2.00	10.00
Liberty 56048	When I Look In Your Eyes / The Winds Of Time	1967	2.00	10.00
Imperial 66379	Spanish Pizza / Jone Cone Phone	1969	1.60	8.00
Imperial 66414	You've Got Me On A Merry-Go-Round / You Better Open Your Eyes	1969	1.60	800

BAGELS, THE

Warner Bros. 5420	I Wanna Hold Your Hair / Yeah, Yeah, Yeah, Yeah	1964	2.00	10.00

BAGGYS, THE

Pipeline 501	El Surfer / El Seagull	1963	7.00	35.00

BAIN, BABETTE

Rendezvous 108	That's It / Graduation Night	1959	2.00	10.00

BAKER, ABIE

Laurel 1010	Moccasin Rock / The Web	1959	3.00	15.00

BAKER, KENNY

Orbit 541	Goodbye, Little Star / I'm Gonna Love You	1959	4.00	20.00

BAKER, PENNY, & THE PILLOWS

Witch 123	Bring Back The Beatles / Gonna Win Him	1964	4.00	20.00

BAKER, RODNEY, & THE CHANTIERS

Jan-Ell 8	Teenage Wedding Song / Graduation	1961	5.00	25.00

BAKER, RONNIE, & THE DELTONES

Laurie 3128	My Story / I Want To Be Loved	1962	5.00	25.00

BAKER, RONNIE

Jell 200	Glory Be / This Big World	196?	3.00	15.00
Laurie 3250	See You In September / Young At Heart	1964	2.00	10.00

Label & Catalog #		A-Side/B-Side	Year	VG	NM

BAKER-GURVITZ ARMY, THE
The Army features Ginger Baker.

Label & Catalog #		A-Side/B-Side	Year	VG	NM
Atco 7043		People /	1974	.40	2.00

BAKER'S AIR FORCE, GINGER
Ginger Baker also recorded with Blind Faith; Cream.

Atco 6750		Man Of Constant Sorrow / Doin' It	1970	.60	3.00

BAKER'S DRUM CHOIR, GINGER

Atco 6816		Attunde / Attunde, Part 2	1970	.60	3.00

BALBOA

Event 200		Jimmy And Janis / Your Love's All Mine	1970	2.00	10.00

BALDRY, LONG JOHN

A&M 974		When The Sun Comes Shinin' Through / Wise To The Ways Of The World	1968	.80	4.00
Warner Bros. 7098		Let The Heartaches Begin / Hey Lord, You Made The Night Too Long	1968	.80	4.00
Warner Bros. 7184		Hold Back The Daybreak / Since I Lost You, Baby	1969	.80	4.00
Warner Bros. 7506		Don't Try To Lay No Boogie Woogie On The King Of Rock And Roll / Mr. Rubin	1971	.60	3.00
Warner Bros. 7516		Don't Try To Lay No Boogie Woogie On The King Of Rock And Roll / Don't Try To Lay No Boogie Woogie, Part 2	1971	.60	3.00
Warner Bros. 7597		Iko Iko / You Can't Judge A Book By Its Cover	1972	.60	3.00
Warner Bros. 7617		Mother Ain't Dead / You Can't Judge A Book By Its Cover	1972	.60	3.00
EMI/America 8018		You've Lost That Loving Feeling / Baldry's Out	1979	.50	2.50
EMI/America 8018	(PS)	You've Lost That Loving Feeling / Baldry's Out	1979	.50	2.50
		("You've Lost That Loving Feeling" is a duet with Kathi McDonald.)			

BALIN, MARTY
Marty balin was the founder of Jefferson Airplane.

Challenge 9146		Nobody But You / You Made Me Fall	1962	6.00	30.00
Challenge 9156		I Specialize In Love / You're Alive With Love	1962	6.00	30.00

BALL, LINDA

Jerden 816		The End / Always You	1966	.80	4.00
Tower 308		Last Train To Clarksville / I Wanna Be Free	1967	1.20	6.00

BALLADEERS, THE

Del-Fi 4123		Morning Star / Tom Gets The Last Laugh	1959	3.00	15.00
Del-Fi 4127		Turtle Dove / Durant Jail	1959	3.00	15.00
Del-Fi 4138		Hurtin' (For The Love Of You) / Roll Call Company J	1960	3.00	15.00

BALLADS, THE

Franwil 5028		Before You Fall In Love / Broke	196?	10.00	50.00

BALLOON FARM, THE

Laurie 3405		A Question Of Temperature / Hurtin' For Your Love	1968	2.00	10.00
Laurie 3445		Hurry Up, Sundown / Farmer Brown	1968	2.00	10.00

BANANA & THE BUNCH
Lowell "Banana" Levinger of The Youngbloods.

Warner Bros. 7621		My True Life Blues / Vanderbilt's Lament	1972	.60	3.00
Warner Bros. 7626		Back In The U.S.A. / Back In The U.S.A.	1972	.60	3.00

BANANA SPLITS, THE

Decca 32391		Wait 'Till Tomorrow / We're The Banana Splits	1968	2.00	10.00
Decca 32429		The Tra La La Song / Toy Piano Melody	1970	2.00	10.00
Decca 32429	(PS)	The Tra La La Song / Toy Piano Melody	1970	3.00	15.00
Decca 21516		Long Live Love / Pretty Painted Carousel	1970	2.00	10.00
Decca 21516	(PS)	Long Live Love / Pretty Painted Carousel	1970	3.00	15.00
		—Extended Play Albums—			
Kellogg's 34578	(DJ)	The Tra-La-La Song	1968	5.00	25.00
Kellogg's 34579	(DJ)	Doin' The Banana Split	1968	5.00	25.00

BAND, THE
The Band was Rick Danko, Garth Hudson, Levon Helm, Richard Manuel and Robbie Robertson. Refer to The Canadian Squires; Bob Dylan; Bob Dylan / The Band; Levon & The Hawks; and Ronnie Hawkins.

Capitol 2041		Jabberwocky / Never Too Much Love	1968	1.00	5.00
Capitol 2269		The Weight / I Shall Be Released	1968	.60	3.00
Capitol 2635		Up On Cripple Creek / The Night They Drove Old Dixie Down	1969	.60	3.00
Capitol 2705		Rag Mama Rag / Unfaithful Servant	1970	.60	3.00
Capitol 2705	(PS)	Rag Mama Rag / Unfaithful Servant	1970	1.00	5.00
Capitol 2879		Time To Kill / The Shape I'm In	1970	.50	2.50
Capitol 3199		Life Is A Carnival / The Moon Struck One	1971	.50	2.50
Capitol 3249		When I Paint My Masterpiece / Where Do We Go From Here	1972	Unreleased?	

Label & Catalog #	A-Side/B-Side	Year	VG	NM
Capitol 3433	Rag Mama Rag / Don't Do It	1973	.50	2.50
Capitol 3500	Caledonia Mission / Hang Up My Rock 'N' Roll Shoes	1973	.40	2.00
Capitol 3758	Ain't Got No Home / Get Up, Jake	1973	.40	2.00
Capitol 3828	Third Man Theme / W.S. Walcott Medicine Show	1974	.40	2.00
Capitol 4230	Ophelia / Hobo Jungle	1976	.40	2.00
Capitol 4316	The Twilight / Acadian Driftwood	1976	.40	2.00
Capitol 4361	Georgia On My Mind /			
	The Night They Drove Old Dixie Down	1976	.40	2.00
Warner Bros. 8592	The Well / Out Of The Blue	1978	.40	2.00

BAND-LONS, THE
Sonic 82661	Miserlou / Honkeytonk	196?	5.00	25.00

BAND WITHOUT A NAME, THE
The Band Without A Name features Davy Allen and may be a pseudonym for The Arrows.
Tower 246	Turn On Your Lovelight / A Perfect Girl	1966	1.60	8.00
Tower 246 (PS)	Turn On Your Lovelight / A Perfect Girl	1966	3.00	15.00
Sidewalk 913	Theme From "Thunder Alley" /			
	Time After Time (I Keep Loving You)	1967	2.00	10.00

BANDITS, THE
Jerden 773	Little Sally Walker / Tell Me	1966	2.00	10.00
Panorama 34	Queen Jane / I Remember The Girl	1966	2.00	10.00

BANGS, THE
The Bangs feature Susanna Hoffs and Debbi and Vicki Peterson, who later recorded as The Bangles.
Downkiddie 001	Getting Out Of Hand / Call On Me	1981	4.00	20.00
Downkiddie 001 (PS)	Getting Out Of Hand / Call On Me	1981	6.00	30.00

BANKS, BESSIE
Tiger 102	Go Now / It Sounds Like My Baby	1964	3.00	15.00

BANKS, DICK
Liberty 55145	Dirty Dog /	195?	4.00	20.00

BANNED
Fontana 1616	It Couldn't Happen Here / Annie Went To Ohio	1968	2.00	10.00
Fontana 1616 (PS)	It Couldn't Happen Here / Annie Went To Ohio	1968	2.00	10.00

BANNERS, THE
MGM 12862	Fortune Teller / Sales Talk	1960	1.60	8.00

BANTAMS, THE
Warner Bros. 5695	Follow Me / Meet Me Tonight, Little Girl	1966	.80	4.00
Warner Bros. 5695 (PS)	Follow Me / Meet Me Tonight, Little Girl	1966	1.00	5.00

BARBARA & THE BELIEVERS
Capitol 5866	When You Wish Upon A Star / What Can Happen To Me Now	1967	3.00	15.00

BARBARA & THE BOYS
Dot 15798	Hooty Sapperticker / Cobra	1958	3.00	15.00

BARBARIANS, THE
Joy 290	Hey, Little Bird / You've Got To Understand	1964	5.00	25.00
Laurie 3308	Are You A Boy Or Are You A Girl? / Take It Or Leave It	1965	2.00	10.00
Laurie 3321	What The New Breed Say / Susie Q	1965	2.00	10.00
Laurie 3326	Moulty / I'll Keep On Seeing You	1966	2.00	10.00

BARBAROSA & THE HISTORIANS
Jade 110/20	When I Fall In Love / Zoom	196?	3.00	15.00

BARBER, GLENN
Starday 249	Shadow My Baby / Feeling No Pain	195?	30.00	150.00

BARBER BROTHERS, THE
Decca 30753	Well, All Right / How Can You Tell If It's Love?	195?	4.00	20.00
Decca 30811	Lovin' Honey / Sunbeam	195?	6.00	30.00

BARBER GREEN, THE
F-Empire 1106	Life / Gliding Ride	196?	2.00	10.00

BARBOUR, KEITH
Epic 10486	Echo Park / Here I Am Losing You	1969	.80	4.00

BARD, ANNETTE
Annette Bard is a pseudonym of former Teddy Bear Annette Kleinbard, who also recorded as Carol Connors.
Imperial 5643	What Difference Does It Make? / Alibi	1960	7.00	35.00

Label & Catalog #		A-Side/B-Side	Year	VG	NM
BARDS, THE					
Piccadilly 224		The Owl And The Pussycat / Light Of Love	1966	1.00	5.00
Piccadilly 232		The Jabberwocky / My Generation	1967	1.00	5.00
Piccadilly 242		Never Too Much Love / Light Of Love	1967	1.00	5.00
Capitol 2041		Never Too Much Love / Jabberwocky	1967	1.00	5.00
Capitol 2148		The Owl And The Pussycat / The Light Of Love	1968	1.20	6.00
Capitol 2148	(PS)	The Owl And The Pussycat / The Light Of Love	1968	3.00	15.00
Jerden 907		Goodtime Charlie's Got The Blues / Tunesmith	1969	1.00	5.00
Parrot 334		Jubilation / Our Love	1969	.60	3.00
Parrot 337		Goodtime Charlie's Got The Blues / Tunesmith	1969	.60	3.00
Parrot 351		Walla Walla / Day By Day	1969	.80	4.00
Burdette 103		I Want You / Freedom Catcher	1971	1.00	5.00
BARE, BOBBY					

After several years of attempts at making it as a rock 'n roller, Bobby Bare signed with RCA Victor in 1962 and while he finally made the pop charts, his RCA recordings moved him into the more lucrative country market.

Capitol 3771		The Livin' End / Beggar	195?	2.00	10.00
Fraternity 861		I'm Hanging Up My Rifle / That's Where I Want To Be	1959	4.00	20.00
Fraternity 867		More Than A Poor Boy Could Give / Sweet Singin' Sam	1960	2.00	10.00
Fraternity 871		No Letter From My Baby / Lynchin' Party	1960	1.25	6.00
Fraternity 878		Book Of Love / Lorena	1961	1.25	6.00
Fraternity 885		Island Of Love / Sailor Man	1961	1.25	6.00
Fraternity 890		Zig Zag / Brooklyn Bridge	1961	1.25	6.00
Fraternity 892		That Mean Old Clock / The Day My Rainbow Fell	1961	1.25	6.00
BARE FAT					
Bang 573		You Can All Join In / Soft	1970	.80	4.00
BARIN, PETE, & THE BELMONTS					
Sabina 504		So Wrong / Broken Heart	1962	10.00	50.00
Sabina 512		The Loneliest Guy In The World / Look For Cindy	1963	6.00	30.00
BARITONES, THE					
Dore 501		After School Rock / Sentimental Baby	1958	8.00	40.00
BARKER, DELBERT					
King 4951		No Good Robin Hood / That's A Sin	195?	3.00	15.00
BARKER BROTHERS, THE					
Kent 302		Hey, Little Mama / I'm In Love With My Teacher	195?	6.00	30.00
BARKLE, AL					
Frantic 108		Muscle Beach / Graduation Party	196?	3.00	15.00
BARNES, BENNY, & THE ECHOES					
Mercury 71284		Moon Over My Shoulder / Lonely Street	1958	3.00	15.00
BARNES, BILL					
Columbia 43491		Sloop John B. / Repeat After Me	1966	.80	4.00
BARNETT, JIM, & THE SILHOUETTES					
Lavender 1454		Kaw-Liga / We Had A Quarrel	196?	2.00	10.00
BARNETT, WES					
Ripcord 127		Pine Ridge Reservation / Pine Ridge Reservation	196?	2.00	10.00
BARNSTORMERS, THE					
Capitol 4692		Big Stomp / Bug Stompin'	1962	3.00	15.00
BARONETS, THE					
Vee Jay 701		Mine All Mine / That's The Way Love Happens	1965	3.00	15.00
BARONS, THE					
Dart 126		Lovely Loretta / Lulu Mae	1962	3.00	15.00
Dart 134		Perfect Love / Until The 13th Chime	1963	3.00	15.00
Bellaire 103		Wanderin' / The Bandit	1963	2.00	10.00
Epic 9586		Pledge Of A Fool / Don't Go Away (Pretty Little Girl)	1963	6.00	30.00
Epic 9747		Remember Rita / Lucky Star	1964	15.00	75.00
Epic 10093		Pledge Of A Fool / Don't Go Away (Pretty Little Girl)	1966	2.00	10.00
BAROQUE BEATLES, THE					
Elektra 45602		You've Got To Hide Your Love Away / Ticket To Ride	1965	1.00	5.00
BAROQUES, THE					
Chess 2001		Mary Jane / Iowa, A Girl's Name	1967	3.00	15.00
BARRACUDAS, THE					
Canjo 104		Hot Rod U.S.A. / Boss Barracuda	1964	4.00	20.00

Label & Catalog #	A-Side/B-Side	Year	VG	NM
BARRACUDAS, THE				
MFI 102	It's Been So Long / Affection	196?	2.00	10.00
BARRAKAT, JOHNNY, & THE VESTELLES				
Dell-Star 103	Happy Tune / Long Ride	1964	5.00	25.00
BARRAN, BOB				
Silver Streak 311	Tom Tom Rock / Mother Goose Hop	1960	10.00	50.00
BARRETT, HUGH, & THE VICTORS				
Madison 164	Got The Bull By The Horns / There Was A Fungus Among Us	1961	4.00	20.00
BARRETTO, RAY				
Tico 419	El Watusi / Ritmo Sabroso	1963	3.00	15.00
BARRI, STEVE				
Steve Barri aslo recorded as The Fantastic Baggys; The Grass Roots; The Imaginations; The Inner Circle; The Lifeguards; The Rally Packs; The Rincon Surfside Band; The Storytellers; The Street Cleaners; and Willie & The Wheels.				
Rona 1003	Down Around The Corner / Please Let It Be You	1961	3.00	15.00
Rona 1004	I Want Your Love / The Story Of The Ring	1961	3.00	15.00
Rona 1005	Two Different Worlds / Don't Run Away From Love	1962	3.00	15.00
Rona 1006	Whenever You Kiss Me / Never Before	1962	3.00	15.00
BARRIES, THE				
Vernon 102	Why Don't You Write Me? / Mary-Ann	1964	8.00	40.00
Ember 1101	Tonight-Tonight / Mary-Ann	1964	6.00	30.00
BARRIES, THE				
Di-Nan 101	When You're Out Of School / Loneliest Man In Town	196?	1.50	8.00
BARRIX, BILLY				
Chess 1662	Cool Off, Baby / Almost	195?	——	——
	(Rare rockabilly. Estimated near mint value $4,000-5,000. Originally issued on a still Shreveport, LA, label. It would be worth even more than the Chess.)			
BARRY, DAVE, & SARA BERNER				
RPM 469	Out Of This World With Flying Saucers / Out Of This World With Flying Saucers, Part 2	1956	4.00	20.00
BARRY, JEFF				
Jeff Barry also recorded with The Raindrops and The Redwoods.				
RCA Victor 47-7477	It's Called Rock And Roll / Hip Couples	1958	4.00	20.00
RCA Victor 47-7797	Lonely Lips / Face From Outer Space	1960	4.00	20.00
RCA Victor 47-7821	All You Need Is A Quarter / Teen Quartet	1960	3.00	15.00
Decca 31037	It Won't Hurt / Never Never	1960	3.00	15.00
Decca 31089	Why Does The Feeling Go Away? / Lenore	1960	3.00	15.00
United Artists 440	We Got Love Money Can't Buy / Welcome Home	1962	2.00	10.00
Red Bird 026	I'll Still Love You / Our Love Can Still Be Saved	1965	2.00	10.00
United Artists 50529	Where It's At / Much Too Young	1969	1.00	5.00
A&M 1422	Walkin' In The Sun / Whatcha Gonna Do?	1972	.80	4.00
BARRY, JOE				
Jin 144	I'm A Fool To Care / I Got A Feeling	1961	3.00	15.00
Smash 1702	I'm A Fool To Care / I Got A Feeling	1961	1.60	8.00
Smash 1710	Teardrops In My Heart / For You, Sunshine	1961	1.60	8.00
Smash 1710 (PS)	Teardrops In My Heart / For You, Sunshine	1961	2.00	10.00
Smash 1745	Why Did You Say Goodbye? / Little Papoose	1962	1.60	8.00
Smash 1762	Just Because / Little Jewel Of The Veaux Carre	1962	1.60	8.00
BARRY, LEN				
Len Barry originally recorded with The Dovells.				
Mercury 72299	Happy Days / Let's Do It Again	1964	1.60	8.00
Cameo 303	Don't Come Back / Jim Dandy	1964	1.20	6.00
Cameo 318	Hearts Are Trump / Little White House	1964	1.60	8.00
Parkway 969	Hearts Are Trump / Little White House	1965	1.00	5.00
Decca 31788	Lip Sync (To The Tongue Twisters) / At The Hop '65	1965	.80	4.00
Decca 31827	1-2-3 / Bullseye	1965	.80	4.00
Decca 31889	Like A Baby / Happiness Is (A Girl Like You)	1966	.80	4.00
Decca 31969	It's That Time Of The Year / Happily Ever After	1966	.80	4.00
Decca 32011	I Struck It Rich / Love Is	1966	.80	4.00
Decca 32054	You Baby / Would I Love You?	1966	.80	4.00
RCA Victor 47-9150	The Moving Finger Writes / Our Love	1967	.80	4.00
RCA Victor 47-9275	All Those Memories / Rainy Side Of The Street	1967	.80	4.00
RCA Victor 47-9348	ABC's Of Love / Come Rain Or Shine	1967	.80	4.00
RCA Victor 47-9464	Sweet And Funky / I Like The Way	1968	.80	4.00
Amy 11026	4-5-6 (Now I'm Alone) / Funky Night	1968	.80	4.00
Amy 11037	Christopher Columbus / You're My Picasso, Baby	1969	.80	4.00

Label & Catalog #		A-Side/B-Side	Year	VG	NM
Amy 11047		A Child Is Born / Wouldn't It Be Beautiful?	1969	.80	4.00
Scepter 12251		Put Out The Fire / Spread It On Like Butter	1966	.60	3.00
Scepter 12263		Keem-O-Sabe / This Old World	1969	1.20	6.00
Scepter 12284		Bob And Carol And Ted And Alice /			
		In My Present State Of Mind	1970	.60	3.00
Buddah 284		Just The Two Of Us / Diggin' Life	1972	.60	3.00
Buddah 284	(PS)	Just The Two Of Us / Diggin' Life	1972	.60	3.00
Paramount 0206		Heaven + Earth / I'm Marching To The Music	197?	.60	3.00
		— Extended Play Albums—			
Decca 74720	(33)	1-2-3 (Jukebox EP)	1968	4.00	20.00

BARRY & THE DEANS
Zirkon 1001		Rock With Me, Baby / I'll Love You	1960	2.00	10.00

BARRY & THE TAMERLANES
Barry is Barry DeVorzon.
Valiant 6034		I Wonder What She's Doing Tonight? / Don't Go	1963	3.00	15.00
Valiant 6040		Roberta / Butterfly	1964	2.00	10.00
Valiant 6046		I Don't Want To Be Your Clown / Lucky Guy	1964	2.00	10.00
Valiant 6050		Pretty Things / A Date With Judy	1964	2.00	10.00
Valiant 6059		Don't Cry, Cindy / Gee	1965	2.00	10.00

BARTLEY, CHRIS
Vando 101		The Sweetest Thing This Side Of Heaven / Love Me, Baby	1967	1.00	5.00
Vando 3000		Baby, It's Wonderful / I'll Be Loving You	196?	1.00	5.00

BASH, OTTO
RCA Victor 47-6426		Later, Alligator / Lookout Mountain	1956	2.00	10.00
RCA Victor 47-6585		The Elvis Blues / Later	1956	5.00	25.00
HDS 2008		My Babe / Straighten Up And Fly Right	1956	2.00	10.00

BASKERVILLE HOUNDS, THE
Tema 128		Space Rock / Space Rock, Part 2	1966	3.00	15.00
Tema 131		Christmas Is Here / Make Me Your Man	1966	3.00	15.00
Tema 131	(PS)	Christmas Is Here / Make Me Your Man	1966	8.00	40.00
Tema 132		All You Had To Do Was Ask / Who Does She Love?	1967	3.00	15.00
Tema 135		Here I Come, Miami / Make Me Your Man	1967	3.00	15.00
Dot 17004		Space Rock / Space Rock, Part 2	1967	1.60	8.00
Dot 17017		Debbie / Jackie's Theme	1967	1.00	5.00

BASICS, THE
Lavender 1851		Basic Surf / Jailer Bring Me Water	196?	3.00	15.00
Lavender 2002		Oh, Lonely Me / Time	196?	2.00	10.00

BASSETT, TONY
Orchid 873		Rockin' Little Mama / Tonight And Always	1961	10.00	50.00

BASSMAN, MR., & THE SYMBOLS
Graphic Arts 1000		Rip Van Winkle / You're The One	196?	3.00	15.00

BATEMAN, GIL
Panorama 12		Wicked Love / Goodnight Irene	1965	1.20	6.00
Jerden 779		Daddy Walked In Darkness / One Eyed Cat	1965	1.20	6.00
Piccadilly 227		Wicked Love / How To Do It	1966	1.20	6.00
Piccadilly 249		The Night Before / The Night Before	1967	1.00	5.00

BATS, THE
HBR 445		Big Bright Eyes / Nothing At All	1965	1.20	6.00

BATS, THE
Flame 5155		Batmobile / Batusi	1966	5.00	25.00
		(Originally released as "Burning Rubber" / "Twin Pipes" credited to Gene Moles.)			

BATTEN, CECILIA
Colonial 431		My Big Brother's Friend / Before	1957	2.00	10.00

BATTIN, SKIP
Refer to The Byrds; Gary & Clyde; The Pledges; and Skip & Flip.
Signpost 70010	(DJ)	Ballad Of Dick Clark / Ballad Of Dick Clark	1973	.60	3.00
		(Stock copies of Signpost 70010 may not exist.)			

BATTYN, SKIP
Aurora 159		The Dating Game Theme / Night Time Girl	196?	1.20	6.00
Groove 0065		Ten Feet Tall / What's Mine Is Mine	195?	1.60	8.00

BAY BOPS, THE
Coral 61975		Joanie / Follow The Rock	1958	8.00	40.00
Coral 62004		My Darling, My Sweet / To The Party	1958	8.00	40.00

Label & Catalog #		A-Side/B-Side	Year	VG	NM

BAY CITY ROLLERS, THE [THE ROLLERS]

Bell 45169		Keep On Dancing / Alright	1972	.60	3.00
Bell 45274		Manana /	1973	.60	3.00
Bell 45481		Shang A Lang /	1974	.60	3.00
Bell 45607		Summer Love Sensation /	1975	.60	3.00
Bell 45618		All Of Me Loves You /	1975	.60	3.00
Arista 120		Bye Bye, Baby / It's For You	1975	.40	2.00
Arista 149		Saturday Night / Marlina	1975	.40	2.00
Arista 149	(PS)	Saturday Night / Marlina	1975	.60	3.00
Arista 170		Money Honey / Maryanne	1976	.40	2.00
Arista 170	(PS)	Money Honey / Maryanne	1976	.60	3.00
Arista 185		Rock And Roll Love Letter / Shanghai'd In Love	1976	.40	2.00
Arista 193		Don't Stop The Music / Don't Stop The Music	1976	.40	2.00
Arista 205		I Only Want To Be With You / Write A Letter	1976	.40	2.00
Arista 216		Yesterday's Hero / My Lisa	1976	.40	2.00
Arista 233		Dedication / Rock 'N Roller	1977	.40	2.00
Arista 233	(PS)	Dedication / Rock 'N Roller	1977	.60	3.00
Arista 256		You Made Me Believe In Magic / Dance, Dance, Dance	1977	.40	2.00
Arista 272		The Way I Feel Tonight / Love Power	1977	.40	2.00
Arista 363		Where Will I Be Now? / If You Were My Woman	1978	.40	2.00
Arista 363	(PS)	Where Will I Be Now? / If You Were My Woman	1978	.60	3.00
Arista 476		Turn On The Radio / Hello And Welcome Home	1978	.40	2.00

BAY RIDGE

Atlantic 2431		I Can't Get Her Out Of My Mind / Back Track	1967	1.00	5.00

BAYLANDERS, THE

Iona 1115		Surfers Rule / Surfer's Blues	1963	8.00	40.00
		(Iona 1115 was also released credited to The Journeymen.)			

BAYMEN, THE

Merri 6000		Bonzai / Daybreak	1963	8.00	40.00

BAYSIDERS, THE

Everest 19366		Over The Rainbow / My Bonnie	1960	2.00	10.00
Everest 19386		Trees / Look For The Silver Lining	1960	2.00	10.00
Everest 19393		Bells Of St. Mary's / Comin' Through The Rye	1960	2.00	10.00

BAYTOVENS, THE

Belfast 101		Such A Fool / Waiting For You	196?	3.00	15.00

BAZOOKA

Bang 559		Boo On You / The Deal	1968	.80	4.00

BE BOP KID, THE
The Be Bop Kid is a pseudonym for Freddy Fender.

Falcon		No Seas Cruel /	1957	20.00	100.00
		("Don't Be Cruel" in Spanish.)			

BEACH, BILL

King 4940		Peg Pants / You're Gonna Like Me, Baby	195?	25.00	125.00

BEACH BOYS, THE

Kapp 289		Bathing Beauty / On The Beach At Sunset	1959	2.00	10.00

BEACH BOYS, THE
The original group consisted of Brian, Dennis and Carl Wilson, Mike Love, and Al Jardine, temporarily replaced by David Marks in 1962 (Capitol 4777-5069). Bruce Johnston joined in 1965, left in 1972 and rejoined in 1980. Blondie Chaplin and Ricki Fataar were official members during the early '70s. With the exception of Jardine, each member has solo records listed in this book. The Honeys appear in on the group's records throughout the '60s with Marilyn Wilson involved with almost everything through 1980. Refer to Annette; Chicago; The Everly Brothers; The Fat Boys; Julio Iglesias; Jan & Dean; Joan Jett; Kenny & The Cadets; The Flame; Charles Lloyd; and the Various Artists EP section.

Brian Wilson collectors note: Beginning in 1967, production credit went to the group; the Brother singles and Capitol 2028, 2068, 2160, 2239 and the a-side of 2530 are nonetheless Brian's. Similarly, assume Brian's handiwork with most of the tracks bearing his songwriting credit (Reprise 0894, 0998, 1047, 1058, 1101, 1138, 1321 and 2118).

Original Capitol singles through 1968 (2160) have orange and yellow swirl labels that read "Mfd. by Capitol Records Inc. U.S.A." along the bottom perimeter. Some titles were repressed in 1968 with identical swirl labels but "Mfd. by Capitol Records Inc. A Subsidiary of Capitol Industries Inc. U.S.A." along the bottom.

"X" 301		Surfin' / Luau	1961	100.00	400.00
Candix 301		Surfin' / Luau	1962	35.00	175.00
		(Original Candix pressings do not mention Era Records on the label.)			
Candix 301	(DJ)	Surfin' / Luau	1962	35.00	175.00
Candix 301		Surfin' / Luau	1962	20.00	100.00
		(Second pressing labels—promo and stock—read "Distributed by Era Records Sales.")			
Candix 331		Surfin' / Luau	1962	30.00	150.00

The Beach Boys' first single was issued on Hite Morgan's tiny "X" Records (not to be confused with the RCA Victor subsidiary). It saw two subsequent pressings on Morgan's Candix, the final one as a follow-up to the group's initial success on Capitol. One of the stops along the path to respectability taken by the "new" Beach Boys was performing at the ultra hip Big Sur Folk Festival, from which a film and album were compiled. Issued as a single, the group's version of *Wouldn't It Be Nice* changed the disdain of many critics, making them new fans. The promo features a mono mix unavailable elsewhere.

Label & Catalog #		A-Side/B-Side	Year	VG	NM
Capitol 4777		**Surfin' Safari / 409**	1962	3.00	15.00
		(Orange & yellow swirl label reads "Mfd. by Capitol Records Inc. U.S.A.")			
Capitol 4777	(PS)	**Surfin' Safari / 409**	1962	10.00	50.00
Capitol 4880		**Ten Little Indians / County Fair**	1962	4.00	20.00
		(Orange & yellow swirl label reads "Mfd. by Capitol Records Inc. U.S.A.")			
Capitol 4880	(PS)	**Ten Little Indians / County Fair**	1962	20.00	100.00
Capitol 4932		**Surfin' U.S.A. / Shut Down**	1963	3.00	15.00
		(Orange & yellow swirl label reads "Mfd. by Capitol Records Inc. U.S.A." *First pressing read "Produced by Nick Venet" and credit Brian Wilson as the a-side songwriter.)*			
Capitol 4932		**Surfin' U.S.A. / Shut Down**	1963	2.00	10.00
		(Orange & yellow swirl label reads "Mfd. by Capitol Records Inc. U.S.A." *Second pressings still list Brian Wilson as the a-side songwriter.)*			
Capitol 4932		**Surfin' U.S.A. / Shut Down**	1963	3.00	15.00
		(Orange & yellow swirl label reads "Mfd. by Capitol Records Inc. U.S.A." *Third pressing labels credit Chuck Berry as the a-side songwriter.)*			
Capitol 5009		**Surfer Girl / Little Deuce Coupe**	1963	2.00	10.00
		(Orange & yellow swirl label reads "Mfd. by Capitol Records Inc. U.S.A.")			
Capitol 5069		**Be True To Your School / In My Room**	1963	1.60	8.00
		(Orange & yellow swirl label reads "Mfd. by Capitol Records Inc. U.S.A.")			
Capitol 5096		**Little Saint Nick / The Lord's Prayer**	1963	3.00	15.00
		(Orange & yellow swirl label reads "Mfd. by Capitol Records Inc. U.S.A.")			
Capitol 5096		**Little Saint Nick / The Lord's Prayer**	1968	4.00	20.00
		(Orange & yellow swirl label reads "A Subsidiary of Capitol Industries U.S.A.")			
Capitol 5096		**Little Saint Nick / The Lord's Prayer**	1969	4.00	20.00
		(Orange & red target label.)			
Capitol 5096		**Little Saint Nick / The Lord's Prayer**	1974	1.60	8.00
		(Orange label with the Capitol logo on the bottom.)			
Capitol 5118		**Fun Fun, Fun / Why Do Fools Fall In Love?**	1964	2.00	10.00
		(Orange & yellow swirl label reads "Mfd. by Capitol Records Inc. U.S.A." *First pressings credit Brian Wilson as the a-side songwriter.)*			
Capitol 5118		**Fun Fun, Fun / Why Do Fools Fall In Love?**	1964	2.00	10.00
		(Orange & yellow swirl label reads "Mfd. by Capitol Records Inc. U.S.A." *Second pressings credit Wilson-Love as the a-side songwriters.)*			
Capitol 5118	(PS)	**Fun Fun, Fun / Why Do Fools Fall In Love?**	1964	5.00	25.00
Capitol 5174		**I Get Around / Don't Worry, Baby**	1964	2.00	10.00
		(Orange & yellow swirl label reads "Mfd. by Capitol Records Inc. U.S.A.")			
Capitol 5174		**I Get Around / Don't Worry, Baby**	1968	4.00	20.00
		(Orange & yellow swirl label reads "A Subsidiary of Capitol Industries U.S.A.")			
Capitol 5174	(PS)	**I Get Around / Don't Worry, Baby**	1964	3.00	15.00
Capitol 5174		**I Get Around / Don't Worry, Baby**	1969	2.00	10.00
		(Orange & red target label.)			
Capitol 5174		**I Get Around / Don't Worry, Baby**	1974	1.60	8.00
		(Orange label with the Capitol logo on the bottom.)			
Capitol 5174		**I Get Around / Don't Worry, Baby**	1978	2.40	12.00
		(Purple label with Capitol's dome logo.)			
Capitol 5245		**When I Grow Up (To Be A Man) / She Knows Me Too Well**	1964	2.40	12.00
		(Orange & yellow swirl label reads "Mfd. by Capitol Records Inc. U.S.A.")			
Capitol 5245		**When I Grow Up (To Be A Man) / She Knows Me Too Well**	1968	4.00	20.00
		(Orange & yellow swirl label reads "A Subsidiary of Capitol Industries U.S.A.")			
Capitol 5245	(PS)	**When I Grow Up (To Be A Man) / She Knows Me Too Well**	1964	4.00	20.00
		(The sleeve has a blue border.)			
Capitol 5245	(PS)	**When I Grow Up (To Be A Man) / She Knows Me Too Well**	1964	5.00	25.00
		(The sleeve has a green border.)			
Capitol 5267	(EP)	**4-By The Beach Boys**	1964	3.00	15.00
		(Orange & yellow swirl label reads "Mfd. by Capitol Records Inc. U.S.A.")			
Capitol 5267	(PS)	**4-By The Beach Boys**	1964	10.00	50.00
Capitol 5306		**Dance, Dance, Dance / The Warmth Of The Sun**	1964	2.00	10.00
		(Orange & yellow swirl label reads "Mfd. by Capitol Records Inc. U.S.A.")			
Capitol 5306	(PS)	**Dance, Dance, Dance / The Warmth Of The Sun**	1964	12.00	60.00
Capitol 5312		**The Man With All The Toys / Blue Christmas**	1964	3.00	15.00
		(Orange & yellow swirl label reads "Mfd. by Capitol Records Inc. U.S.A.")			
Capitol 5372		**Do You Wanna Dance? / Please Let Me Wonder**	1965	2.00	10.00
		(Orange & yellow swirl label reads "Mfd. by Capitol Records Inc. U.S.A.")			
Capitol 5372	(PS)	**Do You Wanna Dance? / Please Let Me Wonder**	1965	4.00	20.00
Capitol 5395		**Help Me, Rhonda / Kiss Me, Baby**	1965	2.00	10.00
		(Orange & yellow swirl label reads "Mfd. by Capitol Records Inc. U.S.A.")			
Capitol 5395	(PS)	**Help Me, Rhonda / Kiss Me, Baby**	1965	2.40	12.00
Capitol 5464		**California Girls / Let Him Run Wild**	1965	2.00	10.00
		(Orange & yellow swirl label reads "Mfd. by Capitol Records Inc. U.S.A.")			
Capitol 5464		**California Girls / Let Him Run Wild**	1968	4.00	20.00
		(Orange & yellow swirl label reads "A Subsidiary of Capitol Industries U.S.A.")			
Capitol 5464	(PS)	**California Girls / Let Him Run Wild**	1965	3.00	15.00
Capitol 5464		**California Girls / Let Him Run Wild**	1969	2.00	10.00
		(Orange & red target label.)			
Capitol 5464		**California Girls / Let Him Run Wild**	1974	1.60	8.00
		(Orange label with the Capitol logo on the bottom.)			

Label & Catalog #		A-Side/B-Side	Year	VG	NM
Capitol 5464		**California Girls / Let Him Run Wild**	1978	2.40	12.00
		(Purple label with Capitol's dome logo.)			
Capitol 5540		**The Little Girl I Once Knew / There's No Other**	1965	2.00	10.00
		(Orange & yellow swirl label reads "Mfd. by Capitol Records Inc. U.S.A.")			
Capitol 5540		**The Little Girl I Once Knew / There's No Other**	1968	4.00	20.00
		(Orange & yellow swirl label reads "A Subsidiary of Capitol Industries U.S.A.")			
Capitol 5540	(PS)	**The Little Girl I Once Knew / There's No Other**	1965	3.00	15.00
Capitol 5561		**Barbara Ann / Girl, Don't Tell Me**	1965	2.00	10.00
		(Orange & yellow swirl label reads "Mfd. by Capitol Records Inc. U.S.A.")			
Capitol 5561		**Barbara Ann / Girl, Don't Tell Me**	1968	4.00	20.00
		(Orange & yellow swirl label reads "A Subsidiary of Capitol Industries U.S.A.")			
Capitol 5561	(PS)	**Barbara Ann / Girl, Don't Tell Me**	1965	15.00	75.00
		(Sleeve has a glossy finish.)			
Capitol 5561	(PS)	**Barbara Ann / Girl, Don't Tell Me**	1965	25.00	125.00
		(Sleeve has a non-glossy finish.)			
Capitol 5602		**Sloop John B. / You're So Good To Me**	1966	2.00	10.00
		(Orange & yellow swirl label reads "Mfd. by Capitol Records Inc. U.S.A.")			
Capitol 5602		**Sloop John B. / You're So Good To Me**	1968	4.00	20.00
		(Orange & yellow swirl label reads "A Subsidiary of Capitol Industries U.S.A.")			
Capitol 5602	(PS)	**Sloop John B. / You're So Good To Me**	1966	2.00	10.00
Capitol 5602		**Sloop John B. / You're So Good To Me**	1969	3.00	15.00
		(Orange & red target label.)			
Capitol 5602		**Sloop John B. / You're So Good To Me**	1974	1.60	8.00
		(Orange label with the Capitol logo on the bottom.)			
Capitol 5602		**Sloop John B. / You're So Good To Me**	1978	2.40	12.00
		(Purple label with Capitol's dome logo.)			
Capitol 5610		**Caroline, No / Summer Means New Love**	1966	3.00	15.00
		(While Capitol 5610 is credited to Brian Wilson, both tracks can be found on Beach Boys' albums. This single was advertised in '66 with a picture sleeve of Brian. Should such a sleeve exist, it could be the rarest and most valuable of all Beach Boys collectibles.)			
Capitol 5706		**Wouldn't It Be Nice / God Only Knows**	1966	2.00	10.00
		(Orange & yellow swirl label reads "Mfd. by Capitol Records Inc. U.S.A.")			
Capitol 5706		**Wouldn't It Be Nice / God Only Knows**	1968	4.00	20.00
		(Orange & yellow swirl label reads "A Subsidiary of Capitol Industries U.S.A.")			
Capitol 5676		**Good Vibrations / Let's Go Away For Awhile**	1966	2.00	10.00
		(Orange & yellow swirl label reads "Mfd. by Capitol Records Inc. U.S.A.")			
Capitol 5676		**Good Vibrations / Let's Go Away For Awhile**	1968	4.00	20.00
		(Orange & yellow swirl label reads "A Subsidiary of Capitol Industries U.S.A.")			
Capitol 5676	(PS)	**Good Vibrations / Let's Go Away For Awhile**	1966	4.00	20.00
Capitol 5826		**Heroes And Villains**	1967	Unreleased	
Capitol 5826	(PS)	**Heroes And Villains**	1967	100.00	500.00
		(Manufactured before the Brother release was announced, these were shipped to oversea markets where it was issued on Capitol. Note that Canadian distributors blacked out Capitol number 5826 and stamped in Brother number 1001 above it.)			
Brother 1001	(DJ)	**Heroes And Villains / You're Welcome**	1967	5.00	25.00
Brother 1001		**Heroes And Villains / You're Welcome**	1967	.80	4.00
		(First pressings erroneously credit Ken Lockert as engineer.)			
Brother 1001		**Heroes And Villains / You're Welcome**	1967	1.20	6.00
		(Later pressings correctly credit Jim Lockert as engineer.)			
Brother 1001	(PS)	**Heroes And Villains / You're Welcome**	1967	8.00	40.00
Brother 1002	(DJ)	**Gettin' Hungry / Devoted To You**	1967	4.00	20.00
Brother 1002		**Gettin' Hungry / Devoted To You**	1967	6.00	30.00
		(While Brother 1002 is credited to Brian Wilson & Mike Love, both tracks can be found on Beach Boys' albums.)			
Capitol P-2028	(DJ)	**Wild Honey / Wind Chimes**	1967	4.00	20.00
Capitol 2028		**Wild Honey / Wind Chimes**	1967	1.60	8.00
		(Orange & yellow swirl label reads "Mfd. by Capitol Records Inc. U.S.A.")			
Capitol P-2068	(DJ)	**Darlin' / Here Today**	1967	4.00	20.00
Capitol 2068		**Darlin' / Here Today**	1967	1.60	8.00
		(Orange & yellow swirl label reads "Mfd. by Capitol Records Inc. U.S.A.")			
Capitol 2068	(PS)	**Darlin' / Here Today**	1967	4.00	20.00
Capitol P-2160	(DJ)	**Friends / Little Bird**	1968	4.00	20.00
Capitol 2160		**Friends / Little Bird**	1968	2.00	10.00
		(Orange & yellow swirl label reads "Mfd. by Capitol Records Inc. U.S.A.")			
Capitol P-2239	(DJ)	**Do It Again / Wake The World**	1968	4.00	20.00
Capitol 2239		**Do It Again / Wake The World**	1968	1.60	8.00
		(Orange & yellow swirl label reads "Mfd. by Capitol Records Inc. U.S.A.")			
Capitol 2239		**Do It Again / Wake The World**	1968	3.00	15.00
		(Orange & yellow swirl label reads "A Subsidiary of Capitol Industries U.S.A.")			
Capitol P-2360	(DJ)	**Bluebirds Over The Mountain / Never Learn Not To Love**	1968	3.00	15.00
Capitol 2360		**Bluebirds Over The Mountain / Never Learn Not To Love**	1968	1.60	8.00
Capitol P-2432	(DJ)	**I Can Hear Music / All I Want To Do**	1969	3.00	15.00
Capitol 2432		**I Can Hear Music / All I Want To Do**	1969	1.60	8.00
Capitol 2530	(DJ)	**Break Away / Celebrate The News**	1969	5.00	25.00
Capitol 2530		**Break Away / Celebrate The News**	1969	1.60	8.00

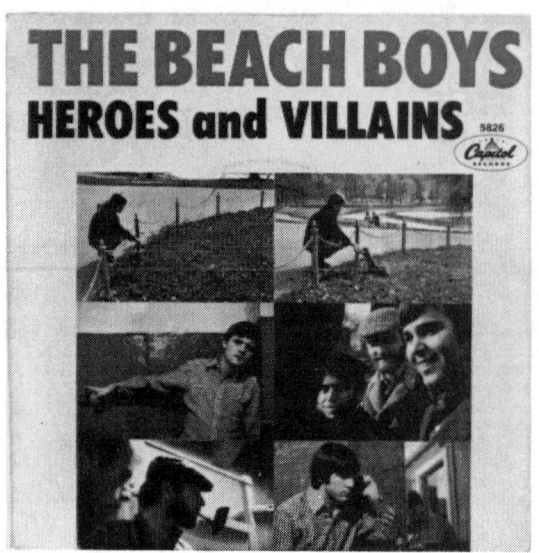

Heroes And Villains was the initial single from *Smile,* the group's scheduled album for the 1966 Christmas season. As Brian Wilson's creation underwent a series of baroque elaborations that led to its continued delay, the single also was put off, missing its original release date only to show up in the summer of '67. Capitol had scheduled the single as 5826 and prepared this sleeve; there is no B-side on the sleeve as the company had been led to believe that the single was to include part I and part 2 of *Heroes.* When the single was released, it was as the maiden single for the group's Brother label with a new picture sleeve. The Capitol sleeve was shipped to various countries where the single would be issued on Capitol.

Label & Catalog #		A-Side/B-Side	Year	VG	NM
Capitol 2765	(DJ)	Cotton Fields / The Nearest Faraway Place	1970	4.00	20.00
Capitol 2765		Cotton Fields / The Nearest Faraway Place	1970	2.00	10.00
Capitol 3924		Surfin' U.S.A. / The Warmth Of The Sun	1974	.80	4.00
Capitol 4093		Little Honda / Hawaii	1975	.60	3.00
Capitol 4110		Barbara Ann / Little Honda	1975	.60	3.00
Capitol 4334		Graduation Day / Be True To Your School	1976	.60	3.00
Capitol 5030		Beach Boys Medley / God Only Knows	1981	.40	2.00
Capitol PB-5595	(DJ)	Rock & Roll To The Rescue / Rock & Roll To The Rescue	1986	.80	4.00
Capitol 5595		Rock & Roll To The Rescue / Good Vibrations	1986	.40	2.00
Capitol 5595	(PS)	Rock & Roll To The Rescue / Good Vibrations	1986	.40	2.00
Capitol 5630		California Dreamin' / Lady Liberty	1986	.40	2.00
Capitol 7PRO-79789	(DJ)	Still Cruisin' / Still Cruisin'	1989	6.00	30.00
Capitol 7PRO-79841	(DJ)	Somewhere Near Japan / Somewhere Near Japan	1989	6.00	30.00

(Stock copies of Capitol 79789 and 79841 were issued as cassettes only.)

— Capitol Starline Reissues —

Most of the Starline singles below remained in print through the years and underwent various label changes: brown, blue, black "rainbow" and purple. These records currently have little collector's value. Note that some pressings of the later brown label and most—if not all—of the blue label pressings, have "Surfer Girl" in binaural stereo instead of mono.

Capitol 6059		Be True To Your School / In My Room	1965	3.00	15.00
Capitol 6059		Be True To Your School / In My Room	1967	1.20	6.00
Capitol 6060		Ten Little Indians / She Knows Me Too Well	1965	3.00	15.00
Capitol 6081		Help Me, Rhonda / Do You Wanna Dance?	1966	2.40	12.00
Capitol 6094		Surfin' U.S.A. / Shut Down	1966	3.00	15.00
Capitol 6095		Surfin' Safari / 409	1966	2.40	12.00

— Original Starline singles above have green swirl labels. —

Capitol 6059		Be True To Your School / In My Room	1967	1.20	6.00
Capitol 6081		Help Me, Rhonda / Do You Wanna Dance?	1967	1.20	6.00
Capitol 6094		Surfin' U.S.A. / Shut Down	1967	1.20	6.00
Capitol 6095		Surfin' Safari / 409	1967	1.60	8.00
Capitol P-6105	(DJ)	Dance, Dance, Dance / The Warmth Of The Sun	1967	4.00	20.00
Capitol 6105		Dance, Dance, Dance / The Warmth Of The Sun	1967	1.00	5.00
Capitol P-6106	(DJ)	Fun, Fun, Fun / Why Do Fools Fall In Love?	1967	4.00	20.00
Capitol 6106		Fun, Fun, Fun / Why Do Fools Fall In Love?	1967	1.20	6.00
Capitol P-6107	(DJ)	Surfer Girl / Little Deuce Coupe	1967	4.00	20.00
Capitol 6107		Surfer Girl / Little Deuce Coupe	1967	1.20	6.00
Capitol 6132		Good Vibrations / Barbara Ann	1968	1.60	8.00

— Starline singles above have red & white labels. —

— Special Promotional Releases —

Capitol (No number)		Spirit Of America / Boogie Woodie	1963	50.00	200.00
Capitol (No number)	(PS)	Spirit Of America	1963	100.00	400.00

(Paper sleeve reads "I Was There KFWB Day! Wallich's Music City South Bay Store Opening Nov. 16, 1963.")

Capitol 2936/37		Salt Lake City / Amusement Parks U.S.A.	1965	35.00	175.00
Capitol 2185/86	(EP)	Complete Selections From "Surfin' Safari"	1962	250.00	750.00

(B-side by Ray Anthony. Issued in a cardboard cover.)

Capitol (No number)	(EP)	Girls On The Beach	1964	—	—

(EP for the film "Girls On The Beach " containing four tracks by the Beach Boys. There is one known copy and no known sleeve. Very rare indeed, with no estimated value at this time, although a near mint copy would easily sell in excess of $1,000.)

Capitol 2754/55	(EP)	Selections From "Beach Boys Concert"	1964	200.00	600.00

(Brian Wilson introduces selections from the group's album and the Hollyridge Strings "Beach Boys Songbook.")

Capitol 2993/94	(EP)	Excerpts From Capitol's "Beach Boys' Party"	1965	150.00	500.00
Capitol SXA-1981	(33)	Surfer Girl (Jukebox EP)	1967	30.00	150.00
Capitol SXA-2027	(33)	Shut Down, Volume 2 (Jukebox EP)	1967	30.00	150.00
Capitol DU-2269	(33)	The Beach Boys Today (Jukebox EP)	1967	25.00	125.00
Capitol DU-2545	(33)	The Best Of The Beach Boys (Jukebox EP)	1967	30.00	150.00
Capitol/LLP-189	(33)	The Best Of The Beach Boys (Jukebox EP in paper sleeve)	1967	5.00	25.00

— Brother/Reprise —

After signing with Warner/Reprise the group revived the Brother label. The singles below are a pale yellow unless noted.

Reprise 0894	(DJ)	Add Some Music To Your Day / Susie Cincinnati	1970	2.00	10.00
Reprise 0894		Add Some Music To Your Day / Susie Cincinnati	1970	1.00	5.00
Reprise 0929	(DJ)	Slip On Through / This Whole World	1970	3.00	15.00
Reprise 0929		Slip On Through / This Whole World	1970	2.00	10.00
Reprise 0957	(DJ)	Tears In The Morning / It's About Time	1970	3.00	15.00
Reprise 0957		Tears In The Morning / It's About Time	1970	4.00	20.00
Reprise 0998	(DJ)	Cool, Cool Water / Cool, Cool Water	1971	10.00	50.00
Reprise 0998	(DJ)	Cool, Cool Water / Forever	1971	12.00	60.00
Reprise 0998		Cool, Cool Water / Forever	1971	15.00	75.00
Ode 66016	(DJ)	Wouldn't It Be Nice / Wouldn't It Be Nice	1971	5.00	25.00
Ode 66016		Wouldn't It Be Nice / (B-side by Merry Clayton)	1971	6.00	30.00
Reprise 1015	(DJ)	Long Promised Road / Deirdre	1971	3.00	15.00
Reprise 1015		Long Promised Road / Deirdre	1971	4.00	20.00
Reprise 1015		Long Promised Road / Deirdre (Brown label)	1971	5.00	25.00

The three promotional versions of the group's Starline Series reissues.

Label & Catalog #		A-Side/B-Side	Year	VG	NM
Reprise 1047	(DJ)	Long Promised Road / Long Promised Road	1971	4.00	20.00
Reprise 1047		Long Promised Road / 'Til I Die	1971	5.00	25.00
Reprise 1047		Long Promised Road / 'Til I Die (Brown label)	1971	6.00	30.00
Reprise 1058	(DJ)	Surf's Up / Don't Go Near The Water	1971	8.00	40.00
Reprise 1058		Surf's Up / Don't Go Near The Water	1971	9.00	45.00
Reprise 1058		Surf's Up / Don't Go Near The Water (Brown label)	1971	10.00	50.00
Reprise 1091	(DJ)	You Need A Mess Of Help To Stand Alone / Cuddle Up	1972	3.00	15.00
Reprise 1091		You Need A Mess Of Help To Stand Alone / Cuddle Up	1972	4.00	20.00
Reprise 1091		You Need A Mess Of Help To Stand Alone / Cuddle Up (Brown label.)	1972	5.00	25.00
Reprise 1101	(DJ)	Marcella / Marcella	1972	3.00	15.00
Reprise 1101		Marcella / Hold On, Dear Brother	1972	4.00	20.00
Reprise 1101		Marcella / Hold On, Dear Brother (Brown label)	1972	5.00	25.00
Reprise 1138	(DJ)	Sail, On Sailor / Only With You	1973	3.00	15.00
Reprise 1138		Sail, On Sailor / Only With You	1973	4.00	20.00
Reprise 1138		Sail, On Sailor / Only With You (Brown label)	1973	5.00	25.00
Reprise 1156	(DJ)	California Saga / California Saga	1973	3.00	15.00
Reprise 1156		California Saga / Funky Pretty	1973	1.20	6.00
Reprise 1156		California Saga / Funky Pretty (Brown label)	1973	4.00	20.00
Reprise 1310	(DJ)	I Can Hear Music / I Can Hear Music	1974	1.20	6.00
Reprise 1310		I Can Hear Music / Let The Wind Blow	1974	3.00	15.00
Reprise 1310		I Can Hear Music / Let The Wind Blow (Brown label)	1974	4.00	20.00
Reprise 1321	(DJ)	Child Of Winter / Child Of Winter	1974	5.00	25.00
Reprise 1321		Child Of Winter / Susie Cincinnati	1974	10.00	50.00
Reprise 1321		Child Of Winter / Susie Cincinnati (Brown label)	1974	10.00	50.00
Reprise 1325	(DJ)	Sail On, Sailor / Sail On, Sailor	1975	2.00	10.00
Reprise 1325		Sail On, Sailor / Only With You	1975	1.20	6.00
Reprise 1325		Sail On, Sailor / Only With You (Brown label)	1975	3.00	15.00
Reprise 1336	(DJ)	Wouldn't It Be Nice / Wouldn't It Be Nice	1975	1.00	5.00
Reprise 1336		Wouldn't It Be Nice / Caroline, No	1975	2.00	10.00
Reprise 1336		Wouldn't It Be Nice / Caroline, No (Brown label)	1975	5.00	25.00
Reprise 1354	(DJ)	Rock And Roll Music / Rock And Roll Music	1976	1.20	6.00
Reprise 1354		Rock And Roll Music / TM Song	1976	.40	2.00
Reprise 1368	(DJ)	It's O.K. / It's O.K.	1976	1.20	6.00
Reprise 1368		It's O.K. / Had To Phone Ya	1976	.40	2.00
Reprise 1375	(DJ)	Susie Cincinnati / Susie Cincinnati	1976	1.00	5.00
Reprise 1375		Susie Cincinnati / Everyone's In Love With You	1976	.80	4.00
Reprise 1389	(DJ)	Honkin' Down The Highway / Honkin' Down The Highway	1977	1.00	5.00
Reprise 1389		Honkin' Down The Highway / Solar System	1977	.60	3.00
Reprise 1394	(DJ)	Peggy Sue / Peggy Sue	1978	1.00	5.00
Reprise 1394		Peggy Sue / Hey, Little Tomboy	1978	.40	2.00

—Brother/Reprise Reissues—

Reprise 0101		Sloop John B. / Wouldn't It Be Nice	1973	1.00	5.00
Reprise 0102		God Only Knows / Caroline, No	1973	1.00	5.00
Reprise 0103		Good Vibrations / Heroes And Villains	1973	.60	3.00
Reprise 0103		Good Vibrations / Heroes And Villains (Brown label)	1973	2.00	10.00
Reprise 0104		Darlin' / Wild Honey	1973	1.20	6.00
Reprise 0105		Friends / Be Here In The Morning	1973	1.20	6.00
Reprise 0106		Do It Again / Cotton Fields	1973	1.40	8.00
Reprise 0107		I Can Hear Music / Bluebirds Over The Mountain	1973	1.20	6.00
Reprise 0118		Rock And Roll Music / It's O.K.	1977	1.20	6.00

—Special/Promotional Releases—

Reprise PRO-422		Sunflower (Radio spots)	1970	30.00	150.00
Reprise 2118	(33)	Mt. Vernon And Fairway (White label) (Released with the stock sleeve.)	1973	4.00	20.00
Reprise 2118	(33)	Mt. Vernon And Fairway (With sleeve) (This EP was taped to the back cover of the "Holland" album.)	1973	2.00	10.00
Reprise PRO-557		Sail On, Sailor / The Trader (Issued with three other singles as Warner/Reprise's January 1973 Preview Pack. Each single included a small insert announcing the upcoming album. The price listed is for the one Beach Boys single and insert alone.)	1973	12.00	60.00
Reprise (No number)		The Beach Boys Radio Special (Promo spot)	1976	6.00	30.00

—Brother/Caribou—

Caribou ZS8-9026	(DJ)	Here Comes The Night / Here Comes The Night	1979	.80	4.00
Caribou ZS8-9026	(DJ)	Here Comes The Night / Here Comes The Night (White label promo reads "DJ Reservice.")	1979	.60	3.00
Caribou ZS8-9026		Here Comes The Night / Baby Blue	1979	.40	2.00
Caribou ZS9-9029	(DJ)	Good Timin' / Good Timin'	1979	1.00	5.00
Caribou ZS9-9029		Good Timin' / Love Surrounds Me	1979	.60	3.00
Caribou ZS9-9030	(DJ)	Lady Lynda / Lady Lynda	1979	.60	3.00
Caribou ZS9-9030		Lady Lynda / Full Sail	1979	.60	3.00
Caribou ZS9-9031	(DJ)	It's A Beautiful Day / It's A Beautiful Day	1979	.60	3.00
Caribou ZS9-9031		It's A Beautiful Day / Sumahama	1979	.40	2.00
Caribou ZS9-9032	(DJ)	Goin' On / Goin' On	1980	.60	3.00
Caribou ZS9-9032		Goin' On / Endless Harmony	1980	.60	3.00

Label & Catalog #		A-Side/B-Side	Year	VG	NM
Caribou ZS9-9033	(DJ)	Livin' With A Heartache / Livin' With A Heartache	1980	.60	3.00
Caribou ZS9-9033		Livin' With A Heartache / Santa Ana Winds	1980	.60	3.00
Caribou 2Z9-9034	(DJ)	School Day / School Day	1981	20.00	100.00
		(Stock copies of Caribou 9034 do not exist.)			
Caribou 2Z5-02633	(DJ)	Come Go With Me / Come Go With Me	1981	.60	3.00
Caribou 2Z5-02633		Come Go With Me / Don't Go Near The Water	1981	.40	2.00
Caribou 2Z4-04913	(DJ)	Getcha Back / Getcha Back	1985	.80	4.00
Caribou 2Z4-04913	(PS)	Getcha Back / Getcha Back	1985	1.20	6.00
Caribou 2Z4-04913		Getcha Back / Male Ego	1985	.40	2.00
Caribou 2Z4-04913	(PS)	Getcha Back / Male Ego	1985	.60	3.00
Caribou 2Z4-05433	(DJ)	It's Gettin' Late / It's Gettin' Late	1985	.80	4.00
Caribou 2Z4-05433	(PS)	It's Gettin' Late / It's Gettin' Late	1985	1.20	6.00
Caribou 2Z4-05433		It's Gettin' Late / It's O.K.	1985	.40	2.00
Caribou 2Z4-05433	(PS)	It's Gettin' Late / It's O.K.	1985	.60	3.00
Caribou 2Z4-05624	(DJ)	She Believes In Love / She Believes In Love	1985	.60	3.00
Caribou 2Z4-05624	(PS)	She Believes In Love Again	1985	1.40	8.00
Caribou 2Z4-05624		She Believes In Love / It's Just A Matter Of Time	1985	.80	4.00
Caribou 2Z4-05624	(PS)	She Believes In Love Again / It's Just A Matter Of Time	1985	1.20	6.00

— 12" Singles—

Label & Catalog #		A-Side/B-Side	Year	VG	NM
Caribou 2Z8-9028	(DJ)	Here Comes The Night (2 versions. Grey label)	1979	2.00	10.00
Caribou 2Z8-9028	(DJ)	Here Comes The Night (2 versions. White label)	1979	1.60	8.00
Caribou 2Z8-9028	(DJ)	Here Comes The Night (2 versions. DJ Reserve)	1979	1.00	5.00
Caribou AS-557	(DJ)	Here Comes The Night (2 versions on blue vinyl)	1979	1.20	6.00
Caribou 2Z8-9028		Here Comes The Night (2 versions)	1979	1.60	8.00

—Special/Promotional Releases—

Label & Catalog #		A-Side/B-Side	Year	VG	NM
W.I.A.A #449/50		What's It All About? Interview	1978	5.00	25.00
W.I.A.A. 1790		What's It All About? Interview	1980	5.00	25.00

BEACH BOYS, THE, & LITTLE RICHARD

Label & Catalog #		A-Side/B-Side	Year	VG	NM
Critique 7-99392	(DJ)	Happy Endings / Happy Endings	1987	.60	3.00
		(White label with a 3:48 a-side and a 4:32 b-side.)			
Critique 7-99392	(DJ)	Happy Endings / Happy Endings	1987	.60	3.00
		(Blue label with a 3:48 a-side and a 4:32 b-side.)			
Critique 7-99392	(DJ)	Happy Endings / Happy Endings	1987	1.00	5.00
		(White label with a 4:03 "hot new mix" a-side and a 4:32 b-side.)			
Critique 7-99392		Happy Endings / California Girls [Live]	1987	.40	2.00
Critique 7-99392	(PS)	Happy Endings / California Girls [Live]	1987	.50	2.50
Elektra 7-69385	(DJ)	Kokomo / Kokomo	1988	.80	4.00
Elektra 7-69385		Kokomo / (B-side by Little Richard)	1988	.40	2.00

BEACH BUMS, THE / D. DODGER
The Beach Bums feature Bob Seger.

Label & Catalog #		A-Side/B-Side	Year	VG	NM
Are You Kidding Me 1010		Florida Time / Ballad Of The Yellow Beret	1966	12.00	60.00
		(One side, "Florida Time," is credited to The Beach Bums; the other side, "Ballad Of The Yellow Beret," is credited to D. Dodger.)			

BEACH GIRLS, THE

Label & Catalog #		A-Side/B-Side	Year	VG	NM
Vault 905		He's My Surfin' Guy / Bobby's The Boy	1963	5.00	25.00
Dyno Vox 202		Skiing In The Snow / Goin' Places	1965	4.00	20.00

BEACH-NIKS, THE

Label & Catalog #		A-Side/B-Side	Year	VG	NM
MMC 007		Like Stoned / Good Things	1965	1.50	8.00
MMC 008		Last Night I Cried / It Was A Nightmare	1965	1.50	8.00

BEACH NUTS, THE

Label & Catalog #		A-Side/B-Side	Year	VG	NM
Coronado 131		Surf Beat '65 / The Last Ride	1963	8.00	40.00
Coronado 131	(PS)	Surf Beat '65 / The Last Ride	1963	12.00	60.00

BEACH NUTS, THE
The Beach Nuts is a pseudonym for members of The Angels, The Belmonts and The Elegants.

Label & Catalog #		A-Side/B-Side	Year	VG	NM
Bang 504		Out In The Sun / Someday Soon	1965	3.00	15.00

BEACHCOMBERS, THE

Label & Catalog #		A-Side/B-Side	Year	VG	NM
Dot 16354		Samoa / Lone Survivor	1962	2.00	10.00

BEACHCOMBERS, THE

Label & Catalog #		A-Side/B-Side	Year	VG	NM
Panorama 11		All To Pieces / The Wheeley	1963	2.00	10.00
Jerden 719		Purple Peanuts / Chinese Bagpiper	1963	2.00	10.00
Jerden 734		Tossin' And Turnin' / The Wheeley	1964	2.00	10.00

BEACHCOMBERS, THE

Label & Catalog #		A-Side/B-Side	Year	VG	NM
Diamond 168		Surfin' The Summer Away / This Is My Love	1964	6.00	30.00
Spar 760		Daytona Darlin' / Daytona Darlin,' Part 2	1965	5.00	25.00

BEACON STREET UNION, THE

Label & Catalog #		A-Side/B-Side	Year	VG	NM
MGM 13865		South End Incident / Speed Kills	1967	1.25	6.00

Label & Catalog #	A-Side/B-Side	Year	VG	NM
MGM 13935	Four Hundred And Five / Blue Suede Shoes	1968	1.25	6.00
MGM 14012	Mayola / May I Light Your Cigarette?	1969	1.25	6.00

BEAGLES, THE

Columbia 43789	I Wanna Capture You / Looking For The Beagles	1967	1.00	5.00

BEAM, TOMMY JIM, & THE FOUR FIFTHS

Hundred Proof 101	My Little Jewel / Bayou	1958	100.00	400.00

BEAR

Verve/Forecast 5096	Greetings / Don't Say A Word	1969	1.00	5.00

BEARD, DEAN, & THE FOUR PALS

Edmoral 1011	Rakin' And Scrapin' / On My Mind Again	1957	25.00	125.00
Atlantic 1137	Rakin' And Scrapin' / On My Mind Again	1957	6.00	30.00

BEARD, DEAN

Challenge 59033	Egad, Charlie Brown / Keeper Of The Key	1959	2.50	12.00
Challenge 59048	Little Lover / Holding On To A Memory	1959	3.00	15.00

BEARER, PAUL, & THE HEARSEMEN

Riverton 105	Route 66 / I've Been Thinking	196?	15.00	75.00

BEAT BROTHERS, THE
No relation to The Beat Brothers who backed Tony Sherida; this may be a clever attempt at a Fab Four rip-off.

MGM 13201	Nick Nack Hully Gully / Lantern Hully Gully	1964	2.00	10.00

BEATIN' PATH, THE

Fontana 1583	The Original Nothing People / I Waited So Long	1968	4.00	20.00

BEATLES, THE

The Beatles' American debut as recording artists happened inauspiciously enough with a mediocre single on Decca issued in 1962 credited to Tony Sheridan & The Beat Brothers (listed separately under Sheridan). The Beat Brothers consisted of John Lennon, Paul McCartney, George Harrison, and drummer Pete Best, who was replaced by Ringo Starr later in 1962. For related listings, refer to the Lee Alan; George Martin; Harv Moore; The Residents; Del Shannon; the Various Artists EP section. There are Beatles "tribute/exploitation" records listed throughout the book.

Decca 31382, the group's first appearance on record in America, is credited to Tony Sheridan & The Beat Brothers; i.e., John, Paul, George and Pete Best. Re-issued on MGM credited to The Beatles With Tony Sheridan.

After Capitol declined the right to release the initial Beatles recordings in 1963 the option was picked up by Vee Jay, who had little success until 1964. Vee Jay also released The Beatles on their subsidiary, Tollie, and their re-issue label, Oldies 45. Vee Jay was followed by Swan MGM and Atco, none of whom were able to break The Beatles until Capitol's entry in January 1964. Swan and Atco were two other labels that enjoyed the fruits of Capitol's misjudgement, leasing the rights to tracks as early as 1963.

Decca 31382	(DJ)	My Bonnie / The Saints *(Pink label)*	1962	——	——
		(Rare. Estimated near mint value $1,500-2,000.)			
Decca 31382		My Bonnie / The Saints *(Black label)*	1962	——	——
		(Rare. Estimated near mint value $8,000-12,000.)			
MGM 13213	(DJ)	My Bonnie / The Saints	1964	50.00	250.00
MGM 13213		My Bonnie / The Saints	1964	6.00	30.00
		(Black label with silver print does not note the album.)			
MGM 13213	(PS)	My Bonnie / The Saints	1964	15.00	75.00
		(Green title sleeve .)			
MGM 13227	(DJ)	Why / Cry For A Shadow	1964	75.00	300.00
MGM 13227		Why / Cry For A Shadow	1964	16.00	80.00
		(Black label reads "From Album E/SE 4215.")			
MGM 13227		Why / Cry For A Shadow	1964	15.00	75.00
		(Black label does not note the album.)			
MGM 13227	(PS)	Why / Cry For A Shadow	1964	60.00	250.00
		(Red title sleeve.)			

The first single released here credited to the Beatles is Vee Jay 498. As the single received virtually no attention from either the radio or the public, it is desperately rare and each version is worth at least four figures on near mint. As can be seen by the staggering array of variations below, the Vee Jay label seemed to have a difficult time keeping their label preference straight... Tollie is a subsidiary of Vee Jay while Oldies was just that, an "oldies" reissue label for Vee Jay.

Vee Jay 498	(DJ)	Please Please Me / Ask Me Why	1963	300.00	900.00
		(White label with the oval logo.)			
Vee Jay 498		Please Please Me / Ask Me Why	1963	330.00	1,000.00
		(Black rainbow label. "VEE JAY" logo in an oval. Group's name is mis-spelled as "Beatles." Catalogue number at the bottom reads "#498.")			
Vee Jay 498		Please Please Me / Ask Me Why	1963	400.00	1,200.00
		(Black rainbow label. "VEE JAY" logo in an oval. Group's name is spelled correctly. Catalogue number at the bottom reads "#498.")			
Vee Jay 498		Please Please Me / Ask Me Why	1963	330.00	1,000.00
		(Black rainbow label. "VEE JAY" logo in an oval. Group's name is mis-spelled as "Beattles." Catalogue number at the bottom reads "VJ 498.")			

Label & Catalog #		A-Side / B-Side	Year	VG	NM
Vee Jay 498		**Please Please Me / Ask Me Why**	1963	400.00	1,200.00
		(Black rainbow label. "VEE JAY" logo in an oval. Group's name is			
		spelled correctly. Catalogue number at the bottom reads "VJ 498.")			
Vee Jay 498		**Please Please Me / Ask Me Why**	1963	500.00	1,500.00
		(Black rainbow label. "VJ" logo in brackets.)			
Vee Jay 522	(DJ)	**From Me To You / Thank You Girl**	1963	75.00	300.00
Vee Jay 522		**From Me To You / Thank You Girl**	1963	75.00	300.00
		(Black rainbow label. "VEE JAY" logo in an oval.)			
Vee Jay 522		**From Me To You / Thank You Girl**	1963	100.00	400.00
		(Black rainbow label. "VJ" logo in brackets.)			
Vee Jay 522		**From Me To You / Thank You Girl**	1963	200.00	600.00
		(Solid black label.)			
Vee Jay 581	(DJ)	**Please Please Me / From Me To You**	1964	100.00	400.00
Vee Jay 581	(PS)	**Please Please Me / From Me To You**	1964	1,000.00	2,500.00
		(Promotional sleeve reads "The Record That Started Beatlemania.")			
Vee Jay 581		**Please Please Me / From Me To You** *(Black rainbow label)*	1964	6.00	30.00
Vee Jay 581		**Please Please Me / From Me To You**	1964	7.00	35.00
		(Black label with two horizontal lines.)			
Vee Jay 581		**Please Please Me / From Me To You** *(Solid black label)*	1964	8.00	40.00
Vee Jay 581		**Please Please Me / From Me To You** *(Yellow label)*	1964	20.00	100.00
Vee Jay 581		**Please Please Me / From Me To You** *(White label)*	1964	40.00	200.00
Vee Jay 581		**Please Please Me / From Me To You** *(Purple label)*	1964	75.00	300.00
Vee Jay 581	(PS)	**Please Please Me / From Me To You**	1964	50.00	250.00
Vee Jay 587	(DJ)	**Do You Want To Know A Secret? / Thank You Girl**	1964	50.00	250.00
Vee Jay 587		**Do You Want To Know A Secret? / Thank You Girl**	1964	4.00	20.00
		(Black rainbow label.)			
Vee Jay 587		**Do You Want To Know A Secret? / Thank You Girl**	1964	7.00	35.00
		(Solid black label. "VJ" logo in brackets.)			
Vee Jay 587		**Do You Want To Know A Secret? / Thank You Girl**	1964	5.00	25.00
		(Solid black label. Plain "VEE JAY" logo.)			
Vee Jay 587		**Do You Want To Know A Secret? / Thank You Girl**	1964	5.00	25.00
		(Solid black label. Plain "VJ" logo.)			
Vee Jay 587		**Do You Want To Know A Secret? / Thank You Girl**	1964	5.00	25.00
		(Black label with two horizontal lines. "VJ" logo in brackets.)			
Vee Jay 587		**Do You Want To Know A Secret? / Thank You Girl**	1964	7.00	35.00
		(Black label with two horizontal lines. Plain "VEE JAY"logo.)			
Vee Jay 587		**Do You Want To Know A Secret? / Thank You Girl**	1964	20.00	100.00
		(Yellow label.)			
Vee Jay 587	(PS)	**Do You Want To Know A Secret? / Thank You Girl**	1964	12.00	60.00
Vee Jay DJ 8	(DJ)	**Ask Me Why / Anna**	1964	——	——
		(Rare. Estimated near mint value $7,000-10,000.)			
Vee Jay	(PS)	**"We Wish You A Merry Christmas" Picture Sleeve**	1964	10.00	50.00
		(Paper sleeve with a die-cut hole and full-color			
		drawings of the Beatles around the border.)			
Swan 4152	(DJ)	**She Loves You / I'll Get You**	1963	75.00	300.00
		(White label promo reads "Promotional Copy Not For Sale.")			
Swan 4152	(DJ)	**She Loves You / I'll Get You**	1963	100.00	400.00
		(White label promo reads "Promotion Copy.")			
Swan 4152		**She Loves You / I'll Get You**	1963	100.00	400.00
		(White label with red print and "Don't Drop Out" on both sides.)			
Swan 4152		**She Loves You / I'll Get You**	1963	100.00	400.00
		(White label with red print. Without "Don't Drop Out.")			
Swan 4152		**She Loves You / I'll Get You** *(White label with blue print)*	1963	150.00	500.00
Swan 4152	(DJ)	**I'll Get You** *(One sided)*	1964	100.00	400.00
		(White label promo without promo markings.)			
Swan 4152	(DJ)	**I'll Get You** *(One sided)*	1964	125.00	500.00
		(White label promo with promo markings.)			
Swan 4152		**She Loves You / I'll Get You**	1964	5.00	25.00
		(Black label with "Don't Drop Out" on both sides.)			
Swan 4152		**She Loves You / I'll Get You**	1964	5.00	25.00
		(Black label with silver print without "Don't Drop Out.")			
Swan 4152	(PS)	**She Loves You / I'll Get You**	1964	10.00	50.00
Swan 4182	(DJ)	**Sie Liebt Dich / I'll Get You**	1964	75.00	300.00
		(White label promo with black print and an "X" on the side.)			
Swan 4182		**Sie Liebt Dich / I'll Get You**	1964	20.00	100.00
		(White label with red print reads "Sie Liebt Dich (She Loves You)"			
		on the same line and has "Virtue Studio" etched in the trail-off.)			
Swan 4182		**Sie Liebt Dich / I'll Get You**	1964	15.00	75.00
		(White label with red print and the English title below the German.)			
Swan 4182		**Sie Liebt Dich / I'll Get You**	1964	15.00	75.00
		(White label with orange print.)			
Tollie 9001		**Twist And Shout / There's A Place**	1964	10.00	50.00
		(Yellow label with green print.)			
Tollie 9001		**Twist And Shout / There's A Place**	1964	4.00	20.00
		(Yellow label with black print and plain "TOLLIE" logo.)			
Tollie 9001		**Twist And Shout / There's A Place**	1964	6.00	30.00
		(Yellow label with black print and a black "tollie" logo in a box.)			

Label & Catalog #		A-Side/B-Side	Year	VG	NM
Tollie 9001		**Twist And Shout / There's A Place**	1964	7.00	35.00
		(Yellow label with black print and a purple "tollie" logo in a box.)			
Tollie 9001		**Twist And Shout / There's A Place**	1964	6.00	30.00
		(Yellow label with black print and "TOLLIE" with a round cornered "E" in a box.)			
Tollie 9001		**Twist And Shout / There's A Place**	1964	10.00	50.00
		(Yellow label with black print and a "TOLLIE" logo in a brackets.)			
Tollie 9001		**Twist And Shout / There's A Place**	1964	10.00	50.00
		(Yellow label with blue print.)			
Tollie 9001		**Twist And Shout / There's A Place**	1964	8.00	40.00
		(Yellow label with purple print.)			
Tollie 9001		**Twist And Shout / There's A Place**	1964	6.00	30.00
		(Yellow label with green print.)			
Tollie 9001		**Twist And Shout / There's A Place**	1964	10.00	50.00
		(Black label with silver print.)			
Tollie 9008	(DJ)	**Love Me Do / P.S. I Love You**	1964	100.00	400.00
Tollie 9008		**Love Me Do / P.S. I Love You** *(Yellow label)*	1964	6.00	30.00
Tollie 9008		**Love Me Do / P.S. I Love You**	1964	8.00	40.00
		(Black label with silver print.)			
Tollie 9008	(PS)	**Love Me Do / P.S. I Love You**	1964	20.00	100.00
Atco 6302	(DJ)	**Sweet Georgia Brown /**			
		Take Out Some Insurance On Me, Baby	1964	40.00	200.00
		(White label promo.)			
Atco 6302		**Sweet Georgia Brown /**			
		Take Out Some Insurance On Me, Baby	1964	30.00	150.00
		(Yellow & white label.)			
Atco 6308	(DJ)	**Ain't She Sweet / Nobody's Child**	1964	50.00	250.00
		(White label promo with "Vocal by John Lennon" at the bottom.)			
Atco 6308		**Ain't She Sweet / Nobody's Child**	1964	7.00	35.00
		(Yellow & white label with both "Vocal by John Lennon" and "Division of Atlantic Records" on the bottom.)			
Atco 6308	(DJ)	**Ain't She Sweet / Nobody's Child**	1964	40.00	200.00
		(White label promo with "Vocal by John Lennon" on the left.)			
Atco 6308		**Ain't She Sweet / Nobody's Child**	1964	6.00	30.00
		(Yellow & white label with "Vocal by John Lennon" on the left and "Division of Atlantic Records" on the bottom.)			
Atco 6308	(PS)	**Ain't She Sweet / Nobody's Child**	1964	75.00	300.00
		(Black & white illustration sleeve with title in blue print.)			
Atco 6308		**Ain't She Sweet / Nobody's Child**	1969	4.00	20.00
		(Yellow & white label with "Mfg. By Atlantic Recording Corp." on the bottom.)			
Oldies OL-149		**Do You Want To Know A Secret? / Thank You Girl**	1964	3.00	15.00
Oldies OL-150		**Please Please Me / From Me To You**	1964	3.00	15.00
Oldies OL-151		**Love Me Do / P.S. I Love You**	1964	3.00	15.00
Oldies OL-152		**Twist And Shout / There's A Place**	1964	3.00	15.00
		(Oldies 149-152 have red labels with a white logo on top.)			

— Extended Play Albums —

Vee Jay 903	(DJ)	**Souvenir Of Their Visit To America**	1964	50.00	250.00
		(The first song on side-2, "Ask Me Why," is in much larger print than the other titles. A few copies were issued in a special paper sleeve, listed and priced separately below.)			
Vee Jay 903	(PS)	**Souvenir Of Their Visit To America**	1964	—	—
		(Promotional sleeve reads "ask me why-the beatles: an E. P. that is selling like a single... at single record prices." Rare. Estimated near mint value $7,000-10,000.)			
Vee Jay 903		**Souvenir Of Their Visit To America**	1964	30.00	150.00
		(Black rainbow label. "VJ" logo in brackets. The first song on side-2, "Ask Me Why," is in much larger print than the other titles.)			
Vee Jay 903	(DJ)	**Souvenir Of Their Visit To America**	1964	50.00	250.00
		(The price is for the promotional record only. "Ask Me Why" is the same size as the other titles.)			
Vee Jay 903		**Souvenir Of Their Visit To America**	1964	12.00	60.00
		(Black rainbow label. "VEE JAY" logo in an oval.)			
Vee Jay 903		**Souvenir Of Their Visit To America**	1964	35.00	175.00
		(Black rainbow label. "VJ" logo in brackets.)			
Vee Jay 903		**Souvenir Of Their Visit To America**	1964	35.00	175.00
		(Solid black label with "VEE JAY" logo.)			
Vee Jay 903		**Souvenir Of Their Visit To America**	1964	25.00	125.00
		(Solid black label with "VEE JAY" logo in an oval.)			

— Capitol Records —

Capitol finally picked up their right to release EMI material in the United Sates in January of 1964 with #5112, "I Want To Hold Your Hand." The rest, as they say, is history... Original Capitol singles through 1968 (2160) have orange and yellow swirl labels that read "Mfd. by Capitol Records Inc. U.S.A." along the bottom perimeter. Some titles were repressed in 1968 with identical swirl labels but "Mfd. by Capitol Records Inc. A Subsidiary of Capitol Industries Inc. U.S.A." along the bottom.

Label & Catalog #		A-Side/B-Side	Year	VG	NM

While most of The Beatles' singles have remained in print since release and gone through a number of label changes, those listed below are the rarest of the most interest to collectors. (Refer to the Apple listings below.) The picture sleeves that accompanied the original release of each single were pressed on different sides of the continent with identifiable traits: those manufactured on the East Coast have the top of each side of the sleeve trimmed straight across, although one side is slightly shorter than the other. Those printed on the West Coast have a die-cut "thumb notch," for easy removal of the record, cut into one side. For the most part, these sleeves have similar values; exceptions are listed.

Every Capitol single and picture sleeve from the '60s has been illegally reproduced. The counterfeit records are on very thin vinyl and have a less glossy label; the sleeves are shot from other sleeves and the reproduction is fuzzy. The note "Printed in U.S.A.," plainly visible on originals, is blurred or lost on the counterfeits. Also, all of the sleeves are reproductions of the East Coast cut as described above.

Label & Catalog #		A-Side/B-Side	Year	VG	NM
Capitol 5112		I Want To Hold Your Hand / I Saw Her Standing There	1964	5.00	25.00
		(Orange & yellow swirl label reads "Mfd. by Capitol Records Inc. U.S.A."			
		First pressings credit Walter Hofer as the music publishers.)			
Capitol 5112		I Want To Hold Your Hand / I Saw Her Standing There	1964	4.00	20.00
		(Orange & yellow swirl label reads "Mfd. by Capitol Records Inc. U.S.A."			
		Second pressings credit George Pincus & Sons as the music publishers.)			
Capitol 5112		I Want To Hold Your Hand / I Saw Her Standing There	1964	3.00	15.00
		(Orange & yellow swirl label reads "Mfd. by Capitol Records Inc. U.S.A."			
		Third pressings credit Gil Music as the music publishers.)			
Capitol 5112	(PS)	I Want To Hold Your Hand / I Saw Her Standing There	1964	8.00	40.00
Capitol 5112	(PS)	I Want To Hold Your Hand WMCA Good Guys Sleeve	1964	——	——
		(Promotional sleeve identical to the commercial release but with			
		the six WMCA "good guys" on the back. Issued with a stock single.			
		Rare. Estimated near mint value $2,000-3,000.)			
Capitol 5112		I Want To Hold Your Hand / I Saw Her Standing There	1968	6.00	30.00
		(Orange & yellow swirl label reads "A Subsidiary of Capitol Industries U.S.A.")			
Capitol 5112		I Want To Hold Your Hand / I Saw Her Standing There	1969	6.00	30.00
		(Red and orange label with the Capitol dome logo on the left.)			
Capitol 5112		I Want To Hold Your Hand / I Saw Her Standing There	1970	3.00	15.00
		(Red and orange label with a round target logo on the left.)			
Capitol 5150		Can't Buy Me Love / You Can't Do That	1964	4.00	20.00
		(Orange & yellow swirl label reads "Mfd. by Capitol Records Inc. U.S.A.")			
Capitol 5150	(PS)	Can't Buy Me Love / You Can't Do That	1964	150.00	600.00
Capitol 5150		Can't Buy Me Love / You Can't Do That	1968	6.00	30.00
		(Orange & yellow swirl label reads "A Subsidiary of Capitol Industries U.S.A.")			
Capitol 5150		Can't Buy Me Love / You Can't Do That	1969	6.00	30.00
		(Red and orange label with the Capitol dome logo on the left.)			
Capitol 5150		Can't Buy Me Love / You Can't Do That	1970	3.00	15.00
		(Red and orange label with a round target logo on the left.)			
Capitol 5222		A Hard Day's Night / I Should Have Known Better	1964	4.00	20.00
		(Orange & yellow swirl label reads "Mfd. by Capitol Records Inc. U.S.A.")			
Capitol 5222	(PS)	A Hard Day's Night / I Should Have Known Better	1964	6.00	30.00
Capitol 5222		A Hard Day's Night / I Should Have Known Better	1968	6.00	30.00
		(Orange & yellow swirl label reads "A Subsidiary of Capitol Industries U.S.A.")			
Capitol 5222		A Hard Day's Night / I Should Have Known Better	1969	6.00	30.00
		(Red and orange label with the Capitol dome logo on the left.)			
Capitol 5222		A Hard Day's Night / I Should Have Known Better	1970	3.00	15.00
		(Red and orange label with a round target logo on the left.)			
Capitol 5234		I'll Cry Instead / I'm Happy Just To Dance With You	1964	4.00	20.00
		(Orange & yellow swirl label reads "Mfd. by Capitol Records Inc. U.S.A.")			
Capitol 5234	(PS)	I'll Cry Instead / I'm Happy Just To Dance With You	1964	15.00	75.00
Capitol 5234		I'll Cry Instead / I'm Happy Just To Dance With You	1968	6.00	30.00
		(Orange & yellow swirl label reads "A Subsidiary of Capitol Industries U.S.A.")			
Capitol 5234		I'll Cry Instead / I'm Happy Just To Dance With You	1969	6.00	30.00
		(Red and orange label with the Capitol dome logo on the left.)			
Capitol 5234		I'll Cry Instead / I'm Happy Just To Dance With You	1970	3.00	15.00
		(Red and orange label with a round target logo on the left.)			
Capitol 5235		And I Love Her / If I Fell	1964	3.00	15.00
		(Orange & yellow swirl label reads "Mfd. by Capitol Records Inc. U.S.A.")			
Capitol 5235	(PS)	And I Love Her / If I Fell	1964	15.00	75.00
Capitol 5235		And I Love Her / If I Fell	1968	6.00	30.00
		(Orange & yellow swirl label reads "A Subsidiary of Capitol Industries U.S.A.")			
Capitol 5235		And I Love Her / If I Fell	1969	6.00	30.00
		(Red and orange label with the Capitol dome logo on the left.)			
Capitol 5235		And I Love Her / If I Fell	1970	3.00	15.00
		(Red and orange label with a round target logo on the left.)			
Capitol 5255		Matchbox / Slow Down	1964	4.00	20.00
		(Orange & yellow swirl label reads "Mfd. by Capitol Records Inc. U.S.A.")			
Capitol 5255	(PS)	Matchbox / Slow Down	1964	16.00	80.00
Capitol 5255		Matchbox / Slow Down	1968	6.00	30.00
		(Orange & yellow swirl label reads "A Subsidiary of Capitol Industries U.S.A.")			
Capitol 5255		Matchbox / Slow Down	1969	6.00	30.00
		(Red and orange label with the Capitol dome logo on the left.)			
Capitol 5255		Matchbox / Slow Down	1970	3.00	15.00
		(Red and orange label with a round target logo on the left.)			

Label & Catalog #		A-Side/B-Side	Year	VG	NM
Capitol 5327		**I Feel Fine / She's A Woman**	1964	3.00	15.00
		(Orange & yellow swirl label reads "Mfd. by Capitol Records Inc. U.S.A.")			
Capitol 5327	(PS)	**I Feel Fine / She's A Woman**	1964	6.00	30.00
Capitol 5327		**I Feel Fine / She's A Woman**	1968	6.00	30.00
		(Orange & yellow swirl label reads "A Subsidiary of Capitol Industries U.S.A.")			
Capitol 5327		**I Feel Fine / She's A Woman**	1969	6.00	30.00
		(Red and orange label with the Capitol dome logo on the left.)			
Capitol 5327		**I Feel Fine / She's A Woman**	1970	3.00	15.00
		(Red and orange label with a round target logo on the left.)			
Capitol 5371		**Eight Days A Week / I Don't Want To Spoil The Party**	1965	3.00	15.00
		(Orange & yellow swirl label reads "Mfd. by Capitol Records Inc. U.S.A.")			
Capitol 5371	(PS)	**Eight Days A Week / I Don't Want To Spoil The Party**	1965	6.00	30.00
		(Sleeve is trimmed straight across the top on both sides.)			
Capitol 5371	(PS)	**Eight Days A Week / I Don't Want To Spoil The Party**	1965	3.00	15.00
		(Sleeve has a thumb notch cut on one side of the top.)			
Capitol 5371		**Eight Days A Week / I Don't Want To Spoil The Party**	1968	6.00	30.00
		(Orange & yellow swirl label reads "A Subsidiary of Capitol Industries U.S.A.")			
Capitol 5371		**Eight Days A Week / I Don't Want To Spoil The Party**	1969	6.00	30.00
		(Red and orange label with the Capitol dome logo on the left.)			
Capitol 5371		**Eight Days A Week / I Don't Want To Spoil The Party**	1970	3.00	15.00
		(Red and orange label with a round target logo on the left.)			
Capitol 5407		**Ticket To Ride / Yes It Is**	1965	3.00	15.00
		(Orange & yellow swirl label reads "Mfd. by Capitol Records Inc. U.S.A.")			
Capitol 5407	(PS)	**Ticket To Ride / Yes It Is**	1965	15.00	75.00
Capitol 5407		**Ticket To Ride / Yes It Is**	1968	6.00	30.00
		(Orange & yellow swirl label reads "A Subsidiary of Capitol Industries U.S.A.")			
Capitol 5407		**Ticket To Ride / Yes It Is**	1969	6.00	30.00
		(Red and orange label with the Capitol dome logo on the left.)			
Capitol 5407		**Ticket To Ride / Yes It Is**	1970	3.00	15.00
		(Red and orange label with a round target logo on the left.)			
Capitol 5476		**Help! / I'm Down**	1965	3.00	15.00
		(Orange & yellow swirl label reads "Mfd. by Capitol Records Inc. U.S.A.")			
Capitol 5476	(PS)	**Help! / I'm Down**	1965	6.00	30.00
Capitol 5476		**Help! / I'm Down**	1968	6.00	30.00
		(Orange & yellow swirl label reads "A Subsidiary of Capitol Industries U.S.A.")			
Capitol 5476		**Help! / I'm Down**	1969	6.00	30.00
		(Red and orange label with the Capitol dome logo on the left.)			
Capitol 5476		**Help! / I'm Down**	1970	3.00	15.00
		(Red and orange label with a round target logo on the left.)			
Capitol 5498		**Yesterday / Act Naturally**	1965	3.00	15.00
		(Orange & yellow swirl label reads "Mfd. by Capitol Records Inc. U.S.A.")			
Capitol 5498	(PS)	**Yesterday / Act Naturally**	1965	6.00	30.00
Capitol 5498		**Yesterday / Act Naturally**	1968	6.00	30.00
		(Orange & yellow swirl label reads "A Subsidiary of Capitol Industries U.S.A.")			
Capitol 5498		**Yesterday / Act Naturally**	1969	6.00	30.00
		(Red and orange label with the Capitol dome logo on the left.)			
Capitol 5498		**Yesterday / Act Naturally**	1970	3.00	15.00
		(Red and orange label with a round target logo on the left.)			
Capitol 5555		**We Can Work It Out / Day Tripper**	1965	3.00	15.00
		(Orange & yellow swirl label reads "Mfd. by Capitol Records Inc. U.S.A.")			
Capitol 5555	(PS)	**We Can Work It Out / Day Tripper**	1965	6.00	30.00
Capitol 5555		**We Can Work It Out / Day Tripper**	1968	6.00	30.00
		(Orange & yellow swirl label reads "A Subsidiary of Capitol Industries U.S.A.")			
Capitol 5555		**We Can Work It Out / Day Tripper**	1969	500.00	1,500.00
		(Red & white Starline label.)			
Capitol 5555		**We Can Work It Out / Day Tripper**	1969	6.00	30.00
		(Red and orange label with the Capitol dome logo on the left.)			
Capitol 5555		**We Can Work It Out / Day Tripper**	1970	3.00	15.00
		(Red and orange label with a round target logo on the left.)			
Capitol 5587		**Nowhere Man / What Goes On**	1966	3.00	15.00
		(Orange & yellow swirl label reads "Mfd. by Capitol Records Inc. U.S.A."			
		First pressings credit Lennon-McCartney as songwriters on the b-side)			
Capitol 5587		**Nowhere Man / What Goes On**	1966	5.00	25.00
		(Orange & yellow swirl label reads "Mfd. by Capitol Records Inc. U.S.A."			
		Second pressings credit Lennon-McCartney-Starkey as the songwriters.)			
Capitol 5587	(PS)	**Nowhere Man / What Goes On**	1966	6.00	30.00
Capitol 5587		**Nowhere Man / What Goes On**	1968	6.00	30.00
		(Orange & yellow swirl label reads "A Subsidiary of Capitol Industries U.S.A.")			
Capitol 5587		**Nowhere Man / What Goes On**	1969	6.00	30.00
		(Red and orange label with the Capitol dome logo on the left.)			
Capitol 5587		**Nowhere Man / What Goes On**	1970	3.00	15.00
		(Red and orange label with a round target logo on the left.)			
Capitol 5651		**Paperback Writer / Rain**	1966	3.00	15.00
		(Orange & yellow swirl label reads "Mfd. by Capitol Records Inc. U.S.A.")			
Capitol 5651	(PS)	**Paperback Writer / Rain**	1966	6.00	30.00
Capitol 5651		**Paperback Writer / Rain**	1968	4.00	20.00
		(Orange & yellow swirl label reads "A Subsidiary of Capitol Industries U.S.A.")			

Label & Catalog #		A-Side/B-Side	Year	VG	NM
Capitol 5651		**Paperback Writer / Rain**	1969	6.00	30.00
		(Red and orange label with the Capitol dome logo on the left.)			
Capitol 5651		**Paperback Writer / Rain**	1970	3.00	15.00
		(Red and orange label with a round target logo on the left.)			
Capitol 5715		**Yellow Submarine / Eleanor Rigby**	1966	3.00	15.00
		(Orange & yellow swirl label reads "Mfd. by Capitol Records Inc. U.S.A.")			
Capitol 5715	(PS)	**Yellow Submarine / Eleanor Rigby**	1966	7.00	35.00
Capitol 5715		**Yellow Submarine / Eleanor Rigby**	1968	6.00	30.00
		(Orange & yellow swirl label reads "A Subsidiary of Capitol Industries U.S.A.")			
Capitol 5715		**Yellow Submarine / Eleanor Rigby**	1970	3.00	15.00
		(Red and orange label with a round target logo on the left.)			
Capitol 5715		**Yellow Submarine / Eleanor Rigby**	1969	6.00	30.00
		(Red and orange label with the Capitol dome logo on the left.)			
Capitol P-5810	(DJ)	**Penny Lane / Strawberry Fields Forever**	1967	50.00	250.00
		(Green label. A-side features a "trumpet-solo ending.")			
Capitol P-5810	(DJ)	**Penny Lane / Strawberry Fields Forever**	1967	125.00	500.00
		(Green label. A-side does not feature the "trumpet-solo ending.")			
Capitol 5810		**Penny Lane / Strawberry Fields Forever**	1967	3.00	15.00
		(Orange & yellow swirl label reads "Mfd. by Capitol Records Inc. U.S.A." First pressings list the a-side's time at 3:00.)			
Capitol 5810		**Penny Lane / Strawberry Fields Forever**	1967	3.00	15.00
		(Orange & yellow swirl label reads "Mfd. by Capitol Records Inc. U.S.A." Second pressings list the a-side's time at 2:57.)			
Capitol 5810	(PS)	**Penny Lane / Strawberry Fields Forever**	1967	10.00	50.00
Capitol 5810		**Penny Lane / Strawberry Fields Forever**	1968	6.00	30.00
		(Orange & yellow swirl label reads "A Subsidiary of Capitol Industries U.S.A.")			
Capitol 5810		**Penny Lane / Strawberry Fields Forever**	1969	6.00	30.00
		(Red and orange label with the Capitol dome logo on the left.)			
Capitol 5810		**Penny Lane / Strawberry Fields Forever**	1970	3.00	15.00
		(Red and orange label with a round target logo on the left.)			
Capitol P-5964	(DJ)	**All You Need Is Love / Baby, You're A Rich Man**	1967	40.00	200.00
Capitol 5964		**All You Need Is Love / Baby, You're A Rich Man**	1967	3.00	15.00
		(Orange & yellow swirl label reads "Mfd. by Capitol Records Inc. U.S.A.")			
Capitol 5964	(PS)	**All You Need Is Love / Baby, You're A Rich Man**	1967	4.00	20.00
Capitol 5964		**All You Need Is Love / Baby, You're A Rich Man**	1968	6.00	30.00
		(Orange & yellow swirl label reads "A Subsidiary of Capitol Industries U.S.A.")			
Capitol 5964		**All You Need Is Love / Baby, You're A Rich Man**	1969	6.00	30.00
		(Red and orange label with the Capitol dome logo on the left.)			
Capitol 5964		**All You Need Is Love / Baby, You're A Rich Man**	1970	3.00	15.00
		(Red and orange label with a round target logo on the left.)			
Capitol P-2056	(DJ)	**Hello, Goodbye / I Am The Walrus**	1967	40.00	200.00
Capitol 2056		**Hello, Goodbye / I Am The Walrus**	1967	4.00	20.00
		(Orange & yellow swirl label reads "Mfd. by Capitol Records Inc. U.S.A." Credits MacLen Music Inc. as the music publisher.)			
Capitol 2056		**Hello, Goodbye / I Am The Walrus**	1967	4.00	20.00
		(Orange & yellow swirl label reads "Mfd. by Capitol Records Inc. U.S.A." Credits Comet Music Inc. as the music publisher.)			
Capitol 2056	(PS)	**Hello, Goodbye / I Am The Walrus**	1967	10.00	50.00
Capitol 2056		**Hello, Goodbye / I Am The Walrus**	1968	6.00	30.00
		(Orange & yellow swirl label reads "A Subsidiary of Capitol Industries U.S.A.")			
Capitol 2056		**Hello, Goodbye / I Am The Walrus**	1969	6.00	30.00
		(Red and orange label with the Capitol dome logo on the left.)			
Capitol 2056		**Hello, Goodbye / I Am The Walrus**	1970	3.00	15.00
		(Red and orange label with a round target logo on the left.)			
Capitol P-2138	(DJ)	**Lady Madonna / The Inner Light**	1968	40.00	200.00
Capitol 2138		**Lady Madonna / The Inner Light**	1968	4.00	20.00
		(Orange & yellow swirl label reads "Mfd. by Capitol Records Inc. U.S.A.")			
Capitol 2138	(PS)	**Lady Madonna / The Inner Light**	1968	6.00	30.00
		(Sleeve is trimmed straight across the top on both sides.)			
Capitol 2138		**Lady Madonna / The Inner Light**	1968	6.00	30.00
		(Orange & yellow swirl label reads "A Subsidiary of Capitol Industries U.S.A.")			
Capitol 2138		**Lady Madonna / The Inner Light**	1969	6.00	30.00
		(Red and orange label with the Capitol dome logo on the left.)			
Capitol 2138		**Lady Madonna / The Inner Light**	1970	3.00	15.00
		(Red and orange label with a round target logo on the left.)			
Capitol 72144		**All My Loving / This Boy** (Red & orange label)	1972	20.00	100.00

—*Capitol Starline Series*—

Label & Catalog #	A-Side/B-Side	Year	VG	NM
Capitol 6061	**Twist And Shout / There's A Place**	1965	15.00	75.00
Capitol 6062	**Love Me Do / P.S. I Love You**	1965	15.00	75.00
Capitol 6063	**Please, Please Me / From Me To You**	1965	15.00	75.00
Capitol 6064	**Do You Want To Know A Secret / Thank You Girl**	1965	15.00	75.00
Capitol 6065	**Roll Over, Beethoven / Misery**	1965	15.00	75.00
Capitol 6066	**Kansas City / Boys**	1965	12.00	60.00

—*Original Starline singles above have green swirl labels.*—

Label & Catalog #	A-Side/B-Side	Year	VG	NM
Capitol 6065	**Roll Over, Beethoven / Misery**	1969	5.00	25.00

—*Red & orange label with the Capitol dome logo on the left.*—

Label & Catalog #		A-Side/B-Side	Year	VG	NM

—Extended Play Albums—

Capitol EAP1-2121		**Four By The Beatles**	1964	**75.00**	**300.00**
Capitol R-6365		**4-By The Beatles**	1964	**50.00**	**200.00**

—Special/Promotional Releses—

Capitol/Holiday Inn		**"A Gift From Your Holiday Inn Keeper" Wraparound**	1964	**250.00**	**750.00**
		(Yellow paper sheet with green print reads "Smash Hit In Travel-Smash Hit In Entertainment" and was stapled around stock picture sleeves.)			
Capitol RB-2637/38		**Music City KFWBeatles / You Can't Do That**	1964	**200.00**	**600.00**
		(Red label. A-side label has the Capitol Custom logo on the right and reads "Limited Pressings-June 5, 1964" beneath title at top.)			
Capitol RB-2637/38	(PS)	**Music City KFWBeatles / You Can't Do That**	1964	**400.00**	**1,200.00**
		(Promotional mailer reads "The Beatles Talk And Sing! Wallichs Music City KFWB/98-Souvenir Record-A Limited Pressing Celebrating The Opening Of Wallichs Music City, Topanga Plaza, Canoga Park.")			
United Artists		**A Hard Day's Night Interview**	1964	**800.00**	**2,000.00**
Capitol PRO-2548/49		**Open-End Interview With The Beatles**	1964	**250.00**	**750.00**
Capitol PRO-2548/49	(PS)	**Open-End Interview With The Beatles**	1964	**400.00**	**1,200.00**
Capitol PRO-2598/99	(33)	**The Beatles' Second Open-End Interview**	1964	**125.00**	**500.00**
Capitol PRO-2598/99	(PS)	**The Beatles' Second Open-End Interview**	1964	**250.00**	**750.00**
Capitol PRO-2720/1		**The Beatles Introduce New Songs**	1964	**800.00**	**2,000.00**
		(John and Paul introduce songs by Cilla Black and Peter & Gordon. Issued without a cover.)			
Capitol/Evatone 8464		**A Surprise Gift From The Beatles, The Beach Boys & The Kingston Trio** *(5" flexidisc)*	1964	**125.00**	**500.00**
Capitol/Evatone 8464		**A Surprise Gift From The Beatles, The Beach Boys & The Kingston Trio** *(6" x 9" mailer)*	1964	**500.00**	**1,500.00**
Capitol/Evatone 8464		**A Surprise Gift From The Beatles, The Beach Boys & The Kingston Trio** *(7" tri-fold vinyl coated card.)*	1964	**150.00**	**600.00**
Capitol SXA-2047	(33)	**Meet The Beatles** *(Jukebox EP)*	1967	**250.00**	**750.00**
Capitol SXA-2080	(33)	**The Beatles' Second Album** *(Jukebox EP)*	1967	**250.00**	**750.00**
Capitol SXA-2108	(33)	**Something New** *(Jukebox EP)*	1967	**330.00**	**1,000.00**

—Official Beatles Fan Club—

(Fan Club)		**1964 Seasons Greetings From The Beatles**	1964	**50.00**	**250.00**
		(Tri-fold vinyl coated card.)			
Lyntone 948		**The Beatles Third Christmas Record**	1965	**30.00**	**150.00**
(Postcard)		**1966 Seasons Greetings From The Beatles**	1966	**35.00**	**175.00**
(Postacrd)		**1967 Seasons Greetings From The Beatles**	1967	**35.00**	**175.00**
(Flexidisc)		**The Beatles 1968 Christmas Record**	1968	**25.00**	**125.00**
Flexidisc H-2041		**Happy Christmas 1969**	1969	**15.00**	**75.00**

—Apple Records—

The Apple reissues of 1971 bore labels that read "Mfd. by Apple Records Inc." A label variation of note is the addition of a black star to the label; this occurred in 1971 and doubles the record's value. Another variation occurred in 1975: a disclaimer that reads "All Rights Reserved. Unauthorized duplication is a violation of applicable laws." These were used briefly and are escalating in value.

Apple 2276		**Hey Jude / Revolution**	1968	**2.00**	**10.00**
		(Label that reads "Mfd. by Capitol Records Inc." on the bottom.)			
Apple 2276		**Hey Jude / Revolution**	197?	**1.00**	**5.00**
		(Labels read "Mfd. by Apple Records Inc." on the bottom.)			
Apple 2490		**Get Back / Don't Let Me Down**	1969	**1.20**	**6.00**
		(Label that reads "Mfd. by Capitol Records Inc." on the bottom. The label credits The Beatles With Billy Preston.)			
Apple 2490		**Get Back / Don't Let Me Down**	197?	**1.00**	**5.00**
		(Labels read "Mfd. by Apple Records Inc." on the bottom.)			
Apple 2531		**Ballad Of John And Yoko / Old Brown Shoe**	1969	**1.20**	**6.00**
		(Label that reads "Mfd. by Capitol Records Inc." on the bottom.)			
Apple 2531		**Ballad Of John And Yoko / Old Brown Shoe**	197?	**1.00**	**5.00**
		(Labels read "Mfd. by Apple Records Inc." on the bottom.)			
Apple 2531	(PS)	**Ballad Of John And Yoko / Old Brown Shoe**	1969	**8.00**	**40.00**
Apple 2654		**Something / Come Together**	1969	**1.60**	**8.00**
		(Label that reads "Mfd. by Capitol Records Inc." on the bottom.)			
Apple 2654		**Something / Come Together**	197?	**1.00**	**5.00**
		(Labels read "Mfd. by Apple Records Inc." on the bottom.)			
Apple 2764		**Let It Be / You Know My Name**	1970	**1.60**	**8.00**
		(Label that reads "Mfd. by Capitol Records Inc." on the bottom.)			
Apple 2764		**Let It Be / You Know My Name**	197?	**1.00**	**5.00**
		(Labels read "Mfd. by Apple Records Inc." on the bottom.)			
Apple 2764	(PS)	**Let It Be / You Know My Name**	1970	**6.00**	**30.00**
Apple 8232		**The Long And Winding Road / For You Blue**	1970	**2.00**	**10.00**
		(Label that reads "Mfd. by Capitol Records Inc." on the bottom. A-side produced by Phil Spector.)			
Apple 8232		**The Long And Winding Road / For You Blue**	197?	**1.00**	**5.00**
		(Labels read "Mfd. by Apple Records Inc." on the bottom.)			
Apple 8232	(PS)	**The Long And Winding Road / For You Blue**	1970	**7.00**	**35.00**

Label & Catalog #		A-Side / B-Side	Year	VG	NM
		—Apple Reissues—			
Apple 5112		I Want To Hold Your Hand / I Saw Her Standing There	1971	3.00	15.00
Apple 5150		Can't Buy Me Love / You Can't Do That	1971	3.00	15.00
Apple 5222		A Hard Day's Night / I Should Have Known Better	1971	3.00	15.00
Apple 5234		I'll Cry Instead / I'm Happy Just To Dance With You	1971	3.00	15.00
Apple 5235		And I Love Her / If I Fell	1971	3.00	15.00
Apple 5255		Matchbox / Slow Down	1971	3.00	15.00
Apple 5327		I Feel Fine / She's A Woman	1971	3.00	15.00
Apple 5371		Eight Days A Week / I Don't Want To Spoil The Party	1971	3.00	15.00
Apple 5407		Ticket To Ride / Yes It Is	1971	3.00	15.00
Apple 5476		Help! / I'm Down	1971	3.00	15.00
Apple 5498		Yesterday / Act Naturally	1971	3.00	15.00
Apple 5555		We Can Work It Out / Day Tripper	1971	3.00	15.00
Apple 5587		Nowhere Man / What Goes On	1971	3.00	15.00
Apple 5651		Paperback Writer / Rain	1971	3.00	15.00
Apple 5715		Yellow Submarine / Eleanor Rigby	1971	3.00	15.00
Apple 5810		Penny Lane / Strawberry Fields Forever	1971	3.00	15.00
Apple 5964		All You Need Is Love / Baby, You're A Rich Man	1971	3.00	15.00
Apple 2056		Hello, Goodbye / I Am The Walrus	1971	3.00	15.00
Apple 2138		Lady Madonna / The Inner Light	1971	3.00	15.00
		—Apple reissues above have a black star printed on the a-side of the label.—			
Apple 5112		I Want To Hold Your Hand / I Saw Her Standing There	1971	1.20	6.00
Apple 5150		Can't Buy Me Love / You Can't Do That	1971	1.20	6.00
Apple 5222		A Hard Day's Night / I Should Have Known Better	1971	1.20	6.00
Apple 5234		I'll Cry Instead / I'm Happy Just To Dance With You	1971	1.20	6.00
Apple 5235		And I Love Her / If I Fell	1971	1.20	6.00
Apple 5255		Matchbox / Slow Down	1971	1.20	6.00
Apple 5327		I Feel Fine / She's A Woman	1971	1.20	6.00
Apple 5371		Eight Days A Week / I Don't Want To Spoil The Party	1971	1.20	6.00
Apple 5407		Ticket To Ride / Yes It Is	1971	1.20	6.00
Apple 5476		Help! / I'm Down	1971	1.20	6.00
Apple 5498		Yesterday / Act Naturally	1971	1.20	6.00
Apple 5555		We Can Work It Out / Day Tripper	1971	1.20	6.00
Apple 5587		Nowhere Man / What Goes On	1971	1.20	6.00
Apple 5651		Paperback Writer / Rain	1971	1.20	6.00
Apple 5715		Yellow Submarine / Eleanor Rigby	1971	1.20	6.00
Apple 5810		Penny Lane / Strawberry Fields Forever	1971	1.20	6.00
Apple 5964		All You Need Is Love / Baby, You're A Rich Man	1971	1.20	6.00
Apple 2056		Hello, Goodbye / I Am The Walrus	1971	1.20	6.00
Apple 2138		Lady Madonna / The Inner Light	1971	1.00	5.00
		—Apple reissues above do not have a black star printed on the label.—			
		—Special/Promotional Releases—			
Apple KAL-1004	(DJ)	Yellow Submarine (Radio spots)	1968	400.00	1,200.00
Americorp		Yellow Submarine / Eleanor Rigby (4" flexi-disc.)	1969	—	—
		(Rare. There are no transactions from which to derive an accurate value.)			
Americom 2276		Hey Jude / Revolution (4" flexi-disc.)	1969	75.00	300.00
Americom 335		Get Back / Don't Let Me Down (4" flexi-disc.)	1969	330.00	1,000.00
Beatles Promo 1970		Dialogue From The Motion Picture "Let It Be" (One sided)	1970	10.00	50.00
United Artists 42370		Let It Be (One sided radio spots)	1970	330.00	1,000.00
		—Capitol Repackages—			
By the mid '70s both the Beatles and Apple were a memory and the release of their material reverted to Capitol...					
Capitol P-4274	(DJ)	Helter Skelter / Helter Skelter	1976	6.00	30.00
Capitol P-4274	(DJ)	Got To Get You Into My Life / Got To Get You Into My Life	1976	6.00	30.00
Capitol 4274		Got To Get You Into My Life / Helter Skelter	1976	1.00	5.00
Capitol 4274	(PS)	Got To Get You Into My Life / Helter Skelter	1976	2.00	10.00
Capitol 4347	(DJ)	Ob-La-Di, Ob-La-Da / Ob-La-Di, Ob-La-Da	1976	7.00	35.00
Capitol 4347		Ob-La-Di, Ob-La-Da / Julia	1976	.80	4.00
Capitol 4347	(PS)	Ob-La-Di, Ob-La-Da / Julia	1976	1.00	5.00
Capitol P-4506	(DJ)	Girl / Girl	1977	30.00	150.00
Capitol 4506	(PS)	Girl	1977	3.00	15.00
Capitol P-4612	(DJ)	Sgt. Pepper-With A Little Help From My Friends / A Day In The Life	1978	7.00	35.00
Capitol 4612		Sgt. Pepper-With A Little Help From My Friends / A Day In The Life (Purple label)	1978	.80	4.00
Capitol 4612	(PS)	Sgt. Pepper-With A Little Help From My Friends / A Day In The Life	1978	2.00	10.00
Capitol PB-5100	(DJ)	The Beatles Movie Medley / Fab Four On Film	1982	5.00	25.00
Capitol B-5100		The Beatles Movie Medley / Fab Four On Film	1982	12.00	60.00
Capitol B-5100	(PS)	The Beatles Movie Medley / Fab Four On Film	1982	4.00	20.00
Capitol B-5107		The Beatles Movie Medley / I'm Happy Just To Dance With You	1982	.40	2.00
Capitol B-5107	(PS)	The Beatles Movie Medley / I'm Happy Just To Dance With You	1982	.80	4.00
Capitol PB-5189	(DJ)	Love Me Do / Love Me Do	1982	3.00	15.00
Capitol B-5189		Love Me Do / P.S. I Love You	1982	.40	2.00
Capitol B-5189	(PS)	Love Me Do / P.S. I Love You	1982	.80	4.00

Label & Catalog #		A-Side/B-Side	Year	VG	NM
Capitol P-5112	(DJ)	I Want To Hold Your Hand / I Saw Her Standing There	1984	3.00	15.00
Capitol 5112		I Want To Hold Your Hand / I Saw Her Standing There	1984	.60	3.00
		(Commemorative reissue: the label reads "Mfd. by Capitol Records. A subsidiary of Capitol Industries Inc. U.S.A." on the left side.)			
Capitol 5112	(PS)	I Want To Hold Your Hand / I Saw Her Standing There	1984	.60	3.00
Capitol B-5439		Leave My Kitten Alone	1985	Unreleased	
Capitol B-5439	(PS)	Leave My Kitten Alone	1985	30.00	150.00
		—12" Singles—			
Capitol SPRO-9758	(DJ)	The Beatles Movie Medley / Fab Four On Film (PC)	1982	12.00	60.00
Ultimix #20		Twist And Shout	1988	30.00	150.00

BEATLES COSTELLO, THE
The Beatles Costello features Andy Paley.

Label & Catalog #		A-Side/B-Side	Year	VG	NM
Pious 310		Washing The Defectives-Soldier Of Love / I Feel Fine-Theme From A Summer Place-Out Of Limits	1978	1.00	5.00
Pious 310	(PS)	Washing The Defectives-Soldier Of Love / I Feel Fine-Theme From A Summer Place-Out Of Limits	1978	1.00	5.00

BEATLETTES, THE [THE BEATLE-ETTES]

Label & Catalog #	A-Side/B-Side	Year	VG	NM
Jubilee 5472	Only Seventeen / Now We're Together	1964	4.00	20.00
Assault 1893	Yes, You Can Hold My Hand / Yes, You Can Hold My Hand, Part 2	1964	4.00	20.00
Jamie 1270	Dance Beatle, Dance / We Were Meant To Be Married	1964	4.00	20.00

BEATNIKS, THE

Label & Catalog #	A-Side/B-Side	Year	VG	NM
Performance 500	Beat Generation / Get Yourself-A-Ready	1959	2.00	10.00

BEATS, THE

Label & Catalog #	A-Side/B-Side	Year	VG	NM
Columbia 41781	Beatnik Bounce / Beatnik Bounce, Part 2	1960	2.00	10.00

BEATSTALKERS, THE

Label & Catalog #	A-Side/B-Side	Year	VG	NM
Press 5001	You Better Get A Hold On / Left Hand Right	1966	2.00	10.00

BEATTY, E. C.

Label & Catalog #	A-Side/B-Side	Year	VG	NM
Colonial 7003	Ski King / I'm A Lucky Man	1959	2.00	10.00

BEAU BRUMMELS, THE
Original group features Ron Elliott, Ron Meagher, Sal Valentino and John Petersen.

Label & Catalog #	A-Side/B-Side	Year	VG	NM
Autumn 8	Laugh Laugh / With You, Baby	1965	1.60	8.00
Autumn 10	Just A Little / They'll Make You Cry	1965	1.60	8.00
Autumn 16	You Tell Me Why / I Want You	1965	1.60	8.00
Autumn 20	Don't Talk To Strangers / In Good Time	1965	1.20	6.00
Autumn 24	Good Time Music / Sad Little Girl	1965	1.20	6.00
Warner Bros. 5813	One Too Many Mornings / She Reigns	1966	1.20	6.00
Warner Bros. 5848	Here We Are Again / Fine With Me	1966	1.00	5.00
Warner Bros. 7014	Two Days 'Til Tomorrow / Don't Make Promises	1967	1.00	5.00
Warner Bros. 7079	Magic Hollow / Lower Lever	1967	1.00	5.00
Warner Bros. 7204	Are You Happy? / Lift Me	1968	1.00	5.00
Warner Bros. 7218	I'm A Sleeper / Long Walk Down To Misery	1968	1.00	5.00
Warner Bros. 7260	Cherokee Girl / Deep Water	1968	1.00	5.00
Warner Bros. 8119	You Tell Me Why / Down To The Bottom	1975	1.40	2.00

BEAU-MARKS, THE

Label & Catalog #	A-Side/B-Side	Year	VG	NM
Shad 5017	Clap Your Hands / Daddy Said	1960	2.00	10.00
Shad 5021	'Cause We're In Love / Billy Went A-Walking	1960	3.00	15.00
Time 1032	Oh, Joan / Rockin' Blues	1961	4.00	20.00
Rust 5035	Classmate / School Is Out	1961	2.00	10.00
Rust 5050	Tender Years / I'll Never Be The Same	1962	2.00	10.00
Port 70029	Lovely Little Lady / Little Miss Twist	1962	2.00	10.00
Mainstream 688	Clap Your Hands / Daddy Said	1968	1.20	6.00

BEAUCHEMINS, THE

Label & Catalog #	A-Side/B-Side	Year	VG	NM
Mustang 3015	My Lovin' Baby / Shenandoah	1966	1.20	6.00

BEAUMONT, JIMMY
Jimmy Beaumont originally recorded with The Skyliners.

Label & Catalog #	A-Side/B-Side	Year	VG	NM
Colpix 607	The End Of A Story / Baion Rhythms	1961	3.00	15.00
May 112	Everybody's Crying / Camera	1961	3.00	15.00
May 115	I Shoulda Listened To Mama / Juarez	1962	3.00	15.00
May 120	Never Say Goodbye / I'm Gonna Try My Wings	1962	4.00	20.00
May 136	I'll Always Be In Love With You / Give Her My Best	1962	3.00	15.00
Bang 510	Tell Me / I Feel I'm Falling In Love	1966	3.00	15.00
Bang 525	I Never Loved Her Anyway / You Got Too Much Going For You	1966	4.00	20.00
Gallant 3007	Please Send Me Someone To Love / There Is No Other Love	196?	4.00	20.00
Gallant 3012	Love Is A Dangerous Game / Just A Little Closer	196?	2.00	10.00

Label & Catalog #	A-Side/B-Side	Year	VG	NM
BEAUMONT, JIMMY, & THE SKYLINERS				
Capitol 3979	Where Have They Gone? / I Could Have Loved You So Well	1974	2.00	10.00
Drive 6250	The Day The Clown Cried / Our Day Is Here	1976	2.00	10.00
BEAUS: Refer to BOBBI & THE BEAUS				
BEAUTIFUL DAZE, THE				
Alfa	City Jungle / City Jungle (Part 2)	196?	4.00	20.00
Spread City 101	City Jungle / City Jungle (Part 2)	196?	2.00	10.00
RPR 101	City Jungle / City Jungle (Part 2)	196?	1.20	6.00
BEAVERS, THE				
Capitol 3956	Rockin' At The Drive In / Sack Dress	1958	3.00	15.00
Capitol 4015	Low As I Can Be / Road To Happiness	1958	2.00	10.00
BECK, BECKY LEE				
Challenge 9372	I Want A Beatle For Christmas / Puppy Dog	1964	4.00	20.00
BECK, JEFF [JEFF BECK GROUP]				
Jeff Beck's original group (Epic 10218-10484) features Rod Stewart and Ron Wood. Refer to Donovan; The Yardbirds.				
Epic 10218	Tally Man / Rock My Plimsoul	1967	2.00	10.00
Epic 10157	Hi Ho Silver Lining / Beck's Bolero	1967	2.00	10.00
Epic 10484	Jailhouse Rock / Plynth	1969	.80	4.00
Epic 50112	You Know What I Mean / Constipated Duck	1975	.40	2.00
Epic 50276	Come Dancing / Head For The Backstage Pass	1975	.40	2.00
BECK, JIMMY				
Champion 1002	Pipe Dreams / Blue Night	1959	2.00	10.00
BECKETT QUINTET, THE				
Gemcor 5003	Baby Blue / No Correspondence	1965	2.40	12.00
A&M 782	Baby Blue / No Correspondence	1965	2.00	10.00
BECKY & THE LOLLIPOPS				
Troy 6493	I Don't Care (What They Say) / Come On Home	1964	3.00	15.00
Epic 9736	I Don't Care (What They Say) / Come On Home	1964	1.60	8.00
BED OF ROSES				
Deltron 813	I Don't Believe You / Hate	196?	5.00	25.00
BEDBUGS, THE				
The Bedbugs feature David Seville a.k.a. Ross Bagdasarian.				
Liberty 55679	Yeah Yeah / Lucy Lucy	1964	3.00	15.00
BEDIENT, JACK, & THE CHESSMEN				
Era 3050	The Mystic One / Questions	1961	2.00	10.00
Trophy 1001	Silver Haired Daddy / Pretty One	1964	2.00	10.00
Palomar 2212	Dream Boy / Drummer Boy	1965	2.00	10.00
Fantasy 595	See The Little Girl / Here I Am	1965	4.00	20.00
Fantasy 598	Double Whammy / I Want You To Know	1965	6.00	30.00
Executive Prod. 21	I've Been Loving You / I Could Never Lose My Love For You	1966	2.00	10.00
Executive Prod. 21	Beautiful / Release Me	1966	2.00	10.00
Rev 104-66	Glimmer Sunshine / Where Did She Go?	1966	6.00	30.00
Columbia 44302	I Could Have Loved You So Well / Love Workshop	1967	1.00	5.00
Columbia 44481	Pretty One / See That Girl	1968	1.00	5.00
Columbia 44565	The Pleasures Of You / It's Over	1968	1.00	5.00
Columbia 44671	My Prayer / Independence Day	1968	1.00	5.00
BEDWELLS, THE				
Del-Fi 4230	Karate / Karate Again	1963	2.00	10.00
BEE, JAY				
Clock 1743	There's No One For Me / I'll Go On	1961	4.00	20.00
BEE, JAY, & THE KATS				
Bangar 00606	Tension / When School Is Through	195?	8.00	40.00
BEE GEES, THE				
The Bee Gees as the brothers Gibb: Barry, Maurice and Robin. Refer to Fut.				
Atco 6487	New York Mining Disaster / I Can't See Nobody	1967	4.00	20.00
	(Original promos were issued without listing the artist's name, capitalizing on the record's Beatles-like sound.)			
Atco 6487	New York Mining Disaster / I Can't See Nobody	1967	1.20	6.00
Atco 6503	To Love Somebody / Close Another Door	1967	1.20	6.00
Atco 6521	Holiday / Every Christian Lion-Hearted Man	1967	1.20	6.00
Atco 6532	Massachusetts / Sir Geoffrey Saved The World	1967	1.20	6.00
Atco 6548	Words / Sinking Ships	1968	1.00	5.00
Atco 6570	Jumbo / The Singer Sang His Song	1968	1.00	5.00

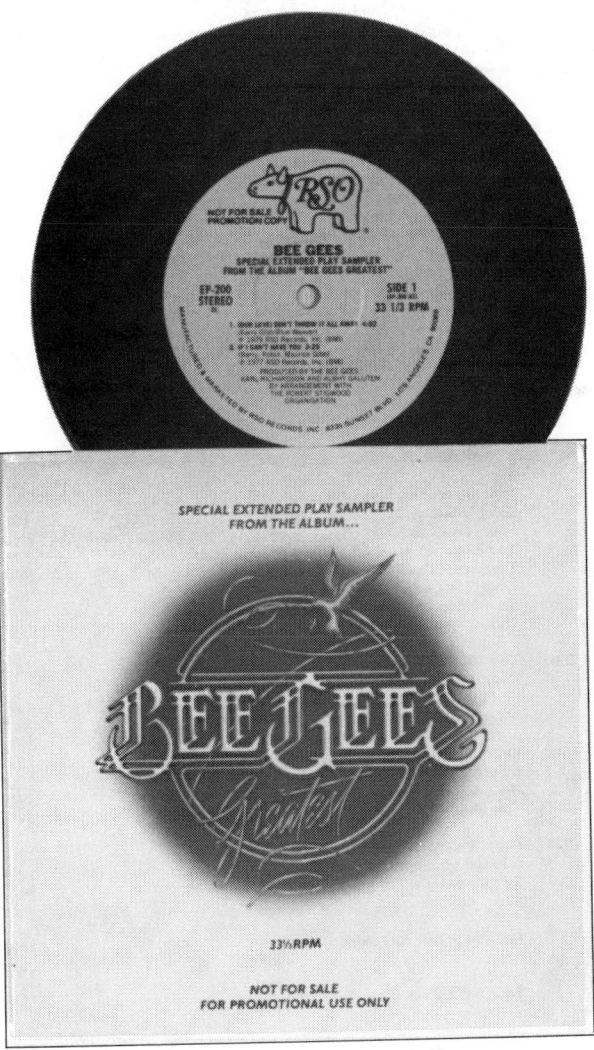

While the extended play album (EP) as a commercial concern was through in the States by the mid '60s, it surfaced in the '70s as a popular promotional item (at least in the majors; among the countless new indie labels it was an obvious medium of expression of the punk/new wave artists). This one placed four of the Bee Gees' hits in a paper picture steeve.

Label & Catalog #		A-Side / B-Side	Year	VG	NM
Atco 6603		I've Gotta Get A Message To You / Kitty Kan	1968	1.00	5.00
Atco 6639		I Started A Joke / Kilburn Towers	1968	1.00	5.00
Atco 6657		First Of May / Lamplight	1969	1.00	5.00
Atco 6682		Tomorrow, Tomorrow / Sun In The Morning	1969	1.00	5.00
Atco 6702		Don't Forget To Remember / The Lord	1969	1.00	5.00
Atco 6702		Don't Forget To Remember / I Lay Down And Die	1969	1.20	6.00
Atco 6741		If I Only Had My Mind On Something Else / Sweetheart	1969	1.00	5.00
Atco 6752		I. O. I. O. / Then You Left Me	1970	1.00	5.00
Atco 6795		Lonely Days / Man For All Seasons	1970	.80	4.00
Atco 6824		How Can You Mend A Broken Heart? / Country Woman	1970	.80	4.00
Atco 6847		Don't Want To Live Inside Myself / Walking Back To Waterloo	1971	.60	3.00
Atco 6871		My World / On Time	1971	.60	3.00
Atco 6896		Run To Me / Road To Alaska	1972	.60	3.00
Atco 6909		Alive / Paper Mache Cabbages And Kings	1972	.60	3.00
RSO 401		Saw A New Morning / My Life Has Been A Song	1973	.40	2.00
RSO 404		Wouldn't I Be Someone? / Elisa	1973	.40	2.00
RSO 408		Mr. Natural / It Doesn't Matter Much To Me	1974	.40	2.00
RSO 410		Throw A Penny / I Can't Let You Go	1974	.40	2.00
RSO 501		Charade / Heavy Breathing	1974	.40	2.00
RSO 510		Jive Talkin' / Wind Of Change	1975	.40	2.00
RSO 515		Nights On Broadway / Edge Of The Universe	1975	.40	2.00
RSO 519		Fanny (Be Tender With My Love) / Country Lanes	1975	.40	2.00
RSO 853		You Should Be Dancing / Subway	1976	.40	2.00
RSO 859		Love So Right / You Stepped Into My Life	1976	.40	2.00
RSO 867		Boogie Child / Lovers	1977	.40	2.00
RSO 880		Edge Of The Universe / Words	1977	.40	2.00
RSO 882		How Deep Is Your Love? / Can't Keep A Good Man Down	1977	.40	2.00
RSO 885		Stayin' Alive / If I Can't Have You	1977	.40	2.00
RSO 889		Night Fever / Down The Road	1978	.40	2.00
SSF 199070		Sesame Street Fever / Trash	1978	.40	2.00
RSO 907		She's Leaving Home / Oh! Darling	1978	.60	3.00
		(B-sides to SSF 199070 and RSO 807 credited to Robin Gibb)			
RSO 913		Too Much Heaven / Rest Your Love On Me	1978	.40	2.00
RSO 918		Tragedy / Until	1979	.40	2.00
RSO 925		Love You Inside Out / I'm Satisfied	1979	.40	2.00
RSO 1066		He's A Liar / He's A Liar, Part 2	1981	.40	2.00
RSO 1067		Living Eyes / I Still Love You	1981	.40	2.00
		— 12" Singles—			
RSO 853	(DJ)	You Should Be Dancing (One sided)	1976	2.00	10.00
RSO PRO-013	(DJ)	Boogie Child-You Stepped Into My Life / You Should Be Dancing-Subway	1976	2.00	10.00
RSO PRO-033	(DJ)	Stayin' Alive / Night Fever / More Than A Woman / You Should Be Dancing	1977	1.60	8.00
RSO PRO-1008	(DJ)	Tragedy / Search Find / Love You Inside Out	1979	1.20	6.00
RSO PRO-1028	(DJ)	He's A Liar / He's A Liar / He's A Liar / He's A Liar	1981	1.20	6.00
RSO PRO-1029	(DJ)	He's A Liar / He's A Liar	1981	1.20	6.00
RSO PRO-209	(DJ)	The Woman In You / The Woman In You	1983	1.20	6.00
		—Extended Play Albums—			
Atco SD-37-264	(33)	Rare, Precious And Beautiful (Jukebox EP)	1968	4.00	20.00
Atco EP-4535	(DJ)	Odessa (Paper title sleeve)	1969	5.00	25.00
RSO 200	(DJ)	The Bee Gees' Greatest (Paper title sleeve)	1979	2.00	10.00

BEECHWOODS, THE

Smash 1843		I'm Not A Kid Anymore / Place	1963	1.60	8.00

BEEDS, THE

Team 519		You Don't Have To / Run To Her	1968	.80	4.00

BEEFCAKE

Deram 85064		You Don't Know / There You Go Again	1970	.60	3.00

BEEFEATERS, THE
The Beefeaters later recorded as The Byrds.

Elektra 45013	(DJ)	Please Let Me Love You / It Won't Be Wrong	1964	25.00	125.00
Elektra 45013		Please Let Me Love You / It Won't Be Wrong	1964	40.00	200.00

BEL-TONES, THE

Del Amo 4647		Back Down / Breaktime	195?	8.00	40.00

BELAIRES, THE

No Sound 1022		Pony Rock / Palmeras	1962	2.00	10.00

BELAIRS, THE (THE BEL-AIRES)

Triumph 54		Kami-Kaze / Vampire	1963	8.00	40.00
Arvee 5034		Mr. Moto / Little Brown Jug	1963	4.00	20.00
Arvee 5054		Volcanic Action / Runaway	1963	20.00	100.00
Lucky Token 107		Baggies / Charlie Chan	1964	6.00	30.00

Label & Catalog #	A-Side/B-Side	Year	VG	NM
BELEW, CARL				
Decca 30947	Cool Gator Shoes / No Regrets	195?	4.00	20.00
BELFAST GYPSYS, THE				
The Belfast Gypsies is a pseudonym for Them with Kim Fowley on vocals.				
Loma 2051	Gloria's Dream (Round And Round) / Secret Police	1966	3.00	15.00
Loma 2060	People, Let's Freak Out / Portland Town	1966	4.00	20.00
BELL, CHRIS				
Chris Bell was formerly a member of Big Star.				
Car 6	I Am The Cosmos / You And Your Sister	1978	10.00	50.00
Car 6 (PS)	I Am The Cosmos / You And Your Sister	1978	10.00	50.00
BELL, DONNIE				
Reece-Rawson 1101	Little Girl Shy / Sugar Baby	196?	2.00	10.00
BELL, EDDIE, & THE ROCK-A-FELLAS				
Coed 512	Countin' The Days / Night Party	1959	3.00	15.00
BELL, EDDY, & THE BEL-AIRES				
Mercury 71677	The Masked Man (Hi-Yo Silver) / Anytime	1960	2.00	10.00
Lucky Four 1012	The Great, Great Pumpkin / I'm Still In Love With You	196?	3.00	15.00
BELL, FREDDIE, & THE BELLBOYS				
Teen 101	Hound Dog / Move Me, Baby	1955	5.00	25.00
Teen 103	5-10-15 Hours / Old Town Hall	1955	4.00	20.00
Wing 90066	Ding Dong / I Said It And I'm Glad	1956	3.00	15.00
Wing 90082	Rompin' And Stompin' / The Hucklebuck	1956	3.00	15.00
Mercury 70919	Stay Loose, Mother Goose / Alright, OK, You Win	1956	4.00	20.00
Mercury 71075	Hey There You / Take The First Train Out Of Town	1957	4.00	20.00
	—*Original Mercury singles above have maroon labels.*—			
Mercury 71105	Rockin' Is My Business / You're Gonna Be Sorry	1957	3.00	15.00
Audicon 103	A Heart For A Heart / The Sound Of My Heart	1959	3.00	15.00
BELL, JOHNNY				
Brunswick 55142	The Third Degree / Flip, Flop And Fly	1959	25.00	125.00
BELL, KAY, & THE SPACEMEN				
Buena Vista 428	Surfer's Blues / Scream Alone	1963	5.00	25.00
BELL, KAY, & THE TUFFS				
Dot 16304	Surfer's Stomp / Surfer's Stomp, Part 2	196?	3.00	15.00
BELL, TOMMY				
Zil 9001	Swamp Gal / Midnight Dreams	195?	20.00	100.00
BELL, VINCENT				
Del Amo 4647	Break Time / Back Down	195?	4.00	20.00
Independent 102	Quicksand / Lead Guitar	195?	6.00	30.00
BELL HOPS, THE				
Tin Pan Alley 153	Merchant Street Blues / Please Don't Say No To Me	1956	8.00	20.00
BELL HOPS, THE				
Barb 100	Angela / Ring Dang Doo Ting A Ling	195?	3.00	15.00
Barb 101/2	Teenage Years / Carmella	195?	3.00	15.00
BELL NOTES, THE				
Time 1004	I've Had It / Be Mine	1958	3.00	15.00
Time 1010	Old Spanish Town / She Went That-A-Way	1959	3.00	15.00
Time 1013	Betty Dear / That's Right	1959	3.00	15.00
Time 1015	You're A Big Girl Now / Don't Ask Me Why	1959	3.00	15.00
Time 1017	No Dice / White Buckskin Sneakers & Checkerboard Socks	1960	3.00	15.00
Madison 136	To Each His Own / Shortenin' Bread	1960	2.00	10.00
Madison 141	Friendly Star / Real Wild Child	1960	2.00	10.00
Autograph 204	Little Girl In Blue / Too Young Or Too Old	1960	2.00	10.00
BELLINGHAM ACCENTS, THE				
Jerden 746	Bacon Fat / Sampan	1965	1.60	8.00
BELLINO, JOHNNY				
Decca 31753	Angel Girl / I Keep Telling Myself	1965	2.00	10.00
BELLTONES, THE				
Olympic 241	(Please Try) To Understand Me / Swinging Little Chickie	1962	10.00	50.00
BELLUS, TONY				
NRC 023	Robbin' The Cradle / Valentine Girl	1959	3.00	15.00

Label & Catalog #	A-Side/B-Side	Year	VG	NM
NRC 035	Hey, Little Darlin' / Only Your Heart	1959	3.00	15.00
NRC 040	Young Girls / Little Dreams	1960	3.00	15.00
NRC 045	Young Girls / Hey, Little Darlin'	1960	3.00	15.00
NRC 051	The End Of My Love / The Echo Of An Old Song	1960	3.00	15.00
NRC 058	The Great Pretender / Give Me A Heart	1960	3.00	15.00

BELMONTS, THE
The Belmonts feature Carlo Mastrangelo. Refer to Pete Barin; Freddy Cannon; Carlo; Dion; and Buddy Sheppard.

Label & Catalog #	A-Side/B-Side	Year	VG	NM
Mohawk 106	Teenage Clementine / Santa Margerita	1957	8.00	40.00
Laurie 3080	We Belong Together / Such A Long Way	1961	5.00	25.00
Surprise 1000	Tell Me Why / Smoke From Your Cigarette	1961	15.00	75.00
Sabrina 500	Tell Me Why / Smoke From Your Cigarette	1961	3.00	15.00
Sabrina 501	Don't Get Around Much Anymore / Searching For A New Love	1961	4.00	20.00
Sabrina 502	I Need Someone / That American Dance	1961	4.00	20.00
Sabrina 503	I Confess / Hombre	1962	4.00	20.00
Sabrina 505	Come On, Little Angel / How About Me?	1962	3.00	15.00
Sabrina 507	Diddle-Dee-Dum (What Happens When Your Love Has Gone?) / Farewell	1962	3.00	15.00
Sabrina 509	Ann-Marie / Accentuate The Positive	1963	3.00	15.00
Sabrina 513	Walk On, Boy / Let's Call It A Day	1963	4.00	20.00
Sabrina 517	More Important Things To Do / Let's Call It A Day	1964	3.00	15.00
Sabrina 517	More Important Things To Do / Let's Call It A Day (Brown vinyl)	1964	5.00	25.00
Sabrina 519	C'mon Everybody / Why?	1964	5.00	25.00
Sabrina 521	Nothing In Return / Wintertime	1964	15.00	75.00
United Artists 809	I Don't Know Why / Summertime	1965	3.00	15.00
United Artists 904	(Then) I Walked Away / My Love Has Gone Away	1965	3.00	15.00
United Artists 966	I Got A Feeling / To Be With You	1965	3.00	15.00
United Artists 5007	Come With Me / You're Like A Mystery	1966	4.00	20.00
Dot 17173	She Only Wants To Do Her Own Thing / Reminiscences	1968	2.00	10.00
Dot 17257	Have You Heard-The Worst That Could Happen / Answer Me, My Love	1969	2.00	10.00
Strawberry 106	Cheek To Cheek / Voyager	1976	.80	4.00
Laurie 3631	A Brand New Song / Story Teller	1975	1.00	5.00

BELVEDERES, THE

Label & Catalog #	A-Side/B-Side	Year	VG	NM
Count Rhapsody 5163	From Out Of Nowhere / Tormented	195?	7.00	35.00
	The McCoy / Tired Out	195?	6.00	30.00

BELTONES THE: *Refer to* RONNIE DOVE & THE BELTONES

BEN & BEA

Label & Catalog #	A-Side/B-Side	Year	VG	NM
Philips 4000	Gee, Baby / Let The Good Times Roll	1962	2.00	10.00

BENDIX, RALPH

Label & Catalog #	A-Side/B-Side	Year	VG	NM
ABC-Paramount 10340	Baby Sittin' Boogie / Sonne, Mond Und Sterne	1962	4.00	20.00

BENEFIELD, MARVIN
Marvin Benefield also recorded as Vince Everett.

Label & Catalog #	A-Side/B-Side	Year	VG	NM
Royalty 505	I'm Snowed /	1958	20.00	100.00

BENNETT, BOYD

Label & Catalog #	A-Side/B-Side	Year	VG	NM
King 1413	Waterloo / I've Had Enough	1955	3.00	15.00
King 1432	Poison Ivy / You Upset Me, Baby	1955	3.00	15.00
King 1443	Everlovin' / Boogie At Midnight	1955	3.00	15.00
King 1470	Seventeen / Little Old You	1955	3.00	15.00
King 1475	Tennessee Rock And Roll / Oo-Oo-Oo	1955	3.00	15.00
King 1494	My Boy, Flat Top / Banjo Rock And Roll	1955	3.00	15.00

—Original King singles above originally have maroon labels.—

Label & Catalog #	A-Side/B-Side	Year	VG	NM
King 4853	The Most / Desperately	1956	2.00	10.00
King 4874	Right Around The Corner / Partners For Life	1956	2.00	10.00
King 4903	Blues Suede Shoes / Mumbles Blues	1956	2.00	10.00
King 4925	The Groovy Age / Let Me Love You	1956	2.00	10.00
King 4953	Hit That Jive, Jack / Rabbit-Eye Pink And Charcoal Black	1956	2.00	10.00
King 4985	Rockin' Up A Storm / A Lock Of Your Hair	1957	2.00	10.00
King 5021	I'm Moving On / Big Jay Shuffle	195?	2.00	10.00
King 5049	Big Boy / Put The Chain On The Door	195?	2.00	10.00
King 5070	Shindig / Hammer Head	195?	2.00	10.00
King 5097	Boy Meets Girl / Sentimental Journey	195?	2.00	10.00
King 5113	Her Momma Doesn't Think It's Right / Signed, Sealed, Delivered	195?	2.00	10.00
King 5115	Move / Click Clack	195?	2.00	10.00
King 5282	High School Hop / Cool Disc Jockey	1959	2.00	10.00
King 5374	Seventeen / My Boy Flat Top	195?	2.00	10.00

—Original King singles above have blue labels.—

Label & Catalog #	A-Side/B-Side	Year	VG	NM
Mercury 71409	Tear It Up / Tight Tights	1959	1.60	8.00
Mercury 71479	Boogie Bear / A Boy Can Tell	1959	1.60	8.00

Label & Catalog #	A-Side/B-Side	Year	VG	NM
Mercury 71537	Naughty Rock And Roll / Lover's Night	1960	1.60	8.00
Mercury 71605	It's Wonderful / Amos, Amas, Amat	1960	1.60	8.00
Mercury 71648	Seventeen / Sarasota	1960	1.60	8.00
Mercury 71724	Big Junior / Hershey Bar	1961	1.60	8.00
Mercury 71813	The Brain / Coffee Break	1961	1.60	8.00
	— Extended Play Albums —			
King 377	Rock And Roll	1957	100.00	400.00
King 383	Rock And Roll	1957	100.00	400.00

BENNETT, CLIFF, & THE REBEL ROUSERS

Capitol 4621	I'm In Love With You / One Way Out	1961	8.00	40.00
Ascot 2146	Everybody Loves A Lover / My Old Stand By	1964	2.00	10.00
Amy 930	If Only You'd Reply / Three Rooms With Running Water	1965	2.00	10.00
ABC 10842	Got To Get You Into My Life / Baby Each Day	1966	2.00	10.00

BENNETT, JERRY

Arch 1617	Report From Outer Space / Report From Outer Space	195?	5.00	25.00

BENNETT, JOE, & THE SPARKLETONES

ABC-Paramount 9837	Black Slacks / Boppin' Rock Boogie	1957	3.00	15.00
ABC-Paramount 9867	Penny Loafers And Bobby Socks / Rocket	1957	3.00	15.00
ABC-Paramount 9885	Cotton Pickin' Rocker / I Dig You, Baby	1958	4.00	20.00
ABC-Paramount 9929	We've Had It / Little Turtle	1958	3.00	15.00
ABC-Paramount 9959	Late Again / Do The Stop	1958	4.00	20.00
Paris 530	Bayou Rock / Beautiful One	1959	4.00	20.00
Paris 537	Boys Do Cry / What The Heck	1959	3.00	15.00
Paris 542	Are You From Dixie? / Beautiful One	1960	3.00	15.00

BENNETT, PETE, & THE EMBERS

Cupid 1212	Tarantella Rock / Bunny Hop	1959	3.00	15.00
Sunset 1002	Fever / Soft	1963	2.00	10.00

BENNETT, RON

Ta-Rh 1	Dingle Dangle Doll / My Only Girl	195?	3.00	15.00

BENNIE & LEE

Todd 1041	Soldier Boy / Johnny's Girl	1959	3.00	15.00

BENNY & THE BEDBUGS

DCP 1008	The Beatle Beat / Roll Over, Beethoven	1964	2.00	10.00

BENSKIN, SAMMY, & THE SPACEMEN

Clock 1018	Neptune / Neptune, Part 2	1960	3.00	15.00

BENSON, JANE

Atco 6151	Growing Up / Surrendering	1959	2.00	10.00

BENTLEY, JAY, & THE JET SET

GNP/Crescendo 332	Watusi '64 / I'll Get You	1964	1.20	6.00
GNP/Crescendo 347	Come On-On / Everybody's Got A Dancing Partner	1965	1.20	6.00

BENTLEYS, THE

Smash 1967	She's My Hot Rod Queen / Why Does Everybody Want To Hold My Baby?	1965	2.00	10.00
Smash 1988	Why Didn't I Listen To Mother? / Lose A Tear	1965	3.00	15.00

BERMUDAS, THE

Era 3125	Donnie / Chu Sen Ling	1964	2.00	10.00
Era 3133	Blue Dreamer / Seeing Is Believing	1964	2.00	10.00

BERNADETTE & THE SWINGING BEARS

Beach 1001	Crazy Yogi / When You're Dancing With Me	1961	2.00	10.00

BERNARD, ROD (& THE TWISTERS)

Carl	Linda Gail / Little Bitta Mama	1957	7.00	35.00
Jin 105	This Should Go On Forever / Pardon, Mr. Gordon	1958	10.00	50.00
Argo 5327	This Should Go On Forever / Pardon, Mr. Gordon	1958	4.00	20.00
Argo 5338	My Life Is A Mystery / You're On My Mind	1959	3.00	15.00
Mercury 71507	One More Chance / Shedding Teardrops Over You	1959	2.50	15.00
Mercury 71592	Let's Get Together Tonight / One Of These Days	1959	2.50	15.00
Mercury 71654	Dance, Fool, Dance / Two Fools In Love	1959	2.50	15.00
Mercury 71689	Strange Kisses / Just A Memory	1960	2.00	10.00
Mercury 71767	Who Knows? / Lonely Hearts Club	1961	2.00	10.00
Mercury 71842	I'm Not Lonely Anymore / Tell Me Sometime	1960	2.00	10.00
Hallway 1902	Colinda / Who's Gonna Rock My Baby?	1962	2.00	10.00
Hallway 1906	Fais De Do / New Orleans Jail	1962	2.00	10.00
Hallway 1915	Forgive / I Want Somebody	1963	2.00	10.00
Hallway 1917	Diggy Liggy Lo / The Clock	1963	2.00	10.00

Label & Catalog #		A-Side/B-Side	Year	VG	NM
Hallway 1922		I Might As Well / My Old Mother-In-Law	1963	2.00	10.00
Hallway/Smash 1806		Wedding Bells / I Had A Girl	1964	1.60	8.00
Teardrop 3044		Our Teenage Love / Doing The Do Wa Woo	1964	1.60	8.00
Teardrop 3052		You're The Reason I'm In Love / My Jole Blon	1964	1.60	8.00
Teardrop 3060		No Money Down / (Jealousy) Little Green Man	1964	1.60	8.00
Teardrop 3178		This Should Go On Forever /	1965	1.20	6.00
Arbee 101		Recorded In England /			
		Somebody Wrote That Song For My Baby	1965	1.20	6.00
Arbee 104		Gimme Back My Cadillac /			
		Don't You Think I've Paid Enough?	1965	1.20	6.00
Arbee 105		These Were Our Songs / Just Another Lie		1.20	6.00

BERRIES, THE

| Epic 7645 | | The King / If I Had The Wings Of A Dove | 1971 | .60 | 3.00 |

BERRY, CHUCK

Chuck Berry's use of county style guitar patterns, his clear, wry phrasing, and his ability to turn a teenage cliche has enabled him to produce the most widely covered and copied body of material in the genre, influencing virtually every single artist who chooses rock & roll for a living.

Chess 1604		Maybellene / Wee Wee Hours	1955	4.00	20.00
Chess 1610		Thirty Days / Together	1955	4.00	20.00
Chess 1615		No Money Down / The Downward Train	1956	5.00	25.00
Chess 1626		Roll Over, Beethoven / Drifting Heart	1956	4.00	20.00
Chess 1635		Too Much Monkey Business / Brown Eyed Handsome Man	1956	4.00	20.00
Chess 1645		You Can't Catch Me / Havana Moon	1956	4.00	20.00
Chess 1653		School Days / Deep Feeling	1957	3.00	15.00
Chess 1664		Oh, Baby Doll / Oh, Juanda	1957	3.00	15.00

— Chess singles above have blue silver top labels.—

Chess 1671		Rock And Roll Music / Blue Feeling	1957	3.00	15.00
Chess 1683		Sweet Little Sixteen / Reelin' And Rockin'	1958	3.00	15.00
Chess 1691		Johnny B. Goode / Around And Around	1958	3.00	15.00
Chess 1697		Beautiful Delilah / Vacation Time	1958	2.00	10.00
Chess 1700		Carol / Hey, Pedro	1958	2.00	10.00
Chess 1700		Carol / Lazy Pedro	1958	3.00	15.00

(Label incorrectly lists the b-side as "Lazy Pedro.")

| Chess 1709 | | Sweet Little Rock And Roller / Jo Jo Gunne | 1958 | 2.00 | 10.00 |
| Chess 1709 | | Sweet Little Rock And Roll / Jo Jo Gunne | 1958 | 3.00 | 15.00 |

(Label incorrectly lists the a-side as "Sweet Little Rock And Roll.")

Chess 1714		Run, Rudolph, Run / Merry Christmas, Baby	1958	3.00	15.00
Chess 1716		Anthony Boy / That's My Desire	1959	2.00	10.00
Chess 1722		Almost Grown / Little Queenie	1959	3.00	15.00
Chess 1729		Back In The U.S.A. / Memphis, Tennessee	1959	3.00	15.00
Chess 1737		Broken Arrow / Childhood Sweetheart	1959	3.00	15.00
Chess 1747		Too Pooped To Pop / Let It Rock	1960	2.00	10.00
Chess 1754		Bye, Bye Johnny / Worried Life Blues	1960	2.00	10.00
Chess 1763		I Got To Find My Baby / Mad Lad	1960	2.00	10.00
Chess 1767		Jaguar And Thunderbird / Our Little Rendezvous	1960	2.00	10.00
Chess 1779		I'm Talking About You / Little Star	1961	2.00	10.00
Chess 1799		Come On / Go, Go, Go	1962	3.00	15.00
Chess 1853		I'm Talking About You / Diploma For Two	1963	3.00	15.00
Chess 1866		Sweet Little Sixteen / Memphis	1963	3.00	15.00
Chess 1883		Nadine (Is It You?) / Orangutang	1964	4.00	20.00

— Chess singles above have blue labels with a vertical "Chess" logo.—

Chess 1799		Come On / Go, Go, Go	1962	1.60	8.00
Chess 1853		I'm Talking About You / Diploma For Two	1963	1.60	8.00
Chess 1866		Sweet Little Sixteen / Memphis	1963	1.60	8.00
Chess 1883		Nadine (Is It You?) / Orangutang	1964	4.00	20.00
Chess 1883		Nadine (Is It You?) / Orangutang	1964	1.60	8.00
Chess 1898		No Particular Place To Go / You Two	1964	1.60	8.00
Chess 1898	(PS)	No Particular Place To Go / You Two	1964	8.00	20.00
Chess 1906		You Never Can Tell / Brenda Lee	1964	1.60	8.00
Chess 1906	(PS)	You Never Can Tell / Brenda Lee	1964	8.00	20.00
Chess 1912		Little Marie / Go, Bobby Soxer	1964	3.00	15.00
Chess 1912	(PS)	Little Marie / Go, Bobby Soxer	1964	1.60	8.00
Chess 1916		Promised Land / Things I Used To Do	1964	1.60	8.00
Chess 1916	(PS)	Promised Land / Things I Used To Do	1964	8.00	20.00
Checker 1089		Chuck's Beat / (B-side by Bo Diddley)	1964	1.60	8.00
Chess 1926		Dear Dad / Lonely School Days	1965	1.60	8.00
Chess 1943		It Wasn't Me / Welcome Back, Pretty Baby	1965	1.60	8.00
Chess 1943	(PS)	It Wasn't Me / Welcome Back, Pretty Baby	1965	4.00	20.00
Chess 1963		Lonely School Days / Ramona, Say Yes	1966	1.60	8.00
Chess 1963		Havana Moon / Ramona, Say Yes	1966	1.60	8.00

— Chess singles above have black labels with a gold "Chess" logo.—

Mercury 72643		Club Nitty Gritty / Laugh And Cry	1966	1.00	5.00
Mercury 72680		Back To Memphis / I Do Really Love You	1967	1.00	5.00
Mercury 72748		It Hurts Me, Too / Feelin' It	1967	1.00	5.00
Mercury 72840		Louie To Frisco / Ma, Dear	1968	1.00	5.00

Label & Catalog #		A-Side/B-Side	Year	VG	NM
Mercury 72963		It's Too Dark In There / Good Lookin' Woman	1969	1.00	5.00
Mercury 72963	(PS)	It's Too Dark In There / Good Lookin' Woman	1969	3.00	15.00
Mercury 30143		Maybellene / Sweet Little Sixteen	1969	1.00	5.00
Mercury 30144		School Days / Memphis, Tennessee	1969	1.00	5.00
Mercury 30145		Roll Over, Beethoven / Back In The U.S.A.	1969	1.00	5.00
Mercury 30146		Rock And Roll Music / Johnny B. Goode	1969	1.00	5.00
Hip Pocket 34		Maybellene / Roll Over, Beethoven (4" flexidisc with jacket)	1969	2.00	10.00
Chess 2090		Tulane / Have Mercy, Judge	1970	.60	3.00
Chess 2131		My Ding-A-Ling / Johnny B. Goode	1972	.60	3.00
Chess 2136		Reelin' And Rockin' / Let's Boogie	1972	.60	3.00
Chess 2140		Bio / Roll 'Em, Pete	1973	.60	3.00
Chess 2169		Shake, Rattle And Roll / Baby, What You Want Me To Do	1973	.60	3.00
Chess 9010		Roll Over, Beethoven / Nadine	1973	.60	3.00
Chess 9020		Maybellene / Rock And Roll Music	1973	.60	3.00
Chess 9021		Sweet Little Sixteen / Johnny B. Goode	1973	.60	3.00
Chess 9030		School Days / Memphis, Tennessee	1973	.60	3.00
Atco 7203		Oh, What A Thrill / California	1979	.60	3.00
		—Extended Play Albums—			
Chess 5118		After School Session	1957	10.00	400.00
Chess 5119		Rock And Roll Music	1957	75.00	300.00
Chess 5121		Sweet Little Sixteen	1958	75.00	300.00
Chess 5124		Pickin' Berries	1958	100.00	400.00
Chess 5126		Sweet Little Rock And Roller	1958	75.00	300.00
		—Original Chess EPs above have silver on black labels.—			

BERRY, DAVE

London 9666		Memphis, Tennessee / My Baby Left Me	1964	2.00	10.00
London 9698		The Crying Game / Don't Gimme No Lip, Child	1964	2.00	10.00
London 9781		This Strange Effect / Now	1964	2.00	10.00

BERRY, JAN: Refer to JAN

BERRY, REED & LOU

Dreem 1001		What A Dolly / Hot Rod	195?	40.00	200.00
20th Century Fox 169		What A Dolly / Hot Rod	195?	15.00	75.00

BERRY, MIKE, & THE OUTLAWS

Coral 62341		Tribute To Buddy Holly / Every Little Kiss	1962	10.00	50.00
Coral 62357		Don't You Think It's Time? / Loneliness	1962	2.00	10.00
Coral 62483		Gonna Fall In Love / It Comes And Goes	1963	2.00	10.00

BERRY KIDS, THE

MGM 12379		Go Go Go Right Into Town / Love Me, Love	195?	3.00	15.00
MGM 12496		Rootie Tootie / You're My Teenage Baby	195?	3.00	15.00
Soo 12		Suzie /	195?	3.00	15.00

BERWICK, BRAD

Clinton 1012		I'm Better Than The Beatles / Walkin' Down Easy Street	1964	3.00	15.00

BEST, PETE

Note that this is not the same Peter Best listed below.

Capitol 2092		Carousel Of Love / I Want You	1968	.40	2.00

BEST, PETER

Peter Best was the original drummer with The Beatles.

Happening 117/8		If You Can't Get Her / The Way I Feel About You	1964	20.00	100.00
Happening 405		If You Can't Get Her / Don't Play With Me (Little Girl)	1964	20.00	100.00
Beatles 800		(I'll Try) Anyway / I Want To Be There	1964	20.00	100.00
Cameo 391	(DJ)	Boys / Kansas City	1966	5.00	25.00
Cameo 391	(PS)	Boys / Kansas City	1966	10.00	50.00
Mr. Maestro 712	(DJ)	Casting My Spell / I'm Blue (Blue vinyl)	1965	20.00	100.00
Mr. Maestro 712		Casting My Spell / I'm Blue	1965	20.00	100.00
Mr. Maestro 711	(DJ)	I Can't Do Without You Now / Keys To My Heart (Blue vinyl)	1964	20.00	100.00
Mr. Maestro 711		I Can't Do Without You Now / Keys To My Heart	1964	20.00	100.00

BETHLEHEM EXIT

Jabberwock 110		Walk Me Out / Blues Concerning My Girl	196?	6.00	30.00

BEVERLY & THE DONUTS

Bobbi 701		Until The Boy Is Yours / Written In The Cards	195?	10.00	50.00

BEVERLY HILLS BLUES BAND, THE

The Beverly Hills Blues Band features Dino Martin, Jr. and Desi Arnaz, Jr. of Dino, Desi & Billy.

Warner Bros. 8191		If I Can Just Get Through The Night / Just Because	1975	.80	4.00

Label & Catalog #	A-Side/B-Side	Year	VG	NM
BIANCO, CAPPY				
Casa Blanca	The Cat / La Donna Riccia	195?	3.00	15.00
ABC-Paramount 10044	The Cat / La Donna Riccia	195?	2.00	10.00
BIG BEATS, THE				
The Big Beats feature Trini Lopez.				
Columbia 41072	Clark's Expedition / Big Boys	1958	3.00	15.00
BIG BO				
Duchess 1013	Big Bo's Twist / Hully Gully Now	1962	1.60	8.00
BIG BOB				
Stacy 952	Wowsville / Wowsville, Part 2	1962	2.00	10.00
BIG BOPPER, THE				
The Big Bopper was a pseudonym for J.P. Richardson.				
"D" 1008	Chantilly Lace / Purple People Eater Meets The Witch Doctor	1958	30.00	150.00
Mercury 71343	Chantilly Lace / Purple People Eater Meets The Witch Doctor	1958	4.00	20.00
Mercury 71375	Big Bopper's Wedding / Little Red Riding Hood	1958	4.00	20.00
Mercury 71416	Walking Through My Dreams / Someone Watching Over You	1959	5.00	25.00
Mercury 71451	It's The Truth, Ruth / That's What I'm Talking About	1959	4.00	20.00
Mercury 71482	Pink Petticoats / The Clock	1959	4.00	20.00
	—*Mercury singles above have maroon or black labels.*—			
BIG BROTHER & THE HOLDING COMPANY				
Big Brother featured Peter Albin, Sam Andrews, David Getz, James Gurley with Janis Joplin. Andrews and Joplin left in 1968; Nick Gravenites and Dave Shallock joined in 1970.				
Mainstream 657	Blindman / All Is Loneliness	1968	1.00	5.00
Mainstream 662	Down On Me / Call On Me	1968	1.00	5.00
Mainstream 666	Bye, Bye Baby / Intruder	1968	1.00	5.00
Mainstream 675	Women Is Losers / Light Is Faster Than Sound	1968	1.00	5.00
Mainstream 678	Coo Coo / Last Mile	1968	1.00	5.00
Columbia 44626	Piece Of My Heart / Turtle Blues	1968	.80	4.00
Columbia 44626 (PS)	Piece Of My Heart / Turtle Blues	1968	3.00	15.00
Columbia 45502	Black Widow Spider / Nu Bugalooo Jam	1969	.80	4.00
BIG DADDY (WITH THE LITTLE SISTERS)				
Royal 1004	Daddy Frog / (B-side by D.H. & The Downbeats)	1959	4.00	20.00
BIG FRAMUS				
Shoreline 2131	Change Your Luck / Put Some Color In Your Life	1965	3.00	15.00
BIG GUYS, THE				
Palette 5110	Walkin' The Board / Faith 7	1964	6.00	30.00
Palette 5114	Zombie / Propulsion	1964	6.00	30.00
Warner Bros. 7047	Hang My Head And Cry / (B-side by The Cookies)	1967	1.00	5.00
BIG INNERS, THE				
Panorama 16	Ethmoiditus Com Polyposis / Do You Wonder	196?	1.20	6.00
BIG JIVE				
Shad 5019	Blue Eyes / Stardust In Her Eyes	1960	10.00	50.00
BIG JOHN & THE FABULOUS BLENDS				
The Fabulous Blends also recorded as The Blends.				
Casa Grande 5001	Baby, You're Wrong, Dead Wrong / Hey, Little Fool	195?	4.00	20.00
BIG MOE & THE PANICS				
Audio Lab 1 (EP)	Big Moe & The Panics	1959	10.00	50.00
BIG MOOSE & THE JAMS				
Age 29113	Off The Hook / Bright Sounds	1962	1.50	8.00
BIG SAM & THE HOUSE WRECKERS				
Eric 7003	The Rains Came / At The Party	1962	3.00	15.00
BIG STAR				
Big Star featured Alex Chilton, previously of The Box Tops, and Chris Bell, who left in 1973..				
Ardent 2902	When My Baby's Beside Me / In The Street	1972	2.00	10.00
Ardent 294	Don't Lie To Me / Watch The Sunrise	1972	2.00	10.00
Ardent 2912	September Gurls / September Gurls	1974	2.00	10.00
BIG WHEELIE & THE HUBCAPS				
Scepter 12375	Elvis Presley Medley / Chuck Berry Medley	1973	1.20	6.00
Scepter 12385	Little Richard Medley / Over The Mountain	1973	1.00	5.00
Scepter 12392	Red Neck Rock & Rollrs / Leader Of The Pack	1974	1.00	5.00

Label & Catalog #	A-Side/B-Side	Year	VG	NM
BIGGS, KENNY				
B/W 615/6	Swingin' Swanee Rock / There's No Excuse	1961	1.60	8.00
BIGHORN				
Bighorn 1	I Get High / Takin' Me Down	195?	4.00	20.00
BIKINIS, THE				
Roulette 4073	Bikini / Boogie Rock And Roll	1958	2.00	10.00
Top Rank 2032	Crazy Vibrations / Spunky	1960	2.00	10.00
BILLIE & MARK				
Demon 1513	Deep Down / Just So You Love Me	1959	2.00	10.00
BILLIE & RICKY				
Sue 711	Baby Doll / Mama, Papa Please	1959	3.00	15.00
BILLIE & THE MOONLIGHTERS				
Crystal Ball 101	You Made Me Cry / Little Indian Girl	197?	.80	4.00
Crystal Ball 101	You Made Me Cry / Little Indian Girl (Red vinyl)	197?	2.00	10.00
Crystal Ball 101	You Made Me Cry / Little Indian Girl (Multi-colored vinyl)	197?	3.00	15.00
BILLION DOLLAR BABIES, THE				
The Billion Dollar Babies were Alice Cooper's band.				
Polydor 14394	Rock 'N' Roll Radio / Wasn't I The One?	1977	.80	4.00
Polydor 14406 (DJ)	Too Young / Too Young	1977	2.00	10.00
	(Stock copies of Polydor 14406 may not exist.)			
BILLY & EDDIE				
Top Rank 2017	The King Is Coming Back / Come Back, Baby	1959	3.00	15.00
BILLY & SUE				
Billy & Sue are Oliver and Leslie Gore.				
Crewe 343 (DJ)	Come Softly To Me / Billy 'N Sue's Love Scene	1970	1.00	5.00
Crewe 343	Come Softly To Me / Billy 'N Sue's Love Scene	1970	2.00	10.00
BILLY & THE ECHOES				
Gala 121	Bodacious Twist / Come Softly	1962	1.50	8.00
BILLY & THE ESSENTIALS [LITTLE BILLY & THE ESSENTIALS]				
"Little" Billy Carl also recorded with The Heatwaves and Marshmallow Way.				
Landa 691	The Dance Is Over / Steady Girl	1962	6.00	30.00
	(Landa 691 credits Little Billy & The Essentials.)			
Jamie 1229	The Dance Is Over / Steady Girl	1962	3.00	15.00
Jamie 1239	Over The Weekend / Maybe You'll Be There	1962	4.00	20.00
Mercury 72127	Lonely Weekend / Young At Heart	1963	3.00	15.00
Mercury 72210	Last Dance / Yes, Sir, That's My Baby	1963	3.00	15.00
Cameo 344	Remember Me, Baby / The Actor	1965	——	——
	(Rare white doowop. Estimated near mint value $250-500.)			
Smash 2045	My Way Of Saying / Baralu's Wedding Day	1966	3.00	15.00
Smash 2071	Don't Cry (Sing Along With The Music) / Baby, Go Away	1966	3.00	15.00
BILLY & THE FLEET				
Arlen 514	Nobody Wants To Give Me What I Want / Power Shift	1963	3.00	15.00
BILLY & THE KIDS				
Lute 6016	Take A Chance On Love / The Way It Used To Be	1961	6.00	30.00
Harmike 1300	(Theme Of The) Nightrider / The Long Wait	1962	6.00	30.00
Triangle 2	(Theme Of The) Nightrider / The Long Wait	1962	5.00	25.00
	(Originally released on Adara as "Nightrider" / "The Big Disappointment" credited to The Chapelles.)			
BILLY & THE KIDS				
Julian 104	Say You Love Me / It's Not The Same	1965	3.00	15.00
Julian 109	When I See You / Do You Need Me?	1965	3.00	15.00
Decca 31951	Shut Down Again / Troubles Of My Own	1966	3.00	15.00
BILLY JOE & THE CHECKMATES				
Dore 620	Percolator (Twist) / Round And Round And Round And Round	1961	2.00	10.00
Dore 636	Twist That Thing / Rocky's Theme	1962	2.00	10.00
BILLY JOE & THE CHESSMEN				
Wolfie 102	Happy Jack / The Loaf	1963	2.00	10.00
BING BONGS, THE: *Refer to DICKY DELL & THE BING BONGS*				
BIRDMEN, THE				
Rock-It 1003	Dance The Jaybird / Dance The Jaybird, Part 2	1961	8.00	40.00

Label & Catalog #		A-Side/B-Side	Year	VG	NM
BIRDS OF A FEATHER					
Page One 21037		Country Comfort / One More Time	1970	.60	3.00
Armour 8426		Elvis, How Could I Resist? / Elvis, How Could I Resist?	1977	.60	3.00
BISCAYNE BAY SURFERS, THE					
Mayhams 214		Surfing Is A Sight To See / Surfing On A Swinging Soiree	1964	5.00	25.00
		(" Surfing Is A Sight To See" was originally issued as "Surfin' On A Swingin' Soiree" credited to Prof. Marcell Collegians.)			
BISCAYNES, THE					
The Biscaynes feature Scott Engel, Gary Leeds and John Maus a.k.a. John Stewart, later The Walker Brothers.					
Northridge 1001		Church Key / (B-side by The Surfaris)	1963	7.00	35.00
Reprise 2047		Church Key / (B-side by The Surfaris)	1963	5.00	25.00
Co-En 01		Midnight In Montevideo / (B-side by The Co-Encidentals)	196?	6.00	30.00
BISHOP, ELVIN					
Fillmore 7002		So Fine / So Fine	197?	.60	3.00
Fillmore 7003		Don't Fight It, Feel It / Don't Fight It, Feel It	197?	.60	3.00
Fillmore 7004		I Just Can't Go On / I Just Can't Go On	197?	.60	3.00
Capricorn 0202		Travelin' Shoes / Fishin'	1974	.40	2.00
Capricorn 0237		Sure Feels Good / Arkansas Line	1975	.40	2.00
Capricorn 0243		Juke Joint Jump / Calling All Cows	1975	.40	2.00
Capricorn 0248		Silent Night / Silent Night, Part 2	1976	.40	2.00
Capricorn 0252		Fooled Around And Fell In Love / Slick Titty Boom	1976	.40	2.00
Capricorn 0252		Fooled Around And Fell In Love / Have A Good Time	1976	.40	2.00
Capricorn 0256		Struttin' My Stuff / Grab All The Love	1976	.40	2.00
Capricorn 0266		Spend Some Time / Sugar Dumplin'	1976	.40	2.00
Capricorn 0269		Keep It Cool / Yes, Sir	1977	.40	2.00
Capricorn 0285		Rock My Soul / Yes, Sir	1978	.40	2.00
BITTER SWEETS, THE					
Original 70		Another Chance / In The West	196?	3.00	15.00
Cameo 368		What A Lonely Way To Start The Summertime / Mark My Words	1965	2.00	10.00
BJORN & BENNY (WITH ANNA & FRIEDA)					
Bjorn Ulvaeus and Benny Anderson with Anna Faltsko and Anni-Frid Lingstad, later Abba.					
Playboy 50014		People Need Love / Merry-Go-Round	1973	4.00	20.00
Playboy 50018		Another Town, Another Train / I Am Just A Girl	1973	4.00	20.00
Playboy 50025		Rock 'N Roll Band / Another Town, Another Train	1973	4.00	20.00
BLACK, BILL [BILL BLACK'S COMBO]					
Bill Black originally recorded with Elvis Presley.					
Hi 2007		Blue Tango / Willie	1959	1.25	8.00
Hi 2018		Smokie / Smokie, Part 2	1959	1.25	8.00
Hi 2021		White Silver Sands / The Wheel	1960	.80	6.00
Hi 2022		Josephine / Dry Bones	1960	.80	6.00
Hi 2022	(PS)	Josephine / Dry Bones	1960	2.00	10.00
Hi 2026		Don't Be Cruel / Rollin'	1960	.80	6.00
Hi 2026	(PS)	Don't Be Cruel / Rollin'	1960	2.00	10.00
Hi 2027		Blue Tango / Willie	1960	.80	6.00
Hi 2027	(PS)	Blue Tango / Willie	1960	2.00	10.00
Hi 2028		Hearts Of Stone / Royal Blue	1961	1.20	6.00
Hi 2030		Do, Lord / When The Roll Is Called Up Yonder	1961	1.20	6.00
Hi 2031		Down By The Riverside / It Is No Secret	1961	1.20	6.00
Hi 2033		Just A Closer Walk With Thee / This Old House	1961	1.20	6.00
Hi 2036		Yogi / Ole Buttermilk Sky	1961	1.20	6.00
Hi 2036	(PS)	Yogi / Ole Buttermilk Sky	1961	1.60	8.00
Hi 2038		Movin' / Honky Train	1961	1.25	6.00
Hi 2042		Twist-Her / My Girl Josephine	1961	1.20	6.00
Hi 2052		Twistin' White Silver Sands / My Babe	1962	1.20	6.00
Hi 2052	(PS)	Twistin' White Silver Sands / My Babe	1962	1.60	8.00
Hi 2055		So What / Blues For The Red Boy	1962	1.20	6.00
Hi 2059		Joey's Song / Hot Taco	1962	1.20	6.00
Hi 2064		Do It-Rat Now! / Little Jaspar	1963	1.20	6.00
Hi 2069		Monkey Shine / Long Gone	1963	1.20	6.00
Hi 2072		Comin' On / Soft Winds	1964	1.20	6.00
Hi 2077		Tequila / Raunchy	1964	1.20	6.00
Hi 2079		Little Queenie / Boo Ray	1964	1.20	6.00
Hi 2085		Come On Home / He'll Have To Go	1965	1.20	6.00
Hi 2094		Spootin' / Crazy Feel	1965	1.20	6.00
Hi 2106		Hey, Good Lookin' / Mountain Of Love	1966	.60	3.00
Hi 2115		Rambler / You Call Everybody Darling	1966	.60	3.00
Hi 2124		Son Of Smokie / Peg Leg	1967	.60	3.00
Hi 2145		Turn On Your Love Light / Ribbon Of Darkness	1968	.60	3.00
Hi 2153		Bright Lights, Big City / Red Light	1968	.60	3.00
Hi 2168		Creepin' Around / Son Of Hicory Holer's Tramp	1969	.60	3.00
Hi 2185		Closin' Time / No More	1969	.60	3.00

Label & Catalog #		A-Side/B-Side	Year	VG	NM
Hi 2208		Daylite / Four A.M.	1970	.60	3.00
Hi 2234		Mighty Fine / Smokey Bourbon Street	1970	.60	3.00
Columbia 44867		Slow Action / But It's Alright	1969	.60	3.00
Columbia 44983		California Dreamin' / Funky Train	1970	.60	3.00
Columbia 45092		Heaven Knows / 1518 Chelsea	1971	.60	3.00
Columbia 45162		Keep The Customer Satisfied / 1518 Chelsea	1971	.60	3.00
Mega 0052		Oh Happy Day / Sugar Cured	1972	.60	3.00
Mega 0070		Harlem Nocturne / Sassy Pants	1972	.60	3.00
Mega 0086		Night Train / Bluff City Cookin'	1972	.60	3.00
Mega 0117		Memphis Shuffle / Satin Sheets	1973	.60	3.00
Mega 201		Smokie: Part II / Tequila	1974	.60	3.00
Mega 207		Oh Happy Day / Listen To The Music	1974	.60	3.00
Hi 2277		Soul Serenade / Pickin'	1974	.60	3.00
Hi 2283		Boilin' Cabbage / Truck Stop	1974	.60	3.00
Hi 2291		Back Up And Push / Almost Persuaded	1975	.60	3.00
Hi 2301		Fire On The Bayou / Memphis Stroll	1975	.60	3.00
Hi 2311		Jump Back, Joe Joe / I Can Help	1975	.60	3.00
Hi 2317		Red Neck Rock / Yakety Sax	1975	.60	3.00
Hi 78508		Cashin' In (A Tribute To Luther Perkins) / L.A. Blues	1978	.60	3.00
		—Extended Play Albums—			
Hi 22002		Solid And Raunchy	1960	7.00	35.00
Hi 22003		That Wonderful Feeling	1961	7.00	35.00
Hi 1104	(33)	King Of The Road (Jukebox EP)	1968	7.00	15.00
Hi 32127	(33)	Tunes By Chuck Berry (Jukebox EP)	1968	3.00	15.00
Hi 32141	(33)	Bill Black's Beat Goes On (Jukebox EP)	1968	3.00	15.00
Mega 192	(33)	Jukebox Favorites (Jukebox EP)	1972	3.00	15.00

BLACK, CILLA
Refer to the Beatles' Capitol EPs section.

Label & Catalog #		A-Side/B-Side	Year	VG	NM
Capitol 5196		You're My World / Suffer Now I Must	1964	1.00	6.00
Capitol 5258		It's For You / He Won't Ask Me	1964	1.00	5.00
Capitol 5373		Is It Love? / One Little Voice	1965	1.00	5.00
Capitol 5414		I've Been Wrong Before / My Love, Come Home	1965	1.00	5.00
Capitol 5595		Love's Just A Broken Heart / Yesterday	1966	1.00	5.00
Capitol 5595	(PS)	Love's Just A Broken Heart / Yesterday	1966	3.00	15.00
Capitol 5674		Alfie / Night Time Is Here	1966	1.00	5.00
Capitol 5763		Don't Answer Me / The Right One Is Left	1967	1.00	5.00
Capitol 5782		For No One / A Fool Am I	1967	1.00	5.00
Private Stock 45040		I'll Take A Tango / To Know Him Is To Love Him	1975	.80	4.00
Private Stock 45077		Fantasy / It's Now	1975	.80	4.00

BLACK, JAY
Jay Black also recorded with The Empires; The Harbor Lights; Jay & The Americans; and Two Chaps.

Label & Catalog #		A-Side/B-Side	Year	VG	NM
United Artists 50116		What Will My Mary Say? / Return To Me	1967	.80	4.00
United Artists 50116	(PS)	What Will My Mary Say? / Return To Me	1967	1.50	8.00
Private Stock		Every Time You Walk In The Room / I'd Build A Bridge	197?	.80	4.00
Millennium 618		Love Is In The Air / (Don't Go) Please Stay	197?	.80	4.00
Atlantic/Mig. 3273		Running Scared / Dolphins	1975	.80	4.00
Roulette 7198		One Night Affair / Between Two Worlds	1976	1.0	5.00

BLACK, JIMMY CARL
Jimmy Carl Black also recorded with The Mothers Of Invention.

Label & Catalog #		A-Side/B-Side	Year	VG	NM
MCA 1914	(DJ)	Jimmy Carl Black Raps About Geronimo Black	1971	3.00	15.00

BLACK, SHARON

Label & Catalog #	A-Side/B-Side	Year	VG	NM
Philips 40290	Mother Dear, You've Got A Silly Daughter / Under The Smile Of Love	1965	1.20	6.00

BLACK, TERRY

Label & Catalog #		A-Side/B-Side	Year	VG	NM
Tollie 9026		Unless You Care / Can't We Go Somewhere?	1964	1.00	5.00
Tollie 9041		Everyone Can Tell / Say It Again	1965	1.00	5.00
Tollie 9041	(PS)	Everyone Can Tell / Say It Again	1965	2.00	10.00
Dunhill 4005		How Many Guys? / Only Sixteen	1965	.80	4.00

BLACK HAWKS, THE

Label & Catalog #	A-Side/B-Side	Year	VG	NM
Roadhouse 1000	Beatrice, My Darling / Love Me When I'm Old	195?	20.00	100.00

BLACK OAK ARKANSAS

Label & Catalog #	A-Side/B-Side	Year	VG	NM
Atco 6829	Lord Have Mercy On Me / Uncle Lijah	1971	.60	3.00
Atco 6849	Hot And Nasty / Singing The Blues	1972	.60	3.00
Atco 6948	Jim Dandy / Red Hot Lovin'	1973	.60	3.00
Atco 7015	Taxman / Dixie	1973	.60	3.00
MCA 40496	Strong Enough To Be Gentle / Ace In The Hole	1976	.40	2.00
MCA 40536	Great Balls Of Fire / Highway Pirate	1976	.40	2.00
MCA 40586	Fistful Of Love / Storm Of Passion	1976	.40	2.00
MCA 40621	When The Band Was Singin' "Shakin' All Over" / Bad Boy's Back In School	1977	.40	2.00

Label & Catalog #		A-Side/B-Side	Year	VG	NM
Capricorn 0285		Not Fade Away / Feels So Good	1978	.40	2.00
Capricorn 0305		Ride With Me / Wind In Our Sails	1978	.40	2.00

BLACK SABBATH
Black Sabbath was Geezer Butler, Tony Iommi, Ozzie Osbourne and Bill Ward.

Label & Catalog #		A-Side/B-Side	Year	VG	NM
Warner Bros. 7437		Paranoid / The Wizard	1970	1.60	8.00
Warner Bros. 7530		Iron Man / Electric Funeral	1972	1.60	8.00
Warner Bros. 7625		Tomorrow's Dream / Laguna Sunrise	1972	1.20	6.00
Warner Bros. 7764		Sabbath, Bloody Sabbath / Changes	1974	1.20	6.00
Warner Bros. 7802		Iron Man / Electric Funeral	1975	1.20	6.00
Warner Bros. 8315		Rock 'N' Roll Doctor / It's Alright	1976	1.20	6.00

BLACK WATCH, THE

Label & Catalog #		A-Side/B-Side	Year	VG	NM
Fenton 2508		Left Behind / I Wish I Had The Nerve	196?	4.00	20.00

BLACKBURN & SNOW
Blackburn & Snow reportedly features Peter Lewis, Jerry Miller and Don Stephenson of Moby Grape.

Label & Catalog #		A-Side/B-Side	Year	VG	NM
Verve 10478		Stranger In A Strange Land / Uptown, Downtown	1967	2.00	10.00
Verve 10563		Time / Postwar Baby	1967	2.00	10.00

BLACKWELLS, THE

Label & Catalog #		A-Side/B-Side	Year	VG	NM
G&G 126		Here's The Question / Please Don't Come Crying	1959	2.00	10.00
G&G 131		Holy Sombrero / Oh, My Love	1959	2.00	10.00
Guyden 2020		Holy Sombrero / Oh, My Love	1959	2.00	10.00
Jamie 1141		You Are Free / Depot	1959	2.00	10.00
Jamie 1150		Honey, Honey / Always It's You	1960	1.60	8.00
Jamie 1150	(PS)	Honey, Honey / Always It's You	1960	2.00	10.00
Jamie 1157		Mansion On The Hill / Unchained Melody	1960	1.60	8.00
Jamie 1173		Christmas Holiday / Little Match Girl	1960	1.60	8.00
Jamie 1179		Love Or Money / Big Daddy And The Cat	1961	1.20	6.00
Jamie 1199		You Took Advantage Of Me / I	1961	1.20	6.00

BLADES OF GRASS, THE

Label & Catalog #		A-Side/B-Side	Year	VG	NM
Jubilee 5582		Happy / That's What A Boy Likes	1967	.80	4.00
Jubilee 5590		Baby, You're A Real Good Friend Of Mine / Just Another Face	1967	.80	4.00
Jubilee 5605		Help / Just Ah	1968	.80	4.00
Jubilee 5616		You Won't Find That Girl / Charlie And Fred	1968	.80	4.00
Jubilee 5622		You Turned Off The Sun / The Way You'll Never Be	1968	.80	4.00
Jubilee 5635		I Love You, Alice B. Toklas / That's What A Boy Likes	1968	.80	4.00

BLAINE, HAL (& THE YOUNG COUGARS)
Refer to Hal's Angels.

Label & Catalog #		A-Side/B-Side	Year	VG	NM
RCA Victor 47-8147		Hawaii 1963 / East Side Story	1963	3.00	15.00
RCA Victor 47-8223		(Dance With The) Surfin' Band / The Drummer Plays For Me	1963	3.00	20.00
RCA Victor 47-8282		Gear Stripper / Challenger II	1963	3.00	15.00
Dunhill 4006		Topsy '65 / La Bamba	1965	2.00	10.00
Dunhill 4021		Secret Agent Man / Midnight At Pink's	1966	2.00	10.00
Dunhill 4049		Bang Bang Rhythm / Drums A Go Go	1966	3.50	15.00
Dunhill 4074		The Swinger / Drums A Go Go	1966	2.00	10.00
Dunhill 4091		Love In / Wiggy	1967	2.00	10.00
Dunhill 142		Allegro From MacArthur Park / Drums A Go Go	1968	2.00	10.00
Dunhill 4181		Beverly Drive / Midnight At Pink's	1968	2.00	10.00
		—Extended Play Albums—			
Dunhill D-2	(DJ)	Drums A Go Go (Radio sampler)	1965	4.00	20.00

BLAIR, TOM, & THE WEST COASTERS

Label & Catalog #		A-Side/B-Side	Year	VG	NM
Teen Tunes 2469		West Coast / With My Hand On My Heart	1961	7.00	35.00
Decca 31223		West Coast / With My Hand On My Heart	1961	5.00	25.00

BLAKE, BUDDY

Label & Catalog #		A-Side/B-Side	Year	VG	NM
Phillips Inter. 3516		You Passed Me By / Please Convince Me	1958	3.00	15.00

BLAKE, TOMMY
Buddy Blake is a pseudonym for Buddy Cunningham.

Label & Catalog #		A-Side/B-Side	Year	VG	NM
Sun 278		Flat Foot Sam / Lordy Hoody	1957	6.00	30.00
Sun 300		Sweetie Pie / I Dig You, Baby	1958	35.00	175.00

BLANDERS, THE

Label & Catalog #		A-Side/B-Side	Year	VG	NM
Smash 2005		Jitterbug / Desert Sands	1965	6.00	30.00

BLANE, MARCIE

Label & Catalog #		A-Side/B-Side	Year	VG	NM
Seville 120		Bobby's Girl / Time To Dream	1962	3.00	15.00
Seville 123		What Does A Girl Do? / How Can I Tell Him?	1963	2.00	10.00
Seville 126		Little Miss Fool / Ragtime Sound	1963	2.00	10.00
Seville 128		You Gave My Number To Billy / Told You So	1963	2.00	10.00
Seville 130		Why Can't I Get A Guy? / Who's Going To Take My Daddy's Place?	1963	2.00	10.00

Label & Catalog #	A-Side/B-Side	Year	VG	NM
Seville 133	Bobby Did / After The Laughter	1963	2.00	10.00
Seville 137	She'll Break The String / The Hurtin' Kind	1964	2.00	10.00
BLANE & THE JULIANS				
Julian 100	Go On / Don't Say No No	196?	8.00	40.00
BLAVAT, JERRY, & THE YON-TEENS				
Epic 10193	Let's Love Again / Jerry's Theme	1967	1.60	8.00
BLAZERS, THE				
Acree 101	Beaver Patrol / Shore Break	1963	8.00	40.00
Acree 102	Sound Of Mecca / Bangalore	1964	8.00	40.00
BLAZERS, THE				
Mundo 864	Grasshopper / A Little Bit Of Stop	196?	5.00	25.00
Golden Crest	Hula Hoop Party / Viva La Compagne	196?	5.00	25.00
BLAZERS, THE				
Dot 16623	Masked Granma / Summer Session	1964	5.00	25.00
BLAZERS, THE: *Refer to* RODNEY & THE BLAZERS				
BLAZONS, THE				
Bravura 5001	Little Girl / Magic Lamp	196?	10.00	50.00
BLENDAIRS, THE				
Tin Pan Alley 252	My Love Is Just For You / Repetition	195?	10.00	50.00
BLENDELLS, THE				
Rampart 641	La La La La La / Huggie's Bunnies	1964	3.00	15.00
Reprise 0291	La La La La La / Huggie's Bunnies	1964	2.00	10.00
BLENDERS, THE				
RCA Victor 47-6712	New Sensations In Sound / Wake Up To Music	1956	2.00	10.00
BLENDERS, THE				
Wanger 189	Angel / Old MacDonald	196?	3.00	15.00
Witch 117	Boys Think / Squat and Squirm	1963	2.00	10.00
Witch 114	Daughter / Everybody's Got The Right	1963	3.00	15.00
BLENDS, THE				
The Blends also recorded as Big John & The Fabulous Blends.				
Casa Grande 3037	Now It's Your Turn / Someone To Care	1960	6.00	30.00
Casa Grande 5000	Music Maestro, Please / 1,000 Miles Away	1961	4.00	20.00
Skylark 108	Tell Me / The Way I Want You	1961	3.00	15.00
Talent 110	Tell Me / The Way I Want You	1961	3.00	15.00
BLESSING, MICHAEL				
Michael Blessing is a pseudonym for Michael Nesmith.				
Colpix 787	(DJ) The New Recruit / A Journey	1965	5.00	25.00
Colpix 787	The New Recruit / A Journey	1965	10.00	50.00
Colpix 792	(DJ) Until It's Time For You To Go / What's The Trouble, Officer	1965	5.00	25.00
Colpix 792	Until It's Time For You To Go / What's The Trouble, Officer	1965	10.00	50.00
BLEU LITES, THE				
Baysound 67003	Forever / They Don't Know My Heart	195?	6.00	30.00
Baysound 67007	A Lonely Man's Prayer / Bony Marony	195?	4.00	20.00
Baysound 67010	The End Of My Dreams / Yes I Do	195?	3.00	15.00
BLIND HOG				
Vulcan 112	Memphis / I'm A Hog For You, Baby	196?	2.00	10.00
Vulcan	Rockin' Pneumonia And The Boogie Woogie Flu /	196?	2.00	10.00
BLISTERS, THE				
Titanic 5005	Fifty Mile Hike / Recitation	1963	2.00	10.00
BLOBS, THE				
Verve 10675	Son Of Blob / Party Pooper	1969	2.00	10.00
BLOCKBUSTERS, THE				
Crystalette 725	Hi, Hon / Boogie Bop	1959	4.00	20.00
BLOCKBUSTERS, THE				
Rockin' 500	Goodbye, Squaresville / Muddy	1968	1.00	5.00
BLODWYN PIG				
Blodwyn Pig feature Mick Abrahams, formerly of Jethro Tull.				
A&M 1158	Dear Jill / Summer Day	1970	1.00	5.00

Label & Catalog #		A-Side/B-Side	Year	VG	NM
BLOKES, THE					
Wasp 109		Rhythm And Blues / She's Just A Girl In Love	196?	2.00	10.00
BLOND					
Fontana 1673		Deep Inside My Heart /			
		I Will Bring You Flowers In The Morning	1968	1.00	5.00
Fontana 1673	(PS)	Deep Inside My Heart /			
		I Will Bring You Flowers In The Morning	1968	1.25	6.00

BLONDIE

Blondie was Clem Burke, Jim Destri, Debbie Harry as "Blondie," Chris Stein, and Gary Valentine, who was replaced by Frank Infante in 1976. Nigel Harrison joined in 1977. Refer to Rodney & The Brunettes.

Private Stock 45097	(DJ)	X-Offender / In The Sun	1976	2.00	10.00
Private Stock 45097		X-Offender / In The Sun	1976	4.00	20.00
Private Stock 45141	(DJ)	In The Flesh / Man Overboard	1977	2.00	10.00
Private Stock 45141		In The Flesh / Man Overboard	1977	3.00	15.00
Chrysalis 2220		Denis / I'm On E	1977	1.00	5.00
Chrysalis 2251		I'm Gonna Love You, Too / Just Go Away	1978	1.00	5.00
Chrysalis 2271		Hanging On The Telephone / Fade Away And Radiate	1978	.60	3.00
Chrysalis 2271	(PS)	Hanging On The Telephone / Fade Away And Radiate	1978	.60	3.00
Chrysalis 2295		Heart Of Glass / 11:59	1979	.60	3.00
Chrysalis 2295	(PS)	Heart Of Glass / 11:59	1979	.60	3.00
Chrysalis 2336		One Way Or Another / Just Go Away	1979	.60	3.00
Chrysalis 2379		Dreaming / Living In The Real World	1979	.60	3.00
Chrysalis 2408		The Hardest Part / Sound Asleep	1980	.60	3.00
Chrysalis 2408	(PS)	The Hardest Part / Sound Asleep	1980	.60	3.00
Chrysalis 2410		Atomic / Die Young Stay Pretty	1980	.40	2.00
Chrysalis 2410	(PS)	Atomic / Die Young Stay Pretty	1980	.40	2.00
Chrysalis 2414		Call Me / Call Me	1980	.40	2.00
Chrysalis 2414	(PS)	Call Me / Call Me	1980	.40	2.00
Chrysalis 2465		The Tide Is High / Suzy And Jeffrey	1980	.40	2.00
Chrysalis 2465	(PS)	The Tide Is High / Suzy And Jeffrey	1980	.40	2.00
Chrysalis 2485		Rapture / Walk Like Me	1981	.40	2.00
Chrysalis 2485	(PS)	Rapture / Walk Like Me	1981	.40	2.00
Chrysalis 2603		Island Of Lost Souls / Dragonfly	1982	.40	2.00
Chrysalis 2603	(PS)	Island Of Lost Souls / Dragonfly	1982	.40	2.00
		—12" Singles—			
Chrysalis 2275		Heart Of Glass / Heart Of Glass	1979	2.00	10.00
Chrysalis 2414		Call Me / Call Me	1980	2.00	10.00
Salsoul 56341		Llamae (Version Espanol) / Llamae *(Instrumental)*	1980	3.00	15.00

BLOOD, SWEAT & TEARS

Initially the brainchild of Al Kooper with Bobby Colomby, Jim Fielder and Steve Katz, the Koop flew and the band picked up vocalist David Clayton-Thomas.

Columbia 44559		I Can't Quit Her / House In The Country	1968	.80	4.00
Columbia 44776		You've Made Me So Very Happy / Blues (Part II)	1969	.60	3.00
Columbia 44871		Spinning Wheel / More And More	1969	.60	3.00
Columbia 45008		And When I Die / Sometimes In Winter	1969	.60	3.00
Columbia 45204		Hi-De-Ho / The Battle	1970	.60	3.00
Columbia 45235		Lucretia MacEvil / Lucretia's Reprise	1970	.60	3.00
Columbia 45427		Go Down Gamblin' / Valentine's Day	1971	.40	2.00
Columbia 45427	(PS)	Go Down Gamblin' / Valentine's Day	1971	.60	3.00
Columbia 45477		Lisa, Listen To Me / Cowboys And Indians	1971	.40	2.00
Columbia 45661		So Long Dixie / Alone	1972	.40	2.00
Columbia 45661	(PS)	So Long Dixie / Alone	1972	.60	3.00
Columbia 45965		Save Our Ship / Song For John	1973	.40	2.00
Columbia 46059		Tell Me That I'm Wrong / Rock Reprise	1974	.40	2.00
Columbia 10151		Got To Get You Into My Life / Naked Man	1975	.40	2.00
Columbia 10400		You're The One / Heavy Blue	1977	.40	2.00
ABC 12310		Blue Street / Somebody I Trusted	1978	.40	2.00

BLOODROCK					
Capitol 3009		D. O. A. / Children's Heritage	1971	1.60	6.00
Capitol 3089		A Certain Kind / You Gotta Pull	1971	1.60	6.00
Capitol P-3451	(DJ)	Bloodrock Interview *(Paper sleeve)*	1972	3.00	15.00

BLOOM, BOBBY

Bobby Bloom originally recorded as Bobby Mann.

Kama Sutra 229		Love, Don't Let Me Down / Where Is The Woman	1967	1.60	8.00
White Whale 285		All I Wanna Do Is Dance / Taggin' Along	1969	.60	3.00
L&R 157		Montego Bay / Try A Little Harder	1970	.60	3.00
MGM 14212		Make Me Happy / This Thing I've Gotten Into	1971	.40	2.00
MGM 14246		We're All Goin' Home / Careful Not To Break The Spell	1971	.40	2.00
Roulette 7095		Where Are We Going? / Of Yesterday	1971	.40	2.00

BLOOMFIELD, MICHAEL; AL KOOPER, & STEVE STILLS					
Columbia 44657		Season Of The Witch / Albert Shuffle	1968	.80	4.00
Columbia 44678		The Weight / Man's Temptation	1968	.80	4.00

Label & Catalog #		A-Side/B-Side	Year	VG	NM
BLOOS MAGOOS, THE: *Refer to* THE BLUES MAGOOS					
BLOSSOMS, THE					
E.O.E.O.C.		Things Are Changing / Things Are Changing	1965	30.00	150.00
E.O.E.O.C.	(PS)	Things Are Changing / Things Are Changing	1965	30.00	150.00
		(Manufactured for the Equal Opportunity Employment Opportunities Campaign using a Phil Spector production of Brian Wilson's "Don't Hurt My Little Sister" with Brian on piano. The same backing track was used on performances by Jay & The Americans and The Supremes.)			
BLUE BELLS, THE					
Last Chance 1		Atlantis / Moccasin	195?	8.00	40.00
BLUE CHEER					
The original Blue Cheer was Dickie Peterson, Leigh Stephens and Paul Whaley, who left in 1969;. Later members were Ralph Kellogg, Norm Mayell and Bruce Stevens. Refer to Group B.					
Philips 40516		Summertime Blues / Out Of Focus	1968	1.60	8.00
Philips 40516	(PS)	Summertime Blues / Out Of Focus	1968	3.00	15.00
Philips 40541		Just A Little Bit / Gypsy Ball	1968	1.20	6.00
Philips 40561		Feathers From Your Tree / Sun Cycle	1968	1.20	6.00
Philips 40561	(PS)	Feathers From Your Tree / Sun Cycle	1968	4.00	20.00
Philips 40602		West Coast Child Of Sunshine / When It All Gets Old	1969	1.20	6.00
Philips 40651		All Night Long / Fortunes	1969	1.20	6.00
Philips 40664		Natural Men / Hello, L.A., Bye Bye, Birmingham	1960	1.20	6.00
Philips 40682		Ain't That The Way / Fool	1970	1.60	8.00
Philips 40691		Fool / Pilot	1970	1.20	6.00
Philips 40691		Babajai / Pilot	1970	1.20	6.00
BLUE CRYSTALS, THE					
Mercury 71455		Broke Up / Queen Of All The Girls	1959	4.00	20.00
BLUES BROTHERS, THE					
The Blues Brothers were comedians Dan Aykroyd and John Belushi.					
Atlantic 3545		Soul Man / Excusez Moi, Mon Cherie	1978	.60	3.00
Atlantic 3545	(PS)	Soul Man / Excusez Moi, Mon Cherie	1978	.60	3.00
Atlantic 3564		Rubber Biscuit / B-Movie Box Car Blues	1978	.60	3.00
Atlantic 3666		Gimme Some Lovin' / She Caught The Katy	1980	.60	3.00
Atlantic 3666	(PS)	Gimme Some Lovin' / She Caught The Katy	1980	.60	3.00
Atlantic 3758		Jailhouse Rock /	1980	.60	3.00
Atlantic 3884		Expressway To Your Heart / Rubber Biscuit	1981	.60	3.00
BLUE ECHOES, THE					
Itzy 11		Blue Belle Bounce / Tiger Talk	196?	3.00	15.00
BLUE ECHOES, THE					
Raynard 10019		Moonride / What I Say	195?	7.00	35.00
BLUE EYED SOUL					
Blue Eyed Soul features Billy Vera.					
Cameo 401		The Shadow Of Your Love / Look Gently At The Rain	1966	2.00	10.00
Cameo 423		Tonight I Am King / Something New	1966	2.00	10.00
BLUE GIN					
NWI 2767		Light Blue / I'm Glad	1970	1.00	5.00
NWI 2767	(PS)	Light Blue / I'm Glad	1970	1.00	5.00
BLUE JAYS, THE					
Laurie 3037		Sweet Georgia Brown / J.J.'s Blues	1959	3.00	15.00
BLUE JAYS, THE					
Roadhouse 113472		Could I Adore You? / Sweet Pauline	196?	2.00	10.00
Milestone 2008		Lover's Island / You're Gonna Try	1961	3.00	15.00
Milestone 2009		Tears Are Falling / Tree Top Len	1961	4.00	20.00
Milestone 2010		Let's Make Love / Rock, Rock, Rock	1961	3.00	15.00
Milestone 2012		The Right To Love / Rock, Rock, Rock	1962	3.00	15.00
Milestone 2014		Venus, My Love / Tall Len	1962	5.00	25.00
BLUE JEANS, THE					
Souvenir 1006		Cool Martini / Since You've Gone	1961	3.00	15.00
Souvenir 1007		DJ Theme / Moon Mist	1961	3.00	15.00
BLUE MOONS, THE					
Jaguar 1001		A Sunday Kind Of Love / Peace Of Mind	196?	3.00	15.00
BLUE OYSTER CULT					
Columbia 10046		Dominance And Submission / Career Of Evil	1974	1.00	5.00
Columbia 10169		Born To Be Wild / Born To Be Wild	1975	1.00	5.00
Columbia 10384		(Don't Fear) The Reaper / Tattoo Vampire	1976	.60	3.00

Label & Catalog #		A-Side/B-Side	Year	VG	NM
Columbia 10560		This Ain't The Summer Of Love / Debbie Denise	1977	.60	3.00
Columbia 10659		Goin' Through The Motions / Searchin' For Celine	1977	.60	3.00
Columbia 10697		Godzilla / Nosferatu	1978	.60	3.00
Columbia 10841		We Gotta Get Out Of This Place / E. T. I.	1978	.60	3.00
Columbia 11055		In Thee / Lonely Teardrops	1979	.60	3.00
Columbia 11145		You're Not The One (I Was Looking For) / Moon Crazy	1979	.60	3.00
Columbia 02415		Burnin' For You / Vengeance (The Pact)	1981	.60	3.00
Columbia 02415	(PS)	Burnin' For You / Vengeance (The Pact)	1981	.60	3.00

BLUE RAYS, THE
| Philips 40186 | | Who (Will It Be Today)? / Come On, Baby | 1964 | 3.00 | 15.00 |

BLUE RIDGE RANGERS, THE
The Rangers were a one man band: John Fogerty, formerly of Creedence Clearwater Revival.
Fantasy 683		Blue Ridge Mountain Blues / Have Thine Own Way	1972	.80	4.00
Fantasy 683	(PS)	Blue Ridge Mountain Blues / Have Thine Own Way	1972	2.00	10.00
Fantasy 689		Jambalya (On The Bayou) / Workin' On A Building	1972	.80	4.00
Fantasy 700		Hearts Of Stone / Somewhere Listening (For My Name)	1973	.80	4.00
Fantasy 710		Back In The Hills / You Don't Owe Me A Thing	1973	.80	4.00

BLUE RONDOS, THE
| Parkway 937 | | Little Baby / I Go For You | 1964 | 1.20 | 6.00 |

BLUE SKY BOYS, THE
| Blue Sky 101 | | Cherie / Just Another One In Love With You | 196? | 1.20 | 6.00 |

BLUE SONNETS, THE
| Columbia 42793 | | It's Never Too Late / Thank You, Mr. Moon | 1963 | 10.00 | 50.00 |

BLUE STAINS, THE
| Scarlet 501 | | You Don't Know Me / My Wife Can't Cook | 196? | 3.00 | 15.00 |

BLUE THINGS, THE
Ruff 1000		Mary Lou / Your Turn To Cry	1966	4.00	20.00
Ruff 1002		Pretty Thing-Oh / Just Two Days Ago	1966	4.00	20.00
RCA Victor 47-8692		La Do Da Da / I Must Be Doing Something Wrong	1968	3.00	15.00
RCA Victor 47-8860		Man On The Street / Doll House	1968	3.00	15.00
RCA Victor 47-8998		Orange Rooftop Of Your Mind / One Hour Cleaners	1968	5.00	25.00
RCA Victor 47-9203		You Can Live In Our Tree / Twist And Shout	1968	4.00	20.00
RCA Victor 47-9308		Yes, My Friend / Somebody Help Me	1968	3.00	15.00

BLUEBEARDS, THE
| Date 1547 | | Come On-A My House / I'm Home | 1967 | 1.00 | 5.00 |

BLUEBIRD
Burdette 101		Modessa / Goin' Down	1970	.80	4.00
Jerden 918		Billy Drake / I Shall Be Released	1970	.80	4.00
Piccadilley 113		Windy Linda / Touch	1971	1.00	5.00
Piccadilley 115		Here I Am / From The Country	1971	1.00	5.00

BLUEFIELD DOUGHBOYS, THE
| Panorama 1002 | | Flying On The Ground Is Wrong / Lovin' You | 1968 | 2.00 | 10.00 |

BLUENOTES, THE
Brooke 111		I Don't Know What It Is / Summer Love	1959	3.00	15.00
Brooke 116		I'm Gonna Find Out / Forever On My Mind	1960	3.00	15.00
Brooke 119		Summer Love / It Had To Be You	1960	3.00	15.00

BLUENOTES, THE: *Refer to* LITTLE BILL & THE BLUENOTES

BLUERAYS, THE
| Philips 40186 | | Who? / Come On, Baby | 1964 | 2.00 | 10.00 |

BLUES IMAGE, THE
Atco 6718		Lay Your Sweet Love On Me / Outside Was Night	1969	.60	3.00
Atco 6746		Ride Captain, Ride / Pay My Dues	1970	.80	4.00
Atco 6777		Gas Lamps And Clay / Running The Water	1970	.60	3.00
Atco 6798		Rise Up / Take Me Back	1971	.60	3.00

BLUES MAGOOS, THE [THE BLOOS MAGOOS]
Ganin 1000		Who Do You Love? / Let Your Love Ride	1966	4.00	20.00
Verve/Folkways 5006		People Had No Faces / So, I'm Right And You're Wrong *(First pressings credit The Bloos Magoos.)*	1966	3.00	15.00
Verve/Folkways 5006		People Had No Faces / So, I'm Right And You're Wrong *(Second pressings credit The Blues Magoos.)*	1966	2.00	10.00
Verve/Folkways 5044		People Had No Faces / So, I'm Right And You're Wrong	1967	2.00	10.00
Mercury 72590		Tobacco Road / Sometimes	1966	1.00	6.00

Label & Catalog #		A-Side/B-Side	Year	VG	NM
Mercury 72622		(We Ain't Got) Nothin' Yet / Gotta Get Away	1966	1.20	6.00
Mercury 72660		Pipe Dream / There's A Chance We Can Make It	1967	1.20	6.00
Mercury 72660	(PS)	Pipe Dream / There's A Chance We Can Make It	1967	2.00	12.00
Mercury 72692		One By One / Dante's Inferno	1967	1.20	6.00
Mercury 72692	(PS)	One By One / Dante's Inferno	1967	3.00	15.00
Mercury 72707		I Wanna Be There / Summer Is The Man	1967	1.20	6.00
Mercury 72729		There She Goes / Life Is Just A Cher O' Bowlies	1967	1.20	6.00
Mercury 72838		I Can Hear The Grass Grow / Yellow Rose	1968	1.20	6.00
ABC 11250		Never Goin' Back To Georgia /			
		Feelin' Time (I Can Feel It)	1968	.80	4.00

BLUES PROJECT, THE
The original Project included Roy Blumenfeld, Danny Kalb, Steve Katz, Al Kooper and Tommy Flanders, who left in 1966.

Verve/Folkways 5004		Back Door Man / Violets Of Dawn	1966	1.60	8.00
Verve/Folkways 5013		I Want To Be Your Drive / Catch The Wind	1966	1.20	6.00
Verve/Folkways 5019		Where There's Smoke There's Fire / Goin' Down Louisiana	1967	1.20	6.00
Verve/Folkways 5019	(PS)	Where There's Smoke There's Fire / Goin' Down Louisiana	1967	4.00	20.00
Verve/Folkways 5032		I Can't Keep From Crying / The Way My Baby Walks	1966	1.20	6.00
Verve/Folkways 5040		No Time Like The Right Time / Steve's Song	1967	1.00	5.00
Verve/Folkways 5063		Gentle Dreams / Lost In The Shuffle	1967	1.20	6.00

BLUESVILLE
Jerden 788		As Tears Go By / Don't Think Twice	1966	1.25	6.00

BLUM, BOB
Orbit 101		Thanks To You / Where Are The Stars?	196?	1.00	5.00

BO-PETE
Bo-Pete is a pseudonym for Harry Nilsson.

Try 501		Do You Wanna? / Groovie Little Suzie	196?	4.00	20.00

BO STREET RUNNERS, THE
K.R. 0117		Aladdin (One sided)	196?	5.00	25.00

BO-WEEVILS, THE
United States 1934		The Beatles Will Getcha /	1964	3.00	15.00

BOB & BOBBY
Bob is Bob Norberg, who also recorded as Bob & Sheri and The Survivors.

Tower 154		Twelve-O-Four / Baby, What You Want Me To Do	1965	10.00	50.00

BOB & JERRY
Bob Feldman and Jerry Goldstein, who also recorded as The Sheep and The Strangeloves.

Columbia 42162		We're The Guys / Dreamy Eyes	1961	4.00	20.00
Musicor 1018		Chubby (Isn't Chubby Anymore) / Nursery Rhyme Folk	1962	2.00	10.00
Musicor 1018		Chubby / Nursery Rhyme Folk	1962	2.00	10.00

BOB & SHERI
Bob is Bob Norberg, who also recorded as Bob & Bobby and The Survivors. Produced by Brian Wilson.

Safari 101	(DJ)	The Surfer Moon / Humpty Dumpty (White label)	1962	250.00	750.00
Safari 101		The Surfer Moon / Humpty Dumpty (Blue label)	1962	500.00	1,500.00
Safari 101		The Surfer Moon / Humpty Dumpty (Pink label)		Bootleg	
Safari 101		The Surfer Moon / Humpty Dumpty (Blue vinyl)		Bootleg	

BOB & THE AVERONES
Brent 7054		Please Say You Want Me / Patti	1964	3.00	15.00

BOB & THE MESSENGERS
Rust 5069		Splash Down / Bob's Groove	1963	2.00	10.00

BOB B. SOXX & THE BLUE JEANS
Bobb B. is Bobby Sheen, the Blue Jeans are The Blossoms, the producer is Phil Spector.

Philles 107		Zip-A-Dee-Doo-Dah / Flip And Nitty (Orange label)	1962	4.00	20.00
Philles 107		Zip-A-Dee-Doo-Dah / Flip And Nitty	1962	3.00	15.00
Philles 110		Why Do Lovers Break Each Other's Hearts? /			
		Dr. Kaplan's Office	1963	3.00	15.00
Philles 113		Not Too Young To Get Married / Annette	1963	3.00	15.00
		—Philles singles above have blue labels without a company address.—			

BOB-O-LINKS, THE: Refer to THE BOBOLINKS

BOBBI & THE BEAUS
Unart 2009		Losing Game / Melvin	1959	3.00	15.00

BOBBI-PINS, THE
Mercury 72389		Little Wheels / Sad, Sad Girl	1964	3.00	15.00

Label & Catalog #	A-Side/B-Side	Year	VG	NM
BOBBIE & THE PLEASERS				
Jamie 1118	The Monster / The Switch	1959	3.00	15.00
BOBBIES, THE				
Sonny 1001	(She) Put Me Down / (She) Put Me Down, Part 2	1966	1.00	5.00
BOBBY & THE CONSOLES				
Bobby is Bobby Pedrick, Jr.				
Diamond 141	My Jelly Bean / Nita	1963	15.00	75.00
Diamond 141	My Jelly Bean / Nita (Brown vinyl)	1963	20.00	100.00
BOBBY & THE INNKEEPERS				
Tragic 4809	World Of Fantasy / A Change Is Gonna Come	196?	2.00	10.00
BOBBY & THE ORBITS				
Seeco 6005	Felicia / Bandstand Dancing	1959	4.00	20.00
Seeco 6030	Teenage Love / What Do I Say?	1959	3.00	15.00
BOBBY & THE VELVETS				
Bobby is Bobby Sanders. Refer to The Extremes.				
Rason 501	I Promise / Now We Know	1959	10.00	50.00
BOBOLINKS, THE [THE BOB-O-LINKS]				
Key 573	I Wanna Be Elvis Presley's Sergeant /			
	Your Cotton-Pickin' Heart	1958	10.00	50.00
Key 575	Chocolate Ice Cream / Mechanical Man	1959	2.00	10.00
Tune 226	Lonesome Wind / Message From Me	1961	2.00	10.00
Hi Ho 101	I Promise / Mr. Grog	1962	3.00	15.00
BODINE				
MGM 14088	Keep Lookin' Through My Window / Easy To See	1969	2.00	10.00
BODROCKERS, THE				
Bolo 755	I've Waited Far To Long / Born Not To Ramble	1965	2.00	10.00
BOETCHER, CURT [CURT BOETTCHER]				
Curt Boetcher also recorded with or as California; Friar Tuck; Millennium; and Sagittarius. Note: Curt also spelled his name as Betcher and Becher. Both singles were produced by Gary Usher.				
Together 117	Share With Me / Sometimes	1969	2.00	10.00
Elektra 45834	I Love You More Each Day / Such A Lady	1973	1.00	5.00
BOLL WEEVIL				
Funn 1001	Free-Dumb Riders / Free-Dumb Riders, Part 2	196?	2.00	10.00
BOMPERS, THE				
The Bompers feature Carol Connors.				
HBR 441	Do The Bomp / Early Bird	1965	7.00	35.00
BON, JOANN, & THE COQUETTES				
MTA 129	You're Getting Restless / I'll Release You	1967	2.00	10.00
BON-AIRES, THE				
Rust TR3	Blue Beat / Driving Alone	1962	20.00	100.00
Rust 5077	My Love, My Love / Bye Bye	1964	5.00	25.00
Rust 5097	Shrine Of St. Cecilia / Jeanie Baby	1965	7.00	35.00
Catamount 130	New Me / My Heart's Desire	1971	2.00	10.00
Flamingo 1000	Cherry / At Night	1976	2.00	10.00
Flamingo 1001	Out Of Sight, Out Of Mind / I Love You	1976	2.00	10.00
BON BONS, THE				
The Bon Bons later recorded as The Shangri-Las.				
Coral 62402 (DJ)	What's Wrong With Ringo? / Come On, Baby	1964	5.00	25.00
Coral 62402	What's Wrong With Ringo? / Come On, Baby	1964	10.00	50.00
Coral 62435 (DJ)	Everybody Wants My Boyfriend / Each Time	1964	4.00	20.00
Coral 62435	Everybody Wants My Boyfriend / Each Time	1964	8.00	40.00
BOND, BOBBY				
Danceland 1000	Livin' Doll / Sweet Love	1961	2.00	10.00
BOND, EDDIE				
Ekko 1015	Double Dirty Lovin' / Talkin' Off The Wall	1956	20.00	100.00
Diplomat 8566	Monkey And The Baboon /	1956	10.00	50.00
Mercury 70826	Rockin' Daddy / I've Got A Woman	1956	12.00	60.00
Mercury 70882	Slip, Slip, Slippin' In / Flip Flop Mama	1956	12.00	60.00
Mercury 70941	Boppin' Bonnie / Baby, Baby, Baby	1958	12.00	60.00
Mercury 71153	Lovin' You, Lovin' You / Hershey Bar	1957	6.00	30.00
Mercury 71237	Backslidin' / Love, Love, Love	1957	6.00	30.00
Erwin 2001	Here Comes The Train /	1957	8.00	40.00

Label & Catalog #		A-Side/B-Side	Year	VG	NM
Memphis 114		Cold Dark Waters / Raunchy	1957	8.00	40.00
Memphis 115		Here Comes The Train /	1957	8.00	40.00

BOND, JOHNNY
Country singer Bond recorded a few rockabilly tracks along with a novelty number for the pop market.

Columbia 21160		Wildcat / Let Me Go, Devil	195?	2.00	25.00
Columbia 21521		Little Rock & Roll / I'll Be There	195?	3.00	15.00
Columbia 40842		Honky Tonk Fever / Lay It On The Line	195?	2.50	12.00
Starday 678		Hot Rod Surfin' Beatle Hootenanny /			
		Don't Mama Count Anymore?	1964	3.00	15.00

BONDS, GARY "U. S."

Legrand 1003		New Orleans / Please Forgive Me	1960	3.00	15.00
		(Label credits U.S. Bonds.)			
Legrand 1003		New Orleans / Please Forgive Me	1960	3.00	15.00
Legrand 1005		Not Me / Give Me One More Chance	1960	3.00	15.00
	— Legrand 1003 and 1005 originally issued with purple labels; reddish purple labels are reissues.—				
Legrand 1005		Not Me / Give Me One More Chance	196?	2.00	10.00
Legrand 1008		Quarter To Three / Old Time Story	1961	2.00	10.00
Legrand 1008	(PS)	Quarter To Three / Old Time Story	1961	3.00	15.00
Legrand 1009		School Is Out / One Million Years	1961	2.00	10.00
Legrand 1009	(PS)	School Is Out / One Million Years	1961	3.00	15.00
Legrand 1012		School Is In / Trip To The Moon	1961	2.00	10.00
Legrand 1015		Dear Lady / Havin' So Much Fun	1961	2.00	10.00
Legrand 1015		Dear Lady Twist / Havin' So Much Fun	1961	2.00	10.00
Legrand 1018		Twist Twist, Senora / Food Of Love	1962	2.00	10.00
Legrand 1019		Seven Day Weekend / Gettin' A Groove	1962	2.00	10.00
Legrand 1020		Copy Cat / I'll Change That, Too	1962	2.00	10.00
Legrand 1022		I Dig This Station / Mixed Up Faculty	1962	2.00	10.00
Legrand 1025		Do The Limbo With Me / Where Did That Naughty Girl Go?	1963	2.00	10.00
Legrand 1027		I Don't Wanna Wait / What A Dream	1963	2.00	10.00
Legrand 1029		No More Homework / She's Alright	1963	2.00	10.00
Legrand 1030		Perdido / Perdido, Part 2	1964	2.00	10.00
Legrand 1031		My Sweet Ruby Rose / King Kong's Monkey	1964	2.00	10.00
Legrand 1035		Oh Yeah, Oh Yeah / Let Me Go, Lover	1964	2.00	10.00
Legrand 1039		Do The Bumpsie / Beaches, U.S.A.	1965	2.00	10.00
Legrand 1040		Take Me Back To New Orleans / I'm That Kind Of Guy	1965	2.00	10.00
Legrand 1043		Send Her Back To Me / Workin' For My Baby	1965	2.00	10.00
Legrand 1045		Call Me For Christmas / Mixed Up Faculty	1966	2.00	10.00
Legrand 1046		What A Crazy World / Sarah Jane	1966	2.00	10.00
	— Original Legrand singles above have gold, red & white labels; singles with just gold & red labels are reissues.—				
Atco 6689		The Star / You Need A Personal Manager	1969	1.00	5.00
EMI America 8079		This Little Girl / Way Back When	1981	.20	1.00
EMI America 8079	(PS)	This Little Girl / Way Back When	1981	.20	1.00
EMI America 8089		Jole Blon / Just Like A Child	1981	.20	1.00
EMI America 8099		Just Like A Child / Your Love	1981	.20	1.00
EMI America 8117		Out Of Work / Bring Her Back	1981	.20	1.00
EMI America 8117	(PS)	Out Of Work / Bring Her Back	1981	.20	1.00
EMI America 8133		Love's On The Line / Way Back When	1981	.20	1.00
EMI America 8145		Way Back When / Turn The Music Down	1982	.20	1.00

BONDSMEN, THE

Dawn 303		Wipe Out '66 / (B-side by The Derbys)	1966	3.00	15.00
Dawn 303		Wipe Out '66 / (B-side by The Derbys) (Blue vinyl)	1966	6.00	30.00

BONFELLS, THE

Northwestern 2536		Baby / Have You Ever Had The Blues?	1964	8.00	40.00

BONFIRE, MARS

Columbia 44772		Faster Than The Speed Of Life / She	1968	1.20	6.00
Columbia 44888		Lady Moon Walker / In Christina's Arms	1969	1.20	6.00

BONN, SKEETER

RCA Victor 47-6352		Rock-A-Bye Baby / There's No Use	195?	2.00	10.00

BONNER, GARY

Columbia 44306		Heart Of Juliet Jones / Me About You	1967	2.00	10.00
Columbia 44306	(PS)	Heart Of Juliet Jones / Me About You	1967	3.00	15.00
Columbia 44703		Jug Of Wine / Saddest	1968	1.00	5.00

BONNEVILLES, THE

Coral 62273		Freeway U.S.A. / Johnny	1961	3.00	15.00

BONNEVILLES, THE

Question Mark 101		High Noon Stomp / Dirty Herb	1962	7.00	35.00
Question Mark 101	(PS)	High Noon Stomp / Dirty Herb	1962	15.00	75.00
Question Mark 103		Bonneville Stomp / Knock Around	1962	7.00	35.00

Label & Catalog #	A-Side/B-Side	Year	VG	NM
BONNEVILLES, THE				
Whitehall 30002	I Do / Make Believe Lovin'	1959	6.00	30.00
Munich 103	Lorraine / Zu Zu	1960	40.00	200.00
Barry 104	Lorraine / Zu Zu	1962	6.00	30.00
Capri 102	Until You Say We're Through / Give Me Your Love	196?	8.00	40.00
BONNIE & THE BUTTERFLIES				
Smash 1878	I Saw Him Standing There / Dust Storm	1964	3.00	15.00
BONNIE & THE DENIMS				
LLP 101	Class Reunion / Time Will Tell	1965	2.00	10.00
BONNIE & THE TREASURES				
Long believed to feature Veronica Bennett of The Ronettes, "Bonnie" was, in fact, Ms. Charlotte O' Hara.				
Phi-Dan 5005	Home Of The Brave / Our Song	1965	10.00	50.00
	(Produced by Phil Spector.)			
Pablo 7014	Davey, I'm So Glad It Rained / (B-side by Mid-Americans)	196?	6.00	30.00
BONNY, BILLY				
Mark '56 830	Bobby Jean / Bootleg Rock	1959	2.00	10.00
BONO, SONNY: Refer to SONNY				
BONQUETS, TOOTIE				
Parkway 887	You Done Me Wrong / The Conquer	1963	8.00	40.00
BONZO DOG BAND, THE				
Liberty 66345	I'm The Urban Spaceman / Canyons Of Your Mind	1968	2.00	10.00
United Artists 50809	I'm The Urban Spaceman / Canyons Of Your Mind	1971	1.00	5.00
United Artists 50943 (DJ)	Slush / Slush	1972	1.20	6.00
	(Stock copies of U.A. 50943 may not exist.)			
BOO & THE GIRLFRIENDS				
Boo is a pseudonym for Freddy Fender.				
Talent Scout 1010	Something On Your Mind / You Got What It Takes	1960	3.00	15.00
BOO BOO & BUNKIE				
Brent 7045	Turn Around / This Old Town	1963	2.00	10.00
BOOKWORMS, THE				
Titan 1714	Ditchin' / Just Cruisin' Around	1961	2.00	10.00
BOON, BAB				
Poleese 100	Song Titles / (B-side by Peter Goon)	196?	6.00	30.00
BOONE, PAT				
Pat Boone may also have recorded as The Phantom. Some sides below credit Pat & Shirley Boone.				
Republic 7049	Until You Tell Me So / My Heart Belongs To You	1954	3.00	15.00
Republic 7062	Remember To Be Mine / Half Way Chance With You	1954	3.00	15.00
Republic 7084	I Need Someone / Loving You Madly	1954	3.00	15.00
Republic 7119	I Need Someone / My Heart Belongs To You	1955	3.00	15.00
Dot 15338	Two Hearts / Tra La La	1955	2.40	12.00
Dot 15377	Ain't That A Shame / Tennessee Saturday Night	1955	2.40	12.00
Dot 15422	At My Front Door / No Other Arms	1955	2.40	12.00
Dot 15435	Gee Whittakers / Take The Time	1955	2.40	12.00
Dot 15443	I'll Be Home / Tutti Frutti	1956	2.40	12.00
Dot 15457	Long Tall Sally / Just As Long As I'm With You	1956	2.40	12.00
Dot 15472	I Almost Lost My Mind / I'm In Love With You	1956	2.40	12.00
Dot 15490	Friendly Persuasion / Chains Of Love	1956	2.40	12.00
	— Dot singles above have maroon labels. —			
Dot 15338	Two Hearts / Tra La La	1956	2.00	10.00
Dot 15377	Ain't That A Shame / Tennessee Saturday Night	1956	2.00	10.00
Dot 15422	At My Front Door / No Other Arms	1956	2.00	10.00
Dot 15435	Gee Whittakers / Take The Time	1956	2.00	10.00
Dot 15443	I'll Be Home / Tutti Frutti	1956	2.00	10.00
Dot 15457	Long Tall Sally / Just As Long As I'm With You	1956	2.00	10.00
Dot 15472	I Almost Lost My Mind / I'm In Love With You	1956	2.00	10.00
Dot 15490	Friendly Persuasion / Chains Of Love	1956	2.00	10.00
Dot 15521	Don't Forbid Me / Anastasia	1956	2.00	10.00
Dot 15570	Love Letters In The Sand / Bernadine	1957	2.00	10.00
Dot 15570 (PS)	Love Letters In The Sand / Bernadine	1957	3.00	15.00
Dot 15602	Remember You're Mine / There's A Gold Mine In The Sky	1957	2.00	10.00
Dot 15660	April Love / When The Swallows Come Back To Capistrano	1957	2.00	10.00
Dot 15690	A Wonderful Time Up There / It's Too Soon To Know	1958	2.00	10.00
Dot 15750	Sugar Moon / Cherie, I Love You	1958	2.00	10.00
Dot 15750 (PS)	Sugar Moon / Cherie, I Love You	1958	3.00	15.00
Dot 15785	If Dreams Came True / That's How Much I Love You	1958	2.00	10.00
Dot 15825	For My Good Fortune / Gee, But It's Lonely	1958	2.00	10.00

While Pat has more or less avoided the bulk of fads or scenes that have happened since he entered the biz, this obscure number was ol' white bucks' stab at the West Coast sound. Both sides featured harmonies from Bruce Johnston and Terry Melcher and make this one of the hottest of all Boone's many releases among collectors.

Label & Catalog #		A-Side/B-Side	Year	VG	NM
Dot 15840		I'll Remember Tonight / The Mardi Gras March	1958	2.00	10.00
Dot 15840	(PS)	I'll Remember Tonight / The Mardi Gras March	1958	3.00	15.00
Dot 15888		With The Wind And Rain In Your Hair /			
		Good Rocking Tonight	1959	2.00	10.00
Dot S-200	(S)	With The Wind And Rain In Your Hair /			
		Good Rocking Tonight	1959	3.00	15.00
Dot 15914		For A Penny / The Wang Dang Taffy-Apple Tango	1959	2.00	10.00
Dot S-203	(S)	For A Penny / The Wang Dang Taffy-Apple Tango	1959	3.00	15.00
Dot 15955		Twixt Twelve And Twenty / Rock, Boll Weevil	1959	2.00	10.00
Dot 15955	(PS)	Twixt Twelve And Twenty / Rock, Boll Weevil	1959	3.00	15.00
Dot S-207	(S)	Twixt Twelve And Twenty / Rock, Boll Weevil	1959	3.00	15.00
Dot 15982		Fool's Hall Of Fame / The Brightest Wishing Star	1959	2.00	10.00
Dot 15982	(PS)	Fool's Hall Of Fame / The Brightest Wishing Star	1959	3.00	15.00
Dot S-211	(S)	Fool's Hall Of Fame / The Brightest Wishing Star	1959	3.00	15.00
Dot 16006		Beyond The Sunset / My Faithful Heart	1959	2.00	10.00
Dot S-218	(S)	Beyond The Sunset / My Faithful Heart	1959	3.00	15.00
Dot 16015		Journey To The Center Of The Earth /			
		Journey To The Center Of The Earth, part 2	1959	1.00	5.00
Dot 16028		I'll Be Home / Ain't That A Shame	1960	1.00	5.00
Dot 16033		I Almost Lost My Mind / Friendly Persuasion	1960	1.00	5.00
Dot 16034		Don't Forbid Me / April Love	1960	1.00	5.00
Dot 16035		Love Letters In The Sand / A Wonderful Time Up There	1960	1.00	5.00
Dot 16048		(Welcome) New Lovers / Words	1960	2.00	10.00
Dot 16048	(PS)	(Welcome) New Lovers / Words	1960	3.00	15.00
Dot S-220	(S)	(Welcome) New Lovers / Words	1960	3.00	15.00
Dot 16073		Walking The Floor Over You / Spring Rain	1960	2.00	10.00
Dot 16073	(PS)	Walking The Floor Over You / Spring Rain	1960	3.00	15.00
Dot S-221	(S)	Walking The Floor Over You / Spring Rain	1960	3.00	15.00
Dot 16122		Delia Gone / Candy Sweet	1960	2.00	10.00
Dot S-228	(S)	Delia Gone / Candy Sweet	1960	3.00	15.00
Dot 16152		Dear John / Alabam	1960	2.00	10.00
Dot 16176		The Exodus Song (This Land Is Mine) /			
		There's A Moon Out Tonight	1961	2.00	10.00
Dot 16209		Moody River / A Thousand Years	1961	2.00	10.00
Dot S-294	(S)	Moody River / A Thousand Years	1961	3.00	15.00
Dot 16244		Big Cold Wind / That's My Desire	1961	1.20	6.00
Dot S-295	(S)	Big Cold Wind / That's My Desire	1961	3.00	15.00
Dot 16278		Louella /	1961	1.20	6.00
Dot 16284		Johnny Will (If I'm Dreaming) / Just Let Me Dream	1961	1.20	6.00
Dot S-321	(S)	Johnny Will (If I'm Dreaming) / Just Let Me Dream	1961	3.00	15.00
Dot 16312		I'll See You In My Dreams	1962	1.20	6.00
Dot S-325	(S)	I'll See You In My Dreams	1962	3.00	15.00
Dot 16349		Quando, Quando, Quando / Willing And Eager	1962	1.00	5.00
Dot S-348	(S)	Quando, Quando, Quando / Willing And Eager	1962	3.00	15.00
Dot 16368		Speedy Gonzales / The Locket	1962	1.00	5.00
Dot 16391		Ten Lonely Guys / Lover's Island	1962	1.00	5.00
Dot 16406		Blues Stay Away From Me / Every Step Of The Way	1962	1.00	5.00
Dot S-385	(S)	Blues Stay Away From Me / Every Step Of The Way	1962	3.00	15.00
Dot 16416		Mexican Joe / In The Room	1963	1.00	5.00
Dot S-323	(S)	Mexican Joe / In The Room	1963	3.00	15.00
Dot 16439		Meditation (Meditacao) / The Days Of Wine And Roses	1963	.80	4.00
Dot 16474		Always You And Me / Main Attraction	1963	.80	4.00
Dot 16494		Tie Me Kangaroo Down, Sport / I Feel Like Crying	1963	.80	4.00
Dot 16498		Main Attraction / Si, Si, Si	1963	.80	4.00
Dot 16525		Mister Moon / Love Me	1963	.80	4.00
Dot 16547		Santa's Coming In A Whirley Bird / O Holy Night	1963	.80	4.00
Dot 16559		Some Enchanted Evening / That's Me	1963	.80	4.00
Dot 16576		I Like What You Do / Never Put It In Writing	1964	.80	4.00
Dot 16598		I Understand / Rosemarie	1964	.80	4.00
Dot 16626		Side By Side / I'll Never Be Free	1964	.80	4.00
Dot 16641		Sincerely / Don't You Just Know It	1964	.80	4.00
Dot 16658		Beach Girl / Little Honda	1964	5.00	25.00
		(Bruce Johnston and Terry Melcher produce and provide back-up vocals.)			
Dot 16668		Goodbye Charlie / Love, Who Needs It?	1964	.60	3.00
Dot 16684		I'd Rather Die Young / I Want It That Way	1965	.60	3.00
Dot 16699		Blueberry Hill / Heartaches	1965	.60	3.00
Dot 16707		Baby Elephant Walk / Say Goodbye	1965	.60	3.00
Dot 16728		Pearly Shells / Crazy Arms	1965	.60	3.00
Dot 16738		(Welcome) New Lovers / Mickey Mouse	1965	.60	3.00
Dot 16754		Rainy Days / With My Eyes Wide Open I'm Dreaming	1965	.60	3.00
Dot 16785		I Love You So Much It Hurts /			
		Meet Me Tonight In Dreamland	1965	.60	3.00
Dot 16808		Man Alone / Run To Me, Baby	1966	.60	3.00
Dot 16825		As Tears Go By / Judith	1966	.60	3.00
Dot 16836		It Seems Like Yesterday /			
		Well Remembered, Highly Thought Of Love Affair	1966	.60	3.00
Dot 16871		Five Miles From Home /			
		Don't Put Your Feet In The Lemonade	1966	.60	3.00

Label & Catalog #		A-Side/B-Side	Year	VG	NM
Dot 16903		Wreath Of Grapes / You Don't Need Me Anymore	1966	.60	3.00
Dot 16933	(DJ)	Wish You Were Here, Buddy / (B-side by Jimmie Rodgers) (Red vinyl)	1967	2.00	10.00
Dot 16933		Wish You Were Here, Buddy / Love For Love	1967	.60	3.00
Dot 16998		Hurry Sundown / What If They Gave A War And Nobody Came?	1967	.60	3.00
Dot 17018		Have You Heard (It's All Over) / Me	1967	.60	3.00
Dot 17027		In The Mirror Of Your Mind / Swanee Is A River	1967	.60	3.00
Dot 17045		By The Time I Get To Phoenix / Ride, Ride, Ride	1967	.60	3.00
Dot 17056		Green Kentucky Hills Of Home / You Mean All The World To Me	1968	.60	3.00
Dot 17076		Emily / It's A Happening World	1968	.60	3.00
Dot 17098		500 Miles / I Had A Dream	1968	.60	3.00
Dot 17122		Gonna Find Me A Bluebird / Deafening Roar Of Silence	1968	.60	3.00
Dot 17156		Beyond One Memory / September Blues	1968	.60	3.00
Tetragrammaton 1516		July, You're A Woman / Break My Mind	1969	.60	3.00
Tetragrammaton 1529		What's Gnawing At Me / Never Goin' Back To Nashville	1969	.60	3.00
Tetragrammaton 1540		Good Morning, Dear / You Win Again	1969	.60	3.00
Capitol 2763		What Are You Doing For The Rest Of Your Life? / Now I'm Saved	1970	.60	3.00
Capitol 2860		Picking Up Pebbles / Oh, My God	1970	.60	3.00
Lion 106		Mr. Blue / Song Of The Children Of Israel	1971	.60	3.00
Lion 119		I Believe In Music / Children Learn What They Live	1971	.60	3.00
Lion 126		If You're Gonna Make A Fool Of Somebody / Empty Chairs	1972	.60	3.00
MGM 14242		All For The Love Of Sunshine / (B-side by Mike Curb)	1971	.60	3.00
MGM 14282		Where There's A Heartache / C'mon-Give Me A Hand	1971	.60	3.00
MGM 1414470		I Saw The Light / The Great Speckled Bird	1972	.60	3.00
MGM 14476		Did You Give The World Some Love Today, Babe? / Pay The Piper	1973	.60	3.00
MGM 14521		Tying The Pieces Together / Hayden Carter	1973	.60	3.00
MGM 14601		Everything Begins And Ends With You / Golden Rocket	1973	.60	3.00
Buena Vista 487		The Sounds Of Christmas / Little Green Tree	1973	.60	3.00
Melodyland M6001F		Candy Lips / Young Girl	1974	.60	3.00
Melodyland M6005F		Indiana Girl / Young Girl	1975	.60	3.00
Melodyland M6018F		I'd Do It With You / Yester-Me, Yester-You, Yesterday	1975	.60	3.00
Melodyland M6029F		Glory Train / U.F.O.	1975	.60	3.00
Motown M1334F		Viva Espana / When The Love Light Starts Shining Through His Eyes	1975	.60	3.00
Hitsville 6037F		Texas Woman / It's Gone	1976	.40	2.00
Hitsville 6042F		Oklahoma Sunshine / Won't Be Home Tonight	1976	.40	2.00
Hitsville 6047F		Country Days And Country Nights / When The Love Light Starts Shining Through His Eyes	1976	.40	2.00
Hitsville 6054F		Colorado Country Morning / Don't Want To Fall Away From You	1976	.40	2.00
Warner Bros. PRO-720	(DJ)	Watching The River Run / Don't Let The Feeling Get Away	1978	.30	1.50
Warner Bros. PRO-743	(DJ)	When I'm With You I'm Feeling Good / When I'm With You I'm Feeling Good	1978	.30	1.50
Warner Bros. MCP-106	(DJ)	It Feels Good (To Love Again) / It Feels Good (To Love Again)	1978	.30	1.50
Warner Bros. 49097		Midnight / Can You Feel The Love? (Warner Bros. 49097 credited to Pat & Shirley Boone.)	1978	.30	1.50
Warner Bros. 49255		Love's Got A Way Of Hanging On / The Hostage Prayer	1979	.30	1.50
Warner Bros. 49596		Colorado Country Morning / What Ever Happened To Good Old Honky Tonk Music?	1980	.30	1.50
Warner Bros. 49691		Throw It Away / Won't be Home Tonight	1981	.30	1.50

— Extended Play Albums —

Label & Catalog #		A-Side/B-Side	Year	VG	NM
Dot 1049		Pat Boone	1955	6.00	30.00
Dot 1053		Pat On Mike	1956	6.00	30.00
Dot 1054		Friendly Persuasion	1956	6.00	30.00
Dot 1055		A Date With Pat Boone	1956	5.00	25.00
Dot 1056		A Closer Walk With Thee	1956	5.00	25.00
Dot 1057		Four By Pat	1957	5.00	25.00
Dot 1062		Merry Christmas	1957	5.00	25.00
Dot 1064		Tutti Frutti	1957	5.00	25.00
Dot 1069		Star Dust	1958	5.00	25.00
Dot 1075		Mardi Gras	1958	5.00	25.00
Dot 1076		Side By Side	1959	5.00	25.00
Dot 1082		Tenderly	1959	5.00	25.00
Dot 1083		Pat's Greatest Hits	1959	5.00	25.00
Dot 1086		I'm In The Mood For You	1960	5.00	25.00
Dot 1090		Beyond The Sunset	1960	5.00	25.00
Dot 1096		Moonglow	1960	5.00	25.00
Dot 1098		All Hands On Deck	1960	5.00	25.00
Dot 399	(33)	I'll See You In My Dreams (Jukebox EP)	1968	2.00	10.00

BOONE GIRLS, THE
Pat's daughters, featuring Debby.

Label & Catalog #		A-Side/B-Side	Year	VG	NM
Lion 110		Bless The Beast And The Children / Anthem-Revelation	1972	.60	3.00

Label & Catalog #	A-Side/B-Side	Year	VG	NM
BOOT, JOE				
Celestial 111	Rock And Roll Radio / That's Tough	195?	5.00	25.00
BOOTIQUES, THE				
Date 1513	Mr. Man Of The World / Did You Get Your Fun?	1967	1.20	6.00
BOOTLES, THE				
GNP/Crescendo 311	I'll Let You Hold My Hand / Never Till Now	1964	1.20	6.00
BOOTMEN, THE				
Etiquette 10	1, 2, 3, 4 / Black Widow	1964	2.00	10.00
Riverton 101	Love You All I Can / Forevermore	1965	3.00	15.00
Riverton 104	Ain't It The Truth, Babe / Wherever You Hide	1966	5.00	25.00
BORESON, STAN				
Golden Crest 201	Little Green Apples / Honey	196?	1.00	5.00
BOSS FIVE, THE				
Impact 1003	Please, Mr. President / You Cheat Too Much	196?	2.00	10.00
BOSSMEN, THE				
The Bossmen feature Dick Wagner.				
Soft 121	Take A Look / It's A Shame	196?	3.00	15.00
Dicto 1001	Bad Girl / Here's Congratulations	1965	3.00	15.00
Dicto 1002	Wait And See / You're The Girl For Me	1965	3.00	15.00
Lucky Eleven 227	Wait And See / You're The Girl For Me	1966	2.00	10.00
Lucky Eleven 231	Baby Boy / You And I	1966	2.00	10.00
M&L 1809	Help Me, Baby / Thanks To You	196?	3.00	15.00
BOSTON				
Epic 50266	More Than A Feeling / Smokin'	1976	.40	2.00
Epic 50329	Long Time / Let Me Take You Home Tonight	1977	.40	2.00
Epic 50381	Peace Of Mind / Foreplay	1977	.40	2.00
Epic 50590	Don't Look Back / The Journey	1978	.40	2.00
Epic 50638	A Man I'll Never Be / Don't Be Afraid	1978	.40	2.00
Epic 50677	Feelin' Satisfied / Used To Bad News	1979	.40	2.00
BOSTON CRABS, THE				
Capitol 5493	Down In Mexico / Who?	1964	1.20	6.00
Tower 368	You Didn't Have To Be So Nice / Gin House	1966	1.20	6.00
BOSTON TEA PARTY, THE				
Challenge 59368	Words / Spinach	1966	2.00	10.00
Flick Disc 900	Free Service / I'm Tellin' You	196?	1.00	5.00
BOWEN, JIMMY (& THE ORCHIDS)				
Blue Moon	I'm Stickin' With You / (B-side by Buddy Knox)	1957	——	——
	(Although unverified, rumors of this record's existence continue.)			
Triple-D 798	I'm Stickin' With You / (B-side by Buddy Knox)	1957	——	——
	(Rare. Estimated near mint value $500-1,000.)			
Roulette 4001	I'm Stickin' With You / Ever-Lovin' Fingers	1957	4.00	20.00
Roulette 4010	Warm Up To Me, Baby / I Trusted You	1957	3.00	15.00
Roulette 4017	Don't Tell Me Your Troubles / Ever Since That Night	1958	3.00	15.00
Roulette 4023	Cross Over / It's Shameful	1958	3.00	15.00
Roulette 4083	By The Light Of The Silvery Moon / The Two-Step	1958	3.00	15.00
Roulette 4102	My Kind Of Woman / Blue Moon	1958	3.00	15.00
Roulette 4122	Always Faithful / Wish I Were Tied To You	1959	3.00	15.00
Roulette 4175	You're Just Wasting Your Time / Walking On Air	1959	3.00	15.00
Roulette 4224	Your Loving Arms / Oh Yeah, Oh Yeah	1959	3.00	15.00
Crest 1085	Don't Drop / Someone To Love	1961	3.00	15.00
Capehart 5005	Teenage Dream World / It's Against The Law	1962	3.00	15.00
Capehart 5005 (PS)	Teenage Dream World / It's Against The Law	1962	8.00	40.00
	—Extended Play Albums—			
Roulette 302	Jimmy Bowen	1957	50.00	200.00
BOWERS, BOB				
Dart 120	Sandy / Teenage Lonesome	1960	3.00	15.00
BOWERY BOYS, THE				
Hemisphere 102	It's For You / Duck	1969	.80	4.00
BOWIE, DAVID				
Refer to Buzz; Dana Gillespie; Lulu; Mott The Hoople; Iggy Pop; Queen & David Bowie; Lou Reed; The Spiders From Mars.				
Warner Bros. 5815 (DJ)	Can't Help Thinking About Me / And I Say To Myself	1966	50.00	200.00
Warner Bros. 5818	Can't Help Thinking About Me / And I Say To Myself	1966	100.00	400.00
	(Label credits "David Bowie & The Lower Third.")			
Deram 85009	Rubber Band / There Is A Happy Land	1966	12.00	60.00
Deram 85016	Love You Til Tuesday / Did You Ever Have A Dream?	1967	10.00	50.00

Label & Catalog #		A-Side/B-Side	Year	VG	NM
London 20079		The Laughing Gnome / Gospel According To Tony Day	1967	10.00	50.00
		(Reissued in 1973 with the same catalog number.)			
Mercury DJ-156	(DJ)	Space Oddity / Space Oddity	1969	10.00	50.00
Mercury 72949		Space Oddity / The Wild-Eyed Boy From Freecloud	1969	10.00	50.00
Mercury 73075	(DJ)	Memory Of A Free Festival /			
		Memory Of A Free Festival, Part 2	1970	16.00	80.00
Mercury 73075		Memory Of A Free Festival /			
		Memory Of A Free Festival, Part 2	1970	20.00	100.00
Mercury DJ-311	(DJ)	All The Madmen (One sided)	1971	20.00	100.00
Mercury 73173	(DJ)	All The Madmen / All The Madmen	1971	15.00	75.00
		(Stock copies of Mercury 73173 may not exist.)			
RCA Victor 74-0605		Changes / Andy Warhol (Grey label)	1971	2.00	10.00
RCA Victor 74-0605		Changes / Andy Warhol (Orange label)	1971	1.20	6.00
RCA Victor 74-0719		Starman / Suffragette City	1972	1.20	6.00
RCA Victor 74-0719	(PS)	Starman / Suffragette City	1972	5.00	25.00
RCA Victor 74-0838		The Jean Genie / Hang On To Yourself	1972	1.20	6.00
RCA Victor 74-0876		Space Oddity / The Man Who Sold The World	1973	1.20	6.00
RCA Victor 74-0876	(PS)	Space Oddity / The Man Who Sold The World	1973	3.00	15.00
RCA Victor APBO-0001		Time / The Prettiest Star	1973	1.60	8.00
RCA Victor APBO-0001	(PS)	Time / The Prettiest Star	1973	125.00	500.00
RCA Victor APBO-0028		Let's Spend The Night Together / Lady Grinning Soul	1973	1.20	6.00
RCA Victor APBO-0160		Sorrow / Amsterdam	1973	1.20	6.00
RCA Victor APBO-0287		Rebel Rebel / Lady Grinning Soul	1974	1.20	6.00
RCA Victor LPBO-5009		Rebel Rebel / Queen Bitch	1974	5.00	25.00
		(RCA 5009 contains an alternate mix of "Rebel Rebel.")			
RCA Victor APBO-0293		Diamond Dogs / Holy Holy	1974	2.00	10.00
RCA Victor PB-10026		1984 / Queen Bitch	1974	2.00	10.00
RCA Victor PB-10105		Rock 'N Roll With Me / Panic In Detroit	1974	1.20	6.00
RCA Victor LPBO-5021		Rock 'N Roll Suicide / Quicksand	1974	2.00	10.00
		—Original RCA Victor singles above have orange labels.—			
RCA Victor PB-10152		Young Americans / Knock On Wood	1975	1.00	5.00
RCA Victor PB-10320		Fame / Right	1975	1.00	5.00
RCA Victor PB-10441		Golden Years / Can You Hear Me?	1975	1.00	5.00
		—Original RCA Victor singles above have brown labels.—			
RCA Victor PB-10664		TVC 15 / We Are The Dead	1976	.80	4.00
RCA Victor PB-10736		Stay / Word On A Wing	1976	.80	4.00
RCA Victor PB-10905		Sound And Vision / A New Career In A New Town	1977	.80	4.00
RCA Victor PB-11017		Be My Wife / Speed Of Life	1977	.80	4.00
RCA Victor PB-11121		Heroes / V-2 Schneider	1977	.80	4.00
RCA Victor PB-11190		Beauty And The Beast / Sense Of Doubt	1978	.80	4.00
RCA Victor PB-11585		Boys Keep Swinging / Fantastic Voyage	1979	.80	4.00
RCA Victor PB-11661		D.J. / Fantastic Voyage	1979	.80	4.00
RCA Victor PB-11724		Look Back In Anger / Repetition	1979	.80	4.00
RCA Victor PB-11887		John, I'm Only Dancing / Joe The Lion	1979	.80	4.00
RCA Victor JH-12078	(DJ)	Ashes To Ashes (Promo picture sleeve)	1980	3.00	15.00
RCA Victor PB-12078		Ashes To Ashes / It's No Game, Part 1	1980	.40	2.00
RCA Victor PB-12078	(PS)	Ashes To Ashes / It's No Game, Part 1	1980	.60	3.00
RCA Victor JE-12087	(DJ)	Fashion / It's No Game / Teenage Wildlife	1980	75.00	300.00
RCA Victor PB-12134		Fashion / Scream Like A Baby	1980	.40	2.00
RCA Victor PB-12134	(PS)	Fashion / Scream Like A Baby	1980	.60	3.00
MCA 12805	(DJ)	Cat People (Putting Out Fire) (Picture disc)	1982	10.00	50.00
		(Features a Filmex back.)			
MCA 12805	(DJ)	Cat People (Putting Out Fire) (Picture disc)	1982	6.00	30.00
Backstreet 1767	(DJ)	Cat People (Putting Out Fire) / Cat People	1982	1.00	5.00
Backstreet 1767	(PS)	Cat People (Putting Out Fire) / Cat People	1982	1.00	5.00
Backstreet 52024		Cat People (Putting Out Fire) / Paul's Theme	1982	.40	2.00
Backstreet 52024	(PS)	Cat People (Putting Out Fire) / Paul's Theme	1982	.40	2.00
EMI B-8158		Let's Dance / Cat People	1983	.40	2.00
EMI B-8158	(PS)	Let's Dance / Cat People	1983	.40	2.00
EMI B-8165		China Girl / Shake It	1983	.40	2.00
EMI B-8165	(PS)	China Girl / Shake It	1983	.40	2.00
EMI B-8177		Modern Love / Modern Love	1983	.40	2.00
EMI B-8177	(PS)	Modern Love / Modern Love	1983	.40	2.00
EMI B-8190		Without You / Criminal World	1983	.40	2.00
EMI B-8190	(PS)	Without You / Criminal World	1983	.40	2.00
RCA Victor JK-13660	(DJ)	White Light, White Heat (Promo picture sleeve)	1983	1.00	5.00
RCA Victor PB-13660		White Light, White Heat / Cracked Actor	1983	.40	2.00
RCA Victor PB-13660	(PS)	White Light, White Heat / Cracked Actor	1983	.40	2.00
RCA Victor PB-13769		1984 / TVC 15	1984	.40	2.00
RCA Victor PB-13769	(PS)	1984 / TVC 15	1984	.40	2.00
EMI P-B-8231	(DJ)	Blue Jean / Blue Jean (Blue vinyl)	1984	1.20	6.00
EMI B-8231		Blue Jean / Dancing With The Big Boys	1984	.40	2.00
EMI P-8231		Blue Jean / Dancing With The Big Boys (Blue vinyl)	1984	1.00	5.00
EMI B-8231	(PS)	Blue Jean / Dancing With The Big Boys	1984	.40	2.00
EMI B-8246		Tonight / Tumble And Twirl	1984	.40	2.00
EMI B-8246	(PS)	Tonight / Tumble And Twirl	1984	.40	2.00
		—Special/Promotional Releases—			
RCA Victor 45-103	(EP)	David Bowie (With picture sleeve)	1972	6.00	30.00

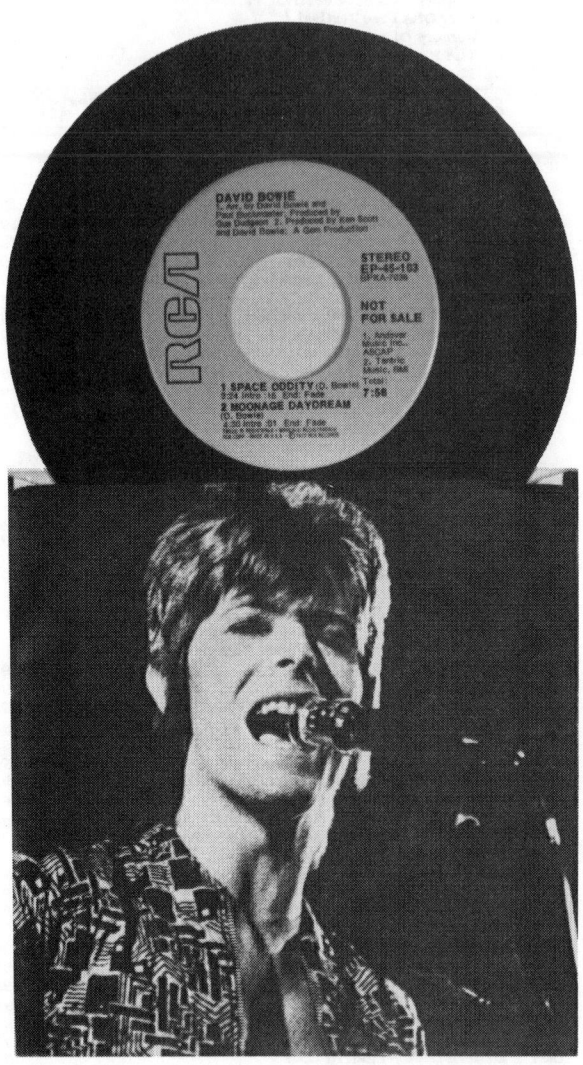

While there are no commercial EPs from Mr. Bowie for American collectors, this promo sampled four tracks from various albums and came in a black & white paper picture sleeve from Bowie's *Ziggy Stardust* period.

Label & Catalog #		A-Side/B-Side	Year	VG	NM
MA-1791	(EP)	What's It All About?	1978	10.00	50.00
		(Interview with Bowie on one side, Frank Zappa on the other.)			
Shubert XXX-01	(EP)	Elephant Man (One sided)	1980	5.00	25.00
		(Promo for Bowie's performance does not feature Bowie on the record.)			
		— 12" Singles—			
RCA Victor JD-11151	(DJ)	"Heroes" / "Heroes"	1977	5.00	25.00
RCA Victor JD-11204	(DJ)	Beauty And The Beast / Fame (PC)	1977	4.00	20.00
RCA Victor PC-11204		Beauty And The Beast / Fame	1977	2.00	10.00
RCA Victor JD-11306	(DJ)	Peter And The Wolf (One sided)	1978	5.00	25.00
RCA Victor DJL1-3255	(DJ)	Star / What In The World / Breaking Glass	1978	8.00	40.00
		(White vinyl issued in a picture cover.)			
RCA Victor JD-11886	(DJ)	John, I'm Only Dancing (Again) / Golden Years	1979	3.00	15.00
RCA Victor PD-11886		John, I'm Only Dancing (Again) / Golden Years	1979	2.00	10.00
RCA Victor DJL1-3795	(DJ)	Space Oddity / Ashes To Ashes / Ashes To Ashes (PC)	1980	4.00	20.00
RCA Victor JD-12140	(DJ)	Fashion / Fashion	1980	3.00	15.00
RCA Victor PD-12145		Fashion / Scream Like A Baby	1980	2.00	10.00
RCA Victor JD-12249	(DJ)	Up The Hill Backwards / Crystal Japan (PC)	1980	4.00	20.00
RCA Victor PD-12249		Up The Hill Backwards / Crystal Japan	1980	4.00	20.00
		(Issued in a picture cover with a 12" sheet of stamps.)			
Backstreet 1759	(DJ)	Cat People (Putting Out Fire) / Cat People (PC)	1982	3.00	15.00
EMI SPRO-9904	(DJ)	Let's Dance / Cat People (Putting Out Fire) (PC)	1983	3.00	15.00
EMI SPRO-9904	(DJ)	Let's Dance / Cat People (Putting Out Fire)	1983	2.00	10.00
EMI V-7805		Let's Dance / Cat People (Putting Out Fire) (PC)	1983	1.25	6.00
EMI SPRO-9952	(DJ)	China Girl / Shake It (PC)	1983	2.00	10.00
EMI V-7809		China Girl / Shake It (PC)	1983	1.25	6.00
EMI SPRO-	(DJ)	Modern Love / Modern Love	1983	2.00	10.00
EMI V-7811		Modern Love / Modern Love (PC)	1983	1.25	6.00
RCA Victor JD-13770	(DJ)	1984 / 1984	1984	3.00	15.00
RCA Victor PD-13770		1984 / TVC 15 (PC)	1984	2.00	10.00
EMI SPRO-9122	(DJ)	Blue Jean / Dancing With The Big Boys (PC)	1984	2.00	10.00
EMI V-7838		Blue Jean / Dancing With The Big Boys (PC)	1984	1.25	6.00
EMI SPRO-9295	(DJ)	Tonight / Tonight	1984	2.00	10.00
EMI-7846		Tonight / Tumble And Twirl / Tonight (PC)	1984	1.25	6.00
EMI SPRO-9985	(DJ)	Day In Day Out / Day In Day Out	1987	2.00	10.00
EMI SPRO-9996	(DJ)	Day In Day Out (4 versions)	1987	1.25	6.00
EMI 19234		Day In Day Out / Day In Day Out / Julie	1987	1.25	6.00
EMI 19247		Time Will Crawl / Time Will Crawl / Girls / Girls	1987	1.25	6.00
EMI 19255		Never Let Me Down (3 versions) / 87 / Cry	1987	1.25	6.00
EMI SPRO-04532	(DJ)	Fame '90 (Five versions)	1990	1.00	5.00

BOWIE, DAVID, & IGGY POP

RCA Victor JT-10956	(12")	Sound And Vision-Sister Midnight (DJ)	1978	10.00	50.00

BOWLEGS, THE

Zab 101		One More Time / One More Time, Part 2	1961	2.00	10.00
Vee Jay 400		One More Time / One More Time, Part 2	1961	1.00	5.00

BOWN, ALAN

Music Factory 402		Technicolor Dream / Toyland	1971	.60	3.00

BOWS & ARROWS, THE

GNP/Crescendo 356		I Don't Believe You / You Know What You Can Do	1965	1.60	8.00

BOX, DAVID

Candix 339		I've Had My Moments / If You Can't Say Something Nice	1962	5.00	25.00

BOX TOPS, THE

The Box Tops feature Alex Chilton. Refer to Big Star.

Mala 565		The Letter / Happy Times	1967	1.20	6.00
Hip Pocket 27		The Letter / Happy Times	1967	2.00	10.00
Mala 580		Neon Rainbow / Everything I Am	1967	1.20	6.00
Mala 593		Cry Like A Baby / The Door You Closed To Me	1968	1.20	6.00
Mala 12005		Choo Choo Train / Fields Of Clover	1968	1.20	6.00
Mala 12017		I Met Her In Church / People Gonna Talk	1968	1.20	6.00
Mala 12035		Sweet Cream Ladies / I See Only Sunshine	1968	1.20	6.00
Mala 12038		I Shall Be Released / I Must Be The Devil	1969	1.20	6.00
Mala 12040		Soul Deep / (The) Happy Song	1969	1.20	6.00
Mala 12042		Turn On A Dream / Together	1969	1.20	6.00
Sphere Sound 77001		The Letter / Happy Times (Blue label)	1968	2.00	10.00
Sphere Sound 77001		The Letter / Happy Times (Silver label)	1969	1.20	6.00
Sphere Sound 77002		Cry Like A Baby / Fields Of Clover (Silver label)	1969	1.20	6.00
Bell 865		You Keep Tightening Up On Me / Come On, Honey	1970	1.20	6.00
Bell 923		Let me Go / Got To Hold On To You	1971	1.20	6.00
Bell 981		King's Highway / Since I Been Gone	1971	1.20	6.00
Hi 2228		Sugar Creek Woman / It's All Over	1971	1.20	6.00
Hi 2242		Angel / Hold On, Girl	1971	1.20	6.00
Stax 0199		Willobee And Dale / It's Gonna Be Alright	1974	1.60	8.00

Label & Catalog #		A-Side/B-Side	Year	VG	NM
BOYCE, TOMMY					
Tommy Boyce also recorded as Christopher Cloud.					
Dot 16117		Give Me The Clue / Gypsy Song	1960	3.00	15.00
RCA Victor 47-7975		Along Came Linda / You Look So Lonely	1961	3.00	15.00
RCA Victor 47-8025		Come Here, Joann / The Way I Used To Be	1962	3.00	15.00
RCA Victor 47-8074		I'll Remember Carol / Too Late For Tears	1962	3.00	15.00
RCA Victor 47-8126		Change Of Heart / Sweet Little Baby	1962	3.00	15.00
RCA Victor 47-8208		Don't Be Afraid / A Million Things To Say	1963	3.00	15.00
Colpix 794		Let's Go Where The Action Is / Let's Go Where The Action Is	1965	3.00	15.00
MGM 13400		I Don't Have To Worry ('Bout You) / Pretty Thing (You're Out Of Sight)	1965	2.00	10.00
MGM 13429		Little Suzie Somethin' / Pee's N Que's	1965	2.00	10.00
A&M 809		Sunday, The Day Before Monday / Green Grass (Is Turning Brown)	1966	2.00	10.00
A&M 826		In Case The Wind Should Blow / Simon Smith	1966	3.00	15.00
R-Dell 111		Betty Jean / I'm Not Sure	196?	3.00	15.00
Wow 345		Is It True? / Little One	196?	3.00	15.00
Capitol 3136		Alice, My Sweet / Eve Laurin	1971	.80	4.00
BOYCE, TOMMY, & BOBBY HART					
Boyce and Hart also recorded with Mickey Dolenz and Davy Jones of The Monkees.					
A&M 858		Out And About / My Little Chickadee	1967	.80	4.00
A&M 858	(PS)	Out And About / My Little Chickadee	1967	1.60	8.00
A&M 874		Sometimes She's A Little Girl / Love Every Day	1967	.80	4.00
A&M 874	(PS)	Sometimes She's A Little Girl / Love Every Day	1967	1.60	8.00
A&M 893		I Wonder What She's Doing Tonight / The Ambushers	1967	1.00	5.00
A&M 893	(PS)	I Wonder What She's Doing Tonight / The Ambushers	1967	2.00	10.00
A&M 919		Goodbye Baby (I Don't Want To See You Cry) / Where Angels Go (Trouble Follows)	1968	.80	4.00
A&M 919	(PS)	Goodbye Baby (I Don't Want To See You Cry) / Where Angels Go (Trouble Follows)	1968	1.60	8.00
A&M 948		Alice Long (You're Still My Favorite Girlfriend) / P. O. Box 9847	1968	.80	4.00
A&M 948	(PS)	Alice Long (You're Still My Favorite Girlfriend) / P. O. Box 9847	1968	2.00	10.00
A&M 993		We're All Going To The Same Place / 6 + 6	1968	.80	4.00
A&M 993	(PS)	We're All Going To The Same Place / 6 + 6	1968	1.60	8.00
A&M 1017		It's All Happening On The Inside / Maybe Somebody Heard	1968	1.60	8.00
A&M 1031		L. U. V. (Let Us Vote) / I Wanna Be Free	1968	.80	4.00
A&M 1031	(PS)	L. U. V. (Let Us Vote) / I Wanna Be Free	1968	1.00	5.00
Aquarian 380		I'll Blow You A Kiss In The Wind / Smilin'	197?	.60	3.00
Aquarian 380	(PS)	I'll Blow You A Kiss In The Wind / Smilin'	197?	1.00	5.00
BOY FRIENDS, THE					
Glaser 1000		Shy Boy / Snake In The Grass	1961	2.00	10.00
BOY FRIENDS, THE: *Refer to* **TERRY CORIN & THE BOY FRIENDS**					
BOYE, FRANNY					
Gone 5095		Rock Around The Clock / I Know That We're In Love	1961	2.00	10.00
BOYFRIENDS, THE					
Kapp 569		Let's Fall In Love / Oh, Lana	1963	10.00	50.00
BOYS BLUE, THE					
Members of Boys Blue later formed The Sorrows.					
ABC-Paramount 10658		Take A Heart / You Got What I Want	1965	6.00	30.00
BOYS FROM NEW YORK CITY, THE					
Laurie 3412		Take It Or Leave It / These Are The Things	1967	1.00	5.00
Laurie 3434		I'm Down, Girl / Mary And John	1968	1.00	5.00
Laurie 3443		Goin' To California / A Little Bit Harder	1968	1.00	5.00
BOYS NEXT DOOR, THE					
Cameo 394		I Could See Me Dancing With You / There's No Greater Sin	1966	2.00	10.00
Atco 6443		Mandy / One Face In The Crowd	1966	2.00	10.00
Atco 6477		See The Way She's Mine / Be Gone Girl	1967	2.00	10.00
BRACELETS, THE					
Congress 104		Waddle, Waddle / I'll Play Along	1962	2.50	12.00
20th Century Fox 539		We're Just Fooling Ourselves / You Better Move On	1964	2.00	10.00
BRADY, JIM, & THE SONICS					
Jerden 913		Goodbye / Near My Soul	1969	.80	4.00
Pulsar 2424		Goodbye / Near My Soul	1969	.80	4.00

Label & Catalog #		A-Side/B-Side	Year	VG	NM
BRADY BUNCH, THE					
The Brady Bunch are Chris Knight, Mike Lookinland and Maureen McCormick.					
Paramount 0062		**Frosty The Snowman / Silver Bells**	1971	2.00	10.00
Paramount 0062	(PS)	**Frosty The Snowman / Silver Bells**	1971	3.00	15.00
Paramount 0141		**Time To Change /**			
		We Can Make The World A Whole Lot Brighter	1972	1.20	6.00
Paramount 0167		**We'll Always Be Friends / Time To Change**	1972	1.20	6.00
Paramount 0205		**Zuckerman's Famous Pig / Charlotte's Web**	1973	1.20	6.00
Paramount 0205	(PS)	**Zuckerman's Famous Pig / Charlotte's Web**	1973	1.00	10.00
BRAGG, DOUG, & CHERI ROBBINS					
Skippy 106		**Teenage Feeling / Juvenile Baby**	1959	5.00	25.00
BRAIN POLICE, THE					
Head 2002		**World Of Wax / Smoking At Windsor Hall**	1965	4.00	20.00
BRAMLETT, DELANEY					
Refer to Lani & Boni.					
GNP/Crescendo 328		**You Never Looked Sweeter / Heartbreak Hotel**	1964	.80	4.00
GNP/Crescendo 339		**Liverpool Lou / You Have No Choice**	1965	.80	4.00
GNP/Crescendo 363		**Without Your Love / Better Man Than Me**	1966	.80	4.00
BRANDON, DON					
Challenge 9183		**Here Comes Trouble / Play The Game**	1963	2.00	10.00
Challenge 59224		**Easy Boy, Don't Get Excited / It's Wonderful Being Young**	1964	2.00	10.00
Dot 16600		**Ballad Of Bonneville / Doin' The Swim**	1964	5.00	25.00
Dot 16644		**The Party Last Night / Cuando La Luna**	1964	5.00	25.00
		(Dot 16600 and 16644 were produced by Gary Usher.)			
BRANDON, JOHNNY					
Laurie 3042		**Santa Claus, Jr. / Theme From Santa Claus, Jr.**	1959	3.00	15.00
Laurie 3042	(PS)	**Santa Claus, Jr. / Theme From Santa Claus, Jr.**	1959	4.00	20.00
BRANDON, KATHY					
Crystalette 759		**Surfin' Doll / A Boy To Love Me**	1963	3.00	15.00
BRASHER, (MISS) CATHY					
Era 3129		**I'll Remember Jimmy / Too Late To Be Lovers**	1964	2.00	10.00
Chattahoochee 690		**Shh... Listen / He Told Me He Loved Me**	1965	2.00	10.00
BRAVE BELT					
Brave Belt features Randy Bachman, formerly of The Guess Who.					
Reprise 1023		**Rock And Roll Band / Any Day Means Tomorrow**	1971	.40	2.00
Reprise 1039		**Crazy Arms, Crazy Eyes / Holy Train**	1971	.40	2.00
Reprise 1061		**Never Comin' Home / Can You Feel It?**	1971	.40	2.00
Reprise 1083		**Another Way Out / Dunrobin's Gone**	1972	.40	2.00
BRAVE NEW WORLD, THE					
Piccadilly 225		**It's Tomorrow / Cried**	1966	4.00	20.00
Epic 10123		**It's Tomorrow / Cried**	1967	3.00	15.00
BREAD					
Bread is David Gates and James Griffin.					
Elektra 45666		**Any Way You Want Me / Dismal Day**	1969	.60	3.00
Elektra 45668		**Could I? / You Can't Measure The Cost**	1969	.60	3.00
Elektra 45686		**Make It With You / Why Do You Keep Me Waiting?**	1970	.60	3.00
Elektra 45701		**It Don't Matter To Me / Call On Me**	1970	.60	3.00
Elektra 45701	(PS)	**It Don't Matter To Me / Call On Me**	1970	.60	3.00
Elektra 45711		**Let Your Love Go / Too Much Love**	1971	.40	2.00
Elektra 45720		**If / Take Comfort**	1971	.40	2.00
Elektra 45720	(PS)	**If / Take Comfort**	1971	.60	3.00
Elektra 45740		**Mother Freedom / Live In Your Love**	1971	.40	2.00
Elektra 45751		**Baby I'm-A Want You / Truckin'**	1971	.40	2.00
Elektra 45765		**Everything I Own / I Don't Love You**	1972	.40	2.00
Elektra 45784		**(I Found Her) Diary / Down On My Knees**	1972	.40	2.00
Elektra 45803		**The Guitar Man / Just Like Yesterday**	1972	.40	2.00
Elektra 45818		**Sweet Surrender / Make It By Yourself**	1972	.40	2.00
Elektra 45832		**Aubrey / Don't Even Know Her Name**	1973	.40	2.00
Elektra 45365		**Lost Without Your Love / Change Of Heart**	1976	.40	2.00
Elektra 45389		**Hooked On You / Our Lady Of Sorrow**	1977	.40	2.00
BREAKAWAYS, THE					
Melbourne 1805		**Granada / The Flipper**	1964	6.00	30.00
London 10526		**That Boy Of Mine / Here She Comes**	1964	3.00	15.00
Cameo 323		**That's How It Goes / He Doesn't Love Me**	1964	3.00	15.00
BREAKERS, THE					
Impact 14		**Surf Bird / Surfin' Tragedy**	1963	3.00	15.00

Label & Catalog #	A-Side/B-Side	Year	VG	NM
Impact 14	Surf Bird / Surfin' Tragedy (Gold vinyl)	1963	5.00	25.00
Marsh 206	Balboa Memories / Long Way Home	1963	6.00	30.00
Brana 1001/2	Kami-Kaze / Surf Breaker	1963	10.00	50.00
DJB 116	Jet Stream / Beach Head	1964	6.00	30.00
DJB 116	Super Jet Rumble / Beach Head	1964	6.00	30.00
	("Super Jet Rumble" and "Jet Stream" are the same track.)			

BREAKERS, THE
| Riverton 102 | All My Nights, All My Days / Better For The Both Of Us | 1965 | 3.00 | 15.00 |
| Jerden 789 | All My Nights, All My Days / Better For The Both Of Us | 1966 | 2.00 | 10.00 |

BREEDEN, GENE & JERRY HILL
| Chance 111 | Poor Broke Mixed-Up Mess Of A Heart / Off My Mind | 196? | 2.00 | 10.00 |

BRENNAN QUARTET, BUDDY
| Warwick 517 | The Chase / Big River (Anniversary Song) | 1959 | 2.00 | 10.00 |

BRENT & THE SPECTRAS
| Spectra | Oh, Darling / Patricia | 196? | 3.00 | 15.00 |

BRENT, FRANKIE
Vik 0322	Cold As Ice / Playing With Fire	1958	3.00	15.00
Strand 25014	No Rock And Rollin' Here / Lover's Lane	1960	3.00	15.00
Cameo 181	More Of Everything / Bangin' On The Bongo	1960	2.00	10.00
Cameo 187	Hi Ho Silver / Amigos	1961	2.00	10.00
Cameo 196	Rang Dang Do / Hold It	1961	2.00	10.00

BRENT, RONNIE
| United Artists 108 | My Sweet Verlena / Love | 1958 | 10.00 | 50.00 |

BRENTWOODS, THE
| Dore 559 | Midnight Star / As I Live From Day To Day | 1960 | 4.00 | 20.00 |

BRET & TERRY
| Prestige 313 | Beatle Fever / The Beatle | 1964 | 4.00 | 20.00 |

BRIANS, ROBIN HOOD
| Fraternity 803 | Dis A Itty Bitty! / Without You | 1958 | 25.00 | 125.00 |

BRIDGE: Refer to BROOKLYN BRIDGE

BRIGADIERS, THE
| Mala 441 | Cry Of The Wild Goose / Dixie Brigade | 196? | 4.00 | 20.00 |

BRIGATI, EDDIE
Eddie Brigati is a former member of The Young Rascals.
| Elektra 45328 | Groovin' / Lost In The Wilderness | 1976 | .60 | 3.00 |
| Elektra 45349 | Gotta Get Next To Somebody / Made In Spain | 1976 | .40 | 2.00 |

BRIGGS, LILLIAN
Epic 9115	I Want You To Be My Baby / Don't Stay Away Too Long	1955	3.00	15.00
Epic 9138	Rock N' Roll-y Poly Santa Claus / Can't Stop	1956	3.00	15.00
Epic 9151	Eddie, My Love / Teen In Jeans From New Orleans	1956	2.00	10.00

BRIGHT, LARRY
Highland 1052	Should I? / Twinkie-Lee	1961	3.00	15.00
Tide 006	Mojo Workout / I'll Change My Ways	1960	4.00	20.00
Tide 008	Should I? / Natural Born Lover	1960	3.00	15.00
Tide 0012	When I'm With You / (I'm A) Mojo Man	1960	3.00	15.00
Tide 0021	Way Down Home / Bloodhound	1961	3.00	15.00
Tide 1083	Please Give Your Love / It Ain't Right	1961	2.00	10.00
Edit 2001	Please Give Your Love / It Ain't Right	1962	2.00	10.00
Del-Fi 4204	Surfin' Queen / My Hands Are Tied	1963	3.00	15.00
Del-Fi 4209	Bacon Fat / Do The Thing	1963	2.00	10.00
Del-Fi 4214	When I Did The Mashed Potatoes With You / Shake That Thing	1963	2.00	10.00
Del-Fi 4234	Got My Mojo Workin' / I'm A Man	1963	2.00	10.00
Bright 0014	She Belongs To Me / La Bomba	1965	2.00	10.00

BRIGHTONES, THE
| Warner Bros. 5472 | Swim, Swim, Swim / Rumors | 1964 | 3.00 | 15.00 |

BRIKS, THE
| Bismark 1013 | Can You See Me? / Foolish Baby | 1966 | 3.00 | 15.00 |
| Dot | Can You See Me? / Foolish Baby | 1966 | 2.40 | 12.00 |

BRINKLEY, JAY, & THE PITTY PATS
| Kliff 100 | I'll Be Your Baby / Guitar Smoke | 1959 | 8.00 | 40.00 |

Label & Catalog #	A-Side/B-Side	Year	VG	NM
BRINSLEY SCHWARZ				
Brinsley Schwarz features Nick Lowe.				
United Artists 50976	Happy Doing What We're Doing / Nervous On The Road	1972	.80	4.00
BRISCOE, JOHNNY, & THE LITTLE BEAVERS				
Atlantic 2822	Why Do Fools Fall In Love? / Sugar Love	1971	1.00	5.00
BRISTOL, BOB				
Riter 105	Humpty Dumpty / Love Flew Away	196?	3.00	15.00
BRITISH ROAD RUNNERS, THE				
Laurie 3426	Do Something To Me / Flower Movement	1968	1.25	6.00
BRITISH WALKERS, THE				
Manchester 651120	Watch Yourself / Bad Lightin'	1964	3.00	15.00
Try 502	Diddley Daddy / I Found You	1964	2.00	10.00
Charger 108	The Girl Can't Help It / Lonely Lover's Prayer	1964	2.00	10.00
Cameo 466	Shake / That Was Yesterday	1964	2.00	10.00
BRITT, DARRYL, & THE BLUE JEANS				
Blue 1199	Lover Lover / Since You're Gone	195?	10.00	50.00
BRITT, LYNN				
Miki 1117	Too Long / Two Times A Stranger	1961	3.00	15.00
Dot 16203	Too Long / Two Times A Stranger	1961	2.00	10.00
BRITT, TOMMY				
Unison 201	Fabulous, Fantastic And Fifteen / Same Girl	1959	2.00	10.00
BROADWELL, JACK				
Spur 100	I'll Be Going Home / Washington Waltz	196?	2.00	10.00
Clover 1002	Where Do I Go From Here? / Washington Waltz	196?	2.00	10.00
BROCK, B., & HIS VIBRATOS				
La Broc 101	Hang Five / Fright	196?	7.00	35.00
BROCK, B., & THE SULTANS				
Crown 5399	Do The Beetle /	1964	2.00	10.00
BROGUES, THE				
The Brogues feature Greg Elmore and Gary Grub a.k.a Gary Duncan, later of Quicksilver Messenger Service.				
Twilight 408	But Now I'm Fine / Someday	1965	8.00	40.00
Twilight 408	But Now I'm Fine / Early Bird	1965	8.00	40.00
Challenge 59316	I Ain't No Miracle Worker / Don't Shoot Me Down	1965	5.00	25.00
BROOK BROTHERS, THE [THE BROOKS]				
London 1987	War Paint / Sometimes	1961	2.00	10.00
London 10501	One Last Kiss / Ain't Gonna Wash For A Week	1961	2.00	10.00
London 10515	Tell Tale / Too Scared	1962	2.00	10.00
London 9668	Once In A While / Poor, Poor Plan	1964	2.00	10.00
BROOKLYN BRIDGE [BRIDGE]				
Brooklyn Bridge features Johnny Maestro, formerly of The Crests.				
Buddah 60	From My Window / Little Red Boat By The River	1968	.80	4.00
Buddah 75	The Worst That Could Happen / Your Kite, My Kite	1968	.80	4.00
Buddah 95	Blessed Is The Rain / Welcome Me, Love	1969	.80	4.00
Buddah 126	Your Husband-My Wife / Everybody's Cookin'	1969	.80	4.00
Buddah 126	Your Husband-My Wife / Upside Down (Inside Out)	1969	.60	3.00
Buddah 139	You'll Never Walk Alone / Minstrel Lady	1969	.60	3.00
Buddah 162	Free As The Wind / He's Not A Happy Man	1970	.60	3.00
Buddah 179	Down By The River / Look Again	1970	.80	4.00
Buddah 193	Day Is Done / Opposites	1970	.80	4.00
Buddah 199	Nights In White Satin / Cynthia	1971	1.20	6.00
Buddah 230	Wednesday In Your Garden /	1971	1.20	6.00
Buddah 293	Bruno's Place / Man In A Band	1972	1.20	6.00
Buddah 317 (DJ)	I Feel Free / I Fee Free	1972	1.00	5.00
	(Buddah 317 credits Bridge. Stock copies may not exist.)			
BROOKS, BOBBY				
RCA Victor EPA-4273 (EP)	Teenagers Dance To Bobby Brooks	1958	8.00	40.00
BROOKS, BONNIE				
United Artists 708	Bring Back My Beatles To Me / A Letter From My Love	1964	3.00	15.00
BROOKS, CHUCK, & THE SHARPIES				
Dub 2844	You Make Me Feel Mean / Spinning My Wheels	1958	40.00	200.00

Label & Catalog #		A-Side / B-Side	Year	VG	NM
BROOKS, DONNIE					
Era 3004		Lil' Sweetheart / If You're Lookin'	1959	2.00	10.00
Era 3007		Sway And Move With The Beat / White Orchid	1960	1.20	6.00
Era 3014		The Devil Ain't A Man / How Long?	1960	1.20	6.00
Era 3018		Mission Bell / Do It For Me	1960	1.20	6.00
Era 3028		Doll House / Round Robin	1960	1.20	6.00
Era 3028	(PS)	Doll House / Round Robin	1960	3.00	15.00
Era 3042		Memphis / That's Why	1961	1.20	6.00
Era 3042	(PS)	Memphis / That's Why	1961	3.00	15.00
Era 3049		All I Can Give / Wishbone	1961	1.20	6.00
Era 3052		Boomerang / How Long?	1961	1.20	6.00
Era 3059		Sweet Lorraine / Up To My Ears In Tears	1961	1.20	6.00
Era 3063		Up To My Ears In Tears / Goodnight, Judy	1961	1.20	6.00
Era 3063		Your Little Boy's Come Home / Goodnight, Judy	1961	1.20	6.00
Era 3071		My Favorite Kind Of Face / He Stole Flo	1962	1.20	6.00
Era 3077		Oh, You Beautiful Doll / Just A Bystander	1962	1.20	6.00
Era 3095		It's Not That Easy / Cries My Heart	1962	1.20	6.00
BROOKS, DUSTY, & HIS TONES					
Sun 182		Tears And Wine / Heaven Or Fire	1953	——	——
		(Rare. Estimated near mint value $1,500-3,000.)			
BROTHERHOOD					
Brotherhood is Smitty, Drake and Fang, formerly of Paul Revere's Raiders.					
RCA Victor 47-9621		Jump Out The Window / Box Guitar	1968	1.00	5.00
RCA Victor 47-9621	(PS)	Jump Out The Window / Box Guitar	1968	2.00	10.00
RCA Victor 74-0216		Don't Let Go / Rose Garden	1969	1.00	5.00
BROTHERS, THE					
Argo 5318		Deep Sleep / Lazy Susan	196?	1.60	8.00
Argo 5329		Deep Sleep / Sioux City Sue	196?	1.60	8.00
Checker 995		My True Love / One Lonely Heart	196?	1.60	8.00
BROTHERS, THE					
White Whale 250		Today Is Today / With The Rain	1967	2.00	10.00
White Whale 255		The Girl's Alright / Love Story	1967	2.00	10.00
BROTHERS & FRIENDS					
Sky		You're Wasting Precious Time / My Little Woman	196?	2.00	10.00
BROUGHAM CLOSET					
Mother Bear 538		Wishing / To Say Goodbye	1968	1.60	8.00
BROWN, AL, & HIS TUNETOPPERS					
Amy 804		The Madison / Mo Madison	1960	2.00	10.00
BROWN, ARTHUR					
Atlantic 2556		Fire / Rest Cure	1968	1.00	5.00
Track 2582		Nightmare / I Put A Spell On You	1969	.80	4.00
BROWN, B., & THE ROCKIN' McVOUTS					
Vest 830		Fannie Mae Is Back / Candied Yams	1960	3.00	15.00
BROWN, BILL					
Custom Sound 164		Tight Levis And Boots /			
		The Heart That You've Been Walking On	195?	8.00	40.00
BROWN, BILLY					
Columbia 41029		Did We Have A Party? / It's Love	1957	5.00	25.00
Columbia 41100		Meet Me In The Alley, Sally / I Wanted You	1958	5.00	25.00
Columbia 41174		Once In A Lifetime / Next	1958	5.00	25.00
Columbia 41297		Echo Mountain / Flip Out	1958	5.00	25.00
BROWN, BOOTS, & HIS BLOCKBUSTERS					
Boots and his band is a pseudonym for West Coast jazz stars Milt Bernhart, Bob Cooper, Roy Harte, Shelly Manne, Gerry					
Mulligan, Frank Patchen, Dave Pell, Shorty Rogers, Howard Rumsey and Bud Shank.					
RCA Victor 47-5110		Block Buster / Shortenin' Bread	1953	4.00	20.00
RCA Victor 47-5228		Blue Fairy Boogie / Breakfast Ball	1953	4.00	20.00
RCA Victor 47-7269		Cerveza / Juicy	1958	3.00	15.00
RCA Victor 47-7399		Trollin' / Jim Twangy	1959	3.00	15.00
RCA Victor 47-7732		Jet Train / El Brasero	1960	3.00	15.00
		— Extended Play Albums —			
RCA Groove EGB-1000		Rock That Beat	1958	10.00	50.00
BROWN, BUSTER					
Fire 1008		Fannie Mae / Lost In A Dream	1960	2.00	10.00

Label & Catalog #	A-Side/B-Side	Year	VG	NM

BROWN, DOUG, & THE OMENS
Doug Brown is a pseudonym for Bob Seger.

Hideout 1008	T. G. I. F. / The First	1965	25.00	125.00

BROWN, GEORGE WASHINGTON
George Washington Brown is a pseudonym for Van Dyke Parks.

Warner Bros. 7026	Donovan's Colours / Donovan's Colours, Part 2	1967	2.00	10.00

BROWN, JAMES

Federal 12258	Please Please Please / Why Do You Do Me? (Silver top label.)	1956	7.00	35.00
Federal 12258	Please Please Please / Why Do You Do Me?	1956	5.00	20.00
Federal 12264	I Don't Know / I Feel That Old Feeling Coming On	1956	5.00	20.00
Federal 12277	No, No, No / Hold My Baby's Hand	1956	5.00	20.00
Federal 12289	Just Won't Do Right / Let's Make It	1956	4.00	20.00
Federal 12290	Chonnie-On-Chon / I Won't Plead No More	1957	4.00	20.00
Federal 12292	Can't Be The Same / Gonna Try	1957	4.00	20.00
Federal 12295	Love Or A Game / Messing With The Blues	1957	4.00	20.00
Federal 12300	You're Mine, You're Mine / I Walked Alone	1957	4.00	20.00
Federal 12311	That Dood It / Baby Cries Over The Ocean	1957	4.00	20.00
Federal 12316	Begging, Begging / That's When I Lost My Heart	1958	4.00	20.00
Federal 12337	Try Me / Tell Me What I Did Wrong	1958	4.00	20.00
Federal 12348	I Want You So Bad / There Must Be A Reason	1959	4.00	20.00
Federal 12352	I've Got To Change / It Hurts To Tell You	1959	4.00	20.00
Federal 12361	Good Good Lovin' / Don't Let It Happen To Me	1959	4.00	20.00
Federal 12364	Got To Cry / It Was You	1959	4.00	20.00
Federal 12369	I'll Go Crazy / I Know It's True (I Found Someone)	1960	3.00	15.00
Federal 12370	Think / You've Got The Power	1960	3.00	15.00
Federal 12378	This Old Heart / Wonder When You're Coming Home	1960	3.00	15.00

BROWN, JAY, & THE JETS

Peach 736	Rockin' The Guitar / Hanky Panky	196?	2.00	10.00

BROWN, LES, JR.

GNP-Crescendo 191	Surfin' And Swingin' / Drum Safari	1962	3.00	15.00

BROWN, LOUISE

Witch 1	Son-In-Law / You Gave Me Misery	1961	2.00	10.00

BROWN, MICHAEL
Michael Brown also recorded with The Left Bank and Stories.

Kama Sutra 563	Circles / Premonitions	1972	.60	3.00

BROWN, RAY, & THE WHISPERS

GNP/Crescendo 357	Fool, Fool, Fool / Pride	1965	1.60	8.00

BROWN, TIMMY

Mercury 72175	Do The Crossfire / Love, Love, Love	1962	2.00	10.00
Mercury 72226	Runnin' Late / If I Loved You	1963	2.00	10.00

BROWN, TOM, & THE TOM TOM'S

Jaro 77023	Tomahawk / Kentucky Waltz	1960	5.00	25.00

BROWN & HARPER

Crystal	The Astronauts / Zounds	196?	4.00	20.00

BROWNSVILLE STATION
Brownsville Station features Kub "The Vinyl Junkie" Koda.

Warner Bros. 7441	Be-Bop Confidential / City Life	1971	.80	4.00
Warner Bros. 7456	Roadrunner / Do The Bosco	1971	.80	4.00
Big Tree 156	The Red Back Spider / Rock With The Music	1972	.60	3.00
Big Tree 161	Let Your Yeah Be Yeah / Mister Robert	1973	.60	3.00
Big Tree 10611	Smokin' In The Boys Room / Barefootin'	1973	1.00	5.00
Big Tree 15005	I'm The Leader Of The Gang / Meet Me On The 4th Floor	1974	.60	3.00
Big Tree 16001	Kings Of The Party / Ostrich	1974	.60	3.00
Big Tree 16029	Mama Don't Allow No Parkin' / I Got It Bad For You	1975	.60	3.00
Private Stock 45149	Lady (Put The Light On Me) / Rockers And Rollers	1977	.60	3.00
Private Stock 45167	The Martian Boogie / Mr. Johnson Sez	1977	.60	3.00

BRUCE, EDWIN [ED BRUCE]

Sun 276	Rock Boppin' Baby / More Than Yesterday	1957	4.00	20.00
Sun 292	Sweet Woman / Part Of My Life	1958	5.00	25.00
Wand 136	The Greatest Man / It's Coming To Me	1963	2.00	10.00
Wand 140	See The Big Man Cry / You Need A New Love	1963	2.00	10.00

BRUCE, LENNY

Warner Bros. PRO-598 (EP)	The Law, The Language & Lenny Bruce (Paper sleeve)	1974	6.00	30.00

Label & Catalog #	A-Side/B-Side	Year	VG	NM
BRUCE & JERRY				
Bruce Johnston and Jerry Cooper.				
Arwin 1003	Take This Pearl / I Saw Her First	1959	5.00	25.00
BRUCE & TERRY				
Bruce Johnston and Terry Melcher				
Columbia 42956	Custom Machine / Makaha At Midnight	1964	5.00	25.00
Columbia 43055	Summer Means Fun / Yeah!	1964	5.00	25.00
Columbia 43238	Carmen / I Love You, Model T	1965	5.00	25.00
Columbia 43378	Raining In My Heart / Four Strong Winds	1965	5.00	25.00
Columbia 43479	Come, Love / Thank You, Baby	1965	5.00	25.00
Columbia 43582	Don't Run Away / Girl, It's All Right Now	1966	6.00	30.00
BRUNO, BRUCE				
Roulette 4386	Hey Little One / Same Time, Same Place	1961	2.00	10.00
Roulette 4427	Dear Joanne / Venus In Blue Jeans	1962	4.00	20.00
BRUNO & THE GLADIATORS				
Vault 901	Warm Is The Sun / Istanbul	1963	4.00	20.00
BRYAN, BILLY				
Billy Bryan is a pseudonym for Gene Pitney.				
Blaze 351	Going Back To My Love / Cradle Of My Arms	196?	2.00	10.00
BRYAN, DORA				
Fontana 427	All I Want For Christmas Is A Beatle / If I Were A Fairy	1964	3.00	15.00
BRYANT, GARY				
Jerden 721	Just A Nobody / Open House	1963	.80	4.00
Panorama 50	Open House / I Don't Really Want To Go	1964	.80	4.00
4 Corners 109	She Was You Again / Crystal Anne	1965	1.00	5.00
Jerden 736	She Was You Again / Crystal Anne	1965	1.00	5.00
Jerden 754	Out Of My Mind / Just A Matter Of Time	1965	.80	4.00
BRYANT, LAURA K.				
Cameo 106	Billy / Part Time Gal	1957	2.00	10.00
Cameo 112	The Kiss I Never Had / I Don't Hurt Anymore	1957	2.00	10.00
Cameo 124	Bobby / Angel Tears	1958	2.00	10.00
BRYANT, LILLIE				
Cameo 122	Good Morning, Baby / The Gambler	1958	2.00	10.00
BUBBLE PUPPY				
International Arts. 128	Hot Smoke And Sassafrass / Lonely	1969	2.00	10.00
International Arts. 133	If I Had A Reason / Beginnings	1969	2.00	10.00
International Arts. 136	Days Of Our Time / Thinkin' About Thinkin'	1969	2.00	10.00
International Arts. 138 (DJ)	What Do You See? / Hurry Sundown (Green vinyl)	1970	5.00	25.00
International Arts. 138	What Do You See? / Hurry Sundown	1970	2.00	10.00
BUBI & BOB				
Sphinx 1201	The Mummy / Biscayne Beat	1959	4.00	20.00
BUCHANAN, BILL				
Gone 5032	The Thing / Oh, Happy Day	1958	5.00	25.00
United Artists 531	The Night Before Halloween / Beware	1962	2.00	10.00
BUCHANAN & ANCELL				
Features Bill Buchanan.				
Flying Saucer 1232	Meet The Creature / The Creature	1957	5.00	25.00
BUCHANAN & CELLA				
Features Bill Buchanan.				
ABC-Paramount 10033	String Along With Pal-O-Mine / More String Along With Pal-O-Mine	1959	3.00	15.00
BUCHANAN & GOODMAN				
Bill Buchanan and Dickie Goodman. Refer to Susan Smith.				
Luniverse 101X	Back To Earth / Back To Earth, Part 2	1956	35.00	175.00
Radioactive 101	The Flying Saucer / The Flying Saucer, Part 2	1956	10.00	50.00
	(Originals have the Luniverse logo on the label.)			
Radioactive 101	The Flying Saucer / The Flying Saucer, Part 2	196?	2.00	10.00
	(Reissues do not have the Luniverse logo on the label.)			
Luniverse 101	The Flying Saucer / The Flying Saucer, Part 2	1956	3.00	15.00
Luniverse 102X	Public Opinion / Public Opinion, Part 2	1956	——	——
	(Rare. The possibility exists that this does not exist.)			
Luniverse 102	On Trial / Crazy	1956	6.00	30.00
Luniverse 103	The Banana Boat Story / The Mystery	1956	5.00	25.00
Luniverse 105	Flying Saucer The Second / Martian Melody	1957	5.00	25.00

Bruce Johnston and Terry Melcher functioned as Columbia's answer to Brian Wilson, recording under a series of guises, including Bruce & Terry, writing, arranging and producing other acts, most of which emulated Wilson's sound with varying degrees of success. Johnston eventually joined the Beach Boys while Melcher became one of the label's more successful staff producers, essentially creating most of the later Paul Revere & The Raiders' singles in collaboration with Mark Lindsay and selected studio musicians.

Label & Catalog #	A-Side/B-Side	Year	VG	NM
Luniverse 107	Santa And The Satellite / Santa And The Satellite, Part 2	1957	5.00	25.00
Luniverse 108	The Flying Saucer Goes West / Saucer Serenade	1958	4.00	20.00
Novelty 301	Frankenstein Of '59 / Frankenstein Returns	1959	4.00	20.00
Comic 500	Flying Saucer The Third / The Cha Cha Lesson	1959	4.00	20.00

BUCHANAN & GREENFIELD
Features Bill Buchanan.

Novel 711	The Invasion / What A Lonely Party (Red label)	1964	4.00	20.00
Novel 711	The Invasion / What A Lonely Party (Red & white label)	197?	1.00	5.00

BUCHANAN BROTHERS, THE
The Buchanan Brothers are Terry Cashman, Gene Pistilli and Tommy West.

Event 3302	Medicine Man / Medicine Man, Part 2	1969	.50	2.50
Event 3305	Son Of A Lovin' Man / I'll Never Get Enough	1969	.50	2.50
Event 3307	Last Time / The Feeling That I Get	1969	.50	2.50
Event 3309	Rosanna / A Sad Song With A Happy Soul	1970	.50	2.50

BUCK, JOHN, & HIS BLAZERS
The Blazers also recorded as Ronny & The Daytonas.

Warner Bros. 5194	Forbidden City / Chi Chi	1961	2.00	10.00

BUCK & THE HUNTERS

Westland 15761	Without Your Love I'm Nobody / The Train Is Leaving Me Behind	1962	3.00	15.00

BUCKINGHAM NICKS
Lindsay Buckingham and Stevie Nicks, later of Fleetwood Mac.

Polydor 14335		Don't Let Me Down Again / Crystal	1976	4.00	20.00
Polydor 14428		Crying In The Night / Stephanie	1977	3.00	15.00
Polydor 14428	(PS)	Crying In The Night / Stephanie	1977	5.00	25.00

BUCKINGHAMS, THE

Laurie 3258	Gonna Say Goodbye / Many Times	1964	1.00	5.00

BUCKINGHAMS, THE
The Buckinghams are Nick Fortune, Carl Giammerse, Marty Grebb, John Poulos, Denny Tufano. Refer to The Centuries; The Falling Pebbles.

U.S.A. 844		Don't Want To Cry / I'll Go Crazy	1966	2.00	10.00
U.S.A. 848		I Call Your Name / Makin' Up And Breakin' Up	1966	2.00	10.00
U.S.A. 853		I've Been Wrong / Love Ain't Enough	1966	2.00	10.00
U.S.A. 860		Kind Of A Drag / You Make Me Feel So Good	1966	2.00	10.00
U.S.A. 869		Lawdy, Miss Clawdy / I Call Your Name	1967	2.00	10.00
U.S.A. 873		I Don't Want To Cry / Summertime	1967	2.00	10.00
SpectraSound 4618		Sweets For My Sweets / Beginner's Love	1967	3.00	15.00
Columbia 44053		Don't You Care? / Why Don't You Love Me?	1967	.80	4.00
Columbia 44053	(PS)	Don't You Care? / Why Don't You Love Me?	1967	1.60	8.00
Columbia 44182		Mercy, Mercy, Mercy / You Are Gone	1967	.80	4.00
Columbia 44182	(PS)	Mercy, Mercy, Mercy / You Are Gone	1967	1.60	8.00
Columbia 44254		Hey, Baby (They're Playing Our Song) / And Our Love	1967	.80	4.00
Columbia 44254	(PS)	Hey, Baby (They're Playing Our Song) / And Our Love	1967	1.60	8.00
Columbia 44378		Susan / Foreign Power	1967	.80	4.00
Columbia 44378	(PS)	Susan / Foreign Power	1967	1.60	8.00
Columbia 44533		Back In Love Again / You Misunderstand Me	1968	.80	4.00
Columbia 44533	(PS)	Back In Love Again / You Misunderstand Me	1968	1.60	8.00
Columbia 44672		Where Did You Come From? / Song Of The Breeze	1968	.80	4.00
Columbia 44672	(PS)	Where Did You Come From? / Song Of The Breeze	1968	2.00	10.00
Columbia 44790		This Is How Much I Love You / Can't Find The Words	1969	1.00	5.00
Columbia 44790	(PS)	This Is How Much I Love You / Can't Find The Words	1969	2.00	10.00
Columbia 44923		It's A Beautiful Day / Difference Of Opinion	1969	1.00	5.00

BUCKINS, MICKEY, & THE NEW BREED

South Camp 7007	Big Boy Pete / Reflections Of Charlie Brown	1967	1.00	5.00

BUCKLEY, TIM

Elektra 45606	Grief In My Soul / Wings	1966	1.00	5.00
Elektra 45612	Aren't You The Girl? / Strange Street Affair Under Blue	1966	1.00	5.00
Elektra 45618	Once Upon A Time / Lady Give Me Your Heart	1966	1.00	5.00
Elektra 45623	Morning Glory / Once I Was	1967	1.00	5.00
Discreet 1187	Quicksand / Stone In Love	1974	1.00	5.00
Discreet 1189	Dolphins / Honey Man	1974	1.00	5.00
Discreet 1311	Wanda Lu / Who Could Deny You?	1975	1.00	5.00

BUDD, LANDON

Alert 1002	Killer Reef / Grunion Run	196?	10.00	50.00

BUDDIES, THE

Comet 2143	Must Be True Love / Hully Gully Mama	196?	3.00	15.00

Label & Catalog #		A-Side/B-Side	Year	VG	NM
BUDDIES, THE					
Swan 4170		The Beatle / Pulsebeat	1964	3.00	15.00
BUDDIES, THE					
The Buddies is a pseudonym for The Tokens.					
Swing 102		On The Go / Only My Friend	1964	7.00	35.00
BUDDIES, THE					
The Buddies feature Gary Usher.					
Decca 31920	(DJ)	Duckman / Duckman (Part 2)	1966	2.00	10.00
Decca 31920		Duckman / Duckman (Part 2)	1966	4.00	20.00
BUDDIES, THE: *Refer to* LITTLE BUTCHIE SAUNDERS & THE BUDDIES					
BUDDY & THE DIMES					
Emi 2440		It's A Sin To Tell A Lie / Sweet Heart	196?	3.00	15.00
BUDDY & THE FADS					
Morocco 1001		Won't You Love Me? / Is It Just A Game?	195?	40.00	200.00
BUDDY & THE HEARTS					
Landa 701		Thirty Days / Let It Rock	1964	3.00	15.00
BUDDY & THE WILDCATS					
Rust 5060		Night Crawl / (The Party's) Over Here	1963	2.00	10.00
BUDGIE					
Kapp 2152		Nude Disintegrating Parachuting Woman / Crash Course	1972	1.00	5.00
Kapp 2185		Whiskey River / Stranded	1972	1.00	5.00
MCA 40367		Honey / I Ain't No Mountain	1975	.80	4.00
BUENA VISTAS, THE					
Swan 4255		Hot Shot / TNT	1966	1.00	5.00
Swan 4269		Foxy / Filet Of Soul	1966	1.00	5.00
BUFFALO NICKEL, THE					
Dome 507		I Could Be So Good To You / Hard To Be Without You	196?	1.00	5.00
BUFFALO REBELS, THE: *Refer to* THE REBELS					
BUFFALO SPRINGFIELD, THE					
The Buffalo Springfield are Richie Furay, Dewey Martin, Bruce Palmer, Steve Stills and Neil Young. Jim Messina replaced Martin in 1967.					
Atco 6428	(DJ)	Nowadays Clancy Can't Even Sing / Go And Say Goodbye	1966	2.00	10.00
Atco 6428		Nowadays Clancy Can't Even Sing / Go And Say Goodbye	1966	4.00	20.00
Atco 6452	(DJ)	Burned / Everybody's Wrong	1966	2.00	10.00
Atco 6452		Burned / Everybody's Wrong	1966	4.00	20.00
Atco 6459		For What It's Worth / Do I Have To Come Right Out And Say It?	1967	1.20	6.00
Atco 6499		Bluebird / Mr. Soul	1967	1.00	5.00
Atco 6519		Rock 'N' Roll Woman / A Child's Claim To Fame	1967	1.00	5.00
Atco 6545		Expecting To Fly / Everydays	1968	1.00	5.00
Atco 6572		Uno Mundo / Merry-Go-Round	1968	.80	4.00
Atco 6602		Kind Woman / Special Care	1968	.80	4.00
Atco 6615		Four Days Gone / On The Way Home	1968	.80	4.00
BUG COLLECTORS, THE					
Catch 103		Beatle Bug / Thief In The Night	1964	3.00	15.00
BUG MEN, THE					
Dot 16592		Beatles, You Bug Me / Bloomin' Bird	1964	3.00	15.00
BUGALOOS, THE					
Capitol 2946		For A Friend / The Senses Of Our World	1969	1.00	5.00
BUGGS, THE					
Soma 1413		The Buggs Vs. The Beatles / She Loves Me	1964	5.00	25.00
BUGS, THE					
Polaris 00001		Pretty Girl / Slide	196?	4.00	20.00
Astor		Pretty Girl / Slide	196?	4.00	20.00
BULLDOG					
Bulldog features Dino Danelli and Gene Cornish of The Young Rascals.					
Decca 32996		Good Times Are Coming / No	1972	.50	2.50
MCA 40014		Are You Really Happy Together? / I'm A Mad Man	1973	.50	2.50
MCA 40050		I Tip My Hat / I'm A Mad Man	1973	.50	2.50

Label & Catalog #	A-Side / B-Side	Year	VG	NM
BULLDOGS, THE				
Mercury 72262	John, Paul, George And Ringo / What Do I See?	1964	4.00	20.00
BUNGLE & KLEEN				
Partee 1302	The UFO Landing / The UFO Landing, Part 2	196?	3.00	15.00
BUMPS, THE				
Piccadilly 238	Baby Blue / Please Come Down	1967	2.00	10.00
Piccadilly 245	Hey Girl / Wake Up, Wake Up	1967	1.60	8.00
Piccadilly 251	It Wasn't Real / Hard Woman	1967	1.60	8.00
Sin-a-Way 301	You Don't Love Me Anymore / Can't Say I Told You So	196?	2.00	10.00
Walrus 001/2	Ode To A Toad / Shining	1969	2.00	10.00
BUOYS, THE				
Wilkes-Barre's biggest shot at the charts!				
Scepter 12275	Timothy / It Feels Good	1971	1.00	5.00
Scepter 12275 (PS)	Timothy / It Feels Good	1971	1.00	5.00
Scepter 12318	Give Up Your Guns / Prince Of Thieves	1971	.80	4.00
Polydor 14201	Liza's Last Ride / Downtown Singer	1973	.80	4.00
BURDEN, RAY				
Cullman 6403	That Kind Of Carrying On /	195?	15.00	75.00
BURDON, ERIC, & THE ANIMALS				
Except for Burdon, this is a completely different band than the original Animals.				
MGM 13582	See See Rider / She'll Return It	1966	1.00	5.00
MGM 13636	Help Me, Girl / That Ain't Where It's At	1967	1.00	5.00
MGM 13721	When I Was Young / A Girl Named Sandoz	1967	1.00	5.00
MGM 13769	San Franciscan Nights / Good Times	1967	1.00	5.00
MGM 13769 (PS)	San Franciscan Nights / Good Times	1967	3.00	15.00
MGM CS11-5 (DJ)	MGM Celebrity Scene: Eric Burdon And The Animals	1967	12.00	60.00
	(Boxed set of five stereo singles, MGM 13791-13795, with a cue sheet, bio and jukebox title strips; the price is for the complete set. The five promo singles are priced separately below.)			
MGM 13791 (DJ)	Don't Bring Me Down / When I Was Young	1967	1.60	8.00
MGM 13792 (DJ)	See See Rider / Hey Gyp	1967	1.60	8.00
MGM 13793 (DJ)	Help Me, Girl / Inside Looking Out	1967	1.60	8.00
MGM 13794 (DJ)	San Franciscan Nights / Good Times	1967	1.60	8.00
MGM 13795 (DJ)	The Other Side Of This Life / It's All Meat	1967	1.60	8.00
MGM 13868	Monterey / Ain't That So	1967	1.00	5.00
MGM 13868 (PS)	Monterey / Ain't That So	1967	2.00	10.00
MGM 13917	Anything / It's All Meat	1968	1.00	5.00
MGM 13939	Sky Pilot / Sky Pilot, Part 2	1968	1.00	5.00
MGM 14013	White Houses / River Deep-Mountain High	1968	1.00	5.00
BURDON, ERIC, & WAR				
MGM 14118	Spill The Wine / Magic Mountain	1970	1.00	5.00
MGM 14118 (PS)	Spill The Wine / Magic Mountain	1970	2.00	10.00
MGM 14196	They Can't Take Away Our Music / Home Cookin'	1970	.80	4.00
Capitol 3997	The Real Me / Letter From The Country Farm	1974	.80	4.00
ABC 12244	Magic Mountain / Home Dream	1977	.80	4.00
BURDON, ERIC, & JIMMY WITHERSPOON				
MGM 14296	Soledad / Headin' For Home	1971	.80	4.00
BURDON BAND, ERIC				
Capitol 3997	The Real Me / Letter From The Country Farm	1974	.80	4.00
Capitol 4007	Ring Of Fire / The Real Me	1974	.80	4.00
BURGESS, DAVE				
Dave Burgess also recorded as Dave Dupree.				
Challenge 1008	I'm Available / Who's Gonna Cry? (Dark blue label)	1957	4.00	20.00
Challenge 59032	Lovey Dovey Baby / I Hang My Head And Cry	1959	3.00	15.00
Challenge 59037	Lulu / I Don't Want To Know	1959	3.00	15.00
Challenge 59045	Everlovin' / Just For Me	1959	3.00	15.00
	—Original Challenge singles above have maroon labels.—			
BURGESS, DAVE, & THE CHAMPS				
Refer to The Champs.				
Challenge 1018	Maybelle / Take This Love	1958	4.00	20.00
BURGESS, SONNY				
Sun 247	Red Headed Woman / We Wanna Boogie	1956	15.00	75.00
Sun 263	Restless / Ain't Got A Thing	1957	8.00	40.00
Sun 285	My Bucket's Got A Hole In It / Sweet Misery	1958	6.00	30.00
Sun 304	Itchy / Thunderbird	1958	3.00	15.00

Label & Catalog #		A-Side/B-Side	Year	VG	NM

BURK, DANNY, & THE INVADERS

| ARA 216 | | Ain't Goin' Nowhere / Till I'm Sure | 196? | 3.00 | 15.00 |

BURK, TOMMY, & THE COUNTS
Refer to The Counts.

Rich-Rose 1001		Cute / Ding-A-Ling	196?	5.00	25.00
Rich-Rose 1003		She Told A Lie / You Took My Heart	196?	10.00	50.00
Rich-Rose 711		Just A Little Bit / (Don't Hafta) Shop Around	196?	6.00	30.00
Atco 6340		Just A Little Bit / You Better Move On	196?	2.00	10.00

BURKE, BUDDY

| Bullseye 1002 | | That Big Old Moon / Street Of Sorrows | 1959 | 25.00 | 125.00 |

BURNETTE, DORSEY
Dorsey was a member of brother Johnny's Rock 'N' Roll Trio.

Abbott 188		The Devil's Queen / Let's Fall In Love	1955	5.00	25.00
Cee Jam 16		Bertha Lou / 'Til The Law Says Stop	1957	6.00	30.00
Imperial 5561		You Came As A Miracle / Try	1959	3.00	15.00
Imperial 5597		Lonely Train / Misery	1959	3.00	15.00
Imperial 5668		Way In The Middle Of The Night / Your Love	1960	5.00	25.00
Imperial 5987		Circle Rock / House With A Tin Rooftop	1960	5.00	25.00
Era 3012		(There Was A) Tall Oak Tree / Juarez Town	1960	2.00	10.00
Era 3019		Hey, Little One / Big Rock Candy Mountain	1960	2.00	10.00
Era 3025		Red Roses / The Ghost Of Billy Maloo	1960	2.00	10.00
Era 3033		The River And The Mountain / This Hotel	1960	2.00	10.00
Era 3033	(PS)	The River And The Mountain / This Hotel	1960	5.00	25.00
Era 3041		(It's No) Sin / Hard Rock Mine	1961	2.00	10.00
Era 3045		Great Shakin' Fever / That's Me Without You	1961	2.00	10.00
Dot 16230		Raining In My Heart / A Full House	1961	2.00	10.00
Dot 16265		Sad Boy / The Feminine Touch	1961	2.00	10.00
		Be A Navy Man	196?	3.00	15.00
	(PS)	Be A Navy Man	196?	5.00	25.00
Reprise 20093		Castle In The Sky / Boys Kept Hanging Around	1962	1.50	8.00
Reprise 20121		Darling Jane / I'm A Waitin' For Ya, Baby	1963	1.50	8.00
Reprise 20177		Invisible Chains / Pebbles	1963	1.50	8.00
Reprise 20208		One Of The Lonely / Where's The Girl?	1963	1.50	8.00
Reprise 0246		Four For Texas / Foolish Pride	1963	1.50	8.00
Reprise 0246	(PS)	Four For Texas / Foolish Pride	1963	3.00	15.00
Mel-o-dy 113		Little Acorn / Cold As Usual	1964	1.50	8.00
Mel-o-dy 116		Everybody's Angel / Jimmy Brown	1964	1.50	8.00
Mel-o-dy 118		Ever Since The World Began / Long, Long Time Ago	1964	1.50	8.00
Smash 2029		In The Morning / To Remember	1966	1.25	6.00
Smash 2039		If You Want To Love Somebody / Teach Me, Little Children	1966	1.25	6.00
Smash 2062		I Just Can't Be Tamed / Tall Oak Tree	1966	1.25	6.00
Music Factory 417		I'll Walk Away / Son, You've Got To Make It Alone	1968	1.25	6.00
Happy Tiger 546		To Be A Man / Fly Away And Hurry Home	1970	2.00	10.00
Happy Tiger 563		Call Me Low Down / One Lump Sum	1970	2.00	10.00
Calliope 8012		Soon As I Touched Her / Dear Hearted Children	1977	.80	3.00

BURNETTE, JOHNNY, & THE ROCK 'N ROLL TRIO
Johnny Burnette, Dorsey Burnette and Paul Burlison. Although technically these are all Johnny Burnette singles and should be listed as such (individual records are credited to The Johnny Burnette Trio, Johnny Burnette & The Rock 'N Roll Trio, or solely to Johnny Burnette), the Rock 'N Roll Trio has achieved an identity, at least with rockabilly collectors, independent of Burnette's solo career.

Von 1006		You're Undecided / Go, Mule, Go	1954	——	——
		(Rare. Estimated near mint value $750-1,500.)			
Coral 61651	(DJ)	Tear It Up / You're Undecided	1956	20.00	100.00
Coral 61651		Tear It Up / You're Undecided	1956	30.00	150.00
Coral 61675	(DJ)	Midnight Train / Oh, Baby Babe	1956	20.00	100.00
Coral 61675		Midnight Train / Oh, Baby Babe	1956	30.00	150.00
Coral 61719	(DJ)	Honey Hush / The Train Kept A Rollin'	1956	15.00	75.00
Coral 61719		Honey Hush / The Train Kept A Rollin'	1956	20.00	100.00
Coral 61758	(DJ)	Lonesome Train (On A Lonesome Track) / I Just Found Out	1956	20.00	100.00
Coral 61758		Lonesome Train (On A Lonesome Track) / I Just Found Out	1956	30.00	150.00
Coral 61829	(DJ)	Eager Beaver Baby / Touch Me	1957	20.00	100.00
Coral 61829		Eager Beaver Baby / Touch Me	1957	30.00	150.00
Coral 61869	(DJ)	Drinkin' Wine Spo-Dee-O-Dee / Butterfingers	1957	20.00	100.00
Coral 61869		Drinkin' Wine Spo-Dee-O-Dee / Butterfingers	1957	30.00	150.00
Coral 61918	(DJ)	Rock Billy Boogie / If You Want It Enough	1957	20.00	100.00
Coral 61918		Rock Billy Boogie / If You Want It Enough	1957	30.00	150.00
Coral 62190	(DJ)	Blues, Stay Away From Me / Midnight Train	1960	15.00	75.00
Coral 62190		Blues, Stay Away From Me / Midnight Train	1960	25.00	125.00

BURNETTE, JOHNNY

Freedom 44001		I'm Restless / Kiss Me	1959	7.00	35.00
Freedom 44001		I'm Restless / Kiss Me	1959	8.00	40.00
Freedom 44011	(DJ)	Gumbo / Me And Bear	1959	7.00	35.00
Freedom 44011		Gumbo / Me And Bear	1959	8.00	40.00

Label & Catalog #		A-Side/B-Side	Year	VG	NM
Freedom 44017	(DJ)	Sweet Baby Doll / I'll Never Love Again	1959	8.00	40.00
Freedom 44017		Sweet Baby Doll / I'll Never Love Again	1959	10.00	50.00
Liberty 55222		Settin' The Woods On Fire / Kentucky Waltz	1960	2.00	10.00
Liberty 55243		Don't Do It / Patrick Henry	1960	2.00	10.00
Liberty 55258		Dreamin' / Cincinnati Fireball	1960	3.00	15.00
Liberty 55285		You're Sixteen / I Beg Your Pardon	1960	3.00	15.00
Liberty 55285	(PS)	You're Sixteen / I Beg Your Pardon	1960	4.00	20.00
Liberty 55298		Little Boy Sad / I Go Down To The River	1961	2.00	10.00
Liberty 55298	(PS)	Little Boy Sad / I Go Down To The River	1961	4.00	20.00
Liberty 55318		Big, Big World / Ballad Of The One-Eyed Jacks	1961	2.00	10.00
Liberty 55318	(PS)	Big, Big World / Ballad Of The One-Eyed Jacks	1961	4.00	20.00
Liberty 55345		I've Got A Lot Of Things To Do / Girls	1961	2.00	10.00
Liberty 55379		God, Country And My Baby / Honestly, I Do	1961	2.00	10.00
Liberty 55416		Why Am I? / Clown Shoes	1962	2.00	10.00
Liberty 55448		The Fool Of The Year / Poorest Boy In Town	1962	2.00	10.00
Liberty 55489		Damn The Defiant / Lonesome Waters	1962	2.00	10.00
Chancellor 1116		I Wanna Thank Your Folks / The Giant	1962	3.00	15.00
Chancellor 1123		Party Girl / Tag Along	1962	3.00	15.00
Chancellor 1129		Remember Me? / Time Is Not Enough	1962	3.00	15.00
Capitol 5023		All Week Long / It Isn't There	1963	2.00	10.00
Capitol 5114		You Taught Me The Way To Love You / The Opposite	1964	2.00	10.00
Capitol 5176		Walkin,' Talkin' Doll / Sweet Suzie	1964	2.00	10.00
Magic Lamp 515		Bigger Man / Less Than A Heartache	1964	5.00	25.00
Magic Lamp 515	(PS)	Bigger Man / Less Than A Heartache	1964	35.00	175.00
Sahara 512		Fountain Of Love / What A Summer Day	1964	2.00	10.00
		—Extended Play Albums—			
Liberty 1004		Dreamin'	1960	20.00	100.00
Liberty 1011		Johnny Burnette Hits	1961	20.00	100.00

BURNETTE, JOHNNY & DORSEY (THE BURNETTE BROTHERS)
Johnny and Dorsey also recorded as The Texans.

Imperial 5509		Warm Love / My Honey	1958	15.00	75.00
Reprise 20153		Hey Sue / It Don't Take Much	1963	3.00	15.00

BURNING SLICKS, THE

Battle 45926		Midnight Drag / Hard Drivin' Man	1963	4.00	20.00
Battle 45926	(PS)	Midnight Drag / Hard Drivin' Man	1963	6.00	30.00
Riverside 4571		Midnight Drag / Hard Drivin' Man	1963	3.00	15.00

BURNS, SONNY

Starday 209		A Real Cool Cat / Frown On The Moon	195?	10.00	50.00

BURRELL, BOZ

Epic 10097		Pinocchio / The Baby Song	1966	2.00	10.00

BURSON ENTERPRISE

Ru Ro 413		Mr. Soul / Got To Be A Reason	1968	1.20	6.00

BURTON, JAMES, & RALPH MOONEY

Capitol 2140		Corn Pickin' / Texas Waltz	1968	1.60	8.00

BURTON, JIMMY
Jimmy Burton also recorded as James Burton, above, and Jimmy Dobro.

Miramar 108		Love Lost / Jimmy's Blues	196?	2.00	10.00

BURTON, WENDY

Columbia 42624		17,000,000 Bicycles / Mommy's Daddy, Daddy's Daddy And Santa Claus	1962	1.60	8.00

BUSEY, GARY

Epic/Am. Int. 50581		Maybe Baby / True Love Ways	1978	.40	2.00
Epic/Am. Int. 50607		Clear Lake Medley / Maybe Baby	1978	.40	2.00

BUSH, KATE

Harvest 8003		Wuthering Heights / Kite	1978	2.00	10.00
Harvest 8003	(PS)	Wuthering Heights / Kite	1978	3.00	15.00
Harvest 8006		The Man With The Child In His Eyes / Moving	1979	2.50	12.00
Harvest 8006	(PS)	The Man With The Child In His Eyes / Moving	1979	3.00	15.00
EMI		Running Up That Hill / Under The Ivy	1985	.60	3.00
EMI		Hounds Of Love / The Burning Bridge	1985	.60	3.00
EMI		The Big Sky / Not This Time	1985	.60	3.00
EMI		Cloudbusting /	1986	.60	3.00
EMI		Experiment IV / Wuthering Heights	1986	.60	3.00
		—12" Singles—			
EMI	(DJ)	Them Heavy People / Them Heavy People	1979	3.00	15.00
EMI	(DJ)	Suspended In Gaffa / Suspended In Gaffa	1982	3.00	15.00
EMI	(DJ)	Running Up That Hill / Running Up That Hill	1985	3.00	15.00
EMI		Running Up That Hill / Under The Ivy	1985	2.00	10.00

The Byrds' first single, *Mr. Tambourine Man,* was issued on red vinyl and shipped to radio stations in this black & white sleeve. While the one side called attention to the group's upcoming appearance on the popular TV show, Hullabaloo, the other side featured this formal group portrait, one of the loveliest photos of any group from the period.

Label & Catalog #		A-Side/B-Side	Year	VG	NM
EMI	(DJ)	Hounds Of Love / Hounds Of Love	1985	3.00	15.00
EMI		The Big Sky / Not This Time	1985	2.00	10.00
EMI		Cloudbusting / Cloudbusting	1986	2.00	10.00
EMI		Experiment IV / December Will Be Magic	1986	2.00	10.00
BUSTERS, THE					
Arlen 735		Bust Out / Astronauts	1963	3.00	15.00
Arlen 740		All American Surfer / Pine Tree Hop	1963	4.00	20.00
Arlen 745		Torrid Zone / Heartaches	1964	3.00	15.00
BUTLER, DAWS					
Merri 6011		Bingo Ringo / Clementine	1964	4.00	20.00
Merri 6011	(PS)	Bingo Ringo / Clementine	1964	5.00	25.00
Mercury 72262		Bingo Ringo / Clementine	1964	3.00	15.00
BUTTERFIELD BLUES BAND, PAUL					
Elektra 45609		Come On In / I Got A Mind To Give Up Living	1967	1.00	5.00
Elektra 45620		Run Out Of Time / One More Heartache	1967	1.00	5.00
Elektra 45620	(PS)	Run Out Of Time / One More Heartache	1967	2.00	10.00
BUTTERFIELD, PAUL					
Bearsville 49706		Living In Memphis /			
		Footprints On The Windshield Upside Down	1981	.40	2.00

BUTTERFLIES, THE: *Refer to* BONNIE & THE BUTTERFLIES

BUTTONS, THE					
Columbia 42834		Foot Stompin' U.S.A. / Walk Away Girl	1963	1.50	8.00
BUTTONS & THE BEAUS, THE					
Zen 104		Never Leave Your Sugar (Standing In The Rain) /			
		Twistin' Blues	1963	3.00	15.00

BUZZ
Buzz features David Bowie.

Coral 62492		I've Gotta Buzz / You're Holding Me Down	1964	40.00	200.00

BUZZ & BUCKY
Buzz Cason and John "Buck" Wilkin of Ronny & The Daytonas. Refer to John Buck & His Blazers.

Amy 924		Bay City / Tiger A-Go-Go	1965	4.00	20.00
BUZZCOCKS, THE					
I.R.S. 9001		Everybody's Happy Nowadays / Why Can't I Touch It?	1979	1.00	5.00
I.R.S. 9001	(PS)	Everybody's Happy Nowadays / Why Can't I Touch It?	1979	1.00	5.00
I.R.S. 9010		Something's Gone Wrong Again / I Believe	1980	1.00	5.00
I.R.S. 9010	(PS)	Something's Gone Wrong Again / I Believe	1980	1.00	5.00
I.R.S. 9017		Why, She's A Girl From The Chain Store /			
		You Are Everything	1980	1.00	5.00
I.R.S. 9017	(PS)	Why, She's A Girl From The Chain Store /			
		You Are Everything	1980	1.00	5.00
I.R.S. 9019		Strange Things / Airwaves Dream	1980	1.00	5.00
I.R.S. 9019	(PS)	Strange Things / Airwaves Dream	1980	1.00	5.00
I.R.S. 9020		Running Free / What Do You Know?	1980	1.00	5.00
I.R.S. 9020	(PS)	Running Free / What Do You Know?	1980	1.00	5.00
BUZZSAW					
RCA Victor 47-8000		Live In The Springtime / I Can Make You Happy	1962	3.00	15.00
BYE BYES, THE					
Mercury 71530		Blonde Hair, Blue Eyes, Ruby Lips / Do You?	1959	2.00	10.00

BYRDS, THE
Originals members were Gene Clark, who left in 1966, Michael Clarke, David Crosby, Chris Hillman and Jim/Roger McGuinn, who originally recorded as The Beefeaters. By 1967 only Hillman and McGuinn were left, joined by Kevin Kelley and Gram Parsons, both from the International Submarine Band. Hillman, Kelley and Parsons left in 1968. Later members were Skip Battin, Gene Parsons, Clarence White and John York.

Columbia 43271	(DJ)	Mr. Tambourine Man / Mr. Tambourine Man *(Red vinyl)*	1965	25.00	125.00
Columbia 43271	(PS)	Mr. Tambourine Man / Mr. Tambourine Man	1965	30.00	150.00
Columbia 43271	(DJ)	Mr. Tambourine Man / I Knew I'd Want You	1965	5.00	25.00
Columbia 43271	(DJ)	Mr. Tambourine Man / I Knew I'd Want You	1965	2.00	10.00
Columbia 43332	(DJ)	Feel A Whole Lot Better / Feel A Whole Lot Better	1965	20.00	100.00
		(Red vinyl)			
Columbia 43332	(DJ)	All I Really Want To Do / All I Really Want To Do	1965	15.00	75.00
		(Red vinyl)			
Columbia 43332	(DJ)	All I Really Want To Do / Feel A Whole Lot Better	1965	5.00	25.00
Columbia 43332		All I Really Want To Do / Feel A Whole Lot Better	1965	2.00	10.00
Columbia 43424	(DJ)	Turn, Turn, Turn / Turn, Turn, Turn *(Red vinyl)*	1965	20.00	100.00
Columbia 43424	(DJ)	Turn, Turn, Turn / She Don't Care About Time	1965	5.00	25.00
Columbia 43424		Turn, Turn, Turn / She Don't Care About Time	1965	2.00	10.00

Label & Catalog #		A-Side/B-Side	Year	VG	NM
Columbia 43501	(DJ)	Set You Free This Time / It Won't Be Wrong	1966	4.00	20.00
Columbia 43501		Set You Free This Time / It Won't Be Wrong	1966	1.60	8.00
Columbia 43578	(DJ)	Eight Miles High / Why?	1966	4.00	20.00
Columbia 43578		Eight Miles High / Why?	1966	1.60	8.00
Columbia 43578	(PS)	Eight Miles High / Why?	1966	3.00	15.00
Columbia 43702	(DJ)	5D (Fifth Dimension) / Captain Soul	1966	4.00	20.00
Columbia 43702		5D (Fifth Dimension) / Captain Soul	1966	1.60	8.00
Columbia 43766	(DJ)	Mr. Spaceman / What's Happening?	1966	4.00	20.00
Columbia 43766		Mr. Spaceman / What's Happening?	1966	1.60	8.00
Columbia 43987	(DJ)	So You Want To Be A Rock And Roll Star / Everybody's Been Burned	1967	4.00	20.00
Columbia 43987		So You Want To Be A Rock And Roll Star / Everybody's Been Burned	1967	1.60	8.00
Columbia 44157	(DJ)	Have You Seen Her Face? / Don't Make Waves	1967	4.00	20.00
Columbia 44157		Have You Seen Her Face? / Don't Make Waves	1967	2.00	10.00
Columbia 44157	(PS)	Have You Seen Her Face? / Don't Make Waves	1967	8.00	40.00
Columbia 44054	(DJ)	My Back Pages / Renaissance Fair	1967	3.00	15.00
Columbia 44054		My Back Pages / Renaissance Fair	1967	1.60	8.00
Columbia 44230	(DJ)	Lady Friend / Old John Robertson	1967	4.00	20.00
Columbia 44230		Lady Friend / Old John Robertson	1967	1.60	8.00
Columbia 44362	(DJ)	Goin' Back / Change Is Now	1967	4.00	20.00
Columbia 44362		Goin' Back / Change Is Now	1967	1.60	8.00
Columbia 44499	(DJ)	You Ain't Goin' Nowhere / Artificial Energy	1968	4.00	20.00
Columbia 44499		You Ain't Goin' Nowhere / Artificial Energy	1968	1.60	8.00
Columbia 44643	(DJ)	Pretty Boy Floyd / I Am A Pilgrim	1968	4.00	20.00
Columbia 44643		Pretty Boy Floyd / I Am A Pilgrim	1968	1.60	8.00
		(Columbia 43987-44643 were produced by Gary Usher.)			
Columbia 44746	(DJ)	Drug Store Truck-Driving Man / Bad Night At The Whiskey	1969	2.00	10.00
Columbia 44746		Drug Store Truck-Driving Man / Bad Night At The Whiskey	1969	1.80	4.00
Columbia 44868	(DJ)	Lay Lady Lay / Old Blue	1969	2.00	10.00
Columbia 44868		Lay Lady Lay / Old Blue	1969	1.80	4.00
Columbia 44990	(DJ)	Ballad Of Easy Rider / Wasn't Born To Follow	1969	2.00	10.00
Columbia 44990	(DJ)	Wasn't Born To Follow / Wasn't Born To Follow	1969	2.00	10.00
Columbia 44990		Ballad Of Easy Rider / Wasn't Born To Follow	1969	.80	4.00
Columbia 45071	(DJ)	Jesus Is Just Alright / It's All Over Now, Baby Blue	1970	2.00	10.00
		(Stock copies of Columbia 45761 may not exist.)			
Columbia 45259	(DJ)	Chestnut Mare / Just A Season	1970	2.00	10.00
Columbia 45259		Chestnut Mare / Just A Season	1970	.80	4.00
Columbia 45440	(DJ)	Glory Glory / Citizen Kane	1971	2.00	10.00
Columbia 45440		Glory Glory / Citizen Kane	1971	.80	4.00
Columbia 45514	(DJ)	Farther Along / America's Great National Pastime	1971	2.00	10.00
Columbia 45514		Farther Along / America's Great National Pastime	1971	.80	4.00
Columbia 45761	(DJ)	Jesus Is Just Alright / Jesus Is Just Alright	1972	2.00	10.00
Columbia SP-1602	(DJ)	Lover Of The Bayou / Goin' Back	1973	2.00	10.00
Asylum 11016		Full Circle / Long Live The King	1973	.40	2.00
Asylum 11019		Cowgirl In The Sand / Long Live The King	1973	.40	2.00
		—Special/Promotional Releases—			
Columbia 2LP116003-4		5D (Fifth Dimension) / The 5D Interview (Paper sleeve)	1966	—	—
		(Rare. Estimated near mint value $300-500.)			
Columbia CV-10287		The Byrds (Paper picture sleeve)	1970	3.00	15.00
		(Compact-33 EP issued through Scholastic Book Services.)			
Columbia SP-284	(DJ)	The World Turns All Around Her / He Was A Friend Of Mine	197?	2.00	10.00
		(From the "promotional Roger McGuinn Airplay Anthology" album.)			

BYRNES, ED "KOOKIE"

Label & Catalog #		A-Side/B-Side	Year	VG	NM
Warner Bros. 5047		Kookie, Kookie (Lend Me Your Comb) / You're The Top	1959	3.00	15.00
Warner Bros. 5047	(PS)	Kookie, Kookie (Lend Me Your Comb) / You're The Top	1959	4.00	20.00
Warner Bros. 5087		Like, I Love You / Kookie's Mad Pad	1959	2.00	10.00
Warner Bros. 5087	(PS)	Like, I Love You / Kookie's Mad Pad	1959	3.00	15.00
Warner Bros. 5114		Kookie's Love Song / Kookie's Love Song, Part 2	1959	2.00	10.00
Warner Bros. 5114	(PS)	Kookie's Love Song / Kookie's Love Song, Part 2	1959	3.00	15.00
Warner Bros. 5121		Yulesville / Lonely Christmas	1959	2.00	10.00
Warner Bros. 5121	(PS)	Yulesville / Lonely Christmas	1959	3.00	15.00
		—Extended Play Albums—			
Warner Bros. 1309		Ed "Kookie" Byrnes	1959	10.00	50.00
Warner Bros. PRO-102	(DJ)	Ed "Kookie" Byrnes (Radio spots issued without a cover)	1959	6.00	30.00

BYRON, JIMMIE

Label & Catalog #	A-Side/B-Side	Year	VG	NM
Teen 113	Sidewalk Rock / Screamin'	1957	6.00	30.00

BYRON, LORD DOUGLAS

Label & Catalog #	A-Side/B-Side	Year	VG	NM
Union 505	Big Bad Ho-Dad / (B-side by The Continentals)	1962	7.00	35.00
Dot 16685	Surfin' Santa / The Drink That Makes You Shrink	1964	4.00	20.00

C.C.S.

Rak 4501	Whole Lotta Love / Boom Boom	1971	1.00	5.00
Rak 4507	Save The World / Tap Turns On The Water	1971	.80	4.00

C.L. & THE PICTURES
C.L. is Curtis Lee.

Dunes 2010	Let's Take A Ride / I'm Asking Forgiveness	1962	3.00	15.00
Dunes 2017	Afraid / Mary Go Round	1962	3.00	15.00
Dunes 2023	I'm Sorry / That's What's Happening	1963	3.00	15.00
Monument 854	He'll Only Hurt You / Talking About My Baby	1964	2.00	10.00
Monument 888	Could This Be Magic? / Yolanda	1964	2.00	10.00
Monument 958	Baby, Not Now / Jigsaw Puzzle	1964	2.00	10.00

C.O.D.'S, THE

Kellmac 1003	Michael / Cry No More	1965	1.60	8.00
Kellmac 1005	I'm A Good Guy / Pretty Baby	1965	1.60	8.00

C-QUINS, THE

Ditto 501	My Only Love / You've Been Crying	1962	3.00	15.00
Chess 1815	My Only Love / You've Been Crying	1962	3.00	15.00

CABBOTT, JOHNNY

Columbia 42283	(DJ)	Night And Day / On My Own Again	1962	5.00	25.00
Columbia 42283		Night And Day / On My Own Again	1962	8.00	40.00
Columbia 42283	(33)	Night And Day / On My Own Again	1962	15.00	75.00

CABLES, THE

Kay Bee 102	Forget It / The Broom	196?	1.50	8.00

CAESAR, IRVING

Buena Vista 477	What! No Mickey Mouse! / What Kind Of Party Is This?	1964	2.00	10.00

CAESAR & CLEO
Caesar & Cleo later recorded as Sonny & Cher.

Vault 909		The Letter / Spring Fever	1963	4.00	20.00
		(Vault 909 was reissued on Vault 916 and credited to Sonny & Cher.)			
Reprise 0308		Do You Want To Dance? / Love Is Strange	1964	3.00	15.00
Reprise 0419		Let The Good Times Roll / Love Is Strange	1965	3.00	15.00
Reprise 0419	(PS)	Let The Good Times Roll / Love Is Strange	1965	6.00	30.00

CAESARS, THE

Lanie 2001	(La La) I Love You / Get Yourself Together	196?	2.00	10.00

CAGLE, AUBREY

House Of Sound 504	Real Cool / Want To Be Wanted Blues	195?	150.00	600.00
Glee 1000	Be-Bop Blues / Just For You	1960	25.00	125.00
Glee 1001	Come Along, Little Girl / Blue Lonely World	196?	15.00	75.00
Glee	Bop 'N Stroll /	196?	10.00	50.00

CAGLE, WADE, & THE ESCORTS

Sun 360	Highland Rock / Groovy Train	1961	2.50	12.00

CAHILL, CRAIG, & THE OFFBEATS: *Refer to* THE OFFBEATS

CAHPERONES, THE: *Refer to* THE CHAPERONES

CAIN, JEFFREY

Altera 001	Lonely Boy / Oh, Tomorrow	196?	2.00	10.00

CAJUNS, THE (WITH JACQUI SHANNON)

Fraternity 836	Just Another Lie / Cajun Blues	1958	5.00	25.00
	(Fraternity 838 was reissued on Sage & Sand credited to Jackie Shannon & The Cajuns.)			

CAKE, THE

Decca 32179		Baby, That's Me / Mockingbird	1967	1.00	5.00
Decca 32212		You Can Have Him / I Know	1967	1.00	5.00
Decca 32212	(PS)	You Can Have Him / I Know	1967	3.00	15.00
Decca 32235		Fire Fly / Rainbow Wood	1967	1.00	5.00
Decca 32347		Have You Heard The News About Miss Molly? / P.T. 280	1968	1.00	5.00

Label & Catalog #	A-Side/B-Side	Year	VG	NM
CAL & IVAN				
Skoop 1052	Lazy / Lazy (Part 2)	1960	3.00	15.00
CALE, JOHN				
John Cale was formerly a member of The Velvet Underground.				
Columbia 45154	Cleo / Fairweather Friend	1970	.80	4.00
Columbia 45266	Big White Cloud / Gideon's Bible	1970	.80	4.00
Reprise 1108	Days Of Steam / Legs Larry At Television Center	1972	.80	4.00
CALENDAR GIRLS, THE				
4 Corners 118	People Will Talk / Sha-Rel-A-Nova	1965	2.00	10.00
CALENDARS, THE				
Coed 564	I'm Gonna Laugh At You / You're Too Fast	1961	40.00	200.00
CALIFORNIA MUSIC [CALIFORNIA]				
California Music/California was a loose aggregation of musicians devoted to mid-'60s California rock/pop: Curt Becher (formerly Boetcher), Kenny Hinkle, Bruce Johnston, Terry Melcher, Chad Stuart and Gary Usher.				
RCA/Equinox 10120	Don't Worry, Baby / Ten Years Harmony	1974	3.00	15.00
RCA/Equinox 10363	Why Do Fools Fall In Love? / Don't Worry, Baby	1975	3.00	15.00
	("Why Do Fools Fall In Love?" was produced by Brian Wilson.)			
RCA/Equinox 10572	Jamaica Farewell / California Music	1976	3.00	15.00
	("Jamaica Farewell " features Brian Wilson on keyboards.)			
Warner/Curb 8253	Music, Music, Music / Happy In Hollywood	1976	2.00	10.00
Warner/Curb 8307	I Love You So / Happy In Hollywood	1976	2.00	10.00
RSO 901	I Can Hear Music / Love's Supposed To Be That Way	1978	2.00	10.00
	— 12" Singles—			
Warner/Curb 8253 (DJ)	Music, Music, Music / Music, Music, Music	1976	2.00	10.00
CALIFORNIA SUNS, THE				
Imperial 66179 (DJ)	Masked Grandma / Little Bit Of Heaven	1964	2.00	10.00
Imperial 66179	Masked Grandma / Little Bit Of Heaven	1964	4.00	20.00
CALLENDER, BOBBY				
Roulette 4471	Little Star / Love And Kisses	1963	2.00	10.00
CALLICUTT, DUDLEY, & THE GO BOYS				
DC 0412	Get Ready, Baby / Heart Trouble	195?	20.00	100.00
CALVEYS, THE				
Comma 84349	I Need Love / The Wind	196?	6.00	30.00
CAMEL DRIVERS, THE				
Top Dog 100	The Grass Looks Greener / It's Gonna Rain	1968	2.00	10.00
Top Dog 103	Sunday Morning 6 O' Clock / Give It A Try	1968	2.00	10.00
Buddah 61	Sunday Morning 6 O' Clock / Give It A Try	1968	1.00	5.00
CAMELOTS, THE				
Aanko 0110	Your Way / Don't Leave Me, Baby	1963	6.00	30.00
Aanko 1004	Sunday Kind Of Love / My Imagination	1963	10.00	50.00
Crimson 1001	Don't Leave Me, Baby / The Letter	1964	2.00	10.00
Cameo 334	Don't Leave Me, Baby / (B-side by The Ebonaires)	1964	3.00	15.00
Ember 1108	Pocahontas / Searching For My Baby	1964	2.00	10.00
Dream 1001	Your Way / I Wonder	1967	2.00	10.00
Times Square 32	Dance Girl / (B-side by The Suns)	196?	2.00	10.00
Times Square 32	Dance Girl / (B-side by The Suns) (Colored vinyl)	196?	3.00	15.00
CAMELOTS, THE				
Comet 2158	Scratch / Charge	196?	2.00	10.00
CAMERONS, THE				
Cousins 1-2	Cheryl / Boom Chic-A-Boom	1960	10.00	50.00
Cousins 1003	Guardian Angel / A Girl I Marry	1961	20.00	100.00
Felsted 8636	Guardian Angel / A Girl I Marry	1961	4.00	20.00
CAMINOS, THE				
Lavender 1925	The Camino Flip / You'll Make Him Mad	196?	2.00	10.00
CAMPANELLA, DAVID, & THE DELLCHORDS				
David Campanella is baseball great Roy's son.				
Kane 25593	Over The Rainbow / Everything's That Way	1959	10.00	50.00

CAMPBELL, GLEN

Glen Campbell struggled through a variety of guises in his early career, including working as a touring Beach Boy. It was this association that led to his most collectible single, "Guess I'm Dumb" (see below). His move to a bland country/pop style reached a broader market; these singles— many of them top 40 hits— are not included in this edition. Refer to The Champs; The Gee Cees; The Green River Boys; Mr. 12 String Guitar; and Sagittarius.

Label & Catalog #		A-Side/B-Side	Year	VG	NM
Capehart 5008		Death Valley / Nothing Better Than A Pretty Woman	196?	5.00	25.00
Ceneco 1324		Dreams For Sale / I've Got To Win	1961	5.00	25.00
Ceneco 1356		I Wonder / You You You	1961	4.00	20.00
Crest 1087		Turn Around, Look At Me / Brenda	1961	4.00	20.00
Crest 1096		Miracle Of Love / Once More	1961	2.00	10.00
Everest 2500		Delight Arkansas / Walk Right In	196?	2.00	10.00
Capitol 4783		Too Late To Worry, Too Blue To Cry / How Do I Tell My Heart Not To Worry?	1962	1.00	5.00
Capitol 4856		Long Black Limousine / Here I Am	1962	1.00	5.00
Capitol 4856	(PS)	Long Black Limousine / Here I Am	1962	5.00	25.00
Capitol 4925		Prima Donna / Oh, My Darling	1963	1.00	5.00
Capitol 5037		As Far As I'm Concerned / Same Old Places	1963	1.00	5.00
Capitol 5172		Through The Eyes Of A Child / Let Me Tell You 'Bout Mary	1964	1.00	5.00
Capitol 5279		Summer, Winter, Spring And Fall / Heartaches Can Be Fun	1964	1.00	5.00
Capitol 5279	(PS)	Summer, Winter, Spring And Fall / Heartaches Can Be Fun	1964	4.00	20.00
Capitol 5360		Tomorrow Never Comes / Woman's World	1965	1.00	5.00
Capitol 5441		Guess I'm Dumb / That's All Right	1965	12.00	60.00

("Guess I'm Dumb," a precursor to the sound and style of "Pet Sounds," was written and produced by Brian Wilson and features The Honeys.)

CAMPBELL, JO ANN
Refer to Jo Ann & Troy.

Eldorado 504		Come On, Baby / Forever Young	195?	5.00	25.00
Eldorado 509		Funny Thing / I Can't Give You Anything But Love	195?	3.00	15.00
Point 4		Wherever You Go / I'm Coming Home Late Tonight	195?	3.00	15.00
Gone 5014		Wait A Minute / I'm In Love With You	195?	3.00	15.00
Gone 5021		Rock And Roll Love / You're Driving Me Mad	1959	4.00	20.00
Gone 5027		Wassa Matter With You? / You Do	1959	3.00	15.00
Gone 5037		I'm Nobody's Baby Now / I Really, Really Love You	1959	3.00	15.00
Gone 5049		Tall Boy / Happy New Year, Baby	1959	3.00	15.00
Gone 5055		Mama (Can I Go Out Tonight?) / Nervous	1959	3.00	15.00

—*Original Gone singles above have black labels with a clown on top.*—

Gone 5068		I Ain't Got No Steady Date / Beachcomber	1959	3.00	15.00
ABC-Paramount 10134		A Kookie Little Paradise / Bobby, Bobby, Bobby	1960	2.50	12.00
ABC-Paramount 10134	(S)	A Kookie Little Paradise / Bobby, Bobby, Bobby	1960	5.00	25.00
ABC-Paramount 10172		Crazy Daisy / But Maybe This Year	1960	2.50	12.00
ABC-Paramount 10200		Motorcycle Michael / Puka Puka Pants	1961	3.00	15.00
ABC-Paramount 10224		Eddie, My Love / It Wasn't Right	1961	3.00	15.00
ABC-Paramount 10258		Mama Don't Want / Duane	1961	2.00	10.00
ABC-Paramount 10300		You Made Me Love You / I Changed My Mind, Jack	1962	2.00	10.00
ABC-Paramount 10335		I Wish It Would Rain All Summer / Amateur Night	1962	2.00	10.00
Cameo 223		(I'm The Girl On) Wolverton Mountain / Sloppy Joe	1962	2.00	10.00
Cameo 237		Mr. Fix-It Man / Let Me Do It My Way	1962	2.00	10.00
Cameo 249		Mother, Please! / Waitin' For Love	1963	2.00	10.00

CAMPI, RAY

TNT 145		Play It Cool / Caterpillar	1957	75.00	300.00
Dot 15617		It Ain't Me / Give That Love To Me	1957	10.00	50.00

CAMPERS, THE [THE CAMPS]
Parkway 974 was released credited to both The Camps and The Campers, pseudonyms for The Crickets.

Parkway 974		The Ballad Of Batman / Batmobile	1965	5.00	25.00
Parkway 974	(PS)	The Ballad Of Batman / Batmobile	1965	5.00	25.00

CANADIAN BEATLES, THE

Tide 2003		Think I'm Gonna Cry / I'll Show You The Way	1964	3.00	15.00
Tide 2006		Love Walked Away / I'm Comin' Home	1964	3.00	15.00

CANADIAN CLASSICS, THE
The Canadian Classics recorded as The Classics in Canada and later as The Collectors.

Valiant 723		I Don't Know / Gone Away	1966	3.00	15.00

CANADIAN ROGUES, THE

Charay		Ooh-Poo-Pa-Doo / Deep In Touch	1966	3.00	15.00
Palmer 5017		Ooh-Poo-Pa-Doo / Deep In Touch	1966	2.00	10.00

CANADIAN SQUIRES, THE
The Canadian Squires later recorded as Levon & The Hawks and The Band.

Ware 6002		Uh-Uh-Uh / Leave Me Alone	1965	5.00	25.00

CANADIAN SWEETHEARTS, THE

A&M 713		Freight Train / Out For Fun	1963	2.00	10.00

CANARIES, THE

Dimension 1047		I'm Sorry, Baby / Runaround Ronnie	1963	2.00	10.00

CANDOLI, PETE

Nan 3004		Beatle Bug Jump / You Made Me Love You	1964	3.00	15.00

Label & Catalog #		A-Side/B-Side	Year	VG	NM
CANDY GIRLS, THE					
Rotate 5001		Tomorrow, My Love / Run	196?	2.00	10.00
Rotate 5005		Runaround (Baby, Baby) / Run	196?	2.00	10.00
CANDYMEN, THE					
ABC 10995		Georgia Pines / Movies In My Mind	1967	.80	4.00
ABC 11077		Candyman / Crowded Room	1968	.80	4.00
Liberty 56172		Happy Tonight / Papers	1970	.80	4.00
CANE, GARY, & HIS FRIENDS					
Shell 717		C'mere, Baby Doll / The Fight	1960	2.00	10.00
Shell 719		I'll Walk The Earth / The Yen Yet Song	1960	2.00	10.00
CANE, STACEY					
Jubilee 5500		Funny Face / Who Are You?	1965	1.20	6.00
CANNED HEAT					
Liberty 55979		Rollin' And Tumblin' / Bullfrog Blues	1967	1.20	6.00
Liberty 55979	(PS)	Rollin' And Tumblin' / Bullfrog Blues	1967	2.00	10.00
Liberty 56038		On The Road Again / Boogie Music	1968	1.20	6.00
Liberty 56077		Going Up The Country / One Kind Favor	1968	1.20	6.00
Liberty 56077	(PS)	Going Up The Country / One Kind Favor	1968	2.00	10.00
Liberty 56079		The Christmas Blues / The Chipmunk Song	1968	2.00	10.00
		(Features The Chipmunks.)			
Liberty 56097		Time Was / Low Down	1969	1.20	6.00
Liberty 56127		Sic 'Em, Pigs / Poor Moon	1969	1.20	6.00
Liberty 56151		Let's Work Together / I'm Her Man	1970	1.20	6.00
Liberty 56180		Future Blues / Going Up The Country	1971	1.20	6.00
Liberty 56217		Wooly Bully / My Time Ain't Long	1973	1.60	8.00
United Artists 167		Rock And Roll Music / Lookin' For My Rainbow	1976	1.00	5.00
CANNED HEAT & LITTLE RICHARD					
United Artists 50892		Rockin' With The King / I Don't Care What You Tell Me	1972	.80	4.00
CANNIBAL & THE HEADHUNTERS					
Aires 1001		Dance By The Light / Means So Much	1964	2.00	10.00
Rampart 642		Land Of 1,000 Dances / Show You How To Love Me	1965	2.00	10.00
Rampart 644		Here Comes Love / Nau Ninny Nau	1965	2.00	10.00
Rampart 646		Follow The Music / I Need Your Loving	1965	2.00	10.00
Rampart 654		Please, Baby, Please / Out Of Sight	1966	2.00	10.00
Date 1516		Zulu King / La Bamba	1966	1.20	6.00
Date 1525		Land Of 1,000 Dances / Love Bird	1966	1.20	6.00
Capitol 2393		Mean So Much / Get It On Up	1969	1.20	6.00
CANNON, ACE					
Fernwood 135		Hoe Down Rock / Summertime	1960	4.00	20.00
Hi 2040		Tuff / Sittin' Tight	1961	.80	4.00
Hi 2051		Blues (Stay Away From Me) / Blues In My Heart	1962	.80	4.00
Hi 2065		Cottonfields / Mildew	1963	.80	4.00
Hi 2065	(PS)	Cottonfields / Mildew	1963	1.00	5.00
Hi 2070		Swanee River / Moanin' The Blues	1963	.80	4.00
Hi 2070	(PS)	Swanee River / Moanin' The Blues	1963	1.00	5.00
Hi 2074		Searchin' / Love Letters In The Sand	1964	.80	4.00
Santo 503		Sugar Blues / .38 Special	1962	1.00	5.00
Santo 506		Big Shot / Rest	1962	1.00	5.00
CANNON, FREDDY					
Freddy Cannon also recorded with Danny & The Juniors.					
Swan 4031		Tallahassee Lassie / You Know	1959	3.00	15.00
Swan 4038		Okefenokee / Kookie Hat	1959	3.00	15.00
Swan 4043		Way Down Yonder In New Orleans / Fractured	1959	3.00	15.00
Swan 4043	(PS)	Way Down Yonder In New Orleans / Fractured	1959	4.00	20.00
Swan 4050		Chattanooga Shoe Shine Boy / Boston	1960	2.00	10.00
Swan 4050	(PS)	Chattanooga Shoe Shine Boy / Boston	1960	3.00	15.00
Swan 4053		The Urge / Jump Over	1960	2.00	10.00
Swan 4053	(PS)	The Urge / Jump Over	1960	3.00	15.00
Swan 4057		Happy Shades Of Blue / Cuernavaca Choo Choo	1960	2.00	10.00
Swan 4057	(PS)	Happy Shades Of Blue / Cuernavaca Choo Choo	1960	3.00	15.00
Swan 4061		Humdinger / My Blue Heaven	1960	2.00	10.00
Swan 4061	(PS)	Humdinger / My Blue Heaven	1960	3.00	15.00
Swan 4066		Muskrat Ramble / Two Thousand 88s	1961	2.00	10.00
Swan 4066	(PS)	Muskrat Ramble / Two Thousand 88s	1961	3.00	15.00
Swan 4071		Buzz Buzz A-Diddle-It / Opportunity	1961	2.00	10.00
Swan 4078		Transistor Sister / Walk On The Moon	1961	2.00	10.00
Swan 4078	(PS)	Transistor Sister / Walk On The Moon	1961	3.00	15.00
Swan 4083		For Me And My Gal / Blue Plate Special	1961	2.00	10.00
Swan 4096		Teen Queen Of The Week / Wild Guy	1962	2.00	10.00
Swan 4106		Palisades Park / June, July And August	1962	2.00	10.00

Label & Catalog #		A-Side/B-Side	Year	VG	NM
Swan 4117		What's Gonna Happen When Summer's Gone? / Broadway	1962	2.00	10.00
Swan 4122		If You Were A Rock And Roll Record / The Truth, Ruth	1962	1.60	8.00
Swan 4132		Four Letter Man / Come On And Love Me	1963	1.60	8.00
Swan 4139		Patty Baby / Betty Jean	1963	1.60	8.00
Swan 4149		Everybody Monkey / Oh, Gloria	1963	1.60	8.00
Swan 4155		Do What The Hippies Do / That's The Way The Girls Are	1963	1.60	8.00
Swan 4166		Sweet Georgia Brown / What A Party	1964	1.60	8.00
Swan 4178		The Ups And Downs Of Love / It's Been Nice	1964	3.00	15.00
Warner Bros. 5409		Abigail Beecher / All American Girl	1964	1.60	8.00
Warner Bros. 5434		O.K. Wheeler, The Used Car Dealer / Odie Cologne	1964	1.60	8.00
Warner Bros. 5448		Summertime U.S.A. / Got A Good Thing Going	1964	2.00	10.00
Warner Bros. 5487		Little Autograph Seeker / Too Much Monkey Business	1964	2.00	10.00
Warner Bros. 5615		Little Miss A-Go-Go / In The Night	1964	1.60	8.00
Warner Bros. 5615	(PS)	Little Miss A-Go-Go / In The Night	1964	4.00	20.00
Warner Bros. 5645		Action / Beachwood City	1965	1.60	8.00
Warner Bros. 5666		Let Me Show You Where It's At / The Old Rag Man	1965	1.60	8.00
Warner Bros. 5673		She's Somethin' Else / Little Bitty Corrine	1965	2.00	10.00
Warner Bros. 5693		The Dedication Song / Come On, Come On	1966	1.60	8.00
Warner Bros. 5810		The Greatest Show On Earth / Hokie Pokie Pal	1966	1.60	8.00
Warner Bros. 5832		Natalie / The Laughing Song	1966	2.00	10.00
Warner Bros. 5859		Run For The Sun / Use Your Imagination	1966	2.00	10.00
Warner Bros. 5876		In My Wildest Dream / A Happy Clown	1967	3.00	15.00
Warner Bros. 7019		Maverick's Flats / Run To The Poet Man	1967	3.00	15.00
Warner Bros. 7075		20th Century Fox / Cincinnati Woman	1967	3.00	15.00
Buddah 242		Rockin' Robin / Red Valley	1967	2.00	10.00
Rock 'N Roll 1601		Rock Around The Clock / Sock It To The Judge	1968	1.20	6.00
Rock 'N Roll 1604		Sea Cruise / She's A Friday Night Fox	1968	1.20	6.00
Royal American 2		Charged Up, Turned Up Rock & Roll Singer / I Ain't Much But I'm Yours	1969	2.00	10.00
Royal American 288		Blossom Dear / Strawberry Wine	1969	2.00	10.00
Sire 4102		If You Give Me A Title / Beautiful Downtown Burbank	1972	1.00	5.00
Metromedia 262		If You've Got The Time / Take Me Back	1972	2.00	10.00
MCA 40269		Rock N Roll A-B-C's / Superman	197?	3.00	15.00
Amhearst 201		Mean Rebel Rouser / Dance To The Bop	1983	.80	4.00

CANNON, FREDDY, & THE BELMONTS

Mirasound 1002		Let's Put The Fun Back In Rock N Roll / Your Mama Ain't Always Right	1981	.80	4.00

CANNON BROTHERS, THE

Ric 107		Surfin' In Bermuda / Look What You've Done	1964	6.00	30.00

CANNONBALLS, THE

Brunswick 55231		Teen Tango / Summer Feeling	1962	1.20	6.00

CANTERBURY FAIR

Koala 8081		Days I Love / Song On A May Morning	196?	2.00	10.00

CANTERBURY TALES, THE

Dot 16893		Gretal / Broken Piece Of Crystal	1966	2.50	12.00
Merrilyn 5302		Rainy Day / Jug Band	1967	1.00	5.00

CANTINA BAND, THE
The Cantina Band features Lou Christie.

Millennium 11818		Summer '81 / Out In California	1981	.80	4.00

CANUCKS, THE

Diadon 116		Rock Around The Barn / Never Before	1960	2.00	10.00

CANYON, RUSTY

Teenerama 1001		Banana-What A Crazy Fruit! / The Storyman	1958	2.00	10.00

CAPEHART, JERRY
Jerry Capehart's guitarist is Eddie Cochran.

Cash 1021		Walkin' Stick Boogie / Rollin'	1956	35.00	175.00
Crest 1101		Song Of New Orleans / The Young And Blue	1962	5.00	25.00

CAPELLO, LENNY, & THE DOTS

Ric 960		Cotton Candy / Tootles	1961	2.00	10.00
Ric 991		Geneveve / 90 Pound Weakling	1962	2.00	10.00

CAPERS, THE

Jani 1263		Get Squared Away / Who Ya Gonna Believe?	196?	2.00	10.00
ANI 1268		I Don't Know / Don't Ask Me Why	196?	3.00	15.00

CAPES OF GOOD HOPE, THE

Round 1001		Shades / Lady Margaret	1966	2.00	10.00

Label & Catalog #	A-Side/B-Side	Year	VG	NM
CAPITOLS, THE Triumph 601	Three O' Clock Rock / Write Me A Love Letter	1959	3.00	15.00
CAPITOLS, THE Gateway 721	Day By Day / Little Things	195?	25.00	125.00
CAPITOLS, THE Pet 807	Angel Of Love / 'Cause I Love You	1958	15.00	75.00
CAPITOLS, THE *The Capitols also recorded with Mickey Tolliver.* Cindy 3002	Rosemary / Millie	195?	35.00	175.00
CAPP, JOE, & THE STARFIRES Roulette 4436	Comic Strip Wobble / It's Wobblin' Time	1962	2.00	10.00
Roulette 4458	Groovy Movie / Scooter Booter	1962	2.00	10.00
CAPREEZ, THE Sound 126	Rosanna / Over You	1966	2.00	10.00
Sound 149	It's Good To Be Home Again / How To Make A Sad Man Glad	1967	2.00	10.00
Sound 171	Time / Soulsation	1967	2.00	10.00
Tower 370	Time / Soulsation	1967	2.00	10.00
CAPRI, BOBBY Ariste 101	One Sided Love / Charm Bracelet	1960	8.00	40.00
Johnson 124	You And I / Cleopatra	1961	3.00	15.00
Johnson 126	The Night / I'm Gonna Be Another Man	1961	8.00	40.00
CAPRI, JOHN Bomarc 306	Love For Me / When I'm Lonely	195?	10.00	50.00
CAPRIS, THE Planet 1010	There's A Moon Out Tonight / Indian Girl	1960	100.00	400.00
Lost Nite 101	There's A Moon Out Tonight / Indian Girl (Pink label)	1960	5.00	25.00
Old Town 1094	There's A Moon Out Tonight / Indian Girl (Blue label)	1960	5.00	25.00
Trommers 101	There's A Moon Out Tonight / Indian Girl	1961	4.00	20.00
Old Town 1099	When I Fell In Love / Some People Think	1961	4.00	20.00
Old Town 1103	Tears In My Eyes / Why Do I Cry?	1961	4.00	20.00
Old Town 1107	Girl Of My Dreams / My Island In The Sun	1961	5.00	25.00
Mr. Peeke 118	Limbo / From The Vine Came The Grape	1963	2.50	12.00
Ambient Sound 02697	There's A Moon Out Again / Morse Code Of Love	1982	1.00	5.00
CAPS, THE White Star 102	Daddy Dean / Red Headed Flea	1959	3.00	15.00
CAPTAIN & TENNILLE, THE *Daryl Dragon and Toni Tennille. Refer to Dennis Wilson & Rumbo.* Butterscotch 001	The Way I Want To Touch You / Disney Girls	1974	3.00	15.00
Joyce 101	The Way I Want To Touch You / Disney Girls	1974	2.00	10.00

CAPTAIN BEEFHEART & THE MAGIC BAND
The Captain is Don Van Vliet; Magic Band members have included Mark Boston, Alex St. Claire, Ry Cooder, Jeff Cotton, John French, Jerry Handley, Bill Harkleroad and ex-Mothers Roy Estrada, Eliot Ingber and Art Tripp III.

Label & Catalog #		A-Side/B-Side	Year	VG	NM
A&M 794	(DJ)	Diddy Wah Diddy / Who Do You Think You're Fooling?	1964	4.00	20.00
A&M 794		Diddy Wah Diddy / Who Do You Think You're Fooling?	1964	6.00	30.00
A&M Test Pressing	(DJ)	Moon Child / Here I Am, I Always Am	1964	40.00	200.00
A&M 818	(DJ)	Moon Child / Frying Pan	1964	4.00	20.00
A&M 818		Moon Child / Frying Pan	1964	6.00	30.00
Buddah 9	(DJ)	Yellow Brick Road / Abba Zabba	1968	2.00	10.00
Buddah 9		Yellow Brick Road / Abba Zabba	1968	3.00	15.00
Buddah 108	(DJ)	Plastic Factory / Where There's Woman	1970	2.00	10.00
Buddah 108		Plastic Factory / Where There's Woman	1970	3.00	15.00
Reprise PRO-514	(DJ)	Click Clack / Glider	1971	4.00	20.00
Reprise PRO-514	(PS)	Click Clack / Glider	1971	6.00	30.00
Reprise 1068		Click Clack / I Wanna Booglarize You, Baby	1971	3.00	15.00
Reprise PRO-547	(DJ)	Too Much Time / Lo Yo-Yo Stuff	1972	4.00	20.00
Reprise PRO-547	(PS)	Too Much Time / Lo Yo-Yo Stuff	1972	6.00	30.00
Reprise 1133		Too Much Time / My Head Is My Only House	1972	3.00	15.00
Mercury 73494	(DJ)	Upon The My O My / I've Got Love On My Mind	1974	1.00	5.00
Mercury 73494		Upon The My O My / I've Got Love On My Mind	1974	1.50	8.00
MCA 40897		Hard Workin' Man / (B-side by Jack Nitzsche)	1978	1.00	5.00
Epic 03190		Ice Cream For Crow / Light Reflected Off The Oceans Of My Mind	1982	1.00	5.00
Epic 03190	(PS)	Ice Cream For Crow / Light Reflected Off The Oceans Of My Mind	1982	1.00	5.00

Label & Catalog #	A-Side/B-Side	Year	VG	NM
CAPTAIN GROOVY & HIS BUBBLEGUM ARMY				
Super-K 4	Capt. Groovy And His Bubblegum Army / Bubblegum March	1969	2.00	10.00
CAPTAIN ZOOM & THE ANDROIDS				
A&M 781	Here Comes Captain Zoom / The Zoom	1965	2.00	10.00
A&M 785	I Really Want You / Long Tall Texan	1965	2.00	10.00
CAPTIVATIONS, THE				
The Captivations are Gary Paxton and Gary Usher.				
Pentacle	Red Hot Scramblers-Go / Speedshift	1964	10.00	50.00
Garpax 44179	Red Hot Scramblers-Go / Speedshift	1964	5.00	25.00
CARAMEN, ART				
Dasa 101	Falling For You / Eternity Of Love	196?	3.00	15.00
CARAMETTA, PHIL				
ABC-Paramount 10308	Pain Set To Music / (B-side by Sonny Giamotta)	1962	3.00	15.00
CARAVELLES, THE				
Joey 6208	One Little Kiss / Twistin' Marie	1962	20.00	100.00
Starmaker 1925	Pink Lips / Angry Angel	196?	4.00	20.00
CARAVELLES, THE				
Smash 1852	You Don't Have To Be A Baby To Cry / Last One To Know	1963	2.00	10.00
Smash 1869	Have You Ever Been Lonely? / Don't Blow Your Cool	1964	2.00	10.00
Smash 1901	How Can I Be Sure? / You Are Here	1964	2.00	10.00
CARDBOARD ZEPPELIN				
Cardboard Zeppelin is a pseudonym for The Regents.				
Laurie 3433	City Lights / Ten Story Building	1968	2.00	10.00
CARDELL, NICK				
Liberty 55556	How Can I Help It? / Arlene	1963	5.00	25.00
Amcan 405	I Stand Alone / Everybody Jump	196?	4.00	20.00
CARDIGAN BROTHERS, THE				
Motion 3000	Everybody Loves A Guy Named Johnny / Say Hello	1962	2.00	10.00
Chairman 4400	I Know, I Know, I Know / Let's Go To The Movies	1962	2.00	10.00
CARDIGANS, THE				
Mercury 71251	Your Graduation Means Goodbye / Bo-Weevil On The Mountain Top	1958	3.00	15.00
Mercury 71349	It's Better That You Love / Wacky Wacky	1958	2.00	10.00
Mercury 71367	Poor Boy / Each Other	1958	2.00	10.00
Spann 6931	Make Up Your Mind / Half Breed	1959	7.00	35.00
CARDINALS, THE				
Cha-Cha 740	Tomato Juice / I Want You	1966	3.00	15.00
Cha-Cha 740 (PS)	Tomato Juice / I Want You	1966	3.00	15.00
Cha-Cha 74?	Hatchet Face / Go Go Girl	1966	4.00	25.00
Cha-Cha 748	I'm Gonna Tell On You / When You're Away	1966	3.00	15.00
CAREFREES, THE				
London Int. 10614	We Love You Beatles / Hot Blooded Lover	1964	2.00	10.00
London Int. 10614 (PS)	We Love You Beatles / Hot Blooded Lover	1964	4.00	20.00
London Int. 10615	Paddy Wack / Aren't You Glad You're You?	1964	2.00	10.00
CARI, EDDIE				
Mermaid 104	Wishing Time / This Love Of Mine	196?	2.00	10.00
CARIANS, THE				
Magenta 04	Only A Dream / Girls	1961	10.00	50.00
Indigo 136	She's Gone / Snooty Friends	1962	10.00	50.00
CARL & THE COMMANDERS				
Cameo 197	Farmer John / Cleanin' Up	1961	2.00	10.00
CARLE, BUDDY, & THE DEL VIKINGS				
Refer to The Del Vikings.				
Eedee 3501	Understand / It's Too Late	196?	2.00	10.00
CARLO				
Carlo Mastrangelo was formerly a member of The Belmonts. Refer to Carlo & Jimmy; Carlo's Crown Jewel; and Endless Pulse.				
Laurie 3151	Write Me A Letter / Baby Doll	1963	6.00	30.00
Laurie 3157	Little Orphan Doll / Mairzy Doats	1963	5.00	25.00
Laurie 3175	Story Of My Love / Five Minutes More	1963	6.00	30.00

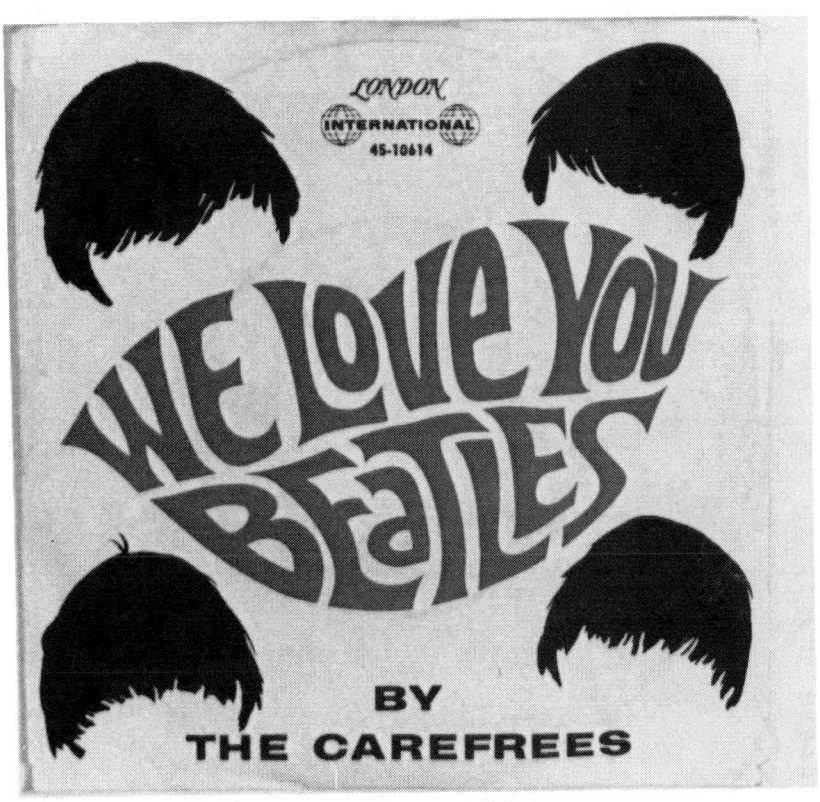

In 1964 the Beatles' haircuts were actually more recognizable in the States than were the Fab Four themselves, as witnessed on this picture sleeve, which promoted their hair, not the unidentified musicians making up the Carefrees!

Label & Catalog #		A-Side/B-Side	Year	VG	NM
Laurie 3227		Stranger In My Arms / Ring-A-Ling	1964	8.00	40.00
Raftis 110		Claudine / Fever	196?	2.00	10.00
Raftis 112		Let There Be Love /	196?	2.00	10.00
CARLO & JIMMY					
Laurie 3063		Happy Tune / Rockin' Rocket	1960	3.00	15.00
CARLO & THE SECRETS					
Thrown 801		Pony Party / 1,000 Pounds Of Potatoes	196?	3.00	15.00
CARLO'S CROWN JEWEL					
Tower 497		It's Alright / Shoo-Fly Pie And Apple Pan Dowdy	1968	1.60	8.00
CARLOS, BARRY, & THE NIGHT-CAPS					
Amber 3537		Are You Running Away? / Don't You Know?	1965	5.00	25.00
CARLOS BROTHERS, THE					
Del-Fi 4112		Come On, Let's Dance / Tonight	1959	2.00	10.00
Del-Fi 4145		It's Time To Go / La Bamba	1961	2.00	10.00
CARLYLE, ROSS					
ABC 9833		Beach Party / Der Becki	1957	3.00	15.00
CARMEL					
MGM 13869		I Can't Shake This Feeling / Let My Child Be Free	1967	2.00	10.00
MGM 13985		They Didn't Believe Me / One Day	1968	2.00	10.00
CARMEL SISTERS, THE					
The Carmel Sisters also recorded as Carol & Cheryl.					
Jubilee 5464		Joey's Comin' Home / The Rumor	1963	4.00	20.00
CARMEL COVERED POPCORN					
Vistone 2055		Suzie-Q / Looking For A Place	1968	3.00	15.00
CARMELETTES, THE					
Alpine 53		My Foolish Heart / Promise Me A Rose	1959	3.00	15.00
Alpine 61		Something Tells Me I'm In Love / Aching For You	1960	3.00	15.00
CARMEN, ERIC					
Eric Carmen also recorded with Cyrus Erie; The Quick; and The Raspberries.					
Epic 10669		It Won't Be The Same Without You / I'll Hold Out My Hand	1970		
Unreleased?					
Arista 0165		All By Myself / Everything	1975	.50	2.50
Arista 0184		Never Gonna Fall In Love Again / No Hard Feelings	1976	.50	2.50
Arista 0200		Sunrise / My Girl	1976	.50	2.50
Arista 0266		She Did It / Someday	1977	.50	2.50
Arista 0266	(PS)	She Did It / Someday	1977	.80	4.00
Arista 0295		Boats Against The Current / Take It Or Leave It	1977	.40	2.00
Arista 0319		I Think I Found Myself / Marathon Man	1978	.40	2.00
Arista 0354		Change Of Heart / Hey, Deanie	1978	.40	2.00
Arista 0384		Baby, I Need Your Loving / Heaven Can Wait	1979	.40	2.00
Arista 0435		Haven't We Come A Long Way, Baby? / End Of The World	1980	.40	2.00
Arista 0506		It Hurts Too Much / You Need Some Lovin'	1980	.40	2.00
Arista 0550		All For Love / Tonight You're Mine	1980	.40	2.00
Arista 0567		Foolin' Myself / Lost In The Shuffle	1980	.40	2.00
Geffen 29188		I Wanna Hear It From Your Lips / Spotlight	1984	.40	2.00
Geffen 29188	(PS)	I Wanna Hear It From Your Lips / Spotlight	1984	.60	3.00
Geffen 29032		I'm Through With Love / Maybe My Baby	1985	.40	2.00
Geffen 29032	(PS)	I'm Through With Love / Maybe My Baby	1985	.60	3.00
RCA Victor 5315		Hungry Eyes / Where Are You Tonight?	1987	.40	2.00
Arista 9686		Make Me Lose Control / That's Rock And Roll	1988	.40	2.00
Arista 9686	(PS)	Make Me Lose Control / That's Rock And Roll	1988	.60	3.00
Arista 9746		Reason To Cry / Sunrise	1988	.40	2.00
Arista 9746	(PS)	Reason To Cry / Sunrise	1988	.60	3.00
Cool 101		The Rock Stops Here / The Rock Stops Here	1988	1.00	5.00
Cool 101	(PS)	The Rock Stops Here / The Rock Stops Here	1988	1.25	6.00
CARMEN, TONY, & THE SPITFIRES					
The Spitfires also recorded as Tony & The Day Dreams.					
Abel 224		Don't Run To Me / Spitfire	196?	2.00	10.00
CARNABY STREET RUNNERS, THE					
Buddah 30		Live And In Person / Dom's Frantic Pandemonium	1968	.80	4.00
Super K 11		While You're Out Looking For Sugar / Makin' Love In A Tree House	1969	.80	4.00
CARNATIONS, THE					
Terry Tone 199		Sleepy Hollow / Barbary Coast	196?	6.00	30.00

Label & Catalog #		A-Side/B-Side	Year	VG	NM
CARNATIONS, THE					
Tilt 780		Scorpion / Fireball Mail	196?	3.00	15.00
Laurie 3163		Funny Time / Punctuation	1963	3.00	15.00
CARO, TONY					
Crystalette 742		Chemistry Of Love / Hard To Get	1960	2.00	10.00
CAROL & CHERYL					
Carol & Cheryl also recorded as The Carmel Sisters.					
Colpix 767		Go Go G.T.O. / Sunny Winter	1965	4.00	20.00
CARONATORS, THE					
Clock 1045		Long Hot Summer / Senorita	1960	2.00	10.00
CAROUSELS, THE					
Gone 5118		You Can Come / Pretty Little Thing	1961	6.00	30.00
Gone 5118		If You Want To / Pretty Little Thing	1961	6.00	30.00
Gone 5131		Never Let Him Go / Dirty Tricks	1962	3.00	15.00
CAROUSELS, THE					
Autumn 13		Beneath The Willow / Sail Away	1965	2.00	10.00
CARPENTER, CHRIS					
United Artists 50266		Waterfall / This World	1968	2.00	10.00
CARPENTER, KAREN					
Magic Lamp 704		I'll Be Yours / Looking For Love	196?	——	——
		(Rare. Estimated near mint value $500-1,000.)			
CARPENTER, STEVE					
Brunswick 55322		You're Putting Me On / Something Good Is Gonna Happen	196?	2.00	10.00
CARPENTER, THELMA					
Coral 62241		Yes, I'm Lonesome Tonight / Gimmie A Little Kiss	1960	2.00	10.00
CARPENTERS, THE					
Karen and Richard Carpenter.					
A&M 1142		Ticket To Ride / Your Wonderful Parade	1969	1.00	5.00
A&M 1183		(They Long To Be) Close To You / I Kept On Loving You	1970	.60	3.00
A&M 1217		We've Only Just Begun / All Of My Life	1970	.60	3.00
A&M 1217	(PS)	We've Only Just Begun / All Of My Life	1970	1.00	5.00
A&M 1236		Merry Christmas, Darling / Mr. Guder	1970	.80	4.00
A&M 1236	(PS)	Merry Christmas, Darling / Mr. Guder	1970	1.00	5.00
A&M 1243		For All We Know / Don't Be Afraid	1971	.60	3.00
A&M 1243	(PS)	For All We Know / Don't Be Afraid	1971	1.00	5.00
A&M 1260		Rainy Days And Mondays / Saturday	1971	.60	3.00
A&M 1260	(PS)	Rainy Days And Mondays / Saturday	1971	.60	3.00
A&M 1289		Superstar / Bless The Beasts And The Children	1971	.60	3.00
A&M 1289	(PS)	Superstar / Bless The Beasts And The Children	1971	.60	3.00
A&M 1322		Hurting Each Other / Maybe It's You	1972	.60	3.00
A&M 1322	(PS)	Hurting Each Other / Maybe It's You	1972	.60	3.00
A&M 1351		It's Going To Take Some Time / Flat Baroque	1972	.60	3.00
A&M 1351	(PS)	It's Going To Take Some Time / Flat Baroque	1972	.60	3.00
A&M 1367		Goodbye To Love / Crystal Lullabye	1972	.60	3.00
A&M 1367	(PS)	Goodbye To Love / Crystal Lullabye	1972	.60	3.00
A&M 1413		Sing / Druscilla Penny	1973	.60	3.00
A&M 1413	(PS)	Sing / Druscilla Penny	1973	.60	3.00
A&M 1446		Yesterday Once More / Road Ode	1973	.60	3.00
A&M 1446	(PS)	Yesterday Once More / Road Ode	1973	.60	3.00
A&M 1468		Top Of The World / Heather	1973	.60	3.00
A&M 1468	(PS)	Top Of The World / Heather	1973	.60	3.00
A&M 1521		I Won't Last A Day Without You / One Love	1974	.60	3.00
A&M 1521	(PS)	I Won't Last A Day Without You / One Love	1974	.60	3.00
A&M 1646		Please Mr. Postman / The Masquerade	1974	.60	3.00
A&M 1646	(PS)	Please Mr. Postman / The Masquerade	1974	.60	3.00
A&M 1648		Santa Claus Is Coming To Town / Merry Christmas, Darling	1974	.60	3.00
A&M 1677		Only Yesterday / Happy	1975	.60	3.00
A&M 1677	(PS)	Only Yesterday / Happy	1975	.60	3.00
A&M 1721		Solitaire / Love Me For What I Am	1975	.60	3.00
A&M 1721	(PS)	Solitaire / Love Me For What I Am	1975	.60	3.00
A&M 1800		There's A Kind Of Hush / Goodbye And I Love You	1976	.60	3.00
A&M 1800	(PS)	There's A Kind Of Hush / Goodbye And I Love You	1976	.60	3.00
A&M 1828		I Need To Be In Love / Sandy	1976	.60	3.00
A&M 1859		Boat To Sail / Goofus	1976	.60	3.00
A&M 1940		All You Get From Love Is A Love Song / I Have You	1977	.60	3.00
A&M 1940	(PS)	All You Get From Love Is A Love Song / I Have You	1977	.60	3.00
A&M 1978		Calling Occupants Of Interplanetary Craft / Can't Smile Without You	1977	.60	3.00

Label & Catalog #		A-Side/B-Side	Year	VG	NM
A&M 1991		The Christmas Song / Merry Christmas, Darling	1977	.60	3.00
A&M 1991	(PS)	The Christmas Song / Merry Christmas, Darling	1977	.60	3.00
A&M 2008		Sweet, Sweet Smile / I Have You	1978	.60	3.00
A&M 2097		I Believe You / B'wana, She No Home	1978	.60	3.00
A&M 2344		Touch Me When We're Dancing / Because We Are In Love	1981	.40	2.00
A&M 2344	(PS)	Touch Me When We're Dancing / Because We Are In Love	1981	.40	2.00
A&M 2370		Somebody's Been Lyin' / (Want You) Back In My Life Again	1981	.40	2.00
A&M 2386		Those Good Old Dreams / When It's Gone	1981	.40	2.00
A&M 2405		Beachwood 4-5789 / Two Sides	1982	.40	2.00
A&M 2585		Make Believe It's Your First Time / Look To Your Dreams	1983	.40	2.00
A&M 2585	(PS)	Make Believe It's Your First Time / Look To Your Dreams	1983	.40	2.00
A&M 2620		Your Baby Doesn't Love You Anymore / Sailing On The Tide	1984	.40	2.00

CARR, TIMOTHY

Hot Biscuit 1454		A Stop Along The Way / Let's Start All Over Again	1967	1.60	8.00

CARR, VALERIE

Roulette 4038		You're The Greatest / Over The Rainbow	1957	2.00	10.00
Roulette 4066		When The Boys Talk About The Girls / Padre	1958	2.00	10.00
Atlas 1258		Rockin' Bed / Make Someone Happy	195?	3.00	15.00

CARR, WOODY

Jerden 799		Hey Little One / Just Another Fool	196?	2.00	10.00
Piccadilly 229		I Should Have Loved You More / I Think I Love	196?	2.00	10.00
Mari 451		Cryin' Town / (B-side by Barbara McBride)	196?	2.00	10.00
Jerden 924		Peace Dance / Undecided Woman	196?	1.60	8.00

CARROLL, ANDREA

Epic 9438		I've Got A Date With Frankie / Young And Lonely	1961	4.00	20.00
Epic 9450		Please Don't Talk To The Lifeguard / Room Of Memories	1961	3.00	15.00
Epic 9523		Miss Happiness / Fifteen Shades Of Pink	1962	3.00	15.00
Big Top 3156		It Hurts To Be Sixteen / Why Am I So Shy?	1963	3.00	15.00
United Artists 50039		Hey, Beach Boy / Why Should We Take The Easy Way Out?	1963	3.00	15.00
United Artists 982		She Gets Everything She Wants / The World Isn't Big Enough	1966	2.00	10.00

CARROLL, BERNADETTE

Julia 1106		My Heart Stood Still / Sweet Sugar Sweet	1962	2.00	10.00
Laurie 3217		All The Way Home I Cried / Nicky	1963	2.00	10.00
Laurie 3238		Party Girl / I Don't Wanna Know	1964	2.00	10.00
Laurie 3278		One Little Lie / The Hero	1964	2.00	10.00

CARROLL, BOB

Bally 1028		Butterfly / Look What You've Done To Me	1957	3.00	15.00

CARROLL, CATHY (& THE EARLS)

Triodex 11		Jimmy Love / Deep In A Young Boys Heart	1961	3.00	15.00
Warner Bros. 5284		Poor Little Puppet / Love And Learn	1962	2.00	10.00

CARROLL, JIMMY

Fascination 2000		Big Green Car /	195?	10.00	50.00
Carousel 44		Angelina / Anita	1959	3.00	15.00
Carousel 44	(S)	Angelina / Anita	1959	5.00	25.00

CARROLL, JOHNNY

Decca 29940		Rock 'N Roll Ruby / Trying To Get To You	1956	7.00	35.00
Decca 29941		Wild, Wild Women / Corrine, Corrina	1956	7.00	35.00

CARROLL, JOHNNY, & THE HOT RODS

Decca 30013		Hot Rock / Crazy, Crazy Lovin'	1956	7.00	35.00

CARROL, LINDA, & THE YOUNG MEN

Camelot 113		I Wanna Go Home / Love Is A Strange Thing	196?	1.00	5.00

CARROLL, PETE

Pete Carroll recorded with The Carroll Brothers.

Cameo 279		You're A Dog / Fiasco	1963	2.00	10.00

CARROLL, RONNIE

Philips 40110		Say Wonderful Things / Please Tell Me Your Name	1963	2.00	10.00

CARROLL, WAYNE

Domain 1018		Cindy Lee / Chicken Out	1957	5.00	25.00

CARROLL, YVONNE

Domain 1018		Gee, What A Guy / Stuck On You	1963	2.00	10.00

Label & Catalog #		A-Side/B-Side	Year	VG	NM
CARROLL BROTHERS, THE					
The Carroll Brothers feature Pete Carroll.					
Felsted 8550		I Found You / Movin' Day	1959	3.00	15.00
Cameo 140		(My Gal Is) Red Hot / Dearly Beloved	1961	10.00	50.00
Cameo 213		Don't Knock The Twist / Bo Diddley	1962	2.00	10.00
Cameo 221		Sweet Georgia Brown / Boot It	1962	2.00	10.00
CARS, THE					
Elektra 45537		My Best Friend's Girl / Don't Cha Stop	1978	.40	2.00
Elektra 45491	(DJ)	Just What I Needed / Just What I Needed (Red vinyl)	1978	.80	4.00
Elektra 45491		Just What I Needed / I'm In Touch With Your World	1978	.40	2.00
Elektra 45491	(PS)	Just What I Needed / I'm In Touch With Your World	1978	.40	2.00
Elektra 46014		Good Times Roll / All Mixed Up	1979	.40	2.00
Elektra 46063		Let's Go / That's It	1979	.40	2.00
Elektra 46546		It's All I Can Do / Got A Lot On My Mind	1979	.40	2.00
Elektra 46546	(PS)	It's All I Can Do / Got A Lot On My Mind	1979	.40	2.00
Elektra 46580		Double Life / Candy-O	1979	.40	2.00
Elektra 47039		Touch And Go / Down Boys	1980	.40	2.00
Elektra 47080		Don't Tell Me No / Don't Go To Pieces	1980	.40	2.00
Elektra 47101		Gimme Some Slack / Don't Go To Pieces	1981	.40	2.00
Elektra 47250		Shake It Up / Cruiser	1981	.40	2.00
Elektra 47250	(PS)	Shake It Up / Cruiser	1981	.40	2.00
Elektra 47433		Since You're Gone / Think It Over	1982	.40	2.00
Elektra 47433	(PS)	Since You're Gone / Think It Over	1982	.40	2.00
CARSON, DON, & THE WHIRLAWAYS					
Crest 1051		Three Carburetors / Smoke Smoke Smoke	1960	2.00	10.00
CARTER, DEAN					
Milky Way 004		Care / The Rockin' Bandit	1966	3.00	15.00
Milky Way		Jailhouse Rock / Rebel Woman	1966	8.00	40.00
CARTOON CANDY CARNIVAL, THE					
Metromedia 105		Everything Is Mickey Mouse / Mickey Mouse Concerto In B Flat	1969	1.00	5.00
CARTOONE					
Atlantic 2598		Mr. Poor Man / Knick Knack Man	1969	.80	4.00
Atlantic 2630		Reflections On A Common Theme / A Penny For The Sun	1970	.60	3.00
CARTOONS, THE					
Tuba 20006		Big Bad Batusi / Batusi	1966	2.00	10.00
CARTRIDGE, FLIP					
Parrot 306		Don't Take The Lovers From The World / Dear Mrs. Applebee	1966	.80	4.00
CARTWRIGHT, DOTTI					
Orbit 112		I'm Gonna Tell You Goodbye / Love Can't Stay Alive This Way	196?	1.00	5.00
CARTY, RIC					
Stars 539		Oooh-Eee / Young Love	1956	25.00	125.00
RCA Victor 47-6751		Oooh-Eee / Young Love	1956	5.00	25.00
CARUSO, DICK					
MGM 12811		Blue Denim / I'll Tell You In This Song	1959	2.00	10.00
MGM 12827		Teenagers Blues / Playing The Field	1959	2.00	10.00
MGM 12852		If I / Dee De Dum	1960	8.00	40.00
CARVELS, THE					
Twirl 2022		Seventeen / Don't Let Him Know	1966	2.00	10.00
CASCADE SWEETHEARTS, THE					
Garland 2016		Taxi Man / Tippy Toeing	196?	2.00	10.00
CASCADES, THE					
Valiant 6021		There's A Reason / Second Chance	1962	2.00	10.00
Valiant 6026		Rhythm Of The Rain / Let Me Be	1962	2.00	10.00
Valiant 6028		Shy Girl / The Last Leaf	1963	2.00	10.00
Valiant 6032		I Wanna Be Your Lover / My First Day Alone	1963	2.00	10.00
RCA Victor 47-8206		A Little Like Lovin' / Cinderella	1963	1.60	8.00
RCA Victor 47-8206	(PS)	A Little Like Lovin' / Cinderella	1963	3.00	15.00
RCA Victor 47-8268		For Your Sweet Love / Jeannie	1963	1.60	8.00
RCA Victor 47-8321		Little Bitty Falling Star / Those Were The Good Old Days	1964	1.60	8.00
RCA Victor 47-8402		I Dare You To Try / Awake	1964	1.60	8.00
Charter 1018		She Was Really Never Mine (To Lose) / My Best Girl	1964	2.00	10.00
Charter 1018		She Was Never Mine (To Lose) / My Best Girl	1964	1.00	5.00

Label & Catalog #	A-Side/B-Side	Year	VG	NM
Liberty 55822	I Bet You Won't Stay / She's In Love Again	1965	1.00	5.00
Arwin 132	Cheryl's Goin' Home / Truly Julie's Blues	1966	1.20	6.00
Arwin 134	All's Fair In Love And War / Midnight Lace	1966	1.20	6.00
Smash 2083	Hey, Little Girl Of Mine / Blue Hours	1967	1.00	5.00
Smash 2101	Flying On The Ground / Main Street	1967	1.00	5.00
Probe 543	Everyone Is Blossoming / Two Sided Man	1968	.80	4.00
Uni 55152	Maybe The Rain Will Fall / Naggin' Cries	1969	.80	4.00
Uni 55169	Big City Country Boy / Indian River	1969	.80	4.00
Uni 55200	But For Love / Hazel Autumn Cocoa Brown	1970	.80	4.00
Uni 55231	April, May, June And July / Big Ugly Sky	1970	.80	4.00
Can-Base 714	Sweet America / I Started A Joke	1972	.60	3.00
London 177	Two Sided Man / The Woman's A Girl	1972	.60	3.00
Renee 105	Pains In My Heart / One That I Can Spare	197?	.60	3.00

CASCADES, THE

Label & Catalog #	A-Side/B-Side	Year	VG	NM
MRC 1018	My Best Girl / She Was Never Mine (To Lose)	1964	7.00	35.00
Charter 1018	My Best Girl / She Was Never Mine (To Lose)	1964	5.00	25.00

CASE, SCOTT RICHARD
Scott Case also recorded as SRC.

Label & Catalog #	A-Side/B-Side	Year	VG	NM
A-Squared 301	I'm So Glad / Who Is That Girl?	196?	5.00	25.00

CASEY, AL (& THE K-C ETTES)
Contrary to popular assumption, The Honeys deny having recorded with Casey as The KC-Ettes. Refer to Dunae Eddy.

Label & Catalog #	A-Side/B-Side	Year	VG	NM
United Artists 158	Keep Talking / The Stinger	1959	3.00	15.00
Highland 1004	Night Beat / The Stinger	1960	3.00	15.00
Challenge 59086	Cocoanut Grove / Alley Cat	1960	3.00	15.00
Stacy 925	Cookin' / Hot Foot	1962	2.00	10.00
Stacy 936	Jivin' Around / Doin' The Shotish	1962	2.00	10.00
Stacy 950	Chicken Feathers / Laughin'	1963	2.00	10.00
Stacy 956	Doin' It / Monte Carlo	1963	2.00	10.00
Stacy 961	Fun House / Indian Love Call	1963	2.00	10.00
Stacy 962	Surfin' Hootenanny / Easy Pickin'	1963	3.00	15.00
Stacy 962	Surfin' Hootenanny / Easy Pickin' *(Red vinyl)*	1963	6.00	30.00
Stacy 964	Surfin' Blues / Guitars, Guitars, Guitars	1963	2.00	10.00
Stacy 971	Cookin' / What Are We Gonna Do In '64?	1964	2.00	10.00

CASH, EDDIE, & THE CASHIERS

Label & Catalog #	A-Side/B-Side	Year	VG	NM
Peak 1001	Land Of Promises / Doing All Right	1958	35.00	175.00

CASH, JOHNNY (& THE TENNESSEE TWO)
Johnny Cash's Sun recordings were fairly unadorned country, making few real concessions to the rock 'n roll market. Since his move to Columbia in 1958, he has enjoyed three decades of success, producing a body of work that has made him an American music standard who has placed over two dozen records on the Top 100.

Label & Catalog #	A-Side/B-Side	Year	VG	NM
Sun 221	Hey, Porter / Cry! Cry! Cry!	1956	5.00	25.00
Sun 232	Folsom Prison Blues / So Doggone Lonesome	1956	4.00	20.00
Sun 241	I Walk The Line / Get Rhythm	1956	4.00	20.00
Sun 258	Train Of Love / There You Go	1956	3.00	15.00
Sun 266	Next In Line / Don't Make Me Go	1957	3.00	15.00
Sun 279	Home Of The Blues / Give My Love To Rose	1957	3.00	15.00
Sun 283	Ballad Of A Teenage Queen / Big River	1958	3.00	15.00
Sun 295	Guess Things Happen That Way / Come In, Stranger	1958	3.00	15.00
Sun 295 (PS)	Guess Things Happen That Way / Come In, Stranger	1958	5.00	25.00
Sun 302	The Ways Of A Woman In Love / You're The Nearest Thing To Heaven	1958	2.00	10.00
Sun 309	It's Just About Time / I Just Thought You'd Like To Know	1958	2.00	10.00
Sun 316	Thanks A Lot / Luther Played The Boogie	1959	2.00	10.00
Sun 321	Katy, Too / I Forgot To Remember To Forget	1959	2.00	10.00
Sun 331	Goodbye, Little Darling / You Tell Me	1959	2.00	10.00
Sun 334	Straight A's In Love / I Love You Because	1960	2.00	10.00
Sun 343	Down The Street To 301 / The Story Of A Broken Heart	1960	2.00	10.00
Sun 347	Mean Eyed Cat / Port Of Lonely Hearts	1960	2.00	10.00
Sun 355	Oh, Lonesome Me / Life Goes On	1960	2.00	10.00
Sun 363	My Treasure / Sugar Time	1961	2.00	10.00
Sun 376	Blue Train / Born To Lose	1962	2.00	10.00
Sun 392	Wide Open Road / Belshazar	1964	2.00	10.00
Sun 1103	Get Rhythm / Hey, Porter	1969	.60	3.00
Sun 1111	Rock Island Line / Next In Line	1969	.60	3.00
Sun 1121	Big River / Come In, Stranger	1969	.60	3.00
	—Extended Play Albums—			
Sun 111	Johnny Cash Sings Hank Williams	1956	10.00	50.00
Sun 112	Johnny Cash	1956	10.00	50.00
Sun 113	I Walk The Line	1956	10.00	50.00
Sun 114	Johnny Cash: His Top Hits	1957	10.00	50.00
Sun 116	Home Of The Blues	1957	10.00	50.00
Sun 117	Johnny Cash	1958	10.00	50.00

Label & Catalog #	A-Side/B-Side	Year	VG	NM
CASHMERES, THE				
Laurie 3078	A Very Special Birthday / I Believe In St. Nick	1960	5.00	25.00
Laurie 3088	I Gotta Go / Singing Waters	1961	3.00	15.00
Laurie 3105	Poppa Said / Life Line	1961	3.00	15.00
Lake 703	Everything's Gonna Be Alright / Four Lonely Nights	1961	3.00	15.00
CASINOS, THE				
Itzy 2	Do You Recall? / The Suns	196?	6.00	30.00
CASINOS, THE				
Terry 115	Gee Whiz / Lovely One	1964	3.00	15.00
Terry 116	Too Good To Be True / That's The Way	1964	3.00	15.00
Fraternity 306	Moon River / Soul Serenade	1966	1.20	6.00
Fraternity 944	Right There Beside You / The Gallop	1965	1.20	6.00
Fraternity 949	She's Out Of Sight / The Gallop	1965	1.20	6.00
Fraternity 977	Then You Can Tell Me Goodbye / I Still Love You	1967	1.60	8.00
Fraternity 985	It's All Over Now / Tailor Made	1967	1.20	6.00
Fraternity 987	Forever And A Night / How Long Has It Been?	1967	1.20	6.00
Fraternity 995	Please Love Me / When I Stop Dreaming	1967	1.20	6.00
Fraternity 1020	Those Are The Things We'll Share / Casinos Having Fun	1969	1.20	6.00
Airtown 886	Too Good To Be True / That's The Way	1967	2.00	10.00
United Artists 50255	Here I Am / Peggy	1968	1.00	5.00
United Artists 50313	Leavin' Makes The Rain Come Down / Nobody's Child	1968	1.00	5.00
Fraternity 1250	Loving Her Was Easier / A Restless Wind	1971	1.00	5.00
Million 13	The Angels Are All Asleep / I'm Walking Behind You	1972	.80	4.00
CASLONS, THE				
Seeco 6078	Anniversary Of Love / The Quiet One	1961	3.00	15.00
Amy 836	For All We Know / Settle Me Down	1962	4.00	20.00
CASSIDY, DAVID				
David Cassidy also recorded with The Partridge Family.				
Bell 45150	Cherish / All I Wanna Do Is Touch You	1972	.80	4.00
Bell 45150 (PS)	Cherish / All I Wanna Do Is Touch You	1972	1.00	5.00
Bell 45187	Could It Be Forever? / Blind Hope	1972	.80	4.00
Bell 45187 (PS)	Could It Be Forever? / Blind Hope	1972	1.00	5.00
Bell 45220	How Can I Be Sure? / Ricky's Tune	1972	.80	4.00
Bell 45260	Rock Me, Baby / Two Time Loser	1972	.80	4.00
Bell 45386	Daydream / Can't Go Home Again	1973	.80	4.00
Bell 45413	Daydreamer / The Puppy Song	1973	.80	4.00
Bell 45605	Please Please Me / Breaking Up Is Hard To Do	1974	.80	4.00
RCA Victor PB-10321	Get It Up For Love / Love In Bloom	1975	1.60	8.00
RCA Victor PB-10405	Darlin' / This Could Be The Night	1975	3.00	1500
RCA Victor PB-10585	Bedtime / Tomorrow	1976	1.60	8.00
RCA Victor PB-10647	On Fire / Breakin' Down Again	1976	1.60	8.00
	(RCA 10321-10647 were produced by Bruce Johnston.)			
RCA Victor PB-10788	Gettin' It In The Street / I'll Have To Go Away (Saying Goodbye)	1977	1.60	8.00
RCA Victor PB-10921	Rosa's Cantina / Saying Goodbye Ain't Easy (We'll Have To Go Away)	1977	.60	3.00
MCA 41101	Hurt So Bad / Once A Fool	1979	.80	4.00
MCA 41101 (PS)	Hurt So Bad / Once A Fool	1979	1.20	6.00
Enigma 334 (DJ)	Lyin' To Myself *(Picture disc)*	1990	.80	4.00
CASSIDY, DAVID, & TODD RUNDGREN & UTOPIA				
Warner Bros. 49640 (DJ)	So Sad About Us / So Sad About Us	1980	1.00	5.00
	(Stock copies of Warner Bros. 49640 may not exist.)			
CASTALEERS, THE				
Felsted 8504	Come Back / Hi Fi Baby	1957	3.00	15.00
Felsted 8512	My Bull Fightin' Baby / Lonely Boy	1958	3.00	15.00
Felsted 8585	You're My Dream / I'll Be Around	1959	3.00	15.00
Planet 44	That's Why I Cry / My Baby's All Right	1961	5.00	25.00
Donna 1349	That's Why I Cry / My Baby's All Right	1961	3.00	15.00
CASTAWAYS, THE				
Assault 1870	I Found You / Hey, There	195?	4.00	20.00
CASTAWAYS, THE				
Bear 2000	(I) Feel So Fine / Hit The Road, Jack	1965	4.00	20.00
Soma 1433	Liar, Liar / Sam	1965	2.00	10.00
Soma 1442	Goodbye Babe / A Man's Gotta Be A Man	1965	2.00	10.00
CASTAWAYS, THE				
Fontana 1615	Walking In Different Circles / Just On High	1966	1.00	5.00
Fontana 1626	What Kind Of Face? / Lavender Popcorn	1968	1.00	5.00

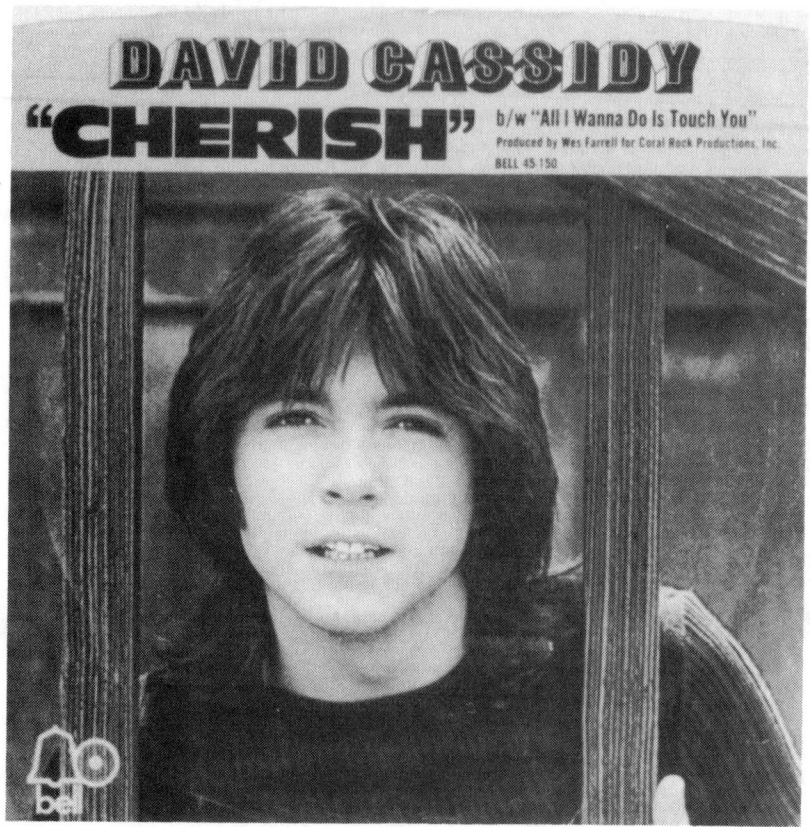

The main fantasy squeeze of millions of post (?) pubescent females in the early '70s (from whence this sleeve), it is David's later work — especially a series of singles on RCA Victor produced by Bruce Johnston — that command the most attention from collectors.

Label & Catalog #	A-Side/B-Side	Year	VG	NM
CASTELLS, THE				
The Castells feature Chuck Girard.				
Era 3038	Little Sad Eyes / Romeo	1961	2.00	10.00
Era 3048	Sacred / Dreamy	1961	2.00	10.00
Era 3057	Make Believe Wedding / My Miracle	1961	2.00	10.00
Era 3064	The Vision Of You / Stiki De Boom Boom	1961	2.00	10.00
Era 3073	So This Is Love / On The Street Of Tears	1962	2.00	10.00
Era 3083	Oh, What It Seemed To Be / Stand There, Mountain	1962	2.00	10.00
Era 3089	Echoes In The Night / Only One	1962	2.00	10.00
Era 3098	Eternal Love, Eternal Spring / Clown Prince	1962	2.00	10.00
Era 3102	Initials / Little Sad Eyes	1963	2.00	10.00
Era 3107	What Do Little Girls Dream Of? / Some Enchanted Evening	1963	2.00	10.00
Warner Bros. 5421	I Do / Teardrops	1964	10.00	50.00
	("I Do" was written and produced by Brian Wilson.)			
Warner Bros. 5445	Could This Be Magic? / Shinny Up Your Own Side	1964	2.00	10.00
Warner Bros. 5486	Love Finds A Way / Tell Her If I Could	1964	2.00	10.00
Decca 31834	Just Walk Away / An Angel Cried	1965	2.00	10.00
Decca 31967	Life Goes On / I Thought You'd Like That	1966	2.00	10.00
CASTELLS, THE				
United Artists 50324	Two Lovers / Jerusalem	1967	1.20	6.00
Laurie 3444	Rocky Ridges / I'd Like To Know	1968	1.20	6.00
CASTLE, JOEY, & THE DADDY-O'S				
Headline 1008	Rock And Roll Daddy-O / Wild Love	1959	100.00	400.00
CASTLE, TONY (& THE RAIDERS)				
Gone 5099	Salty / Hi Lili, Hi Lo	1961	2.00	10.00
Gone 5099	Salty / Salty, Part 2	1961	2.00	10.00
Gone 5105	Sincerely / Tara's Theme	1961	1.60	8.00
Gone 5107	Seems Like Old Times / The Loneliest Girl In The World	1961	1.60	8.00
CASTLE KINGS, THE				
The Castle Kings were produced by Phil Spector.				
Atlantic 2107	You Can Get Him Frankenstein / Loch Lomond	1961	5.00	25.00
CASTLE SISTERS, THE				
Roulette 4220	Will You Love Me Tomorrow? / Thirteen	1960	2.00	10.00
Terrace 7506	Wishing Star / Goodbye, Dad	1962	2.00	10.00
Terrace 7506 (PS)	Wishing Star / Goodbye, Dad	1962	3.00	15.00
CASTLE TONES, THE				
Fire Fly 321	We Met At A Dance / At The Hot Dog Stand	196?	2.00	10.00
CASTLEMEN, THE				
Blue 100	Little Dab / Blue Illusion	196?	2.00	10.00
CASTRO, FRANKIE				
Wing 90051	Steamboat / Why, Baby, Why?	1956	2.00	10.00
CASTRO, VINCE				
Doe 102	Bong Bong (I Love You Madly) / You're My Girl	1958	5.00	25.00
Apt 25007	Bong Bong (I Love You Madly) / You're My Girl	1958	4.00	20.00
Apt 25025	'Cause I Love You / Too Proud To Cry	1958	4.00	20.00
Apt 25047	You're My Girl / Bongo Twist	1959	4.00	20.00
CASUAL THREE, THE				
The Casual Three feature Dickie Goodman.				
Luniverse 109	Invisible Thing / Some Other Fellow	1958	5.00	25.00
CASUAL TONES, THE				
Library 763	Brand "X" / Stackin' Books	196?	2.00	10.00
CASUALAIRS, THE				
Mona Lee 136	At The Dance / Satisfied	195?	6.00	30.00
Craig 5001	Cruising / Bossa Nova Twist	195?	7.00	35.00
CASUALEERS, THE				
Laurie 3407	Open Your Eyes / You Better Be Sure	1968	2.00	10.00
Laurie 3441	Come Back To My Arms / When I'm In Your Arms	1968	2.00	10.00
CASUALS, THE				
Dot 15557	My Love Song For You / Somebody Help Me	1957	3.00	15.00
Dot 15671	Till You Come Back To Me / Hello Love	1958	3.00	15.00
CASUALS, THE				
Sound Stage 7 2534	Mustang 2+2 / Play Me A Sad Song	1964	2.00	10.00
Minaret 109	Money / Big Hammer	196?	2.00	10.00

Label & Catalog #	A-Side/B-Side	Year	VG	NM
CASUALS, THE: *Refer to* THE ORIGINAL CASUALS				
CASULTARS, THE				
Autumn 21	Just For You / This Is A Mean World	1965	1.00	5.00
CASWELL, JOHNNY				
Smash 1833	At The Shore / Gotta Dance	1963	2.00	10.00
Smash 1879	My Girl / Hot Dogs	1963	3.00	15.00
CAT				
RCA Victor 74-0279	Looking Through A Glass Darkly / Light Of Love	1969	.40	2.00
CAT MOTHER & THE ALL-NIGHT NEWSBOYS				
Polydor 14002	Good Old Rock And Roll / Bad News	1969	.40	2.00
Polydor 14007	Can You Dance To It? / Marie	1969	.40	2.00
CATALANO, VINNY				
Hammer 6312	Please, Mr. Juke Box Man / Rags To Riches	196?	2.00	10.00
CATALINAS, THE				
Little 811/2	Castle Of Love / Give Me Your Love	195?	15.00	75.00
CATALINAS, THE				
Rita 1006	Ring Of Stars / Woolie Woolie Willie	1960	2.00	10.00
CATALINAS, THE				
Dee Jay 1010	Bail Out / Bulletin	1963	8.00	40.00
Sims 134	Bail Out / Bulletin	1963	3.00	15.00
20th Century Fox 299	Safari / Pretty Little Nashville Girl	1964	6.00	30.00
Ric 113	Banzai Washout / Beach Walkin'	1964	5.00	25.00
Ric 164	Surfer Boy / Boss Barracuda	1965	5.00	25.00
	(Both Ric singles feature Bruce Johnston.)			
CATALINAS, THE				
Scepter 12188	Tick Tock / You Haven't The Right	1967	2.00	10.00
CATALINAS, THE: *Refer to* VIC & THE CATALINAS				
CATERPILLARS, THE				
Port 70038	The Caterpillar Song / Hello, Happy Happy Goodbye	1964	1.20	6.00
CATES, RONNIE, & THE TRAVELLERS				
Terrace 7501	Old Man River / Long Time	1961	6.00	30.00
CATHY & JOE				
Smash 1929	I See You / It's All Over Now	1964	2.00	10.00
Smash 1959	Bye Bye Love / A Day At A Time	1965	2.00	10.00
CATHY JEAN & THE ROOMATES [CATHY JEAN]				
Valmor 007	Please Love Me Forever / Canadian Sunset	1961	3.00	15.00
Valmor 009	Make Me Smile Again / Sugar Cake	1961	4.00	20.00
Valmor 011	I Only Want You / Only Love	1961	3.00	15.00
Valmor 016	Please Tell Me / Sugar Cake	1962	3.00	15.00
Philips 40014	Believe Me / Double Trouble	1962	3.00	15.00
Philips 40106	My Heart Belongs To Only You / I Only Want You	1963	3.00	15.00
Philips 40143	Believe Me / Double Trouble	1963	3.00	15.00
	(Philips 40106 and 40143 credit Cathy Jean.)			
CAUTIONS, THE				
Ikon 113/4	Surfin' Beach / Groovin'	196?	7.00	35.00
CAVALIERE, FELIX				
Felix Cavaliere originally recorded with The Young Rascals.				
Bearsville 0300	High Price To Pay / Mountain Men	1974	.50	2.50
Bearsville 0302	Everlasting Rain / Future Train	1974	.50	2.50
Bearsville 0305	Never Felt Love Before / Love Came	1975	.50	2.50
Epic 50785	Castles In The Air / Outside Your Window	1980	.40	2.00
Epic 50829	Only A Lonely Heart Sees / You Turned Me Around	1980	.40	2.00
Epic 50880	Dancin' The Night Away / Good To Have Love Back	1980	.40	2.00
CAVALIERS, THE				
Galena 1277	Blowin' Smoke / Ten More Miles	1962	2.00	10.00
CAVELL, MARC, & THE CLASS MATES				
Candix 329	I Didn't Lie / I See It	1962	6.00	30.00
CAVELLO, JIMMY, & HIS HOUSE ROCKERS				
Coral 61689	Soda Shoppe Rock / That's The Groovy Thing	1956	4.00	20.00

Label & Catalog #		A-Side/B-Side	Year	VG	NM
Coral 61728		Rock Rock Rock / The Big Beat	1956	5.00	25.00
Coral 61787		Oooh-Wee / Foot Stompin'	1957	4.00	20.00
CELEBRATION					
Celebration features Mike Love.					
MCA 40891	(DJ)	Almost Summer (KRTH Version) / Almost Summer	1978	1.20	6.00
MCA 40891	(DJ)	Almost Summer / Lookin' Good	1978	1.00	5.00
MCA 40891		Almost Summer / Lookin' Good	1978	.60	3.00
		("Almost Summer" features Brian Wilson.)			
MCA 40930		Summer In The City / Island Girl	1978	.80	4.00
Pacific Arts 105		Gettin' Hungry / Starbaby	1979	2.00	10.00
CELEBRITIES, THE					
Music Makers 101		I Want You / Mambo Daddy	1961	5.00	25.00
CELESTIALS, THE: *Refer to* **BOBBY GEE & THE CELESTIALS**					
CELLIS, RONNIE, & HIS CONTINENTALS					
Valmor 067		Chicken / My Love Is Haunted	196?	2.00	10.00
CENTRAL NERVOUS SYSTEM, THE					
The Central Nervous System features Nicky Addeo.					
Laurie 3446		Alice In Wonderland / Something Happened To Me	1968	2.00	10.00
Laurie 3421		It Takes All Kinds / I'm Still Hung Up On You	1968	2.00	10.00
CENTURIES, THE					
Cleopatra 2	(DJ)	The Outer Limits / Polynesian Paradise (Red vinyl)	1963	6.00	30.00
Cleopatra 2		The Outer Limits / Polynesian Paradise (Black vinyl)	1963	3.00	15.00
Cleopatra 3		Fourth Dimension / Jack 23	1964	5.00	25.00
CENTURIES, THE					
The Centuries later recorded as The Buckinghams.					
SpectraSound 641		It's Alright / I Love You No More	196?	10.00	50.00
CENTURYS, THE					
Bangar 00638		Lonely Heart / Man With The Golden Arm	196?	2.00	10.00
CEPTORS, THE					
Panorama 1001		I Can't Take It / I Need Her	1967	1.60	8.00
CERF, CHRIS					
MGM 13103		The Cheerleader / In The Middle Of The Night	1962	1.20	6.00
CHAD & JEREMY					
Chad Stuart and Jeremy Clyde. Refer to California Music.					
World Artists 1021		Yesterday's Gone / Lemon Tree	1964	1.20	6.00
World Artists 1027		A Summer Song / No Tears For Johnny	1964	1.20	6.00
World Artists 1034		Willow Weep For Me / If She Was Mine	1964	1.20	6.00
World Artists 1034	(PS)	Willow Weep For Me / If She Was Mine	1964	2.00	10.00
World Artists 1041		If I Loved You / Dona Donna	1965	1.00	5.00
World Artists 1041	(PS)	If I Loved You / Dona Donna	1965	2.00	10.00
World Artists 1052		What Do You Want With Me? / A Very Good Year	1965	1.00	5.00
World Artists 1056		From A Window / My Colouring Book	1965	1.00	5.00
World Artists 1060		September In The Rain / Only For The Young	1965	1.00	5.00
Columbia 43277	(DJ)	Before And After / Fare Thee Well (Red vinyl)	1965	3.00	15.00
Columbia 43277		Before And After / Fare Thee Well	1965	1.00	5.00
Columbia 43277	(PS)	Before And After / Fare Thee Well	1965	2.00	10.00
Columbia 43339		I Don't Wanna Lose You, Baby / Pennies	1965	1.00	5.00
Columbia 43339	(PS)	I Don't Wanna Lose You, Baby / Pennies	1965	2.00	10.00
Columbia 43414		I Have Dreamed / Should I?	1965	1.00	5.00
Columbia 43414	(PS)	I Have Dreamed / Should I?	1965	2.00	10.00
Columbia 43490		Teenage Failure / Early Morning Rain	1966	1.00	5.00
Columbia 43490	(PS)	Teenage Failure / Early Morning Rain	1966	2.00	10.00
Columbia 43682		Distant Shores / Last Night	1966	1.00	5.00
Columbia 43682	(PS)	Distant Shores / Last Night	1966	2.00	10.00
Columbia 43807		You Are She / I Won't Cry	1966	1.00	5.00
Columbia 43807	(PS)	You Are She / I Won't Cry	1966	2.00	10.00
Columbia 44379		Painted Dayglow Smile / Editorial	1967	1.00	5.00
Columbia 44525		Rest In Peace / Sister Marie	1967	1.00	5.00
Columbia 44660	(PS)	Paxton Quigley's Had The Course (Promo)	1967	3.00	15.00
		(Promo picture sleeve depicts a Nazi militray rally.)			
Columbia 44660		Paxton Quigley's Had The Course / You Need Feet	1967	1.00	5.00
		(Columbia 44379, 44525 and 44660 were produced by Gary Usher.)			
Rocshire 9505		Bite The Bullet / Interview	1983	.60	3.00
CHADONS, THE					
Chattahoochee 643		All I Do Is Dream Of You / We're In Love	1964	2.00	10.00
Chattahoochee 664		Start All Over Again / It's A Crying Shame	1965	2.00	10.00

Label & Catalog #	A-Side / B-Side	Year	VG	NM
CHAFFIN, ERNIE				
Sun 262	Lonesome For My Baby / Feelin' Low	1957	4.00	20.00
Sun 275	I'm Lonesome / Laughin' And Jokin'	1957	3.00	15.00
Sun 307	My Love For You / Born To Lose	1958	3.00	15.00
Sun 320	Don't Ever Leave Me / Miracle Of You	1959	3.00	15.00
CHAIN REACTION				
Earl 1003	Chain Reaction / Sometimes I Think About	196?	2.00	10.00
CHAINS, THE				
HBR 460	Carol's Got A Cobra / I Hate To See You Crying	1966	3.00	15.00
CHALETS, THE				
Tru-Lite 1001	Who's Laughing, Who's Crying? / Fat Fat Fat Mom-Mi-O	1961	5.00	25.00
Dart 1026	Who's Laughing, Who's Crying? / Fat Fat Fat Mom-Mi-O	1961	3.00	15.00
Musicnote 1001	Who's Laughing, Who's Crying? / Fat Fat Fat Mom-Mi-O	1961	2.00	10.00
CHALLENGERS, THE				
Tri Phi 1020	Every Day / I Hear An Echo	1962	3.00	15.00
Tri Phi 1012	Stay With Me / Honey, Honey, Honey	1962	3.00	15.00
Challenge 1105	The Butterfly / Who Shot The Hole In My Sombrero?	1962	3.00	15.00
CHALLENGERS, THE				
The Challengers also recorded as The Clee Shays and The Good Guys.				
Vault 900	Torquay / Bulldog	1963	2.00	10.00
Vault 902	Moondog / Tidal Wave	1963	2.00	10.00
Vault 904	Foot Tapper / On The Move	1963	2.00	10.00
Vault 910	Hot Rod Hootenanny / Maybellene	1964	2.00	10.00
Vault 913	K-39 / Hot Rod Show	1964	2.00	10.00
Vault 918	Channel Nine / Can't Seem To Get Over You	1965	2.00	10.00
Vault 1075	Wipe Out / One-Oh Seven Five Dash	1965	3.00	15.00
Princess 53	Mr. Moto '65 / Chieflado	1965	3.00	15.00
	(Princess 53 was also released credited to The Spartans.)			
Princess 55	Pipeline / Come Right Back To Me	1965	4.00	20.00
Dot 16757	You Can't Sit Down / (B-side by the Surfaris)	1965	7.00	35.00
Triumph 55	Atlantis / Steve's Tune	1965	3.00	15.00
Triumph 64	The Dating Game / The Dating Game, Part 2	1965	3.00	15.00
Triumph 1/2 (DJ)	Pipeline / Asphalt Spinner	1965	4.00	20.00
GNP/Crescendo 362	The Man From U.N.C.L.E. / The Streets Of London	1966	1.20	6.00
GNP/Crescendo 362	The Man From U.N.C.L.E. / Summer Nights	1966	1.20	6.00
GNP/Crescendo 368	Walk With Me / How Could I?	1966	1.20	6.00
GNP/Crescendo 376	Wipeout / North Beach	1966	1.20	6.00
GNP/Crescendo 380	Milord / What If It Should Rain?	1966	1.00	5.00
GNP/Crescendo 396	The Water Country / Everything To Me	1968	1.00	5.00
GNP/Crescendo 400	Color Me In / Before You	196?	1.00	5.00
GNP/Crescendo 412	Chitty Chitty Bang Bang / Lonely Little Girl	1969	1.00	5.00
CHALLENGERS, THE				
Triodex 107	Deadline / Cry Of The Goose	1964	1.00	5.00
Triodex 102	Goofus / Lazy Twist	1964	2.00	10.00
CHAMBERMEN, THE				
Chambermen 1292	Louie Go Home / Midnight Hour	196?	2.00	10.00
CHAMP, BILLY				
ABC-Paramount 10518	Hush-A-Bye / Believe Me	1964	3.00	15.00
CHAMPAGNES, THE				
Skymac 1002	Cash / Crazy	1963	3.00	15.00
Laurie 3189	Cash / Crazy	1963	2.00	10.00
CHAMPS, THE				
The original Champs were Glen Aldin, Dave Burgess, Bob Morris, Dale Norris and Chuck Rio. Later members included Glen Campbell, Dash Crofts and Jimmy Seals. Refer to Dave Burgess.				
Challenge 1016	Tequila / Train To Nowhere	1958	4.00	20.00
Challenge 59007	El Rancho Rock / Midnighter	1958	3.00	15.00
Challenge 59018	Chariot Rock / Subway	1958	3.00	15.00
Challenge 59026	Rockin' Mary / Turnpike	1958	3.00	15.00
Challenge 59035	Gone Train / Beatnik	1959	3.00	15.00
Challenge 59043	Caramba! / Moonlight Bay	1959	3.00	15.00
Challenge 59049	Night Train / The Rattler	1959	3.00	15.00
Challenge 59053	Double Eagle Rock / Sky High	1959	3.00	15.00
Challenge 59063	Too Much Tequila / Twenty Thousand Leagues	1960	3.00	15.00
Challenge 59076	Red Eye / The Little Matador	1960	3.00	15.00
Challenge 59086	Alley Cat / Coconut Grove	1960	3.00	15.00
Challenge 59097	Tough Train / The Face	1960	3.00	15.00
Challenge 59103	Hokey Pokey / Jumping Bean	1961	3.00	15.00
	—Original Challenge singles above have maroon labels.—			

Label & Catalog #		A-Side/B-Side	Year	VG	NM
Challenge 9113		Sombrero / The Shoddy Shoddy	1961	2.00	10.00
Challenge 9116		Cantina / Panic Button	1961	2.00	10.00
Challenge 9131		Tequila Twist / Limbo Rock	1962	2.00	10.00
Challenge 9140		La Cucaracha / Experiment In Terror	1962	2.00	10.00
Challenge 9143		I've Just Seen Her / What A Country	1962	2.00	10.00
Challenge 9143	(PS)	I've Just Seen Her / What A Country	1962	4.00	20.00
Challenge 9162		Limbo Dance / Latin Limbo	1962	2.00	10.00
Challenge 9174		Varsity Rock / That Did It	1962	2.00	10.00
Challenge 9180		Mr. Cool / 3/4 Mash	1962	2.00	10.00
Challenge 9189		Shades / Nik Nak	1963	2.00	10.00
Challenge 9199		Cactus Juice / Roots	1963	2.00	10.00

— Original Challenge singles above have green labels that read "Dist. by Warner Bros."—

Challenge 59219	San Juan / Jalisco	1963	2.00	10.00
Challenge 59236	Only The Young / Switzerland	1964	2.00	10.00
Challenge 59263	Kahlua / Fraternity Waltz	1964	2.00	10.00
Challenge 59277	Bright Lights, Big City / French 75	1965	2.00	10.00
Challenge 59314	The Man From Durango / Red Pepper	1965	2.00	10.00
Challenge 59322	Buckaroo / Anna	1965	2.00	10.00

— Extended Play Albums—

Challenge 7100	Tequila	1958	40.00	200.00
Challenge 57101	Caramba!	1959	30.00	150.00

CHAN-DELLS, THE

Arc 8101/2	Sand Surfer / Louie Louie	1963	7.00	35.00

CHANCE, LARRY

Barry 110	Let Them Talk / Promise Her Anything	1964	10.00	50.00

CHANCE, WAYNE

Whirlybird 2006	Send Her To Me / Just A Little Bit O' Lovin'	195?	5.00	25.00

CHANCELLORS, THE

Port 5000	Tell Me You Love Me / There Goes My Girl	1958	10.00	50.00

CHANCELLORS, THE

Fenton 2066	Once In A Million / Journey	196?	2.00	10.00
Fenton 2072	Dear John / Five Minus Three	196?	2.00	10.00
Soma 1421	Yo Yo / Little Latin Lupe Lu	1963	2.00	10.00
Soma 1435	I'm A Man / So Fine	1964	2.00	10.00

CHANCELLORS, THE

Chandel 101	Blackout / Diamond In The Sky	196?	2.00	10.00

CHANCELLORS, THE
The Chancellors were produced by Bobby Fuller.

Eastwood 120	Judy / I Can No Longer Pretend	1964	5.00	25.00

CHANCERS, THE

Dot 15870	Shirley Ann / My One	1958	3.00	15.00

CHANDELLES, THE

Dot 16553	Jester / El Gato	1963	4.00	20.00

CHANDLER, BARBARA

Kapp 542	It Hurts To Be Sixteen / Running, Running Johnny	1963	2.00	10.00

CHANDLER, KENNY

United Artists 342	The Magic Ring / Drums	1961	2.00	10.00
United Artists 384	What Kind Of Love Is Yours? / Please, Mr. Mountain	1961	2.00	10.00
Laurie 3140	Man On The Run / Leave Me If You Want To	1963	2.00	10.00
Laurie 3158	Heart / Wait For Me	1963	2.00	10.00
Laurie 3181	I Can't Stand Tears At A Party / I Tell Myself	1963	2.00	10.00

CHANEY JR., LON

Tower 114	Monster Holiday / Yuletide Jerk	1964	5.00	25.00

CHANGIN' TIMES, THE

Philips 40320	The Pied Pier / Thank You, Babe	1965	2.00	10.00
Philips 40341	How Is The Air Up There? / Young And Innocent Girl	1965	3.00	15.00
Philips 40368	I Should Have Brought Her Home / Goin' Lovin' With Her	1966	2.00	10.00
Philips 40401	All In The Mind Of A Young Girl / Aladdin	1966	2.00	10.00
Bell 675	Free Spirit (She Comes On) / You Just Seem To Know	196?	1.00	5.00
Bell 711	When The Good Sun Shines / Show Me The Way To Go Home	196?	1.00	5.00

CHANGING COLORS, THE

Tower 457	Girl For All Seasons / Want You By My Side	1968	2.00	10.00
Tower 492	Da Da Da Da / Gimme Back	1969	2.00	10.00

Label & Catalog #		A-Side/B-Side	Year	VG	NM
CHANNEL, BRUCE					
King 5294		Slow Down, Baby / Will I Ever Love Again?	196?	6.00	30.00
Teenager 601		Run Romance, Run / Don't Leave Me	1962	5.00	25.00
Manco 1035		Run Romance, Run / Don't Leave Me	1962	2.00	10.00
LeCam 953		Hey! Baby / Dream Girl	1962	6.00	30.00
Smash 1731		Hey! Baby / Dream Girl	1962	3.00	15.00
Smash 1752		Number One Man / If Only I Had Known	1962	2.00	10.00
Smash 1769		Come On, Baby / Mine Exclusively	1962	2.00	10.00
Smash 1780		Somewhere In This Town / Stand Tough	1962	2.00	10.00
Smash 1780	(PS)	Somewhere In This Town / Stand Tough	1962	3.00	15.00
Smash 1792		Let's Hurt Together / Oh, Baby	1963	2.00	10.00
Smash 1826		Night People / No Other Baby	1963	2.00	10.00
Smash 1826	(PS)	Night People / No Other Baby	1963	3.00	15.00
Smash 1838		Send Her Home / Dipsy Doodle	1963	2.00	10.00
Smash 1838	(PS)	Send Her Home / Dipsy Doodle	1963	3.00	15.00
LeCam 122		Going Back To Louisiana / Forget Me Not	1964	2.00	10.00
LeCam 125		My Baby / Blue Monday	1964	2.00	10.00
Mel-o-dy 114		You Make Me Happy / You Never Looked Better	1964	2.00	10.00
Mala 579		Mr. Bus Driver / It's Me	1967	2.00	10.00
LeCam 1117		A Presley Medley / A Man Without A Woman	1977	.60	3.00
LeCam 7277		The King Is Free (Love Me) / (B-side by Andy & The Dude)	1977	.60	3.00
Elektra 46587		One More Last Chance / That's The Truth, Ruth	1980	.50	2.50
CHANTAYS, THE					
The Chantays also recorded as The Ill Winds and The Leaping Ferns.					
Downey 104		Pipeline / Move It	1962	6.00	30.00
Dot 16440		Pipeline / Move It	1963	3.00	15.00
Downey 108		Monsoon / Scoth's High	1963	3.00	15.00
Dot 16492		Monsoon / Scoth's High	1963	2.00	10.00
Downey 116		Space Probe / Continental Missile	1963	3.00	15.00
Downey 120		Only If You Care / Love Can Be Cruel	1964	3.00	15.00
Downey 126		Beyond / I'll Be Back Someday	1964	4.00	20.00
Downey 130		Three Coins In The Fountain / Greenz	1965	3.00	15.00
Dot 104	(DJ)	Pipeline / Move It (Green vinyl)	1966	30.00	150.00
Dot 104		Pipeline / Move It	1966	2.00	10.00
CHANTEERS, THE					
Mercury 71979		She's Coming Home / Mr. Zebra	1962	4.00	20.00
Mercury 72037		I Waited / Just A Little Boy	1962	6.00	30.00
CHANTELLES, THE					
GNP-Crescendo 415		Out Of My Mind / More To Love	1968	1.00	5.00
CHANTIERS, THE					
DJB 112		Dear Mr. Clock / Peppermint	1964	4.00	20.00
CHANTIERS, THE: *Refer to* **RODNEY BAKER & THE CHANTIERS**					
CHANTONES, THE					
Carlton 485		Five Little Numbers / It's Just A Summer Love	1958	6.00	30.00
Top Rank 2066		Don't Open That Door / Tangerock	1960	3.00	15.00
Capitol 4661		Stormy Weather / Sweet Georgia Brown	1961	4.00	20.00
CHANTS, THE					
Capitol 3949		Close Friends / Lost And Found	1958	2.00	10.00
Capitol 3949	(PS)	Close Friends / Lost And Found	1958	4.00	20.00
Tru Eko 3567/77		Respectable / Kiss Me Goodbye	1961	3.00	15.00
MGM 13008		Respectable / Kiss Me Goodbye	1961	2.00	10.00
U.W.R. 4243		Respectable / Rockin' Santa	1962	2.00	10.00
Verve 10244		Dick Tracy / Choo-Choo	1963	2.00	10.00
Cameo 268		I Don't Care / Come Go With Me	1963	4.00	20.00
Cameo 277		I Don't Care / Come Go With Me	1963	2.00	10.00
Cameo 297		A Thousand Stars / I Could Write A Book	1964	4.00	20.00
Interphon 7703		She's Mine / Then I'll Be Home	1964	2.00	10.00
CHANTS, THE					
Nite Owl 40		Heaven And Paradise / When I'm With You	196?	5.00	25.00
CHANTS, THE					
Checker 1209		Surfside / Chicken N' Gravy	1968	.80	4.00
CHAPARRALS, THE					
Roulette 4229		Leapin' Guitar / Beer Barrel Rock	1960	2.00	10.00
CHAPEL, JEAN					
Sun 244		I Won't Be Rockin' Tonight / Welcome To The Club	1956	7.00	35.00
RCA Victor 47-6681		I Won't Be Rockin' Tonight / Welcome To The Club	1956	5.00	25.00

Label & Catalog #		A-Side/B-Side	Year	VG	NM
CHAPELLES, THE					
Adara 101		Night Rider / The Big Disappointment	1961	7.00	35.00
		(Adara 101 was reissued on Triangle as "Nightrider" / "The Long Wait" credited to Billy & The Kids.)			
CHAPERONES, THE [THE CAHPERONES]					
Josie 880		Dance With Me / Cruise To The Moon	1961	3.00	15.00
		(Label misprint credits the groups as The Cahperones.)			
Josie 880		Dance With Me / Cruise To The Moon	1961	3.00	15.00
Josie 885		Shining Star / My Shadow And Me	1961	4.00	20.00
Josie 891		Blueberry Sweet / The Man From The Moon	1961	5.00	25.00
CHAPIN, HARRY					
Elektra 45770		Taxi / Empty	1972	.40	2.00
Elektra 45792		Could You Put Your Light On, Please / Any Old Kind Of Day	1972	.40	2.00
Elektra 45811		Sunday Morning Sunshine / Burning Herself	1972	.40	2.00
Elektra 45828		Better Place To Be / Winter Song	1972	.40	2.00
Elektra 45874		W-O-L-D / Short Stories	1973	.40	2.00
Elektra 45203		Cat's In The Cradle / Vacancy	1974	.40	2.00
Elektra 45893		What Made America Famous? / Old College Avenue	1974	.40	2.00
Elektra 45236		I Wanna Learn A Love Song / She Sings The Songs Without Words	1975	.40	2.00
Elektra 45264		Dreams Go By / Stop Singing Those Sad Songs	1975	.40	2.00
Elektra 45285		Tangled Up Puppet / Dirt Gets Under The Fingernails	1975	.40	2.00
Elektra 45327		Better Place To Be / Better Place To Be, Part 2	1976	.40	2.00
Elektra 45368		Corey's Coming / If My Mary Were Here	1976	.40	2.00
Elektra 45445		My Old Lady / I Do It For You, Jane	1976	.40	2.00
Elektra 45066		Taxi / W-O-L-D	1976	.40	2.00
Elektra 45067		Cat's In The Cradle / What Made America Famous?	1976	.40	2.00
Elektra 45426		Dance Band On The Titanic / I Wonder What Happened To Him	1977	.40	2.00
Elektra 45497		If You Want To Feel / I Wonder What Would Happen To This World	1978	.40	2.00
Elektra 45524		Flowers Are Red / Jenny	1978	.40	2.00
Boardwalk 5700		Sequel / I Finally Found It, Baby	1980	.40	2.00
Boardwalk 5705		Remember When The Music? / Northwest 222	1981	.40	2.00
CHAPINS, THE					
The Chapins feature Harry Chapin.					
Rock-Land 664		Old Time Movies / Not Your Kind	1966	2.00	10.00
Rock-Land 664	(PS)	Old Time Movies / Not Your Kind	1966	2.00	10.00
CHAPLIN, BLONDIE					
Blondie Chaplin was formerly a member of The Flame and The Beach Boys.					
Asylum 45400		Gimme More Rock 'N Roll / Woman, Don't Cry	1977	.60	3.00
CHAPLAIN, PAUL					
Harper 100		Shortenin' Bread / Nicotine	1961	3.00	15.00
CHARADES, THE					
United Artists 132		Make Me Happy Now / Shang Lang A Ding Dong	1958	3.00	15.00
United Artists 183		Bright Red Skinny Pants / Let Me Love You	1959	3.00	15.00
CHARADES, THE					
Ava 154		Please Be My Love Tonight / Turn Him Down	1963	4.00	20.00
Original Sound 47		Close To Me / Take A Chance	1964	3.00	15.00
Warner Bros. 5415		He's Not Your Boyfriend / Hey, Operator	1964	2.00	10.00
OKeh 7195		Love Of My Life / Can't Make It Without You	1964	2.00	10.00
Mercury 72414		Power Of Love / You're With Me All The Way	1965	2.00	10.00
CHARADES, THE					
Skylark 502		Flamingo / Someone In The Kitchen With Dinah	1964	2.00	10.00
CHARADES BAND, THE					
Northridge 1002		Surf 'N Stomp / For You	1963	6.00	30.00
Impact 32		Sophia / Christina	1964	6.00	30.00
CHARGERS, THE					
B.E.A.T. 1006		The Last Charge / Miss Letha Jones	196?	2.00	10.00
CHARIOTS, THE					
Time 1006		Gloria / A Sunday Morning Love *(Blue label)*	1959	6.00	30.00
Time 1006		Gloria / A Sunday Morning Love *(Red label)*	1959	3.00	15.00
CHARIOTS, THE					
RSVP 1105		Open House / Tiger In Your Tank	196?	2.00	10.00

Label & Catalog #		A-Side / B-Side	Year	VG	NM
CHARITY SHAYNE					
Autumn 22		Ain't It, Babe? / Then You Try	1965	2.00	10.00
CHARLATANS, THE					
Kapp 779		32:20 / The Shadow Knows	1966	4.00	20.00
Kapp 779	(PS)	32:20 / The Shadow Knows	1966	6.00	30.00
Philips 40610		High Coin / When We Go Sailin' By	1969	3.00	15.00
Philips 44824		Date: May 19, 1969 (One sided)	1969	12.00	60.00
CHARLES, CALIRE, & THE TERRYTONES					
Refer to The Terrytones.					
Wye 1002		You're My Ideal / Ah Do Me Kitchie	1960	5.00	25.00
CHARLES, RAY					
Swingtime 250		(Ooh Baby) Baby, Let Me Hold Your Hand / (I'm Just A) Lonely Boy	1951	——	——
Swingtime 274		Kiss Me, Baby (All Night Long) / I'm Glad For Your Sake	1951	——	——
Swingtime 276		Changeable Woman Blues / Moonrise	1951	——	——
Swingtime 297		Baby, Won't You Please Come Home / Hey, Now	1951	——	——
Swingtime 300		Guitar Blues / Baby, Let Me Hear You Call My Name	1952	——	——
Swingtime 326		Misery In My Heart (I'm Going Down To The River) / The Snow Is Falling (I Used To Be So Happy)	1952	——	——
Sittin' in With 641		Baby Let Me Hear You Call My Name / Guitar Blues	1952	——	——
Sittin' in With 651		I Can't Do No More / (B-side by Rufus Beacham)	1952	——	——
Rockin' 504		Walkin' And Talkin' (To Myself) / I'm Wonderin' And Wonderin'	1952	——	——
		(The singles above on Swingtime, Sittin' In With and Rockin' may exist. If so, they are rare with an estimated near mint value of $250-750.)			
Atlantic 976		Roll With Me, Baby / The Midnight Hour	1952	30.00	150.00
Atlantic 984		The Sun's Gonna Shine Again / Jumpin' In The Mornin'	1952	30.00	150.00
Atlantic 999		Mess Around / Funny But I Still Love You	1953	20.00	100.00
Atlantic 1008		Feelin' Sad / Heartbreaker	1954	8.00	40.00
Atlantic 1021		It Should Have Been Me / Sinner's Prayer	1954	5.00	25.00
Atlantic 1037		Don't You Know (Baby?) / Losing Hand	1954	5.00	25.00
Atlantic 1050		I['ve] Got A Woman / Come Back, Baby	1955	5.00	25.00
Atlantic 1063		This Little Girl Of Mine / A Fool About You	1955	4.00	20.00
Atlantic 1076		Greenbacks / Blackjack	1955	4.00	20.00
		— Original Atlantic singles above have yellow & black labels without the spinner.—			
Atlantic 1085		I'll Drown In My Own Tears / Mary Ann	1956	3.00	15.00
Atlantic 1096		Hallelujah, I Love Her So / What Would I Do Without You?	1956	3.00	15.00
Atlantic 1108		Lonely Avenue / Leave My Woman Alone	1957	3.00	15.00
Atlantic 1124		Ain't That Love / I Want To Know	1957	3.00	15.00
Atlantic 1143		Get On The Right Track / It's All Right	1957	3.00	15.00
Atlantic 1154		Swanee River Rock / I Want A Little Girl	1957	3.00	15.00
Atlantic 1172		Talkin' 'Bout You / That's Enough	1958	3.00	15.00
Atlantic 1180		Yes, Indeed / I Had A Dream	1958	3.00	15.00
Atlantic 1196		You Be My Baby / My Bonnie	1958	3.00	15.00
Atlantic 2006		Rockhouse / Rockhouse, Part 2	1958	3.00	15.00
Atlantic 2010		The Right Time / Tell All The World About You	1959	3.00	15.00
Atlantic 2022		That's Enough / Tell Me, How Do You Feel?	1959	3.00	15.00
Atlantic 2031		What'd I Say / What'd I Say, Part 2	1959	3.00	15.00
Atlantic 2043		I'm Movin' On / I Believe To My Soul	1959	3.00	15.00
Atlantic 2047		Let The Good Times Roll / Don't Let The Sun Catch You Crying	1959	3.00	15.00
Atlantic 2055		Just For A Thrill / Heartbreaker	1960	3.00	15.00
Atlantic 2068		Tell The Truth / Sweet Sixteen Bars	1960	2.00	10.00
Atlantic 2084		Come Rain Or Come Shine / Tell Me You'll Wait For Me	1960	2.00	10.00
Atlantic 2094		Early In The Morning / A Bit Of Soul	1961	2.00	10.00
Atlantic 2106		It Should've Been Me / Am I Blue?	1961	2.00	10.00
Atlantic 2118		Hard Times (No One Knows Better Than I) / I Wonder Who	1962	2.00	10.00
Atlantic 2174		Carrying That Load / Feelin' Sad	1962	2.00	10.00
Atlantic 2239		Talkin' 'Bout You / In A Little Spanish Town	1964	2.00	10.00
Atlantic 2470		Come Rain Or Come Shine / Tell Me You'll Wait For Me	1966	5.00	
		— Extended Play Albums—			
Atlantic 567		Ray Charles	1956	30.00	150.00
Atlantic 587		Ray Charles	1957	30.00	150.00
Atlantic 597		The Great Ray Charles	1957	20.00	100.00
Atlantic 607		Rock With Ray Charles	1958	20.00	100.00
Atlantic 614		Soul Brothers	1958	20.00	100.00
Atlantic 619		The Genius Of Ray Charles	1959	20.00	100.00
Atlantic 8029	(33)	What'd I Say	1968	4.00	20.00
CHARLES, SONNY, & THE CHECKMATES					
A&M 1053		Black Pearl / Lazy Susan	1969	1.00	5.00
A&M 1127		Proud Mary / Spanish Harlem	1969	1.00	5.00
A&M 1130		Proud Mary / Do You Love Your Baby?	1969	1.00	5.00
		("Black Pearl" and "Proud Mary" were produced by Phil Spector.)			

Label & Catalog #		A-Side / B-Side	Year	VG	NM
CHARLES, TOMMY					
Decca 92717		Our Love Affair / If You Were Me	1956	2.00	10.00
Decca 29946		After School / I'll Wait For Your Call	1956	2.00	10.00
CHARLIE & CHAN					
Kapp 582		Rickshaw Drag Race / My Boyfriend's Learning Karate	1964	2.00	10.00
CHARMETTES, THE					
Hi 2003		Skating In The Blue Light / My Love	196?	3.00	15.00
Marlin 16001		Surrender, My Love / One More Time	196?	3.00	15.00
Tri-Disc 103		On A Night Like Tonight / Why, Oh Why?	1962	3.00	15.00
Kapp 547		Please Don't Kiss Me Again / What Is A Tear?	1963	3.00	15.00
Kapp 570		0021-0021-Ooh / He's A Wise Guy	1964	2.00	10.00
Mala 491		My Lover Is A Boy Scout / Mailbox	1964	2.00	10.00
World Artists 1055		Stop The Wedding / Sugar Boy	1965	2.00	10.00
CHARTBUSTERS, THE					
Mutual 502		She's The One / Slippin' Through Your Fingers	1964	2.50	12.00
Mutual 508		Why (Doncha Be My Girl?) / Stop The Music	1964	2.50	12.00
Mutual 511		You're Breakin' My Heart / Can't You Hear Me Calling?	1965	2.50	12.00
Crusader 118		Lonely Surfer Boy / New Orleans	1965	4.00	20.00
CHASTAIN, JODY					
Kay 1002		My My / Jody's Beat	1960	10.00	50.00
CHATEAUS, THE					
Coral 62364		Honest I Will / Summer's Here	1963	3.00	15.00
CHATEAUS, THE					
Boss 9912		I'm The One / The Bells Of Rhymney	1965	2.00	10.00
Sound Stage-7 2536		Moanin' / Seven Comes Eleven	1965	2.00	10.00
Jam 114		Summer Has Come And Gone / Count On Me	1965	2.00	10.00
CHATER, KERRY					
Kerry Chater originally recorded as a member of The Outcasts and The Union Gap.					
Warner Bros. 8591		Leave Well Enough Alone / Well On My Way To Loving You	1978	.60	3.00
Warner Bros. 8591		Leave Well Enough Alone / Ain't Nothin' But A Heartache	1978	.60	3.00
CHATHAM TRIO, THE					
Virgelle 709		Wanders End / Madame Jeanette	196?	1.00	5.00
CHAVIS BROTHERS, THE [THE FIVE CHAVIS BROTHERS]					
Clock 1025		So Tired / I Love You	1959	3.00	15.00
Coral 62270		Baby, Don't Leave Me / Old Time Rock And Roll	1962	6.00	30.00
CHAYNS, THE					
International Arts. 114		Night Time / Live With The Moon	1967	2.00	10.00
International Arts. 119		There's Nothing Wrong / See It Through	1967	2.00	10.00

CHECKER, CHUBBY

In 1960 Chubby Checker covered an obscure Hank Ballard side and, for all intents and purposes, invented modern popular dancing. "The Twist," which reached #1 in 1960 and then soared backed to the top in 1962, not only was the first internationally popular dance where partners did not depend on one another's movements, it also affected the way R&B and pop records were made for years. Unfortunately, over the sourse of time Checker's association with dance crazes totally overshadowed his considerable singing ability and his non-twisting career suffered. Refer to Bobby Rydell.

Parkway 804		The Class / School Days, Oh, School Days	1959	5.00	25.00
Parkway 806		The Jet / Ray Charles-ton	1959	6.00	30.00
Parkway 808		Samson And Delilah / Whole Lotta Laughin'	1959	5.00	25.00
Parkway 810		Dancing Dinosaur / Those Private Eyes (Keep Watching Me)	1960	4.00	20.00
Parkway 811		The Twist / Toot	1960	3.00	15.00
Parkway 811	(DJ)	The Twist / Twistin' U.S.A. (Red vinyl)	1961	30.00	150.00
Parkway 811	(DJ)	The Twist / Twistin' U.S.A. (Yellow vinyl)	1961	15.00	75.00
Parkway 811		The Twist / Twistin' U.S.A.	1961	2.00	10.00
Parkway 811	(PS)	The Twist / Twistin' U.S.A.	1961	2.00	10.00
Parkway 813		The Hucklebuck / Whole Lotta Shaking Goin' On	1961	2.00	10.00
Parkway 818		Pony Time / Oh, Susannah	1961	2.00	10.00
Parkway 822		Dance The Mess Around / Good, Good Lovin'	1961	2.00	10.00
Parkway 824		Let's Twist Again / Everything's Gonna Be Alright	1961	2.00	10.00
		(Copies of Parkway 824 on colored vinyl are bootlegs from 1978.)			
Parkway 824	(PS)	Let's Twist Again / Everything's Gonna Be Alright	1961	3.00	15.00
Parkway 830		The Fly / That's The Way It Goes	1962	2.00	10.00
Parkway 830	(PS)	The Fly / That's The Way It Goes	1962	3.00	15.00
Parkway 835		Slow Twistin' / La Paloma Twist	1962	2.00	10.00
Parkway 835	(PS)	Slow Twistin' / La Paloma Twist	1962	3.00	15.00
		("Slow Twistin'" features Dee Dee Sharp.)			
Parkway 842		Dancin' Party / Gotta Get Myself Together	1962	2.00	10.00
Parkway 842	(PS)	Dancin' Party / Gotta Get Myself Together	1962	3.00	15.00

Label & Catalog #		A-Side/B-Side	Year	VG	NM
Parkway 849		Limbo Rock / Popeye (The Hitch-Hiker)	1962	2.00	10.00
Parkway 849	(PS)	Limbo Rock / Popeye (The Hitch-Hiker)	1962	3.00	15.00
Parkway 862		Twenty Miles / Let's Limbo Some More	1963	2.00	10.00
Parkway 862	(PS)	Twenty Miles / Let's Limbo Some More	1963	3.00	15.00
Parkway 873		Birdland / Black Cloud	1963	2.00	10.00
Parkway 873	(PS)	Birdland / Black Cloud	1963	3.00	15.00
Parkway 879		Surf Party / Twist It Up	1963	2.00	10.00
Parkway 879	(PS)	Surf Party / Twist It Up	1963	3.00	15.00
Parkway 890		Loddy Lo / Hooka Tooka	1963	2.00	10.00
Parkway 890	(PS)	Loddy Lo / Hooka Tooka	1963	3.00	15.00
Parkway 907		Hey Bobba Needle / Spread Joy	1964	2.00	10.00
Parkway 907	(PS)	Hey Bobba Needle / Spread Joy	1964	3.00	15.00
Parkway 920		Lazy Elsie Molly / Rosie	1964	2.00	10.00
Parkway 920	(PS)	Lazy Elsie Molly / Rosie	1964	3.00	15.00
Parkway 922		She Wants To Swim / You Better Believe It, Baby	1964	2.00	10.00
Parkway 922	(PS)	She Wants To Swim / You Better Believe It, Baby	1964	3.00	15.00
Parkway 936		Lovely Lovely / The Weekend's Here	1965	2.00	10.00
Parkway 936	(PS)	Lovely Lovely / The Weekend's Here	1965	3.00	15.00
Parkway 949		Do The Freddie / (At The) Discoteque	1965	2.00	10.00
Parkway 949		Let's Freddie / (At The) Discoteque	1965	2.00	10.00
Parkway 959		Everything's Wrong / Cu Ma La Be-Stay	1965	2.00	10.00
Parkway 965		You Just Don't Know / Two Hearts Make One Love	1965	3.00	15.00
Parkway 989		Hey, You! Little Boo-Ga-Loo / Pussy Cat	1966	2.00	10.00
Parkway 105		You Got The Power / Looking At Tomorrow	1966	2.00	10.00
Parkway 112		Karate Monkey / Her Heart	1966	2.00	10.00
Buddah 100		Back In The U.S.S.R. / Windy Cream	1969	2.00	10.00
20th Century Fox 2040		Reggae My Way / Gypsy	1973	1.00	5.00
20th Century Fox 2075		She's A Bad Woman / Happiness Is A Girl Like You	1974	1.00	5.00
Amherst 716		The Rub / Move It	1976	.60	3.00
MCA 52015		Tonight's The Night / Running	1982	.60	3.00
MCA 52043		Harder Than Diamond / Your Love	1982	.60	3.00
Sea Bright 5128		Read You Like A Book /	1986	.60	3.00
		—12" Singles—			
Amherst D-4		The Rub / Move It	1976	2.00	10.00
Sea Bright 5128		Read You Like A Book / Read You Like A Book	1986	2.00	10.00
		—Extended Play Albums—			
Parkway 5001		Chubby Checker (Paper cut-out sleeve)	1961	6.00	30.00

CHECKERS, THE

Arvee 5035		Skooby Doo / Skooby Doo (Part 2)	196?	2.00	10.00
Arvee 5037		Swingin' Summer / Skooby Doo	196?	2.00	10.00
Dottie 1001		Buzz / Big Cat	196?	2.00	10.00
Audio 108		Feel Alright / Persuasion	196?	2.00	10.00
Jerden 710		Black Cat / Soft Blue	1963	2.00	10.00

CHECKERS, THE

Skyla 1120		Blue Saturday / Cascade	1962	2.00	10.00

CHECKMATES, THE

The Checkmates also recorded with Tommy Vance and King George.

Audio 113		Blue Star / Work Song	196?	2.00	10.00
Ruff 1003		Hey Girl / All The Time Now	1966	2.00	10.00

CHECKMATES, LTD, THE: Refer to SONNY CHARLES & THE CHECKMATES

CHEERIOS, THE

Infinity 011		Where Are You Tonight? / Ding Dong Honeymoon	1963	100.00	400.00
Infinity 1		Where Are You Tonight? / Ding Dong Honeymoon	1963	2.00	10.00

CHEERLEADERS, THE: Refer to FRANK & MAC

CHEETAHS, THE

Philips 40239		That Goodnight Kiss / Mecca	1964	2.00	10.00

CHER [CHERILYN]

Cher also recorded as, or with, Bonnie Jo Mason; Allman & Woman; Caesar & Cleo; and Sonny & Cher.

Imperial 66081		Dream Baby / Stan Quetzal	1964	5.00	25.00
		(Imperial 66081 credits Cherilyn.)			
Imperial 66114		All I Really Want To Do / I'm Gonna Love You	1965	1.20	6.00
Imperial 66136		Where Do You Go? / See See Blues	1965	1.00	5.00
Imperial 66160		Bang Bang / Our Day Will Come	1966	1.00	5.00
Imperial 66192		Alfie / She's Not Better Than Me	1966	1.00	5.00
Imperial 66217		Behind The Door / Magic In The Air	1966	1.00	5.00
Imperial 66223		Dream Baby / Behind The Door	1967	1.00	5.00
Imperial 66223	(PS)	Dream Baby / Behind The Door	1967	3.00	15.00
Imperial 66252		Hey, Joe / Our Day Will Come	1967	1.00	5.00
Imperial 66261		You Better Sit Down, Kids / Elusive Butterfly	1967	1.00	5.00
Imperial 66261		You Better Sit Down, Kids / Mama	1967	1.00	5.00

Label & Catalog #	A-Side/B-Side	Year	VG	NM
Imperial 66282	But I Can't Love You More / Click Song #1	1967	1.00	5.00
Imperial 66307	Take Me For A Little While / Song Called Children	1967	1.00	5.00
Atlantic 6684	Chastity's Song / Gilded Splinters	1969	1.00	5.00
Atco 6658	Yours Until Tomorrow / The Very Thought Of You	1969	.50	2.50
Atco 6684	Chastity's Song / Guilded Splinters	1969	.50	2.50
Atco 6704	For What It's Worth / Hangin' On	1969	.50	2.50
Atco 6713	You Made Me So Very Happy / The First Time	1969	.50	2.50
Atco 6793	Superstar / The First Time	1970	.50	2.50
Atco 6868	Lay Lady Lay / Hangin' On	1971	.50	2.50
Kapp 2134	Don't Put It On Me / Classified 1A	1971	.50	2.50
Kapp 2146	Gypsies, Tramps And Thieves / He'll Never Know	1971	.50	2.50
Kapp 2158	The Way Of Love / Don't Put It On Me	1972	.50	2.50
Kapp 2171	Living In A House Divided / One Honest Man	1972	.50	2.50
Kapp 2184	Don't Hide Your Love / The First Time	1972	.50	2.50
United Artists 50864	Will You Love Me Tomorrow? / Reason To Believe	1971	.50	2.50
United Artists 50974	Our Day Will Come / Ol' Man River	1972	.50	2.50
United Artists XW511	Sunny / Alfie	1972	.50	2.50
MCA 40039	Am I Blue? / How Long Has This Been Going On?	1973	.40	2.00
MCA 40102	Half-Breed / Melody	1973	.40	2.00
MCA 40161	Dark Lady / Two People Clinging To A Thread	1973	.40	2.00
MCA 40245	Train Of Thought / Dixie Girl	1974	.40	2.00
MCA 40273	I Saw A Man And He Danced With His Wife / I Hate To Sleep Alone	1974	.40	2.00
MCA 40324	Carousel Man /	1975	.40	2.00
MCA 40375	Rescue Me / Dixie Girl	1975	.40	2.00
Warner Spector 0400	Baby, I Love You / A Woman's Story ("Baby, I Love You" was produced by Phil Spector.)	1974	1.00	5.00
Warner Bros. 8096	These Days / Geronimo's Cadillac	1975	.20	1.00
Warner Bros. 8263	Borrowed Time / Long Distance Love Affair	1976	.20	1.00
Warner Bros. 8311	Pirate / Send The Man Over	1977	.20	1.00
Warner Bros. 8366	War Paint And Soft Feathers / Send The Man Over	1977	.20	1.00
Casablanca 2208	Hell On Wheels / Get Down (Guitar Groupie)	1979	.20	1.00
Casablanca 2228	Holdin' Out For Love / Boys And Girls	1979	.20	1.00
Casablanca 965	Take Me Home / My Song (Too Far Gone)	1979	.20	1.00
Casablanca 987	It's Too Late To Love Me Now / Wasn't It Good?	1979	.20	1.00
	— 12" Singles—			
Casablanca 20150	Take Me Home / My Song (Too Far Gone)	1979	2.00	10.00
Casablanca 20168	It's Too Late To Love Me Now / Wasn't It Good?	1979	2.00	10.00

CHER & NILSSON

Label & Catalog #	A-Side/B-Side	Year	VG	NM
Warner Spector 0402	A Love Like Yours / Just Enough To Keep Me Hangin' ("A Love Like Yours" was produced by Phil Spector.)	1975	1.00	5.00

CHEROKEES, THE

Label & Catalog #	A-Side/B-Side	Year	VG	NM
Challenge 9135	Cherokee Stomp / Uprisin'	1961	2.00	10.00

CHEROKEES, THE

Label & Catalog #	A-Side/B-Side	Year	VG	NM
MGM 13334	Seven Daffodils / A Wondrous Place	1964	3.00	15.00
MGM 13433	Turn My Back On You / Dig A Little Deeper	1965	4.00	20.00

CHERRY FIZZ

Label & Catalog #	A-Side/B-Side	Year	VG	NM
Fat Chance 101	Tinker Tailor / Lie Around	1968	4.00	20.00

CHERRY PEOPLE, THE

Label & Catalog #		A-Side/B-Side	Year	VG	NM
Heritage 801		And Suddenly / Imagination	1968	1.00	5.00
Heritage 801	(PS)	And Suddenly / Imagination	1968	1.00	5.00

CHERRY SLUSH, THE

The Cherry Slush features Dick Wagner.

Label & Catalog #	A-Side/B-Side	Year	VG	NM
U.S.A. 895	I Cannot Stop You / Don't Walk Away	1968	1.20	6.00
U.S.A. 904	Day Don't Come / Gotta Take It Easy	1968	1.20	6.00

CHERUBS, THE

Label & Catalog #	A-Side/B-Side	Year	VG	NM
Dore 545	Julie, Julie / They Go Ape	1960	2.00	10.00

CHESSMAN SQUARE

Label & Catalog #		A-Side/B-Side	Year	VG	NM
Lion 1002		Circles / Try	196?	4.00	20.00
Lion 1002	(PS)	Circles / Try	196?	25.00	125.00

CHESSMEN, THE

Label & Catalog #	A-Side/B-Side	Year	VG	NM
Mirasonic 1002	I Live For You / Do Wop	195?	25.00	125.00
Safari 1011	The Keeper Of My Love /	195?	100.00	400.00
AMC 101	Mr. Cupid / What's To Become Of Me?	1962	3.00	15.00
Amy 841	Stormy Dreams / Pick It Up	1962	2.00	10.00
G-Clef 707	Voyage / Sorry	196?	3.00	15.00

CHESSMEN, THE

Label & Catalog #	A-Side/B-Side	Year	VG	NM
GMA 12	Touchdown / Glory Be	196?	7.00	35.00

Label & Catalog #	A-Side/B-Side	Year	VG	NM
CHESSMEN, THE				
The Chessmen also recorded with Jack Bedient.				
Fantasy 595	See The Little Girl / Looking For A Good Love	196?	4.00	20.00
CHESSMEN, THE				
Golden Crest 2661	Bells Bells / Prayer Of Love	196?	2.00	10.00
Jerden 743	Mustang / Mr. Meadowlands	196?	2.00	10.00
CHESSMEN, THE				
Mercury 72498	Love Didn't Die / You Lost Your Game	1965	2.00	10.00
Mercury 72559	What's Causing This Sensation / Running Wild	1966	2.00	10.00
Chess 1950	Nothing But You / Why Can't I Be Your Man?	1966	2.00	10.00
CHESTER, GARY				
Coral 62379	Rockin' Drummer / Sing Sing Sing	1963	1.20	8.00
CHESTNUTS, THE				
Night Train 906	Rock 'N Roll Tragedy / I'm So Blue	196?	3.00	15.00
CHEVELLE FIVE, THE				
UMI 100	I'm Sorry, Girl / Come Back Bird	1966	2.00	10.00
Titan 1737	Dangling Little Friends / Stone And Steel Men	1967	5.00	25.00
Titan 1737 (PS)	Dangling Little Friends / Stone And Steel Men	1967	10.00	50.00
CHEVELLES, THE				
Bangar 603	Blue Chevelle / Mala Boo	196?	8.00	40.00
Bangar 616	Chevelle Stomp / Dear Sue	196?	8.00	40.00
CHEVELL'S, THE				
Chevell 101	Let There Be Surf / Rip Tide	1963	8.00	40.00
CHEVELS, THE				
Musicland 20101	Play Me A Sad Song / Devil's Little Angels	196?	3.00	15.00
Gass 1001	Hootenanny Ho-Down / Hendersonville	1963	2.00	10.00
CHEVRONS, THE				
Brent 7000	Don't Be Heartless / That Comes With Love	1959	3.00	15.00
Brent 7007	Lullabye / Day After Forever	1959	3.00	15.00
Brent 7015	Little Darlin' / Little Star	1960	3.00	15.00
Time 1	Come Go With Me / I'm In Love Again	1961	4.00	20.00
CHEVRONS, THE				
Cuca 6381	For Your Love / Good Good Lovin'	1961	4.00	20.00
Sara 6462	Please Don't Make Me Cry / Still In Love With You	1962	3.00	15.00
CHEYENNE				
Current 1001	I'm Not A Rich Man / We're Losin'	196?	.60	3.00

CHICAGO [THE CHICAGO TRANSIT AUTHORITY]
The C.T.A.'s original members were Pete Cetera, Terry Kath, Robert Lamm, Lee Loughnane, James Pankow, Walt Parazaider, Walt Perry and Danny Seraphine (Columbia 44909 and 45011), at which point Perry left. Later members include Laudir De Olivetra (1974); Donnie Dacus (1978-79), Chris Pinnick (1979-81) and Bill Champlin, who joined in 1981.

Columbia 44909	Questions 67 & 68 / Listen	1969	.80	4.00
Columbia 45011	Beginnings / Poem 58	1969	.80	4.00
Columbia 45127	Make Me Smile / Colour My World	1970	.60	3.00
Columbia 45194	25 Or 6 To 4 / Where Do We Go From Here?	1970	.60	3.00
Columbia 45264	Does Anybody Really Know What Time It Is? / Listen	1970	.60	3.00
Columbia 45264 (PS)	Does Anybody Really Know What Time It Is? / Listen	1970	1.00	5.00
Columbia 45331	Free / Free Country	1971	.60	3.00
Columbia 45331 (PS)	Free / Free Country	1971	.80	4.00
Columbia 45370	Lowdown / Loneliness Is Just A Word	1971	.60	3.00
Columbia 45370 (PS)	Lowdown / Loneliness Is Just A Word	1971	.80	4.00
Columbia 45417	Beginnings / Colour My World	1971	.60	3.00
Columbia 45417 (PS)	Beginnings / Colour My World	1971	.80	4.00
Columbia 45467	Questions 67 & 68 / I'm A Man	1971	.40	2.00
Columbia 45657	Saturday In The Park / Alma Mater	1972	.40	2.00
Columbia 45717	Dialogue / Now That You've Gone	1972	.40	2.00
Columbia 45717 (PS)	Dialogue / Now That You've Gone	1972	.80	4.00
Columbia 33210	Colour My World / I'm A Man	1972	.60	3.00
Columbia 45880	Feelin' Stronger Every Day / Jenny	1973	.40	2.00
Columbia 45933	Just You 'N' Me / Critics Choice	1973	.40	2.00
Columbia 46020	(I've Been) Searchin' So Long / Byblos	1974	.40	2.00
Columbia 46062	Call On Me / Prelude To Air	1974	.40	2.00
Columbia 10049	Wishing You Were Here / Lifesaver	1974	.60	3.00
	("Wishing You Were Here" features vocals by Carl and Dennis Wilson and Al Jardine.)			
Columbia 10092	Harry Truman / Till We Meet Again	1975	.40	2.00
Columbia 10092 (PS)	Harry Truman / Till We Meet Again	1975	.60	3.00

Label & Catalog #		A-Side/B-Side	Year	VG	NM
Columbia 10131		Old Days / Hideaway	1975	.40	2.00
Columbia 10200		Brand New Love Affair / Hideaway	1975	.40	2.00
Columbia 10360		Another Rainy Day In New York City / Hope For Love	1976	.40	2.00
Columbia 10390		If You Leave Me Now / Together Again	1976	.40	2.00
Columbia 10523		You Are On My Mind / Gently I'll Wake You	1977	.40	2.00
Columbia 10620	(PS)	Baby, What A Big Surprise (Promo picture sleeve)	1977	.60	3.00
Columbia 10620		Baby, What A Big Surprise / Takin' It On Uptown	1977	.40	2.00
Columbia 10683		Little One / Till The End Of Time	1977	.40	2.00
Columbia 10737		Take Me Back To Chicago / Policeman	1978	.40	2.00
Columbia 10845		Alive Again / Love Was New	1978	.40	2.00
Columbia 10879		No Tell Lover / Take A Chance	1979	.40	2.00
Columbia 10935		Gone Long Gone / The Greatest Love On Earth	1979	.40	2.00
Columbia 11061		Must Have Been Crazy / Closer To You	1979	.40	2.00
Columbia 11124		Street Player / Window Dreamin'	1979	.40	2.00
Columbia 11345		Thunder And Lightning / I'd Rather Be Rich	1980	.40	2.00
Columbia 11376		Song For You / The American Dream	1980	.40	2.00
Full Moon/Epic 29979		Hard To Say I'm Sorry / Sonny, Think Twice	1982	.40	2.00
		— 12" Singles—			
Columbia 11138		Street Player / Window Dreamin'	1980	1.60	8.00
		—Special/Promotional Releases—			
Columbia 30110	(33)	Chicago III (Jukebox EP)	1970	4.00	20.00
Columbia 32400	(33)	Chicago IV (Jukebox EP)	1973	4.00	20.00
Columbia A6S-178		Chicago IX (Greatest Hits)	1975	6.00	30.00
		(Boxed set of six singles; the price is for the complete set. The six promo singles are priced separately below.)			
Columbia AS-179	(DJ)	Beginnings / Beginnings	1975	.80	4.00
Columbia AS-180	(DJ)	Wishing You Were Here / (I've Been) Searching So Long	1975	.80	4.00
Columbia AS-181	(DJ)	Just You 'N' Me / Call On Me	1975	.80	4.00
Columbia AS-182	(DJ)	Saturday In The Park / Feelin' Stronger Everyday	1975	.80	4.00
Columbia AS-183	(DJ)	Make Me Smile / 25 Or 6 To 4	1975	.80	4.00
Columbia AS-184	(DJ)	Does Anybody Really Know What Time It Is? / Colour My World	1975	.80	4.00

CHICAGO, ARTIE
Artie Chicago is a pseudonym for Ernie Maresca.

Laurie 3424		The Wanderer / Please Don't Play Me A-7	1968	2.00	10.00

CHICAGO FIRE, THE

U.S.A. 898		Candy And Me / Come See What I Got	1968	.80	4.00

CHICAGO LOOP, THE

DynoVoice 226		She Comes To Me (When She Needs Good Lovin') / This Must Be The Place	1966	1.20	6.00
DynoVoice 230		Richard Cory / Cloudy	1967	1.20	6.00
Mercury 72755		Can't Find The Words / Saved	1967	1.00	5.00
Mercury 72802		Technicolor Thursday / Beginning At The End	1968	1.00	5.00

CHICK & RICK

Kenco 5018		Dear Mr. TV Picture Eye / Back To School	1961	1.20	6.00

CHICK & THE NOBLES

U.S.A. 772		I Cry / Island For Two	1965	3.00	15.00

CHICKEN SHACK

Epic 10414		Worried About My Woman / Six Nights In Seven	1968	1.00	5.00
Blue Horizon 100		Tears In The Wind / The Things You Put Me Through	1970	1.00	5.00
Blue Horizon 302		Diary Of Your Life / Maudie	1972	1.00	5.00
Deram 7537		As Time Goes Passing By /	1973	.80	4.00

CHICKS, THE: *Refer to KELL OSBORNE & THE CHICKS*

CHIEFS, THE

Greenwich 408		Apache / Dee's Dream	196?	3.00	15.00
Greenwich 410		Moments To Remember / Enchiladas	196?	3.00	15.00
Valiant 6038		Tom Tom / Howl	1964	3.00	15.00

CHILDREN, THE

Sweet Smoke 2		Jumping Jack Flash / Good Feeling	1968	2.00	10.00

CHILDREN OF PARADISE

Columbia 44265		Hey, You Got Somethin' / What Am I Doing Here?	1967	2.00	10.00

CHILDREN OF STONE

Love 146		Mary, Can You See? / He Is Mine	1966	3.00	15.00

CHIMES, THE

Limelight 3000		Angel Child / Cry, Cry Baby	1957	3.00	15.00
Limelight 3002		Du Wap / Stop, Look And Listen	1958	3.00	15.00

Label & Catalog #		A-Side/B-Side	Year	VG	NM
Tag 444		Oh, How I Love You / Once In A While	1960	10.00	50.00
Tag 444		Summer Night / Once In A While	1960	4.00	20.00
Tag 445		I'm In The Mood For Love / Only Love	1961	3.00	15.00
Tag 447		Let's Fall In Love / Dream Girl	1961	3.00	15.00
Tag 450		Paradise / My Love	1962	4.00	20.00
Metro 1		Who's Heart Are You Breakin' Now? / Baby's Comin' Home	1963	4.00	20.00
Laurie 3211		Who's Heart Are You Breakin' Now? / Baby's Comin' Home	1963	2.00	10.00

CHIP & DAVE

Dun Star 5005		Soon Another Day / Seventh Round	1965	2.00	10.00
Jerden 771		Soon Another Day / Seventh Round	1965	1.00	5.00
Decca 32073		Everybody's Laughing / Who's To Say?	1967	2.00	10.00

CHIP & THE QUARTERTONES

Carlton 604		You Were My Baby / Simple Simon	1962	35.00	175.00

CHIPMUNKS, THE
The Chipmunks are Alvin, Simon and Theodore under the direction of David Seville. Refer to Canned Heat.

Liberty 55168		The Chipmunk Song / Almost Good	1958	3.00	15.00
Liberty 55179		Alvin's Harmonica / Mediocre	1959	3.00	15.00
Liberty 55200		Ragtime Cowboy Joe / Flip Side	1959	3.00	15.00
Liberty 55200	(PS)	Ragtime Cowboy Joe / Flip Side	1959	4.00	20.00
Liberty 77200	(S)	Ragtime Cowboy Joe / Flip Side	1959	5.00	25.00
Liberty 55250		The Chipmunk Song / Alvin's Harmonica	1959	3.00	15.00
Liberty 55250	(PS)	The Chipmunk Song / Alvin's Harmonica	1959	4.00	20.00
Liberty 77250	(S)	The Chipmunk Song / Alvin's Harmonica	1959	5.00	25.00
Liberty 55233		Alvin's Orchestra / Copyright 1960	1960	2.00	10.00
Liberty 55233	(PS)	Alvin's Orchestra / Copyright 1960	1960	4.00	20.00
Liberty 55246		Comin' 'Round The Mountain / Sing A Goofy Song	1960	2.00	10.00
Liberty 55246	(PS)	Comin' 'Round The Mountain / Sing A Goofy Song	1960	5.00	25.00
Liberty 55277		Alvin For President / Sack Time	1960	2.00	10.00
Liberty 55277	(PS)	Alvin For President / Sack Time	1960	5.00	25.00
Liberty 55289		Rudolph The Red Nosed Reindeer / Spain	1960	2.00	10.00
Liberty 55289	(PS)	Rudolph The Red Nosed Reindeer / Spain	1960	3.50	18.00
Liberty 55424		The Alvin Twist / I Wish I Could Speak French	1962	2.00	10.00
Liberty 55452		America The Beautiful / My Wild Irish Rose	1962	2.00	10.00
Liberty 55544		Alvin's All-Star Chipmunk Band / Old MacDonald Cha Cha Cha	1963	2.00	10.00
Liberty 55544	(PS)	Alvin's All-Star Chipmunk Band / Old MacDonald Cha Cha Cha	1963	5.00	25.00
Liberty 55632		Effin Alvin / (B-side by David Seville)	1963	2.00	10.00
Liberty 55635		The Night Before Christmas / Wonderful Day	1963	2.00	10.00
Liberty 55635	(PS)	The Night Before Christmas / Wonderful Day	1963	4.00	20.00
Liberty 55734		All My Lovin' / Do You Want To Know A Secret?	1964	2.00	10.00
Columbia (No number)		Happy Birthday (5" cardboard picture disc)	1964	4.00	20.00
Liberty 55773		Supercalifragilisticexpialidoucious / Do-Re-Mi	1965	1.20	6.00
Liberty 55832		I'm Henry VIII, I Am / What's New, Pussycat?	1965	1.20	6.00
Dot 16997		Sorry About That, Herb / Apple Picker	1966	3.00	15.00
Sunset 61002		Talk To The Animals / My Friend The Doctor	1968	1.00	5.00
Sunset 61002	(PS)	Talk To The Animals / My Friend The Doctor	1968	3.00	15.00
Sunset 61003		Chitty Chitty Bang Bang / Hushabye Mountain	1968	1.00	5.00
Sunset 61003	(PS)	Chitty Chitty Bang Bang / Hushabye Mountain	1968	2.00	10.00
		—Extended Play Albums—			
Liberty LSX-1007		Alvin's Harmonica	1959	12.00	60.00
Liberty LSX-1008		Let's All Sing With The Chipmunks	1960	10.00	50.00
Liberty LSX-1015		The Chipmunk Songbook	1962	6.00	30.00
Liberty LSX-1016		Christmas With The Chipmunks	1962	6.00	30.00
Liberty LST-7388		The Chipmunks Sing The Beatles Hits	1964	6.00	30.00

CHIPPENDALES, THE

Andie 5013		Drip Drop / What A Night	1959	3.00	15.00
Rust 5033		Voodoo / The Day Will Come	1961	2.00	10.00

CHIPS, THE

Clifton 54		When I'm With You / Everyone's Laughing	195?	8.00	40.00

CHIPS, THE

Ember 1077		Bye Bye, My Love / What A Lie	1961	3.00	15.00
Strand 25027		Darling / You're On My Mind	1961	3.00	15.00
Tollie 9042		Party People / Long Lonely Winter	1965	2.00	10.00

CHIYO & THE CRESCENTS
Chiyo & The Crescents also recorded as The Crescents Featuring Chiyo.

Break Out 3/4		Devil Surf / Pink Dominoes	1963	7.00	35.00

CHOCOLATE TELEPHONE POLE, THE

Jack O' Diamonds 1011		Let's Tranquilize With Color / One By One	1967	3.00	15.00

Prior to the success of the Chipmunks as animated cartoon characters, the drawings for the Liberty single sleeves and album covers featured three different rodents, cruder but livelier than the more familiar ones.

Label & Catalog #		A-Side / B-Side	Year	VG	NM
CHOCOLATE TUNNEL, THE					
Era 3185		Ostrich People / Highly Successful Young Rupert White	1967	3.00	15.00
CHOCOLATE WATCH BAND, THE					
The Chocolate Watch Band originally recorded as The Hogs.					
Uptown 740	(DJ)	Baby Blue / Sweet Young Thing	1966	6.00	30.00
Uptown 740		Baby Blue / Sweet Young Thing	1966	8.00	40.00
Uptown 749	(DJ)	Misty Lane / She Weaves A Tender Trap	1966	6.00	30.00
Uptown 749		Misty Lane / She Weaves A Tender Trap	1966	8.00	40.00
Tower 373	(DJ)	Are You Gonna Be There (At The Love-In)? / No Way Out	1967	6.00	30.00
Tower 373		Are You Gonna Be There (At The Love-In)? / No Way Out	1967	8.00	40.00
CHOIR, THE					
The Choir features Jim Bonfanti, Bob Wally Bryson and Dave Smalley, later of The Raspberries. Contrary to previous assumptions, Eric Carmen did not record with The Choir.					
Canadian Am. 203		It's Cold Outside / I'm Going Home	1967	5.00	25.00
Roulette 4738		It's Cold Outside / I'm Going Home	1967	3.00	15.00
Roulette 4760		No One Here To Play With / Don't You Feel A Little Sorry For Me?	1967	3.00	15.00
Roulette 47005		Changin' My Mind / When You Were With Me	1968	3.00	15.00
Intrepid 75020		Gonna Have A Good Time Tonight / So Much Love	1970	4.00	20.00
— Extended Play Albums—					
Bomp 104		The Choir (Paper picture sleeve)	1976	2.00	10.00
CHORD-O-ROYS, THE: *Refer to* BOBBY ROY & THE CHORD-O-ROYS					
CHOSEN FEW, THE					
North Beach 1003		Nobody But Me / I Think It's Time	1966	3.00	15.00
Autumn 17		Nobody But Me / I Think It's Time	1966	2.00	10.00
CHOSEN FEW, THE					
Power International		Another Goodbye / Forget About The Past	1966	1.60	8.00
Dart 1080		We Walk Together / Foolin' Around With Me	1967	1.60	8.00
Liberty 55919		Synthetic Man / Last Man Alive	1967	1.60	8.00
Denim 1092		Pink Clouds And Lemonade / Stop In The Name Of Love	1968	1.20	6.00
Roulette 7015		You Can Never Be Wrong / Footsee	1968	1.20	6.00
Carusa 504		Hey Joe / Summer's Love	196?	3.00	15.00
Playboy 106		I've Had It / Ask Me, Baby	196?	2.00	10.00
Co-op 510		La La La La La La / Why Can't I Love You?	196?	1.06	8.00
Canyon 1000		Taking All Of The Love I Can / Birth Of A Playboy	196?	2.00	10.00
Crystal 1107		You're A Big Girl Now / You're A Big Girl Now	196?	2.00	10.00
CHOSEN LOT, THE					
Sidra 9004		Time Was / If You Want To	196?	2.00	10.00
CHRIS & KATHY					
Chris Montez and Kathy Young.					
Monogram 517		All You Had To Do (Was Tell Me) / Love Me	1963	3.00	15.00
Monogram 520		Shoot That Curl / It Takes Two	1963	4.00	20.00
Monogram 520	(PS)	Shoot That Curl / It Takes Two	1963	20.00	100.00
CHRISTIAN, BOBBY					
Mercury 72102		The Spider And The Fly / Cha Cha Hop	1963	2.00	10.00
CHRISTIAN, ROGER					
Roger Christian was the lyricist for most of Brian Wilson's car songs.					
Rendezvous 195		Little Mary Christmas / The Meaning Of Christmas	1962	2.00	10.00
NBI 100		The Last Drag / Big Bad Ho-Dad	1964	10.00	50.00
CHRISTIAN'S CRUSADERS					
RCA Victor 47-8828		That's Nice / She's Got The Action	1965	1.60	8.00
CHRISTIE, DEAN					
Top Flight 113		So Much / Oh, What A Love	196?	4.00	20.00
SWL 1607		Heartbreaker / Mashed Potato Twist	1962	1.20	6.00
Select 715		Heartbreaker / I'm A Loser	1962	1.20	6.00
Select 718		Teenage Jezebel / Shake	1962	1.20	6.00
Mercury 72140		Mona / City Boy	1963	1.20	6.00
Mercury 72228		Get With It / That's My Girlfriend	1964	1.20	6.00
CHRISTIE, LYNN, & THE DECKERS					
Nar 225		Oh, Where Did You Go? / What Did I Do?	1957	5.00	25.00
CHRISTIE, LOU (& THE CLASSICS)					
Lou Christie also recorded with, or as, The Cantina Band; Chic Christy; The Classics; Lugee & The Lions; D.C. Larue; Marcy Jo; Sacco; and The Tammys.					
C&C 102		The Gypsy Cried / Red Sails In The Sunset	1962	25.00	125.00
Am. Music Makers 006		The Jury / Little Did I Know	1962	3.00	15.00
Roulette 4457		The Gypsy Cried / Red Sails In The Sunset	1963	2.00	10.00

Label & Catalog #		A-Side / B-Side	Year	VG	NM
Roulette 4481		Two Faces Have I / All That Glitters Isn't Gold	1963	2.00	10.00
Roulette 4504		How Many Teardrops? / You And I	1963	2.00	10.00
Roulette 4527		Shy Boy / It Can Happen	1963	2.00	10.00
Roulette 4545		Stay / There They Go	1964	2.00	10.00
Roulette 4554		When You Dance / Maybe You'll Be There	1964	2.00	10.00
Alcar 207		Close Your Eyes / Funny Thing	1964	5.00	25.00
		(Alcar 207 was originally issued on Starr credited to The Classics.)			
Alcar 208		You're With It / Tomorrow Will Come	1964	3.00	15.00
Colpix 735		Merry Go Round / Guitars And Bongos	1964	2.00	10.00
Colpix 753		Have I Sinned? / Pot Of Gold	1964	2.00	10.00
Colpix 770		Make Summer Last Forever / Why Did You Do It, Baby	1965	2.00	10.00
Colpix 778		A Teenager In Love / Backtrack	1965	2.00	10.00
Colpix 799		Big Time / Cryin' On My Knees	1966	2.00	10.00
Colpix 799	(PS)	Big Time / Cryin' On My Knees	1966	3.00	15.00
MGM 13412		Lightnin' Strikes / Cryin' In The Streets	1965	1.20	6.00
MGM 13473		Rhapsody In The Rain / Trapeze	1966	8.00	40.00
		("Rhapsody In The Rain" was originally released with the lyrics "We were makin' out in the rain.")			
MGM 13473		Rhapsody In The Rain / Trapeze	1966	1.20	6.00
		("Rhapsody In The Rain" was reissued with "We fell in love in the rain.")			
MGM 13473	(PS)	Rhapsody In The Rain / Trapeze	1966	2.00	10.00
MGM 13533		Painter / Du Ronda	1966	1.20	6.00
MGM 13533	(PS)	Painter / Du Ronda	1966	3.00	15.00
MGM 13576		If My Car Could Talk / Song Of Lita	1966	1.20	6.00
MGM 13576	(PS)	If My Car Could Talk / Song Of Lita	1966	3.00	15.00
MGM 13623		Since I Don't Have You / Wild Life's In Season	1966	1.20	6.00
Co&Ce 235		Outside The Gates Of Heaven / All That Glitters Isn't Gold	1966	1.00	5.00
World 1002		The Jury / Little Did I Know	1966	1.25	6.00
Columbia 44062		Shake Hands And Walk Away Cryin' / Escape	1967	1.20	6.00
Columbia 44177		Self Expression / Back To The Days Of The Romans	1967	1.20	6.00
Columbia 44240		Gina / Escape	1967	1.20	6.00
Columbia 44338		Don't Stop Me / Back To The Days Of The Romans	1967	1.20	6.00
Buddah 65		Genesis And The Third Verse / Rake Up The Leaves	1968	1.60	8.00
Buddah 76		Saints Of Aquarius / Canterbury Road	1968	1.60	8.00
Buddah 116		I'm Gonna Make You Mine / I'm Gonna Get Married	1969	1.00	5.00
Buddah 149		Are You Getting Any Sunshine? / It'll Take Time	1969	1.00	5.00
Buddah 163		She Sold Me Magic / Love Is Over	1970	1.00	5.00
Buddah 192		Indian Lady / Glory River	1970	1.00	5.00
Buddah 235		Waco / Lighthouse	1971	1.20	6.00
Buddah 257	(DJ)	Mickey's Monkey / Wonderful Dream	1971	2.00	10.00
Buddah 257		Mickey's Monkey / Wonderful Dream	1971	6.00	30.00
Buddah 285		Sing Me, Sing Me / The Paper Song	1972	1.00	5.00
Buddah 285	(PS)	Sing Me, Sing Me / The Paper Song (Promo picture sleeve)	1972	2.00	10.00
Buddah 312	(DJ)	Shuffle On Down To Pittsburgh / I'm Gonna Get Married	1973	2.00	10.00
Buddah 312		Shuffle On Down To Pittsburgh / I'm Gonna Get Married	1973	4.00	20.00
Three Brothers 400		Blue Canadian Rocky Dream / Wilma Lee And Stony	1973	1.00	5.00
Three Brothers 402		Beyond The Blue Horizon / Saddle The Wind	1974	1.00	5.00
Three Brothers 403		You Were The One / Good Mornin'	1974	1.00	5.00
Three Brothers 405		Sunbeam / Hey, You Cajun	1975	1.50	8.00
Epic 50244		Ridin' In My Van / Summer In Malibu	1976	1.00	5.00
Slipped Disc 45270		Summer Days / The One And Only Original Sunshine Kid	1976	3.00	15.00
Midsong Inter. 10848		You're Gonna Make Love To Me / Fantasies	1976	1.00	5.00
Midsong Inter. 10959		Spanish Wine / Dancing In The Sand	1978	1.00	5.00
Midsong Inter. 72013		Don't Knock My Love / Don't Knock My Love	1980	1.00	5.00
		(Duet with Pia Zadora.)			
Plateau 101		Guardian Angels / Guardian Angels	1981	5.00	25.00
		— 12" Singles —			
Plateau 101		Guardian Angels / Guardian Angels	1981	3.00	15.00

CHRISTIE, LOU, & LESLEY GORE

Label & Catalog #		A-Side / B-Side	Year	VG	NM
Manhattan 50039		Since I Don't Have You / It's Only Make Believe	1986	.60	3.00

CHRISTIE, SUSAN
Refer to Chic Christy.

Label & Catalog #		A-Side / B-Side	Year	VG	NM
Columbia 43595	(PS)	I Love Onions (Promo picture sleeve)	1966	2.00	10.00
Columbia 43595		I Love Onions / Take Me As You Find Me	1966	.80	4.00

CHRISTMAS, JOHNNY, & THE DYNAMIICS

Label & Catalog #		A-Side / B-Side	Year	VG	NM
PDQ 001		Soft Lips / Dum Dum (The Lollipop Song)	196?	2.00	10.00

CHRISTMAS SPIRIT
Christmas Spirit is Linda Ronstadt with The Turtles.

Label & Catalog #		A-Side / B-Side	Year	VG	NM
White Whale 290	(DJ)	Christmas Is My Time Of Year / Will You Still Believe In Me?	1968	5.00	25.00
White Whale 290		Christmas Is My Time Of Year / Will You Still Believe In Me?	1968	10.00	50.00

CHRISTOPHER & THE CHAPS

Label & Catalog #		A-Side / B-Side	Year	VG	NM
Fontana 1530		It's Alright Ma, I'm Only Bleeding / They Just Don't Care	1965	3.00	15.00

Label & Catalog #		A-Side/B-Side	Year	VG	NM
CHRISTOPHER MILK					
United Arts. SP-66	(EP)	Christopher Milk	1971	3.00	15.00
CHRISTY, CHARLES					
HBR 455		Cherry Pie / Will I Find Her?	1966	1.20	6.00
HBR 473		Young And Beautiful / In The Arms Of A Girl	1966	1.20	6.00
CHRISTY, CHIC					
Chic Christy features Lou and Susan Christie.					
Hac 103		With This Kiss / My Billet-Doux To You	1961	4.00	20.00
CHRISTY, DON					
Don Christy is a pseudonym for Sonny Bono.					
Specialty 672		One Little Answer / Wearing Black	1959	3.00	15.00
Go 1001		As Long As You Love Me / I'll Always Be Grateful	1960	3.00	15.00
Name 3		As Long As You Love Me / I'll Always Be Grateful	1960	3.00	15.00
Fidelity 3020		Don't Have To Tell Me / Wearing Black	1960	3.00	15.00
Rush 1001		I'll Change / Try It Out On Me	196?	2.00	10.00
Rush 1004		Little Miss Cool /	196?	2.00	10.00
CHUCK & BETTY					
Decca 30671		Bobby Socks Baby / Jelly Beans	1958	3.00	15.00
Decca 30875		Walking In My Dreams / Win Or Lose	1958	3.00	15.00
Decca 30985		Sissy Britches / Come Back, Little Girl	1959	3.00	15.00
CHUCK & JOE					
Chuck Girard and Joe Kelley.					
Decca 31805	(DJ)	Feel So Fine (Feel So Good) / Can't Fool Me Twice	1965	2.00	10.00
Decca 31805		Feel So Fine (Feel So Good) / Can't Fool Me Twice	1965	4.00	20.00
Decca 31871	(DJ)	Harlem Shuffle / I Wish You Didn't Treat Me So Well	1965	2.00	10.00
Decca 31871		Harlem Shuffle / I Wish You Didn't Treat Me So Well	1965	4.00	20.00
CHUCK & JOHNNY					
Diamond 121		You're My Girl / (B-side by Bobby Vinton)	1962	2.00	10.00
CHUCK-A-LUCKS, THE					
Lin 5014		The Magic Of First Love / Disc Jockey Fever	1958?	4.00	20.00
Bow 305		Heaven Knows / Chuck-A-Luck	196?	4.00	20.00
Warner Bros. 5198		I'm Hospitalized Over You / Cotton Pickin' Love	1961	3.00	15.00
Warner Bros. 5198		Long John / Pick Up And Deliver	1961	3.00	15.00
Jubilee 5415		Unconditional Surrender / Tarzan's Date	1961	3.00	15.00
CHUCKENDOES, THE					
Toppa 1097		Butter Fingers / Liebestraum	196?	2.00	10.00
CHUCKLES, THE					
West Side 1019		On The Street Where You Live / I'll Wait	196?	3.00	15.00
CHUG & DOUG					
Charger 101		Ringo Comes To Town / My Girl	1964	3.00	15.00
CICCONE, DON					
Don Ciccone also recorded with Don & The Chevells; The Critters; and The Four Seasons.					
Kama Sutra 506		Down When It's Up, Up When It's Down / There's Got To Be A Word	1970	1.00	5.00
CINDERELLAS, THE					
Decca 30925		I Was Only Fifteen / You Never Shoulda Gone Away	1959	3.00	15.00
Decca 30830		Mister Dee-Jay / Yum Yum Yum	1959	3.00	15.00
Mercury 72394		Fairy Tale / Mr. Happy Love Joy	1965	2.00	10.00
CINDERELLAS, THE					
Dimension 1026		Baby, Baby (I Still Love You) / Please Don't Wake Me	1964	6.00	30.00
CINDY & LINDY					
ABC-Paramount 9847		The Language Of Love / Brigette's Song	1957	3.00	15.00
Coral 62008		I'll String Along With You / The Wonder That Is You	1959	3.00	15.00
Coral 62165		Let's Go Steady / There Are Such Things	1960	3.00	15.00
Pilgrim 702		Let's Go Steady / The Wedding Is Over	1960	3.00	15.00
Pilgrim 705		Lovin' And Being Loved / Hungry Heart	1960	3.00	15.00
CINDY & SANDY					
Tailspin 102		Make Believe Baby / Why Not?	1960	2.00	10.00
CINERAMAS, THE					
Rhapsody 71963/4		Crying For You / I'm Sorry, Baby	1960	4.00	20.00
Champ 103		Life Can Be Beautiful / It Must Be Love	1960	5.00	25.00
Clifton 4		Is This All Mine? / Crying For You	1974	1.00	5.00

Label & Catalog #		A-Side/B-Side	Year	VG	NM
CINNAMONS, THE					
B.T. Puppy 503		Strange, Strange Feeling / I'm Not Gonna Worry	1965	1.00	5.00
B.T. Puppy 508		Dance To The Music / Mr. Cupid '65	1965	1.00	5.00
CITATIONS, THE					
Canadian Am. 136		Magic Eyes / Mystery Of Love	1961	6.00	30.00
CITATIONS, THE					
Sara 3301		Moon Race / Slippin' And Slidin'	1963	5.00	25.00
Epic 9603		Moon Race / Slippin' And Slidin'	1963	3.00	15.00
CITATIONS, THE					
Vangee 301		The Girl Next Door / Ten Miles From Nowhere	1967	6.00	30.00
Fraternity 992		The Girl Next Door / Ten Miles From Nowhere	1967	3.00	15.00
CITY					
City features Carole King.					
Ode 113		Paradise Alley / Snow Queen	1968	2.00	10.00
Ode 119		That Old Sweet Roll / Why Are You Leaving?	1969	2.00	10.00
CITY LIMITS, THE					
Uptown 728		Stagger Lee / Backyard Compost	196?	2.00	10.00
CITY SURFERS, THE					
Capitol 5002		Beach Ball / Sun Tan Baby	1963	5.00	25.00
Capitol 5052		Powder Puff / 50 Miles To Go	1963	5.00	25.00
CITY ZU, THE					
Columbia 44342		Give A Little Bit / I'll Find Another	1967	1.00	5.00
Dot 17166		Eeny Meeny / Too Much, Too Soon, Too Fast	1969	1.00	5.00
Dot 17266		Quick Like A Bunny / Stop Running Away	196?	1.00	5.00
CLAIRE, NANCY					
Rona 1007		Danny / Yes	196?	.60	3.00
Rona		Little Baby / Cheatin' On Me	196?	.60	3.00
CLANTON, IKE					
Ace 583		Down The Aisle / I'm Sorry	1960	2.00	10.00
Mercury 71975		Sugar Plum / Guilty	1962	2.00	10.00
CLANTON, JIMMY					
Jimmy Clanton also recorded as Jimmy Dale.					
Ace 537		I Trusted You / That's You, Baby	1958	3.00	15.00
Ace 546		Just A Dream / You Aim To Please	1958	3.00	15.00
Ace 551		A Letter To An Angel / A Part Of Me	1958	3.00	15.00
		—Ace singles above have white labels with the catalog number on the bottom.—			
Ace 537		I Trusted You / That's You, Baby	1959	2.00	10.00
Ace 546		Just A Dream / You Aim To Please	1959	2.00	10.00
Ace 551		A Letter To An Angel / A Part Of Me	1959	2.00	10.00
Ace 560		A Ship On A Stormy Sea / My Love Is Strong	1959	2.00	10.00
Ace 567		My Own True Love / Little Boy In Love	1959	2.00	10.00
Ace 567	(PS)	My Own True Love / Little Boy In Love	1959	6.00	30.00
Ace 567	(S)	My Own True Love / Little Boy In Love	1959	6.00	30.00
Ace 575		Go, Jimmy, Go / I Trusted You *(Purple label)*	1959	3.00	15.00
Ace 575		Go, Jimmy, Go / I Trusted You	1959	2.00	10.00
Ace 575	(PS)	Go, Jimmy, Go / I Trusted You	1959	6.00	30.00
Ace 585		Another Sleepless Night / I'm Gonna Try	1960	2.00	10.00
Ace 585	(PS)	Another Sleepless Night / I'm Gonna Try	1960	5.00	25.00
Ace 600		Come Back / Wait	1960	2.00	10.00
Ace 600	(PS)	Come Back / Wait	1960	5.00	25.00
Ace 607		What Am I Gonna Do? / If I	1961	2.00	10.00
Ace 607	(PS)	What Am I Gonna Do? / If I	1961	5.00	25.00
Ace 616		Down The Aisle / No Longer Blue	1961	2.00	10.00
Ace 616	(PS)	Down The Aisle / No Longer Blue	1961	5.00	25.00
Ace 622		I Just Wanna Make Love / Don't Look At Me	1961	2.00	10.00
Ace 622	(PS)	I Just Wanna Make Love / Don't Look At Me	1961	5.00	25.00
Ace 634		Lucky In Love With You / Not Like A Brother	1961	2.00	10.00
Ace 634	(PS)	Lucky In Love With You / Not Like A Brother	1961	5.00	25.00
Ace 641		Twist On, Little Girl / Wayward Love	1962	2.00	10.00
Ace 641	(PS)	Twist On, Little Girl / Wayward Love	1962	5.00	25.00
Ace 655		Just A Moment / Because I Do	1962	2.00	10.00
Ace 655	(PS)	Just A Moment / Because I Do	1962	5.00	25.00
Ace 664	(DJ)	Venus In Blue Jeans / Highway Bound	1962	5.00	25.00
		—Ace singles above have white labels with the catalog number on the right.—			
Ace 8001		Venus In Blue Jeans / Highway Bound	1962	3.00	15.00
Ace 8005		Darkest Street In Town / Dreams Of A Fool	1963	1.60	8.00
Ace 8006		Endless Night / Another Day, Another Heartache	1963	1.60	8.00
Ace 8006	(PS)	Endless Night / Another Day, Another Heartache	1963	3.00	15.00

Label & Catalog #		A-Side/B-Side	Year	VG	NM
Ace 8007		Cindy / I Care Enough	1963	1.60	8.00
Vin 1028		What Am I Living For? / Wedding Blues	196?	1.00	5.00
Philips 40161		All The Words In The World / Red Don't Go With Blue	1963	1.00	5.00
Philips 40181		I'll Step Aside / I Won't Cry Anymore	1964	1.00	5.00
Philips 40181	(PS)	I'll Step Aside / I Won't Cry Anymore	1964	2.50	12.00
Philips 40208		If I'm A Fool (For Loving You) / A Million Drums	1964	1.00	5.00
Philips 40219		Follow The Sun / Lock The Windows, Lock The Doors	1964	1.00	5.00
Mala 500		Hurting Each Other / Don't Keep Your Friends Away	1965	1.00	5.00
Mala 516		Everything I Touch Turns To Tears / That Special Way	1965	1.00	5.00
Imperial 66242		The Absence Of Lisa / C'mon Jim	1967	.80	4.00
Imperial 66274		I'll Be Loving You / Calico Junction	1967	.80	4.00
Laurie 3508		Curly / I'll Never Forget Your Love	1969	.80	4.00
Laurie 3534		Tell Me / I'll Never Forget Your Love	1969	.80	4.00
Spiral 3406		Coolest Hot Pants / Coolest Hot Pants (Inst.)	1971	.80	4.00
Starcrest 078	(DJ)	Old Rock 'N Roller / Old Rock 'N Roller	197?	.80	4.00
Starfire 104		I Wanna Go Home / You Kissed A Fool Goodbye	197?	.60	3.00
		—Extended Play Albums—			
Ace 101		Jimmy Clanton	1959	35.00	175.00
		(Ace EP 101 features four songs from the film "Go, Johnny, Go!")			
Ace 102		Thinking Of You	1959	25.00	125.00
Ace 103		I'm Always Chasing Rainbows	1959	25.00	125.00
Ace 642		Teenage Millionaire	1961	25.00	125.00

CLAPTON, ERIC
Eric Clapton also recorded with Cream; Derek & The Dominos; John Mayall; and The Yardbirds.

Label & Catalog #		A-Side/B-Side	Year	VG	NM
Atco 6738		Teasing / Souling	1970	.80	4.00
Atco 6784		After Midnight / Easy Now	1970	.60	3.00
Polydor 15049		Let It Rain / Easy Now	1972	.60	3.00
Polydor 15056		Bell Bottom Blues / Little Wing	1973	.60	3.00
RSO 409		I Shot The Sheriff / Give Me Strength	1974	.60	3.00
RSO 500		I Shot The Sheriff / Give Me Strength	1974	.40	2.00
RSO 503		Willie And The Hand Jive / Mainline Florida	1974	.40	2.00
RSO 509		Pretty Blue Eyes / Swing Down, Sweet Chariot	1975	.40	2.00
RSO 513		Knockin' On Heaven's Door / Someone Like You	1975	.40	2.00
RSO 861		All Our Past Times / Hello, Old Friend	1976	.40	2.00
RSO 868		Hungry / Carnival	1977	.40	2.00
RSO 886		Lay Down, Sally / Next Time You See Her	1977	.40	2.00
RSO 895		Wonderful Tonight / Peaches And Diesel	1978	.40	2.00
RSO 910		Promises / Watch Out For Lucy	1978	.40	2.00
RSO 928		Cocaine / Tulsa Time	1979	.40	2.00
RSO 1039		Tulsa Time / Cocaine	1980	.40	2.00
RSO 1051		Blues Power / Early In The Morning	1980	.40	2.00
RSO 1060		I Can't Stand It / Black Rose	1981	.40	2.00
RSO 1064		Another Ticket / Rita Mae	1981	.40	2.00
RSO 1064	(PS)	Another Ticket / Rita Mae	1981	.40	2.00

CLARK, DAVE [THE DAVE CLARK FIVE]
Dave Clark with Lenny Davidson, Rick Huxley, Dennis Payton and Mike Smith. Refer to the Various Artists EP section.

Label & Catalog #		A-Side/B-Side	Year	VG	NM
Laurie 3188		I Walk The Line / First Love	1963	10.00	50.00
Rust 5078		I Walk The Line / First Love	1964	7.00	35.00
Jubilee 5476		Chaquita / In Your Heart	1964	3.00	15.00
Congress 212		I Knew It All The Time / That's What I Said	1964	3.00	15.00
Congress 212	(PS)	I Knew It All The Time / That's What I Said	1964	6.00	30.00
Epic 9656		Glad All Over / I Know You	1964	2.00	10.00
Epic 9656	(PS)	Glad All Over / I Know You	1964	3.00	15.00
Epic 9671		Bits And Pieces / All Of The Time	1964	2.00	10.00
Epic 9678		Do You Love Me? / Chaquita	1964	2.00	10.00
Nabisco 245		Do You Love Me? (One sided)	1964	4.00	20.00
Epic 9692		Can't You See That She's Mine? / No Time To Lose	1964	2.00	10.00
Epic 9692	(PS)	Can't You See That She's Mine? / No Time To Lose	1964	3.00	15.00
Epic 9704		Because / Theme Without A Name	1964	2.00	10.00
Epic 9704	(PS)	Because / Theme Without A Name	1964	3.00	15.00
Epic 9722		Everybody Knows / Ol' Sol	1964	2.00	10.00
Epic 9722	(PS)	Everybody Knows / Ol' Sol	1964	3.00	15.00
Epic 9739		Any Way You Want It / Crying Over You	1964	2.00	10.00
Epic 9763		Come Home / Your Turn To Cry	1965	2.00	10.00
Epic 9763	(PS)	Come Home / Your Turn To Cry	1965	3.00	15.00
Epic 9786		Reelin' And Rockin' / I'm Thinking	1965	2.00	10.00
Epic 9811		I Like It Like That / Hurtin' Inside	1965	2.00	10.00
Epic 9811	(PS)	I Like It Like That / Hurtin' Inside	1965	3.00	15.00
Epic 9833		Catch Us If You Can / On The Move	1965	2.00	10.00
Epic 9833	(PS)	Catch Us If You Can / On The Move	1965	3.00	15.00
Epic 9863	(DJ)	Over And Over / Over And Over (Red vinyl)	1965	7.00	35.00
Epic 9863	(PS)	Over And Over / Over And Over	1965	7.00	35.00
Epic 9863		Over And Over / I'll Be Yours (My Love)	1965	2.00	10.00
Epic 9863	(PS)	Over And Over / I'll Be Yours (My Love)	1965	3.00	15.00
Epic 9882		At The Scene / Miss You	1966	2.00	10.00
Epic 9882	(PS)	At The Scene / Miss You	1966	3.00	15.00

If you believed the teen 'zines of 1964, the Beatles' main competition for the charts (and spendable cash) of American youth was Herman's Hermits and the Dave Clark Five... While the DC5's career as hit makers in the U.S. was all but over by 1967, their later singles are rather rare, especially stock copies. Many of the picture sleeves from post '66 are also tough, although they often accompanied the promotional release; *Nineteen Days* was a modest hit in some parts of the country at the end of 1966.

Label & Catalog #		A-Side / B-Side	Year	VG	NM
Epic 10004		Try Too Hard / All Night Long	1966	1.60	8.00
Epic 10004	(PS)	Try Too Hard / All Night Long	1966	3.00	15.00
Epic 10031		Please Tell Me Why / Look Before You Leap	1966	1.60	8.00
Epic 10031	(PS)	Please Tell Me Why / Look Before You Leap	1966	2.00	10.00
Epic 10053		Satisfied With You / Don't Let Me Down	1966	1.60	8.00
Epic 10053	(PS)	Satisfied With You / Don't Let Me Down	1966	3.00	15.00
Epic 10076		Nineteen Days / Sitting Here, Baby	1966	1.60	8.00
Epic 10076	(PS)	Nineteen Days / Sitting Here, Baby	1966	3.00	15.00
Epic 10114		I've Got To Have A Reason / Good Time Baby	1967	1.60	8.00
Epic 10114	(PS)	I've Got To Have A Reason / Good Time Baby	1967	3.00	15.00
Epic 10144		You Got What It Takes / Doctor Rhythm	1967	1.60	8.00
Epic 10144	(PS)	You Got What It Takes / Doctor Rhythm	1967	3.00	15.00
Epic 10179		You Must Have Been A Beautiful Baby / Man In The Pin-Stripe Suit	1967	1.60	8.00
Epic 10179	(PS)	You Must Have Been A Beautiful Baby / Man In The Pin-Stripe Suit	1967	4.00	20.00
Epic 10209	(DJ)	A Little Bit Now / You Don't Play Me Around	1967	1.60	8.00
Epic 10209		A Little Bit Now / You Don't Play Me Around	1967	2.00	10.00
Epic 10209	(PS)	A Little Bit Now / You Don't Play Me Around	1967	2.00	10.00
Epic 10244	(DJ)	Red And Blue / Concentration Baby	1967	1.60	8.00
Epic 10244		Red And Blue / Concentration Baby	1967	2.00	10.00
Epic 10244	(PS)	Red And Blue / Concentration Baby	1967	4.00	20.00
Epic 10260/65		Everybody Knows / (B-side by Lulu)	1967	4.00	20.00
Epic 10265	(DJ)	Everybody Knows / Inside And Out	1967	1.60	8.00
Epic 10265		Everybody Knows / Inside And Out	1967	2.00	10.00
Epic 10265	(PS)	Everybody Knows / Inside And Out	1967	5.00	25.00
Epic 10325	(DJ)	Please Stay / Forget	1968	1.60	8.00
Epic 10325		Please Stay / Forget	1968	2.00	10.00
Epic 10375	(DJ)	The Red Balloon / Maze Of Love	1968	1.60	8.00
Epic 10375		The Red Balloon / Maze Of Love	1968	2.00	10.00
Epic 10375	(PS)	The Red Balloon / Maze Of Love	1968	4.00	20.00
Epic 10474	(DJ)	Paradise / 34-06	1969	1.60	8.00
Epic 10474		Paradise / 34-06	1969	2.00	10.00
Epic 10474	(PS)	Paradise / 34-06	1969	5.00	25.00
Epic 10509	(DJ)	If Somebody Loves You / Best Day's Work	1969	1.60	8.00
Epic 10509		If Somebody Loves You / Best Day's Work	1969	2.40	12.00
Epic 10547	(DJ)	Bring It On Home To Me / Darling, I Love You	1970	1.60	8.00
Epic 10547		Bring It On Home To Me / Darling, I Love You	1970	2.00	10.00
Epic 10547	(PS)	Bring It On Home To Me / Darling, I Love You	1970	2.00	10.00
Epic 10635	(DJ)	Here Comes Summer / Five By Five	1970	1.60	8.00
Epic 10635		Here Comes Summer / Five By Five	1970	2.00	10.00
Epic 10684	(DJ)	Good Old Rock & Roll / One Night-Lawdy, Miss Clawdy	1970	1.60	8.00
Epic 10684		Good Old Rock & Roll / One Night-Lawdy, Miss Clawdy	1970	3.00	15.00
Epic 10684	(PS)	Good Old Rock & Roll / One Night-Lawdy, Miss Clawdy	1970	5.00	25.00
Epic 10704	(DJ)	Southern Man / Southern Man	1971	3.00	15.00
Epic 10704	(DJ)	Southern Man / If You Wanna See Me Cry	1971	4.00	20.00
Epic 10704		Southern Man / If You Wanna See Me Cry	1971	6.00	30.00
Epic 10768	(DJ)	Won't You Be My Lady? / Won't You Be My Lady?	1971	2.00	10.00
Epic 10768	(DJ)	Won't You Be My Lady? / Into Your Life	1971	2.00	10.00
Epic 10768		Won't You Be My Lady? / Into Your Life	1971	3.00	15.00
Epic 10894	(DJ)	Rub It In / Rub It In	1972	2.00	10.00
Epic 10894	(DJ)	Rub It In / I'm Sorry, Baby	1972	2.00	10.00
Epic 10894		Rub It In / I'm Sorry, Baby	1972	3.00	15.00
—Epic "Memory Lane" Reissues—					
Epic 2225	(DJ)	Glad All Over / Bits And Pieces	1972	1.50	8.00
Epic 2225		Glad All Over / Bits And Pieces	1972	.40	2.00
Epic 2230	(DJ)	Because / Do You Love Me?	1972	1.50	8.00
Epic 2230		Because / Do You Love Me?	1972	.40	2.00
Epic 2234	(DJ)	Any Way You Want It / Can't You See That She's Mine?	1972	1.50	8.00
Epic 2234		Any Way You Want It / Can't You See That She's Mine?	1972	.40	2.00
Epic 2239	(DJ)	I Like It Like That / Everybody Knows	1972	1.50	8.00
Epic 2239		I Like It Like That / Everybody Knows	1972	.40	2.00
Epic 2248	(DJ)	Over And Over / Catch Us If You Can	1972	1.50	8.00
Epic 2248		Over And Over / Catch Us If You Can	1972	.40	2.00
Epic 2294	(DJ)	Bring It On Home To Me / If Somebody Loves You	1972	1.50	8.00
Epic 2294		Bring It On Home To Me / If Somebody Loves You	1972	.40	2.00
Epic 2313	(DJ)	I Like It Like That / Can't You See That She's Mine?	1972	1.50	8.00
Epic 2313		I Like It Like That / Can't You See That She's Mine?	1972	.40	2.00
Epic 2316	(DJ)	Come Home / You Got What It Takes	1972	1.50	8.00
Epic 2316		Come Home / You Got What It Takes	1972	.40	2.00
—Special/Promotional Releases—					
Auravision	(DJ)	The Dave Clark Five Sing (5" cardboard picture disc) (Issued by Pond's Cold Cream.)	1964	10.00	50.00
Epic 26185	(33)	The Dave Clark Five's Greatest Hits (Jukebox EP)	1967	5.00	25.00
Epic 26221	(33)	More Greatest Hits (Jukebox EP)	1968	5.00	25.00

Label & Catalog #		A-Side/B-Side	Year	VG	NM

CLARK, GENE
The late, great Gene Clark also recorded with The Byrds and Dillard & Clark.

Columbia 43903		Echoes / I Found You	1966	2.00	10.00
Columbia 43903	(PS)	Echoes / I Found You	1966	5.00	25.00
Columbia 44088		So You Say You Lost Your Baby / Is Yours Is Mine	1967	2.00	10.00
Asylum 45222		Life's Greatest Fool / From A Silver Phial	1974	.80	4.00
RSO 876		Home Run King / Comely Saturday	1977	.60	3.00

CLARK, PETULA
Refer to the Various Artists section.

Coral 60971		Tell Me Truly / Song Of A Mermaid	1953	3.00	15.00
Coral 61077		Where Did My Snowman Go? / Three Little Kittens	1954	3.00	15.00
King 1371		The Little Shoemaker / Helpless	1954	3.00	15.00
MGM 12049		The Pendulum Song / Romance In Rome	1955	2.00	10.00
Imperial 5582		Baby Lover / Ever Been In Love?	1959	2.00	10.00
Imperial 5655		Where Are You (Now That I Need You)? / I Love A Violin	1960	2.00	10.00
Warwick 652		Isn't This A Lovely Day? / Romeo	1961	2.00	10.00
London 10504		With All My Love / My Friend The Sea	1962	1.60	8.00
London 10510		I'm Counting On You / Some Other World	1962	1.60	8.00
London 10516		Whistlin' For The Moon / Tender Love	1962	1.60	8.00
Laurie 3143		The Road / Jumble Sale	1962	1.20	6.00
Laurie 3156		I Will Follow Him / Darling Cheri	1963	1.20	6.00
Laurie 3316		In Love / Darling Cheri	1964	1.20	6.00
Warner Bros. 5494		Downtown / You'd Better Love Me	1964	1.20	6.00
Warner Bros. 5612		I Know A Place / Jack And John	1965	1.20	6.00
Warner Bros. 5643		You'd Better Come Home / Heart	1965	1.20	6.00
Warner Bros. 5661		'Round Every Corner / Two Rivers	1965	1.20	6.00
Warner Bros. 5684		My Love / Where Am I Going?	1965	1.20	6.00
Warner Bros. 5802		A Sign Of The Times / Time For Love	1966	1.20	6.00
Warner Bros. 5835		I Couldn't Live Without Your Love / Your Way Of Life	1966	1.20	6.00
Warner Bros. 5863		Who Am I? / Love Is A Long Journey	1966	1.20	6.00
Warner Bros. 5882		Color My World / Take Me Home Again	1966	1.20	6.00
Warner Bros. 7002		This Is My Song / High	1967	1.20	6.00
Warner Bros. 7049		Don't Sleep In The Subway / Here Comes The Morning	1967	1.20	6.00
Warner Bros. 7073		The Cat In The Window (The Bird In The Sky) / Fancy Dancin' Man	1967	1.20	6.00
Warner Bros. 7097		The Other's Man's Grass Is Always Greener / At The Crossroads	1967	1.20	6.00
Warner Bros. 7170		Kiss Me Goodbye / I've Got Love Going For Me	1968	1.20	6.00
Warner Bros. 7216		Don't Give Up / Every Time I See A Rainbow	1968	1.20	6.00
Warner Bros. 7244		American Boys / Look To The Sky	1968	1.20	6.00
Warner Bros. 7275		Happy Heart / Love Is The Only Thing	1969	.80	4.00
Warner Bros. 7310		Look At Mine / You And I	1969	.80	4.00
Warner Bros. 7343		No One Better Than You / Things Bright And Beautiful	1969	.80	4.00
Warner Bros. 7422		Beautiful Sounds / The Song Is Love	1970	.80	4.00
Warner Bros. 7467		Couldn't Sleep / The Song Of My Life	1970	.80	4.00
Warner Bros. 7484		I Don't Know How To Love Him / Maybe	1970	.80	4.00
MGM 14392		My Guy / Little Bit O' Lovin'	1972	.60	3.00
MGM 14431		Wedding Song (There Is Love) / Song Without End	1972	.60	3.00
MGM 14511		Serenade Of Love / I Can't Remember How It Was Before	1973	.60	3.00
MGM 14577		Gratification / I Can't Remember How It Was Before	1973	.60	3.00
MGM 14673		Silver Spoon / Fixing To Live	1973	.60	3.00
MGM 14708		In The Old Fashioned Way / Come On Home	1974	.60	3.00
Dunhill 15007		Never Was A Horse / I'm The Woman You Need	1974	.60	3.00
Dunhill 15019		Loving Arms / I'm The Woman You Need	1974	.60	3.00
Scotti 02676		Natural Love / Because I Love Him	1981	.60	3.00
Scotti 02979		Blue Eyes Cryin' In The Rain / Love Won't Always Pass You By	1982	.60	3.00
Scotti 03171		Dreamin' With My Eyes Wide Open / Afterglow	1982	.60	3.00
		—Extended Play Albums—			
Warner Bros. 1743	(33)	Petula (Jukebox EP)	1968	3.00	15.00
Warner Bros. 1765	(33)	Petula Clark's Greatest Hits (Jukebox EP)	1968	3.00	15.00

CLARK, SANFORD

MCI 1003		The Fool / Lonesome For A Letter	1956	30.00	150.00
Dot 15481		The Fool / Lonesome For A Letter	1956	6.00	30.00
Dot 15516		A Cheat / Usta Be My Baby	1956	4.00	20.00
		—Original Dot singles above have maroon labels.—			
Dot 15481		The Fool / Lonesome For A Letter	1957	3.00	15.00
Dot 15516		A Cheat / Usta Be My Baby	1957	3.00	15.00
Dot 15534		Ooo Baby / 9 Lb. Hammer	1957	3.00	15.00
Dot 15556		The Glory Of Love / Darling Dear	1957	3.00	15.00
Dot 15585		Love Charms / Lou Be Doo	1957	3.00	15.00
Dot 15646		Swanee River Rock / The Man Who Made An Angel Cry	1957	4.00	20.00
Dot 15738		Modern Romance / Travelin' Man	1958	30.00	150.00
Jamie 1107		Sing 'Em Some Blues / Still As The Night	1958	4.00	20.00
		("Sing 'Em Some Blues" features Duane Eddy.)			
Jamie 1120		Bad Luck / My Jealousy	1950	3.00	15.00

Label & Catalog #	A-Side/B-Side	Year	VG	NM
Jamie 1129	Run Boy, Run / New Kind Of Fool	1959	3.00	15.00
Jamie 1153	Pledging My Love / Go On Home	1960	3.00	15.00
Trey 3016	It Hurts Me, Too / Guess It's Love	1961	3.00	15.00
Ramco 1872	The Fool / Step Aside	1966	3.00	15.00

CLARKE, ALLAN
Allan Clarke also recorded with The Hollies.

Epic 10914	Ruby / Baby, It's Alright With Me	1972	.60	3.00
Atlantic 3459	(I Will Be Your) Shadow In The Street / The Passenger	1977	.40	2.00
Atlantic 3497	I Wasn't Born Yesterday /			
	The Man Who Manufactured Daydreams	1977	.40	2.00
Atlantic 3522	I'm Betting My Life On You / Who's Goin' Out The Back Door	1978	.40	2.00
Asylum 45313	If You Think You Know How To Love Me / Light A Light	1979	.40	2.00
Asylum 46617	Slipstream / Imagination's Child	1979	.40	2.00
Asylum 47019	The Only Ones / Driving The Doomsday Cars	1980	.40	2.00

CLASS-AIRS, THE

Honey Bee	Tears Start To Fall / Too Old To Cry	195?	75.00	300.00

CLASS CUTTERS, THE: *Refer to* **HERBIE & THE CLASS CUTTERS**

CLASS MATES, THE

Marquee 101	High School / Don't Make Me Cry	1960	3.00	15.00
Marquee 102	Until Then / Pretty Little Pet	1960	3.00	15.00
Seg-Way 104	Here Comes Suzy / Homework	1961	3.00	15.00

CLASS MATES, THE: *Refer to* **MARK CAVELL & THE CLASS MATES**

CLASSIC FOUR, THE

Algonquin 1651	True Story / What Would I Do?	1962	8.00	40.00
Twist 1001	Island Of Paradise / What Will I Do Without You?	1962	8.00	40.00
Twist 1003	Heavenly Bliss / Please Be Mine	1962	50.00	200.00

CLASSICS, THE
The Classics feature Lou Christie.

Starr 508	Close Your Eyes / Funny Things	1960	30.00	150.00

CLASSICS, THE
The Classics also recorded with Herb Lance.

Dart 1015	Cinderella / So In Love	1960	5.00	25.00
Dart 1024	Life Is But A Dream / That's The Way	1960	25.00	125.00
Dart 1032	Angel Angela / Eenie Minie Mo	1960	4.00	20.00
Mercury 71829	Life Is But A Dream / That's The Way	1960	5.00	25.00
Stream Line 1028	Life Is But A Dream / That's The Way	1960	5.00	25.00
Music Note 118	P.S. I Love You / Wrap Your Troubles In A Dream	1963	3.00	15.00
Music Note 1116	Till Then / Eenie Minie Mo	1963	2.00	10.00
Musictone 1114	Cinderella / So In Love	196?	2.00	10.00
Musictone 6131	Too Young / Who's Laughing, Who's Crying?	196?	3.00	15.00
Stork 2	You'll Never Know / Dancing With You	1964	3.00	15.00
Piccolo 500	I Apologize / Love For Today	1965	5.00	25.00

CLASSICS, THE

Jerden 742	Till I Met You / I Didn't Take Much	1964	1.20	6.00

CLASSICS IV, THE [THE CLASSICS]

Arlen 746	It's Too Late / Don't Make Me Wait	1964	3.00	15.00
Capitol 5710	Pollyanna / Cry Baby	1966	3.00	15.00
	(Capitol 5710 credits The Classics.)			
Capitol 5816	Little Darling / Nothing To Lose	1967	3.00	15.00
Imperial 66259	Spooky / Poor People	1967	1.00	5.00
Imperial 66294	Soul Train / Strange Changes	1968	1.00	5.00
Imperial 66328	Stormy / 24 Hours Of Loneliness	1968	1.00	5.00
Imperial 66352	Traces / Mary, Mary, Row Your Boat	1969	1.00	5.00
Imperial 66378	Everyday With You Girl / Sentimental Lady	1969	.60	3.00
Imperial 66393	Change Of Heart / Rainy Day	1969	.60	3.00
Imperial 66424	Midnight / The Comic	1969	.60	3.00
Imperial 66439	The Funniest Thing / Nobody Loves You But Me	1970	.60	3.00
Liberty 56182	God Knows I Loved Her / We Miss You	1970	.40	2.00
Liberty 56200	Where Did All The Good Times Go? / Ain't It The Truth	1970	.40	2.00
United Artists 50777	Most Of All / It's Time For Love	1971	.40	2.00
United Artists 50805	Cherry Hill Park / Pick Up The Pieces	1971	.40	2.00
MGM/South 7002	What Am I Crying For? / All In Your Mind	1972	.40	2.00
MGM/South 7012	Rosanna / One Man Show	1973	.40	2.00
MGM/South 7016	Make Me Believe It / Save The Sunlight	1973	.40	2.00
MGM/South 7027	It's Now Winter's Day / Losing My Mind	1973	.40	2.00

Label & Catalog #		A-Side/B-Side	Year	VG	NM
CLASSMATES, THE					
King 1487		A Kiss Is Not A Kiss / What Am I Gonna Do?	1955	5.00	25.00
Silhouette 509		Gotta Go And See My Baby / Washed My Heart Of Love	1956	5.00	25.00
Dot 15460		Return My Heart / Who's Gonna Take You To The Prom?	1956	3.00	15.00
Dot 15464		Break Down And Love Me / Two Straws In The Wind	1956	3.00	15.00
Dot 15504		Friends / I Want My Love Close By	1957	3.00	15.00
Dot 15589		You Aren't The Only One / You Do Soomething To Me	1957	3.00	15.00
Seg-Way 104		Homework / Here Comes Suzy	1961	2.00	10.00
Stacy 935		Did You Ever? / Will You Love Me Tomorrow?	1962	2.00	10.00
Radar 2624		Teenage Twister / Graduation	1962	2.00	10.00
CLASS MATES, THE: *Refer to* RONNIE JONES & THE CLASS MATES					
CLASSMEN, THE					
Limelight 3012		My Special Angel / Love Is Gone	1963	2.00	10.00
Limelight 3012		Do You Want To Dance? / All Time Fool	1963	2.00	10.00
CLASSMEN, THE					
Impact 1012		Everything Is Alright / Susie Jones	1966	4.00	20.00
CLAY, CASSIUS					
Columbia 43007		I Am The Greatest / Stand By Me	1964	2.00	10.00
Columbia 43007	(PS)	I Am The Greatest / Stand By Me	1964	5.00	25.00
CLAY, CHRIS					
Veltone 111		Santa Under Analysis / Santa Under Analysis, Part 2	195?	5.00	25.00
CLAY, JOE					
Vik 0211		Duck Tail / Sixteen Chicks	195?	10.00	50.00
CLAYTON, RICH, & THE RUMBLES					
The Rumbles also recorded as The Fabulous Rumbles.					
Dawn Cory 1003		Wail It / Flip Side	1963	8.00	40.00
CLAYTON-THOMAS, DAVID, & THE SHAYS					
David Clayton-Thomas later recorded with Blood, Sweat & Tears.					
Atco 6347		Hey, Hey, Hey / Walk That Walk	1965	3.00	15.00
Tower 206		Out Of The Sunshine / Take Me Back	1966	2.00	10.00
CLAYTON-THOMAS, DAVID, & THE BOSSMEN					
Tower 263		Born With The Blues / Brainwashed	1966	2.00	10.00
CLAYTON-THOMAS, DAVID					
Roulette 7048		No No No / Monopoly	1969	2.00	10.00
Decca 32556		Say Boss Man / Done Somebody Wrong	1969	2.00	10.00
Columbia 45569		Sing A Song / We're All Meat From The Same Bone	1972	.80	4.00
Columbia 45603		Magnificent Sanctuary Band / North Beach Race Track	1972	.80	4.00
CLEAR LIGHT					
Elektra 45622		She's Ready To Be Free / Black Roses	1967	2.00	10.00
CLEE-SHAYS, THE					
The Clee-Shays is a pseudonym for The Challengers.					
Triumph 65		Dynamite / The Man From U.N.C.L.E.	1966	2.00	10.00
CLEFS OF LAVENDER HILL, THE					
Thames		Stop! Get A Ticket / First Tell Me Why	1966	4.00	20.00
Date 1510		Stop! Get A Ticket / First Tell Me Why	1966	2.00	10.00
Date 1530		One More Time / So I'll Try	1966	2.00	10.00
Date 1533		It Won't Be Long / Play With Fire	1966	2.00	10.00
CLEMENT, JACK					
Sun 291		Ten Years / Your Lover Boy	1958	3.00	15.00
Sun 311		The Black Haired Man / Wrong	1958	3.00	15.00
CLICK CLACKS, THE					
Apt 25010		Roma Rocka-Rolla / Pretty Little Pearlie	1958	3.00	15.00
Apt 25032		Kiss Goodbye / Rocket Roll	1959	3.00	15.00
CLIENTELLS, THE					
MBS 007		Church Bells May Ring / My Love	195?	4.00	20.00
CLIFF TRIO, BENNY					
Drift 1441		Shake Um Up Rock / The Breaking Point	1959	——	——
		(Rare. Estimated near mint value $1,500-3,000.)			

Label & Catalog #		A-Side/B-Side	Year	VG	NM
CLIFFORD, BUZZ (& THE TEENAGERS)					
Columbia 41774		Hello, Mr. Moonlight / Blue Lagoon	1960	2.50	12.00
Columbia 41774	(PS)	Hello, Mr. Moonlight / Blue Lagoon	1960	5.00	25.00
Columbia 41876		Baby Sitter Boogie / Driftwood	1960	5.00	25.00
Columbia 41876		Baby Sittin' Boogie / Driftwood	1960	2.50	12.00
Columbia 41876	(PS)	Baby Sittin' Boogie / Driftwood	1960	4.00	20.00
Columbia 41876	(33)	Baby Sittin' Boogie / Driftwood	1960	4.00	20.00
Columbia 41979		Three Little Fishes / Simply Because	1961	3.00	15.00
Columbia 41979	(PS)	Three Little Fishes / Simply Because	1961	4.00	20.00
Columbia 42019		I'll Never Forget / The Awakening	1961	6.00	30.00
Columbia 42019	(PS)	I'll Never Forget / The Awakening	1961	7.00	35.00
Columbia 42019	(33)	I'll Never Forget / The Awakening	1961	7.00	35.00
Columbia 42177		Moving Day / Loneliness	1961	2.00	10.00
Columbia 42177	(PS)	Moving Day / Loneliness	1961	4.00	20.00
Columbia 42177	(33)	Moving Day / Loneliness	1961	4.00	20.00
Columbia 42290		Forever / Magic Circle	1962	3.00	15.00
Columbia 42290	(PS)	Forever / Magic Circle	1962	4.00	20.00
Columbia 42290	(33)	Forever / Magic Circle	1962	4.00	20.00
A&M 878		Just Can't Wait / On My Way	1967	.80	4.00
CLIFFORD, DOUG					
Doug Clifford originally recorded with Creedence Clearwater Revival.					
Fantasy 686		Latin Music / Take A Train	1973	1.00	5.00
CLIFFTERS, THE					
Philips 40050		Django / Amapola	1962	2.00	10.00
CLIFTON, BILL					
London 9638		Beatle Crazy / Little Girl Dressed In Blue	1964	3.00	15.00
CLIMATES, THE					
Sun 404		No You For Me / Breaking Up Again	1958	3.00	15.00
CLINGER SISTERS, THE					
Tollie 9020		Shoop Shoop De Shoop, Rama Lama Ding Dong, Yeah Yeah Yeah / Lipstick Song	1964	2.00	10.00
Tollie 9035		Golly, Mom / Puppet	1964	1.20	6.00
Tollie 9038		What Can I Give Him? / Jingle Dingle Do	1964	1.20	6.00
CLINKING BEARD, THE					
Jerden 992		Pay Yourself, Loretta / Funky Man	196?	1.00	5.00
CLIQUE, THE					
ABC-Paramount 10655		She Ain't No Good / Time Time Time	1965	2.00	10.00
CLIQUE, THE					
Cinema 001		Stay By Me / Splash One	1967	4.00	20.00
Scepter 12202		Stay By Me / Splash One	1967	2.00	10.00
Scepter 12212		Love Ain't Easy / Gotta Get Away	1968	2.00	10.00
White Whale 312		Shadow Of Your Love / Superman	1969	.80	4.00
White Whale 323		Sugar On Sunday / Superman	1969	.80	4.00
White Whale 333		I'll Hold Out My Hand / Soul Mates	1969	.80	4.00
White Whale 335		My Darkest Hour / Shadow Of Your Love	1969	.80	4.00
White Whale 338		Sparkle And Shine / I'm Alive	1970	.80	4.00
White Whale 361		Memphis / Southbound Wind	1970	.80	4.00
White Whale 367	(DJ)	Judy Judy Judy / Judy Judy Judy	1970	1.00	5.00
		(Stock copies of W.W. 367 may not exist.)			
CLOCK-WORK ORANGE					
Rust 5126		What Am I Without You? / Image Of You	1964	2.00	10.00
CLOCKWORK ORANGES, THE					
Liberty 55887		Ready Steady / After Tonight	1966	2.00	10.00
CLOUD, CHRISTOPHER					
Christopher Cloud is a pseudonym for Tommy Boyce.					
Chelsea 0101		Thank God For Rock And Roll / Thank God For Rock And Roll	1972	1.00	5.00
Chelsea 0118		Zip A Dee Doo Dah / Zip A Dee Doo Dah	1973	1.00	5.00
CLOUDS, THE					
Round 1008		Darling, I Love You / TV Mix Up	1959	8.00	40.00
CLOUDS, THE					
The Clouds feature Bill Medley.					
Medley 1001		Night Owl / My Tears Will Go Away	1960	5.00	25.00

Label & Catalog #		A-Side/B-Side	Year	VG	NM
COACHMEN, THE					
MMC 010		Mr. Moon / Nothing At All	1965	2.00	10.00
MMC 010		Mr. Moon / Nothing At All (Blue vinyl)	1965	4.00	20.00
MMC 013		My generation / No Answer	1965	5.00	25.00
Bear 1974		Mr. Moon / Nothing At All	1965	2.00	10.00
Bear 1976		Linda Lou / I'm A King Bee	1966	2.00	10.00
Capitol 5896		Seasons In The Sun / Garrielle	1967	1.00	5.00
MMC 014		Time Won't Change / Tell Her No	1967	2.00	10.00
Target 1001		Girl In The Wind / The News Is Out	1969	.60	3.00
COASTLINERS, THE					
Dear 1300		I See Me / California On My Mind	196?	3.00	15.00
Astro 109		The Lonely Sea / Big Mike, The Sidewalk Surfer	1965	8.00	40.00
Back Beat 554		Alright / Wonderful You	1965	3.00	15.00
Back Beat 566		She's My Girl / I'll Be Home	1966	4.00	20.00
COBRAS, THE					
Casino 13409		La La / Goodbye, Molly	1964	7.00	35.00
Swan 4176		La La / Goodbye, Molly	1964	3.00	15.00
COCHISE					
United Artists 50756		Love's Made A Fool Of You / Words Of A Dying Man	1971	.60	3.00
		—Extended Play Albums—			
United Artists SP-50	(33)	Swallow Tales (Jukebox EP)	1971	1.60	8.00

COCHRAN, EDDIE

Eddie Cochran also recorded with, or as, Jerry Capehart; The Cochran Brothers; The Gee Cees; Bo Davis; Lee Denson; The Galaxies; Jewel & Eddie; Jerry Neal; and Ray Stanley.

Crest 1026	(DJ)	Skinny Jim / Half Loved	1956	25.00	125.00
Crest 1026		Skinny Jim / Half Loved	1956	50.00	200.00
Crest 1026		Skinny Jim / Half Loved (Red vinyl)	1956	150.00	600.00
Liberty 55056		Sittin' In The Balcony / Dark Lonely Street	1957	4.00	20.00
Liberty 55070		Mean When I'm Mad / One Kiss	1957	4.00	20.00
Liberty 55070	(PS)	Mean When I'm Mad / One Kiss	1957	330.00	1,000.00
Liberty 55087		Am I Blue? / Drive-In Show	1957	5.00	25.00
Liberty 55112		Twenty Flight Rock / Cradle Baby	1957	15.00	75.00
Liberty 55123		Jeannie Jeannie Jeannie / Pocketful Of Hearts	1958	4.00	20.00
Liberty 55138		Pretty Girl / Teresa	1958	5.00	25.00
Liberty 55144		Summertime Blues / Love Again	1958	4.00	20.00
Liberty 55166		C'mon Everybody / Don't Ever Let Me Go	1958	4.00	20.00
Liberty 55177		Teenage Heaven / I Remember	1959	5.00	25.00
Liberty 55203		Something Else / Boll Weevil Song	1959	4.00	20.00
Liberty 55217		Hallelujah, I Love Her So / Little Angel	1959	4.00	20.00
Liberty 55242		Cut Across, Shorty / Three Steps To Heaven	1960	5.00	25.00
Liberty 55278		Sweetie Pie / Lonely	1960	4.00	20.00
Liberty 55389		Weekend / Lonely	1961	4.00	20.00
		—Original Liberty singles above have green labels.—			
Capehart 5003		Rough Stuff / Our Love	1960	5.00	25.00
Capehart 5003	(PS)	Rough Stuff / Our Love	1960	50.00	200.00
		—Extended Play Albums—			
Liberty 3061-1		Singin' To My Baby (Volume 1)	1958	50.00	250.00
Liberty 3061-2		Singin' To My Baby (Volume 2)	1958	50.00	250.00
Liberty 3061-3		Singin' To My Baby (Volume 3)	1958	50.00	250.00
COCHRAN, JACKIE LEE					
Sims 107		Hip Shakin' Mama / Riverside Jump	1956	35.00	175.00
Decca 30206		Mama, Don't You Think I Know? / Ruby Pearl	1957	15.00	75.00
Viv 988		I Want You / Buy A Car	1957	30.00	150.00
Viv 102		I Want You / Buy A Car	1958	15.00	75.00
ABC-Paramount 9930		I Want You / Buy A Car	1958	12.00	60.00
Jaguar 3031		I Wanna See You / Georgia Lee Brown	1959	15.00	75.00
Spry 120		Endless Love / Pity Me	1960	75.00	300.00
COCHRAN, WAYNE (& THE C. C. RIDERS)					
Scottie 1303		My Little Girl / The Coo	1959	2.00	10.00
King 5856		Last Kiss / I Dreamed, I Gambled, I Lost	1964	1.20	6.00
Soft 779		Harlem Shuffle / Somebody Please	1965	1.20	6.00
Mercury 72507		Harlem Shuffle / Somebody Please	1965	1.00	5.00
Mercury 72507	(PS)	Harlem Shuffle / Somebody Please	1965	2.00	10.00
Mercury 72552		Get Down With It / No Rest For The Wicked	1966	1.00	5.00
Mercury 72623		Goin' Back To Miami / I'm In Trouble	1967	1.00	5.00
Chess 2020		When My Baby Cries / Some A Your Sweet Lovin'	1967	1.20	6.00
Chess 2020	(PS)	When My Baby Cries / Some A Your Sweet Lovin'	1967	2.00	10.00
Epic 10859		Do You Like The Sound Of Music? / Somebody's Been Cuttin' In On My Groove	1972	.80	4.00
Epic 10893		Long, Long Day / Sleepless Nights	1972	.80	4.00

Label & Catalog #		A-Side/B-Side	Year	VG	NM
COCHRAN BROTHERS, THE					
The Cochran Brothers feature Eddie Cochran.					
Ekko 1003		Mr. Fiddle / Two Blue Singing Stars	1955	40.00	200.00
Ekko 1005		Guilty Conscience / Your Tomorrow Never Comes	1955	40.00	200.00
Ekko 3001		Tired And Sleepy / Fool's Paradise	1956	50.00	250.00
COCKER, JOE					
Joe Cocker originally recorded as Vance Arnold.					
A&M 928		Marjorie / New Age Of The Lily	1968	.60	3.00
A&M 991		With A Little Help From My Friends / Something's Coming In	1968	.60	3.00
A&M 1063		Feeling Alright / Sandpaper Cadillac	1969	.60	3.00
A&M 1112		Delta Lady / She's So Good To Me	1969	.40	2.00
A&M 1147		She Came In Through The Bathroom Window / Change In Louise	1969	.60	3.00
A&M 1147	(PS)	She Came In Through The Bathroom Window / Change In Louise	1969	1.00	5.00
A&M 1174		The Letter / Space Captain	1970	.60	3.00
A&M 1174	(PS)	The Letter / Space Captain	1970	.60	3.00
A&M 1200		Cry Me A River / Give Peace A Chance	1970	.40	2.00
A&M 1200	(PS)	Cry Me A River / Give Peace A Chance	1970	.60	3.00
A&M 1258		High Time We Went / Black-Eyed Blues	1971	.40	2.00
A&M 1258	(PS)	High Time We Went / Black-Eyed Blues	1971	.60	3.00
A&M 1370		Midnight Rider / Woman To Woman	1972	.40	2.00
A&M 1370	(PS)	Midnight Rider / Woman To Woman	1972	.60	3.00
A&M 1407		Pardon Me, Sir / St. James Infirmary Blues	1973	.40	2.00
A&M 1407	(PS)	Pardon Me, Sir / St. James Infirmary Blues	1973	.60	3.00
A&M 1539		Put Out The Light / If I Love You	1974	.40	2.00
A&M 1539	(PS)	Put Out The Light / If I Love You	1974	.60	3.00
A&M 1626		I Can Stand A Little Rain / I Get Mad	1974	.40	2.00
A&M 1641		You Are So Beautiful / It's A Sin When You Love Somebody	1975	.40	2.00
A&M 1758		It's All Over But The Shoutin' / Forgive Me Now	1975	.40	2.00
A&M 1830		The Jealous Kind / You Came Along	1976	.40	2.00
A&M 1855		You Came Along / I Broke Down	1976	.40	2.00
COE, JAMIE, & THE GIGOLOS					
Addison 15001		Summertime Symphony / There's Gonna Be A Day	196?	3.00	15.00
ABC-Paramount 10203		I'm Getting Married / Two Dozen And A Half	1961	2.00	10.00
ABC-Paramount 10267		Little Dear, Little Darling / How Low Is Low?	1961	2.00	10.00
Big Top 3107		But Yesterday / Cleopatra	1962	2.00	10.00
Big Top 3139		The Fool / Got That Feeling	1963	2.00	10.00
Enterprise 5005		The Dealer / Close Your Eyes	1964	2.00	10.00
Enterprise 5055		I Was The One / Good Enough For You	1964	2.00	10.00
Reprise 0295		The Dealer / Close Your Eyes	1964	2.00	10.00
COEDS, THE					
The Coeds is a pseudonym for The Tokens.					
Swing 101		Mark My Words / You're My First Love	1964	3.00	15.00
COEDS, THE: *Refer to* **JOHNNY MAESTRO**					
COFF, DENNIS, & THE LYMAN WOODWARD TRIO					
Maverick 1007		It's Your Thing / Rover Rogue	1967	3.00	15.00
COL-LEE-JETS, THE					
Northwestern 2477		Phony Baby / Jam And Jelly	196?	4.00	20.00
Shadow 7711		Jo Ann / A Minor Mood	196?	2.00	10.00
Shadow 7712		Cynthia / Blind Date	196?	2.00	10.00
COLD BLOOD					
San Francisco 60		You Got Me Hummin' / If You Will	1970	.80	4.00
San Francisco 61		I Wish I Knew How It Would Feel To Be Free / I'm A Good Woman	1970	.80	4.00
San Francisco 62		Too Many People / I Can't Stay	1970	.80	4.00
San Francisco 66		Understanding / Shop Talk	1970	.80	4.00
Reprise 1092		Down To The Bone / Valdez Down In The Country	1972	.60	3.00
Reprise 1157		Baby, I Love You / Livin' Your Dream	1973	.60	3.00
COLDER, BEN					
MGM 13147		Goin' Surfin' / Still #2	1963	2.00	10.00
COLE, CARMEN					
Groove 0057		Bobby, Darlin' / I Just Don't Understand	1955	3.00	15.00
COLE, CINDY					
Tower 145		A Love Like Yours / He's Sure The Boy I Love	1965	1.60	8.00
Tower 302		Lonely City Blue Boy / Just Being Your Baby	1966	1.60	8.00

Label & Catalog #	A-Side/B-Side	Year	VG	NM

COLE, CLAY
Imperial 5804 — Twist Around The Clock / Don't Twist (With Anyone Else But Me) — 1962 — 1.60 — 8.00

Label & Catalog #	A-Side/B-Side	Year	VG	NM
COLE, CLAY				
Imperial 5804	Twist Around The Clock / Don't Twist (With Anyone Else But Me)	1962	1.60	8.00
COLE, DON & ALLYNE				
Son Ray 101	Something's Got A Hold On Me / Poor Fool	1965	1.60	8.00
COLE, FRED				
Lois 101	Big Boots / Hey, Little Lover	1961	3.00	15.00
COLE, JERRY, & HIS SPACEMEN				
Refer to the Various Artists EP section.				
Capitol 5056	Midnight Mary / Land Of Dreams	1963	2.00	10.00
Capitol 5106	Pokey / One Color Blues	1964	2.00	10.00
Capitol 5141	Night Rumble / Boss Dance	1964	2.00	10.00
Capitol 5256	Meet Me On The Corner / Life Will Go On	1964	2.00	10.00
Capitol PRO-2649 (DJ)	Movin' Surf / Racing Waves	1964	3.00	15.00
	(Capitol PRO-2649 was issued in a special "pocket" on the cover of Dick Dale's "Surf Age" album.)			
COLE, JERRY, & TRINITY				
Warner Bros. 8101	Susanna's Song (In The California Morning) / Child Of The Times	1975	.60	3.00
Warner Bros. 8156	Liberated Lady / In The Pocket	1975	.60	3.00
COLE, JOHNNY, & THE REPTILES				
Radiant 1503	Wrap My Heart In Velvet / Lizard Gizzard	1961	40.00	200.00
COLE, LEE				
Mist 1010	Cool Baby / Suzy Ann	1959	20.00	100.00
COLE, SONNY, & THE RHYTHM ROAMERS				
Excel 123	I Dreamed I Was Elvis / Curfew Cops	195?	20.00	100.00
Rollin' Rock 001	I Dreamed I Was Elvis / Curfew Cops	197?	2.00	10.00
COLEMAN, JOE				
Rem 304	Rock All Night / Rock All Night, part 2	1960	2.00	10.00
COLEMAN, LENNY (WITH NINO & THE EBB-TIDES)				
Laurie 3290	Four Seasons / Shake It Easy	1965	5.00	25.00
COLL, BRIAN, & THE PLATTERMEN				
Parrot 10818	I'm In Love Again / I'll Take You Home Again, Kathleen	1966	2.00	10.00
COLLAGE				
Coliseum *(No number)*	Girl Don't Tell Me / Best Friend	1967	3.00	15.00
Smash 2150	Anyday's A Sunday Afternoon / Driftin'	1968	.80	4.00
Smash 2170	The Story Of Rock And Roll / Virginia Day's Ragtime Stories	1968	.80	4.00
COLLECTION				
Hot Biscuit 1455	Both Sides Now / Tomorrow Is A Window	1968	1.00	5.00
RCA Victor 47-9463	Paper Crown Of Gold / Aquarius	1968	2.00	10.00
COLLECTORS, THE				
The Collectors originally recorded in the U.S. as The Canadian Classics.				
Valiant 760	Looking At A Baby / Old Man	1967	2.00	10.00
Warner Bros. 7059	Fisherwoman / Listen To The Words	1968	1.00	5.00
Warner Bros. 7159	Make It Easy / Fat Bird	1968	1.00	5.00
Warner Bros. 7194	Lydia Purple / She (Will O' The Wisp)	1968	1.00	5.00
Warner Bros. 7194	Lydia Purple / I Ain't No Rich Man	1968	1.00	5.00
Warner Bros. 7300	Early Morning / My Love Delights Me	1969	1.00	5.00
COLLEGIANS, THE				
X-Tra 108	Let's Go For A Ride / Heavenly Night	1958	7.00	35.00
Winley 224	Zoom Zoom Zoom / On Your Merry Way	1957	7.00	35.00
	(Label has small print; thick vinyl)			
Winley 224	Zoom Zoom Zoom / On Your Merry Way	1957	4.00	20.00
	(Label has large print; thin vinyl)			
Winley 261	Oh, I Need Your Love / Tonite, Oh Tonite	1961	3.00	15.00
Winley 263	Right Around The Corner / Teenie Weenie Little Bit	1961	3.00	15.00
Post 10002	I'm Ready / Grandma Told Me So	1962	4.00	20.00
Times Square 11	Let's Go For A Ride / Heavenly Night	1963	2.00	10.00
COLLEGIATES, THE				
Heritage 105	I Had A Dream / Growing Up	1961	3.00	15.00

Label & Catalog #	A-Side/B-Side	Year	VG	NM
COLLEY, KEITH				
Era 3054	It's Nice Out Tonight / Zing Went The Strings	1961	1.20	6.00
Era 3067	Put Em Down / (And Her Name Is) Scarlet	1962	1.20	6.00
Era 3078	Someone To Take Your Place / The Number	196?	1.20	6.00
Unical 3004	Heartbreaker, U.S.A. / Heartbreaker, U.S.A.	196?	1.00	5.00
Unical 3006	Enamorado / No Joke Shame Shame	196?	1.00	5.00
Unical 3013	Aladdin / Cuando La Luna	196?	1.00	5.00
Unical 3011	Queridita Mia / Ramblin' Bee	196?	1.00	5.00
Vee Jay 682	Billy Girl / Welcome Home Baby	1965	1.20	6.00
Challenge 9344	Tonight I'm Telling You / Up Off My Knees	1966	.80	4.00
Columbia 44410	Shame, Shame, Shame / Enamorado	1968	.80	4.00
	(Produced by Gary Usher.)			
COLLINS, CAROL				
Carol Collins is a pseudonym for Carol Connors.				
Dunes 2005	Dear One / Johnny, Oh, Johnny	1961	7.00	35.00
COLLINS, JIMMY				
Orbit 110	Straight Shift / Fluid Drive	196?	3.00	15.00
COLONIALS, THE				
Tru-Lite 127	Little Miss Muffet / Do Pop Si	196?	8.00	40.00
COLORING BOOK, THE				
Challenger 118	Smokestack Lightnin' / You Make Me Feel So Good	196?	2.00	10.00
COLOURS				
Dot 17060	Brother Lou's Love Colony / Lovin'	1968	.80	4.00
Dot 17132	Love Heals / Bad Day At Black Rock Bay	1968	.80	4.00
Dot 17181	Hyannisport Soul / Run Away From Here	1969	.80	4.00
COLT, STEVE, & THE 45'S				
Big Beat 1001	Hey Girl, How Ya Gonna Act? / I've Been Loving You	196?	2.00	10.00
Big Beat 1006	Dynamite / Take Away	196?	2.00	10.00
RCA Victor 47-8913	Just A Little Bit Of Soul / So Far Away	1966	2.00	10.00
COLTON, TONY, & THE CONCORDS				
Roulette 4475	Goodbye Cindy, Goodbye / Tell The World	1963	1.20	6.00
COLUMBUS, RAY, & THE INVADERS				
Philips 40189	I Wanna Be Your Man / Cat's Eye	1964	1.20	6.00
Philips 40326	Where Have You Been? / She's Back	1965	1.20	6.00
Philips 40340	She's A Mod / The Cruel Sea	1965	1.20	6.00
Colstar 1001	She's A Mod / Kick Me	1967	1.00	5.00
Colstar 1002	We Want A Beat /	1967	2.00	10.00
Colstar 1003	In The Morning Of Today / I Would Rather Blow A Bagpipe	1967	1.00	5.00
COMANCHEROES, THE				
Teen 1052	TP / VW	196?	6.00	30.00
COMMANCHES, THE				
Hickory 1264	Tomorrow / Missed Your Lovin'	1964	1.20	6.00
COMMITTEE, THE				
White Whale 257	California My Way / You For Weren't It If	1967	1.20	6.00
COMMUNICATION AGGREGATION, THE				
Our Bag 101	Freakout U.S.A. / Off The Wall	1966	3.00	15.00
RCA Victor 47-8930	Freakout U.S.A. / Off The Wall	1966	2.00	10.00
COMO, NICKY (WITH THE DEL SATINS)				
Tang 1231	Your Guardian Angel / Just A Little While	195?	6.00	30.00
COMPANIONS, THE				
The Companions is a pseudonym for The Tokens.				
Columbia 42279	I'll Always Love You / A Little Bit Of Blue	1962	5.00	25.00
COMPETITORS, THE				
Dot 16560	Little Stick Nomad / Power Shift	1963	8.00	40.00
	(Produced by Gary Usher.)			
COMRADE X				
Era 3048	Spacenik / Theme From Spacenik	1961	2.00	10.00
COMSTOCK, BOBBY				
Lawn 202	Let's Stomp / I Want To Do It	1965	3.00	15.00
Ascot 2216	Can't Judge A Book / Out Of Sight	1966	2.00	10.00

Label & Catalog #	A-Side/B-Side	Year	VG	NM
CONCEPTS, THE				
Catamount 112	**The Vow / You Me Pregunto**	1966	2.00	10.00
CONCORDS, THE				
The Concords also recorded as The Sherwoods; The Snowmen.				
RCA Victor 47-7911	**Again / The Boy Most Likely**	1961	4.00	20.00
Gramercy 304	**Cross My Heart / Our Last Goodbye**	1961	75.00	300.00
Gramercy 305	**My Dreams / Scarlet Ribbons**	1962	8.00	40.00
Herald 576	**Marlene / Our Love Wasn't Meant To Be**	1962	3.00	15.00
Herald 578	**Cold And Frosty Morning / Don't Go Now**	1962	3.00	15.00
Rust 5048	**One Step From Heaven / Away**	1962	3.00	15.00
Epic 9697	**Should I Cry? / It's Our Wedding Day**	1964	6.00	30.00
Boom 60021	**Down The Isle Of Love / Feel A Love Comin' On**	1966	3.00	15.00
Polydor 14036	**Down The Isle Of Love / Feel A Love Comin' On**	1970	2.00	10.00
CONDELLO, MIKE				
Blitz KPHO-TV 005 (EP)	**Commodore Condello's Salt River Navy Band**	196?	5.00	25.00
Blitz Cheap 006 (EP)	**Commodore Condello's Salt River Navy Band**	196?	5.00	25.00
	(Both EPs issued with a black & white paper sleeve.)			
Scepter 12261	**Goodnight / Long**	1967	2.00	10.00
CONEY ISLAND KIDS, THE				
Jubilee 5215	**Moonlight Beach / Baby, Baby You**	1955	3.00	15.00
Josie 791	**Red Light, Green Light / I Love It**	1956	3.00	15.00
Josie 802	**We Want A Rock And Roll President /**			
	Thwistle Rock And Thwistle Roll	1956	3.00	15.00
Josie 809	**Popcorn And Candy / Not You, Pie Face**	1956	3.00	15.00
CONFESSIONS, THE				
Epic 4974	**Be Bop Baby / Before You Change Your Mind**	1961	3.00	15.00
CONLON, CHUCK				
Marlin 16007	**Won't You Say Yes To Me, Girl? / Midnight Reader**	196?	3.00	15.00
CONLON & THE CRAWLERS				
Features Chuck Conlon. The Crawlers later recorded as The Nightcrawlers.				
Marlin 16006	**I Won't Tell /**	196?	6.00	30.00
CONN, TONY				
Decca 30813	**Like Wow! / Dangerous Doll**	1958	5.00	25.00
Decca 30865	**You Pretty Thing / Run Rabbit Run**	1959	5.00	25.00
CONNELL, DOUG, & THE HOT RODS				
Alton 600	**On Our Way From School / You're My Girl**	196?	3.00	15.00
CONNIE & THE BELLHOPS				
"R" 505	**Bop Sticks / Shot Rod**	195?	5.00	25.00
CONNIE & THE CONES				
NRC 5006	**I See The Image Of You / Let Us Pretend**	1959	3.00	15.00
Roulette 4223	**I Love My Teddy Bear / Lonely Girl's Prayer**	1960	3.00	15.00
Roulette 4313	**Take All The Kisses / No Time For Tears**	1961	3.00	15.00
CONNORS, CAROL [CAROL CONNORS & THE CYCLES]				
Carol Connors originally recorded as Annette Kleinbard with The Teddy Bears. Refer to Annette Bard; Carol Collins; The Surfettes.				
Columbia 41976	**My Diary / You Are My Answer**	1961	2.00	10.00
Columbia 41976 (33)	**My Diary / You Are My Answer**	1961	5.00	25.00
Columbia 42155	**My Special Boy / Listen To The Beat**	1961	2.00	10.00
Columbia 42155 (33)	**My Special Boy / Listen To The Beat**	1961	5.00	25.00
Columbia 42337	**What Do You See In Him? / That's All It Takes**	1962	2.00	10.00
Columbia 42337 (33)	**What Do You See In Him? / That's All It Takes**	1962	5.00	25.00
Era 3084	**Big, Big Love / Two Rivers**	1962	4.00	20.00
Era 3096	**Tommy, Go Away / I Wanna Know**	1962	4.00	20.00
Capitol 5152	**Never / Angel, My Angel**	1964	3.00	15.00
N.T.C. RJ80 (DJ)	**Yum Yum Yamaha** *(One sided)*	1964	5.00	25.00
N.T.C. RJ80 (PS)	**Yum Yum Yamaha**	1964	35.00	175.00
	(The N.T.C. disc credits Carol Connors & The Cycles.)			
Mira 219	**Lonely Little Beach Girl /**			
	My Baby Looks But He Don't Touch	1966	3.00	15.00
Mira 219 (PS)	**Lonely Little Beach Girl /**			
	My Baby Looks But He Don't Touch	1966	12.00	60.00
CONNORS, GREG				
Trey 3003	**Tears Me Up / Caught In The Act**	1960	2.00	10.00
CONNOTATIONS, THE				
Technichord 1000	**Two Hearts Fall In Love / Before I Go** *(Red vinyl)*	195?	40.00	200.00

Carol Connors was one of many pseudonyms used by former Teddy Bear Carol Kleinbard (she also recorded as Annette Bard, Carol Collins and the Surfettes) as she attempted to breach the wall of masculinity in the surf music field. *Yum Yum Yamaha* was cut for the motor bike company and included a picture sleeve.

Label & Catalog #	A-Side/B-Side	Year	VG	NM
CONQUERORS, THE				
Lu Pine 108	Duchess Conquers Duke / Billy Is My Boyfriend	1962	8.00	40.00
CONNY				
Capitol 4526	This Little Girl's Gone Rockin' / Midi, Midinette	1961	3.00	15.00
CONRAD & THE HURRICANE STRINGS				
Daytone 6401	Hurricane / Sweet Love	1963	6.00	30.00
Era 3130	Hurricane / Sweet Love	1963	4.00	20.00
CONROY, BERT, & THE MISFITS				
Deb-Co 1000	Debbie / That Old Gang Of Mine	196?	4.00	20.00
CONSOLES, THE: *Refer to* BOBBY & THE CONSOLES				
CONSORTS, THE				
Cousins 1004	Please Be Mine / Time After Time	1961	40.00	200.00
Apt 25066	Please Be Mine / Time After Time	1961	6.00	30.00
CONSTELLATIONS, THE				
Process 127	Quoidas /	196?	6.00	30.00
CONSTELLATIONS, THE				
Chattahoochee 656	Rise 'N Shine / Johnny B. Goode	1964	2.00	10.00
CONTE III, THE				
Ra-O 101	Hey, Miss Fanny / Pupalina	196?	2.00	10.00
CONTENDERS, THE				
Blue Sky 105	Mr. Dee Jay / Yes I Do	1959	3.00	15.00
CONTENDERS, THE				
Chattahoochee 644	The Dune Buggy / Go Ahead	1964	3.00	15.00
Chattahoochee 656	Rise And Shine / Johnny B. Goode	1964	3.00	15.00
Beth 1001	Ambassador Of Love / I'll Show You How To Love	1965	3.00	15.00
CONTINENTAL COUSINS, THE				
Palette 5081	Buddha / Kana Kapila	1961	8.00	40.00
CONTINENTAL ROCKERS, THE				
Nimbo 1774	Flashback / Heat Wave	1964	2.00	10.00
CONTINENTALS, THE				
Penguin 1002	Cool Penguin / Soap Sudz	1959	2.00	10.00
Era 3003	Cool Penguin / Soap Sudz	1959	2.00	10.00
Bolo 720	I'm Coming Home / The Turnaround	196?	2.00	10.00
CONTINENTALS, THE				
Union 505	Coffee House / (B-side by Lord Douglas Byron)	1962	7.00	35.00
CONTINENTALS, THE				
Lifetime 1019	Cathy's Clown / Maybe Baby	1966	1.20	6.00
CONTINENTALS, THE: *Refer to* JOEY & THE CONTINENTALS; RICHIE & THE CONTINENTALS				
CONTRAILS, THE				
Millage 104	Feel So Fine / Make Me Love You	196?	3.00	15.00
Diamond 213	Someone / Mummy Walk	1966	3.00	15.00
CONTRASTS, THE: *Refer to* BILLY VERA & THE CONTRASTS				
CONVERTERS, THE				
Star-Hi 10560	Dave's Place / Lost City	196?	1.60	8.00
COOK, JACK				
Ramco 1721	Walk Another Mile / My Evil Mind	1962	2.00	10.00
Ramco 1739	Run Boy, Run Boy / I Got A Book	1962	2.00	10.00
Ruby 1	Walk Another Mile / My Evil Mind	1963	2.00	10.00
COOK, KEN				
Philips Inter. 3534	I Was A Fool / Crazy Baby	1958	7.00	35.00
	("I Was A Fool " is a duet with Roy Orbison.)			
COOKIE & THE CRUMBS				
Vest 55	My Dream Of You / Someday Baby	1966	2.00	10.00

Label & Catalog #		A-Side/B-Side	Year	VG	NM
COOKIES, THE					
Warner Bros. 7025		All My Trials / Wounded	1967	1.00	5.00
Warner Bros. 7047		Mrs. Cupid / (B-side by The Big Guys)	1967	1.00	5.00
COOL, CALVIN					
Charter 7		Beach Bash / El Tocolote	1963	5.00	25.00
COOL, FRANK, & THE NIGHT RAIDERS					
Julian 111		People Ask Me / Just Wishing	196?	.80	4.00
COOL HEAT					
Forward 152		Groovin' With Mr. Bloe / Are You Nuts?	1970	1.00	5.00
		("Groovin' With Mr. Bloe" was released on Life 200 credited to Wind.)			
COOL-TONES, THE					
Warwick 505		Movin' Out / Ginchy	1959	3.00	15.00
Radiant 1510		The Dixie Blues / Daylight In Dixie	195?	2.00	10.00
COOLEY, EDDIE, & THE DIMPLES					
Royal Roost 621		Priscilla / Got A Little Woman	1956	2.00	10.00
Royal Roost 626		A Spark Met A Flame / Driftwood	1957	2.00	10.00
Royal Roost 628		Hey, You / Pull Pull	1957	2.00	10.00
Roulette 4272		Priscilla / A Spark Met A Flame	1960	2.00	10.00

COOPER, ALICE [THE ALICE COOPER GROUP]
Originally a group, Alice Cooper was Glen Buxton, Mike Bruce, Dennis Dunaway, Neal Smith and Vince Furnier as "Alice." When Furnier broke the band up in 1974, the others recorded as The Billion Dollar Babies. Refer to The Nazz; The Spiders.

Label & Catalog #		A-Side/B-Side	Year	VG	NM
Straight 101	(DJ)	Reflected / Living	1969	5.00	25.00
		(Stock copies of Straight 101 may not exist.)			
Warner Bros. 7141		Eighteen / Caught In A Dream	1970	1.00	5.00
Warner Bros. 7398		Shoe Salesman / Return Of The Spiders	1970	3.00	15.00
Warner Bros. 7449		Eighteen / (This Is My) Body	1971	1.00	5.00
Warner Bros. 7490		Caught In A Dream / Hallowed Be My Name	1971	1.00	5.00
Warner Bros. 7529		Under My Wheels / Desperado	1971	1.00	5.00
Warner Bros. 7568		Be My Lover / Yeah, Yeah, Yeah	1972	1.00	5.00
Warner Bros. 7596		School's Out / Gutter Cat	1972	1.00	5.00
Warner Bros. 7596	(PS)	School's Out / Gutter Cat	1972	1.00	10.00
Warner Bros. 7631		Elected / Luney Tune	1972	1.00	5.00
Warner Bros. 7631	(PS)	Elected / Luney Tune	1972	1.00	10.00
Warner Bros. 7673		Hello Hooray / Generation Landslide	1973	1.00	5.00
Warner Bros. 7691		No More Mr. Nice Guy / Raped And Freezin'	1973	1.00	5.00
Warner Bros. 7724		Billion Dollar Babies / Mary Ann	1973	1.00	5.00
Warner Bros. 7762		Teenage Lament '74 / Hard Hearted Alice	1973	1.00	5.00
Warner Bros. 7783		Muscle Of Love / Crazy Little Child	1974	1.00	5.00
Atlantic 3254		Only Women / Cold Ethyl	1975	.80	4.00
Atlantic 3280		Department Of Youth / Some Folks	1975	.80	4.00
Atlantic 3298		Welcome To My Nightmare / Cold Ethyl	1975	.80	4.00
Warner Bros. 8023		I'm Eighteen / Muscle Of Love	1975	60	3.00
Warner Bros. 8228		I Never Cry / Go To Hell	1976	.60	3.00
Warner Bros. 8349		You And Me / It's Hot Tonight	1977	.60	3.00
Warner Bros. 8349	(PS)	You And Me / It's Hot Tonight	1977	.60	3.00
Warner Bros. 8448		(No More) Love At Your Convenience / I Never Wrote Those Songs	1977	.60	3.00
Warner Bros. 8607		School's Out (Live) / School's Out	1977	.60	3.00
Warner Bros. 8695		How You Gonna See Me Now? / No Tricks	1978	.60	3.00
Warner Bros. 8760		From The Inside / Nurse Rozetta	1979	.60	3.00
Warner Bros. 49204		Clones (We're All) / Model Citizen	1980	.60	3.00
Warner Bros. 49204	(PS)	Clones (We're All) / Model Citizen	1980	.60	3.00
Warner Bros. 49526		Talk Talk / Dance Yourself To Dance	1980	.60	3.00
Warner Bros. 49780		You Want It, You Got It / Who Do You Think We Are?	1981	.40	2.00
Warner Bros. 29828		I Am The Future / Tag, You're It	1982	.40	2.00
Warner Bros. 29928		I Like Girls / Zorro's Ascent	1982	.40	2.00
MCA 52904		He's Back (The Man Behind The Mask) / Billion Dollar Babies	1986	.40	2.00
MCA 53212		Freedom / Time To Kill	1987	.40	2.00
MCA 53212	(PS)	Freedom / Time To Kill	1987	.40	2.00
Epic 08114		I Got A Line On You / (B-side by Brittany Fox)	1989	.20	1.00
Epic 68958		Poison / Trash	1989	.20	1.00
Epic 73085		House Of Fire / Ballad Of Dwight Fry (Live)	1990	.20	1.00
		— 12" Singles—			
Warner Bros. 864	(DJ)	(We're All) Clones / (We're All) Clones	1980	2.00	10.00
Warner Bros. 1059	(DJ)	I Like Girls / I Like Girls	1985	1.20	6.00
MCA 17177	(DJ)	He's Back (The Man Behind The Mask) / Billion Dollar Babies	1986	1.20	6.00
MCA 17205	(DJ)	Give It Up / Give It Up	1986	1.20	6.00
Epic EAS-1347	(DJ)	I Got A Line On You / I Got A Line On You	1989	1.20	6.00
Epic EAS-1663	(DJ)	Poison / Poison	1989	1.20	6.00

Label & Catalog #		A-Side/B-Side	Year	VG	NM
Epic EAS-1686	(DJ)	**Trash / Trash**	1989	1.20	6.00
Epic EAS-1890	(DJ)	**I'm Your Gun / I'm Your Gun**	1989	1.20	6.00
		— Extended Play Albums—			
Warner Bros. 208	(33)	**Billion Dollar Babies** (Jukebox EP)	1973	8.00	40.00
Warner Bros. 235	(33)	**Muscle Of Love** (Jukebox EP)	1973	8.00	40.00

COOPER, BO
Bo Cooper is a pseudonym for Ron Dante.

Bell 460		**Don't Call It Love / Christian**	1973	.80	4.00

COOPER, CHRISTINE

Parkway 971		**S.O.S. Heart In Distress / Say What You Feel**	1966	1.20	6.00
Parkway 983		**Heartaches Away, My Boy / A Bad Boy**	1966	1.20	6.00

COOPER, DAVE, & THE CONTINENTALS

Westco 7		**Church Key / Continental Surf**	195?	6.00	30.00

COOPER, JOHNNY

Ermine 37		**Rivalry / I Found Love With You**	1962	3.00	15.00
Ermine 38		**Little Bride / Dumb, Dumb Bunny**	1962	4.00	20.00
Ermine 40		**Digetty Dogetty / While You're Young**	1962	3.00	15.00
Ermine 44		**Flame Of Love / Oreo**	1963	4.00	20.00

COPAS, LLOYD

Dot 15686		**Circle Rock / My Little Red Wagon**	195?	15.00	75.00

COPESETICS, THE

Premium 409		**Believe In Me / Collegian**	1956	25.00	125.00

COPELAND, KEN

Lin 5007		**Pledge Of Love /** (B-side by the Mints)	1957	5.00	25.00
Lin 5017		**Fanny Brown / Chaser Of Hearts**	1957	6.00	30.00
Imperial 5432		**Pledge Of Love /** (B-side by the Mints)	1957	3.00	15.00
Imperial 5453		**Teenage / Bed Of Lies**	1957	3.00	15.00

COPPERHEAD
Copperhead features John Cippolina, formerly of Quicksilver Messenger Service.

Columbia 45810		**Chameleon / Roller Derby Star**	1973	3.00	15.00

COPS 'N ROBBERS

Parrot 9716		**There's Got To Be A Reason / St. James Infirmary**	1964	1.20	6.00
Coral 62460		**I Could Have Danced All Night / Keep Right On**	1965	1.20	6.00

COQUETTES, THE

RCA Victor 47-6143		**Crew Cut And Baby Blue Eyes / That Naughty Waltz**	1955	3.00	15.00

CORBETTA, JERRY: Refer to THE FOUR SEASONS; SUGARLOAF

CORCORAN, NOREEN

Vee Jay 555		**Why Can't A Boy And Girl Just Stay In Love**	1963	4.00	20.00

CORDEL, PAT, & THE CRESCENTS

Club 1011		**Darling, Come Back / My My Tears**	1956	100.00	400.00
Michelle 503		**Darling, Come Back / My My Tears**	1959	7.00	35.00
		(The Michelle reissue credits Pat Cordell & The Elegants.)			
Victory 1001		**Darling, Come Back / My My Tears** (Red vinyl)	1961	5.00	25.00

CORDELL, RICHIE

Rori 707		**Tick Tock / Please Don't Tell Her**	1962	8.00	40.00
Amy 882	(DJ)	**Georgiana / Better Lovin'** (Blue vinyl)	1964	5.00	25.00
Amy 882		**Georgiana / Better Lovin'**	1964	3.00	15.00
Street Car 101		**Thinking Of You / Raindrops**	196?	3.00	15.00
Street Car 400		**I Wish It Could Be / Maybe Baby, I'm Blue**	196?	3.00	15.00

CORDELLS, THE

Ador 6402		**Happy Time / I Love How You Love Me**	1964	5.00	25.00

CORDIALS, THE

Seven Arts 707		**Dawn Is Almost Here / Keep An Eye**	1961	8.00	40.00
Felsted 8653		**Once In A Lifetime / What Kind Of Fool Am I?**	1962	5.00	25.00
Reveile 106		**Eternal Love / The International Twist**	1962	50.00	200.00
Whip 276		**Listen My Heart / My Heart's Desire**	196?	30.00	150.00
Liberty 55484		**Oh, How I Love Her / You Can't Believe In Love**	1965	3.00	15.00

CORDING, HENRY

Columbia 40762		**Rock And Roll Mops / Hiccough Rock**	1957	20.00	100.00

This relatively obscure Vee Jay girl group sound by Noreen Corcoran has raised the eyebrows of many collectors due to its lavish production and the songwriting credit to a "O. Spector."

Label & Catalog #	A-Side / B-Side	Year	VG	NM
CORDOVANS, THE				
Johnson 731	My Heart / Come On, Baby	1960	5.00	25.00
CORDUROYS, THE				
Planet 122	Tick Tock / Too Much Of A Woman	1967	2.00	10.00
COREY, ED				
Mala 443	Lindy Hop / Dingy Dong	1962	1.20	6.00
COREY, HERB				
Top Rank 2018	This Could Be The Night / Midnight Blues	1959	3.00	15.00
COREY, JOHN (WITH THE FOUR SEASONS)				
Vee Jay 466	Pollyanna / I'll Forget	1962	5.00	25.00
CORIN, TERRY, & THE BOY FRIENDS				
Terry Corin also recorded as Terry & The Mellos.				
Colony 110	Dream Date / Sick Sick Sick	1960	5.00	25.00
CORLEY, BOB				
Stars 4773	Number One Street /	1955	3.00	15.00
RCA Victor 47-6438	Jury Duty / Income Tax	1956	3.00	15.00
CORNELL, DOUG				
Deb 1000	Hong Kong Rock / Toddling	1959	5.00	25.00
CORNELLS, THE				
The Cornells feature Peter Lewis, later of Moby Grape.				
Garex 100	Mama's Little Baby / Wak-A-Cha	1962	5.00	25.00
Garex 102	Malibu Surf / Agua Caliente	1963	5.00	25.00
Garex 201	Beachbound / Lone Star Stomp	1963	5.00	25.00
Garex 206	Surf Fever / Do The Slauson	1963	5.00	25.00
CORNISH, GENE, & THE UNBEATABLES				
The Unbeatables later recorded as The Young Rascals.				
Dawn 550	Do The Capri / Lonely Will I Stay	1964	4.00	20.00
Dawn 557	I Wanna Be A Beetle / Oh, Misery	1964	5.00	25.00
CORONA				
Regina 106	I'd Do Anything For You / Paula's English	196?	2.50	12.00
CORONADOS, THE				
Arlingwood 6467	Florida Sun /	196?	7.00	35.00
CORPORATE IMAGE, THE				
MGM 13614	Not Fade Away / I'm Not The Same	1966	3.00	15.00
CORRENTE, SAL				
Roulette 4673	Run Run Run / Love Me	1966	3.00	15.00
CORT SKIFFLE GROUP, BOB				
London 1713	Don't You Rock Me, Daddy-O / It Takes A Worried Man	195?	3.00	15.00
CORVELLS, THE				
Century Custom 19805	Vic's Tune / Dunebuggy Ride	1964	4.00	20.00
CORVETS, THE				
20th Century Fox 223	Shark In The Park / Only Last Night	1960	2.00	10.00
CORVETTES, THE				
Sheraton 201	In The Chapel / The Swinging Smitty	196?	7.00	35.00
CORVETTES, THE				
Arco 104	Rockin' Round The Mountain / Shasta	1959	4.00	20.00
CORVETTES, THE				
The Corvettes were produced by Michael Nesmith.				
Dot 17283	Level With Your Senses / Beware Of Time	1969	2.00	10.00
Dot 17244	Lion In Your Heart / Back Home Girl	1969	2.00	10.00
CORWINS, THE				
Gilmar 222	Little Star / When	196?	3.00	15.00
COSTELLO, ELVIS (& THE ATTRACTIONS)				
Columbia 10641	Alison / Miracle Man	1977	3.00	15.00
Columbia 10696	Watching The Detectives /			
	Blame It On Cane-Mystery Dance	1977	3.00	15.00
Columbia 10705	Alison / Watching The Detectives	1978	2.00	10.00

Elvis Costello, a record collector himself, has provided his fans with a multitude of odds and ends throughout his career, including this EP, issued commercially with copies of his third album, *Armed Forces,* containing tracks cut live and unavailable elsewhere.

Label & Catalog #		A-Side/B-Side	Year	VG	NM
Columbia 10762		This Year's Girl / Big Tears	1978	1.00	5.00
Columbia AE7-1172	(DJ)	My Funny Valentine / What's So Funny 'Bout Peace, Love And Understanding? (Red vinyl)	1979	2.00	10.00
Columbia 10919		Accidents Will Happen / Sunday's Best	1979	.80	4.00
Columbia 11194		I Can't Stand Up For Falling Down / Girls Talk	1980	.80	4.00
Columbia 11284		New Amsterdam / Wednesday Week	1980	.60	3.00
Columbia 11389		Gettin' Mighty Crowded / Radio Sweetheart	1980	.60	3.00
Columbia 60519		Watch Your Step / Luxembourg	1980	.60	3.00
Columbia 60519	(PS)	Watch Your Step / Luxembourg	1980	.80	4.00
Columbia 02629		A Good Year For The Roses / Your Angel Steps Out Of Heaven	1981	.40	2.00
Columbia 03202		Man Out Of Time / Man Out Of Time	1981	.40	2.00
Columbia 03269		Man Out Of Time (One sided)	1982	1.00	5.00
Columbia 04045	(PS)	Everyday I Write The Book (Promo picture sleeve)	1983	1.00	5.00
Columbia 04045		Everyday I Write The Book / Heathen Town	1983	.40	2.00
Columbia 04045	(PS)	Everyday I Write The Book / Heathen Town	1983	.60	3.00
Columbia 04266		Let Them All Talk / Shipbuilding	1983	.40	2.00
Columbia 04502	(PS)	The Only Flame In Town (Promo picture sleeve)	1984	1.00	5.00
Columbia 04502		The Only Flame In Town / Turning The Town Red	1984	.40	2.00
Columbia 04502	(PS)	The Only Flame In Town / Turning The Town Red	1984	.60	3.00
Columbia 04625		I Wanna Be Loved / Love Field	1984	.40	2.00
Columbia 05809		Don't Let Me Be Misunderstood / Brand New Hairdo	1986	.40	2.00
Columbia 06059		Loveable / Get Yourself Another Fool	1986	.40	2.00
		(Columbia 05809 and 06059 credit The Costello Show.)			
Columbia 06135		Seven Day Weekend / (B-side by Jimmy Cliff)	1986	.40	2.00
Columbia 06135	(PS)	Seven Day Weekend / (B-side by Jimmy Cliff)	1986	.60	3.00
		(Label credits Jimmy Cliff and Elvis Costello.)			
Columbia 06326		Tokyo Storm Warning / Tokyo Storm Warning, Part 2	1986	.40	2.00
Warner Bros. 22981		Veronica / You're No Good	1989	.20	1.00
Warner Bros. 22981	(PS)	Veronica / You're No Good	1989	.40	2.00
		—12" Singles—			
Columbia AS-443	(DJ)	Cruel To Be Kind / Radio Radio (PC)	1978	3.00	15.00
		(The a-side features one track by Nick Lowe, the second by Elvis; the b-side, on the Capitol label, is by Mink DeVille.)			
Columbia AS-529	(DJ)	Live At Hollywood High (EP)	1978	3.00	15.00
Columbia AS-847	(DJ)	Taking Liberties (EP)	1980	3.00	15.00
Columbia AS-1510	(DJ)	Man Out Of Time / Beyond Belief	1982	2.00	10.00
Columbia 04115		Everyday I Write The Book / Heathen Town / Night Time (PC)	1983	2.00	10.00
Columbia 05081		The Only Flame In Town / Baby, It's You / Pump It Up (PC)	1984	2.00	10.00
		("Baby, It's You" is a duet with Nick Lowe.)			
Columbia CAS-2310	(DJ)	Don't Let Me Be Misunderstood (Live) / Don't Let Me Be Misunderstood (Live) (PC)	1986	2.00	10.00
Columbia CAS-2371	(DJ)	Loveable / Loveable	1986	1.00	5.00
		(Columbia 2310 and 2371 credit The Costello Show)			
Columbia CAS-2380	(DJ)	Seven Day Weekend / Seven Day Weekend	1987	1.00	5.00
		(Label credits Jimmy Cliff and Elvis Costello.)			
		—Extended Play Albums—			
Columbia AE7-1171	(DJ)	Live At Hollywood High	1978	2.00	10.00
Columbia AE7-1171		Live At Hollywood High	1978	1.20	6.00
Columbia 11251	(DJ)	I Can't Stand Up For Falling Down	1980	2.00	10.00
Columbia 11251		I Can't Stand Up For Falling Down	1980	1.20	6.00

COTILLIONS, THE

Alley 1003		Surf Twist / Sahara	1962	3.00	15.00

COTTON, JAMES

Sun 199		My Baby / Straighten Up, Baby	1954	330.00	1,000.00
Sun 206		Hold Me In Your Arms / Cotton Crop Blues	1954	500.00	1,500.00

COTTON MOUTH

Sabina 4		Mr. Fisker's Glory / Sunshine Saleslady	196?	2.00	10.00

COUNT & THE COLONY

Pa-Go-Go 121		Can't You See? / That's The Way	196?	6.00	30.00
S.S.S. Int. 711		Say What You Think / Symptoms Of Love	196?	1.00	5.00

COUNT FIVE

Double Shot 104		Psychotic Reaction / They're Gonna Get You	1966	2.00	10.00
Double Shot 106		Peace Of Mind / The Morning After	1966	2.00	10.00
Double Shot 110		You Must Believe Me / Teeny Bopper, Teeny Bopper	1967	3.00	15.00
Double Shot 115		Contrast / Merry-Go-Round	1967	2.00	10.00
Double Shot 125		Declaration Of Independence / Revelation In Slow Motion	1968	3.00	15.00
Double Shot 141		Pretty Big Mouth / Mailman	1968	2.00	10.00

COUNT LORRY & THE BITERS

Dragon 4406		Frankenstein Stomp / Groovin' With Drac	1965	2.00	10.00

Label & Catalog #	A-Side/B-Side	Year	VG	NM

COUNTDOWNS, THE
The Countdowns later recorded as New Dawn.

Summit 0004	Lost Horizon / It Hurts	196?	6.00	30.00

COUNTRY BOYS, THE
The Country Boys feature David Gates.

Del-Fi 4245	Okie Surfer / Blue Surf	1964	5.00	25.00

COUNTRY COUSINS, THE

Souvenir 1009	I Just Thought I'd Call You Up / Don't Stay Out Late	1960	2.00	10.00

COUNTRY HAMS, THE
The Country Hams is a pseudonym for Paul and Linda McCartney.

EMI 3977	(DJ)	Walking In The Park With Louise / Bridge On The River Suite	1974	8.00	40.00
EMI 3977		Walking In The Park With Louise / Bridge On The River Suite	1974	10.00	50.00
EMI 3977	(PS)	Walking In The Park With Louise / Bridge On The River Suite	1974	10.00	50.00

COUNTRY JOE & THE FISH
Country Joe McDonald's original Fish were Bruce Barthol, David Cohen, Chicken Hirsch and Barry Melton.

Vanguard 35052		Not So Sweet Martha Lorraine / The Masked Matador	1967	1.20	6.00
Vanguard 35059		Janis / Janis, Part 2	1967	1.20	6.00
Vanguard 35061		Who Am I? / Thursday	1968	1.00	5.00
Vanguard 35061	(PS)	Who Am I? / Thursday	1968	4.00	20.00
Vanguard 35068		Rock And Soul Music / Rock And Soul Music, Part 2	1968	1.00	5.00
Vanguard 35090		Here I Go Again / Baby, You're Driving Me Crazy	1969	1.00	5.00
Vanguard 35112		I-Feel-Like-I'm-Fixin'-To-Die-Rag / Janis	1970	1.00	5.00
	—Extended Play Albums—			
Rag Baby 1001		Talking Issue *(Paper enrleope sleeve)*	1965	30.00	150.00
Rag Baby 1002		Country Joe & The Fish *(Paper enrleope sleeve)*	1965	30.00	150.00
Rag Baby 1002		Country Joe & The Fish *(Cardboard cover with script print)*	1965	30.00	150.00
Rag Baby 1002		Country Joe & The Fish *(Cardboard cover with block print)*	196?	10.00	50.00

COUNTRY JOE (McDONALD)

Vanguard 35133	Hold On, It's Coming / Playing With Fire	1971	.60	3.00
Vanguard 35150	Hang On / Hand Of Man	1973	.60	3.00
Vanguard 35161	Fantasy / I Seen A Rocket	1973	.60	3.00
Vanguard 35181	Doctor Hip / Satisfactory Blues	1974	.60	3.00
Vanguard 35184	Chile / Jesse James	1975	.60	3.00
Fantasy 758	Breakfast For Two / Lost My Connection	1975	.50	2.50
Fantasy 765	Save The Whales! / Oh, Jamaica	1975	.50	2.50
Fantasy 780	Love Is A Fire / This And That	1976	.50	2.50
Fantasy 814	Coyote / Southern Cross	1978	.50	2.50
Fantasy 822	Bring Back The '60s, Man / Sunshine	1978	.50	2.50
Fantasy 876	Private Parts / Take Time Out	1980	.50	2.50
Rag Baby 101	Voyage Of The Good Ship Undersize / Voyage Of The Good Ship Undersize (Part 2)	1980	.40	2.00
Rag Baby 102	Peace On Earth / Santa Claus Rag	1983	.40	2.00
	—Extended Play Albums—			
Rag Baby 1003	Resist!	1971	6.00	30.00

COUNTRYMEN, FREDDY

La Rae 501	Back Up And Push / The Raven	196?	7.00	35.00
	(LaRae 501 was also released as "Hot Doggin'" / "The Falcon" credited to Freddy & Lonnie.)			

COUNTS, THE
The Counts also recorded with Tommy Burk.

Nat 100	Counted Out / You'll Feel It, Too	1962	6.00	30.00
Nat 101	Stormy Weather / True Love's Gone	1963	6.00	30.00
Smash 1821	Stormy Weather / True Love's Gone	1963	2.50	12.00

COUNTS, THE

Manco 1060	Surfer's Paradise / Chug-A-Lug	196?	8.00	40.00
Count 5	Beat / After Beat	196?	4.00	20.00

COUNTS, THE

Sea Crest 6003	Turn On Song / Enchanted Sea	1964	3.00	15.00
Sea Crest 6004	Doggin' / And Then I Cried	1964	2.00	10.00
Panorama 9	Chitlins, Etc. / Clyde, Clyde, The Cow's Outside	1965	1.00	5.00
Panorama 33	Come Now / Since I Fell For You	1966	1.20	6.00

COUSINS, THE

Chancellor 1074	What'd I Say / (B-side by The Playboys)	1961	2.00	10.00

Label & Catalog #		A-Side / B-Side	Year	VG	NM

COVELLE, BUDDY
Buddy Covelle also recorded as Valine Hackert.

Coral 62181	(DJ)	Lorraine / I'll Go On Loving You	1960	50.00	200.00
Coral 62181		Lorraine / I'll Go On Loving You	1960	100.00	400.00

COWSILLS, THE

Philips 40382		Most Of All / Siamese Cat	1966	1.00	5.00
Philips 40382	(PS)	Most Of All / Siamese Cat	1966	3.00	15.00
Philips 40406		Party Girl / What's It Gonna Be Like?	1966	1.00	5.00
Philips 40437		Could It Be, Let Me Know / Most Peculiar Man	1967	1.00	5.00
MGM 13810		The Rain, The Park And Other Things / River Blue	1967	1.00	5.00
MGM 13810	(PS)	The Rain, The Park And Other Things / River Blue	1967	1.20	6.00
MGM 13886		We Can Fly / Time For Remembrance	1968	1.00	5.00
MGM 13886	(PS)	We Can Fly / Time For Remembrance	1968	1.20	6.00
MGM 13909		In Need Of A Friend / Mister Flynn	1968	1.00	5.00
MGM 13944		Indian Lake / Newspaper Blanket	1968	1.00	5.00
MGM 13944	(PS)	Indian Lake / Newspaper Blanket	1968	1.20	6.00
MGM 13981		Poor Baby / Meet Me At The Wishing Well	1968	.80	4.00
MGM 14011		Candy Kid / Impossible Years	1969	.80	4.00
MGM 14026		Hair / What Is Happy?	1969	1.00	5.00
MGM 14063		The Prophecy Of Daniel And John The Divine (Six-Six-Six) / Gotta Get Away From It All	1969	.80	4.00
MGM 14084		Silver Threads And Golden Needles / Love American Style	1969	.80	4.00
MGM 14084	(PS)	Silver Threads And Golden Needles / Love American Style	1969	3.00	15.00
MGM 14106		Start To Love / Two By Two	1970	.80	4.00
London 149		On My Side / There Is No Child	1971	1.00	5.00
London 153		You / Crystal Claps	1972	1.00	5.00
London 170		Blue Road / Covered Wagon	1972	1.00	5.00

BILL COWSILL

MGM 14166		When Everybody's Here / I Wish I Could Say The Same About You	1970	.80	4.00

JOHN COWSILL

MGM 14003		Captain Sad And His Ship Of Fools / Path Of Love	1968	.80	4.00

COX, JERRY

Buz 100		Lover Man / Maria	195?	10.00	50.00
Frantic 751		Debbie Jean / Sherry	1959	20.00	100.00

CRADDOCK, CRASH
Like more than a few contemporary country singers, Billy "Crash" Craddock got his start with rock & roll. His sole charting record, "Don't Destroy Me," barely scratched the nether regions of the charts. He has, of course, pursued a successful career as a country/western artist, with an occasional cross-over hit, mainly with ABC.

Colonial 721		Bird Doggin' / Millionaire	1958	3.00	15.00
Date 1007		Ah, Poor Little Baby / Lulu Lee	1958	3.00	15.00
Columbia 41316		Am I To Be The One? / I Miss You So Much	1959	2.00	10.00
Columbia 41367		Blabbermouth / Sweetie Pie	1959	2.00	10.00
Columbia 41470		Don't Destroy Me / Boom Boom Baby	1959	2.00	10.00
Columbia 41470	(PS)	Don't Destroy Me / Boom Boom Baby	1959	7.00	35.00
Columbia 41536		Since She Turned Seventeen / I Want That	1960	2.00	10.00
Columbia 41619		All I Want Is You / Letter Of Love	1960	2.00	10.00
Columbia 41619	(PS)	All I Want Is You / Letter Of Love	1960	8.00	40.00
Columbia 41677		One Last Kiss / Is It True Or False?	1960	4.00	20.00
Columbia 41822		Good Time Billy / Heavenly Love	1960	2.00	10.00
Mercury 71811		True Love / How Lonely He Must Be	1961	2.00	10.00
King 5912		Bitty Betty / Right Around The Corner	1964	2.00	10.00
King 5924		My Baby's Got Flat Feet / One Heartache Too Many	1964	2.00	10.00

CRAFT, MORTY

Tod 122		All Mixed Up / Guessin' Games	1957	5.00	25.00

CRAFTSMEN, THE
The Craftsmen is a pseudonym for Johnny & The Hurricanes.

Warwick 538		Goofus / Rock Along	1960	3.00	15.00
Warwick 586		Tweedle Dee / Walkin' With Mr. Lee	1962	3.00	15.00
Warwick 678		McBoing Boing / What's The Matter With Grownups?	1963	3.00	15.00

CRAFTYS, THE
The Craftys also recorded as The Halos.

Seven Arts 708		L-O-V-E / Heart Breaking World	1961	4.00	20.00
Elmor 310		Zoom Zoom Zoom / I Went To A Party	1962	6.00	30.00

CRAIG, JIMMY

Brill 1		All For You / Gonna Love My Baby	1959	3.00	15.00

CRAIG, THE

Fontana 1579		I Must Be Mad / Suspense	1967	4.00	20.00

Label & Catalog #		A-Side/B-Side	Year	VG	NM
CRAIG & MICHAEL					
Downey 140		Drifty / That Kind Of Girl	1967	2.00	10.00
CRAIN, JIMMY					
Spangle 2009		Shing-A-Shang / Will You Tell Me?	1958	10.00	50.00
CRAMPS, THE					
Vengeance 666		Surfin' Bird / The Way I Walk	1978	4.00	20.00
Vengeance 666	(PS)	Surfin' Bird / The Way I Walk	1978	5.00	25.00
Vengeance 668		Domino / Human Fly	1978	4.00	20.00
Vengeance 668	(PS)	Domino / Human Fly	1978	5.00	25.00
Illegal 09014		Drug Train / Garbage Man	1980	2.00	10.00
Illegal 09014	(PS)	Drug Train / Garbage Man	1980	3.00	15.00
I.R.S. 9021		Goo Goo Muck / She Said	1981	1.00	5.00
I.R.S. 9021	(PS)	Goo Goo Muck / She Said	1981	1.00	5.00
CRANE, CAROL					
Challenge 59292		(Mother, It's A) Frightful Situation / What Else Do You Do For Kicks?	1961	2.00	10.00
CRANE, SHERRY					
Sun 328		Willie, Willie / Winnie The Parakeet	1959	3.00	15.00
CRAWFORD, BOBBY					
Del-Fi 4211		Mrs. Smith, Please Wake Up Joan / That Little Old Lovemaker Me	1963	2.00	10.00
CRAWFORD, JOHNNY					
Wynne 124		Dance With The Dolly / Ask	1961	2.00	10.00
Del-Fi 4162		Daydreams / So Goes The Story	1961	2.00	10.00
Del-Fi 4162	(PS)	Daydreams / So Goes The Story	1961	3.00	15.00
Del-Fi 4165		Your Love Is Growing Cold / Treasure	1961	2.00	10.00
Del-Fi 4165	(PS)	Your Love Is Growing Cold / Treasure	1961	3.00	15.00
Del-Fi 4172		Patti Ann / Donna	1962	2.00	10.00
Del-Fi 4178		Cindy's Birthday / Something Special	1962	2.00	10.00
Del-Fi 4178	(PS)	Cindy's Birthday / Something Special	1962	3.00	15.00
Del-Fi 4181		Your Nose Is Gonna Grow / Mr. Blue	1962	1.60	8.00
Del-Fi 4181	(PS)	Your Nose Is Gonna Grow / Mr. Blue	1962	3.00	15.00
Del-Fi 4188		Rumors / No One Really Loves A Clown	1962	1.60	8.00
Del-Fi 4188	(PS)	Rumors / No One Really Loves A Clown	1962	3.00	15.00
Del-Fi 4193		Proud / Lonesome Town	1962	1.60	8.00
Del-Fi 4203		When I Fall In Love / Cry On My Shoulder	1963	1.60	8.00
Del-Fi 4215		What Happened To Janie? / Petite Chanson	1963	1.60	8.00
Del-Fi 4221		Cindy's Gonna Cry / Debbie	1963	1.60	8.00
Del-Fi 4229		Sandy / Ol' Shorty	1963	2.00	10.00
Del-Fi 4231		Judy Loves Me / Living In The Past	1964	2.00	10.00
Del-Fi 4242		The Girl Next Door / Sittin' And Watchin'	1964	2.00	10.00
Sidewalk 932		Angelica / Everybody Has Their Day	1968	2.00	10.00
Sidewalk 941		Good Guys Finish Last / Everyone Should Own A Dream	1968	2.00	10.00
CRAWFORD BROTHERS, THE					
Bobby and Johnny Crawford.					
Del-Fi 4191		Good Buddies / You Gotta Wear Shoes	1962	1.60	8.00
Del-Fi 4191	(PS)	Good Buddies / You Gotta Wear Shoes	1962	3.00	15.00
CRAZY ELEPHANT					
Bell 763		Gimme Gimme Good Lovin' / Dark Part Of My Mind	1969	1.00	5.00
Bell 804		Sunshine, Red Wine / Pam	1969	.80	4.00
Bell 817		Gimme Some More / My Baby (Honey Pie)	1969	.80	4.00
Bell 846		There's A Better Day A Comin' / Space Buggy	1970	.80	4.00
Bell 875		There Ain't No Umbopo / Land Rover	1970	1.00	5.00
		("There Ain't No Umbopo" features 10CC.)			
Sphere Sound 005		Gimme Gimme Good Lovin' / Dark Part Of My Mind	1969	1.00	5.00
CRAZY GIRLS, THE					
Capitol 5050		Hey Hey, Ha Ha / Joe The Guitar Man	1963	2.00	10.00
CRAZY HORSE					
Original members consisted of Ralph Molina, Jack Nitzsche, Billy Talbot and Danny Whitten with Nils Lofgren; George Whitesell joined after Whitten's death in 1972. Refer to Danny & The Memories; The Rockets; Neil Young.					
Reprise 1025		Dance, Dance, Dance / Carolay	1971	.80	4.00
Reprise 1046		Dirty Dirty / Beggar's Day	1971	.80	4.00
Reprise 1075		All Alone Now / One Thing I Love	1972	.60	3.00
CRAZY JACKS, THE					
London 10024		Liszt Stomp / Paganinni Stomp	1963	1.20	6.00

Label & Catalog #		A-Side/B-Side	Year	VG	NM
CRAZY KATS, THE					
Deauville 1005		Makin' Whoopee / The Candy Stick Twist	1962	1.20	6.00
CRAZY LUKE					
Do Brooks 1		Karate / Tea And Rice	1963	1.20	6.00
CRAZY MORLEY					
Cameo 147		As Long As We're Happy Together / I Chicken Out	1958	3.00	15.00
CREAM					
Cream was Ginger Baker, Jack Bruce and Eric Clapton with occasional assistance from producer Felix Pappalardi.					
Atco 6462		I Feel Free / N.S.U.	1967	1.60	8.00
Atco 6488		Strange Brew / Tales Of Brave Ulysses	1967	1.20	6.00
Atco 6522		Spoonful / Spoonful, Part 2	1967	1.00	5.00
Atco 6544		Sunshine Of Your Love / S.W.L.A.B.R.	1967	1.00	5.00
Atco 6575		Anyone For Tennis? / Pressed Rat And Warthog	1968	1.00	5.00
Atco 6617		White Room / Those Were The Days	1968	1.00	5.00
Atco 6646		Crossroads / Passing The Time	1969	1.00	5.00
Atco 6668		Badge / What A Bringdown	1969	1.00	5.00
Atco 6708		Sweet Wine / Lawdy Mama	1969	1.20	6.00
		—*Extended Play Albums*—			
Atco 4525	(DJ)	Wheels Of Fire *(Paper picture sleeve)*	1967	15.00	75.00
CREATION					
Planet 116		Making Time / Try And Stop Me	1966	4.00	20.00
Planet 119		Piff! Bang! Pow! / Painter Man	1966	4.00	20.00
Decca 32155		If I Stay Too Long / Nightmares	1967	5.00	25.00
Decca 32227		How Does It Feel? / Life Is Just Beginning	1967	6.00	30.00
CREATIONS, THE					
The Creations also recorded with Johnny Angel.					
Tip Top 400		Every Night I Pray / Mommy And Daddy	1956	4.00	20.00
Tip Top 501		There Goes The Girl I Love / You Are My Darling	1956	4.00	20.00
Jamie 1197		The Bells / Shang Shang	1960	3.00	15.00
Mel-o-dy 101		This Is Our Night / You're My Inspiration	1962	3.00	15.00
Meridian *(No number)*		The Wedding / I've Got A Feeling	1962	3.00	15.00
Penny 9022		We're In Love / Lady Luck	1962	3.00	15.00
Pine Crest 101		Wake Up In The Morning / Strolling Through The Park	1961	4.00	20.00
Take Ten 1501		We're In Love / Lady Luck	1963	3.00	15.00
CREATIONS, THE					
Top Hat 1003		Crash / Chickie Darling	196?	8.00	40.00
Top Hat 1003	(PS)	Crash / Chickie Darling	196?	15.00	75.00
CREATIONS IV, THE					
HBR 440		Dance In The Sand / Little Girl	1965	1.20	6.00
CREATORS, THE					
Dooto 463		I've Had You / Drafted, Volunteered, Enlisted	1961	4.00	20.00
Hi-Q 5021		Wear My Ring / Booga Bear	1961	4.00	20.00
Time 1038		Do You Remember? / There's Going To Be An Angel	1961	4.00	20.00
T-Kay 110		Boy, He's Got It! / I'll Never, Never Do It Again	1962	4.00	20.00
Philips 40058		Boy, He's Got It! / I'll Never, Never Do It Again	1963	4.00	20.00
Philips 40060		I'll Stay Home (New Year's Eve) / Shoom Ba Boom	1963	40.00	200.00
Epic 9605		Cross Fire / Crazy Love	1963	3.00	15.00
CREATURES, THE					
Columbia 43480		Turn Out The Light / It Must Be Love	1966	2.00	10.00
Columbia 43689		String Along / The Night Is Warm	1966	2.00	10.00
Columbia 43884		Looking At Tomorrow / Someone Needs You	1966	2.00	10.00
Columbia 44145		Hurtin' All Over / Love Is A Funny Little Game	1967	2.00	10.00
CREDIBILTY GAP, THE					
Capitol 2246		Comin' Into My Own / Bein' Like The Birdies	1968	.80	4.00
CREEDENCE CLEARWATER REVIVAL					
CCR features Doug Clifford, Stu Cook, John and Tom Fogerty. Refer to Tom Fogerty & The Blue Velvets; The Golliwogs.					
Scorpio 412		Porterville / Call It Pretending	1967	10.00	50.00
Fantasy 616		Susie Q / Susie Q, Part 2	1968	1.20	6.00
Fantasy 617		I Put A Spell On You / Walk On Water	1968	1.00	5.00
Fantasy 619		Proud Mary / Born On The Bayou	1969	1.00	5.00
Fantasy 622		Bad Moon Rising / Lodi	1969	1.00	5.00
Fantasy 625		Green River / Commotion	1969	1.00	5.00
Fantasy 634		Down On The Corner / Fortunate Son	1969	1.00	5.00
Fantasy 634	(PS)	Down On The Corner / Fortunate Son	1969	2.00	10.00
Fantasy 2838	(DJ)	45 Revolutions Per Minute	1969	8.00	40.00
Fantasy 2838	(PS)	45 Revolutions Per Minute	1969	8.00	40.00

Label & Catalog #		A-Side/B-Side	Year	VG	NM
Fantasy 637		Travelin' Band / Who'll Stop The Rain?	1970	1.00	5.00
Fantasy 637	(PS)	Travelin' Band / Who'll Stop The Rain?	1970	2.00	10.00
Fantasy 641		Up Around The Bend / Run Through The Jungle	1970	1.00	5.00
Fantasy 641	(PS)	Up Around The Bend / Run Through The Jungle	1970	2.00	10.00
Fantasy 645		Lookin' Out My Back Door / Long As I Can See The Light	1970	1.00	5.00
Fantasy 645	(PS)	Lookin' Out My Back Door / Long As I Can See The Light	1970	2.00	10.00
Fantasy 655		Have You Ever Seen The Rain? / Hey Tonight	1971	1.00	5.00
Fantasy 665		Sweet Hitch-Hiker / Door To Door	1971	1.00	5.00
Fantasy 665	(PS)	Sweet Hitch-Hiker / Door To Door	1971	2.00	10.00
Fantasy 676		Someday Never Comes / Tearin' Up The Country	1972	.80	4.00
Fantasy 759		I Heard It Through The Grapevine / Good Golly Miss Molly	1976	.40	3.00
Fantasy 759	(PS)	I Heard It Through The Grapevine / Good Golly Miss Molly	1976	.60	3.00
Fantasy 908		Tombstone Shadow / Commotion	1981	.40	2.00
Fantasy 917		Medley U.S.A. / Bad Moon Rising	1981	.40	2.00
Fantasy 920		Cotton Fields / Lodi	1981	.40	2.00
		— 12" Singles—			
Fantasy 759-D-LP	(DJ)	I Heard It Through The Grapevine / Good Golly Miss Molly	1976	4.00	20.00

CREELS, THE
Judd 1005		See Me Once Again / Do You Wanta Jump?	1958	3.00	15.00

CREME & GODLEY
Lol Creme and Kevin Godley of 10CC.
Mercury 73965		The Flood / 5 O' Clock In The Morning	1977	.60	3.00

CRESCENDOS, THE
The Crescendos feature Dale Ward.
Nasco 6005		Oh, Julie / My Little Girl	1957	4.00	20.00
Nasco 6005	(PS)	Oh, Julie / My Little Girl	1957	10.00	50.00
Nasco 6009		School Girl / Crazy Love	1957	3.00	15.00
Nasco 6009	(PS)	School Girl / Crazy Love	1957	6.00	30.00
Nasco 6021		Young And In Love / Rainy Sunday	1958	4.00	20.00
Nasco 6021	(PS)	Young And In Love / Rainy Sunday	1958	6.00	30.00
Scarlet 4007		Let's Take A Walk / Strange Love	1960	4.00	20.00
Scarlet 4009		I'm So Ashamed / Angel Face	1961	8.00	40.00

CRESCENDOS, THE
Domain 1025		A Fellow Needs A Girl / Black Cat	196?	3.00	15.00

CRESCENDOS, THE
Impro 5006		Tidal Wave / Crescendo Special	1962	5.00	25.00
Nu Sound 1007		Count Down / The Hawk Walk	196?	4.00	20.00
Nu Sound 1014		Movin' Wild / Sweet Talk	196?	4.00	20.00

CRESCENTS, THE
Hamilton 50033		Hey There / When You Wish Upon A Star	1960	5.00	25.00
Arlen 743		Smoke Gets In Your Eyes / Johnny Won't Run Around	1964	3.00	15.00

CRESCENTS, THE: *Refer to* PAT CORDELL & THE CRESCENTS

CRESCENTS (FEATURING CHIYO), THE
Refer to Chiyo & The Crescents.
Era 3116		Breakout / Pink Dominoes	1963	3.00	15.00

CRESENT SIX, THE
Rust 5102		Nightmare / And Then	1965	3.00	15.00

CRESHENDOES, THE
The Creshendoes feature Chuck Rio a.k.a. Danny Flores. Refer to The Champs; The Cruchendoes; The Persuaders;.
Saturn 404		Surfing Strip / Hanging Ten	1963	7.00	35.00

CRESCHENDOS, THE
Music City 831		My Heart's Desire / Take My Heart *(Maroon label)*	1957	15.00	75.00
Music City 839		Teenage Prayer / *(Maroon label)*	1957	15.00	75.00
Gone 5100		My Heart's Desire / Take My Heart	195?	4.00	20.00

CRESTERS, THE
Capitol 5238		Put Your Arms Around Me / Do It With Me	1964	2.00	10.00

CRESTRIDERS, THE
Crystalette 756		Surf Stomp / Surfin' Fever	1960	4.00	20.00

(Originally released as "Boomerang" / "Slave Chain," credited to The Spinners. "Surf Stomp" was also released as "The Lion," credited to Duke Mitchell.)

CRESTS, THE [JOHNNY MAESTRO & THE CRESTS]
The Crests are Jay Carter, Tommy Gough, Johnny Maestro and Harold Torres.
Joyce 103		My Juanita / Sweetest One	1957	50.00	250.00

(First pressing labels feature the "JoYce" logo.)

Label & Catalog #	A-Side/B-Side	Year	VG	NM
Joyce 103	My Juanita / Sweetest One	195?	8.00	40.00
	(Second pressing labels feature the "Joyce" logo.)			
Joyce 105	No One To Love / Wish She Was Mine	1957	50.00	200.00
Coed 501	Pretty Little Angel / I Thank The Moon	1958	20.00	100.00
	(First pressing labels have "Coed" in red print.)			
Coed 501	Pretty Little Angel / I Thank The Moon	1959	6.00	30.00
	(Second pressing labels have "Coed" in red & black print.)			
Coed 506	Sixteen Candles / Beside You	1959	6.00	30.00
	(First pressings credit Coronation Music Publishers.)			
Coed 506	Sixteen Candles / Beside You	1959	4.00	20.00
	(Second pressings credit January Music Publishers.)			
Coed 509	Six Nights A Week / I Do	1959	4.00	20.00
Coed 511	The Flower Of Love / Molly Mae	1959	4.00	20.00
Coed 515	The Angels Listened In / I Thank The Moon	1959	4.00	20.00
Coed 521	A Year Ago Tonight / Paper Clown	1959	4.00	20.00
Coed 525	Step By Step / Gee (But I'd Give The World)	1960	4.00	20.00
Coed 531	Trouble In Paradise / Always You	1960	4.00	20.00
	— Original Coed singles above have red & black labels.—			
Coed 506	Sixteen Candles / Beside You	1960	2.00	10.00
Coed 509	Six Nights A Week / I Do	1960	2.00	10.00
Coed 511	The Flower Of Love / Molly Mae	1960	2.00	10.00
Coed 515	The Angels Listened In / I Thank The Moon	1960	2.00	10.00
Coed 521	A Year Ago Tonight / Paper Clown	1960	2.00	10.00
Coed 525	Step By Step / Gee (But I'd Give The World)	1960	2.00	10.00
Coed 531	Trouble In Paradise / Always You	1960	2.00	10.00
Coed 535	Journey Of Love / If My Heart Could Write A Letter	1960	2.00	10.00
Coed 537	Isn't It Amazing? / Molly Mae	1960	2.00	10.00
Coed 543	I Remember (The Still Of The Night) / Good Golly Miss Molly	1961	2.00	10.00
Coed 561	Little Miracles / Baby, I Gotta Know	1962	3.00	15.00
	—Coed singles above have black labels.—			
United Artists 474	50,000,000 Heartbeats / Before I Loved Her	1962	8.00	40.00
Musictone 1106	Sweetest One / My Juanita	1962	2.00	10.00
Trans Atlas (No number)	The Actor / Three Tears In A Bucket	1962	4.00	20.00
Selma 311	Guilty / Number One With Me	1962	4.00	20.00
Selma 4000	Did I Remember? / Tears Will Fall	1963	5.00	25.00
Times Square 2	No One To Love / Wish She Was Mine	1963	2.00	10.00
Times Square 6	Baby / I Love You So	1963	2.00	10.00
Times Square 97	Baby / I Love You So	196?	2.00	10.00
Coral 62403	You Blew Out The Candles / A Love To Last A Lifetime	1964	5.00	25.00
Scepter 12112	I'm Stepping Out Of The Picture / Afraid Of Love	1965	2.00	10.00
Parkway 118	My Time / Is It You?	1965	2.00	10.00
Parkway 987	Try Me / Heartburn	1966	2.00	10.00
Parkway 999	Come See Me / I Care About You	1967	2.00	10.00
	(The Parkway sides credit Johnny Maestro & The Crests.)			
	—Extended Play Albums—			
Coed 101	The Angels Listened In	1959	75.00	300.00

CREW, THE

Brass 194	Hot Wire / Big Junk	1963	2.00	10.00

CREW CUTS, THE

Mercury 70341	Crazy 'Bout You, Baby / Angela Mia	1954	3.00	15.00
Mercury 70404	Sh-Boom / I Spoke Too Soon	1954	4.00	20.00
Mercury 70443	Oop Shoop / Do Me Good, Baby	1954	3.00	15.00
Mercury 70490	All I Wanna Do / The Barking Dog	1954	3.00	15.00
Mercury 70491	Dance, Mr. Snowman, Dance	1954	3.00	15.00
Mercury 70494	The Whiffenpoof Song / Varsity Drag	1954	3.00	15.00
Mercury 70529	Earth Angel / Ko Ko Mo	1955	4.00	20.00
Mercury 70597	Don't Be Angry / Chop Chop Boom	1955	3.00	15.00
Mercury 70598	Unchained Melody / Two Hearts, Two Kisses	1955	3.00	15.00
Mercury 70634	A Story Untold / Carmen's Boogie	1955	3.00	15.00
Mercury 70668	Gum Drop / Present Arms	1955	3.00	15.00
Mercury 70668	Gum Drop / Song Of The Fool	1955	3.00	15.00
Mercury 70710	Slam Bam / Are You Having Any Fun?	1955	3.00	15.00
Mercury 70741	Angels In The Sky / Mostly Marsha	1955	3.00	15.00
Mercury 70782	Seven Days / That's Your Mistake	1956	3.00	15.00
Mercury 70840	Out Of The Picture / Honey Hair, Sugar Lips, Eyes Of Blue	1956	3.00	15.00
Mercury 70890	Tell Me Why / Rebel In Town	1956	3.00	15.00
Mercury 70922	Thirteen Going On Fourteen / Bei Mir Bist Du Schoen	1956	3.00	15.00
Mercury 70977	Love In A Home / Keeper Of The Flame	1956	3.00	15.00
Mercury 70988	Halls Of Ivy / Varsity Drag	1956	3.00	15.00
Mercury 71022	Young Love / Little By Little	1957	3.00	15.00
Mercury 71076	Angelus / Whatever, Whenever, Whoever	1957	3.00	15.00
	—Original Mercury singles above have maroon labels.—			
Mercury 70341	Crazy 'Bout You, Baby / Angela Mia	1957	2.00	10.00
Mercury 70404	Sh-Boom / I Spoke Too Soon	1957	2.00	10.00
Mercury 70443	Oop Shoop / Do Me Good, Baby	1957	2.00	10.00

Label & Catalog #	A-Side/B-Side	Year	VG	NM
Mercury 70490	All I Wanna Do / The Barking Dog	1957	2.00	10.00
Mercury 70491	Dance, Mr. Snowman, Dance	1957	2.00	10.00
Mercury 70494	The Whiffenpoof Song / Varsity Drag	1957	2.00	10.00
Mercury 70529	Earth Angel / Ko Ko Mo	1957	2.00	10.00
Mercury 70597	Don't Be Angry / Chop Chop Boom	1957	2.00	10.00
Mercury 70598	Unchained Melody / Two Hearts, Two Kisses	1957	2.00	10.00
Mercury 70634	A Story Untold / Carmen's Boogie	1957	2.00	10.00
Mercury 70668	Gum Drop / Present Arms	1957	2.00	10.00
Mercury 70668	Gum Drop / Song Of The Fool	1957	2.00	10.00
Mercury 70710	Slam Bam / Are You Having Any Fun?	1957	2.00	10.00
Mercury 70741	Angels In The Sky / Mostly Marsha	1957	2.00	10.00
Mercury 70782	Seven Days / That's Your Mistake	1957	2.00	10.00
Mercury 70840	Out Of The Picture / Honey Hair, Sugar Lips, Eyes Of Blue	1957	2.00	10.00
Mercury 70890	Tell Me Why / Rebel In Town	1957	2.00	10.00
Mercury 70922	Thirteen Going On Fourteen / Bei Mir Bist Du Schoen	1957	2.00	10.00
Mercury 70977	Love In A Home / Keeper Of The Flame	1957	2.00	10.00
Mercury 70988	Halls Of Ivy / Varsity Drag	1957	2.00	10.00
Mercury 71022	Young Love / Little By Little	1957	2.00	10.00
Mercury 71076	Angelus / Whatever, Whenever, Whoever	1957	2.00	10.00
Mercury 71125	Susie Q / Such A Shame	1957	2.40	12.00
Mercury 71168	I Sit In My Window / Hey, You Face	1957	2.40	12.00
Mercury 71223	Be My Only Love / I Like It Like That	1957	2.40	12.00
	—Mercury singles above have black labels.—			
RCA Victor 47-7320	Hey, Stella! / Forever, My Darling	1958	2.00	10.00
RCA Victor 47-7359	Baby Be Mine / That's My Desire	1958	2.00	10.00
RCA Victor 47-7446	Can You Hear Me? / Fraternity Pin	1959	2.00	10.00
RCA Victor 47-7509	Gone, Gone, Gone / Someone In Heaven	1959	2.00	10.00
RCA Victor 47-7577	Bermuda / Kin-Ni-Ki-Nic	1959	2.00	10.00
RCA Victor 47-7667	It's No Secret / No, No Nevermore	1960	2.00	10.00
RCA Victor 47-7734	American Beauty Rose / The Shrine On The Top Of The Hill	1960	2.00	10.00
RCA Victor 47-7759	Going To Church On Sunday / Aura Lee	1960	2.00	10.00
Warwick 623	Legend Of Gunga Din / Number One With Me	1961	2.00	10.00
Whale 507	Electric Chair / Twistin' All Around The World	1962	2.00	10.00
Whale 508	Laura Love / Little Donkey	1962	2.00	10.00
Whale 509	Electric Chair / Twistin' All Around The World	1962	2.00	10.00
Vee Jay 569	Hush, Little Baby / Ti' Pi' Tum	1963	2.00	10.00
ABC-Paramount 10450	Hip-Huggers / You're A Star, Donna Donna	1964	2.00	10.00
Chess 1892	Yea Yea, She Wants Me / Ain't That Nice	1964	2.00	10.00
Firebird 1805	You've Been In / My Heart Belongs To Only You	1970	1.00	5.00
	—Extended Play Albums—			
Mercury 13261	Crazy 'Bout You, Baby	1954	10.00	50.00
Mercury 13274	Three Cheers For The Crew Cuts (Volume 1)	1954	10.00	50.00
Mercury 13275	Three Cheers For The Crew Cuts (Volume 2)	1954	10.00	50.00
Mercury 13290	Tops In Pops	1954	10.00	50.00
Mercury 13325	The Crew Cuts Go Longhair	1954	10.00	50.00
Mercury 13326	Longhair Swing With The Crew Cuts	1954	10.00	50.00
Mercury 13327	The Crew Cuts Swing The Masters	1954	10.00	50.00

CREWNECKS, THE

Label & Catalog #	A-Side/B-Side	Year	VG	NM
Rhapsody 71960	I'll Never Forget You /	1959	3.00	15.00
Rhapsody 71961	Rockin' Zombie / When I First Fall In Love	1959	3.00	15.00

CRIBBINS, BERNARD

Label & Catalog #	A-Side/B-Side	Year	VG	NM
Capitol 5933	When I'm Sixty Four / Oh, My Word	1967	1.60	8.00

CRICKETS, THE

Buddy Holly with Jerry Allison, Sonny Curtis and Jerry Naylor. Holly appears on Brunswick 55034-55094 and 62238. Later members, after Holly's death, included Tommy Allsup, Glen Hardin, Joe Mauldin, Jerry Naylor and Nikki Sullivan. Refer to The Camps; Jim Pewter; Bobby Vee.

Label & Catalog #		A-Side/B-Side	Year	VG	NM
Brunswick 9-55009	(DJ)	That'll Be The Day / I'm Lookin' For Someone To Love	1957	20.00	100.00
Brunswick 9-55009		That'll Be The Day / I'm Lookin' For Someone To Love	1957	6.00	30.00
Brunswick 9-55035	(DJ)	Oh, Boy / Not Fade Away	1957	20.00	100.00
Brunswick 9-55035		Oh, Boy / Not Fade Away	1957	6.00	30.00
Brunswick 9-55053	(DJ)	Maybe Baby / Tell Me How	1958	20.00	100.00
Brunswick 9-55053		Maybe Baby / Tell Me How	1958	5.00	25.00
Brunswick 9-55072	(DJ)	Think It Over / Fools Paradise	1958	20.00	100.00
Brunswick 9-55072		Think It Over / Fools Paradise	1958	5.00	25.00
Brunswick 9-55094	(DJ)	It's So Easy / Lonesome Tears	1959	20.00	100.00
Brunswick 9-55094		It's So Easy / Lonesome Tears	1959	6.00	30.00
Brunswick 9-55124	(DJ)	Love's Made A Fool Of You / Someone, Someone	1959	15.00	75.00
Brunswick 9-55124		Love's Made A Fool Of You / Someone, Someone	1959	5.00	25.00
Brunswick 9-55153	(DJ)	When You Ask About Love / Deborah	1959	15.00	75.00
Brunswick 9-55153		When You Ask About Love / Deborah	1959	5.00	25.00
		—Original Brunswick singles have maroon labels with machine stamped numbers in the trail-off vinyl.—			
Brunswick 9-55009		That'll Be The Day / I'm Lookin' For Someone To Love	1960	3.00	15.00
Brunswick 9-55035		Oh, Boy / Not Fade Away	1960	3.00	15.00
Brunswick 9-55053		Maybe Baby / Tell Me How	1960	3.00	15.00
Brunswick 9-55072		Think It Over / Fools Paradise	1960	3.00	15.00

Label & Catalog #		A-Side/B-Side	Year	VG	NM
Brunswick 9-55094		It's So Easy / Lonesome Tears	1960	3.00	15.00
Brunswick 9-55124		Love's Made A Fool Of You / Someone, Someone	1960	3.00	15.00
Brunswick 9-55153		When You Ask About Love / Deborah	1960	3.00	15.00
— Brunswick singles have orange labels with machine stamped numbers in the trail-off vinyl.—					
Brunswick 9-55009		That'll Be The Day / I'm Lookin' For Someone To Love	1963	2.00	15.00
Brunswick 9-55035		Oh, Boy / Not Fade Away	1963	2.00	10.00
Brunswick 9-55053		Maybe Baby / Tell Me How	1963	2.00	10.00
Brunswick 9-55072		Think It Over / Fools Paradise	1963	2.00	10.00
Brunswick 9-55094		It's So Easy / Lonesome Tears	1963	2.00	10.00
Brunswick 9-55124		Love's Made A Fool Of You / Someone, Someone	1963	2.00	10.00
Brunswick 9-55153		When You Ask About Love / Deborah	1963	2.00	10.00
— Brunswick singles have black labels with machine stamped numbers in the trail-off vinyl.—					
Coral 62198		More Than I Can Say / Baby My Heart	1960	4.00	20.00
Coral 62238		Peggy Sue Got Married / Don'cha Know?	1960	5.00	25.00
Liberty 55392		I'm Feeling Better / He's Old Enough To Know Better	1961	3.00	15.00
Liberty 55441		Don't Ever Change / I'm Not A Bad Guy	1962	3.00	15.00
Liberty 55495		Little Hollywood Girl / Parisian Girl	1962	2.00	10.00
Liberty 55540		Teardrops Like Rain / My Little Girl	1963	3.00	15.00
Liberty 55603		April Avenue / Don't Say You Love Me	1963	3.00	15.00
Liberty 55668		From Me To You / Please Please Me	1964	6.00	30.00
Liberty 55696		All Over You / La Bamba	1964	3.00	15.00
Liberty 55742		I Think I've Caught The Blues / We Gotta Get Together	1965	3.00	15.00
Liberty 55767		Ev'rybody's Got A Little Problem / Now Hear This	1965	3.00	15.00
Million 415		A Million Miles Apart / Million Dollar Movie	196?	1.25	6.00
Music Factory 415		A Million Miles Apart / Million Dollar Movie	1968	3.00	15.00
Barnaby ZS7-2061		True Love Ways / Rockin' 50's Rock 'N Roll	1972	4.00	20.00
—Extended Play Albums—					
Brunswick EB-71036		The Chirping Crickets	1957	100.00	400.00
Brunswick EB-71038		The Sound Of The Crickets	1958	75.00	300.00
Coral EC-81192		The Crickets	1963	50.00	200.00
(Brunswick 71036, 71038 and Coral 81192 feature Buddy Holly.)					
Holly Memorial 100		The Crickets Live	1978	2.00	10.00

CRISS, GARY
Strand 25044		Good Golly, Miss Molly / I'll Love Only You	1962	3.00	15.00

CRISS, PETER
Peter Criss is a member of Kiss.
Casablanca 961		You Still Matter To Me / Hooked On Rock N' Roll	1978	1.20	6.00
Casablanca 2311		By Myself / I Found Love	198?	1.00	5.00

CRITERIONS, THE
Celilia 1010		Don't Say Goodbye / Crying The Blues Over Me	1959	8.00	40.00
Celilia 1208		I Remain Truly Yours / You, Just You	1959	4.00	20.00
Laurie 3305		I Remain Truly Yours / You, Just You	1965	2.00	10.00

CRITTERS, THE
Design 2640		In Time / You Better Slow Down	196?	1.20	6.00

CRITTERS, THE
The Critters feature Don Ciccone.
Kapp 752		Younger Girl / Gone For Awhile	1966	1.00	5.00
Kapp 769		Mr. Dieingly Sad / It Just Won't Be That Way	1966	1.00	5.00
Kapp 769	(PS)	Mr. Dieingly Sad / It Just Won't Be That Way	1966	3.00	15.00
Kapp 793		Bad Misunderstanding / Forever Or No More	1966	.60	3.00
Kapp 805		Marryin' Kind Of Love / New York Bound	1967	.60	3.00
Kapp 838		Don't Let The Rain Fall On Me / Walk Like A Man Again	1967	.60	3.00
Kapp 858		Little Girl / Dancing In The Streets	1967	.60	3.00
Project-3 1326		Good Morning Sunshine / Moment Of Being With You	1967	.80	4.00
Project-3 1349		Cool Sunday Morning / Lisa, But Not The Same	1968	.80	4.00
Project-3 1363		I Just Want To Sit Right Here And Look At You /			
		She Said She Loved Him	1968	.80	4.00

CROCE, JIM
ABC 11328		You Don't Mess Around With Jim /			
		Photographs And Memories	1972	.80	4.00
ABC 11335		Operator (That's Not The Way It Feels) /			
		Rapid Roy (The Stock Car Boy)	1972	.60	3.00
ABC 11346		One Less Set Of Footsteps / It Doesn't Have To Be That Way	1973	.60	3.00
ABC 11359		Bad Bad Leroy Brown / A Good Time Man Like Me			
		Ain't Got No Business (Singin' The Blues)	1973	.80	4.00
ABC 11389		I Got A Name / Alabama Rain	1973	.80	4.00
ABC 11405		Time In A Bottle / Hard Time Losin' Man	1973	.80	4.00
ABC 11413		It Doesn't Have To Be That Way / Roller Derby Queen	1973	.60	3.00
ABC 11413	(PS)	It Doesn't Have To Be That Way / Roller Derby Queen	1973	.60	3.00
ABC 11424		I'll Have To Say I Love You In A Song / Salon And Saloon	1974	.80	4.00
ABC 11447		Workin' At The Car Wash Blues / Thursday	1974	.60	3.00
ABC 12015		Workin' At The Car Wash Blues / Thursday	1974	.60	3.00

Label & Catalog #		A-Side/B-Side	Year	VG	NM
Lifesong 45001		Chain Gang Medley / Stone Walls	1975	.60	3.00
Lifesong 45005		Mississippi Lady / Maybe Tomorrow	1976	.60	3.00

CROCKETT BROTHERS, THE

| Del-Fi 4213 | | Mother, Mother, Can I Go Surfin'? / After I've Been So True | 1963 | 6.00 | 30.00 |
| Donna 1389 | | Fastest Car In Town / Why? | 1963 | 6.00 | 30.00 |

CROME SYRCUS

Merrilyn 5303		White Korte Feather / Blue Morning	196?	2.00	10.00
Jerden 921		Lord In Black / Elevator Operator	1970	2.00	10.00
Piccadilly 256		Lord In Black / Long Hard Road	197?	.80	4.00
Command 4511		Take It Like A Man / Crystals	197?	1.00	5.00
Command 4511		Take It Like A Man / Cover Up	197?	1.00	5.00
Command	(DJ)	The Pain I Feel / We're A Winner	197?	2.00	10.00

CROSBY, DAVID

David Crosby, an original Byrd, also recorded with Steve Still, Graham Nash and Neil Young as CS&N and CSN&Y.

| Atlantic 2729 | | Music Is Love / Laughing | 1971 | .60 | 3.00 |
| Atlantic 2809 | | Orleans / Traction In The Rain | 1971 | .60 | 3.00 |

CROSBY, DAVID, & GRAHAM NASH

Atlantic 2873		Immigration Man / Whole Cloth	1972	.60	3.00
Atlantic 2892		Southbound Train / The Wall Song	1972	.60	3.00
ABC 12140		Carry Me / Mama Lion	1975	.40	2.00
ABC 12165		Take The Money And Run / Bittersweet	1976	.40	2.00
ABC 12185		Love Work Out / Bittersweet	1976	.40	2.00
ABC 12199		Out Of The Darkness / Broken Bird	1976	.40	2.00
ABC 12217		Spotlight / Foolish Man	1977	.40	2.00

CROSBY, GARY

Decca 29527		Truly Do / His And Her's	1955	2.00	10.00
Gregmark 11		That's All Right, Baby / Who?	1962	3.00	15.00
		(Gregmark 11 features The Paris Sisters.)			

CROSBY, STILLS & NASH

Atlantic 2652		Marrakesh Express / Helplessly Hoping	1969	.60	3.00
Atlantic 2676		Suite: Judy Blue Eyes / Long Time Gone	1969	.60	3.00
Atlantic 3401		Just A Song Before I Go / Dark Star	1977	.40	2.00
Atlantic 3401	(PS)	Just A Song Before I Go / Dark Star	1977	.40	2.00
Atlantic 3432		Fair Game / Anything At All	1977	.40	2.00
Atlantic 3453		Carried Away /	1977	.40	2.00
Atlantic 4058		Wasted On The Way / Delta	1982	.40	2.00
Atlantic 4058	(PS)	Wasted On The Way / Delta	1982	.40	2.00
Atlantic 89969		Southern Cross / Into The Darkness	1982	.40	2.00

CROSBY, STILLS, NASH & YOUNG

David Crosby, Steve Stills, Graham Nash and Neil Young.

Atlantic 2723		Woodstock / Helpless	1970	.60	3.00
Atlantic 2735		Teach Your Children / Carry On	1970	.60	3.00
Atlantic 2740		Ohio / Find The Cost Of Freedom	1970	.60	3.00
Atlantic 2740	(PS)	Ohio / Find The Cost Of Freedom	1970	.60	3.00
Atlantic 2760		Our House / Deja Vu	1970	.60	3.00
Atlantic 89003		American Dream / Compass	1988	.40	2.00
Atlantic 89003	(PS)	American Dream / Compass	1988	.40	2.00
Atlantic 88966		Got It Made / This Old House	1988	.40	2.00
Atlantic 88966	(PS)	Got It Made / This Old House	1988	.40	2.00
		—Extended Play Albums—			
Atlantic 7200	(33)	Deja Vu (Jukebox EP)	1970	4.00	20.00

CROSS, JIMMY

Recordo 502		Pretty Girls Everywhere / Suntan Sally	1961	2.00	10.00
Tollie 9039		I Want My Baby Back / Play The Other Side	1964	2.00	10.00
Tollie 9044		Ballad Of James Bond / Play The Other Side Again	1964	2.00	10.00
Red Bird 042		Hey, Little Girl / Super-Duper Man	1965	2.00	10.00
Chicken 101		Hey, Little Girl / Hey, Little Girl (Part 2)	1965	2.00	10.00

CROSS COUNTRY

Cross Country is Mitch Margo, Phil Matgo and Jay Siegel of The Tokens.

Atco 6932		Rock And Roll Music / Just A Thought	1973	.80	4.00
Atco 6934		In The Midnight Hour / A Smile Song	1973	.80	4.00
Atco 6947		Tastes So Good To Me / A Ball Song	1973	.80	4.00
Atco 7009		Penny Whistle Band / Lord, Can't Sing A Solo	1974	.80	4.00

CROSSFIRES, THE

Crossfire later recorded as The Turtles.

| Capco 104 | | Fiberglass Jungle / Dr. Jekyll And Mr. Hyde | 1963 | 10.00 | 50.00 |
| Lucky Token 112 | | One Potato, Two Potato / That'll Be The Day | 1965 | 5.00 | 25.00 |

Label & Catalog #		A-Side/B-Side	Year	VG	NM
CROW					
Amaret 112		Evil Woman, Don't Play Your Games With Me /			
		Gonna Leave A Mark	1969	.80	4.00
Amaret 119		Busy Day / Cottage Cheese	1970	.60	3.00
Amaret 119		Slow Down / Cottage Cheese	1970	.60	3.00
Amaret 125		Don't Try To Lay No Boogie-Woogie On The King			
		Of Rock And Roll / Satisfied	1970	.60	3.00
Amaret 129		Watching Can Waste Up The Time / Yellow Dawg	1971	.60	3.00
Amaret 133		Something In Your Blood / Yellow Dawg	1971	.60	3.00
Amaret 145		Everything Has To Be Free / Mobile Blue	1972	.60	3.00
Amaret 148		If It Feels Good, Do It / Cado Queen	1972	.60	3.00
CROWN, BOBBY, & THE KAPERS					
Felco 102		One-Way Ticket / Your Conscience	1960	75.00	300.00
CROWNS, THE					
Chordette 1001		Party Time / Amazon Basin Pop	1962	2.00	10.00
CROWNS, THE					
Old Town 1171		Possibility / Watch Out *(Blue label)*	1963	7.00	35.00
CRUCHENDOES, THE					
The Cruchendoes, who also recorded as The Creshendoes, feature Chuck Rio.					
Toppa 1097		Butter Fingers / Lieber Straum	196?	4.00	20.00
CRUISERS, THE					
Era 1052		A Ring Around A Chain / Buoys And Gulls	1957	4.00	20.00
Finch 353		Baby, What A Fool I've Been / *(B-side by LeRoy Jones)*	1957	4.00	20.00
Zebra 119		There's A Girl / Foolish Me	195?	25.00	125.00
Arch 1611		I Want Your Love / I Said Hear	1959	3.00	15.00
Coda 3005		Betty Ann / You Made A Fool Out Of Me	1959	3.00	15.00
Winston 1033		Cruisin' / My Mary Lou	1959	3.00	15.00
Pharaoh 128		Another Lonely Night / Please Let Me Be	196?	3.00	15.00
CRUM, SIMON					
Simon Crum is a pseudonym for Ferlin Husky.					
Capitol 3460		Bop Cat, Bop / Muki Ruki	1962	5.00	25.00
Capitol 4966		Don't Be Mad / Little Red Webb	1963	5.00	25.00
CRUSADERS, THE					
DKR		Busted Surfboard / Seminole	196?	6.00	30.00
CRYAN' SHAMES, THE					
Destination 624		Sugar And Spice / Ben Franklin's Almanac	1966	2.00	10.00
Columbia 43836		I Wanna Meet You / We Could Be Happy	1966	1.00	5.00
Columbia 44037		Mr. Unreliable / Georgia	1967	1.00	5.00
Columbia 44191		It Could Be We're In Love / I Was Lonely When	1967	1.00	5.00
Columbia 44191	(PS)	It Could Be We're In Love / I Was Lonely When	1967	2.00	10.00
Columbia 44457		Sailing Ship / Up On The Roof	1967	.80	4.00
Columbia 44545		Young Birds Fly / Sunshine Psalm	1968	.80	4.00
Columbia 44638		Greenburg, Glickstein, Charles, David Smith & Jones /			
		The Warm	1968	.80	4.00
Columbia 44759		First Train To California / A Master's Fool	1968	.80	4.00
Columbia 45027		Rainmaker / Bits And Pieces	1970	.80	4.00
CRYIN' SHAMES, THE					
London 1001		Please Stay (Don't Go) / What's New, Pussy Cat?	1968	1.00	5.00
CRYSTAL, CATHY					
Day Dell 1001		Jimmy / Sing A Song Of Loneliness	196?	1.20	6.00
CRYSTAL, LOU					
SFAZ 1001		Sheila Baby / Dreaming Of An Angel	1962	5.00	25.00
CRYSTAL FOREST					
Poole 1315		We Wonder Why / I've Been Lonely	196?	2.00	10.00
CRYSTAL MANSION, THE					
Capitol 2275		Thought Of Loving You / Hallelujah	1968	.80	4.00
Capitol 2424		For The First Time / I Got Something For You	1968	.80	4.00
Capitol 2543		Everything's In Love Today / Country	1969	.80	4.00
CRYSTAL TEARDROP					
Garland 2027		Findin' My Own Kind Of Song / Dorchester Summer	1970	2.00	10.00
CRYSTAL TONES, THE					
M.Z. 007		A Girl I Love / Debra-Lee	1959	50.00	200.00

Label & Catalog #		A-Side/B-Side	Year	VG	NM
CRYSTALS, THE					
Indigo 114		**Dreams And Wishes / Mr. Brush**	1961	3.00	15.00
CRYSTALS, THE					

The Crystals are Barbara Alston, Dolores Brooks, Dee Kennibrew and Pat Wright. Philles 105 is actually The Blossoms with Darlene Love, who also sang lead on Philles 108.

Philles 100		**There's No Other / Oh Yeah, Maybe Baby**	1961	4.00	20.00
Philles 102		**Uptown / What A Nice Way To Turn 17**	1962	4.00	20.00
Philles 105		**He Hit Me / No One Ever Tells Me**	1962	4.00	20.00
Philles 106		**He's A Rebel / I Love You, Eddie**	1962	4.00	20.00
		— Original Philles singles above have orange labels.—			
Philles 105		**He Hit Me / No One Ever Tells Me**	1962	4.00	20.00
Philles 106		**He's A Rebel / I Love You, Eddie**	1962	4.00	20.00
		—Philles singles above have blue laels with the company address.—			
Philles 109		**He's Sure The Boy I Love / Walking Along**	1962	3.00	15.00
Philles 109X		**He's Sure The Boy I Love / Walking Along**	1962	3.00	15.00
Philles 111	(DJ)	**Do The Screw / Do The Screw**	1963	——	——
		(Rare. Estimated near mint value $3,000-5,000.)			
Philles 112		**Da Doo Ron Ron / Git It**	1963	3.00	15.00
Philles 115		**Then He Kissed Me / Brother Julius**	1963	3.00	15.00
		—Philles singles above have blue labels.—			
Philles 119		**Little Boy / Harry And Milt**	1964	4.00	20.00
Philles 119X		**Little Boy / Harry And Milt**	1964	3.00	15.00
Philles 122		**All Grown Up / Irving**	1964	3.00	15.00
United Artists 994		**Are You Trying To Get Rid Of Me? / I Got A Man**	1965	2.00	10.00
United Artists 927		**You Can't Tie A Good Girl Down / My Place**	1965	2.00	10.00
CUFF LINKS, THE					

The Cuff Links feature Ron Dante.

Decca 32533		**Tracy / Where Do You Go To?**	1969	.80	4.00
Decca 32533	(PS)	**Tracy / Where Do You Go To?**	1969	2.00	10.00
Decca 32592		**When Julie Comes Around / Sally Ann**	1969	.60	3.00
Decca 32639		**Run, Sally, Run / I Remember**	1970	.60	3.00
Decca 32732		**Thank You, Pretty Baby / Kiss**	1970	.60	3.00
CUFFLINKS, THE					
Gait 1445		**Only One Love / Next To You**	195?	25.00	125.00
CUNICO, GINO					
Kama Sutra		**Yesterday's Too Many Dreams Away / No Strings**	1973	1.60	8.00
Kama Sutra 597		**Melanie / Melanie**	1974	1.20	6.00
		(Stock copies of K.S. 597 may not exist.)			
CUNNINGHAM, BUDDY					
Sun 208		**Right Or Wrong / Why Do I Cry?**	1954	——	——
		(Rare. Estimated near mint value $500-1,000.)			
CUPCAKES, THE					
Time 1011		**Deutsche Rock And Roll / It's Willy**	1959	2.00	10.00
Diamond 177		**Pied Piper / Winter Blue**	1964	1.20	6.00
CUPIDS, THE: *Refer to* DARWIN & THE CUPIDS					
CUPS, THE					
Tetragrammaton 1538		**Good As Gold / My Life And Times**	1969	.80	4.00
CURB, MIKE, & THE CURBSTONES					
Reprise 0287		**Velocita / Hot Dawg**	1964	4.00	20.00
SIDEWALK SOUNDS, THE [MIKE CURB & THE SIDEWALK SOUNDS]					
Tower 352		**Billy Jack's Theme / Born Loser's Theme**	1967	1.20	6.00
Tower 480		**Eight Young Men (Devil's Eight Theme) / Let's Go**	1968	1.20	6.00
CURB CONGREGATION, MIKE					

Mike Curb, future reactionary Gov. of CA, also recorded as The Sidewalk Sounds.

Tower 202		**Sunshine / Suzie Darling**	1969	1.00	5.00
MGM 14140		**Long Haired Lover From Liverpool / Sweet Gingerbread Man**	1970	.60	3.00
MGM 14151		**Burning Bridges / We'll Sing In The Sunshine**	1970	.60	3.00
MGM 14242		**M.I.A.-P.O.W. /** *(B-side by Pat Boone)*	1971	.60	3.00
MGM 14243		**I Was Born In Love With You / Sweet Gingerbread Man**	1971	.60	3.00
MGM 14265		**Fly Me A Place For The Summer / Sweet Gingerbread Man**	1971	.60	3.00
MGM 14336		**Forty Days And Forty Nights / Softly Whispering I Love You**	1971	.60	3.00
MGM 14366		**I Saw The Light / Take Up The Hammer Of Hope**	1971	.60	3.00
MGM 14391		**See You In September / Very Same Time Next Year**	1971	.60	3.00
MGM 14442		**I Understand / This Land Is Your Land**	1972	.60	3.00
MGM 14494		**It's A Small, Small World / Shinin' On Me**	1972	.60	3.00

Label & Catalog #	A-Side/B-Side	Year	VG	NM
CURBSTONES, THE				
The Curbstones is another creative offshoot from the fertile imagination of Gov. Curb.				
MGM 14449	Children's Marching Song / Kid Power Title Song	1972	.60	3.00
MGM 14525	Everybody's Got Fingers / Scrumpdillyishus	1973	.60	3.00
CURLEY & THE JADES				
Reprise 20046	Boom Stix / Bull Fighter	1961	5.00	25.00
CURLS, THE				
Everest 19319	Imaginez Vouz / Why Didn't I Go?	1959	3.00	15.00
Everest 19350	He's My Hero / Like A Waterfall	1960	3.00	15.00
CURRENTS, THE				
Laurie 3205	Night Run / Riff Raff	1963	4.00	20.00
CURRIE, CHERIE & MARIE				
Cherie and Marie Currie originally recorded with The Runaways.				
Capitol 4754	Since You've Been Gone / Longer Than Forever	1979	.80	4.00
Capitol 4754 (PS)	Since You've Been Gone / Longer Than Forever	1979	2.00	10.00
CURRY, TIM				
Ode 66117 (DJ)	Baby Love / Baby Love	1976	.80	4.00
Ode 66117	Baby Love / Just 14	1976	3.00	15.00
	("Just 14" features Brian Wilson on backing vocal.)			
CURTIS, MAC				
King 4927	If I Had Me A Woman / Just So You Call Me	1956	10.00	50.00
King 4947	Grandaddy's Rockin' / Half Hearted Love	1956	10.00	50.00
King 4965	You Ain't Treatin' Me Right / The Low Road	1956	7.00	35.00
King 4995	That Ain't Nothin' But Right / Don't You Love Me?	1956	7.00	35.00
King 5059	I'll Be Gentle / Say So	1957	7.00	35.00
King 5107	You Are My Special Baby / What You Want	1957	7.00	35.00
King 5121	Little Miss Linda / Missy Ann	1957	7.00	35.00
Felsted 8592	Come Back, Baby / No Never Alone	1960	3.00	15.00
Dot 16315	You're The One / Dance Her By Me	1961	3.00	15.00
CURTIS, SONNY				
Sonny Curtis was a member of Buddy Holly's Crickets.				
Dot 15754	Wrong Again / Laughing Stock	1958	6.00	30.00
Dot 15799	Willa Mae Jones / A Pretty Girl	1958	5.00	25.00
Coral 62207	Red Headed Stranger / Talk About My Baby	1960	7.00	35.00
Dimension 1017	So Used To Lovin' You / Last Song I'm Ever Gonna Sing	1963	4.00	20.00
	("So Used To Lovin' You" was produced by Jan Berry.)			
Dimension 1023	You Don't Belong In This Place / Unsaintly Judy	1963	3.00	15.00
Dimension 1024	A Beatle I Want To Be / So Used To Lovin' You	1964	5.00	25.00
Liberty 55710	I Pledge My Love To You / Bo Diddley Beach	1964	4.00	20.00
Viva 602	My Way Of Life / Last Call	1966	3.00	15.00
Viva 607	Destiny's Child / The Collector	1966	3.00	15.00
Viva 617	I Wanna Go Bumming Around / I'm A Gypsy Man	1967	3.00	15.00
Viva 626	Atlanta, Georgia Stray / Day Drinker	1968	3.00	15.00
Viva 630	The Straight Life / How Little Men Care	1968	3.00	15.00
Viva 634	Holiday For Clowns / Day Gig	1969	4.00	20.00
Viva 636	Girl Of The North / Hung Up In Your Eyes	1969	4.00	20.00
Ovation 1006	Love Is All Around / Here, There And Everywhere	1970	4.00	20.00
Ovation 1023	You Don't Belong In This Place / Unsaintly Judy	1970	3.00	15.00
Mercury 73438	Rock And Roll, I Gave You The Best Years Of My Life / My Mama Sure Left Me Some Good Old Days	1972	3.00	15.00
A&M 1352	Sunny Mornin' / The Lights Of L.A.	1972	4.00	20.00
Capitol 4158	Lovesick Blues / It's Only A Question Of Time	1975	2.00	10.00
Capitol 4227	It's Only A Question Of Time / When It's Just You And Me	1976	2.00	10.00
Capitol 4240	Where's Patricia Now? / When It's Just You And Me	1976	3.00	15.00
Elektra 46526	Cheatin' Clouds / The Cowboy Singer	1979	.60	3.00
Elektra 46568	Do You Remember "Roll Over, Beethoven?" / Walk Right Back	1979	.60	3.00
Elektra 46616	The Real Buddy Holly Story / Ain't Nobody Honest	1980	.80	4.00
Elektra 46663	Love Is All Around / The Clone Song	1980	.60	3.00
CURTISS, DAVE, & THE TREMORS				
Karate 514	How I Cry / Que Sera Sera	1965	1.20	6.00
CURTISS, JIMMY				
Laurie 3312	You're What's Happening, Baby / Not For You	1965	2.00	10.00
Laurie 3315	The Girl From The Land Of 1,000 Dances / Let's Dance	1965	6.00	30.00
	(Laurie 3315 features The Regents.)			
CURTOLA, BOBBY				
Del-Fi 4163	My Heart's Tongue-Tied / Don't You Sweetheart Me	1961	2.00	10.00
Del-Fi 4177	Fortune Teller / Johnny Take Your Time	1962	2.00	10.00

Label & Catalog #		A-Side/B-Side	Year	VG	NM
Del-Fi 4182		I Cry And Cry / Big Time Spender	1962	2.00	10.00
Del-Fi 4182	(PS)	I Cry And Cry / Big Time Spender	1962	4.00	20.00
Del-Fi 4185		Aladdin / I Don't Want To Go On Without You	1962	2.00	10.00
Del-Fi 4185	(PS)	Aladdin / I Don't Want To Go On Without You	1962	4.00	20.00
Del-Fi 4195		Destination Love / Hitch Hiker	1963	2.00	10.00
Del-Fi 4223		Three Rows Over / How'm I Gonna Tell You?	1963	2.00	10.00

CUSTER & THE SURVIVORS

Golden State 1657		I Saw Her Walking / Flapjacks	196?	2.00	10.00

CUSTOMS, THE
The Customs later recorded as The Surfaris.

Regano 1062		Steppin' Out / Hi Hat	1962	10.00	50.00
		(Regano 1062 was reissued as "Surfin' '63" / "Boss Beat" and credited to The Original Surfaris.)			

CUSTOMS, THE

Arlen 511		Because Of Love / Earthquake	1963	2.00	10.00

CUT-UPS, THE

Mecca 2500		Twant / The Cup-Up Walk	196?	2.00	10.00

CUTE TEENS, THE

Aladdin 3458		When My Teenage Days Are Over / From This Day Forward	1959	4.00	20.00

CYCLONE III
Cyclone III is a pseudonym for The Statens and features Frankie Valli on backing vocals.

Philips 40258		Surfananny / You've Got A Bomb	1965	8.00	40.00

CYCLONES, THE

Trophy 500		Bullwhip Rock / Nelda Jane	1958	7.00	35.00

CYMBAL, JOHNNY
Johnny Cymbal later recorded as, or with, Derek; Milk; and Taurus.

MGM 12935		It'll Be Me / Always, Always	1960	3.00	15.00
MGM 12978		The Water Was Red / Bunny	1960	3.00	15.00
Kedlen 2001		Bachelor Man / Growing Up With You	1963	3.00	15.00
Vee Jay 495		Bachelor Man / Growing Up With You	1963	2.00	10.00
Kapp 503		Mr. Bass Man / Sacred Lover's Vow	1963	3.00	15.00
Kapp 524		Teenage Heaven / Cinderella Baby	1963	3.00	15.00
Kapp 539		Tiajuana / Dum Dum Dee Dum	1963	3.00	15.00
Kapp 556		Hurdy Gurdy Man / Marshmallow	1963	2.00	10.00
Kapp 576		There Goes A Bad Girl / Refreshment Time	1964	2.00	10.00
Kapp 614		Little Miss Lonely / Connie	1964	2.00	10.00
DCP 1135		Go VW, Go / Sorrow And Pain	1965	4.00	20.00
DCP 1146		Summertime's Here At Last / My Last Day	1965	3.00	15.00
Amaret 110		Big River / Girl From River County	1969	.80	4.00

CYNICS, THE

Bear		Train Kept A' Rollin' / You're A Better Man Than I	196?	4.00	20.00

CYRKLE, THE
Refer to the Various Artists EP section.

Columbia 43589	(DJ)	Red Rubber Ball / Red Rubber Ball (Red vinyl)	1966	5.00	25.00
Columbia 43589		Red Rubber Ball / How Can I Leave Her?	1966	1.20	6.00
Columbia 43589	(PS)	Red Rubber Ball / How Can I Leave Her?	1966	5.00	25.00
Columbia 43729	(DJ)	Turn Down Day / Turn Down Day (Red vinyl)	1966	4.00	20.00
Columbia 43729		Turn Down Day / Big Little Woman	1966	1.20	6.00
Columbia 43729	(PS)	Turn Down Day / Big Little Woman	1966	1.20	6.00
Columbia CSM-466	(DJ)	Camaro / (B-side by Paul Revere & The Raiders)	1967	1.20	6.00
Columbia CSM-466	(PS)	Camaro / SS 396	1967	2.00	10.00
Columbia 43871		Please Don't Ever Leave Me / Money To Burn	1967	.80	4.00
Columbia 43965		I Wish You Could Be Here / The Visit (She Was Here)	1967	.80	4.00
Columbia 43965	(PS)	I Wish You Could Be Here / The Visit (She Was Here)	1967	1.25	6.00
Columbia 44108		We Had A Good Thing Goin' / Two Rooms	1967	.80	4.00
Columbia 44224		Penny Arcade / The Words	1967	.80	4.00
Columbia 44426		Friends / Reading Her Paper	1968	.80	4.00

CYRUS ERIE

Epic 10451		Sparrow / Get The Message	1969	2.00	10.00

D.

D'ACCORDS, THE
Don-El 110 | Runnin' Around / Who's Been Loving You? | 196? | 4.00 | 20.00

D'AGOSTIN, DICK
Dot 15773 | Nancy Lynne / Afraid To Take A Chance | 1958 | 10.00 | 50.00

D'AMBRA, JOE, & THE EMBERS
Mercury 71725 | Don't Forget To Write / Please Come Home | 1960 | 3.00 | 15.00

D'ANTREA, BOB
Tribute 261 | Falling From Paradise / Equator | 196? | 2.50 | 12.00

D. H. & THE DOWNBEATS
Royal 1004 | Bus Ride / (B-side by Big Daddy) | 1959 | 4.00 | 20.00

D-MEN, THE
The D-Men later recorded as The Fifth Estate.
Veep 1206 | Don't You Know? / No Hope For Me | 1966 | 2.00 | 10.00
Veep 1209 | Just Don't Care / Mousin' Around | 1966 | 2.00 | 10.00
Kapp 691 | So Little Time / Every Minute Of Every Day | 1965 | 2.00 | 10.00

DA-PREES
Twist 70913 | Payday / Sometimes | 195? | 20.00 | 100.00

DABETTES, THE
Advance 3933 | One Dab Man / Why Do You Care? | 1962 | 3.00 | 15.00

DACHE, BERTELL
Bertell Dache is a pseudonym for Tony Orlando and features Carole King on backing vocals.
United Artists 260 | All The World Loves A Lover / You Gotta Have Chicks | 1961 | 4.00 | 20.00
United Artists 290 | Love Eyes / Not Just Tomorrow But Always | 1961 | 4.00 | 20.00
Diamond 201 | Anchors Aweigh, Girl / Don't Stop The World For Me | 196? | 3.00 | 15.00

DADDY O'S, THE
Cabot 122 | Got A Match? / Have A Cigar | 1958 | 1.50 | 8.00

DAHILLS, THE
Musicor 1041 | Michelle / Why Do We Have To Say Goodnight? | 196? | 4.00 | 20.00
Crystal Ball 107 | She's My Angel / I Who Love You | 196? | 1.20 | 6.00

DAHL, DICK
Original Sound 53 | Untrue / Don't Let The Little Girl Cry | 1965 | 1.60 | 8.00

DAILEY, JACK
Guyden 2038 | Little Charmer / Please Understand | 1960 | 2.00 | 10.00
Jamie 1162 | Little Charmer / Please Understand | 1960 | 1.60 | 8.00

DAILY FLASH, THE
Parrot 308 | Queen Jane Approximately / Jack Of Diamonds | 1966 | 3.00 | 15.00
Uni 55001 | The French Girl / Green Rocky Road | 1967 | 3.00 | 15.00

DAKIL COMBO, FLOYD
Jetstar 103 | Dance, Franny, Dance / Look What You've Gone And Done | 1964 | 6.00 | 30.00
Guyden 2111 | Dance, Franny, Dance / Look What You've Gone And Done | 1965 | 3.00 | 15.00
Earth 402 | Bad Boy / Stoppin' Traffic | 1965 | 8.00 | 40.00
Earth 403 | Kitty Kitty / It Takes A Lot To Hurt | 1965 | 6.00 | 30.00
Earth 404 | Stronger Than Dirt / You're The Kind Of Girl | 1965 | 6.00 | 30.00

DAKOTAS, THE
The Dakotas also recorded with Billy J. Kramer.
Liberty 55618 | The Cruel Surf / The Millionaire | 1963 | 5.00 | 25.00

DAKUS, WES, & THE REBELS
Gallio 102 | Surfs You Right / Dogfood | 1963 | 6.00 | 30.00
Kapp 806 | Armful Of Teddy Bears / (B-side by Barry Allen) | 1967 | 2.00 | 10.00
Kapp 815 | See Saw / (B-side by Dennis Paul) | 1967 | 2.00 | 10.00

DALE, DENNY, & THE HONEYMOONS
Soma 1447 | Mr. Moon / Why Did You Leave Me? | 1966 | 2.00 | 10.00

Label & Catalog #		A-Side/B-Side	Year	VG	NM
DALE, DICK, & THE DEL-TONES					
Refer to The Exiles; the Various Artists EPs section.					
Deltone 5012		Ooh Whee, Marie / Breaking Heart	1959	10.00	50.00
Deltone 5013		Stop Teasin' / Without Your Love	1959	10.00	50.00
Deltone 5014		Jessie Pearl / St. Louis Blues	1960	15.00	75.00
Cupid 106		We'll Never Hear The End Of It / Fairest Of Them All	1960	4.00	20.00
Deltone 5016		Ooh Whee, Marie / Without Your Love	1951	4.00	20.00
Deltone 5017		Let's Go Trippin' / Del-Tone Rock	1961	3.00	15.00
Deltone 5018		Jungle Fever / Shake-N-Stomp	1962	3.00	15.00
Deltone 5019		Miserlou / Eight Till Midnight	1962	3.00	15.00
Deltone 5020		Peppermint Man / Surf Beat	1962	3.00	15.00
Deltone 5028		Lovin' On My Brain / Run For Your Life	1963	5.00	25.00
U.S. Army 1301/2		Enlistment Twist / (B-side by Craig Adams) (Blue vinyl)	196?	10.00	50.00
U.S. Army 1301/2		Enlistment Twist / (B-side by Craig Adams)	196?	4.00	20.00
U.S. Army 1301/2	(PS)	Enlistment Twist / (B-side by Craig Adams)	196?	6.00	30.00
Capitol 4939		Miserlou / Eight Till Midnight	1963	3.00	15.00
Capitol 4940		Peppermint Man / Surf Beat	1963	3.00	15.00
Capitol PRO-2320	(33)	Peppermint Man / Open End Interview-Misirlou	1963	10.00	50.00
Capitol PRO-2320	(PS)	Peppermint Man / Open End Interview-Misirlou	1963	20.00	100.00
Capitol 5010		King Of The Surf Guitars / Hava Nagila	1963	3.00	15.00
Capitol 5010	(PS)	King Of The Surf Guitars / Hava Nagila	1963	8.00	40.00
Saturn 401		We'll Never Hear The End Of It / Fairest Of Them All	1963	5.00	25.00
Yes 7014		We'll Never Hear The End Of It / Fairest Of Them All	1963	5.00	25.00
Yes 7014	(PS)	We'll Never Hear The End Of It / Fairest Of Them All	1963	7.00	35.00
Concert Room 371		We'll Never Hear The End Of It / Fairest Of Them All	1963	4.00	20.00
Capitol 5048		The Scavenger / Wild Ideas	1963	3.00	15.00
Capitol 5098		The Wedge / Night Rider	1963	3.00	15.00
Capitol 5140		The Victor / Mr. Eliminator	1964	3.00	15.00
Capitol 5187		Grudge Run / Wild, Wild Mustang	1964	3.00	15.00
Capitol PRO-2647	(DJ)	Thunder Wave / Spanish Kiss	1964	3.00	15.00
		(Capitol PRO-2647 was issued in a special "pocket" on the cover of Jerry Cole's "Surf Age" album.)			
Capitol 5225		Glory Wave / Never On Sunday	1964	3.00	15.00
Capitol 5290		Who Can He Be? / Oh, Marie	1964	2.00	10.00
Capitol 5389		Let's Go Trippin' '65 / Watusi Jo	1965	2.00	10.00
Cougar 711		Ramblin' Man / You're Hurtin' Now	1967	3.00	15.00
Cougar 712		Taco Wagon / Spanish Kiss	1967	3.00	15.00
Accent 1243		Eyes Of A Child / Just A Waitin'	1968	2.00	10.00
GNP-Crescendo 804		Let's Go Trippin' / Those Memories Of You	1975	1.00	5.00
Columbia 07340		Pipeline / (B-side by S.R. Vaughan)	1987	.80	4.00
Columbia 07340	(PS)	Pipeline / (B-side by S.R. Vaughan)	1987	1.20	6.00
DALE, JIMMY					
Jimmy Dale is a pseudonym for Jimmy Clanton.					
Drew-Blan 1003		Emma Lee / My Pride And Joy	1958	5.00	25.00
DALE & GRACE					
Michelle 921		I'm Leaving It Up To You / Foolin' Around	1963	2.00	10.00
Michelle 923		Stop And Think It Over / Bad Luck	1963	1.60	8.00
Michelle 928		The Loneliest Night / I'm Not Free	1964	1.60	8.00
Montel 921		I'm Leaving It Up To You / Foolin' Around	1963	1.00	5.00
Montel 923		Stop And Think It Over / Bad Luck	1963	1.00	5.00
Montel 928		The Loneliest Night / I'm Not Free	1964	1.00	5.00
Montel 942		What Am I Living For? / Something Special	1964	1.00	5.00
Montel 989		So Fine / It Keeps Right On A Hurtin'	1967	1.00	5.00
DALES, THE					
Crest 1069		Rockin' Nellie / Sweet Annie	1960	3.00	15.00
DALTON, DANNY					
Teen 505		Who's Gonna Hold Your Hand? / Walkin'	1959	3.00	15.00
DALTON BOYS, THE					
The Dalton Boys feature Danny Dalton.					
Skyla 1124		Much More Stronger / I'm Thinkin'	1962	2.00	10.00
DALTON BROTHERS, THE					
The Dalton Brothers is a pseudonym for Scott Engel and John Stewart, later of The Walker Brothers.					
Martay 2001		I Only Came To Dance With You / Without You, Love	1964	4.00	20.00
DAMASCANS, THE					
Pyramid 6372		Go 'Way, Girl /	196?	4.00	20.00
DAMERON, DONNA					
Dart 113		Bopper 486609 / Big Love	1959	8.00	40.00
DAMIANO, JOE					
Chancellor 1339		I Cried / Sittin' On The Shelf	1959	2.00	10.00

Label & Catalog #		A-Side/B-Side	Year	VG	NM
DAMON, RUSS					
ABC-Paramount 10664		Cry, Big Boy, Cry / Let Me Go	1965	1.20	6.00
DAMPHIER, TOM (WITH THE TOKENS)					
Kirshner 4264		Mister Radio Man / Everybody Tries	1976	1.20	6.00
DAN-RAYS, THE					
Regency 105		Surfin' Granny / Monkey Chile	195?	6.00	30.00
DAN & DALE					
Tifton 125		Batman's Theme / Robin's Theme	1966	3.00	15.00
Tifton 125	(PS)	Batman's Theme / Robin's Theme	1966	5.00	25.00
DANA, JEFF					
Fleetwood 1011		Oh, Gina / A Boy Can Dance	196?	3.00	15.00
DANDELION WINE					
Sussex 502		Some Kind Of Summer / Hot Dog	196?	1.00	5.00
DANE T & THE DEL RAYS					
Refer to The Del Rays.					
Carousel 213		Girl In My Heart / Scooter Town	195?	15.00	75.00
DANETTA & THE STARLETS					
OKeh 7155		You Belong To Me / Impression	196?	4.00	20.00
DANIELLE					
Danielle features Ginger Blake of The Honeys.					
Casablanca 2276		Let's Have A Party Tonight / Say I Laid Eyes On You	1980	.80	4.00
		— 12" Singles—			
Casablanca		Let's Have A Party Tonight / Let's Have A Party Tonight	1980	1.00	5.00
DANIELS, JEFF					
Meladee 117		Daddy-O-Rock / Hey Woman	1958	100.00	400.00
Astro 108		Foxy Dan / Someday You'll Remember	196?	20.00	100.00
Big Howdy 8121		Foxy Dan / Someday You'll Remember	196?	20.00	100.00
DANIELS, RAY					
Aura 4511		Geraldine / *(B-side by Rick & The Ravens)*	1965	10.00	50.00
DANNY & THE ACCENTS					
Valli 307		Her Diary / She Can't Be Real	196?	2.00	10.00
DANNY & THE CROWNS					
Mercury 72096		The Story Of Jack And Jill / Night Moon	1962	2.00	10.00
DANNY & THE DREAMERS					
Dream 7		Forgive Me / Venus	195?	6.00	30.00
DANNY & THE HITMAKERS					
Cavalcade 1001		Bimba Rock / Orangutang Rock	1964	2.00	10.00
DANNY & THE JUNIORS					
Danny Rapp with Frank Mattei, Joe Terranova and Dave White as The Juniors.					
Singular 711		At The Hop / Sometimes (When I'm All Alone)	1957	125.00	500.00
ABC-Paramount 9871		At The Hop / Sometimes (When I'm All Alone)	1957	4.00	20.00
ABC-Paramount 9888		Rock & Roll Is Here To Stay / School Boy Romance	1958	4.00	20.00
ABC-Paramount 9926		Dottie / In The Meantime	1958	3.00	15.00
ABC-Paramount 9953		Crazy Cave / A Thief	1958	3.00	15.00
ABC-Paramount 9978		I Feel So Lonely / Sassy Fran	1959	3.00	15.00
ABC-Paramount 10004		Do You Love Me? / Somehow I Can't Forget	1959	3.00	15.00
ABC-Paramount 10052		Playing Hard To Get / Of Love	1959	3.00	15.00
Swan 4060		Twistin' U.S.A. / A Thousand Miles Away	1960	3.00	15.00
Swan 4064		Candy Cane, Sugary Plum / O Holy Night	1960	2.00	10.00
Swan 4064	(PS)	Candy Cane, Sugary Plum / O Holy Night	1960	25.00	125.00
Swan 4068		Pony Express / Day Dreamer	1961	3.00	15.00
Swan 4072		Cha Cha Go-Go / Mr. Whisper	1961	3.00	15.00
Swan 4082		Back To The Hop / Charleston Fish	1961	2.00	10.00
Swan 4082	(PS)	Back To The Hop / Charleston Fish	1961	10.00	50.00
Swan 4092		Twistin' All Night Long / Some Kind Of Nut	1962	2.00	10.00
		("Twistin' All Night Long" features Freddy Cannon.)			
Swan 4100		Doin' The Continental Walk / Do The Mashed Potato	1962	2.00	10.00
Swan 4113		We Got Soul / Funny	1962	2.00	10.00
Top Rank 604		Twistin' England / Twistin' All Night Long	1962	2.00	10.00
Guyden 2076		Oo-La-La-Limbo / Now And Then	1963	3.00	15.00
Mercury 72220		Sad Girl / Let's Go Ski-ing	1963	3.00	15.00
Ronn 24		I Can't See Nobody / Mr. 'Reen	1968	1.00	5.00

Label & Catalog #	A-Side/B-Side	Year	VG	NM
Luv 252	Rock And Roll Is Here To Stay / Sometimes (When I'm All Alone)	1968	.80	4.00
Crunch 018001	At The Hop / Let The Good Times Roll	1973	1.00	5.00

—Extended Play Albums—

ABC-Paramount 11	At The Hop	1957	100.00	400.00

DANNY & THE MEMORIES
Danny is Danny Whitten, later of The Rockets and Crazy Horse.

Valiant 6049	Don't Go / Can't Help Lovin' That Girl Of Mine	1964	5.00	25.00

DANNY & THE SAINTS

Fanelle 101	Big Lulu /	196?	5.00	25.00
Warner Bros. 5134	No One Has Eyes For Me / Peggy's Party	1959	2.00	10.00

DANNY & THE SENIORS

Panorama 26	Wicked Girl / Oh Devil	1966	1.20	6.00

DANNY & THE VELAIRES

Ramco 1983	I Found A Love / It's Over	195?	8.00	40.00
Brent 7072	What Am I Livin' For? / Shaggy Dog	1967	3.00	15.00

DANTE

Tide 003	My Aching Heart / My Lament	1960	3.00	15.00
Decca 31178	If You Don't Know / Leave Your Tears Behind You	1960	2.50	12.00
Decca 31268	Bye Bye, Baby / That's Why	1961	2.50	12.00
Decca 31319	Ring Or Write Or Call / Say It To Me	1961	2.50	12.00
A&M 788	Speedoo / Sweet Lover	1966	2.00	10.00

DANTE, DAVID

RCA Victor 47-7943	Garden Of Eden / Juanita	1961	2.00	10.00
RCA Victor 47-8056	K-K-K-Katy / Speedy Gonzales	1962	2.00	10.00

DANTE, RON [RONNIE DANTE]
Ron Dante also recorded with, or as, The Archies; Bo Cooper; The Cuff Links; Dante's Inferno; The Detergents; Ronnie & The Dirt Riders; C.G. Rose; and The Webspinners.

Almont 307		Little Lollypop /	1963	3.00	15.00
Music Voice 503		If You Love Me, Laurie / Don't Stand Up In A Canoe	1964	2.00	10.00
Musicor 1058		Look At Me / There's Love	1965	1.20	6.00
Musicor 1090		In The Rain / Poor Boys	1965	1.20	6.00
Musicor 1105		If You Love Me, Laurie / Don't Stand Up In A Canoe	1965	1.20	6.00
Musicor 1135		Hey Mom, Hey Pop / Heart Stop Calling Her Name	1965	1.20	6.00
Columbia 43720		Think / 221 East Maple	1966	1.20	6.00
Columbia 43862		Janie Janie / I'll Give You Things	1966	1.20	6.00
Dot 17023		Gypsy Be Mine / The Absence Of Liza	1967	1.20	6.00
Mercury 72812		Raining In My Sunshine / Follow A Dream	1968	1.00	5.00
Kirshner 1010		Let Me Bring You Up / How Do You Know?	1970	.80	4.00
Kirshner 1010	(PS)	Let Me Bring You Up / How Do You Know?	1970	2.00	10.00
Kirshner 5007		C'mon Girl / Sweet Taste Of Love	1970	.80	4.00
Scepter 12333	(DJ)	That's What Life Is All About / That's What Life Is All About (Stock copies of Scepter 12333 may not exist.)	1972	.60	3.00
Bell 610		Charmer / Yesterday Dreamin'	1974	1.00	5.00
Bell 619		Midnight Show / Christian	1974	1.00	5.00
RCA Victor 10340		Sugar Sugar / Sugar Sugar, Part 2	1975	.60	3.00
RCA Victor 10898		Skywriter / How Am I To Know?	1977	.60	3.00
Handshake 02107		Show And Tell / God Bless Rock 'N' Roll	1980	.60	3.00
Handshake 02552		Letter From Zowie /	1980	.60	3.00

DANTE & HIS FRIENDS
Refer to Dante & The Evergreens.

Imperial 5798	Something Happens / Are You Just My Friend?	1961	3.00	15.00
Imperial 5827	Miss America / Now I've Got You	1962	3.00	15.00

DANTE & THE EVERGREENS
Dante Drowty with Tony Moon, Frank Rosenthal and Bill Young. Also recorded as Dante & His Friends.

Madison 130	Alley-Oop / The Right Time	1960	3.00	15.00
Madison 135	Time Machine / Dream Land	1960	3.00	15.00
Madison 143	What Are You Doing New Year's Eve? / Yeah, Baby	1960	3.00	15.00
Madison 154	Think Sweet Thoughts / Da Doo	1961	3.00	15.00

DANTE'S INFERNO
Dante's Inferno features Ron Dante.

Infinity 50008	Ain't Misbehavin' / 'Round About Midnight	1979	.60	3.00
Infinity 50018	Fire Island / They're Playing Our Song	1979	.60	3.00
Infinity 50038	Brand New Key / They're Playing Our Song	1979	.60	3.00

—12" Singles—

Infinity 16003	Ain't Misbehavin' / 'Round About Midnight	1979	.80	4.00
Infinity 16005	Fire Island / They're Playing Our Song	1979	.80	4.00

Label & Catalog #		A-Side/B-Side	Year	VG	NM
DANTES, THE					
Courtney 713		Zebra Shoot / Dragon Walk	1964	6.00	30.00
Rotate 5008		Top Down Time / How Many Times?	1964	3.00	15.00
Jamie 1314		80-96 / Can't Get Enough Of Your Love	1966	2.00	10.00
Cameo 431		Under My Thumb / Can I Get A Witness?	1966	2.00	10.00
Main Line 1366		Connection / Satisfaction	1967	3.00	15.00
DANZIG, GLENN					
Glenn Danzig is a member of The Misfits.					
Plan-9 1015		Who Killed Marilyn? / Spook City USA *(Black vinyl)*	1981	10.00	50.00
Plan-9 1015		Who Killed Marilyn? / Spook City USA *(Purple vinyl)*	1981	15.00	75.00
Plan-9 1015		Who Killed Marilyn? / Spook City USA *(Black/purple vinyl)*	1981	20.00	100.00
Plan-9 1015	(PS)	Who Killed Marilyn? / Spook City USA	1981	10.00	50.00
DARIN, BOBBY [BOB DARIN]					
Decca 29883		Rock Island Line / Timber *(Lines label)*	1956	4.00	20.00
Decca 9-29883		Rock Island Line / Timber *(Star label)*	1956	3.00	15.00
Decca 9-29922		Silly Willy / Blue-Eyed Mermaid *(Lines label)*	1956	4.00	20.00
Decca 9-29922		Silly Willy / Blue-Eyed Mermaid *(Star label)*	1956	3.00	15.00
Decca 9-30031		Hear Them Bells / The Greatest Builder *(Lines label)*	1956	4.00	20.00
Decca 9-30031		Hear Them Bells / The Greatest Builder *(Star label)*	1956	3.00	15.00
Decca 9-30225		Dealer In Dreams / Help Me *(Lines label)*	1957	4.00	20.00
Decca 9-30225		Dealer In Dreams / Help Me *(Star label)*	1957	3.00	15.00
Decca 9-30737		Silly Willy / Dealer In Dreams *(Star label)*	1958	4.00	20.00
Decca 9-30737		Dealer In Dreams / Help Me *(Star label)*	1959	3.00	15.00
Atco 6092		I Found A Million Dollar Baby / Talk To Me Something	1957	3.00	15.00
Atco 6103		Don't Call My Name / Pretty Baby	1957	3.00	15.00
Atco 6109		Just In Case You Change Your Mind / So Mean	1958	3.00	15.00
Atco 6117		Splish Splash / Judy, Don't Be Moody	1958	3.00	15.00
Brunswick 9-55073	(DJ)	Early In The Morning / Now We're One	1958	20.00	100.00
Brunswick 9-55073		Early In The Morning / Now We're One	1958	10.00	50.00
		(Brunswick 55073 credits The Ding Dongs.)			
Atco 6121		Early In The Morning / Now We're One	1958	6.00	30.00
		(First pressings of Atco 6121 credit The Rinky Dinks.)			
Atco 6121		Early In The Morning / Now We're One	1958	3.00	15.00
		(Second pressings credit Bobby Darin & The Rinky Dinks.)			
Atco 6127		Queen Of The Hop / Lost Love	1958	3.00	15.00
Atco 6128		Mighty, Might Man / You're Mine	1958	6.00	30.00
		(First pressings of Atco 6128 credit The Rinky Dinks.)			
Atco 6128		Mighty, Might Man / You're Mine	1958	3.00	15.00
		(Second pressings credit Bobby Darin & The Rinky Dinks.)			
Atco 6133		Plain Jane / While I'm Gone	1959	3.00	15.00
Atco 6133	(PS)	Plain Jane / While I'm Gone	1959	4.00	20.00
Atco 6133	(S)	Plain Jane / While I'm Gone	1959	5.00	25.00
Atco 6140		Dream Lover / Bullmoose	1959	3.00	15.00
Atco 6140	(PS)	Dream Lover / Bullmoose	1959	4.00	20.00
Atco 6147		Mack The Knife / Was There A Call For Me	1959	3.00	15.00
Atco 6147	(PS)	Mack The Knife / Was There A Call For Me	1959	4.00	20.00
Atco 6158		Beyond The Sea / That's The Way Love Is	1960	3.00	15.00
Atco 6158	(PS)	Beyond The Sea / That's The Way Love Is	1960	4.00	20.00
Atco 6161		Clementine / Tall Story	1960	3.00	15.00
Atco 6161	(PS)	Clementine / Tall Story	1960	4.00	20.00
Atco SPD	(DJ)	She's Tanfastic / Moment Of Love	1960	3.00	15.00
Atco 6167		Won't You Come Home, Bill Bailey / I'll Be There	1960	2.00	10.00
Atco 6167	(PS)	Won't You Come Home, Bill Bailey / I'll Be There	1960	3.00	15.00
Atco 6173		Beachcomber / Autumn Blues	1960	2.00	10.00
Atco 6173	(PS)	Beachcomber / Autumn Blues	1960	3.00	15.00
Atco 6179		Artificial Flowers / Somebody To Love	1960	2.00	10.00
Atco 6179	(PS)	Artificial Flowers / Somebody To Love	1960	3.00	15.00
Atco 6183		Christmas-Auld Lang Syne / Child Of God	1960	2.00	10.00
Atco 6183	(PS)	Christmas-Auld Lang Syne / Child Of God	1960	3.00	15.00
Colpix CP 1		That's How It Went All Right / What Happened On Stage Five?	1960	2.00	10.00
Atco 6188		Lazy River / Oo-Ee Train	1961	1.60	8.00
Atco 6188	(PS)	Lazy River / Oo-Ee Train	1961	2.00	10.00
Atco 6196		Nature Boy / Look For My True Love	1961	1.60	8.00
Atco 6196	(PS)	Nature Boy / Look For My True Love	1961	2.00	10.00
Atco 6200		Theme From "Come September" / Walk Back To Me	1961	1.60	8.00
Atco 6200	(PS)	Theme From "Come September" / Walk Back To Me	1961	2.00	10.00
Atco 6206		You Must Have Been A Beautiful Baby / Sorrow Tomorrow	1961	1.60	8.00
Atco 6206	(PS)	You Must Have Been A Beautiful Baby / Sorrow Tomorrow	1961	2.00	10.00
Atco 6211		Ave Maria / O Come All Ye Faithful	1961	1.60	8.00
Atco 6211	(PS)	Ave Maria / O Come All Ye Faithful	1961	25.00	125.00
Atco 6214		Irresistible You / Multiplication	1961	1.60	8.00
Atco 6214	(PS)	Irresistible You / Multiplication	1961	2.00	10.00
Atco 6221		What'd I Say / What'd I Say, Part 2	1962	1.60	8.00
Atco 6221	(PS)	What'd I Say / What'd I Say, Part 2	1962	2.00	10.00
Atco 6229		Things / Jailer, Bring Me Water	1962	1.20	6.00

Label & Catalog #		A-Side/B-Side	Year	VG	NM
Atco 6236		Baby Face / You Know How	1962	1.20	6.00
Atco 6244		I Found A New Baby / Keep A Walkin'	1962	1.20	6.00
Atco 6297		Milord / Golden Earrings	1964	1.20	6.00
Atco 6316		Swing Low, Sweet Chariot / Similau	1964	1.20	6.00
Atco 6334		Minnie The Moocher / Hard Hearted Hannah	1965	1.20	6.00
		—Original Atco singles above do not have the company's street address on the label and have "AT" etched in the trail-off vinyl.—			
Capitol 4837		If A Man Answers / A True, True Love	1962	.80	4.00
Capitol 4837	(PS)	If A Man Answers / A True, True Love	1962	1.20	6.00
Capitol 4897		You're The Reason I'm Living / Now You're Gone	1963	.80	4.00
Capitol 4897	(PS)	You're The Reason I'm Living / Now You're Gone	1963	1.20	6.00
Capitol 4970		18 Yellow Roses / Not For Me	1963	.80	4.00
Capitol 4970	(PS)	18 Yellow Roses / Not For Me	1963	1.20	6.00
Capitol 5019		Treat My Baby Good / Down So Long	1963	.80	4.00
Capitol 5079		Be Mad, Little Girl / Since You Been Gone	1963	.80	4.00
Capitol PRO-2354		Sally Was A Good Old Girl / Who Can I Count On?	1963	1.00	5.00
Capitol PRO-2354	(PS)	Sally Was A Good Old Girl / Who Can I Count On?	1963	2.00	10.00
Capitol 5126		I Wonder Who's Kissing Her Now / As Long As I'm Singing	1964	.80	4.00
Capitol 5257		The Things In This House / Wait By The Water	1964	.80	4.00
Capitol 5359		Hello Dolly / Goodbye Charlie	1965	.80	4.00
Capitol 5399		A World Without You / Venice	1965	.80	4.00
Capitol 5443		When I Get Home / Lonely Road	1965	.80	4.00
Capitol 5443	(PS)	When I Get Home / Lonely Road	1965	1.20	6.00
Capitol 5481		That Funny Feeling / Gyp The Cat	1965	.80	4.00
Atlantic 2305		Funny What Love Can Do / We Didn't Ask To Be Brought Here	1965	.80	4.00
Atlantic 2317		The Breaking Point / Silver Dollar	1966	.80	4.00
Atlantic 2329		Mame / Walking In The Shadow Of Love	1966	.80	4.00
Atlantic 2341		Who's Afraid? / Merci, Cherie	1966	.80	4.00
Atlantic 2350		If I Were A Carpenter / Rainin'	1966	.80	4.00
Atlantic 2367		The Girl That Stood Beside Me / Reason To Believe	1966	.80	4.00
Atlantic 2376		Lovin' You / Amy	1967	.80	4.00
Atlantic 2395		The Lady Came From Baltimore / I Am	1967	.80	4.00
Atlantic 2420		Darling Be Home Soon / Hello, Sunshine	1967	.80	4.00
Atlantic 2433		Talk To The Animals / She Knows	1967	.80	4.00
Atlantic 2433		Talk To The Animals / After Today	1967	.80	4.00
Direction 350		Long Line Rider / Change	1969	1.00	5.00
Direction 351		Me And Mr. Hohner / Song For A Dollar	1969	1.00	5.00
Direction 352		Distractions (Part 1) / Jive	1969	1.00	5.00
Direction 4001		Baby May / Sweet Reasons	1969	1.00	5.00
Direction 4002		Maybe We Can Get It Together / Rx-Pyro (Prescription: Fire)	1970	1.00	5.00
Motown 1183		Someday We'll Be Together / Melodie	1971	.60	3.00
Motown 1193	(DJ)	Simple Song Of Freedom / Simple Song Of Freedom	1971	.60	3.00
Motown 1203		Sail Away / Hard Headed Woman	1972	.60	3.00
Motown 1212		Average People / Something In Her Love	1972	.60	3.00
Motown 1217		Happy / Something In Her Love	1972	.60	3.00
Motown Y572F		Mack The Knife / If I Were A Carpenter	1974	.40	2.00
Atlantic 7-89166		Mack The Knife / Beyond The Sea	198?	.40	2.00
Atlantic 13055		Splish Splash / Queen Of The Hop	198?	.40	2.00
Atlantic 13056		Mack The Knife / Beyond The Sea	198?	.40	2.00
Atlantic 13057		Dream Lover / If I Were A Carpenter	198?	.40	2.00
Atlantic 13147		Things / Won't You Come Home, Bill Bailey	198?	.40	2.00
Atlantic 13148		Artificial Flowers / Multiplication	198?	.40	2.00
		—Extended Play Albums—			
Decca ED-2676		Hear Them Bells	1957	20.00	100.00
Atco 4502		Bobby Darin	1959	10.00	50.00
Atco 4504		That's All	1959	10.00	50.00
Atco 4505		Bobby Darin	1959	10.00	50.00
Atco 4508		This Is Darin	1960	10.00	50.00
Atco 4512		Darin At The Copa	1960	10.00	50.00
Atco SP-1001	(DJ)	For Teenagers Only (Paper picture sleeve)	1960	20.00	100.00
Atco 4513		For Teenagers Only	1960	15.00	75.00
Capitol MB-2849	(DJ)	Scripto Presents Bobby Darin	1962	3.00	15.00
Capitol MB-2850		Bobby Darin	1962	6.00	30.00
Capitol 1866		You're The Reason I'm Loving	1963	6.00	30.00
Capitol 2262		18 Yellow Roses	1963	6.00	30.00

DARLENE & THE JOKERS

| Danco 115 | | Frankie / Love Me, Love Me | 1960 | 2.00 | 10.00 |

DARLENES, THE

| Stacy 965 | | (I'm Afraid) You Hurt Me / I Still Like Rock And Roll | 196? | 2.00 | 10.00 |

DARLINGS, THE

Dore 663		To Know Him Is To Love Him / Train Out Of Memphis	1963	2.00	10.00
Dore 677		He Played 1, 2, 3, 4 / My Pillow	1963	2.00	10.00
Mercury 72185		Two Time Loser / Please Let Me Know	1963	2.00	10.00

Label & Catalog #		A-Side/B-Side	Year	VG	NM
DARNELL, BUDDY					
Columbia 44197		Beggar's Parade / My World Of Make Believe	196?	3.00	15.00
DARNELL & THE DREAMS					
West Side 1020		The Day Before Yesterday / I Had A Love	1964	7.00	35.00
DARNELS, THE: *Refer to* DEBBIE & THE DARNELS					
DARRAGH, DAVE					
Dara 1		I Try, I Cry, I Die / Teen Age Dream	196?	2.00	10.00
DARRELL, GUY "DADDY COOL"					
Warwick 614		Daddy Cool, Daddy Cool / Nobody Else But You	1961	3.00	15.00
DARRELL & THE OXFORDS					
Darrell & The Oxfords is a pseudonym for The Tokens.					
Roulette 4174		Picture In My Wallet / Roses Are Red	1959	3.00	15.00
Roulette 4230		Can't You Tell? / Your Mother Said No	1960	4.00	20.00
DARRELLS, THE					
Lyco 1003		So Tenderly / Without Warning	196?	4.00	20.00
DARREN, JAMES [JIMMY DARREN]					
Colpix 102		There's No Such Thing / Mighty Pretty Territory	1958	2.00	10.00
Colpix 102	(PS)	There's No Such Thing / Mighty Pretty Territory	1958	3.00	15.00
Colpix 113		Gidget / You	1959	2.00	10.00
Colpix 119		Angel Face / I Don't Wanna Lose Ya	1959	2.00	10.00
Colpix 119	(S)	Angel Face / I Don't Wanna Lose Ya	1959	4.00	20.00
Colpix 128		I Ain't Sharin' Sharon / Love Among The Young	1959	1.60	8.00
Colpix 130		Teen Age Years / Let There Be Love	1959	1.60	8.00
Colpix 138		You Are My Dream / Your Smile	1960	1.60	8.00
Colpix 142		Because They're Young / Tears In My Eyes	1960	1.60	8.00
Colpix 145		P.S. I Love You / Love Theme From "La Strada"	1960	1.60	8.00
Colpix 155		How Sweet You Are / All The Young Men	1960	1.60	8.00
Colpix 168		Man About Town / Come On, My Love	1960	1.60	8.00
		(Colpix 102-168 credit Jimmy Darren.)			
Colpix 181		Goodbye Cruel World / Walking My Baby Back Home	1960	2.00	10.00
Colpix 185		Fool's Paradise / Gotta Have Love	1960	1.60	8.00
Colpix 189		Gidget Goes Hawaiian / Wild About The Girl	1960	2.00	10.00
Colpix 609		Goodbye Cruel World / Valerie	1961	1.60	8.00
Colpix 609	(PS)	Goodbye Cruel World / Valerie	1961	3.00	15.00
Colpix 622		Her Royal Majesty / If I Could Only Tell You	1962	2.00	10.00
Colpix 630		Conscience / Dream Big	1962	1.00	5.00
Colpix 644		Mary's Little Lamb / Life Of The Party	1962	1.00	5.00
Colpix 655		Hail To The Conquering Hero / Too Young To Go Steady	1962	1.00	5.00
Colpix 664		Hear What I Wanna Hear / I'll Be Loving You	1962	1.00	5.00
Colpix 672		Pin A Medal On Joey / Diamond Head	1963	1.00	5.00
Colpix 685		They Should Have Given You The Oscar / Blame It On My Youth	1963	1.00	5.00
Colpix 696		Gegetta / Grande Luna, Italiana	1963	1.00	5.00
Colpix 708		Back Stage / Under The Yum Yum Tree	1963	1.00	5.00
Colpix 758		Just Think Of Tonight / Punch And Judy	1964	1.00	5.00
Colpix 765		A Married Man / Baby, Talk To Me	1964	1.00	5.00
Warner Bros. 5648		Because You're Mine / Millions Of Roses	1966	.60	3.00
Warner Bros. 5689		I Want To Be Lonely / Tom Hawk	1966	.60	3.00
Warner Bros. 5812		Where Did We Go Wrong? / Counting The Cracks	1966	.80	4.00
Warner Bros. 5838		Crazy Me / They Don't Know	1966	.60	3.00
Warner Bros. 5874		All / Misty Morning Eyes	1966	.60	3.00
Warner Bros. 7071		House Song / They Don't Know	1967	.60	3.00
Warner Bros. 7152		Cherie / Wait Until Dark	1967	.60	3.00
Warner Bros. 7206		Each And Every Part Of Me / Little Bit Of Heaven	1967	.60	3.00
Buddah 177		That's My World / Wheeling, West Va.	1970	.60	3.00
Kirshner 1012		I Think Somebody Loves Me / Ain't Been Home In A Long Time	1970	.60	3.00
Kirshner 5013		Bring Me Down Slow / More And More	1970	.60	3.00
Kirshner 5015		As Long As You Love Me / Mammy Blue	1971	.60	3.00
Kirshner 5025		Brian's Song / Thank Heaven For Little Girls	1971	.60	3.00
MGM 14558		Let The Heartaches Begin / Sad Song	1973	.60	3.00
MGM 14667		Sad Eyed Romany Woman / Stay	1973	.60	3.00
Private Stock 050		Love On The Screen / Losing You	197?	.40	2.00
Private Stock 064		One Has My Heart, The Other Has My Name / Sleepin' In A Bed Of Lies	197?	.40	2.00
Private Stock 136		You Take My Heart Away / You Take My Heart Away *(Disco)*	197?	.40	2.00
Private Stock 152		Only A Dream Away / Only A Dream Away	197?	.40	2.00
		(Stock copies of P.S. 152 may not exist.)			
RCA Victor PB-11316		California / Let Me Take You In My Arms Again	1982	.60	3.00
RCA Victor PB-11419		Next Time / Something Like Nothing Before	1983	.40	2.00

Label & Catalog #	A-Side/B-Side	Year	VG	NM
DARROW, JAY				
Keen 82124	Girl In My Dreams / I Love That Girl	1960	3.00	15.00
DART				
Garland 2004	Genevieve / I Can't Understand	196?	2.00	10.00
Garland 2019	Don't Cry No More / Lead Me On	196?	2.00	10.00
DARTELLS, THE				
Arlen 509	Hot Pastrami / Dartell Stomp	1963	4.00	20.00
Arlen 513	Dance, Everybody, Dance / The Scoobie Song	1963	3.00	15.00
Dot 16453	Hot Pastrami / Dartell Stomp	1963	2.00	10.00
Dot 16502	Dance, Everybody, Dance / The Scoobie Song	1963	2.00	10.00
Dot 16551	Sweet Pea / Convicted	1963	1.00	5.00
Dot 16546	Swiss Cheese / Dartell Stomp	1964	1.00	5.00
HBR 457	Clap Your Hands / Where Do We Stand?	1966	1.00	5.00
DARTELLS, THE				
Sande 103	The Girl Can't Help It / Stranger On The Shore	196?	3.00	15.00
DARTS, THE				
Dot 15752	Sweet Little Baby / Gee-Ver-Men-Nee-Vers	1958	3.00	15.00
Apt 25023	On My Mind / Well, Baby	1958	3.00	15.00
Tempus 1506	Gone Too Long / Shimmy Shimmy	1958	3.00	15.00
DARVELL, BARRY				
Colt-45 107	Geronimo Stomp / How Will It End?	1959	6.00	30.00
Colt-45 110	Butterfly Baby / Send Me Some Lovin'	1960	4.00	20.00
Colt-45 301	All I Need Is You / Run, Little Billy	1961	3.00	15.00
Cub 9088	Little Angel Lost / Fountain Of Love	1961	8.00	40.00
Atlantic 2128	Lost Love / Silver Dollar	1961	3.00	15.00
Atlantic 2138	Adam And Evil / King For Tonight	1962	3.00	15.00
DARVELS, THE				
Eddies 69	I Lost My Baby / Gone	196?	7.00	35.00
DARWIN & THE CUPIDS				
Jerden 1	Chloe / How Long	1960	1.00	5.00
Jerden 9	Goodnight My Love / Won't You Give Me A Chance	1960	1.00	5.00
DATE WITH SOUL, THE				
York 408 (DJ)	Yes Sir, That's My Baby / Bee Side Soul	1967	6.00	30.00
York 408	Yes Sir, That's My Baby / Bee Side Soul	1967	10.00	50.00
	("Yes Sir, That's My Baby" was originally issued on Apogee, credited to Hale & The Hushabyes.)			
DAULPHINS, THE: *Refer to* DAVY JONES & THE DAULPHINS				
DAVE				
Nite Rider	Tornado / She's Mine	196?	8.00	40.00
DAVE & BOB				
M&F 169	Two Old Sparrows / Whoa, Bessie	196?	5.00	25.00
DAVE & LEE				
David Gates and Leon Russell.				
London 197	Sad September / Tryin' To Be Someone	196?	5.00	25.00
DAVE & THE CARDIGANS				
Bay 216	My Falling Star / Cha Cha Baby	196?	4.00	20.00
DAVE & THE CUSTOMS				
DAC 500	Ali Baba / Shortenin' Bread	1963	15.00	75.00
DAC 501	The Local / You Should Be Glad	1963	15.00	75.00
DAC 502	Mizeriou / Boney Moroney	1963	15.00	75.00
DAC 503	He Was A Friend Of Mine / I Ask You Why	1964	4.00	20.00
DAVE & THE MARKSMEN [THE MARKSMEN]				
Dave is David Marks. Refer to The Beach Boys; The Moon; and Matthew Moore.				
Westco 10	Down The Tubes / Ooh Poo Poh Doo	1963	7.00	35.00
Westco 10	Down The Tubes / Ooh Poo Poh Doo (Yellow vinyl)	1963	15.00	75.00
	(Westco 10 credits The Marksmen.)			
A&M 730	Cruisin' / Kustom Car Show	1964	10.00	50.00
A&M 745	Do You Know What Lovers Say? / Food Fair	1964	6.00	30.00
Warner Bros. 5485	I Wanna Cry / I Could Make You Mine	1964	4.00	20.00
DAVE & THE ORBITS				
American Arts 14	Cheeta's Uncle / Chili Beans	1964	7.00	35.00

Label & Catalog #		A-Side/B-Side	Year	VG	NM
DAVE & THE SAINTS					
Band Box 341		Leavin' Surf City / Fever	1963	3.00	15.00
DAVE & THE SHADOWS					
Check Mate 1011		Blue Down / Hereafter	1962	3.00	15.00
Fenton 942		Faith / Playboy	1962	4.00	20.00
DAVE & THE STEREOS					
Pennant 1001		Roamin' Romeo / This Must Be Love	196?	3.00	15.00
DAVE, STAN & ROBIN					
Startime 106		Day Tripper / Get Off Of My Cloud	1966	2.00	10.00
DAVI (WITH THE SPIDELS)					
Stark 110		Reason For Love / Go, Charley, Go	195?	50.00	200.00
DAVID, JOHNNY					
Dot 16078		Race With The Devil / I Met A Girl	1960	4.00	20.00
DAVID & FREDDIE					
Bullseye 1010		Oy Vah / (B-side by David Ellin)	1958	3.00	15.00
DAVID & GOLIATH					
Tomaro 101		Like Strangers / I'm Still Loving You	196?	2.00	10.00
DAVID & JONATHAN					
20th Century Fox 641		Modesty / Willie Waltz	1966	.80	4.00
Capitol 5563		Michelle / How Bitter The Taste Of Love	1966	.80	4.00
Capitol 5563	(PS)	Michelle / How Bitter The Taste Of Love	1966	.80	4.00
Capitol 5625		Speak Her Name / I Know	1966	.60	3.00
Capitol 5625	(PS)	Speak Her Name / I Know	1966	.60	3.00
Capitol 5700		Lovers Of The World Unite / Oh, My Word	1966	.60	3.00
Capitol 5777		Time / The Magic Book	1967	.60	3.00
Capitol 5870		Lookin' For My Life / Ten Stories High	1967	.60	3.00
Capitol 5934		She's Leaving Home / One More Every Minute	1967	.60	3.00
Amy 11012		Softly Whispering I Love You / Something's Gotten Hold Of My Heart	1968	.80	4.00
DAVIDS, JANIE, & THE FOUR LETTERMEN					
Key 576		Gonna Get Even With Elvis Presley's Sergeant / Big Deal	1958	7.00	35.00
DAVIES, BOB					
Click 14		Rock N' Roll Show / With You Tonight	1963	2.00	10.00
DAVIES, DAVE					
Dave Davies first two "solo" singles, Reprise 0614 and 0660, are from Kinks' sessions, and are listed under the group.					
RCA Victor PB-12089		Imagination's Real / Wild Man	1980	.40	2.00
RCA Victor PB-12089	(PS)	Imagination's Real / Wild Man	1980	2.00	10.00
RCA Victor JB-12147		Doing The Best For You / Nothing More To Lose	1980	.40	2.00
Warners Brothers 29425		Mean Disposition / Cold Winter	1983	.40	2.00
Warners Brothers 29509		Love Gets You / One Night With Her	1983	.40	2.00
DAVIS, BO					
Crest 1027	(DJ)	Let's Coast Awhile / Drownin' All My Sorrows	1956	10.00	50.00
Crest 1027		Let's Coast Awhile / Drownin' All My Sorrows (Crest 1027 features Eddie Cochran on guitar.)	1956	15.00	75.00
DAVIS, HARLEY, & THE TEEN-AIRES					
Wildcat 0064		Mad Lover / My Definition Of You	196?	2.00	10.00
DAVIS, HAYWARD					
Christy 103		Bubble Gum / Rock My Rockin' Chair	1960	2.00	10.00
DAVIS, JAN					
Aljo 104		The Surfing Matador / Scramble	1963	7.00	35.00
Smash 1863		The Snow Surfing Matador / Scramble	1964	3.00	15.00
A&M 733		Boss Machine / Fugitive	1964	2.00	10.00
A&M 744		Unwanted / Guitar Star	1964	2.00	10.00
White Whale 226		Run For Your Life / Lost In Space	1965	2.00	10.00
DAVIS, JESSE ED					
Columbia AE7-1067	(DJ)	Exclusive Interview With Jesse Ed Davis	1970	2.00	10.00
Atco 6807		Every Night Is Saturday Night / Golden Sun Goddess	1972	.60	3.00
Atco 6873		Sue Me, Sue You Blues / My Captain	1972	.60	3.00
Atco 6889		Ululu / Alcatraz	1972	.60	3.00
DAVIS, JOHNNY					
Smash 1839		Red Capris / Lazy Guitar	1963	2.00	10.00

Label & Catalog #	A-Side/B-Side	Year	VG	NM
DAVIS, JOYCE				
United Artists 339	**Stop Giving Your Man Away / When Boy Meets Girl**	1960	2.00	10.00
DAVIS, LAURIE				
Guaranteed 218	**Don' Cha Shop Around /**			
	Red Blooded, True Blue American Boy	196?	3.00	15.00
DAVIS, LINK				
Starday 242	**Sixteen Chicks / Grasshopper Rock**	195?	8.00	40.00
Kook 1026	**Beatle Bug / I Keep Wanting You More**	1964	4.00	20.00
DAVIS, MYLER				
Cameo 210	**MD Twist / Let's Twist Again**	1962	2.00	10.00
DAVIS, RAY (WITH THE COACHMEN FIVE)				
Janson 100	**Oh, Joan / This I Know**	196?	5.00	25.00
DAVIS, SPENCER [THE SPENCER DAVIS GROUP]				
The original line-up through 1967 was Spencer Davis, Pete York and Muff and Stevie Winwood.				
Fontana 1960	**I Can't Stand It / Midnight Train**	1964	1.20	6.00
Atco 6400	**Keep On Running / High Time Baby**	1966	1.20	6.00
Atco 6416	**Somebody Help Me / Stevie's Blues**	1966	1.20	6.00
United Artists 50108	**Gimme Some Lovin' / Blues In F**	1966	1.20	6.00
United Artists 50144	**I'm A Man / Can't Get Enough Of It**	1967	1.20	6.00
United Artists 50162	**Somebody Help Me / On The Green Light**	1967	1.20	6.00
United Artists 50202	**Time Seller / Don't Want You No More**	1967	1.00	5.00
United Artists 50202 (PS)	**Time Seller / Don't Want You No More**	1967	3.00	15.00
United Artists 50286	**After Tea / Looking Back**	1967	1.00	5.00
United Artists 50922	**Sunday Walk In The Rain / Listen To The Rhythm**	1972	1.00	5.00
United Artists 50993	**Rainy Season / Tumble-Down Tenement Row**	1972	1.00	5.00
Vertigo 110	**Don't You Let It Bring You Down /**			
	Today Gluggo, Tomorrow The World	1973	.60	3.00
Vertigo 112	**Living In A Back Street / Need A Helping Hand**	1973	.60	3.00
DAWN				
Dawn originally recorded as The Five Discs.				
Laurie 3388	**I'm Afraid They're All Talking About Me / Lover's Melody**	1967	1.00	5.00
Laurie 3417	**Sandy / For The Love Of Money**	1967	1.00	5.00
Rust 5128	**Bring It On Home / Baby, I Love You**	1968	1.00	5.00
DAWN, BILLY				
Coed 516	**Gotta Find My Baby / Whip It Up**	1959	2.00	10.00
DAWN, GINGER				
Lee 1001	**Rockin' With Santa / Madness**	196?	2.00	10.00
DAWNS, THE				
Apt 25088	**Can't Get Him Off Of My Mind / Two Of A Kind**	196?	2.00	10.00
DAWNS, THE				
Atco 6296	**It Seems Like Yesterday / From You, Only You**	1964	2.00	10.00
DAWNS, THE				
Climax 104	**How Deep Is The Ocean? / Why Did You Let Me Love You?**	196?	3.00	15.00
DAY, CAROLINE				
Dimension 1025	**Teenage Prayer / Steam**	1964	2.00	10.00
DAY, DARLENE				
Music Makers 106	**I Love You So / Will**	1961	15.00	75.00
DAY, TERRY				
Terry Day is a pseudonym for Terry Melcher.				
Columbia 42427	**I Waited Too Long / That's All I Want**	1963	3.00	15.00
Columbia 42427 (PS)	**I Waited Too Long / That's All I Want**	1963	7.00	35.00
Columbia 42678	**Be A Soldier / I Love You, Betty**	1963	4.00	20.00
Columbia 42678 (PS)	**Be A Soldier / I Love You, Betty**	1963	8.00	40.00
Columbia 42678 (33)	**Be A Soldier / I Love You, Betty**	1963	8.00	40.00
	(Columbia 42678 was produced by Phil Spector.)			
DAY BLINDNESS				
Day Blindness features Sammy Hagar.				
Studio 2494	**A House And A Dog / Middle Class Lament**	1969	3.00	15.00
DAYCHORDS, THE				
Donel 110	**Runnin' Around / Who's Been Loving You?**	195?	5.00	25.00
Donel 120	**One More Time / Too Bad**	195?	6.00	30.00

Label & Catalog #		A-Side/B-Side	Year	VG	NM
DAYE, BILLIE					
Bliss 1002		When A Girl Gives Her Heart To A Boy /	196?	3.00	15.00
DAYE, CAROLYN					
Challenge 9150		Fragile / Alone At The Prom	1962	2.00	10.00
DAYTONAS, THE					
Amy 961		Hey Little Girl / Please Go Aawy	1965	3.00	15.00
DAYTONAS, THE: *Refer to* **RONNY & THE DAYTONAS**					
DAYE, FRANKIE, & THE KNIGHTS					
Studio 9904		Dance Party Rock / Drag It	1959	2.00	10.00
DE-FENDERS, THE					
World Pacific 382		Wild One / (Dance To The) Yakety Sax	1963	4.00	20.00
Del Fi 4226		Little Deuce Coupe / (B-side by The Deuce Coupes)	1963	3.00	15.00
DE-LIGHTS, THE					
Ad Lib 0207		I'm Comin' Home / One, Two, Button My Shoe	196?	4.00	20.00
DEACON & THE ROCK 'N' ROLLERS					
Nau-Voo 804		Rockin' On The Moon / I Don't Wanna Leave	1959	4.00	20.00
DEACONS, THE					
Camelot 131		You Can Make It If You Try / You Can Make It From Here	196?	2.00	10.00
DEAD BOYS, THE					
The Dead Boys are Stiv Bators, Johnny Blitz, Cheetah Chrome, Jeff Magnum and Jimmy Zero.					
Sire 1004		Sonic Reducer / Down In Flames	1977	1.00	5.00
Sire 1004	(PS)	Sonic Reducer / Down In Flames	1977	2.00	10.00
Sire 1029		Tell Me / Not Anymore / Ain't Nothin' To Do	1978	1.00	5.00
Sire 1029	(PS)	Tell Me / Not Anymore / Ain't Nothin' To Do	1978	2.00	10.00
DEAL, BILL, & THE RHONDELLS					
Heritage 803		May I? / Day By Day My Love Grows Stronger	1968	1.20	6.00
Heritage 812		I've Been Hurt / I've Got My Needs	1969	1.20	6.00
Heritage 817		What Kind Of Fool Do You Think I Am? /			
		Are You Ready For This?	1969	1.20	6.00
Heritage 818		Swingin' Tight / Tuck's Theme	1969	1.20	6.00
Heritage 818	(PS)	Swingin' Tight / Tuck's Theme	1969	2.00	10.00
Heritage 821		Nothing Succeeds Like Success / Swingin' Tight	1970	1.20	6.00
Heritage 824		Hey Bulldog / I'm Gonna Make You Love Me	1970	1.00	5.00
Buddah 318		It's Too Late / So What If It Rains	1971	.80	4.00
Buddah 330		Everybody's Got Something To Hide / I Live In The Night	1971	.80	4.00
Polydor 14103		Can You Make It? / Sea Of Love	1973	.80	4.00
DEAL, DON					
Era 1039		Unfaithful Diane / Devil Of Deceit	1967	3.00	15.00
Era 1051		My Blind Date / Even Then	1957	3.00	15.00
Era 1060		She Was Here, But Now She's Gone /			
		You'd Look Good With A Tear In Your Eye	1958	3.00	15.00
DEAL, HARRY, & THE GALAXIES					
Eclipse 6000		You're Always In My Mind / I Still Love You	1970	1.00	5.00
DEAN, BOBBY					
Profile 4006		Just Between Teens / It's A Fad	195?	8.00	40.00
Chess 1710		Go, Mr. Dillon / I'm Ready	196?	4.00	20.00
DEAN, DEBBIE					
Motown 1025		Everybody's Talking About My Baby / I Cried All Night	1962	3.00	15.00
Motown 1025	(PS)	Everybody's Talking About My Baby / I Cried All Night	1962	7.00	35.00
DEAN, DONNIE					
Drift 1451		Ruby Lee / Frankie And Johnny	1959	8.00	40.00
Apt 25082		Movie Star / Ridin' On A Rainbow	1960	3.00	15.00
DEAN, JAMES					
Romeo 100		Dean's Lament / Jungle Rhythm	195?	5.00	25.00
Romeo 100	(PS)	Dean's Lament / Jungle Rhythm	195?	10.00	50.00
DEAN, LARRY					
Brunswick 55056		Pony Tail / All The Time	1958	3.00	15.00
DEAN, LENNY, & THE ROCKIN' CHAIRS					
Refer to The Rockin' Chairs.					
Recorte 412		Memories Of Love / Girl Of Mine	1959	5.00	25.00

Label & Catalog #	A-Side/B-Side	Year	VG	NM
DEAN, RICKY				
Emmy 1013	Little Girl / Blue Tears	196?	5.00	25.00
Del Fi 4190	Little Girl / Blue Tears	196?	3.00	15.00
DEAN, RITCHIE				
Am Can 400	Now You Tell Me / Schagone (She's Gone)	196?	4.00	20.00
Imperial 5953	How Come? / Answer Me	1963	2.00	10.00
DEAN & JEAN				
Ember 1054	Never Let Your Love Fade Away / Turn It Off	1964	1.00	5.00
Rust 5067	Tra La La La Suzy / I Love The Summertime	1964	1.00	5.00
Rust 5075	Hey Jean, Hey Dean / Please Don't Tell Me Now	1964	3.00	15.00
	(Rust 5075 features The Del Satins.)			
Rust 5081	I Wanna Be Loved / Thread Your Needle	1965	1.00	5.00
Rust 5085	Goddess Of Love / The Man Who Will Never Grow Old	1965	2.00	10.00
Rust 5089	In My Way / Sticks And Stones	1965	1.00	5.00
Rust 5100	Goddess Of Love / Lovingly Yours	1965	1.00	5.00

DEAN & MARC: *Refer to* DEAN & MARC MATHIS

Label & Catalog #	A-Side/B-Side	Year	VG	NM
DEANE, JANET (WITH THE SKYLINERS)				
Gateway 719	Another Night Alone / I'm Glad I Waited	196?	4.00	20.00
DEANS, THE				
Mohawk 114	My Heart Is Low / I'll Love You Forever	1960	5.00	25.00
Mohawk 119	Humpty Dumpty / La Chaim (Good Luck)	1961	5.00	25.00
Mohawk 126	I Don't Want To Wait / It's You	1961	6.00	30.00
Laurie 3114	I Don't Want To Wait / Little White Gardenia	1961	4.00	20.00

DEANS, THE: *Refer to* BARRY & THE DEANS

Label & Catalog #	A-Side/B-Side	Year	VG	NM
DEARLY BELOVEDS, THE				
Columbia 43797	Peep Peep Pop Pop / It Is Better	1966	1.20	6.00
Columbia 43959	You Ain't Gonna To Do What You Did To Him To Me /			
	Wait Till The Morning	1966	1.20	6.00
DEATON, FRANK, & THE MAD LADS				
Bally 1042	My Love For You / Just A Little Bit More	1957	10.00	50.00
DEB-TONES, THE				
RCA Victor 47-7242	Miss Lonely Hearts / Cuddly Baby	1958	3.00	15.00
RCA Victor 47-7384	Give It Up / Rock A Bye	1958	3.00	15.00
RCA Victor 47-7539	I'm In Love Again / Knock Knock, Who's There?	1959	3.00	15.00
DEBBIE & THE DARNELS				
Vernon 100	The Time / Why, Why?	1962	3.00	15.00
Vernon 101	This Time / Santa, Teach Me To Dance	1962	5.00	25.00
Columbia 42530	Daddy / Mr. Johnny Jones	1962	2.00	10.00
DeBERRY, JIMMY				
Sun 185	Take A Little Chance / Time Has Made A Change	1953	——	——
	(Rare. Estimated near mint value $1,500-3,000.)			
DEBONAIRES, THE [THE FIVE DEBONAIRES]				
Herald 509	Darling / Whispering Blues	1957	25.00	125.00
	(First pressings of Herald 509 credit The Five Debonaires.)			
Herald 509	Darling / Whispering Blues	1958	5.00	25.00
	(Second pressings credit to The Debonaires.)			
Gee 1054	Well Wait / Make Believe Lover	1959	5.00	25.00
Dore 592	Every Once In A While / Gert's Skirt	1961	4.00	20.00
Dore 654	Hold Back The Dawn / Mama Don't Care	1962	4.00	20.00
Dore 712	Everybody's Movin' / Mama Don't Care	1964	4.00	20.00
DEBONAIRS, THE				
Winter 502	Crazy Kind Of Love / To Be Without You	196?	3.00	15.00
Elmont 1004	This Must Be Paradise / I Need You, Darling	196?	5.00	25.00

DeBREE, PETER, & THE WANDERERS
The Wanderers also recorded as Jimmy Gartin & The Swingers.

Label & Catalog #	A-Side/B-Side	Year	VG	NM
Fortune 134	Hey! Mr. Presley / Long Tall You	1958	7.00	35.00
DEBS, THE				
Josie 833	(We Like) Crew Cuts / (B-side by The Pastels)	1958	3.00	15.00
DECADES, THE				
Daytone 1306	Dance Forevermore / Louie De Loop	196?	7.00	35.00
Daytone 6403	Lonely Drummer / The Phantom Strikes Back	1964	7.00	35.00
Janie 10645	Strange Worlds / C'mon, Pretty Baby	1966	10.00	50.00

Label & Catalog #		A-Side/B-Side	Year	VG	NM
DECKELMAN, BUD					
Meteor 5014		Daydreamin' / Let's Not Pretend	1954	10.00	50.00
DECKERS, THE: *Refer to* LYNN CHRISTIE & THE DECKERS					
DECOU, ART					
Form 100		I Cried A Million Tears / Where Are You?	1959	2.00	10.00
DEDICATIONS, THE					
C&A 506		Shining Star / Mary Lou	195?	40.00	200.00
Card 335/6		Why Don't You Write Me? / Boppin' Around	195?	5.00	25.00
Card 335/6	(PS)	Why Don't You Write Me? / Boppin' Around	195?	7.00	35.00
DEDICATIONS, THE					
Spokane 4003		When / (B-side by Scott English)	1963	5.00	25.00
DEDICATIONS, THE					
The Dedications is a pseudonym for The Turtles					
White Whale 340	(DJ)	Teardrops / Teardrops	1970	6.00	30.00
		(Stock copies of W.W. 340 may not exist.)			
DEE, BILLY, & THE SUPERCHARGERS					
Westford 101		Curb Service /	1963	2.00	10.00
DEE, DAVE; DOZY, BEAKY, MICK & TICH					
Refer to Dozy, Beaky, Mick & Tich.					
Fontana 1537		No Time / You Make It Move	1966	1.00	5.00
Fontana 1545		Hold Tight / You Know What I Want	1966	1.00	5.00
Fontana 1553		Hideaway / Here's A Heart	1966	1.00	5.00
Fontana 1559		Bend It / She's So Good To Me	1966	1.00	5.00
Fontana 1569		Save Me / Shame	1967	1.00	5.00
Fontana 1591		Okay / Master Llewellyn	1967	1.00	5.00
Imperial 66270		Zabadak / The Sun Goes Down	1967	.80	4.00
Imperial 66287		Legend Of Xanadu / Please	1968	.80	4.00
Fontana 4406		Tonight Today / Bad News	1970	.80	4.00
Atlantic 89757		Staying With It /	1983	.60	3.00
DEE, DAVE					
Bell 906		Annabella / Kelly	1970	.80	4.00
DEE, JACKIE					
Jackie Dee is a pseudonym for Jackie DeShannon.					
Gone 5008		I'll Be True / How Wrong I Was	1957	5.00	25.00
Liberty 55148		Buddy / Stolypso Dance	1958	4.00	20.00
DEE, JIMMY (& THE OFFBEATS)					
TNT 148		Henrietta / Don't Cry No More	1957	8.00	40.00
		(TNT 148 credits Jimmy Dee & The Offbeats.)			
Dot 15664		Henrietta / Don't Cry No More	1957	3.00	15.00
TNT 152		You're Late, Miss Kate / Here I Come	1958	8.00	40.00
Dot 15721		You're Late, Miss Kate / Here I Come	1958	3.00	15.00
TNT 161		I Feel Like Rockin' / Rock Tick Tock	1959	8.00	40.00
Cutie 1400		You Beat Me To The Punch / I've Got A Secret	1963	2.00	10.00
DEE, JOE, & HIS TOP HANDS					
Refer to The Tremonts.					
Pat Riccio 105		Honky-Tonk Guitar / Blind Heart	196?	2.00	10.00
Pat Riccio 107		I Thought I Heard You Calling My Name /			
		Some Of These Nights	196?	2.00	10.00
DEE, JOEY [JOEY DEE & THE STARLITERS]					
Joey Dee also recorded as The Hawk. Refer to the Various Artists EP section.					
Bonus 7009		Lorraine / The Girl I Walk To School	196?	2.00	10.00
Bonus 7009	(PS)	Lorraine / The Girl I Walk To School	196?	4.00	20.00
Scepter 1210		The Face Of An Angel / Shimmy, Baby	1960	3.00	15.00
Monument	(DJ)	The Yaya Twist / (B-side by Dion)	1961	4.00	20.00
Roulette 4401		Peppermint Twist / Peppermint Twist, Part 2	1961	3.00	15.00
Roulette 4408		Hey, Let's Twist / Roly Poly	1962	1.00	5.00
Roulette 4408	(PS)	Hey, Let's Twist / Roly Poly	1962	2.00	10.00
Roulette 4416		Shout / Shout, Part 2	1962	1.00	5.00
Roulette 4416	(PS)	Shout / Shout, Part 2	1962	2.00	10.00
Roulette 4431		Everytime / Everytime, Part 2	1962	1.00	5.00
Roulette 4438		What Kind Of Love Is This? / Wing Ding	1962	1.00	5.00
Roulette 4438	(PS)	What Kind Of Love Is This? / Wing Ding	1962	2.00	10.00
Roulette 4456		I Lost My Baby / Keep Your Mind On What You're Doing	1962	1.00	5.00
Roulette 4456	(PS)	I Lost My Baby / Keep Your Mind On What You're Doing	1962	2.00	10.00
Roulette 4467		Baby You're Driving Me Crazy / Help Me Pick Up The Pieces	1963	1.00	5.00
Roulette 4488		Hot Pastrami With Mashed Potatoes /			

Label & Catalog #		A-Side/B-Side	Year	VG	NM
		Hot Pastrami With Mashed Potatoes, Part 2	1963	1.00	5.00
Roulette 4503		Dance, Dance, Dance / Let's Have A Party	1963	1.20	6.00
Roulette 4525		Fannie Mae / Ya Ya	1964	1.00	5.00
Roulette 4539		Down By The Riverside / Getting Nearer	1964	4.00	20.00
		("Getting Nearer" features backing vocals by The Ronettes.)			
Roulette 4617		Cry A Little Sometimes / Wing Ding	1965	1.20	6.00
Vaseline Hair Tonic		Learn To Dance The Authentic Peppermint Twist /			
		Learn To Dance The Authentic Peppermint Twist, Part 2	1962	2.00	10.00
Vaseline Hair Tonic	(PS)	Learn To Dance The Authentic Peppermint Twist /			
		Learn To Dance The Authentic Peppermint Twist, Part 2	1962	2.00	10.00
Jubilee 5532	(DJ)	Feel Good About It / Feel Good About It, Part 2	1965	1.60	8.00
Jubilee 5539	(DJ)	Dancin' On The Beach / Good Little You	1965	1.60	8.00
Jubilee 5554	(DJ)	She's So Exceptional / It's Got You	1965	2.00	10.00
Jubilee 5566	(DJ)	You Can't Sit Down / Put Your Heart In It	1965	1.60	8.00
		(Stock copies of Jubilee 5532, 5539, 5554 and 5566 may not exist.)			
Little 813/4		Lorraine / The Girl I Walk To School	196?	.80	4.00

DEE, JOEY, & THE NEW STARLIGHTERS

Caneil 100		How Can I Forget / How Can I Forget, Part 2	1974	.80	4.00
Tonsil 0003		Roses And Candy / Raw Meat	1974	.80	4.00

DEE, JOHNNY

Johnny Dee is a pseudonym for John D. Loudermilk.

Colonial 430		Sittin' In The Balcony / A+ In Love	1957	2.00	10.00
Colonial 433		Teenage Queen / It's Gotta Be You	1957	3.00	15.00
Dot 15699		Somebody Sweet / They Were Right	1958	2.00	10.00

DEE, RICKY, & THE EMBERS

Newtown 5001		Workout / Workout (Part 2)	1962	2.00	10.00

DEE, RONNIE

Back Beat 522		Action Packed / Make The Move	1962	4.00	20.00

DEE, SANDRA

Decca 31042		When I Fall In Love / Dear Johnny	196?	2.00	10.00
Decca 31063		Do It While You're Young / Questions	196?	2.00	10.00
Decca 31063	(PS)	Do It While You're Young / Questions	196?	4.00	20.00
Decca 31265		Let's Fall In Love / Tammy Tell Me True	196?	2.00	10.00

DEE, SONNY

Kapp 421		Here I Stand / I'm Not The One For You	1961	4.00	20.00

DEE, TOMMY

Crest 1057		Three Stars / I'll Never Change	1959	3.00	15.00
Crest 1057	(S)	Three Stars / I'll Never Change	1959	7.00	35.00
Crest 1061		The Chair / Hello, Lonesome	1959	3.00	15.00
Crest 1067		Angel Of Love / Merry Christmas, Mary	1959	3.00	15.00
Challenge 59087		Ballad Of A Drag Race / The Story Of Susie	1960	3.00	15.00
Pike 5905		Look Homeward, Dear Angel / A Little Dog Cried	196?	3.00	15.00
Sims 260		Missing While Surfing / Goodbye High School	1966	5.00	25.00

DEE, TONY, & THE PAGEANTS

Du-Well 101		Make Me Your Queen / Saturday Romance	1963	20.00	100.00
Arlen 731		Make Me Your Queen / Saturday Romance	1963	5.00	25.00

DEE CALS, THE

Coed 1960		Stars In The Blue, What Should I Do? / A Wonderful Day	1959	10.00	50.00
Kayhams 1960		Stars In The Blue, What Should I Do? / A Wonderful Day	1961	4.00	20.00

DEE JAY & THE RUNAWAYS

IGL 100		Jenny Jenny /	1965	50.00	200.00
Coulee 109		Love Bug Crawl /	1966	20.00	100.00
Smash 2034		Three Steps To Heaven / Peter Rabbit	1966	2.00	10.00
Smash 2049		She's A Big Girl Now / He's Not Your Friend	1966	2.00	10.00
Sonic 155		And I Know / Sunshine Morning	1968	2.00	10.00

DEE JAYES, THE

Highland 1031		Bongo Beach Party / Mr. Bongo Man	1962	7.00	35.00

DEEP PURPLE

Original members of Deep Purple were Ritchie Blackmore, Rod Evans, Jon Lord, Ian Paice and Nick Semper. Evans and Semper were replaced by Ian Gillan and Roger Glover in 1969, both of whom were replaced by David Coverdale and Glenn Hughes in 1973. Blackmore left in 1975, briefly replaced by Tommy Bolin. Refer to Episode Six.

Tetragrammaton 1503		Hush / One More Rainy Day	1968	2.00	10.00
Tetragrammaton 1503	(PS)	Hush / One More Rainy Day	1968	6.00	30.00
Tetragrammaton 1508		Kentucky Woman / Hard Road	1968	2.00	10.00
Tetragrammaton 1508	(PS)	Kentucky Woman / Hard Road	1968	2.50	12.00
Tetragrammaton 1514		River Deep-Mountain High / Listen, Learn, Read On	1969	1.50	8.00

Label & Catalog #	A-Side/B-Side	Year	VG	NM
Tetragrammaton 1519	The Bird Has Flown / Emmaretta	1969	1.50	8.00
Tetragrammaton 1537	Hallelujah (I Am The Preacher) / April	1969	1.50	8.00
Warner Bros. 7504	Black Night / Into The Fire	1970	1.00	5.00
Warner Bros. 7528	Fireball / I'm Alone	1971	1.00	5.00
Warner Bros. 7572	River Deep-Mountain High / Listen, Learn, Read On	1972	1.00	5.00
Warner Bros. 7595	Strange Kind Of Woman / I'm Alone	1972	1.00	5.00
Warner Bros. 7634	Highway Star / Highway Star	1973	1.00	5.00
Warner Bros. 7672	Woman From Tokyo / Super Trouper	1973	1.00	5.00
Warner Bros. 7710	Smoke On The Water / Smoke On The Water	1973	1.00	5.00
Warner Bros. 7737	Super Trouper / Woman From Tokyo	1973	1.00	5.00
Warner Bros. 7784	Might Just Take Your Life / Coronarias Redig	1974	1.00	5.00
Warner Bros. 7809	Burn / Coronarias Redig	1974	1.00	5.00
Warner Bros. 8049	You Can't Do It Right (With The One You Love) / High Ball Shooter	1975	1.00	5.00
Warner Bros. 8069	Stormbringer / Love Don't Mean A Thing	1975	1.00	5.00
Warner Bros. 8182	Getting Tighter / Love Child	1975	1.00	5.00

DEEP SIX, THE

Soft 960	Last Time Around / One And One	1965	2.00	10.00
Saw Man 101	Rising Sun / Strollin' Blues	1965	2.00	10.00
Liberty 55380	Rising Sun / Strollin' Blues	1965	1.60	8.00
Liberty 55858	Things We Say / I Wanna Shout	1966	2.00	10.00
Liberty 55882	Counting / When Morning Breaks	1966	1.60	8.00
Liberty 55901	What Would You Wish From The Golden Fish? / Why Say Goodbye?	1966	1.60	8.00
Liberty 55926	Image Of A Girl / C'mon Baby	1966	2.00	10.00

DEEPEST BLUE

Blue Fin 102	Pretty Little Thing / Somebody's Girl	1966	2.00	10.00

DEERFIELD, JOHNNY, & THE DEL-ITES

Dell 616	Hey, Little Mary / Feelings	196?	2.00	10.00

DEFENDERS, THE

Realm 001	Beatles, We Want Our Girls Back Now /	1964	4.00	20.00

DEFENDERS, THE

Parkway 926	I Laughed So Hard / Island Of Love	1964	3.00	15.00

DEFIANT ONES, THE

Essar 1002	Defiant Drums / Rebel Rouser	1961	7.00	35.00
Real Fine 834	Defiant Drums #2 / Defiant Theme	1961	6.00	30.00

DEFIANTS, THE

Baronet 5	Surfer's Twist / Twistin' And Stompin'	1962	3.00	15.00

DEL & THE ESCORTS
Refer to The Escorts.

Rome 103	Someone To Watch Over Me / Baby Doll	195?	7.00	35.00

DEL-AIRES, THE
The Del-Aires also recorded as Ronnie & The Del-Atres.

Coral 62370	Elaine / Just Wigglin' And Wobblin'	1963	4.00	20.00
Coral 62404	My Funny Valentine / Drag	1963	8.00	40.00
Coral 62419	Arlene / I'm Your Baby	1964	10.00	50.00

DEL-AIRES, THE

Delsey 302	It Took A Long Time / Ma Ma Marie	196?	7.00	35.00

DEL-AIRS, THE

M.B.S. 001	While Walking / Lost My Job	1960	10.00	50.00

DEL-AIRS, THE

Arrawak 1003	Why Did He Leave? / I'm Lonely	1962	3.00	15.00

DEL CADES, THE

United Sound 175		World's Fair U.S.A. / It Takes Two To Fall In Love	1964	3.00	15.00
United Sound 175	(PS)	World's Fair U.S.A. / It Takes Two To Fall In Love	1964	5.00	25.00

DEL CAPRIS, THE

Almont 304	Speak To Me Of Love / Theresa	196?	5.00	25.00

DEL CAPRIS, THE

Ronjerdon 39	Hey Little Girl / Forever My Girl	1967	2.00	10.00
Kama Sutra 235	Hey Little Girl / Forever My Girl	1967	1.00	5.00

DEL CHORDS, THE: *Refer to DONNIE & THE DEL CHORDS*

Label & Catalog #	A-Side/B-Side	Year	VG	NM
DEL CONTE, DAVE				
Merri 6003	Lonely Surfer / Don't Cry	196?	7.00	35.00
DEL FOURS, THE				
Zenith 250	Beatle Song / Dare Me	1964	3.00	15.00
DEL-LARKS, THE				
East West 116	Remember The Night / Lady Love	1958	8.00	40.00
DEL-LOURDS, THE				
Solar 1001	All Alone / Gloria	1963	4.00	20.00
Solar 1003	All Alone / Gloria	1963	4.00	20.00
DEL-MARS, THE				
ABC-Paramount 10426	That's My Desire / You Know	1963	2.00	10.00
Mercury 72244	Snacky Poo / Snacky Poo, Part 2	1964	2.00	10.00
DEL RAYS				
The Del Rays also recorded as Dane T & The Del Rays.				
Planet 52	Lorraine / The Bounce	196?	8.00	40.00
DEL RAYS, THE				
Teislo/Del Ray 6142	Wipe Out / Pipeline	1964	8.00	40.00
DEL RICOS, THE				
"620" 1008	The Beatle Crawl / Beatle Hootenanny	1964	4.00	20.00
DEL RIOS, THE				
Big 613	The Vines Of Love / Session	1968	15.00	75.00
Rust 5066	Valerie / Mystery	1963	5.00	25.00
DEL SATINS, THE [THE DELL SATINS]				
The Del Satins feature Nicky Como; Stosh Ziska. Refer to Dean & Jean; Foreign Intrigue; Ernie Maresca.				
End 1096	I'll Pray For You / I Remember The Night	1961	25.00	125.00
Win 702	Counting Teardrops / Remember	196?	10.00	50.00
Laurie 3132	Teardrops Follow Me / Best Wishes, Good Luck, Goodbye	1962	4.00	20.00
Laurie 3149	Does My Heart Stand A Chance? / Ballad Of A D.J.	1962	5.00	25.00
Columbia 42802	Feelin' No Pain / Who Cares?	1963	5.00	25.00
Mala 475	Two Broken Hearts / Believe In Me	1964	3.00	15.00
B.T. Puppy 506	My Candy Apple Vette / Hang Around	1965	2.00	10.00
B.T. Puppy 509	Sweets For My Sweet / A Girl Named Arlene	1965	2.00	10.00
B.T. Puppy 514	Relief / The Throwaway Song	1965	2.00	10.00
B.T. Puppy 515	I Can't Find The Girl On My Mind / Oh, Kathy	1965	3.00	15.00
B.T. Puppy 563	I'll Do My Crying Tomorrow / A Girl Named Arlene	1967	3.00	15.00
Diamond 216	A Little Rain Must Fall / Love, Hate, Revenge	1967	2.00	10.00
Diamond 216	A Little Rain Must Fall / Love, Hate, Revenge (Brown vinyl)	1967	4.00	20.00
DEL SHAYS, THE				
Charger 102	I'll Love You Forever / Fake It	1964	25.00	125.00
DEL-TINOS, THE				
The Del-Tinos feature Cub Koda later of Brownsville Station..				
Conic 1451	Nightlife / Pa Pa Ooh Mau Mau	196?	2.00	10.00
DEL-TONES, THE: Refer to DICK DALE				
DEL-VETTS, THE				
Seeburg 3018	Ram Charger / Little Latin Lupe Lou	1965	7.00	35.00
Dunwich 125	Last Time Around / Every Time	1965	5.00	25.00
Dunwich 142	I Call May Baby STP / That's The Way It Is	1966	2.00	10.00
Dunwich 142 (PS)	I Call May Baby STP / That's The Way It Is	1966	4.00	20.00
	(Some copies of the picture sleeve included an STP decal.)			
DEL VIKINGS, THE [THE DELL VIKINGS]				

The Del Vikings were most prominent integrated rock 'n roll/rhythm 'n blues group of the '50s. The original group includes Gus Backus, Dave Lerchy, Clarence Quick and Norm Wright with Kripps Johnson joining in 1957. Numerous changes followed, including the addition of Chuck Jackson. Refer to Buddy Carle.

Label & Catalog #	A-Side/B-Side	Year	VG	NM
Fee Bee 902	True Love / Baby, Let Me Know	1956	25.00	125.00
Fee Bee 205	Come Go With Me / How Can I Find True Love?	1956	25.00	125.00
Fee Bee 205	Come Go With Me / Whispering Bells	195?	4.00	20.00
Fee Bee 206	Down In Bermuda / Maggie	1956	25.00	125.00
Fee Bee 210	What Made Maggie Run? / Uh, Uh Baby	1956	20.00	100.00
Fee Bee 210	What Made Maggie Run? / Down By The Stream	1956	20.00	100.00
Fee Bee 214	Whispering Bells / Don't Be A Fool	1957	20.00	100.00
Fee Bee 218	You Say You Love Me / I'm Spinning	1957	25.00	125.00
Fee Bee 221	Willette / I Want To Marry You	1957	20.00	100.00
Fee Bee 221	Willette / Woke Up This Morning	1957	15.00	75.00
	—Fee Bee singles above have orange labels with a bee on top and two thick horizontal lines.—			

Label & Catalog #	A-Side/B-Side	Year	VG	NM
Luniverse 106	Hey, Senorita / Over The Rainbow	1957	20.00	100.00
Luniverse 114	There I Go / Girl, Girl	1957	15.00	75.00
Dot 15538	Come Go With Me / How Can I Find True Love?	1957	4.00	20.00
Dot 15571	What Made Maggie Run? / Little Billy Boy	1957	3.00	15.00
Dot 15592	Whispering Bells / Don't Be A Fool	1957	4.00	20.00
Dot 15636	When I Come Home / I'm Spinning	1957	3.00	15.00
	—Dot singles above have black labels.—			
Mercury 71132	Cool Shake / Jitterbug Mary	1957	3.00	15.00
Mercury 71180	Come Go With Me / What 'Cha Gotta Lose?	1957	3.00	15.00
Mercury 71198	I'm Spinning / When I Come Home	1957	3.00	15.00
Mercury 71241	Your Book Of Love / Snowbound	1957	3.00	15.00
Mercury 71266	Can't Wait / The Voodoo Man	1958	3.00	15.00
Mercury 71345	You Cheated / Pretty Little Things Called Girls	1958	3.00	15.00
	—Mercury singles above have black labels.—			
Alpine 66	Pistol Packin' Mama / The Sun	1960	15.00	75.00
ABC-Paramount 10208	Bring Back Your Heart / I'll Never Stop Crying	1961	5.00	25.00
ABC-Paramount 10248	I Hear Bells / Don't Get Slick On Me	1961	10.00	50.00
ABC-Paramount 10278	Kiss Me / Face The Music	1962	4.00	20.00
Gateway 743	I've Got To Know / We Three	1964	4.00	20.00
Scepter 12367	Come Go With Me / When You're Asleep	1972	1.00	5.00
Bim Bam Boom 111	I Want To Marry You / Cold Feet	1972	1.00	5.00
	—Extended Play Albums—			
Dot 1058	Come Go With Us	1957	100.00	400.00
Mercury 3359	They Sing-They Swing (Volume 1)	1957	50.00	200.00
Mercury 3362	They Sing-They Swing (Volume 2)	1957	50.00	200.00
Mercury 3363	They Sing-They Swing (Volume 3)	1957	50.00	200.00

DELACARDOS, THE

Dimension 1040	Forget About The Guy / Dance, Gypsy, Dance	1964	2.00	10.00

DELACARDOS, THE

Elgey 1001	Letter To A School Girl / I'll Never Let You Down	1959	6.00	15.00
United Artists 276	I Got It / Thing-A-Ma-Jig	1960	2.00	10.00
United Artists 310	Hold Back The Tears / Mr. Dillon	1961	2.00	10.00
Shell 308	Dream Girl / I Just Want To Know	1961	3.00	15.00
Shell 311	Girl-Girl / Love Is The Greatest Thing	1962	3.00	15.00
Imperial 5992	On The Beach / Everybody's Rockin'	1963	2.00	10.00
Atlantic 2368	She's The One I Love / Got No One	1966	2.00	10.00
Atlantic 2389	I Know I'm Not Much / You Don't have To See Me	1967	2.00	10.00
Atlantic 2419	They Put A Spell On You / A Fool For You	1967	2.00	10.00

DELANCEYS, THE

ABC 10353	High Voltage / The Scratch	1962	4.00	20.00

DELFONICS, THE

Fling 727	There They Go / Over And Over	1962	3.00	15.00

DELICATES, THE

Unart 2017	Black And White Thunderbird / Ronnie Is My Lover	1959	4.00	20.00
Unart 2024	Ring A Ding / Mensurry	1959	4.00	20.00
United Artists 210	Your Happiest Years / Flip Flip	1960	3.00	15.00
United Artists 228	Too Young To Date / The Kiss	1960	3.00	15.00
Roulette 4321	Not Tomorrow / Little Ship	1961	3.00	15.00
Roulette 4360	Little Boy Of Mine / Dickie Went And Did It	1961	3.00	15.00
Roulette 4387	I Don't Know Why / Strange Love	1961	3.00	15.00
Challenge 59232	C'mon Everybody / I've Been Hurt	1964	2.40	12.00
Challenge 59267	I Want To Get Married / I've Been Hurt	1965	2.40	12.00
Challenge 59304	Stop Shovin' Me Around / Comin' Down With Love	1965	2.40	12.00

DELL, DICKEY, & THE BING BONGS
The Bing Bongs also recorded as The Troys.

Dragon 10205	Ding-A-Ling-A-Ling-Ding-Dong / The Cling	195?	25.00	125.00

DELL, DON, & THE MONTEREYS

Roman 2963	Make Believe Love / I Want You, I Need You, I Love You	196?	5.00	25.00

DELL, DON, & THE UPSTARTS

East Coast 102	Time / May It Be My Fortune	196?	7.00	35.00
East Coast 106	A Special Love / Someone For Me	196?	30.00	150.00

DELL, JIMMY

RCA Victor 47-7134	She Won't Pet / Teeny Weeny	1958	3.00	15.00
RCA Victor 47-7194	Cool It, Baby / The Message	1958	4.00	20.00

DELL, LENNY
Lenny Dell originally recorded with The Demensions.

United Artists 50311	I'll Come Home / Love Came By	1968	1.00	5.00
United Artists 50314	Don't Say Goodbye / Over The Rainbow	1968	1.00	5.00

Label & Catalog #	A-Side/B-Side	Year	VG	NM
DELL, TONY				
King 5766	Magic Wand / My Girl	1963	7.00	35.00
DELL SATINS, THE: *Refer to* THE DEL SATINS				
DELLCHORDS, THE: *Refer to* DAVID CAMPANELLA				
DELLS, THE: *Refer to* JOE SOUTH				
DELLWOODS, THE				
Big Top 3137	Don't Put Onions On Your Hamburger / Her Mustache	1963	4.00	20.00
DELMAR, EDDIE (WITH THE BOB KNIGHT FOUR)				
Madison 168	Love Bells / Blanche	195?	7.00	35.00
Vegas 628	Garden In The Rain / My Heart Beckons You	195?	5.00	25.00
DELMONICOS, THE				
Musictone 6122	Until You / World's Biggest Fools	196?	4.00	20.00
Aku *(No number)*	There They Go / You Can Call	196?	5.00	25.00
DELMONICOS, THE: *Refer to* DENISE GERMAINE				
DELMONICS, THE				
Musicnote 6122	Until You / World's Biggest Fool	196?	4.00	20.00
DELONGS, THE				
Art Flow 3906	I Want Your Love / You're Never Too Young	196?	4.00	20.00
DELRAYS, INC., THE				
Salen 002	I'm A Lovin' / Billy Beat	196?	3.00	15.00
DELRONS, THE: *Refer to* REPARATA & THE DELRONS				
DELTAS, THE				
Cambridge 124	Goodnight, My Love / Give My Love A Chance	195?	7.00	35.00
DELTAS, THE				
Philips 40023	The Work Song / My Own True Love	1962	4.00	20.00
Philips 40023	Hold Me, Thrill Me, Kiss Me / My Own True Love	1962	3.00	15.00
DELTONES, THE: *Refer to* RONNIE BAKER				
DELVONS, THE				
J.D.F. 760	Please Stay / Stay Clear Of Love	1967	3.00	15.00
DELVY, RICHARD				
Triumph 55	Atlantic / Steve's Theme	1963	7.00	35.00
DeMARCO, LOU				
Ferris 320	Careless Love / My Lady Fair	196?	3.00	15.00
DeMARCO, RALPH				
Guaranteed 202	More Than Riches / Old Shep	1959	4.00	20.00
Guaranteed 202 *(PS)*	More Than Riches / Old Shep	1959	6.00	30.00
DeMATTEO, NICKY, & THE SORROWS				
Guyden 2024	Suddenly / More Than Riches	1960	2.00	10.00
Cameo 407	I Wanna Be Lonely / Little Red Kitten	1965	2.50	12.00
DEMENSIONS, THE				
The Demensions feature Lenny Dell.				
Mohawk 116	Over The Rainbow / Nursery Rhyme Rock	1960	4.00	20.00
Mohawk 120	Don't Take Your Love Away From Me /			
	Zing! Went The Strings Of My Heart	1960	4.00	20.00
Mohawk 121	Ave Maria / God's Christmas	1960	4.00	20.00
Mohawk 123	A Tear Fell / Theresa	1961	4.00	20.00
Coral 62277	Again / Count Your Blessings Instead Of Sheep	1961	3.00	15.00
Coral 62293	As Time Goes By / Seven Days	1962	4.00	20.00
Coral 62323	Young At Heart / Your Cheatin' Heart	1962	3.00	15.00
Coral 62344	Just One More Chance / My Foolish Heart	1963	5.00	25.00
Coral 62359	Fly Me To The Moon / You'll Never Know	1963	4.00	20.00
Coral 62382	Just A Shoulder To Cry On / Don't Worry About Bobby	1963	5.00	25.00
Coral 62392	A Little White Gardenia / Don't Cry, Pretty Baby	1964	4.00	20.00
Coral 62432	This Time Next Year / My Old Girl Friend	1964	4.00	20.00
Coral 62444	Once A Day / Ting Aling Ting Toy	1964	4.00	20.00
Coral 65559	Zing! Went The Strings Of My Heart / Over The Rainbow	1962	3.00	15.00
Coral 65611	As Time Goes By / My Foolish Heart	1967	1.00	5.00

Label & Catalog #	A-Side / B-Side	Year	VG	NM
DEMILLES, THE				
Laurie 3230	Donna Lee / Um Ba Pa	1964	4.00	20.00
Laurie 3247	Cry And Be On Your Way / Lazy Love	1964	10.00	50.00
DEMOLYRS, THE				
UWR 900	Rain / Hey Little Rosie	195?	100.00	400.00
DEMOTRONS, THE				
Enrica 1003	Rock-A-Way Special / Bugle Boy	195?	7.00	35.00
DEMOTRONS, THE				
Radar 2615	Hombre / Swingin' Soiree	1962	2.00	10.00
Radar 2616	The Pretzel Twist / Meet Mr. Calahan	1962	2.00	10.00
Radar 2621	Sticks And Stones / Adventures In Paradise	1962	2.00	10.00
DEMOTRONS, THE				
Cameo 456	Beg, Borrow And Steal / Midnight In New York	1966	1.20	6.00
Rust 5025	Rockin' With Mother Goose / Home On The Pad	196?	1.00	5.00
Scepter 12174	Brother, Where Are You? / Take This Love I Have	1966	1.00	5.00
DENELS, THE				
Bamboo 517	Here Comes The Ho-Dads / Massacre Stomp	1962	6.00	30.00
Union 502	Here Comes The Ho-Dads / Massacre Stomp	1962	4.00	20.00
DENISON, HOMER				
Brunswick 55150	Chickie Run / March Slave Boogie	1959	2.50	12.00
DENNIS & THE EXPLORERS: *Refer to* THE EXPLORERS				
DENNIS & THE SUPERTONES				
Smash 1809	Doin' The Superman / Superman	1963	1.20	6.00
DENNY & THE DEDICATIONS				
Susan 111	Lost Love / I'll Show You How To Love Me	196?	3.00	15.00
DENNY & THE LP'S				
Rockit 001	Why Not Give Me Your Heart? / Slide-Cha-Lypso	195?	40.00	200.00
DENOTATIONS, THE				
Lawn 253	Lone Stranger / Nena	1965	30.00	150.00
DENSON, LEE				
Vik 0281	New Shoes / Climb Love Mountain	1956	15.00	75.00
	("New Shoes" features Eddie Cochran on guitar.)			
DENTON, BOB [BOBBY DENTON]				
Dot 15833	Playboy / Twenty Four Hour Night	1958	3.00	15.00
Judd 1001	Sweet And Innocent / Back To School	1959	3.00	15.00
Judd 1013	Lover's Plea / I'll Always Be Yours	1959	3.00	15.00
DENTON, MICKEY				
Big Top 3078	Steady Kind / Now You Can't Give Them Away	1961	2.00	10.00
DERBYS, THE				
Dawn 303	People Say / (B-side by The Bondsmen)	1966	3.00	15.00
Dawn 303	People Say / (B-side by The Bondsmen) (Blue vinyl)	1966	6.00	30.00
DEREK				
Derek is a pseudonym for Johnny Cymbal.				
Bang 558	Cinnamon / This Is My Story	1968	.80	4.00
Bang 566	Back Door Man / Sell Your Soul	1969	.60	3.00
Bang 571	Inside Out-Outside In / Sell Your Soul	1969	.60	3.00
DEREK & THE DOMINOS				
Derek is Eric Clapton; The Dominos feature Duane Allman.				
Atco 6780 (DJ)	Tell The Truth / Roll It Over	1970	2.00	10.00
	("Tell The Truth" was produced by Phil Spector. Stock copies of Atco 6780 may not exist.)			
Atco 6803	Bell Bottom Blues / Keep On Crying	1971	1.00	5.00
Atco 6809	Layla / I Am Yours	1971	1.00	5.00
RSO 400	Why Does Love Got To Be So Sad? / Presence Of The Lord	1973	1.00	5.00
DeRIEUX, LARRY				
Arco 102	Chicken Session / Darlene	195?	10.00	50.00
DESDA				
Del-Fi 4174	Splish Splash Twist / Sittin' In The Corner	1962	2.00	10.00

Label & Catalog #		A-Side/B-Side	Year	VG	NM
DESERT RATS, THE					
Mink 5001		High Noon / Sohonie	195?	8.00	40.00
DeSHANNON, JACKIE					
Jackie DeShannon also recorded as Jackie Dee and Jackie Shannon and with The Cajuns and Hale & The Hushabyes					
Edison Int. 416		I Wanna Go Home / So Warm	1960	3.00	15.00
Edison Int. 418		Put My Baby Down / The Foolish One	1960	3.00	15.00
Liberty 55288		Lonely Girl / Teach Me	1961	2.00	10.00
Liberty 55342		Think About You / Heaven Is Being With You	1961	2.00	10.00
Liberty 55358		Wish I Could Find A Boy / I Won't Turn You Down	1961	2.00	10.00
Liberty 55387		Baby (When Ya Kiss Me) / Ain't That Love?	1961	2.00	10.00
Liberty 55425		I'll Drown In My Tears / The Prince	1962	2.00	10.00
Liberty 55425		That's What Boys Are Made Of / The Prince	1962	2.00	10.00
Liberty 55484		Just Like In The Movies / Guess Who?	1962	2.00	10.00
Liberty 55497		You Won't Forget Me / I Don't Think So Much Of Myself	1962	2.00	10.00
Liberty 55526		Faded Love / Dancing Silhouettes	1963	1.20	6.00
Liberty 55526	(PS)	Faded Love / Dancing Silhouettes	1963	3.00	15.00
Liberty 55563		Needles And Pins / Did He Call Today, Mom?	1963	1.20	6.00
Liberty 55602	(DJ)	Little Yellow Roses / Little Yellow Roses *(Yellow vinyl)*	1963	5.00	25.00
Liberty 55602		Little Yellow Roses / Oh, Sweet Chariot	1963	1.20	6.00
Liberty 55602		Little Yellow Roses / 500 Miles	1963	1.20	6.00
Liberty 55645		When You Walk In The Room / Till You Say You're Mine	1964	1.20	6.00
Liberty 55678		Oh, Boy! / I'm Lookin' For Someone To Love	1964	1.20	6.00
Liberty 55705		She Don't Understand Him Like I Do /			
		Hold Your Head High	1964	1.20	6.00
Liberty 55730		He's Got The Whole World In His Hands / It's Love, Baby	1964	1.20	6.00
Liberty 55735		Over You / When You Walk In The Room	1964	1.20	6.00
Liberty 56187		It's So Nice / Mediterranean Sky	1965	1.20	6.00
Imperial 66110		What The World Needs Now Is Love / Remember The Boy	1965	1.20	6.00
Imperial 66132		A Lifetime Of Loneliness / Don't Turn Your Back On Me	1965	.80	4.00
Imperial 66171		Come And Get Me / Splendor In The Grass	1966	.80	4.00
Imperial 66202		I Can Make It With You / To Be Myself	1966	.80	4.00
Imperial 66224		Come On Down / Find Me, Love	1966	.80	4.00
Imperial 66236		Where Does The Sun Go? / The Wishing Doll	1967	.80	4.00
Imperial 66251		It's All In The Game / Changin' My Mind	1967	.80	4.00
Imperial 66301		Nobody's Home To Go Home To / Nicole	1967	.80	4.00
Imperial 66312		I Didn't Want To Have To Do It / Splendor In The Grass	1968	.80	4.00
Imperial 66313		The Weight / Effervescent Blue	1968	.80	4.00
Imperial 66342		Laurel Canyon / Holly Would	1968	.80	4.00
Imperial 66370		Trust Me / What Is This?	1969	.80	4.00
Imperial 66385		Put A Little Love In Your Heart / Always Together	1969	1.00	5.00
Imperial 66419		Love Will Find A Way / Completely	1969	.80	4.00
Imperial 66430		Do You Know How Christmas Trees Are Grown? /			
		One Christmas	1969	1.00	5.00
Imperial 66438		Brighton Hill / You Can Come To Me	1970	.80	4.00
Imperial 66452		You Keep Me Hangin' On-Hurt So Bad /			
		What Was Your Day Like?	1970	.80	4.00
Capitol 3130		Keep Me Warm / Salinas	1971	.40	2.00
Capitol 3185		Stoned Cold Soul / West Virginia Mine	1971	.40	2.00
Atlantic 2871		Vanilla O' Lay / Only Love Can Break Your Heart	1972	.40	2.00
Atlantic 2895		Paradise / I Wanna Roo You	1972	.40	2.00
Atlantic 2919		Speak Out To Me / Sweet Sixteen	1972	.40	2.00
Atlantic 2924		Chains On My Soul / Peaceful In My Soul	1972	.40	2.00
Atlantic 2994		Your Baby Is A Lady / (If You Never Have A Big Hit Record)			
		You're Still Gonna Be A Star	1973	.40	2.00
Atlantic 3041		Jimmie, Just Sing Me One More Song / You've Changed	1974	.40	2.00
Columbia 10221	(DJ)	Boat To Sail / Boat To Sail	1975	.60	3.00
Columbia 10221		Boat To Sail / Let The Sailors Dance	1975	2.00	10.00
		("Boat To Sail" features Brian Wilson on backing vocal.)			
Columbia 10340		All Night Desire / Fire In The City	1976	.60	3.00
Amherst 725		Don't Let The Flame Burn Out / I Don't Think I Can Wait	1978	.40	2.00
Amherst 733		You're The Only Dancer / Tonight You're Doin' It Right	1978	.40	2.00
DESIRES, THE					
The Desires also recorded as The Regents.					
20th Century Fox 195		I Don't Know Why / Longing	1960	3.00	15.00
Smash 1763		There I Go Again / I Never Loved Like This	1962	3.00	15.00
Dasa 102		Phyllis Beloved / The Girl For Me	1962	4.00	20.00
Seville 118		I Ask You / Story Of Love	1962	5.00	25.00
DeSOTO, BOBBY					
Claro 5914		The Cheater / Don't Talk, Just Kiss	1959	2.50	12.00
DESTINAIRES, THE					
Old Timer 609		Rag Doll / Tear Drops	1965	1.20	6.00
Old Timer 610		Chapel Bells / It's Better This Way	1965	1.20	6.00
Old Timer 613		Diamonds And Pearls / More	1965	1.20	6.00
Old Timer 614		You're Cheating On Me / (B-side by The Lancers)	1965	1.20	6.00

Label & Catalog #		A-Side/B-Side	Year	VG	NM
DESTINATIONS, THE					
Destination 638		**Hello Girl / With You**	1967	1.20	6.00
DESTINEERS, THE					
RCA Victor 47-8049		**So Young / Take A Look**	1962	2.40	12.00
DETERGENTS, THE					
The Detergents feature Ron Dante.					
Roulette 4590		**Leader Of The Laundromat / Ulcers**	1964	2.00	10.00
Roulette 4590	(PS)	**Leader Of The Laundromat / Ulcers**	1964	5.00	25.00
Roulette 4603		**Double-O Seven / The Blue Kangaroo**	1965	1.60	8.00
Roulette 4616		**Mrs. Jones (How 'Bout It) / Tea And Crumpets**	1966	1.60	8.00
Roulette 4626		**Little Dum-Dum / Soldier Boy**	1966	1.60	8.00
Roulette 4642		**Here She Comes / Bad Girl**	1966	1.60	8.00
Kapp 735		**I Can Never Eat Home Anymore / Igor's Cellar**	1966	2.00	10.00
Kapp 753		**Some Sunday Morning / Pushin' The Panic Button**	1967	1.60	8.00
DETOURS, THE					
McSherry 1285		**Bring Back My Beatles To Me / Money**	1964	5.00	25.00
DETROIT					
Detroit features Mitch Ryder.					
Paramount 0094		**It Ain't Easy / Long Neck Goose**	1971	1.20	6.00
Paramount 0133		**Rock 'N Roll / Box Of Old Roses**	1971	1.20	6.00
Paramount 0158		**Oo La La Dee Da Doo / Gimme Shelter**	1972	1.20	6.00
DETROIT WHEELS, THE					
Mitch Ryder's Detroit Wheels later recorded as The Rockets.					
Inferno 5002		**Linda Sue Dixon / Tally Ho**	1968	1.20	6.00
Inferno 5003		**Think / Think, Part 2**	1968	1.20	6.00
DEUCE COUPES, THE					
Del-Fi 4226		**Hayburner / (B-side by The De-Fenders)**	1963	3.00	15.00
DEUCES OF RHYTHM & THE TEMPO TOPPERS, THE					
The D.O.R.&.T.T.T. feature Little Richard.					
Peacock 1616		**Ain't That Good News / A Fool At The Wheel** *(Red label)*	1953	40.00	200.00
Peacock 1628		**Rice, Red Beans And Turnip Greens / Always** *(Red label)*	1954	40.00	200.00
DEUCES WILD, THE					
Specialty 654		**I'm In A Whirl / The Meaning Of Love**	1959	7.00	35.00
Sheen 108		**By Golly Gee / Just The Boy Next Door**		3.00	15.00
DEVERONS, THE					
Raynard 1406		**On The Road Again / Unnoticed**	1966	2.00	10.00
DeVILLE SISTERS, THE					
Imperial 5539		**Hula Hoop / Deep In Love**	1958	3.00	15.00
DEVILLES, THE					
Jerden 107		**Mary Lee / Searching For Love**	1961	1.60	8.00
DEVLIN, JOHNNY					
Coral 62334		**Stayin' Up Late / Angel Of Love**	1962	4.00	20.00
DEVO					
Booji Boy 703-1		**(I Can't Get No) Satisfaction /**			
		(I Saw My Baby Getting) Sloppy	1977	2.00	10.00
Booji Boy 7033-14		**Mongoloid / Jocko Homo**	1977	2.00	10.00
Booji Boy 7033-14	(PS)	**Mongoloid / Jocko Homo**	1977	2.00	10.00
Bomp 72843		**(I Can't Get No) Satisfaction /**			
		(I Saw My Baby Getting) Sloppy	1978	.60	3.00
Bomp 72843	(PS)	**(I Can't Get No) Satisfaction /**			
		(I Saw My Baby Getting) Sloppy	1978	.60	3.00
DEVONS, THE					
The Devons were produced by Gary Usher and feature Chuck Girard as lead singer.					
Decca 31777	(DJ)	**Honda Bike / Free Fall**	1965	8.00	40.00
Decca 31777		**Honda Bike / Free Fall**	1965	16.00	80.00
Decca 31822	(DJ)	**It's All Over Now, Baby Blue / Are You Really Real?**	1965	3.00	15.00
Decca 31822		**It's All Over Now, Baby Blue / Are You Really Real?**	1965	6.00	30.00
Decca 31899	(DJ)	**Come On / A Little Extra Effort**	1965	3.00	15.00
Decca 31899		**Come On / A Little Extra Effort**	1965	6.00	30.00
DEVONS, THE					
The Devons also recorded as The Sir Douglas Quintet.					
Pic One 111		**Wine, Wine, Wine / Joey's Guitar**	1966	15.00	75.00

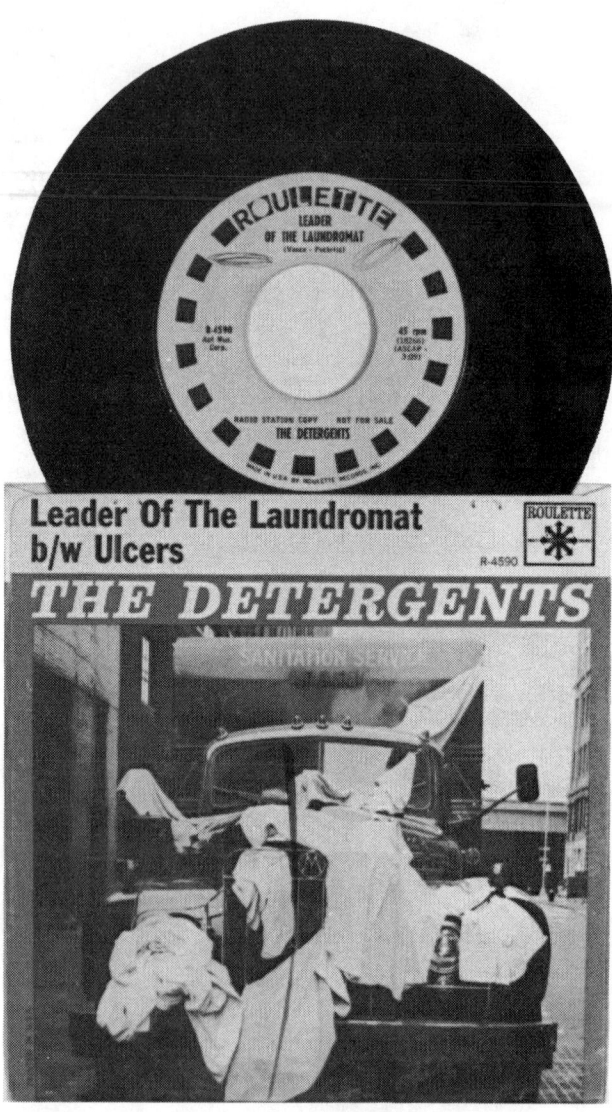

One of the best of the many "answer records" of the '60s, the Detergents' *Leader Of The Laundromat* was a rather witty send-up of *The Leader Of The Pack,* by the quintessential girl group, the Shangri-La's.

Label & Catalog #		A-Side/B-Side	Year	VG	NM
DeVORZON, BARRY					
Refer to Barry & The Tamerlanes.					
RCA Victor 47-7124		Baby Doll / Barbara Jean	1957	3.00	15.00
RCA Victor 47-7406		Honey Bunny / Too Soon	1958	4.00	20.00
RCA Victor 47-7510		Cora Lee / Blue, Green And Gold	1959	3.00	15.00
Columbia 41612		Rosemary / Hey Little Darlin'	1960	3.00	15.00
DEVOTIONS, THE					
Delta 1001		Rip Van Winkle / I Love You For Sentimental Reasons	1961	20.00	100.00
Roulette 4406		Rip Van Winkle / I Love You For Sentimental Reasons	1961	5.00	25.00
Roulette 4541		Rip Van Winkle / I Love You For Sentimental Reasons	1961	3.00	15.00
Roulette 4556		Sunday Kind Of Love / Tears From A Broken Heart	1962	4.00	20.00
Roulette 4580		Snow White / Zindy Lou	1962	5.00	25.00
DEWEY, GEORGE & JACK					
Raven 700		Flying Saucers Have Landed /			
		Flying Saucers Have Landed, Part 2	195?	6.00	30.00
DEY, TRACEY (& THE FOUR-EVERS)					
Vee Jay 467		Jerry (I'm Your Sherry) / Once In A Blue, Blue Moon	1962	3.00	15.00
Liberty 55604		Teen Age Cleopatra / Who's That?	1963	3.00	15.00
		(Liberty 55604 features The Four-Evers.)			
Amy 894		Here Comes The Boy / Teddy's The Boy I Love	1963	2.00	10.00
Amy 901		Gonna Get Along Without You Now / Go Away	1964	2.00	10.00
Amy 908		Hanging On To My Baby / Ska-Doo-Dee-Yah	1964	2.00	10.00
Amy 912		I Won't Tell / Any Kind Of Love	1964	2.00	10.00
DIAL TONES, THE					
Lawn 203		So Young / Chicago Bird	1963	6.00	30.00
DIALS, THE					
Time 1068		Monkey Dance / Monkey Walk	1963	2.00	10.00
DIALTONES, THE					
Dandy Dan 1		Cherry Pie / Again	1959	7.00	35.00
DIALTONES, THE					
The Dialtones is a pseudonym for Randy & The Rainbows.					
Goldisc 3005		Till I Heard It From You / Johnny	1960	4.00	20.00
Goldisc 3020		Till I Heard It From You / Johnny	1961	3.00	15.00
DIAMOND, BRIAN, & THE CUTTERS					
Hickory 1321		Big Bad Wolf / See If I Care	1965	2.00	10.00
DIAMOND, GERRY					
Dwain 811		Nancy / A Little Rock, A Little Roll	1960	2.00	10.00
DIAMOND, NEIL					
Refer to Neil & Jack.					
Columbia 42809	(DJ)	Clown Town / At Night	1963	30.00	150.00
Columbia 42809		Clown Town / At Night	1963	75.00	300.00
Bang 519		Solitary Man / Do It	1966	1.20	6.00
Bang 528		Cherry, Cherry / I'll Come Running	1966	1.20	6.00
Bang 536		I Got The Feeling (Oh No No) / The Boat That I Row	1966	1.20	6.00
Bang 540		You Got To Me / Someday, Baby	1967	1.20	6.00
Bang 542		Girl, You'll Be A Woman Soon / You'll Forget	1967	1.20	6.00
Hip Pocket 5		Girl, You'll Be A Woman Soon / Cherry, Cherry	1967	3.00	15.00
		(4" flexidisc with a picture envelope.)			
Hip Pocket 17		Solitary Man / You Got To Me	1967	3.00	15.00
		(4" flexidisc with a picture envelope.)			
Bang 547		Thank The Lord For The Night Time / The Long Way Home	1967	1.20	6.00
Bang 551		Kentucky Woman / The Time Is Now	1967	1.20	6.00
Bang 554		New Orleans / Hanky Panky	1968	1.00	5.00
Bang 556		Red, Red Wine / Red Rubber Ball	1968	1.00	5.00
Bang 561		Shilo / La Bamba	1968	1.00	5.00
Bang 575		Shilo / La Bamba	1968	1.00	5.00
Bang 578		Solitary Man / The Time Is Now	1970	1.00	5.00
Bang 580		Do It / Hanky Panky	1970	1.00	5.00
Bang 586		I'm A Believer / Crooker Street	1971	1.00	5.00
Bang 703		The Long Way Home / Monday, Monday	1973	1.00	5.00
Bang 105		Cherry, Cherry / Girl, You'll Be A Woman Soon	1973	.60	3.00
Bang 108		Solitary Man / I'm A Believer	1973	.60	3.00
Uni 55065		Brooklyn Roads / Holiday Inn	1968	1.00	5.00
Uni 55075	(DJ)	Two Bit Manchild / Broad Old Woman *(Red vinyl)*	1968	10.00	50.00
Uni 55075		Two Bit Manchild / Broad Old Woman	1968	1.00	5.00
Uni 55075	(PS)	Two Bit Manchild / Broad Old Woman	1968	4.00	20.00
Uni 55084		Sunday Sun / Honey Drippin' Time	1968	.80	4.00

Label & Catalog #		A-Side/B-Side	Year	VG	NM
Uni 55109		Brother Love's Traveling Salvation Show /			
		Modern Day Versions Of Love	1969	.80	4.00
Uni 55136		Sweet Caroline / Dig In	1969	.80	4.00
Uni 55175		Holly Holy / Hurtin' You Don't Come Easy	1969	.80	4.00
Uni 55204		Until It's Time For You To Go / The Singer Sings His Songs	1970	.80	4.00
Uni 55224		Soolaimon (African Trilogy II) /			
		And The Grass Won't Pay No Mind	1970	.80	4.00
Uni 55224	(PS)	Soolaimon (African Trilogy II) /			
		And The Grass Won't Pay No Mind	1970	3.00	15.00
Uni 55250		Cracklin' Rosie / Lordy	1970	.80	4.00
Uni 55264		He Ain't Heavy, He's My Brother / Free Life	1970	.80	4.00
Uni 55278		I Am... I Said / Done Too Soon	1971	.80	4.00
Uni 55310		Stones / Crunchy Granola Suite	1971	.80	4.00
Uni 55326		Song Sung Blue / Gitchy Goomy	1972	.80	4.00
Uni 55346		Play Me / Porcupine Pie	1972	.80	4.00
Uni 55352		Walk On Water / High Rolling Man	1972	.80	4.00
MCA 40017		Cherry Cherry / Morningside	1973	.60	3.00
MCA 40092		The Last Thing On My Mind / Canta Libra	1973	.60	3.00
Columbia 45942		Be / Flight Of The Gull	1973	.60	3.00
Columbia 45998		Skybird / Lonely Looking Sky	1974	.60	3.00
Columbia 10043		Longfellow Serenade / Rosemary's Wine	1974	.60	3.00
Columbia 10084		I've Been This Way Before / Reggae Strut	1975	.60	3.00
Columbia 10138		The Last Picasso / The Gift Of Song	1975	.60	3.00
Columbia 10366		If You Know What I Mean / Street Life	1976	.60	3.00
Columbia 10405		Don't Think... Feel / Home Is A Wounded Heart	1976	.60	3.00
Columbia 10452		Beautiful Noise / Signs	1976	.60	3.00
Columbia 10657		Desiree / Once In A While	1978	.60	3.00
Columbia 10840		You Don't Bring Me Flowers / You Don't Bring Me Flowers	1978	.60	3.00
Columbia 10897		Forever In Blue Jeans / Remember Me	1979	.60	3.00
Columbia 10945		Say Maybe / Diamond Girls	1979	.60	3.00
Columbia 11175		September Morn' / I'm A Believer	1979	.60	3.00
Columbia 11232		The Good Lord Loves You /			
		The Sun Ain't Gonna Shine Anymore	1979	.60	3.00
Capitol 4939		Love On The Rocks / Acapulco	1980	.30	1.50
Capitol 4939	(PS)	Love On The Rocks / Acapulco	1980	.40	2.00
Capitol 4960		Hello Again / Amazed And Confused	1980	.30	1.50
Capitol 4960	(PS)	Hello Again / Amazed And Confused	1980	.40	2.00
Capitol 4994		America / Songs Of Life (Picture label)	1980	.40	2.00
Capitol 4994		America / Songs Of Life (Blue label)	1980	.30	1.50
Capitol 4994	(PS)	America / Songs Of Life	1980	.40	2.00
Columbia 02604		Yesterday's Songs / Guitar Heaven	1981	.30	1.50
Columbia 02604	(PS)	Yesterday's Songs / Guitar Heaven	1981	.40	2.00
Columbia 02712		On The Way To The Sky / Save Me	1981	.30	1.50
Columbia 02712	(PS)	On The Way To The Sky / Save Me	1981	.40	2.00
Columbia 03219		Heartlight / You Don't Know Me	1982	.30	1.50
Columbia 03219	(PS)	Heartlight / You Don't Know Me	1982	.40	2.00
Columbia 03345		Heartlight (One sided)	1982	1.00	5.00
Columbia 03503		I'm Alive /	1982	.30	1.50
Columbia 03801		Front Page Story /	1983	.30	1.50
Columbia 03801	(PS)	Front Page Story /	1983	.40	2.00
Columbia 04541		Turn Around /	1984	.30	1.50
Columbia 04541	(PS)	Turn Around /	1984	.30	1.50
Columbia 06136		The Story Of My Life /	1986	.30	1.50
Columbia 06136	(PS)	The Story Of My Life /	1986	.40	2.00
		—Extended Play Albums—			
Uni LLP-127	(33)	Neil Diamond Gold (Jukebox EP)	1970	6.00	30.00
Uni LLP	(33)	Stones (Jukebox EP)	1971	6.00	30.00
Columbia 32919	(DJ)	Serenade (Issued without a cover)	1974	5.00	25.00

DIAMONDS, THE

Label & Catalog #		A-Side/B-Side	Year	VG	NM
Coral 61502		Black Denim Trousers And Motorcycle Boots / Nip Sip	1955	3.00	15.00
Coral 61577		Be My Lovin' Baby / Smooch Me	1955	3.00	15.00
Mercury 70790		Why Do Fools Fall In Love? / You, Baby, You	1956	4.00	20.00
Mercury 70835		The Church Bells May Ring / Little Girl Of Mine	1956	4.00	20.00
Mercury 70899		Love, Love, Love / Ev'ry Night About This Time	1956	4.00	20.00
Mercury 70934		Soft Summer Breeze / Ka-Ding-Dong	1956	4.00	20.00
Mercury 71021		A Thousand Miles Away / Ev'ry Minute Of The Day	1956	4.00	20.00
Mercury 71060		Little Darlin' / Faithful And True	1957	5.00	25.00
Mercury 71060		Little Darlin' / Faithful And True (Brown vinyl)	1957	10.00	50.00
		—Original Mercury singles above have maroon labels.—			
Mercury 70790		Why Do Fools Fall In Love? / You, Baby, You	1957	2.00	10.00
Mercury 70835		The Church Bells May Ring / Little Girl Of Mine	1957	2.00	10.00
Mercury 70899		Love, Love, Love / Ev'ry Night About This Time	1957	2.00	10.00
Mercury 70934		Soft Summer Breeze / Ka-Ding-Dong	1957	2.00	10.00
Mercury 71021		A Thousand Miles Away / Ev'ry Minute Of The Day	1957	2.00	10.00
Mercury 71060		Little Darlin' / Faithful And True	1957	2.00	10.00
Mercury 71128		Words Of Love / Don't Say Goodbye	1957	2.00	10.00
Mercury 71165		Zip Zip / Oh, How I Wish	1957	2.00	10.00

Label & Catalog #		A-Side/B-Side	Year	VG	NM
Mercury 71197		Silhouettes / Daddy Cool	1957	2.00	10.00
Mercury 71242		The Stroll / Land Of Beauty	1957	2.00	10.00
Mercury 71291		High Sign / Chick-Lets (Don't Let Me Down)	1958	2.00	10.00
Mercury 71291	(PS)	High Sign / Chick-Lets (Don't Let Me Down)	1958	15.00	75.00
Mercury 71330		Kathy-O / Happy Years	1958	2.00	10.00
Mercury 71366		Walking Along / Eternal Lovers	1958	2.00	10.00
Mercury 71404		She Say (Oom Dooby Doom) /			
		From The Bottom Of My Heart	1959	2.00	10.00
Mercury 71449		Gretchen / A Mother's Love	1959	2.00	10.00
Mercury 71468		Holding Your Hand / Sneaky Alligator	1959	2.00	10.00
Mercury 71505		Young In Years / The Twenty Second Day	1959		
Mercury 71534		Batman, Wolfman, Frankenstein Or Dracula /			
		Walkin' The Stroll	1959	2.00	10.00
Mercury 71586		Real True Love / Tell The Truth	1960	2.00	10.00
Mercury 71633		Pencil Song / Slave Girl	1960	2.00	10.00
Mercury 71735		The Crumble / You'd Be Mine	1960	2.00	10.00
Mercury 71782		I Sho' Lawd Will / You Short Changed Me	1961	2.00	10.00
Mercury 71818		The Munch / Woomai-Ling	1961	2.00	10.00
Mercury 71831		One Summer Night / It's A Doggone Shame	1961	2.00	10.00
Mercury 71956		The Horizontal Lieutenant / Vanishing American	1962	2.00	10.00
		—Extended Play Albums—			
Brunswick 71031		The Diamonds	1956	50.00	200.00
Mercury 3356		The Diamonds (Volume 1)	1956	25.00	125.00
Mercury 3357		The Diamonds (Volume 2)	1956	25.00	125.00
Mercury 3358		The Diamonds (Volume 3)	1957	25.00	125.00
Mercury 3367		The Diamonds	1957	25.00	125.00
Mercury 3390		The Stroll	1957	25.00	125.00
Mercury 4038		The Diamonds' Golden Hits	1958	20.00	100.00

DIANE & THE DARLETTES

Dunes 2016	Just You / The Wobble	1962	3.00	15.00

DIATONES, THE

Bandera 2509	Oh, Baby, Come Dance With Me / Ruby, Be Gone	195?	6.00	30.00

DICK & DEE DEE
Features Dick St. John.

Lama 7778		The Mountain's High / I Want Someone	1961	4.00	20.00
Lama 7780		Goodbye To Love / Swing Low	1961	3.00	15.00
Lama 7783		Tell Me / Will You Always Love Me?	1961	3.00	15.00
Liberty 55350		The Mountain's High / I Want Someone	1961	2.00	10.00
Liberty 55382		Goodbye To Love / Swing Low	1961	1.20	6.00
Liberty 55412		Tell Me / Will You Always Love Me?	1962	1.20	6.00
Liberty 55478		All I Want / Life's Just A Play	1962	1.20	6.00
Warner Bros. 5320		The River Took My Baby / My Lonely Self	1963	1.00	5.00
Warner Bros. 5320	(PS)	The River Took My Baby / My Lonely Self	1963	5.00	25.00
Warner Bros. 5342		Young And In Love / Say To Me	1963	1.00	5.00
Warner Bros. 5364		Love Is A Once In A Lifetime Thing /			
		Chug-A-Chug-A-Choo-Choo	1963	1.00	5.00
Warner Bros. 5383		Where Did The Good Times Go? /			
		Guess Our Love Must Show	1963	1.00	5.00
Warner Bros. 5396		Turn Around / Don't Leave Me	1963	1.00	5.00
Warner Bros. 5411		All My Trials / Don't Think Twice, It's Alright	1964	1.00	5.00
Warner Bros. 5426		The Gift / Not Fade Away	1964	1.00	5.00
Warner Bros. 5451		You Were Mine / Remember Then?	1964	1.00	5.00
Warner Bros. 5470		Without Your Love / The Riddle Song	1964	1.00	5.00
Warner Bros. 5482		Thou Shalt Not Steal / River 'Round The Bend	1964	1.00	5.00
Warner Bros. 5482	(PS)	Thou Shalt Not Steal / River 'Round The Bend	1964	5.00	25.00
Warner Bros. 5608		Be My Baby / Room 404	1965	1.00	5.00
Warner Bros. 5627		When Blue Turns To Grey /			
		Some Things Just Stick In Your Mind	1965	1.00	5.00
Warner Bros. 5652		The World Is Waiting / Vini Vini	1965	1.00	5.00
Warner Bros. 5671		Use What You've Got / P.S. 1402 (Your Local Charm School)	1965	2.00	10.00
Warner Bros. 5680		New Orleans / Use What You've Got	1965	1.00	5.00
Warner Bros. 5699		Sha-La / Till	1966	1.00	5.00
Warner Bros. 5860		Make Up Before We Break Up /			
		Can't Get Enough Of Your Love	1967	1.00	5.00
Warner Bros. 7017		Long, Lonely Nights / I'll Always Be Around	1967	1.00	5.00
Warner Bros. 7069		One In A Million / Baby, I Need You	1967	1.00	5.00
Dot 17145		The Escape Suite / I'm Not Gonna Get Hung Up About It	1969	3.00	15.00
Dot 17261		We'll Sing In The Sunshine / In The Season Of Our Love	1969	1.60	8.00
Dot 17305		Do I Love You / You Come Back To Haunt Me	1970	1.60	8.00

DICK & DON
Dick and Don Addrisi.

Valiant 742	Excuse Me / You're Bad	1966	1.20	6.00

Label & Catalog #	A-Side/B-Side	Year	VG	NM
DICKENS, THE				
The Dickens is a pseudonym for NRBQ.				
Scepter 12322	Sho Need Love / Don't Talk About My Music	1971	2.00	10.00
DICKEY DOO & THE DON'TS				
Dickey Doo is Gerry Granahan.				
Swan 4001	Click Clack / Did You Cry?	1958	2.00	10.00
Swan 4006	Nee Nee Na Na Na Na Nu Nu / Flip Top Box	1958	3.00	15.00
Swan 4014	Leave Me Alone (Let Me Cry) / Wild Party	1958	2.00	10.00
Swan 4025	Teardrops Will Fall / Come With Us	1959	1.60	8.00
Swan 4033	Dear Heart, Don't Cry / Ballad Of A Train	1959	1.60	8.00
Swan 4046	Wabash Cannonball / The Drums Of Richard A-Doo	1959	1.60	8.00
United Artists 238	Teen Scene / Pity Pity	1960	1.60	8.00
United Artists 362	The Judge / A Little Dog Cried	1961	1.60	8.00
Ascot 2178	Click Clack '65 / Don't Count Me Out	1965	1.60	8.00
Danna 4001	The Judge / Doo Plus Two	1967	1.60	8.00
DICKIE & THE DEBONAIRES				
Valli 302	Yo Yo Girl / Please, Mr. Disc Jockey	196?	40.00	200.00
Asta 101	Debonaire Rock / The Stomp	1961	6.00	30.00
DICTATORS, THE				
Asylum 45420	Hey, Boys / Disease	1977	1.00	5.00
DIDDLEY, BO				
Bo Diddley is a pseudonym for Ellis McDaniel.				
Checker 814	Bo Diddley / I'm A Man	1955	7.00	35.00
Checker 819	Diddley Daddy / She's Fine, She's Fine	1955	8.00	40.00
	(A-side features The Moonglows on backing vocals.)			
Checker 827	Pretty Thing / Bring It To Jerome	1955	6.00	30.00
Checker 832	Diddy Wah Diddy / I'm Looking For A Woman	1956	6.00	30.00
Checker 842	Who Do You Love? / In Bad	1956	6.00	30.00
	(First pressing erroneously prints the title as "In Bad.")			
Checker 842	Who Do You Love? / I'm Bad	1956	6.00	30.00
Checker 850	Cops And Robbers / Down Home Special	1956	6.00	30.00
Checker 860	Hey! Bo Diddley / Mona	1957	6.00	30.00
	(Checker singles above have maroon labels with silver web on top.)			
Checker 878	Say! Boss Man / Before You Accuse Me	1957	3.00	15.00
Checker 896	Hush Your Mouth / Dearest Darling	1958	3.00	15.00
Checker 907	Willie And Lillie / Bo Meets The Monster	1958	3.00	15.00
Checker 914	I'm Sorry / Oh, Yeah	1959	3.00	15.00
Checker 924	Crackin' Up / The Great Grandfather	1959	4.00	20.00
Checker 931	Say, Man / The Clock Strikes Twelve	1959	4.00	20.00
Checker 936	Say, Man, Back Again / She's All Right	1959	2.00	10.00
Checker 942	Road Runner / My Story	1960	3.00	15.00
Checker 951	Walkin' And Talkin' / Crawdad	1960	2.00	10.00
Checker 965	Gunslinger / Signifyin'	1960	2.00	10.00
Checker 976	Not Guilty / Aztec	1961	2.00	10.00
Checker 985	Call Me / Pills	1961	4.00	20.00
Checker 997	Bo Diddley / I'm A Man	1962	2.00	10.00
Checker 1019	You Can't Judge A Book By Its Cover / I Can Tell	1962	2.00	10.00
Checker 1045	Surfer's Love Call / Greatest Lover In The World	1963	2.00	10.00
Checker 1083	Jo Ann / Mama, Keep Your Big Mouth Shut	1963	2.00	10.00
Checker 1089	Bo's Beat / (B-side by Chuck Berry)	1964	2.00	10.00
Checker 1098	Hey Good Lookin' / You Ain't Bad	1964	1.60	8.00
Checker 1123	500% More Man / Let The Kids Dance	1964	1.60	8.00
Checker 1200	Another Sugar Daddy / I'm High Again	1965	1.60	8.00
	—Extended Play Albums—			
Checker 5125	Bo Diddley (Cardboard cover)	1958	40.00	200.00
Checker 5125	Bo Diddley (Paper sleeve cover)	1958	30.00	150.00
DILL, DANNY				
ABC-Paramount 9734	Hungry For Your Lovin' / The Stranger Of Abilene	1956	10.00	50.00
DILLARD & CLARK				
Doug Dillard and Gene Clark.				
A&M 1033	Don't Be Cruel / Lyin' Down The Middle	1969	2.00	10.00
A&M 1087	Why Not Your Baby? / Radio Song	1969	1.00	5.00
A&M 1165	Don't Let Me Down / Rocky Top	1970	.80	4.00
DILLARDS, THE				
Elektra 45003	Dooley / Dong's Love	1964	1.60	8.00
Elektra 45006	Hootin' Banjo / Polly Vaughn	1965	1.60	8.00
Elektra 45641	Reason To Believe / Nobody Knows	1967	.80	4.00
Elektra 45661	Listen To The Sound / The Biggest Whatever	1968	.80	4.00
Elektra 45679	Rain Maker / West Montana Hanna	1969	.80	4.00

Label & Catalog #	A-Side/B-Side	Year	VG	NM
DILLON, ZIG				
"R" 512	Bird Song Boogie / Beetle Bug	195?	3.00	15.00
DIMENSIONS, THE				
Mohawk 116	Over The Rainbow / Nursery Rhyme Rock *(Maroon label)*	1960	8.00	40.00
Mohawk 116	Over The Rainbow / Nursery Rhyme Rock *(Brown label)*	196?	4.00	20.00
Mohawk 116	Over The Rainbow / Nursery Rhyme Rock *(Red label)*	196?	3.00	15.00
Mohawk 120	Zing Went The Strings Of My Heart /			
	Don't Take Your Love From Me	1960	3.00	15.00
Mohawk 121	Ave Maria / God's Christmas	1960	6.00	30.00
Mohawk 123	A Tear Fell / Theresa	1961	10.00	50.00
DIMENSIONS, THE				
Washington Square 2025	Treat Me Right / We're Doing Fine	196?	2.00	10.00
DIMENSIONS, THE				
Carram 105	Surfside / To Be Young	196?	8.00	40.00
DIMENSIONS, THE				
Panorama 25	She's Boss / Penny	1966	3.00	15.00
HBR 1477	She's Boss / Penny	1966	2.00	10.00
Panorama 41	Baby What Do You Say / Knock You Flat	1967	2.00	10.00
DIMINISHED FIFTH, THE				
Hush 231	Doctor Dear / Do You Hear?	1966	4.00	20.00
DIMPLES, THE				
Era 1079	Toy Telephone / Gimme Jimmy	1958	4.00	20.00
Dore 517	Invitation To A Party / My Sister's Beau	1959	4.00	20.00
Era 3079	Toy Telephone / Gimme Jimmy	1962	2.00	10.00
Cameo 325	Dreaming Of You / Please Don't Be Angry With Me	1964	2.00	10.00
DIMPLES, THE: *Refer to* EDDIE COOLEY & THE DIMPLES				
DING DONGS, THE: *Refer to* BOBBY DARIN				
DINKS, THE				
Sully 925	Ugly Girl / Rocka-Mow-Mow	1966	2.00	10.00
DINNING, MARK				
MGM 12553	When You're Tired Of Breaking Other Hearts / School Fool	1957	3.00	15.00
MGM 12732	Secretly In Love With You / The Blackeyed Gypsy	1958	3.00	15.00
MGM 12775	Cutie Cutie / Life Of Love	1959	3.00	15.00
MGM 12845	Teen Angel / Bye Now, Baby	1961	3.00	15.00
MGM 12888	A Star Is Born (A Love Has Died) / You Win Again	1960	2.00	10.00
MGM 12929	The Lovin' Touch / Come Back To Me	1960	2.00	10.00
MGM 12929 (PS)	The Lovin' Touch / Come Back To Me	1960	3.00	15.00
MGM 12958	She Cried On My Shoulder / The World Is Gettin' Smaller	1960	1.60	8.00
MGM 12980	Top Forty News, Weather And Sports / Suddenly	1961	1.60	8.00
MGM 13007	Another Lonely Girl / Can't Forget	1961	1.60	8.00
MGM 13024	Lonely Island / Turn Me On	1961	1.60	8.00
MGM 13061	All Of This For Sally / The Pickup	1962	1.60	8.00
DINO, PAUL				
Promo 2180	Ginnie Bell / Bye Bye	1960	2.00	10.00
DINO & THE DELTONES				
Cobra 1112	Sticks And Stones / The Living End	1965	4.00	20.00
Cobra 1117	Daydream / Slapstick	1965	4.00	20.00
DINO & THE DIPLOMATS				
Vida 0100/1	Hush-A-Bye, My Love / Homework	196?	5.00	25.00
Vida 0102/3	Such A Fool For You / Soft Wind	196?	5.00	25.00
Laurie LR-3103	I Can't Believe / My Dream	1961	6.00	30.00
Laurie 3103	I Can't Believe / My Dream	1961	3.00	15.00
DINO & THE HEARTSPINNERS				
Starlight 9	I Believe In You / Gee	196?	2.00	10.00
Starlight 11	The Lover's Plea / Mexico	196?	2.00	10.00
Starlight 13	The Bells Of Love /	196?	2.00	10.00
Pyramid 164	Flames / Shirley	196?	2.00	10.00
Bam Boom 108	Cry Like I Cried / That's My Girl	1973	1.20	6.00
Bam Boom 112	I Love You So / Two Kinds Of People In The World	1973	1.20	6.00
Bam Boom 119	Hey Senorita / I'm Not A Know It All	1973	1.20	6.00
Robin Hood 141	Zoom! / Let's Go Back To Yesterday	1974	1.20	6.00
Robin Hood 142	Who Do You Think You Are? / A Thousand Miles Away	1974	1.20	6.00

Label & Catalog #		A-Side/B-Side	Year	VG	NM

DINO, DESI & BILLY
Dino Martin, Jr., Desi Arnaz, Jr., and Billy Hinsche. Refer to The Beverly Hills Blues Band.

Label & Catalog #		A-Side/B-Side	Year	VG	NM
Reprise 0324		Since You Broke My Heart / We Know	1965	1.20	6.00
Reprise 0367		I'm A Fool / So Many Ways	1965	1.20	6.00
Reprise 0367	(PS)	I'm A Fool / So Many Ways	1965	2.00	10.00
Reprise 0401		Not The Lovin' Kind / Chimes Of Freedom	1965	1.00	5.00
Reprise 0401	(PS)	Not The Lovin' Kind / Chimes Of Freedom	1965	2.00	10.00
Reprise 0426		Please Don't Fight It / The Rebel Kind	1965	1.00	5.00
Reprise 0426	(PS)	Please Don't Fight It / The Rebel Kind	1965	2.00	10.00
Reprise 0444		I Can't Get Her Off My Mind / Superman	1966	1.00	5.00
Reprise 0462		It's Just The Way You Are / Tie Me Down	1966	1.00	5.00
Reprise 0496		Look Out Girls (Here We Come) / She's So Far Out She's In	1966	1.00	5.00
Reprise 0529		I Hope She's There Tonight / Josephine	1966	1.20	6.00
Reprise 0544		If You're Thinkin' What I'm Thinkin' / Pretty Flamingo	1967	1.20	6.00
Reprise 0579		Two In The Afternoon / Good Luck, Best Wishes To You	1967	1.20	6.00
Reprise 0619		Kitty Doyle / Without Hurtin' Someone	1967	1.60	8.00
Reprise 0653		My, What A Shame / The Inside Outside Caspar Milquetoast Eskimo Flash	1968	1.60	8.00
Reprise 0653	(PS)	My, What A Shame / The Inside Outside Caspar Milquetoast Eskimo Flash	1968	3.00	15.00
Reprise 0698		Tell Someone You Love Them / General Outline	1968	1.60	8.00
Reprise 0965		Lady Love / A Certain Sound	1970	5.00	25.00
		("Lady Love" was written by Brian Wilson.)			
Uni 55127		Thru Spray Colored Glasses / Someday	1969	1.60	8.00

DIO, RONNIE, & THE PROPHETS
Ronnie Dio also recorded with Elf.

Atlantic 2145		Love Pains / The Ooh Poo Pah Doo	1962	5.00	25.00
Lawn 218		Gonna Make It Alone / Singin' Street	1963	4.00	20.00
Swan 4165		Mr. Misery / Our Year	1964	2.00	10.00
Kapp 725		Dear Darlin' / Smiling By Day	1965	2.00	10.00
Kapp 770		The Way Of Love / Walking Alone	1966	2.00	10.00
Parkway 143		Ten Days With Brenda / Walking In Different Circles	1967	3.00	15.00

DION & THE TIMBERLANES
Features Dion DiMucci.

Mohawk 105		The Chosen Few / Out In Colorado	1957	10.00	50.00
Jubilee 5294		The Chosen Few / Out In Colorado	1957	6.00	30.00

DION & THE BELMONTS
Dion DiMucci with Angelo D'Aleo, Carlo Mastrangelo and Fred Milano. D'Aleo left in 1959 and was replaced by Frank Lyndon in 1960. Refer to The Belmonts.

Laurie 3013		I Wonder Why / Teen Angel *(Grey label)*	1958	5.00	25.00
Laurie 3013		I Wonder Why / Teen Angel	1958	4.00	20.00
Laurie 3015		No One Knows / I Can't Go On (Rosalie)	1958	4.00	20.00
		—Original Laurie singles above have blue labels.—			
Laurie 3013		I Wonder Why / Teen Angel	1959	3.00	15.00
Laurie 3015		No One Knows / I Can't Go On (Rosalie)	1959	3.00	15.00
Laurie 3021		Don't Pity Me / Just You	1959	3.00	15.00
Laurie 3027		A Teenager In Love / I've Cried Before	1959	4.00	20.00
Laurie 3027	(S)	A Teenager In Love / I've Cried Before	1959	7.00	35.00
Laurie 3035		Every Little Thing I Do / A Lover's Prayer	1959	2.00	10.00
Laurie 3035	(PS)	Every Little Thing I Do / A Lover's Prayer	1959	4.00	20.00
Laurie 3044		Where Or When / That's My Desire	1959	3.00	15.00
Laurie 3044	(PS)	Where Or When / That's My Desire	1959	4.00	20.00
Laurie 3052		When You Wish Upon A Star / Wonderful Girl	1960	3.00	15.00
Laurie 3052	(PS)	When You Wish Upon A Star / Wonderful Girl	1960	4.00	20.00
Laurie 3059		In The Still Of The Night / A Funny Feeling	1960	3.00	15.00
Laurie 3059	(PS)	In The Still Of The Night / A Funny Feeling	1960	4.00	20.00
		—Laurie singles above have red & white labels.—			
ABC 10868		My Girl / The Month Of May	1966	2.00	10.00
ABC 10896		Movin' Man / For Bobbie	1967	2.00	10.00
		—Extended Play Albums—			
Laurie LEP-302		Where Or When	1959	25.00	125.00

DION (& THE WANDERERS)
Dion DiMucci. Refer to Dion & The Belmonts; Dion & The Timberlanes.

Laurie 3070		Lonely Teenager / Little Miss Blue	1960	2.00	10.00
Laurie 3070	(PS)	Lonely Teenager / Little Miss Blue	1960	3.00	15.00
Laurie 3070	(S)	Lonely Teenager / Little Miss Blue	1960	6.00	30.00
Laurie 3081		Havin' Fun / Northeast End Of The Corner	1961	2.00	10.00
Laurie 3081	(PS)	Havin' Fun / Northeast End Of The Corner	1961	3.00	15.00
Laurie 3090		Kissin' Game / Heaven Help Me	1961	2.00	10.00
Laurie 3090	(PS)	Kissin' Game / Heaven Help Me	1961	3.00	15.00
Laurie 3101		Somebody Nobody Wants / Could Somebody Take My Place Tonight?	1961	2.00	10.00
Laurie 3110		Runaround Sue / Runaway Girl	1961	2.00	10.00
Laurie 3110	(PS)	Runaround Sue / Runaway Girl	1961	3.00	15.00

Label & Catalog #		A-Side/B-Side	Year	VG	NM
Laurie 3110	(S)	Runaround Sue / Runaway Girl	1961	6.00	30.00
Laurie 3115		The Wanderer / The Majestic	1961	2.00	10.00
Laurie 3115	(PS)	The Wanderer / The Majestic	1961	3.00	15.00
Monument	(DJ)	Runaround Sue / (B-side by Joey Dee)	1961	4.00	20.00
Laurie 3123		Lovers Who Wander / (I Was) Born To Cry	1962	2.00	10.00
Laurie 3123	(PS)	Lovers Who Wander / (I Was) Born To Cry	1962	3.00	15.00
Laurie 3134		Little Diane / Lost For Sure	1962	2.00	10.00
Laurie 3134	(PS)	Little Diane / Lost For Sure	1962	3.00	15.00
Laurie 3145		Love Came To Me / Little Girl	1962	2.00	10.00
Laurie 3153		Sandy / Faith	1963	2.00	10.00
Laurie 3171		Come Go With Me / King Without A Queen	1963	2.00	10.00
Laurie 3187		Lonely World / Tag Along	1963	2.00	10.00
Laurie 3225		Then I'll Be Tired Of You / After The Dance	1964	3.00	15.00
Laurie 3240		Shout / Little Girl	1964	3.00	15.00
Laurie 3303		I Got The Blues / (I Was) Born To Cry	1965	2.00	10.00
		—Original Laurie singles above have red & white labels.—			
Columbia 42662		Ruby Baby / He'll Only Hurt You	1963	1.60	8.00
Columbia 42662	(PS)	Ruby Baby / He'll Only Hurt You	1963	2.00	10.00
Columbia 42776		This Little Girl / The Loneliest Man In The World	1963	1.60	8.00
Columbia 42810	(DJ)	Be Careful Of Stones That You Throw /			
		Be Careful Of Stones That You Throw (Blue vinyl)	1963	7.00	35.00
Columbia 42810		Be Careful Of Stones That You Throw /			
		I Can't Believe (That You Don't Love Me Anymore)	1963	1.60	8.00
Columbia 42852	(DJ)	Donna, The Prima Donna / Donna The Prima Donna	1963	7.00	35.00
		(Red vinyl.)			
Columbia 42852		Donna, The Prima Donna / You're Mine	1963	1.60	8.00
Columbia 42917		Drip Drop / No One's Waiting For Me	1963	1.60	8.00
Columbia 42977		I'm Your Hootchy Kootchy Man / The Road I'm On	1964	1.60	8.00
Columbia 42977	(PS)	I'm Your Hootchy Kootchy Man / The Road I'm On	1964	3.00	15.00
Columbia 43096		Johnny B. Goode / Chicago Blues	1964	1.00	5.00
Columbia 43213		Unloved, Unwanted Me / Sweet, Sweet Baby	1965	2.00	10.00
Columbia 43293		Spoonful / Kickin' Child	1965	2.00	10.00
Columbia 43423		Tomorrow Won't Bring The Rain / You Move Me, Babe	1966	2.00	10.00
Columbia 43423	(PS)	Tomorrow Won't Bring The Rain / You Move Me, Babe	1966	4.00	20.00
Columbia 43483		Time In My Heart For You / Wake Up, Baby	1966	2.00	10.00
Columbia 43692		Two Ton Feather / So Much Younger	1966	2.00	10.00
		(Columbia 43423, 43483 and 44719 credit Dion & The Wanderers.)			
Columbia 44719		I Can't Help But Wonder Where I'm Bound / Southern Train	1968	2.00	10.00
Laurie 3464		Abraham, Martin And John / Daddy Rollin' (In Your Arms)	1968	1.00	5.00
Laurie 3478		Purple Haze / The Dolphins	1969	1.00	5.00
Laurie 3495		Both Sides Now / Sun Fun Song	1969	1.60	8.00
Laurie 3504		Loving You Is Sweeter Than Ever / He Looks A Lot Like Me	1969	1.60	8.00
Warner Bros. 7356		Natural Man / If We Only Have Love	1970	.80	4.00
Warner Bros. 7401		Your Own Back Yard / Sit Down, Old Friend	1970	.80	4.00
Warner Bros. 7469		Close To It All / Let It Be	1970	.80	4.00
Warner Bros. 7491		Josie / Sunniland	1971	.80	4.00
Warner Bros. 7537		Sanctuary / Brand New Morning	1971	.80	4.00
Warner Bros. 7537	(PS)	Sanctuary / Brand New Morning	1971	2.00	10.00
Warner Bros. 537	(DJ)	Suite For Late Summer	1972	3.00	15.00
Warner Bros. 7663		Running Close Behind You / Seagull	1972	.80	4.00
Warner Bros. 7704		Doctor Rock And Roll / Sunshine Lady	1973	.80	4.00
Warner Bros. 7793		New York City Song / Richer Than A Rich Man	1974	.80	4.00
Warner/Spector 0403		Make The Woman Love Me / Running Close Behind You	1975	2.00	10.00
		("Make The Woman Love Me" was produced by Phil Spector.)			
Big Tree/Spector 16063		Born To Be With You / Running Close Behind You	1976	2.00	10.00
		("Born To Be With You" was produced by Phil Spector.)			
Warner Bros. 8234		Hey, My Love / Lover Boy Supreme	1976	.60	3.00
Warner Bros. 8258		The Way You Do The Things You Do / Lover Boy Supreme	1976	.60	3.00
Warner Bros. 8293		The Queen Of '59 / Oh, The Night	1976	.60	3.00
Warner Bros. 8406		Young Virgin Eyes (I'm All Wrapped Up) / Oh, The Night	1977	.60	3.00
Warner Bros. 814	(DJ)	The Wanderer / The Wanderer	1977	5.00	25.00
Lifesong 45082		Fire In The Night / Street Mama	1978	5.00	25.00
Lifesong 1765		Heart Of A Saturday Night /			
		You've Awakened Something In Me	1978	1.00	5.00
Lifesong 1770		Midtown American Street Gang / Guitar Queen	1978	1.00	5.00
Lifesong 1785		(I Used To Be A) Brooklyn Dodger / Streetheart Theme	1979	1.00	5.00

Label & Catalog #		A-Side/B-Side	Year	VG	NM
DIPLOMATS, THE					
Arock 1000		Unchained Melody / Cards On The Table	1964	2.00	10.00
Arock 1004		Here's A Heart / He's Got You Now	1964	2.00	10.00
Arock 1008		Help Me / Hey, Mr. Taxi Driver	1964	2.00	10.00
DIPLOMETTES, THE					
Diplomacy 24		My Intuition / Sit Yourself Down	196?	2.00	10.00
DIRT BAND, THE: *Refer to* THE NITTY GRITTY DIRT BAND					
DIRTY FILTHY MUD					
Worex 2340		The Forest Of Black / Morning Sunflower	1969	4.00	20.00
Worex 2340	(PS)	The Forest Of Black / Morning Sunflower	1969	6.00	30.00
DISCHORDS, THE					
Bonneville		Wipeout / Mary's Little Lamb	1963	6.00	30.00
DISCIPLES OF SHAFTESBURY, THE					
International Arts. 109		My Cup Is Full / Times Gone By	1966	3.00	15.00
DISCOTAYS, THE					
Scepter 1295		Monkey In A Cage / (B-side by The Guess Who)	1965	6.00	30.00
DISENTRI, TURNER					
Turner Disentri is a pseudonym for Bob Gaudio. Refer to The Royal Teens and The Four Seasons.					
Topix 6001		10,000,000 Tears / Spanish Lace	1960	20.00	100.00
DISRAELI					
Mantra 113		Spinnin' Round / What Will The New Day Bring	1968	1.20	6.00
Mantra 114		Say You Love Me / I've Seen Her One Time	1969	1.20	6.00
Mantra 115		The Lonely One / You Can't Do That	196?	1.20	6.00
Mantra		Tomorrow's Day / Humidity	196?	1.20	6.00
DIXON, BILLY, & THE TOPICS					
Refer to The Topics.					
Topix 6002		I Am All Alone / Trance	1960	30.00	150.00
Topix 6008		Lost Lullabye / Trance	1960	30.00	150.00
DIXON, WEBB					
Astro 102		Rock Awhile / Rock And Roll Angel	1959	5.00	25.00
DOBKINS, CARL, JR.					
Fraternity 794		Take Hold Of My Hand / That's Why I'm Asking	1958	4.00	20.00
Decca 30803		My Heart Is An Open Book / My Pledge To You	1959	3.00	15.00
Decca 30856		If You Don't Want My Lovin' / Love Is Everything	1959	3.00	15.00
Decca 31020		Lucky Devil / In My Heart	1959	3.00	15.00
Decca 31020	(PS)	Lucky Devil / In My Heart	1959	4.00	20.00
Decca 31088		Exclusively Yours / One Little Girl	1960	2.00	10.00
Decca 31143		Genie / A Different Kind Of Love	1960	2.00	10.00
Decca 31182		Love Light / Take Time Out	1960	2.00	10.00
Decca 31260		That's What I Call True Love / Pretty Little Girl In The Yellow Dress	1961	2.00	10.00
Decca 31301		Chance To Belong / Sawdust Dolly	1961	2.00	10.00
Decca 31353		Promise Me / Ask Me No Questions	1962	2.00	10.00
Atco 6283		If Teardrops Were Diamonds / I'm So Sorry, Little Girl	1963	2.00	10.00
Colpix 762		A Little Bit Later Down The Line / His Loss Is My Gain	1965	2.00	10.00
DOBRO, JIMMY					
Jimmy Dobro is a pseudonym for James Burton.					
Philips 40137		Swamp Fever / Everybody Listen To The Dobro	1963	5.00	25.00
DOBRO COMBO, LON					
Troy 1003		Mid-Night Surf / Undercurrent	1963	7.00	35.00
DR. JOHN (THE NIGHT TRIPPER)					
Dr. John is a pseudonym for Mac Rebennack.					
Atco 6882		Iko Iko / Huey Smith Medley	1972	1.00	5.00
Atco 6900		Let The Good Times Roll / Stack-A-Lee	1972	.80	4.00
Atco 6914		Right Place, Wrong Time / I Been Hoodooed	1973	.80	4.00
Atco 6937		Such A Night / Cold Cold Cold	1973	.80	4.00
Atco 6957		(Everybody Wanna Get Rich) Rite Away / Mos' Scocious	1974	.80	4.00

Label & Catalog #		A-Side/B-Side	Year	VG	NM
DOCTOR ROSS					
Sun 193		Come Back, Baby / Chicago Breakdown	1953	75.00	300.00
Sun 212		The Boogie Disease / Juke Box Boogie	1954	——	——
		(Rare. Estimated near mint value $500-1,000.)			
DR. SHOCK					
Greentree 1701		The Bloody / Let There Be Fright	196?	2.40	12.00
DR. WEST'S MEDICINE (SHOW & JUNK) BAND					
Dr. West features Norman Greenbaum.					
Go Go 00100		The Eggplant That Ate Chicago /			
		You Can't Fight City Hall Blues	1966	1.00	5.00
Go Go 00102		Gondoliers, Shakespeares, Overseers, Playboys			
		And Bums / Daddy, I Know	1967	1.00	5.00
Go Go 00102	(PS)	Gondoliers, Shakespeares, Overseers, Playboys			
		And Bums / Daddy, I Know	1967	2.00	10.00
Go Go 00104		You Can Fly / The Circus Left Town Today	1967	1.00	5.00
Go Go 00106		Bullets Laverne / Jigsaw	1968	1.00	5.00
DODD, DICK					
Dick Dodd originally recorded with The Standells.					
Tower 447		Little Sister / Lonely Weekends	1968	2.00	10.00
Tower 447	(PS)	Little Sister / Lonely Weekends	1968	4.00	20.00
Tower 490		Fanny / Don't Be Ashamed To Call My Name	1968	2.00	10.00
Attarack 102		Guilty / Requiem 820	1970	2.00	10.00
DODD, JIMMY: *Refer to* ANNETTE					
DODGERS, THE					
Island 058		Don't Let Them Be Wrong / Get To You	1978	.80	4.00
Polydor 14515		Love On The Rebound / Come Out Fighting	1978	.80	4.00
DODO, JOE, & THE GROOVERS					
RCA Victor 47-7207		Goin' Steady / Groovy	1958	2.00	10.00
DODSON, HERB					
Stacey 954		Disc Jockey's Christmas Eve / What Is A Disc Jockey?	1962	2.00	10.00
DOGG, REDD					
Del-Fi 4152		Who's Lonesome Tonight, Act 3? (Part 1) /			
		Who's Lonesome Tonight, Act 3? (Part 2)	1961	3.00	15.00
DOHERTY, DENNY					
Denny Doherty originally recorded with The Mugwumps and The Mamas & The Papas.					
Paramount 0286		You'll Never Know / Good Night And Good Morning	1972	.80	4.00
Columbia 45779		Baby, Catch The Moon / Indian Girl	1973	1.00	5.00
Columbia 45866		My Song / Indian Girl	1973	1.00	5.00
Playboy 6066	(DJ)	Simone / Simone	1976	1.00	5.00
		(Stock copies of Playboy 6066 may not exist.)			
DOLENZ, MICKEY					
Mickey Dolenz also recorded with The Monkees and Starship.					
Challenge 59353		Don't Do It / Plastic Symphony III	1967	3.00	15.00
Challenge 59353	(PS)	Don't Do It / Plastic Symphony III	1967	4.00	20.00
Challenge 59372		Huff Puff / (The Obvious) Fate	1967	3.00	15.00
Challenge 59372	(PS)	Huff Puff / (The Obvious) Fate	1967	8.00	40.00
MGM 14309	(DJ)	Easy On You / Oh, Someone	1971	2.00	10.00
MGM 14309		Easy On You / Oh, Someone	1971	4.00	20.00
MGM 14395	(DJ)	A Lover's Prayer / Unattended In The Dungeon	1972	2.00	10.00
MGM 14395		A Lover's Prayer / Unattended In The Dungeon	1972	4.00	20.00
Romar 710	(DJ)	Daybreak / Love War	1973	2.00	10.00
Romar 710		Daybreak / Love War	1973	4.00	20.00
Romar 715	(DJ)	Buddy Holly Tribute / Oh, She's Young	1974	2.00	10.00
Romar 715		Buddy Holly Tribute / Oh, She's Young	1974	4.00	20.00
Chrysalis 2297		Alicia / Love Light	1979	1.00	5.00
DOLENZ & JONES					
Mickey Dolenz and Davey Jones of The Monkees.					
Bell 986	(DJ)	Do It In The Name Of Love / Lady Jane	1972	4.00	20.00
Bell 986		Do It In The Name Of Love / Lady Jane	1972	8.00	40.00
MCA	(UK)	Gotta Get Up / Lifeline / It's A Jungle Out There	1978	3.00	15.00
DOLENZ, JONES, BOYCE & HART					
Mickey Dolenz, Davey Jones, Tommy Boyce and Bobby Hart.					
Capitol 4180		I Remember The Feeling / You And I	1975	2.00	10.00
Capitol 4271		I Love You (And I'm Glad I Said It) / Savin' My Love For You	1975	2.00	10.00

Label & Catalog #		A-Side/B-Side	Year	VG	NM
DOLENZ, JONES & TORK					
Mickey Dolenz, Davey Jones and Peter Tork of The Monkees.					
Fan Club/CDS 700		Christmas Is My Time Of Year / White Christmas	1976	4.00	20.00
Fan Club/CDS 700	(PS)	Christmas Is My Time Of Year / White Christmas	1976	6.00	30.00
DOLPHINS, THE					
Shad 5020		Tell Tale Kisses / I Found True Love	1960	7.00	35.00
Empress 102		One More For The Road / Rainbow's End	1961	3.00	15.00
Fraternity 937		I Don't Want To Go On Without You / Hey-Da-Da-Now	1964	3.00	15.00
Fraternity 940		Little Donna / Beautiful Woman	1965	3.00	15.00
DOLPHINS, THE					
Gemini 501		Dance / Pony Race	1962	3.00	15.00
Laurie 3202		Hang On / Swingin' Soiree	1963	4.00	20.00
Yorkshire 125		Surfing East Coast / I Should Have Stayed	196?	6.00	30.00
DOMINEERS, THE					
Roulette 4245		Nothing Can Go Wrong / Richie, Come On Down	1960	5.00	25.00
DOMINIONS, THE					
Graves 1091		Spanish Harlem / I Need Her	196?	3.00	15.00
DOMINO, BOBBY					
Donna 1339		Marilyn / Your Love For Me	195?	5.00	25.00
DOMINO, FATS					
Imperial 5099		Korea Blues / Every Night About This Time	1950	150.00	600.00
Imperial 5114		Tired Of Crying / What's The Matter, Baby?	1950	100.00	400.00
Imperial 5123		Don't You Lie To Me / Sometimes I Wonder	1951	100.00	400.00
Imperial 5138		No, No Baby / Right From Wrong	1951	100.00	400.00
Imperial 5167		You Know I Miss You / I'll Be Gone	1952	100.00	400.00
Imperial 5180		Goin' Home / Reeling And Rocking	1952	75.00	300.00
Imperial 5197		Poor, Poor Me / Trust In Me	1952	30.00	150.00
Imperial 5209		How Long / Dreaming	1952	12.00	60.00
Imperial 5209		How Long / Dreaming (Red vinyl)	1952	40.00	200.00
Imperial 5220		Nobody Loves Me / Cheatin'	1953	12.00	60.00
Imperial 5220		Nobody Loves Me / Cheatin' (Red vinyl)	1953	40.00	200.00
Imperial 5231		Going To The River / Mardis Gras In New Orleans	1953	15.00	75.00
Imperial 5231		Going To The River / Mardis Gras In New Orleans (Red vinyl)	1953	75.00	300.00
Imperial 5240		Please Don't Leave Me / The Girl I Love	1953	8.00	40.00
Imperial 5251		Rose Mary / You Said You Loved Me	1953	9.00	45.00
Imperial 5262		Somethin' Wrong / Don't Leave Me This Way	1954	7.00	35.00
Imperial 5272		You Done Me Wrong / Little Schoolgirl	1954	9.00	45.00
Imperial 5283		Baby, Please / Where Did You Stay?	1954	9.00	45.00
		— Original Imperial singles above have blue labels with script print.—			
Imperial 5301		You Can Pack Your Suitcase / I Lived My Life	1954	5.00	25.00
Imperial 5313		Love Me / Don't You Hear Me Callin' You?	1954	5.00	25.00
Imperial 5323		I Know / Thinking Of You	1955	7.00	35.00
Imperial 5323		I Know / Thinking Of You (Red vinyl)	1955	100.00	400.00
Imperial 5340		Don't You Know / Helping Hand	1955	6.00	30.00
Imperial 5348		Ain't It A Shame / La La	1955	5.00	25.00
Imperial 5357		All By Myself / Trouble Of My Own	1955	10.00	50.00
		— Original Imperial singles above have red labels with script print.—			
Imperial 5357		All By Myself / Trouble Of My Own	1955	4.00	20.00
Imperial 5369		Poor Me / I Can't Go On	1955	4.00	20.00
Imperial 5375		Don't Blame It On Me / Bo Weevil	1956	4.00	20.00
Imperial 5386		I'm In Love Again / My Blue Heaven	1956	4.00	20.00
Imperial 5396		When My Dreamboat Comes Home / So Long	1956	4.00	20.00
Imperial 5407		Blueberry Hill / Honey Chile	1956	4.00	20.00
Imperial 5417		Blue Monday / What's The Reason I'm Not Pleasing You?	1957	4.00	20.00
Imperial 5428		I'm Walkin' / I'm In The Mood For Love	1957	4.00	20.00
Imperial 5428	(PS)	I'm Walkin' / I'm In The Mood For Love	1957	8.00	40.00
Imperial 5442		Valley Of Tears / It's You I Love	1957	4.00	20.00
Imperial 5454		What Will I Tell My Heart / When I See You	1957	4.00	20.00
		— Original Imperial singles above have red or maroon labels with block print.—			
Imperial 5467		Wait And See / I Still Love You	1957	4.00	20.00
Imperial 5477		The Big Beat / I Want You To Know	1958	4.00	20.00
Imperial 5477	(PS)	The Big Beat / I Want You To Know	1958	10.00	50.00
Imperial 5492		Yes, My Darling / Don't You Know I Love You?	1958	4.00	20.00
Imperial 5515		Sick And Tired / No, No	1958	4.00	20.00
Imperial 5526		Little Mary / Prisoner's Song	1958	4.00	20.00
Imperial 5537		It Must Be Love / Young School Girl	1958	4.00	20.00
Imperial 5553		Whole Lotta Loving / Coquette	1959	4.00	20.00
		— Original Imperial singles above have red, maroon or black labels with block print.—			
Imperial 5569		When The Saints Go Marching In / Telling Lies	1959	2.00	10.00
Imperial 5585		I'm Ready / Margie	1959	2.00	10.00

Label & Catalog #		A-Side/B-Side	Year	VG	NM
Imperial 5606		I Want To Walk You Home / I'm Gonna Be A Wheel Some Day	1959	2.00	10.00
Imperial 5606	(PS)	I Want To Walk You Home / I'm Gonna Be A Wheel Some Day	1959	8.00	40.00
Imperial 5629		Be My Guest / I've Been Around	1959	2.00	10.00
Imperial 5629	(PS)	Be My Guest / I've Been Around	1959	7.00	35.00
Imperial 5645		Country Boy / If You Need Me	1960	2.00	10.00
Imperial 5660		Tell Me That You Love Me / Before I Grow Too Old	1960	2.00	10.00
Imperial 5675		Walking To New Orleans / Don't Come Knockin'	1960	2.00	10.00
Imperial 5687		Put Your Arms Around Me, Honey / Three Nights A Week	1960	2.00	10.00
Imperial 5704		My Girl Josephine / Natural Born Lover	1960	2.00	10.00
Imperial 5723		What A Price / Ain't That Just Like Women	1961	2.00	10.00
Imperial 5734		Shu Rah / Fell In Love On Monday	1961	2.00	10.00
Imperial 5753		It Keeps Rainin' / I Just Cry	1961	2.00	10.00
Imperial 5764		Let The Four Winds Blow / Good Hearted Man	1961	2.00	10.00
Imperial 5779		What A Party / Rockin' Bicycle	1961	2.00	10.00
Imperial 5796		I Hear You Knockin' / Jambalaya	1961	2.00	10.00
Imperial 5816		You Win Again / Ida Jane	1962	2.00	10.00
Imperial 5833		My Heart Is Breaking / My Real Name	1962	2.00	10.00
Imperial 5863		Nothing New / Dance With Mr. Domino	1962	2.00	10.00
Imperial 5875		Did You Ever See A Dream Walk? / Stop The Clock	1962	2.00	10.00
Imperial 5895		Won't You Come On Back / Hands Across The Table	1963	2.00	10.00
Imperial 5909		Hum Diddy Doo / Those Eyes	1963	2.00	10.00
Imperial 5937		You Always Hurt The One You Love / Trouble Blues	1963	2.00	10.00
Imperial 5959		Isle Of Capri / True Confession	1963	2.00	10.00
Imperial 5980		One Night / I Can't Go On This Way	1963	2.00	10.00
Imperial 5999		Your Cheatin' Heart / Goin' Home	1963	2.00	10.00
Imperial 66005		I Can't Give You Anything But Love / Goin' Home	1964	2.00	10.00
Imperial 66016		Your Cheatin' Heart / When I Was Young	1964	2.00	10.00
ABC-Paramount 10444		There Goes My Heart Again / Can't Go On Without You	1963	1.60	8.00
ABC-Paramount 10475		When I'm Walking / I've Got A Right To Cry	1963	1.60	8.00
ABC-Paramount 10484		Red Sails In The Sunset / Songs For Rosemary	1963	1.60	8.00
ABC-Paramount 10512		Who Cares? / Just A Lonely Man	1963	1.60	8.00
ABC-Paramount 10531		Lazy Lady / I Don't Want To Set The World On Fire	1964	1.60	8.00
ABC-Paramount 10545		Something You Got, Baby / If You Don't Know What Love Is	1964	1.60	8.00
ABC-Paramount 10567		Mary, Oh Mary / Packin' Up	1964	1.60	8.00
ABC-Paramount 10584		Sally Was A Good Old Girl / For You	1964	1.60	8.00
ABC-Paramount 10596		Heartbreak Hill / Kansas City	1964	1.60	8.00
ABC-Paramount 10644		Let Me Call You Sweetheart / Good Night, Sweetheart	1965	1.60	8.00
ABC-Paramount 10631		Why Don't You Do Right? / Wigs	1965	1.60	8.00
ABC-Paramount 10902		I'm Living Right / I Don't Want To Set The World On Fire	1967	1.60	8.00
Mercury 72463		I Done Got Over It / I Left My Heart In San Francisco	1965	1.60	8.00
Mercury 72485		It's Never Too Late / That's What You Got	1965	1.60	8.00
Mercury 72485	(PS)	It's Never Too Late / That's What You Got	1965	4.00	20.00
Reprise 0696		Honest Papas Love Their Mamas Better / One For The Highway	1968	2.00	10.00
Reprise 0763		Lady Madonna / One For The Highway	1968	2.00	10.00
Reprise 0775		Lovely Rita / Wait Till It Happens To You	1968	2.00	10.00
Reprise 0810		Everybody's Got Something To Hide Except For Me And My Baby / So Swell When You're Well	1968	2.00	10.00
Reprise 0891		Have You Seen My Baby? / Let Me Belong To You	1968	2.00	10.00
Reprise 0944		New Orleans Ain't The Same / Sweet Patootie	1968	2.00	10.00
		—Extended Play Albums—			
Imperial 127		Fats Domino (Red label with script print)	1955	40.00	200.00
Imperial 127		Fats Domino (Maroon label)	1955	30.00	150.00
Imperial 138		Fats Domino	1956	20.00	100.00
Imperial 139		Fats Domino	1956	20.00	100.00
Imperial 140		Fats Domino	1956	20.00	100.00
Imperial 141		Rock And Rollin'	1956	20.00	100.00
Imperial 142		Rock And Rollin'	1956	20.00	100.00
Imperial 143		Rock And Rollin'	1956	20.00	100.00
Imperial 144		This Is Fats Domino	1956	20.00	100.00
Imperial 145		This Is Fats Domino	1956	20.00	100.00
Imperial 146		This Is Fats Domino	1956	20.00	100.00
Imperial 147		Here Comes Fats	1957	20.00	100.00
Imperial 148		Here Stands Fats Domino	1957	20.00	100.00
Imperial 149		Here Stands Fats Domino	1957	20.00	100.00
Imperial 150		Here Stands Fats Domino	1957	20.00	100.00
Imperial 151		Cookin' With Fats	1955	20.00	100.00
Imperial 152		Rockin' With Fats	1957	20.00	100.00
ABC 479	(33)	Fats On Fire (Jukebox EP)	1968	4.00	20.00
ABC 510	(33)	Getaway With Fats Domino (Jukebox EP)	1968	4.00	20.00

DON & DEWEY
Don is Salvatore Bono a.k.a. Sonny Bono.

Specialty 672		The Letter / Koko Joe	1960	3.00	15.00
Rush 1002		Soul Motion / Stretchin' Out	196?	2.00	10.00
Rush 1003		Don't Ever Leave Me /	196?	2.00	10.00

Label & Catalog #		A-Side/B-Side	Year	VG	NM
DON & JUAN					
Big Top 3079		What's Your Name? / Chicken Necks	1962	3.00	15.00
Big Top 3106		Two Fools Are We / Pot Luck	1962	3.00	15.00
Big Top 3121		Magic Wand / What I Really Meant To Say	1962	7.00	35.00
Big Top 3145		True Love Never Runs Smooth / Is It Alright If I Love You?	1963	10.00	50.00
Mala 447		Peddling My Love / Molinda	1963	2.00	10.00
Mala 469		Could This Be Love? / Lonely Man	1963	2.00	10.00
DON & HIS ROSES					
Dot 15755		Since You Went Away To School / Right Now	1958	10.00	50.00
Dot 15874		Leave Those Cats Alone / Don't Try To Change Me	195?	10.00	50.00
DON & THE CHEVELLS					
Don is Don Ciccone, who later recorded with The Critters and The Four Seasons.					
Speedway 1000		Inner Limits / The Only Girl	196?	7.00	35.00
DON & THE GALAXIES					
Fox/Fidel 3		Sundown / Avalanche	1962	2.00	10.00
Fox/Fidel 3	(PS)	Sundown / Avalanche	1962	6.00	30.00
DON & THE GOODTIMES					
Don is Don Galucci. Refer to The Kingsmen; Touch; Jim Valley.					
Wand 165		Turn On / Make It			
Wand 184		Straight Scepter / There's Something On Your Mind	1965	.80	4.00
Jerden 762		Little Sally Tease / You'll Never Walk Alone	1965	.80	4.00
Dunhill 4008		Little Sally Tease / Little Green Thing	1965	1.00	5.00
Dunhill 4015		I'll Be Down Forever / Big Big Knight	1965	.80	4.00
Dunhill 4022		Hey There, Mary Mae / Sweets For My Sweet	1965	1.00	5.00
Piccadilly 223		You Were A Child / I Hate To Hate You	1966	.80	4.00
Jerden 805		Blue Turns To Grey / I'm Real	1966	.80	4.00
Jerden 808		You Were A Child / I Hate To Hate You	1966	.80	4.00
Epic 10145		I Could Be So Good To You / And It's So Good	1967	.80	4.00
Epic 10145	(PS)	I Could Be So Good To You / And It's So Good	1967	2.00	10.00
Epic 10199		Happy And Me / If You Love Her Cherish Her And Such	1967	.80	4.00
Epic 10241		Sally!! (Studio-A At 6 O' Clock In The Morning) / Bambi	1967	.80	4.00
Epic 10280		May My Heart Be Cast In Stone / Ball Of Fire	1968	.80	4.00
Burdette 3		Colors Of Life / You Did It Before	1968	1.00	5.00
DON RAYS, THE					
Capco 103		Pacific Honky Tonk / (B-side by Cleve Herman)	1963	6.00	30.00
DONATO, MIKE					
PM 101		Dora / Summertime Love	196?	4.00	20.00
DONEGAN, LONNIE					
London 1650		Rock Island Line / John Henry	1956	2.00	10.00
Mercury 70872		Lost John / Stewball	1956	2.00	10.00
Dot 15911		Does Your Chewing Gum Lose Its Flavor (On The Bedpost Over Night?) / Aunt Rhody	1959	2.00	10.00
Dot 15953		Fort Worth Jail / Whoa Back, Buck	1959	1.20	6.00
Dot 16263		Light From The Lighthouse / Whoa Back, Buck	1961	1.20	6.00
Atlantic 2058		My Old Man's A Dustman / The Golden Vanity	1960	1.20	6.00
Atlantic 2063		Take This Hammer / Nobody Understands Me	1960	1.20	6.00
Atlantic 2081		Junco Partner / Lorelei	1960	1.20	6.00
Atlantic 2108		Have A Drink On Me / Beyond The Sunset	1961	1.20	6.00
Atlantic 2123		Wreck Of The John B. / Sorry, But I'm Gonna Have To Pass	1961	1.20	6.00
Hickory 1274		Bad News / Interstate 40	1964	.80	4.00
Hickory 1267		Fisherman's Luck / There's A Big Wheel	1964	.80	4.00
DONLAYS, THE					
Brent 7033		Bad Boy / Devil In His Heart	1962	4.00	20.00
DONNA MARIE					
Coral 62445		Eddie Wasn't There / Mankiller	1965	2.00	10.00
Columbia 44402		The Penthouse / Pretty Thing	1968	.80	4.00
Columbia 44402	(PS)	The Penthouse / Pretty Thing	1968	.80	4.00
DONNELL, DOUG, & THE HOT RODS					
Alton 602		On Our Way From School / You're My Girl	1959	3.00	15.00
DONNER, RAL (& THE STARFIRES)					
Scottie 1310		Tell Me Why / That's All Right With Me	1959	10.00	50.00
Gone 5102		Girl Of My Best Friend / It's Been A Long Time (First pressings have a black label.)	1960	5.00	25.00
Gone 5102		Girl Of My Best Friend / It's Been A Long Time	1961	3.00	15.00
Gone 5108		To Love / And Then	1961	5.00	25.00
Gone 5108		You Don't Know What You've Got (Until You Lose It) / So Close To Heaven	1961	3.00	15.00

Label & Catalog #		A-Side/B-Side	Year	VG	NM
Gone 5114		Please Don't Go / I Didn't Figure On Him To Come Back	1961	3.00	15.00
Gone 5119		School Of Heartbreakers / Because They're Young	1961	5.00	25.00
Gone 5121		She's Everything (I Wanted You To Be) / Will You Love Me In Heaven?	1961	3.00	15.00
Gone 5121		She's Everything (I Wanted You To Be) / Because We're Young	1961	4.00	20.00
Gone 5125		(What A Sad Way) To Love Someone / Will You Love Me In Heaven?	1962	3.00	15.00
Gone 5129		Loveless Life / Bells Of Love	1962	3.00	15.00
Gone 5133		To Love / Sweetheart	1962	3.00	15.00
		—Gone singles above have multi-color label with a clown logo.—			
End GG-19		You Don't Know What You've Got (Until You Lose It) / She's Everything	1963	4.00	20.00
Tau 105		Loneliness Of A Star / And Then	1963	5.00	25.00
Reprise 20135		(These Are The Things That Make Up) Christmas Day / Second Miracle	1963	5.00	25.00
Reprise 20141		I Got Burned / A Tear In My Eye	1963	5.00	25.00
Reprise 20141	(PS)	I Got Burned / A Tear In My Eye	1963	30.00	150.00
Reprise 20176		I Wish This Night Would Never End / Don't Put Your Heart In His Hand	1963	6.00	30.00
Reprise 20192		Run, Little Linda / Beyond The Heartbreak	1963	6.00	30.00
Fontana 1502		You Finally Said Something Good / Poison Ivy League	1964	4.00	20.00
Fontana 1502		Tear In My Eye / Poison Ivy League	1964	4.00	20.00
Fontana 1515		Good Lovin' / The Other Side Of Me	1964	4.00	20.00
Smash 34774	(DJ)	Good Lovin' / The Other Side Of Me	1964	6.00	30.00
		(Stock copies of Smash 34774 may not exist.)			
Red Bird 057		Love Isn't Like That / It Will Only Make You Love Me More	1965	7.00	35.00
Rising Sons 714		Just A Little Sunshine In The Rain / If I Promise	1968	2.00	10.00
MJ 222		(All Of A Sudden) My Heart Sings / Lovin' Place	1971	1.00	5.00
MJ 222	(PS)	(All Of A Sudden) My Heart Sings / Lovin' Place	1971	1.00	5.00
Sunlight 1006		Wait A Minute / Don't Let It Slip Away	1972	1.60	8.00
Starfire 100		Wait A Minute / Don't Let It Slip Away (White vinyl)	1972	1.60	8.00
Chicago Fire 7402		The Wedding Song / Godfather Per Me	1974	1.60	8.00
Mid-Eagle 101		(If I Had My) Life To Live Over / Lost	1974	2.00	10.00
Mid-Eagle 275		The Wedding Song / Godfather Per Me	1974	1.20	6.00
Thunder 7801		The Day The Beat Stopped / Rock On Me	1978	1.00	5.00
Starfire 103		Christmas Day / (Green vinyl)	1978	.60	3.00
Starfire 103	(PS)	Christmas Day / (Green vinyl)	1978	.60	3.00
Starfire 114		Rip It Up / Don't Leave Me Now	1979	.60	3.00
Starfire 114	(PS)	Rip It Up / Don't Leave Me Now	1979	.60	3.00
Starfire 114		Rip It Up / Don't Leave Me Now Picture Disc	1979	2.00	10.00

DONNIE & THE COR-VETS

Label & Catalog #		A-Side/B-Side	Year	VG	NM
Aertaun 1104		Some Little Someone / The Skip	1965	1.20	6.00

DONNIE & THE DARLINGTONS

Label & Catalog #		A-Side/B-Side	Year	VG	NM
ABC-Paramount 10633		Poppin' My Clutch / Since Grandpa Got A Rail Job	1965	4.00	20.00

DONNIE & THE DEL CHORDS [DONNIE & THE DELCHORDS]

Label & Catalog #		A-Side/B-Side	Year	VG	NM
Taurus 352		So Lonely / When You're Alone	1961	4.00	20.00
Epic 9495		So Lonely / When You're Alone	1962	2.00	10.00
Taurus 357		I Don't Care / I'll Be With You In Apple Blossom Time	1963	4.00	20.00
Taurus 361		That Old Feeling / Transylvania Mist	1963	4.00	20.00
Taurus 363		I Found Heaven / Be With You	1963	4.00	20.00
Taurus 364		I'm In The Mood For Love / I've Got A Woman	1963	3.00	15.00

DONNIE & THE DREAMERS

Label & Catalog #		A-Side/B-Side	Year	VG	NM
Decca 31312	(DJ)	Ruby, My Love / Carole	1961	6.00	30.00
Decca 31312		Ruby, My Love / Carole	1961	10.00	50.00
Whale 500		Count Every Star / Dorothy	1961	4.00	20.00
Whale 505		My Memories Of You / Teenage Love	1961	5.00	25.00

DONNY & THE BI-LANGOS

Label & Catalog #		A-Side/B-Side	Year	VG	NM
Colton 101		I'm Not A Know-It-All /	196?	5.00	25.00

DONOVAN (DONOVAN LEITCH)

Label & Catalog #		A-Side/B-Side	Year	VG	NM
Hickory 1309		Catch The Wind / Why Do You Treat Me Like You Do?	1965	1.20	6.00
Hickory 1324		Colours / Josie	1965	1.20	6.00
Hickory 1338		Universal Soldier / Do You Hear Me Now?	1965	1.20	6.00
Hickory 1375		Little Tin Soldier / You're Gonna Need Somebody On Your Mind	1965	1.20	6.00
Hickory 1402		To Try For The Sun / Turquoise	1965	1.20	6.00
Hickory 1417		Hey Gyp / The War Drags On	1966	1.20	6.00
Hickory 1470		Sunny Goodge Street / Summer Day Reflection Song	1966	1.20	6.00
Hickory 1492		Why Do You Treat Me Like You Do? / Do You Hear Me Now?	1965	1.20	6.00
Epic 10045		Sunshine Superman / The Trip	1966	1.00	5.00
Epic 10045	(PS)	Sunshine Superman / The Trip	1966	2.00	10.00

Label & Catalog #		A-Side / B-Side	Year	VG	NM
Epic 10098		Mellow Yellow / Sunny South Kensington	1966	1.00	5.00
Epic 10098	(PS)	Mellow Yellow / Sunny South Kensington	1966	2.00	10.00
Epic 10127		Epistle To Dippy / Preachin' Love	1967	.80	4.00
Epic 10127	(PS)	Epistle To Dippy / Preachin' Love	1967	1.20	6.00
Epic 10212		There Is A Mountain / Sand And Foam	1967	.80	4.00
Epic 10253		Wear Your Love Like Heaven / Oh, Gosh	1967	.80	4.00
Epic 10253	(PS)	Wear Your Love Like Heaven / Oh, Gosh	1967	1.20	6.00
Epic 10300		Jennifer Juniper / Poor Cow	1968	.80	4.00
Epic 10300	(PS)	Jennifer Juniper / Poor Cow	1968	1.20	6.00
Epic 10345		Hurdy Gurdy Man / Teen Angel	1968	.80	4.00
Epic 10345	(PS)	Hurdy Gurdy Man / Teen Angel	1968	1.20	6.00
Epic 10393		Lalena / Aye, My Love	1968	.80	4.00
Epic 10393	(PS)	Lalena / Aye, My Love	1968	1.20	6.00
Epic 10434		Atlantis / To Susan On The West Coast Waiting	1969	.80	4.00
Epic 10434	(PS)	Atlantis / To Susan On The West Coast Waiting	1969	1.20	6.00
Epic 10510		Goo Goo Barabajagal / Trudi	1969	.80	4.00
Epic 10510	(PS)	Goo Goo Barabajagal / Trudi	1969	1.20	6.00
		("Goo Goo Barabajagal" features The Jeff Beck Group.)			
Epic 10649		Riki Tiki Tavi / Roots Of Oak	1970	.80	4.00
Epic 10649	(PS)	Riki Tiki Tavi / Roots Of Oak	1970	1.20	6.00
Epic 10694		Celia Of The Seals / Song Of The Wandering Aengus	1971	.80	4.00
Epic 10694	(PS)	Celia Of The Seals / Song Of The Wandering Aengus	1971	1.20	6.00
Epic 10983		I Like You / Earth Sign Man	1973	.40	2.00
Epic 11023		Maria Magenta / Intergalactic Laxative	1973	.40	2.00
Epic 11108		Sailing Homeward / Yellow Star	1974	.40	2.00
Epic 50016		Rock 'N' Roll With Me / Divine Daze Of Deathless Delight	1974	.40	2.00
Epic 50077		Rock And Roll Soldier / How Silly	1975	.40	2.00
Epic 50237		Dark-Eyed Blue Jean Angel / Well Known Has-Been	1976	.40	2.00
Arista 0280		Dare To Be Different / International Man	1977	.40	2.00

DONS, THE

Label & Catalog #		A-Side / B-Side	Year	VG	NM
Heartbeat 1		Dream Girl / Marcheta	196?	2.00	10.00

DOO, DICKEY, & THE DON'TS

Label & Catalog #		A-Side / B-Side	Year	VG	NM
Swan 4001		Click-Clack / Did You Cry?	1957	3.00	15.00
Swan 4006		Flip Top Box / Nee Nee Na Na Na Na Nu Nu	1958	3.00	15.00
Swan 4014		Leave Me Alone / Wild Party	1958	3.00	15.00
Swan 4025		Teardrops Will Fall / Come With Us	1959	3.00	15.00
Swan 4033		Ballad Of A Train / Dear Heart, Don't Cry	1959	3.00	15.00
Swan 4046		Wabash Cannon Ball / Drums Of Richard A. Doo	1959	3.00	15.00
United Artists 238		Teen Scene / Pity Pity	1960	2.00	10.00
United Artists 362		The Judge / Little Dog Cried	1961	2.00	10.00
Ascot 2178		Click Clack '65 / Don't Count Me Out	1965	1.00	5.00

DOOR NOBS, THE

Label & Catalog #		A-Side / B-Side	Year	VG	NM
Viv 4625		Hi-Fi Baby / I Need Your Lovin'	1965	4.00	20.00

DOORS, THE

The Doors are John Densmore, Robbie Krieger, Ray Manzarek and Jim Morrison.

Label & Catalog #		A-Side / B-Side	Year	VG	NM
Elektra 45611		Break On Through / End Of The Night (Yellow label)	1966	4.00	20.00
Elektra 45611		Break On Through / End Of The Night	1967	2.00	10.00
Elektra 45611	(PS)	Break On Through / End Of The Night	1967	8.00	40.00
Elektra 45615		Light My Fire / Crystal Ship	1967	1.60	8.00
Elektra 45621		People Are Strange / Unhappy Girl	1967	1.60	8.00
Elektra 45621	(PS)	People Are Strange / Unhappy Girl	1967	4.00	20.00
Elektra 45624		Love Me Two Times / Moonlight Drive	1967	1.60	8.00
Elektra 45628		The Unknown Soldier / We Could Be So Good Together	1968	2.00	10.00
Elektra 45628	(PS)	The Unknown Soldier / We Could Be So Good Together	1968	3.00	15.00
Elektra 45635		Hello, I Love You / Love Street	1968	1.20	6.00
Elektra 45646		Touch Me / Wild Child	1968	1.20	6.00
Elektra 45656		Wishful, Sinful / Who Scared You?	1969	1.20	6.00
Elektra 45663		Tell All The People / Easy Ride	1969	1.20	6.00
Elektra 45663	(PS)	Tell All The People / Easy Ride	1969	3.00	15.00
Elektra 45675		Runnin' Blue / Do It	1969	1.00	5.00
Elektra 45685		You Make Me Real / Roadhouse Blues	1970	1.00	5.00
Elektra 45726		Love Her Madly / (You Need Meat) Don't Go No Further	1971	1.00	5.00
Elektra 45738		Riders On The Storm / Changeling	1971	1.00	5.00
Elektra 45757		Tightrope Ride / Variety Is The Spice Of Life	1971	1.00	5.00
Elektra 45768		Ships With Sails / In The Eye Of The Sun	1972	1.00	5.00
Elektra 45793		Get Up And Dance / Treetrunk	1972	1.00	5.00
Elektra 45807		The Mosquito / It Slipped My Mind	1972	1.00	5.00
Elektra 45825		Piano Bird / Good Rockin'	1972	1.00	5.00
		(Elektra 45757-825 do not feature Jim Morrison.)			
Elektra 46005		Roadhouse Blues / Albinoni / Adagio	1979	.60	3.00
Elektra 12400		The End / Delta	1980	.60	3.00
Elektra 69770		Gloria / Love Me Two Times	1983	.60	3.00
Elektra 69770	(PS)	Gloria / Love Me Two Times	1983	.60	3.00

Label & Catalog #	A-Side/B-Side	Year	VG	NM
DOREN, VAN				
Hickory 1262	Surfin' Liza / Huntington Beach	1964	2.00	10.00
DORIES, THE				
Dore 528	Tragedy Of Love / I Loved Him So	1960	5.00	25.00
Dore 556	They Go Ape / Don't Jump	1960	2.00	10.00
Dore 629	Stompin' Sh-Boom / Breakup	1962	3.00	15.00
DORMAN, HAROLD				
Rita 1003	Mountain Of Love / To Be With You	1960	3.00	15.00
Rita 1008	River Of Tears / I'll Come Running	1960	3.00	15.00
Rita 1012	Moved To Kansas City / Take A Chance On Me	1960	3.00	15.00
Sun 362	There They Go / I'll Stick By You	1961	3.00	15.00
Sun 370	Uncle Jonah's Place / Just One Step	1961	3.00	15.00
Sun 377	Wait 'Til Saturday Night / In The Beginning	1962	3.00	15.00
DORSALS, THE (WITH THE GATORMEN)				
Camelot 120	Namu / Killer Whale	196?	1.20	6.00
DORSEY, GERRY				
Gerry Dorsey later recorded as Englebert Humperdinck.				
Hickory 1337	Baby, Turn Around / Do The Things	1965	2.00	10.00
DORSEY, MEL				
Orbit 105	I Ain't Gonna Take It No More / Here In My Heart	195?	10.00	50.00
DOTS, THE: *Refer to* **LENNY CAPELLO**				
DOTSON BROTHERS, THE				
Loran 1027	Rock-In Ricksha / Orbit	195?	7.00	35.00
DOUBLE DATERS, THE				
Carlton 457	Hey! Blondie Baby / The Senior Stroll	1958	3.00	15.00
Dot 15780	Beach Umbrella / Summer In The Mountains	1958	3.00	15.00
DOUBLE IV				
Capitol 4902	Magic Star (Telstar) / Is There Anything I Can Do For You?	1963	2.00	10.00
DOUBLE IMAGE				
Amy 985	Power Of Love / Say You Love Me	1967	2.00	10.00
DOUBLEDAY, BORIS, & HIS COMMAND PILOTS				
Pilotune 1	Go Go, You Pilots / Go Go, You Pilots (Part 2)	196?	2.00	10.00
DOUCET, SUZANNE				
Interphon 7704	Sei Mein Baby (Be My Baby) / Das Geht Doch Keinen	1964	2.50	12.00
DOUG & FREDDIE (WITH THE PYRAMIDS)				
Finer Arts 1001	Take A Chance On Love / I Know You're Lyin'	195?	15.00	75.00
Rendezvous 111	A Lover's Plea / I Believe In Love	195?	7.00	35.00
DOUGIE & THE DOLPHINS				
Angletone 542	Yesterday's Dreams / Double Date	196?	6.00	30.00
DOUGLAS, BOBBY, & THE CONSPIRACY				
Conspiracy 101	You Walked Into My Life / Together	196?	2.00	10.00
DOUGLAS, GARY				
Antique 0013	Santa Goofed / Santa Caught A Cold	1960	2.00	10.00
DOUGLAS, RONNY				
Everest 19413	Run, Run, Run / You Say	1961	2.00	10.00
Everest 19425	Candy And Gum / You'll Come Back	1961	2.00	10.00
Epic 9843	Say Didd-I-Lee Hey / Worth Waiting For	1965	2.00	10.00
DOUGLAS, SCOTT				
Apogee 105	The Beatles' Barber / The Wall Paper Song	1964	3.00	15.00
DOUGLAS, SCOTT, & THE VENTURE QUINTET				
The Quintet is The Ventures.				
Blue Horizon 102	Hold Me, Thrill Me, Kiss Me / No Next Time	1960	20.00	100.00
DOUGLAS, SHERRI LEE, & THE GONDOLIERS				
Maverick 601	Chime Bells / Grey Skies	196?	3.00	15.00
DOUGLAS, STEVE, & HIS MERRY MEN				
Philles 104	Yes Sir, That's My Baby / Lt. Colonel Bogey's Parade	1962	4.00	20.00
	("Yes Sir, That's My Baby" was produced by Phil Spector.)			

Label & Catalog #		A-Side/B-Side	Year	VG	NM

DOUGLAS, WAYNE
Wayne Douglas is a pseudonym for Doug Sahm.

Label & Catalog #		A-Side/B-Side	Year	VG	NM
Mercury 73098	(DJ)	Be Real / I Don't Want To Go Home	1970	2.00	10.00
Mercury 73098		Be Real / I Don't Want To Go Home	1970	4.00	20.00

DOVAL, JIM, & THE GAUCHOS [JIM SANDOVAL]

Dot 16468		Fire Ball / Good And Bad	1963	2.00	10.00
Dot 16548		Love Me One More Time / Love Me One More Time, Part 2	1964	2.00	10.00
Dot 16571		Barracuda / The Scrub	1964	2.00	10.00
Diplomacy 1000		Love Me One More Time / Love Me One More Time, Part 2	1964	2.00	10.00
		(Diplomacy 1000 credits Jim SanDoval & The Gauchos.)			
Diplomacy 3		Donna / The Scrub	1964	2.00	10.00
Diplomacy 5		Stranded In The Pool / Right Now	1964	2.00	10.00
Diplomacy 6		Beatles Rule / Pink Elephant	1964	3.00	15.00
Diplomacy 7		She's A Very Nice Girl / Bony Maronie	1964	2.00	10.00
Diplomacy 8		The Good And The Bad / Fireballed	1965	2.00	10.00
Diplomacy 17		She's So Fine / Mama, Keep Your Big Mouth Shut	1965	4.00	20.00
ABC-Paramount 10621		Out Of Sight / Annie Ya Ya	1965	1.00	5.00
ABC-Paramount 10637		I Know You're Fooling Around / Uptown Caballero	1965	1.00	5.00

DOVE, RONNIE & THE BELTONES

Decca 31288		Party Doll / Yes Darling, I'll Be Around	1961	3.00	15.00
Jalo 1406		No Greater Love / Saddest Hour	1962	3.00	15.00

DOVELLS, THE
The Dovells are Danny Brooks, Mike Dennis, Arnie Satin and Jerry Summers featuring Len Barry.

Parkway 819		No, No, No / Letters Of Love	1961	3.00	15.00
Parkway 827		Bristol Stomp / Out In The Cold Again	1961	3.00	15.00
Parkway 827		Bristol Stomp / Letters Of Love	1961	2.00	10.00
Parkway 833		Doin' The New Continental / Mope-Itty Mope Stomp	1962	1.60	8.00
Parkway 833	(PS)	Doin' The New Continental / Mope-Itty Mope Stomp	1962	3.00	15.00
Parkway 838		Bristol Twistin' Annie / The Actor	1962	2.00	10.00
Parkway 838	(PS)	Bristol Twistin' Annie / The Actor	1962	3.00	15.00
Parkway 845		Hully Gully Baby / Your Last Chance	1962	1.60	8.00
Parkway 845	(PS)	Hully Gully Baby / Your Last Chance	1962	3.00	15.00
Parkway 855		The Jitterbug / Kissin' In The Kitchen	1962	1.20	6.00
Parkway 855	(PS)	The Jitterbug / Kissin' In The Kitchen	1962	3.00	15.00
Parkway 861		You Can't Run Away From Yourself / Help Me, Baby	1963	1.20	6.00
Parkway 861	(PS)	You Can't Run Away From Yourself / Help Me, Baby	1963	3.00	15.00
Parkway 867		You Can't Sit Down / Wildwood Days	1963	1.20	6.00
Parkway 867	(PS)	You Can't Sit Down / Wildwood Days	1963	2.00	10.00
Parkway 867		You Can't Sit Down / Stompin' Everywhere	1963	1.20	6.00
Parkway 867	(PS)	You Can't Sit Down / Stompin' Everywhere	1963	2.00	10.00
Parkway 882		Betty In Bermudas / Dance The Fro	1963	1.20	6.00
Parkway 882	(PS)	Betty In Bermudas / Dance The Fro	1963	2.00	10.00
Parkway 889		Stop Monkeyin' Aroun' / No, No, No	1963	1.20	6.00
Parkway 889	(PS)	Stop Monkeyin' Aroun' / No, No, No	1963	2.00	10.00
Parkway 901		Be My Girl / Dragster On The Prowl	1964	2.00	10.00
Parkway 911		Happy Birthday Just The Same / One Potato, Two Potato	1964	1.20	6.00
Parkway 925		Watusi With Lucy / What In The World's Come Over You?	1964	1.60	8.00
Parkway 925	(PS)	Watusi With Lucy / What In The World's Come Over You?	1964	4.00	20.00
Swan 4231		Happy / Alright	1965	4.00	20.00
Jamie 1369		One Winter Love / Blue	196?	1.00	5.00
MGM 13628		There's A Girl / Love Is Everywhere	1966	1.00	5.00
MGM 13946		Here Comes The Judge / (B-side by The Magistrates)	1968	1.00	5.00
Decca 32919		Kiss The Hurt Away / He Cries Like A Baby	1970	.80	4.00
Event 3310		Roll Over, Beethoven / Something About You, Boy	1970	1.00	5.00
Abkco 4029		Baby Workout / Hully Gully Baby	1972	1.50	8.00
Verve 10701		Sometimes / Far Away	1972	1.00	5.00
MGM 14568		Mary's Magic Show / Don't Vote For Luke McCabe	1973	1.00	5.00
Event 216		Dancing In The Street / Back On The Road Again	1974	1.00	5.00
Paramount 0134		L-O-V-E, Love / We're All In This Together	197?	1.00	5.00

DOVER, ARNOLD

Yale 247		You Can't Play Tag With My Head / The House I Live In	196?	6.00	30.00

DOVERS, THE

Valentine 1000		Alice, My Love / A Lovely Lady	195?	50.00	200.00
New Horizon 501		Devil You May Be /	195?	4.00	20.00

DOWD, LARRY, & THE ROCKATONES

Spinning 6009		Blue Swingin' Mama / Pink Cadillac	1959	35.00	175.00

DOWELL, JOE

Smash 1708		Wooden Heart / Little Bo Peep	1961	1.60	8.00
Smash 1708	(PS)	Wooden Heart / Little Bo Peep	1961	2.40	12.00
Smash 1717		The Bridge Of Love / Just Love Me	1961	1.20	6.00

Label & Catalog #		A-Side/B-Side	Year	VG	NM
Smash 1728		(I Wonder) Who's Spending Christmas With You / A Kiss For Christmas	1961	1.20	6.00
Smash 1730		Sound Of Sadness / Thorn On The Rose	1962	1.20	6.00
Smash 1759		Little Red Rented Rowboat / One I Left For You	1962	1.20	6.00
Smash 1759	(PS)	Little Red Rented Rowboat / One I Left For You	1962	1.20	6.00
Smash 1786		Poor Little Cupid / No Secrets	1962	1.20	6.00
Smash 1799		Our School Days / Bringa-Branga-Brought	1963	1.20	6.00
Smash 1816		Bobby Blue Loves Linda Lou / My Darling Wears White Today	1963	1.20	6.00

DOWLANDS, THE

Tollie 9002		All My Loving / Hey Sally	1964	3.00	15.00

DOWN CHILDREN, THE

Philips 40441		Night Time Girl / I Can Tell	1967	5.00	25.00

DOWNBEATS, THE

Gee 1019		My Girl / China Doll	1956	8.00	40.00

DOWNBEATS, THE

Wilco 9		Alfalfa / Red X	196?	2.00	10.00
Dynamite 1011		Downbeat / Rug Cuttin'	1962	2.00	10.00
Dynamite 243		You Gotta Tell Me / It Won't Be Easy	196?	2.00	10.00

DOWNES, JACK E., & HIS FRIENDS

Jedco 5001		Surfin' Way Out / Strictly Drums	196?	7.00	35.00
Jedco 5002		Strictly Drums / Strictly Drums, Part 2	196?	7.00	35.00

DOWNES, VINNIE

Transcontinental 1011		Foolish Pride / An Angel Never Cries	196?	3.00	15.00

DOWNLINERS SECT, THE

Smash 1954		Little Egypt / Sect Appeal	1964	5.00	25.00

DOYLE, DICKIE

Wye 1009		My Little Angel / Dreamland Last Night	195?	25.00	125.00
Viking 4226		Little Baby Lee / The Simple Things Of Life	195?	10.00	50.00

DOZY, BEAKY, MICK & TICH
Refer to Dave Dee, Dozy, Beaky, Mick & Tich.

Cotillion 44061		Bad News / Tonight Today	1970	1.00	5.00

DRAG KINGS, THE

United Artists 676		Nitro / Bearing Burners	1964	4.00	20.00

DRAGONS, THE
The Dragons features Daryl Dragon. Refer to The Captain & Tennille and Dennis Wilson & Rumbo.

Capitol 5278		Troll / Elephant Stomp	1964	3.00	15.00

DRAKE, MANN

Bethlehem 3049		Horror Movie / Vampire's Ball	1962	2.00	10.00

DRAPER, RONNIE (& THE FOUR-DO-MATICS)

Virgelle 712		Summer Of '62 / How It Lies, How It Lies, How It Lies	196?	2.00	10.00
Crossroad 3007		Banjo Boogie / I Won't Go Huntin'	196?	2.00	10.00

DRASTICS, THE

Bolo 738		Sadness In My Heart / Smok Smok	196?	2.00	10.00

DREAM GIRLS, THE
The Dream Girls also recorded with Bobbie Smith.

Cameo 165		Don't Break My Heart / Oh, This Is Why	1959	4.00	20.00
Metro 20029		Crying In The Night / I'm In Love With You	1959	3.00	15.00
Metro 20034		Heartaches / Love Him	1960	3.00	15.00
Big Top 3059		Don't Break My Heart / I Could Write A Book	1960	3.00	15.00

DREAMERS, THE

Guaranteed 219		Canadian Sunset / Mary Mary	1960	5.00	25.00
Apt 25053		I Sing This Song / Mary's Little Lamb	1960	4.00	20.00
Cousins 1005		Because Of You / Little Girl	1961	20.00	100.00
May 133		Because Of You / Little Girl	1961	4.00	20.00
Goldisc 3015		Teenage Vows Of Love / Natalie	1961	5.00	25.00

DREAMERS, THE: *Refer to* DONNIE & THE DREAMERS

DREAMS, THE

Smash 1748		Too Late / Inexperience	1962	3.00	15.00

Label & Catalog #		A-Side/B-Side	Year	VG	NM
DRESSLER, LEN					
Mercury 70774		Chain Gang / These Hands	1956	3.00	15.00
Capitol 5055		Tell Him / Just Because	1963	2.00	10.00

DRIFTERS, THE

The Drifters' first six singles were credited to Clyde McPhatter & The Drifters (Atlantic 1006-1055) and are listed under his name; Johnny Moore took over as lead tenor after McPhatter's departure (1078-1161). In 1959 the entire group was fired and replaced by The Crowns featuring lead singer Ben E. King (2025-2087). Later leads include Rudy Lewis (2105-2225) and Johnny Moore again (2237-2624).

Label & Catalog #		A-Side/B-Side	Year	VG	NM
Atlantic 1078		Adorable / Steamboat	1955	6.00	30.00
		(Yellow & black label without a spinner.)			
Atlantic 1078		Adorable / Steamboat	1955	4.00	20.00
Atlantic 1089		Ruby Baby / Your Promise To Be Mine	1956	4.00	20.00
Atlantic 1101		Soldier Of Fortune / I Got To Get Myself A Woman	1956	4.00	20.00
Atlantic 1123		Fools Fall In Love / It Was A Tear	1957	4.00	20.00
Atlantic 1141		Hypnotized / Drifting Away From You	1957	3.00	15.00
Atlantic 1161		I Know / Yodee Yankee	195?	3.00	15.00
Atlantic 1187		Drip Drop / Moonlight Bay	1958	3.00	15.00
Atlantic 2025		There Goes My Baby / Oh, My Love	1959	3.00	15.00
Atlantic 2040		Dance With Me / True Love, True Love	1959	2.00	10.00
Atlantic 2050		This Magic Moment / Baltimore	1960	2.00	10.00
Atlantic 2062		Lonely Winds / Hey, Senorita	1960	2.00	10.00
Atlantic 2071		Save The Last Dance For Me / Nobody But Me	1960	2.00	10.00
Atlantic 2087		I Count The Tears / Suddenly There's A Valley	1960	2.00	10.00
		— Atlantic singles above have red & black labels without a spinner.—			
Atlantic 2096		Some Kind Of Wonderful / Honey Bee	1961	1.20	6.00
Atlantic 2105		Please Stay / No Sweet Lovin'	1961	1.20	6.00
Atlantic 2117		Sweets For My Sweet / Loneliness Or Happiness	1961	1.20	6.00
Atlantic 2127		Room Full Of Tears / Somebody New Dancin' With You	1961	1.20	6.00
Atlantic 2134		When My Little Girl Is Smiling / Mexican Divorce	1962	1.20	6.00
Atlantic 2143		Stranger On The Shore / What To Do	1962	1.20	6.00
Atlantic 2151		Sometimes I Wonder / Jackpot	1962	1.20	6.00
Atlantic 2162		Up On The Roof / Another Night With The Boys	1962	1.20	6.00
Atlantic 2182		On Broadway / Let The Music Play	1963	1.20	6.00
Atlantic 2191		Rat Race / If You Don't Come Back	1963	1.20	6.00
Atlantic 2201		I'll Take You Home / I Feel Good All Over	1963	1.20	6.00
Atlantic 2216		Vaya Con Dios / In The Land Of Make Believe	1964	1.00	5.00
Atlantic 2225		One Way Love / Didn't It	1964	1.00	5.00
Atlantic 2237		Under The Boardwalk / I Don't want To Go On Without You	1964	1.00	5.00
Atlantic 2253		(I've Got) Sand In My Shoes / He's Just A Playboy	1964	1.00	5.00
Atlantic 2260		Saturday Night At The Movies / Spanish Lace	1964	1.00	5.00
Atlantic 2260	(PS)	Saturday Night At The Movies / Spanish Lace	1964	3.00	15.00
Atlantic 2261		The Christmas Song / I Remember Christmas	1964	1.00	5.00
Atlantic 2261	(PS)	The Christmas Song / I Remember Christmas	1964	3.00	15.00
Atlantic 2268		At The Club / Answer The Phone	1965	1.00	5.00
Atlantic 2285		Come On Over To My Place / Chains Of Love	1965	1.00	5.00
Atlantic 2292		Follow Me / The Outside World	1965	1.00	5.00
Atlantic 2298		I'll Take You Where The Music's Playing / Far From The Maddening Crowd	1965	1.00	5.00
Atlantic 2310		Nylon Stockings / We Gotta Sing	1965	1.00	5.00
Atlantic 2325		Memories Are Made Of This / My Islands In The Sun	1966	1.00	5.00
		— Atlantic singles above have red & black labels with a spinner.—			
		—Extended Play Albums—			
Atlantic 534		The Drifters Featuring Clyde McPhatter	195?	100.00	400.00
Atlantic 592		The Drifters	195?	75.00	300.00
Atlantic 8113	(33)	I'll Take You Where The Music's Playing	1968	6.00	30.00
Atlantic 8115	(33)	The Drifters' Golden Hits	1968	3.00	15.00
DRIFTWOODS, THE					
DBS 163		Wobble Willie /	195?	7.00	35.00
DRIVERS, THE					
Comet 2142		High Gear / Low Gear	1961	3.00	15.00
DRONGOS, THE					
White Whale 235		If You Want To Know / Under My Thumb	1966	4.00	20.00
DU-KANES, THE					
HSH 501		Our Star / Shock Treatment	1964	7.00	35.00
DU SHON, JEAN					
Atco 6198		Talk To Me, Talk To Me / Tired Of Trying	1961	2.00	10.00
		("Talk To Me, Talk To Me" was produced by Phil Spector.)			
DUAL TONES, THE					
Sabre 204		Bubble Gum Bop / I'll Belong To You	1960	2.00	10.00

Label & Catalog #	A-Side/B-Side	Year	VG	NM
DUALS, THE				
Arc 4446	Nearest To My Heart / Bye Bye	196?	3.00	15.00
DUALS, THE				
Star Revue 1031	Stick Shift / Cruisin'	1961	——	——
	(Rare. Estimated near mint value $250-500.)			
Sue 745	Stick Shift / Cruisin'	1961	4.00	20.00
DUCAN, LESLEY				
Jerden 755	I Want A Steady Guy / Moving Away	196?	.80	4.00
DUCANES, THE				
Goldisc 3024	Little Did I Know / I'm So Happy (Tra-La-La)	1961	5.00	25.00
	("Little Did I Know" was produced by Phil Spector.)			
DUDES, THE				
Sue 723	Rudolph The Red Nosed Reindeer / Jingle Bells	1959	2.00	10.00
Sue 725	Mack The Knife / Organ Grinder Swing	1960	2.00	10.00
DUDLEY				
Arvee 587	El Pizza / Lone Prairie Rock	1960	3.00	15.00
DUGAN, TOMMY				
Rivers 1010	Remember Me / Worried Mind	196?	2.00	10.00
DUGOSH, EDDIE, & THE REDTOPS				
Award 116	Release My Heart /	195?	6.00	30.00
DUKES OF STRATOSPEAR, THE				
The Dukes is a pseudonym for XTC.				
Geffen PRO-2840 (12")	Vanishing Girl / Vanishing Girl (DJ)	1987	1.20	6.00
DUNE, LORNA				
Select 730	Midnight Joey / I'm Going With Bobby	1964	2.00	10.00
DUNES, THE				
Madison 156	Lonely Sands / Sloppy Jalopy	1961	3.00	15.00
DUNHILLS, THE				
Royal 110	Sounds Of The Wind / Ricochet	195?	6.00	30.00
DUPONTS, THE				
Roulette 4060	Screamin' At Dracula's Ball / Half Past Nothing	1958	3.00	15.00
DUPREE, DAVE				
Dave Dupree is a pseudonym for Dave Burgess.				
Challenge 1001	Don't Cry, For You I Love / Fire In The Eyes	1957	4.00	20.00
Challenge 1002	Flame Of Love / Well, It Isn't Fair	1957	4.00	20.00
Challenge 1005	A Job Well Done / Our Tomorrow	1957	4.00	20.00
	— Original Challenge singles above have dark blue labels.—			
DUPREE, SIMON, & THE BIG SOUND				
Simon is Derek Shulman of Gentle Giant.				
Tower 377	Kites / Like The Sun, Like The Fire	1969	1.20	6.00
DUPREES, THE				
The Duprees featuring Joey Vann also recorded as The Italian Asphalt & Pavement Company.				
Coed 569	You Belong To Me / Take Me As I Am	1962	2.00	10.00
Coed 571	My Own True Love / Ginny	1962	2.00	10.00
Coed 574	I'd Rather Be Here In Your Arms /	1962	2.00	10.00
	I Wish I Could Believe You			
Coed 576	Gone With The Wind / Let's Make Love Again	1963	2.00	10.00
Coed 580	Take Me As I Am / I Gotta Tell Her Now	1963	2.00	10.00
Coed 584	The Things I Love / Why Don't You Believe Me?	1963	3.00	15.00
Coed 584	My Dearest One / Why Don't You Believe Me?	1963	2.00	10.00
Coed 585	Have You Heard? / Love Eyes	1963	2.00	10.00
Coed 587	(It's No) Sin / The Sand And The Sea	1963	2.00	10.00
Coed 591	Please Let Her Know / Where Are You?	1964	2.00	10.00
Coed 593	So Many Have Told Me / Unbelievable	1964	2.00	10.00
Coed 595	It Isn't Fair / So Little Time	1964	2.00	10.00
Coed 596	I'm Yours / Wedding Ring	1964	2.00	10.00
Columbia 43336	Around The Corner / They Said It Couldn't Be Done	1965	2.00	10.00
Columbia 43464	She Waits For Him / Norma Jean	1965	2.00	10.00
Columbia 43577	Let Them Talk / Exodus Song	1966	3.00	15.00
Columbia 43802	It's Not Time Now / Don't Want To Have To Do It	1966	3.00	15.00
Columbia 44078	Be My Love / I Understand	1967	3.00	15.00
Heritage 804	My Special Angel / Ring Of Love	1968	1.60	8.00

Label & Catalog #		A-Side/B-Side	Year	VG	NM
Heritage 805		Goodnight, My Love / Ring Of Love	1968	1.60	8.00
Heritage 805	(PS)	Goodnight, My Love / Ring Of Love	1968	1.60	8.00
Heritage 808		My Love, My Love / The Sky's The Limit	1969	1.60	8.00
Heritage 808	(PS)	My Love, My Love / The Sky's The Limit	1969	1.60	8.00
Heritage 811		Two Different Worlds / Hope	1969	1.60	8.00
Heritage 811	(PS)	Two Different Worlds / Hope	1969	1.60	8.00
Heritage 826		Have You Heard? / My Love, My Love	1970	1.60	8.00
RCA Victor PB-10407		The Sky's The Limit / Delicious	1975	2.00	10.00

DURKEE, RAY
| Jubilee 5422 | | The Cosmonaut / The Cosmonaut, Part 2 | 1962 | 3.00 | 15.00 |

DUROCS, THE
| Capitol 4756 | | It Hurts To Be In Love / No Fool, No Fun | 1979 | .80 | 4.00 |
| Capitol 4787 | | Saving It All Up For Larry / Lie To Me | 1979 | .80 | 4.00 |

DUSK
Dusk features Peggy Santiglia, formerly of The Angels.
Bell 961		Angel Baby / If We Just Leave Today	1970	.80	4.00
Bell 961		Angel Baby / Reach Out And Speak My Name	1970	.80	4.00
Bell 990		I Hear Those Church Bells Ringing / I Cannot See To See You	1970	.80	4.00
Bell 45148		Suburbia U.S.A. / Treat Me Like A Good Piece Of Candy	1971	.80	4.00
Bell 45207	(DJ)	Point Of No Return / Point Of No Return	1972	.80	4.00
		(Stock copies of Bell 45207 may not exist.)			

DUVALL, HUELYN
Starfire 600		It's No Wonder /	195?	10.00	50.00
Challenge 1012		Teen Queen / Comin' Or Goin' *(Blue label)*	1958	20.00	100.00
Challenge 1012		Teen Queen / Comin' Or Goin' *(Maroon label)*	1959	7.00	35.00
Challenge 59002		Hum-Dinger / You Knock Me Out	1959	7.00	35.00
Challenge 59014		Little Boy Blue / Three Months To Kill	1959	8.00	40.00
Challenge 59025		Friday Night On A Dollar Bill / Juliet	1959	7.00	35.00
Challenge 59069		Pucker Paint / Boom Boom Baby	1960	7.00	35.00

DUVALS, THE
| Prelude 110 | | The Last Surf / Ferny Roast | 1963 | 4.00 | 20.00 |

DUVELLS, THE
| Rust 5045 | | Danny Boy / How Come? | 1963 | 3.00 | 15.00 |

DYLAN, BOB
Refer to Alan Ginsberg; The Traveling Wilburys; the Various Artists EP section.
Columbia 42656	(DJ)	Mixed Up Confusion / Corrina, Corrina	1963	75.00	300.00
Columbia 42656		Mixed Up Confusion / Corrina, Corrina	1963	———	———
		(Rare. Estimated near mint value $500-1,000.)			
Columbia ?????	(DJ)	Blowin' In The Wind / Don't Think Twice	1963	75.00	300.00
		(White label promo reads "Special album excerpt.")			
Columbia 42856	(PS)	Blowin' In The Wind / Don't Think Twice	1963	150.00	600.00
		(Promotional title sleeve with a "rebel with a cause" theme.)			
Columbia 42856	(DJ)	Blowin' In The Wind / Don't Think Twice	1963	50.00	250.00
		(Regular white label promo.)			
Columbia 42856		Blowin' In The Wind / Don't Think Twice	1963	75.00	300.00
Columbia 43242	(DJ)	Subterranean Homesick Blues / Subterranean Homesick Blues *(Red vinyl)*	1965	50.00	200.00
Columbia 43242	(PS)	Subterranean Homesick Blues	1965	———	———
		(Black & white sleeve with a photo of The Beatles on the back. Rare. Estimated near mint value $500-1,000.)			
Columbia 43242	(DJ)	Subterranean Homesick Blues / She Belongs To Me	1965	8.00	40.00
Columbia 43242		Subterranean Homesick Blues / She Belongs To Me	1965	1.60	8.00
Columbia 43242		Subterranean Homesick Blues / She Belongs To Me	197?	5.00	25.00
		(Grey label reissue from the early '70s.)			
Columbia 43346	(DJ)	Like A Rolling Stone / Like A Rolling Stone *(Red vinyl)*	1965	35.00	175.00
Columbia 43346	(DJ)	Like A Rolling Stone / Like A Rolling Stone (Part 1)	1965	15.00	75.00
Columbia 43346	(DJ)	Like A Rolling Stone (Part 1) / Like A Rolling Stone (Part 2)	1965	8.00	40.00
Columbia 43346		Like A Rolling Stone / The Gates Of Eden	1965	1.60	8.00
Columbia 43389	(DJ)	Positively 4th Street / From A Buick 6	1965	8.00	40.00
Columbia 43389		Positively 4th Street / From A Buick 6	1965	1.60	8.00
Columbia 43389	(PS)	Positively 4th Street / From A Buick 6	1965	8.00	40.00
Columbia 43389		Positively 4th Street / From A Buick 6	1965	40.00	200.00
		(Red label mispressing issued in the Los Angeles area contains a slow, alternate take of "Can You Please Crawl Out Your Window," although the label reads "Positively 4th Street." Must be heard to identify.)			
Columbia 43389		Positively 4th Street / From A Buick 6 *(Grey label)*	197?	5.00	25.00
Columbia 43477	(DJ)	Can You Please Crawl Out Your Window? / Highway 61 Revisited	1965	8.00	40.00
Columbia 43477		Can You Please Crawl Out Your Window? / Highway 61 Revisited	1965	2.00	10.00

Label & Catalog #		A-Side/B-Side	Year	VG	NM
Columbia 43541	(DJ)	One Of Us Must Know / Queen Jane Approximately	1966	8.00	40.00
Columbia 43541		One Of Us Must Know / Queen Jane Approximately	1966	2.00	10.00
Columbia 43592	(DJ)	Rainy Day Women 12 x 35 / Pledging My Time (Red vinyl)	1966	35.00	175.00
Columbia 43592	(DJ)	Rainy Day Women 12 x 35 / Pledging My Time	1966	8.00	40.00
Columbia 43592		Rainy Day Women 12 x 35 / Pledging My Time	1966	1.60	8.00
Columbia 43683	(DJ)	I Want You / I Want You (Red vinyl)	1966	35.00	175.00
Columbia 43683	(DJ)	I Want You / Just Like Tom Thumb's Blues	1966	8.00	40.00
Columbia 43683		I Want You / Just Like Tom Thumb's Blues	1966	1.60	8.00
Columbia 43683	(PS)	I Want You / Just Like Tom Thumb's Blues	1966	7.00	35.00
Columbia 43792	(DJ)	Just Like A Woman / Just Like A Woman (Red vinyl)	1966	35.00	175.00
Columbia 43792	(DJ)	Just Like A Woman / Obviously Five Believers	1966	8.00	40.00
Columbia 43792		Just Like A Woman / Obviously Five Believers	1966	1.60	8.00
Columbia 44069	(DJ)	Leopard-Skin Pillbox Hat / Most Likely You Go Your Way & I'll Go Mine	1967	8.00	40.00
Columbia 44069		Leopard-Skin Pillbox Hat / Most Likely You Go Your Way & I'll Go Mine	1967	3.00	15.00
Columbia 44826	(DJ)	I Threw It All Away / Drifter's Escape	1969	3.00	15.00
Columbia 44826		I Threw It All Away / Drifter's Escape	1969	1.00	5.00
Columbia 44926	(DJ)	Lay Lady Lay / Peggy Day	1969	3.00	15.00
Columbia 44926		Lay Lady Lay / Peggy Day	1969	1.00	5.00
Columbia 45004	(DJ)	Tonight I'll Be Staying Here With You / Country Pie	1969	3.00	15.00
Columbia 45004		Tonight I'll Be Staying Here With You / Country Pie	1969	1.00	5.00
Columbia 45199	(DJ)	Wigwam / Copper Kettle	1970	2.00	10.00
Columbia 45199		Wigwam / Copper Kettle	1970	.60	3.00
		(Red label with "Columbia Records" in pale white repeated in horizontal rows on the entire label.)			
Columbia 45199		Wigwam / Copper Kettle (Red label with black print)	1970	.60	3.00
Columbia 45199		Wigwam / Copper Kettle	1970	.60	3.00
		(Red label with "Columbia Records" in white around label edge.)			
Columbia AE-25	(DJ)	All The Tired Horses / All The Tired Horses	1970	6.00	30.00
Columbia 45409	(DJ)	Watching The River Flow / Watching The River Flow	1971	2.00	10.00
Columbia 45409		Watching The River Flow / Spanish Is The Loving Tongue	1971	.80	4.00
Columbia 1039	(DJ)	If Not For You / Tomorrow Is A Long Time	1971	6.00	30.00
Columbia 45516	(DJ)	George Jackson / George Jackson	1971	3.00	15.00
Columbia 45516		George Jackson / George Jackson	1971	2.00	10.00
Columbia 45913	(DJ)	Knockin' On Heaven's Door / Knockin' On Heaven's Door	1973	2.00	10.00
Columbia 45913		Knockin' On Heaven's Door / Turkey Chase	1973	.60	3.00
Columbia 45982	(DJ)	A Fool Such As I / A Fool Such As I	1973	2.00	10.00
Columbia 45982		A Fool Such As I / Lily Of The West	1973	.60	3.00
Asylum 11033	(DJ)	On A Night Like This / You Angel, You	1974	2.00	10.00
Asylum 11033		On A Night Like This / You Angel, You	1974	.40.	2.00
Asylum 11035	(DJ)	Something There Is About You / Tough Mama	1974	2.00	10.00
Asylum 11035		Something There Is About You / Tough Mama	1974	.40.	2.00
Asylum 45212	(DJ)	All Along The Watchtower / It Ain't Me, Babe	1974	2.00	10.00
Asylum 45212		All Along The Watchtower / It Ain't Me, Babe	1974	3.00	15.00
Columbia 10106	(DJ)	Tangled Up In Blue (Long) / Tangled Up In Blue (Short)	1975	3.00	15.00
Columbia 10106	(DJ)	Tangled Up In Blue (Mono) / Tangled Up In Blue (Stereo)	1975	2.00	10.00
Columbia 10106		Tangled Up In Blue / If You See Her Say Hello	1975	.80	4.00
Columbia 10217	(DJ)	Million Dollar Bash / Million Dollar Bash	1975	3.00	15.00
Columbia 10217		Million Dollar Bash / Tears Of Rage	1975	2.00	10.00
Columbia 10245	(DJ)	Hurricane, Part 1 / Hurricane, Part 1	1975	2.00	10.00
Columbia 10245	(PS)	Hurricane, Part 1 (Promo picture sleeve)	1975	4.00	20.00
Columbia 10245	(DJ)	Hurricane (Mono) / Hurricane (Stereo)	1975	1.00	5.00
Columbia 10245	(DJ)	Hurricane / Hurricane ("Special Rush Re-Service")	1975	1.00	5.00
Columbia 10245		Hurricane / Hurricane, Part 2	1975	.60	3.00
Columbia 10245	(PS)	Hurricane / Hurricane	1975	.60	3.00
Columbia 10298	(DJ)	Mozambique / Mozambique	1976	.80	4.00
Columbia 10298		Mozambique / Oh, Sister	1976	.60	3.00
Columbia 10454	(DJ)	Stuck Inside Of Mobile With The Memphis Blues Again / Stuck Inside Of Mobile With The Memphis Blues Again	1977	1.00	5.00
Columbia 10454		Stuck Inside Of Mobile With The Memphis Blues Again / Rita May	1977	.80	4.00
Columbia 10454	(PS)	Stuck Inside Of Mobile With The Memphis Blues Again / Rita May	1977	1.00	5.00
Columbia 10805	(DJ)	Baby, Stop Crying / Baby, Stop Crying	1978	1.00	5.00
Columbia 10805		Baby, Stop Crying / New Pony	1978	.60	3.00
Columbia 10851	(DJ)	Changing Of The Guards / Changing Of The Guards	1978	1.00	5.00
Columbia 10851		Changing Of The Guards / Senor	1978	.60	3.00
Columbia 11072	(DJ)	Gotta Serve Somebody / Gotta Serve Somebody	1979	1.00	5.00
Columbia 11072		Gotta Serve Somebody / Trouble In Mind	1979	.80	4.00
Columbia 11168	(DJ)	Man Gave Names To All The Animals / Man Gave Names To All The Animals	1979	1.00	5.00
Columbia 11168		Man Gave Names To All The Animals / When You Gonna Wake Up?	1979	1.00	5.00
Columbia 11235	(DJ)	Slow Train / Slow Train	1980	.60	3.00
Columbia 11235	(PS)	Slow Train (Promo picture sleeve)	1980	6.00	30.00
Columbia 11235		Slow Train / Do Right To Me, Baby	1980	.30	1.50
Columbia 11235	(PS)	Slow Train / Do Right To Me, Baby	1980	.30	1.50

Label & Catalog #		A-Side/B-Side	Year	VG	NM
Columbia 11370	(DJ)	Saved / Saved	1980	1.00	5.00
Columbia 11370		Saved / Are You Ready?	1980	5.00	25.00
Columbia 11318	(DJ)	Solid Rock / Covenant Woman	1980	1.00	5.00
Columbia 11318		Solid Rock / Covenant Woman	1980	.80	4.00
Columbia 02510	(DJ)	Heart Of Mine / Heart Of Mine	1981	.60	3.00
Columbia 02510		Heart Of Mine / The Groom's Still Waiting At The Altar	1981	.60	3.00
Columbia 02510	(PS)	Heart Of Mine / The Groom's Still Waiting At The Altar	1981	.60	3.00
Columbia 04301	(DJ)	Sweetheart Like You / Sweetheart Like You	1983	.60	3.00
Columbia 04301		Sweetheart Like You / Union Sundown	1983	.30	1.50
Columbia 04301	(PS)	Sweetheart Like You / Union Sundown	1983	.60	3.00
Columbia 04425	(DJ)	Joker Man / Joker Man	1983	.60	3.00
Columbia 04425		Joker Man / Isis	1983	.80	4.00
Columbia 04933	(DJ)	Tight Connection To My Heart / Tight Connection To My Heart	1985	.60	3.00
Columbia 04933		Tight Connection To My Heart / We Better Talk This Over	1985	.30	1.50
Columbia 04933	(PS)	Tight Connection To My Heart / We Better Talk This Over	1985	.30	1.50
Columbia 05697	(DJ)	Emotionally Yours / Emotionally Yours	1985	.60	3.00
Columbia 05697		Emotionally Yours / When The Night Comes Falling From The Sky	1985	.40	2.00
MCA 52811		Band Of The Hand /	1986	.60	3.00
MCA 52811	(PS)	Band Of The Hand /	1986	.60	3.00
		— 12" Singles—			
Columbia AS-???	(DJ)	Renaldo And Clara (TC)	1976	7.00	35.00
		(Very convincing counterfeits flooded the market in the late '70s.)			
Columbia AS-798	(DJ)	Solid Rock / Are You Ready / What Can I Do For You?	1980	3.00	15.00
Columbia AS-1263	(DJ)	Shot Of Love / Heart Of Mine / Trouble / Every Grain Of Sand	1981	3.00	15.00
Columbia AS-1975	(DJ)	Highway 61 Revisited / Highway 61 Revisited	1984	2.00	10.00
Columbia CAS-2086	(DJ)	Tight Connection To My Heart / Tight Connection To My Heart	1985	.80	4.00
Columbia CAS-2242	(DJ)	Emotionally Yours / Emotionally Yours	1985	1.00	5.00
Columbia CAS-2169	(DJ)	When The Night Comes Falling From The Sky / When The Night Comes Falling From The Sky	1985	1.00	5.00
Columbia CAS-2443	(DJ)	Got My Mind Made Up / Brownsville Girl (PC)	1986	3.00	15.00
		(Tri-fold picture cover with promotional title strips attached.)			
Columbia CAS-2492	(DJ)	You Wanna Ramble? / You Wanna Ramble?	1986	1.00	5.00
		—Extended Play Albums—			
Columbia 7-9128	(33)	Bringing It All Back Home (Jukebox EP)	1967	100.00	400.00

DYLAN, BOB / THE BAND

Label & Catalog #		A-Side/B-Side	Year	VG	NM
Asylum 11043	(DJ)	Most Likely You Go Your Way And I'll Go Mine / Stage Fright	1974	.60	3.00
Asylum 11043		Most Likely You Go Your Way And I'll Go Mine / Stage Fright	1974	.40	2.00

DYNA-SORES, THE

Label & Catalog #	A-Side/B-Side	Year	VG	NM
Rendezvous 120	Alley-Oop / Jungle Walk	1960	2.00	10.00

DYNAMICS, THE [JIMMY HANNA & THE DYNAMICS]
The Dynamics feature Jimmy Hanna and Larry Coryell.

Label & Catalog #	A-Side/B-Side	Year	VG	NM
Penguin 1006	Baby / Aces Up	1959	5.00	25.00
Guaranteed 201	Baby / Aces Up	1959	4.00	20.00
Seafair 100	Onion Salad / Lonesome Llama	1960	2.00	10.00
Seafair 107	At The Mardi Gras / J.A.J.	1961	2.00	10.00
Bolo 730	At The Mardi Gras / J.A.J.	1962	1.20	6.00
Bolo 735	Wild Child / Spongy	1962	1.20	6.00
Bolo 737	Genevieve / Moonlight In Vermont	1963	1.20	6.00
Bolo 740	Tennessee Boy / Tough Talk	1963	1.20	6.00
Bolo 747	Where Does Love Go? / Busybody	1964	1.20	6.00
Bolo 751	Knee Poppin' / Who's Afraid Of Virginia Wolf?	1964	1.20	6.00
Bolo 752	Leaving Here / Someone Somewhere	1965	1.20	6.00
	(Bolo 737, 747 and 752 credited to Jimmy Hanna & The Dynamics.)			
Jerden 800	I'll Be Standing There / All She Said	1966	1.00	5.00
Panorama 51	Stop And Take A Look Around / Stop And Take A Look Around	1967	1.00	5.00

DYNAMICS, THE

Label & Catalog #	A-Side/B-Side	Year	VG	NM
Capri 104	Always I Have Loved You / No One But You	1959	4.00	20.00
Arc 4450	Enchanted Love / Happiness And Love	1959	7.00	35.00
Decca 31046	Seems Like Only Yesterday / How Should I Feel?	1960	3.00	15.00
Decca 31129	The Girl By The Gate / At The End Of Each Day	1960	3.00	15.00
Decca 31450	Seems Like Only Yesterday / How Should I Feel?	1962	2.00	10.00

DYNAMICS, THE

Label & Catalog #	A-Side/B-Side	Year	VG	NM
Seeco 6008	Someone / Moonlight	1959	3.00	15.00
Delta 1002	Blue Moon / Pidgeion-Toed	1959	4.00	20.00
Dynamic 504	The Girl I Met Last Night / Nobody's Going Out With Me	1962	8.00	40.00
Dynamic (No number)	Dream Girl / Christmas Plea	1962	6.00	30.00

Label & Catalog #	A-Side / B-Side	Year	VG	NM
Dynamic 1002	Delsinia / So Fine	1963	5.00	25.00
Reprise 20183	Delsinia / So Fine	1963	3.00	15.00
Impala 501	Moonlight / Someone	196?	10.00	50.00
Liban 1006	If I Give My Heart To You / Blind Date	196?	4.00	20.00
Lavere 186	I Can't Give You Anything But Love /			
	Wrap Your Troubles In Dreams	196?	3.00	15.00
Cindy 3005	Gone Is My Love / Saints Come Marching In	196?	15.00	75.00
DYNAMICS, THE				
Liberty 55628	Chapel On A Hill / Conquistador	1963	6.00	30.00
DYNAMICS, THE				
Big Top 3161	Misery / I'm A Man	1963	3.00	15.00
Big Top 516	I Wanna Know / And That's A Natural Fact	1964	3.00	15.00
DYNAMICS, THE				
Top Ten 100	Yes, I Love You, Baby / Soul Sloopy	196?	2.00	10.00
Top Ten 927	Whenever I'm Without You / Love To A Guy	196?	2.00	10.00
DYNAMICS, THE				
Farrall 964	Later On / Departure	196?	7.00	35.00
DYNAMOS, THE				
Press 101	Teen Blues / The Harem	1961	4.00	20.00
DYNASTYS				
Jerden 783	It's Been a Long, Long Time / Forever And A Day	196?	2.00	10.00
DYNATONES, THE				
St. Clair 117	Fife Piper / And I Always Will	1966	3.00	15.00
HBR 494	Fife Piper / And I Always Will	1966	.80	4.00
DYNATONES, THE				
Alto 2020	The Skunk / The Skunk, Part 2	1966	.80	4.00

E.

E-TYPES, THE

Link 1		I Can't Do It / Long Before	1966	5.00	25.00
Link 1	(PS)	I Can't Do It / Long Before	1966	5.00	25.00
Dot 16864		I Can't Do It / Long Before	1966	3.00	15.00
Sunburst 101		The Love Of The Loved / She Moves Me	196?	3.00	15.00
Uptown 754		Back To Me / Big City	1967	3.00	15.00
Tower 325		Put The Clock Back On The Wall / 4th Street	1967	4.00	20.00

EAGER, JOHNNY

End 1061		I Understand / Blessing Of Love	1959	3.00	15.00

EAGLES, THE

Smash 1837		Christine / Stalactite	1963	2.00	10.00

EARL-JEAN

Colpix 729		I'm Into Somethin' Good / We Love And Learn	1964	2.00	10.00
Colpix 748		Randy / They're Jealous Of Me	1964	2.00	10.00

EARLS, THE

Rome 101		Life Is But A Dream / It's You	1961	7.00	35.00
Rome 101		Life Is But A Dream / Without You	1961	5.00	25.00
Rome 102		Lookin' For My Baby / Cross My Heart	1961	4.00	20.00
Rome 5117		My Heart's Desire / I'll Never Cry	1962	8.00	40.00
Barry 1021		I Believe / Don't Forget	1963	7.00	35.00
Old Town 1130		Remember Then / Let's Waddle	1963	4.00	20.00
Old Town 1133		Never / I Keep A Telling You	1963	4.00	20.00
Old Town 1141		Eyes / Look My Way	1963	3.00	15.00
Old Town 1145		Kissin' / Cry Cry Cry	1963	3.00	15.00
Old Town 1149		I Believe / Don't Forget	1963	5.00	25.00
Old Town 1169		Oh, What A Time / Ask Anybody	1964	3.00	15.00
Old Town 1181		Remember Me, Baby / Amor	1965	5.00	25.00
Old Town 1182		Remember Me, Baby / Amor	1965	3.00	15.00
		—Original Old Town singles above have blue labels.—			
Mr. G 801		If I Could Do It Over Again / Papa	196?	3.00	15.00
ABC 11109		It's Been A Long Time Coming / My Lonely, Lonely Room	1968	3.00	15.00
Clifton 39		Lookin' For My Baby / Cross My Heart	1974	.80	4.00
Clifton 47		Dreams Come True / My Heart's Desire	1974	.80	4.00
Columbia 10225		Goin' Uptown / Mrs. Woman	1976	1.60	8.00
Rome 111		Stormy Weather / (B-side by The Pretenders)	1976	.80	4.00
Rome 112/3		Little Boy And Girl / Lost Love	1976	.80	4.00
Rome 112/3		Little Boy And Girl / Lost Love (Colored vinyl)	1976	1.60	8.00
Rome 114/5		All Through Our Teens / Whoever You Are	1976	.80	4.00
Rome 114/5		All Through Our Teens / Whoever You Are (Colored vinyl)	1976	1.60	8.00
Woodbury 101		Tonight (Could Be The Night) / Meditation	1977	1.60	8.00
Harvey 100	(DJ)	Sunday Kind Of Love / Teenager's Dream (Colored vinyl)	197?	2.00	10.00
Harvey 100		Sunday Kind Of Love / Teenager's Dream	197?	1.20	6.00
Power-Martin 1005		Stormy Weather / (B-side by The Pretenders)	197?	1.00	5.00

EARLS, JACK, & THE JIMBOS

Sun 240		Slow Down / A Fool For You	1956	7.00	35.00

EARTH OPERA

Earth Opera features Billy Mundi, who also recorded with The Mothers Of Invention and Rhinocerous.

Elektra 45650		Home To You / Alfie Finney	1967	1.25	6.00

EARTHQUAKE

Beserkley 5701		Friday On My Mind / (B-side by Jonathan Richman)	1975	.80	4.00
Beserkley 5701	(PS)	Friday On My Mind / (B-side by Jonathan Richman)	1975	1.00	5.00

EASYBEATS, THE

The Easybeats were Dick Diamonde, Harry Vanda, Steve Wright and George Young. Refer to The Marcus Roll Band.

Ascot 2214		Women / In My Book	1966	2.00	10.00
Ascot 2214	(PS)	Women / In My Book	1966	5.00	25.00
United Artists 50106		Friday On My Mind / Made My Bed	1967	2.00	10.00
United Artists 50187		Pretty Girl / Heaven And Hell	1967	1.20	6.00
United Artists 50206		Falling Off The Edge Of The World / Sam	1968	1.20	6.00
United Artists 50289		Hello, How Are You? / Come In, You'll Get Pneumonia	1968	1.20	6.00
United Artists 50488		Good Times / Lay Down And Die	1968	1.20	6.00
Rare Earth 5009		St. Louis / Can't Find Love	1969	1.00	5.00

EBB-TIDES, THE: *Refer to* NINO & THE EBB-TIDES

Label & Catalog #	A-Side/B-Side	Year	VG	NM
EBB-TIDES, THE				
R&R 303	Low Tide / Ballad Of Jed Clampett	1963	8.00	40.00
R&R 304	Mr. Moto / Surfin' '69	196?	8.00	40.00
EBBS, THE				
Dore 521	Cartoons / Vicki Sue	1959	3.00	15.00
EBBTIDES, THE				
Monument 520	Come On And Cry / Straightaway	1962	2.00	10.00
EBBTONES, THE				
Dart 70026	Rockin' On The Range / Ram Induction	1963	3.00	15.00
EBONAIRES, THE				
Cameo 334	Love Call / (B-side by The Camelots)	1964	3.00	15.00
ECCENTRICS, THE				
Fresh 32	Podunk Holler /	196?	2.00	10.00
ECHO TIMES, THE				
Dart 1009	So In Love / My Baby Doll	196?	5.00	25.00
ECHOES, THE				
The Echoes later recorded as The Innocents.				
Andex 22102	Dee Dee Di Oh / Time	1959	4.00	20.00
ECHOES, THE				
Dolton 18	Born To Be With You / My Guiding Light	1960	2.00	10.00
ECHOES, THE				
SRG 101	Baby Blue / Boomerang	1961	50.00	200.00
Seg-Way 103	Baby Blue / Boomerang	1961	2.00	10.00
Seg-Way 102	Gee Oh Gee / Angel Of My Heart	1961	3.00	15.00
Seg-Way 106	Sad Eyes / It's Rainin'	1961	3.00	15.00
Smash 1766	Bluebirds Over The Mountain / A Chicken Ain't Nothin' But A Bird	1962	2.00	10.00
Smash 1807	Keep An Eye On Her / A Million Miles From Nowhere	1963	2.00	10.00
Smash 1850	Annabelle Lee / If Love Is	1963	2.00	10.00
Ascot 2188	I Love Candy / Paper Roses	196?	10.00	50.00
ECHOES, THE: Refer to FRANKIE & THE ECHOES				
ECHOMORES, THE				
Rocket 1042	Cute Chick / Little Chick	195?	25.00	125.00
ECSTASIES, THE				
Amy 853	That Lucky Old Sun / A Time For Love	1962	10.00	50.00
EDDIE, JASON, & THE CENTERMEN				
Capitol 5727	Singing The Blues / True To You	1966	3.00	15.00
EDDIE & THE EVERGREENS				
Eddie & The Evergreens is a pseudonym for Sha-Na-Na.				
Kama Sutra 578 (DJ)	In The Still Of The Night / In The Still Of The Night (Stock copies of K.S. 578 may not exist.)	197?	3.00	15.00
EDDIE & BETTY				
Six Thousand 601	Sweet Someone / One Little Dream Of You	1957	4.00	20.00
Lark 4512	Sweet Someone / You Took Your Love From Me	1959	3.00	15.00
Warner Bros. 5054	Sweet Someone / Saturday Night Fish Fry	1959	2.00	10.00
Warner Bros. 5079	Embarcadero Boogie / Give Up Your Twin Pipe, Mother	1959	2.00	10.00
EDDIE & THE SHOWMEN				
Liberty 55566	Toes On The Nose / Border Town	1963	6.00	30.00
Liberty 55608	Squad Car / Scratch	1963	5.00	25.00
Liberty 55659	Movin' On / Mr. Rebel	1963	5.00	25.00
Liberty 55695	Lanky Bones / Far Away Places	1964	6.00	30.00
Liberty 55720	We Are The Young / Young And Lively	1964	6.00	30.00
	—Extended Play Albums—			
Moxie 1031	Eddie & The Showmen	1980	2.00	10.00
EDDY, DUANE				
Duane Eddy also recorded with Sanford Clark; The Gigolos; and Jimmy & Duane.				
Ford 500	Ramrod / Caravan (Label credits Duane Eddy & His Rock-A-Billies. Rare. Estimated near mint value $500-1,000.)	1957	—	—
Jamie 1101	Movin' 'N' Groovin' / Up And Down (Pink label)	1958	5.00	25.00
Jamie 1101	Movin' 'N' Groovin' / Up And Down	1958	3.00	15.00

Label & Catalog #		A-Side / B-Side	Year	VG	NM
Jamie 1104		Rebel 'Rouser / Stalkin'	1958	3.00	15.00
Jamie 1109		Ramrod / The Walker	1958	4.00	20.00
		—Original Jamie singles above have yellow labels with "JAMIE" logo on top.—			
Jamie 1111		Cannonball / Mason Dixon Line	1958	3.00	15.00
Jamie 1117		The Lonely One / Detour	1959	3.00	15.00
Jamie 1117	(S)	The Lonely One / Detour	1959	7.00	35.00
Jamie 1122		Yep! / Three 30 Blues	1959	3.00	15.00
Jamie 1122	(PS)	Yep! / Three 30 Blues	1959	6.00	30.00
		—Original Jamie singles above have yellow labels with "Jamie" logo on top.—			
Jamie 1126		Forty Miles Of Bad Road / The Quiet Three	1959	2.00	10.00
Jamie 1126	(PS)	Forty Miles Of Bad Road / The Quiet Three	1959	6.00	30.00
Jamie 1126	(S)	Forty Miles Of Bad Road / The Quiet Three	1959	7.00	35.00
Jamie 1130		Some Kind-A Earthquake / First Love, First Tears	1959	2.00	10.00
Jamie 1130	(PS)	Some Kind-A Earthquake / First Love, First Tears	1959	6.00	30.00
Jamie 1130	(S)	Some Kind-A Earthquake / First Love, First Tears	1959	7.00	35.00
Jamie 1144		Bonnie, Come Back / Lost Island	1959	2.00	10.00
Jamie 1144	(PS)	Bonnie, Come Back / Lost Island	1959	5.00	25.00
Jamie 1151		Shazam! / The Secret Seven	1960	2.00	10.00
Jamie 1151	(PS)	Shazam! / The Secret Seven	1960	6.00	30.00
Jamie 1156		Because They're Young / Rebel Walk	1960	2.00	10.00
Jamie 1156	(PS)	Because They're Young / Rebel Walk	1960	5.00	25.00
Jamie 1163		Komotion / Theme For Moon Children	1960	2.00	10.00
Jamie 1163	(PS)	Komotion / Theme For Moon Children	1960	5.00	25.00
Jamie 1168		Peter Gunn / Along The Navajo Trail	1960	2.00	10.00
Jamie 1168	(PS)	Peter Gunn / Along The Navajo Trail	1960	5.00	25.00
Jamie JLP-73	(33)	Peter Gunn / Along The Navajo Trail (S)	1960	15.00	75.00
		(Compact-33, Living Stereo single.)			
Jamie 1175		Pepe / Lost Friend	1960	2.00	10.00
Jamie 1175	(PS)	Pepe / Lost Friend (Red sleeve)	1960	6.00	30.00
Jamie 1175	(PS)	Pepe / Lost Friend (Yellow sleeve)	1960	5.00	25.00
Jamie 1183		Theme From Dixie / Gidget Goes Hawaiian	1961	2.00	10.00
Jamie 1183	(PS)	Theme From Dixie / Gidget Goes Hawaiian	1961	5.00	25.00
Jamie 1187		Ring Of Fire / Bobby	1961	2.00	10.00
Jamie 1187	(PS)	Ring Of Fire / Bobby	1961	6.00	30.00
Jamie 1195		Drivin' Home / Tammy	1961	2.00	10.00
Jamie 1195	(PS)	Drivin' Home / Tammy	1961	5.00	25.00
Jamie 1200		My Blue Heaven / Along Came Linda	1961	2.00	10.00
Jamie 1200	(PS)	My Blue Heaven / Along Came Linda	1961	5.00	25.00
Jamie 1206		The Avenger / Londonberry Air	1962	2.00	10.00
Jamie 1209		The Battle / Trombone	1962	2.00	10.00
Jamie 1224		Runaway Pony / Trombone	1962	2.00	10.00
Gregmark 5		Caravan / Caravan, Part 2	1961	3.00	15.00
		(While the label to Gregmark 5 lists Duane Eddy, this is an Al Casey record.)			
RCA Victor 47-7999		Deep In The Heart Of Texas / Saints And Sinners	1962	1.60	8.00
RCA Victor 47-7999	(PS)	Deep In The Heart Of Texas / Saints And Sinners	1962	3.00	15.00
RCA Victor 47-8047		The Ballad Of Paladin / The Wild Westerners	1962	1.60	8.00
RCA Victor 47-8047	(PS)	The Ballad Of Paladin / The Wild Westerners	1962	3.00	15.00
RCA Victor 47-8087		(Dance With The) Guitar Man / Stretchin' Out	1962	3.00	15.00
RCA Victor 47-8087	(PS)	(Dance With The) Guitar Man / Stretchin' Out	1962	5.00	25.00
		("(Dance With The) Guitar Man" features The Honeys as The Rebel-Ettes.)			
RCA Victor 47-8131		Boss Guitar / The Desert Rat	1963	2.00	10.00
RCA Victor 47-8131	(PS)	Boss Guitar / The Desert Rat	1963	3.00	15.00
RCA Victor 47-8180		Lonely Boy, Lonely Guitar / Joshin'	1963	1.60	8.00
RCA Victor 47-8180	(PS)	Lonely Boy, Lonely Guitar / Joshin'	1963	3.00	15.00
RCA Victor 47-8214		Your Baby's Gone Surfin' / Shuckin'	1963	3.00	15.00
RCA Victor 47-8214	(PS)	Your Baby's Gone Surfin' / Shuckin'	1963	4.00	20.00
		(Although uncredited, "Your Baby's Gone Surfin'" features The Honeys.)			
RCA Victor 47-8276		The Son Of Rebel Rouser / The Story Of Three Loves	1964	1.60	8.00
RCA Victor 47-8276	(PS)	The Son Of Rebel Rouser / The Story Of Three Loves	1964	3.00	15.00
RCA Victor 47-8335		Guitar Child / Jerky Jalopy	1964	2.00	10.00
RCA Victor 47-8335	(PS)	Guitar Child / Jerky Jalopy	1964	3.00	15.00
RCA Victor 47-8376		Theme From A Summer Place / Water Skiing	1964	1.60	8.00
RCA Victor 47-8376	(PS)	Theme From A Summer Place / Water Skiing	1964	3.00	15.00
RCA Victor 47-8442		Guitar Star / The Iguana	1964	1.60	8.00
RCA Victor 47-8442	(PS)	Guitar Star / The Iguana	1964	3.00	15.00
RCA Victor 47-8507		Moonshot / Roughneck	1965	1.60	8.00
RCA Victor 47-8507	(PS)	Moonshot / Roughneck	1965	4.00	20.00
Colpix 779		Trash / South Phoenix	1965	2.00	10.00
Colpix 788		Don't Think Twice, It's Alright / House Of The Rising Sun	1966	2.00	10.00
Colpix 788	(PS)	Don't Think Twice, It's Alright / House Of The Rising Sun	1966	7.00	35.00
Colpix 795		El Rancho Grande / Poppa's Movin' On (I'm Movin' On)	1966	2.00	10.00
Reprise 0504		Daydream / This Guitar Was Made For Twangin'	1966	1.00	5.00
Reprise 0557		Monsoon / Roarin'	1966	1.00	5.00
Reprise 0622		Guitar On My Mind / Wicked Woman From Wickenburg	1967	1.00	5.00
Reprise 0662		This Town / There Is A Mountain	1967	1.00	5.00
Reprise 0690		Velvet Night / Niki Hokey	1968	1.00	5.00
Reprise 0690		Satin Hours / Niki Hokey	1968	1.00	5.00
Congress 6010		Put A Little Love In Your Heart / Freight Train	1970	2.00	10.00

Label & Catalog #		A-Side/B-Side	Year	VG	NM
Uni 55237		The Five Seventeen / Something	1970	2.00	10.00
Big Tree 157		Renegade / Nightly News	1972	1.50	8.00
Elektra 45359		You Are My Sunshine / 7 To 8	1977	.80	4.00
Capitol 44018		Spies / Spies	1987	.40	2.00
Capitol 44018	(PS)	Spies / Spies	1987	.40	2.00
		— Extended Play Albums—			
Jamie 100		Duane Eddy	1958	15.00	75.00
Jamie 301		Detour	1959	12.00	60.00
Jamie 302		Yep!	1959	12.00	60.00
Jamie 303		Shazam!	1959	12.00	60.00
Jamie 304		Because They're Young	1959	12.00	60.00
RCA Victor VLP-2993	(33)	Twangin' The Golden Hits (Jukebox EP)	1967	5.00	25.00

EDDY, JIM

Dore 537		Teen Age Angel / Everglades	1959	2.00	10.00

EDEN ROCKERS, THE

Cannady 100		The Cruise / Wasted	1959	2.00	10.00

EDEN ROCKS, THE

Nugget 1006		Eden Rock / Rockin' With Satan	1959	2.00	10.00

EDMUNDS, DAVE

MAM 3601		I Hear You Knocking / Black Bill	1970	.80	4.00
MAM 3608		I'm Coming Home / Country Roll	1971	1.00	5.00
MAM 3611		Blue Monday / I'll Get Along	1971	1.00	5.00
RCA Victor APBO-5000		Born To Be With You / Pick Axe Rag	1973	1.00	5.00
RCA Victor 74-0882		Baby I Love You / Maybe	1973	1.00	5.00
RCA Victor PB-10118		Let It Be Me / Need A Shot Of Rhythm And Blues	1974	1.00	5.00

EDWARDS, CHUCK, & THE FIVE CROWNS

Alanna 557		If I Were King / Lucy And Jimmy Got Married	1959	5.00	25.00

EDWARDS, JOHNNY, & THE WHITE CAPS

Northland 7002		Rock And Roll Saddles / Why'd You Leave Me?	195?	50.00	200.00

EDWARDS, VERN

Probe 100		Cool, Cool Baby / Glenda	1959	50.00	200.00

EELY, JACK, & THE COURTMEN
Jack Eely is a pseudonym for Jack E. Lee of The Kingsmen.

Bang 520		Louie, Louie '66 / David's Mood	1966	2.00	10.00
Bang 534		Louie Go Home / Ride Ride Baby	1966	2.00	10.00

EGGHEADS, THE

Decca 31079		What Did Unda Wear? / Cellars Of Paris	1960	2.00	10.00

EGYPTIAN COMBO, THE

Norman 549		Gale Winds / Rockin' Little Egypt	1964	2.00	10.00

EGYPTIANS, THE

Chance 100		Twin Son / My Little Girl	1965	3.00	15.00

EL CAMINOS, THE
The El Caminos also recorded with Mr. Lee.

Camelot 107		My Woman / I'm A Hog For You Baby	196?	2.00	10.00

EL CLOD

Challenge 9159		Tijuana Border / Pedro's Piano Roll Twist	1962	1.60	8.00
Mercury 72082		He's Not A Rebel / Holiday In Havana	1963	2.00	10.00
Vee Jay 647		Tijuana Watusi / Gringo	1965	1.60	8.00

EL REYS, THE

Ideal (No number)		Diamonds And Pearls / Rocket Of Love	1965	4.00	20.00
Ideal (No number)		Angalie / Beverly	1965	4.00	20.00

EL SIERROS, THE

Times Square 29		Valerie / I Love You So	1964	4.00	20.00
Times Square 101		Life Is But A Dream / Pretty Little Girl	1964	4.00	20.00
Yussels 7702		Sunday Kind Of Love / Daddy's Comin' Home	196?	3.00	15.00

ELECTRIC FLAG, THE

Sidewalk 929		Peter's Trip / Green And Gold	1967	3.00	15.00
Columbia 44307		Groovin' Is Easy / Over Lovin' You	1967	1.00	5.00
Columbia 44307	(PS)	Groovin' Is Easy / Over Lovin' You	1967	2.00	10.00
Columbia 44376		Sunny / Soul Searchin'	1967	1.00	5.00

Label & Catalog #		A-Side/B-Side	Year	VG	NM
ELECTRIC INDIAN, THE					
Marmaduke 4001		Keem-O-Sabe / Broad Street	1969	2.00	10.00
United Artists 50563		Keem-O-Sabe / Broad Street	1969	1.00	5.00
United Artists 50613		Land Of 1,000 Dances / Geronimo	1969	.80	4.00
ELECTRIC LIGHT ORCHESTRA, THE (E.L.O.)					
ELO was Bev Bevan, Jeff Lynne, Rick Price and Roy Wood, (i.e., The Move). Price and Wood left after the first single,					
leaving Bevan and Lynne the nucleus of an ever-changing line-up. Refer to Olivia Newton-John.					
United Artists 50914		10538 Overture / (Battle Of) Marston Moor	1972	.60	3.00
United Artists 173		Roll Over Beethoven / Queen Of The Hours	1973	.50	2.50
United Artists 337		Showdown / In Old England Town	1973	.50	2.50
United Artists 405		Ma Ma Ma Belle / Daybreaker	1974	.50	2.50
United Artists 573		Can't Get It Out Of My Head / Illusion In G Major	1974	.50	2.50
United Artists 573	(PS)	Can't Get It Out Of My Head / Illusion In G Major	1974	.60	3.00
United Artists 634		Boy Blue / Eldorado	1974	.50	2.50
United Artists 729		Evil Woman / 10538 Overture	1975	.50	2.50
United Artists 770		Strange Magic / New World Rising	1976	.50	2.50
United Artists 770	(PS)	Strange Magic / New World Rising	1976	.60	3.00
United Artists 888		Livin' Thing / Ma Ma Ma Belle	1976	.50	2.50
United Artists 939		Do Ya / Nightrider	1977	.50	2.50
United Artists 1000		Telephone Line / Poor Boy *(Green vinyl)*	1977	.50	2.50
United Artists 1000		Telephone Line / Poor Boy	1977	.50	2.50
United Artists 1000	(PS)	Telephone Line / Poor Boy	1977	.60	3.00
United Artists 1177		Evil Woman / Livin' Thing	1977	.50	2.50
U.A./Jet 1099		Turn To Stone / Mister Kingdom	1978	.40	2.00
U.A./Jet 1099	(PS)	Turn To Stone / Mister Kingdom	1978	.50	2.50
U.A./Jet 1145		Sweet Talking Woman / Fire On High *(Purple vinyl)*	1978	.60	3.00
U.A./Jet 1145		Sweet Talking Woman / Fire On High	1978	.40	2.00
U.A./Jet 1145	(PS)	Sweet Talking Woman / Fire On High	1978	.50	2.50
U.A./Jet 5050		Mr. Blue Sky / One Summer Dream	1978	.40	2.00
U.A./Jet 5052		It's Over / The Whale	1978	.40	2.00
U.A./Jet 5057		Shine A Little Love / Jungle	1979	.40	2.00
U.A./Jet 5057	(PS)	Shine A Little Love / Jungle	1979	.50	2.50
U.A./Jet 5060		Don't Bring Me Down / Dreaming Of 4,000	1979	.40	2.00
U.A./Jet 5064		Confusion / Poker	1979	.40	2.00
U.A./Jet 5067		Last Train To London / Down Home Train	1979	.40	2.00
MCA 41246		I'm Alive / Drum Dreams	1980	.40	2.00
MCA 41246	(PS)	I'm Alive / Drum Dreams	1980	.40	2.00
MCA 41285		Xanadu / Whenever You're Away From Me	1980	.40	2.00
MCA 41285	(PS)	Xanadu / Whenever You're Away From Me	1980	.40	2.00
MCA 41289		All Over The World / Drum Dreams	1980	.40	2.00
MCA 41289	(PS)	All Over The World / Drum Dreams	1980	.40	2.00
Jet 02408		Hold On Tight / When Time Stood Still	1981	.40	2.00
Jet 02559		Twilight / Julie Don't Live Here	1981	.40	2.00
Jet 02693		Rain Is Falling / Another Heart Breaks	1981	.40	2.00
Jet 03694		Rock 'N Roll Is King / After All	1983	.40	2.00
Jet 04130		Four Little Diamonds / Letter From Spain	1983	.40	2.00
Jet 04208		Stranger / Train Of Gold	1983	.40	2.00
CBS 05766		Calling America / Caught In A Trap	1986	.30	1.50
CBS 05766	(PS)	Calling America / Caught In A Trap	1986	.30	1.50
CBS 05892		So Serious / Endless Lies	1986	.30	1.50
CBS 05892	(PS)	So Serious / Endless Lies	1986	.30	1.50
		— 12" Singles—			
Jet SP-137	(DJ)	Livin' Thing / (One-sided on blue vinyl)	1977	2.00	10.00
Jet AS-474	(DJ)	Mr. Blue Sky / Mr. Blue Sky	1978	1.25	6.00
Jet AS-1252	(DJ)	Hold On Tight / Pre-Release Montage	1981	1.00	5.00
Jet AS-1319	(DJ)	Twilight / Julie Don't Live Here	1981	1.00	5.00
Jet AS-1724	(DJ)	Rock N Roll Is King / (B-side by Quiet Riot)	1983	1.25	6.00
Jet AS-1736	(DJ)	Four Little Diamonds / Secret Messages	1983	1.00	5.00
CBS ZAS-2254	(DJ)	Calling America / Calling America	1986	.80	4.00
CBS ZAS-2321	(DJ)	So Serious / So Serious	1986	.80	4.00
ELECTRIC PRUNES, THE					
Reprise 0473		Ain't It Hard? / Little Olive	1966	3.00	15.00
Reprise 0532		I Had Too Much To Dream Last Night / Lovin'	1966	2.00	10.00
Reprise 0564		Get Me To The World On Time / Are You Lovin' Me More?	1967	2.00	10.00
Reprise 0594		Dr. Do Good / Hideaway	1967	2.00	10.00
Reprise 0607		The Great Banana Hoax / Wind-Up Toys	1967	2.00	10.00
Reprise 0652		You Never Had It Better /			
		Everybody Knows You're Not In Love	1968	3.00	15.00
Reprise PRO-277	(DJ)	Sanctus / Credo	1968	3.00	15.00
Reprise 0833		Violet Rose / Sell	1969	2.00	10.00
ELEGANT IV, THE					
Cousins 1005		Time to Say Goodbye / I'm Tired	1961	4.00	20.00
Mercury 72516		Time to Say Goodbye / I'm Tired	1965	2.00	10.00

Label & Catalog #		A-Side/B-Side	Year	VG	NM
ELEGANTS, THE [VITO & THE ELEGANTS]					
The Elegants feature Vito Picone. Refer to The Beach Nuts; Pat Cordel.					
Apt 25005		Little Star / Getting Dizzy	1958	6.00	40.00
		(First pressings have black labels with silver print.)			
Apt 25005		Little Star / Getting Dizzy	1959	5.00	25.00
Apt 25017		Please Believe Me / Goodnight	1959	5.00	25.00
Apt 25029		True Love Affair / Payday	1959	5.00	25.00
		—Apt singles above have multi-color labels.—			
Apt 25005		Little Star / Getting Dizzy	1960	2.00	10.00
Apt 25017		Please Believe Me / Goodnight	1960	2.00	10.00
Apt 25029		True Love Affair / Payday	1960	2.00	10.00
		—Apt singles above have two-color labels.—			
Hull 732		Little Boy Blue / Get Well Soon	1960	20.00	100.00
United Artists 230		Let My Prayers Be With You / Speak Low	1960	4.00	20.00
United Artists 295		Happiness / Spiral	1961	8.00	40.00
ABC-Paramount 10219		Tiny Cloud / I've Seen Everything	1961	5.00	25.00
Photo 2662		Dressin' Up / A Dream Can Come True	1963	10.00	50.00
Photo 2662	(PS)	Dressin' Up / A Dream Can Come True	1963	20.00	100.00
Laurie 3283		Barbara Beware / A Letter From Vietnam	1965	5.00	25.00
Laurie 3298		Wake Up / Bring Back Wendy	1965	8.00	40.00
Laurie 3324		Belinda / Lazy Love	1965	3.00	15.00
		(Laurie 3324 credits Vito & The Elegants.)			
Bim Bam Boom 121		Lonesome Weekend / It's Just A Matter Of Time	1974	.80	4.00
Bim Bam Boom 121		Lonesome Weekend / It's Just A Matter Of Time	1974	1.25	6.00
		(Colored vinyl.)			
ELEGANTS, THE					
Bangar 613		Minor Chaos / Lost Souls	196?	7.00	35.00
ELEKTRAS, THE					
United Artists 594		All I Want To Do Is Run / It Ain't As Easy As That	1963	2.00	10.00
ELEPHANT'S MEMORY					
Elephant's Memory also recorded with John Lennon and Yoko Ono.					
Buddah 98		Crossroads Of The Stepping Stones / Jungle Gym At The Zoo	1969	.80	4.00
Metromedia 182		Mongoose / I Couldn't Dream	1970	.80	4.00
Metromedia 182	(PS)	Mongoose / I Couldn't Dream	1970	.80	4.00
Apple 1854		Liberation Special / Power Boogie	1972	75.00	300.00
		(Pulled immediately after release.)			
Apple 1854		Liberation Special / Madness	1972	.80	4.00
Apple 1854	(PS)	Liberation Special / Madness	1972	3.00	15.00
RCA Victor 74-268		Rock 'N' Roll Streaker / Angels Forever	1974	.60	3.00
ELF					
Elf features Ronnie Dio.					
MGM 14752		L.A. 59 / (B-side by Hank Lochlin)	1971	2.00	10.00
Epic 10933		Hoochie Koochie Lady / First Avenue	1972	2.00	10.00
ELGINS, THE					
Titan 1724		Extra, Extra / My Illness	1961	40.00	200.00
Congress 214		The Times We've Wasted / Rita Mae	1964	3.00	15.00
Congress 225		Here In My Heart / We're Gonna Have A Good Time	1964	6.00	30.00
Valiant 712		Scene / You Found Yourself Another Fool	1965	2.00	10.00
ELITE, THE					
Charay 17		One Potato / Two Potato	1966	7.00	35.00
Charay 31		My Confusion / Come To You	1966	7.00	35.00
Charay 56		Bye Bye Baby / All I Want Is You	1966	7.00	35.00
ELITES, THE					
Abel 225		Northern Star / The Little Chapel	1959	8.00	40.00
ELITES, THE					
Hi-Lite 106		You Mean So Much To Me /	195?	6.00	30.00
ELLIN, DAVID					
Bullseye 1010		Quackety Quack / (B-side by David & Freddie)	1958	3.00	15.00
ELLIOT, BILL, & THE ELASTIC OZ BAND					
Apple P-1835	(DJ)	God Save Us / God Save Us	1971	6.00	30.00
Apple 1835		God Save Us / Do The Oz	1971	2.00	10.00
Apple 1835	(PS)	God Save Us / Do The Oz	1971	3.00	15.00
		("Do The Oz" features John Lennon on lead vocal.)			
ELLIOT, BERN, & THE FENMEN					
London 9670		New Orleans / Everybody Needs A Little Love	1964	3.00	15.00
London 9722		Money / Nobody But Me	1964	3.00	15.00

Label & Catalog #	A-Side / B-Side	Year	VG	NM
ELLIS, DON, & THE ROYAL DUKES				
Bee 201	Party Doll / A Woman's Love	196?	3.00	15.00
ELLIS, JIMMY				
Jimmy Ellis also recorded as Orion.				
Dradco 1892	Don't Count Your Chickens / Love Is But Love	1964	3.00	15.00
MCA 40060	There Ya Go / Here Comes That Wonderful Feeling	1974	.80	4.00
Boblo	The Closer He Gets /	1976	.80	4.00
Boblo 526	Tupelo Woman /	1977	.80	4.00
Boblo 531	There You Go / Here Comes That Wonderful Feeling	1977	.80	4.00
Boblo 532	Movin' On / My Baby's Out Of Sight	1977	.80	4.00
Boblo 536	I'm Not Trying To Be Like Elvis / Games You've Been Playing	1978	.80	4.00
Boblo 536 (PS)	I'm Not Trying To Be Like Elvis / Games You've Been Playing	1978	1.00	5.00
Sun 1129	That's All Right / Blue Moon Of Kentucky *(First pressing of Sun 1129 do not credit an artist.)*	1978	.80	4.00
Sun 1129	That's All Right / Blue Moon Of Kentucky *(Second pressings credit Jimmy Ellis.)*	1978	.50	2.50
Sun 1131	I Use Her To Remind Me Of You / Changing	1978	.50	2.50
Sun 1136	D.O.A. / Misty / That's All Right / Blue Moon Of Kentucky	1978	.80	4.00
ELMO, SUNNIE, & THE MINOR CHORDS				
Refer to The Minor Chords.				
Flick 005	Bad Bulldog / Fire	195?	4.00	20.00
Flick 009	Let Me / Indian Love Call	195?	8.00	40.00
ELMORE, RUSS				
Panorama 3	Don't Run Johnny / My Silent Heart	196?	2.00	10.00
Trek 1	House Of Dreams / (Here Come The Teardrops) Ready Or Not	196?	2.00	10.00
ELMORE, RUSS & RUSSANNE				
Dolton 14	What Does Santa Claus Want For Christmas? / Big Words	1960	1.00	5.00
EMANONS, THE				
Winley 226	Dear One / We Teenagers (Know What We Want) *(First pressings of have 1/4" print on the label.)*	1958	10.00	50.00
Winley 226	Dear One / We Teenagers (Know What We Want) *(Second pressings have larger print on the label.)*	1958	3.00	15.00
ABC-Paramount 9913	Dear One / We Teenagers (Know What We Want)	1958	2.00	10.00
EMBERGLOWS, THE				
Dore 591	Have You Found Someone New? / Sack And Chemise Gang Fight	1961	5.00	25.00
Amazon 1005	Sentimental Reasons / Make Up Your Mind	1962	4.00	20.00
EMBERS, THE				
Suemi 4553	I'm Goin Surfin' / Why Am I So Blue?	196?	8.00	40.00
EMBERS, THE: *Refer to JOE D'AMBRA*				
EMCEES, THE				
Cimaron 4044	Wine, Wine, Wine / Hot Rock	1960	4.00	20.00
EMERALDS, THE				
DC 179	Emerald Surf / Surfin' Around The World	1964	7.00	35.00
Moonglow 232	Moonlight Surf / Little D Special	1964	5.00	25.00
Moonglow 232	Moonlight Surf / Little D Special *(Green vinyl)*	1964	15.00	75.00
Todd 7734	Roadrunner / Silver	1964	7.00	35.00
Riviera 714/5	Search For Love / Little D Special	1964	7.00	35.00
EMERGENCY EXIT, THE				
Ru-Ro 412	Maybe Too Late / Why Girl	1966	3.00	15.00
Dunhill 4060	Maybe Too Late / Why Girl	1966	2.00	10.00
Dunhill 4082	It's Too Late Baby / You've Been Changing Your Mind	1967	2.00	10.00
EMERSON, BILLY "THE KID"				
Sun 195	No Teasing Around / If Lovin' Is Believing	1954	75.00	300.00
Sun 203	I'm Not Going Home / The Woodchuck	1954	125.00	500.00
Sun 214	When It Rains, It Really Pours / Move Baby, Move	1954	8.00	40.00
Sun 219	Red Hot / No Greater Love	1955	10.00	50.00
Sun 233	Little Fine Healthy Thing / Something For Nothing	1956	8.00	40.00
EMJAYS, THE				
Greenwich 411	This Is My Love / Waitin' (The Pitty Pat Song)	1959	2.00	10.00
Greenwich 412	Cross My Heart / All My Love, All My Life	1959	2.00	10.00
Paris 538	Over The Rainbow / Cookie Jar	1960	2.00	10.00

Label & Catalog #	A-Side / B-Side	Year	VG	NM
EMOTIONS, THE				
Fury 1010	It's Love / Candlelight	1957	8.00	40.00
Card 600	(By The Light Of The) Silvery Moon / Do You Love Me?	1962	30.00	150.00
EMOTIONS, THE				
Kapp 490	Echo / Come Dance, Baby	1962	3.00	15.00
Kapp 513	L-O-V-E / A Million Reasons	1963	3.00	15.00
Laurie 3167	Starlit Night / Fool's Paradise	1963	5.00	25.00
20th Century Fox 430	A Story Untold / One Life, One Love, One You	1963	3.00	15.00
20th Century Fox 452	Rainbow / Little Miss Blue	1963	3.00	15.00
20th Century Fox 478	Boomerang / I Love You Madly	1964	3.00	15.00
20th Century Fox 623	Heart Strings / Every Time	1964	3.00	15.00
Karate 506	I Wonder / Hey Baby	1964	4.00	20.00
Calla 122	She's My Baby / Baby, I Need Your Lovin'	1965	3.00	15.00
Johnson 746	You're A Better Man Than I / Are You Real?	196?	2.00	10.00
EMPALA SIX, THE				
Blue Moon 417	Double Time / Travelin'	1960	8.00	40.00
Blue Moon 419	Sweet And Sour / Empala Rock	1960	7.00	35.00
EMPERORS, THE				
Wickwire 13003	Searchin' 'Round The World / Laughing Linda	1964	3.00	15.00
EMPERORS, THE				
Mala 543	Karate / I've Got To Have Her	1966	2.00	10.00
EMPIRES, THE				
Chavis 1026	Love You So Bad / Come Home, Girl	196?	7.00	35.00
EMPIRES, THE				
Lake 711	Over The Summer Vacation / You're So Popular	196?	3.00	15.00
EMPIRES, THE				
The Empires feature Jay Black.				
Epic 9527	A Time And A Place / Punch Your Nose	1962	5.00	25.00
EMPIRES, THE				
The Empires also recorded as Eddie Friend & The Empires.				
Calico 121	Only In My Dreams / Definition Of Love	1960	3.00	15.00
Colpix 680	Three Little Fishes / Everybody Knew But Me	1963	4.00	20.00
EMPIRES, THE				
DCP 116	Love Is Strange / Have Mercy	1964	2.00	10.00
EMS, THE				
Virgelle 711	Punchappy /	196?	2.00	10.00
ENCHANTERS, THE				
Members of The Enchanters later recorded as The Safaris.				
Orbit 532	Touch Of Love / Cafe Bohemian	1959	7.00	35.00
ENCHANTERS, THE				
Stardust 102	Spellbound By The Moon / Know It All	196?	125.00	500.00
Bald Eagle 3001	Come, My Baby, Let's Do The Stroll / Rock Around	1958	6.00	30.00
Orbit 532	Touch Of Love / Cafe Bohemia	1961	10.00	50.00
Bamboo 513	Touch Of Love / Cafe Bohemia	1961	6.00	30.00
Musitron 1072	I Lied To My Heart / Talk While You Walk (Blue label)	1961	8.00	40.00
JJ&M (No number)	Oh, Rosemarie / Bewildered	1962	20.00	100.00
Epsom 103	I Need Your Love / Goddess Of Love	1962	6.00	30.00
ENCHANTERS, THE				
Confederate	Everybody Rock / No Parking	1963	8.00	40.00
Tom-Tom 301	Surf Blast / Tum Tiki	1963	8.00	40.00
ENCHANTERS, THE				
Vargo 10	You Worry Me / So Much	196?	2.00	10.00
ENCHANTMENTS, THE				
Romac 1001	Lonely Heart / Popeye	1962	5.00	25.00
Gone 5130	(I Love You) Sherry / Come On Home	1962	3.00	15.00
Ritz 17003	I Love My Baby / Pains In My Heart	1963	15.00	75.00
Rogue (No number)	I Could Never Love Another / Good Old Acappella	196?	4.00	20.00
ENCHANTMENTS, THE				
Faro 620	I'm In Love With Your Daughter / I'm In Love With Your Daughter, Part 2	1964	2.00	10.00

Label & Catalog #		A-Side/B-Side	Year	VG	NM
ENCHANTONES, THE					
Poplar 116		My Picture Of You / We Fell In Love	1962	10.00	50.00
ENCHORDS, THE					
Laurie 3089		Zoom Zoom Zoom / I Need You, Baby	1961	10.00	50.00
ENCOUNTERS, THE					
Swan 4205		Don't Stop / A Place In Your Heart	1965	8.00	40.00
ENDELLS, THE					
Heigh Ho 605		Vicky / The Monkey Dance	1963	2.00	10.00
END					
Cha-Cha		Not Fade Away / Memorandum	1966	7.00	35.00
END, THE					
The End was produced by Bill Wyman.					
Philips 40323		I Can't Get My Joy / Hey, Little Girl	1965	2.00	10.00
London 1016		Shades Of Orange / Loving, Sacred Loving	1968	3.00	15.00
		(The two sides of London 1016 are often bootlegged as outakes from The Rolling Stones "Their Satanic Majesties Request" album.)			
ENDELS, THE					
Heigh-Ho 604/5		The Monkey Dance / Vicky	1963	2.00	10.00
ENDLESS PULSE					
Endless Pulse features Carlo Mastrangelo.					
Laurie 3448		Time Is A Wastin' / Ghost Town	1968	2.00	10.00
Laurie 3468		You Turned Me Over / Just You	1968	2.00	10.00
Laurie 3488		Nowhere Chick / Wake Me, Shake Me	1969	2.00	10.00
ENEMYS, THE [CORY WELLS & THE ENEMYS]					
The Enemys feature Danny Hutton and Cory Wells, later of Three Dog Night.					
Valiant 714		Say Goodbye To Donna / Sinner Man	1965	3.00	15.00
		(Valiant 714 credits Cory Wells & The Enemys.)			
MGM 13252		Hey, Joe / My Dues Have Been Paid	1966	2.00	10.00
MGM 13485		Glitter And Gold / Too Much Monkey Business	1966	2.00	10.00
MGM 13573		Mojo Woman / My Dues Have Been Paid	1966	2.00	10.00
ENERGIZERS, THE					
Kef 4458		(Save Our Energy) That's What Simon Says / Energy Rock	196?	3.00	15.00
ENGEL, BUTCH, & THE SHOWMEN					
MEA 4505		Tell Me, Please / You Know All I Want	1964	3.00	15.00
ENGEL, BUTCH, & THE STYX					
Refer to The Styx.					
Loma 2065		I Like Her / Going Home	1966	3.00	15.00
ENGEL, JOANNE					
Sabina 508		Mirror Mirror On The Wall / Set Me Free	1963	2.00	10.00
ENGEL, SCOTT					
Scott Engel also recorded with, or as, The Dalton Brothers; The Moongooners; The Newporters; The Routers; Scott Walker; and The Walker Brothers.					
Orbit 506		The Livin' End / Good For Nothin'	1958	3.00	15.00
Orbit 506	(PS)	The Livin' End / Good For Nothin'	1958	6.00	30.00
Orbit 511		Charley Bop / All I Do Is Dream	1958	4.00	20.00
Orbit 511	(PS)	Charley Bop / All I Do Is Dream	1958	10.00	50.00
Orbit 512		Bluebell / Paper Doll	1958	3.00	15.00
Orbit 512	(PS)	Bluebell / Paper Doll	1958	6.00	30.00
Orbit 537		Golden Rule Of Love / Sunday	1959	3.00	15.00
Orbit 537	(PS)	Golden Rule Of Love / Sunday	1959	6.00	30.00
Orbit 545		Comin' Home / I Don't Wanna Know	1959	3.00	15.00
Liberty 55312		Mr. Jones / Anything Will Do	1962	3.00	15.00
Liberty 55428		Forevermore / Anything Will Do	1962	2.00	10.00
Martay 2004		Devil Surfer / Your Guess	1963	5.00	25.00
Challenge 9206		Devil Surfer / Your Guess	1963	3.00	15.00
ENGLER, JERRY, & THE FOUR EKKOS					
Brunswick 55037		Unfaithful One / Sputnik (Satellite Girl)	1957	10.00	50.00
ENGLISH, SCOTT (& THE ACCENTS)					
Dot 16099		White Cliffs Of Dover / 4,000 Miles Away	1960	5.00	25.00
Joker 777		When / Ugly Pills (You're Takin')	1962	7.00	35.00
Sultan 5500		Rags To Riches / Where Can I Go?	1963	10.00	50.00
Spokane 4003		High On A Hill / (B-side by The Dedications)	1963	5.00	25.00
Spokane 4007		Here Comes The Pain / All I Want Is You	1964	4.00	20.00

Label & Catalog #	A-Side/B-Side	Year	VG	NM
Janus 171	Brandy / Lead Me Back	1971	2.00	10.00
Janus 192	Woman In My Life / Ballad Of The Unloved	1972	.50	2.50

ENJOYABLES, THE

Capitol 5321	Push A Little Harder / We'll Make A Way	1964	2.00	10.00

ENO (BRIAN ENO)
Eno was a member of Roxy Music.

Island 036 (DJ)	The Lion Sleeps Tonight (Wimoweh) / The Lion Sleeps Tonight (Wimoweh)	1975	3.00	15.00
Island 036	The Lion Sleeps Tonight (Wimoweh) / I'll Come Running (To Tie Your Shoes)	1975	5.00	25.00

ENTERTAINERS, THE

Demand 2932	How Much Do You Love Me? / Danny Boy	196?	4.00	20.00
Catch 101	Marianne / Fuddy Duddy Walk	1963	2.00	10.00

ENYA

Geffen 27633	Orinoco Flow (Sail Away) / Out Of The Blue	1989	.40	2.00
Geffen 27633 (PS)	Orinoco Flow (Sail Away) / Out Of The Blue	1989	.40	2.00

EPAE, JAY

Capitol 5029	Little Big Horn / Wiped Out	1963	4.00	20.00

EPIKS, THE

Process 146	When We're Apart / Give Me A Chance	196?	4.00	20.00

EPISODE SIX
Episode Six features Ian Gillian, later of Deep Purple.

Warner Bros. 5851	Here, There And Everywhere / Mighty Morris Ten	1966	5.00	25.00
Compass 7007	Morning Dew / Sunshine Girl	1967	3.00	15.00
Elektra 45617	Love-Hate-Revenge / Baby, Baby, Baby	1967	3.00	15.00

EPISODES, THE

Four Seasons	Where Is My Love? / Christmas Tree	195?	30.00	150.00

EPPS, PRESTON

Original Sound 4	Bongo Rock / Bongo Party	1959	2.00	10.00
Original Sound 4 (S)	Bongo Rock / Bongo Party	1959	4.00	20.00
Original Sound 9	Bongo Bongo Bongo / Hully Gully Bongo	1960	2.00	10.00
Original Sound 14	Bongo In The Congo / Bongo Shuffle	1960	2.00	10.00
Original Sound 17	Jungle Drums / Bongo Rocket	1961	2.00	10.00
Top Rank 2067	Bongola / Blue Bongo	1960	2.00	10.00
Majesty 1300	Bongo Boogie / Flamenco Boogie	196?	2.00	10.00
Polo 214	Say Yeah / My Lost Love	196?	2.00	10.00
	—Extended Play Albums—			
Original Sound 1001	Bongo Rock	1959	15.00	75.00

ERNIE & THE EMPEROR

Reprise 0414	Meet Me At The Corner / Got A Lot I Want To Say	1965	6.00	30.00

ERNIE & THE HALOS

Guyden 2085	Girl From Across The Sea (Angel Marie) / Darling, Don't Make Me Cry	1965	15.00	75.00

ERVIN, FRANKIE, & THE SPEARS

Don 202	Why Did It End? / Try To Care	195?	40.00	200.00

ERWIN, BILL, & THE FOUR JACKS

Pel 501	Too Young To Be Blue / High School Days	1962	5.00	25.00
Fairlane 21020	Too Young To Be Blue / High School Days	1962	5.00	25.00

ESCORTS, THE [GOLDIE & THE ESCORTS]

Coral 62302	Gloria / Seven Wonders Of The World	1962	7.00	35.00
Coral 62317	As I Love You / Guadamaus (Blue label)	1962	15.00	75.00
Coral 62317	As I Love You / Guadamaus	1962	6.00	30.00
Coral 62336	Somewhere / Submarine Race Watching	1962	3.00	15.00
Coral 62349	One Hand, One Heart / I Can't Be Free	1963	3.00	15.00
	(Coral 62349 credits Goldie & The Escorts.)			
Coral 62372	Back Home Again / Something Has Changed Him	1963	3.00	15.00
Coral 62385	My Heart Cries For You / Give Me Tomorrow	1963	6.00	30.00
	—Coral singles above have orange labels.—			

ESCORTS, THE

Boomerang 621	Little Big Horn / Wiped Out	1962	8.00	40.00

Label & Catalog #	A-Side/B-Side		Year	VG	NM
ESCORTS, THE					
Fontana 1912	Dizzy Miss Lizzie / All I Want Is You		1964	2.00	10.00
Fontana 1512	C'mon Home, Baby / She Gets No Lovin' That Way		1965	2.00	10.00
ESQUIRE, KENNY, & THE STARLITES					
Ember 1011	Pretty Brown Eyes / They Call Me A Dreamer		1956	8.00	40.00
Ember 1021	Tears Are Just For Fools / Boom Chica Boom		1956	10.00	50.00
ESQUIRES, THE					
The Esquires also recorded with Laughing Gravy.					
Durco 1001	Flashin' Red / What A Burn!		1964	6.00	30.00
ESQUIRES, THE					
Rite 1490	You've Got Another Thing Coming /		196?	5.00	25.00
ESSENTIALS, THE: *Refer to* BILLY & THE ESSENTIALS					
ESSEX, THE					
Best 101	Cemetery Stomp / Pray For Surf		196?	7.00	35.00
ETHICS, THE					
Graves 1099	She's A Deceiver / It's O.K.		196?	3.00	15.00
EUNIQUES, THE					
"620" 1003	Pretty Baby /		195?	10.00	50.00
"620" 1006	Cry Cry Cry / Chicken (Yeah)		195?	6.00	30.00
EUPHORIA					
Mainstream 655	No Me Tomorrow / Hungry Women		1968	3.00	15.00
EUPHORIA					
Heritage 831	You Must Forget / Ride The Magic Carpet		1969	1.60	8.00
EVANS, JERRY, & THE OFF KEYS					
Refer to The Off Keys.					
Rowe 002	Oh, Little Girl / You Are		1962	10.00	50.00
EVANS, PAUL					
RCA Victor 47-6906	What Do You Know? / Dorothy		1957	3.00	15.00
RCA Victor 47-6992	Poor Broken Heart / Caught		1957	3.00	15.00
Atco 6138	At My Party / Beat Generation		1959	3.00	15.00
Atco 6170	Long Gone / Mickey, My Love		1960	3.00	15.00
Guaranteed 200	Seven Little Girls Sitting In The Back Seat / Worshipping An Idol		1959	2.00	10.00
Guaranteed 205	Midnight Special / Since I Met You, Baby		1959	2.00	10.00
Guaranteed 208	Happy-Go-Lucky Me / Fish In The Ocean		1960	2.00	10.00
Guaranteed 210	The Brigade Of Broken Hearts / Twins		1960	2.00	10.00
Guaranteed 213	Hushabye, Little Guitar / Blind Boy		1960	2.00	10.00
Carlton 539	Show Folk / I Love To Make Love To You		1961	2.00	10.00
Carlton 543	Not Me / After The Hurricane		1961	2.00	10.00
Carlton 554	Just Because I Love You / This Pullover		1961	2.00	10.00
Carlton 558	Over The Mountain, Across The Sea / Sisal Twine		1962	2.00	10.00
Kapp 473	Feelin' No Pain / Picture Of You		1963	1.60	8.00
Kapp 527	Ten Thousand Years / Even Tan		1963	1.60	8.00
EVERETT, VINCE					
Vince Everett is a pseudonym for Marvin Benefield.					
Town 1964	Buttercup / Land Of No Return		1960	7.00	35.00
ABC-Paramount 10313	Such A Night / Don't Go		1962	8.00	40.00
ABC-Paramount 10360	I Ain't Gonna Be Your Low Down Dog No More / Sugar Bee		1962	8.00	40.00
ABC-Paramount 10472	Baby, Let's Play House / Livin' High		1963	10.00	50.00
ABC-Paramount 10624	To Have, To Hold And Let Go / Big Brother		1963	7.00	35.00
EVERLY BROTHERS, THE					
Don and Phil Everly. Refer to The Beach Boys; the Various Artists section.					
Columbia 21496	(DJ)	The Sun Keeps Shining / Keep A Loving Me	1956	50.00	250.00
Columbia 21496		The Sun Keeps Shining / Keep A Loving Me	1956	100.00	400.00
Cadence 1315		Bye, Bye, Love / I Wonder If I Care As Much	1957	3.00	15.00
Cadence 1337		Wake Up, Little Susie / Maybe Tomorrow	1957	3.00	15.00
Cadence 1337	(PS)	Wake Up, Little Susie / Maybe Tomorrow	1957	35.00	175.00
Cadence 1342		This Little Girl Of Mine / Should We Tell Him?	1958	3.00	15.00
Cadence 1348		All I Have To Do Is Dream / Claudette	1958	3.00	15.00
Cadence 1350		Bird Dog / Devoted To You	1958	3.00	15.00
Cadence 1355		Problems / Love Of My Life	1958	3.00	15.00
Cadence 1355	(PS)	Problems / Love Of My Life	1958	5.00	25.00
Cadence 1364		Take A Message To Mary / Poor Jenny	1959	3.00	15.00
Cadence 1369		('Til) I Kissed You / Oh, What A Feeling	1959	3.00	15.00
Cadence 1369	(PS)	('Til) I Kissed You / Oh, What A Feeling	1959	5.00	25.00

Label & Catalog #		A-Side/B-Side	Year	VG	NM
Cadence 1376		Let It Be Me / Since You Broke My Heart	1959	3.00	15.00
Cadence 1376	(PS)	Let It Be Me / Since You Broke My Heart	1959	5.00	25.00
Cadence 1380		When Will I Be Loved? / Be-Bop A-Lula	1960	3.00	15.00
Cadence 1388		Like Strangers / Brand New Heartache	1960	3.00	15.00
Cadence 1429		I'm Here To Get My Baby Out Of Jail / Lightning Express	1962	3.00	15.00
Cadence 1429	(PS)	I'm Here To Get My Baby Out Of Jail / Lightning Express	1962	5.00	25.00
Warner Bros. 5151	(DJ)	Cathy's Clown / Always It's You (Gold vinyl)	1960	20.00	100.00
Warner Bros. 5151		Cathy's Clown / Always It's You	1960	2.00	10.00
Warner Bros. 5151	(PS)	Cathy's Clown / Always It's You	1960	4.00	20.00
Warner Bros. S-5151	(S)	Cathy's Clown / Always It's You	1960	10.00	50.00
Warner Bros. 5163	(DJ)	So Sad / Lucille (Gold vinyl)	1960	20.00	100.00
Warner Bros. 5163		So Sad / Lucille	1960	2.00	10.00
Warner Bros. 5163	(PS)	So Sad / Lucille	1960	3.00	15.00
Warner Bros. 5199	(DJ)	Ebony Eyes / Walk Right Back (Gold vinyl)	1961	20.00	100.00
Warner Bros. 5199		Ebony Eyes / Walk Right Back	1961	2.00	10.00
Warner Bros. 5199	(PS)	Ebony Eyes / Walk Right Back	1961	3.00	15.00
Warner Bros. 5220		Temptation / Stick With Me, Baby	1961	2.00	10.00
Warner Bros. 5220	(PS)	Temptation / Stick With Me, Baby	1961	4.00	20.00
Warner Bros. 5250		Crying In The Rain / I'm Not Angry	1961	2.00	10.00
Warner Bros. 5250	(PS)	Crying In The Rain / I'm Not Angry	1961	2.00	10.00
Warner Bros. 5273		That's Old Fashioned / How Can I Meet Her?	1962	2.00	10.00
Warner Bros. 5273	(PS)	That's Old Fashioned / How Can I Meet Her?	1962	4.00	20.00
Warner Bros. 5297		Don't Ask Me To Be Friends / No One Can Make My Sunshine Smile	1962	3.00	15.00
Warner Bros. 5297	(PS)	Don't Ask Me To Be Friends / No One Can Make My Sunshine Smile	1962	4.00	20.00
Warner Bros. 5346		So It Always Will Be / Nancy's Minuet	1963	1.60	8.00
Warner Bros. 5362		I'm Afraid / It's Been Nice	1963	1.60	8.00
Warner Bros. 5389		Love Her / The Girl Sang The Blues	1963	2.00	10.00
Warner Bros. 5422		Hello, Amy / Ain't That Loving You, Baby	1964	2.00	10.00
Warner Bros. 5441		The Ferris Wheel / Don't Forget To Cry	1964	1.60	8.00
Warner Bros. 5466		You're The One I Love / Ring Around My Rosie	1964	2.00	10.00
Warner Bros. 5478		Gone, Gone, Gone / Torture	1964	1.60	8.00
Warner Bros. 5501		Don't Blame Me / Muskrat	1965	2.00	10.00
Warner Bros. 5501	(PS)	Don't Blame Me / Muskrat	1965	3.00	15.00
Warner Bros. 5600		You're My Girl / Don't Let The World Know	1965	2.00	10.00
Warner Bros. 5611		That'll Be The Day / Give Me A Sweetheart	1965	2.00	10.00
Warner Bros. 5628		The Price Of Love / It Only Costs A Dime	1965	2.00	10.00
Warner Bros. 5635		I'll Never Get Over You / Follow Me	1965	2.00	10.00
Warner Bros. 5649		Love Is Strange / A Man With Money	1965	2.00	10.00
Warner Bros. 5649	(PS)	Love Is Strange / A Man With Money	1965	5.00	25.00
Warner Bros. 5682		It's All Over / I Used To Love You	1965	2.00	10.00
Warner Bros. 5698		The Doll House Is Empty / Lovey Kravezit	1966	3.00	15.00
Warner Bros. 5808		The Power Of Love / Leave My Girl Alone	1966	2.00	10.00
Warner Bros. 5833		Somebody Help Me / Hard, Hard Year	1966	2.00	10.00
Warner Bros. 5857		Fifi The Flea / Like Every Time Before	1966	2.00	10.00
		(Although uncredited, Warner 5833 and 5857 feature The Hollies on instrumental and vocal backing.)			
Warner Bros. 5901		She Never Smiles Anymore / Devil Child	1967	2.00	10.00
Warner Bros. 7020		Bowling Green / I Don't Want To Love You	1967	1.00	5.00
Warner Bros. 7062		Mary Jane / Talking To The Flowers	1967	1.60	8.00
Warner Bros. 7088		Love Of The Common People / Voice Within	1967	1.60	8.00
Warner Bros. 7192		Empty Boxes / It's My Time	1968	1.00	5.00
Warner Bros. 7226		Lord Of The Manor / Milk Train	1968	2.00	10.00
Warner Bros. 7290		I'm On My Way Home Again / Cuckoo Bird	1969	2.00	10.00
Warner Bros. 7262		T For Texas / I Wonder If I Care As Much	1969	2.00	10.00
Warner Bros. 7326		Carolina On My Mind / My Little Yellow Bird	1969	1.60	8.00
Warner Bros. 7425		Yves / Human Race	1970	3.00	15.00
RCA Victor 74-0717		Stories We Could Tell / Ridin' High	1972	.80	4.00
RCA Victor 74-0849		Lay It Down / Paradise	1972	.80	4.00
RCA Victor 74-0901		Not Fade Away / Ladies Love Outlaws	1973	.80	4.00
Mercury 880 423		The Story Of Me /	1984	.50	2.50
		—Extended Play Albums—			
Cadence 104		The Everly Brothers (Volume 1)	1957	10.00	50.00
Cadence 105		The Everly Brothers (Volume 2)	1957	10.00	50.00
Cadence 107		The Everly Brothers (Volume 3)	1957	10.00	50.00
Cadence 108		Songs Our Daddy Taught Us (Volume 1)	1958	8.00	40.00
Cadence 109		Songs Our Daddy Taught Us (Volume 2)	1958	8.00	40.00
Cadence 110		Songs Our Daddy Taught Us (Volume 3)	1958	8.00	40.00
Cadence 111		The Everly Brothers	1959	8.00	40.00
Cadence 118		The Everly Brothers	1959	8.00	40.00
Cadence 121		The Very Best Of The Everly Brothers	1960	5.00	25.00
Cadence 333		Rockin' With The Everly Brothers	1961	5.00	25.00
Warner Bros. PRO-135	(DJ)	Souvenir Sampler	1964	8.00	40.00
		(Album sampler with ten drastically edited songs.)			
Warner Bros. 1554	(33)	The Very Best Of The Everly Brothers (Jukebox EP)	1968	3.00	15.00

Label & Catalog #		A-Side/B-Side	Year	VG	NM
EVERLY BROTHERS & BEACH BOYS, THE					
Capitol 44297	(DJ)	Don't Worry, Baby / Don't Worry, Baby	1988	.40	2.00
Capitol 44297	(PS)	Don't Worry, Baby / Don't Worry, Baby	1988	.60	3.00
Capitol 44297		Don't Worry, Baby / (B-side by Dave Grusin)	1988	2.00	10.00
EVERLY, DON					
Don Everly also recorded as Adrian Kimberly.					
Ode 66009		Tumbling Tumbleweeds / Only Me	1970	1.00	5.00
Ode 66046		Warmin' Up The Band / Evelyn Swing	1973	1.00	5.00
ABC/Hickory 368		Never Like This / Yesterday Just Passed My Way Again	1975	.60	3.00
ABC/Hickory 54002		Love At Last Sight / Oh, I'd Like To Go Away	1976	.60	3.00
ABC/Hickory 54005		Deep Water / Since You Broke My Heart	1976	.60	3.00
ABC/Hickory 54012		Brother Jukebox / Oh, What A Feeling	1977	.60	3.00
Polydor 315		Let's Put Our Hearts Together / So Sad	1981	.60	3.00
EVERLY, PHIL					
Refer to Lou Giordano.					
Pye 0064		God Bless Older Ladies / Sweet Grass Country	1973	.80	4.00
Pye 71014		Old Kentucky River / Summershine	1975	.80	4.00
Pye 71036		Better Than Now / New Old Song	1974	.80	4.00
Pye 71050		Better Than Now / Friends	1975	.80	4.00
Pye 71055		Words In Your Eyes /			
		Back When The Bands Played In Ragtime	1975	.80	4.00
Elektra 46007		Don't Say You Don't Love Me / (B-side by Sondra Locke)	1979	.80	4.00
Elektra 46519		Living Alone / I Just Don't Feel Like Dancing	1979	.80	4.00
Elektra 46556		You Broke It / Buy Me A Beer	1979	.80	4.00
Curb 5401	(DJ)	Dare To Dream Again / Dare To Dream Again	1980	1.00	5.00
Curb 5401		Dare To Dream Again / Lonely Days, Lonely Nights	1980	2.00	10.00
Curb 02116	(DJ)	Sweet Southern Love / Sweet Southern Love	1981	1.00	5.00
Curb 02116		Sweet Southern Love / In Your Eyes	1981	2.00	10.00
Capitol 5197		Who's Gonna Keep Me Warm? /			
		One Way Love (On A Two Way Street)	1983	2.00	10.00
EVERPRESENT FULLNESS, THE					
White Whale 233		Doin' A Number / Wild About My Lovin'	1966	2.00	10.00
White Whale 233		Fine And Dandy / Wild About My Lovin'	1966	2.00	10.00
White Whale 248		Yeah! / Darlin,' You Can Count On Me	1967	2.00	10.00
EVERY MOTHER'S SON					
MGM 13733		Come On Down To My Boat / I Believe In You	1967	1.20	6.00
MGM 13788		Put Your Mind At Ease / Proper Four Leaf Clover	1967	.80	4.00
MGM 13844		Pony With The Golden Mane / Dolls In The Clock	1968	.80	4.00
MGM 13844	(PS)	Pony With The Golden Mane / Dolls In The Clock	1968	2.00	10.00
MGM 13887		No One Knows / What Became Of Mary	1968	.80	4.00
MGM 13987		Rainflowers / For Brandy	1968	.80	4.00
EVERYDAY HUDSON					
Decca 732634		Love Is The Word / Laugh, Funny Funny	1970	1.20	6.00
EVERYTHING IS EVERYTHING					
Vanguard 35082		Witchi Tai To / Ooo Baby	1969	1.00	5.00
EXCELLENTS, THE					
Blast 205		Coney Island Baby / You Baby You (Red label)	1962	5.00	25.00
Blast 205		Coney Island Baby / You Baby You (Blue label)	1962	3.00	15.00
Blast 205		Coney Island Baby / You Baby You (Color label)	1962	3.00	15.00
Blast 207		I Hear A Rhapsody / Why Did You Laugh?	1963	4.00	20.00
EXCELLENTS, THE					
The Excellents later recorded as The Excellons.					
Mermaid 106		Love No One But You / Red Red Robin	196?	25.00	125.00
Old Timer 601		Helene (Your Wish Came True) / Sunday Kind Of Love	196?	3.00	15.00
EXCELLONS, THE					
The Excellons originally recorded as The Excellents.					
Bobby 601		Helene (Your Wish Came True) / Sunday Kind Of Love	1964	6.00	30.00
EXCELS, THE					
Central 2601		You're Mine Forever / Baby Doll	1957	7.00	35.00
R.S.V.P. 111		Can't Help Lovin' That Girl Of Mine / Til You	1961	4.00	20.00
EXCEPTIONS, THE					
Pro 1		Down By The Ocean / Pancho's Villa	1965	20.00	100.00
Cameo 378		Down By The Ocean / Pancho's Villa	1965	5.00	25.00
EXCEPTIONS, THE					
Quill 114		Girl From New York / As Far As I Can See	1967	5.00	25.00
Capitol 5982		Girl From New York / As Far As I Can See	1967	2.00	10.00

Label & Catalog #	A-Side / B-Side	Year	VG	NM

EXECS, THE
Fargo 1055 — Walking In The Rain / Palladium — 1958 — 30.00 — 150.00

EXILES, THE
The Exiles are believed to feature Dick Dale, although Dale denies having played on it.
Campus 111 — Take It Off / Ten Little Indians — 196? — 10.00 — 50.00

EXODUS
Exodus originally recorded as The Four Epics.
Wand 11248 — Silhouettes / You Cheated — 1972 — 2.00 — 10.00

EXOTICS, THE
Jerden 6	Four Banger / Cat Hairs	1960	3.00	15.00
Bolo 722	Oasis / Chattanooga Choo Choo	1961	2.00	10.00
Seafair 108	Ginger Snap /	1963	2.00	10.00
Seafair 113	Jerk Time / For The Winds	1963	2.00	10.00

EXPLOITS, THE: *Refer to* BOBBY MAXWELL

EXPLORERS, THE [DENNIS & THE EXPLORERS]
Coral 62147	Vision Of Love / On A Clear Night	1959	6.00	30.00
Coral 62175	Don't Be A Fool / In The Wee Small Hours Of The Morning	1960	7.00	35.00
Coral 62295	Remember / Every Road	1962	5.00	25.00
	(Coral 62295 credits Dennis & The Explorers.)			
Coral 65575	Vision Of Love / Don't Be A Fool	1963	2.00	10.00

EXPORTS, THE
King 5917 — Car Hop / Seat Belts, Please — 1964 — 2.00 — 10.00

EXPRESS, THE
Piccadilly 226 — You Gotta Understand / Long Green — 1966 — 2.00 — 10.00

EXPRESSIONS, THE
| Teen 101 | Now That You're Gone / Crazy | 195? | 50.00 | 200.00 |
| Arliss 1012 | My Love, My Love / The Sign Of Happiness | 196? | 8.00 | 40.00 |

EXPRESSIONS, THE
| Smash 1848 | Karen / Thrill | 1963 | 3.00 | 15.00 |
| Parkway 892 | On The Corner / To Cry | 1963 | 2.00 | 10.00 |

EXPRESSIONS, THE
| Guyden 2122 | Be Bop A Lula / Skinny Minnie | 1965 | 2.00 | 10.00 |
| Reprise 0360 | One Plus One / Playboy | 1965 | 4.00 | 20.00 |

EXTERMINATORS, THE
Chancellor 1148 — Beatle Bomb / Stomp 'Em Out — 1964 — 4.00 — 20.00

EXTREMES, THE
The Extremes feature Bobby Sanders.
| Everlast 5013 | Let's Elope / Come Next Spring | 1958 | 5.00 | 25.00 |
| Paro 733 | The Bells / That's All I Want | 1962 | 50.00 | 200.00 |

EXZELS, THE
Crossfire 1914 — Canadian Sunset / Hit Talk — 196? — 8.00 — 40.00

EZRA & THE IVIES
United Artists 165 — Comic Book Crazy / Rockin' Shoes — 1959 — 3.00 — 15.00

F.

FABARES, SHELLEY

Colpix 621		Johnny Angel / Where's It Gonna Get Me?	1962	3.00	15.00
Colpix 621	(PS)	Johnny Angel / Where's It Gonna Get Me?	1962	20.00	100.00
Colpix 638		Johnny Loves Me / I'm Growing Up	1962	3.00	15.00
Colpix 638	(PS)	Johnny Loves Me / I'm Growing Up	1962	20.00	100.00
Colpix 654		The Things We Did Last Summer /			
		Breaking Up Is Hard To Do	1962	3.00	15.00
Colpix 667		Big Star / Telephone (Won't You Ring?)	1962	3.00	15.00
Colpix 682		Ronnie, Call Me When You Get A Chance /			
		I Left A Note To Say Goodbye	1963	3.00	15.00
Colpix 705		Welcome Home / Billy Boy	1963	3.00	15.00
Colpix 721		He Don't Love Me / Football Season's Over	1963	10.00	50.00
		("He Don't Love Me" was produced by Jan Berry.)			
Vee Jay 632	(DJ)	I Know You'll Be There / Lost Summer Love	1965	4.00	20.00
Vee Jay 632		I Know You'll Be There / Lost Summer Love	1965	8.00	40.00
		(Vee Jay 632 features The Fantastic Baggies.)			
Dunhill 4001		My Prayer / Pretty Please	1965	4.00	20.00
Dunhill 4041		See Ya' Round On The Rebound / Pretty Please	1965	4.00	20.00

FABARES, SHELLEY, & PAUL PETERSEN

Colpix 631		What Did They Do Before Rock And Roll? / Very Unlikely	1962	3.00	15.00
Colpix 631	(PS)	What Did They Do Before Rock And Roll? / Very Unlikely	1962	15.00	75.00

FABIAN (& THE FABULOUS FOUR)

Chancellor 1020		Shivers / I'm In Love	1958	3.00	15.00
Chancellor 1024		Lilly Lou / Be My Steady Date	1958	3.00	15.00
Chancellor 1029		I'm A Man / Hypnotized	1959	3.00	15.00
Chancellor 1029	(PS)	I'm A Man / Hypnotized	1959	5.00	25.00
Chancellor 1033		Turn Me Loose / Stop, Thief!	1959	3.00	15.00
		—Original Chancellor singles above have pink labels.—			
Chancellor 1020		Shivers / I'm In Love	1959	2.00	10.00
Chancellor 1024		Lilly Lou / Be My Steady Date	1959	2.00	10.00
Chancellor 1029		I'm A Man / Hypnotized	1959	3.00	15.00
Chancellor 1029	(PS)	I'm A Man / Hypnotized	1959	6.00	30.00
Chancellor 1029	(S)	I'm A Man / Hypnotized	1959	6.00	30.00
Chancellor 1033		Turn Me Loose / Stop, Thief!	1959	3.00	15.00
Chancellor 1033	(PS)	Turn Me Loose / Stop, Thief!	1959	6.00	30.00
Chancellor 1033	(S)	Turn Me Loose / Stop, Thief!	1959	6.00	30.00
Chancellor 1037		Tiger / Mighty Cold (To A Warm, Warm Heart)	1959	3.00	15.00
Chancellor 1037	(PS)	Tiger / Mighty Cold (To A Warm, Warm Heart)	1959	6.00	30.00
Chancellor 1037	(S)	Tiger / Mighty Cold (To A Warm, Warm Heart)	1959	6.00	30.00
Chancellor 1041		Come On And Get Me / Got The Feeling	1959	3.00	15.00
Chancellor 1041	(PS)	Come On And Get Me / Got The Feeling	1959	6.00	30.00
Chancellor 1041	(S)	Come On And Get Me / Got The Feeling	1959	6.00	30.00
Chancellor 1044		Hound Dog Man / This Friendly World	1959	3.00	15.00
Chancellor 1044	(PS)	Hound Dog Man / This Friendly World	1959	6.00	30.00
		(There are two different sleeves for this title.)			
Chancellor 1044	(S)	Hound Dog Man / This Friendly World	1959	6.00	30.00
Chancellor 1047		About This Thing Called Love / String Along	1960	2.00	10.00
Chancellor 1047	(PS)	About This Thing Called Love / String Along	1960	6.00	30.00
Chancellor 1047	(S)	About This Thing Called Love / String Along	1960	6.00	30.00
Chancellor 1051		Strollin' In The Springtime /			
		I'm Gonna Sit Right Down And Write Myself A Letter	1960	2.00	10.00
Chancellor 1051	(PS)	Strollin' In The Springtime /			
		I'm Gonna Sit Right Down And Write Myself A Letter	1960	6.00	30.00
Chancellor 1055		Tomorrow / King Of Love	1960	2.00	10.00
Chancellor 1055	(PS)	Tomorrow / King Of Love	1960	6.00	30.00
Chancellor 1061		Kissin' And Twistin' / Long Before	1960	2.00	10.00
Chancellor 1061	(PS)	Kissin' And Twistin' / Long Before	1960	6.00	30.00
Chancellor 1067		You Know You Belong To Somebody Else / Hold On	1961	2.00	10.00
Chancellor 1067	(PS)	You Know You Belong To Somebody Else / Hold On	1961	6.00	30.00
Chancellor 1072		Grapevine / David And Goliath	1961	2.00	10.00
Chancellor 1079		The Love That I'm Giving To You / You're Only Young Once	1961	4.00	20.00
Chancellor 1079	(PS)	The Love That I'm Giving To You / You're Only Young Once	1961	7.00	35.00
Chancellor 1084		A Girl Like You / Dream Factory	1961	2.00	10.00
Chancellor 1084	(PS)	A Girl Like You / Dream Factory	1961	6.00	30.00
Chancellor 1086		Tongue-Tied / Kansas City	1961	3.00	15.00
Chancellor 1092		Wild Party / Made You	1961	3.00	15.00
Chancellor 1092	(PS)	Wild Party / Made You	1961	7.00	35.00
		(Chancellor 1079, 1086 and 1092 feature The Fabulous Four.)			
Dot 16413		Break Down And Cry / She's Stayin' Inside With Me	1962	1.00	5.00

Label & Catalog #		A-Side/B-Side	Year	VG	NM
Cream 7717		The American East / Ease On Into My Life	197?	.80	4.00
Cream 7717	(PS)	The American East / Ease On Into My Life	197?	.80	4.00
		—Extended Play Albums—			
Chancellor A5003		Hold That Tiger (Volume 1)	1959	15.00	75.00
Chancellor B5003		Hold That Tiger (Volume 2)	1959	15.00	75.00
Chancellor C5003		Hold That Tiger (Volume 3)	1959	15.00	75.00
Chancellor A5005		The Fabulous Fabian (Volume 1)	1959	15.00	75.00
Chancellor B5005		The Fabulous Fabian (Volume 2)	1959	15.00	75.00
Chancellor C5005		The Fabulous Fabian (Volume 3)	1959	15.00	75.00
Chancellor A5006		Hound Dog Man	1959	15.00	75.00

FABIO & BRUNO

Vim 509	That's Why / Do You Know?	196?	2.00	10.00

FABS, THE

Cottonball 3604	Dinah Wants Religion / That's The Bag I'm In	1966	30.00	150.00

FABULAIRES, THE

Chelsea 103	Wedding Song / Lonely Days, Lonely Nights	1963	20.00	100.00
	(First pressing labels read "Distributed by Chelsea.")			
Chelsea 103	Wedding Song / Lonely Days, Lonely Nights	1963	5.00	25.00
	(Second pressings read "Distributed by Red Fox.")			

FABULONS, THE
The Fabulons also recorded with The Tikis.

Tower 259	Since You've Been Gone / Don't Ask Me	1966	2.00	10.00

FABULOUS BLENDS, THE: *Refer to* BIG JOHN & THE FABULOUS BLENDS

FABULOUS CHANCELLORS, THE

Ecco 1002	Hey Girl / Raindrops	196?	2.00	10.00
Chandal 101	Black Out / Diamond In The Sky	1963	2.00	10.00
Dot 16535	Black Out / Diamond In The Sky	1963	2.00	10.00

FABULOUS CONTINENTALS, THE

CB 5003	Undertow / Return To Me	1963	3.00	15.00
CB 5007	Let's Get Goin' / New York Walk	1963	3.00	15.00
Sioux 42061	Rockinental / Venus	1964	3.00	15.00
Rori 709	Breakin' Up / Venus	1964	3.00	15.00

FABULOUS FOUR, THE
The Fabulous Four also recorded with Fabian.

Chancellor 1062	In The Chapel In The Moonlight / Mr. Twist	1960	3.00	15.00
Chancellor 1068	Precious Moments / Let's Try Again	1960	4.00	20.00
Chancellor 1078	The Sound Of Summer / Why Do Fools Fall In Love?	1961	5.00	25.00
Chancellor 1085	Betty Ann / Prisoner Of Love	1961	10.00	50.00
Chancellor 1090	I'm Comin' Home / Everybody Knows	1961	4.00	20.00
Chancellor 1098	Everybody Knows / Mr. Twist	1961	4.00	20.00
Chancellor 1102	Forever / It's No Sin	1962	5.00	25.00
Melic 4114	Welcome Me Home / Oop Shoobee Doop	196?	10.00	50.00
Coral 62479	Now You Cry / Got To Get Her Back	1964	3.00	15.00
Brass 311	Now You Cry / Got To Get Her Back	1964	2.00	10.00
Brass 314	Who Could It Be? / Happy	1964	2.00	10.00
Brass 316	I'm Always Doing Something Wrong / Young Blood	1964	2.00	10.00

FABULOUS FUTURAS, THE

Okon	When You Ask About Love / La Doo Da Da	196?	3.00	15.00

FABULOUS GARDENIAS, THE [THE GARDENIAS]

Liz 1004	What's The Matter With Me? / Darling, It's You You You	1961	6.00	30.00
Fairlane 21019	What's The Matter With Me? / Darling, It's You You You	1962	3.00	15.00
	(Fairlane 21019 credits The Gardenias.)			

FABULOUS McCLEVERTYS, THE

Verve 10029	Don't Blame It On Elvis / Tickle, Tickle	1956	5.00	25.00

FABULOUS PACK, THE: *Refer to* TERRY KNIGHT & THE PACK

FABULOUS PEARL DEVINES, THE

Alco 101	You've Been Gone / So Lonely	1963	25.00	125.00

FABULOUS PEPS, THE [THE PEPS]
Refer to Tom Storm & The Peps.

Ge Ge 503	This Love I Have For You / She's Going To Leave You	1965	3.00	15.00
D-Town 1049	You Never Had It So Good / Detroit, Michigan	1965	2.00	10.00
D-Town 1060	Thinking About You / This I Pray	1965	2.00	10.00
	(D-Town 1049 and 1060 credit The Peps.)			
D-Town 1065	My Love Looks Good On You / Speak Your Peace	1966	2.00	10.00

Label & Catalog #	A-Side/B-Side	Year	VG	NM
Premium Stuff 1	I Can't Get Right / Why Are You Blowing My Mind?	1967	1.60	8.00
Premium Stuff 3	So Fine / I'll Never Be The Same Again	1967	1.60	8.00
Premium Stuff 7	Gypsy Woman / Why Are You Blowing My Mind?	1967	1.60	8.00
Wee-3 233	I've Been Trying / With These Eyes	1967	1.60	8.00
FABULOUS PLAYBOYS, THE				
Catalina 1069	Cheater Stomp / Shortenin' Bread	1962	6.00	30.00
FABULOUS ROYALS, THE				
Aegis 1006	I Only Have Eyes For You / Land Of 1,000 Dances	196?	2.00	10.00
FABULOUS RUMBLES, THE				
The Fabulous Rumbles also recorded with Rich Clayton.				
Soma 1448	Echoing Past / I'll Be Gone	196?	6.00	30.00
FABULOUS SHADOWS, THE				
Shadow 1256	Puff Stuff / Walking The Dog	196?	2.00	10.00
FACENDA, TOMMY				
LeGrande 1001	High School U.S.A. / Give Me Another Chance	1959	6.00	15.00
	(Purple label)			
Atlantic 45-51	High School U.S.A.-Virginia / Plea Of Love	1959	6.00	30.00
Atlantic 45-52	High School U.S.A.-New York City / Plea Of Love	1959	6.00	30.00
Atlantic 45-53	High School U.S.A.-North & South Carolina / Plea Of Love	1959	6.00	30.00
Atlantic 45-54	High School U.S.A.-Washington, DC / Plea Of Love	1959	6.00	30.00
Atlantic 45-55	High School U.S.A.-Philadelphia / Plea Of Love	1959	6.00	30.00
Atlantic 45-56	High School U.S.A.-Detroit / Plea Of Love	1959	6.00	30.00
Atlantic 45-57	High School U.S.A.-Pittsburgh / Plea Of Love	1959	6.00	30.00
Atlantic 45-58	High School U.S.A.-Minneapolis & St. Paul / Plea Of Love	1959	6.00	30.00
Atlantic 45-59	High School U.S.A.-Florida / Plea Of Love	1959	6.00	30.00
Atlantic 45-60	High School U.S.A.-Newark, NJ / Plea Of Love	1959	6.00	30.00
Atlantic 45-61	High School U.S.A.-Boston / Plea Of Love	1959	6.00	30.00
Atlantic 45-62	High School U.S.A.-Cleveland / Plea Of Love	1959	6.00	30.00
Atlantic 45-63	High School U.S.A.-Buffalo / Plea Of Love	1959	6.00	30.00
Atlantic 45-64	High School U.S.A.-Hartford / Plea Of Love	1959	6.00	30.00
Atlantic 45-65	High School U.S.A.-Nashville / Plea Of Love	1959	6.00	30.00
Atlantic 45-66	High School U.S.A.-Indianapolis / Plea Of Love	1959	6.00	30.00
Atlantic 45-67	High School U.S.A.-Chicago / Plea Of Love	1959	6.00	30.00
Atlantic 45-68	High School U.S.A.-New Orleans / Plea Of Love	1959	6.00	30.00
Atlantic 45-69	High School U.S.A.-St. Louis & Kansas City / Plea Of Love	1959	6.00	30.00
Atlantic 45-70	High School U.S.A.-Georgia & Alabama / Plea Of Love	1959	6.00	30.00
Atlantic 45-71	High School U.S.A.-Cincinnati / Plea Of Love	1959	6.00	30.00
Atlantic 45-72	High School U.S.A.-Memphis / Plea Of Love	1959	6.00	30.00
Atlantic 45-73	High School U.S.A.-Los Angeles / Plea Of Love	1959	6.00	30.00
Atlantic 45-74	High School U.S.A.-San Francisco / Plea Of Love	1959	6.00	30.00
Atlantic 45-75	High School U.S.A.-Texas / Plea Of Love	1959	6.00	30.00
Atlantic 45-76	High School U.S.A.-Seattle & Portland / Plea Of Love	1959	6.00	30.00
Atlantic 45-77	High School U.S.A.-Denver / Plea Of Love	1959	6.00	30.00
Atlantic 45-78	High School U.S.A.-Oklahoma / Plea Of Love	1959	6.00	30.00
	("High School U.S.A." is the same track with the names of different cities and schools dubbed in for regional play.)			
Atlantic 2057	Little Baby / I Don't Know	1959	3.00	15.00
Nasco 6108	Little Baby / You Are My Everything	1959	3.00	15.00
FACES, THE				
Regina 1326	What Is This Dream? / Skeeter Jones	1965	5.00	25.00
Regina 1328	I'll Walk Alone / I Didn't Want Her	1965	5.00	25.00
Iguana 601	Christmas / New Year's Resolution	1965	40.00	200.00
FACES, THE: *Refer to* **THE SMALL FACES**				
FACETS, THE				
Terrible Tommy's 2675	Ruby Baby / Hanging By A String	196?	2.00	10.00
Atra 1000	Opposites / Pure Camp	196?	2.00	10.00
FADS, THE				
Mercury 72542	Just Like A Woman / The Problem Is	1966	2.00	10.00
FAIR, CARLO				
Express 801	Beetle Bounce /	1964	3.00	15.00
FAIRBURN, WERLY				
Savoy 1503	All The Time / I'm A Fool About Your Love	1956	4.00	20.00
Savoy 1521	Telephone Baby / No Blues Tomorrow	1957	4.00	20.00
FAIRLANES, THE				
Radiant 101	Baby Baby / Tell Me	195?	40.00	200.00
Lucky Seven 102	Seventeen Steps / Johnny Rhythm	1959	7.00	35.00

Label & Catalog #		A-Side/B-Side	Year	VG	NM
Argo 5357		Comin' After You / Little Girl, Little Girl	1960	6.00	30.00
Continental 1001		Writing This Letter / Playboy	196?	6.00	30.00
FAIRLANES, THE					
Minaret 103		I'm Not The Kind Of Guy / The Dagwood	1962	3.00	15.00
Reprise 20213		Surf Train / Lonely Weekends	1963	4.00	20.00
FAIRMOUNTS, THE					
Planet 53		Times And Places / Lucky Guy	195?	8.00	40.00
FAIRPORT CONVENTION					
A&M 1108		Fotheringay / I'll Keep It With Mine	1972	1.00	5.00
A&M 1333		Journeyman's Grace / The World Has Surely Lost Its Head	1972	1.00	5.00
A&M 1348		The Time Is Near / John Lee	1972	1.00	5.00
A&M 1155		Si Tu Dois Partiri / Genesis Hall	1971	1.00	5.00
FAITH, ADAM					
Cub 9061		What Do You Want? / From Now Until Forever	1959	2.00	10.00
Cub 9068		Poor Me / The Reason	1959	2.00	10.00
Cub 9074		I Did What You Told Me / Johnny Comes Marching Home	1960	2.00	10.00
Dot 16405		Don't That Beat All / Mix Me A Person	1962	2.00	10.00
Amy 895		So Long, Baby / The First Time	1964	2.00	10.00
Amy 899		We Are In Love / What Now?	1964	2.00	10.00
Amy 913		It's Alright / I Just Don't Know	1965	2.00	10.00
Amy 922		Talk About Love / Stop Feeling Sorry For Yourself	1965	2.00	10.00
Capitol 5543		I Don't Need That Kind Of Lovin' / I'm Used To Losing You	1965	1.00	5.00
Capitol 5699		I Don't Need That Kind Of Lovin' / I'm Used To Losing You	1965	1.00	5.00
FAITH BAND, THE					
Village 202		Dancin' Shoes / Desire	1978	1.00	5.00
FAITHFULL, MARIANNE					
London 9697		As Tears Go By / Greensleeves	1964	1.20	6.00
London 9731		Come And Stay With Me / What Have I Done Wrong?	1965	1.20	6.00
London 9759		This Little Bird / Morning Sun	1965	1.20	6.00
London 9780		Summer Nights / The Sha-La-La Song	1965	1.20	6.00
London 9802		Go Away From My World / Oh, Look Around You	1965	1.20	6.00
London 9802	(PS)	Go Away From My World / Oh, Look Around You	1965	2.00	10.00
London 20012		Counting / Tomorrow's Calling	1966	1.20	6.00
London 20012	(PS)	Counting / Tomorrow's Calling	1966	2.00	10.00
London 21022	(DJ)	Sister Morphine / Something Better	1969	10.00	50.00
London 21022		Sister Morphine / Something Better	1969	20.00	100.00
		("Sister Morphine" features a backing track recorded for The Rolling Stones "Beggar's Banquet" album.)			
Island 49121		Broken English / Brain Drain	1979	.40	2.00
		—Extended Play Albums—			
London 452	(33)	Go Away From My World	1966	3.00	15.00
FALCONE, TOMMY, & THE CENTURIES					
Design 841		Like Weird / Ship To Shore	1959	2.00	10.00
FALTSKOG, AGNETHA					
Agnetha Faltskog also recorded as a member of Abba.					
Polydor 815230		Can't Shake Loose / Man	1983	.30	2.00
Polydor 815230	(PS)	Can't Shake Loose / Man	1983	.30	2.00
Atlantic 89145		I Wasn't The One / Maybe It Was Magic	1988	.30	2.00
Atlantic 89055		Let It Shine / Maybe It Was Magic	1988	.30	2.00
Atlantic 89055	(PS)	Let It Shine / Maybe It Was Magic	1988	.30	2.00
		—12" Singles—			
Polydor 216-1		Can't Shake Loose (AOR remix)	1983	.80	4.00
FALLEN ANGELS, THE					
Tollie 9049		Up On The Mountain / So Young, So Fine	1965	3.00	15.00
Laurie 3343		Everytime I Fall In Love / I Have Found	1966	2.00	10.00
Laurie 3369		A Little Love From You Will Do / Have You Ever Lost A Love?	1966	2.00	10.00
FALLING PEBBLES, THE					
The Falling Pebbles later recorded as The Buckinghams.					
Alley Cat 201		Lawdy, Miss Clawdy / Virginia Wolf	196?	5.00	25.00
FALLING STARS, THE					
Black 101		Batman / Real Batman	1966	3.00	15.00
FALLOWS, SCOTT, & THE EBBTIDES					
Dot 16577		Surfing Boop-Boop A-Doo / King Of Lovers	1964	4.00	20.00

Label & Catalog #	A-Side/B-Side	Year	VG	NM
FAME, GEORGIE (& THE BLUE FLAMES)				
Imperial 66086	Yeh, Yeh / Preach And Teach	1965	1.20	6.00
Imperial 66106	In The Meantime / Let The Sunshine In	1965	1.00	5.00
Imperial 66125	Like We Used To Be / Blue Monday	1965	1.00	5.00
Imperial 66189	Get Away / El Bandido	1966	1.20	6.00
Imperial 66299	Last Night / Funny How Time Slips Away	1967	1.00	5.00
Epic 10283	Ballad Of Bonnie And Clyde / Beware Of The Dog	1968	.80	4.00
Epic 10347	Hideaway / Kentucky Child	1968	.60	3.00
Epic 10402	Someone To Watch Over Me / For Your Pleasure	1969	.60	3.00
Epic 10640	The Movie Star Song / Fire And Rain	1970	.60	3.00
Island 035	Everlovin' Woman / Ozone	1975	.50	2.50
FAME & PRICE				
Georgie Fame and Alan Price.				
Reprise 1014	Rosetta / John And Mary	1971	.60	3.00
FAMILY, THE				
U.S.A. 886	Face The Autumn / So Much To Remember	1968	2.00	10.00
Vanguard 144101	Saigon Girls / Water Music	196?	1.00	5.00
FAMILY TREE, THE				
Mira 228	Prince Of Dreams / Live Your Own Life	1966	2.00	10.00
RCA Victor 47-9184	Do You Have The Time? / Keepin' A Secret	1967	1.00	5.00
RCA Victor 47-9565	Slippin' Through My Fingers / Miss Butters	1968	1.00	5.00
RCA Victor 47-9671	She Had To Fly / He Spins Around	1968	1.00	5.00
Paula 329	Electric Kangaroo / Terry Tommy	1968	1.00	5.00
FANNY				
Fanny features Joan and June Millington.				
Reprise 0901	Ladies Choice / New Day	1970	.60	3.00
Reprise 0938	Nowhere To Run / One Step At A Time	1970	.60	3.00
Reprise 0963	Changing Horse / Conversation With A Cop	1971	.60	3.00
Reprise 1033	Charity Ball / Place In The Country	1971	.60	3.00
Reprise 1080	Ain't That Peculiar / Think About The Children	1972	.60	3.00
Reprise 1097	Wonderful Feeling / Rock Bottom Blues	1972	.60	3.00
Reprise 1119	Knock On My Door / Young And Dumb	1973	.60	3.00
Reprise 1148	All Mine / I Need You Need Me	1973	.60	3.00
Reprise 1162	Last Night I Had A Dream / Beside Myself	1973	.60	3.00
FANS, THE				
Dot 16688	I Want A Beetle For Christmas / How Far Should My Heart Go?	1964	3.00	15.00
FANTASTIC BAGGYS, THE				
The Baggys — Steve Barri and P. F. Sloan — also recorded with Shelly Fabares and Jan & Dean.				
Imperial 66047	Tell 'Em I'm Surfin' / A Surfer Boy's Dream	1964	6.00	30.00
Imperial 66072	Anywhere The Girls Are / Debbie, Be True	1964	6.00	30.00
Imperial 66092	Alone On The Beach / It Was I	1965	7.00	35.00
FANTASTICS, THE				
Scorpio 407	Dance For An Un-Named Gypsy Queen / Malaguena	1966	3.00	15.00
FANTASYS, THE				
Shirle 4	Surf's Up / I've Been Good To You	196?	6.00	30.00
FARLOWE, CHRIS (& THE THUNDERBIRDS)				
MGM 13567	Out Of Time / Baby, Make It Soon	1966	2.00	10.00
Immediate 5002	Paint It Black / You're So Good To Me	1967	1.20	6.00
Immediate 5005	Handbags And Gladrags / Everybody Makes A Mistake	1968	1.20	6.00
Immediate 5011	Paint It Black / What Have I Been Doing?	1968	1.20	6.00
FARMER, DONNY				
Roulette 4139	My Bride / A Boy, A Girl And A Breeze	1959	3.00	15.00
FARNER, MARK, & DON BREWER				
Farner and Brewer also recorded with Terry Knight & The Pack and Grand Funk Railroad.				
Lucky Eleven 74011	We Gotta Have Love / Harlem Shuffle	1968	2.00	10.00
FARNER BAND, MARK				
Atlantic 3448	You And Me, Baby / Second Chance To Dance	1977	.60	3.00
Atlantic 3510	When A Man Loves A Woman / It Took All Day	1978	.80	4.00
Atlantic 3529	Just One Look / Crystal Eyes	1978	.60	3.00
FARR, GARY, & THE T-BONES				
Epic 9832	Give All She's Got / Don't Stop And Stare	1965	2.00	10.00
FARR, LITTLE JOEY				
Band Box 286	Rock And Roll Santa / Big White Cadillac	1961	25.00	125.00

Label & Catalog #	A-Side/B-Side	Year	VG	NM
FARRAR, TONY				
Trans Atlas 001	**A Blast From The Past / Following You**	1961	5.00	25.00
FARRELL, MICKEY, & THE DYNAMICS				
Bethlehem 3080	**Baby Mine / I'm Calling On You**	1964	3.00	15.00
FARRELL, TONY				
Time 1000	**A Flame In My Heart / Stumpy Stump**	1958	5.00	25.00
FARRELL & THE FLAMES				
Fransil 14	**You'll Be Sorry / Dreams And Memories**	195?	100.00	400.00
FASCINATORS, THE				
Capitol 4053	**Chapel Bells / I Wonder Who**	1958	25.00	125.00
Capitol 4137	**Who Do You Think You Are? / Come To Paradise**	1959	20.00	100.00
	(First pressings have technical info etched in trail-off vinyl.)			
Capitol 4137	**Who Do You Think You Are? / Come To Paradise**	1959	5.00	25.00
	(Second pressings have the info stamped in trail-off vinyl.)			
Capitol 4247	**Oh, Rose Marie / Fried Chicken And Macaroni**	1959	40.00	200.00
Capitol 4544	**Chapel Bells / I Wonder Who**	1960	15.00	75.00
Btm Bam Boom 110	**Oh, Rose Marie / Forgive Me, My Darling**	197?	2.00	10.00
FASHIONETTES, THE				
GNP/Crescendo 322	**Daydreamin' Of You / Only Love**	1966	4.00	20.00
FASHIONS, THE				
Elmor 301	**Please, Let It Be Me / Fairy Tales**	195?	5.00	25.00
FASHIONS, THE				
Felsted 8689	**Surfer's Memories / Surfin' Back To School**	1963	7.00	35.00
FAT BOYS & THE BEACH BOYS, THE				
Tin Pan Apple 885960	**Wipeout / Question**	1987	.40	2.00
Tin Pan Apple 885960 *(PS)*	**Wipeout / Question**	1987	.40	2.00
FATHOMS, THE				
Thumbs Down 1001	**Down To The Sea / Heart Breakin' Baby**	196?	2.00	10.00
FEATHERS, CHARLIE				
Flip 503	**Peeping Eyes / I've Been Deceived**	1955	150.00	500.00
Sun 503	**Peeping Eyes / I've Been Deceived**	1956	100.00	400.00
Sun 231	**Defrost Your Heart / Wedding Gown Of White**	1956	150.00	600.00
Meteor 5032	**Tongue Tied Jill / Get With It** *(Maroon label)*	1956	——	——
	(Rare. Estimated near mint value $500-1,000.)			
Meteor 5032	**Tongue Tied Jill / Get With It** *(Black label)*	195?	75.00	300.00
King 4971	**Can't Hardly Stand It / Everybody's Lovin' My Baby**	1956	75.00	300.00
King 4997	**One Hand Loose / Bottle To The Baby**	1956	50.00	250.00
King 5022	**When You Decide / Nobody's Woman**	1957	30.00	150.00
King 5043	**Too Much Alike / When You Come Around**	1957	30.00	150.00
Kay 1001	**Jungle Fever / Why Don't You?**	1960	40.00	200.00
Wal-May 101	**Dinky John / South Of Chicago**	1960	40.00	200.00
Memphis 103	**Wild, Wild Party / Today And Tomorrow**	1961	20.00	100.00
Holiday Inn 114	**Nobody's Darlin' / Deep Elm Blues**	1963	25.00	125.00
FEATHERS, THE				
Team 518	**Tryin' To Get To You / My Baby's Soul Good**	1968	1.20	6.00
FEDERALS, THE				
Capitol 5526	**Bucket Full Of Love / Leah**	1965	1.20	6.00
FEELIES, THE				
Jerden 904	**Louie Louie / Warm Woman**	1968	2.00	10.00
Jerden 910	**Happy / Look At Me**	1969	1.00	5.00
FELDER'S ORIOLES				
Mercury 72480	**Down Home Girl / Misty**	1965	2.00	10.00
FELICITY, THE				
Felicity features Don Henley.				
Wilson 101	**Hurtin' / I'll Try It**	1965	6.00	30.00
FELIX & THE ESCORTS				
The Escorts later recorded as The Young Rascals.				
Jag 685	**The Syracuse / Save**	1964	25.00	125.00
FELTS, NARVEL				
Mercury 71140	**Kiss-A-Me, Baby / Foolish Thoughts**	1957	4.00	20.00
Mercury 71190	**Cry, Baby, Cry / Lonesome Feeling**	1957	4.00	20.00

Label & Catalog #	A-Side / B-Side	Year	VG	NM
Mercury 71249	Dream World / Rocket Ride	1957	4.00	20.00
Mercury 71249	Dream World / Rocket Ride Stroll	1957	3.00	15.00
Pink 701	Cutie Baby / 3,000 Miles	1959	3.00	15.00
Pink 702	Honey Love / Genavee	1960	3.00	15.00
Groove 0029	Mountain Of Love / End Of My World	1963	3.00	15.00

FEMALE BEATLES, THE

20th Century Fox 531	I Want You / I Don't Want To Cry	1964	3.00	15.00

FENCEMEN, THE

Liberty 55509	Swingin' Gates / Bach 'N' Roll	1962	2.00	10.00
Liberty 55535	Sour Grapes / Sunday Stranger	1963	2.00	10.00

FENDER, FREDDY

Freddy's discography below is an interesting combination of rock and rhythm 'n blues, often with an Hispanic flavor. In 1975 he crashed the country charts, where he has enjoyed a healthy career as a country artist. Freddy also recorded as The Be Bop Kid; Boo & The Girlfriends; Satan & The Disciples; Scotty Wayne.

Duncan 1000	Mean Woman / Holy One	1959	5.00	25.00
Duncan 1001	Wasted Days And Wasted Nights / San Antonio Rock	1959	4.00	20.00
Duncan 1002	Crazy Baby / The Wild Side Of Life	1959	4.00	20.00
Duncan 1004	Since I Met You, Baby / Little Mama	1959	4.00	20.00
Talent Scout 1002	Crazy Baby / The Wild Side Of Life	1959	3.00	15.00
Talent Scout 1007	Find Someone New / Lonely Night	1960	3.00	15.00
Talent Scout 1013	Wasted Days And Wasted Nights / San Antonio Rock	1960	3.00	15.00
Talent Scout 1014	A Man Can Cry / You're Something Else	1961	3.00	15.00
Imperial 5659	Mean Woman / Holy One	1960	4.00	20.00
Imperial 5670	Wasted Days And Wasted Nights / I Can't Remember (When I Didn't Love You)	1960	3.00	15.00
Argo 5375	A Man Can Cry / You're Something Else	1961	2.00	10.00
Norco 100	Love Light Is An Ember / The New Stroll	1963	2.00	10.00
Norco 102	Never Trust A Cheating Woman / You Made Me Cry	1963	2.00	10.00
Norco 103	Going Out With The Tide / Coming Home Soon	196?	1.60	8.00
Norco 104	Just A Little Bit / You Made Me A Fool	196?	1.60	8.00
Norco 106	Ooh Poo Pah Doo / Three Wishes	196?	1.60	8.00
Norco 107	The Magic Of Love / Bony Maronie	196?	1.60	8.00
Norco 108	In The Still Of The Night / You Don't Have To Go	196?	1.60	8.00
Norco 111	Donna / Lover's Quarrel	196?	1.60	8.00
ARV 5083	Crazy Arms / She Thinks I Still Care	196?	1.60	8.00
Pa Go Go 115	Cool Mary Lou / You Are My Sunshine	1967	1.20	6.00
Goldband 1214	My Train Of Love / Carmella	196?	1.20	6.00
Goldband 1272	Three Wishes / Me And My Bottle Of Rum	196?	1.20	6.00
Goldband 1264	Bye Bye, Little Angel / Oh My Love	196?	1.20	6.00
Instand 3332	Today's Your Wedding Day / Some People Say	1969	1.00	5.00
Pacemaker 1973	Wasted Days And Wasted Nights / Bidin' My Time	197?	.80	4.00

FENDER IV, THE

The Fender IV features Randy Holden, later of The Other Half.

Imperial 66061	Mar Gaya / You Better Tell Me Now	1964	8.00	40.00
Imperial 66098	Malibu Run / Everybody Up	1965	8.00	40.00

FENDERMEN, THE

Cuca 1003	Mule Skinner Blues / Torture	1960	30.00	150.00
Soma 1137	Mule Skinner Blues / Torture	1960	3.00	15.00
Soma 1142	Don't You Just Know It? / Beach Party	1960	2.00	10.00
Soma 1155	Can't You Wait? / Heartbreakin' Special	1960	2.00	10.00
Dab 102	Rain Drop / Fas-Nacht-Kuechel	196?	2.00	10.00

FENTON, SHANE, & THE FENTONES

20th Century Fox 439	Don't Do That / I'll Know	1963	3.00	15.00
Laurie 3287	Don't Do That / I'll Know	1965	2.00	10.00

FENWAYS, THE

Ricky L 106	Nothing To Offer You / The #1 Song In The Country	1964	10.00	50.00
Beu Mar 401	Nothing To Offer You / Humpty Dumpty	1964	4.00	20.00
Beu Mar 402	Be Careful, Little Girl / Be Careful, Little Girl, Part 2	1964	4.00	20.00
Roulette 4573	Be Careful, Little Girl / Be Careful, Little Girl, Part 2	1964	2.00	10.00
Blue Cat 116	Hard Road Ahead / The Fight	1964	2.00	10.00
Chess 1901	Nothing To Offer You / Humpty Dumpty	1964	4.00	20.00
Imperial 66082	Walk / Whip And Jerk	1964	2.00	10.00
Co&Ce 233	I'm A Mover / Satisfied	1966	2.00	10.00
Co&Ce 241	I Move Around / A Go-Go	1966	2.00	10.00
Co&Ce 243	I'm Your Toy / Theme For Pammy	1966	2.00	10.00

FERGUSON, JOHNNY

MGM 12789	Waitin' For The Sandman / Afterglow	1959	2.00	10.00
MGM 12855	Angela Jones / Blue Serge And White Lace	1960	2.00	10.00
MGM 12905	I Understand Just How You Feel / Flutter Flutter	1960	2.00	10.00

Label & Catalog #		A-Side/B-Side	Year	VG	NM
FERN, BILL					
Sport 505		Big Game / Stolen Bases	196?	3.00	15.00
FERRA, TINA					
Limelight 3027		R (Is For Ringo) / Modern Youth	1964	3.00	15.00
FERRIER, AL					
Excello 2105		I'm The Man / Hey Baby	195?	15.00	75.00
FERRIER, GARRY					
Academy 112		Ringo-Deer / Just My Luck	1964	3.00	15.00
FERRIS & THE WHEELS					
Bambi 801		I Want To Dance (Every Night) / Chop Chop	1961	5.00	25.00
United Artists 458		Moments Like This / He Was A Fortune Teller	1962	10.00	50.00
FEVER TREE					
Mainstream 661		Hey, Mister / I Can Beat Your Drum	1967	2.00	10.00
Mainstream 665		Girl, Oh Girl (Don't Push Me) / Steve Lenore	1967	2.00	10.00
Uni 55060	(DJ)	San Francisco Girls (Return Of The Native) / San Francisco Girls (Return Of The Native) (*Blue vinyl*)	1968	4.00	20.00
Uni 55060		San Francisco Girls (Return Of The Native) / Come With Me (Rain Song)	1968	1.20	6.00
Uni 55095		Where Do You Go? / What Time Did You Say It Was In Salt Lake City?	1968	1.20	6.00
Uni 55146		Love Makes The Sun Rise / Filigree And Shadow	1969	1.20	6.00
Uni 55172		Clancy / The Sun Also Rises	1969	1.20	6.00
Uni 55202		Catcher In The Rye / What Time Did You Say It Is In Salt Lake City?	1969	1.20	6.00
Uni 55228	(DJ)	I Am / I Am	1970	2.00	10.00
		(Stock copies of Uni 55228 may not exist.)			
Ampex 11013		She Comes In Colors / You're Not The Same Baby	1970	1.20	6.00
Ampex 11028	(DJ)	I Put A Spell On You / Hey Joe	1970	2.00	10.00
		(Stock copies of Ampex 11028 may not exist.)			
FI-DELLS, THE					
Imperial 5780		What Is Love? / Don't Let Me Love You	1961	3.00	15.00
FIDELITONES, THE					
Marlo 1518		Playboy / Say Hey, Pretty Baby	196?	4.00	20.00
FIDELLS, THE					
Warner 1014		No Other / Come Back To Me	196?	3.00	15.00
FIELD, JERRY, & THE (PHILADELPHIA) LAWYERS					
Arch		The Trial / Herb B. Lou And The Legal Eagles	1959	4.00	20.00
Parkway 801		The Trial / Easy Steppin'	1959	3.00	15.00
FIENDS, THE					
Dan-D F1/F2		Thank You, Thing / Quetzal Quake	1965	4.00	20.00
GNP/Crescendo 335		Theme From "The Addams Family" / Quetzal Quake	1965	4.00	20.00
FIFTH ESTATE, THE					
The Fifth Estate originally recorded as The D-Men.					
Red Bird 064		Love Is All A Game / Like I Love You	1966	2.00	10.00
Jubilee 5573		Ding Dong! The Witch Is Dead / The Rub-A-Dub	1967	1.00	5.00
Jubilee 5588		Lost Generation / The Goffin Song	1967	.60	3.00
Jubilee 5595		Heigh-Ho / It's Waiting There For You	1967	.60	3.00
Jubilee 5607		Morning, Morning / Tomorrow Is My Turn	1967	.60	3.00
Jubilee 5617		Do Drop Inn / That's Love	1967	.60	3.00
Jubilee 5627		Coney Island Sally / Tomorrow Is My Turn	1967	.60	3.00
Jubilee 5655		Mickey Mouse Club March / I Knew You Before I Met You	1968	1.00	5.00
Jubilee 5683	(DJ)	Parade Of The Wooden Soldiers / Parade Of The Wooden Soldiers	1969	2.00	10.00
Jubilee 5683	(DJ)	Parade Of The Wooden Soldiers / I Knew You Before I Met You	1969	2.00	10.00
		(Stock copies of Jubilee 5683 may not exist.)			
FILES, THE					
The Files feature Larry Norman.					
Capitol 2429		Blow In My Ear And I'll Follow You Anywhere / I Got A Letter Today From The President	1969	4.00	20.00
FINDERS KEEPERS					
Fontana 1609		Friday Kind Of Monday / On The Beach	1968	1.00	5.00

Label & Catalog #		A-Side/B-Side	Year	VG	NM
FINNEGAN, LARRY					
Coral 62313		There Ain't Nothin' In This World / I'll Be Back, Jack	1962	2.00	10.00
Old Town 1113		Dear One / Candy Lips	1962	2.00	10.00
Old Town 1120		Pretty Little Sunshine / The Walkin' Talkin' Blues	1963	2.00	10.00
Ric 146		A Tribute To Ringo Starr / When My Love Passes By	1964	2.00	10.00
FINNEGAN, MIKE, & THE SERFS					
Parkway 113		Bread And Water / Help Me, Somebody	196?	1.00	5.00
FINN, MICKEY, & THE BLUE MEN					
United Artists 1048		This Sporting Life / Night Comes Down	1965	2.00	10.00
FIRE					
Wall Of Sound 208		Happy Spring Time / Sorry For Tryin'	1968	2.00	10.00
FIRE ESCAPE, THE					
GNP-Crescendo 384		Love Special Delivery / Blood Beat	1967	2.00	10.00

FIREBALLS, THE [JIMMY GILMER & THE FIREBALLS]
The Fireballs feature George Tomsco, Chuck Tharp and Jimmy Gilmer. The following singles, all of which are by The Fireballs, have either or both sides credited to Jimmy Gilmer or Jimmy Gilmer & The Fireballs: Warwick 547 and 592; Hamilton 50037; Dot 16487, 539, 583, 609, 642, 666, 768, 687, 714, 743, 768, 786, 833, 881 and 992; Atco 6583 and 6716. Refer to Guitars Inc.; Buddy Holly; Lupe.

Label & Catalog #		A-Side/B-Side	Year	VG	NM
Kapp 248		Fireball / I Don't Know	1958	4.00	20.00
Top Rank 2008		Torquay / Cry Baby	1959	3.00	15.00
Top Rank 2026		Bulldog / Nearly Sunrise	1959	2.00	10.00
Top Rank 2038		Foot Pattern / Kissin'	1960	2.00	10.00
Top Rank 2038	(S)	Foot Pattern / Kissin'	1960	7.00	35.00
Top Rank 2054		Vaquero / Chief Whoopen Koff	1960	2.00	10.00
Top Rank 2081		Almost Paradise / Sweet Talk	1960	2.00	10.00
Top Rank 3003		Rik-A-Tik / Yacky Doo	1961	2.00	10.00
Lucky 0012		Long, Long Ponytail / Let There Be Love	1960	35.00	175.00
Jaro 77029		Long, Long Ponytail / Let There Be Love	1960	10.00	50.00
		(The Lucky and Jaro singles credit Chuck Tharp & The Fireballs.)			
Warwick 547		True Love Ways / Wishing	1960	3.00	15.00
Warwick 592		Good, Good Lovin' / Do You Think?	1960	3.00	15.00
Warwick 630		Rik-A-Tik / Yacky Doo	1961	2.00	10.00
Warwick 644		Quite A Party / Gunshot	1961	2.00	10.00
7 Arts 714		Call In The Sheriff / Don't Stop	196?	2.00	10.00
7 Arts 714	(PS)	Call In The Sheriff / Don't Stop	196?	6.00	30.00
Hamilton 50036		Blacksmith Blues / Tuff-A-Nuff	1963	2.00	10.00
Hamilton 50037		I'm Gonna Go Walking / Won't Be Long	1963	2.00	10.00
Dot 16487		Sugar Shack / My Heart Is Free	1963	1.60	8.00
Dot 16493		Torquay / Two Peg Legs	1963	1.60	8.00
Dot 16539		Daisy Petal Pickin' / When My Tears Have Dried	1963	1.60	8.00
Dot 16583		Ain't Gonna Tell Anybody / Young Am I	1964	1.60	8.00
Dot 16591		Daytona Drag / Gently Gently	1964	2.00	10.00
Dot 16609		Look At Me / I'll Send For Her	1964	1.60	8.00
Dot 16642		What Kinda Love? / Wishing	1964	1.60	8.00
Dot 16661		Dumbo / Mr. Reed	1964	2.00	10.00
Dot 16666		Cry Baby / Thunder And Lightnin'	1964	1.60	8.00
Dot 16692		Baby, What's Wrong? / Yummie Yama Papa	1964	2.00	10.00
Dot 16715		More Than I Can Say / The Beating Of My Heart	1965	2.00	10.00
Dot 16745		Campusology / Ahhh, Soul	1965	2.00	10.00
Dot 16768		Come To Me / Codine	1965	1.60	8.00
Dot 16834		Jada / What I Am	1966	2.00	10.00
Dot 16687		Break His Heart For Me / Cinnamon Cindy	1965	1.60	8.00
Dot 16714		Lonesome Tears / Born To Be With You	1965	1.60	8.00
Dot 16743		The Fool / Somebody Stole My Watermelon	1965	1.60	8.00
Dot 16768		Codine / Come To Me	1965	1.60	8.00
Dot 16786		Ramblers Blues / She Belongs To Me	1965	1.60	8.00
Dot 16833		Hungry, Hungry, Hungry / White Roses	1966	1.60	8.00
Dot 16881		All I Do Is Dream Of You / Ain't That Rain	1966	1.60	8.00
Dot 16918		Torquay Two / Say I Am	1966	2.00	10.00
Dot 16992		Shy Girl / I Think I'll Catch A Bus	1967	1.60	8.00
Atco 6491		Bottle Of Wine / Can't You See I'm Trying?	1967	1.20	6.00
Atco 6569		Goin' Away / Groovy Motions	1968	1.00	5.00
Atco 6583		Three Squares / Baby	1968	1.00	5.00
Atco 6595		Chicken Little / Three Minutes Time	1968	1.00	5.00
Atco 6614		Come On, React! / Woman, Help Me	1968	1.00	5.00
Atco 6651		Long Green / Light In The Window	1969	1.00	5.00
Atco 6678		Watch Her Walk / Good Morning Shame	1970	1.00	5.00
Atco 6716		Model Child / Sugar In The Woods	1969	1.00	5.00
		—Extended Play Albums—			
Top Rank 1000		The Fireballs	1960	50.00	200.00

Label & Catalog #		A-Side/B-Side	Year	VG	NM
FIREFLIES, THE					
The Fireflies feature Richie Adams.					
Ribbon 6901		You Were Mine (For Awhile) / Stella Got A Fella	1959	2.00	10.00
Ribbon 6904		I Can't Say Goodbye / What Did I Do Wrong?	1969	2.00	10.00
Ribbon 6906		My Girl / Because Of My Pride	1960	2.00	10.00
Canadian Am. 117		Give All Your Love To Me / Marianne	1960	3.00	15.00
Taurus 355		You Were Mine (For Awhile) / One O' Clock Twist	1962	3.00	15.00
Taurus 366		My Prayer For You / Good Friends	1964	3.00	15.00
Taurus 376		Runaround / Could You Mean More?	1965	3.00	15.00
Taurus 380		Tonight / A Time For Us	1965	3.00	15.00
FIRESIGN THEATRE, THE					
Columbia 45052		Station Break / Forward Into The Past	1969	2.00	10.00
Columbia 45052	(PS)	Station Break / Forward Into The Past	1969	8.00	40.00
Columbia AE-34	(DJ)	This Side *(One sided)*	1970	2.00	10.00
Columbia AE7-1022	(DJ)	The Holygram Song / Mr. President	1970	2.00	10.00
Columbia AE7-1041	(DJ)	Live From The Senate Bar (If You Call That Living!) /			
		40 Great Unclaimed Melodies	1972	2.00	10.00
Columbia AE7-1059	(DJ)	Live From The Senate Bar (If You Call That Living!) /			
		Mr. President	1972	2.00	10.00
Rhino RNPD-904		Reagan Vs. Carter *(Picture disc)*	1980	1.00	5.00
		—*Extended Play Albums*—			
Columbia AS-89	(DJ)	For Your Ears Only	1970	4.00	20.00
Mercury PRO-388	(DJ)	DJ Bites From "Eat Or Be Eaten"	1985	3.00	15.00
FIRST EDITION, THE					
The First Edition later recorded country/pop as Kenny Rogers & The First Edition.					
Reprise 0625		Tell It All, Brother / Just Remember You're My Sunshine	1967	.80	4.00
Reprise 0628		I Found A Reason / Ticket To Nowhere	1967	.80	4.00
Reprise 0655		Just Dropped In (To See What Condition My Condition			
		Was In) / Shadow In The Corner Of Your Mind	1968	1.20	6.00
Reprise 0638		Dream On / Only Me	1968	.80	4.00
Reprise 0693		Look Around, I'll Be There / Charlie The Fer De Lance	1968	.80	4.00
Reprise 0773		If I Could Only Change Your Mind /			
		My Thoughts Are With You	1969	.80	4.00
Reprise 0799		But You Know I Love You / Home Made Lies	1969	.80	4.00
Reprise 0822		Good Time Liberator / Once Again She's All Alone	1969	.80	4.00
FIRST ROW BACK, THE					
Graves 1100		Please Don't Go / Destination Train	196?	2.00	10.00
FISHER, GENE, & THE MYSTICS					
Plateau 101		Remember (You're My Girl) / Listen To Me	196?	25.00	125.00
FISHER, JOHNNY					
Park Avenue 125		Tan Dan / Every Time You Cry	1963	7.00	35.00
FISHER, TOMMY					
B&D 1314		Rock And Roll Robin Hood / Audrey	1962	3.00	15.00
FISHER BROTHERS, THE					
Columbia 42522		Girls Cry Over Boys / Thunder And Lightnin'	1962	2.00	10.00
FITZHUGH, SAMMY					
Poplar 115		Linda, Baby / Sadie Mae	1959	6.00	30.00
FIVE AMERICANS, THE [MICHAEL RABON & THE FIVE AMERICANS]					
ABC-Paramount 10686		Love Love Love / Show Me	1965	3.00	15.00
HBR 454		I See The Light / The Outcast	1966	2.00	10.00
HBR 468		Evol-Not Love / Don't You Dare Blame Me	1966	1.60	8.00
HBR 468		Evol-Not Love / Don't Blame Me	1966	1.60	8.00
HBR 468	(PS)	Evol-Not Love / Don't Blame Me	1966	3.00	15.00
HBR 483		Good Times / Losing Game	1966	1.60	8.00
Abnak 106	(DJ)	Say That You Love Me / Without You *(Colored vinyl)*	1965	3.00	15.00
Abnak 106		Say That You Love Me / Without You	1965	1.60	8.00
Abnak 109		I See The Light / The Outcast	1967	1.60	8.00
Abnak 114	(DJ)	Reality / Sympathy *(Colored vinyl)*	1966	4.00	20.00
Abnak 114		Reality / Sympathy	1966	1.60	8.00
Abnak 116	(DJ)	If I Could / Now That It's Over *(Colored vinyl)*	1967	4.00	20.00
Abnak 116		If I Could / Now That It's Over	1967	1.60	8.00
Abnak 118	(DJ)	Western Union / Now That It's Over *(Colored vinyl)*	1967	4.00	20.00
Abnak 118		Western Union / Now That It's Over	1967	1.60	8.00
Abnak 120	(DJ)	Sound Of Love / Sympathy *(Colored vinyl)*	1967	4.00	20.00
Abnak 120		Sound Of Love / Sympathy	1967	1.60	8.00
Abnak 123	(DJ)	Zip Code / Sweet Bird Of Youth *(Colored vinyl)*	1967	4.00	20.00
Abnak 123		Zip Code / Sweet Bird Of Youth	1967	1.60	8.00

Label & Catalog #		A-Side/B-Side	Year	VG	NM
Abnak 125	(DJ)	Stop Light / Tell Ann I Love Her (Colored vinyl)	1967	4.00	20.00
Abnak 125		Stop Light / Tell Ann I Love Her	1967	1.60	8.00
Abnak 125	(PS)	Stop Light / Tell Ann I Love Her	1967	3.00	15.00
Abnak 126	(DJ)	7:30 Guided Tour / See-Saw Man (Colored vinyl)	1968	4.00	20.00
Abnak 126		7:30 Guided Tour / See-Saw Man	1968	1.60	8.00
Abnak 126	(PS)	7:30 Guided Tour / See-Saw Man	1968	3.00	15.00
Abnak 128	(DJ)	Rain Maker / No Communication (Colored vinyl)	1968	4.00	20.00
Abnak 128		Rain Maker / No Communication	1968	1.60	8.00
Abnak 128	(PS)	Rain Maker / No Communication	1968	3.00	15.00
Abnak 131	(DJ)	Lovin' Is Lovin' / Can Man (Colored vinyl)	1968	4.00	20.00
Abnak 131		Lovin' Is Lovin' / Can Man	1968	1.60	8.00
Abnak 132	(DJ)	Generation Gap / The Source (Colored vinyl)	1968	4.00	20.00
Abnak 132		Generation Gap / The Source	1968	1.60	8.00
Abnak 135	(DJ)	Virginia Girl / Call On Me (Colored vinyl)	1969	4.00	20.00
Abnak 135		Virginia Girl / Call On Me	1969	1.60	8.00
Abnak 137	(DJ)	Scrooge / (Colored vinyl)	1969	4.00	20.00
Abnak 137		Scrooge / Ignert Woman	1969	1.60	8.00
Abnak 139	(DJ)	I See The Light '69 / Red Cape (Colored vinyl)	1969	4.00	20.00
Abnak 139		I See The Light '69 / Red Cape	1969	1.60	8.00
Abnak 142	(DJ)	She's Good To Me / Molly Black (Colored vinyl)	1969	4.00	20.00
Abnak 142		She's Good To Me / Molly Black	1969	1.60	8.00
Jetstar 104		I'm Gonna Leave Ya / It's You, Girl	1965	4.00	20.00
Jetstar 105		I'm Feeling O.K. / Slippin' And Slidin'	1965	6.00	30.00

FIVE & DIME
Laurie 3452	Rain / Penny Candy	1968	2.00	10.00

FIVE BLOBS, THE
Columbia 41250	The Blob / Saturday Night In Tijuana	1958	3.00	15.00
Joy 226	Rockin' Pow Wow / From The Top Of Your Guggle	1960	2.00	10.00
Joy 230	Young And Wild / Juliet	1960	2.00	10.00

FIVE BY FIVE
Paula 261	Shake A Tail Feather / Tell Me What You Do	1967	2.00	10.00
Paula 283	Harlem Shuffle / You Really Got A Hold On Me	1967	2.00	10.00
Paula 302	Fire / Hung Up	1967	3.00	15.00
Paula 311	She Digs My Love / Ain't Gonna Be Your Fool No More	1968	2.00	10.00
Paula 319	Apple Cider / Fruit Stand Man	1968	2.00	10.00
Paula 322	Too Much Tomorrow / Ain't Gonna Be Your Fool No More	1966	2.00	10.00
Paula 326	15 Goin' On 20 / Penthouse Pauper	1969	2.00	10.00
Paula 328	Good Connection / Never	1970	2.00	10.00

FIVE CARD STUDS
Red Bird 802	Everybody Needs Somebody / Be-Bop-A-Lula	1966	2.00	10.00
Smash 2080	Beg Me / Once	1967	2.00	10.00

FIVE CHAVIS BROTHERS, THE: Refer to THE CHAVIS BROTHERS

FIVE CHORDS, THE: Refer to JOHNNY JONES

FIVE CLASSICS, THE
Pova 6142	Love Me / Mississippi Mud	1961	5.00	25.00
"A" 317	My Imagination / Come On, Baby	1961	7.00	35.00
Arc 4454	My Imagination / Come On, Baby	1961	4.00	20.00
Medieval 204	Old Cape Cod / Magic Star	196?	4.00	20.00

FIVE COACHMEN, THE
Janson 100	Oh, Joan / This I Know	195?	8.00	40.00

FIVE COUNTS, THE
Vistar 1000	Going Away From You / Shame, Shame	196?	2.00	10.00

FIVE CRYSTALS, THE
Kane 25592	Hey, Landlord / Good Looking Out	1959	8.00	40.00

FIVE DEBONAIRES, THE: Refer to THE DEBONAIRES

FIVE DISCS, THE
The Five Discs also recorded with Adrian Allen, Frankie Gee and later as Dawn.

Emge 1004	I Remember / The World Is A Beautiful Place	1958	7500	300.00
Vik 0327	I Remember / The World Is A Beautiful Place	1958	10.00	50.00
Dwain 6072	Roses / My Chinese Girl	1959	75.00	300.00
Dwain 803	Roses / My Chinese Girl	1959	15.00	75.00
Yale 243/4	Come On, Baby / I Don't Know What I'll Do	1961	50.00	200.00
Calo 202	Adios / My Baby Loves Me (Green label)	1961	25.00	125.00
Calo 202	Adios / My Baby Loves Me (White label)	1962	15.00	75.00
Cheer 1000	Never Let You Go / That Was The Time (Black label)	1962	15.00	75.00
Cheer 1000	Never Let You Go / That Was The Time (Red label)	1963	6.00	30.00

Label & Catalog #	A-Side/B-Side	Year	VG	NM
Rust 5027	I Remember / The World Is A Beautiful Place	1963	3.00	15.00
Mello Mood 1002	Roses / My Chinese Girl	1964	2.00	10.00
Laurie 3601	Rock And Roll Revival / Gypsy Women	1971	3.00	15.00
Pyramid 166	That Was The Time / Let's Fall In Love	197?	1.00	5.00
Crystal Ball 114	Mirror Mirror / Most Of All I Wonder Why	197?	.60	3.00
Crystal Ball 120	Unchained Melody / Shrine Of St. Cecilia	197?	.60	3.00

FIVE EMPREES, THE [THE FIVE EMPRESSIONS]

Freeport 1001	Little Miss Sad / Hey, Lover	1965	3.00	15.00
	(First pressings of Freeport 1001 credit The Five Empressions.)			
Freeport 1001	Little Miss Sad / Hey, Lover	1965	2.00	10.00
Freeport 1007	Little Miss Happiness / Over The Mountain	1966	2.00	10.00
Freeport 1009	Pretty Face / Pretty Face	1966	2.00	10.00
Freeport 1010	Johnny B. Goode / Hey, Lover	1966	2.00	10.00

FIVE EMPRESSIONS, THE: *Refer to* THE FIVE EMPREES

FIVE GENTS, THE

Viking 101	Sandy / Baby Doll	195?	40.00	200.00

FIVE HUNDREDS, THE

Mercury 72291	Run Little Rabbit / Wheel's Last Ride	1964	2.00	10.00

FIVE KINGS, THE

Columbia 43060	Don't Send Me Away / Light Bulb	1964	15.00	75.00
Yvette 101	Here Comes My Baby / Tina	196?	4.00	20.00

FIVE MAN ELECTRICAL BAND, THE
The Five Man Electrical Band originally recorded as The Staccatos.

Capitol 2368	Private Train / It Never Rains On Maple Lane	1969	.80	4.00
Capitol 2517	Baby / Lovin' Look	1969	.80	4.00
Capitol 2562	Sunrise To Sunset / Little Bit Of Love	1969	.80	4.00
Capitol 2628	Riverboat / Good	1969	.80	4.00
MGM 14149	Moonshine / Forever Together	1970	.80	4.00
MGM 14182 (DJ)	Signs / Hello Melinda, Goodbye	1970	1.20	6.00
	(Stock copies of MM 14182 may not exist.)			
Lionel 3213	Signs / Hello Melinda, Goodbye	1970	1.00	5.00
Lionel 3220	Absolutely Right / Butterfly	1971	.60	3.00
Lion 127	Money Back Guarantee / Find The One	1972	.60	3.00
Lion 149	I'm A Stranger Here / Doin' The Best We Can	1973	.60	3.00
Lion 160	Baby Wanna Boogie / Sweet Paradise	1973	.60	3.00
Polydor 14221	Werewolf / Country Angel	1974	.60	3.00
Polydor 14263 (Can)	Johnnie Get A Gun / And The World Goes Round	1974	1.00	5.00

FIVE MORE

Tondy 205	Avalanche / I'm No Good	195?	7.00	35.00

FIVE PLAYBOYS, THE

Fee Bee 213	When We Were Young / Pages Of My Scrapbook	1957	6.00	30.00
Dot 15605	When We Were Young / Pages Of My Scrapbook	1957	5.00	25.00
Mercury 71269	Why Be A Fool? / Time Will Allow	1958	4.00	20.00
Petite 504	She's My Baby / Mr. Echo	195?	4.00	20.00

FIVE REASONS, THE

Cub 9006	Go To School / 3 O' Clock Rock	1958	15.00	75.00

FIVE SECRETS, THE [THE SECRETS]

Decca 30350	See You Next Year / Queen Bee	1957	12.00	60.00
	(First pressings credit The Five Secrets.)			
Decca 30350	See You Next Year / Queen Bee	1958	8.00	40.00
	(Second pressings credit The Secrets.)			

FIVE SHARKS, THE

Times Square 35	Stormy Weather *(Long version)* / If You Love Me	1964	6.00	30.00
Times Square 35	Stormy Weather *(Short version)* / If You Love Me	1964	4.00	20.00
Amber 852	The Lion Sleeps Tonight / Land Of 1,000 Dances	1966	2.00	10.00

FIVE SHARKS, THE

Old Timer 605	I'll Never Let You Go / Stand By Me	1964	3.00	15.00
Old Timer 611	Gloria / Flames	1964	3.00	15.00
Siamese 404	Gloria / Flames	196?	2.00	10.00

FIVE SOUNDS, THE

Baritone 0941	That's When I Fell In Love / Good Time Baby	196?	3.00	15.00
Epic 9856	Baby, Please Don't Cry / Loadin' Coal	1965	2.00	10.00

FIVE SPARKS, THE

Jimbo 1	A Million Tears / Little Bo Peep	1959	10.00	50.00

Label & Catalog #	A-Side/B-Side	Year	VG	NM
FIVE SPOTS, THE				
Soma 1147	**Black Rock / Mr. Fortune**	196?	5.00	25.00
FIVE SUPERIORS, THE				
Garpax 44170	**There's A Fool Born Every Day / Big Shot**	1962	25.00	125.00
FIVE TEENBEATS, THE				
Big Top 3062	**Autumn Mood / Time To Rock**	1960	2.00	10.00
FIVE TINOS, THE				
Sun 222	**Sitting By My Window / Don't Do That**	1955	150.00	500.00
FIVE VETS, THE				
Allstar 713	**You're In Love / Right Now**	195?	25.00	125.00
FLAGMEN, THE				
Limelight 3014	**Drag Strip U.S.A. / Mary**	1964	2.50	12.00
FLAME, THE				
The Flame features Blondie Chaplin and Rickie Fataar, later of The Beach Boys.				
Brother 3500	**See The Light / Got Your Mind Made Up**	1970	1.00	5.00
Brother 3501	**Another Day Like Heaven / I'm So Happy**	1970	1.60	8.00
FLAMES, THE: *Refer to* ALLAN & THE FLAMES				
FLAMIN' GROOVIES, THE				
Epic 10507	**Rockin' Pneumonia And The Boogie Woogie Flu /**			
	The First One's Free	1969	2.00	10.00
Epic 10564	**Somethin' Else / Laurie Did It**	1970	2.00	10.00
Kama Sutra 527	**Have You Seen My Baby? / Yesterday's Numbers**	1971	2.00	10.00
Sire 731	**Teenage Confidential / I Can't Hide**	1976	1.00	5.00
FLANDERS, TOMMY				
Tommy Flanders originally recorded with The Blues Project.				
Verve/Folkways 3075	**The Moonstone / Between Purple And Blue**	1969	1.00	5.00
FLAVOR				
Columbia 44521	**Sally Had A Party / Shop Around**	1968	.80	4.00
FLEAS, THE				
Challenge 9115	**Scratchin' / Tears**	1961	2.00	10.00
FLEET & FREDDY				
Arlen 1002	**Drag Race Boogie / Sunset Till Dawn**	1961	3.00	15.00
FLEETWOOD, MICK				
RCA Victor PB-13621	**I Want You Back / Put Me Right**	1983	.20	1.00
RCA Victor PB-13621 (PS)	**I Want You Back / Put Me Right**	1983	.20	1.00
FLEETWOOD MAC				
Aside from Mick Fleetwood and John McVie, members have included Lindsey Buckingham, Peter Green, Christine McVie, Stevie Nicks, Jeremy Spencer and Bob Welch. Refer to Rob Grill.				
Epic 10351	**Black Magic Woman / Long Grey Mare**	1968	2.00	10.00
Epic 10368	**Stop Messin' Around / Need Your Love So Bad**	1968	2.00	10.00
Epic 10436	**Albatross / Jigsaw Puzzle Blues**	1969	1.20	6.00
Epic 11029	**Black Magic Woman / Albatross**	1973	1.20	6.00
Reprise 0860	**Coming Your Way / Rattlesnake Shake**	1969	1.00	5.00
Reprise 0883	**Oh, Well / Oh, Well (Part 2)**	1970	1.00	5.00
Reprise 0925	**Green Manalishi / World In Harmony**	1970	1.00	5.00
Reprise 0984	**Jewel-Eyed Lady / Station Man**	1971	1.00	5.00
Reprise 1057	**Sands Of Time / Lay It All Down**	1971	1.00	5.00
Reprise 1079	**Oh, Well / Green Manalishi**	1971	1.00	5.00
Reprise 1093	**Sentimental Lady / Sunny Side Of Heaven**	1972	1.00	5.00
Reprise 1159	**Remember Me / Dissatisfied**	1973	1.00	5.00
Reprise 1172	**Did You Ever Love Me? / Revelation**	1973	1.00	5.00
Reprise 1188	**For Your Love / Hypnotized**	1973	1.00	5.00
Reprise 1317	**Heroes Are Hard To Find / Born Enchanter**	1974	1.00	5.00
Reprise 1339	**Over My Head / I'm So Afraid**	1975	.40	2.00
Reprise 1345	**Rhiannon (Will You Ever Win?) / Sugar Daddy**	1976	.40	2.00
Reprise 1356	**Say You Love Me / Monday Morning**	1976	.40	2.00
Warner Bros. 8304	**Go Your Own Way / Silver Springs**	1977	1.00	5.00
Warner Bros. 8371	**Dreams / Songbird**	1977	.30	1.50
Warner Bros. 8413	**Don't Stop / Never Going Back Again**	1977	.30	1.50
Warner Bros. 8413 (PS)	**Don't Stop / Never Going Back Again**	1977	.50	2.00
Warner Bros. 8483	**You Make Loving Fun / Gold Dust Woman**	1977	.30	1.50
Warner Bros. 49077	**Tusk / Never Make Me Cry**	1979	.20	1.00
Warner Bros. 49077 (PS)	**Tusk / Never Make Me Cry**	1979	.50	2.00

Label & Catalog #		A-Side/B-Side	Year	VG	NM
Warner Bros. 49150		Sara / That's Enough For Me	1979	.20	1.00
Warner Bros. 49150	(PS)	Sara / That's Enough For Me	1979	.20	1.00
Warner Bros. 49196		Think About Me / Save Me A Place	1979	.20	1.00
Warner Bros. 49196	(PS)	Think About Me / Save Me A Place	1979	.20	1.00
Warner Bros. 49660		Fireflies / Over My Head	1981	.20	1.00
Warner Bros. 49660	(PS)	Fireflies / Over My Head	1981	.50	2.00
Warner Bros. 49700		The Farmer's Daughter / Monday Morning	1981	.20	1.00
Warner Bros. 49700	(PS)	The Farmer's Daughter / Monday Morning	1981	.50	2.00
Warner Bros. 29966		Hold Me / Eyes Of The World	1982	.20	1.00
Warner Bros. 29966	(PS)	Hold Me / Eyes Of The World	1982	.50	2.00
Warner Bros. 29918		Gypsy / Cool Water	1982	.20	1.00
Warner Bros. 29918	(PS)	Gypsy / Cool Water	1982	.50	2.00

FLEETWOODS, THE

Liberty 55188		Come Softly To Me / I Care So Much	1959	3.00	15.00
Liberty 77188	(S)	Come Softly To Me / I Care So Much	1959	6.00	30.00
Dolphin 1		Come Softly To Me / I Care So Much	1959	2.00	10.00
Dolton 3		Graduation's Here / Oh, Lord, Let It Be	1959	2.00	10.00
Dolton 3	(S)	Graduation's Here / Oh, Lord, Let It Be	1959	6.00	30.00
Dolton 5		Mr. Blue / You Mean Everything To Me	1959	2.00	10.00
Dolton 15		Outside My Window / Magic Star	1960	2.00	10.00
Dolton 22		Runaround / Truly Do	1960	2.00	10.00
Dolton 22	(PS)	Runaround / Truly Do	1960	4.00	20.00
Dolton 27		The Last One To Know / Dormilona	1960	1.60	8.00
Dolton 30		Confidential / I Love You So	1961	1.60	8.00
Dolton 40		Tragedy / Little Miss Sad One	1961	2.00	10.00
Dolton 45		(He's) The Great Imposter / Poor Little Girl	1961	1.60	8.00
Dolton 49		Billy, Old Buddy / Trouble	1962	1.60	8.00
Dolton 62		Lovers By Night, Strangers By Day / They Tell Me It's Summer	1962	1.60	8.00
Dolton 74		You Should Have Been There / Sure Is Lonesome Downtown	1963	1.60	8.00
Dolton 75		Goodnight, My Love / Jimmy, Beware	1963	1.60	8.00
Dolton 86		What'll I Do? / Baby, Bye-O	1963	1.20	6.00
Dolton 93		Lonesome Town / Ruby Red, Baby Blue	1964	1.20	6.00
Dolton 97		Ten Times Blue / Ska Light, Ska Bright	1964	1.20	6.00
Dolton 98		Mr. Sandman / This Is My Prayer	1964	1.20	6.00
Dolton 302		Before And After / Lonely Is As Lonely Does	1965	1.20	6.00
Dolton 307		I'm Not Jimmy / Come Softly To Me	1965	1.20	6.00
Dolton 310		Rainbow / Just As I Needed You	1965	1.20	6.00
Dolton 315		For Lovin' Me / This Is Where I See Her	1966	1.20	6.00
		—Extended Play Albums—			
Dolton 502		The Fleetwoods	1960	15.00	75.00

FLEMING, FRANK

Laurie 3131		All By Myself Alone / School Bus	1961	6.00	30.00
Amy 879		All By Myself / Blue Heartaches	1963	4.00	20.00
		(Amy 879 credits Frankie Fleming Jr.)			

FLINDERS, MATT

Jerden 914		Picking Up Pebbles / Susan Walks Away	1969	.60	3.00

FLINTALES, THE

Flick 429		D-Rail / Flintales' Rock	196?	2.00	10.00

FLINTSTONE, FRED

Epic 9475		Stone Age Rock / Bed Rock Beat	1961	3.00	15.00
B-H 001		Quarry Stone Rock / (A Night In) Bedrock Forest	1962	3.00	15.00
B-H 001	(PS)	Quarry Stone Rock / (A Night In) Bedrock Forest	1962	5.00	25.00

FLINTSTONES, THE

HBR 7021	(EP)	Goldi Rocks And The Three Bearosauruses	1965	3.00	15.00
HBR 7031	(EP)	The Three Little Pigs	1965	3.00	15.00

FLIPS, THE

Mercury 71426		Gone Away / It Will Never Be The Same	1959	4.00	20.00

FLO & EDDIE

Flo & Eddie are Mark Volman and Howard Kaylan. Refer to The Crossfires; The Dedications; The Turtles; Frank Zappa.

Reprise 1113		Goodbye Surprise / Nikki Hoi	1972	.60	3.00
Reprise 1142		Afterglow / Carlos And De Bull	1973	.60	3.00
Reprise 1160		If We Only Had The Time / You're A Lady	1973	.60	3.00
Columbia 10028		Let Me Make You Love Me / Come To My Rescue	1974	.50	2.50
Columbia 10204		Let Me Make You Love Me / Come To My Rescue	1975	.50	2.50
Columbia 10264		Rebecca / Illegal, Immoral And Fattening	1976	.50	2.50
Columbia 10425		Elenore / The Love You Gave Me	1977	.50	2.50
Columbia 10458		Keep It Warm / Hot	1977	.50	2.50
		—Extended Play Albums—			
Warner Bros. PRO-564	(33)	Flo & Eddie	196?	3.00	15.00

Label & Catalog #	A-Side/B-Side	Year	VG	NM
FLOATERS, THE				
Audio 122	**Baby, Cut It Out / Take My Hand**	196?	1.20	6.00
FLOATING BRIDGE, THE				
Vault 947	**Brought Up Wrong / Watch Your Step**	1968	2.00	10.00
Vault 953	**Don't Mean A Thing / Mr. Jaybird**	1969	2.00	10.00
FLOCK, THE				
Destination 628	**Can't You See? / Hold On To My Mind**	1967	2.00	10.00
Destination 631	**Are You The Kind? / I Like You**	1967	2.00	10.00
Destination 635	**Take Me Back / Each Day Is A Lonely Night**	1967	2.00	10.00
U.S.A. 910	**What Would You Do If The Sun Died? / Magical Wings**	1968	2.00	10.00
Columbia 45021	**Tired Of Waiting / Store Bought, Store Thought**	1970	1.00	5.00
FLOWER CHILDREN, THE				
The Flower Children features Simon Stokes.				
Castil 101	**Mini-Skirt Blues / Marching Lovers**	1967	3.00	15.00
Allied 101	**Mini Skirt Blues / Marching Lovers**	1967	3.00	15.00
FLOWER POT, THE				
Vault 935	**Mr. Zig Zag Man / Black Moto**	1967	2.00	10.00
FLOWER POT MEN, THE				
Deram 7516	**A Walk In The Sky / Am I Losing You?**	1967	2.00	10.00
Deram 85051	**Young Birds Fly / In A Moment Of Madness**	1969	2.00	10.00
FLOWER POTS, THE				
Deram 7513	**Let's Go To San Francisco /**			
	Let's Go To San Francisco (Part 2)	1967	2.00	10.00
FLOWER POWER				
Tune-Kel 608	**You Make Me Fly / Sunshine Day**	1969	3.00	15.00
Tune-Kel 612	**Trivialities / Mr. Olympus**	1969	3.00	15.00
Tune-Kel 614	**Stop! Check It! / Orange Skies**	1969	3.00	15.00
FLOWER SHOPPE, THE				
Spring 111	**You've Come A Long Way, Baby / Kill The Monster**	196?	2.00	10.00
FLOYD & JERRY & THE COUNTERPOINTS				
Presta 1003	**Girl / Believe In Things**	1966	1.20	6.00
FLUORESCENTS, THE				
Hanover 4520	**Facts Of Love / Shoopy-Pop-A-Doo**	1959	8.00	40.00
FLYING BURRITO BROTHERS, THE				
The original Flying Burrito Brothers featured Chris Hillman and Gram Parsons.				
A&M 1166	**If You Gotta Go, Go Now / Cody, Cody**	1969	1.60	8.00
A&M 1???	**The Train Song / Hot Buritto #1**	1969	1.60	8.00
A&M 1189	**Down In The Churchyard / Older Guys**	1970	1.60	8.00
A&M 1277	**Colorado / White Line Fever**	1972	1.60	8.00
FLYING CIRCUS, THE				
MTA 117	**I'm Gone / Midnight Highway**	1967	2.00	10.00
MTA 130	**Green Eyes, Green World / Got To Learn To Love**	1967	2.00	10.00
Rock Bottom 670	**Pony Rider / Betty June**	1970	2.00	10.00
FLYING CIRCUS, THE				
Capitol 3694	**Jabber Jabber / Gypsy Road**	1973	1.00	5.00
FLYING MACHINE, THE				
Congress 6000	**Smile A Little Smile For Me /**			
	Maybe We've Been Loving Too Long	1969	.80	4.00
Congress 6012	**Baby, Make It Soon / There She Goes**	1970	.80	4.00
FLYS, THE				
Myskatonic 100	**Got To Get Away / Reality Composition #1**	1966	3.00	15.00
Myskatonic 101	**Be What You Is / The Way Things Are**	1966	3.00	15.00
FOGERTY, JOHN				
John Fogerty also recorded with brother Tommy Fogerty & The Blue Velvets; The Golliwogs; Creedence Clearwater Revival; and as The Blue Ridge Rangers.				
Fantasy 7171	**Comin' Down The Road / Comin' Down The Road**	1973	.80	4.00
Asylum 45274	**Rockin' All Over The World / The Wall**	1975	.60	3.00
Asylum 45291	**Almost Saturday Night / Sea Cruise**	1975	.60	3.00
Asylum 45309	**You Got The Magic / Evil Thing**	1976	.60	3.00

Label & Catalog #		A-Side/B-Side	Year	VG	NM

FOGERTY, TOM, & THE BLUE VELVETS
Tom & The Velvets later recorded as The Golliwogs and Creedence Clearwater Revival.

Orchestra 617		Come On, Baby / Oh! My Love	1961	15.00	75.00
Orchestra 617		Have You Ever Been Lonely? / Bonita	1961	15.00	75.00
Orchestra		Yes, You Did / Now You're Not Mine	1962	15.00	75.00

FOGERTY, TOM
Tom Fogerty also recorded with The Golliwogs; Creedence Clearwater Revival.

Fantasy 661		Goodbye, Media Man / Goodbye, Media Man	1971	.80	4.00
Fantasy 661	(PS)	Goodbye, Media Man / Goodbye, Media Man	1971	2.00	10.00
Fantasy 680		Cast The First Stone / Lady Of Fatima	1972	.80	4.00
Fantasy 702		Joyful Resurrection / Heartbeat	1973	.80	4.00
Fantasy 737		Sweet Things To Come / There Was A Time	1973	.80	4.00

FOGGY DOGS, THE

| Beejay 6902 | | The Fool / Fannie Mae | 196? | 2.00 | 10.00 |

FOLAND, BILL, & THE SURFS

| Tishman 903 | | Surfin' Trumpets / | 196? | 8.00 | 40.00 |

FONTAINE, EDDIE

| Sunbeam 105 | | Nothin' Shakin' / Oh, Wonderful Night | 1959 | 7.00 | 35.00 |
| Argo 5309 | | Nothin' Shakin' / Oh, Wonderful Night | 1959 | 5.00 | 25.00 |

FONTANA, WAYNE, & THE MINDBENDERS
Refer to The Mindbenders.

Fontana 1917		Stop, Look And Listen / Road Runner	1965	1.60	8.00
Fontana 1503		The Game Of Love / Since You've Been Gone	1965	1.20	6.00
Fontana 1509		The Game Of Love / One More Time	1965	1.20	6.00
Fontana 1514		It's Just A Little Bit Too Late / A Long Time Comin'	1965	1.00	5.00
Fontana 1524		She Needs Love / Like I Did	1965	1.00	5.00

FONTANA, WAYNE

MGM 13456		It Was Easier To Hurt Her / You Made Me What I Am Today	1966	.80	4.00
MGM 13516		Come On Home / My Eyes Break Out In Tears	1966	.80	4.00
MGM 13661		Pamela, Pamela / Something Keeps Calling Me Back	1967	.80	4.00
MGM 13762		24 Sycamore / From A Boy To A Man	1967	.80	4.00
Metromedia 133		Say Goodbye To Yesterday / Dayton, Ohio	1969	.80	4.00

FORCE FIVE

| Ascot 2206 | | I Want You, Babe / Gee Too Tiger | 1966 | 10.00 | 50.00 |

FORCIER, JUDY

| Spur 111 | | Pay The Piper / Make A Happy Face | 196? | 2.00 | 10.00 |

FORD, DANBY

| Accent 1196 | | Long Tall Texan / Draft Dodger Rag | 1966 | 1.20 | 6.00 |

FORD, FRANKIE

Ace 549		Cheatin' Woman / The Last One To Cry	1958	3.00	15.00
Ace 554		Sea Cruise / Roberta	1959	4.00	20.00
Ace 566		Alimony / Can't Tell My Heart (What To Do)	1959	3.00	15.00
Ace 580		Time After Time / I Want To Be Your Man	1960	3.00	15.00
Ace 592		Chinatown / What's Goin' On?	1960	3.00	15.00
Ace 592	(PS)	Chinatown / What's Goin' On?	1960	5.00	25.00
Imperial 5686		You Talk Too Much / If You've Got Troubles	1960	2.00	10.00
Imperial 5706		My Southern Belle / The Groom	1960	2.00	10.00
Imperial 5735		Seventeen / Doghouse	1961	2.00	10.00
Imperial 5749		Saturday Night Fish Fry / Love Don't Love Nobody	1961	2.00	10.00
Imperial 5775		What Happened To You? / Let Them Talk	1961	2.00	10.00
Imperial 5819		A Man Only Does / They Said It Couldn't Be Done	1962	2.00	10.00
Ace 8009		Ocean Full Of Tears / Hours Of Need	1963	2.00	10.00
White Cliffs 210		Basin Street Blues / Lonesome Road	1963	2.00	10.00
Constellation 101		China Town / Ocean Full Of Tears	1964	2.00	10.00
Doubloon 101		Half A Crown / I Can't face Tomorrow	1967	2.00	10.00
Paula 351		Peace Of Mind / I'm Proud Of What I Am	1968	1.00	5.00
Cinnamon 752		When I Stop Dreamin' / I'm Proud Of What I Am	1972	1.00	5.00
Cuinnamon 767		Talk To A Carpenter / When I Stop Dreamin'	1973	1.00	5.00
ABC 11431		Blue Monday / All Alone Am I	1974	1.00	5.00
Briarmeade 7600		I've Found Someone Of My Own / Battle Hymn Of The Republic	1976	1.00	5.00
Briarmeade 7701		Desperado / Mardi Gras In New Orleans	1977	1.00	5.00
Briarmeade 7901		Halfway To Paradise / I'm Proud Of What I Am	1979	1.00	5.00
SYC 1227		Growing Pains / Ups And Downs	1982	.80	4.00
SYC 1228		My Prayer / Gospel Ship	1983	.80	4.00
		—*Extended Play Albums*—			
Ace		Sea Cruise	1959	30.00	150.00
Imperial 5105		The Best Of Frankie Ford	195?	20.00	100.00

Label & Catalog #	A-Side/B-Side	Year	VG	NM
FORD, JIM				
Drumfire 2	The Story Of Elvis Presley / Desert Walk	1960	6.00	30.00
Mustang 3025	Linda Comes Running / Sing With Linda	1967	2.00	10.00
FORD, NEAL, & THE FANATICS				
Gina 118	I Will Not Be Lonely / Mine	1965	8.00	40.00
Hickory 1433	Shame On You / Gonna Be My Girl	1968	2.00	10.00
Hickory 1450	Wait For Me / Brand New Girl	1968	2.00	10.00
Hickory 1468	Get Together With Me / Pain	1968	2.00	10.00
Hickory 1490	That Girl Of Mine / I Have Thoughts Of You	1968	2.00	10.00
Hickory 1500	Little World Girl / Movin' Along	1968	2.00	10.00
Hickory 1506	Love's Not Only For The Heart	1968	2.00	10.00
Hickory 1516	I'll Put My Boots On Backwards / Buttercup	1968	2.00	10.00
FOREIGN INTRIGUE				
Foreign Intrigue is a pseudonym for Ernie Maresca & The Del Satins.				
E.M. 1001	The Wanderer / Blind Date	196?	3.00	15.00
FORMATIONS, THE				
Bank 1007	At The Top Of The Stairs / Magic Melody	1968	3.00	15.00
MGM 13899	At The Top Of The Stairs / Magic Melody	1968	1.00	5.00
MGM 13963	Love's Not Only For The Heart / Lonely Voice Of Love	1968	1.00	5.00
MGM 14009	Don't Get Close / There's No Room	1969	1.00	5.00
FORREST, SONNY				
Atco 6157	Diddy Bop / Knock Down	1960	3.00	15.00
FORSAKEN				
M.T.A. 106	Babe / She's Alright	1956	2.00	10.00
FORTE FOUR, THE				
The Forte Four were produced by Gary Usher.				
Decca 31979	Can't You See I'm Trying / Don't Let The Sun Shine On Me	1966	1.60	8.00
Decca 32029	I Don't Wanna Say Goodnight / The Climb	1966	1.60	8.00
FORTUNE, DIANE				
Brunswick 55074	House Of Cards / Set Me Free	1958	3.00	15.00
FORTUNE, GAYLE, & THE TERYTONES				
Refer to The Terrytones.				
Way 1003	I Cry The Blues / Teenage Night Theme	1960	5.00	25.00
FORTUNE, JOHNNY (& THE PARAMOURS)				
Johnny Fortune also recorded with The Sweet Souls.				
Emmy 1001	If You Love Me / Alone And Cryin'	1960	5.00	25.00
Emmy 1001	If You Love Me / Almost Crying	1960	5.00	25.00
Emmy 1002	Gee, But I Miss You / I'm In Heaven	1960	5.00	25.00
Arhaven 1001	Gee, But I Miss You / I'm A Fool For You	1962	3.00	15.00
Arena 102	Gee, But I Miss You / I'm A Fool For You	1963	3.00	15.00
Park Avenue 103	Surfer's Trip / Soul Traveler	1963	3.00	15.00
Park Avenue 104	Need You / One Less Angel	1963	2.00	10.00
Park Avenue 110	Soul Surfer / Midnight Surf	1963	3.00	15.00
Park Avenue 126	Surfer's Trip / Soul Traveler	1963	2.00	10.00
Park Avenue 130	Siboney / Dragster	1963	3.00	15.00
Park Avenue 4905	I'm Talking About You / My Wandering Love	1963	3.00	15.00
Crusader 104	Gee, But I Miss You / If You Love Me	1964	2.00	10.00
United Artists 720	Juarez / It Ain't Necessarily So	1964	2.00	10.00
United Artists 780	Don't Stay Out After Midnight / Don't You Lie To Me	1964	2.00	10.00
Current 101	Say You Will / Come On And Love Me	1965	2.00	10.00
Current 104	You Want Me To Be Your Baby / Dan Stole My Girl	1965	2.00	10.00
Current 105	I'm Lonely For You / I'll Never Let You Go	1965	2.00	10.00
Beaver 111	Stay One More Day / I'm Requesting A Love Song	1966	2.00	10.00
Vault 954	Your True Love / Tell Me You Love Me	1970	1.20	6.00
FORTUNE SEEKERS, THE				
Trident 9966	Why I Cry / Break Loose	195?	1.20	6.00
FORTUNE TELLERS, THE				
Sheryl 340	Just A Little Bit Of Your Love / School Prom	195?	3.00	15.00
FORTUNEERS, THE				
Skytone 1000	Look-A-There / Oh, Woh, Baby	195?	3.00	15.00
FORTUNES, THE				
Cub 9123	You Don't Know (What I've Been Through) / Ghoul In School	1963	3.00	15.00
FORTUNES, THE				
Press 9773	You've Got Your Troubles / I've Gotta Go	1965	1.60	8.00

Label & Catalog #	A-Side/B-Side	Year	VG	NM
Press 9798	Here It Comes Again / Things I Should Have Known	1965	1.20	6.00
Press 9811	This Golden Ring / Someone To Care	1966	1.20	6.00
Press 60001	Silent Street / Gone From My Mind	1967	1.20	6.00
United Artists 50211	His Smile Was A Lie / The Idol	1967	1.00	5.00
United Artists 50280	Fire Brigade / Painting A Shadow	1968	1.00	5.00
World Pacific 77937	That Same Old Feeling / Lifetime Of Love	1970	.80	4.00
Capitol 3086	Here Comes That Rainy Day Feeling Again / Bad Side Of Town	1971	.80	4.00
Capitol 3179	Freedom Comes, Freedom Goes / There's A Man	1972	.60	3.00
Capitol 3445	Wait Until September / Don't Sing To Me	1972	.60	3.00
Capitol 3626	Whenever It's A Sunday / Give Me Some Room	1973	.80	4.00

FORUM, THE

Penthouse 504	The River Is Wide / The River Is Wide	1966	3.00	15.00
Mira 232	The River Is Wide / A Girl Without A Boy	1966	1.60	8.00
Mira 232	The River Is Wide / I Fall In Love	1966	1.20	6.00

FOSTER, JOHN, & SONS BLACK DYKE MILLS BAND

Apple 1800	Thingumybob / Yellow Submarine	1968	30.00	150.00
	(The sliced apple side of the label features "Thingumybob.")			
Apple 1800	Yellow Submarine / Thingumybob	1968	35.00	175.00
	(The sliced apple side of the label features "Yellow Submarine." Both sides were produced by Paul McCartney.)			

FOTHERINGAY

A&M 1223	Ballad Of Ned Kelly / Sea	1970	1.20	6.00

FOTOMAKER

Fotomaker features Dino Danelli and Gene Cornish, formerly of The Young Rascals.

Atlantic 3471	Where Have You Been All My Life? / Say The Same For You	1978	.40	2.00
Atlantic 3483	The Other Side / The Pain	1978	.40	2.00
Atlantic 3531	Miles Away / Snow Blind	1978	.40	2.00
Atlantic 3561	Love Me Forever / Can She Dance?	1979	.40	2.00
Atlantic 3621	Love Me Forever / Fooled Again	1979	.40	2.00

FOUR

Clark 225	Lonely Surfer Boy / Now Is The Time	1965	6.00	30.00

FOUR BELOW ZERO

Double Shot 108	It's Sally's Birthday Today / Don't Send Me Away	1967	.80	4.00
Jerden 903	Getting Thru To You / Happiness	1968	1.00	5.00

FOUR BLADES, THE

Gateway 1170	I Want You To Be My Girl / Can You Find It In Your Heart?	195?	20.00	100.00
Gateway 1174	Church Bells May Ring / Stardust	195?	25.00	125.00
Alert 422	You Didn't Sign Your Letter With Love / Bake That Chicken Pie	195?	12.00	60.00

FOUR BUDDIES, THE

Coral 62217	Hurt / Moonglow	1960	4.00	20.00
Coral 62325	The Light / Cin Cin	1962	3.00	15.00
Philips 40122	Lonely Summer / Slow Locomotion	1963	4.00	20.00
Imperial 66018	I Want To Be The Boy You Love / Just Enough Of Your Love	1964	7.00	35.00

FOUR CAL-QUETTES, THE [THE FOUR COUQUETTES]

Capitol 4534	Sparkle And Shine / In This World	1961	3.00	15.00
	(Capitol 4534 credits The Four Couquettes.)			
Capitol 4574	Starbright / Billy, My Billy	1961	3.00	15.00
Capitol 4657	Most Of All / I'm Gonna Love Him Anyway	1961	3.00	15.00
Capitol 4725	I'll Never Come Back (Silly Boy) / Again	1962	3.00	15.00
Liberty 55549	I Cried / Movie Magazines	1963	2.00	10.00

FOUR CHEERS, THE

End 1034	Fatal Charms Of Love / Perriwinkle Blue	1958	30.00	150.00

FOUR CHEVELLES, THE

Bandbox 357	Darling, Forever / This Is Our Wedding Day	1957	5.00	25.00
Bandbox 358	I Know / I Can't Believe	1957	5.00	25.00

FOUR CLEFS, THE

B.J. 1000	Please Be Mine / Time After Time	1966	3.00	15.00

FOUR COACHMEN, THE

Castle 507	If You Believe / Nothing But Love, Love, Love	1959	3.00	15.00
Adonis 102	That Thing Called A Girl / Wintertime	1960	3.00	15.00
Adonis 106	Swamp Legend / Shalom	1960	3.00	15.00
Dot 16297	Swamp Legend / Shalom	1961	2.00	10.00

Label & Catalog #	A-Side / B-Side	Year	VG	NM
FOUR COUNTS, THE				
Dart 1014	Young Hearts / I'm Gonna Love Ya	1960	4.00	20.00
FOUR COUQUETTES, THE: *Refer to* THE FOUR CAL-QUETTES				
FOUR DATES, THE				
Chancellor 1014	I'm Happy / Eloise	1958	3.00	15.00
Chancellor 1019	Hey, Roly Poly / I Say, Babe	1958	3.00	15.00
Chancellor 1024	Be My Steady Date / Lilly Lou	1958	3.00	15.00
Chancellor 1027	Teenage Neighbor / I Feel Good	1958	3.00	15.00
FOUR DIMENSIONS, THE				
Goldust 5013	Sand Surfin' / I Love You For What You Are	196?	7.00	35.00
FOUR DIRECTIONS, THE				
Coral 62456	Tonight We Love / Arthur	1964	10.00	50.00
FOUR DOTS, THE				
Freedom 44002	It's Heaven / (B-side by *Jeff Stone*)	1958	7.00	35.00
Freedom 44005	Pledging For Your Love / Don't Wake Up The Kids	1959	10.00	50.00
FOUR EPICS, THE				
The Four Epics also recorded as Exodus and The Vespers.				
Heritage 109	I'm On My Way / When The Music Ends	1962	20.00	100.00
Laurie 3155	Again / I Love You, Diane	1963	5.00	25.00
Laurie 3183	How I Wish I Was Single Again / Dance, Joanne	1963	6.00	30.00
FOUR ESCORTS, THE				
Skyla 1113	Don't You Remember? / My Special Girl	1962	3.00	15.00
FOUR-EVERS, THE				
The Four-Evers also recorded with Vic Thomas.				
Columbia 42303	You Belong To Me / Such A Good Night For Dreaming	1962	15.00	75.00
Columbia 42303 (33)	You Belong To Me / Such A Good Night For Dreaming	1962	25.00	125.00
Josie 901	I Confess / Sooner Or Later	1962	4.00	20.00
Smash 1853	Lover, Come Back To Me / It's Love	1963	2.00	10.00
Smash 1887	Please Be Mine / If I Were A Magician	1964	6.00	30.00
Smash 1887	Be My Girl / If I Were A Magician	1964	1.60	8.00
	("Be My Girl" and "Please Be Mine" are the same track.)			
Smash 1921	Everlasting / Doo Be Dum	1964	2.00	10.00
Constellation 151	Stormy / I'm Walkin' (Into The Crowd)	1965	6.00	30.00
Red Bird 078	You Never Had It So Good / What A Scene	1966	4.00	20.00
Columbia 43886	A Lovely Way To Spend An Evening / The Girl I Want	1966	3.00	15.00
Columbia 43886	A Lovely Way To Say Goodbye / The Girl I Wanna Bring Home	1966	2.00	10.00
FOUR-EVERS, THE				
Jamie 1247	One More Time / Everybody's South Street	1963	3.00	15.00
Chattahoochee 630	Come Up In The World / Colors	1964	2.00	10.00
FOUR-FIFTHS, THE				
Hudson 8101	After Graduation / Come On, Girl	196?	15.00	75.00
Hudson 8101	After Graduation / Come On, Girl (*Blue vinyl*)	196?	30.00	150.00
FOUR-FIFTHS, THE				
Columbia 43913	If You Still Want Me / Have You Ever Loved A Girl?	1966	4.00	20.00
FOUR FROGS, THE				
Frog Death 2	Mr. Big / I Think I'm Losing You	196?	2.00	10.00
Frog Death 2 (PS)	Mr. Big / I Think I'm Losing You	196?	5.00	25.00
FOUR GENTS, THE				
Nite Owl 50	You're Just A Little Too Young / Please Don't Ask Me	196?	2.00	10.00
FOUR GRADUATES, THE				
The Four Graduates is a pseudonym for The Happenings.				
Rust 5062	A Lovely Way To Spend An Evening / Picture Of An Angel	1963	15.00	75.00
Rust 5084	Candy Queen / A Boy In Love	1963	30.00	150.00
Crystal Ball 116	May I Have This Dance? / Caught In A Lie	197?	.60	3.00
Crystal Ball 119	Your Initials / Every Year About This Time	197?	.60	3.00
FOUR HOLIDAYS, THE				
Verve 10204	I Don't Wanna Go To School / Love Ya	1960	3.00	15.00
FOUR HORSEMEN, THE				
United Artists 134	My Heartbreak / A Long, Long Time	1958	25.00	125.00
FOUR IMPERIALS, THE				
Chant 10067	My Girl / Teen Age Fool	1958	10.00	50.00

Label & Catalog #		A-Side/B-Side	Year	VG	NM
Lorelei 4444		Lazy Bonnie / Let's Make A Scene	1958	8.00	40.00
Dot 15737		Lazy Bonnie / Let's Make A Scene	1958	4.00	20.00
Fox 102		Give Me One More Chance / Look Up And Live	1958	5.00	25.00
Dial 101		Valley Of Tears / Time Out	1959	12.00	60.00
Twirl 2005		Seven Lonely Days / Santa's Got A Coupe De Ville	196?	3.00	15.00

FOUR IN THE MORNING

Cross Road 7002		Yesterday / LSD	196?	3.00	15.00

FOUR J'S, THE

Herald 528		Dreams Are A Dime A Dozen / Kissin' At The Drive-In	1958	6.00	30.00
United Artists 125		Rock And Roll Age / Be Nice, Don't Fight	1958	10.00	50.00
4-J 506		Will You Be My Love? / Nursery	1963	2.00	10.00
Jamie 1274		By Love Possessed / My Love, My Love	1964	3.00	15.00
Jamie 1267		Here I Am, Broken Hearted / She Said That She Loved Me	1964	4.00	20.00
Congress 6003		Dreamin' / Love My Love	1969	2.00	10.00

FOUR JACKS, THE

Gateway 1136		Gum Drop / R-O-C-K	196?	3.00	15.00
Gateway 1147		Only You /	196?	4.00	20.00
Gateway 1211		Little Darlin' /	196?	4.00	20.00

FOUR JACKS & A JILL

RCA 47-9473		Master Jack / I Looked Back	1968	1.00	5.00
RCA 47-9572		Mister Nico / Hamba Liliwam	1968	.80	4.00

FOUR JETS, THE

Capitol 4270		Driftin' / Jet Black	1959	3.00	15.00

FOUR JOKERS, THE

The Four Jokers feature Nervous Norvous.

Apollo 1163		Catalina Leana / The Little Green Man	1950	7.00	35.00
MGM 11815		Tell Me Now / Caring	1954	6.00	30.00
Diamond 3004		Transfusion / You Did	1956	5.00	25.00

FOUR KINGS, THE

Canadian American 173	(DJ)	One Night (One sided)	1964	4.00	20.00
Canadian American 173		One Night / Lonely Lovers	1964	8.00	40.00

FOUR KNIGHTS WITH THE BLUE JEANS, THE

Souvenir 1008		I Need A Woman / These Things I Hear	1961	3.00	15.00

FOUR LARKS, THE

Tower 402		I Still Love (From The Bottom Of My Heart) / Groovin' At The Go-Go	1968	1.20	6.00

FOUR LOVERS, THE

The Four Lovers later recorded as The Four Seasons.

RCA Victor 47-6518		You're The Apple Of My Eye / The Girl In My Dreams	1956	6.00	30.00
RCA Victor 47-6519		Honey Love / Please Don't Leave Me	1956	5.00	25.00
RCA Victor 47-6646		Jambalaya / Be Lovey Dovey	1956	6.00	30.00
RCA Victor 47-6768		Never Never / Happy Am I	1957	6.00	30.00
RCA Victor 47-6812		Shake A Hand / The Stranger	1957	8.00	40.00
Epic 9255	(DJ)	My Life For Your Love / Pucker Up	1957	75.00	300.00
Epic 9255		My Life For Your Love / Pucker Up	1957	——	——
		(Rare. Estimated near mint value $500-1,000.)			
Decca 30994		It May Be Wrong / Please Take A Chance	196?	*Bootleg*	
		— Extended Play Albums —			
RCA Victor EPA-869		The Four Lovers	1956	100.00	400.00
RCA Victor EPA-871		Joyride	1956	75.00	300.00
RCA Victor 47-6768	(DJ)	The Four Lovers / Homer & Jethro (No cover)	1956	25.00	125.00
RCA Victor DJ-64	(DJ)	The Four Lovers / Teddi King (No cover)	1956	15.00	75.00

FOUR MINTS, THE

Decca 30464		Ruby Baby / Gold	1957	3.00	15.00
NRC 003		Teenage Wonderland / Hey, Little Neil	1958	3.00	15.00
NRC 011		You Belong To My Heart / Wolf	1958	3.00	15.00
NRC 037		Tomorrow Night / Pina Colada	1959	3.00	15.00

FOUR MOST, THE

Milo 107		The Breeze And I / I Love You	196?	7.00	35.00
Milo 107		The Breeze And I / I Love You (Blue vinyl)	196?	2.00	10.00

FOUR NATURALS, THE [THE NATURALS]

Red Top 113		How Strange / Blue Moon	195?	10.00	50.00
		(Red Top 113 credits The Naturals.)			
Red Top 119		I Hear A Rhapsody /	195?	4.00	20.00
Red Top 125		The Thought Of You, Darling / Long, Long Ago	195?	8.00	40.00

Label & Catalog #	A-Side/B-Side	Year	VG	NM
FOUR OF A KIND				
Cameo 154	You Were Made To Love / Love Every Moment	1958	3.00	15.00
Bomarc 302	I Care For You / It's Better That Way	1959	3.00	15.00
Melba 101	Dedicated To You / Hock My Heart	195?	3.00	15.00
FOUR OF US				
Hideout 1003	You're Gonna Be Mine / Free Fall	1965	4.00	20.00
Hideout 1003	You're Gonna Be Mine / Batman	1966	4.00	20.00
Hideout 1012	Feel A Whole Lot Better / I Can't Live Without Your Love	1966	4.00	20.00
FOUR PAGES, THE				
Plateau 101	Autograph Book / Much As I Do	1962	3.00	15.00
FOUR PEARLS, THE				
Dolton 26	Look At Me / It's Almost Tomorrow	1960	5.00	25.00
FOUR PLAYBOYS, THE [THE PLAYBOYS]				
Souvenir 1001	Hawaiian War Chant / Believe It Or Not	1959	3.00	15.00
Souvenir 1002	Stay With Me / Send Me Some Lovin'	1959	4.00	20.00
Dolton 8	Icy Fingers / Party Time	1959	2.00	10.00
SRC 1221	Rave On / The Name Is Love	196?	20.00	100.00
SRC 1237	Lonely Playboy / Jungle Stomp	196?	4.00	20.00
Nite Owl 30	Southbound Express / Cross My Heart	196?	5.00	25.00
FOUR PREPS, THE				
Capitol 3576	Dreamy Eyes / Fools Will Be Fools	1956	2.00	10.00
Capitol 3621	Moonstruck In Madrid / I Cried A Million Tears	1957	2.00	10.00
Capitol 3699	Falling Star / Where Wuz You?	1957	2.00	10.00
Capitol 3761	Promise Me, Baby / Again 'N Again ' Again	1957	2.00	10.00
Capitol 3775	Band Of Angels / How About That?	1957	2.00	10.00
Capitol 3845	26 Miles (Santa Catalina) / It's You	1958	2.00	10.00
Capitol 3960	Big Man / Stop, Baby	1958	2.00	10.00
Capitol 4023	Lazy Summer Night / Summertime Lies	1958	2.00	10.00
Capitol 4078	Cinderella / Gidget	1958	2.00	10.00
Capitol 4126	She Was Five And He Was Ten / Riddle Of Love	1959	2.00	10.00
Capitol 4218	Big Surprise / Try My Arms	1959	2.00	10.00
Capitol 4256	I Ain't Never / Memories, Memories	1959	2.00	10.00
	—Original Capitol singles above have purple labels with the Capitol dome on top.—			
Capitol 4312	Down By The Station / Listen, Honey	1959	1.60	8.00
Capitol 4362	Got A Girl / (Wait 'Til You) Hear It From Me	1960	1.60	8.00
Capitol 4400	Sentimental Kid / Madelina	1960	1.60	8.00
Capitol 4435	Kaw-Liga / The Sand And The Sea	1960	1.60	8.00
Capitol 4478	I've A' Ready Started In / Balboa	1961	1.60	8.00
Capitol 4508	Calcutta / Gone Are The Days	1961	1.60	8.00
Capitol 4568	Grounded / Dream Boy, Dream	1961	1.60	8.00
Capitol 4599	More Money For You And Me / Swing Down Chariot	1961	2.00	10.00
Capitol 4641	More Money For You And Me *(Edited)* / Swing Down Chariot	1961	1.60	8.00
Capitol 4659	Once Around The Block / The Seine	1961	1.60	8.00
	—Original Capitol singles above have purple labels with the Capitol dome on the left.—			
Capitol 4716	The Big Draft / Sunny Cockroach	1962	1.60	8.00
Capitol 4792	Alice / Goodnight, Sweetheart	1962	1.20	6.00
Capitol 4974	Charmaine / Hi Hi, Anybody Home?	1963	1.20	6.00
Capitol 5020	Oh Where, Oh Where / Demons And Witches	1963	1.20	6.00
Capitol 5074	The Greatest Surfing Couple / I'm Falling In Love With A Girl	1963	3.00	15.00
Capitol 5143	A Letter To The Beatles / College Cannonball	1964	1.20	6.00
Capitol 5178	I've Known You All My Life / What Kind Of Bird Is That?	1964	1.20	6.00
Capitol 5236	Girl Without A Top / Two Wrongs Don't make A Right	1964	1.20	6.00
Capitol 5274	My Love, My Love / How To Succeed In Love	1964	1.20	6.00
Capitol 5351	I'll Set My Love To Music / Everlasting	1965	1.20	6.00
Capitol 5450	Our First American Dance / Now I'll Never Be The Same	1965	1.20	6.00
Capitol 5687	Girl In The Shade Of A Striped Umbrella / Let's Call It A Day, Girl	1966	1.20	6.00
Capitol 5609	Something To Remember You By / Annie In Her Granny	1966	1.20	6.00
Capitol 5819	Love Of The Common People / What I Don't Know Can't Hurt Me	1966	1.20	6.00
Capitol 5921	Draftdodger Rag / Hitchhiker	1966	1.20	6.00
	—Extended Play Albums—			
Capitol EAP-826	Dreamy Eyes *(10" EP)*	1957	10.00	50.00
Capitol EPO-1015	26 Miles (Santa Catalina)	1958	8.00	40.00
Capitol EPO-1064	Big Man	1958	8.00	40.00
Capitol EPO-1139	Lazy Summer Night	1958	8.00	40.00
FOUR QUEENS, THE				
ABC-Paramount 10409	Black Stockings / It's Too Late	1963	2.00	10.00
FOUR SEASONS, THE				
Alanna 555	I'm Still In Love With You, Baby / That's The Way The Ball Bounces	1959	4.00	20.00

Label & Catalog #		A-Side / B-Side	Year	VG	NM
Alanna 555		Don't Sweat It, Baby / That's The Way The Ball Bounces	1959	3.00	15.00
Alanna 558		Hot Water Bottle / Love Knows No Season	1959	4.00	20.00

FOUR SEASONS, THE

Members have included Frankie Valli, Bob Gaudio, Bob Ciccone, Jerry Corbetta, Hank Majewski and Nick Massi. Refer to Alex Alda; John Corey; Turner Disentri; Billy Dixon & The Topics; The Four Lovers; Johnny Halo; Tony Hayes; Hal Miller & The Rays; Joey Reynolds; The Royal Teens; Larry Santos; Sugarloaf; The Topics; Van Trevor; The Village Voices; The Wonder Who? Also refer to the Various Artists EPs section.

Label & Catalog #		A-Side / B-Side	Year	VG	NM
Gone 5122	(DJ)	Bermuda / Spanish Lace	196?	8.00	40.00
Gone 5122		Bermuda / Spanish Lace	196?	10.00	50.00
Vee Jay 456		Sherry / I've Cried Before *(Black label)*	1962	3.00	15.00
Vee Jay 456		Sherry / I've Cried Before *(Black rainbow label)*	1962	2.00	10.00
Vee Jay 465		Big Girls Don't Cry / Connie-O *(Black rainbow label)*	1962	2.00	10.00
Vee Jay 478		Santa Claus Is Coming To Town / Christmas Tears	1962	3.00	15.00
Vee Jay 485		Walk Like A Man / Lucky Ladybug	1963	2.00	10.00
Vee Jay 512		Ain't That A Shame? / Soon	1963	2.00	10.00
Vee Jay 539		Candy Girl / Marlena	1963	2.00	10.00
Vee Jay 539	(PS)	Candy Girl / Marlena	1963	10.00	50.00
Vee Jay 562	(DJ)	New Mexican Rose / That's The Way It Is	1963	4.00	20.00
		(Misprint on b-side title.)			
Vee Jay 562		New Mexican Rose / That's The Only Way	1963	2.00	10.00
Vee Jay 576	(DJ)	Peanuts *(One sided)*	1963	20.00	100.00
Vee Jay 576	(DJ)	Peanuts / Stay	1963	15.00	75.00
Vee Jay 576		Peanuts / Stay	1963	20.00	100.00
Vee Jay 582	(DJ)	Stay / Goodnight My Love	1964	3.00	15.00
Vee Jay 582		Stay / Goodnight My Love	1964	2.00	10.00
Vee Jay 597		Alone / Long, Lonely Nights *(Yellow label)*	1964	4.00	20.00
Vee Jay 597		Alone / Long, Lonely Nights *(Black label)*	1964	3.00	15.00
Vee Jay 597		Alone / Long, Lonely Nights *(Black rainbow label)*	1964	2.00	10.00
Vee Jay 597	(PS)	Alone / Long, Lonely Nights	1964	5.00	25.00
Vee Jay 608		Sincerely / One Song	1964	3.00	15.00
Vee Jay 618		Happy, Happy Birthday, Baby / You're The Apple Of My Eye	1964	3.00	15.00
Vee Jay 626		I Saw Mommy Kissing Santa Claus / Christmas Tears	1964	3.00	15.00
Vee Jay 626	(PS)	I Saw Mommy Kissing Santa Claus / Christmas Tears	1964	5.00	25.00
WABC Radio 77	(DJ)	Cousin Brucie Go Go *(One sided on yellow vinyl)*	1964	35.00	175.00
		(Theme song for DJ Cousin Brucie's show.)			
Columbia 6675	(DJ)	Big Man's World *(Cardboard sheet)*	1964	60.00	30.00
Vee Jay 639		Never On Sunday / Connie-O	1965	1.60	8.00
Vee Jay 664		Since I Don't Have You / Tonite, Tonite	1965	2.00	10.00
Vee Jay 713		Little Boy (In Grown Up Clothes) / Silver Wings	1965	3.00	15.00
		(Maroon label)			
Vee Jay 713		Little Boy (In Grown Up Clothes) / Silver Wings	1965	2.00	10.00
		(Black label)			
Gorda 500		Rag Doll / *(B-side by Little Royal)*	1965	2.00	10.00
Vee Jay 719		My Mother's Eyes / Stay	1966	2.00	10.00
Philips 40166		Dawn / No Surfing Today	1964	1.60	8.00
Philips 40185		Ronnie / Born To Silence	1964	1.60	8.00
Philips 40185	(PS)	Ronnie / Born To Silence	1964	2.00	10.00
Philips 40211		Rag Doll / Silence Is Golden	1964	1.60	8.00
Philips 40211	(PS)	Rag Doll / Silence Is Golden	1964	2.00	10.00
Philips 40225		Save It For Me / Funny Face	1964	1.60	8.00
Philips 40238		Big Man In Town / Little Angel	1964	1.60	8.00
Philips 40238	(PS)	Big Man In Town / Little Angel	1964	2.00	10.00
Philips 40260		Bye, Bye, Baby (Baby Goodbye) / Searching Wind	1965	1.60	8.00
Philips 40260	(PS)	Bye, Bye, Baby (Baby Goodbye) / Searching Wind	1965	3.00	15.00
Philips 40278		Toy Soldier / Betrayed	1965	1.60	8.00
Philips 40278	(PS)	Toy Soldier / Betrayed	1965	2.00	10.00
Philips 40305		Girl Come Running / Cry Myself To Sleep	1965	1.60	8.00
Philips 40305	(PS)	Girl Come Running / Cry Myself To Sleep	1965	2.00	10.00
Philips 40317		Let's Hang On! / On Broadway Tonight	1965	1.60	8.00
Philips 40350		Working My Way Back To You / Too Many Memories	1966	1.60	8.00
Philips 40370		Opus 17 (Don't You Worry 'Bout Me) / Beggar's Paradise	1966	1.60	8.00
Philips 40370	(PS)	Opus 17 (Don't You Worry 'Bout Me) / Beggar's Paradise	1966	2.00	10.00
Philips 40393		I've Got You Under My Skin / Huggin' My Pillow	1966	1.60	8.00
Philips 40393	(PS)	I've Got You Under My Skin / Huggin' My Pillow	1966	2.00	10.00
Philips 40412		Tell It To The Rain / Snow Girl	1966	1.60	8.00
Philips 40412	(PS)	Tell It To The Rain / Snow Girl	1966	2.00	10.00
Philips 40433		Beggin' / Dody	1967	1.60	8.00
Philips 40433	(PS)	Beggin' / Dody	1967	2.00	10.00
Philips 40460		C'mon, Marianne / Let's Ride Again	1967	1.60	8.00
Philips 40460	(PS)	C'mon, Marianne / Let's Ride Again	1967	2.00	10.00
Philips 40490		Watch The Flowers Grow / Raven	1967	1.60	8.00
Philips 40490	(PS)	Watch The Flowers Grow / Raven	1967	2.00	10.00
Philips 40500	(Can)	Donneybrook / Around And Around	1968	3.00	15.00
Philips 40523		Will You Love Me Tomorrow? / Around And Around	1968	1.60	8.00
Philips 40542		Saturday's Father / Goodbye Girl	1968	1.60	8.00
Philips 40542	(PS)	Saturday's Father / Goodbye Girl	1968	2.00	10.00
Philips 40542	(PS)	Saturday's Father / Goodbye Girl *(Fold open sleeve)*	1968	4.00	20.00

Label & Catalog #		A-Side/B-Side	Year	VG	NM
Philips 40577		Electric Stories / Pity	1968	1.20	6.00
Philips 40597		Idaho / Something's On Her Mind	1969	1.20	6.00
Philips 40597	(PS)	Idaho / Something's On Her Mind	1969	1.60	8.00
Philips 40661		You've Got Your Troubles / A Dream Of Kings	1970	1.60	8.00
Philips 40662		A Patch Of Blue / She Gives Me Light	1970	1.20	6.00
Philips 40662	(PS)	A Patch Of Blue / She Gives Me Light	1970	1.20	6.00
Bob Crewe DJP-71	(DJ)	Lay Me Down (Wake Me Up) / Lay Me Down (Wake Me Up)	1970	3.00	15.00
Philips 40688	(DJ)	Lay Me Down (Wake Me Up) / Lay Me Down (Wake Me Up)	1970	3.00	15.00
Philips 40688		Lay Me Down (Wake Me Up) / Heartches And Rainbows	1970	3.00	15.00
Philips 40694	(DJ)	Where Are My Dreams? / Where Are My Dreams?	1971	3.00	15.00
Philips 40694		Where Are My Dreams? / Any Day Now-Happy Day	1971	4.00	20.00
Crewe 333		And That Reminds Me (My Heart Reminds Me) / The Singles Game	1969	.60	3.00
Warner Bros. 16107	(Eng)	Sleeping Man / Whatever You Say	1971	15.00	75.00
Seasons 4 Ever 777		Trance / I Am All Alone	1971	1.60	8.00
Seasons 4 Ever 777		Trance / I Am All Alone (Colored vinyl)	1971	3.00	15.00
Mowest 5026		Walk On, Don't Look Back / Sun County	1972	1.20	6.00
Motown 1255		How Come / Life And Breath	1973	1.20	6.00
Motown 1288		Hickory / Charisma	1973	1.20	6.00
Warner Brothers 8168		December 1963 (Oh, What A Night) / Slip Away	1975	.60	3.00
Warner Brothers 8122		Who Loves You? / Who Loves You?	1975	.60	3.00
Warner Brothers 8203		Silver Lake / Mystic Mr. Sun	1976	.60	3.00
Warner Brothers 8407		Down The Hall / I Believe In You	1977	1.60	8.00
		—Extended Play Albums—			
Vee Jay 901		The Four Seasons Sing	1964	10.00	50.00
Vee Jay 902		The Four Seasons Sing (Cardboard cover)	1964	10.00	50.00
Vee Jay 902		The Four Seasons Sing (Paper sleeve)	1964	8.00	40.00
Philips 2705	(33)	Edizone D'Oro (Jukebox EP)	1968	5.00	25.00

FOUR SEASONS, THE, & THE BEACH BOYS

Label & Catalog #		A-Side/B-Side	Year	VG	NM
F.B.I. 7701	(DJ)	East Meets West / East Meets West	1986	2.00	10.00
F.B.I. 7701	(DJ)	East Meets West / Rhapsody	1986	3.00	15.00
F.B.I. 7701		East Meets West / Rhapsody	1986	4.00	20.00

FOUR SHARPS, THE

Sharp 5064		Surf Guitar / Drag Strip	196?	7.00	35.00

FOUR SHARPS, THE

Donna 1330		Church Key / Very Muddy Waters	1961	7.00	35.00
		(Donna 1330 was also released credited to The Gonzos.)			

FOUR SPEEDS, THE
The Four Speeds are a studio creation of Gary Usher.

Challenge 9187	(DJ)	R.P.M. / My Sting Ray	1963	5.00	25.00
Challenge 9187		R.P.M. / My Sting Ray	1963	10.00	50.00
Challenge 9202	(DJ)	Four On The Floor / Cheater Slicks	1963	5.00	25.00
Challenge 9202		Four On The Floor / Cheater Slicks	1963	10.00	50.00

FOUR STAGS, THE

Topaz 1301		Confession / Flame Of Love	196?	.80	4.00

FOUR STARS, THE

Era 3021		Blue Dawn / The Frog (Blue vinyl)	1960	2.00	10.00
Era 3021	(PS)	Blue Dawn / The Frog	1960	2.00	10.00

FOUR TEENS, THE

Challenge 59021		Spark Plug / Go Little Go Cat (Green label)	1958	15.00	75.00
Challenge 59021		Spark Plug / Go Little Go Cat (Black label)	1958	5.00	25.00

FOUR TEMPTATIONS, THE: Refer to THE TEMPTATIONS

FOUR TOWNSMEN, THE

Artflow 145		It Wasn't So Long Before / Sometimes	195?	30.00	150.00

FOUR UNIQUES, THE

Adam 9002		Looking For A Love / Too Young	1961	30.00	150.00
Adam 9004		She's The Only Girl / Twistin' Around	1962	8.00	40.00
200.00					

FOUR UPSETTERS, THE

Sun 381		Crazy Arms / Midnight Soiree	1962	1.60	8.00
Sun 386		Surfin' Calliope / Wabash Cannonball	1963	3.00	15.00

FOUR WHEELS, THE

Delaware 1703		Sneaky Little Helper / Ratchet	1964	6.00	30.00
Soma 1428		Central High Playmate / Colt 45	1965	3.00	15.00

Label & Catalog #	A-Side/B-Side	Year	VG	NM
FOUR WINDS, THE				
Vik 221	Find Someone New / Colorado Moon	1956	2.00	10.00
Decor 175	Five Minutes More / Short Shorts	1957	2.00	10.00
Warwick 633	Daddy's Home / Bull Moose Stomp	1961	8.00	40.00
Derby 10022	Playgirl / Jennifer	196?	6.00	30.00
FOUR WINDS, THE				
Westland 15771/2	The Enemy / Hear The Sound	1962	1.00	5.00
FOUR WINDS, THE				
The Four Winds is a pseudonym of The Tokens.				
Swing 100	Remember Last Summer / Strange, Strange Feeling	1964	4.00	20.00
B.T. Puppy 555	Let It Ride / One Face In The Crowd	1969	1.20	6.00
Crystal Ball 102	Come Softly To Me / Judy	196?	1.00	5.00
Crystal Ball 105	Arlene / Goodbye, Maureen	196?	2.00	10.00
Crystal Ball 105	Arlene / Goodbye, Maureen *(Colored vinyl)*	196?	2.00	10.00
FOUR YOUNG MEN, THE				
Dore 621	Garden In The Rain / That Man Paul	1961	4.00	20.00
Crest 1076	You Been Torturing Me / See Them Laugh	1961	3.00	15.00
Crest 1083	Just For Tonight / Sweetheart In Senior High	1961	3.00	15.00
FOURLANES, THE				
Reprise 20213	Surf Train / Lonely Weekends	1963	3.00	15.00
FOURMOST, THE				
Atco 6280	Hello, Little Girl / Just In Case	1963	2.00	10.00
Atco 6285	Respectable / I'm In Love	1964	1.60	8.00
Atco 6307	If You Cry / A Little Bit Of Loving	1964	1.60	8.00
Atco 6317	How Can I Tell Her? / You Got That Way	1964	1.60	8.00
Capitol 5591	Why Do Fools Fall In Love? / Girls, Girls, Girls	1966	1.20	6.00
Capitol 5738	Here, There And Everywhere / You've Changed	1966	3.00	15.00
FOURTH DIMENSION, THE				
Columbia 43778	Rainy Day / Land Of Make Believe	1966	1.20	6.00
FOWLER, JIMMY				
Dart 118	Let's Rock And Roll / Please Answer My Call	1959	3.00	15.00
FOWLEY, KIM				
Refer to The Gamblers; Hollywood Argyles; King Lizard; The Renegades; and Rocky & The Border Guards.				
Audition	Astrology /	1963	5.00	25.00
Corby 216	The Trip / Big Sur, Bear Mountain, Ciros, Flip Side, Protest Song	1965	5.00	25.00
Mira 209	American Dream / The Statue	1965	2.00	10.00
Living Legend 721	Mr. Responsibility / My Foolish Heart	1965	3.00	15.00
Living Legend 725	Underground Lady / Pop Art '66	1966	3.00	15.00
Loma 2064	Something New And Different / Lights	1966	2.00	10.00
Reprise 0569	Strangers From The Sky / Don't Be Cruel	1967	2.00	10.00
Tower 342	Love Is Alive And Well / Reincarnation	1967	2.00	10.00
Imperial 66326	Born To Be Wild / Space Odyssey	1968	1.60	8.00
Imperial 66349	Wildfire / Bubble Gum	1968	1.60	8.00
Capitol 3403	I'm Bad / Forbidden Love	1972	.80	4.00
Capitol 3534	International Heroes / E.S.P. Reader	1973	.80	4.00
Capitol 3662	Born Dancer / Something New	1973	.80	4.00
FRAGILE LIME, THE				
Sabina 003	Fairyland / I Know What It Is	196?	2.00	10.00
Sabina 005	Day In The Sun / I Need Your Love	196?	2.00	10.00
Warner Bros. 7424	Angie / I'm Gonna Get You	1970	.60	3.00
Thunder Tummy 1017	Happy Song / She Got Me Shakin'	1972	.80	4.00
Metromedia 266	Happy Song / She Got Me Shakin'	1972	.60	3.00
FRAMPTON'S CAMEL				
Frampton's Camel features Peter Frampton. Refer to The Herd; Humble Pie; The Tages.				
A&M 1456	All Night Long / Don't Fade Away	1973	1.00	5.00
A&M 1470	Which Way The Wind Blows / I Believe	1973	1.00	5.00
FRANCE, LARRY				
Landa 700	Last Kiss / Germ City	1964	2.00	10.00
FRANCIS, CONNIE				
MGM 12015	Freddy / Didn't I Love You Enough?	1955	4.00	20.00
MGM 12056	Make Him Jealous / Goody Goodbye	1955	3.00	15.00
MGM 12122	Are You Satisfied? / My Treasure	1956	3.00	15.00
MGM 12191	My First Real Love / Believe In Me	1956	3.00	15.00
MGM 12251	Send For My Baby / Forgetting	1956	3.00	15.00

Label & Catalog #		A-Side/B-Side	Year	VG	NM
MGM 12335		My Sailor Boy / Everyone Needs Someone	1956	3.00	15.00
MGM 12375		I Never Had A Sweetheart / Little Blue Wren	1957	3.00	15.00
MGM 12440		No Other One / I Leaned On A Man	1957	2.50	12.00
MGM 12490		Eighteen / Faded Orchid	1957	2.00	10.00
MGM 12555		You, My Darlin,' You / The Majesty Of Love	1957	2.00	10.00
MGM 12588		Who's Sorry Now? / You Were Only Fooling	1958	2.00	10.00
MGM 12647		I'm Sorry I Made You Cry / Lock Up Your Heart	1958	2.00	10.00
MGM 12683		Stupid Cupid / Carolina Moon	1958	2.00	10.00
MGM 12713		Fallin' / Happy Days And Lonely Nights	1958	2.00	10.00
MGM 12738		My Happiness / Never Before	1958	2.00	10.00
MGM 12738	(PS)	My Happiness / Never Before (Pink sleeve)	1958	3.00	15.00
MGM 12738	(PS)	My Happiness / Never Before (White sleeve)	1958	3.00	15.00
MGM SK-50117	(S)	My Happiness / Never Before	1958	5.00	25.00
MGM 12769		If I Didn't Care / Toward The End Of The Day	1959	2.00	10.00
MGM 12769	(PS)	If I Didn't Care / Toward The End Of The Day	1959	3.00	15.00
MGM 12793		Lipstick On Your Collar / Frankie	1959	2.00	10.00
MGM 12824		You're Gonna Miss Me / Plenty Good Lovin'	1959	2.00	10.00
MGM 12841		Among My Souvenirs / God Bless America	1959	2.00	10.00
		—Original MGM singles above have yellow labels.—			
MGM 12841		Among My Souvenirs / God Bless America	1959	2.00	10.00
MGM SK-50133	(S)	Among My Souvenirs / God Bless America	1959	3.00	15.00
MGM SB-9	(S)	Rock-A-Bye Your Baby With A Dixie Melody / Ciao Ciao Bambina	1960	3.00	15.00
MGM SB-10	(S)	I Almost Lost My Mind / Come Back To Sorrento	1960	3.00	15.00
MGM 12787		Mama / Teddy	1960	1.60	8.00
MGM 12899		Everybody's Somebody's Fool / Jealous Of You	1960	1.60	8.00
MGM 12899	(PS)	Everybody's Somebody's Fool / Jealous Of You	1960	2.00	10.00
MGM 12923		My Heart Has A Mind Of Its Own / Malaguena	1960	1.60	8.00
MGM 12923	(PS)	My Heart Has A Mind Of Its Own / Malaguena	1960	2.00	10.00
MGM 12964		Many Tears Ago / Senza Mama (With No One)	1960	1.60	8.00
MGM 12964	(PS)	Many Tears Ago / Senza Mama (With No One)	1960	2.00	10.00
MGM 12971		Where The Boys Are / No One	1961	1.60	8.00
MGM 12971	(PS)	Where The Boys Are / No One	1961	2.00	10.00
MGM 12995		Breakin' In A Brand New Heart / Someone Else's Boy	1961	1.60	8.00
MGM 12995	(PS)	Breakin' In A Brand New Heart / Someone Else's Boy	1961	2.00	10.00
MGM 13005		Swanee / Atashi No	1961	1.60	8.00
MGM 13019		Together / Too Many Rules	1961	1.60	8.00
MGM 13019	(PS)	Together / Too Many Rules	1961	2.00	10.00
MGM 13039		(He's My) Dreamboat / Hollywood	1961	1.60	8.00
MGM 13039	(PS)	(He's My) Dreamboat / Hollywood	1961	2.00	10.00
MGM 13051		When The Boy In Your Arms (Is The Boy On Your Heart) / Baby's First Christmas	1961	1.60	8.00
MGM 13051	(PS)	When The Boy In Your Arms (Is The Boy On Your Heart) / Baby's First Christmas	1961	2.00	10.00
MGM 13059		Don't Break The Heart That Loves You / Drop It, Joe	1962	1.60	8.00
MGM 13059	(PS)	Don't Break The Heart That Loves You / Drop It, Joe	1962	2.00	10.00
MGM 13074		Second Hand Love / Gonna Git That Man	1962	2.00	10.00
MGM 13074	(PS)	Second Hand Love / Gonna Git That Man	1962	2.00	10.00
		("Second Hand Love" was produced by Phil Spector.)			
MGM 13087		Vacation / The Biggest Sin Of All	1962	1.60	8.00
MGM 13087	(PS)	Vacation / The Biggest Sin Of All	1962	2.00	10.00
MGM 13096		I Was Such A Fool (To Fall In Love With You) / He Thinks I Still Care	1962	1.00	5.00
MGM 13096	(PS)	I Was Such A Fool (To Fall In Love With You) / He Thinks I Still Care	1962	1.20	6.00
MGM 13116		I'm Gonna Be Warm This Winter / La Di La	1962	1.00	5.00
MGM 13116	(PS)	I'm Gonna Be Warm This Winter / La Di La	1962	1.20	6.00
MGM 13127		Follow The Boys / Waiting For Billy	1962	1.00	5.00
MGM 13127	(PS)	Follow The Boys / Waiting For Billy	1962	1.20	6.00
MGM 13143		If My Pillow Could Talk / You're The Only One Who Can Hurt Me	1963	1.00	5.00
MGM 13143	(PS)	If My Pillow Could Talk / You're The Only One Who Can Hurt Me	1963	1.20	6.00
MGM 13160		Drownin' My Sorrows / Mala Femmena	1963	1.00	5.00
MGM 13160	(PS)	Drownin' My Sorrows / Mala Femmena	1963	1.20	6.00
MGM 13176		Your Other Love / Whatever Happened To Rosemarie?	1963	1.00	5.00
MGM 13176	(PS)	Your Other Love / Whatever Happened To Rosemarie?	1963	1.20	6.00
MGM 13203		In The Summer Of His Years / My Buddy	1963	1.00	5.00
MGM 13203	(PS)	In The Summer Of His Years / My Buddy	1963	1.20	6.00
MGM 13214		Blue Winter / You Know You Don't Want Me	1964	1.00	5.00
MGM 13214	(PS)	Blue Winter / You Know You Don't Want Me	1964	1.20	6.00
MGM 13237		Be Anything (But Be Mine) / Tommy	1964	1.00	5.00
MGM 13237	(PS)	Be Anything (But Be Mine) / Tommy	1964	1.00	5.00
MGM 13256		Looking For Love / This Is My Happiest Moment	1964	1.00	5.00
MGM 13256	(PS)	Looking For Love / This Is My Happiest Moment	1964	1.00	5.00
MGM 13287		Don't Ever Leave Me / We Have Something More	1964	1.00	5.00
MGM 13287	(PS)	Don't Ever Leave Me / We Have Something More	1964	1.00	5.00

Label & Catalog #		A-Side/B-Side	Year	VG	NM
MGM 13303		Whose Heart Are You Breaking Tonight? / C'mon, Jerry	1965	1.00	5.00
MGM 13303	(PS)	Whose Heart Are You Breaking Tonight? / C'mon, Jerry	1965	2.00	10.00
MGM 13325		For Mama / She'll Be Coming 'Round The Mountain	1965	1.00	5.00
MGM 13331		Wishing It Was You / You're Mine	1965	1.00	5.00
MGM 13331	(PS)	Wishing It Was You / You're Mine	1965	2.00	10.00
MGM 13363		Forget Domani / No One Sends Me Roses	1965	1.00	5.00
MGM 13389		Roundabout / Bossa Nova Hand Dance	1965	1.00	5.00
MGM 13420		Jealous Heart / Can I Rely On You?	1965	1.00	5.00
MGM 13470		Love Is Me, Love Is You / I'd Let You Break My Heart All Over Again	1966	1.00	5.00
MGM 13470	(PS)	Love Is Me, Love Is You / I'd Let You Break My Heart All Over Again	1966	2.00	10.00
MGM 13505		It's A Different World / Empty Chapel	1966	1.00	5.00
MGM 13505	(PS)	It's A Different World / Empty Chapel	1966	2.00	10.00
MGM 13545		A Letter From A Soldier (Dear Mama) / Somewhere, My Love	1966	.80	4.00
MGM 13578		All The Love In The World / So Nice	1966	.80	4.00
MGM 13610		Spanish Nights And You / Games That Lovers Play	1966	1.00	5.00
MGM 13610	(PS)	Spanish Nights And You / Games That Lovers Play	1966	2.00	10.00
MGM 13665		Another Page / Souvenir D'Italie	1967	.80	4.00
MGM CS-5	(DJ)	Connie Francis	1967	12.00	60.00
		(Boxed set of five stereo singles, MGM 13708-12, with a cue sheet, bio and jukebox title strips. The price is for the complete set. The five promo singles are priced separately below.)			
MGM 13708	(DJ)	Mama / Never On Sunday	1967	1.60	8.00
MGM 13709	(DJ)	My Happiness / La Di La	1967	1.60	8.00
MGM 13710	(DJ)	Malaguena / I Love You Much Too Much	1967	1.60	8.00
MGM 13711	(DJ)	Once In A Lifetime / Oh Lonesome Me	1967	1.60	8.00
MGM 13712	(DJ)	Jealous Heart / Will You Still Be Mine?	1967	1.60	8.00
MGM 13718		Time Alone Will Tell / Born Free	1967	.80	4.00
MGM 13773		My Heart Cries For You / Someone Took The Sweetness Out Of Sweetheart	1967	1.00	5.00
MGM 13773	(PS)	My Heart Cries For You / Someone Took The Sweetness Out Of Sweetheart	1967	3.00	15.00
MGM 13814		Lonely Again / When You Care A Lot For Someone	1967	.80	4.00
MGM 13876		My World Is Slipping Away / Till We're Together	1967	.80	4.00
MGM 13923		Why Say Goodbye? / Adios, Mi Amore	1968	.80	4.00
MGM 13948		Somebody Else Is Taking My Place / Brother, Can You Spare A Dime?	1968	.80	4.00
MGM 14004		I Don't Wanna Play House / The Welfare Check	1968	.80	4.00
MGM 14034		The Wedding Cake / Over Hill, Under Ground	1969	.60	3.00
MGM 14058		Gone Like The Wind / Am I Blue?	1969	.60	3.00
MGM 14058	(PS)	Gone Like The Wind / Am I Blue?	1969	4.00	20.00
MGM 14089		Invierno Trieste / Noches Espanolas Y Tu	1969	Unreleased?	
MGM 14091		My Love / Zingara	1969	1.00	5.00
MGM 14091	(PS)	My Love / Zingara	1969	5.00	25.00
		— *Extended Play Albums*—			
MGM 1599		Connie Francis	1958	10.00	50.00
MGM 1603		Who's Sorry Now?	1958	10.00	50.00
MGM 1604		Who's Sorry Now?	1958	10.00	50.00
MGM 1605		Who's Sorry Now?	1958	10.00	50.00
MGM 1655		My Happiness	1959	8.00	40.00
MGM 1662		If I Didn't Care	1959	8.00	40.00
MGM 1663		The Exciting Connie Francis	1959	8.00	40.00
MGM 1664		The Exciting Connie Francis	1959	8.00	40.00
MGM 1665		The Exciting Connie Francis	1959	8.00	40.00
MGM HC5-6	(DJ)	Heart Circuit Interview (No cover)	1959	10.00	50.00
MGM 1687		Connie Francis	1960	8.00	40.00
MGM 1688		Connie's Greatest Hits	1960	8.00	40.00
MGM 1689		Connie's Greatest Hits	1960	8.00	40.00
MGM 1690		Connie's Greatest Hits	1960	8.00	40.00
MGM 1691		Rock 'N Roll Million Sellers	1960	8.00	40.00
MGM 1692		Rock 'N Roll Million Sellers	1960	8.00	40.00
MGM 1693		Rock 'N Roll Million Sellers	1960	8.00	40.00
MGM 1964		Country & Western Golden Hits	1960	8.00	40.00
MGM 1965		Country & Western Golden Hits	1960	8.00	40.00
MGM 1966		Country & Western Golden Hits	1960	8.00	40.00
MGM 1703		Connie Francis	1961	8.00	40.00
MGM SLM-3776	(33)	My Thanks To You (Jukebox EP)	1968	4.00	20.00
MGM SLM-4145	(33)	Greatest American Waltzes (Jukebox EP)	1968	4.00	20.00

FRANK & MAC / THE CHEERLEADERS
Frank is Frankie Ford.

Spinnett 1000		True Love / Chinese Bandits	1959	4.00	20.00

FRANKIE & JOHNNY
Frankie and Johnny Sardo.

Lido 604		Big Clem / Together Tonight	1958	3.00	15.00

Label & Catalog #	A-Side/B-Side	Year	VG	NM
FRANKIE & JOHNNY				
Blast Off 100	Please Be My Love Tonight / Piccadilly Rose	196?	2.00	10.00
FRANKIE & THE ECHOES				
Savoy 1544	Come Back, Baby / Until We Meet Again	1958	2.50	12.00
FRANKIE & THE FLIPS				
Savoy 1602	Devil Dog Rock / Popeye Twist	1961	2.00	10.00
FRANKIE & THE TIMEBREAKERS				
Mercury 72837	I'll Be Home / Is There Anybody?	1968	2.00	10.00
FRANKLIN, DOUG				
Colonial 7777	My Lucky Love / Drizzlin' Rain	1958	2.00	10.00
Colonial 8888	I Wonder Who's Kissing Her Now? / I Used To Wonder	1958	2.00	10.00
FRANTICS, THE				
Dolton 2	Straight Flush / Young Blues	1959	3.00	15.00
Dolton 6	Fog Cutter / Black Sapphire	1959	3.00	15.00
Dolton 13	Werewolf / Checkerboard	1960	3.00	15.00
Dolton 16	Werewolf / No Werewolf	1960	3.00	15.00
Dolton 24	The Whip / Delilah	1960	1.25	6.00
Dolton 31	Yankee Doodlin' / One Minute Of Flamenco	1961	1.25	6.00
Dolton 33	San Antonio Rose / Trees	1961	1.25	6.00
Seafair 111	San Francisco Swim / Blue Day	196?	1.00	5.00
Bolo 728	Meet Me In Seattle / Bony Moronie	1962	1.00	5.00
Bolo 736	Oh Yeah / Let Our Love Roll On	1962	1.00	5.00
FRATERNITY BROTHERS, THE				
Date 1528	Big Town / Sad Little Boy	1960	3.00	15.00
FRECKLES, THE				
Madison 158	Little Star / Freckle Face	1961	2.00	10.00
FRED, JOHN (& HIS PLAYBOY BAND)				
Montel 904	Down In New Orleans / I Love You	1959	3.00	15.00
Montel 1002	Shirley / My Love For You	1959	3.00	15.00
Montel 1007	Good Lovin' / You Know You Made Me Cry	1961	2.00	10.00
Montel 2001	Mirror Mirror (On The Wall) / To Have And To Hold	1962	2.00	10.00
Jewel 730	Dial 101 / There Goes That Train	1964	2.00	10.00
Jewel 743	Wrong To Me / How Can I Prove?	1965	2.00	10.00
Jewel 737	My First Love / Boogie Children	1965	2.00	10.00
	(Jewel 737 credits The Playboys.)			
N-Joy 1005	My First Love / Boogie Children	1965	2.00	10.00
Paula 225	Fortune Teller / Making Love To You	1966	.80	4.00
Paula 234	Can't I Get A Word In? / Sun City	1966	.80	4.00
Paula 244	Doin' The Best I Can / Leave Her Never	1966	.80	4.00
Paula 247	Outta My Head / Love Comes In Time	1966	.80	4.00
Paula 259	Wind-Up Doll / Up And Down	1967	.80	4.00
Paula 273	Agnes English / Sad Story	1967	1.00	5.00
Paula 282	Judy In Disguise (With Glasses) / When The Lights Go Out (White label)	1967	1.00	5.00
Paula 282	Judy In Disguise (With Glasses) / When The Lights Go Out (Pink label)	1967	1.00	5.00
Paula 282	Judy In Disguise (With Glasses) / When The Lights Go Out (Yellow label)	1967	1.00	5.00
Paula 294	Hey, Hey Bunny / No Letter Today	1968	1.00	5.00
Paula 303	We Played Games / Lonely Are The Lonely	1968	.80	4.00
Paula 310	Little Dum Dum / Tissue Paper	1969	.80	4.00
Paula 315	Sometimes You Just Can't Win / What Is Happiness?	1969	1.00	5.00
Uni 55135	Silly Sarah Carter (Eating On A Moonpie) / Back In The U.S.S.R.	1969	.80	4.00
Uni 55160	Three Deep In A Feeling / Open Doors	1969	.80	4.00
Uni 55187	Love My Soul / Julia, Julia	1970	.80	4.00
Uni 55220	Where's Everybody Going? / Miss Knocker	1970	.80	4.00
Sugarcane 1001	Keep It Hid / You Had To Be A Woman	1975	.80	4.00
Sugarcane 1002	Jukebox Shirley / Hey, Good Lookin'	1975	.80	4.00
	(Sugarcane 1002 credits John Fred.)			
FRED, JOHN, & THE CREEPERS				
The Creepers is a pseudonym for The Playboys.				
Bell 382	I'm In Love Again / In The Mood / Bayou Country	1973	.60	3.00
FREDDIE & THE DREAMERS				
Capitol 5053	I'm Telling You Now / What Have I Done To You?	1963	2.00	10.00
Capitol 5137	You Were Made For Me / Send A Letter To Me	1964	2.00	10.00
Tower 125	I'm Telling You Now / What Have I Done To You?	1964	1.00	5.00
Tower 127	You Were Made For Me / So Fine	1964	1.00	5.00

Label & Catalog #		A-Side/B-Side	Year	VG	NM
Tower 163		Send A Letter To Me / (B-side by Just Four Men)	1965	1.00	5.00
Mercury 72327		Don't Do That To Me / Just For You	1965	.80	4.00
Mercury 72377		I Understand (Just How You Feel) / I Will	1965	.80	4.00
Mercury 72428		Do The Freddie / Tell Me When	1965	.80	4.00
Mercury 72462		A Little You / Things I'd Like To Say	1965	.80	4.00
Mercury 72487		I Don't Know / Windmill In Old Amsterdam	1965	.80	4.00
Mercury 72487	(PS)	I Don't Know / Windmill In Old Amsterdam	1965	2.00	10.00
Super-K 146		She Needs Me / Susan's Tuba	1970	1.00	5.00
		—Extended Play Albums—			
Mercury 661	(33)	Fun Lovin' Freddie (Jukebox EP)	1966	3.00	15.00

FREDDIE & THE PARLIAMENTS
Twirl 1003		Darlene / That Girl	1959	20.00	100.00

FREDDIE & THE VOXPOPPERS
Warwick 589		Lonely For You / Helen Isn't Tellin'	196?	3.00	15.00

FREDDY & CLAIRE
Reprise 2049		After School / Love Is A Game	1962	3.00	15.00

FREDDY & THE FAT BOYS
Fat Man 101		Why Do Fools Fall In Love? / Ballad Of Freddy And Rich	195?	6.00	30.00

FREDDY & LONNIE
La Rae 501		Hot Doggin' / The Falcon	196?	7.00	35.00
		(LaRae 501 was also released as "Back Up & Push" / "The Raven" credited to Freddy Countryman.)			

FREE
Marque 448		What Makes You? / Decision For Lost Soul Blue	1969	4.00	20.00
Atco		What Makes You? / Decision For Lost Soul Blue	1969	2.50	12.00
A&M 1206		All Right Now / Mouthful Of Grass	1970	.60	3.00
A&M 1230		The Stealer / Lying In The Sunshine	1970	.60	3.00
A&M 1230	(PS)	The Stealer / Lying In The Sunshine	1970	.60	3.00
A&M 1352		Little Bit Of Love / Sail On	1971	.60	3.00
Island 1212		Wishing Well / Let Me Show You	1972	.60	3.00

FREE, SCOTT
Alanna 559		Love's Lost / You're My Girl	1960	2.00	10.00

FREE FOR ALL
Challenge		Show Me The Way / Come To My World	196?	3.00	15.00

FREE SPIRITS, THE
ABC 10872		Girl Of The Mountain / Tattoo Man	1966	2.00	10.00

FREED, ALAN; AL COLLINS, & THE MODERNAIRES
Coral 61693		The Space Man / Jazzbo's Theory	1956	5.00	25.00

FREED BAND, ALAN
Coral 61626		Right Now, Right Now / Tina's Canteen	1956	6.00	30.00
Coral 61660		The Camel Rock / I Don't Need Lotsa Money	1956	6.00	30.00
Coral 61749		Rock And Roll Boogie / The Grey Bear	1956	6.00	30.00
Coral 61818		Sentimental Journey / Stop! Look! And Run!	1958	6.00	30.00

FREEWAYS, THE
Hiback 107		I Need Love /	1966	2.00	10.00

FREEWHEELERS, THE
Epic 9725		Beach Boy / Annie	1964	2.00	10.00

FREHLEY, ACE
Ace Frehley is a member of Kiss.
Casablanca 941		New York Groove / Snow Blind	1978	1.00	5.00
Megaforce 89255		Into The Night / Fractured, Too	198?	.80	4.00
Megaforce 89072		Insane / The Acorn Is Spinning	198?	.80	4.00

FRENCH, DON
Lancer 104		Lonely Saturday Night / Goldilocks	1959	3.00	15.00
Lancer 105		Little Blonde Girl / I Look Into My Heart	1959	5.00	25.00

FRENCHY & THE CHESSMEN
Temple 2081		Beetle Bebop / El Tacos	1964	2.00	10.00

FRETS, THE
Uptown 104-2		Do You Want To Dance? / Sunday Drive	196?	.80	4.00

Label & Catalog #	A-Side/B-Side	Year	VG	NM
FRIAR TUCK				
Friar Tuck is a pseudonym for Curt Boetcher.				
Banshee 100	The Return Of Robin Hood /	195?	3.00	15.00
Mercury 72684	Alley Oop / Sweet Pea	1967	2.00	10.00
FRIDA				
Frida is a pseudonym of Annt-frid Lyngstad of Abba.				
Atlantic 89984	I Know There's Something Going On / Threnody	1982	.40	2.00
Atlantic DMD-361 (12")	I Know There's Something Going On /			
	I Know There's Something Going On	1982	1.00	5.00
FRIEDLES				
Bat 1004	Don't Tell Me What To Do / She Can Go	1966	3.00	15.00
Hanna 1001	I Lost Her / I'm So Glad	1966	3.00	15.00
FRIEL, BILL, & THE FABULOUS FURIES				
Joker 1009	Ft. Lauderdale, U.S.A. / Johnny, Come Home	195?	7.00	35.00
FRIEND, EDDIE, & THE EMPIRES				
Refer to The Empires.				
Colpix 112	Tears In My Eyes / Single And Free	1959	50.00	200.00
FRIEND & LOVER				
ABC 10910	Town Called Love / If Tomorrow	1967	.80	4.00
Verve/Forecast 5069	Reach Out In The Darkness / Time Is On Your Side			
	(You're Only Fifteen Years Old)	1968	1.00	5.00
Verve/Forecast 5091	If Love Is In Your Heart / Zig Zag	1968	.80	4.00
Verve/Forecast 5100	I Want To Be Free / Circus	1968	.80	4.00
Cadet/Concept 7019	Hard Lovin' / Coloroad Exile	196?	.80	4.00
Cadet/Concept 7019 (PS)	Hard Lovin' / Coloroad Exile	196?	2.00	10.00
FRIENDS OF WHITNEY SUNDAY, THE				
Capitol 2714	Ballad Of Thunder Road / Love Will Conquer All	1969	1.00	5.00
FRIESMAN, MAGEL				
Sun 294	I Feel So Blue / Memories Of You	1958	3.00	15.00
FRIJID PINK				
Parrot 334	Tell Me Why / Cryin' Shame	1969	1.00	5.00
Parrot 340	God Gave Me You / Drivin' Blues	1970	1.00	5.00
Parrot 341	House Of The Rising Sun / Drivin' Blues	1970	1.20	6.00
Parrot 349	Sing A Song For Freedom / End Of The Line	1970	1.00	5.00
Parrot 352	Heartbreak Hotel / Bye Bye Blues	1970	1.00	5.00
Parrot 355	Music For The People / Sloony	1971	.80	4.00
Parrot 358	We're Gonna Be There / Shorty Kline	1971	.80	4.00
Parrot 360	I Love Her / Lost Son	1971	.80	4.00
Lion 115	Earth Omen / Lazy Day	1972	1.00	5.00
FROGMEN, THE				
Astra 1009	Underwater / The Mad Rush	1961	8.00	40.00
Astra 1010	Beware Below / Tioga	1961	8.00	40.00
Candix 314	Underwater / The Mad Rush	1961	4.00	20.00
Candix 326	Beware Below / Tioga	1961	4.00	20.00
Scott 101	Seahorse Flats / Tioga	1961	7.00	35.00
Scott 102	Underwater / Beware Below	1961	7.00	35.00
Tee Jay 131	Sea Haunt / Diamond Back *(Blue vinyl)*	1962	10.00	50.00
FRONT END, THE				
Smash 2172	Go On Home / Beverly	1968	1.20	6.00
Smash 2199	Remember Walking In The Sand? / The Real Thing	1968	1.20	6.00
FRONT LINE, THE				
York 9000	I Don't Care / Got Love	1966	3.00	15.00
FRONT LINE, THE				
Titan 2001	Saigon Girl / Three Day Pass	1967	2.00	10.00
FRONTIERS, THE				
King 5481	Why Pretend? / Ding Dong Doo	1961	3.00	15.00
King 5534	Nearest Thing To Heaven / Oh, Nurse	1961	3.00	15.00
King 5609	Each Night I Pray / You Shake Me Up	1962	3.00	15.00
FRONTIERS, THE				
The Frontiers feature Roger Koob.				
Philips 40113	I Only Have Eyes For You / Don't Come Crying	1963	4.00	20.00
Philips 40148	I Just Want You / I'm Still Loving You	1963	3.00	15.00
MGM 13722	You / When I See You	1967	2.00	10.00

Label & Catalog #	A-Side/B-Side	Year	VG	NM
FROST				
Frost originally recorded as Dick Wagner & The Frosts.				
Vanguard 35089	Mystery Man / Stand In The Shadows	1969	1.20	6.00
Vanguard 35111 (PS)	Rock And Roll Music / Donny's Blues (DJ)	1969	2.00	10.00
Vanguard 35111	Rock And Roll Music / Donny's Blues	1969	1.00	5.00
FROST, MAX, & THE TROOPERS				
Max Frost & The Troopers is a pseudonym for Davie Allan & the Arrows.				
Tower 419	Shapes Of Things To Come / Free Lovin'	1968	2.00	10.00
Tower 478	Sittin' In Circles / Paxton Quigley's Had The Course	1968	2.00	10.00
Sidewalk 938	Stomper's Ride / There Is A Party Going On	1968	2.00	10.00
FROST, THOMAS & RICHARD				
Imperial 66405	She's Got Love / The Word Is Love	1969	1.00	5.00
Liberty 56191	Open Up Your Heart / Where Did Yesterday Go	1965	1.00	5.00
Liberty 66451	Hello Stranger / Fairy Tale Affair	1965	1.00	5.00
FRUGAL SOUND, THE				
Red Bird 052	Norwegian Wood / Cruel To Be Kind	1966	2.00	10.00
FRUIT OF THE LOOM				
Loom 101	One Hand In Darkness / A Little Bit Of Bach	196?	4.00	20.00
FRUMMOX				
ABC/Probe 470	There You Go / Mary Martin	1970	.80	4.00
FRUMIOUS BANDERSNATCH				
Muggles Gram. (EP)	Frumious Bandersnatch (Purple vinyl)	1967	50.00	250.00
	(Copies on any other color vinyl are bootlegs.)			
FUGATIVES, THE				
Trophy 2666	We Gotta Run / Don't Pretend	196?	3.00	15.00
FUGITIVES, THE				
Sims 115	Freeway / Fugitive	1960	3.00	15.00
Arvee 5014	Freeway / Fugitive	1960	2.00	10.00
FUGITIVES, THE				
D-Town 1034	A Fugitive / A Fugitive	196?	2.00	10.00
D-Town 1044	Let's Get On With It / On Trial	196?	2.00	10.00
Westchester 1002	You Can't Make Me Lonely / I Don't Wanna Talk	196?	2.00	10.00
Columbia 43261	I'll Be A Man / Mean Woman	1965	2.00	10.00
Trend 101	Come On And Clap / You're The Kind Of Girl	1966	4.00	20.00
FUGS, THE				
ESP 4507	Frenzy / I Want To Know	1966	2.00	10.00
FULLER FOUR, BOBBY [BOBBY FULLER & THE FANATICS]				
Bobby and Randy Fuller with DeWayne Quirico and Jim Reese. Refer to The Chancellors; David Haynes & The Pawns; Jay Horton; The Sherwoods; The Shindigs.				
Yucca 140	You're In Love / Guess We'll Fall In Love (Slow version)	1961	15.00	75.00
Yucca 140	You're In Love / Guess We'll Fall In Love (Fast version)	1961	8.00	40.00
Yucca 144	My Heart Jumped / Gently, My Love	1962	15.00	75.00
Eastwood 345	Not Fade Away / Nervous Breakdown	1962	20.00	100.00
Todd 1090	Saturday Night / Stinger	1963	20.00	100.00
Exeter 122	King Of The Beach / Wine, Wine, Wine	1964	50.00	200.00
Exeter 124	I Fought The Law / She's My Girl	1964	75.00	300.00
Exeter 126	Fool Of Love / Shakedown	1964	25.00	125.00
Donna 1403	Those Memories Of You / Our Favorite Martian	1964	50.00	200.00
	(Donna 1403 credits Bobby Fuller & The Fanatics.)			
Mustang 3004	Take My Word / She's My Girl	1965	5.00	25.00
Mustang 3006	Let Her Dance / Another Sad And Lonely Night	1965	3.00	15.00
Liberty 55812	Let Her Dance / Another Sad And Lonely Night	1965	5.00	25.00
Mustang 3011	Never To Be Forgotten / You Kiss Me	1965	3.00	15.00
Mustang 3012	Let Her Dance / Another Sad And Lonely Night	1965	2.00	10.00
Mustang 3014	I Fought The Law / Little Annie Lou	1966	2.00	10.00
Mustang 3016	Love's Made A Fool Of You / Don't Ever Let Me Know	1966	2.00	10.00
Mustang 3018	The Magic Touch / My True Love	1966	2.00	10.00
ABC 2614	I Fought The Law / Little Annie Lou	197?	.80	4.00
Eric 136	I Fought The Law / Love's Made A Fool Of You	197?	.60	3.00
	(These are early versions of both recordings.)			
Lost Nite 257	I Fought The Law / Little Anne Loa	197?	.60	3.00
FULLER, JERRY				
Lin 5011	Blue Memories / I Found A New Love	1958	3.00	15.00
Lin 5012	Teenage Love / Do You Love Me?	1958	3.00	15.00
Lin 5015	Angel From Above / A Certain Smile	1959	3.00	15.00
Lin 5017	Fanny Brown / Chaser Of Hearts	1959	3.00	15.00

Label & Catalog #		A-Side/B-Side	Year	VG	NM
Lin 5019		Lipstick And Rouge / Mother Goose At The Bandstand	1959	4.00	20.00
Challenge 59052		Betty, My Angel / Memories Of You	1959	2.00	10.00
Challenge 59057		Tennessee Waltz / Charlene	1959	2.00	10.00
Challenge 59068		I Dreamed About My Lover / Two Loves Have I	1960	2.00	10.00
Challenge 59074		Above And Beyond / One Heart	1960	2.00	10.00
Challenge 59085		Gone For The Summer / Anna From Louisiana	1960	2.00	10.00
Challenge 59104		Shy Away / Heavenly	1961	2.00	10.00

FULLER, RANDY
Randy Fuller, Bobby's brother, also recorded with The Shindigs.

Label & Catalog #		A-Side/B-Side	Year	VG	NM
Mustang 3020		It's Love / Come What May	1966	5.00	25.00
Mustang 3023		The Things You Do /	1966	5.00	25.00
Show Town 466		It's Love, Come What May / Revelation	1967	3.00	15.00
Show Town 466	(PS)	It's Love, Come What May / Revelation	1967	6.00	30.00
Show Town 482	(DJ)	1,000 Miles In Space / 1,000 Miles In Space	1967	3.00	15.00
		(Stock copies of Show Town 482 may not exist.)			

FUN & GAMES

Label & Catalog #	A-Side/B-Side	Year	VG	NM
Mainstream 671	Today-Tomorrow / Someone Must Have Lied	1967	3.00	15.00
Uni 55086	Elephant Candy / The Way She Smiles	1968	1.00	5.00
Uni 55098	The Grooviest Girl In The World /			
	It Must Of Been The Wind	1968	1.00	5.00
Uni 55128	We / Gotta Say Goodbye	1969	1.20	6.00

FUN SONS, THE
The Fun Sons is a pseudonym for ? & The Mysterians.

Label & Catalog #	A-Side/B-Side	Year	VG	NM
Cameo 478	Hang Ten / Don't Hold It Against Me	1967	6.00	30.00

FUNNY BUNNIES, THE

Label & Catalog #	A-Side/B-Side	Year	VG	NM
Dore 542	Midnight Sun / Sick Song	1960	2.00	10.00

FURY, BILLY

Label & Catalog #	A-Side/B-Side	Year	VG	NM
London 1857	Maybe Tomorrow / Gonna Type A Letter	1959	3.00	15.00
London 1925	Baby, How I Cried / Colette	1960	3.00	15.00
London 9594	Like I've Never Been Gone / Because Of Love	1964	1.20	6.00
London 9682	It's Only Make Believe / Baby, What Do You Want Me To Do?	1964	1.20	6.00
London 9740	Go Ahead And Ask Her / I'm Lost Without You	1965	1.20	6.00

FURY FOUR, THE

Label & Catalog #	A-Side/B-Side	Year	VG	NM
Santana	City Girl / (B-side by The New Yorkers)	1967	2.40	12.00

FURYS, THE

Label & Catalog #	A-Side/B-Side	Year	VG	NM
Manor	Lost Caravan / Running Wild	196?	7.00	35.00

FURYS, THE

Label & Catalog #	A-Side/B-Side	Year	VG	NM
Lavender 1805	Parchman Farm / Beachin'	1963	2.00	10.00
Lavender 1926	Maryann / Sand Flea	1963	2.00	10.00

FURYS, THE

Label & Catalog #	A-Side/B-Side	Year	VG	NM
Studio-City 1026	Little Queenie / Baby, What's Wrong?	1966	4.00	20.00

FUT
Fut features Maurice Gibb of The Bee Gees.

Label & Catalog #	A-Side/B-Side	Year	VG	NM
Beacon 160	Have You Heard The Word? / Futting	1970	2.00	10.00
Fut 160	Have You Heard The Word? / Futting	1976	1.00	5.00

FUTURAS, THE

Label & Catalog #	A-Side/B-Side	Year	VG	NM
Arjay 115	Mile Zero / Storm Surf	1964	10.00	50.00

G-CLEFS, THE

Pilgrim 715	Darla, My Darlin' / Ka-Ding Dong	1956	5.00	25.00
Pilgrim 720	Please Write While I'm Away / 'Cause You're Mine	1956	5.00	25.00
Paris 502	Symbol Of Love /			
	Love Her In The Morning And Love Her In The Night	1957	4.00	20.00
Paris 506	Is This The Way? / Zing Zang Zoo	1957	4.00	20.00
Terrace 7500	I Understand (Just How You Feel) / Little Girl, I Love You	1961	3.00	15.00
Terrace 7503	A Girl Has To Know / Lad	1962	2.00	10.00
Terrace 7507	Make Up Your Mind / They'll Call Me Away	1962	3.00	15.00
Terrace 7510	Sitting In The Moonlight /			
	Lover's Prayer (All Through The Night)	1962	3.00	15.00
Terrace 7514	All My Trials / Big Train	1963	3.00	15.00
Regina 1314	I Believe In All I Feel / To The Winner Goes The Prize	1964	2.00	10.00
Regina 1319	Angel, Listen To Me / Nobody But Betty	1964	3.00	15.00
Veep 1218	I Have / On The Other Side Of Town	1965	2.00	10.00
Veep 1226	This Time / On The Other Side Of Town	1965	2.00	10.00
Loma 2034	Little Lonely Boy / Party '66	1966	2.00	10.00
Loma 2048	I Can't Stand It / The Whirlwind	1966	2.00	10.00
Ditto 503	I'll Remember All Your Kisses / Ka-Ding Dong	196?	2.00	10.00

G-MEN, THE

Groove 009	Johnny And The Mermaid / Raunchy Twist	1961	2.00	10.00

G-NOTES, THE

Tender 510	I Would / Ronnie	1958	5.00	25.00
Jackpot 48000	I Would / Ronnie	1959	3.00	15.00
Guyden 2012	Johnny, Johnny, Johnny / Broken Down Merry-Go-Round	1959	3.00	15.00
Form 102	If They Only Knew / Say You're Mine	1959	3.00	15.00

G.T.O.'S, THE

Claridge 312	She Rides With Me / Rudy Vadoo	1966	4.00	20.00
	(Previously issued on Claridge 304 credited to Joey & The Continentals.)			
Parkway 108	Girl From New York City / Missing Out On The Fun	1966	3.00	15.00

GABRIEL & THE TEENAGE CHOIR

Dunhill 4039	Tweedle Dum's Drive-In / Tweedle Dum's Drive-In	1966	.80	4.00
Dunhill 4058	Chocolate On Sunday / Christmas Is Love	1966	.80	4.00

GADABOUTS, THE

Wing 90008	Two Things I Love / Glass Heart	195?	3.00	15.00
Wing 90043	If You Only Had A Heart / Teenage Rock	195?	3.00	15.00
Mercury 70495	By The Waters Of Minnetonka / Giuseppe Madolino	1954	3.00	15.00
Mercury 70581	Go Boom Boom / Oochi Pachi	1955	3.00	15.00
Mercury 70823	All My Love Belongs To You / Busy Body Rock	1956	3.00	15.00
Mercury 70898	Stranded In The Jungle / Blues Train	1956	3.00	15.00

GADSON, MEL

Big Top 3034	Comin' Down With Love / I'm Getting Sentimental Over You	1960	2.00	10.00

GAINES, RONNIE

Vanco 1005	Willow Road / Gone With The Wind	196?	2.00	10.00

GALAXIES, THE

Guaranteed 216	My Tattle Tale / Love Has Its Way	1960	10.00	50.00
	(Features Eddie Cochran on guitar.)			

GALAXIES, THE

Richie 458	Dear Someone / The Leopard	195?	15.00	75.00

GALAXIES, THE

Capitol 4427	The Big Triangle / Until The Next Time	1960	3.00	15.00
Dot 16212	Tremble / My Blue Heaven	1961	3.00	15.00

GALAXIES, THE

Seafair 110	Shaken / Tacoma	1961	3.00	15.00
Etiquette 4	Stompin' Willie / Doin' The Seaside	1965	1.60	8.00
Etiquette 17	I'm A Worker / Make Love To Me, Baby	1965	2.00	10.00
Etiquette 20	On The Beach / She Said I Do	1965	2.00	10.00
Etiquette 25	I Am Yours / I Who Have Nothing	1966	2.00	10.00
Panorama 54	She Said I Do / Along Comes The Man	1967	1.60	8.00

Label & Catalog #		A-Side/B-Side	Year	VG	NM
GALENS, THE					
Challenge 9212		Baby, I Do Love You / Love Bells	1963	2.00	10.00
Challenge 59253		Chinese Lanterns / Stranger In Paradise	1964	1.20	6.00
Challenge 59402		Young Dreams / I Love You More Than You Know	1965	1.20	6.00
GALES, THE					
Winn 916		I Love You / Squeeze Me	195?	40.00	200.00
J-V-B 34		Don't Let The Sun Catch You Crying /			
		My Eyes Keep Me In Trouble	196?	3.00	15.00
J-V-B 35		Darling Patricia / All Is Well, All Is Well	196?	3.00	15.00
GALLAHADS, THE					
Starla 15		Keeper Of Dreams / Sad Girl	1960	4.00	20.00
Del-Fi 4137		Lonely Guy / Jojo The Big Wheel (Green label)	1960	6.00	30.00
Del-Fi 4137		Lonely Guy / Jojo The Big Wheel (Black label)	196?	3.00	15.00
Del-Fi 4148		I'm Without A Girlfriend / Be Fair (Green label)	1960	6.00	30.00
Del-Fi 4148		I'm Without A Girlfriend / Be Fair (Black label)	196?	3.00	15.00
Donna 1322		Lonely Guy / Jojo The Big Wheel	1960	6.00	30.00
Donna 1361		This Letter To You / The Answer To Love	1961	8.00	40.00
Rendezvous 153		Gone / Why Do Fools Fall In Love?	1961	6.00	30.00
GALLAHADS, THE (& THE COUNTS)					
Sea Crest 6005		Have Love, Will Travel / My Offering	1964	2.00	10.00
Nite Owl 20		Gone / So Long	196?	2.00	10.00
GALLANT, BILLY					
Dee Dee 501		Thinking, Hoping, Wishing / Scribbling On The Wall	195?	10.00	50.00
Goldisc 6		Thinking, Hoping, Wishing / Scribbling On The Wall	195?	4.00	20.00
GALLION, BOB					
MGM 12195		My Square Dancin' Mama /			
		Your Wild Life's Gonna Get To You	195?	5.00	25.00
GAMBLERS, THE					
The Gamblers feature Kim Fowley, Bruce Johnston and Sandy Nelson.					
World Pacific 815		Moon Dawg / LSD-25	1960	7.00	35.00
Last Chance 2		Teen Machine / Tonky	1961	4.00	20.00
Last Chance 108		Teen Machine / Tonky	1962	3.00	15.00
GANTS, THE					
Liberty 55829		Road Runner / My Baby Don't Care	1965	2.00	10.00
Liberty 55844		Dr. Feelgood / Crackin' Up	1966	1.60	8.00
Liberty 55853		Little Boy Sad / Smoke Rings (You Can't Blow)	1966	1.60	8.00
GARCIA, JERRY					
Jerry Garcia is a member of The Grateful Dead. Refer to Howard Wales.					
Warner Bros. PRO-514	(DJ)	Deal / The Wheel	1972	2.00	10.00
Warner Bros. PRO-514	(PS)	Deal / The Wheel	1972	3.00	15.00
Warner Bros. 7551		Deal / The Wheel	1972	1.60	8.00
Warner Bros. 7569		Sugaree / Deep Hour	1972	1.60	8.00
Round 4504		Let It Rock / Midnight Town	1974	1.00	5.00
GARCIA, JERRY / ROBERT HUNTER					
Round		Sample For Dead Heads (With postcard)	1974	4.00	20.00
GARDEN OF EDEN, THE					
Verve 10541		Flower Man / Samantha	1967	1.00	5.00
GARDENIAS, THE: Refer to THE FABULOUS GARDENIAS					
GARI, FRANK					
Ribbon 6903		Your Only Love / Lil' Girl	1959	3.00	15.00
Crusade 1020		I Ain't Got A Girl / Utopia	1960	3.00	15.00
Crusade 1021		Lullabye Of Love / Tonight Is Our Last Night	1961	1.60	8.00
Crusade 1021	(PS)	Lullabye Of Love / Tonight Is Our Last Night	1961	2.00	10.00
Crusade 1022		Princess / The Last Bus Left At Midnight	1961	1.60	8.00
Crusade 1022	(PS)	Princess / The Last Bus Left At Midnight	1961	2.00	10.00
Crusade 1024		You Better Keep Running /			
		There's Lots More Where This Came From	1962	1.60	8.00
Crusade 1024	(PS)	You Better Keep Running /			
		There's Lots More Where This Came From	1962	2.00	10.00
GARNER, (BIG) BILL					
Panorama 5		Ka Ha Huna / Moonbeams	1964	2.00	10.00
Cross Road 3003		I'll See You In My Dreams / Paden Town	196?	.60	3.00
Wasp 112		In A Shanty In Old Shantytown / Wide World Of Country	196?	.60	3.00

Label & Catalog #	A-Side/B-Side	Year	VG	NM
GARNER, JOHNNY				
Imperial 5536	Kiss Me Sweet / Little Starry Eyes	1958	4.00	20.00
Imperial 5548	Fool / Didi Didi	1958	8.00	40.00
GARNETT, GALE				
RCA Victor 47-8388	We'll Sing In The Sunshine / Prism Song	1964	1.00	5.00
RCA Victor 47-8472	Lovin' Place / I Used To Live Here	1964	.80	4.00
RCA Victor 47-8549	I'll Cry Alone / Where Do You Go To Go Away?	1965	.80	4.00
RCA Victor 47-8668	I'm Gonna Sit Right Down And Write Myself A Letter /			
	Why Am I Standing At The Window?	1965	.80	4.00
GARR, ARTIE				
Artie Garr is a pseudonym for Art Garfunkel. Refer to Simon & Garfunkel; Tom & Jerry.				
Warwick 515	Dream Alone / Beat Love	1959	8.00	40.00
Octavia 8002	Private World / Forgive Me	1960	6.00	30.00
GARRET, SCOTT				
OKeh 7104	The Day I Died / In My Heart	1960	3.00	15.00
GARRETT, JOHNNY, & THE RISING SONS				
Uni 55179	Get Around, Downtown Girl / Good People	1969	1.60	8.00
GARRETT, ROBIN				
Mutual 510	Ringo's Revenge / You Run Around	1964	2.00	10.00
GARRETT, SCOTT				
Laurie 3023	A House Of Love / So Far So Good	1959	3.00	15.00
GARRETT, SCOTT, & THE MYSTICS				
Laurie 3029	Love Story / Graduation Souvenirs	1959	8.00	40.00
GARTIN, JIMMY, & THE SWINGERS				
The Swingers also recorded as Peter DeBree & The Wanderers.				
Fortune 134	Hey! Mr. Presley / Honey, Won't You Love Me?	1958	3.00	15.00
GARY & CLYDE				
Gary Paxton and Clyde "Skip" Battin., who also recorded as Skip & Flip.				
Rev 3523	Why Not Confess? / Johnny Risk	1959	5.00	25.00
GARY & DAVE				
Features David Gates.				
London 200	Could You Ever Love Me Again? /			
	Where Do We Go From Here?	196?	3.00	15.00
GARY & THE HORNETS				
Smash 2061	Hi Hi, Hazel / Patti Girl	1966	.60	3.00
Smash 2061 (PS)	Hi Hi, Hazel / Patti Girl	1966	1.00	5.00
Smash 2078	That's All For Now / A Kind Of Hush	1967	.60	3.00
Smash 2078 (PS)	That's All For Now / A Kind Of Hush	1967	1.00	5.00
Smash 2090	Baby, It's You / Tall Tale	1967	.60	3.00
Smash 2145	Turn The World On / Holdin' Back	1968	.60	3.00
GARY & THE KNIGHT LITES				
Prima 1016	I Can't Love You Anymore / Will You Go Steady?	196?	20.00	100.00
Bell 643	A Lonely Soldier's Pledge / So Far Away From Home	1966	3.00	15.00
GARY & THE NITE LITES				
Gary & The Nite Lites later recorded as The American Breed.				
Seeburg Jukebox 3016	Sweet Little Sixteen / Take Me Back	1965	5.00	25.00
Seeburg Jukebox 3017	Bony Moronie / Glad You're Mine	1965	5.00	25.00
U.S.A. 833	I Don't Need Your Help / Big Bad Wolf	1966	4.00	20.00
GARY & THE WOMBATS				
Regina 291	Summer's Over / Squidgy Bad	1963	3.00	15.00
Regina 297	So Tough / Winter Dream	1963	3.00	15.00
GAS COMPANY, THE				
Mirwood 501	Blow Your Mind / Your Time's Up	1965	2.00	10.00
Reprise 0464	You're All Alone / You'll Need Love	1966	1.60	8.00
Reprise 0512	Get Out Of My Life / We Need A Lot More Of Jesus	1966	1.60	8.00
Reprise 0598	First Night Flight / If You Know What I Mean	1967	1.60	8.00
GAS COMPANY, THE				
Beutone 800	I Couldn't Make Up My Mind / I See	1968	1.20	6.00

Label & Catalog #	A-Side/B-Side	Year	VG	NM
GATES, DAVID (& THE ACCENTS)				
Refer to Del Ashley; Bread; The Country Boys; Dave & Lee; Gary & Dave; and The Manchesters.				
East West 123	Swingin' Baby Doll / Walkin' And Talkin'	1959	30.00	150.00
Mala 413	You'll Be My Baby / What's This I Hear?	1960	6.00	30.00
Mala 418	The Happiest Man Alive / The Road Leads To Love	1960	6.00	30.00
Mala 427	The Teardrops In My Heart / Jo, Baby	1961	6.00	30.00
Robbins 1008	Lovin' At Night / Jo, Baby	1961	20.00	100.00
	(Robbins 1008 credits David Gates & The Accents.)			
Perspective	Lovin' At Night / Jo, Baby	1961	8.00	40.00
Del-Fi 4206	No One Really Loves A Clown / You Have It Comin' To You	1964	5.00	25.00
Jads 301	My Baby's Gone Away / Kiss And Tell	1964	5.00	25.00
Planetary 108	Once Upon A Time / Let You Go	1965	4.00	20.00
GSP 1	Sad September / Tryin' To Be Someone	196?	4.00	20.00
Elektra 45857	Clouds / I Use The Soap	1973	.60	3.00
Elektra 45868	Sail Around The World / Help Is On The Way	1973	.60	3.00
Elektra 45223	Never Let Her Go / Watch Out	1975	.60	3.00
Elektra 45245	Part Time Love / Chain Me	1976	.60	3.00
Elektra 45450	Sunday Rider / Goodbye Girl	1977	.60	3.00
Elektra 45500	Took The Last Train / Ann	1978	.60	3.00
Elektra 46588	Where Does The Lovin' Go? / Starship Ride	1980	.60	3.00
Elektra 46646	Can I Can You? / Chingo	198?	.60	3.00
Elektra 47011	Falling In Love Again / Sweet Desire	198?	.60	3.00
GATORMEN, THE				
The Gatormen also recorded with The Dorsals.				
Camelot 119	On Honey / Hey Girl	196?	2.00	10.00
Camelot 124	You See / A Love Not True	196?	2.00	10.00
GAVIN, JIMMY				
Cameo 113	I Sit In My Window / Lonely Chair	1957	3.00	15.00
GAY, BEN, & THE SILLY SAVAGES				
Elm 103	The Ballad Of Ben Gay / Silly Savage Serenade	1974	1.00	5.00
GAYLADS, THE				
Audan 120	Popeye The Sailor Man / Ah So	1961	5.00	25.00
GAYLE, MELVIN				
Castle 1602	Some Of Your Love /	1962	10.00	50.00
Castle 1604	The Kruschev Twist / You're In Love	1962	2.00	10.00
GAYS, THE				
Decca 30988	Alone At The Harbor / Command My Heart	1960	3.00	15.00
GEDDINS & SONS				
Jumpin 50001	Space Moon / Irma Special	196?	3.00	15.00
GEE, BOBBY, & THE CELESTIALS				
Stacy 922	Julie Is Mine / Blue Jean	1959	5.00	25.00
XYZ 611	Sealed With A Kiss / Little Miss Fantasy	1960	4.00	20.00
GEE, FRANKIE (WITH THE FIVE DISCS)				
Claridge 410	Date With The Rain / Ya Ya	1977	4.00	20.00
GEE, SONNY, & THE STANDELS				
Arlen 506	Tidal Wave / Ingrid	1963	2.00	10.00
GEE CEES, THE				
The Gee Cees feature Glen Campbell and Eddie Cochran.				
Crest 1088	Annie Had A Party / Buzzsaw Twist	1961	6.00	30.00
GEE SISTERS, THE				
Palette 5101	(Help Me) Telstar / Andy	1963	2.00	10.00
GEM, FRANKIE				
U.S.A. 713	Crystal Rock / Return To Me	1961	5.00	25.00
GEMS, THE				
Lavender 1941	Shout / Cry About You Baby	196?	1.60	8.00
Uptown 1001	Slave Girl / Hernando's Hideaway	196?	3.00	15.00
Virgelle 711	Punchappy / Bread 'N Butter Twist	196?	2.00	10.00
GENE & DEBBIE				
Gene Thomas.				
TRX 5002	Go With Me / The Torch I Carry	1967	1.20	6.00
TRX 5006	Playboy / I'll Come Running	1968	1.20	6.00
TRX 5010	Lovin' Season / Love Will Give Us Wings	1968	1.20	6.00
TRX 5014	Rings Of Gold / Making Noise Like Love	1968	1.20	6.00

Label & Catalog #		A-Side/B-Side	Year	VG	NM
GENE & THE ESQUIRES					
GNP/Crescendo 345		Rave On / Space Race	1965	2.00	10.00
GENE & TOMMY					
ABC 10981		Can't Get To Stoppin' / Richard And Me	1967	1.20	6.00
GENE THE HAT					
Deauville 1007		(Pass) The Bug / (Pass The) Bug, Part 2	1962	2.00	10.00
GENELS, THE					
Dewey 101		Rainy Night / Linda, Please Wait	195?	8.00	40.00
GENESIS					
Ripcord 004		Window Of Sand / Would You Like To?	1967	2.00	10.00
GENESIS					
Mercury 72806		Angeline / Suzanne	1968	2.00	10.00
GENESIS					
Original members were Tony Banks, Peter Gabriel, Anthony Phillips, Mike Rutherford and Chris Stewart. Later members include Steve Hackett, Phil Collins and Bill Bruford.					
Charisma 26002		I Know What I Like /	1973	4.00	20.00
Charisma 103		Watcher Of The Skies / Willow Farm	1973	4.00	20.00
Atco 7050		Entangled / Ripples	1977	2.00	10.00
Atco 7076		Your Own Special Way / In That Quiet Earth	1977	2.00	10.00
		— Extended Play Albums —			
Charisma	(DJ)	Nursery Cryme	197?	40.00	200.00
GENEVIEVE					
Cadence 1354		I'm Never Gonna Kiss You / Cherie, Cherie	1958	4.00	20.00
		(Features Johnny Tillotson.)			
GENOVA, TOMMY, & THE PRECISIONS					
Bella 606		What Has Happened To You? / The Lover	1961	4.00	20.00
GENTEELS, THE					
Stag 4949		The Force Of Gravity / Springboard	1962	6.00	30.00
Stag 2930/31		Take It Off / Hitch Hiker	1962	6.00	30.00
Capitol 4798		Take It Off / Hitch Hiker	1962	5.00	25.00
GENTLE GIANT					
Gentle Giant features Derek, Phil and Ray Shulman, formerly of Simon Dupree & The Big Sound.					
Columbia AE7-1057	(DJ)	Prologue-Working All Day / Three Friends	1972	1.60	8.00
Capitol 4484		I'm Turning Around / Cogs In Cogs	1977	1.00	5.00
Capitol SPRO-8951	(DJ)	Words From The Wise / Spooky Boogie *(Orange vinyl)*	1978	2.00	10.00
Capitol 4652		Words From The Wise / Spooky Boogie	1978	1.00	5.00
GENTLEMAN JIM & THE HORSEMEN					
Jerden 732		Soul Searchin' / Sharon	1964	1.20	6.00
GENTLEMEN WILD, THE					
NWI 2694		You Gotta Leave / I Believe	1967	1.50	8.00
GENTRY, RAY, & THE ROVIN' GAMBLERS					
Maverick 614		Willie Was A Bad Boy / Do The Fly	195?	100.00	400.00
GENTRYS, THE					
Kado 0074		Moments / Wild	195?	20.00	100.00
GENTRYS, THE					
Youngstown 600		Sometimes / Little Drops Of Water	1965	4.00	20.00
Youngstown 601		Keep On Dancing / Make Up Your Mind	1965	5.00	25.00
MGM 13379		Keep On Dancing / Make Up Your Mind	1965	1.25	6.00
MGM 13432		Spread It On Thick / Brown Paper Sack	1965	1.25	6.00
MGM 13432	(PS)	Spread It On Thick / Brown Paper Sack	1965	2.00	10.00
MGM 13495		Everyday I Have To Cry / Don't Let It Be (This Time)	1966	1.00	5.00
MGM 13561		A Woman Of The World /			
		There Are Two Sides To Every Story	1966	1.00	5.00
MGM 13690		There's A Love / You Make Me Feel So Good	1967	4.00	20.00
MGM 13749		I Can See / 90 Lb. Weakling	1967	1.00	5.00
Bell 753		Tell Me You Care / Midnight Train	1968	.80	4.00
Bell 740		Thinking Like A Child / Silky	1968	.80	4.00
Bell 720		You Better Come Home / I Can't Go Back To Denver	1968	.80	4.00
Sun 1108		Why Should I Cry? / I Need Love	1970	.80	4.00
Sun 1114		Cinnamon Girl / I Just Got The News	1970	.80	4.00
Sun 1118		He'll Never Love You / I Hate To See You Go	1971	.80	4.00
Sun 1120		Goddess Of Love / Friends	1971	.80	4.00
Sun 1122		Wild World / Sunshine	1971	.80	4.00

Label & Catalog #		A-Side/B-Side	Year	VG	NM
Sun 1126		God Save Our Country / Love You All My Life	1971	.80	4.00
Capitol 3459		Changin' / Let Me Put This Ring On Your Finger	1972	.60	3.00
Stax 0223		Little Hung Up On You / Little Gold Band	1974	.60	3.00
Stax 0242		High Flyer / Little Gold Band	1974	.60	3.00
GENTS, THE					
Nite Owl 10		Moonlight Surf / Lazy Day	1960	7.00	35.00
E.V.E. 5153		Surfin' All Day /	196?	7.00	35.00
GENTS, THE					
Times Square 98		Island Of Love / (B-side by The Teen Five)	1964	3.00	15.00
Times Square		I'll Never Let You Go / (B-side by The Teen Five)	1964	2.00	10.00
GEORGE & EARL					
Mercury 70852		Done Gone / Better Stop, Look And Listen	1956	10.00	50.00
GEORGE & LOUIS					
Sun 301		The Return Of Jerry Lee / The Return Of Jerry Lee, Part 2	1958	3.00	15.00
Sun 301		The Return Of Jerry Lee / (B-side by Jerry Lee Lewis)	1958	3.00	15.00
		("The Return Of Jrerry Lee" is a break-in using snippets of Lewis' hits.)			
GEORGE, LOWELL					
Lowell George was a member of Little Feat.					
Warner Bros. 8847		What Do You Want The Girl To Do? / 20 Million Things	1979	.80	4.00
GEORGE, JOHNNY					
Coed 555		A Fiddle And A Bow / Flying Blues Angels	1961	2.00	10.00
GEORGIE PORGIE & THE CRY BABIES					
Jubilee 5578		He's Just Like That / Holdin' On	196?	2.00	10.00
GERARDI, BOB, & THE CLASSICS FOUR					
Recorte 441		Nobody Wants You Anymore / You're Everything To Me	1960	4.00	20.00
GERBER, VINCE					
Jerden 726		Torquila / Cyclone	1964	1.25	6.00
GERMAINE, DENISE (WITH THE DELMONICOS)					
Aku 6139		I'm Fed Up / Teenage Idol	196?	8.00	40.00
GERMS, THE					
What? 01		Forming / Live	1977	3.00	15.00
What? 01	(PS)	Forming / Live	1977	6.00	30.00
		(First pressing records have a label on one side only and the sleeve reads "This record causes ear cancer.")			
What? 01		Forming / Live	1978	1.00	5.00
What? 01	(PS)	Forming / Live	1978	1.00	5.00
		(Second pressing records have labels on both sides.)			
Slash 101		Lexicon Devil / Circle One	1978	12.00	60.00
Slash 101	(PS)	Lexicon Devil / Circle One	1978	12.00	60.00
GERMZ, THE					
The Germz feature Carole King.					
Vertigo 8001		Boy Girl Love / No Easy Way Down	196?	5.00	25.00
GERRI & SHERRI					
RCA Victor 47-8096		Jelly Bean / Gotta Make It Grow	1962	2.00	10.00
GERRY & THE PACEMAKERS					
Gerry Marsden with Pacemakers John Chadwick, Les Maguire and Freddie Marsden.					
Laurie 3162		How Do You Do It? / Away From You	1963	2.00	10.00
Laurie 3196		I Like It / It Happened To Me	1963	2.00	10.00
Laurie 3218		You'll Never Walk Alone / It's Alright	1963	2.00	10.00
Laurie 3233		I'm The One / How Do You Do It?	1963	2.00	10.00
Laurie 3233		I'm The One / It's Alright	1964	1.60	8.00
Laurie 3251		Don't Let The Sun Catch You Crying / I'm The One	1964	2.00	10.00
Laurie 3251		Don't Let The Sun Catch You Crying / Away From You	1964	1.60	8.00
Laurie 3261		How Do You Do It? / You'll Never Walk Alone	1964	1.60	8.00
Laurie 3271		I Like It / Jambalaya	1964	1.60	8.00
Laurie 3279		I'll Be There / You, You, You	1964	1.60	8.00
Laurie 3284		Ferry Across The Mersey / Pretend	1965	1.60	8.00
Laurie 3293		It's Gonna Be Alright / Skinny Minnie	1965	1.20	6.00
Laurie 3302		You'll Never Walk Alone / Away From You	1965	1.20	6.00
Laurie 3313		Give All Your Love To Me / You're The Reason	1965	1.20	6.00
Laurie 3323		Walk Hand In Hand / Dreams	1965	1.20	6.00
Laurie 3337		La La La / Without You	1966	1.20	6.00
Laurie 3354		Girl On A Swing / The Way You Look Tonight	1966	1.20	6.00
Laurie 3370		Looking For My Life / Big, Bright Green Pleasure Machine	1966	1.60	8.00

Label & Catalog #	A-Side/B-Side	Year	VG	NM
GESTICS, THE				
Surfer 106	Let's Go Trippin' / Kahuna	1963	7.00	35.00
Surfer 114	Rockin' Fury / Invasion	1964	6.00	30.00
GESTURES, THE				
Soma 1417	Run Run Run / It Seems To Me	1964	2.00	10.00
Soma 1426	Don't Mess Around / Candlelight	1965	3.00	15.00
GHETTO-PACIFIC				
Challenger 121	Leopard Skin Pillbox Hat / You Can't Judge A Book By Its Cover	1967	2.00	10.00
GHOST RIDERS, THE				
Newland 1001	Ghost Rider's Theme / Mental Revenge	196?	8.00	40.00
GIANT JELLYBEAN COPOUT, THE				
Poppy 504	Awake In A Dream / Look At The Girls	1968	5.00	25.00
GIANT SUNFLOWER, THE				
Take 6 1000	February Sunshine / More Sunshine	1967	2.00	10.00
Ode '70 102	February Sunshine / More Sunshine	1967	1.20	6.00
Ode '70 104	What's So Good About Goodbye? / Mark Twain	1967	1.20	6.00
GIBB, MAURICE				
Maurice Gibb is a member of The Bee Gees.				
Atco 6757	Railroad / I've Come Back	1970	1.00	5.00
GIBB, ROBIN				
Robin Gibb is a member of The Bee Gees.				
Atco 6698	Saved By The Bell / Mother And Jack	1969	.80	4.00
Atco 6727	One Million Years / Weekend	1969	.80	4.00
Atco 6737	August October / Give Me A Smile	1969	.80	4.00
Polydor 810-895	Juliet / Hearts On Fire	1983	.60	3.00
GIBSON, BOBBY, & THE VOYAGERS				
Gibson 6003	B-52 /	196?	7.00	35.00
GIBSON, JILL				
Jill Gibson was produced by Jan Berry.				
Imperial 66068 (DJ)	It's As Easy As 1-2-3 / It's As Easy As 1-2-3	1964	4.00	20.00
Imperial 66068	It's As Easy As 1-2-3 / Jilly's Flip Side	1964	8.00	40.00
GIBSON, JOHNNY				
Big Top 3088	Midnight / Chuck-A-Luck	1962	2.00	10.00
GIFFORD, BOB, & THE JOINT RETURN				
Julian 112	Nancy, Darling / Blame It On A Woman	196?	2.00	10.00
GIFTS, THE				
Ballad 6001	Lovin' You / Rock My Soul	1966	2.00	10.00
Ballad 6002	Goodbye, My Love / Soul Dust	1966	2.00	10.00
Ballad 6003	You Can't Keep Love In A Broken Heart /	1966	2.00	10.00
GIGI				
Seg Way 1010	This Time Next Summer / Little Bit Of Lovin'	1961	2.00	10.00
GIGOLOS, THE				
Broadway 1000	Black And Blue /	196?	3.00	15.00
Enterprise 5000	Don't You Just Know It / Movin' Out	196?	3.00	15.00
GIGOLOS, THE				
The Gigolos feature Duane Eddy on guitar.				
Daynite 1	Swingin' Saints / Night Crawlers	196?	5.00	25.00
GILL, RONNIE, & THE PASTEL KEYS				
Expedite 2853	Geraldine / Standing On The Mountain	1958	35.00	175.00
Rip 108	Geraldine / Standing On The Mountain	1958	10.00	50.00
Rip 129	Geraldine / Standing On The Mountain	1958	10.00	50.00
GILLESPIE, DANA				
RCA Victor 2446	Andy Warhol / Dizzy Heights	1974	.80	4.00
	("Andy Warhol" was produced by David Bowie and Mick Ronson.)			
GILLEY, MICKEY				
Minor 106	Oo-ee, Baby / Tell Me Why	195?	40.00	200.00
Dot 15706	Call Me Shorty / Come On, Baby	1957	10.00	50.00
Rex 1007	Grapevine / That's How It's Got To Be	1959	3.00	15.00
Lynn 503	Everything Turned To Love / Your Selfish Pride	1960	3.00	15.00

Label & Catalog #	A-Side/B-Side	Year	VG	NM
Lynn 508	Lonely Lonely Nights / My Baby's Cheatin' Again	1960	3.00	15.00
Lynn 508	Turn Around / My Baby's Cheatin' Again	1960	2.00	10.00
Lynn 512	Slippin' And Slidin' / (It's The) End Of The Line	1961	3.00	15.00
Khoury's 712	Drive In Movie / Give Me A Chance	1961	6.00	30.00
Astro 102	Lonely Wine / Down The Line	196?	25.00	125.00
Astro 103	Is It Wrong? / Turn Around	196?	3.00	15.00
Astro 104	Susie Q / Night After Night	196?	3.00	15.00
Astro 106	Lotta Lovin' / I Miss You So	196?	3.00	15.00
Astro 110	A Certain Smile / If I Didn't have A Dime	196?	3.00	15.00
Astro 112	Little Egypt / If I Didn't Have A Dime	196?	3.00	15.00
Goldband 1223	I Ain't Going Home / No Greater Love	196?	2.00	10.00
Act-1 101	Say No More / Make Me Believe	196?	2.00	10.00
Potomac 901	Is It Wrong / No Greater Love	196?	3.00	15.00
Sabra 518	Valley Of Tears / I Need Your Love	196?	3.00	15.00
Princess 4004	Drive In Movie / Your First Time	196?	3.00	15.00
Princess 4006	Wild Side Of Life / Caught In The Middle	196?	3.00	15.00
Princess 4011	I'll Keep On Dreaming / I'll Keep Searching	196?	3.00	15.00
Princess 4015	World Of My own / I Still Care	196?	3.00	15.00
Supreme 101	Now That I Have You / Happy Birthday	196?	1.60	8.00
Supreme 1022	Everything Turned To Love / No One Will Ever Know	196?	1.60	8.00
San 1513	I Ain't No Bo Diddley / I'm To Blame	196?	2.00	10.00
Daryl 101	What Have I Done? / Three's A Crowd	196?	1.60	8.00

GILMER, JIMMY
Jimmy Gilmer also recorded with The Fireballs.

Decca 30942	Look Alive / Because I Need You	1959	3.00	15.00

GILREATH, JAMES

Joy 274	Little Band Of Gold / I'll Walk With You	1963	2.00	10.00

GINGER
Ginger Blake, who also recorded as or with Danielle; Ginger & The Snaps; The Honeys; Sugar; and Gary Usher.

Titan	Dry Tears / Spare Time	1960	15.00	75.00

GINGER & THE CHIFFONS

Groove 0003	Where Were You Last Night? / She	1961	6.00	30.00

GINGER & THE SNAPS
Ginger Blake, Diane Rovell and Marilyn Wilson, a.k.a. The Honeys.

Tore 1008	Love Me The Way That I Love You / Truly	1961	10.00	50.00
MGM 13413 (DJ)	Seven Days In September / Growing Up Is Hard To Do	1965	15.00	75.00
MGM 13413	Seven Days In September / Growing Up Is Hard To Do	1965	30.00	150.00

GINGER-SNAPS, THE

Dunhill 4003	The Sh-Down-Down Song / I've Got Faith In Him	1965	3.00	15.00

GINGERSNAPS, THE

Kapp 226	Gingerbread / Lenny, Lenny	1958	4.00	20.00

GINO

Parnaso 102	She Looks So Tough / Grouch	196?	4.00	20.00

GINO & GINA

Mercury 71283	(It's Been A Long, Long Time) Pretty Baby / Love's A Carousel	1958	2.50	12.00
Mercury 71346	She Belongs To Me / Rainin,' Rainin'	1958	2.00	10.00

GINSBERG, ALAN

Evatone Soundsheet	September On Jessore Road *(Flexidisc with Bob Dylan)*	1972	8.00	40.00

GIORDANO, LOU
Produced by Buddy Holly and Phil Everly, both of whom played on the A-side and sang on the B-side.

Brunswick 9-55115 (DJ)	Stay Close To Me / Don't Cha Know	1959	100.00	400.00
Brunswick 9-55115	Stay Close To Me / Don't Cha Know *(Maroon label)*	1959	200.00	600.00

GIRARD, CHUCK
Chuck, best known as the lead singer for The Hondells, also provided vocals for The Castells; Chuck & Joe; The Devons; The Go Go's; Six The Hard Way; The Timers; and The Toads.

GIRLS FROM SYRACUSE, THE

Palmer 5001	Love Is Happening To Me Now / You Could Have Had Me All Along	1965	3.00	15.00

GLASS MENAGERIE, THE

Revolvo 208	End Of The Line / Troubled Mind	196?	3.00	15.00

Label & Catalog #		A-Side/B-Side	Year	VG	NM
GLEAMS, THE					
Kip 236		I Don't Know Why You Sent For Me / You Broke My Heart	196?	4.00	20.00
Kapp 565		Mr. Magic Moon / Pile Driver	1963	3.00	15.00
GLEAVES, CLIFF					
Liberty 55263		Long Black Hearse / You And Your Kind	1961	2.00	10.00
GLEEMS, THE					
Parkway 893		Sandra, Baby / You Are The One	1963	3.00	15.00
GLEN & DELLA					
Virgelle 734		Blue Love / I'm Talking At You	196?	2.00	10.00
GLEN & DELMAY					
Wasp 121		Hear Cindy Sing / Sin City	196?	2.00	10.00
GLENS, THE					
Ro-Nan 1002		Image Of Love / I Feel So Blue	195?	10.00	50.00
GLENWOODS, THE					
Jubilee 5402		Elaine / That's The Way It'll Be	1960	6.00	30.00
GLOBETROTTERS, THE					
Kirshner 5006		Cheer Me Up / Gravy	1970	1.60	8.00
Kirshner 5006	(PS)	Cheer Me Up / Gravy	1970	2.00	10.00
Kirshner 5008		Rainy Day Bells / Meadowlark	1970	1.60	8.00
Kirshner 5012		Duke Of Earl / Everybody's Got Hot Pants	1971	1.60	8.00
Kirshner 5016		Everybody Needs Love / ESP	1971	1.60	8.00
GLYN, RICHARD					
Dot 15927		High School Fool / It Seems To Me	1959	2.00	10.00
GO-BOYS, THE					
DC 0418		Flippin' / Ramble	1959	3.00	15.00
GO-CARTS, THE					
Hope 1003		Blue Moon Of Kentucky / Rockin' Liza	1961	3.00	15.00
GO GO'S, THE					
RCA Victor 47-8370		Chicken Of The Sea / Lonely Girl	1964	2.00	10.00
RCA Victor 47-8435	(DJ)	Saturday's Hero / Wild One	1964	3.00	15.00
RCA Victor 47-8435		Saturday's Hero / Wild One	1964	6.00	30.00
		(RCA 8435 was produced by Gary Usher and features Chuck Girard.)			
GO-TOGETHERS, THE					
Coast 100		Time After Time / Train	196?	4.00	20.00
GO ZOO BAND, THE					
Go Go 101		Oh, Baby Mine (I Get So Lonely) / Sid's Lid	1966	2.00	10.00
GODCHAUX, KEITH & DONNA: *Refer to* KEITH & DONNA					
GODFREY DANIEL					
Nostalgia 102		Hey, Jude / Shop Around	196?	.80	4.00
GOINS, HERBIE, & THE NIGHTRIDERS					
Capitol 5978		The Incredible Miss Brown / Comin' Home To You	1967	1.20	6.00
GOLD					
Paramount 0013		Lovin' You Is A Groove / I Was Gonna Leave Today	1969	2.00	10.00
GOLD					
Golden State 501		Summertime / No Parking	1969	3.00	15.00
GOLD BUGS, THE					
Coral 62453		Stop That Wedding / It's So Nice	1965	8.00	40.00
GOLDBERG REUNION, BARRY					
Buddah 59		Hole In My Pocket / Sittin' In Circles	1968	.80	4.00
GOLDBERG-MILLER BLUES BAND, THE					
Barry Goldberg and Steve Miller.					
Epic 9865	(DJ)	More Soul Than Soulful / More Soul Than Soulful (Blue vinyl)	1965	5.00	25.00
Epic 9865	(PS)	More Soul Than Soulful (Promo picture sleeve)	1965	5.00	25.00
Epic 9865		More Soul Than Soulful / The Mother Song	1965	2.00	10.00
Epic 10033		Whole Lotta Shakin' Goin' On / Ginger Man	1965	2.00	10.00

Label & Catalog #		A-Side/B-Side	Year	VG	NM
GOLDEN EARRING(S), THE					
Atlantic 2710		Eight Miles High / One Huge Road	1970	1.20	6.00
Track 40202		Radar Love / Just Like Vince Taylor	1974	1.00	5.00
Track 40309		Candy's Going Bad / She Flies On Strange Wings	1974	.80	4.00
Track 40369		Lucky Numbers / Ce Soir	1975	.80	4.00
Track 40412		The Switch / The Lonesome D.J.	1975	.80	4.00
MCA 40513		Sleep Walkin' / Babylon	1975	.60	3.00
MCA 40802		Radar Love / Radar Love	1978	.60	3.00
GOLDEN HORIZON, THE					
Fontana 1666		Dear Emily / Love Is The Only Answer	1969	1.00	5.00
GOLDEN NUGGETS, THE					
Hawk 105/6		Surf Everybody / Everybody Bird	1963	7.00	35.00
GOLDIE, DON (WITH THE SIR DOUGLAS QUINTET)					
Teardrop 3070		We'll Take Our Last Walk Tonight / Walking The Streets	1966	5.00	25.00
GOLDIE & THE ESCORTS: *Refer to* **THE ESCORTS**					
GOLDIE & THE GINGERBREADS					
Atco 6354		That's Why I Love You / What Kind Of Man Are You?	1965	2.00	10.00
Atco 6475		Walking In Different Circles / Song Of The Moon	1967	2.00	10.00
GOLDSBORO, BOBBY					
Laurie 3130		Lonely Traveler / You Better Go Home	1962	1.20	6.00
Laurie 3148		Molly / Honey Baby	1962	1.20	6.00
Laurie 3159		The Runaround / The Letter	1962	1.20	6.00
Laurie 3168		That's What Love Will Do /			
		Light The Candles (Throw The Rice)	1963	1.20	6.00
United Artists 672		See The Funny Little Clown / Hello, Loser	1963	1.00	5.00
United Artists 710		Whenever He Holds You / If She Was Mine	1964	.80	4.00
United Artists 710	(PS)	Whenever He Holds You / If She Was Mine	1964	2.00	10.00
United Artists 742		Me Japanese Boy, I Love You / Everyone But Me	1964	.80	4.00
United Artists 781		I Don't Know You Anymore / Little Drops Of Water	1964	.80	4.00
United Artists 810		Little Things / I Can't Go On Pretending	1964	.80	4.00
United Artists 862		Voodoo Woman / It Breaks My Heart	1965	.80	4.00
United Artists 908		If You've Got A Heart / If You Wait For Love	1965	.80	4.00
United Artists 925		Broomstick Cowboy / Ain't Got Time For Happy	1965	.80	4.00
United Artists 980		It's Too Late / I'm Going Home	1966	.80	4.00
United Artists 50018		I Know You Better Than That / When Your Love Has Gone	1966	.80	4.00
United Artists 50018	(PS)	I Know You Better Than That / When Your Love Has Gone	1966	1.20	6.00
United Artists 50044		Longer Than Forever / Take Your Love	1966	.80	4.00
United Artists 50056		It Hurts Me / Pity The Fool	1966	.80	4.00
United Artists 50087		Blue Autumn / I Just Don't Love You Anymore	1966	.80	4.00
United Artists 50318		The Autumn Of My Life / She Chased Me	1968	.60	3.00
United Artists 50318	(PS)	The Autumn Of My Life / She Chased Me	1968	1.20	6.00
United Artists 50470		Look Around You (It's Christmas Time) / Christmas Wish	1968	.80	4.00
GOLDTONES, THE					
A&R 714		Gutterball / Strike	1963	6.00	30.00
A&R 714	(PS)	Gutterball / Strike	1963	6.00	30.00
GOLLIWOGS, THE					
The Golliwogs originally recorded as Tom Fogerty & The Blue Velvets, later, as Creedence Clearwater Revival.					
Fantasy 590		Don't Tell Me No Lies / Little Girl, Does Your Mama Know?	1964	8.00	40.00
Fantasy 597		You Came Walking / Where You Been?	1965	8.00	40.00
Fantasy 599		You Got Nothin' On Me / You Can't Be True	1965	8.00	40.00
Scorpio 404		Brown Eyed Girl / You Better Be Careful	1965	8.00	40.00
Scorpio 405		Fight Fire / Fragile Girl	1966	8.00	40.00
Scorpio 408		Walking On The Water / You Better Get It	1966	8.00	40.00
Scorpio 412	(DJ)	Porterville / Call It Pretending	1967	10.00	50.00
		(Stock copies of Scorpio 412 may not exist.)			
GOMEZ, JOHNNY RAY, & THE U-NEEKS					
Applause 1000		Romp Out / Our Love Is Over	195?	7.00	35.00
Applause 1001		Kick Off / Looking For Love	195?	7.00	35.00
GONE ALL-STARS, THE					
Gone 5016		7-11 / Down Yonder	1958	2.50	12.00
GONGETTES, THE					
Original Sound 21		Gong Gong, I'm Blue / Trouble	1962	1.50	8.00
GONN					
Emir SS-9217		Blackout Of Gretely / Pain In My Heart	1966	40.00	200.00
Merry Jaine IT-2316		You're Looking Fine / Come With Me	1967	20.00	100.00

Label & Catalog #		A-Side/B-Side	Year	VG	NM
GONZALES, ZIGGY					
Pop Side 5		Let Me Walk You Home / Cherokee	1961	2.00	10.00
GONZOS, THE					
Donna 1330		Church Key / Very Muddy Waters	1961	7.00	35.00
		(Donna 1330 was also released credited to The Four Sharps.)			
GOOBERS, THE					
Surf 1001		Hawaiian Holiday / Buyer Beware	1963	8.00	40.00
GOOD GUYS, THE					
The Good Guys is a pseudonym for The Challengers.					
GNP/Crescendo 326		Asphalt Wipe Out / Scratch	1964	4.00	20.00
GOOD SHIP LOLLIPOP, THE					
Ember 701		Maxwell's Silver Hammer / How Does It Feel?	1969	1.00	5.00
GOODIES, THE					
Blue Cat 117		The Dum Dum Ditty / Sophisticated Boom Boom	1964	2.00	10.00
GOODMAN, DICKIE					
Refer to Hickey Badman; Buchanan & Goodman; The Casual Three; Joel Langran; The Pennsylvania Players.					
Mark X 8009		The Touchables / Martian Melody (Yellow label)	1961	3.00	15.00
Mark-X 8010		The Touchables In Brooklyn / Mystery	1961	3.00	15.00
Rori 601		Horror Movies / Whoa, Mule	1961	4.00	20.00
Rori 602		The Berlin Top Ten / Little Tiger	1961	4.00	20.00
Rori 701		Santa And The Touchables / North Pole Rock	1961	3.00	15.00
M.D. 101		Shmonanza / Backwards Theme	1961	3.00	15.00
J.D.M. 001		Ben Crazy / Flip Side	1962	4.00	20.00
Diamond 119		Ben Crazy / Flip Side	1962	2.00	10.00
20th Century Fox 443		Senate Hearing / Lock Up	1963	2.00	10.00
Audio Spectrum 75		Presidential Interview (Flying Saucer '64) / Paul Revere	1964	7.00	35.00
Red Bird 058		Batman And His Grandmother / Suspense	1966	2.00	10.00
Twirl 20915		James Bomb / Seventh Theme	1966	2.00	10.00
Davy Jones 663		White House Happening / President Johnson	1966	4.00	20.00
Davy Jones 663	(PS)	White House Happening / President Johnson	1966	6.00	30.00
Cotique 158		On Campus / (B-side by Johnny Colo)	1969	.80	4.00
Cotique 173		Luna Trip / (B-side by Joey Pastrana)	1969	1.20	6.00
Ramgo 501		Speaking Of Ecology / Dayton's Theme	1970	4.00	20.00
Rainy Wednesday 202		Watergate / Friends	1973	.80	4.00
Rainy Wednesday 204		Purple People Eater / Ruthie's Socks	1973	.80	4.00
Rainy Wednesday 205		The Constitution / The End	1974	.80	4.00
Rainy Wednesday 206		Energy Crisis '74 / The End	1974	.80	4.00
Rainy Wednesday 206		Energy Crisis '74 / Ruthie's Theme	1974	1.25	6.00
Rainy Wednesday 207		Mr. President / Popularity	1974	.80	4.00
Rainy Wednesday 208		Gerry Ford / Robert	1975	.80	4.00
Rainy Wednesday 209		Inflation In The Nation / Jon And Jed's Theme	1975	.80	4.00
Cash 451		Mr. Jaws / Irv's Theme	1975	.80	4.00
Janus 271		Star Warts / The Boys Tune	1975	1.00	5.00
Shock 6		Kong / Ed's Tune	1977	.80	4.00
Hotline 1017		Energy Crisis '79 / Pain	1979	.80	4.00
Prelude 8018		Election '80 /	1980	1.00	5.00
Wacko 1381		America '81 /	1981	1.20	6.00
Extran 601		Hey, E.T. / Get A Job	1982	.80	4.00
Montage 1200	(DJ)	Hey, E.T. / The Ride Of Paul Revere	1982	.80	4.00
Montage 1200		Hey, E.T. / The Ride Of Paul Revere	1982	2.00	10.00
Rhino 019		Radio Russia / Washington Inside Out	1983	.50	2.50
Shell 711		Election '84 / Herb's Theme	1984	.50	2.50
Z-100 100	(DJ)	Attack Of The Z Monster / Mystery	1984	1.00	5.00
Wacko 1001		Mr. President / Dancin' U.S.A.	198?	.60	3.00
Wacko 1002		Super Duper Man / Robert's Tune	198?	.60	3.00
Goodname 7100		Safe Sex Report / Safety First	1988	2.00	10.00
GOODTIME WASHBOARD THREE, THE					
Fantasy 582		Don't Blame PG&E, Pal / Oakland	1967	1.20	6.00
GOOFERS, THE					
Coral 61305		Hearts Of Stone / You're The One	1954	3.00	15.00
Coral 61383		Flip, Flop And Fly / My Babe	1955	3.00	15.00
Coral 61431		Goofy Dry Bone / Nare	1955	3.00	15.00
Coral 61480		Dee-Do, Dee-Do / What Does That Dream Mean?	1955	3.00	15.00
Coral 61545		Sick Sick Sick / Twenty One	1955	3.00	15.00
Coral 61593		Crave Me / Oh, How I Miss You Tonight	1956	3.00	15.00
Coral 61650		Teardrop Motel / Tennessee Rock And Roll	1956	3.00	15.00
Coral 61664		I'm Gonna Rock And Roll 'Til I Die / Our Miss Brooks	1956	3.00	15.00
GOON, PETER					
Poleese 100		Whistler / (B-side by Bab Boon)	196?	6.00	30.00

Label & Catalog #		A-Side/B-Side	Year	VG	NM
GORDEN					
Uptown 730		Greensleeves / Send For Me	1967	1.20	6.00
Piccadilly 234		Greensleeves / Send For Me	1967	1.00	5.00
GORDON, MIKE, & THE AGATES					
Dore 681		Rumble At Newport Beach / Last Call For Dinner	1963	6.00	30.00
GORDON, ROSCOE					
Flip 227		Just Love Me, Baby / Weeping Blues	1955	50.00	200.00
Flip 237		The Chicken (Dance With You) / Love For You, Baby	1956	6.00	30.00
Sun 227		Just Love Me, Baby / Weeping Blues	1955	50.00	200.00
Sun 237		The Chicken (Dance With You) / Love For You, Baby	1956	25.00	125.00
Sun 257		Shoobie Oobie / Cheese And Crackers	1956	3.00	15.00
Sun 305		Sally Jo / Torro	1958	3.00	15.00
GORDON & SUE (WITH THE ALGONQUINS)					
Carlton 595		Surfin' Sax / Surfin' Sal And Charmin' Willie	1963	4.00	20.00
GORE, LESLEY					
Refer to Billy & Sue; Lou Christie & Lesley Gore; the Various Artists section.					
Mercury 72119		It's My Party / Danny	1963	2.00	10.00
Mercury 72119	(PS)	It's My Party / Danny	1963	3.00	15.00
Mercury 72143		Judy's Turn To Cry / Just Let Me Cry	1963	2.00	10.00
Mercury 72143	(PS)	Judy's Turn To Cry / Just Let Me Cry	1963	3.00	15.00
Mercury 72180		She's A Fool / The Old Crowd	1963	2.00	10.00
Mercury 72180	(PS)	She's A Fool / The Old Crowd	1963	3.00	15.00
Mercury 72206		You Don't Own Me / Run, Bobby, Run	1963	2.00	10.00
Mercury 72206	(PS)	You Don't Own Me / Run, Bobby, Run	1963	3.00	15.00
Mercury 72245		Je Nais Sais Plus / Je N'ose Pas	1963	2.00	10.00
Mercury 72259		That's The Way Boys Are / That's The Way The Ball Bounces	1964	1.60	8.00
Mercury 72259	(PS)	That's The Way Boys Are / That's The Way The Ball Bounces	1964	3.00	15.00
Mercury 72270		I Don't Wanna Be A Loser / It's Gotta Be You	1964	1.60	8.00
Mercury 72270	(PS)	I Don't Wanna Be A Loser / It's Gotta Be You	1964	3.00	15.00
Mercury 72309		Maybe I Know / Wonder Boy	1964	1.60	8.00
Mercury 72309	(PS)	Maybe I Know / Wonder Boy	1964	3.00	15.00
Mercury 72352		Sometimes I Wish I Were A Boy / Hey Now	1964	1.60	8.00
Mercury 72352	(PS)	Sometimes I Wish I Were A Boy / Hey Now	1964	3.00	15.00
Mercury 72372		The Look Of Love / Little Girl, Go Home	1964	1.60	8.00
Mercury 72372	(PS)	The Look Of Love / Little Girl, Go Home	1964	3.00	15.00
Mercury 72412		All Of My Life / I Cannot Hope For Anyone	1965	1.60	8.00
Mercury 72412	(PS)	All Of My Life / I Cannot Hope For Anyone	1965	3.00	15.00
Mercury 72433		Sunshine, Lollipops And Roses / You've Come Back	1965	1.60	8.00
Mercury 72433	(PS)	Sunshine, Lollipops And Roses / You've Come Back	1965	3.00	15.00
Mercury 72475		My Town, My Guy And Me / A Girl In Love	1965	1.60	8.00
Mercury 72475	(PS)	My Town, My Guy And Me / A Girl In Love	1965	3.00	15.00
Mercury 72513		I Won't Love You Anymore (Sorry) / No Matter What You Did	1965	1.60	8.00
Mercury 72513	(PS)	I Won't Love You Anymore (Sorry) / No Matter What You Did	1965	3.00	15.00
Mercury 72530		We Know We're In Love / That's What I'll Do	1966	1.60	8.00
Mercury 72553		Young Love / I Just Don't Know If I Can	1966	1.60	8.00
Mercury 72580		Off And Running / I Don't Care	1966	1.60	8.00
Mercury 72611		Treat Me Like A Lady / Maybe Now	1966	1.60	8.00
Mercury 72649		California Nights / I'm Going Out	1967	1.60	8.00
Mercury 72649	(PS)	California Nights / I'm Going Out	1967	3.00	15.00
Mercury 72683		Summer And Sandy / I'm Fallin' Down	1967	1.60	8.00
Mercury 72683	(PS)	Summer And Sandy / I'm Fallin' Down	1967	3.00	15.00
Mercury 72726		Brink Of Disaster / On A Day Like This	1967	1.00	5.00
Mercury 72759		It's A Happening World / Magic Colors	1968	1.60	8.00
Mercury 72787		Small Talk / Say What You See	1968	1.60	8.00
Mercury 72819		He Gives Me Love (La La La) / A Brand New Me	1968	1.60	8.00
Mercury 72842		I Can't Make It Without You / Where Can I Go?	1969	1.60	8.00
Mercury 72867		Look The Other Way / I'll Be Standing There	1969	1.60	8.00
Mercury 72892		Take Good Care / You Sent Me Silver Bells	1969	2.00	10.00
Mercury 72892		Take Good Care / I Can't Make It Without You	1969	2.00	10.00
Mercury 72931	(DJ)	98.6 Summer Day / Summer Symphony	1970	1.60	8.00
Mercury 72931		98.6 Summer Day / Summer Symphony	1970	3.00	15.00
Mercury 72969	(DJ)	Wedding Bell Blues / One By One	1970	1.60	8.00
Mercury 72969		Wedding Bell Blues / One By One	1970	3.00	15.00
Crewe 338	(DJ)	Tomorrow's Children / Why Doesn't Love Make Me Happy?	1970	1.00	5.00
Crewe 338		Tomorrow's Children / Why Doesn't Love Make Me Happy?	1970	2.00	10.00
Crewe 344	(DJ)	When Yesterday Was Tomorrow / Why Me, Why You?	1970	1.00	5.00
Crewe 344		When Yesterday Was Tomorrow / Why Me, Why You?	1970	2.00	10.00
Mowest 5029	(DJ)	The Road I Walk / She Said That	1972	1.00	5.00
Mowest 5029		The Road I Walk / She Said That	1972	2.00	10.00
Mowest 5042		Give It To Me, Sweet Thing / Don't Want To Be One	1973	*Unreleased*	
A&M 1710		Give It To Me, Sweet Thing / Immortality	1975	1.00	5.00
A&M 1710	(PS)	Give It To Me, Sweet Thing / Immortality	1975	1.00	5.00

Label & Catalog #		A-Side/B-Side	Year	VG	NM
GORGEOUS HILL					
Sun 397		Carlene / Too Late To Right My Wrong	196?	2.00	10.00
GOTHAM CITY CRIME FIGHTERS, THE					
Batwing 1001		That's Life / Who Stole The Batmobile?	1966	4.00	20.00
GOTHAM CITY TEENS, THE					
RMT 1000		Holy Ravioli /	1966	3.00	15.00
GOTHICS, THE					
Carol 4115		My Dream / Love You Too Much	195?	25.00	125.00
GOULD, SANDRA					
Philips 40138		My Son The Surfer / Hello, Melvin	1963	3.00	15.00
GOWANS, SONNY					
United Artists 114		Kissin' At The Drive-In / Rockin' By Myself	1957	20.00	100.00
GRABEAU, BOBBY (& THE TEENETTES)					
Crest 1059		There's Something About Your Kiss / Lolita	1959	2.00	10.00
Crest 1064		Back To School, Back To You / Don't Ever Let Me Go	1959	4.00	20.00
GRACIE, CHARLIE					
Cameo 105		Butterfly / Ninety-Nine Ways	1957	4.00	20.00
Cameo 107		Fabulous / Just Lookin'	1957	3.00	15.00
Cameo 111		I Love You So Much It Hurts / Wanderin' Eyes	1957	3.00	15.00
Cameo 118		Cool Baby / You've Got A Heart Like A Rock	1957	3.00	15.00
Cameo 127		Dressin' Up / Crazy Girl	1958	3.00	15.00
Cameo 141		Love Bird / Trying	1958	3.00	15.00
		—Original Cameo singles above have orange labels.—			
Coral 62073		Doodlebug / Hurry Up, Buttercup	1959	2.00	10.00
Coral 62115		Angel Of Love / I'm A Fool, That's Why	1959	3.00	15.00
Coral 62141		Oh-Well-A / Because I Love You So	1959	2.00	10.00
Roulette 4255		The Race / I Look For You	1959	2.00	10.00
Roulette 4312		Sorry For You / Scenery	1961	2.00	10.00
Felsted 8629		W-Wow / Makin' Whoopee	1961	2.00	10.00
President 825		Pretty Baby / Night And Day, U.S.A.	1962	2.00	10.00
20th Century Fox 5033		My Baby Loves Me / Head Home, Honey	1965	1.20	6.00
Diamond 178		He'll Never Love You Like I Do / Keep My Love Next To Your Heart	1965	1.20	6.00
GRADUATES, THE					
Corsican 0058		What Good Is Graduation? / Lonely	1959	6.00	30.00
Shan-Todd 0055		Ballad Of A Girl And A Boy / Care	1959	4.00	20.00
GRADUATES, THE					
GNP/Crescendo 404		Shapes Of Things To Come / Listen To The Music	1968	1.00	5.00
GRADY, DON					
Don Grady also recorded with The Yellow Balloon.					
Capitol 5181		A Broken Heart Knows Better / I Think You're Thru	1964	1.60	8.00
Challenge 69328		Don't Let It Happen / Out	1966	1.60	8.00
Canterbury 507	(DJ)	Leaving It Up To You / Impressions With Syvonne	1966	1.60	8.00
		(Stock copies of Canterbury 507 may not exist.)			
Canterbury 581		The Children Of St. Monica / A Good Man To Have Around	1966	1.00	5.00
Canterbury 581	(PS)	The Children Of St. Monica / A Good Man To Have Around	1966	2.00	10.00
GRADY, DON, & THE PALACE GUARD					
Refer to The Palace Guard.					
Orange Empire 9164		Summertime Game / Little People	1965	2.00	10.00
GRAHAM, LOU, & THE SADDLEMEN					
Gotham 429		A Sweet Bunch Of Roses / I'm Lonesome	195?	6.00	30.00
GRANAHAN, GERRY					
Gerry Granahan also recorded with Dicky Doo & The Don'ts.					
Atco 6122		Confess It To Your Heart / Sweet Affection	1958	3.00	15.00
Sunbeam 102		No Chemise, Please / Girl Of My Dreams	1958	2.00	10.00
Sunbeam 108		Baby, Wait / Completely	1958	2.00	10.00
Sunbeam 112		As Ready As I'll Ever Be / Nobody Can Handle This Job	1958	2.00	10.00
Sunbeam 122		King Size / I'm Afraid You'll Never Know	1959	3.00	15.00
Sunbeam 127		A Ring, A Bracelet, A Heart / You're Adorable	1959	2.00	10.00
Gone 5065		Let The Rumors Fly / Put Me Anywhere	1959	2.00	10.00
Gone 5081		Look For Me / It Hurts	1960	2.00	10.00
Gone 5081	(PS)	Look For Me / It Hurts	1960	3.00	15.00
Canadian Am. 116		In My Heart / When Irish Eyes Are Smiling	1960	2.00	10.00
Canadian Am. 119		Where's The Girl? / You'll Never Walk Alone	1960	2.00	10.00
Canadian Am. 121		Short Skirts / I'm Afraid I'll Never Know	1960	2.00	10.00

Label & Catalog #	A-Side/B-Side	Year	VG	NM
Caprice 106	Dancing Man / Unchained Melody	1961	2.00	10.00
Caprice 108	Dance, Girl, Dance / Too Big For Her Bikini	1961	2.00	10.00

GRANAHAN, GERRY, WITH THE WILDWOODS
The Wildwoods is a pseudonym for The Five Satins.

Caprice 102	Dance Girl, Dance / Too Big For Her Bikini	1961	30.00	150.00

GRAND, K.C., & THE SHADES

Matt 0003	Lookie Lookie Lookie /	195?	10.00	50.00

GRAND FUNK RAILROAD [GRAND FUNK]
Grand Funk is Don Brewer, Mark Farner and Mel Schacher, who originally recorded as Terry Knight & The Pack. They were joined by Craig Frost in 1972. The reformed group of 1981 consisted of Brewer, Farner and Dennis Bellinger.

Capitol 2567	Time Machine / High On A Horse	1969	1.00	5.00
Capitol 2691	Mr. Limousine Driver / High Falootin' Woman	1969	1.00	5.00
Capitol 2732	Heartbreaker / Please Don't Worry	1970	.80	4.00
Capitol 2816	Nothing Is The Same / Sin's A Good Man's Brother	1970	.80	4.00
Capitol 2877	Closer To Home / Aimless Lady	1970	.80	4.00
Capitol 2996	Mean Mistreater / Mark Says Alright	1970	.80	4.00
Capitol 3095	Feelin' Alright / I Want Freedom	1971	.80	4.00
Capitol 3160	Gimme Shelter / I Can Feel Him In The Morning	1971	.80	4.00
Capitol 3217	Save The Land / People, Let's Stop The War	1971	.80	4.00
Capitol 3255	Footstompin' Music / I Come Tumblin'	1971	.80	4.00
Capitol 3255 (PS)	Footstompin' Music / I Come Tumblin'	1971	1.00	5.00
Capitol 3316	Upsetter / No Lies	1972	.80	4.00
Capitol 3316 (PS)	Upsetter / No Lies	1972	1.00	5.00
Capitol 3363	Rock 'N' Soul / Flight Of The Phoenix	1972	.80	4.00
Capitol 3660	We're An American Band / Creepin' (Gold vinyl)	1973	1.25	6.00
Capitol 3660	We're An American Band / Creepin'	1973	.60	3.00
Capitol 3660 (PS)	We're An American Band / Creepin'	1973	.80	4.00
Capitol 3760	Walk Like A Man / The Railroad	1973	.60	3.00
Capitol 3760 (PS)	Walk Like A Man / The Railroad	1973	.80	4.00
Capitol 3840	The Loco-Motion / Destitute And Losin'	1974	.60	3.00
Capitol 3840 (PS)	The Loco-Motion / Destitute And Losin'	1974	.80	4.00
Capitol 3917	Shinin' On / Mr. Pretty Boy	1974	.60	3.00
Capitol 3917 (PS)	Shinin' On / Mr. Pretty Boy	1974	.80	4.00
Capitol 4002	Some Kind Of Wonderful / Wild	1974	.60	3.00
Capitol 4002 (PS)	Some Kind Of Wonderful / Wild	1974	.80	4.00
Capitol 4046	Bad Time / Good And Evil	1975	.60	3.00
Capitol 4199	Take Me / Genevieve	1975	.60	3.00
Capitol 4199 (PS)	Take Me / Genevieve	1975	.80	4.00
Capitol 4235	Sally / Love Is Dyin'	1976	.60	3.00
Capitol 4235 (PS)	Sally / Love Is Dyin'	1976	.80	4.00
MCA 40590	Can You Do It? / 1976	1976	.60	3.00
MCA 40590 (PS)	Can You Do It? / 1976	1976	.80	4.00
MCA 4641	Just Couldn't Wait / Out To Get You	1977	.60	3.00
Warner Bros. 49823	Y-O-U / Testify	1981	.40	2.00
Warner Bros. 49823 (PS)	Y-O-U / Testify	1981	.60	3.00

GRAND PREES, THE

Haral 780	Alone / I'm Gone	196?	10.00	50.00
Candi 1020	Sit And Cry / Jungle Fever	196?	3.00	15.00

GRAND PRIX, THE

Vault 906	Candy Apple Buggy / '41 Ford	1963	3.00	15.00

GRAND PRIX MACHINE, THE

Laurie 3512	Cynthia / Theme From Cynthia	1969	1.20	6.00

GRANGER, GERRI

Big Top 3150	Just Tell Him Jane Said Hello / What's Wrong With Me?	1963	2.00	10.00

GRANT, JANIE

Caprice 104	Triangle / She's Going Steady With You	1961	1.60	8.00
Caprice 109	Romeo / Roller Coaster	1961	1.60	8.00
Caprice 111	I Wonder Who's Kissing Him Now? / Unhappy Birthday	1961	1.60	8.00
Caprice 113	Oh, Johnny / Oh, My Love	1962	1.60	8.00
Caprice 115	That Greasy Kid Stuff / Trying To Forget You	1962	1.60	8.00
Caprice 119	Two's Company And Three's A Crowd / Peggy Got Engaged	1962	1.60	8.00
United Artists 616	Who's Heart Are You Breaking Now? / Tell Me, Mama	1963	1.60	8.00
United Artists 649	That Kind Of Boy / Priceless Possession	1963	1.60	8.00

GRANT, JOHNNY

Panorama 17	It Doesn't Matter Anymore / Cryin', Wishin', Hopin'	196?	2.00	10.00

GRANT'S BLUEBOYS

Garland 2014	Love Is Such A Game / If I Were A Carpenter	1969	2.00	10.00

Label & Catalog #		A-Side/B-Side	Year	VG	NM
GRANTS, LITTLE GUY					
Lawn 103		So Young / It's You	1959	4.00	20.00
GRAPEFRUIT					
Equinox 70000		Dear Delilah / Dead Boot	1968	1.00	5.00
Equinox 70005		Elevator / Yes	1968	1.00	5.00
GRAPEVINE					
MGM 13933		I Can't Get Enough Of You / Independent Me	1968	1.20	6.00
GRASS ROOTS, THE					

The original group (Dunhill 4103-4053) was a creation of Steve Barri and Phil Sloan. In 1967, Rick Coonce, Warren Entner, Rob Grill and Creed Bratton, replaced by Dennis Provisor in 1968, took over the name and the recording.

Dunhill 4013		You're A Lonely Girl / Mr. Jones	1966	3.00	15.00
Dunhill 4029		Where Were You When I Needed You? / (These Are) Bad Times	1966	3.00	15.00
Dunhill 4043		Only When You're Lonely / This Is What I Was Made For	1966	3.00	15.00
Dunhill 4053		Look Out, Girl / Tip Of My Tongue	1967	3.00	15.00
Dunhill 4084		Let's Live For Today / Depressed Feeling	1967	1.20	6.00
Dunhill 4094		Things I Should Have Said Today / Tip Of My Tongue	1967	1.20	6.00
Dunhill 4094	(PS)	Things I Should Have Said Today / Tip Of My Tongue	1967	3.00	15.00
Dunhill 4105		Wake Up, Wake Up / No Exit	1967	1.00	5.00
Dunhill 4122		Melody For You / Hey, Friend	1968	1.00	5.00
Dunhill 4129		Feelings / Here's Where You Belong	1968	1.00	5.00
Dunhill 4144		Midnight Confessions / Who Will You Be Tomorrow?	1968	1.00	5.00
Dunhill 4162		Bella Linda / Hot Bright Blues	1968	.80	4.00
Dunhill 4180		Lovin' Things / You And Love Are The Same	1969	.80	4.00
Dunhill 4187		The River Is Wide / (You Gotta) Live For Love	1969	.80	4.00
Dunhill 4198		I'd Wait A Million Years / Fly Me To Havana	1969	.80	4.00
Dunhill 4217		Heaven Knows / Don't Remind Me	1969	.80	4.00
Dunhill 4227		Walking Through The Country / Truck Drivin' Man	1970	.80	4.00
Dunhill 4237		Baby Hold On / Get It Together	1970	.80	4.00
Dunhill 4237	(PS)	Baby Hold On / Get It Together	1970	1.25	6.00
Dunhill 4249		Come On And Say It / Something's Comin' Over Me	1970	.60	3.00
Dunhill 4249	(PS)	Come On And Say It / Something's Comin' Over Me	1970	1.00	5.00
Dunhill 4263		Temptation Eyes / Keepin' Me Down	1970	.60	3.00
Dunhill 4279		Sooner Or Later / I Can Turn Off The Rain	1971	.60	3.00
Dunhill 4289		Two Divided By Love / Let It Go	1971	.60	3.00
Dunhill 4302		Glory Bound / Only One	1972	.60	3.00
Dunhill 4316		The Runaway / Move Along	1972	.60	3.00
Dunhill 4325		Any Way The Wind Blows / Monday Blues	1972	1.25	6.00
Dunhill 4335		Love Is What You Make It / Someone To Love	1973	.60	3.00
Dunhill 4345		Where There's Smoke There's Fire / Look But Don't Touch	1973	.60	3.00
Dunhill 4371		We Can't Dance To Your Music / Look But Don't Touch	1973	.60	3.00
Dunhill 15006		Stealin' Love (In The Night) / We Almost Made It Together	197?	.60	3.00
Haven 7015		Mamacita / Last Time Around	197?	.60	3.00
Haven 7021		Naked Man / Nothing Good Comes Easy	197?	.60	3.00
Haven 802		Out In The Open / Optical Illusion	1976	.60	3.00
MCA 52058		Here Comes That Feeling Again /	1982	.40	2.00
MCA 52104		She Don't Know Me / Keeps On Burning	1982	.40	2.00
GRATEFUL DEAD, THE					

The Dead are Jerry Garcia, Bill Kreutzmann, Phil Lesh, Ron "Pigpen" McKernan (who died in 1973), Bob Weir, lyricist Robert Hunter and Mickey Hart (1967-70, 1973 to the present). Other members include Tom Constanten, 1968-70; Keith and Donna Godchaux, 1971-79; and Brent Mydland, who joined in 1979 (and who died in 1989).

Scorpio 201		Stealin' / Don't Ease Me In	1966	50.00	200.00
Warner Bros. 7016		The Golden Road (To Unlimited Devotion) / Cream Puff War	1967	3.00	15.00
Warner Bros. 7186		Dark Star / Born Cross-Eyed	1968	3.00	15.00
Warner Bros. 7186	(PS)	Dark Star / Born Cross-Eyed	1968	20.00	100.00
Warner Bros. 7324		Dupree's Diamond Blues / Cosmic Charlie	1969	3.00	15.00
Warner Bros. 7410		Uncle John's Band / New Speedway Boogie	1970	2.00	10.00
Warner Bros. 7464		Truckin' / Ripple	1970	2.00	10.00
Warner Bros. 7627	(DJ)	Johnny B. Goode / Johnny B. Goode	1972	3.00	15.00
Warner Bros. 7627	(DJ)	Johnny B. Goode / (B-side by The Elvin Bishop Group)	1972	4.00	20.00
Warner Bros. 7667		Sugar Magnolia / Mr. Charlie	1973	1.20	6.00
Grateful Dead 01		Let Me Sing Your Blues Away / Here Comes Sunshine	1973	2.00	10.00
Grateful Dead 02		Eyes Of The World / Weather Report, Part 1	1974	2.00	10.00
Grateful Dead 03	(PS)	U.S. Blues / U.S. Blues	1974	4.00	20.00
Grateful Dead 03		U.S. Blues / Loose Lucy	1974	1.20	6.00
Grateful Dead 718		The Music Never Stopped / Help On The Way	1975	1.60	8.00
Grateful Dead 762	(DJ)	Franklin's Tower / Franklin's Tower	1976	2.50	12.00
Arista 0276		Dancin' In The Streets / Terrapin Station	1977	.60	3.00
Arista 0291		Passenger / Terrapin Station	1977	.60	3.00
Arista 383		Good Lovin' / Stagger Lee	1978	.60	3.00
Arista 410		Shakedown Street / Stagger Lee	1978	.60	3.00
Arista 519		Alabama Getaway / Far From Me	1980	.60	3.00
Arista 519	(PS)	Alabama Getaway / Far From Me	1980	.80	4.00
Arista 546		Don't Ease Me In / Far From Me	1980	.40	2.00

Label & Catalog #		A-Side/B-Side	Year	VG	NM
Arista 116		Alabama Getaway / Shakedown Street	1981	.40	2.00
Arista 9606	(DJ)	Touch Of Grey / My Brother Esau *(Grey vinyl)*	1988	.60	3.00
Arista 9606		Touch Of Grey / My Brother Esau *(Grey vinyl)*	1988	.40	2.00
Arista 9606		Touch Of Grey / My Brother Esau	1988	.30	1.50
Arista 9606	(PS)	Touch Of Grey / My Brother Esau	1988	.40	2.00
Arista 9643		Throwing Stones / When Push Comes To Shove	1988	.30	1.50
		— 12" Singles—			
Arista 9606	(DJ)	Touch Of Grey / My Brother Esau	1988	1.50	8.00
		—Extended Play Albums—			
Warner Bros. PRO-226	(33)	American Beauty *(Jukebox EP)*	1970	6.00	30.00
Warner Bros. PRO-544	(33)	Europe '72 *(Jukebox EP)*	1972	6.00	30.00

GRAVES, BILLY
| Monument 401 | | The Shag (Is Totally Cool) / Uncertain | 1959 | 2.00 | 10.00 |
| Monument 404 | | Long Journey Home / Midnight Bus | 1959 | 2.00 | 10.00 |

GRAVES, JOE
| Parkway 964 | | Beautiful Girl / See Saw | 1965 | 1.20 | 6.00 |

GRAY, GENE, & THE STINGRAYS
| Linda 110 | | Surf Bunny / Surfer's Mood | 1963 | 4.00 | 20.00 |
| Dot 16478 | | Surf Bunny / Surfer's Mood | 1963 | 2.00 | 10.00 |

GRAY, MAUREEN
Chancellor 1082		Crazy Over You / Today's The Day	1961	3.00	15.00
Chancellor 1091		I Don't Want To Cry / Come On And Dance	1961	2.00	10.00
Chancellor 1100		I'm So Young / There Is A Boy	1962	2.00	10.00
Landa 689		Dancin' The Strand / Oh, My	1962	2.00	10.00
Landa 692		People Are Talking / Oh, My	1962	2.00	10.00
Mercury 72131		Story Of My Love / Summertime Is Near	1963	2.00	10.00
Mercury 72227		Goodbye Baby / I'm A Happy Girl (Tra La La)	1963	3.00	15.00

GRAYZELL, RUDY
Sun 290		Judy / I Think Of You	1958	7.00	35.00
Starday 241		Duck Tail / You're Gone	1956	10.00	50.00
Starday 270		Jig-Ga-Lee-Ga / You Hurt Me So	1956	10.00	50.00
Starday 321		Let's Get Wild / I Love You So	1957	10.00	50.00

GREASE BAND, THE
| Shelter 7304 | | Laughed At The Judge / Let It Be Gone | 1971 | .80 | 4.00 |

GREASERS, THE
| Jaye Joseph 1002 | | Movin' Out / Greasy | 1963 | 8.00 | 40.00 |

GREAT LOVE TRIP, THE
| Uni 55163 | | Why Can't We Be? / Noah | 1969 | 1.00 | 5.00 |

GREAT SOCIETY, THE
The Great Society features Grace Slick, later of Jefferson Airplane.
| North Beach 1001 | | Someone To Love / Free Advice | 1966 | 30.00 | 150.00 |
| Columbia 44583 | | Sally Go 'Round The Roses / Didn't Think So | 1968 | 3.00 | 15.00 |

GREAT TRAIN ROBBERY, THE
| ABC 11205 | | Heartless Hurdy Gurdy / Wasted | 1969 | 1.20 | 6.00 |

GREATS, THE
| Ebb 145 | | Marching Elvis / Fiddler's Rock | 1958 | 5.00 | 25.00 |

GRECO, JOHNNY, & THE DAVIES
| Pageant 602 | | Why Don't You Love Me? / Rocket Ride | 195? | 6.00 | 30.00 |
| Sonic 813 | | High School Dance / Hogwash | 1959 | 3.00 | 15.00 |

GREEK FOUNTAINS, THE
| Philips 40255 | | Blue Jean / Countin' The Steps | 1966 | 1.20 | 6.00 |

GREEK BEANS, THE
| Tower 237 | | Knock On My Door / Who Needs You? | 1966 | 2.00 | 10.00 |

GREEN, DE ROY, & THE COOL GENTS
| Cee Jay 584 | | Beggar To A Queen / At The Teen Center | 196? | 4.00 | 20.00 |

GREEN, KEITH
Decca 31799		The Way I Used To Be / A Go-Go Getter	1965	2.00	10.00
Decca 31859		Girl Don't Tell Me / How To Be Your Guy	1965	4.00	20.00
Decca 31973		You're What's Happening, Baby / Home Town Girls	1966	2.00	10.00
		(The Decca sides were produced by Gary Usher.)			
Era 3210		Fantastic / L.A. Smog Blues	1967	1.00	5.00
Era 108		Country Store / Sgt. Pepper's Epitaph	1968	1.20	6.00

Label & Catalog #	A-Side/B-Side	Year	VG	NM

GREEN RIVER BOYS, THE
The Green River Boys feature Glen Campbell

Capitol 4867	Kentucky Means Paradise / Truck Driving Man	1962	2.00	10.00
Capitol 4990	Dark As A Dungeon / Divorce Me C.O.D.	1963	2.00	10.00

GREENBAUM, NORMAN
Norman Greenbaum also recorded with Dr. West's Medicine Show & Junk Band.

Gregar 00107	Twentieth Century Fox / Nancy Whiskey	1969	.80	4.00
Reprise 0885	Spirit In The Sky / Milk Cow	1970	.80	4.00
Reprise 0919	Canned Ham / Junior Cadillac	1970	.40	2.00
Reprise 0956 (PS)	I. J. Foxx / I. J. Foxx (Promo)	1970	2.00	10.00
Reprise 0956	I. J. Foxx / Rhode Island Red	1970	.40	2.00
Reprise 1008	California Earthquake / Rhode Island Red	1971	.40	2.00

GREENBEATS, THE

Jerden 757	If This World Were Mine / You Must Be The One	196?	1.20	6.00
Jerden 763	So Sad / I'm On Fire	196?	1.20	6.00

GREENBERG, STEVE

Trip 3000	Run To You / Big Bruce	1969	.80	4.00

GREENLEE, LEE

Brent 7003	Cherry, I'm In Love With You, Baby / Starlight	1959	3.00	15.00

GREENSTREETS, THE

Corsair 400	Moon Shot / Locust Run	1963	7.00	35.00

GREENWICH, ELLIE
Ellie Greenwich also recorded with Meantime.

Red Bird 034	You Don't Know / Baby	1965	6.00	30.00
United Artists 50151	I Want You To Be My Baby / Goodnight, Goodnight	1967	2.00	10.00
Bell 855	Ain't That Peculiar? / I Don't Wanna Be Left Outside	1969	1.50	8.00
Verve 10719	Maybe I Know / Today I Met The Boy I'm Gonna Marry	1972	1.25	6.00
Verve 10724	Chapel Of Love / River Deep, Mountain High	1973	1.25	6.00

GREGG, BOBBY (& HIS FRIENDS)

Cotton 1003	The Jam / The Jam, Part 2	1962	1.60	8.00
Cotton 1006	Potato Peeler / Sweet Georgia Brown	1962	1.60	8.00
Epic 9541	Let's Jam Again / Let's Jam Again (Part 2)	1962	1.00	5.00
Epic 9579	Walk On / Drummer Man	1963	1.00	5.00
Epic 9601	Take Me Out To The Ball / Game Scarlet O' Hara	1963	1.00	5.00
Epic 9616	Kangaroo (Part 2) / Kootanda	1963	1.00	5.00

GREGORY, HARRISON

Cordella 047	Twistin' Raindrops / I'm Alone (Features Paul Simon)	196?	6.00	30.00

GREGORY, IVAN & THE BLUE NOTES

G&G 110	Elvis Presley Blues / Kathy	1956	35.00	175.00

GRIEVES, GRANT

Big K 1002	Four In The Floor / Married Woman	196?	3.00	15.00
Big K 1003	Honky Tonk Fever / Drinkin' And Drivin'	196?	3.00	15.00
Big K 1007	Shake It, Baby / If I Ever Stop Laughing	196?	3.00	15.00
Injun 106	Four In The Floor / M1 Automatic	196?	2.00	10.00
Cracker Box 10075	Good Time Girl / I've Got You	196?	2.00	10.00
Cracker Box 10076	I'll Get To You / From Nine To Five	196?	2.00	10.00

GRIFFIN, JIMMY

Dot 15223	A Love Like You / You Took My Loving	1955	5.00	25.00
Atco 606	She's A Woman / Somebody Take Me	1956	4.00	20.00
Atco 6068	Little Mary / I'm Getting Right	1956	4.00	20.00

GRIFFIN, JIMMY [JAMES GRIFFIN]
James Griffin also recorded with Bread.

Reprise 20114	Girls Grow Up Faster Than Boys / It's A Free Country	1963	3.00	15.00
Reprise 20161	What Kind Of Girl Are You? / A Little Like Lovin' You	1963	3.00	15.00
Reprise 20178	Summer Holiday / Love Letters In The Sand	1963	3.00	15.00
Reprise 20221	Little Miss Cool / Marie Is Moving	1963	3.00	15.00
Reprise 0286	My Baby Made Me Cry / All My Loving	1964	2.00	10.00
Reprise 0280	Running To You / Gotta Lotta Love (Ciribiribin)	1964	2.00	10.00
Reprise 0304	Try / You're Nobody Till Somebody Loves You	1964	2.00	10.00
Imperial 66108	These Are The Times / Walking To New Orleans	1965	1.60	8.00
Imperial 66152	Hard Row To Hoe / He Will Break Your Heart	1966	1.60	8.00
Viva 527	The Light Of Your Mind / Thank You, Love	1968	1.00	5.00
Viva 611	Lookin' So Much Better / The Miracle Worker	1967	1.00	5.00
Viva 642	The Miracle Worker / Thank You, Love	1970	1.00	5.00
Polydor 14213	Breakin' Up Is Easy / Melody Maker	1973	.40	2.00
Polydor 14282	How Do You Say Goodbye? / Treat Her Right	1975	.40	2.00

Label & Catalog #	A-Side/B-Side	Year	VG	NM
GRIFFITH, PEGGI				
Now 1008	Rockin' The Blues / I Played The Fool	196?	8.00	40.00
Dolton 23	After My Laughter Came Tears /			
	That's All I Really Want From You	1960	1.00	5.00
GRILL, ROB				
Rob Grill originally recorded with The Grass Roots.				
Mercury 76009	Rock Sugar / Have Mercy	1979	.60	3.00
	("Rock Sugar" features Lindsay Buckingham, Mick Fleetwood and John McVie.)			
Mercury 76068	Where Were You When I Needed You? /			
	Rockin' On The Road Again	1979	.40	2.00
GRIMMS, THE				
DJM 1001	Back Breaker / Masked Poet	1973	1.25	6.00
GRIN				
Grin features Nils Lofgren.				
Spindizzy 4001	If I Were A Song / See What A Love Can Do?	1971	.50	2.50
Spindizzy 4002	Everybody's Missing The Sun / Eighteen-Faced Lover	1971	.50	2.50
Spindizzy 4005	White Lies / Just To Have You	1972	.50	2.50
Spindizzy 4006	End Unkind / Slippery Fingers	1972	.50	2.50
Thunder 4000	We All Sung Together / See What A Love Can Do	197?	.50	2.50
GROGAN, TOBY				
Vee Jay 560	Angel / Just A Friend	1963	6.00	30.00
GROOTNA				
Columbia 45461	Full Time Woman / Is It All Over?	1971	1.00	5.00
Columbia 45538	Waitin' For My Ship / That's What You Get	1971	1.00	5.00
GROOVE, THE				
20th Century Fox 6671	Love Is Getting Better / The Light Of Love	1966	1.20	6.00
Wand 1163	Love Is Getting Better / The Light Of Love	1967	1.00	5.00
GROOVY GOOLIES, THE				
RCA Victor 74-0383	The First Annual Semi-Formal Combination			
	Celebration Meet-The-Monster Population Party /			
	Save Your Good Lovin' For Me	1970	1.00	5.00
GROUNDHOGS, THE				
Interphon 7715	Rock Me / Shake It	1965	2.00	10.00
Planet 104	I'll Never Fall In Love Again / Over You, Baby	196?	2.00	10.00
GROUNDSPEED				
Decca 32344	In A Dream / L-12 East	1968	2.00	10.00
GROUP, THE				
The Group features Gary Zekley.				
Warner Bros. 5840	Baby, Baby, It's You / Can't Get Enough Of Your Love	196?	3.00	15.00
GROUP B				
Members of Group B later recorded as Blue Cheer.				
Scorpio 402	Stop Calling Me / She's Gone	196?	5.00	25.00
Scorpio 406	I Never Really Knew / I Know Your Name, Girl	196?	5.00	25.00
GRUMP				
Magic Carpet 901	I'll Give You Love / Heartbreak Hotel	1969	2.00	10.00
GRUNION HUNTERS, THE				
Highland 1035	The Four-Eyed, Tongue-Tied, Swimmin' Surfer Biter /			
	Sing Along To The Swimmin' Surfer Biter	1963	8.00	40.00
GRUNIONS, THE				
Jocko 505	Surfin' Psycho / Big Noise From Winnetka	1963	7.00	35.00
GUERCIO, JAMES WILLIAM				
Columbia 45886	Tell Me / Prelude	1970	1.00	5.00
GUERRERO, LALO				
L&M 101	Elvis Perez / Lola	1956	5.00	25.00
L&M 1000	Pound Dog / Pancho Claus	1956	5.00	25.00
GUESS WHO, THE				
Members included Chad Allan, Randy Bachman and Burton Cummings, none of whom are on the Elektra or Hilltak sides.				
Scepter 1295	Shakin' All Over / (B-side by The Discotays)	1965	6.00	30.00
Scepter 1295	Shakin' All Over / Till We Kissed	1965	2.50	12.00
Scepter 12108	Goodnight, Goodnight / Hey, Ho, What You Do To Me	1965	2.50	12.00
Scepter 12118	Hurting Each Other / Baby's Birthday	1965	3.00	15.00
Scepter 12131	Baby Feelin' / Believe Me	1966	3.00	15.00

Label & Catalog #		A-Side/B-Side	Year	VG	NM
Scepter 12144		Clock On The Wall / One Day	1966	3.00	15.00
Amy 967	(DJ)	She's All Mine / All Right	1967	5.00	25.00
Amy 976	(DJ)	His Girl / It's My Pride	1967	5.00	25.00
		(Stock copies of Amy 967 and 976 may not exist)			
Fontana 1597	(DJ)	This Time Long Ago / There's No Getting Away From You	1969	3.00	15.00
Fontana 1597		This Time Long Ago / There's No Getting Away From You	1969	6.00	30.00
RCA Victor 74-0102		These Eyes / Lightfoot	1969	.60	3.00
RCA Victor 74-0195		Laughing / Undun	1969	.60	3.00
RCA Victor 74-0223	(DJ)	Friends Of Mine / Friends Of Mine, Part 2	1969	2.00	10.00
RCA Victor 74-0300		No Time / Proper Stranger	1969	.60	3.00
RCA Victor 74-0325		American Woman / No Sugar Tonight	1970	.60	3.00
RCA Victor 74-0367		Hand Me Down World / Runnin' Down The Street	1970	.60	3.00
RCA Victor 74-0388		Share The Land / Bus Rider	1970	.60	3.00
RCA Victor 74-0388	(PS)	Share The Land / Bus Rider	1970	1.00	5.00
RCA Victor 74-0414		Hang On To Your Life / Do You Miss Me, Darlin'?	1971	.60	3.00
RCA Victor 74-0414	(PS)	Hang On To Your Life / Do You Miss Me, Darlin'?	1971	7.00	35.00
RCA Victor 74-0458		Albert Flasher / Broken	1971	.60	3.00
RCA Victor 74-0522		Rain Dance / One Divided	1971	.60	3.00
RCA Victor 74-0578		Sour Suite / Life In The Bloodstream	1971	.60	3.00
RCA Victor 74-0659		Heartbroken Bopper / Arrivederci, Girl	1972	.60	3.00
RCA Victor 74-0708		Guns, Guns, Guns / Heaven Moved Only Once Yesterday	1972	1.00	5.00
RCA Victor 74-0803		Runnin' Back To Saskatoon / New Mother Nature	1972	1.00	5.00
RCA Victor 74-0880		Follow Your Daughter Home / Bye Bye, Baby	1973	1.00	5.00
RCA Victor 74-0926		The Watcher / Orly	1973	1.00	5.00
RCA Victor 74-0977		Glamour Boy / Lie Down	1973	1.00	5.00
RCA Victor APBO-0217		Star Baby / Musicione	1974	.80	4.00
RCA Victor APBO-0324		Clap For The Wolfman / Road Food	1974	.60	3.00
RCA Victor PB-10075		Dancin' Fool / Seems Like I Can't Live With You But I Can't Live Without You	1974	.60	3.00
RCA Victor PB-10216		Loves Me Like A Brother / Hoedown Time	1975	.60	3.00
RCA Victor PB-10360		Rosanne / Dreams	1975	.60	3.00
RCA Victor PB-10410		When The Band Was Singin' "Shakin' All Over" / Woman	1975	1.00	5.00
RCA Victor PB-10716		Silver Bird / Runnin' Down The Street	1976	1.20	6.00
Hilltak 7803		C'mon, Little Mama / Moon Wave Maker	1978	.80	4.00
Hilltak 7807		Sweet Young Thing / It's Getting Pretty Bad	1979	.80	4.00
		—RCA Gold Standard Rissues—			
RCA Victor 447-0833		These Eyes / No Time	1973	1.00	5.00
RCA Victor 447-0834		Laughing / Undun	1973	1.00	5.00
RCA Victor 447-0835		American Woman / No Sugar Tonight	1973	1.00	5.00
RCA Victor 447-0887		Share The Land / Bus Rider	1973	1.00	5.00
RCA Victor 447-0888		Hang On To Your Life / Hand Me Down World	1973	1.00	5.00
RCA Victor 447-0906		Albert Flasher / Broken	1973	1.20	6.00
RCA Victor 447-0926		Rain Dance / Sour Suite	1973	1.20	6.00
		—Original Gold Standard singles above have red labels.—			

GUILLOTEENS, THE

HBR 446		I Don't Believe / Hey You	1965	2.00	10.00
HBR 451		For My Own / Don't Let The Rain Get You Down	1965	2.00	10.00
HBR 451	(PS)	For My Own / Don't Let The Rain Get You Down	1965	3.00	15.00
HBR 486		I Sit And Cry / Crying All Over My Time	1966	2.00	10.00
Columbia 43852		Wild Child / You Think You're Happy	1966	2.00	10.00

GUISE, THE

Musicland 20011		Long Haired Music / When You're Sorry	196?	1.00	5.00
Musicland 7058		Half A Man / Chumpy McGee	196?	1.00	5.00
Atco 6599		Girl, Make Up Your Mind / Nothing Else But Love	196?	1.00	5.00

GUITAR, BILLY, & THE NIGHT HAWKS

Decca 30634		Here Comes The Night / You Should Have Loved Her More	1958	20.00	100.00

GUITAR RAMBLERS, THE

Columbia 4-42928		Surf Beat / El Torito	1964	2.00	10.00

GUITARS INC.

Guitars Inc. is a pseudonym for The Fireballs.

Hamilton 50035		Little Toy / Holiday Love	1963	3.00	15.00

GULLIVER

Gulliver features Daryl Hall.

Elektra 45689		Angelina / Every Day's Lovely Day	1970	.80	4.00
Elektra 45689		Truly Good Song / Every Day's Lovely Day	1970	1.00	5.00

GUM DROPS, THE

King 1496		Don't Take It So Hard / Gum Drop	1956	4.00	20.00
King 1499		Don't Take It So Hard / I'll Wait For One More Train	1956	4.00	20.00
King 4913		I'll Follow You / I Wonder And Wonder	1956	3.00	15.00
King 4963		Chapel Of Hearts / Natural Born Loser	1956	3.00	15.00

Label & Catalog #		A-Side/B-Side	Year	VG	NM
King 5051		Pigeon / Ba-Bee Da Boat Is Leaving	1956	3.00	15.00
Decca 30584		You're The One / Gun Drop Shoes And Bells In Her Hair	1958	3.00	15.00
Coral 62003		My Own True Love / On The Wings Of The Wind	1958	3.00	15.00
Coral 62102		I Spoke Too Soon / Sie Tu	1959	3.00	15.00
Coral 62138		It Happens Every Day / They Wake Me	1959	3.00	15.00
GUN					
Epic 10413		Race With The Devil / Sunshine	1969	.80	4.00
Epic 10593		Long Hair Wildman / Drown Yourself In The River	1970	.80	4.00
GUNTER, HARDROCK					
Sun 201		Gonna Dance All Night / Fallen Angel	1954	——	——
		(Rare. Estimated near mint value $600-1,000.)			
Emperor 57		Whoo! I Mean Whee! /	195?	50.00	200.00
Emperor 112		Whoo! I Mean Whee! /	195?	15.00	75.00
GURUS, THE					
United Artists 50089		Come Girl / Blue Snow Night	1966	1.60	8.00
United Artists 50089	(PS)	Come Girl / Blue Snow Night	1966	4.00	20.00
United Artists 50140		It Just Won't Be That Way /			
		Everybody's Got To Be Alone Sometime	1967	1.60	8.00
GUY, BOB					
Donna 1380		Dear Jeepers / Letter From Jeepers	1963	30.00	150.00
		("Dear Jeepers" was co-written by Frank Zappa.)			
GYPSY					
Metromedia 202		Gypsy Queen / Dead And Gone	1970	.80	4.00
RCA Victor 74-0862		Day After Day / Lean On Me	1972	.60	3.00

H.

H. B. & THE CHECKMATES
Lavender 1936		Louise, Louise / Summertime	196?	2.00	10.00

H. P. LOVECRAFT
Philips 40464		Any Way That You Want Me / It's All Over For You	1967	1.00	5.00
Philips 40491		Wayfaring Stranger / The Time Machine	1967	1.00	5.00
Philips 40491	(PS)	Wayfaring Stranger / The Time Machine	1967	3.00	15.00
Philips 40506		White Ship / White Ship, Part 2	1967	1.00	5.00
Philips 40578		Keeper Of The Keys / Blue Jack Of Diamonds	1968	1.00	5.00

HACKERT, VELINE
Veline Hackert is a pseudonym for Buddy Covelle.
Brunswick 55151	(DJ)	Show Me How / Billy Boy	1959	15.00	75.00
Brunswick 55151		Show Me How / Billy Boy	1959	30.00	150.00

HAGAN, SAMMY, & THE VISCOUNTS
Capitol 3772	Out Of Your Heart / Smoochie Poochie	1957	6.00	30.00
Capitol 3818	Don't Cry / Wild Bird	1957	6.00	30.00
Capitol 3885	Tail Light / Snuggle Bunny	1958	5.00	25.00

HAGEN, DON
Sea Gull 103	Surfin' Son Of A Gun /	196?	8.00	40.00

HAGGETT, JIMMY
Sun 236	No More / They Call Our Love A Sin	1956	125.00	500.00
Meteor 5043	Gonna Shut You Off, Baby / Tell her True	1957	100.00	400.00

HAIG, RONNIE
Note 11010		Don't You Hear Me Calling, Baby? / Traveler Of Love	1958	5.00	25.00
Note 11014		Rockin' With Rhythm And Blues /			
		Money Is A Thing Of The Past	1958	15.00	75.00
ABC-Paramount 9912	(DJ)	Don't You Hear Me Calling, Baby? / Traveler Of Love	1958	4.00	20.00
ABC-Paramount 9912		Don't You Hear Me Calling, Baby? / Traveler Of Love	1958	8.00	40.00
ABC-Paramount 10209	(DJ)	Don't You Hear Me Calling, Baby? / Traveler Of Love	1961	3.00	15.00
ABC-Paramount 10209		Don't You Hear Me Calling, Baby? / Traveler Of Love	1961	6.00	30.00

HAINES, GARY, & THE FIVE SEQUINS
Kapp 383	Another Girl Like You / Tse Tse Fly	1961	6.00	30.00

HAIRCUTS, THE
Parkway 899		She Loves You / Love Me Do	1964	4.00	20.00
Parkway 899	(PS)	She Loves You / Love Me Do	1964	8.00	40.00

HAL & JEAN
Capitol 5041	Hey, You Standing There / Don't Tell Me Lies	1963	2.00	10.00

HAL'S ANGELS
Hal is Hal Blaine.
Dunhill 4080	The Invaders / Secret Agent Man	1967	3.00	15.00

HALE & THE HUSHABYES
"Yes Sir, That's My Baby" features Brian Wilson., Jackie DeShannon, Sonny & Cher, Darlene Love and The Blossoms and was reissued on York credited to A Date With Soul.
Apogee 104	(DJ)	Yes Sir, That's My Baby / 900 Quetzals	1964	20.00	100.00
Apogee 104		Yes Sir, That's My Baby / 900 Quetzals	1964	40.00	200.00
Reprise 0299	(DJ)	Yes Sir, That's My Baby / Jack's Theme	1964	10.00	50.00
Reprise 0299		Yes Sir, That's My Baby / Jack's Theme	1964	20.00	100.00

HALEY, BILL, & THE SADDLEMEN
Holiday 105	Rocket 88 / Tearstains On My Heart	1951	125.00	500.00
Holiday 108	Green Tree Boogie / Down Deep In My Heart	1951	125.00	500.00
Holiday 110	I'm Crying / Pretty Baby	1951	125.00	500.00
Holiday 111	A Year Ago This Christmas /			
	Don't Want To Be Alone This Holiday	1951	125.00	500.00
Holiday 113	Jukebox Cannonball / Sundown Boogie	1952	125.00	500.00
Essex 303	Rock The Joint / Icy Heart (Block label)	1952	10.00	50.00
Essex 303	Rock The Joint / Icy Heart (Script label)	1952	8.00	40.00
Essex 303	Rock The Joint / Icy Heart (Red vinyl)	1952	330.00	1,000.00
Essex 305	Rockin' Chair On The Moon / Dance With The Dolly			
	(With A Hole In Her Stocking)	1952	8.00	40.00

Label & Catalog #		A-Side/B-Side	Year	VG	NM
HALEY, BILL, & THE COMETS					

There have been many Comets, some of whom recorded independently as The Kingsmen; The Lifeguards; The Merri-Men. Refer to Joey Weltz; the Various Artists EP section.

Label & Catalog #		A-Side/B-Side	Year	VG	NM
Essex 310		Real Rock Drive / Stop Beatin' 'Round The Mulberry Bush (Orange and blue label)	1952	20.00	100.00
Essex 310		Real Rock Drive / Stop Beatin' 'Round The Mulberry Bush (Script label)	1952	12.00	60.00
Essex 321		Crazy Man, Crazy / Whatcha Gonna Do?	1953	6.00	30.00
Essex 327		Fractured / Pat-A-Cake	1953	6.00	30.00
Essex 332		Live It Up / Farewell, So Long, Goodbye	1953	6.00	30.00
Essex 340		I'll Be True / Ten Little Indians	1953	6.00	30.00
Essex 348		Straight Jacket / Chattanooga Choo-Choo	1953	8.00	40.00
Essex 374		Sundown Boogie / Jukebox Cannonball	1954	12.00	60.00
Essex 381		Rocket 88 / Green Tree Boogie	1954	20.00	100.00
Essex 399		Rock The Joint / Farewell, So Long, Goodbye	1954	10.00	50.00
Essex 102		Rock Around The Clock / Crazy, Ma, Crazy	1955	10.00	50.00
Essex 102		Rock Around The Clock / Crazy, Ma, Crazy (Blue vinyl)	1955	20.00	100.00
		(Essex 102 is, in fact, a very early—and highly collectible—bootleg.)			
TransWorld 718		Real Rock Drive / Yes, Indeed	1954	20.00	100.00
Decca 29124	(DJ)	Rock Around The Clock / Thirteen Women (Orange label)	1954	20.00	100.00
Decca 29124	(DJ)	Rock Around The Clock / Thirteen Women (Pink label)	1954	15.00	75.00
Decca 29124		Rock Around The Clock / Thirteen Women (Lines label)	1954	6.00	30.00
Decca 29124		Rock Around The Clock / Thirteen Women (Star label)	1954	4.00	20.00
Decca 29204		Shake, Rattle And Roll / ABC Boogie (Lines label)	1954	5.00	25.00
Decca 29204		Shake, Rattle And Roll / ABC Boogie (Star label)	1954	4.00	20.00
Decca 29317		Dim, Dim The Lights / Happy Baby (Lines label)	1954	5.00	25.00
Decca 29317		Dim, Dim The Lights / Happy Baby (Star label)	1954	4.00	20.00
Decca 29418		Mambo Rock / Birth Of The Boogie (Lines label)	1955	5.00	25.00
Decca 29418		Mambo Rock / Birth Of The Boogie (Star label)	1955	4.00	20.00
Decca 29552		Razzle-Dazzle / Two Hound Dogs (Lines label)	1955	5.00	25.00
Decca 29552		Razzle-Dazzle / Two Hound Dogs (Star label)	1955	4.00	20.00
Decca 29713		Burn That Candle / Rock-A-Beatin' Boogie (Lines label)	1955	5.00	25.00
Decca 29713		Burn That Candle / Rock-A-Beatin' Boogie (Star label)	1955	4.00	20.00
Decca 29791		See You Later, Alligator / The Paper Boy (Lines label)	1955	5.00	25.00
Decca 29791		See You Later, Alligator / The Paper Boy (Star label)	1955	4.00	20.00
Decca 29870		R-O-C-K / The Saints' Rock 'N' Roll (Lines label)	1956	5.00	25.00
Decca 29870		R-O-C-K / The Saints' Rock 'N' Roll (Star label)	1956	4.00	20.00
Decca 29948		Hot Dog Buddy Buddy / Rockin' Through The Rye (Lines label)	1956	4.00	20.00
Decca 29948		Hot Dog Buddy Buddy / Rockin' Through The Rye (Star label)	1956	3.00	15.00
Decca 30028		Rip It Up / Teenager's Mother (Lines label)	1956	4.00	20.00
Decca 30028		Rip It Up / Teenager's Mother (Star label)	1956	3.00	15.00
Decca 30085		Rudy's Rock / Blue Comet Blues (Lines label)	1956	4.00	20.00
Decca 30085		Rudy's Rock / Blue Comet Blues (Star label)	1956	3.00	15.00
Decca 30148		Don't Knock The Rock / Choo Choo Ch' Boogie (Lines label)	1956	4.00	20.00
Decca 30148		Don't Knock The Rock / Choo Choo Ch' Boogie (Star label)	1956	3.00	15.00
Decca 30214		Forty Cups Of Coffee / Hook, Line And Sinker (Lines label)	1957	4.00	20.00
Decca 30214		Forty Cups Of Coffee / Hook, Line And Sinker (Star label)	1957	3.00	15.00
Decca 30314		Billy Goat / Rockin,' Rollin' Rover (Lines label)	1957	4.00	20.00
Decca 30314		Billy Goat / Rockin,' Rollin' Rover (Star label)	1957	3.00	15.00
Decca 30314	(PS)	Billy Goat / Rockin,' Rollin' Rover	1957	20.00	100.00
Decca 30394		The Dipsy Doodle / Miss You (Lines label)	1957	4.00	20.00
Decca 30394		The Dipsy Doodle / Miss You (Star label)	1957	3.00	15.00
Decca 30461		Rock The Joint / How Many? (Lines label)	1957	4.00	20.00
Decca 30461		Rock The Joint / How Many? (Star label)	1957	3.00	15.00
Decca 30530		Mary, Mary Lou / It's A Sin (Lines label)	1957	4.00	20.00
Decca 30530		Mary, Mary Lou / It's A Sin (Star label)	1957	3.00	15.00
Decca 30530	(PS)	Mary, Mary Lou / It's A Sin	1957	8.00	40.00
Decca 30592		Skinny Minnie / Sway With Me (Lines label)	1958	5.00	25.00
Decca 30592		Skinny Minnie / Sway With Me (Star label)	1958	4.00	20.00
Decca 30681		Lean Jean / Don't Nobody Move (Lines label)	1958	4.00	20.00
Decca 30681		Lean Jean / Don't Nobody Move (Star label)	1958	3.00	15.00
Decca 30741		Whoa, Mabel / Chiquita Lina (Lines label)	1958	4.00	20.00
Decca 30741		Whoa, Mabel / Chiquita Lina (Star label)	1958	3.00	15.00
Decca 30781		Corrine, Corrina / B.B. Plenty	1958	3.00	15.00
Decca 30844		I Got A Woman / Charmane	1959	3.00	15.00
Decca 30873		A Fool Such As I / Where'd You Go Last Night?	1959	3.00	15.00
Decca 30926		Caldonia / Shaky	1959	3.00	15.00
Decca 30956		Ooh! Look-A There, Ain't She Pretty / Joey's Song	1959	3.00	15.00
Decca 31030		Skokiaan (South African Song) / Puerto Rican Peddler	1960	3.00	15.00
Decca 31080		Music, Music, Music / Strictly Instrumental	1960	3.00	15.00
		—Original Decca singles abobe have silver on black labels.—			
Warner Bros. 5145		Candy Kisses / Tamiami	1960	3.00	15.00
Warner Bros. 5154		Chick Safari / Hawk	1960	3.00	15.00
Warner Bros. 5171		So Right Tonight / Let The Good Times Roll	1960	3.00	15.00
Warner Bros. 5228		Flip, Flop And Fly / Honky Tonk	1961	3.00	15.00
Gone 5111		The Spanish Twist / My Kind Of Woman	1961	5.00	25.00

Label & Catalog #		A-Side / B-Side	Year	VG	NM
Gone 5116		Riviera / War Paint	1961	5.00	25.00
Logo 7006		The A.B.C. Boogie / (Non-Haley b-side)	1961	3.00	15.00
Newtown 5013		Up Goes My Love / Tenor Man	1963	3.00	15.00
New Hits 5014		Midnight In Washington / White Parakeet	1963	3.00	15.00
Newtown 5024		Dance Around The Clock /			
		What Can I Say After I Say I'm Sorry?	1963	3.00	15.00
Nicetown 5025		Tandy / You Call Everybody Darling	1963	3.00	15.00
Decca 31650		The Green Door / Yeah! She's Evil	1964	2.00	10.00
Decca 25751		Corrine, Corrina / The Green Door	1964	2.00	10.00
Apt 25081		Burn That Candle / Stop, Look And Listen	1965	4.00	20.00
Apt 25087		Haley A-Go-Go / Tongue-Tied Tony	1965	5.00	25.00
United Artists 50483		That's How I Got To Memphis / Ain't Love Funny	1968	2.00	10.00
Radio Active Gold 46		Shake, Rattle And Roll / Rock-A-Beatin' Boogie	1970	1.00	5.00
Radio Active Gold 47		See You Later, Alligator / Rudy's Rock	1970	1.00	5.00
Radio Active Gold 48		Saint's Rock'n Roll / Skinny Minnie	1970	1.00	5.00
Radio Active Gold 49		Razzle-Dazzle / Rip It Up	1970	1.00	5.00
Kama Sutra 508		Framed / Rock Around The Clock	1970	2.00	10.00
Buddah 169		Framed / Rock Around The Clock	1970	1.00	5.00
Janus 162		Travelin' Band / Little Piece At A Time	1971	2.00	10.00
Warner Bros. 7124		Rock Around The Clock / Shake, Rattle And Roll	1971	3.00	15.00
MCA 60025		Rock Around The Clock / Thirteen Women	1973	1.00	5.00
MCA 60067		See You Later, Alligator / Shake, Rattle And Roll	197?	.60	3.00
Kasey 7006		Rock Around The Clock / ABC Boogie	197?	1.00	5.00
Kasey 7006	(PS)	Rock Around The Clock / ABC Boogie	197?	5.00	25.00
Orfeon 9001		Land Of A Thousand Dances / No Matter	197?	.60	3.00
Rag 50		Crazy Man Crazy / Framed	197?	.60	3.00
Forever Oldies 21089		Rock Around The Clock / Shake, Rattle And Roll	197?	.60	3.00
Forever Oldies 21090		See You Later, Alligator / Skinny Minnie	197?	.60	3.00
Arzee 4677		Yodel Your Blues Away / Within This Broken Heart Of Mine	1978	5.00	25.00
Old Gold 9220		Rock Around The Clock / Thirteen Women	1982	.80	4.00
Old Gold 9221		Shake, Rattle And Roll / See You Later, Alligator	1982	.80	4.00
		— Extended Play Albums —			
Essex EP-102		For Your Dance Party	1954	20.00	100.00
Essex EP-102		Bill Haley's Dance Party	1954	20.00	100.00
		(Essex 102 was issued with two different titles.)			
Essex EP-117		Rock With Bill Haley & The Comets (Volume 1)	1954	20.00	100.00
Essex TWEP-117		Rock With Bill Haley & The Comets (Volume 1)	1955	20.00	100.00
Essex EP-118		Rock With Bill Haley & The Comets (Volume 2)	1954	20.00	100.00
Essex ESEP-118		Rock With Bill Haley & The Comets (Volume 2)	1954	20.00	100.00
		(Essex ESEP-118 is credited to Bill Haley & Haley's Comets.)			
Essex TWEP-118		Rock With Bill Haley & The Comets (Volume 2)	1955	20.00	100.00
Essex EP-119		Rock With Bill Haley & The Comets (Volume 3)	1954	20.00	100.00
Essex TWEP-119		Rock With Bill Haley & The Comets (Volume 3)	1955	20.00	100.00
TransWorld TWEP-117		Rock With Bill Haley And His Comets	1955	20.00	100.00
TransWorld TWEP-118		Rock With Bill Haley & The Comets (Volume 2)	1955	20.00	100.00
TransWorld TWEP-119		Rock With Bill Haley & The Comets (Volume 3)	1955	20.00	100.00
		(The TransWorld EPs are reissues of the Essex EPs.)			
Somerset 1300		Bill Haley & The Comets	1954	20.00	100.00
Somerset EX-5600		Rock With Bill Haley & The Comets	1954	20.00	100.00
Decca 2168		Shake, Rattle And Roll	1956	15.00	75.00
Decca 2209		Dim, Dim The Lights	1956	15.00	75.00
Decca 2322		Rock And Roll	1956	15.00	75.00
Decca 2398		Music For The Boyfriend	1956	10.00	50.00
Decca 2416		Rock And Roll Stage Show (Volume 1)	1956	10.00	50.00
Decca 2417		Rock And Roll Stage Show (Volume 2)	1956	10.00	50.00
Decca 2418		Rock And Roll Stage Show (Volume 3)	1956	10.00	50.00
Decca 2532		Rockin' The Oldies	1957	10.00	50.00
Decca 2533		Rock 'N' Roll Party	1957	10.00	50.00
Decca 2534		Rockin' And Rollin'	1957	10.00	50.00
Decca 2564		Rockin' Around The World	1958	10.00	50.00
Decca 2576		Rockin' Around Europe	1958	10.00	50.00
Decca 2577		Rockin' Around The Americas	1958	10.00	50.00
Decca 2615		Rockin' The Joint (Volume 1)	1959	10.00	50.00
Decca 2616		Rip It Up	1959	10.00	50.00
Decca 2638		Bill Haley's Chicks	1959	10.00	50.00
Decca 2670	(S)	Bill Haley & His Comets	1959	20.00	100.00
Decca 72670		Bill Haley & His Comets	1959	20.00	100.00
Decca 2670	(S)	Bill Haley & His Comets	1959	10.00	50.00
Decca 72671		Strictly Instrumental	1959	10.00	50.00
Claire 4779		Rock Around The Clock	1979	6.00	30.00
HALEY, BILL / SHORTY LONG					
Arzee R2-137		Bill Haley Sings	1979	20.00	100.00
HALF A SIXPENCE					
Mike 4005		Mr. Zero / Can It Be?	1966	3.00	15.00

Label & Catalog #	A-Side/B-Side	Year	VG	NM
HALF DOZEN, THE				
Soma 1453	The Angels Listened In / Heat Wave	1966	2.00	10.00
Dunwich	The Angels Listened In / Another Day	1966	2.00	10.00
HALL, BRENDA				
Loma 2020	Soldier Baby Of Mine / Oh Eddy, My Baby	1965	3.00	15.00
HALL, DARYL				
Daryl Hall also recorded with Gulliver.				
Amy 11049	Princess & The Soldier / Princess & The Soldier, Part 2	196?	1.00	5.00
HALL, LARRY				
Hot 1	Sandy / Lovin' Tree	1959	8.00	40.00
Strand 25007	Sandy / Lovin' Tree	1959	4.00	20.00
Strand 25013	Rosemary / A Girl Like You	1960	3.00	15.00
Strand 25016	For Every Boy / I'll Stay Single	1960	3.00	15.00
Strand 25025	Kool Luv / The Girl I Left Behind	1960	3.00	15.00
Strand 25029	Sweet Lips / Rebel Heart	1960	3.00	15.00
Strand 25048	The One You Left Behind / Ladder Of Love	1961	3.00	15.00
HALL, LINDA				
Cuca 1044	You Don't Have A Wooden Heart / Treat Me Nice	1961	4.00	20.00
Cuca 1070	Almost Always True / G. L. Guy	1962	4.00	20.00
Artcraft 007	Beach Boy / All Summer Long	1965	7.00	35.00
HALL, ROY				
Refer to The Hunt Sisters.				
Decca 29697	Whole Lotta Shakin' Goin' On / All By Myself	1955	7.00	35.00
Decca 29786	Don't Stop Now / See Ya Later, Alligator	1956	8.00	40.00
Decca 29880	Luscious / Blue Suede Shoes	1956	8.00	40.00
Decca 30060	Three Alley Cats / Diggin' The Boogie	1956	7.00	35.00
HALLOWAY, LARRY				
Parkway 903	Beatle Teen Beat / Going Up	1964	4.00	20.00
HALO, JOHNNY (WITH THE FOUR SEASONS)				
Topix 6004	More Lovin,' Less Talk / Betty Jean	1962	10.00	50.00
HALOS, THE: *Refer to* JOHNNY ANGEL; ERNIE & THE HALOS				
HALLYDAY, JOHNNY				
Philips 40014	Shake The Hand Of A Fool / Hold Back The Sun	1962	3.00	15.00
Philips 40024	Be Bop A Lula / I Got A Woman	1962	3.00	15.00
Philips 40024 (PS)	Be Bop A Lula / I Got A Woman	1962	5.00	25.00
Philips 40043	Hey, Little Girl / Caravan Of Lonely Men	1962	3.00	15.00
HAMILTON, BOBBY				
Apt 25002	Crazy Eyes For You / While Walking Together	1958	2.00	10.00
Apt 25018	Oh Yeah / How Come?	1959	2.00	10.00
Diana 100	Uh Huh / Lonesome Blues	1959	2.00	10.00
HAMILTON, DANNY				
Regency 12	Weekend At The Beach / No Top	1964	7.00	35.00
HAMILTON, DAVE				
Fortune 861	Beatle Walk / The Argentina	1964	2.00	10.00
HAMILTON IV, GEORGE				
After scoring a number of chart successes in the late '50s, including "The Teen Commandments" as a trio with Paul Anka and Johnny Nash, George switched to RCA Victor, pursuing a successful career in the country/western market.				
Colonial 420	A Rose And A Baby Ruth / If You Don't Know	1956	15.00	75.00
Colonial 451	I've Got A Secret / Sam	1956	15.00	75.00
ABC-Paramount 9765	A Rose And A Baby Ruth / If You Don't Know	1956	4.00	20.00
ABC-Paramount 9782	Only One Love / If I Possessed A Printing Press	1957	3.00	15.00
ABC-Paramount 9838	High School Romance / Everybody's Baby	1957	3.00	15.00
ABC-Paramount 9862	Why Don't They Understand? / Even To	1957	2.00	10.00
ABC-Paramount 9898	Now And For Always / One Heart	1958	2.00	10.00
ABC-Paramount 9924	I Know Where I'm Going / Who's Taking You To The Prom	1958	2.00	10.00
ABC-Paramount 9946	When Will I Know? / Your Cheatin' Heart	1958	2.00	10.00
ABC-Paramount 9966	The Two Of Us / Lucy, Lucy	1959	2.00	10.00
ABC-Paramount 10009	Steady Game / Can You Blame Us?	1959	2.00	10.00
ABC-Paramount 10028	Gee / I Know Your Sweetheart	1959	2.00	10.00
HAMILTON, JUDD, & FURYS				
Julian 101	I'm Not Around Any More / Little Lost Angel	196?	2.00	10.00

Label & Catalog #		A-Side/B-Side	Year	VG	NM
HAMILTON, RUSS					
Kapp 184		Rainbow / We Will Make Love	1957	2.00	10.00
Kapp 194		Wedding Ring / I Still Belong To You	1957	2.00	10.00
HAMMAN, JEFF, & THE SURF TEENS					
Westco 9		Moment Of Truth / Moonshine	196?	7.00	35.00
Westco 9		Moment Of Truth / Moonshine (Gold vinyl)	196?	15.00	75.00
HAMMEL, KARL, JR.					
Arliss 1007		Summer Souvenirs / The Magic Of Summer	1961	3.00	15.00
Arliss 1011		Sitting Alphabetic'ly / A Smile And A Tear	1962	7.00	35.00
HAMMOND, WAYNE, & THE STARFIRES					
Gala 105		Can't See Why / Carolyn	195?	8.00	40.00
HAMPTON, JOHNNY					
Rose 003		Beatle Dance / I Can't Get Along With You	1964	2.00	10.00
HAMPTON, PAUL					
Columbia 41145		Live A Life Of Love / Slam Bam, Thank You, Ma'am	1958	5.00	25.00
HANDY, WAYNE					
Renown 102		Say Yeah / Could It Be?	196?	5.00	25.00
HANNA, JIMMY [THE JIMMY HANNA BIG BAND]					
Jimmy Hanna also recorded with The Dynamics.					
Bolo 756		The Happy Hour / Lonely Man	1965	1.20	6.00
Bolo 758		New York Philly / Sunny	1966	1.20	6.00
Bolo 759		Year Of The Dove / Chinese Crackers	1966	1.20	6.00
Bolo 760		Baby, Don't Lose Your Cool /			
		Baby, Don't Lose Your Cool, Part 2	1966	1.20	6.00
HANNAN, JIMMY					
Atlantic 2247		Beach Ball / You Gotta Have Love	1964	4.00	20.00
HANSEN, DOUG, & THE HOT DOGGERS					
Eva 104		Surfin' Movies / Surfin' On Tears	1963	7.00	35.00
HANSON, JERRY					
Colpix 137		Cool Man / Why Not Cha Cha Cha?	1961	2.00	10.00
HAPPENINGS, THE					
The Happenings, who also recorded as The Four Graduates and The Honor Society, feature Bob Miranda.					
B.T. Puppy 517		Girls On The Go / Go-Go	1966	1.00	5.00
B.T. Puppy 520		See You In September / He Thinks He's A Hero	1966	1.00	5.00
B.T. Puppy 522		Go Away, Little Girl / Tea Time	1966	1.00	5.00
B.T. Puppy 523		Goodnight, My Love / Lilies By Monet	1966	1.00	5.00
B.T. Puppy 181	(DJ)	Have Yourself A Merry Christmas /			
		Have Yourself A Merry Christmas	1966	2.00	10.00
B.T. Puppy 527		I Got Rhythm / You're In A Bad Way	1967	1.00	5.00
B.T. Puppy 530		My Mammy / I Believe In Nothing	1967	.80	4.00
B.T. Puppy 532		Why Do Fools Fall In Love? / When Summer Is Through	1967	.80	4.00
B.T. Puppy 532	(PS)	Why Do Fools Fall In Love? / When Summer Is Through	1967	2.00	10.00
B.T. Puppy 538		Music Music Music / When I Lock My Door	1968	.80	4.00
B.T. Puppy 540		Randy / Love Song Of Mom And Dad	1968	.80	4.00
B.T. Puppy 542		Sealed With A Kiss / Anyway	1968	.80	4.00
B.T. Puppy 543		Breaking Up Is Hard To Do / Anyway	1968	1.00	5.00
B.T. Puppy 544		Girl On A Swing / When I Lock My Door	1968	1.00	5.00
B.T. Puppy 545		Crazy Rhythm / Love Song Of Mom And Dad	1969	1.00	5.00
B.T. Puppy 549		That's All I Want From You / He Thinks He's A Hero	1969	1.00	5.00
Jubilee 5666		Where Do I Go Medley / New Day Comin'	1969	.80	4.00
Jubilee 5677		El Paso County Jail / Won't Anybody Listen?	1969	.80	4.00
Jubilee 5686		Answer Me, My Love / I Need A Woman	1970	.80	4.00
Jubilee 5698		Tomorrow Today Will Be Yesterday / Chain Of Hands	1970	.80	4.00
Jubilee 5702		Crazy Love / Chain Of Hands	1970	.80	4.00
Jubilee 5712		Lullabye In The Rain / I Wish You Could Know Me (Naomi)	1971	.80	4.00
Jubilee 5721	(DJ)	Make Your Own Kind Of Music /			
		Make Your Own Kind Of Music	1971	.80	4.00
		(Stock copies of Jubilee 5721 may not exist.)			
Big Tree 146		Strawberry Morning / Working My Way Back To You	1972	.60	3.00
Big Tree 153		Me Without You / God Bless JoAnn	1972	.60	3.00
Midland Int. 10897		That's Why I Love You / Beyond The Hurt	1976	.60	3.00
Midsong Int. 11127		Let Me Stay / Someone Special	1977	.60	3.00
HAPPY JESTERS, THE					
Dot 15566		Just Because / Heart Of My Heart	1957	3.00	15.00

Label & Catalog #		A-Side/B-Side	Year	VG	NM
HAPPYTONES, THE					
Colpix 693		Summertime Nights / Papa Shame	1963	2.00	10.00
HARBINGER COMPLEX, THE					
Brent 7056		I Think I'm Down / My Dear And Kind Sir	1966	3.00	15.00
HARBOR LITES, THE					
The Harbor Lites feature Jay Black.					
Mala 422		Angel Of Love / Tick-A Tick-A Tock	1960	8.00	40.00
Jaro 77020		What Would I Do Without You? / Is That Too Much To Ask?	1960	7.00	35.00
HARLAND, BILLY					
Brunswick 55066	(DJ)	School House Rock / I Wanna Bop	1958	20.00	100.00
Brunswick 55066		School House Rock / I Wanna Bop	1958	35.00	175.00
HARLEY & THE NIGHT RIDERS					
Manhattan 806		The Wild Angels Ride Tonight / Won't You Help Me?	1967	8.00	40.00
HARMONICA FRANK					
Harmonica Frank Floyd.					
Sun 205		Rockin' Chair Daddy / The Great Medical Menagerist	1954	——	——
		(Rare. Estimated near mint value $3,000-5,000.)			
HARPER, CHUCK					
Chuck Harper also recorded as Chuck Fassett with The Regents.					
Felsted 8658		Summer Is Thru / Call On Me	1962	4.00	20.00
HARPER, REED, & THE THREE NOTES					
Pyramid 4012		Oh, Elvis! / O Sole Mia Rock & Roll	196?	3.00	15.00
HARPERS BIZARRE					
Warner Bros. 5890		The 59th Street Bridge Song (Feeling Groovy) / Lost My Love Today	1967	1.00	5.00
Warner Bros. 7028		Come To The Sunshine / Debutante's Ball	1967	.80	4.00
Warner Bros. 7063		Anything Goes / Malibu U	1967	.80	4.00
Warner Bros. 7090		Chattanooga Choo Choo / Hey, You In The Crowd	1967	.80	4.00
Warner Bros. 7172		Virginia City / Cotton Candy Sandman	1968	.60	3.00
Warner Bros. 7200		Both Sides Now / Small Talk	1968	.60	3.00
Warner Bros. 7223		Battle Of New Orleans / Green Apple Tree	1968	.80	4.00
Warner Bros. 7238		I Love You, Alice B. Toklas / Look To The Rainbow	1969	.60	3.00
Warner Bros. 7296		Witchi Tai To / Knock On Wood	1969	.60	3.00
Warner Bros. 7377		Poly High / Soft Soundin' Music	1970	.60	3.00
Warner Bros. 7388		Anything Goes / Virginia City	1970	.60	3.00
Warner Bros. 7399		If We Ever Needed The Lord Before / Mad	1970	.60	3.00
HARRIS, DAVE					
Town 2004		Elvis And The Unmentionables / (B-side by The Mad DJ)	1962	3.00	15.00
HARRIS, GAIL (GAYLE HARRIS)					
Etiquette 3		Be My Baby / So Much	1961	2.00	10.00
Dep 1144		Here I Go Again /	196?	2.00	10.00
Carlton 584		Here Comes The Hurt / Don't You Love Me No More	1965	1.20	6.00
HARRIS, GENEE					
ABC-Paramount 9900		Bye, Bye Elvis / You're Like A Jumping Jack	1958	7.00	35.00
HARRIS, LESLIE					
Shad 5006		Come On, Little Sarah / I Hung My Head And Cried	1960	3.00	15.00
HARRIS, MIKE, & THE HI-TIDES					
Grimmie 0024		I'm A Grimmie, Baby / I'm So Proud	1963	7.00	35.00
HARRIS, NICK, & THE SOUNDBARRIERS					
Fleetwood 7004		Hootin' And Surfin' / Freeway Hot Rod	196?	6.00	30.00
HARRIS, RAY					
Sun 254		Come On, Little Mama / Where'd You Stay Last Night?	1956	20.00	100.00
Sun 272		Greenback Dollar, Watch And Chain / Foolish Heart	1957	15.00	75.00
HARRIS, ROLF					
20th Century Fox 207		Tie Me Kangaroo Down, Sport / Nick Teen And Al K. Hall	1960	3.00	15.00
20th Century Fox 230		Big Black Hat / Lost Little Boy	1961	2.00	10.00
Epic 9567		Sun Arise / Someone's Pinched My Winkles	1963	1.20	6.00
Epic 9596		Tie Me Kangaroo Down, Sport / Big Black Hat	1963	1.20	6.00
Epic 9596	(PS)	Tie Me Kangaroo Down, Sport / Big Black Hat	1963	2.00	10.00
Epic 9615		Nick Teen And Al K. Hall / I Know A Man	1963	1.00	5.00
Epic 9615	(PS)	Nick Teen And Al K. Hall / I Know A Man	1963	2.00	10.00

Label & Catalog #		A-Side/B-Side	Year	VG	NM
Epic 9641		Lost Little Boy / Six White Boomers	1964	1.00	5.00
Epic 9641	(PS)	Lost Little Boy / Six White Boomers	1964	2.00	10.00
Epic 9682		Court Of King Caractus / Two Buffalos	1964	1.00	5.00
Epic 9721		Ringo For President / Click Go The Shears	1964	3.00	15.00
Epic 9756		The Thing / Wild Colonial Boy	1965	1.00	5.00
Epic 9780		Tie My Hunting Dog Down, Jed / Five Young Apprentices	1965	1.00	5.00
Epic 10037		Big Dog / Jake The Peg	1966	1.00	5.00
MGM 14103		Two Little Boys / I Love My Love	1970	.80	4.00

HARRIS, SHAWN
Shawn Harris originally recorded with The West Coast Pop Art Experimental Band.

Capitol 3697		I'll Cry Out / Color Of Your Eyes	1973	1.00	5.00

HARRIS, TONY, & THE WOODIES

Triumph 60		Go, Go, Little Scrambler / Poor Boy	1965	6.00	30.00

HARRISON, DANNY

Coral 62450		Speak Of The Devil / I'm A Rollin' Stone	1964	2.00	10.00

HARRISON, GEORGE
George Harrison originally recorded with The Beatles; later, The Traveling Wilburys.

Label & Catalog #		A-Side/B-Side	Year	VG	NM
Apple 2995		My Sweet Lord / Isn't It A Pity (Star label)	1970	3.00	15.00
Apple 2995		My Sweet Lord / Isn't It A Pity (Starless label)	1970	1.20	6.00
Apple 2995	(PS)	My Sweet Lord / Isn't It A Pity	1970	6.00	3000
Apple 1828		What Is Life / Apple Scruffs (Star label)	1971	1.20	6.00
Apple 1828		What Is Life / Apple Scruffs (Starless label)	1971	1.00	5.00
Apple 1828	(PS)	What Is Life / Apple Scruffs	1971	6.00	30.00
Apple P-1836	(DJ)	Bangla Desh / Deep Blue	1971	4.00	20.00
Apple 1836		Bangla Desh / Deep Blue (Star label)	1971	3.00	15.00
Apple 1836		Bangla Desh / Deep Blue (Starless label)	1971	1.00	5.00
Apple 1836	(PS)	Bangla Desh / Deep Blue	1971	4.00	20.00
Apple P-1862	(DJ)	Give Me Love / Give Me Love	1973	8.00	40.00
Apple 1862		Give Me Love / Miss O' Dell	1973	1.20	6.00
Apple P-1877	(DJ)	Dark Horse / Dark Horse	1974	8.00	40.00
Apple 1877		Dark Horse / I Don't Care Anymore (Photo label)	1974	1.60	8.00
Apple 1877		Dark Horse / I Don't Care Anymore (White label)	1974	1.20	6.00
Apple 1877	(PS)	Dark Horse / I Don't Care Anymore	1974	15.00	75.00
Apple 1879	(DJ)	Ding Dong, Ding Dong / Ding Dong, Ding Dong	1974	6.00	30.00
Apple 1879		Ding Dong, Ding Dong / Hari's On Tour (Black and white photo label.)	1974	1.00	5.00
Apple 1879		Ding Dong, Ding Dong / Hari's On Tour (Blue and white photo label.)	1974	15.00	75.00
Apple 1879	(PS)	Ding Dong, Ding Dong / Hari's On Tour	1974	4.00	20.00
Apple P-1884	(DJ)	You / You	1975	8.00	40.00
Apple 1884		You / World Of Stone	1975	1.00	5.00
Apple 1884	(PS)	You / World Of Stone	1975	3.00	15.00
Apple 1885	(DJ)	This Guitar / This Guitar	1975	7.00	35.00
Apple 1885		This Guitar / Maya Love	1975	2.00	10.00
Dark Horse 8294	(DJ)	This Song / This Song	1976	4.00	20.00
Dark Horse 8294	(PS)	This Song / This Song	1976	8.00	40.00
Dark Horse 8294	(DJ)	"The Story Behind This Song" Insert	1976	6.00	30.00
Dark Horse 8294		This Song / Learning How To Love You (Brown label)	1976	1.20	6.00
Dark Horse 8294		This Song / Learning How To Love You (White label)	1976	.80	4.00
Dark Horse 8294	(PS)	This Song / Learning How To Love You	1976	5.00	25.00
Dark Horse 8313	(DJ)	Crackerbox Palace / Crackerbox Palace	1977	3.00	15.00
Dark Horse 8313		Crackerbox Palace / Learning How To Love You	1977	.60	3.00
Dark Horse 8763	(DJ)	Blow Away / Blow Away	1979	3.00	15.00
Dark Horse 8763		Blow Away / Soft Hearted Hanna	1979	.60	3.00
Dark Horse 8763	(PS)	Blow Away / Soft Hearted Hanna	1979	1.00	5.00
Dark Horse 8844	(DJ)	Love Comes To Everyone / Love Comes To Everyone	1979	3.00	15.00
Dark Horse 8844		Love Comes To Everyone / Soft Touch	1979	.80	4.00
Dark Horse 8844	(PS)	Love Comes To Everyone / Soft Touch	1979	150.00	600.00
Dark Horse C0410		All Those Years / Teardrops	1981	.60	3.00
Dark Horse 49725	(DJ)	All Those Years / All Those Years	1981	3.00	15.00
Dark Horse 49725		All Those Years / Writings On The Wall	1981	.40	2.00
Dark Horse 49725	(PS)	All Those Years / Writings On The Wall	1981	.80	4.00
Dark Horse 49785	(DJ)	Teardrops / Teardrops	1981	3.00	15.00
Dark Horse 49785		Teardrops / Save The World	1981	.80	4.00
Dark Horse 29864	(DJ)	Wake Up My Love / Wake Up My Love	1982	3.00	15.00
Dark Horse 29864		Wake Up My Love / Greece	1982	1.00	5.00
Dark Horse 29744	(DJ)	I Really Love You / I Really Love You	1983	3.00	15.00
Dark Horse 29744		I Really Love You / Circles	1983	5.00	25.00
Columbia 38-04887	(DJ)	I Don't Want To Do It / I Don't Want To Do It	1985	3.00	15.00
Columbia 38-04887		I Don't Want To Do It / Queen Of The Hop	1985	2.00	10.00
		— 12" Singles—			
Dark Horse PRO-949	(DJ)	All Those Years / All Those Years (TC)	1981	7.00	35.00
Dark Horse 29864	(DJ)	Wake Up My Love / Wake Up My Love (TC)	1982	6.00	30.00
Columbia CAS-2034	(DJ)	I Don't Want To Do It (+ two other artists)	1985	3.00	15.00

Label & Catalog #		A-Side/B-Side	Year	VG	NM
Columbia CAS-2085	(DJ)	I Don't Want To Do It / I Don't Want To Do It	1985	3.00	15.00
		— Extended Play Albums —			
Apple 791	(DJ)	Concert For Bangla Desh (Radio spots)	1971	250.00	750.00

HARRISON, JIM & BOB

Smash 1803		Little Schoolgirl / Baby, I Love You	1963	2.00	10.00

HARRISON, NOEL

London 9755		One Too Many Mornings / Barbara Allen	1965	.80	4.00
London 9795		A Young Girl / The Future Mrs. 'Awkins	1965	.80	4.00
London 9815		It's All Over Now, Baby Blue / Much As I Love You	1966	.80	4.00
London 20011		The Man Behind The Red Balloon / Marlene	1966	.80	4.00
London 20017		Cheryl's Going Home / In A Dusty Old Room	1966	.80	4.00
London 20021		Out For The Day / Fly Sing Song	1967	.80	4.00
Reprise 0599		Sign Of The Queen / Mrs. Williams' Rose	1967	.80	4.00
Reprise 0615		Suzanne / Life Is A Dream	1967	.80	4.00
Reprise 0682		Santa Monica Pier / In Your Childhhod	1967	.80	4.00
Reprise 0758		The Windmills Of Your Mind / Leitch On The Beach	1968	.80	4.00
Reprise 0795		The Great Electric Experiment Is Over /			
		I'll Be Your Baby Tonight	1968	.80	4.00
Reprise 0914		Another Virgin Spring / Tin Wedding	1970	.80	4.00

HARRY & THE CROCODILES

RCA Victor 47-8244		Cheeta / Jungle Hootenanny	1963	2.00	10.00

HARSHMAN, ROBERT LUKE
Robert Harshman later recorded as Bobby Hart.

Guyden 2022		Is You Or Is You Ain't My Baby? / Girl Of My Of Dreams	1959	6.00	30.00
Radio 122		Love Whatcha Doin' To Me / Stop Talkin,' Start Lovin'	1960	8.00	40.00

HART, BILLY & DON

Roulette 4172		Blabbermouth / Check Mated And Bingoed	1959	4.00	20.00

HART, BOBBY
Refer to Robert Luke Harshman; Tommy Boyce & Bobby Hart; Dolenz, Jones, Boyce & Hart.

Reel 100		Girl In The Window / Journey Of Love	1960	3.00	15.00
Bamboo 507		Girl I Used To Know / The Spider And The Fly	1961	5.00	25.00
Era 3039		Girl In The Window / Journey Of Love	196?	2.00	10.00
Infinity 017		Too Many Teardrops / The People Next Door	1962	3.00	15.00
Infinity 022		Lovesick Blues / I Think It's Called A Heartache	1962	3.00	15.00
DCP 1113		That'll Be The Day / Turn On Your Lovelight	1964	2.00	10.00
DCP 1142		Jealous Feeling / Baby, Let Your Hair Down	1965	3.00	15.00
DCP 1152		Around The Corner / Cry My Eyes Out	1966	2.00	10.00
Chelsea 0026		Easy Evil / California	1972	.60	3.00
Warner Bros. 8058		Hard Core Man / To Keep From Crying	1974	.60	3.00
Warner Bros. 8058	(PS)	Hard Core Man / To Keep From Crying	1974	1.00	5.00
Warner Bros. 49079		Loneliest Night / Sometimes Love	197?	.60	3.00
Ariola 809		Lovers For The Night /	1980	.60	3.00

HART, DON

Reserve 118		Presley On Her Mind / Pledge Of Love	1957	10.00	50.00

HART, JUDY

Staccato 101		That's Enough / Didn't He Ramble?	1962	2.00	10.00

HART, MICKEY
Mickey Hart is a member of The Grateful Dead.

Warner Bros. 7644		Blind John / Pump Song	1972	1.60	8.00

HART, RITCHIE

Felsted 8593		The Great Duane / I'm Hypnotized	1959	5.00	25.00

HART, ROCKY, & THE PASSIONS

Glo 216		I Play The Part Of A Fool /			
		Someone Stole My Baby While Doing The Twist	1960	50.00	200.00

HART, ROCKY, & THE PASSIONS

Cub 9052		Every Day / Come With Me	1960	5.00	25.00
Big Top 3069		Crying /	1961	5.00	25.00

HART, RON

Columbia 42866		Calhoun The Elephant / Ghost Of Glory	1963	2.00	10.00

HARTFORD, KEN

Southern Sound 119		Jay Walker / Little Joe, Go Lightly	1963	5.00	25.00
		(Features Frankie Valli.)			

Label & Catalog #	A-Side/B-Side	Year	VG	NM

HARTLEY, AL, & THE HEARTBEATS

Imperial 5986	Ain't You Glad It's Summertime? / Counterfeit Love	196?	4.00	20.00

HARVEY, PHIL

Phil Harvey is a pseudonym for Phil Spector.

Imperial 5583	Bumbershoot / Willy Boy	1959	25.00	125.00

HARVEY & DOC, WITH THE DWELLERS

Harvey is Phil Spector, who also produced.

Annette 1002	Oh, Baby / Uncle Kev	1964	30.00	150.00

HASKELL, JIMMY

Imperial 5491	I'm All Woke Up / B.E.M.S	1958	3.00	15.00
Capitol 4954	The James Bond Theme / Bye Bye Birdie	1963	1.00	5.00

HASSAN, ALI

Philles 103	Malaguena / Chop Sticks	1962	4.00	20.00

HASSLES, THE

The Hassles feature Billy Joel.

United Artists 50215		You've Got Me Hummin' / I'm Thinkin'	1967	2.00	10.00
United Artists 50215	(PS)	You've Got Me Hummin' / I'm Thinkin'	1967	3.00	15.00
United Artists 50258		Every Step I Take (Every Move I Make) / I Hear Voices	1967	2.00	10.00
United Artists 50450		4 O' Clock In The Morning /			
		Let Me Bring You To The Sunshine	1968	2.00	10.00
United Artists 50586		Great Balls Of Fire / Traveling Band	1969	2.00	10.00

HATFIELD, BOBBY

Bobby Hatfield also recorded with The Paramours and The Righteous Brothers, where his first "solo" single is listed.

Verve 10598	Hung Up / Soul Cafe	1968	.60	3.00
Verve 10621	Brothers / What's The Matter, Baby?	1968	.60	3.00
Verve 10634	Only You (And You Alone) / The Wonder Of You	1968	.80	4.00
Verve 10639	I Wish I Didn't Love You So / My Prayer	1968	.60	3.00
Verve 10641	Answer Me, My Love / I Only Have Eyes For You	1968	.60	3.00
Warner Bros. 7566	Oo Wee Baby, I Love You / Rock 'N' Roll Woman	1972	.60	3.00
Warner Bros. 7649	Stay With Me / Rock 'N' Roll Woman	1972	.60	3.00

HATFUL OF RAIN

Sentar 1208	Have You Ever Loved Somebody? / Peculiar Situation	1967	2.00	10.00

HAUNTED, THE

Amy 959	1-2-5 / Eight O' Clock This Morning	1965	5.00	25.00
Jet 4002	I'm Gonna Blow My Little Mind To Bits / Mona	1967	5.00	25.00

HAVENS, THE

Poplar 123	Only Once / Want You	196?	2.00	10.00

HAWK

Hawk is a pseudonym for Joey Dee.

Sunburst 521	Wasn't It A Heavy Summer? /	196?	1.00	5.00

HAWK, THE

The Hawk is a pseudonym for Jerry Lee Lewis.

Philips Inter. 3559	In The Mood / I Get The Blues When It Rains	1960	6.00	30.00

HAWK & THE RANDELLAS

Riverton 103	I Don't Wanna Know / One Like Me	1965	3.00	15.00
Uptown 811	I Don't Wanna Know / Need I Say More?	1965	2.00	10.00

HAWKINS, DALE

Checker 843		See You Soon, Baboon / Four Letter Word	1957	5.00	25.00
Checker 863		Susie-Q / Don't Treat Me This Way	1957	5.00	25.00
Checker 876		Baby, Baby / Mrs. Merguitory's Daughter	1957	5.00	25.00
Checker 892		Little Pig / Tornado	1957	3.00	15.00
Checker 900		La-Do-Da-Da / Cross Ties	1958	3.00	15.00
Checker 906		A House, A Car And A Wedding Ring / My Babe	1958	3.00	15.00
Checker 913		Take My Heart / Someday, One Day	1959	3.00	15.00
Checker 916		Class Cutter (Yeah Yeah) / Lonely Nights	1959	3.00	15.00
Checker 923		Ain't That Lovin' You, Baby / My Dream	1959	3.00	15.00
Checker 929		Our Turn / Lifeguard Man	1959	3.00	15.00
Checker 934		Liza Jane / Back To School Blues	1959	3.00	15.00
Checker 940		Hot Dog / Don't Break Your Promise To Me	1960	3.00	15.00
Checker 944		Every Little Girl / Poor Little Rhode Island	1960	3.00	15.00
Checker 944	(PS)	Every Little Girl / Poor Little Rhode Island	1960	15.00	75.00
Checker 962		Linda / Who?	1960	3.00	15.00
Checker 970		Grandma's House / I Want To Love You	1960	3.00	15.00
Atlantic 2126		I Can't Erase You (Out Of My Heart) / Stay At Home, Lulu	1961	2.00	10.00
Atlantic 2150		With A Feeling / Women, That's What's Happening	1962	2.00	10.00

Label & Catalog #	A-Side/B-Side	Year	VG	NM
Tilt 781	The Same Old Way / Money Honey	1962	2.00	10.00
Tilt 783	Forbidden Love / Wish I Hadn't Called Home	1962	2.00	10.00
Tilt 785	Hawk Blows, Band Plays / Hawk Blows, Band Plays (Part 2)	1962	2.00	10.00
Lincoln 002	Baby, We Had It / Johnny B. Goode	196?	1.60	8.00
ABC-Paramount 10668	The La-La Song / I'll Fly High	1965	1.60	8.00
Bell 807	Little Rain Cloud / Back Street	1969	1.60	8.00
Bell 827	Heavy On My Mind / Joe	1969	1.60	8.00
Paula 424	First Cut Is The Deepest / Nothing Left To Do But Say Goodbye	196?	1.00	5.00
Abnak 110	The Flag / And I Believe You	197?	.80	4.00
Zonk 1002	Gotta Dance / Peaches	1973	.80	4.00

HAWKINS, GLENDA

Orbit 107	No One Can Take Your Place / You Don't Know What Your Heart Wants To Do	196?	1.20	6.00

HAWKINS, JIMMIE

Kem 2751	Sure Do / Back To School Blues (Red vinyl)	1957	4.00	20.00

HAWKINS, RONNIE (& THE HAWKS)
On many of the Roulette sides, Hawkins is backed by The Hawks, a.k.a. The Band. Refer to John Lennon; Rockin' Ronald.

Quality 6128	(Can)	Hey, Bo Diddley / Love Me Like You Can	1959	30.00	150.00
Roulette 4154		Forty Days / One Of These Days	1959	3.00	15.00
Roulette 4154	(S)	Forty Days / One Of These Days	1959	7.00	35.00
Roulette 4177		Mary Lou / Need Your Lovin'	1959	3.00	15.00
Roulette 4177	(S)	Mary Lou / Need Your Lovin'	1959	7.00	35.00
Roulette 4209		Southern Love / Love Me Like You Can	1959	2.00	10.00
Roulette 4228		Lonely Hours / Clara	1960	2.00	10.00
Roulette 4231		The Ballad Of Caryl Chessman / Death Of Floyd Collins	1960	3.00	15.00
Roulette 4249		Ruby Baby / Hayride	1960	2.00	10.00
Roulette 4267		Summertime / Mister And Mississippi	1960	2.00	10.00
Roulette 4311		Cold, Cold Heart / Nobody's Lonesome For Me	1961	2.00	10.00
Roulette 4400		Come, Love / I Feel Good	1961	2.00	10.00
Roulette 4483		Bo Diddley / Who Do You Love?	1963	2.00	10.00
Roulette 4502		High Blood Pressure / There's A Screw Loose	1963	2.00	10.00
Cotillion 44060		Down In The Alley / Matchbox	1970	1.00	5.00
Cotillion 44067		Forty Days / Bitter Green	1970	1.00	5.00
Cotillion 44076		One More Night / Little Bird	1970	1.00	5.00
Monument 8548		Lawdy, Miss Clawdy / Cora Mae	1972	.80	4.00
Monument 8561		Lonesome Town / Kinky	1972	.80	4.00
Monument 8571		Diddley Daddy / Cora Mae	1973	.80	4.00
Monument 8573		Bo Diddley / Lonely Hours	1973	.80	4.00

HAWKS, MICKEY

Profile 4002	Bip Bop Boom / Rock And Roll Rhythm	195?	5.00	25.00

HAWKS, THE

ABC-Paramount 10116	The Grasshopper / The Grissle	1960	2.00	10.00

HAWLEY, DEANE

Dore 524	Pretty Little Mary / New Fad	1959	1.00	5.00
Dore 536	Good Morning, Mr. Sun / Bossman	1960	1.00	5.00
Dore 543	I'll Never Be A Fool Again / Where Is My Angel?	1960	1.00	5.00
Dore 554	Look For A Star / Bossman	1960	1.00	5.00
Dore 569	Like A Fool / Stay At Home Blues	1960	1.00	5.00
Dore 577	Rainbow / Hey, There	1961	1.00	5.00
Liberty 55359	Pocketful Of Rainbows / That Dream Could Never Be	1961	2.00	10.00
Liberty 55446	Queen Of The Angels / You Conquered ("Queen Of The Angels" was produced by Jan Berry.)	1961	2.00	10.00
Sundown 111	Love Of The Common People / I Hate To See Me Go	196?	1.20	6.00
Valor 005	The Mummy's Bracelet / Don't Keep Me Guessing	196?	.80	4.00

HAYDOCK, RON, & THE BOPPERS

Cha Cha 701	Be-Bop-A-Jean / 99 Chicks (White label)	195?	75.00	300.00

HAYES, JIMMY, & THE SOUL SURFERS

Imperial	Summer Surfer / Down To The Beach	1963	4.00	20.00

HAYES, TOMMY (WITH THE FOUR SEASONS)

Philips 40259	Trance / Glistening Lights	1965	6.00	30.00

HAYNES, DAVID, & THE PAWNS
David Haynes & The Pawns were produced by Bobby Fuller.

Exeter 127	Lonely / Meet Me Here	1964	6.00	30.00
Coronado 127	Lonely / Meet Me Here	1965	5.00	25.00
Coronado 132	Lonely Weekends / What Do The Voices Say?	1965	5.00	25.00

Label & Catalog #	A-Side/B-Side	Year	VG	NM
HAYS, TIMOTHY				
RCA Victor 47-7945	That's What Girls Are Made For / Breakaway	1961	1.20	6.00
HAYWARD, JUSTIN				
Deram 5741	Lay It On Me / Songwriter, Part 2	1977	.60	3.00
Deram 7542	Country Girl / Songwriter, Part 2	1977	.60	3.00
Columbia 10799	Forever Autumn / The Fighting Machine	1978	.60	3.00
Columbia 11148	The Eye Of The War / Horsell Common And The Heat Ray	1979	.60	3.00
Deram 401	Night Flight / Suitcase	1980	.60	3.00
Deram 402	A Face In The Crowd / It's Not On	1980	.60	3.00
	—12" Singles—			
Towerbell 71-A	Is It Just A Game? / Lost And Found /			
	Take Your Chances / Silverbird	1985	.80	4.00
HAYWARD, JUSTIN, & JOHN LODGE				
Justin Hayward and John Lodge are members of The Moody Blues.				
Threshold 67019	I Dreamed Last Night / Remember Me, My Friend	1975	.60	3.00
Threshold 67021	Blue Guitar / When You Wake Up	1975	.60	3.00
Threshold 67021 (PS)	Blue Guitar / When You Wake Up	1975	.60	3.00
HEAD, ROY (& THE TRAITS)				
TNT 194	One More Time / Don't Be Blue	1965	2.00	10.00
Scepter 12116	Just A Little Bit / Treat Me Right	1965	1.00	5.00
Scepter 12124	Get Back / Get Back, Part 2	1965	1.00	5.00
Back Beat 543	Teenage Letter / Pain	1965	1.00	5.00
Back Beat 546	Treat Her Right / So Long, My Love	1965	2.00	10.00
Back Beat 555	Apple Of My Eye / I Pass The Day	1965	1.00	5.00
Back Beat 560	My Baby / Pain	1966	1.00	5.00
Back Beat 563	Driving Wheel / Wigglin' And Gigglin'	1966	1.00	5.00
Back Beat 571	To Make A Big Man Cry / Don't Cry No More	1966	1.00	5.00
Back Beat 576	You're (Almost) Tuff / Tush Hog	1967	2.00	10.00
Back Beat 583	Nobody But Me / A Good Man Is Hard To Find	1967	.80	4.00
Mercury 72799	Turn Out The Lights / Broadway Walk	1968	.60	3.00
Mercury 72848	Ain't Goin' Down Right / Lovin' Man On Your Hands	1968	.60	3.00
TMI 9000	Puff Of Smoke / Lord Take A Bow	1972	.60	3.00
TMI 9010	Bitty By Bit / Wait Till I Arrive	1973	.60	3.00
HEADHUNTERS, THE				
Fenton 2518	Times We Share / Think What You've Done	196?	2.00	10.00
HEARD, THE				
Garland 2006	Walk In The Sunlight / Itchin' In My Heart	196?	2.00	10.00
HEARD, LONNIE				
Arlis 1006	A Sunday Kind Of Love / Romance In The Dark	196?	3.00	15.00
HEART				
Look 5023	Give Me A Happy Heart / Now	1969	.80	4.00
Look 5029	I Love You / Love	1970	.80	4.00
HEART				
Heart features Ann and Nancy Wilson. Refer to Ann Wilson & The Heartbreakers.				
Mushroom 7011	Magic Man / How Deep It Goes	1976	.60	3.00
Mushroom 7021	Crazy On You / Dreamboat Annie	1976	.60	3.00
Mushroom 7023	Dreamboat Annie / Sing Child	1976	.60	3.00
Mushroom 7031	Heartless / Just The Wine	1978	.60	3.00
Mushroom 7035	Without You / Her Song	1978	.60	3.00
Mushroom 7043	Magazine / Devil Delight	1979	.60	3.00
Portrait 70004	Barracuda / Cry To Me	1977	.40	2.00
Portrait 70008	Little Queen / Treat Me Well	1977	.40	2.00
Portrait 70010	Kick It Out / Go On, Cry	1977	.40	2.00
Portrait 70020	Straight On / Lighter Touch	1978	.40	2.00
Portrait 70025	Dog And Butterfly / Minstral Wind	1979	.40	2.00
Epic 50847	Even It Up / Pilot	1980	.40	2.00
Epic 50874	Raised On You / Down On Me	1980	.40	2.00
Epic 50892	Bebe Le Strange / Silver Wheels	1980	.40	2.00
Epic 50950	Tell It Like It Is / Strange Euphoria	1980	.40	2.00
Epic 51010	Unchained Melody / Mistral Wind	1981	.40	2.00
Epic 02925	This Man Is Mine	1982	.40	2.00
	—12" Singles—			
Mushroom 7023	Dreamboat Annie / Sing Child	1976	1.00	5.00
Portrait 16445	Straight On / Straight On	1978	1.00	5.00
HEART BREAKERS, THE				
Vik 261	One, Two, I Love You / Without A Cause	1957	25.00	125.00
Vik 299	Love You Till / My Love	1957	40.00	200.00

Label & Catalog #		A-Side/B-Side	Year	VG	NM
HEARTATTACKS, THE					
Remus 5000		Babba Diddy Baby / I'm Angry, Baby	196?	2.00	10.00
HEARTBEATS, THE					
Jubilee 5202		Finally / Boil And Bubble	1955	6.00	30.00
HEARTBREAKERS, THE					
MGM 13129		It's Hard Being A Girl / Special Occasions	1963	2.00	10.00
HEARTBREAKERS, THE					
Brent 7037		Corrida Mash / I'm Leaving It All Up To You	1962	2.00	10.00
Atco 6258		You Had Time / Willow Wept	1963	2.00	10.00
Linda 114		Please Answer / She Is My Baby	1964	2.00	10.00
HEARTBREAKERS, THE					
Donna 1381		Every Time I See You / Cradle Rock	1964	25.00	125.00
		("Every Time I See You" features Frank Zappa on guitar.)			
HEARTS & FLOWERS					
Capitol 5829		Rock And Roll Gypsies / Road To Nowhere	1967	1.20	6.00
Capitol 5897		Please / View From Ward 3	1967	1.00	5.00
Capitol 2167		Tin Angel (Will You Ever Come Down) /			
		She Sang Hymns Out Of Tune	1968	1.00	5.00
HEARTSPINNERS, THE: *Refer to* **DINO & THE HEARTSPINNERS**					
HEATH, JOYCE					
Ms. Heath also recorded as Joyce & The Privateers.					
Dragon 412		Our First Kiss / A Letter To A Disc Jockey	1960	2.00	10.00
Laurie 3062		Johnny Fair / Rain On The River	1960	2.00	10.00
HEATHENS, THE					
Vibra 104		The Other Way Around / Problems	196?	8.00	40.00
HEATWAVES, THE					
The Heatwaves feature Billy Carl. Refer to Billy & The Essentials.					
Philtown 4001		Bad Girl / So Much About My Baby	196?	4.00	20.00
Josie 941		I'll Do My Crying Tomorrow / No Where To Go	1965	2.00	10.00
HECK QUINTET, TOMMY					
Chariot 513		Lost World / Blue 22	196?	7.00	35.00
HEDGEHOPPERS ANONYMOUS					
Hedgehoppers Anonymous features Jonathan King.					
Parrot 9800		It's Good News Week / Afraid Of Love	1965	2.00	10.00
Parrot 9817		Don't Push Me / Please Don't Hurt	1965	2.00	10.00
Parrot 3002		Baby (You're My Everything) / Remember	1966	2.00	10.00
HEFTI, NEAL					
RCA Victor 47-8755		Batman Theme / Batman Chase	1966	1.00	5.00
RCA Victor 47-8755	(PS)	Batman Theme / Batman Chase	1966	3.00	15.00
RCA Victor 9011		Batman Theme / Batman Chase	1989	.40	2.00
RCA Victor 9011	(PS)	Batman Theme / Batman Chase	1989	.40	2.00
		—Extended Play Albums—			
RCA Victor VLP-3573	(33)	Batman Theme (Jukebox EP)	1966	4.00	20.00
HEGARTHY, JERRY					
Topaz 1321		Too Much Monkey Business / Please Handle With Care	196?	2.00	10.00
HEIGHT, RONNIE					
Dore 516		Come Softly To Me / So Young, So Wise	1959	2.00	10.00
Era 3000		It's Not That Easy / Portrait Of Linda	1959	2.00	10.00
Era 3005		Juvenile / Mr. Blues, I Presume	1959	2.00	10.00
Era 3009		A Kiss To Build A Dream On / Maybe Tomorrow	1959	2.00	10.00
Era 3017		Mem'ries And Habits / One Finger Symphony	1960	2.00	10.00
Era 3031		No Date / Mr. Blues, I Presume	1961	2.00	10.00
Bamboo 500		I'm Confessin' / Dolores	1961	2.00	10.00
HEIGHTSMEN, THE					
Imperial 5848		Kretchma / Johnny Reb	1962	2.00	10.00
HEINZ					
Heinz features session guitarist James Page.					
Tower 195		Don't Worry, Baby / Heart Full Of Sorrow	1965	6.00	30.00
HEIRS, THE					
Panorama 39		You Better Slow Down / Do You Want Me	1966	3.00	15.00

Label & Catalog #		A-Side/B-Side	Year	VG	NM
HELL, RICHARD, & THE VOIDOIDS					
Richard Hell originally recorded with Television.					
Ork 81976		**Blank Generation / Love Comes In Spurts**	1977	2.00	10.00
Ork 81976	(PS)	**Blank Generation / Love Comes In Spurts**	1977	3.00	15.00
Sire 1003		**Blank Generation / Love Comes In Spurts**	1977	1.20	6.00
Sire 1003	(PS)	**Blank Generation / Love Comes In Spurts**	1977	1.20	6.00
HELLO PEOPLE, THE					
Philips 40522		**Stranger At The Door / Paisley Teddy Bear**	1968	.80	4.00
Philips 40522	(PS)	**Stranger At The Door / Paisley Teddy Bear**	1968	1.00	5.00
Philips 40531		**It's A Monday Kind Of Tuesday /**			
		(As I Went Down To) Jerusalem	1968	.80	4.00
Philips 40585		**Anthem / Jelly Jam**	1968	.80	4.00
Dunhill 15023		**Future Shock / Destiny**	1975	.60	3.00
ABC 12160		**Book Of Love / How High Is The Moon?**	1976	.60	3.00
HELMS, JIMMIE					
East West 114		**Senior Class Ring / It Was Ours**	1958	5.00	25.00
HENDRIX, AL					
Tally 119		**Rhonda Lee / Go, Daddy, Rock**	1957	15.00	75.00
ABC-Paramount 9901		**Rhonda Lee / Go, Daddy, Rock**	1957	5.00	25.00
HENDRIX, JIMI [THE JIMI HENDRIX EXPERIENCE]					
The Experience (1967-69) included Mitch Mitchell and Noel Redding.					
Audio Fidelity 167		**No Such Animal / No Such Animal, Part 2**	196?	2.00	10.00
Audio Fidelity 167	(PS)	**No Such Animal / No Such Animal, Part 2**	196?	4.00	20.00
Reprise 0572	(DJ)	**Hey Joe / 51st Anniversary**	1967	6.00	30.00
Reprise 0572		**Hey Joe / 51st Anniversary**	1967	8.00	40.00
Reprise 0572	(PS)	**Hey Joe / 51st Anniversary**	1967	50.00	200.00
Reprise 0597		**Purple Haze / The Wind Cries Mary**	1967	2.00	10.00
Reprise 0641		**Foxy Lady / Hey, Joe**	1967	2.00	10.00
Reprise 0665		**Up From The Skies / One Rainy Wish**	1968	3.00	15.00
Reprise 0767		**All Along The Watchtower / Burning Of The Midnight Lamp**	1968	2.00	10.00
Reprise 0792		**Crosstown Traffic / Gypsy Eyes**	1968	2.00	10.00
Reprise 0853		**If 6 Was 9 / Stone Free**	1969	2.00	10.00
Reprise 0905	(DJ)	**Stepping Stone / Izabella**	1970	10.00	50.00
Reprise 0905		**Stepping Stone / Izabella**	1970	15.00	75.00
Reprise 1000		**Freedom / Angel**	1971	2.00	10.00
Reprise 1044		**Dolly Dagger / Star-Spangled Banner**	1971	5.00	25.00
Reprise 1118		**The Wind Cries Mary / Little Wing**	1972	2.00	10.00
Reprise 14286		**Hear My Train / Rock Me, Baby**	1973	2.00	10.00
Reprise PRO-840		**Auld Lang Syne Little Drummer Boy / Silent Night**	1974	10.00	50.00
Guitar Player 7375XS		**Beginnings** *(Flexi-disc)*	1981	.60	3.00
Reprise 29845		**Fire / Little Wing**	1981	.60	3.00
Reprise GRE0728		**Purple Haze / Foxy Lady**	1983	.60	3.00
Reprise 1082	(DJ)	**Johnny B. Goode / Johnny B. Goode**	1983	2.00	10.00
Reprise 1082		**Johnny B. Goode / Lover Man**	1983	.60	3.00
		— *Extended Play Albums* —			
Reprise PRO-???	(DJ)	**And A Happy New Year** *(Paper sleeve)*	1979	25.00	125.00
Reprise EP-2293	(33)	**Gloria** *(Paper sleeve)*	1985	1.50	8.00
		(Issued with the "Essential Jimi Hendrix" album.)			
		— *12" Singles* —			
Reprise PRO-595	(DJ)	**And A Happy New Year** *(PC)*	1979	15.00	75.00
HENHOUSE FIVE + TWO					
The Henhouse Five is a pseudonym for Ray Stevens.					
Warner Bros. 8301		**In The Mood / Classical Cluck**	1977	.60	3.00
HENLEY, LARRY					
Larry Henley also recorded with The Newbeats.					
Hickory 1198		**It's Happening Again / Little Lips (Tell Big Lies)**	1964	1.20	6.00
Hickory 1216		**Just As Much As Ever / Conflicting Reports**	1964	1.20	6.00
Hickory 1272		**My Reasons For Living / Sticking Up For My Baby**	1964	1.20	6.00
Hickory 1298		**His Girl / Eastman Prison Farm**	1965	1.20	6.00
Hickory 1354		**I'd Be A-Lyin' / I Wouldn't Trade It For The World**	1966	1.20	6.00
Viking 1003	(DJ)	**My God And I / My God And I**	1973	1.00	5.00
		(Stock copies of Viking 1003 may not exist.)			
HENN, RICK					
Rick Henn originally recorded with The Sunrays.					
Epic 11036	(DJ)	**Girl On The Beach / Girl On The Beach**	1974	1.00	5.00
Epic 11036		**Girl On The Beach / I Live For The Sun**	1974	3.00	15.00
HENRY, JAMES, & THE OLYMPICS					
Jerden 753		**My Girl Sloopy / Here I Stand**	1965	1.20	6.00
Jerden 778		**Well, Baby / Here I Stand**	1965	1.00	5.00

Label & Catalog #		A-Side/B-Side	Year	VG	NM
HEP CATS, THE					
Del-Fi 4159		What In The World Can I Do? / The Dilly Up	1961	2.00	10.00
HEP STARS, THE					
Cameo 376		Cadillac / Farmer John	1965	3.00	15.00
HEP STARS, THE					
The Hep Stars feature Benny Andersson. Refer to Abba; Bjorn & Benny.					
Dunhill 4040		No Response / Sunny Girl	1966	5.00	25.00
Chartmaker 414		Musty Dusty / It's Now Winter's Day	1969	4.00	20.00
HERBIE & THE CLASS CUTTERS					
RCA Victor 47-7649		Just A Summer Kick / Like Those Ivy Walls	1959	2.00	10.00
HERD, THE					
The Herd features Peter Frampton.					
Fontana 1588		I Can Fly / Understand Me	1967	2.00	10.00
Fontana 1602		From The Underground / Sweet William	1967	2.00	10.00
Fontana 1602	(PS)	From The Underground / Sweet William	1967	8.00	40.00
		(Promotional, fold-open picture sleeve.)			
Fontana 1610		Come On, Believe Me / Paradise Lost	1967	2.00	10.00
Fontana 1618		I Don't Want Our Loving To Die / Our Fairy Tale	1968	2.00	10.00
Fontana 1646		Beauty Queen / The Game	1968	2.00	10.00
HERMAN, CLEVE					
Capco 103		In This Corner / (B-side by The Don Rays)	1963	6.00	30.00
HERMAN'S HERMITS					
The Hermits are Karl Greene, Keith Hopwood, Derek Leckenby, Barry Whitham and Peter Noone as "Herman."					
MGM 13280		I'm Into Something Good / Your Hand In Mine	1964	1.00	5.00
MGM 13310		Can't You Hear My Heart Beat? / I Know Why	1965	.80	4.00
MGM 13310	(PS)	Can't You Hear My Heart Beat? / I Know Why	1965	2.00	10.00
MGM 13332		Silhouettes / Walkin' With My Angel	1965	.80	4.00
MGM 13341		Mrs. Brown, You've Got A Lovely Daughter /			
		I Gotta Dream On	1965	.80	4.00
MGM 13341	(PS)	Mrs. Brown, You've Got A Lovely Daughter /			
		I Gotta Dream On	1965	.80	4.00
MGM 13354		Wonderful World / Traveling Light	1965	.80	4.00
MGM 13354	(PS)	Wonderful World / Traveling Light	1965	1.60	8.00
MGM 13367		I'm Henry VIII, I Am / The End Of The World	1965	.80	4.00
MGM 13367	(PS)	I'm Henry VIII, I Am / The End Of The World	1965	1.60	8.00
MGM 13398		Just A Little Bit Better / Sea Cruise	1965	.80	4.00
MGM 13398	(PS)	Just A Little Bit Better / Sea Cruise	1965	1.60	8.00
MGM 13437		A Must To Avoid / The Man With The Cigar	1965	.80	4.00
MGM 13462		Listen People / Got A Feeling	1966	.80	4.00
MGM 13500		Leaning On A Lamp Post / Hold On	1966	.80	4.00
MGM 13548		This Door Swings Both Ways / For Love	1966	.80	4.00
MGM 13603		Dandy / My Reservations	1966	.80	4.00
MGM 13603	(PS)	Dandy / My Reservations	1966	1.60	8.00
MGM 13639		East West / What Is Wrong, What Is Right?	1966	.80	4.00
MGM 13681		There's A Kind Of Hush / No Milk Today	1967	.80	4.00
MGM 13681	(PS)	There's A Kind Of Hush / No Milk Today	1967	1.60	8.00
MGM 13761		Don't Go Out In The Rain / Moonshine Men	1967	.80	4.00
MGM 13761	(PS)	Don't Go Out In The Rain / Moonshine Men	1967	2.00	10.00
MGM 13787		Museum / The Last Bus Home	1967	.80	4.00
MGM 13787	(PS)	Museum / The Last Bus Home	1967	2.00	10.00
MGM 13885		I Can Take Or Leave Your Loving / Marcels	1968	.80	4.00
MGM 13934		Sleepy Joe / Just One Girl	1968	.80	4.00
MGM 13973		Sunshine Girl / Nobody Needs To Know	1968	.80	4.00
MGM 13994		The Most Beautiful Thing In Life / Ooh! She's Done It Again	1968	1.00	5.00
MGM 14035		Something's Happening /			
		Little Miss Sorrow, Child Of Tomorrow	1969	1.00	5.00
MGM 14060		My Sentimental Friend / My Lady	1969	1.00	5.00
MGM 14100		It's Alright Now / The Star	1969	1.00	5.00
Private Stock 45019		Ginny Go Softly / Blond-Haired Blue-Eyed Boy	1974	1.00	5.00
Buddah 516		Lonely Situation (Love Is All I Need) /			
		Blond-Haired Blue-Eyed Boy	1976	1.00	5.00
Roulette 7213		Heart, Get Ready For Love / Truck Stop Mama	1977	2.00	10.00
HERROLD, DENNIS					
Imperial 5482		Hip Hip Baby / Make With The Lovin'	195?	15.00	75.00
HEWITT, BEN					
Mercury 71413		I Ain't Givin' Up Nothin' (If I Can't Get Something			
		From You) / You Break Me Up	1959	5.00	25.00
Mercury 71472		For Quite Awhile / Patricia June	1959	5.00	25.00

Label & Catalog #		A-Side/B-Side	Year	VG	NM
HEYBURNERS, THE					
Titan 5009		Bird Walk / Speedway	1963	3.00	15.00
HI FI FOUR, THE					
King 4856		Band Of Gold / Davy, You Upset My Life	1956	5.00	25.00
HI-FIVES, THE					
Decca 30576		My Friend / How Can I Win?	1958	5.00	25.00
Decca 30657		Just A Shoulder To Cry On / Dorothy	1958	6.00	30.00
Decca 30744		Lonely / What's New, What's New?	1958	7.00	35.00
HI-FIVES, THE					
Bingo 1006		Felicia / Windy City Special	1960	5.00	25.00
HI-FIVES, THE					
Bell 634		Son Of Raunchy / Julie	195?	6.00	30.00
HI FIVES, THE					
Era 193		Cold Wind / Mean Old Woman	196?	2.00	10.00
Jerden 730		Goin' Away / Tort	1964	1.20	6.00
HI-HATS, THE					
Hi Hat 123		The Big Wake /	196?	7.00	35.00
HI-JACKS, THE					
ABC-Paramount 9742		Wonderful One / The Letter I Wrote Today	1956	3.00	15.00
HI-LIGHTERS, THE					
Cannon 369		At The Hippity Hop / Jeanne	1959	4.00	20.00
Cannon 371/2		Mi Amor / Sweet Little Baby Of Mine	1959	4.00	20.00
HI-LITERS, THE: *Refer to* **BUDDY ROBERTS**					
HI-TONES, THE					
King 5414		Fool, Fool, Fool / Let's Have A Good Time	1960	3.00	15.00
Candix 307		The Special Day / I've Never Seen A Straight Banana	1960	3.00	15.00
Fonsca 201		Lover's Quarrel / Just For You	1961	10.00	50.00
Fonsca 202		No More Pain / I Don't Know Why	1961	10.00	50.00
Eon 101		That Was The Cause Of It All /	196?	3.00	15.00
HICKEY, ERSEL					
Apollo 761		Upside Down Love / The Millionaire	195?	10.00	50.00
Epic 9263		Bluebirds Over The Mountain / Hangin' Around	1958	4.00	20.00
Epic 9278		Goin' Down The Road / Lover's End	1958	3.00	15.00
Epic 9298		You Never Can Tell / Wedding Day	1958	3.00	15.00
Epic 9309		Don't Be Afraid Of Love / You Threw A Dart	1958	3.00	15.00
Epic 9357		What Do You Want? / Love In Bloom	1959	3.00	15.00
Kapp 372		Teardrops At Dawn / I Guess You Could Call It Love	1961	3.00	15.00
Laurie 3165		Put Your Mind At Ease / Some Enchanted Evening	1963	3.00	15.00
Toot 602		Tryin' To Get To You / Blues Station	196?	2.00	10.00
Janus 151		Bluebirds Over The Mountain / Self Made Man	1971	.60	3.00
		—Extended Play Albums—			
Epic EG-7206		In Lover's Land	1958	75.00	300.00
HICKMAN, DUANE					
ABC-Paramount 9908		Pretty Baby-O / School Dance	1958	2.00	10.00
ABC-Paramount 9908	(PS)	Pretty Baby-O / School Dance	1958	4.00	20.00
Capitol 4445		I'm A Lover Not A Fighter / I Pass Your House	195?	2.00	10.00
HICKS, BOB					
Mirasonic 1001		Rock, Baby, Rock / Baby Sittin' All The Time	1959	15.00	75.00
HICKS, DAN, & HIS HOT LICKS					
Blue Thumb 211		Moody Richard / Walkin' One And Only	1973	.60	3.00
Blue Thumb 213		I'm An Old Cowhand / Woe, The Luck	1973	.60	3.00
Blue Thumb 235		My Old Timey Baby / Cheaters Don't Win	1974	.60	3.00
HIGH & MIGHTY, THE					
ABC 10821		Tryin' To Stop Cryin' / Escape From Cuba	1966	1.25	6.00
HIGH NUMBERS, THE					
The High Numbers later recorded as The Who.					
Fontana 480	(UK)	I'm The Face / Zoot Suit	1964	125.00	500.00
Polydor DJ-570	(DJ)	I'm The Face / Zoot Suit	1980	.80	4.00
Polydor DJ-570	(PS)	I'm The Face / Zoot Suit	1980	.80	4.00

Label & Catalog #		A-Side/B-Side	Year	VG	NM
HIGH SEAS, THE					
DMG 4000	(DJ)	Sunday Kind Of Love / We Go Together	1960	10.00	50.00
DMG 4000		Sunday Kind Of Love / We Go Together (Red label)	1960	20.00	100.00
HIGH TENSIONS, THE					
Hitt 591/2		Tampico Rage / Lost Horizon	196?	7.00	35.00
HIGHLIGHTS, THE [FRANK PIZANI & THE HIGHLIGHTS]					
Bally 1016		City Of Angels / Listen, My Love	1956	3.00	15.00
Bally 1027		To Be With You / Will I Ever Know?	1957	3.00	15.00
Bally 1040		Every Time / Angry	1957	4.00	20.00
Bally 1044		Turn Around Shoes / Indiana Style	1958	3.00	15.00
HIGHLIGHTS, THE					
Arcade 190		All The Way With LBJ / Hot To Trot	1964	1.00	5.00
HIGHMINDED, THE					
Raio & Raio 1006		The New E / I Set You Free	196?	7.00	35.00
HIGHSCHOOL CHANTERS, THE					
Fashion 001		Hoodoo The Voodoo / Teenage Chant	1959	2.00	10.00
HIGHWAYMEN, THE					
United Artists 258		Michael / Santiano	1961	1.00	5.00
United Artists 370		Cotton Fields / The Gypsy Rover	1961	.80	4.00
United Artists 439		I'm On My Way / Whiskey In The Jar	1962	.80	4.00
United Artists 475		The Bird Man / Cindy, Oh Cindy	1962	.80	4.00
United Artists 801		Michael '65 / Puttin' On The Style	1965	.80	4.00
HILDRETH, SHOTGUN RED					
Wasp 110		Pistol Packin' Mama / Somebody Loses, Somebody Wins	196?	1.00	5.00
HILL, BUNKER					
Mala 451		Hide And Go Seek / Hide And Go Seek, Part 2	1965	2.00	10.00
Mala 457		Red Ridin' Hood And The Wolf / Nobody Knows	1965	2.00	10.00
Mala 464		The Girl Can't Dance / You Can't Make Me Doubt My Baby	1965	2.00	10.00
HILL, DAVE					
Apogee 106		The Only Boy On The Beach / New Orleans	1964	6.00	30.00
HILL, DAVID					
Kapp 266		Two Brothers / Deep Goes My Love	1959	2.00	10.00
Kapp 293		Living Doll / Keep The Miracle Going	1959	2.00	10.00
HILL, JACKIE					
Mar-Brit 301		Won't You Come Closer? / My Man, He's Everything	196?	3.00	15.00
HILL, JAYCEE					
Epic 9185		Romp Stompin' Boogie / A Love So Fine	1957	10.00	50.00
HILL, RAYMOND					
Sun 204		Bourbon Street Jump / The Snuggle	1954	150.00	600.00
HILL, KENNY, & THE SENTINALS					
Point 5100		Over You / The Bee	1961	5.00	25.00
		(Originally issued on Westco credited to Kenny Hinkle's Friends.)			
HILLMAN, CHRIS					
Chris Hillman also recorded with The Byrds; The Flying Burrito Brothers; McGuinn, Clark & Hillman.					
Asylum 45330		Step On Out / Take It On The Run	1976	.40	2.00
Asylum 45350		Falling Again / Love Is The Sweetest Amnesty	1976	.40	2.00
Asylum 45428		Heartbreaker / Lucky In Love	1977	.40	2.00
HIM					
Him is a pseudonym for Doug Sahm.					
Teardrop 3074		It's A Man Down There / 4 A.M.	1966	5.00	25.00
HINKLE'S FRIENDS, KENNY					
Kenny Hinkle also recorded as Kenny Karter. Refer to California Music; Kenny Hill & The Sentinals; and The Sentinals.					
Westco 5		The Bee / Over You	1962	5.00	25.00
HINSON, DON, & THE RIGORMORTICIANS					
Capitol 5314		The Monster Jerk / Riboflavin-Flavored, Non-Carbonated, Polyunsaturated Blood	1964	1.60	8.00
HIPPIES, THE					
The Hippies originally recorded as The Stereos.					
Parkway 863		Memory Lane / (B-side by Reggie Harrison)	1963	2.00	10.00

Label & Catalog #		A-Side/B-Side	Year	VG	NM

HISTORIANS, THE: *Refer to* BARBASO & THE HISTORIANS

HITMAKERS, THE
Original Sound 01		Chapel Of Love / Cool School	1958	20.00	100.00
Angletone 1104		I Can't Take It Anymore / Too Cool	1959	15.00	75.00

HITMAKERS, THE
Dore 738		How To Make A Hit Record / Buttermilk	1965	2.00	10.00

HITPACK, THE
Colpix 745		Summer Fever / Mr. Big Wheels	1964	5.00	25.00

HIX, CHUCK, & THE COUNT DOWNS
Verve 10169		Sandy / Sixteen	1959	3.00	15.00
Verve 10190		Is You Is? / Ballad Of A Bad Man	1959	3.00	15.00
Flair 101		Loretta / Cookie Duster	1961	3.00	15.00

HO-DADS, THE
Imperial 660011		Honky / Legends	1963	4.00	20.00
Imperial 66023		Space Race / After Dark	1964	4.00	20.00

HOBBITS, THE
Zar 25		Frodo Lives / Jolly Good Fellow	1967	3.00	15.00
Decca 32226		Sunny Day Girl / Daffodil Days	1968	1.00	5.00
Decca 32270		Strawberry Children / Pretty Young Thing	1968	1.00	5.00

HOCKADAY, BOB
Audio 103		Chattanooga Shoeshine Boy /	196?	2.00	10.00

HODGE, CHRIS
Apple 1850		We're On Our Way / Supersoul	1972	.80	4.00
Apple 1850	(PS)	We're On Our Way / Supersoul	1972	1.00	5.00
Apple 1858		Goodbye, Sweet Lorraine / Constant Love	1973	1.00	5.00

HODGE, GARY
Dolton 7		Too Old To Cry / Not For Love Or Money	196?	2.00	10.00

HODGES, EDDIE
Eddie Hodges also recorded with Hayley Mills.
Cadence 1397		I'm Gonna Knock On Your Door /			
		Ain't Gonna Wash For A Week	1961	2.00	10.00
Cadence 1397	(PS)	I'm Gonna Knock On Your Door /			
		Ain't Gonna Wash For A Week	1961	3.00	15.00
Cadence 1410		Bandit Of My Dreams / Mugmates	1962	3.00	15.00
Cadence 1421		Made To Love (Girls, Girls, Girls) / I Make Believe It's You	1962	2.00	10.00
Columbia 42649		Seein' Is Believin' / Secret	1962	1.20	6.00
Columbia 42697		Would You Come Back? / Too Soon To Know	1963	1.20	6.00
Columbia 42811		Rainin' In My Heart / Halfway	1963	1.20	6.00
MGM 13219		Just A Kid In Love / Avalanche	1964	1.20	6.00
MGM 13219	(PS)	Just A Kid In Love / Avalanche	1964	1.20	6.00
Aurora 150		Across The Street (Is A Million Miles Away) /			
		She Doesn't Love Me	1965	1.00	5.00
Aurora 156		Love Minus Zero / The Water Is Over My Head	1965	1.00	5.00
Aurora 161		Hitch Hike / Old Rag Man	1966	1.00	5.00

HOG HEAVEN
Hog Heaven is a pseudonym for The Shondells without Tommy James.
Roulette 7091	(DJ)	Theme From A Thought / Theme From A Thought	1970	1.20	6.00
		(Stock copies of Roulette 7091 may not exist.)			
Roulette 7101		Happy / Prayer	1971	1.20	6.00
Roulette 7106		It Feels Good, Do It / It Feels Good, Do It (Part 2)	1971	1.20	6.00

HOGS, THE
The Hogs later recorded as The Chocolate Watch Band. "Loose Lip Sync Ship" was produced by Frank Zappa.
HBR 511	(DJ)	Blues Theme / Loose Lip Sync Ship	1966	15.00	75.00
HBR 511		Blues Theme / Loose Lip Sync Ship	1966	30.00	150.00

HOLDEN GROUP, DAVE
Bolo 723		This Is Our Love / Around The World In 80 Days	1960	2.00	10.00
Camelot 121		Hold Me / Hog	196?	3.00	15.00
Camelot 125		Hundred Pounds Of Clay / The Old Country	196?	2.00	10.00
Hemlock 1		Dog Catcher Blues / Bingo Playin' Grandma	196?	2.00	10.00

HOLIDAY, CONNIE
Smash 1764		Who'll Be The Boy This Summer? /			
		I'll Be At Your Command	1962	2.00	10.00
Capitol 5447		Mrs. James, I'm Mrs. Brown's Daughter / Old Friend	1965	2.00	10.00

Label & Catalog #		A-Side/B-Side	Year	VG	NM
HOLIDAY, DANNY					
Nolta 356		Just To Satisfy You / Little Queenie	196?	2.00	10.00
HOLIDAY, JOHNNY					
Lawn 208		The Ballad Of A Boy And A Girl / Goodbye, My Love	1963	3.00	15.00
HOLIDAYS, THE					
Andie 5019		Stars Will Remember / Who Knows, Who Cares	1960	10.00	50.00
HOLIDAYS, THE					
Brent 7018		Come Back To Me / No Other Love	1961	3.00	15.00
HOLIDAYS, THE					
Nix 537		One Little Kiss / My Girl (Small "Nix" logo)	1961	6.00	30.00
Nix 537		One Little Kiss / My Girl (Large "Nix" logo)	196?	2.00	10.00
HOLIDAYS, THE: Refer to TONY & THE HOLIDAYS					
HOLLAND, RAY					
Margo 101		Surfboard Stag / My Summer Baby	1963	5.00	25.00
HOLLER, DICK, & HIS ROCKETS					
Ace 540		Uh-Uh-Baby / Livin' By The Gun	1958	4.00	20.00
HOLLERS, WAYNE					
Del-Fi 4121		Dance In The Sand / Why?	1959	2.00	10.00

HOLLIES, THE

The original recording group consisted of Alan Clarke, Eric Haydock, Tony Hicks, Graham Nash and Bobby Elliott. Haydock was replaced by Bernie Calvert in 1966 and in 1968 Terry Sylvester joined after Nash's departure. On Epic 10951, 10989 and 11025, Clarke was replaced by Mikael Rikfors. Refer to The Everly Brothers; Peter Sellers.

Liberty 55674	(DJ)	Stay / Now's The Time	1964	4.00	20.00
Liberty 55674		Stay / Now's The Time	1964	8.00	40.00
Imperial 66026		Just One Look / Keep Off That Friend Of Mine	1964	2.00	10.00
Imperial 66044		Here I Go Again / Lucille	1964	2.00	10.00
Imperial 66070		We're Through / Come On Back	1964	2.00	10.00
Imperial 66099		Yes I Will / Nobody	1965	3.00	15.00
Imperial 66119		I'm Alive / You Know He Did	1965	2.00	10.00
Imperial 66134		Look Through Any Window / So Lonely	1965	2.00	10.00
Imperial 66158		I Can't Let Go / I've Got A Way Of My Own	1966	2.00	10.00
Imperial 66186		Bus Stop / Don't Run And Hide	1966	2.00	10.00
Imperial 66214		Stop, Stop, Stop / It's You	1966	2.00	10.00
Imperial 66231		On A Carousel / All The World Is Love	1967	2.00	10.00
Imperial 66231	(PS)	On A Carousel / All The World Is Love	1967	6.00	30.00
Imperial 66240		Pay You Back With Interest / Whatcha Gonna Do About It?	1967	2.00	10.00
Imperial 66258		Just One Look / Running Through The Night	1967	2.00	10.00
Imperial 66271		If I Needed Someone / Yes I Will	1967	2.00	10.00
Epic 10180		Carrie-Anne / Signs That Will Never Change	1967	1.20	6.00
Epic 10180	(PS)	Carrie-Anne / Signs That Will Never Change	1967	3.00	15.00
Epic 10234		King Midas In Reverse / Water On The Brain	1967	1.20	6.00
Epic 10234	(PS)	King Midas In Reverse / Water On The Brain	1967	3.00	15.00
Epic 10251		Dear Eloise / When Your Light's Turned On	1967	1.20	6.00
Epic 10251	(PS)	Dear Eloise / When Your Light's Turned On	1967	3.00	15.00
Epic 10298		Jennifer Eccles / Try It	1968	1.00	5.00
Epic 10361		Do The Best You Can / Elevated Observation	1968	1.00	5.00
Epic 10400		Listen To Me / Everything Is Sunshine	1968	1.00	5.00
Epic 10454		Sorry, Suzanne / Not That Way At All	1969	1.00	5.00
Epic 10532		He Ain't Heavy, He's My Brother / 'Cos You Like To Love Me	1969	1.00	5.00
Epic 10613		I Can't Tell The Bottom From The Top / Mad Prof. Blyth	1970	.60	3.00
Epic 10677		Gasoline Alley Bred / Dandelion Wine	1970	.60	3.00
Epic 10716		Survival Of The Fittest / Man Without A Heart	1971	.60	3.00
Epic 10754		Hey, Willie / Row The Boat Together	1971	.60	3.00
Epic 10842		The Baby / Oh, Granny	1972	.60	3.00
Epic 10842	(PS)	The Baby / Oh, Granny	1972	2.00	10.00
Epic 10871		Long Cool Woman (In A Black Dress) / Look What We've Got	1972	.60	3.00
Epic 10921		Long Dark Road / Indian Girl	1972	.60	3.00
Epic 10951		Magic Woman Touch / Blue In The Morning	1973	.60	3.00
Epic 10989		Jesus Was A Crossmaker / I Had A Dream	1973	.60	3.00
Epic 11025		Slow Down / Won't We Feel Good In The Morning	1973	.60	3.00
Epic 11051		The Day That Curly Billy Shot Crazy Sam McGee / Born A Man	1973	.60	3.00
Epic 11110		The Air That I Breathe / No More Riders	1974	.60	3.00
Epic 50029		Don't Let Me Down / Layin' To The Music	1974	.60	3.00
Epic 50086		Sandy / Second Hand Hangups	1975	.60	3.00
Epic 50110		Another Night / Time Machine Jive	1975	.60	3.00
Epic 50144		I'm Down / Look Out Johnny	1975	.60	3.00
Epic 50204		Write On / Crocodile Woman	1976	.40	2.00

After riding a seemingly endless string of hits into the tops of the British charts, the Hollies issued their most striking production — and, arguably, their finest single, *King Midas In Reverse,* only to suffer a major set back in terms of position and sales. Nonetheless, this remains a benchmark of baroque flower-power from the main psychedelic era.

Label & Catalog #		A-Side/B-Side	Year	VG	NM
Epic 50422		Draggin' My Heels / I Won't Move Over	1977	.40	2.00
Epic 50522		Writing On The Wall / Burn Out	1978	.40	2.00
Atlantic 89819		Stop! In The Name Of Love / Musical Pictures	1983	.40	2.00
Atlantic 89819	(PS)	Stop! In The Name Of Love / Musical Pictures	1983	.40	2.00
Atlantic 89784		Someone Else's Eyes / If The Lights Go Out	1983	.40	2.00
		— 12" Singles—			
Epic ASD-387	(DJ)	Draggin' My Heels / I Won't Move Over	1977	2.00	10.00

HOLLY, BUDDY (& THE THREE TUNES)

Early Decca singles credit Buddy Holly & The Three Tunes, who were the embryonic Crickets. Decca singles were pressed on a black label with lines on each side of the Decca logo on top and with the later black label with a star beneath the logo. Coral 61852-62210 were originally released as blue label promos; they were reissued on yellow labels in 1962-63 in an effort to stimulate sales. Coral 62329 and 62448 features over-dubbed backing by The Fireballs. Finally, Buddy also did session work with Lou Giordano, Ivan, Waylon Jennings, and the Norman Petty Trio.

Label & Catalog #		A-Side/B-Side	Year	VG	NM
Decca 9-29854	(DJ)	Blue Days, Black Nights / Love Me	1956	50.00	250.00
Decca 9-29854		Blue Days, Black Nights / Love Me (Lines label)	1956	40.00	200.00
Decca 9-29854		Blue Days, Black Nights / Love Me (Star label)	1956	30.00	150.00
Decca 9-30166	(DJ)	Modern Don Juan / You Are My One Desire	1956	50.00	250.00
Decca 9-30166		Modern Don Juan / You Are My One Desire (Lines label)	1956	40.00	200.00
Decca 9-30166		Modern Don Juan / You Are My One Desire (Star label)	1956	30.00	150.00
Decca 9-30434	(DJ)	That'll Be The Day / Rock Around With Ollie Vie	1958	50.00	250.00
Decca 9-30434		That'll Be The Day / Rock Around With Ollie Vie (Lines label.)	1958	40.00	200.00
Decca 9-30434		That'll Be The Day / Rock Around With Ollie Vie (Star label.)	1958	30.00	150.00
Decca 9-30543	(DJ)	Love Me / You Are My One Desire	1958	40.00	200.00
Decca 9-30543		Love Me / You Are My One Desire (Lines label)	1958	20.00	100.00
Decca 9-30543		Love Me / You Are My One Desire (Star label)	1958	15.00	75.00
Decca 9-30650	(DJ)	Girl On My Mind / Ting-A-Ling	1958	40.00	200.00
Decca 9-30650		Girl On My Mind / Ting-A-Ling (Lines label)	1958	20.00	100.00
Decca 9-30650		Girl On My Mind / Ting-A-Ling (Star label)	1958	15.00	75.00
Coral 9-61852	(DJ)	Mailman, Bring Me No More Blues / Words Of Love	1957	50.00	250.00
Coral 9-61852		Mailman, Bring Me No More Blues / Words Of Love	1957	75.00	300.00
Coral 9-61885	(DJ)	Peggy Sue / Everyday	1957	40.00	200.00
Coral 9-61885		Peggy Sue / Everyday	1957	5.00	25.00
Coral 9-61947	(DJ)	I'm Gonna Love You, Too / Listen To Me	1957	30.00	150.00
Coral 9-61947		I'm Gonna Love You, Too / Listen To Me	1957	5.00	25.00
Coral 9-61985	(DJ)	Rave On / Take Your Time	1958	30.00	150.00
Coral 9-61985		Rave On / Take Your Time	1958	5.00	25.00
Coral 9-62006	(DJ)	Early In The Morning / Now We're One	1958	30.00	150.00
Coral 9-62006		Early In The Morning / Now We're One	1958	5.00	25.00
Coral 9-62051	(DJ)	Heartbeat / Well, All Right	1958	30.00	150.00
Coral 9-62051		Heartbeat / Well, All Right	1958	5.00	25.00
Coral 9-62074	(DJ)	It Doesn't Matter Anymore / Raining In My Heart	1959	20.00	100.00
Coral 9-62074		It Doesn't Matter Anymore / Raining In My Heart	1959	5.00	25.00
Coral 9-62134	(DJ)	Peggy Sue Got Married / Crying, Waiting, Hoping	1960	20.00	100.00
Coral 9-62134		Peggy Sue Got Married / Crying, Waiting, Hoping	1960	15.00	75.00
Coral 9-62210	(DJ)	True Love Ways / That Makes It Tough	1960	20.00	100.00
Coral 9-62210		True Love Ways / That Makes It Tough	1960	10.00	50.00
		—Original Coral singles above have orange labels; promos have blue labels.—			
Coral 9-61852	(DJ)	Mailman, Bring Me No More Blues / Words Of Love	1962	15.00	75.00
Coral 9-61852		Mailman, Bring Me No More Blues / Words Of Love	1962	2.00	10.00
Coral 9-61885	(DJ)	Peggy Sue / Everyday	1962	15.00	75.00
Coral 9-61885		Peggy Sue / Everyday	1962	2.00	10.00
Coral 9-61947	(DJ)	I'm Gonna Love You, Too / Listen To Me	1962	15.00	75.00
Coral 9-61947		I'm Gonna Love You, Too / Listen To Me	1962	2.00	10.00
Coral 9-61985	(DJ)	Rave On / Take Your Time	1962	15.00	75.00
Coral 9-61985		Rave On / Take Your Time	1962	2.00	10.00
Coral 9-62006	(DJ)	Early In The Morning / Now We're One	1962	15.00	75.00
Coral 9-62006		Early In The Morning / Now We're One	1962	2.00	10.00
Coral 9-62051	(DJ)	Heartbeat / Well, All Right	1962	15.00	75.00
Coral 9-62051		Heartbeat / Well, All Right	1962	2.00	10.00
Coral 9-62074	(DJ)	It Doesn't Matter Anymore / Raining In My Heart	1962	15.00	75.00
Coral 9-62074		It Doesn't Matter Anymore / Raining In My Heart	1962	2.00	10.00
Coral 9-62134	(DJ)	Peggy Sue Got Married / Crying, Waiting, Hoping	1962	7.00	35.00
Coral 9-62134		Peggy Sue Got Married / Crying, Waiting, Hoping	1962	15.00	75.00
Coral 9-62210	(DJ)	True Love Ways / That Makes It Tough	1962	7.00	35.00
Coral 9-62210		True Love Ways / That Makes It Tough	1962	2.00	10.00
Coral 9-62283	(Can)	You're So Square / Valley Of Tears	1962	20.00	100.00
Coral 9-62329	(DJ)	Reminiscing / Wait Til The Sun Shines, Nellie	1962	15.00	75.00
Coral 9-62329		Reminiscing / Wait Til The Sun Shines, Nellie	1962	5.00	25.00
Coral 9-62352	(DJ)	True Love Ways / Bo Diddley	1963	10.00	50.00
Coral 9-62352		True Love Ways / Bo Diddley	1963	10.00	50.00
Coral 9-62369	(DJ)	Brown-Eyed Handsome Man / Wishing	1963	10.00	50.00
Coral 9-62369		Brown-Eyed Handsome Man / Wishing	1963	8.00	40.00
Coral 9-62390	(DJ)	Rock Around With Ollie Vie / I'm Gonna Love You, Too	1964	10.00	50.00
Coral 9-62390		Rock Around With Ollie Vie / I'm Gonna Love You, Too	1964	6.00	30.00

Label & Catalog #		A-Side/B-Side	Year	VG	NM
Coral 9-62407	(DJ)	Maybe Baby / Not Fade Away	1964	10.00	50.00
Coral 9-62407		Maybe Baby / Not Fade Away	1964	6.00	30.00
Coral 9-62448	(DJ)	Slippin' And Slidin' / What To Do	1965	10.00	50.00
Coral 9-62448		Slippin' And Slidin' / What To Do	1965	15.00	75.00
Coral 9-62554	(DJ)	Rave On / Early In The Morning	1968	5.00	25.00
Coral 9-62554		Rave On / Early In The Morning	1968	5.00	25.00
Coral 9-62558	(DJ)	Love Is Strange / You're The One	1969	5.00	25.00
Coral 9-62558		Love Is Strange / You're The One	1969	3.00	15.00
Coral 9-62558	(PS)	Love Is Strange / You're The One	1969	5.00	25.00
Coral 9-65618		That'll Be The Day / I'm Looking For Someone To Love	1971	3.00	15.00
		—Coral singles above have black labels; promos have yellow labels.—			
MCA 60000		That'll Be The Day / I'm Looking For Someone To Love	1973	2.00	10.00
MCA 60004		Peggy Sue / Everyday	1973	2.00	10.00
MCA 40905		It Doesn't Matter Anymore / Peggy Sue	1978	.80	4.00
MCA 40905	(PS)	It Doesn't Matter Anymore / Peggy Sue	1978	.80	4.00
		—Extended Play Albums—			
Decca ECD-2575		That'll Be The Day	1958	250.00	750.00
		(The back cover has liner notes.)			
Decca ECD-2575		That'll Be The Day	1958	150.00	600.00
		(The back cover has ads for other Coral EPs.)			
Coral EC-81169		Listen To Me	1958	100.00	400.00
Coral EC-81182		The Buddy Holly Story	1959	100.00	400.00
Coral EC-81191		Buddy Holly	1962	100.00	400.00
Coral EC-81193		Brown-Eyed Handsome Man	1963	100.00	400.00

HOLLY TWINS, THE

Label & Catalog #	A-Side/B-Side	Year	VG	NM
Liberty 55048	I Want Elvis For Christmas / The Tender Age	1957	7.00	35.00

HOLLYHAWKS, THE
The Hollyhawks feature Nikki Sullivan of The Crickets.

Label & Catalog #	A-Side/B-Side	Year	VG	NM
Jubilee 5441	I Cry All The Time / When Came The Fall	1963	8.00	40.00

HOLLYHOCKS, THE

Label & Catalog #	A-Side/B-Side	Year	VG	NM
Nasco 6001	Don't Say Tomorrow / You For Me	1957	7.00	35.00

HOLLYWOOD ARGYLES, THE [THE ARGYLES]
The Hollywood Argyles, featuring Gary Paxton and Kim Fowley, later recorded as The New Hollywood Argyles.

Label & Catalog #		A-Side/B-Side	Year	VG	NM
Brent 7004		Vacation Days Are Over / It Takes Time	1959	8.00	20.00
		(Brent 7004 credits The Argyles.)			
Lute 5905		Alley-Oop / Sho Know A Lot About Love	1960	2.00	10.00
Lute 5908		Gun Totin' Critter Named Jack / Bur Eye	1960	2.00	10.00
Lute 6002		Hully Gully / So Fine	1960	2.00	10.00
Paxley 752		You've Been Torturing Me / The Grubble	1960	2.00	10.00
Finer Arts 1002		The Morning After / See You In The Morning	1961	2.00	10.00
Felsted 8674		Bossynover / Find Another way	1963	2.00	10.00
Wham 7037		Alley-Oop /	196?	2.00	10.00
Wham 7037	(PS)	Alley-Oop /	196?	4.00	20.00
Kammy 105		Alley Oop '66 / Do The Funky Foot	1966	3.00	15.00
		(Kammy 105 credits The New Hollywood Argyles.)			

HOLLYWOOD PERSUADERS, THE [THE PERSUADERS]

Label & Catalog #	A-Side/B-Side	Year	VG	NM
Original Sound 39	Tijuana / Grunion Run	1963	10.00	50.00
	("Grunion Run" was written by Frank Zappa, who also played guitar.)			
Original Sound 50	Drums A-Go-Go / Agua Caliente	1963	2.00	10.00

HOLLYWOOD PLAYBOYS, THE
The Hollywood Playboys feature Nick Massi of The Four Seasons.

Label & Catalog #	A-Side/B-Side	Year	VG	NM
Sure 105	Talk To Audrey / Ding Dong, School Is Out	1960	6.00	30.00

HOLLYWOOD REBELS, THE

Label & Catalog #	A-Side/B-Side	Year	VG	NM
Impact 18	Rebel Stomp / Thriller	1962	2.00	10.00

HOLLYWOOD SUNSETS BAND, THE

Label & Catalog #		A-Side/B-Side	Year	VG	NM
Rainbow 1001	(EP)	Teenage World Of Music	1964	7.00	35.00

HOLLYWOOD TORNADOES, THE: Refer to THE TORNADOES

HOLT, DAVEY, & THE HUBCAPS

Label & Catalog #	A-Side/B-Side	Year	VG	NM
United Artists 110	Pittery Pat / You Move Me	1958	4.00	20.00

HOMBRES, THE

Label & Catalog #	A-Side/B-Side	Year	VG	NM
Verve/Forecast 5058	Let It All Hang Out / Go Girl, Go	1967	1.25	6.00
Verve/Forecast 5058	Let It Out (Let It All Hang Out) / Go Girl, Go	1967	1.00	5.00
Verve/Forecast 5076	It's A Gas / Am I High?	1967	.80	4.00
Verve/Forecast 5083	The Prodigal / Mau Mau Mau	1968	.80	4.00
Verve/Forecast 5093	Take My Overwhelming Love / Pumpkin Man	1968	.80	4.00
Sun 1104	If This Ain't Love You, Baby / You Made Me What I Am	1969	1.00	5.00

Label & Catalog #		A-Side/B-Side	Year	VG	NM
HOMETOWNERS, THE					
Fraternity 838		Ding Dong / I Wanna Go Home	1959	3.00	15.00
HONDAS, THE					
Eden 4		Send It / Twelve Feet High	1962	8.00	40.00
HONDELLS, THE					

The Hondells were essentially a studio creation. Mercury tracks produced by Gary Usher—72324, 72366, 72563, 72605 and 72626—feature Chuck Girard as lead singer.

Mercury 72324		Little Honda / Hot Rod High (Black label)	1964	3.00	15.00
Mercury 72324		Little Honda / Hot Rod High (Maroon label)	1964	2.00	10.00
Mercury 72366		My Buddy Seat / You're Gonna Ride With Me (Black label)	1964	6.00	30.00
Mercury 72366		My Buddy Seat / You're Gonna Ride With Me (Maroon label)	1964	2.00	10.00
Mercury 72366	(PS)	My Buddy Seat / You're Gonna Ride With Me ('My Buddy Seat" was produced by Brian Wilson.)	1964	2.00	10.00
Mercury 72405		Little Sidewalk Surfer Girl / Come On (Black label)	1965	5.00	25.00
Mercury 72405		Little Sidewalk Surfer Girl / Come On (Maroon label)	1965	3.00	15.00
Mercury 72443		Sea Of Love / Do As I Say (Black label)	1965	4.00	20.00
Mercury 72443		Sea Of Love / Do As I Say (Maroon label)	1965	2.00	10.00
Mercury 72479		You Meet The Nicest People On A Honda / Sea Cruise (Black label)	1965	4.00	20.00
Mercury 72479		You Meet The Nicest People On A Honda / Sea Cruise (Maroon label)	1965	2.00	10.00
Mercury 72479	(PS)	You Meet The Nicest People On A Honda / Sea Cruise	1965	4.00	20.00
Mercury 72523		Follow Your Heart / Endless Sleep (Black label)	1966	5.00	25.00
Mercury 72523		Follow Your Heart / Endless Sleep (Maroon label)	1966	3.00	15.00
Mercury 72563		Younger Girl / All-American Girl	1966	2.00	10.00
Mercury 72605		Kissin' My Life Away / A Country Love	1967	2.00	10.00
Mercury 72626		Sheryl's Goin' Home / Show Me, Girl	1967	2.00	10.00
Columbia 44361	(DJ)	Just One More Chance / Yes To You	1967	1.00	5.00
Columbia 44361		Just One More Chance / Yes To You	1967	2.00	10.00
Columbia 44557	(DJ)	Atlanta Georgia Stray / Another Woman	1968	1.00	5.00
Columbia 44557		Atlanta Georgia Stray / Another Woman (Columbia sides were produced by Gary Usher.)	1968	2.00	10.00
Amos 131		Shine On Ruby Mountain / Follow The Bouncing Ball	1969	2.00	10.00
Amos 150		Shine On Ruby Mountain / Legend Of Frankie And Johnny	1970	2.00	10.00
HONEY BEES, THE					

Contrary to previous reports, The Honeybees are not The Honeys.

Vee Jay 611		One Girl, One Boy / No Guy	1964	5.00	25.00
HONEYBEES, THE					

The Honeybees feature Carole King.

Fontana 1939		One Wonderful Night / She Don't Deserve You	1964	4.00	20.00
Smash 1939		One Wonderful Night / She Don't Deserve You	1964	3.00	15.00
Wand 1141		Let's Get Back Together / Never In A Million Years	1966	3.00	15.00
HONEYBROOKS, THE					
Wasp 129		Less Of Me / Tacoma	196?	1.00	5.00
HONEYCOMBS, THE					
Interphon 7707		Have I The Right? / Please Don't Pretend Again	1964	1.20	6.00
Interphon 7713		I Can't Stop / I'll Cry Tomorrow	1964	1.20	6.00
Interphon 7713	(PS)	I Can't Stop / I'll Cry Tomorrow	1964	3.00	15.00
Interphon 7716		That's The Way / Color Slide	1964	1.20	6.00
Interphon 7716	(PS)	That's The Way / Color Slide	1964	3.00	15.00
Warner Bros. 5634		I'll See You Tomorrow / Something Better Beginning	1965	1.00	5.00
Warner Bros. 5655		I Can't Get Through To You / That's The Way	1965	1.00	5.00
Warner Bros. 5803		How Will I Know? / Who Is Sylvia?	1966	1.00	5.00
HONEYCONES, THE					
Ember 1033		Betty Moretti / Cool It, Baby	1958	2.00	10.00
Ember 1036		Vision Of You / Op	1958	2.00	10.00
Ember 1042		Gee Whiz / Rockin' In The Knees	1959	2.00	10.00
Ember 1049		Tell Me, Baby / Your face	1959	2.00	10.00
HONEYCUTT, GLENN					
Sun 264		I'll Be Around / I'll Wait Forever	1957	4.00	20.00
HONEYS, THE					

All tracks produced by Brian Wilson. The Honeys—Ginger Blake, Diane Rovell and Marilyn Rovell—also recorded as Ginger; Ginger & The Snaps; and Spring. They also recorded with Annette; Glen Campbell; Duane Eddy; Paul Petersen; Sharon Marie; The Surfaris; and Gary Usher.

Capitol 4952		Shoot The Curl / Surfin' Down The Swanee River	1963	20.00	100.00
	(PS)	Shoot The Curl / Surfin' Down The Swanee River	1963	150.00	500.00
Capitol 5034		Pray For Surf / Hide, Go Seek	1963	35.00	175.00

While the girls who sang with the Beach Boys are best known for their releases on Capitol, it is their sole Warner Bros. single that is the rarest and most sought after, especially the almost impossible-to-find stock copy (unfortunately, not pictured here).

Label & Catalog #		A-Side/B-Side	Year	VG	NM
Capitol 5093		The One You Can't Have / From Jimmy With Tears	1963	35.00	175.00
Warner Bros. 5430	(DJ)	He's A Doll / The Love Of A Boy And A Girl	1964	30.00	150.00
Warner Bros. 5430		He's A Doll / The Love Of A Boy And A Girl	1964	———	———
		(Rare. Estimated near mint value $250-500.)			
Capitol P-2454	(DJ)	Tonight You Belong To Me / Goodnight, My Love	1969	8.00	40.00
Capitol 2454		Tonight You Belong To Me / Goodnight, My Love	1969	10.00	50.00

HONG KONG WHITE SOX, THE
| TransWorld 6906 | | Cholley-Oop / He'd Better Go | 1960 | 2.00 | 10.00 |

HONG KONGS, THE
| Counsel 050 | | Surfin' On The China Sea / Popeye | 1963 | 8.00 | 40.00 |
| Melody Mill 303 | | Surfin' On The China Sea / Popeye | 1963 | 7.00 | 35.00 |

HONOR SOCIETY, THE
The Honor Society is a pseudonym for The Happenings.
| Jubilee 5703 | | Sweet September / Condition Red | 1969 | 2.00 | 10.00 |

HONORABLES, THE
| Honor 100 | | Castle In The Sky / | 195? | 15.00 | 75.00 |

HOOK
Uni 55057		Plug Your Head In / Son Of Fantasy	1968	1.00	5.00
Uni 55077		Homes / Love Theme In E	1968	1.00	5.00
Uni 551459		In The Beginning / Show You The Way	1969	1.00	5.00

HOPE, DEE D.
| Jolum 2501 | | California Surfer / A Boy Of My Own | 1963 | 8.00 | 40.00 |

HOPEFUL, THE
| Mercury 72637 | | 6 O' Clock News-Silent Night / 6 O' Clock News-America The Beautiful | 1966 | 1.00 | 5.00 |

HOPKIN, MARY
Apple 1801		Those Were The Days / Turn, Turn, Turn	1968	1.20	6.00
Americom 238		Those Were The Days / Turn, Turn, Turn (4" flexidisc)	1968	125.00	500.00
Apple 1806		Goodbye / Sparrow	1969	1.20	6.00
Apple 1806	(PS)	Goodbye / Sparrow	1969	2.00	10.00
Apple 1816		Temma Harbour / Lont Ano Dagli Ochli	1970	1.20	6.00
Apple 1816	(PS)	Temma Harbour / Lont Ano Dagli Ochli	1970	1.50	8.00
Apple 1823		Que Sera Sera / Fields Of Etienne	1970	1.20	6.00
Apple 1825		Think About Your Children / Heritage	1970	1.20	6.00
Apple 1825	(PS)	Think About Your Children / Heritage	1970	2.00	10.00
Apple 1843		Water, Paper And Clay / Streets Of London	1971	1.20	6.00
Apple 1855		Knock, Knock, Who's There? / International	1972	1.20	6.00
RCA Victor PB-10694		If You Love Me / Tell Me Now	1976	1.00	3.00

HORIZONS, THE
| Regina 1321 | | Hey Now, Baby / Strange On Strange | 1964 | 2.00 | 10.00 |

HORIZONS, THE: *Refer to* **SUNNY & THE HORIZONS**

HORN, HAROLD
| Jerden 750 | | Miss Ann / Dew B Dewey | 196? | 1.00 | 5.00 |

HORNETS, THE
| Emerald 501 | | Runt / Breakfast In Bed | 196? | 6.00 | 30.00 |

HORNETS, THE
| Liberty 55688 | | On The Track / Motorcycles U.S.A. | 1964 | 2.00 | 10.00 |

HORSES
Horses features Don Johnson, later of Miami VVice.
| White Whale 301 | | Class Of '69 / Country Boy | 1969 | 3.00 | 15.00 |
| White Whale 320 | | Freight Train / | 1969 | 3.00 | 15.00 |

HORTON, JAMIE
Joy 234		My Little Marine / Missin'	1960	2.00	10.00
Joy 241		Robot Man / We're Through, We're Finished	1960	2.00	10.00
Joy 258		They're Playing Our Song / Going, Going, Gone	1961	2.00	10.00

HORTON, JAY (WITH THE BOBBY FULLER FOUR)
| Mustang 3010 | | I Trip On You / | 1965 | 6.00 | 30.00 |
| Mustang 3021 | | It's Love / Come What May | 1966 | 6.00 | 30.00 |

HOSEA, DON
| Sun 368 | | Since I Met You / U Huh Unh | 1961 | 2.00 | 10.00 |

Label & Catalog #	A-Side/B-Side	Year	VG	NM
HOSS, CHARLEY, & THE PONIES				
Columbia 41855	Madison Twist / Raunchy Twist	1960	1.60	8.00
HOT CHOCOLATE BAND, THE				
Apple 1812	Give Peace A Chance / Living Without Tomorrow	1969	2.00	10.00
HOT PEPPERS, THE				
Sea Horn 501	New Orleans Surf / Surfin' With The Monkey	1963	1.00	5.00
HOT ROCKS, THE: *Refer to* JOHNNY CARROLL				
HOT RODS, THE: *Refer to* DOUG DONNELL				
HOT SHOT LOVE				
Sun 196	Wolf Call Boogie / Harmonica Jam	1954	——	——
	(Rare. Estimated near mint value $2,000-3,000.)			
HOT TAMALES, THE				
Alpine 68	Mexican Twist / The Pony	1960	2.00	10.00
HOT-TODDYS, THE				
The Hot-Toddys later recorded as The Buffalo Rebels; The Rebels; and The Rockin' Rebels.				
Shan-Todd 0056	Rockin' Crickets / Shakin' And Stompin'	1959	6.00	30.00
Corsican 0056	Rockin' Crickets / Shakin' And Stompin'	1959	5.00	25.00
Strand 25011	Hoe-Down / Nan-Je-Di	1959	3.00	15.00
HOT TUNA				
Hot Tuna features Jack Cassady and Jorma Kaukonen of Jefferson Airplane.				
Grunt 0502	Water Song / Keep On Truckin'	1971	.80	4.00
Grunt 0502	(PS) Water Song / Keep On Truckin'	1971	2.00	10.00
Grunt 0528	Been So Long / Candy Man	1971	.80	4.00
Grunt 10443	Hot Jelly Roll Blues / Surface Tension	1975	.60	3.00
Grunt 10776	It's So Easy / I Can't Be Satisfied	1976	.60	3.00
HOTLEGS				
Hotlegs is Lol Creme, Kevin Godley, Graham Gouldman and Eric Stewart, who later recorded as 10CC.				
Capitol 3043	Run, Baby, Run / How Many Times?	1970	2.00	10.00
Capitol 2886	Neanderthal Man /			
	You Didn't Like It Because You Didn't Think Of It	1970	1.00	5.00
HOUR GLASS, THE				
The Hour Glass features Duane and Gregg Allman.				
Liberty 56002	Nothing But Tears / Heartbeat	1967	1.20	6.00
Liberty 56002	(PS) Nothing But Tears / Heartbeat	1967	3.00	15.00
Liberty 56029	Power Of Love / I Still Want Your Love	1968	1.20	6.00
Liberty 56053	Changing Of The Guard / D-I-V-O-R-C-E	1968	1.20	6.00
Liberty 56091	I've Been Trying / Silently	1969	1.20	6.00
HOUSTON, DAVID				
Sun 403	Sherry's Lips / Miss Brown	1966	2.00	10.00
HOWARD, DANNY				
Birthstone 1035	Two Lonely Weeks / Dating An Angel	196?	2.00	10.00
Birthstone 1035	(PS) Two Lonely Weeks / Dating An Angel	196?	2.00	10.00
HUBBELL, FRANK, & HIS HUBB-CAPS				
Topix 6005	Broken Date / Broken Date, Part 2	1958	6.00	30.00
HUBBELS, THE				
Audio Fidelity 150	Hippy Dippy Funky Monkey Double Bubble Sitar Man /			
	City Woman	1969	1.00	5.00
HUBCAPS, THE				
The Hubcaps feature Ernie Maresca.				
Laurie 3219	Hot Rod City / Hot Rod City	1965	3.00	15.00
HUDDLE, JACK				
Petsy 207	Starlight / Believe Me	1959	100.00	400.00
Kapp 207	Starlight / Believe Me	1959	30.00	150.00
HUGHES, LINDA				
Panorama 43	Does She Or Doesn't She / Keep A Messin' With My Guy	1966	1.00	5.00
Panorama 46	The Cheat / I Been Wishin'	196?	1.00	5.00
Jerden 782	What Am I Livin' For? / Look Up My History	1966	1.00	5.00
Jerden 920	The Man Who Could Be So Good To Me /			
	Funny How Time Slips Away	1970	.60	3.00
Great Northwest 714	Elvis Won't Be Here For Christmas /			
	Here Comes That Hurt Again	1977	.60	3.00

Label & Catalog #		A-Side/B-Side	Year	VG	NM
HUGHES, LYNNE Mercury 73059		Freeway Gypsy / Never Stop A Dream	1970	1.00	5.00
HUGHES, MARVIN Capitol 4950		Blast Off / Nashville Bossa Nova	1963	1.20	6.00
HUGHLEY, GEORGE Gaye 004		Do The Beatle / My Love Is True	1964	2.00	10.00
HUHN, BILLY, & THE CATALINAS Lesley 1923		Baltimore / Freshman Queen	196?	6.00	30.00
HULLABALOOS, THE Roulette 4587		I'm Gonna Love You, Too / Party Doll	1964	2.00	10.00
Roulette 4587	(PS)	I'm Gonna Love You, Too / Party Doll	1964	4.00	20.00
Roulette 4593		Did You Ever? / Beware	1965	2.00	10.00
Roulette 4593	(PS)	Did You Ever? / Beware	1965	4.00	20.00
Roulette 4612		Learning The Game / Don't Stop	1965	2.00	10.00
Roulette 4612	(PS)	Learning The Game / Don't Stop	1965	4.00	20.00
Roulette 4662		I Won't Turn Away Now / My Heart Keeps Telling Me	1965	2.00	10.00
Roulette 4662	(PS)	I Won't Turn Away Now / My Heart Keeps Telling Me	1965	4.00	20.00
HUMAN BEINGS, THE Impact 1022		I Can't Tell / Yessir, That's My Baby	1965	2.00	10.00
Warner Bros. 5622		Because I Love Her / Ain't That Lovin' You, Baby	1965	2.00	10.00
HUMAN BEINZ, THE Gateway 828		Gloria / The Times They Are A-Changin'	1967	3.00	15.00
Gateway 838		You Can't Make Me Cry / Pied Piper	1967	3.00	15.00
Capitol 5990		Nobody But Me / Sueno	1967	1.60	8.00
Capitol 2119		Turn On Your Lovelight / It's Fun To Be Clean	1968	1.60	8.00
Capitol 2119	(PS)	Turn On Your Lovelight / It's Fun To Be Clean	1968	3.00	15.00
Capitol 2198		Every Time Woman/ The Face	1968	1.60	8.00
Capitol 2431		This Little Girl Of Mine / I've Got To Keep On Pushin'	1969	1.60	8.00
HUMAN EXPRESSION, THE Accent 1214		Every Night / Love At A Psychedelic Velocity	1967	4.00	20.00
HUMAN INSTINCT, THE Time 503		Pink Dawn / Renaissance Fair	1967	3.00	15.00
HUMBLE PIE *Humble Pie features Peter Frampton and Steve Marriott. Refer to The Small Faces.*					
Immediate 001		Natural Born Woman / I'll Go Alone	1969	.80	4.00
A&M 1282		I Don't Need No Doctor / A Song For Jenny	1971	.60	3.00
A&M 1282	(PS)	I Don't Need No Doctor / A Song For Jenny	1971	1.20	6.00
A&M 1349		Hot 'N' Nasty / You're So Good For Me	1972	.60	3.00
A&M 1349	(PS)	Hot 'N' Nasty / You're So Good For Me	1972	1.20	6.00
A&M 1366		Thirty Days In The Hole / Sweet Peace And Time	1972	.50	2.50
A&M 1406	(PS)	Black Coffee / Say No More *(Promo)*	1972	2.00	10.00
A&M 1406		Black Coffee / Say No More	1972	.50	2.50
A&M 1440		Get Down To It / Honky Tonk Woman	1973	.50	2.50
A&M 1530		Ninety-Nine Pounds / Rally With Ali	1974	.50	2.50
A&M 1711		Rock And Roll Music / Road Hog	1975	.50	2.50
HUMBLEBUMS, THE United Artists 50711		All The Best People Do / Cruisin'	1971	1.00	5.00
HUMDINGERS, THE Dale 106		Necklace Of Teardrops / The Clock In Lovers Lane	1957	5.00	25.00
HUMMINGBIRDS, THE Jerden 727		La Dee Dah / Fern	1964	1.00	5.00
Jerden 740		Lotta Lovin' / Bluebirds Over The Mountain	1964	1.00	5.00
HUNG JURY, THE Colgems 1010		Buses / Let The Good Times In	1967	2.00	10.00
HUNGER! Public 1001		Colors / Mind Machine	196?	3.00	15.00
Public 101/2		She Let Him Continue / Mind Machine	196?	3.00	15.00
HUNGRY TIGER White Whale 313		Fee Fi Fo Fum / Fum Fo Fi Fee	1969	2.00	10.00
HUNT, LANNY, & THE THEMES Star		Over Easy /	1965	2.00	10.00
Panorama 42		Stay / Suzie Q	1966	2.00	10.00

Label & Catalog #	A-Side/B-Side		Year	VG	NM
HUNT SISTERS & MARK					
Mark is Roy Hall.					
Fortune 210	Elvis Is Rocking Again / Teardrops		1960	10.00	50.00
HUNTER, CHRISTINE					
Roulette 4589	Santa Bring Me Ringo / Where Were You, Daddy?		1964	2.00	10.00
HUNTER, ROBERT					
Robert Hunter is the lyricist for The Grateful Dead. Refer to Jerry Garcia.					
Round 4505	It Must Have Been The Roses / Rum Runners		1974	1.60	8.00
HUNTER, ROBERT / PHIL LESH & NED LAGIN					
Round	Sample For Dead Heads *(With postcard)*		1974	4.00	20.00
HUNTER, TAB					
Dot 15533	Young Love / Red Sails In The Sunset		1956	3.00	15.00
Dot 15548	Ninety-Nine Ways / Don't Get Around Much Anymore		1957	3.00	15.00
Dot 15657	I'm Alone Because I Love You / Don't Let It Get Around		1957	3.00	15.00
Dot 16036	Young Love / 99 Ways		1957	3.00	15.00
Warner Bros. 5008	Jealous Heart / Lonesome Road		1958	2.00	10.00
Warner Bros. 5032	I'll Be With You In Apple Blossom Time / My Only Love		1959	2.00	10.00
Warner Bros. 5032	I'll Be With You In Apple Blossom Time / My Only Love	(S)	1959	3.00	15.00
Warner Bros. 5051	There's No Fool Like A Young Fool / I'll Never Smile Again		1959	2.00	10.00
Warner Bros. 5051	There's No Fool Like A Young Fool / I'll Never Smile Again	(S)	1959	3.00	15.00
Warner Bros. 5093	Our Love / Waitin' For Fall		1960	2.00	10.00
Warner Bros. 5093	Our Love / Waitin' For Fall	(PS)	1960	3.00	15.00
HUNTINGTONS, THE					
Wasp 106	You Better Mend Your Ways / I Told The World		196?	2.00	10.00
HUSAK, GEORGE W.					
Wind Jammer-3 1	I'm Surfing /		196?	7.00	35.00
HUSTLERS, THE					
House of Note 69/70	Hangin' Five / Barefoot Adventure		1964	7.00	35.00
Downey 118	Inertia / Eight Ball		1964	4.00	20.00
Downey 125	Kopout / Migraine		1964	4.00	20.00
Rich 113/4	Wipe Out / Linda		1965	8.00	40.00
HUTCH, BILLY					
Time 1067	Effin-Nanny Stomp / Effin-Nanny Monkey		1963	1.50	8.00
HUTTON, DANNY					
Danny Hutton also recorded with The Enemys; Basil Swift & The Seegrams; and Three Dog Night.					
Almo 213	Why Don't You Love Me Anymore? / Home In Pasadena		1965	2.00	10.00
HBR 447	Roses And Rainbows / Monster Shindig, Part 1		1965	2.00	10.00
HBR 447	Roses And Rainbows / Monster Shindig, Part 1	(PS)	1965	4.00	20.00
HBR 453	Big Bright Eyes / Monster Shindig, Part 2		1965	2.00	10.00
MGM 13502	Funny How Love Can Be / Dreamin' Isn't Good For You		1966	1.20	6.00
MGM 13502	Funny How Love Can Be / Dreamin' Isn't Good For You	(PS)	1966	3.00	15.00
MGM 13613	Hang On To A Dream / Hit The Wall		1966	1.20	6.00
HYLAND, BRIAN					
Leader 801	Rosemary / Library Love Affair		1960	3.00	15.00
Leader 805	Itsy Bitsy Teenie Weenie Yellow Polkadot Bikini / Don't Dilly Dally, Sally		1960	3.00	15.00
Kapp 342	Itsy Bitsy Teenie Weenie Yellow Polkadot Bikini / Don't Dilly Dally, Sally		1960	2.00	10.00
Kapp 342	Itsy Bitsy Teenie Weenie Yellow Polkadot Bikini / Don't Dilly Dally, Sally	(PS)	1960	3.00	15.00
Kapp 352	(The Clickety Clack Song) Four Little Heels / That's How Much		1960	1.60	8.00
Kapp 352	(The Clickety Clack Song) Four Little Heels / That's How Much	(PS)	1960	3.00	15.00
Kapp 363	I Gotta Go / Lopsided, Over Loaded		1960	1.60	8.00
Kapp 363	I Gotta Go / Lopsided, Over Loaded	(PS)	1960	3.00	15.00
Kapp 401	Lipstick On Your Lips / When Will I Know?		1961	1.60	8.00
ABC-Paramount 10236	Let Me Belong To You / Let It Die		1961	1.00	5.00
ABC-Paramount 10262	I'll Never Stop Wanting You / The Night I Cried		1961	1.00	5.00
ABC-Paramount 10262	I'll Never Stop Wanting You / The Night I Cried	(PS)	1961	3.00	15.00
ABC-Paramount 10294	Ginny Come Lately / I Should Be Getting Better		1962	1.25	6.00
ABC-Paramount 10294	Ginny Come Lately / I Should Be Getting Better	(PS)	1962	3.00	15.00
ABC-Paramount 10336	Sealed With A Kiss / Summer Job		1962	1.00	5.00
ABC-Paramount 10336	Sealed With A Kiss / Summer Job	(PS)	1962	3.00	15.00
ABC-Paramount 10359	Warmed Over Kisses / Walk A Lonely Mile		1962	1.00	5.00
ABC-Paramount 10359	Warmed Over Kisses / Walk A Lonely Mile	(PS)	1962	3.00	15.00
ABC-Paramount 10374	I May Not Live To See Tomorrow / It Ain't That Way		1962	1.00	5.00
ABC-Paramount 10374	I May Not Live To See Tomorrow / It Ain't That Way	(PS)	1962	3.00	15.00

Label & Catalog #		A-Side/B-Side	Year	VG	NM
ABC-Paramount 10400		If Mary's There / Remember Me	1963	1.00	5.00
ABC-Paramount 10400	(PS)	If Mary's There / Remember Me	1963	3.00	15.00
ABC-Paramount 10427		Somewhere In The Night / I Wish Today Was Yesterday	1963	1.00	5.00
ABC-Paramount 10452		I'm Afraid To Go Home / Save Your Heart For Me	1963	1.00	5.00
ABC-Paramount 10494		Nothing Matters But You / Let Us Make Our Own Mistakes	1963	1.00	5.00
ABC-Paramount 10549		Out Of Sight, Out Of Mind / Act Naturally	1964	1.00	5.00
Philips 40179		Here's To Our Love / Two Kinds Of Girls	1963	.80	4.00
Philips 40179	(PS)	Here's To Our Love / Two Kinds Of Girls	1963	1.50	8.00
Philips 40203		Devoted To You / Pledging My Love	1963	.80	4.00
Philips 40203	(PS)	Devoted To You / Pledging My Love	1963	1.50	8.00
Philips 40221		Now I Belong To You / One Step Forward, Two Steps Back	1964	.80	4.00
Philips 40263		He Don't Understand You / Love Will Find A Way	1964	.80	4.00
Philips 40263	(PS)	He Don't Understand You / Love Will Find A Way	1964	1.50	8.00
Philips 40306		Stay Away From Her / I Can't Keep A Secret	1965	.80	4.00
Philips 40354		3,000 Miles / Sometimes They Do, Sometimes They Don't	1966	.80	4.00
Philips 40377		The Joker Went Wild / I Can Hear The Rain	1966	.80	4.00
Philips 40405		Run, Run, Look And See / Why Did You Do It?	1966	.80	4.00
Philips 40424		Hung Up In Your Eyes / Why Mine?	1966	.80	4.00
Philips 40424	(PS)	Hung Up In Your Eyes / Why Mine?	1966	1.25	6.00
Philips 40444		Holiday For Clowns / Yesterday I Had A Girl	1967	.60	3.00
Philips 40472		Get The Message / Kinda Groovy	1967	.60	3.00
Dot 17050		Apologize / Words On Paper	1968	.60	3.00
Dot 17176		Tragedy / You'd Better Stop And Think It Over	1969	.60	3.00
Dot 17222		A Million To One / It Could All Begin Again	1969	.60	3.00
Dot 17258		Stay And Love Me All Summer / Rainy April Morning	1969	.60	3.00
Uni 55240		Gypsy Woman / You And Me #2	1970	.60	3.00
Uni 55272		Lonely Teardrops / Lorraine	1970	.60	3.00
Uni 55287		No Place To Run / So Long, Marianne	1971	.60	3.00
Uni 55306		Out Of The Blue / Oh, You Came Back	1971	.60	3.00
Uni 55323		With My Eyes Wide Open / I Love Every Little Thing About You	1972	.60	3.00
Uni 55334		Only Wanna Make You Happy / When You're Lovin' Me	1972	.60	3.00

HYPO DERMICS, THE

Titanic 5002		Blues Till News / Operation Twisted	1962	2.00	10.00

HYSTERICS, THE

Ra-O 103		You've Got Me All Wrong / St. James Infirmary	196?	3.00	15.00

I.

I, JAN, I: *Refer to* JAN

I. V. LEAGUERS, THE
Porter 1004	Ring Chimes / The Story	1957	7.00	35.00
Dot 15677	Ring Chimes / The Story	1957	4.00	20.00
Nau-Voo 803	Told By The Stars / Jim Jam	1959	100.00	400.00

IAN, JANIS
Verve VK-5027	Society's Child / Letter To Jon	1966	1.00	5.00
Verve/Forecast 5027	Society's Child / Letter To Jon	1966	.60	3.00
Verve/Forecast 5041	I'll Give You A Stone If You'll Throw It / Younger Generation Blues	1967	.60	3.00
Verve/Forecast 5059	Friends Again / Lady Of The Night	1968	.60	3.00
Verve/Forecast 5072	Insanity Comes Quietly To The Structured Mind / Sunflakes Fall, Snowrays Call	1968	.60	3.00
Verve/Forecast 5079	Song For All The Seasons Of Your Mind / Lonely One	1968	.80	4.00
Verve/Forecast 5099	Everybody Knows / Janey's Blues	1968	.60	3.00
Capitol 3107	He's A Rainbow / Here In Spain	1971	.60	3.00
Columbia 10154	At Seventeen / Stars	1975	.40	2.00
Columbia 10331	I Would Like To Dance / Goodbye To Morning	1976	.40	2.00
Columbia 10297	Boy, I Really Tied One On / Aftertones	1976	.40	2.00
Columbia 10228	In The Winter / Thank Yous	1976	.40	2.00
Columbia 10391	Roses / Love Is Blind	1976	.40	2.00
Columbia 10484	Miracle Row / Take It To The Sky	1977	.40	2.00
Columbia 10526	I Want To Make You Love Me / Candlelight	1977	.40	2.00
Columbia 10813	That Grand Illusion / Jopper Painting	1978	.40	2.00
Columbia 10864	The Bridge / Do You Wanna Dance?	1978	.40	2.00
Columbia 10979	Here Comes The Night / Tonight Will Last Forever	1979	.40	2.00
Columbia 11111	Fly Too High / Night Rains	1979	.40	2.00

IAN & THE ZODIACS
Philips 40244		Cryin' Game / Lovin' Wreck	1964	1.20	6.00
Philips 40277		Message To Martha / Good Morning, Little Schoolgirl	1965	1.20	6.00
Philips 40291		So Much In Love With You / This Empty Space	1965	1.20	6.00
Philips 40291	(PS)	So Much In Love With You / This Empty Space	1965	3.00	15.00
Philips 40343		Why Can't It Be Me? / Leave It To Me	1966	1.20	6.00
Philips 40369		Where Were You? / No Money, No Honey	1966	1.20	6.00
		—Extended Play Albums—			
Philips 807	(33)	Ian And The Zodiacs (*Jukebox EP*)	1967	6.00	30.00

ICE CREAM
Capitol 2321	Chewing Gum Kid / Epitaph To Marie	1968	1.00	5.00

ICEMEN, THE
ABC 11038	How Can I Get Over A Fox Like You? / Loogaboo	1968	1.00	5.00

ICHABOD & THE CRANES
Coral 62401	The Turtle / Supermarket Of Love	1964	3.00	15.00

ID
RCA Victor 47-9136	Short Circuit / Boil The Kettle, Mother	1967	3.00	15.00
RCA Victor 47-9195	Wild Times / The Rake	1967	3.00	15.00

IDAHO, KEN
Fame 506	School Of Love / From Loving You	1959	2.00	10.00

IDEALS, THE
Decca 30720	My Girl / Annie Was A Stroller	1958	5.00	25.00
Decca 30800	Ivy League Lover / Don't Be A Baby, Baby	1959	3.00	15.00
Stars Of Hollywood 1001	Please, Jan / Always Yours	1959	7.00	35.00
Checker 920	Knee Socks / Mary Lamb	1959	3.00	15.00
Checker 979	Knee Socks / Mary Lamb	1961	2.00	10.00
Paso 6401	Together /	1961	6.00	30.00
Paso 6402	Magic / Teens	1961	7.00	35.00
Cortland 110	Don Juan / The Gorilla	1963	2.00	10.00
Cortland 115	Mo Gorilla / Feeling Of A Kiss	1963	2.00	10.00
St. Lawrence 1020	I Got Lucky / Tell Her I Apologize	1966	2.00	10.00

Label & Catalog #	A-Side/B-Side	Year	VG	NM
IDES OF MARCH, THE [THE I'DES OF MARCH]				
Parrot 304	You Wouldn't Listen / I'll Keep Searching	1966	2.00	10.00
	(Parrot 304 credits the groups as The I'des Of March.)			
Parrot 310	Roller Coaster / Things Aren't Always What They Seem	1966	2.00	10.00
Parrot 312	Sha-La-La-La-La-La-Lee / You Need Love	1966	2.00	10.00
Parrot 321	Give Your Mind Wings / My Foolish Pride	1967	2.00	10.00
Parrot 326	Hole In My Soul / Girls Don't Grow On Trees	1967	2.00	10.00
Warner Bros. 7334	One Woman Man / High On A Hillside	1969	.60	3.00
Warner Bros. 7378	Vehicle / Lead Me Home Gently	1970	.60	3.00
Warner Bros. 7403	Superman / Home	1970	.40	2.00
Warner Bros. 7426	Melody / The Sky Is Falling	1970	.40	2.00
Warner Bros. 7466	L. A. Goodbye / Mrs. Grayson's Farm	1971	.40	2.00
Warner Bros. 7507	Friends Of Feeling / Tie-Dye Princess	1971	.40	2.00
Warner Bros. 7526	Giddy-Up, Ride Me / Freedom Sweet	1971	.40	2.00
RCA Victor 74-0052	Heavy On The Country / Hot Water	197?	.40	2.00
RCA Victor 74-0850	Mother America / Landlady	197?	.40	2.00
IDIOTS & CO., THE [THE IDIOTS]				
Riverside 4505	School For Airplane Pirates / The Sportscaster	1961	1.20	6.00
IDLE RACE, THE				
The Idle Race feature Jeff Lynne, later of The Electric Light Orchestra and The Traveling Wilburies.				
Liberty 55997	Here We Go Round The Lemon Tree / My Father's Son	1967	3.00	15.00
IDLERS, THE				
Audio Spectrum 68	The Chase / Ja-Da	1964	2.00	10.00
IDOLS, THE				
E-Z 1	Jeannine / Can't Tag Along	195?	6.00	30.00
IDYLLS, THE				
Spinning 6012	Annette / Love Me Again	1960	6.00	30.00
IF				
Capitol 2090	Raise The Level Of Your Conscious Mind / What Did I Say About The Box, Jack?	1970	.80	4.00
Capitol 2909	Promised Land / I'm Reaching Out On All Sides	1970	.80	4.00
Capitol 3068	Your City Is Falling / Woman, Can't You See?	1971	.80	4.00
Capitol 3932	I Believe In Rock And Roll / Still Alive	1973	.80	4.00
IGLESIAS, JULIO, & THE BEACH BOYS				
Columbia 38-04726 (DJ)	Air That I Breathe / Air That I Breathe	1984	1.00	5.00
Columbia 38-04726 (PS)	Air That I Breathe (Promo picture sleeve)	1984	1.00	5.00
	(Brian Wilson arrangements with vocals by The Beach Boys. Stock copies of Columbia 04725 may not exist)			
IGOR & THE MANICS				
Dolton 29	The Bog Green / Gung Ho	1960	2.00	10.00
IGUANAS, THE				
Dunhill 4004	Don't Come Running To Me / This Is What I Was Made For	1965	1.00	5.00
Dunhill 4056	Diana / This Is What I Was Made For	1966	1.00	5.00
Dunhill 3001	Michelle / Meet Me Tonight, Little Girl	1966	1.00	5.00
ILFORD SUBWAY, THE				
Equinox 70001	New Song / Third Prophecy	1967	2.00	10.00
ILL WIND				
ABC 11107	In My Dark World / Walkin' And Singin'	1968	1.00	5.00
ILL WINDS, THE				
The Ill Winds is a pseudonym for The Chantays.				
Reprise 423	So Be On Your Way (I Won't Cry) / Fear Of The Rain	1965	2.00	10.00
Reprise 492	I Idolize You / A Letter	1966	2.00	10.00
ILLINOIS SPEED PRESS, THE				
Columbia 44564	Get In The Wind / Get In The Wind (Part 2)	1968	.80	4.00
Columbia 44564 (PS)	Get In The Wind / Get In The Wind (Part 2)	1968	2.00	10.00
Columbia 45166	Sadly Out Of Place / Country Dumplin'	1970	.80	4.00
ILLUSION, THE				
Steed 718	Did You See Her Eyes? / Falling In Love	1969	.80	4.00
Steed 721	How Does It Feel? / Once In A Lifetime	1969	.80	4.00
Steed 722	Together / Don't Push It	1969	.80	4.00
Steed 726	Let's Make Each Other Happy / Beside You	1970	.80	4.00
Steed 732	Wait A Minute / Collection	1971	.80	4.00

Label & Catalog #	A-Side/B-Side	Year	VG	NM
ILLUSIONS, THE				
Coral 62173	The Letter / Henry And Henrietta	1960	8.00	40.00
ILLUSIONS, THE				
Ember 1071	Can't We Fall In Love? / How High Is The Mountain?	1961	6.00	30.00
ILLUSIONS, THE				
Malt 104	Hey, Boy / Lonely Soldier	1962	7.00	35.00
Sheraton 104	Hey, Boy / Lonely Soldier	1962	3.00	15.00
ILLUSIONS, THE				
Laurie 3245	In The Beginning / Maybe	1964	5.00	25.00
ILLUSIONS, THE				
Round 1018	Jezebel / Nightmare	1963	10.00	50.00
VP 201	Ooh Pah Doo / (B-side by Marlow Stewart)	1964	7.00	35.00
ILLUSIONS, THE				
Columbia 43700	I Know / Take My Heart	1966	2.00	10.00
ILLUSIONS, THE				
Kape 1001	The Closer You Are / For Sentimental Reasons	196?	2.00	10.00
IMAGINATIONS, THE				
Music Makers 103	The Search Is Over / Goodnight Baby	1961	3.00	15.00
Music Makers 108	Guardian Angel / Hey You	1961	3.00	15.00
Ballad 500	Mama's Little Baby / Wait A Little Longer, Son	1962	3.00	15.00
Bo Marc 301	Mama's Little Baby / Wait A Little Longer, Son	1962	2.00	10.00
IMAGINATIONS, THE				
The Imaginations feature Steve Barri and Phil Sloan.				
Dunhill 4092	Summer In New York / I Love You When You're Mad	1967	2.00	10.00
IMPACS, THE				
King 5851	Jo-Ann / Two Strangers	1964	3.00	15.00
King 5851	Shimmy Shimmy / Zot	1964	2.00	10.00
King 5891	She Didn't Even Say Hello / Kool It	1964	2.00	10.00
King 5910	Don't Cry, Baby / Ain't That The Way Life Is	1964	2.00	10.00
King 5965	Your Mama Put The Hurt On Me / Cape Kennedy, Florida	1965	2.00	10.00
IMPACTS, THE				
Watts 5599	Now Is The Time / Soup	1959	15.00	75.00
RCA Victor 47-7583	Croc-O-Doll / Bobby Sox Squaw	1959	3.00	15.00
RCA Victor 47-7609	They Say / Canadian Sunset	1959	7.00	35.00
Carlton 548	Darling, Now You're Mine / Help Me, Somebody	1961	7.00	35.00
Watts 5600	They Say / Canadian Sunset	197?	Bootleg	
IMPACTS, THE				
Anderson 104	Summer / Lindae	196?	7.00	35.00
IMPACTS, THE				
Kip 1890	Burnt Valves / Chrome Reverse	196?	5.00	25.00
IMPACTS, THE				
Parkway 865	Tears In My Heart / I'm Gonna Make You Cry	1963	3.00	15.00
IMPACT EXPRESS, THE [THE IMPACTS]				
NWI 2660	Leavin' Here / A Little Bit More	1965	3.00	15.00
Lavender 2005	Don't You Dare / Green Green Fields	1967	2.00	10.00
Lavender 2006	I'm Gonna Change The World / You Get Your Kicks	1967	2.00	10.00
Lavender 2007	Don't You Dare / Sunshine Day	1968	2.00	10.00
Lavender 2008	A Little Love / Fly With Me	1968	1.60	8.00
IMPACT V				
Agar 7171	Riptide / Island Of Love	196?	7.00	35.00
IMPAKS, THE				
Express 716	Make Up Your Mind / Climb Upon Your Rockin' Chair	1962	4.00	20.00
IMPAX, THE				
Warner Bros. 5153	Baby, You're My Love / Cool Breeze	1960	3.00	15.00
IMPERIAL GENTS, THE				
Laurie 3540	Little Darlin' / The Imperial Gents Stomp	1970	2.00	10.00
IMPERIALITES, THE				
Imperial 66015	Let's Get One / Have Love, Will Travel	1964	4.00	20.00

Label & Catalog #		A-Side/B-Side	Year	VG	NM
IMPERIALS, THE					
Capitol 4924		I'm Still Dancing / Bermuda Wonderful	1963	3.00	15.00
IMPERIALS, THE					
Jerden 745		Backyard Compost / The Slip	1964	1.20	6.00
IMPERIALS, THE					
Audio 104		The Bottle Green / Crossfiring	196?	1.20	6.00
IMPOSSIBLES, THE					
Blanche 029		Chapel Bells / Little By Little	195?	50.00	200.00
IMPOSSIBLES, THE					
RMP 501		Everywhere I Go / Well, It's Alright '66 (Black label)	196?	3.00	15.00
RMP 1030		Mr. Maestro / Well, It's Alright	196?	2.00	10.00
IMPOSSIBLES, THE					
Reprise 0305		Lonely Bluebird / Paint Me A Pretty Picture	1964	2.00	10.00
IMPOSTERS, THE					
Frog Death 1		Wipe In / Tulsa	1964	5.00	25.00
IMPROPER BOSTONIANS, THE					
Minuteman 207		How Many Tears? / I Still Love You	1966	2.00	10.00
Minuteman 208		Set You Free This Time / Come To Me, My Baby	1967	2.00	10.00
Minuteman 209		Out Of My Mind / You Made Me A Giant	1967	2.00	10.00
Coral 62543		Gee, I'm Gonna Miss You / Victim Of Environment	1967	1.20	6.00
IMUS, JAY JAY, & FREDDY FORD					
Challenge 59248		I'm A Hot Rodder / The Boogaloo	1963	2.00	10.00
IN BETWEEN SETS, THE					
Rust 5125		Walkin' In The Rain / The One Who Really Loves You	1965	2.00	10.00
IN-BE-TWEENS, THE					
The In-Be-Tweens later recorded as Slade.					
Highland 1173		Girl Child, I Am An Evil Witchman / Security	1966	15.00	75.00
IN CROWD, THE					
Musicor 1111		Do The Surfer Jerk / Girl In The Black Bikini	1965	2.00	10.00
Abnak 121	(DJ)	Big Cities / Inside Out (Yellow vinyl)	1967	2.00	10.00
Abnak 121		Big Cities / Inside Out	1967	1.00	5.00
Abnak 129	(DJ)	Hangin' From Your Lovin' Tree / Let's Take A Walk (Yellow vinyl)	1968	2.00	10.00
Abnak 129		Hangin' From Your Lovin' Tree / Let's Take A Walk	1968	1.00	5.00
IN CROWD, THE					
Brent 7046		Cat Dance / Grapevine	1965	2.00	10.00
Viva 604		Questions And Answers / Happiness In My Heart	1966	1.20	6.00
Viva 610		If I Knew A Magic Word / Never Ending Symphony	1967	1.20	6.00
IN CROWD, THE					
Tower 147		Things She Says / That's How Strong My Love Is	1965	5.00	25.00
Tower 196		Why Must They Criticize? / I Don't Mind	1965	5.00	25.00
IN CROWD, THE					
Hickory 1378		Speed Queen / Cry, Baby, Cry	1966	3.00	15.00
Hickory 1413		In The Midnight Hour / Just Give Me Time	1966	2.00	10.00
IN CROWD, THE					
Abnak 121		Big Cities / Inside Out	1967	1.00	5.00
INCIDENTALS, THE					
Gar-Lo 1000		Barbara / Where's My True Love?	1961	3.00	15.00
INCIDENTALS, THE					
Ford 134		Driving Guitars / All Night	1964	7.00	35.00
Ford 138		Fireside / Lucille	1964	6.00	30.00
INCOGNITOS, THE					
Zee 001		Dee Jay's Dilemma / Forget It	1961	5.00	25.00
INCONCEIVABLES, THE					
Columbia 43894		Hamburger Patti / Patti's Theme	1966	2.00	10.00
INCREDABLES, THE					
Kelrich 851		If You Gave A Party / Little Bitty Bandit	196?	4.00	20.00

Label & Catalog #	A-Side/B-Side	Year	VG	NM
INCREDIBLE INVADERS, THE				
Prophonics 2028	This Time / The Boy Is Gone	196?	2.00	10.00
INDIVIDUALS, THE				
Gold Seal 1000	Please Baby, Be Mine / Not Me	196?	5.00	25.00
INDIVIDUALS, THE				
The Individuals also recorded with Chuck Rio.				
Tequila 101	La Bamba / Heartbreak Hotel	196?	3.00	15.00
INDIVIDUALS, THE				
21 Label 451	Table Talk / Happiness Is Just A Thing Called Joe	197?	.80	4.00
INDUSTRIAL IMAGE, THE				
Epic 10096	Living In The Middle Ages / Put My Mind At Ease	1966	1.20	6.00
INELIGIBLES, THE				
Anderson 109	Tiger Paws /	196?	2.00	10.00
INFATUATORS, THE				
Destiny 504	I Found My Love / Where Are You?	1961	25.00	125.00
Vee Jay 395	I Found My Love / Where Are You?	1961	5.00	25.00
INFERNOS, THE				
Hawk 13500	Goin' Cruisin' /	1963	2.00	10.00
INITIALS, THE				
Dee 1001	Bells Of Joy / You	195?	50.00	200.00
Sherry 667	Bells Of Joy / You	195?	8.00	40.00
INMAN, JIMMY				
NRC 5004	Loved Her The Whole Week Through / Saving My Love	1959	3.00	15.00
INNER CIRCLE, THE				
The Inner Circle features Steve Barri and Phil Sloan.				
Dunhill 4128	So Long, Marianne / Goes To Show You	1968	3.00	15.00
INNER CITY MISSION, THE				
Kama Sutra 510	Get Back, John / Got So Many Songs	1970	1.00	5.00
INNOCENCE, THE				
The Innocence is Pete Anders and Vinnie Poncia.				
Kama Sutra 214	There's Got To Be A Word! / It's Not Gonna Take Too Long	1966	.80	4.00
Kama Sutra 222	Mairzy Doats / A Lifetime Lovin' You	1967	.80	4.00
Kama Sutra 228	All I Do Is Think About You / Whence I Make Thee Mine	1967	.80	4.00
Kama Sutra 232	Someone Got Caught In My Eye / Your Show Is Over	1967	.80	4.00
Kama Sutra 237	Day Turns Me On / It's Not Gonna Take Too Long	1967	.80	4.00
INNOCENTS, THE				
TransWorld 7001	Tick Tock / The Rat	1960	2.00	10.00
INNOCENTS, THE				
The Innocents originally recorded as The Echoes. Refer to Kathy Young.				
Indigo 105	Honest I Do / My Baby Hully Gullys	1960	3.00	15.00
Indigo 111	Gee Whiz / Please, Mr. Sun	1960	3.00	15.00
Indigo 116	Kathy / In The Beginning	1961	3.00	15.00
Indigo 124	Beware / Because I Love You So	1961	3.00	15.00
Indigo 128	Donna / You Got Me Goin'	1961	3.00	15.00
Indigo 132	Pains In My Heart / When I Become A Man	1962	3.00	15.00
Indigo 141	Dee Dee Di Oh / Time	1962	3.00	15.00
Decca 31519	Come On, Lover / Don't Cry	1963	3.00	15.00
Reprise 20112	Be Mine / Oh, How I Miss My Baby	1963	3.00	15.00
Reprise 20125	You're Never Satisfied / Oh, How I Miss My Baby	1963	3.00	15.00
Warner Bros. 5450	My Heart Stood Still / Don't Call Me Lonely Anymore	1964	4.00	20.00
INRHODES, THE				
Dunhill 4055	Hold The High Ground / Looking Around	1966	2.00	10.00
Dunhill 4078	Try And Stop Me / Looking Around	1967	1.00	5.00
INSECTS, THE				
Applause 1002	Let's Bug The Beatles / (B-side by The Little Lady Beatles)	1964	3.00	15.00
INSIDE-OUTS, THE				
Palmer 5012	My Love (I'll Be True To You) / Gunfred Goon	1967	2.00	10.00
INSIDERS, THE				
Red Bird 055	Chapel Bells Are Calling / I'm Stuck On You	1966	2.00	10.00

Label & Catalog #	A-Side/B-Side	Year	VG	NM
INSPIRATIONS, THE				
Sparkle 102	**Angel In Disguise / Stool Pigeon**	1960	15.00	75.00
Al-Brite 1651	**Angel In Disguise / Stool Pigeon**	1960	10.00	50.00
Gone 5097	**Angel In Disguise / Stool Pigeon**	1961	4.00	20.00
Jamie 1212	**Dry Your Eyes / Good Bye** (Black label)	1961	10.00	50.00
Jamie 1212	**Dry Your Eyes / Good Bye** (Color label)	196?	3.00	15.00
Sultan 1	**The Genie / The Feeling Of Her Kiss**	196?	6.00	30.00
INSPIRATIONS, THE: *Refer to* RONNIE VARE & THE INSPIRATIONS				
INTENTIONS, THE				
Philips 40428	**Night Rider / Don't Forget That I Love You**	1967	1.20	6.00
Uptown 710	**Time / Cool Summer Night**	196?	2.00	10.00
INTERIORS, THE				
Worthy 1008	**Darling Little Angel / Voodoo Doll**	1961	25.00	125.00
Worthy 1009	**Echoes /**	1961	10.00	50.00
INTERLUDES, THE				
RCA Victor 47-7281	**I Shed A Million Tears / Oo-Wee**	1958	5.00	25.00
ABC-Paramount 10213	**Beautiful, Wonderful, Heavenly You / #1 In The Nation**	1961	3.00	15.00
INTERNATIONAL BRICK				
Camelot 137	**You Should Be So High / Flower Children**	196?	2.00	10.00
INTERNATIONAL SUBMARINE BAND, THE				
The International Submarine Band feature Gram Parsons and Kevin Kelley, later of The Byrds.				
Ascot 2218 (DJ)	**The Russians Are Coming / Truck Driving Man**	1966	3.00	15.00
Ascot 2218	**The Russians Are Coming / Truck Driving Man**	1966	6.00	30.00
Columbia 43935 (DJ)	**Sum Up Broke / One Day Week**	1967	3.00	15.00
Columbia 43935	**Sum Up Broke / One Day Week**	1967	6.00	30.00
LHI 1205	**Luxury Liner / Blue Eyes**	1968	3.00	15.00
LHI 1217	**Miller's Cave / I Must Be Somebody Else You've Known**	1968	3.00	15.00
INTERNATIONALS, THE				
ABC-Paramount 9964	**Goin' To A Party / I Love You So**	1958	4.00	20.00
INTERPRETERS, THE				
Gemini 100	**I Get The Message / Stop That Man**	1965	2.00	10.00
INTERVALS, THE				
Ad 104	**Side Street / I Still Love That Man**	1959	4.00	20.00
Apt 25019	**Side Street / I Still Love That Man**	1959	3.00	15.00
INTIMATES, THE				
Amcan 402	**Got You Where I Want You** (One sided)	196?	5.00	25.00
Amcan 402	**Got You Where I Want You / Only Girl For Me**	196?	15.00	75.00
Epic 9743	**Smart, Too Late / I've Got A Tiger In My Tank**	1964	3.00	15.00
INTREPIDES, THE				
Mascio 120	**Golash / Donna**	1965	7.00	35.00
INTRUDERS, THE				
Sahara 101	**Wild Goose / Trombone**	1963	3.00	15.00
Anderson 103	**Surfin' Green / The Intruder**	196?	7.00	35.00
INVADERS, THE				
Bamboo 501	**Davey Jones' Rocker / Trouble On Main Street**	1961	8.00	40.00
Whingding 950	**Disc Jockey / Burma Road**	1961	7.00	35.00
INVADERS, THE				
Philips 40189	**I Wanna Be Your Man / Cat's Eyes**	1964	2.00	10.00
Instro 1000	**Invasion / Pam**	196?	4.00	20.00
INVADERS, THE				
Mohawk 139	**The Id / One Step Into Darkness**	1965	3.00	15.00
INVADERS, THE				
Capitol 2292	**California Sun / Love And Hate**	1968	2.00	10.00
U.S.A. 902	**Flower Song / With A Tear**	1968	2.00	10.00
INVASION				
Dynamic Sound 2004	**I Want To Thank You / The Invasion Is Coming**	1967	2.00	10.00
INVICTAS, THE				
Jack Bee 1003	**Gone So Long / Nellie**	1959	4.00	20.00
20th Century Fox 493	**Breakout / Missing**	1964	4.00	20.00

Label & Catalog #		A-Side/B-Side	Year	VG	NM
IRIDESCENTS, THE					
Hudson 8102		Three Coins In The Fountain / Strong Love	1963	5.00	25.00
Hudson 8102		Three Coins In The Fountain / Strong Love (Blue vinyl)	1963	25.00	125.00
Ultrasonic 109		I Know / The Angels Sang	196?	4.00	20.00
IRON BUTTERFLY, THE					
Atco 6573		Unconscious Power / Possession	1968	.60	3.00
Atco 6606		In-A-Gadda-Da-Vida / Iron Butterfly Theme	1968	.80	4.00
Atco 6647		Soul Experience / In The Crowd	1969	.60	3.00
Atco 6676		The Time Of Our Lives / It Must Be Love	1969	.60	3.00
Atco 6712		I Can't Help But Deceive You, Little Girl / To Be Alone	1969	.60	3.00
Atco 6782		Easy Rider (Let The Wind Pave The Way) / Soldier In Our Town	1970	.60	3.00
Atco 6818		Stone Believer / Silly Sally	1971	.60	3.00
MCA 40379		Searchin' Circles / Pearly Gates	1975	.40	2.00
MCA 40493		Get It Out / Beyond The Milky Way	1975	.40	2.00
IRON GATE, THE					
Mobile 3429		You Must Believe Me / Get Ready	1968	1.20	6.00
IRRIDESCENTS, THE					
Hawk 4001		Bali Ha'i / Swamp Surfer	1963	8.00	40.00
Infinity 037		Bali Ha'i / Swamp Surfer	1963	5.00	25.00
Oldies 183		Bali Ha'i / Swamp Surfer	1964	2.00	10.00
ISABEL, RUSTY					
Brent 7001		Firewater / The Blast	1959	4.00	20.00
Brent 7006		Manhunt / I Give Up	1959	2.00	10.00
ISLE, JIMMY					
Bally 1034		Baby-O / Hassle	1957	3.00	15.00
Roulette 4065		Going Wild / You And Johnny Smith	1958	4.00	20.00
Everest 19320		Billy Boy / Oh, Judy	1959	3.00	15.00
Sun 306		I've Been Waiting / Diamond Ring	1958	3.00	15.00
Sun 318		Time Will Tell / Without A Love	1959	3.00	15.00
Sun 332		What A Life / Together	1960	2.00	10.00
Mala 459		Everybody Got A Little Girl But Me / Our Town	196?	2.00	10.00
ITALIAN ASPHALT & PAVEMENT COMPANY, THE [IA&P CO.]					
IA&P Co. originally recorded as The Duprees.					
Colossus 110		The Sky's The Limit / Check Yourself	1970	.80	4.00
Colossus 110	(PS)	The Sky's The Limit / Check Yourself	1970	.80	4.00
ITELS, THE					
Magnifico 101		Stars Of Paradise / Chubby Isn't Chubby Anymore	1961	8.00	40.00
IT'S A BEAUTIFUL DAY					
It's A Beautiful Day features David LaFlamme.					
Columbia 44928		White Bird / Wasted Union Blues	1969	1.20	6.00
Columbia 45152		Soapstone Mountain / Do You Remember The Sun?	1970	1.00	5.00
Columbia 45309		The Dolphins / Do You Remember The Sun?	1971	1.00	5.00
Columbia 45536		Anytime / Oranges And Apples	1972	1.00	5.00
Columbia 45788		White Bird / Wasted Union Blues	1973	1.00	5.00
Columbia 45853		Time / Ain't That Lovin' You, Baby	1973	1.00	5.00
San Francisco Sound 11680		Aquarian Dream / Bulgaria	198?	2.00	10.00
IVAN					
Ivan is a pseudonym for Jerry Allison of The Crickets.					
Coral 62017	(DJ)	Real Wild Child / Oh, You Beautiful Doll	1958	15.00	75.00
Coral 62017		Real Wild Child / Oh, You Beautiful Doll (Features Buddy Holly.)	1958	30.00	150.00
Coral 62081	(DJ)	That'll Be Alright / Frankie Frankenstein	1959	30.00	150.00
Coral 62081		That'll Be Alright / Frankie Frankenstein	1959	75.00	300.00
Coral 65607		That'll Be Alright / Frankie Frankenstein	1967	10.00	50.00
IVES, JIMMY					
Comet 21		My Tumbling Heart / Settle Down	195?	5.00	25.00
IVEYS, THE					
The Iveys later recorded as Badfinger.					
Apple 1803		Maybe Tomorrow / Daddy's A Millionaire (Star label)	1969	6.00	30.00
Apple 1803		Maybe Tomorrow / Daddy's A Millionaire (Starless label)	1969	4.00	20.00
Americom 301		Maybe Tomorrow / Daddy's A Millionaire (4" flexidisc)	1969	150.00	600.00
IVIES, THE					
Roulette 4183		I Really Want To Know / Voodoo	1959	3.00	15.00

Label & Catalog #		A-Side/B-Side	Year	VG	NM
IVOLEERS, THE					
Buzz 101		Lover's Quarrel / Come With Me	1959	50.00	200.00
IVORIES, THE					
Mercury 71239		Me And You / I'm In Love	1957	4.00	20.00
IVORYS, THE					
Sparta 001		Why Don't You Write Me? / Deep Freeze	1962	10.00	50.00
IVY JIVIES, THE					
Jaro 77036		Million Dollar Girl / Knockout	1960	5.00	25.00
IVY LEAGUE, THE					
Cameo 343		What More Do You Want? / Your Love Is All I Want	1965	2.00	10.00
Cameo 356		Funny How Love Can Be / Lonely Room	1965	2.00	10.00
Cameo 365		A Girl Like You / That's Why I'm Crying	1965	2.00	10.00
Cameo 377		Graduation Day / Tossin' And Turnin'	1965	2.00	10.00
Cameo 388		Our Love Is Slipping Away / I Could Make You Fall In Love	1966	2.00	10.00
Cameo 388	(PS)	Our Love Is Slipping Away / I Could Make You Fall In Love	1966	3.00	15.00
Cameo 449		My World Fell Down / When You're Young	1966	2.00	10.00
IVY THREE, THE					
Shell 720		Was Judy There? / Yogi	1960	3.00	15.00
Shell 723		Hush, Little Baby / Alone In The Chapel	1960	3.00	15.00
Shell 302		Nine Out Of Ten / I've Cried Enough For Two	1961	3.00	15.00
Shell 306		Bagoo / Suicide	1961	3.00	15.00
IVY TONES, THE					
Red Top 105		Oo-Wee, Baby / Each Time *(Blue label)*	1958	5.00	25.00
Red Top 105		Oo-Wee, Baby / Each Time	195?	3.00	15.00
IVYS, THE					
Coed 518		All I Want / Lost Without You	1959	4.00	20.00

J.

J. B. K. FOUR, THE
Quest 301	Clap Your Hands / Go, Go	196?	2.00	10.00

J. R. & THE ATTRACTIONS
Hunch 928	Bristol Stomp / I'm Yours	196?	5.00	25.00

JACKASSES, THE
Bray 2626	Sugaree / Shake It Up	1964	4.00	20.00

JACKSON, JILL
Ms. Jackson also recorded as part of Jill & Ray and Paul & Paula.
Reprise 0294	All Over Again / Hey, Handsome Boy	196?	2.00	10.00
Reprise 0325	Pixie Girl / Just Don't Know What To Do With Myself	196?	2.00	10.00
Reprise 0365	Born Too Late / Here Comes The Night	196?	2.00	10.00
Reprise 0415	Treasure Of Love / I'll Love You For A While	196?	2.00	10.00

JACKSON, PYTHON LEE
Python Lee's vocalist was Rod Stewart.
GNP/Crescendo 449	In A Broken Dream / Doin' Fine	1973	1.00	5.00
GNP/Crescendo 462	Cloud Nine / Rod's Blues	1973	1.00	5.00

JACKSON, WANDA
After a series of country singles for Decca (not included here), Wanda Jackson signed with Capitol and proceeded to record some of the toughest rock 'n roll ever cut, earning her the title of "Queen of Rockabilly." These records do essentially define female rockabilly. By 1962 she had returned to her roots and has recorded country and gospel since.
Capitol 3485	I Gotta Know / Half As Good A Girl	1956	5.00	25.00
Capitol 3575	Hot Dog! That Made Him Mad / Silver Thread And Golden Needles	1956	5.00	25.00
Capitol 3637	Cryin' Through The Night / Baby Loves Him	1957	7.00	35.00
Capitol 3683	Let Me Explain / Don A Wanna	1957	4.00	20.00
Capitol 3764	Cool Love / Did You Miss Me?	1957	4.00	20.00
Capitol 3843	Fujiyama Mama / No Wedding Bells For Joe	1957	5.00	25.00
Capitol 3941	Honey Bop / Just A Queen For A Day	1958	5.00	25.00
Capitol 4026	Mean Mean Man / Our Song	1958	5.00	25.00
Capitol 4081	Rock Your Baby / Sinful Heart	1958	4.00	20.00
Capitol 4142	Savin' My Love / I Wanna Waltz	1959	4.00	20.00
	—Capitol singles above have purple labels with the Capitol logo on top.—			
Capitol 4397	Let's Have A Party / Cool Love	1960	5.00	25.00
	(A-side features backing by Gene Vincent's Blue Caps.)			
Capitol 4553	Right Or Wrong / Tunnel Of Love	1961	3.00	15.00
Capitol 4635	In The Middle Of A Heartache / I'd Be Ashamed	1961	2.00	10.00
	—Capitol singles above have purple labels with the Capitol logo on the left.—			
Capitol 4681	A Little Bitty Tear / I Don't Wanta Go	1962	2.00	10.00
Capitol 4723	If I Cried Every Time You Hurt Me / Let My Love Walk In	1962	2.00	10.00
Capitol 4723 (PS)	If I Cried Every Time You Hurt Me / Let My Love Walk In	1962	4.00	20.00

JADES, THE
The Jades feature Lou Reed, later of The Velvet Underground.
Time 1002	Leave Her For Me / So Blue	1957	25.00	125.00

JADES, THE
Oxboro 2002	Surfin' Crow / Blue Black Hair	1963	7.00	35.00
Gaity 2-23-64	Surfin' Crow '64 / Blue Black Hair	1964	7.00	35.00

JAMES, BOBBY
Jolum 102	Let's Surf / Take This Lollipop	196?	7.00	35.00

JAMES, DEVINY
Deviny James later recorded as Jim Pewter.
Beta 1006	Little Girl / Blue, Blue Denims	1959	5.00	25.00
Studio City 1002	That's All Right, Mama / Baby Child	1961	3.00	15.00

JAMES, TOMMY, & THE SHONDELLS
The Shondells on the first two sides were a different group than the one James fronted after the belated success of "Hanky Panky." These later Shondells also recorded as Hog Heaven.
Snap 102	Hanky Panky / Thunderbolt	1963	8.00	40.00
	(First pressings of Snap 102 make no mention of Red Fox Records.)			
Snap 102	Hanky Panky / Thunderbolt	1963	6.00	30.00
	(Second pressings read "Dist. by Red Fox Records.")			
Red Fox 110	Hanky Panky / Thunderbolt	1966	8.00	40.00
	(The Snap and Red Fox labels credit The Shondells.)			

Label & Catalog #		A-Side/B-Side	Year	VG	NM
Roulette 4686		Hanky Panky / Thunderbolt	1966	1.20	6.00
Roulette 4695		Say I Am (What I Am) / Lots Of Pretty Girls	1966	1.00	5.00
Roulette 4695	(PS)	Say I Am (What I Am) / Lots Of Pretty Girls	1966	2.00	10.00
Roulette 4710		It's Only Love / Ya Ya	1966	2.00	10.00
Roulette 4710		It's Only Love / Don't Let My Love Pass You By	1966	1.00	5.00
Roulette 4720		I Think We're Alone Now / Gone, Gone, Gone	1967	1.00	5.00
Roulette 4720	(PS)	I Think We're Alone Now / Gone, Gone, Gone	1967	2.00	10.00
Roulette 4736		Mirage / Run, Run, Run	1967	1.00	5.00
Roulette 4736	(PS)	Mirage / Run, Run, Run	1967	2.00	10.00
Roulette 4756		I Like The Way / I Can't Take It No More	1967	1.00	5.00
Roulette 4762		Gettin' Together / Real Girl	1967	1.00	5.00
Roulette 4762	(PS)	Gettin' Together / Real Girl	1967	2.00	10.00
Roulette 4775		Out Of The Blue / Love's Closin' In On Me	1967	1.00	5.00
Hip Pocket 1		Mirage / I Think We're Alone Now	1967	2.00	10.00
		(4" flexidisc issued with a picture envelope.)			
Hip Pocket 2		Hanky Panky / Gettin' Together	1967	2.00	10.00
		(4" flexidisc issued with a picture envelope.)			
Roulette 7000		Get Out Now / Wish It Were You	1968	1.00	5.00
Roulette 7008		Mony Mony / One, Two, Three And I Fell	1968	1.20	6.00
Roulette 7016		Somebody Cares / Do Unto Me	1968	1.00	5.00
Roulette 7024		Do Something To Me / Gingerbread Man	1968	1.00	5.00
Roulette 7028	(DJ)	Crimson And Clover / (I'm) Taken	1968	3.00	15.00
Roulette 7028		Crimson And Clover / Some Kind Of Love	1968	1.20	6.00
Roulette 7039		Sweet Cherry Wine / Breakaway	1969	1.00	5.00
Roulette 7050		Crystal Blue Persuasion / I'm Alive	1969	1.00	5.00
Roulette 7060		Ball Of Fire / Makin' Good Time	1969	1.00	5.00
Roulette 7066		She / Loved One	1969	1.00	5.00
Roulette 7071		Gotta Get Back To You / Red Rover	1970	1.00	5.00
Roulette 7076		Come To Me / Talkin' And Signifyin'	1970	1.00	5.00

JAMES, TOMMY

Label & Catalog #		A-Side/B-Side	Year	VG	NM
Roulette 7084		Ball And Chain / Candy Maker	1970	.60	3.00
Roulette 7093		Church Street Soul Revival / Draggin' The Line	1970	1.00	5.00
Roulette 7100		Adrienne / Light Of Day	1971	.60	3.00
Roulette 7103		Draggin' The Line / Bits And Pieces	1971	.60	3.00
Roulette 7110		I'm Comin' Home / Sing, Sing, Sing	1971	.60	3.00
Roulette 7114		Nothing To Hide / Walk A Country Mile	1971	.60	3.00
Roulette 7119		Tell 'Em Willie Boy's A' Comin' / Forty Days And Forty Nights	1972	.60	3.00
Roulette 7126		Cat's Eyes In The Night / Dark Is The Night	1972	.60	3.00
Roulette 7130		Love Song / Kingston Highway	1972	.60	3.00
Roulette 7135		Celebration / The Last One To Know	1972	.60	3.00
Roulette 7140		Boo, Boo, Don'tcha Be Blue / Rings And Things	1973	.60	3.00
Roulette 7147		Calico / Hey, My Lady	1973	.60	3.00
MCA 40289		Glory Glory / Coming Down	1976	1.00	5.00
Fantasy 761		I Love You Love Me Love / Devil Gale Drive	1976	.60	3.00
Fantasy 761	(PS)	I Love You Love Me Love / Devil Gale Drive	1976	1.00	5.00
Fantasy 776		Tighter And Tighter / Coming Down	1976	1.00	5.00
Fantasy 811		Midnight Rider / Love Will Find A Way	1977	1.00	5.00
Fantasy 996		Tighter And Tighter / Coming Down	1978	.80	4.00
Millennium 11785		Three Times In Love / I Just Wanna Play The Music	1977	.60	3.00
Millennium 11787		No Hay Dos Sin Tres / I Just Wanna Play The Music	1977	.80	4.00
Millennium 11787	(PS)	No Hay Dos Sin Tres / I Just Wanna Play The Music	1977	1.60	8.00
		("No Hay Dos Sin Tres" is a Spanish version of "Three Times In Love.")			
Millennium 11788		You Got Me / It's All Right Now	1980	.50	2.50
Millennium 11802		You're So Easy To Love / Halfway To Heaven	1981	.50	2.50
Millennium 11814		Lady In White / Paying For My Lover's Mistake	1981	.50	2.50
21 Records 105		Say Please / Two Time Lover	1983	.50	2.50
21 Records 105	(PS)	Say Please / Two Time Lover	1983	.50	2.50

JAMESON, BOBBY

Label & Catalog #		A-Side/B-Side	Year	VG	NM
Penthouse 503		Gotta Find My Roogalator /	1962	15.00	75.00
		("Gotta Find My Roogalator" was arranged by Frank Zappa.)			
Talamo 1834		I Wanna Love You / I'm Lonely	1964	1.00	5.00

JAMIE & JANE
Gene Pitney and Ginny Arnell.

Label & Catalog #		A-Side/B-Side	Year	VG	NM
Decca 30862		Strolling (Thru The Park) / Snuggle Up, Baby	1959	3.00	15.00
Decca 30934		Faithful Our Love / Classical Rock And Roll	1959	3.00	15.00

JAN
Jan Berry. Refer to Sonny Curtis; Shelley Fabares; Jill Gibson; Deane Hawley; Jan & Arni; Jan & Dean; and The Matadors..

Label & Catalog #		A-Side/B-Side	Year	VG	NM
Ripple 6101		Tomorrow's Teardrops / My Midsummer Night's Dream	1961	8.00	40.00
		(Ripple 6101 credits Jan "Barry.")			
Liberty 55845		The Universal Coward / I Can't Wait To Love You	1966	3.00	15.00
Liberty 55845	(PS)	The Universal Coward / I Can't Wait To Love You	1966	20.00	100.00
Ode 66023	(DJ)	Mother Earth / Blue Moon Shuffle	1973	3.00	15.00
		(Issued with an insert letter from Jan.)			

Label & Catalog #		A-Side/B-Side	Year	VG	NM
Ode 66023		Mother Earth / Blue Moon Shuffle	1973	4.00	20.00
Ode 66034	(DJ)	Blue Moon Shuffle / Blue Moon Shuffle	1973	3.00	15.00
Ode 66034		Blue Moon Shuffle / Don't You Just Know It	1973	7.00	35.00
		(Brian Wilson shares lead vocals with Berry on "Don't You Just Know It.")			
Ode 66050	(DJ)	Tinsel Town / Blow Up Music	1973	3.00	15.00
Ode 66050		Tinsel Town / Blow Up Music	1973	4.00	20.00
		(Ode 66050 credits "I, Jan, I.")			
Ode 66111	(DJ)	Fun City / Fun City	1974	3.00	15.00
Ode 66111		Fun City / Totally Wild	1974	4.00	20.00
		(Ode 66111 credits Jan & Dean.)			
Ode 66120	(DJ)	Sing Sang A Song / Sing Sang A Song	1974	3.00	15.00
Ode 66120		Sing Sang A Song / Sing Sang A Song	1974	4.00	20.00
A&M 1957	(DJ)	Little Queenie / Little Queenie	1977	2.00	10.00
A&M 1957		Little Queenie / That's The Way It Is	1977	3.00	15.00
A&M 2020	(DJ)	Skateboard Surfin' U.S.A. / Skateboard Surfin' U.S.A.	1978	2.00	10.00
A&M 2020		Skateboard Surfin' U.S.A. / How, How I Love Her	1978	3.00	15.00

JAN & ARNIE
Jan Berry and Arnie Ginsberg. Refer to The Rituals.

Label & Catalog #		A-Side/B-Side	Year	VG	NM
Arwin 108		Jennie Lee / Gotta Get A Date	1958	5.00	25.00
Arwin 111		Gas Money / Bonnie Lou	1958	5.00	25.00
Arwin 113		I Love Linda / The Beat That Can't Be Beat	1958	12.00	60.00
Dot 16116		Gas Money / Gotta Get A Date	1960	6.00	30.00
		—Extended Play Albums—			
Dot 1097		Jan And Arnie	1960	100.00	400.00

JAN & DEAN
Jan Berry and Dean Torrence. In attempting to keep their name alive, both Jan and Dean have issued essentially solo singles using the two names: Columbia 44036 and the Warner sides are Jan's recordings while the Magic Lamp, J&D and Jan & Dean sides are Jan's. Refer to Laughing Gravy; The Legendary Masked Surfers; Mike Love & Dean Torrence; The Phaetons; The Rally Packs; the Various Artists section. Liberty 55672-923 feature vocal backing by The Fantastic Baggys.

Label & Catalog #		A-Side/B-Side	Year	VG	NM
Dore 522		Baby Talk / Jeanette, Get Your Hair Done	1959	75.00	300.00
		(Although this is a Jan & Dean record, first pressings credit Jan & Arnie.)			
Dore 522		Baby Talk / Jeanette, Get Your Hair Done	1959	4.00	20.00
		(Second pressings correctly credit Jan & Dean.)			
Dore 531		There's A Girl / My Heart Sings	1959	3.00	15.00
Dore 539		Clementine / My Heart Sings	1960	3.00	15.00
Dore 548		Cindy / White Tennis Sneakers	1960	3.00	15.00
Dore 555		We Go Together / Rosilane	1960	3.00	15.00
Dore 555	(PS)	We Go Together / Rosilane	1960	10.00	50.00
Dore 555		We Go Together / Rosie Lane	1960	3.00	15.00
Dore 576		Gee / Such A Good Night For Dreamin'	1960	3.00	15.00
Dore 576	(PS)	Gee / Such A Good Night For Dreamin'	1960	35.00	175.00
Dore 583		Baggy Pants / Judy's An Angel	1961	5.00	25.00
Dore 610		Julie / Don't Fly Away	1961	5.00	25.00
Challenge 9111		Those Words / Heart And Soul	1961	5.00	25.00
Challenge 9111		My Midsummer Night's Dream / Heart And Soul	1961	3.00	15.00
Challenge 59111		My Midsummer Night's Dream / Heart And Soul	1961	3.00	15.00
Challenge 9120		Something A Little Bit Different / Wanted: One Girl	1961	3.00	15.00
Liberty 55397		A Sunday Kind Of Love / Poor Little Puppet	1962	3.00	15.00
Liberty 55454		Tennessee / Your Heart Has Changed My Mind	1962	3.00	15.00
Liberty 55496		My Favorite Dream / Who Put The Bomp?	1962	7.00	35.00
Liberty 55522	(DJ)	She's Still Talking Baby Talk / Frosty The Snowman	1962	15.00	75.00
Liberty 55522		She's Still Talking Baby Talk / Frosty The Snowman	1962	30.00	150.00
Liberty 55531		Linda / When I Learn How To Cry	1963	2.00	10.00
Liberty 55580		Surf City / She's My Summer Girl	1963	2.00	10.00
Liberty 55580	(PS)	Surf City / She's My Summer Girl	1963	4.00	20.00
		("Surf City" features Brian Wilson.)			
Liberty 55613		Honolulu Lulu / Someday	1963	2.00	10.00
Liberty 55613	(PS)	Honolulu Lulu / Someday	1963	4.00	20.00
Liberty 55641		Drag City / Schlock Rock	1963	2.00	10.00
Liberty 55641	(PS)	Drag City / Schlock Rock	1963	5.00	25.00
Liberty 55672		Dead Man's Curve / The New Girl In School	1964	2.00	10.00
Liberty 55672	(PS)	Dead Man's Curve / The New Girl In School	1964	4.00	20.00
Liberty 55704		Little Old Lady From Pasadena / My Mighty G.T.O.	1964	2.00	10.00
Liberty 55704	(PS)	Little Old Lady From Pasadena / My Mighty G.T.O.	1964	3.00	15.00
Liberty 55724		Ride The Wild Surf / The Anaheim, Azusa And Cucamonga Sewing Circle, Book Review And Timing Association	1964	2.00	10.00
Liberty 55724	(PS)	Ride The Wild Surf / The Anaheim, Azusa And Cucamonga Sewing Circle, Book Review And Timing Association	1964	5.00	25.00
Liberty 55727		Sidewalk Surfin' / When It's Over	1964	2.00	10.00
Liberty 55727	(PS)	Sidewalk Surfin' / When It's Over	1964	6.00	30.00
Liberty 55766		From All Over The World / Freeway Flyer	1965	2.00	10.00
Liberty 55766	(PS)	From All Over The World / Freeway Flyer	1965	25.00	125.00
Liberty 55792		You Really Know How To Hurt A Guy / It's As Easy As 1-2-3	1965	2.00	10.00
Liberty 55792	(PS)	You Really Know How To Hurt A Guy / It's As Easy As 1-2-3	1965	3.00	15.00
Liberty 55833		I Found A Girl / It's A Shame To Say Goodbye	1965	2.00	10.00

Label & Catalog #		A-Side/B-Side	Year	VG	NM
Liberty 55849		Folk City / A Beginning From An End	1965	2.00	10.00
Liberty 55849	(PS)	Folk City / A Beginning From An End	1965	6.00	30.00
Liberty 55860		Batman / Bucket T	1966	3.00	15.00
Liberty 55866		Popsicle / Norwegian Wood	1966	2.00	10.00
Liberty 55905		Fiddle Around / A Surfer's Dream	1966	2.00	10.00
Liberty 55923		The New Girl In School / School Day	1966	2.00	10.00
Magic Lamp 401		California Lullabye / Summertime	1966	6.00	30.00
J&D 401		California Lullabye / Summertime, Summertime	1966	6.00	30.00
J&D 402		Like A Summer Rain / Louisiana Man	1966	8.00	40.00
Jan & Dean 10		Hawaii / Tijuana	1966	15.00	75.00
Jan & Dean 11		Fan Tan / Love And Hate	1966	25.00	125.00
Columbia 4-44036		Yellow Balloon / A Taste Of Rain	1967	5.00	25.00
Warner Bros. 7151	(DJ)	Love And Hate / Only A Boy	1967	4.00	20.00
Warner Bros. 7151		Love And Hate / Only A Boy	1967	8.00	40.00
Warner Bros. 7219	(DJ)	I Know My Mind / Laurel And Hardy	1968	5.00	25.00
Warner Bros. 7219		I Know My Mind / Laurel And Hardy	1968	10.00	50.00
Warner Bros. 7240	(DJ)	Girl, You're Blowing My Mind / In The Still Of The Night	1968	15.00	75.00
		(Stock copies of Warner Bros. 7240 may not exist.)			
United Artists 50859		Jenny Lee / Vegetables	1972	3.00	15.00
United Artists 50859	(PS)	Jenny Lee / Vegetables	1972	5.00	25.00
		("Vegetables" is a reissue of the Laughing Gravy side with new vocals by Brian Wilson and Spring.)			
United Artists 092	(DJ)	Dead Man's Curve / Dead Man's Curve	1972	3.00	15.00
		(Stock copies of U.A. 092 may not exist.)			
United Artists 670		Sidewalk Surfing / Gonna Hustle You	1976	3.00	15.00

JARVIS, FELTON

Viva 1001		Don't Knock Elvis / Honest John	1959	3.00	15.00

JAY, MORTY, & THE SURFING CATS

Legend 124		Salt Water Taffy / (B-side by Jerry Norrell)	1963	5.00	25.00

JAY, II, IRA

Sun 351		You Don't Love Me / More Than Anything	1960	2.00	10.00

JAY & THE AMERICANS

U.A. 353-566 features John Traynor as "Jay." After that, the lead singer is Jay Black.

United Artists 353		Tonight / The Other Girls	1962	1.20	6.00
United Artists 415		She Cried / Dawning	1962	2.00	10.00
United Artists 479		This Is It / It's My Turn To Cry	1962	1.20	6.00
United Artists 504		Tomorrow / Yes	1963	1.20	6.00
United Artists 566		What's The Use? / Strangers Tomorrow	1963	1.20	6.00
United Artists 626		Only In America / My Clair De Lune	1963	.80	4.00
United Artists 629	(DJ)	Baby, This Is Rock & Roll / Baby, This Is Rock & Roll	1963	2.00	10.00
		(U.A. used #629 commercially for a Garnett Mimms & The Enchanters single.)			
United Artists 669		Come Dance With Me / Look In My Eyes, Marie	1963	.80	4.00
United Artists 693		To Wait For Love / Friday	1964	.80	4.00
United Artists 759		Come A Little Bit Closer / Goodbye, Boys, Goodbye	1964	.80	4.00
United Artists 805		Let's Lock The Door (And Throw Away The Key) / I'll Remember You	1964	.80	4.00
United Artists 845		Think Of The Good Times / If You Were Mine, Girl	1965	.80	4.00
United Artists 881		Cara Mia / When It's All Over	1965	.80	4.00
United Artists 919		Some Enchanted Evening / Girl	1965	.80	4.00
United Artists 919	(PS)	Some Enchanted Evening / Girl	1965	2.00	10.00
United Artists 948		Sunday And Me / Through This Door	1965	.80	4.00
E.O.E.O.C.		Things Are Changing / Things Are Changing	1965	20.00	100.00
E.O.E.O.C.	(PS)	Things Are Changing / Things Are Changing	1965	20.00	100.00
		(Manufactured for the Equal Opportunity Employment Opportunities Campaign using a Phil Spector production of Brian Wilson's "Don't Hurt My Little Sister" with Brian on piano. The same backing track was used on performances by The Blossoms and The Supremes.)			
United Artists 992		Why Can't You Bring Me Home? / Baby, Stop Your Crying	1966	.80	4.00
United Artists 50016		Crying / I Don't Need A Friend	1966	.80	4.00
United Artists 50016	(PS)	Crying / I Don't Need A Friend	1966	2.00	10.00
United Artists 50046		Livin' Above Your Head / Look At Me, What Do You See?	1966	.80	4.00
United Artists 50046	(PS)	Livin' Above Your Head / Look At Me, What Do You See?	1966	2.00	10.00
United Artists 50086		Stop The Clock / Baby, Stay Home	1966	.60	3.00
United Artists 50094		(He's) Raining In My Sunshine / The Reason For Living	1966	.60	3.00
United Artists 50139		Nature Boy / You Ain't As Hip As All That, Baby	1967	.60	3.00
United Artists 50196		Got Hung Up Along The Way / Yellow Forest	1967	.60	3.00
United Artists 50222		French Provincial / Shanghai Noodle Factory	1967	.60	3.00
United Artists 50282		No Other Love / No, I Don't Know Her	1968	.60	3.00
United Artists 50448		You Ain't Gonna Wake Up Crying / Gemini	1968	.60	3.00
United Artists 50475		This Magic Moment / Since I Don't Have You	1968	.80	4.00
United Artists 50510		When You Dance / No, I Don't Know Her	1969	.60	3.00
United Artists 50535		Hushabye / Gypsy Woman	1969	.60	3.00
United Artists 50567		Learnin' How To Fly / For The Love Of A Lady	1969	.60	3.00
United Artists 50605		Walkin' In The Rain / For The Love Of A Lady	1969	.60	3.00

Label & Catalog #		A-Side/B-Side	Year	VG	NM
United Artists 50654		Capture The Moment / Do You Ever Think Of Me?	1970	.60	3.00
United Artists 50683		Do I Love You? / Tricia (Tell Your Daddy)	1970	.60	3.00
United Artists 50858		There Goes My Baby / Solitary Man	1970	.80	4.00

JAY & THE DELTAS
Jay is a pseudonym for Jim Waller.

Warner Bros. 5404	(DJ)	Bells Are Ringing / Superhawk	1963	5.00	25.00
Warner Bros. 5404		Bells Are Ringing / Superhawk	1963	10.00	50.00

JEAN, BOBBIE

Sun 342		You Burned The Bridges / Cheaters Never Win	1960	2.00	10.00

JEANNIE & THE MILLER SISTERS: *Refer to* **THE MILLER SISTERS**

JEFFERSON AIRPLANE
The original recording group features Signe Anderson, Marty Balin, Jack Casady, Paul Kantner, Jorma Kaukonen, and Alexander "Skip" Spence. Anderson and Spence left in late '66, replaced by Grace Slick and Spencer Dryden. When Dryden left in 1970, Joey Covington joined. Refer to The Great Society; Hot Tuna; Moby Grape.

RCA Victor 47-8769		It's No Secret / Runnin' 'Round This World	1966	2.00	10.00
RCA Victor 47-8848		Come Up The Years / Blues From An Airplane	1966	2.00	10.00
RCA Victor 47-8967		Bringing Me Down / Let Me In	1966	2.00	10.00
RCA Victor 47-9063		My Best Friend / How Do You Feel?	1967	2.00	10.00
RCA Victor 47-9140		Somebody To Love / She Has Funny Cars	1967	1.20	6.00
RCA Victor 47-9248		White Rabbit / Plastic Fantastic Lover	1967	1.20	6.00
RCA Victor 47-9297		Ballad Of You And Me And Pooneil / Two Heads	1967	1.00	5.00
RCA Victor 47-9389		Watch Her Ride / Martha	1968	1.00	5.00
RCA Victor 47-9496		Greasy Heart / Share A Little Joke	1968	1.00	5.00
RCA Victor 47-9644		Crown Of Creation / Lather	1968	1.00	5.00
RCA Victor 47-9644	(PS)	Crown Of Creation / Lather	1968	3.00	15.00
RCA Victor 74-0150		The Other Side Of This Life / Plastic Fantastic Lover	1969	.80	4.00
RCA Victor 74-0150	(PS)	The Other Side Of This Life / Plastic Fantastic Lover	1969	3.00	15.00
RCA Victor 74-0245		Volunteers / We Can Be Together	1970	.80	4.00
RCA Victor 74-0245	(PS)	Volunteers / We Can Be Together	1970	2.00	10.00
RCA Victor 74-0343		Have You Seen The Saucers? / Mexico	1970	.80	4.00
RCA Victor 74-0343	(PS)	Have You Seen The Saucers? / Mexico	1970	2.00	10.00
RCA Victor447-0796		Somebody To Love / White Rabbit (Red label)	1975	1.00	5.00
Grunt 0500		Pretty As You Feel / Wild Turkey	1971	.60	3.00
Grunt 0500	(PS)	Pretty As You Feel / Wild Turkey	1971	1.20	6.00
Grunt 0506		Long John Silver / Milk Train	1971	.60	3.00
Grunt 0506	(PS)	Long John Silver / Milk Train	1971	2.00	10.00
Grunt 0511		Twilight Double Header / Trial By Fire	1972	.60	3.00
Grunt 10988	(DJ)	White Rabbit / White Rabbit (White vinyl)	1977	5.00	25.00
RCA Victor 5156-7-RAB		White Rabbit / White Rabbit (White vinyl)	1988	.80	4.00
RCA Victor 5156-7-RAB	(PS)	White Rabbit / White Rabbit	1988	.80	4.00

JEFFERSON HANDKERCHIEF

Challenge 59371		I'm Allergic To Flowers / Little Matador	1967	1.60	8.00

JEFFERSON STARSHIP, THE
The Starship has featured Balin, Casady, Kantner, Kaukonen, and Slick with John Barbata, Papa John Creach, David Freiberg, Peter Kaukonen, Craig Chaquico, and Mickey Thomas, among others.

RCA Victor 74-0426		A Child Is Coming / Let's Go Together	1971	.60	3.00
RCA Victor 74-0426	(PS)	A Child Is Coming / Let's Go Together	1971	1.00	5.00
		(RCA 0425 credits Paul Kantner & The Jefferson Starship.)			
Grunt 0503		China / Sunfighter	1971	.60	3.00
Grunt 0503	(PS)	China / Sunfighter	1971	1.00	5.00
Grunt 10080		Ride The Tiger / Devil's Den	1974	.40	2.00
Grunt 10206		Caroline / Be Young	1975	.40	2.00
Grunt 10367		Miracles / There Is Love	1975	.40	2.00
Grunt 10456		Play On Love / I Want To See Another World	1975	.40	2.00
Grunt 10746		With Your Love / Switch Blade	1976	.40	2.00
Grunt 10791		St. Charles / Love, Lonely Love	1976	.40	2.00
Grunt 11196		Count On Me / Show Yourself	1978	.40	2.00
Grunt 11196	(PS)	Count On Me / Show Yourself	1978	.40	2.00
Grunt 11274		Runaway / Hot Water	1978	.40	2.00
Grunt 11274	(PS)	Runaway / Hot Water	1978	.40	2.00
Grunt 11374		Crazy Feelin' / Love Too Good	1978	.40	2.00
Grunt 11374	(PS)	Crazy Feelin' / Love Too Good	1978	.40	2.00
Grunt 11426		Light The Sky On Fire / Hyperdrive	1978	.40	2.00
Grunt 11426	(PS)	Light The Sky On Fire / Hyperdrive	1978	.40	2.00
Grunt 11750		Jane / Freedom At Point Zero	1979	.40	2.00
Grunt 11750	(PS)	Jane / Freedom At Point Zero	1979	.40	2.00

JELLY BEANS, THE

Red Bird 003		I Wanna Love Him So Bad / So Long	1964	2.00	10.00
Red Bird 011		Baby, Be Mine / The Kind Of Boy You Can't Forget	1964	2.00	10.00
Eskee 001		I'm Hip To You / You Don't Mean No Good To Me	196?	2.00	10.00

Released in tandem with the two-disc compilation, *2400 Fulton Street,* an overview of what may have been America's best '60s group, this white vinyl reissue of *White Rabbit* included this lovely psychedelic sleeve.

The first appearance of the Jefferson Starship was with Paul Kantner's *Blows Against The Empire* album. As science fiction it was lame, but as the sleeve accompanying the single illustrates, it could have worked as a comic book or animated short.

Label & Catalog #		A-Side/B-Side	Year	VG	NM
JELLY BEAN					
EMI B-9297		**Sidewalk Talk / The Mexican**	1984	2.00	10.00
EMI 501791	(12")	**Sidewalk Talk** (Four versions)	1984	2.00	10.00
		("Sidewalk Talk" features backing vocals by Madonna.)			
JENNIFER (JENNIFER WARNES)					
Parrot 324		**Here, There And Everywhere / Sunny Day Blue**	1968	1.00	5.00
Parrot 328		**The Park / Chelsea Morning**	1969	1.00	5.00
Parrot 333		**I Am Waiting / The Leaves**	1969	1.00	5.00
Parrot 336		**Easy To Be Hard / Let The Sunshine In**	1969	1.00	5.00
Parrot 343		**We're Not Gonna Take It / The Weather's Better**	1970	1.00	5.00
Parrot 346		**Cajun Train / Old Folks**	1970	1.00	5.00
JENNINGS, WAYLON					

Waylon Jennings toured as Buddy Holly's bass player, which led to Holly's producing his first side. He recorded several singles that were influenced by the folk scene of the early '60s. In 1965 he signed with RCA, where his records were aimed at the country market. By the early '70s he had introduced some of rock's attitudes in his music, which led to country's "outlaw" sound, influencing most young country artists—and not a few rockers—since.

Label & Catalog #		A-Side/B-Side	Year	VG	NM
Brunswick 9-55130	(DJ)	**Jole Blon / When Sin Stops**	1959	30.00	150.00
Brunswick 9-55130		**Jole Blon / When Sin Stops**	1959	50.00	250.00
		(A-side produced by Buddy Holly, who plays guitar.)			
Trend 102		**Another Blue Day / Never Again**	1962	5.00	25.00
Trend 106		**The Stage / My Baby Walks All Over Me**	1963	20.00	100.00
Bat 121639		**Dream Baby / Crying**	1962	6.00	30.00
A&M 722		**Rave On / Love Denied**	1963	3.00	15.00
A&M 739		**Four Strong Winds / Just To Satisfy You**	1964	2.00	10.00
JENSEN, DICK (& THE SWAMP MEN)					
Maholo 1012		**Surfin' In Hawaii / Doin' The Tamure**	1963	7.00	35.00
Amber 7001		**Swamped / Waikiki Rumble**	196?	2.00	10.00
JERRY & JEFF					
Jerry Kasenetz and Jeff Katz.					
Super-K 7		**Sweet Charity / Voodoo Medicine Man**	1969	1.20	6.00
Super-K 101		**Sweet, Sweet Lovin' You / Mr. Jensen**	1969	1.20	6.00
JERRY & THE DIAMONDS					
Arc 7456		**Sea-N-Shore / Metal Flakes**	1964	8.00	40.00
JESTERS, THE (JIM MESSINA & THE JESTERS)					
Ultima 705		**Drag Like Boogie / A-Rab**	1964	5.00	25.00
Feature 101		**Panther Pounce / Tiger Tail**	1964	6.00	30.00
JESTERS, THE					
Jerden 741		**Amazon / Alki Point**	1965	1.20	6.00
JESTERS, THE					
Sun 400		**My Babe / Cadillac Man**	1966	4.00	20.00
JET CITY FIVE, THE					
Thumbs Down 1005		**Do You Wonder / Oh Julie**	196?	1.20	6.00
JETHRO TULL					

Jethro Tull features Ian Anderson and Mick Abrahams. Refer to Blodwyn Pig.

Label & Catalog #		A-Side/B-Side	Year	VG	NM
Reprise 0815	(DJ)	**Love Story / Song For Jeffrey**	1968	3.00	15.00
Reprise 0845	(DJ)	**Living In The Past / Driving Song**	1969	3.00	15.00
Reprise 0886	(DJ)	**Reasons For Waiting / Sweet Dream**	1969	3.00	15.00
Reprise 0886		**Back To The Family / Sweet Dream**	1969	.80	4.00
Reprise 0899	(DJ)	**Teacher / Witch's Promise**	1970	3.00	15.00
Reprise 0927		**Inside / Time For Everything**	1970	.80	4.00
Reprise 1024		**Hymn 43 / Mother Goose**	1971	.60	3.00
Chrysalis 2006		**Living In The Past / Christmas Song**	1972	.60	3.00
Chrysalis 2012		**A Passion Play (Edit #8) / A Passion Play (Edit #9)**	1973	.80	4.00
Chrysalis 2017		**A Passion Play (Edit #6) / A Passion Play (Edit #10)**	1973	.60	3.00
Chrysalis 2101	(DJ)	**Bungle In The Jungle / Bungle In The Jungle**	1974	2.00	10.00
Chrysalis 2101	(PS)	**Bungle In The Jungle / Bungle In The Jungle**	1974	2.00	10.00
Chrysalis 2101		**Bungle In The Jungle / Back Door Angel**	1974	.60	3.00
Chrysalis 2103		**Skating Away (On The Thin Ice Of A New Day) / Sea Lion**	1975	.60	3.00
Chrysalis 2106		**Minstrel In The Gallery / Summer Day Sands**	1975	.60	3.00
Chrysalis 2110		**Locomotive Breath / Fat Man**	1976	.60	3.00
Chrysalis 2114		**Too Old To Rock And Roll (Too Young To Die) / Bad Eyed And Loveless**	1976	.60	3.00
Chrysalis 2135		**The Whistler / Strip Cartoon**	1977	.60	3.00
Chrysalis 2387		**Home / Warm Sporran**	1979	.60	3.00
Chrysalis 2613		**Fallen On Hard Times / Pussy Willow**	1982	.60	3.00
		— 12" Singles—			
Chrysalis 3PDJ	(DJ)	**Ring Out, Solstice Bells / March The Mad Scientists / X-Mas Song / Pan Dance**	1976	3.00	15.00

Label & Catalog #		A-Side/B-Side	Year	VG	NM
Chrysalis 18PDJ	(DJ)	Dark Ages / Dark Ages	1976	2.00	10.00
		— Extended Play Albums—			
Chrysalis 1044		Aqualung	1971	4.00	20.00

JEWEL & EDDIE
Jewel Aikens. Eddie Cochran is believed to play guitar.

Silver 1004		Doin' The Hully Gully / Opportunity	1960	5.00	25.00
Silver 1004		Strollin' Guitar / Opportunity	1960	3.00	15.00
Silver 1008		Sixteen Tons / My Eyes Are Crying For You	1960	5.00	25.00

JILL & RAY
Jill & Ray also recorded as Paul & Paula.

Le Cam 979		Hey, Paula / Bobbie Is The One	1962	6.00	30.00

JIMMY & DUANE
Features Duane Eddy.

EBX Preston 212		Soda Fountain Girl /	195?	50.00	200.00

JIMMY & THE ILLUSIONS

Jolyon 36		Undertow / Karen	1963	5.00	25.00

JIMMY & WALTER

Sun 180		Easy / Before Long	1953	—	—
		(Rare. Estimated near mint value $1,000-2,000.)			

JIVIN' GENE & THE JOKERS

Mercury 71485		Breakin' Up Is Hard To Do / My Need For Love	1959	2.00	10.00
Mercury 71561		You're Jealous / Go On, Go On	1960	2.00	10.00
Mercury 71680		Release Me / Going Out With The Tide	1960	2.00	10.00
Mercury 71751		Poor Me / That's What It's Like	1961	2.00	10.00

JO

Capitol 4745		I Don't Want To Be Another Good Luck Charm /			
		She Can Have You	1962	3.00	15.00

JO ANN & TROY
Features Jo Ann Campbell.

Atlantic 2256		I Found A Love, Oh What A Love / Who Do You Love?	1965	2.00	10.00

JODIMARS, THE

Capitol 3285		Let's All Rock Together / Well Now, Dig This	1955	3.00	15.00
Capitol 3360		Dance The Bop / Boom, Boom My Bayou Baby	1956	3.00	15.00
Capitol 3436		Rattle My Bones / Lotsa Love	1956	3.00	15.00
Capitol 3512		Eat Your Heart Out, Annie / Rattle Shakin' Daddy	1956	3.00	15.00
Capitol 3588		Clarabella / Midnight	1956	3.00	15.00
Capitol 3633		Cloud 99 / Later	1957	3.00	15.00

JOE & JUMA

Jerden 108		Mr. Wind / She's The Girl For Me	1960	1.20	6.00

JOE & RITA

Wasp 120		The Only Thing You Need Is Love / Papa Saus	196?	1.00	5.00

JOE & THE FURIES

Parliament 9770-5		Weasel / Broken Arrow	196?	7.00	35.00

JOEL, BILLY
Billy Joel also recorded with The Hassles.

Family 0900		She's Got A Way / Everybody Loves You Now	1973	2.00	10.00
Family 0906		Tomorrow Is Today / Everybody Loves You Now	1973	2.00	10.00

JOEY & THE CONTINENTALS

Claridge 304		She Rides With Me / Rudy Vadoo	196?	5.00	25.00
		(Reissued on Claridge 312 credited to The G.T.O.'s.)			
Laurie 3294		Sad Girl / Baby	1965	1.50	8.00

JOEY & DANNY

Swan 4157		Underwater Surfers / I Got Rid Of The Rats	1963	3.00	15.00

JOHN, ELTON
Elton also recorded with Neil Sedaka.

DJM 70008	(DJ)	Lady Samantha / All Across The Heavens	1969	10.00	50.00
DJM 70008		Lady Samantha / All Across The Heavens	1969	30.00	15000
Congress 6017	(DJ)	Lady Samantha / It's Me That You Need	1970	5.00	25.00
Congress 6017		Lady Samantha / It's Me That You Need	1970	10.00	50.00
Congress 6022	(DJ)	Border Song / Bad Side Of The Moon	1970	5.00	25.00
Congress 6022		Border Song / Bad Side Of The Moon	1970	10.00	50.00

Label & Catalog #		A-Side/B-Side	Year	VG	NM
Viking 1010	(DJ)	From Denver To L.A. / From Denver To L.A.	1970	5.00	25.00
Viking 1010		From Denver To L.A. / (B-side by Barbara Moore Singers)	1970	10.00	50.00
Uni 55246		Border Song / Bad Side Of The Moon	1970	.80	4.00
Uni 55265		Take Me To The Pilot / Your Song	1970	.80	4.00
Uni 55277		Friends / Honey Roll	1971	.80	4.00
Uni 55314		Levon / Goodbye	1971	.80	4.00
Uni 55318		Tiny Dancer / Razor Face	1972	.80	4.00
Uni 55328		Rocket Man / Suzie (Dramas)	1972	.80	4.00
Uni 55343		Honky Cat / Slave	1972	.80	4.00
MCA 40000		Crocodile Rock / Elderberry Wine (Solid black label)	1972	.80	4.00
MCA 40000		Crocodile Rock / Elderberry Wine	1972	.60	3.00
MCA 40046		Daniel / Skyline Pigeon	1973	.60	3.00
MCA 40105		Saturday Night's Alright For Fighting / Jack Rabbit-Whenever You're Ready	1973	.60	3.00
MCA 40148		Goodbye Yellow Brick Road / Young Man's Blues	1973	.60	3.00
MCA 65018		Step Into Christmas / Ho! Ho! Ho! Who'd Be A Turkey At Christmas?	1973	.60	3.00
MCA 40198		Bennie And The Jets / Harmony	1974	.60	3.00
MCA 40259		Don't Let The Sun Go Down On Me / Sick City	1974	.60	3.00
MCA 40297		Bitch Is Back, The / Cold Highway	1974	.60	3.00
MCA 40344		Lucy In The Sky With Diamonds / One Day At A Time	1974	.60	3.00
MCA 40344	(PS)	Lucy In The Sky With Diamonds / One Day At A Time	1974	1.50	8.00
MCA 40364	(PS)	Philadelphia Freedom (Promo picture sleeve.)	1975	4.00	20.00
MCA 40364		Philadelphia Freedom / I Saw Her Standing There	1975	.60	3.00
MCA 40364	(PS)	Philadelphia Freedom / I Saw Her Standing There	1975	.80	4.00
Polydor 002	(DJ)	Pinball Wizard / (B-side by Tina Turner)	1975	5.00	25.00
MCA 40421		Someone Saved My Life Tonight / House Of Cards	1975	.60	3.00
MCA 40461		Island Girl / Sugar On The Floor	1975	.60	3.00
MCA 40505		Grow Some Funk Of Your Own / I Feel Like A Bullet	1976	.60	3.00
MCA/Rocket 40645		Sorry Seems To Be The Hardest Word / Shoulder Holster	1976	.60	3.00
MCA 1938	(DJ)	Love Song / Love Song	1976	4.00	20.00
MCA 40677		Bite Your Lip (Get Up And Dance) / Chameleon	1977	.60	3.00
MCA 40892		Ego / Flintstone Boy	1978	.60	3.00
MCA 40892	(PS)	Ego / Flintstone Boy	1978	.60	3.00
		—Original MCA singles above have black labels with a rainbow.—			
MCA 40973		Part-Time Love / I Cry At Night	1978	.40	2.00
MCA 40973	(PS)	Part-Time Love / I Cry At Night	1978	.40	2.00
MCA 40993		Song For Guy / Lovesick	1979	.40	2.00
MCA 40993	(PS)	Song For Guy / Lovesick	1979	.40	2.00
MCA 41042		Mama Can't Buy You Love / Three-Way Love Affair	1979	.40	2.00
MCA 41042	(PS)	Mama Can't Buy You Love / Three-Way Love Affair	1979	.40	2.00
MCA 41126		Victim Of Love / Strangers	1979	.40	2.00
MCA 41159		Johnny B. Goode / Georgia	1979	.40	2.00
		—Original MCA singles above have tan labels with a rainbow.—			
MCA 41236		Little Jeannie / Conquer The Sun (Picture label)	1980	.40	2.00
MCA 41236	(PS)	Little Jeannie / Conquer The Sun	1980	.40	2.00
MCA 41293		Don't Ya Wanna Play This Game No More? / Cartier / White Man Danger	1980	.40	2.00
Geffen 49722		Nobody Wins / Fools In Fashion	1981	.30	1.50
Geffen 49722	(PS)	Nobody Wins / Fools In Fashion	1981	.30	1.50
Geffen 49788		Chloe / Tortured	1981	.30	1.50
Geffen 50049		Empty Garden / Take Me Down To The Ocean	1982	.30	1.50
Geffen 50049	(PS)	Empty Garden / Take Me Down To The Ocean	1982	.30	1.50
Geffen 29954		Blue Eyes / Hey Papa Legba	1982	.30	1.50
Geffen 29954	(PS)	Blue Eyes / Hey Papa Legba	1982	.30	1.50
Geffen 29846		Ball & Chain / Where Have All The Good Times Gone	1982	.30	1.50
Geffen 29639		I'm Still Standing / Love So Cold	1983	.30	1.50
Geffen 29639	(PS)	I'm Still Standing / Love So Cold	1983	.30	1.50
Geffen 29568		Kiss The Bride / Choc Ice Goes Mental	1983	.30	1.50
Geffen 29568	(PS)	Kiss The Bride / Choc Ice Goes Mental	1983	.30	1.50
Geffen 29460		I Guess That's Why They Call It The Blues / The Retreat	1983	.30	1.50
Geffen 29460	(PS)	I Guess That's Why They Call It The Blues / The Retreat	1983	.30	1.50
Geffen 29292		Sad Songs / A Simple Man	1984	.30	1.50
Geffen 29189		Who Wears These Shoes? / Lonely Boy	1984	.30	1.50
Geffen 29189	(PS)	Who Wears These Shoes? / Lonely Boy	1984	.30	1.50
Geffen 29111		In Neon / Tactics	1984	.30	1.50
Geffen 28873		Wrap Her Up / The Man Who Never Died	1985	.30	1.50
Geffen 28873	(PS)	Wrap Her Up / The Man Who Never Died	1985	.30	1.50
Geffen 28800		Nikita / Restless	1985	.30	1.50
Geffen 28800	(PS)	Nikita / Restless	1985	.30	1.50
Geffen 28578		Heartache All Over The World / Highlander	1986	.20	1.00
Geffen 28578	(PS)	Heartache All Over The World / Highlander	1986	.20	1.00
MCA 53196		Candle In The Wind / Sorry Seems To Be The Hardest Word	1987	.20	1.00
MCA 53196	(PS)	Candle In The Wind / Sorry Seems To Be The Hardest Word (White sleeve)	1987	.60	3.00
MCA 53196	(PS)	Candle In The Wind / Sorry Seems To Be The Hardest Word (Yellow sleeve)	1987	.40	2.00

Label & Catalog #		A-Side/B-Side	Year	VG	NM
MCA 53260		Take Me To The Pilot / Tonight	1988	.20	1.00
MCA 53260	(PS)	Take Me To The Pilot / Tonight	1988	.20	1.00
MCA 53345		I Don't Wanna Go On With You Like That / Rope Around A Fool	1988	.20	1.00
MCA 53345	(PS)	I Don't Wanna Go On With You Like That / Rope Around A Fool	1988	.20	1.00
		—12" Singles—			
MCA 1172	(DJ)	Bite Your Lip / Bite Your Lip (TC)	1977	1.60	8.00
MCA 1174	(DJ)	Get Up And Dance (TC. Blue vinyl)	1977	3.00	15.00
MCA 1979	(DJ)	Ego / Ego	1978	1.60	8.00
MCA 1848	(DJ)	Victim Of Love Box	1979	15.00	75.00
		(Individually numbered boxed set of four promotional 12" singles.)			
MCA 1850	(DJ)	Victim Of Love / Victim Of Love	1979	1.60	8.00
MCA 1854	(DJ)	Johnny B. Goode / Johnny B. Goode	1979	1.60	8.00
Geffen 948	(DJ)	Nobody Wins / Nobody Wins (PC)	1981	2.00	10.00
Geffen 1463	(DJ)	Empty Garden / Empty Garden	1982	2.00	10.00
		(Issued with a lyric sheet.)			
Geffen 2025	(DJ)	I'm Still Standing / I'm Still Standing(PC)	1983	1.20	6.00
Geffen 2066	(DJ)	Kiss The Bride / Kiss The Bride(PC)	1983	1.20	6.00
Geffen ?	(DJ)	I Guess That's Why They Call It The Blues / I Guess That's Why They Call It The Blues(PC)	1983	1.20	6.00
Geffen 2160	(DJ)	Sad Songs / Sad Songs (PC)	1984	1.20	6.00
Geffen 2176	(DJ)	Sasson Presents Elton John	1984	3.00	15.00
Geffen 2374	(DJ)	Wrap Her Up / Wrap Her Up(PC)	1985	1.20	6.00
Geffen 2569	(DJ)	Heartache All Over The World / Heartache All Over The World(PC)	1986	1.20	6.00
MCA 17458	(DJ)	Candle In The Wind / Candle In The Wind	1987	1.00	5.00
Geffen 20563		Heartache All Over The World / Highlander & Heartache All Over The World	1986	.60	3.00
MCA 17475	(DJ)	Take Me To The Pilot / Tonight	1988	1.00	5.00
MCA 23870	(DJ)	I Don't Wanna Go On With You Like That / I Don't Wanna Go On With You Like That	1988	.80	4.00
Geffen 2324	(DJ)	Act Of War, Part 1 / Act Of War, Part 2(PC)	1985	1.00	5.00
		—Extended Play Albums—			
Uni LLP-143	(33)	Tumbleweed Connection (Jukebox EP)	1971	6.00	30.00
MCA LLP-207	(33)	Don't Shoot Me, I'm Only The Piano Player (Jukebox EP)	1972	6.00	30.00

JOHN, ELTON, & KIKI DEE

| MCA 40585 | | Don't Go Breaking My Heart / Snow Queen | 1976 | .60 | 3.00 |
| MCA 40585 | (PS) | Don't Go Breaking My Heart / Snow Queen | 1976 | .60 | 3.00 |

JOHNNY & THE HURRICANES
Johnny Parts with Butch Mattice, Don Staczek, Paul Tesluk and David Yorko, who also recorded as The Craftsmen.

Twirl 1001		Crossfire / Lazy	1959	8.00	40.00
Warwick 502		Crossfire / Lazy	1959	3.00	15.00
Warwick 509		Red River Rock / Buckeye	1959	2.00	10.00
Warwick 509	(S)	Red River Rock / Buckeye	1959	6.00	30.00
Warwick 513		Reville Rock / Time Bomb	1959	2.00	10.00
Warwick 513	(S)	Reville Rock / Time Bomb	1959	6.00	30.00
Warwick 520		Beatnik Fly / Sand Storm	1960	2.00	10.00
Warwick 520	(PS)	Beatnik Fly / Sand Storm	1960	4.00	20.00
Warwick 611		Red River Rock / Wheels	1961	1.00	5.00
Big Top 3036	(PS)	Down Yonder / Sheba	1960	4.00	20.00
Big Top 3051		Rocking Goose / Revival	1960	2.00	10.00
Big Top 3051	(PS)	Rocking Goose / Revival	1960	4.00	20.00
Big Top 3056		You Are My Sunshine / Molly-O	1960	2.00	10.00
Big Top 3056	(PS)	You Are My Sunshine / Molly-O	1960	4.00	20.00
Big Top 3063		Ja-Da / Mr. Lonely	1961	2.00	10.00
Big Top 3063	(PS)	Ja-Da / Mr. Lonely	1961	4.00	20.00
Big Top 3076		Old Smokie / High Voltage	1961	2.00	10.00
Big Top 3076	(PS)	Old Smokie / High Voltage	1961	4.00	20.00
Big Top 3090		Traffic Jam / Farewell, Farewell	1961	2.00	10.00
Big Top 3103		Miserlou / Salvation	1961	2.00	10.00
Big Top 3113		San Antonio Rose / Come On, Train	1962	2.00	10.00
Big Top 3125		Sheik Of Arabee / Minnesota Fats	1962	2.00	10.00
Big Top 3132		What Ever Happened To Baby Jane? / Greens And Beans	1962	2.00	10.00
Big Top 3146		James Bond Theme / Hungry Eyes	1963	2.00	10.00
Big Top 3159		Kaw Liga / Rough Road	1963	2.00	10.00
Jeff 211		Saga Of The Beatles / Rene	1964	3.00	15.00
Mala 470		It's A Mad, Mad, Mad, Mad World / Shadows	1965	1.60	8.00
Mala 483		That's All / Money Honey	1965	1.60	8.00
Atila 211		Saga Of The Beatles / Rene	1967	1.25	6.00
Atila 214		I Love You / Judy's Moody	1967	1.25	6.00
Atila 215		Because I Love Her / Wisdom's Fifth Take	1967	1.25	6.00
Atila 216		Red River Rock '67 / The Psychedelic Lion	1967	1.25	6.00
		—Extended Play Albums—			
Warwick 700		Johnny & The Hurricanes	1959	30.00	150.00

Label & Catalog #		A-Side/B-Side	Year	VG	NM
JOHNNY & THE MARK IV					
Charay 95		Sounds Of Malibu / Down The Pike	196?	7.00	35.00
Revue 11056		Sounds Of Malibu / Down The Pike	196?	.80	4.00
JOHNNY & THE TOKENS					
Warwick 658		The Taste Of A Tear / Never Till Now	1961	3.00	15.00
JOHNNY & THE VELVETONES					
Jerden 714		Hitch Hiking Home / S.O. S.	1963	1.20	6.00
JOHNSON, BILL					
Sun 340		Bobaloo / Bad Times Ahead	1960	2.00	10.00
JOHNSON, CLIFF					
Columbia 40865		Go 'Way, Hound Dog / Twenty Four Hours A Day	1956	10.00	50.00
JOHNSON, JACKIE (WITH LEON SMITH)					
Willamette 102		Star Light, Star Bright / Please Please	195?	10.00	50.00
JOHNSON, JESS					
Cross Roads 1002		Pretty One / Here I Am	196?	3.00	15.00
JOHNSON, KAY					
Willamette 104		Baby, Don't Step On Me / Within A Heartbeat	196?	2.00	10.00

JOHNSTON, BRUCE [THE SURF STOMPERS]
Refer to The Beach Boys; Bruce & Jerry; Bruce & Terry; California; California Music; David Cassidy; The Catalinas; The Gamblers; The Kustom Kings; The Legendary Masked Surfers; Terry Melcher; Sandy Nelson; The Renegades; The Reveres; The Rip Chords; The Rogues; Sagittarius; The Sidewalk Surfers; Bob Sled & The Toboggans; Kip Tyler & The Flips; The Vettes; and the Various Artists EP section.

Del-Fi 4202	(DJ)	The Original Surfer Stomp / Pajama Party	1961	12.00	60.00
		(Promo copies of Del-Fi 4202 credit The Surf Stompers.)			
Del-Fi 4202		Pajama Party / The Original Surfer Stomp	1961	5.00	25.00
Ronda 1003		Do The Surfer Stomp / Do The Surfer Stomp, Part 2	1962	6.00	30.00
Donna 1354	(DJ)	Do The Surfer Stomp / Do The Surfer Stomp, Part 2	1962	10.00	50.00
		(Promo copies of Donna 1354 credit The Surf Stompers.)			
Donna 1354		Do The Surfer Stomp / Do The Surfer Stomp, Part 2	1962	4.00	20.00
Donna 1354	(PS)	Do The Surfer Stomp / Do The Surfer Stomp, Part 2	1962	7.00	35.00
Donna 1364		Soupy Shuffle Stomp / Moon Shot	1962	6.00	30.00
Columbia 10568	(DJ)	Pipeline / Pipeline	1977	.80	4.00
Columbia 10568		Pipeline / Disney Girls	1977	1.60	8.00
		— 12" Singles—			
Columbia 10567	(DJ)	Pipeline / Deirdre	1977	1.00	5.00
Columbia 10567		Pipeline / Deirdre	1977	2.00	10.00

JOKERS, THE: *Refer to* DARLENE & THE JOKERS: TY STEWART

JOLLY GREEN GIANTS, THE					
Redcoat 101		Caught You Redhanded / Busy Bobby	196?	3.00	15.00
JONES, DAVY, & THE DAULPHINS					
Sinclair 1005		Annabelle Lee / Dance, Dance, Little Girl, Dance	1961	3.00	15.00

JONES, DAVY [DAVID JONES]
Davy Jones also recorded with The Monkees; Dolenz, Jones, Boyce & Hart; and Dolenz, Jones & Tork.. Note: Colpix singles credit David Jones.

Colpix 764		Dream Girl / Take Me To Paradise	1965	3.00	15.00
Colpix 764	(PS)	Dream Girl / Take Me To Paradise	1965	5.00	25.00
Colpix 784		What Are We Going To Do? / This Bouquet	1965	3.00	15.00
Colpix 784	(PS)	What Are We Going To Do? / This Bouquet	1965	5.00	25.00
Colpix 789		Girl From Chelsea / Theme For A New Love	1965	3.00	15.00
Colpix 789	(PS)	Girl From Chelsea / Theme For A New Love	1965	6.00	30.00
Bell 45111		Rainy Jane / Welcome To My Love	1971	2.00	10.00
Bell 45136		I Really Love You / Sitting In The Apple Tree	1971	2.00	10.00
Bell 45154	(DJ)	Girl / Take My Love	1971	6.00	30.00
Bell 45154		Girl / Take My Love	1971	12.00	60.00
Bell 45154	(DJ)	I'll Believe In You / The Road To Love	1971	2.00	10.00
Bell 45154		I'll Believe In You / The Road To Love	1971	4.00	20.00
MGM 14458	(DJ)	You're A Lady / Who Was It?	1972	3.00	15.00
MGM 14458		You're A Lady / Who Was It?	1972	6.00	30.00
MGM 14524	(DJ)	Rubberene / Who Was It?	1973	3.00	15.00
MGM 14524		Rubberene / Who Was It?	1973	6.00	30.00
JONES, DAVY, & THE DOLPHINS					
Sinclair 1005		Dance Dance, Little Girl, Dance / Annabelle-Lee	1961	4.00	20.00
Audicon 116		The Bullfight / Strictly Polynesian	1961	7.00	35.00
Tower 4527		Hell's Angels / The Only Way To Fly	1967	3.00	15.00

Label & Catalog #		A-Side/B-Side	Year	VG	NM
JONES, JOHN PAUL					
Vitality		The Wahoo /	196?	2.00	10.00
JONES, JOHN PAUL					
Parkway 915		Baja / Foggy Day In Vietnam	1964	5.00	25.00
JONES, JOHNN					
Dore 682		Surfer Smash / Sing Along With Surfer Smash	1963	4.00	20.00
JONES, JOHNNY, & THE FIVE CHORDS					
Jamie 1110		Love Is Like Music / Don't Just Stand There	1958	4.00	20.00
JONES, ROCKY					
Wasp 116		T For Texas / Break The News	196?	1.20	6.00
Wasp 108		Mule Skinner Blues / Put The Bottle On The Table	196?	3.00	15.00
JONES, RONNIE, & THE CLASS MATES					
End 1002		Little Girl Next Door / Teenage Rock	1957	4.00	20.00
End 1014		Lonely Boy / My Baby Cries	1958	4.00	20.00
End 1125		Lonely Boy / Teenage Rock	1964	2.00	10.00
JONES, SHIRLEY					
Ms. Jones was a "member" of The Partdridge Family.					
Bell 45119		Everybody's Reachin' Out For Someone /			
		I've Still Got My Heart, Joe	1970	2.00	10.00
JONES, TOM					
Tower 126		Little Lonely One / That's What We'll All Do	1965	1.00	5.00
Tower 126	(PS)	Little Lonely One / That's What We'll All Do	1965	2.00	10.00
Tower 176		I Was A Fool / Lonely Joe	1966	1.00	5.00
Tower 176	(PS)	I Was A Fool / Lonely Joe	1966	2.00	10.00
Tower 190		Chills And Fever / Baby, I'm In Love	1966	1.00	5.00
Parrot 9737		It's Not Unusual /			
		To Wait For Love (Is To Waste Your Life Away)	1965	.80	4.00
Parrot 9765		What's New, Pussycat? / Once Upon A Time	1965	.80	4.00
Parrot 9765	(PS)	What's New, Pussycat? / Once Upon A Time	1965	.80	4.00
Parrot 9787		With These Hands / Some Other Guy	1965	.80	4.00
Parrot 9787	(PS)	With These Hands / Some Other Guy	1965	.80	4.00
Parrot 9801		Thunderball / Key To My Heart	1965	.80	4.00
Parrot 9801	(PS)	Thunderball / Key To My Heart	1965	3.00	15.00
		(First pressings sleeves depicts a dead female and a spear gun.)			
Parrot 9801	(PS)	Thunderball / Key To My Heart	1965	.80	4.00
Parrot 9809		Promise Her Anything / Little You	1966	.80	4.00
Parrot 40006		Not Responsible / Once There Was A Time	1966	.80	4.00
Parrot 40007		Till /	1966	.80	4.00
Parrot 40008		City Girl / What A Party	1966	.80	4.00
Parrot 40009		Green, Green Grass Of Home / If I Had You	1966	.80	4.00
Parrot 40012		Detroit City / Ten Guitars	1967	.80	4.00
Parrot 40014		Funny Familiar Forgotten Things / I'll Never Let You Go	1967	.80	4.00
Parrot 40016		Sixteen Tons / Things I Wanna Do	1967	.80	4.00
Parrot 40018		I'll Never Fall In Love Again / Once Upon A Time	1967	.80	4.00
Parrot 40024		I'm Coming Home / Lonely One	1967	.80	4.00
Parrot 40025		Delilah / Smile Away Your Blues	1968	.80	4.00
Parrot 40029		Help Yourself / Day By Day	1968	.80	4.00
Parrot 40035		A Minute Of Your Time / Looking Out My Window	1968	.80	4.00
Parrot 40038		Love Me Tonight / Hide And Seek	1969	.80	4.00
Parrot 40038	(PS)	Love Me Tonight / Hide And Seek	1969	.80	4.00
Parrot 40045		Without Love (There Is Nothing) /			
		The Man Who Knows Too Much	1969	.80	4.00
Parrot 40045	(PS)	Without Love (There Is Nothing) /			
		The Man Who Knows Too Much	1969	.80	4.00
Parrot 40048		Daughter Of Darkness / Tupelo Mississippi Flash	1970	.60	3.00
Parrot 40048	(PS)	Daughter Of Darkness / Tupelo Mississippi Flash	1970	.60	3.00
Parrot 40051		I (Who Have Nothing) / Stop Breaking My Heart	1970	.60	3.00
Parrot 40051	(PS)	I (Who Have Nothing) / Stop Breaking My Heart	1970	.60	3.00
Parrot 40056		Can't Stop Loving You / Never Give Away Love	1970	.60	3.00
Parrot 40056	(PS)	Can't Stop Loving You / Never Give Away Love	1970	.60	3.00
Parrot 40058		She's A Lady / My Way	1971	.60	3.00
Parrot 40058	(PS)	She's A Lady / My Way	1971	.60	3.00
Parrot 40062		Puppet Man / Every Mile	1971	.60	3.00
Parrot 40064		Puppet Man / Resurrection Shuffle	1971	.60	3.00
Parrot 40064	(PS)	Puppet Man / Resurrection Shuffle	1971	.60	3.00
Parrot 40067		Till / One Day Soon	1971	.60	3.00
Parrot 40070		The Young New Mexican Puppeteer /			
		All That I Need Is Time	1973	.60	3.00
Parrot 40074		Letter To Lucille / Thank The Lord	1973	.60	3.00
Parrot 40078		La, La, La (Just Having You Here) / Love, Love, Love	1973	.60	3.00
Parrot 40080		Somethin' 'Bout You, Baby, I Like / Keep A 'Talkin' ' Love	1973	.60	3.00

Label & Catalog #		A-Side/B-Side	Year	VG	NM
Parrot 40081		Pledging My Love / I'm Gone Too Far	197?	.60	3.00
Parrot 40083		Ain't No Love / When The Band Goes Home	197?	.60	3.00
Parrot 40084		I Got Your Number / The Pain Of Love	197?	.60	3.00
Parrot 40086		Memories Don't Leave Like People Do / Helping hand	197?	.60	3.00

JONES BROTHERS, THE

Sun 213		Look To Jesus / Every Night	1955	4.00	20.00

JONES QUARTET, DAVY

Shepherd 2205		My Son The Surfer / Beach Boy	1963	7.00	35.00

JONES TRIO, GAY

Celestial 113		Swinging On Nothing / Chicago	196?	2.00	10.00

JORDAN BROTHERS, THE

Mer-Bri 101		Beach Party /	1965	6.00	30.00

JOSIE & THE PUSSYCATS
The Pussycats feature Cheryl Ladd.

Capitol CP 59-2		With Every Beat Of My Heart / Josie	1972	3.00	15.00
Capitol CP 59-2	(PS)	With Every Beat Of My Heart / Josie	1972	5.00	25.00
Capitol CP 60-3		Voodoo / If That Isn't Love	1972	3.00	15.00
Capitol CP 60-3	(PS)	Voodoo / If That Isn't Love	1972	5.00	25.00
Capitol 2967		With Every Beat Of My Heart / It's Alright With Me	1972	3.00	15.00

JOURNEYMEN, THE

Iona 1111		Work Out / Bag's Groove	1961	7.00	35.00
Iona 1115		Surfer's Blues / Surfer's Rule	1963	7.00	35.00
		(Iona 1115 was also released credited to The Baylanders.)			

JOURNEYMEN, THE
The Journeymen were John and Michelle Philip, later of The Mamas & The Papas, and Scott McKenzie.

Capitol 4625		River She Comes Down / 500 Miles	1961	2.00	10.00
Capitol 4678		Kumbaya / Soft Blow The Summer Winds	1962	2.00	10.00
Capitol 4737		Don't Turn Around / Hush Now, Sally	1962	2.00	10.00
Capitol 4829		What'll I Do? / Loadin' Coal	1962	2.00	10.00
Capitol 4943		Rag Mama / I Never Will Marry	1963	2.00	10.00
Capitol 5031		Ja Da / Kumbaya	1963	2.00	10.00

JOY & THE BOYS

Seafair 104		Meet Me In Seattle / Stephen Foster Medley	196?	1.00	5.00

JOY DIVISION

Rough Trade		Love Will Tear Us Apart / These Days	1980	2.00	10.00
Rough Trade	(PS)	Love Will Tear Us Apart / These Days	1980	2.00	10.00
Factory 28		Komakino / Incubation / Untitled (Flexidisc)	1980	2.00	10.00
Factory 28		Komakino / Incubation (Flexidisc)	1980	4.00	20.00
Factory 28	(PS)	Komakino / Incubation (Flexidisc)	1980	6.00	30.00
		—12" Singles—			
Rough Trade 2		She's Lost Control / Atmosphere	1980	3.00	15.00

JOYCE [HEATH] & THE PRIVATEERS

Agon 1003		Honor Roll Of Love / The Bunny Tale	195?	10.00	50.00

JULY FOUR, THE

Cameo 480		Frightened Little Girl / Mr. Miff	1967	2.00	10.00
		("Mr. Miff" is the same track as Love Potion's "Moby Binks")			

JUST FOUR MEN

Tower 163		There's Not One Thing / (B-side by Freddie & Dreamers)	1964	.80	4.00

JUSTICE V

Panorama 55		Things Get Worse / That Certain Tenderness	1967	1.20	6.00

JUSTIS, BILL

Phillips Inter. 3519		Raunchy / Midnight Man	1957	4.00	20.00
Phillips Inter. 3522		College Man / The Stranger	1958	3.00	15.00
Phillips Inter. 3525		Scroungie / Wild Rice	1958	3.00	15.00
Phillips Inter. 3529		Summer Holiday / Cattywampus	1958	3.00	15.00
Phillips Inter. 3535		Bop Train / String Of Pearls	1958	3.00	15.00
Phillips Inter. 3544		Cloud Nine / Flea Circus	1959	3.00	15.00

JUVENILES, THE

Jerden 770		Bo Diddley / Yes, I Believe	1965	2.00	10.00
Jerden 795		Baby, Baby / I've Searched	1966	2.00	10.00
Panorama 50		You Gotta Understand / Long Green	196?	2.00	10.00

K.

KAC-TIES, THE

Kape 702		Donald Duck / Over The Rainbow	196?	3.00	15.00
Kape 501		Happy Birthday / Girl In My Heart	196?	2.00	10.00

KACT-TIES, THE

Shelly 165		Oh, What A Night / Let Me In Your Life	1964	3.00	15.00
Atco 6299		Oh, What A Night / Let Me In Your Life	1964	2.40	12.00

KAE, RONNY, & THE SAINTS

Band Box 362		Swimming Drums / The Lurch	1964	3.00	15.00

KAI, LANI

Keen 2023		Beach Party / Little Brown Girl	1958	6.00	30.00

KALIN TWINS, THE

Decca 30552		Jumpin' Jack / Walkin' To School	1958	2.00	10.00
Decca 30642		When / Three O' Clock Thrill	1958	2.00	10.00
Decca 30745		Forget Me Not / Dream Of Me	1958	2.00	10.00
Decca 30807		It's Only The Beginning / Oh! My Goodness	1959	2.00	10.00
Decca 30868		When I Look In The Mirror / Cool	1959	2.00	10.00
Decca 30911		Sweet Sugar Lips / Moody	1959	2.00	10.00
Decca 30997		Why Don't You Believe? / The Meaning Of The Blues	1959	2.00	10.00
Decca 30997	(PS)	Why Don't You Believe? / The Meaning Of The Blues	1959	3.00	15.00
Decca 31064		Loneliness / Chicken Thief	1960	2.00	10.00
Decca 31111		True To You / Blue, Blue Town	1960	2.00	10.00
		— Extended Play Albums —			
Decca 2623		When?	1958	16.00	80.00
Decca 2641		Forget Me Not	1958	16.00	80.00

KAMEN, NICK

Sire 28435		Eachtime You Break My Heart / Eachtime You Break My Heart (Instrumental)	1986	2.00	10.00
Sire 20598	(12")	Eachtime You Break My Heart (Three versions) (PC)	1986	2.00	10.00
Sire 20632	(12")	Eachtime You Break My Heart (Three versions) (PC)	1986	2.00	10.00
		("Eachtime You Break My Heart" features Madonna.)			

KAN DELLS, THE

Boss 6501		Cloudburst / Cry Girl	196?	8.00	40.00

KANE, BERNIE, & THE ROCKIN' RHYTHMS

Tabb 9133		High Tide / Pink Lady	1966	6.00	30.00

KANE, PAUL

Tribute 128		He Was My Brother / Carlos Dominguez	197?	2.00	10.00
		(Label reads "Paul Simon writing under the name Paul Kane.")			

KANSAS STANDARD, THE

Nolta 357		Morning Glory / Whisper Soft	196?	2.00	10.00
Nolta 358		I Can Come To You / Oriental Box	196?	2.00	10.00

KAPP, HUB, & THE WHEELS

Take Five 631		Let's Really Hear It / Work, Work	1963	2.00	10.00
Take Five 631	(PS)	Let's Really Hear It / Work, Work	1963	4.00	20.00
Capitol 5215		Sigh, Cry, Almost Die / Bony Marony	1964	2.00	10.00
Capitol 5215	(PS)	Sigh, Cry, Almost Die / Bony Marony	1964	4.00	20.00

KARTER, KENNY

Kenny Karter also recorded as Kenny Hinkle with The Sentinals.

Westco 8		Surfing With Boney Moroney / Blue Booze (Yellow vinyl)	1962	6.00	30.00
Point 5101		Surfing With Boney Moroney / Blue Booze	1962	4.00	20.00

KAY, JOHN

John Kay also recorded with Sparrow and Steppenwolf.

Dunhill 4309		I'm Movin' On / Walk Beside Me	1972	.60	3.00
Dunhill 4319		Somebody / You Win Again	1972	.60	3.00
Dunhill 4351		Moonshine / Nobody Lives Here Anymore	1973	.60	3.00
Dunhill 4360		Easy Evil / Dance To My Song	1973	.60	3.00
Mercury 74004		Give Me Some News I Could Use / Say You Will	1974	.60	3.00

KAYLAN, HOWARD, & MARK VOLMAN: *Refer to* FLO & EDDIE

Label & Catalog #		A-Side/B-Side	Year	VG	NM
KAYO & TRINITIES					
Souvenir 1004		**Walking To School With My Love / Kathy Jo**	1959	2.00	10.00
KEEGAN, SKY					
Claridge 406		**Memphis Miracle / Rock And Roll Heaven**	1975	.60	3.00
KEENS, THE: *Refer to* RICK & THE KEENS					
KEITH					
Mercury 72596		**Ain't Gonna Lie / It Started All Over Again**	1966	.80	4.00
Mercury 72596	(PS)	**Ain't Gonna Lie / It Started All Over Again**	1966	1.00	5.00
Mercury 72639		**98.6 / Teenie Bopper Song**	1966	.80	4.00
Mercury 72639	(PS)	**98.6 / Teenie Bopper Song**	1966	1.00	5.00
Mercury 72652		**Tell Me To My Face / Pretty Little Shy One**	1967	.60	3.00
Mercury 72652	(PS)	**Tell Me To My Face / Pretty Little Shy One**	1967	1.00	5.00
Mercury 72695		**Daylight Savin' Time / Happy Walking Around**	1967	.60	3.00
Mercury 72695	(PS)	**Daylight Savin' Time / Happy Walking Around**	1967	1.00	5.00
Mercury DJ-90	(DJ)	**Sugar Man / Sugar Man**	1967	.80	4.00
Mercury DJ-90	(PS)	**Sugar Man / Sugar Man**	1967	1.20	6.00
Mercury 72715		**Sugar Man / Easy As Pie**	1967	.60	3.00
Mercury 72715	(PS)	**Sugar Man / Easy As Pie**	1967	1.00	5.00
Mercury 72746		**Candy, Candy / I'm So Proud**	1968	.60	3.00
Mercury 72746	(PS)	**Candy, Candy / I'm So Proud**	1968	1.00	5.00
Mercury 72794		**The Pleasure Of Your Company / Hurry**	1968	.60	3.00
Mercury 72794	(PS)	**The Pleasure Of Your Company / Hurry**	1968	1.00	5.00
RCA Victor 74-0140		**Marstand / The Problem**	1969	.60	3.00
RCA Victor 74-0222		**Fairy Tale Or Two / Trixon's Election**	1969	.60	3.00
KEITH, DAVID: *Refer to* ELVIS PRESLEY					
KEITH & DONNA / OLD & IN THE WAY					
Keith and Donna Godchaux also recorded with The Grateful Dead.					
Round		**Sample For Dead Heads** *(With postcard)*	1974	4.00	20.00
KELLY, LEE					
Wasp 104		**False Or True / No Letter Today**	196?	1.20	6.00
KELLY, LEON, & THE RHYTHM ROCKERS					
Space 795		**You Put My Heart In Orbit / Rockaway**	196?	3.00	15.00
KELLY FOUR, THE					
Silver 1001		**Strollin' Guitar / Guybo**	1959	5.00	25.00
Silver 1006		**Annie Has A Party / So Fine, Be Mine**	1960	5.00	25.00
		(Silver 1001 and 1006 feature Eddie Cochran on guitar.)			
Candix 325		**Annie Has A Party / Sweet Angelina**	1963	2.00	10.00
KEN & THE BUSHMEN					
Captain 8716		**Running And Jumping / Little Girl**	196?	2.00	10.00
KENNEDY, CINDY					
Bel Fair 103		**Skate Board /**	196?	2.00	10.00
KENNEDY, DAVE, & THE BLAZERS					
Bolo 721		**Where Did My Darling Go? / Please Don't Leave Me Alone**	196?	2.00	10.00
KENNY & THE BEACH FIENDS: *Refer to* KENNY & THE FIENDS					
KENNY & THE CADETS					
Kenny & The Cadets feature Brian and Carl Wilson of The Beach Boys.					
Randy 422		**Barbie / What Is A Young Man Made Of?** *(Pink label)*	1962	50.00	250.00
Randy 422		**Barbie / What Is A Young Man Made Of?** *(Red & gold vinyl)*	1962	250.00	750.00
Randy 422		**Barbie / What Is A Young Man Made Of?** *(White label)*	1962	*Bootleg*	
KENNY & THE DRASTICS					
Bolo 739		**Sadness In My Heart / Smok Smok**	196?	2.00	10.00
KENNY & THE FIENDS [KENNY & THE BEACH FIENDS]					
Posae 871		**House On Haunted Hill / Green Door**	1963	4.00	20.00
Princess 51		**House On Haunted Hill / House On Haunted Hill, Part 2**	1963	3.00	15.00
Dot 16568		**House On Haunted Hill / House On Haunted Hill, Part 2**	1963	2.00	10.00
Dot 16596		**Moon Shot / One-Two-Three-Four**	1963	2.00	10.00
KENNY & THE HO-DADDIES					
Indigo 134		**Surf Dance / Goofy Guitar**	1961	3.00	15.00

Label & Catalog #	A-Side / B-Side	Year	VG	NM
KENNY & THE KASUALS				
Mark-IV 911	Nothin' Better To Do / Floatin'	1966	5.00	25.00
Mark-IV 1003	It's All Right / You Make Me Feel So Good	1966	5.00	25.00
Mark-IV 1006	Journey To Tyme / I'm Gonna Make It	1967	8.00	40.00
	—Extended Play Albums—			
Mark-IV 400	Kenny And The Kasuals Are Back	1979	3.00	15.00
Mark-IV 400	Kenny And The Kasuals Are Back (Clear vinyl)	1979	3.00	15.00
KENNY & THE NIGHT RIDERS				
Bristol 102	Swamp Rat / Andromeda	196?	6.00	30.00
KENNY & THE SOCIALITES				
Crosstown 001	King Tut Rock / I'll Have To Decide	196?	5.00	25.00
KENNY & THE SULTANS				
Garllo 1	The Wipeout / With Vigor	1963	8.00	40.00
KESSLER, KEITH				
M.T.W. 102	Don't Crowd Me / Sunshine Morning	196?	2.00	10.00
M.T.W. 102 (PS)	Don't Crowd Me / Sunshine Morning	196?	3.00	15.00
KEY MEN, THE				
EM 1002	Sun-Burstin' / Up To News	196?	5.00	25.00
KEYTONES, THE				
Chelsea 1002	Don't Tell William / Parking Field 4	1961	3.00	15.00
Chelsea 1013	One, Two, Three / Sweet Chariot	1962	3.00	15.00
Chelsea 101	I Don't Care / La Do Da Da	1962	3.00	15.00
KIM, ANDY				
United Artists 591	I Love You Once / Love Me, Love Me	1963	1.00	5.00
TCF 5	Give Me Your Love / Li'l Liz	196?	1.00	5.00
20th Century 6709	Give Me Your Love / That Girl	196?	1.00	5.00
Red Bird 040	I Hear You Say I Love You / Falling In Love	1965	1.00	5.00
Steed 707	How'd We Ever Get This Way / Are You Ever Comin' Home	1968	.80	4.00
Steed 710	Shoot 'Em Up, Baby / Ordinary Kind Of Girl	1968	.80	4.00
Steed 711	Rainbow Ride / Ressurection	1968	.80	4.00
Steed 715	Foundation Of My Soul / Tricia, Tell Your Dad	1969	.80	4.00
Steed 716	Baby, I Love You / Gee, Girl	1969	.80	4.00
Steed 720	So Good Together / Got To Know	1969	.80	4.00
Steed 723	A Friend In The City / You	1970	.80	4.00
Steed 727	It's Your Life / To Be Continued	1970	.80	4.00
Steed 729	Be My Baby / Love That Little Woman	1970	.80	4.00
Steed 731	I Wish I Were / Walkin' My La De Da	1971	.80	3.00
Steed 734	I Been Moved / I Had You	1971	.80	3.00
Uni 55332	Who Has The Answers? / Sandy Hollow Dreamer	1972	.60	3.00
Uni 55353	Love The Poor Boy / Love Song	1972	.60	3.00
Uni 55356	Oh, What A Day / Sunshine	1972	.60	3.00
Capitol 3895	Rock Me Gently / Rock Me Gently, Part 2	1974	.60	3.00
Capitol 3962	Fire, Baby I'm On Fire / Here Comes Mornin'	1974	.40	2.00
Capitol 4032	Essence Of Joan / Hang Up Those Rock & Roll Shoes	1975	.40	2.00
Capitol 4096	You Are My Everything / Mary Ann	1975	.40	2.00
Capitol 4130	(She Got Me) Dancin' / Baby, You're All I Got	1976	.40	2.00
Capitol 4234	Oh, Pretty Woman / Baby, You're All I Got	1976	.40	2.00
KIMBERLY, ADRIAN				
Adrian Kimberly is a pseudonym for Don Everly.				
Calliope 6501	Pomp And Circumstance / Black Mountain Stomp	1961	5.00	25.00
Calliope 6503	God Bless America / Greensleeves	1961	5.00	25.00
Calliope 6504	When You Wish Upon A Star / Draggin' Dragon	1961	5.00	25.00
KIMBERLY & THE TERRIERS				
Jerden 749	Humpty Dumpty / Naomi Wise	1965	3.00	15.00
KING, CAROLE				
Carole King also recorded with City; The Germz; The Honeybees; The Palisades.				
ABC-Paramount 9921	Goin' Wild / The Right Girl	1958	10.00	50.00
ABC-Paramount 9986	Baby Sittin' / Under The Stars	1959	10.00	50.00
RCA Victor 47-7560	Queen Of The Beach / Short Mort	1959	15.00	75.00
Alpine 57	Oh, Neil! / A Very Special Boy	1960	50.00	250.00
Companion 2000	It Might As Well Rain Until September / Nobody's Perfect	1962	15.00	75.00
Dimension 1000	It Might As Well Rain Until September / Nobody's Perfect	1962	2.00	10.00
Dimension 1004	School Bells Are Ringing / I Didn't Have Any	1963	3.00	15.00
Dimension 1009	He's A Bad Boy / We Grew Up Together	1963	4.00	20.00
Tomorrow 7502	A Road To Nowhere / Some Of Your Lovin'	1966	8.00	40.00

Label & Catalog #		A-Side/B-Side	Year	VG	NM
KING, HIAL					
MBK 104		Malibu Sunset / War Path	1963	7.00	35.00
KING, JONATHAN					
Jonathan King also recorded with Hedgehoppers Anonymous.					
Parrot 9774		Everyone's Gone To The Moon / Summer's Coming	1965	1.60	8.00
Parrot 9804		Where The Sun Has Never Shone / Green Is The Grass	1965	1.00	5.00
Parrot 3005		Just Like A Woman / Land Of The Golden Tree	1966	1.00	5.00
Parrot 3008		Icicles (Fell From The Heart Of A Bluebird) /			
		In A Hundred Years From Now	1966	1.00	5.00
Parrot 3011		Round Round / Time And Motion	1967	1.00	5.00
Parrot 3021		(Message To The Political Candidates) 1968 /			
		Colloquial Sex	1968	1.00	5.00
Parrot 3027		Lazybones / I Just Want To Say Thank You	1970	.80	4.00
Parrot 3029		Hooked On A Feeling / I Don't Want To Be Gay	1971	.80	4.00
Parrot 3030		Flirt / Hey, Jim	1972	.80	4.00
UK 49002		Learned Tax Council / A Tall Order For A Short Guy	1973	.60	3.00
UK 49014		Mary, My Love / A Tall Order For A Short Guy	1974	.60	3.00
UK 49018		The Kung Fu Anthem / A Little Bit Left Of Right	1974	.60	3.00
UK 49034		The Way You Look Tonight /			
		The True Story Of Molly Malone	1974	.60	3.00
KING BISCUIT ENTERTAINERS, THE					
KBE 1		Courtship Of Priscilla Brown / Now Baby I Love You	1968	1.20	6.00
Burdette 7		Stormy / Pride	1968	.80	4.00
Burdette 9		Ride My Soul Away / Take My Thoughts Away	1968	.80	4.00
Revue 11066		Rollin' Free Man / Sunset Blues	1968	1.00	5.00
KING CRIMSON					
Atlantic 3016		The Night Watch / The Great Deceiver	1974	1.00	5.00
Warner Bros. 29964		Heartburn / Requiem	1982	.80	4.00
Warner Bros. 29309		Sleepless / Man With An Open Heart	1984	.80	4.00
		— 12" Singles —			
Warner Bros. PRO-1005	(DJ)	Elephant Talk (Dance Remix) / Thela Hun /			
		Ginjeet / Matte Kudasai	1981	2.00	10.00
Warner Bros. PRO-1045	(DJ)	Heartburn / Neal And Jack And Me /			
		Sartori In Tangier (TC)	1984	2.00	10.00
Warner Bros. PRO-2013	(DJ)	Sleepless (Dance mix) / Sleepless	1984	2.00	10.00
Warner Bros. PRO-2131	(DJ)	Sleepless / Sleepless (PC)	1984	2.00	10.00
Warner Bros. PRO-2158	(DJ)	Three Of A Perfect Pair / Man With An Open Heart (PC)	1984	2.00	10.00
		— Extended Play Albums —			
Atlantic PR-190	(33)	Larks Tongue In Aspic (Paper sleeve)	1969	8.00	40.00
KING GEORGE & THE CHECKMATES					
Refer to The Checkmates.					
Panorama 20		Miss Galore / What A Fool	1965	1.20	6.00
Jerden 768		Miss Galore / What A Fool	1965	1.20	6.00
Jerden 790		Yo Yo / You Must Be The One	1966	1.20	6.00
KING LIZARD					
King Lizard is a pseudonym for Kim Fowley.					
Original Sound 99		Big Bad Cadillac / Man Without A Count	1970	3.00	15.00
KING PINS, THE					
MGM 13535		Door Banger / Rod Hot Rod	1966	7.00	35.00
Larse 101		94 Second Turf / Rod Hot Rod	1966	6.00	30.00
KINGSLEY, ROBIN					
Tower 109		In And Out / Dreamin' Of You	1965	2.00	10.00
Jerden 767		Whispers / I'd Have To Be Out Of My Mind	1965	2.00	10.00
Tower 182		Whispers / I'd Have To Be Out Of My Mind	1965	2.00	10.00
KINGSMEN, THE					
The Kingsmen is a pseudonym for members of Bill Haley's Comets. Refer to The Lifeguards; The Merri-Men.					
East / West 115		Weekend / Better Believe It	1958	5.00	25.00
East / West 120		The Cat Walk / Congo Rock	1958	5.00	25.00
KINGSMEN, THE					
Gary Abbot, Lynn Easton, Don Galluci, Mike Mitchell and Norm Sundholm. Refer to Don & The Goodtimes.					
Jalynne 108		Lady's Choice / Dig This	1963	3.00	15.00
Jerden 712		Louie, Louie / Haunted Castle	1963	10.00	50.00
		(Original copies of Jerden 712 do not have "340" etched in the trail-off vinyl. Copies on colored vinyl are bootlegs.)			
Wand 143		Louie, Louie / Haunted Castle	1963	3.00	15.00
Wand 143		Louie, Louie '64-'65-'66 / Haunted Castle	1966	2.00	10.00
Wand 150		Money / Bent Scepter	1964	1.60	8.00
Wand 157		Little Latin Lupe Lu / David's Mood	1964	1.60	8.00

Label & Catalog #		A-Side/B-Side	Year	VG	NM
Wand 164		Death Of An Angel / Searching For Love	1964	1.60	8.00
Wand 172		The Jolly Green Giant / Long Green	1965	1.60	8.00
Wand 183		The Climb / I'm Waiting	1965	1.60	8.00
Wand 189		Annie Fanny / Give Her Lovin'	1965	1.60	8.00
Wand 1107		The Gamma Goochee / It's Only The Dog	1966	2.00	10.00
Wand 1115		Killer Joe / Little Green Thing	1966	2.00	10.00
Wand 1118		The Krunch / The Climb	1966	2.00	10.00
Wand 1118	(PS)	The Krunch / The Climb	1966	5.00	25.00
Wand 1127		Little Sally Tease / My Wife Can't Cook	1966	.80	4.00
Wand 1137		If I Needed Someone / Grass Is Green	1966	.80	4.00
Wand 1147		Trouble / Daytime Shadows	1967	.80	4.00
Wand 1154		Wolf Of Manhattan / Children's Caretaker	1967	1.00	5.00
Wand 1157		Don't Say No / (I Have Found) Another Girl	1967	1.00	5.00
Wand 1164		Bo Diddley Bach / Just Before The Break Of Day	1967	1.20	6.00
Wand 1174		Get Out Of My Life, Woman / Since You've Been Gone	1968	1.00	5.00
Wand 1180		I Guess I Was Only Dreamin' / Oh, Love	1968	1.20	6.00
Capitol 3576		You'd Better Do Right / You'd Better Do Right	1972	.80	4.00

KINGSTON TRIO, THE

The major recording members consisted of the original KT, Dave Guard, Nick Reynolds and Bob Shane (1957-1961); and the second Trio, Reynolds, Shane and John Stewart (1961-1967). Refer to the Various Artists EP section.

Label & Catalog #		A-Side/B-Side	Year	VG	NM
Capitol 3970		Scarlet Ribbons / Three Jolly Coachmen	1958	3.00	15.00
Capitol 4049		Tom Dooley / Ruby Red	1958	3.00	15.00
Capitol 4114		Raspberries, Strawberries / Sally	1959	3.00	15.00
Capitol 4167		Tijuana Jail / Oh, Cindy	1959	3.00	15.00
Capitol 4167	(S)	Tijuana Jail / Oh, Cindy	1959	6.00	30.00
Capitol 4221		M.T.A. / All My Sorrows	1959	3.00	15.00
Capitol 4271		A Worried Man / San Miguel	1959	3.00	15.00
		—Capitol singles above have purple labels with the Capitol logo on top.—			
Capitol 4303		Coo Coo-U / Green Grasses	1959	2.00	10.00
Capitol 4338		El Matador / Home From The Hill	1960	2.00	10.00
Capitol 4338	(PS)	El Matador / Home From The Hill	1960	3.00	15.00
Capitol 4379		Bad Man Blunder / The Escape Of Old John Webb	1960	2.00	10.00
Capitol 4441		Everglades / This Mornin,' This Evenin,' So Soon	1960	2.00	10.00
Capitol 4475		Somerset Gloucestershire Wassail / Goodnight, My Baby	1960	2.00	10.00
Capitol 4475	(PS)	Somerset Gloucestershire Wassail / Goodnight, My Baby	1960	4.00	20.00
Capitol 4514		Tom Dooley / M.T.A.	1961	5.00	25.00
Capitol 4536		You're Gonna Miss Me / En El Agua	1961	2.00	10.00
Capitol 4642		Coming From The Mountains / Nothing More To Look Forward To	1961	2.00	10.00
Capitol 4671		Where Have All The Flowers Gone? / O Ken Karanga	1962	2.00	10.00
		—Original Capitol singles above have purple labels with the Capitol logo on the left.—			
Capitol 4671		Where Have All The Flowers Gone? / O Ken Karanga	1962	2.00	10.00
Capitol 4740		Scotch And Soda / Jane, Jane, Jane	1962	1.60	8.00
Capitol 4740	(PS)	Scotch And Soda / Jane, Jane, Jane	1962	3.00	15.00
Capitol 4808		C'mon Betty Home / Old Joe Clark	1962	1.60	8.00
Capitol 4842		One More Town / She Was Good To Me	1962	1.60	8.00
Capitol 4842	(PS)	One More Town / She Was Good To Me	1962	3.00	15.00
Capitol 4898		Greenback Dollar / The New Frontier	1963	1.60	8.00
Capitol 4898	(PS)	Greenback Dollar / The New Frontier	1963	3.00	15.00
Capitol 4951		Reverend Mr. Black / One More Round	1963	1.60	8.00
Capitol 5005		Desert Pete / Ballad Of The Thresher	1963	1.60	8.00
Capitol 5078		Ally Ally Oxen Free / Marcelle Vahine	1963	1.60	8.00
Capitol 5132		Last Night I Had The Strangest Dream / The Patriot Game	1964	1.60	8.00
Capitol 5166		Seasons In The Sun / If You Don't Look Around	1965	1.60	8.00
Capitol 6046		A Worried Man / Scotch And Soda	1964	1.60	8.00
Capitol 6071		Greenback Dollar / Reverend Mr. Black	1965	1.60	8.00
		—Original Capitol singles above have yellow & orange swirl labels with the Capitol logo on the left.—			
Decca 31702		My Rambling Boy / Hope You Understand	1964	2.00	10.00
Decca 31730		I'm Going Home / Little Play Soldiers	1965	1.60	8.00
Decca 31790		Yes, I Can Feel It / Stay Awhile	1965	1.50	8.00
Decca 31860		Runaway Song / Parchment Farm Blues	1965	1.60	8.00
Decca 31922		Norwegian Wood / Put Your Money Away	1966	1.60	8.00
Decca 31961		The Spinnin' Of The World / A Little Soul Is Born	1966	1.60	8.00
Decca 32010		Lock All The Windows / Hit And Run	1966	1.60	8.00
Decca 32040		Texas Across The River / Babe, You've Been On My Mind	1966	2.00	10.00
Tetragrammaton 1526		One Too Many Mornings / Scotch And Soda	1969	1.00	5.00
Capitol 3149		Tell The Riverboat Captain / Windy Wakefield	1971	1.00	5.00
		(Capitol 3149 credits The New Kingston Trio.)			
Mountain Creek 301/2	(DJ)	Big Ship Glory / Johnson Party Of Four	1977	5.00	25.00
Nautilus NR2-45	(DJ)	Aspen Gold / Longest Beer Of The Night	1979	1.00	5.00
Xeres 10004		Looking For The Sunshine / Reverend Mr. Black	1982	.80	4.00
Xeres 10004	(PS)	Looking For The Sunshine / Reverend Mr. Black	1982	.80	4.00
		—Extended Play Albums—			
Capitol 996		The Kingston Trio	1958	8.00	40.00
Capitol 1119		M.T.A.	1958	8.00	40.00
Capitol 1129		Tijuana Jail	1958	8.00	40.00

Label & Catalog #		A-Side/B-Side	Year	VG	NM
Capitol 1136		Tom Dooley	1958	· 8.00	40.00
Capitol 1182		Raspberries, Strawberries	1959	8.00	40.00
Capitol 1-1199		The Kingston Trio At Large (Part 1)	1959	6.00	30.00
Capitol 2-1199		The Kingston Trio At Large (Part 2)	1959	6.00	30.00
Capitol 3-1199		The Kingston Trio At Large (Part 3)	1959	6.00	30.00
Capitol 1-1258		Here We Go Again (Part 1)	1959	6.00	30.00
Capitol 2-1258		Here We Go Again (Part 2)	1959	6.00	30.00
Capitol 3-1258		Here We Go Again (Part 3)	1959	6.00	30.00
Capitol 1332		A Worried Man	1960	6.00	30.00
Capitol 1-1352		Sold Out (Part 1)	1960	6.00	30.00
Capitol 2-1352		Sold Out (Part 2)	1960	6.00	30.00
Capitol 3-1352		Sold Out (Part 3)	1960	6.00	30.00
Capitol 1-1407		String Along (Part 1)	1960	6.00	30.00
Capitol 2-1407		String Along (Part 2)	1960	6.00	30.00
Capitol 3-1407		String Along (Part 3)	1960	6.00	30.00
Capitol 1-1446		The Last Month Of The Year (Part 1)	1960	6.00	30.00
Capitol 2-1446		The Last Month Of The Year (Part 2)	1960	6.00	30.00
Capitol 3-1446		The Last Month Of The Year (Part 3)	1960	6.00	30.00
Capitol 1-1474		Make Way (Part 1)	1961	6.00	30.00
Capitol 2-1474		Make Way (Part 2)	1961	6.00	30.00
Capitol 3-1474		Make Way (Part 3)	1961	6.00	30.00
Capitol 1-1642		Close-Up (Part 1)	1961	6.00	30.00
Capitol 2-1642		Close-Up (Part 2)	1961	6.00	30.00
Capitol 3-1642		Close-Up (Part 3)	1961	6.00	30.00
Capitol PRO-2230	(DJ)	New Frontier / (B-side by Frank Sinatra)	1962	5.00	25.00
Capitol PRO-2529/30	(DJ)	From "Time To Think"	1963	5.00	25.00
Capitol SXA-1577	(33)	The Kingston Trio (Jukebox EP)	1968	5.00	25.00
Capitol SXA-1809	(33)	New Frontier (Jukebox EP)	1968	5.00	25.00
Capitol SXA-1871	(33)	#16 (Jukebox EP)	1968	5.00	25.00
		—Special/Promotional Releases—			
Capitol PRO-856		The Merry Minuet / Tic, Tic, Tic	1959	5.00	25.00
Capitol 2782/3		Molly Dee / Haul Away	1959	2.00	10.00
Capitol 2782/3	(PS)	Molly Dee / Haul Away	1959	3.00	15.00
USAF 79/80		A Worried Man / (B-side by Sonny James)	1959	2.50	12.00
Capitol PRO-1211/2	(EP)	Selections From The Kingston Trio's Three Hit Albums	1959	8.00	40.00
Capitol 2670/1	(EP)	Cool Cargo	1960	5.00	25.00
Capitol X1-1407	(33)	When I Was Young / Leave My Woman Alone	1960	2.00	10.00
Capitol X2-1407	(33)	This Mornin,' This Evenin,' So Soon / Everglades	1960	2.00	10.00
Capitol X3-1407	(33)	Buddy, Better Get On Down The Line / South Wind	1960	2.00	10.00
Capitol X4-1407	(33)	Who's Gonna Hold Her Hand / Tomorrow	1960	2.00	10.00
Capitol X5-1407	(33)	Colorado Trail / The Tattooed Lady	1960	2.00	10.00
		(Capitol 1407 X1-5 are stereo jukebox singles.)			
Capitol XE1-1446	(33)	We Wish You A Merry Christmas / Last Month Of The Year	1960	2.00	10.00
Capitol XE2-1446	(33)	Sing We Noel / Go Where I Send Thee	1960	2.00	10.00
Capitol XE3-1446	(33)	The White Snows Of Winter / All Through The Night	1960	2.00	10.00
Capitol XE4-1446	(33)	Follow Now, O Shepherds /			
		Somerset Gloucestershire Wassail	1960	2.00	10.00
Capitol XE5-1446	(33)	Bye Bye, Thou Little Tiny Child / Mary Mild	1960	2.00	10.00
		(Capitol 1446 XE1-5 are stereo jukebox singles.)			
Capitol 2006/7		Farewell Adelita / Corey, Corey	1960	2.00	10.00
Capitol 2006/7	(PS)	Farewell Adelita / Corey, Corey	1960	3.00	15.00
USAF 129/130		Everglades / (B-side by The Four Preps)	1960	5.00	55.00
USAF 103/104		El Matador / (B-side by Dinah Shore)	1960	5.00	25.00
Capitol SM-1705	(33)	Billy Goat Hill / Take Her Out Of Pity	1962	2.00	10.00
		(Capitol 1705 is a stereo jukebox single.)			
Capitol SXE1-1809	(33)	Some Fool Made A Soldier Of Me / To Be Redeemed	1962	2.00	10.00
Capitol SXE2-1809	(33)	Honey, Are You Mad At Your Man? / Adios Farewell	1962	2.00	10.00
Capitol SXE3-1809	(33)	Poor Ellen Smith / My Lord, What A Mornin'	1962	2.00	10.00
Capitol SXE4-1809	(33)	Long Black Veil / Genny Glen	1962	2.00	10.00
Capitol SXE5-1809	(33)	The First Time / Dogie's Lament	1962	2.00	10.00
		(Capitol 1809 SXE1-5 are stereo jukebox singles.)			

KINKS, THE

The original Kinks are Ray and Dave Davies with Mick Avory and Pete Quaife, who left in 1969. Later members include John Dalton, 1969-77, and Jon Gosling, 1970-78. Refer to The Turtles.

Cameo 308	(DJ)	Long Tall Sally / I Took My Baby Home	1964	20.00	100.00
Cameo 308		Long Tall Sally / I Took My Baby Home	1964	30.00	150.00
Cameo 345	(DJ)	Long Tall Sally / I Took My Baby Home	1964	10.00	50.00
Cameo 345		Long Tall Sally / I Took My Baby Home	1964	15.00	75.00
Cameo 348	(DJ)	You Still Want Me / You Do Something To Me	1965	15.00	75.00
Cameo 348		You Still Want Me / You Do Something To Me	1965	25.00	125.00
Reprise 0306	(DJ)	You Really Got Me / It's Alright	1964	6.00	30.00
Reprise 0306		You Really Got Me / It's Alright	1964	5.00	25.00
		(First pressings have a pinkish two-tone label.)			
Reprise 0306		You Really Got Me / It's Alright	1964	5.00	25.00
Reprise 0334	(DJ)	All Day And All Of The Night / I Gotta Move	1964	2.00	10.00
Reprise 0334		All Day And All Of The Night / I Gotta Move	1964	5.00	25.00

Label & Catalog #		A-Side/B-Side	Year	VG	NM
Reprise 0347	(DJ)	Tired Of Waiting For You / Come On Now	1965	5.00	25.00
Reprise 0347		Tired Of Waiting For You / Come On Now	1965	2.00	10.00
Reprise 0366	(DJ)	Ev'rybody's Gonna Be Happy / Who'll Be The Next In Line?	1965	5.00	25.00
Reprise 0366		Ev'rybody's Gonna Be Happy / Who'll Be The Next In Line?	1965	2.00	10.00
Reprise 0379	(DJ)	Set Me Free / I Need You	1965	5.00	25.00
Reprise 0379		Set Me Free / I Need You	1965	2.00	10.00
Reprise 0409	(DJ)	See My Friends / Never Met A Girl Like You	1965	5.00	25.00
Reprise 0409		See My Friends / Never Met A Girl Like You	1965	2.00	10.00
Reprise 0420	(DJ)	A Well Respected Man / Such A Shame	1965	5.00	25.00
Reprise 0420		A Well Respected Man / Such A Shame	1965	2.00	10.00
Reprise 0454	(DJ)	'Til The End Of The Day / Where Have All The Good Times Gone?	1966	5.00	25.00
Reprise 0454		'Til The End Of The Day / Where Have All The Good Times Gone?	1966	2.00	10.00
Reprise 0471	(DJ)	Dedicated Follower Of Fashion / Sittin' On My Sofa	1966	5.00	25.00
Reprise 0471		Dedicated Follower Of Fashion / Sittin' On My Sofa	1966	2.00	10.00
Reprise 0497	(DJ)	Sunny Afternoon / I'm Not Like Everybody Else	1966	5.00	25.00
Reprise 0497		Sunny Afternoon / I'm Not Like Everybody Else	1966	2.00	10.00
Reprise 0540	(DJ)	Dead End Street / Big Black Smoke	1967	3.00	15.00
Reprise 0540		Dead End Street / Big Black Smoke	1967	4.00	20.00
Reprise 0587	(DJ)	Mr. Pleasant / Harry Rag	1967	3.00	15.00
Reprise 0587		Mr. Pleasant / Harry Rag	1967	4.00	20.00
Reprise 0612	(DJ)	Waterloo Sunset / Two Sisters	1967	3.00	15.00
Reprise 0612		Waterloo Sunset / Two Sisters	1967	4.00	20.00
Reprise 0614	(DJ)	Death Of A Clown / Love Me Til The Sun Shines	1967	3.00	15.00
Reprise 0614		Death Of A Clown / Love Me Til The Sun Shines	1967	4.00	20.00
Reprise 0647	(DJ)	Autumn Almanac / David Watts	1967	3.00	15.00
Reprise 0647		Autumn Almanac / David Watts	1967	4.00	20.00
Reprise 0660	(DJ)	Susannah's Still Alive / Funny Face	1968	3.00	15.00
Reprise 0660		Susannah's Still Alive / Funny Face	1968	4.00	20.00
		(Reprise 0614 and 0660, both from Kinks' sessions, credit Dave Davies.)			
Reprise 0691	(DJ)	Wonderboy / Polly	1968	3.00	15.00
Reprise 0691		Wonderboy / Polly	1968	4.00	20.00
Reprise 0762	(DJ)	Days / She's Got Everything	1968	3.00	15.00
Reprise 0762		Days / She's Got Everything	1968	4.00	20.00
Reprise 0806	(DJ)	Starstruck / Picture Book	1969	3.00	15.00
Reprise 0806		Starstruck / Picture Book	1969	4.00	20.00
Reprise 0847	(DJ)	Village Green Preservation Society / Do You Remember Walter?	1969	3.00	15.00
Reprise 0847		Village Green Preservation Society / Do You Remember Walter?	1969	4.00	20.00
Reprise 0863	(DJ)	Victoria / Brainwashed	1969	3.00	15.00
Reprise 0863		Victoria / Brainwashed	1969	3.00	15.00
Reprise 0930	(DJ)	Lola / Mindless Child Of Motherhood	1970	3.00	15.00
Reprise 0930		Lola / Mindless Child Of Motherhood	1970	1.00	5.00
Reprise 0979	(DJ)	Apeman / Rats	1970	3.00	15.00
Reprise 0979		Apeman / Rats	1970	1.60	8.00
Reprise 1017	(DJ)	God's Children / The Way Love Used To Be	1971	3.00	15.00
Reprise 1017		God's Children / The Way Love Used To Be	1971	3.00	15.00
Reprise 1094	(DJ)	King Kong / Waterloo Sunset	1972	3.00	15.00
Reprise 1094		King Kong / Waterloo Sunset	1972	3.00	15.00
		(Many of the Reprise singles from the latter '60s were pressed on polystyrene, while the white label promos continued to be pressed on vinyl.)			
RCA Victor 74-0620	(DJ)	20th Century Man / Skin And Bones	1971	1.60	8.00
RCA Victor 74-0620		20th Century Man / Skin And Bones	1971	.60	3.00
RCA Victor 74-0807	(DJ)	Supersonic Rocket Ship / You Don't Know My Name	1972	1.60	8.00
RCA Victor 74-0807		Supersonic Rocket Ship / You Don't Know My Name	1972	.60	3.00
RCA Victor 74-0852	(DJ)	Celluloid Heroes / Hot Potatoes	1972	1.60	8.00
RCA Victor 74-0852		Celluloid Heroes / Hot Potatoes	1972	.60	3.00
RCA Victor 74-0940	(DJ)	One Of The Survivors / Scrapheap City	1973	1.60	8.00
RCA Victor 74-0940		One Of The Survivors / Scrapheap City	1973	.60	3.00
RCA Victor LPBO-5001	(DJ)	Sitting In The Midday Sun / Sweet Lady Genevieve	1973	1.60	8.00
RCA Victor LPBO-5001		Sitting In The Midday Sun / Sweet Lady Genevieve	1973	.80	4.00
RCA Victor APBO-0275	(DJ)	Money Talks / Money Talks	1974	1.60	8.00
RCA Victor APBO-0275		Money Talks / Here Comes Flash	1974	.60	3.00
RCA Victor PB-10019	(DJ)	Mirror Of Love / Mirror Of Love	1974	1.60	8.00
RCA Victor PB-10019		Mirror Of Love / He's Evil	1974	.60	3.00
RCA Victor PB-10121	(DJ)	Preservation / Preservation	1974	1.60	8.00
RCA Victor PB-10121		Preservation / Salvation Road	1974	.60	3.00
RCA Victor PB-10251	(DJ)	Starmaker / Starmaker	1975	1.60	8.00
RCA Victor PB-10251		Starmaker / Ordinary People	1975	.60	3.00
RCA Victor PB-10551	(DJ)	I'm In Disgrace / I'm In Disgrace	1975	1.60	8.00
RCA Victor PB-10551		I'm In Disgrace / The Hard Way	1975	.60	3.00
Arista SP-5	(DJ)	Sleepwalker / All The Kids On The Street (Yellow vinyl)	1977	3.00	15.00
Arista 0240		Sleepwalker / Full Moon	1977	.40	2.00
Arista 0247		Jukebox Music / Life Goes On	1977	.40	2.00
Arista 0296	(DJ)	Father Christmas / Father Christmas	1977	1.00	5.00
Arista 0296	(PS)	Father Christmas (Promo picture sleeve)	1977	1.00	5.00

Label & Catalog #		A-Side/B-Side	Year	VG	NM
Arista 0296		**Father Christmas / Prince Of Punks**	1977	.40	2.00
Arista 0296	(PS)	**Father Christmas / Prince Of Punks**	1977	1.00	5.00
Arista 0342		**A Rock 'N Roll Fantasy / Get Up**	1978	.40	2.00
Arista 0342		**A Rock 'N Roll Fantasy / Live Life**	1978	.60	3.00
Arista 0372		**Black Messiah / Live Life**	1978	.40	2.00
Arista 0409		**Superman / Low Budget**	1979	.40	2.00
Arista 0448		**A Dollar Of Gas / Low Budget**	1979	.40	2.00
Arista 0458		**Catch Me Now I'm Falling / Low Budget**	1979	.40	2.00
Arista 0541		**Celluloid Heroes / Lola**	1980	.40	2.00
Arista 0541	(PS)	**Celluloid Heroes / Lola**	1980	.80	4.00
Arista 0577		**You Really Got Me / Attitude**	1980	.40	2.00
Arista 0619		**Destroyer / Back To Front**	1981	.40	2.00
Arista 0649		**Better Things / Yo-Yo**	1981	.40	2.00
Arista 9085		**Don't Forget To Dance / Young Conservatives**	1983	.40	2.00
Arista 1054		**Come Dancing / Noise**	1983	.40	2.00
Arista 9334		**Summer's Gone / Going Solo**	1984	.50	2.50
		— 12" Singles —			
Arista CP-700		**Superman / Low Budget**	1979	1.00	5.00
Arista 9085	(DJ)	**Don't Forget To Dance / Don't Forget To Dance**	1983	1.00	5.00

KISS

Original members of Kiss were Peter Criss, Ace Frehley, Gene Simmons and Paul Stanley.

Label & Catalog #		A-Side/B-Side	Year	VG	NM
Casablanca NEB 0004		**Nothin' To Lose / Love Theme From Kiss**	1974	2.00	10.00
Casablanca NEB 0011		**Kissin' Time / Nothin' To Lose**	1974	2.00	10.00
Casablanca NEB 0015		**Strutter / 100,000 Years**	1974	2.00	10.00
Casablanca NB 823		**Let Me Go, Rock 'N Roll / Hotter Than Hell**	1974	2.00	10.00
Casablanca NB 829		**Rock And Roll All Nite / Getaway**	1975	2.00	10.00
Casablanca NB 841		**C'mon And Love Me / Getaway**	1975	2.00	10.00
Casablanca NB 850		**Rock And Roll All Nite / Rock And Roll All Nite**	1975	1.20	5.00
Casablanca NB 854		**Shout It Out Loud / Sweet Pain**	1976	1.20	5.00
Casablanca NB 858		**Flaming Youth / God Of Thunder**	1976	2.00	10.00
Casablanca NB 858	(PS)	**Flaming Youth / God Of Thunder**	1976	7.00	35.00
Casablanca NB 863		**Detroit Rock City / Beth**	1976	1.00	5.00
Casablanca NB 873		**Hard Luck Woman / Mr. Speed**	1976	1.00	5.00
Casablanca NB 880		**Calling Dr. Love / Take Me**	1977	1.00	5.00
Casablanca NB 889		**Christine Sixteen / Shock Me**	1977	1.00	5.00
Casablanca NB 895		**Love Gun / Hooligan**	1977	1.00	5.00
Casablanca NB 906		**Shout It Out Loud / Nothin' To Lose**	1978	1.00	5.00
Casablanca NB 915		**Rocket Ride / Tomorrow And Tonight**	1978	1.00	5.00
Casablanca NB 928		**Strutter '78 / Shock Me**	1978	1.00	5.00
Casablanca NB 983		**I Was Made For Lovin' You / Hard Times**	1979	.80	4.00
Casablanca NB 2205		**Sure Know Something / Dirty Livin'**	1979	.80	4.00
Casablanca NB 2282		**Shandi / She's So European**	1980	.80	4.00
Casablanca NB 2299		**Tomorrow / Naked City**	1980	.80	4.00
Casablanca NB 2343		**A World Without Heroes / Dark Light**	1981	.80	4.00
Casablanca NB 2365		**I Love It Loud / Danger**	1981	.80	4.00
Casablanca NB 2365	(PS)	**I Love It Loud / Danger**	1981	3.00	15.00
Casablanca 814 671		**Lick It Up / Dance All Over Your Face**	1983	.60	3.00
Casablanca 818 216		**All Hell's Breakin' Loose / Young And Wasted**	1983	.60	3.00
Casablanca 818 216		**Heaven's On Fire / Lonely Is The Hunter**	1984	.60	3.00
Casablanca 880 535		**Thrills In The Night / Burn, Bitch, Burn**	1984	.60	3.00
Casablanca 884 141		**Tears Are Falling / Anyway You Slice It**	1985	.60	3.00
Casablanca 884 141	(PS)	**Tears Are Falling / Anyway You Slice It**	1985	.60	3.00
Casablanca 888 796		**Crazy Nights / No, No, No**	1987	.60	3.00
Casablanca 888 796	(PS)	**Crazy Nights / No, No, No**	1987	.60	3.00
Casablanca 870 022		**Reason To Live / Thief In The Night**	1987	.60	3.00
Casablanca 870 022	(PS)	**Reason To Live / Thief In The Night**	1987	.60	3.00
Casablanca 870 215		**Turn On The Night / Hell Or High Water**	1987	.60	3.00
Casablanca 870 215	(PS)	**Turn On The Night / Hell Or High Water**	1987	.60	3.00
Casablanca 872 246		**Let's Put The X In Sex / Calling Dr. Love**	1988	.80	4.00
Casablanca 872 246	(PS)	**Let's Put The X In Sex / Calling Dr. Love**	1988	.80	4.00
Casablanca 876 146		**Hide Your Heart / Betrayed**	1989	.50	2.50
Casablanca 876 716		**Forever / The Street Giveth And The Street Taketh Away**	1989	.50	2.50
		— 12" Singles —			
Casablanca NB 298	(DJ)	**I Was Made For Lovin' You** *(One sided)*	1978	4.00	20.00
Casablanca NB 298		**I Was Made For Lovin' You / Charisma**	1978	3.00	15.00
Casablanca PRO-229	(DJ)	**Lick It Up / Lick It Up**	1983	3.00	15.00
Casablanca PRO-244	(DJ)	**All Hell's Breakin' Loose / All Hell's Breakin' Loose**	1983	2.00	10.00
Casablanca PRO-311	(DJ)	**Heaven's On Fire / Heaven's On Fire**	1984	3.00	15.00
Casablanca PRO-326	(DJ)	**Thrills In The Night / Thrills In The Night**	1984	2.00	10.00
Casablanca PRO-377	(DJ)	**Tears Are Falling / Tears Are Falling**	1985	2.00	10.00
Casablanca PRO-395	(DJ)	**Uh! All Night / Uh! All Night**	1985	2.00	10.00
Casablanca PRO-531	(DJ)	**Crazy Nights / Crazy Nights**	1987	2.00	10.00
Casablanca PRO-559	(DJ)	**Reason To Live / Reason To Live**	1987	2.00	10.00
Casablanca PRO-572	(DJ)	**Turn On The Night / Turn On The Night**	1987	2.00	10.00
Casablanca	(DJ)	**Let's Put The X In Sex / Let's Put The X In Sex / Let's Put The X In Sex / Let's Put The X In Sex**	1988	4.00	20.00

Label & Catalog #	A-Side/B-Side	Year	VG	NM
KISS INC.				
Bell 931	**Hey, Mr. Holy Man / Kids Are Crying**	1973	2.00	10.00
KJR ORCHESTRA, THE				
Reprise 0469	**Jet City / Wonder Mother**	1966	1.20	6.00
KLEIN, GEORGE				
Sun 358	**U. T. Party / U. T. Party, Part 2**	1961	2.00	10.00
KLEIN, MO, & THE SERGEANTS				
Crystalette 722	**Alright, Private / Flying Loxbox**	1958	5.00	25.00

KNICKERBOCKERS, THE
The Knickerbockers are Beau Charles, John Charles, Buddy Randell and Jimmy Walker. Refer to The Righteous Brothers.

Challenge 59268	**Bite, Bite, Barracuda / All I Need Is You**	1965	1.00	5.00
Challenge 59293	**Jerktown / Room For One More**	1965	1.00	5.00
Challenge 59321	**Lies / The Coming Generation**	1965	2.00	10.00
Challenge 59326	**One Track Mind / I Must Be Doing Something Right**	1966	1.00	5.00
Challenge 59332	**High On Love / Stick With Me**	1966	1.00	5.00
Challenge 59335	**Chapel In The Fields / Just One Girl**	1966	1.00	5.00
Challenge 59341	**Rumors, Gossip, Words Untrue / Love Is A Bird**	1966	1.00	5.00
Challenge 59359	**Sweet Green Fields / What Does That Make You?**	1967	1.00	5.00
Challenge 59366	**Come And Get It / Wishful Thinking**	1967	1.00	5.00
Challenge 59380	**I Can Do Better Than That / You'll Never Walk Alone**	1967	1.00	5.00
Challenge 59384	**They Ran For Their Lives / As A Matter Of Fact**	1967	1.00	5.00

KNICKERBOCKERS, THE: *Refer to* BUDDY RANDELL

KNIGHT, CHRIS
Chris Knight was a member of The Brady Bunch.

Paramount 0177	**Over And Over / Good For Each Other**	1972	2.00	10.00
Paramount 0177 (PS)	**Over And Over / Good For Each Other**	1972	3.00	15.00

KNIGHT, TERRY, & THE PACK [THE FABULOUS PACK; THE PACK]
After recording under various versions of The Pack, featured Don Brewer and Mark Farner, the group changed their name and, with Knight as manager, recorded as Grand Funk Railroad.

Wingate 007	**Tears Come Rollin' / Color Of Our Love**	1964	3.00	15.00
Lucky Eleven 003	**I've Got News / Harlem Shuffle**	1965	2.00	10.00
Lucky Eleven 007	**Does It Matter To You, Girl? / Widetrackin'**	1965	2.00	10.00
Lucky Eleven 007 (PS)	**Does It Matter To You, Girl? / Widetrackin'**	1965	3.00	15.00
	(Wingate 007 and L.E. 003 and 007 credits The Fabulous Pack.)			
Lucky Eleven 225	**I've Been Told / How Much More?**	1966	1.20	6.00
Lucky Eleven 228	**Lady Jane / Lovin' Kind**	1966	1.20	6.00
Lucky Eleven 229	**A Change On The Way / What's On Your Mind?**	1966	1.20	6.00
Lucky Eleven 230	**(I) Who Have Nothing / Numbers**	1966	1.20	6.00
Lucky Eleven 235	**Love, Love, Love, Love, Love / This Precious Time**	1967	1.20	6.00
Lucky Eleven 236	**One Monkey Don't Stop No Show / The Train**	1967	1.20	6.00
Lucky Eleven 1141	**Better Man Than I / Got Love**	196?	1.20	6.00
Cameo 482	**Lizabeth Peach / Forever And A Day**	1967	1.00	5.00
Capitol 2174	**Without A Woman / Next To Your Fire**	1968	2.00	10.00
	(Capitol 2174 credits The Pack.)			
Capitol 2409	**Such A Lonely Life / Lullaby**	1969	1.00	5.00
Capitol 2506	**The Legend Of St. Paul / The Legend Of William And Mary**	1969	1.00	5.00

KNIGHT TRAINS, THE

Hart-Van 126	**Surfin' On The Rocks / Beach Head**	196?	7.00	35.00

KNIGHTS, THE
The Knights are a studio creation of Gary Usher.

Capitol 5302	**Hot Rod High / Theme For Teen Love**	1964	8.00	40.00

KNOCKOUTS, THE

Shad 5013	**Darling Lorraine / Riot In Room 3C**	1959	5.00	25.00
	("Darling Lorraine" features a long ending.)			
Shad 5013	**Darling Lorraine / Riot In Room 3C**	1959	3.00	15.00
	("Darling Lorraine" features a shorter ending.)			
Shad 5018	**Please Be Mine / Rich Boy, Poor Boy**	1960	3.00	15.00

KNOX, BUDDY (& THE RHYTHM ORCHIDS)

Blue Moon	**Party Doll** / *(B-side by Jimmy Bowen)*	1957	——	——
	(Although unverified, rumors of this record's existence continue.)			
Triple-D 798	**Party Doll** / *(B-side by Jimmy Bowen)*	1957	——	——
	(Rare. Estimated near mint value $500-1,000.)			
Roulette 4002	**Party Doll / My Baby's Gone**	1957	6.00	30.00
Roulette 4009	**Rock Your Little Baby To Sleep / Don't Make Me Cry**	1957	5.00	25.00
	—*Original Roulette singles above have white labels with criss-crossed color bars.*—			
Roulette 4002	**Party Doll / My Baby's Gone**	1957	3.00	15.00
Roulette 4009	**Rock Your Little Baby To Sleep / Don't Make Me Cry**	1957	3.00	15.00

Label & Catalog #		A-Side/B-Side	Year	VG	NM
Roulette 4018		Hula Love / Devil Woman	1957	3.00	15.00
Roulette 4042		Swingin' Daddy / Whenever I'm Lonely	1958	3.00	15.00
Roulette 4082		Somebody Touched Me / C'mon, Baby	1958	3.00	15.00
Roulette 4120		Teasable, Pleasable You / That's Why I Cry	1959	3.00	15.00
Roulette 4140		I Think I'm Gonna Kill Myself / To Be With You	1959	3.00	15.00
Roulette 4179		I Ain't Sharin' Sharon / Taste Of The Blues	1959	3.00	15.00
Roulette 4262		Long, Lonely Nights / Storm Clouds	1960	3.00	15.00
		—Roulette singles above have orange labels.—			
Liberty 55290		Lovey Dovey / I Got You	1960	2.00	10.00
Liberty 55305		Ling-Ting-Tong / The Kisses	1961	1.60	8.00
Liberty 55305	(PS)	Ling-Ting-Tong / The Kisses	1961	4.00	20.00
Liberty 55366		All By Myself / Three-Eyed Man	1962	1.60	8.00
Liberty 55411		Chi-Hua-Hua / Open	1962	1.20	6.00
Liberty 55473		She's Gone / Now There's Only Me	1962	1.20	6.00
Liberty 55503		Three Way Love Affair / Dear Abby	1962	1.20	6.00
Liberty 55592		Tomorrow Is A Comin' / Shadaroom	1963	1.20	6.00
Liberty 55650		Hitch-Hike Back To Georgia / Thanks A Lot	1963	1.20	6.00
Liberty 55694		Good Lovin' / All Time Loser	1963	1.20	6.00
Liberty 54525		Lovey Dovey / Ling-Ting-Tong	1963	.60	3.00
Reprise 0395		Good Time Girl / Livin' In A House Full Of Love	1965	1.20	6.00
Reprise 0431		A Lover's Question / You Said Goodbye	1965	1.20	6.00
Reprise 0463		A White Sport Coat (And A Pink Carnation) / That Don't Do Me No Good	1966	1.20	6.00
Reprise 0501		Love Has Many Ways / 16 Feet Of Patio	1966	1.20	6.00
Ruff 1001		Jo-Ann / Don't Make A Ripple	1966	1.00	5.00
United Artists 50301		Gypsy Man / This Time Tomorrow	1968	1.00	5.00
United Artists 50463		Tonight My Sleepless Night's Gone To Town / A Million Years Or So	1968	1.00	5.00
United Artists 50526		Night Runners / God Knows I Love You	1969	1.00	5.00
United Artists 50596		Salt Lake City / I'm Only Rockin'	1969	1.00	5.00
United Artists 50644		Back To New Orleans / Yesterday Is Gone	1970	1.00	5.00
United Artists 50722		Glory Train / White Dove	1970	1.00	5.00
United Artists 50789		Travelin' Light / Come Softly To Me	1971	1.00	5.00
		—Extended Play Albums—			
Roulette 301		Buddy Knox	195?	50.00	200.00

KOO KREW, THE

Ascot 2225		Wet And Wild / Down To Earth	196?	6.00	30.00

KOOB, ROGER

Birth 102		Give Me The Love I'm Needing / You'll Be Alone	1970	1.20	6.00

KRAMER, BILLY J., & THE DAKOTAS
Refer to The Dakotas.

Liberty 55586		Do You Want To Know A Secret? / I'll Be On My Way	1963	2.00	10.00
Liberty 55626		Bad To Me / I Call Your Name	1964	2.00	10.00
Liberty 55643		I'll Keep You Satisfied / I Know	1964	2.00	10.00
Liberty 55667		Do You Want To Know A Secret? / Bad To Me	1964	2.00	10.00
Imperial 66027		Little Children / Bad To Me	1964	1.60	8.00
Imperial 66048		I'll Keep You Satisfied / I Know	1964	1.60	8.00
Imperial 66051		From A Window / I'll Be On My Way	1965	1.60	8.00
Imperial 66051	(PS)	From A Window / I'll Be On My Way	1965	3.00	15.00
Imperial 66095		It's Gotta Last Forever / They Remind Me Of You	1965	1.20	6.00
Imperial 66115		Trains And Boats And Planes / That's The Way I Feel	1965	1.20	6.00
Imperial 66135		Irresistible You / Twilight Time	1965	1.20	6.00
Imperial 66143		I'll Be Doggone / Neon City	1965	1.20	6.00
Imperial 66210		Take My Hand / You Make Me Feel Like Someone	1966	1.20	6.00

KUBAN, BOB, & THE IN MEN

Norman 558		Turn On Your Love Light / Jerkin' Time	1966	1.20	6.00
Musicland 20001		The Cheater / Try Me, Baby	1966	1.20	6.00
Musicland 20006		The Teaser / All I Want	1966	1.20	6.00
Musicland 20007		Pretzel Party / The Pretzel	1967	1.20	6.00
Musicland 20013		Harlem Shuffle / Theme From "Virginia Wolfe"	1967	1.20	6.00
Musicland 20017		Batman Theme / You Better Run, You Better Hide	1967	1.60	8.00

KURT & THE KAPERS

V-Lee 211		Mongoose / Trapped	196?	7.00	35.00

KUSTOM KINGS, THE

Smash 1883	(DJ)	In My '40 Ford / Clutch Rider	1964	4.00	20.00
Smash 1883		In My '40 Ford / Clutch Rider	1964	8.00	40.00
		("In My '40 Ford" features Bruce Johnston.)			

L.

L.A. TEENS, THE
The L.A. Teens were produced by Gary Usher.

Decca 31763	(DJ)	You'll Come Running Back / I'm Gonna Get You	1965	2.00	10.00
Decca 31763		You'll Come Running Back / I'm Gonna Get You	1965	4.00	20.00
Decca 31813	(DJ)	All I Really Want To Do / Saturday's Child	1965	2.00	10.00
Decca 31813		All I Really Want To Do / Saturday's Child	1965	4.00	20.00

LaBEEF, SLEEPY
Sleepy is a pseudonym for Tommy LaBeef. Refer to the Various Artists EP section.

Crescent 102	Turn Me Loose /	195?	20.00	100.00
Starday 292	I'm Through / All Alone	1957	50.00	150.00
Mercury 71112	I'm Through / All Alone	1957	15.00	75.00
Mercury 71179	All The Time / Lonely	1957	15.00	75.00
Columbia 44068	Sure Beats The Heck Out Of Settlin' Down / Schneider	1967	2.00	10.00
Columbia 44261	Completely Destroyed / Go Ahead On, Baby	1967	2.00	10.00
Columbia 44455	Every Day / If I Go Right I'm Wrong	1968	2.00	10.00
Plantation 55	Too Much Monkey Business / Got You On My Mind	1970	.80	4.00
Plantation 74	Blackland Farmer / Got You On My Mind	1970	.80	4.00
Sun 1132	Thunder Road / Hundred Pounds Of Lovin'	1971	.60	3.00
Sun 1133	Ghost Riders In The Sky /	1971	.60	3.00
Sun 1134	There Ain't Much After Texas / Hundred Pounds Of Lovin'	1971	.60	3.00
Sun 1137	Good Rockin' Boogie / Mathilda	1978	.60	3.00
Sun 1145	Flying Saucers Rock 'N' Roll / Boogie Woogie Country Girl	1979	.60	3.00

LaBEEF, TOMMY
Tommy also recorded as Sleepy LaBeef.

Wayside 1651	Ride On, Josephine /	1959	50.00	250.00
Wayside 1652	Walkin' Slowly /	1959	50.00	250.00
Wayside 1654	Tore Up /	1959	50.00	250.00
Picture 1937	Ride On, Josephine /	1959	20.00	100.00

LaFLAMME, DAVID
David LaFlamme originally recorded with It's A Beautiful Day.

Amherst 717		White Bird / Spirit Of America	1976	.40	2.00
Amherst 717	(PS)	White Bird / Spirit Of America	1976	.40	2.00

LAINE, DENNY
Denny Laine originally recorded with The Moody Blues.

Deram 7509	Ask The People / Say You Don't Mind	1967	1.00	5.00
Capitol 4340	I'm Lookin' For Someone To Love /			
	It's So Easy-Listen To Me	1976	1.00	5.00
Capitol 4425	Heartbeat / Moondreams	1977	1.00	5.00
	(Capitol 4340 and 4425 were produced by Paul McCartney.)			
Arista 511	Japanese Tears / Guess I'm Only Falling	1980	.60	3.00

LAKE, KAREN

Big Top 3077	I'd Like To Miss My Graduation / Airmail Special	1961	3.00	15.00
	(Produced by Phil Spector.)			

LAMARR, GENE

Spry 113	That Crazy Little House / You Don't Love Me Anymore	1959	20.00	100.00
Spry 114	You Can Count On Me / Just A Little Bit Longer	1959	20.00	100.00
Spry 115	Close To Me / Mooneyes	1959	20.00	100.00

LANCASTRAINS, THE

Jerden 798	The World Keeps Going Round / Not The Same	196?	1.20	6.00
Capitol 5501	There'll Be No More Goodbyes /			
	Never Gonna Come On Home	1964	1.00	5.00

LANCE & THE LEGENDS

Impression 109	Baby, Without You / I Cried	196?	2.00	10.00

LANCE, HERB, & THE CLASSICS
Refer to The Classics.

Promo 1010	Blue Moon / Little Boy Lost	1961	3.00	15.00

LANCE, LARRY, & THE SKY RIDERS

Monkswell 3101	Bright Orange Light / Tickled Pink	196?	3.00	15.00
Monkswell 3106	Puddin' And Pie / One Lone Tugger At The Dock	196?	3.00	15.00

Label & Catalog #	A-Side/B-Side	Year	VG	NM
LANCERS, THE				
Cloud 500	Baja / When Johnny Comes Draggin' Home	196?	8.00	40.00
Old Timer 604	Baja / When Johnny Comes Draggin' Home	1975	1.00	5.00
Old Timer 604	Baja / When Johnny Comes Draggin' Home (Red vinyl)	1975	2.00	10.00
Old Timer 614	The Spy / (B-side by The Destinaires)	1975	1.00	5.00
LANCERS, THE				
Lancelot	See You In Seattle /	196?	2.00	10.00
Lancelot 122	Can't Help Falling In Love With You / Heart Of A Clown	196?	2.00	10.00
LANDIS, JERRY				
Jerry Landis is a pseudonym for Paul Simon.				
MGM 12822	Anna Belle / Loneliness	1959	8.00	40.00
Warwick 552	Just A Boy / Shy	1960	8.00	40.00
Warwick 588	Just A Boy / I'd Like To Be	1960	8.00	40.00
Warwick 616	Play Me A Sad Song / It Means A Lot To Them	1961	8.00	40.00
Canadian American 130	I'm Lonely / I Wish I Weren't In Love	1961	15.00	75.00
Amy 875	Lisa / The Lone Teen Ranger	1962	10.00	50.00
LANDON, MICHAEL				
Fono Graf 1240	Gimme A Little Kiss / Be Patient With Me	196?	3.00	15.00
Fono Graf 1240 (PS)	Gimme A Little Kiss / Be Patient With Me	196?	5.00	25.00
LANE, MICKEY				
Laurie 3071	Nightcap / Dum Dee Dee Dum	1960	4.00	20.00
LANG, JULIE				
DeLuxe 6111	Elvis / Woman Need De Man	1957	3.00	15.00
LANGRAN, JOEL				
Rori 714	I Really Want To Be A Singer / Young And Foolish (Written and produced by Dickie Goodman.)	1964	2.00	10.00
LANHAM, RICHARD				
Acme 712	Dance Of Love / On Your Radio	1957	4.00	20.00
Acme 722	Wishing All The Time / The Day I Met You	1957	6.00	30.00
Josie 985	Don't Believe Him / Have A Little Faith	1965	1.20	6.00
LANI & BONI				
Delaney and Bonnie Bramlett.				
Garpax 4084	Cherry Pie / Hey, Mr. Weatherman	1964	2.00	10.00
LARADOS, THE				
The Larados also recorded with Danny Zella.				
Fox (No number)	Bad Bad Guitar Man / Now The Parting Begins	1957	5.00	25.00
LARADOS, THE				
Madog 801	Will You Love Me Tomorrow? / You Didn't Care	196?	5.00	25.00
LARRY & THE CROSSFIRES				
Searcy 711	Torquay '65 / Wee Wee Hours	1965	6.00	30.00
LARRY & THE LOAFERS				
Shurfine 017	Let's Go To The Beach / Who?	196?	7.00	35.00
LARUE, D.C.				
Pyramid 8009	Don't Keep It In The Shadows / Bad News (Features Lou Christie.)	1977	1.00	5.00
LAST, THE				
Backlash 001	She Don't Know Why I'm Here / Bombing Of London	1977	8.00	40.00
Backlash 002	Every Summer Day / Slave Driver	1978	8.00	40.00
Bomp 119	She Don't Know Why I'm Here / Bombing Of London	1978	2.00	10.00
Bomp 126	Every Summer Day / Slave Driver (Different version of "Every Summer Day.")	1979	1.60	8.00
Backlash 003	L.A. Explosion / Hitler's Brother	1979	4.00	20.00
	— Extended Play Album —			
Warf Rat 1082	Up In The Air	1982	2.00	10.00
LAST FIVE, THE				
Wand 1122	Kicking You / Weatherman	1966	2.00	10.00
LAUGHING GRAVY, THE				
Laughing Gravy is Dean Torrence with The Esquires. The basic track to "Vegetables" is a Brian Wilson "Smile" remnant.				
White Whale 261 (DJ)	Vegetables / Vegetables	1967	20.00	100.00
White Whale 261	Vegetables / Snow Flakes On Laughing Gravy's Whiskers	1967	30.00	150.00

Label & Catalog #		A-Side/B-Side	Year	VG	NM
LAW FOUR, JOHNNY					
Providence 419		There Ought To Be A Law / Call On Me	196?	3.00	15.00
Providence 421		Since I Don't Have You / Underdog	196?	3.00	15.00
LAWRENCE, SYD					
Cosmic 1001		The Answer To The Flying Saucer / (B-side by Billy Mure)	1956	4.00	20.00
LAWRENCE, WALT					
Hollywood Inter. 2/3		Cascade / Twilight Adrift	195?	6.00	30.00
LAZAR, BILLY, & THE WOODY WAGONERS					
Scarlett 1		Surfin' Around /	196?	7.00	35.00
LEAHY ORCHESTRA, JOE					
Ring-A-Ding 704		The Happy Surfer / Goodnight Dream Boy	1963	6.00	30.00
LEAPING FERNS, THE					
The Leaping Ferns is a pseudonym for The Chantays.					
X-Panded Sound 103		It Never Works Out For Me / Maybe Baby	1965	4.00	20.00
LEARY, DR. TIMOTHY					
Mercury 72713		Turn On, Tune In, Drop Out / Turn On, Tune In, Drop Out, Part 2	1968	3.00	15.00
LEATHER BOY, THE					
Parkway 125		Jersey Thursday / Black Friday	1966	4.00	20.00
MGM 13724		I'm A Leather Boy / Shadows	1967	4.00	20.00
MGM 13724	(PS)	I'm A Leather Boy / Shadows	1967	8.00	40.00
MGM 13790		Soulin' / On The Go	1967	4.00	20.00
Flower 100		My Prayer / You Gotta Have Soul	196?	6.00	30.00
LEAVES, THE					
Mira 202		Love Minus Zero-No Limit / Too Many People	1965	2.00	10.00
Mira 207		Hey, Joe, Where You Gonna Go? / Be With You	1965	3.00	15.00
Mira 213		A Different Story / You Better Move On	1966	1.25	6.00
Mira 220		Funny Little World / Be With You	1966	1.00	5.00
Mira 222		Hey, Joe / Funny Little World	1966	1.20	6.00
Mira 227		Too Many People / Girl From The East	1966	1.20	6.00
Mira 231		Get Out Of My Life Woman / Girl From The East	1966	1.00	5.00
Mira 234		Be With You / You Better Move On	1966	1.00	5.00
Capitol 5799		Twilight Sanctuary / Lemon Princess	1967	1.00	5.00
LED ZEPPELIN					
Led Zeppelin is John Bonham, John Paul Jones, Jimmy Page and Robert Plant. Refer to Listen; The Yardbirds.					
Atlantic 2613	(DJ)	Good Times Bad Times / Good Times Bad Times	1969	8.00	40.00
Atlantic 2613		Good Times Bad Times / Communication Breakdown	1969	3.00	15.00
Atlantic 2690	(DJ)	Living, Loving Maid (She's Just A Woman) (One sided)	1969	30.00	150.00
Atlantic 2690	(DJ)	Whole Lotta Love (5:33) / Whole Lotta Love (3:12)	1969	8.00	40.00
Atlantic 2690	(DJ)	Whole Lotta Love / Whole Lotta Love	1969	6.00	30.00
Atlantic 2690		Whole Lotta Love / Living, Loving Maid (She's Just A Woman)	1969	1.00	5.00
Atlantic 2777	(DJ)	Immigrant Song (One sided)	1970	30.00	150.00
Atlantic 2777	(DJ)	Immigrant Song / Immigrant Song	1970	5.00	25.00
Atlantic 2777		Immigrant Song / Hey, Hey, What Can I Do?	1970	2.00	10.00
Atlantic 2849	(DJ)	Black Dog / Black Dog	1971	5.00	25.00
Atlantic 2849		Black Dog / Misty Mountain Hop	1971	1.00	5.00
Atlantic 2865	(DJ)	Rock And Roll / Rock And Roll	1972	5.00	25.00
Atlantic 2865		Rock And Roll / Four Sticks	1972	1.00	5.00
Atlantic 2970	(DJ)	Over The Hills And Far Away / Over The Hills And Far Away	1973	4.00	20.00
Atlantic 2970		Over The Hills And Far Away / Dancing Days	1973	1.00	5.00
Atlantic 2986	(DJ)	D'yer Maker / D'yer Maker	1973	4.00	20.00
Atlantic 2986		D'yer Maker / The Crunge	1973	1.00	5.00
Swan Song 70102	(DJ)	Trampled Underfoot / Trampled Underfoot	1974	2.00	10.00
Swan Song 70102		Trampled Underfoot / Black Country Woman	1974	.80	4.00
Swan Song 70110	(DJ)	Candy Store Rock / Candy Store Rock	1977	2.00	10.00
Swan Song 70110		Candy Store Rock / New Orleans	1977	.80	4.00
Swan Song 71003	(DJ)	Fool In The Rain / Fool In The Rain	1979	2.00	10.00
Swan Song 71003		Fool In The Rain / Hot Dog	1979	.80	4.00
		—Special/Promotional Releases—			
Atco 6779		Whole Lotta Love / (B-side by King Curtis)	1969	8.00	40.00
Atlantic 1019	(33)	Dazed And Confused / Babe, I'm Gonna Leave You (Issued with a paper sleeve.)	1969	100.00	400.00
Atlantic 171	(33)	Led Zeppelin IV (Jukebox EP)	1970	50.00	200.00
Atlantic PR	(33)	Gallow's Pole (Jukebox single)	197?	30.00	150.00
Atlantic PR-175		Stairway To Heaven / Stairway To Heaven	1973	10.00	50.00
Atlantic PR-175	(PS)	Stairway To Heaven / Stairway To Heaven	1973	25.00	125.00
Atlantic PR-213	(33)	Houses Of The Holy (Jukebox EP)	1973	20.00	100.00
Atlantic PR-269		Stairway To Heaven (No cover)	1973	10.00	50.00

Label & Catalog #		A-Side/B-Side	Year	VG	NM

LEE: Refer to LEE MARENO

LEE, ARTHUR, & THE L.A.G.'S

| Capitol 4980 | | The Ninth Wave / Rumble-Still-Skins | 1963 | 5.00 | 25.00 |

LEE, ARTHUR

Arthur Lee also recorded with The L.A.G.'s (above); The American Four; Love; Ronnie & The Pomona Casuals.

A&M 1361		Everybody's Gotta Live /			
		Love Jumped Through My Window	1972	.60	3.00
A&M 1381		Sad Song / You Want Change For Your Rerun	1972	.60	3.00

LEE, BILLY, & THE RIVIERAS

Billy Lee & The Rivieras later recorded as Mitch Ryder & The Detroit Wheels.

| Hyland 3016 | | Won't You Dance With Me? / You Know | 196? | 4.00 | 20.00 |

LEE, BRENDA

Refer to the Various Artists EP section.

Apollo 490		Ain't Gonna Give Nobody None / If I Ever Get Rich	1956	6.00	30.00
Decca 30050		Jambalaya / Bigelow-6200	1956	3.00	15.00
Decca 30107		Christy Christmas / I'm Gonna Lasso Santa Claus	1956	3.00	15.00
Decca 30107	(PS)	Christy Christmas / I'm Gonna Lasso Santa Claus	1956	7.00	35.00
Decca 30198		One Step At A Time / Fairyland	1957	3.00	15.00
Decca 30333		Dynamite / Love You 'Til I Die	1957	3.00	15.00
Decca 30411		Ain't That Love? / One Teenager To Another	1957	3.00	15.00
Decca 30535		Rock The Bop / Rock-A-Bye Baby Blues	1958	3.00	15.00
Decca 30673		Ring-A My Phone / Little Jonah	1958	4.00	20.00
Decca 30776		Rockin' Around The Christmas Tree / Papa Noel	1958	3.00	15.00
Decca 30776	(PS)	Rockin' Around The Christmas Tree / Papa Noel	1958	4.00	20.00
Decca 30806		Bill Bailey, Won't You Please Come Home? /			
		Hummin' The Blues	1959	3.00	15.00
Decca 30885		Let's Jump The Broomstick / Some Of These Days	1959	4.00	20.00
Decca 30967		Sweet Nothin's / Weep No More, My Baby	1959	2.00	10.00
Decca 30967	(PS)	Sweet Nothin's / Weep No More, My Baby	1959	15.00	75.00
Decca 31093		I'm Sorry / That's All You Gotta Do	1960	2.00	10.00
Decca 31093	(PS)	I'm Sorry / That's All You Gotta Do	1960	3.00	15.00
Decca 31149		I Want To Be Wanted / Just A Little	1960	2.00	10.00
Decca 31149	(PS)	I Want To Be Wanted / Just A Little	1960	3.00	15.00
Decca 31195		Emotions / I'm Learning About Love	1961	2.00	10.00
Decca 31195	(PS)	Emotions / I'm Learning About Love	1961	3.00	15.00
Decca 31231		You Can Depend On Me / It's Never Too Late	1961	2.00	10.00
Decca 31231	(PS)	You Can Depend On Me / It's Never Too Late	1961	3.00	15.00
Decca 31272		Dum Dum / Eventually	1961	2.00	10.00
Decca 31272	(PS)	Dum Dum / Eventually	1961	3.00	15.00
Decca 31309		Fool #1 / Anybody But Me	1961	2.00	10.00
Decca 31309	(PS)	Fool #1 / Anybody But Me	1961	3.00	15.00
Decca 31348		Break It To Me Gently / So Deep	1962	2.00	10.00
Decca 31348	(PS)	Break It To Me Gently / So Deep	1962	3.00	15.00
Decca 31379		Everybody Loves Me But You / Here Comes That Feelin'	1962	2.00	10.00
Decca 31407		Heart In Hand / It Started All Over Again	1962	2.00	10.00
Decca 31424		All Alone Am I / Save All Your Lovin' For Me	1962	2.00	10.00
Decca 31424	(PS)	All Alone Am I / Save All Your Lovin' For Me	1962	3.00	15.00
Decca 31454		Your Used-To-Be / She'll Never Know	1963	2.00	10.00
Decca 31454	(PS)	Your Used-To-Be / She'll Never Know	1963	3.00	15.00
Decca 31478		Losing You / He's So Heavenly	1963	2.00	10.00
Decca 31478	(PS)	Losing You / He's So Heavenly	1963	3.00	15.00
Decca 31510		My Whole World Is Falling Down / I Wonder	1963	2.00	10.00
Decca 31510	(PS)	My Whole World Is Falling Down / I Wonder	1963	3.00	15.00
Decca 31539		The Grass Is Greener / Sweet, Impossible You	1963	2.00	10.00
Decca 31539	(PS)	The Grass Is Greener / Sweet, Impossible You	1963	3.00	15.00
Decca 31570		As Usual / Lonely, Lonely, Lonely Me	1963	2.00	10.00
Decca 31599		Think / The Waiting Game	1964	1.60	8.00
Decca 31599	(PS)	Think / The Waiting Game	1964	2.00	10.00
Decca 31628		Alone With You / My Dreams	1964	1.60	8.00
Decca 31628	(PS)	Alone With You / My Dreams	1964	2.00	10.00
Decca 31654		When You Loved Me / He's Sure To Remember Me	1964	1.60	8.00
Decca 31654	(PS)	When You Loved Me / He's Sure To Remember Me	1964	2.00	10.00
Decca 31687		Jingle Bell Rock / Winter Wonderland	1964	1.60	8.00
Decca 31687	(PS)	Jingle Bell Rock / Winter Wonderland	1964	2.00	10.00
Decca 31688		This Time Of Year / Christmas Will Be Just Another Day	1964	1.60	8.00
Decca 31688	(PS)	This Time Of Year / Christmas Will Be Just Another Day	1964	2.00	10.00
Decca 31690		Is It True? / Just Behind The Rainbow	1964	1.00	5.00
Decca 31690	(PS)	Is It True? / Just Behind The Rainbow	1964	2.00	10.00
Decca 31728		Thanks A Lot / The Crying Game	1965	1.00	5.00
Decca 31762		Truly, Truly True / I Still Miss Someone	1965	1.00	5.00
Decca 31762	(PS)	Truly, Truly True / I Still Miss Someone	1965	2.00	10.00
Decca 31792		Too Many Rivers / No One	1965	1.00	5.00
Decca 31849		Rusty Bells / If You Don't	1965	1.00	5.00
Decca 31917		Too Little Time / Time And Time Again	1965	1.00	5.00

Label & Catalog #		A-Side/B-Side	Year	VG	NM
Decca 31970		Ain't Gonna Cry No More / It Takes One To Know One	1966	1.00	5.00
Decca 32018		Coming On Strong / You Keep Coming Back To Me	1966	1.00	5.00
Decca 32079		Ride, Ride, Ride / Lonely People Do Foolish Things	1967	1.00	5.00
Decca 32119		Take Me / Born To Be By Your Side	1967	1.00	5.00
Decca 32161		My Heart Keeps Hangin' On / Where Love Is	1967	1.00	5.00
Decca 32213		Where's The Melody? / Save Me For A Rainy Day	1968	1.00	5.00
Decca 32248		Fantasy / That's All Right	1968	1.00	5.00
Decca 32299		Cabaret / Mood Indigo	1968	1.00	5.00
Decca 32330		Each Day Is A Rainbow / Kansas City	1968	1.00	5.00
Decca 32428		Johnny One Time / I Must Have Been Out Of My Mind	1969	1.00	5.00
Decca 32428	(PS)	Johnny One Time / I Must Have Been Out Of My Mind	1969	3.00	15.00
Decca 32491		You Don't Need Me For Anything Anymore /			
		Bring Me Sunshine	1969	1.00	5.00
Decca 32560		Let It Be Me / You Better Move On	1969	1.00	5.00
Decca 32675		I Think I Love You Again / Hello, Love	1970	.80	4.00
Decca 32734		Sisters In Sorrow / Do Right Woman, Do Right Man	1970	.80	4.00
Decca 32848		If This Is Out Last Time /			
		Everybody's Reaching Out For Someone	1971	.80	4.00
Decca 32918		Misty Memories / I'm A Memory	1972	.80	4.00
Decca 32975		Always On My Mind / That Ain't Right	1972	.80	4.00
		—Special/Promotional Releases—			
Decca (No number)	(DJ)	Sincerely, Brenda Lee	1967	10.00	50.00
		(Boxed set of five stereo singles, Verve 10520-10524, with a cue sheet, bio and jukebox title strips. The price is for the complete set. The five promo singles are priced separately below.)			
Decca 38275	(DJ)	If You Love Me / Just Another Lie	1967	1.00	5.00
Decca 38276	(DJ)	When I Fall In Love / Crazy Talk	1967	1.00	5.00
Decca 38277	(DJ)	Swanee River Rock / Around The World	1967	1.00	5.00
Decca 38278	(DJ)	Will You Love Me Tomorrow / Georgia On My Mind	1967	1.00	5.00
Decca 38279	(DJ)	I'm In The Mood For Love / Cry	1967	1.00	5.00
Decca (No number)	(DJ)	Emotions	1967	10.00	50.00
		(Boxed set of five stereo singles, Verve 10520-10524, with a cue sheet, bio and jukebox title strips. The price is for the complete set. The five promo singles are priced separately below.)			
Decca 34060	(DJ)	Lazy River / You Always Hurt	1967	1.00	5.00
Decca 34061	(DJ)	It's The Talk Of The Town / You've Got Me Crying Again	1967	1.00	5.00
Decca 34062	(DJ)	How Deep Is The Ocean? / Send Me Some Lovin'	1967	1.00	5.00
Decca 34063	(DJ)	Fools Rush In / I'll Always Be In Love With You	1967	1.00	5.00
Decca 34064	(DJ)	I'll Be Seeing You / Hold Me	1967	1.00	5.00
Decca 34370	(DJ)	Open-End Interview With Brenda Lee	1972	4.00	20.00
		—Extended Play Albums—			
Decca 2661		Brenda Lee	1959	12.00	60.00
Decca 2678		Sweet Nothin's	1960	10.00	50.00
Decca 2682		Brenda Lee	1960	10.00	50.00
Decca 2683		I'm Sorry	1960	10.00	50.00
Decca 2702		Brenda Lee	1960	10.00	50.00
Decca 2704		Lover, Come Back To Me	1961	10.00	50.00
Decca 2712		Brenda Lee	1961	10.00	50.00
Decca 2716		Brenda Lee	1961	10.00	50.00
Decca 2725		Everybody Loves Me But You	1962	10.00	50.00
Decca 2730		Brenda Lee	1962	10.00	50.00
Decca 2738		Brenda Lee	1962	10.00	50.00
Decca 2745		Brenda Lee	1962	10.00	50.00
Decca 2755		Brenda Lee	196?	10.00	50.00
Decca 2764		Brenda Lee	196?	10.00	50.00

LEE, BUDDY, & THE SATELLITES

Columbia 4-43125		Count Down / Way Out	1964	3.00	15.00

LEE, CURTIS

Curtis Lee also recorded as C.L. & The Pictures.

Hot 7		I Never Knew What Love Could Do / Gotta Have You	195?	15.00	75.00
Warrior 1555		With All My Heart / Pure Love	195?	6.00	30.00
Sabra 517		I'm Asking Forgiveness / Let's Take A Ride	1960	4.00	20.00
Dunes 2001		Special Love / In Love	1960	2.00	10.00
Dunes 2003		Pledge Of Love / Then I'll Know	1960	2.00	10.00
Dunes 2007		Pretty Little Angel Eyes / Gee, How I Wish	1961	3.00	15.00
Dunes 2008		Under The Moon Of Love / Beverly Jean	1961	3.00	15.00
		(Dunes 2007 and 2008 were produced by Phil Spector.)			
Dunes 2010		I'm Asking Forgiveness / Let's Take A Ride	1961	2.00	10.00
Dunes 2012		Just Another Fool / A Night At Daddy G's	1962	2.00	10.00
Dunes 2015		Does He Mean That Much To You? / The Wobble	1962	2.00	10.00
Dunes 2017		Afraid / Mary Go Round	1962	2.00	10.00
Dunes 2020		Lonely Weekends / Better Him Than Me	1963	2.00	10.00
Dunes 2021		Pickin' Up The Pieces Of My Heart / Mr. Mistaken	1963	2.00	10.00
Dunes 2023		I'm Sorry / That's What's Happening	1963	2.00	10.00

Label & Catalog #		A-Side/B-Side	Year	VG	NM
LEE, DICKEY (& THE COLLEGIATES)					
Tampa 131		Stay True, Baby / Dream Boy	195?	6.00	30.00
Sun 280		Memories New Grow Old / Good Lovin'	1957	3.00	15.00
Sun 297		Fool, Fool, Fool / Dreamy Nights	1958	3.00	15.00
Dot 16087		Why Don't You Write Me? / Life In A Teenage World	1960	2.00	10.00
Smash 1758		Patches / More Or Less	1962	1.00	5.00
Smash 1791		I Saw Linda Yesterday / The Girl I Can't Forget	1962	.80	4.00
Smash 1808		Don't Wanna Think About Paula / Just A Friend	1963	.80	4.00
Smash 1822		I Go Lonely / Ten Million Faces	1963	.80	4.00
Smash 1844		She Wants To Be Bobby's Girl / The Day The Sawmill Closed	1964	.80	4.00
Smash 1871		To The Aisle / Mother Nature	1964	.80	4.00
Smash 1913		Me And My Teardrops / Only Trust In Me	1964	.80	4.00
Hallway 1924		Big Brother / She's Walking Away	1964	.80	4.00
TCF Hall 102		Laurie (Strange Things Happen) / Party Doll	1965	.80	4.00
TCF Hall 111		The Girl From Peyton Place / The Girl I Used To Know	1965	.80	4.00
TCF Hall 118		Good Girl Goin' Bad / Pretty White Dress	1965	.80	4.00
TCF Hall 128		Good Guy /	1965	.80	4.00
Atco 6546		Red, Green, Yellow And Blue / Run Right Back	196?	.80	4.00
LEE, JACK E., & THE SQUIRES					
Jack E. Lee is a pseudonym for Jack Ely.					
RCA Victor 47-8452		Love That Louie / Octavepuss	1964	1.20	6.00
LEE, JENNY, & THE STARLETS					
Refer to The Starlets.					
Congress 107		What I Gotta Do / Show Me A Man	196?	1.00	5.00
LEE, JUDY					
Wasp 114		Blaming It All On You / I Need You Now	196?	1.20	6.00
LEE, LARRY, & THE LEESURES					
Camelot 111		Boot And Soul / Mo-Jo	196?	2.00	10.00
LEE, LORRY, & DELLA					
Mecca 2699		Let Him Go, Go, Go / Because (I Love You)	196?	1.00	5.00
LEE, PETER					
Topaz 1324		Do You Know / Teardrop	196?	2.00	10.00
LEE, WALLY					
Now 1010		Oh No, Daddy O / Just A Little Bit Lonely	195?	5.00	25.00
LEFT BANKE, THE					
The Left Banke features Michael Brown and Steve Martin					
Smash 2041		Walk Away, Renee / I Haven't Got The Nerve	1966	2.00	10.00
Smash 2074		Pretty Ballerina / Lazy Day	1966	2.00	10.00
Smash 2089		Ivy, Ivy / And Suddenly	1967	2.00	10.00
Smash 2097		She May Call You Up Tonight / Barterers And Their Wives	1967	2.00	10.00
Smash 2119		Desiree / I've Got Something On My Mind	1967	2.00	10.00
Smash 2119	(PS)	Desiree / I've Got Something On My Mind	1967	10.00	25.00
Smash 2165		Dark Is The Bark / My Friend Today	1968	2.00	10.00
Smash 2189		Goodbye, Holly / Sing, Little Bird, Sing	1968	2.00	10.00
Smash 2209		Bryant Hotel / Give The Man A Hand	1969	2.00	10.00
Smash 2226		Nice To See You / There's Gonna Be A Storm	1969	2.00	10.00
Smash 2243		Myrah / Pedestal	1969	8.00	40.00
Smash 2243	(PS)	Myrah / Pedestal	1969	Bootleg	
Camerica 005		Queen Of Paradise / And One Day	1978	1.00	5.00
LEGENDARY MASKED SURFERS, THE					
The Masked Surfers are Bruce Johnston, Terry Melcher and Dean Torrence.					
United Artists 50958		Gonna Hustle You / Summertime, Summertime	1972	5.00	25.00
United Artists 270		Summer Means Fun / Gonna Hustle You	1973	5.00	25.00
United Artists 270	(PS)	Summer Means Fun / Gonna Hustle You	1973	5.00	25.00
LEGENDARY STARDUST COWBOY, THE					
Psycho Suave 1033		Paralyzed / Who's Knocking On My Door?	1968	6.00	30.00
Mercury 72862		Paralyzed / Who's Knocking On My Door?	1968	3.00	15.00
Mercury 72891		Down In The Wrecking Yard / I Took A Trip On A Gemini Spaceship	1969	2.00	10.00
Mercury 72912		Everything's Getting Bigger But Our Love / Kiss And Run	1969	2.00	10.00
LEGENDS, THE					
Ermine 39		My Love For You / Say Mama	1962	8.00	40.00
Ermine 41		Late Train / Lariat	1962	8.00	40.00
Ermine 43		I Wish I Knew / Bop-A-Lena	1962	10.00	50.00
Ermine 45		Temptation / Marionette	1962	8.00	40.00
Jamie 1228		Tell The Truth / You'll Never See The Forest	1962	3.00	15.00
Capitol 5014		Run To The Movies / Summertime Blues	1963	3.00	15.00

The Legendary Masked Surfers — Dean Torrence's reworking of an older Jan & Dean track with the capable assistance of Bruce & Terry and Brian and former L.A. session greats Glen Campbell, Leon Russell and Larry Knechtel — issued one single before sinking into oblivion.

Label & Catalog #		A-Side/B-Side	Year	VG	NM

LEGENDS, THE
| Caldwell 410 | | Jungle Lullaby / Go Away With Me | 1962 | 3.00 | 15.00 |

LEGENDS, THE
| Doc Holliday 107 | | Surf's Up / Dance With The Drummer Man | 1963 | 7.00 | 35.00 |
| Doc Holliday 107 | (PS) | Surf's Up / Dance With The Drummer Man | 1963 | 7.00 | 35.00 |

LEGENDS, THE
The Legends feature Dan Hartman.
UP 2202		Baby, Get Your Head Screwed On / Why?	1968	10.00	50.00
Bridge Society 2204		Keep On Running / Cheating	1968	8.00	40.00
Railroad House 12003		High Towers / Fever Games	1969	4.00	20.00
Railroad House 12003	(PS)	High Towers / Fever Games	1969	4.00	20.00
Flexidisc	(DJ)	Sometimes I Can't Help It / Jefferson Strongbox	1970	10.00	50.00
Heart 7672		Rock And Roll Woman / Problems	1972	4.00	20.00
Epic 10937		Rock And Roll Woman / Problems	1972	1.20	6.00

LEIGH, STAN
| Celestial 114 | | What Will I Tell My Heart? / Was It Rain | 196? | 2.00 | 10.00 |

LEMON PIPERS, THE
Carol 107		Quiet Please / Monaural 78	196?	3.00	15.00
Buddah 11		Turn Around And Take A Look / Danger	1967	1.00	5.00
Buddah 23		Green Tambourine / No Help From Me	1967	1.20	6.00
Buddah 31		Rice Is Nice / Blueberry Blue	1968	1.00	5.00
Buddah 31	(PS)	Rice Is Nice / Blueberry Blue	1968	2.00	10.00
Buddah 41		Jelly Jungle (Of Orange Marmalade) / Shoeshine Boy	1968	1.00	5.00
Buddah 63		Lonely Atmosphere / Wine And Violet	1968	1.00	5.00
Buddah 136		I Was Born Not To Follow / Rainbow Tree	1968	1.00	5.00

LEMONS, ROBIN
| Dilley 111 | | Take A Ride In The Country / Paisley Trees | 196? | 2.00 | 10.00 |

LENNON, FREDDIE
John Lennon's father.
| Jerden 792 | | That's My Life (My Love And My Home) / The Next Time You Feel Important | 1965 | 12.00 | 60.00 |

LENNON, JOHN (& THE PLASTIC ONO BAND)
For additional listings refer to The Beatles; Bill Elliott; and Nilsson.
Apple 1809		Give Peace A Chance / (B-side by Yoko Ono)	1969	1.00	5.00
Apple 1809	(PS)	Give Peace A Chance / (B-side by Yoko Ono)	1969	2.00	10.00
Apple 1813		Cold Turkey / (B-side by Yoko Ono)	1969	.80	4.00
Apple 1813	(PS)	Cold Turkey / (B-side by Yoko Ono) (Black sleeve with picture and print in white.)	1969	12.00	60.00
Apple 1818	(DJ)	Instant Karma (We All Shine On) (One sided)	1970	50.00	200.00
Apple 1818		Instant Karma (We All Shine On) / (B-side by Yoko Ono) (Apple label reads "Mfd. by Capitol Records" below the apple.)	1970	1.60	8.00
Apple 1818		Instant Karma (We All Shine On) / (B-side by Yoko Ono) (Apple label reads "Mfd. by Apple Records Inc" below the apple.)	1970	1.00	5.00
Apple 1818	(PS)	Instant Karma (We All Shine On) / (B-side by Yoko Ono)	1970	2.00	10.00
Apple 1827		Mother / (B-side by Yoko Ono) (Star label)	1970	2.00	10.00
Apple 1827		Mother / (B-side by Yoko Ono) (Starless label)	1970	1.00	5.00
Apple 1827	(PS)	Mother / (B-side by Yoko Ono)	1970	30.00	150.00
Apple 1830		Power To The People / (B-side by Yoko Ono) (Star label)	1971	1.25	6.00
Apple 1830		Power To The People / (B-side by Yoko Ono)	1971	1.00	5.00
Apple 1830	(PS)	Power To The People / (B-side by Yoko Ono)	1971	6.00	30.00
Apple 1840		Imagine / It's So Hard (Brown label)	1971	1.25	6.00
Apple 1840		Imagine / It's So Hard (Green label)	1971	1.00	5.00
Apple S-45X-47663	(DJ)	Happy X-mas (War Is Over) / (B-side by Yoko Ono)	1971	150.00	600.00
Apple 1842		Happy X-mas (War Is Over) / (B-side by Yoko Ono) (Photo label on green vinyl.)	1971	2.00	10.00
Apple 1842		Happy X-mas (War Is Over) / (B-side by Yoko Ono) (Apple label on green vinyl.)	1971	1.60	8.00
Apple 1842	(PS)	Happy X-mas (War Is Over) / (B-side by Yoko Ono)	1971	4.00	20.00
Apple 1848		Woman Is The Nigger Of The World / (B-side by Yoko Ono)	1972	.80	4.00
Apple 1848	(PS)	Woman Is The Nigger Of The World / (B-side by Yoko Ono) (Apple 1848 features Elephant's Memory.)	1972	5.00	25.00
Apple P-1868	(DJ)	Mind Games / Mind Games	1973	8.00	40.00
Apple 1868		Mind Games / Meat City	1973	1.00	5.00
Apple 1868	(PS)	Mind Games / Meat City	1973	2.00	10.00
Apple P-1874	(DJ)	Whatever Gets You Through The Night / Whatever Gets You Through The Night	1974	8.00	40.00
Apple 1874		Whatever Gets You Through The Night / Beef Jerky	1974	1.00	5.00
Apple P-1878	(DJ)	What You Got / What You Got	1974	30.00	150.00
Apple P-1878	(DJ)	#9 Dream / #9 Dream	1974	8.00	40.00
Apple 1878		#9 Dream / What You Got	1974	1.00	5.00
Apple P-1883	(DJ)	Ain't That A Shame / Ain't That A Shame	1975	50.00	200.00

Label & Catalog #		A-Side/B-Side	Year	VG	NM
Apple P-1883	(DJ)	Slippin' And Slidin' / Slippin' And Slidin'	1975	50.00	200.00
Apple P-1881	(DJ)	Stand By Me / Stand By Me	1975	8.00	40.00
Apple 1881		Stand By Me / Move Over Mrs. L	1975	1.00	5.00
Capitol 1842		Happy X-mas (War Is Over) / (B-side by Yoko Ono)	1976	4.00	20.00
Capitol 1878		#9 Dream / What You Got	1976	4.00	20.00
		—Capitol singles above have orange labels.—			
Geffen 49604	(DJ)	(Just Like) Starting Over / (Just Like) Starting Over	1980	3.00	15.00
Geffen 49604		(Just Like) Starting Over / (B-side by Yoko Ono)	1980	.40	2.00
Geffen 49604	(PS)	(Just Like) Starting Over / (B-side by Yoko Ono)	1980	.60	3.00
Geffen 49644	(DJ)	Woman / (B-side by Yoko Ono)	1981	3.00	15.00
Geffen 49644		Woman / (B-side by Yoko Ono)	1981	.40	2.00
Geffen 49644	(PS)	Woman / (B-side by Yoko Ono)	1981	.80	4.00
Geffen 49695	(DJ)	Watching The Wheels / (B-side by Yoko Ono)	1981	3.00	15.00
Geffen 49695		Watching The Wheels / (B-side by Yoko Ono)	1981	.40	2.00
Geffen 49695	(PS)	Watching The Wheels / (B-side by Yoko Ono)	1981	.80	4.00
Geffen 29855	(DJ)	Happy X-mas (War Is Over) / Happy X-mas (War Is Over)	1982	3.00	15.00
Geffen 29855		Happy X-mas (War Is Over) / (B-side by Yoko Ono)	1982	.40	2.00
Geffen 29855	(PS)	Happy X-mas (War Is Over) / (B-side by Yoko Ono)	1982	.80	4.00
Polydor 821-107-7	(DJ)	I'm Stepping Out / I'm Stepping Out	1984	3.00	15.00
Polydor 821-107-7		I'm Stepping Out / (B-side by Yoko Ono)	1984	.40	2.00
Polydor 821-107-7	(PS)	I'm Stepping Out / (B-side by Yoko Ono)	1984	.80	4.00
Polydor 821-204-7	(DJ)	Borrowed Time / Borrowed Time	1984	3.00	15.00
Polydor 821-204-7		Borrowed Time / (B-side by Yoko Ono)	1984	.60	3.00
Polydor 821-204-7	(PS)	Borrowed Time / (B-side by Yoko Ono)	1984	.80	4.00
Polydor 817-254-7	(DJ)	Nobody Told Me / Nobody Told Me (Red label on opaque black vinyl.)	1985	3.00	15.00
Polydor 817-254-7	(DJ)	Nobody Told Me / Nobody Told Me (Red label on transluscent purple vinyl; light will shine through.)	1985	4.00	20.00
Polydor 817-254-7		Nobody Told Me / (B-side by Yoko Ono) (Label reads "Mfg. by Polygram.")	1985	.40	2.00
Polydor 817-254-7		Nobody Told Me / (B-side by Yoko Ono) (Label reads "Mfg. by Polydor.")	1985	3.00	15.00
Polydor 817-254-7	(PS)	Nobody Told Me / (B-side by Yoko Ono)	1985	.80	4.00
Polydor 881-378-7	(DJ)	Every Man Has A Woman Who Loves Him / Every Man Has A Woman Who Loves Him	1984	3.00	15.00
Polydor 881-378-7		Every Man Has A Woman Who Loves Him / (B-side by Sean Ono Lennon)	1984	1.00	5.00
Polydor 881-378-7	(PS)	Every Man Has A Woman Who Loves Him	1984	1.00	5.00
Capitol 44230	(DJ)	Jealous Guy / Jealous Guy	1988	3.00	15.00
Capitol 44230		Jealous Guy / Give Peace A Chance	1988	.80	4.00
Capitol 44230		Jealous Guy / Give Peace A Chance	1988	.80	4.00
		—Special/Promotional Releases—			
Americom 435		Give Peace A Chance / (B-side by Yoko Ono) (4" flexi-disc)	1969	330.00	1,000.00
Atlantic PRO-104/5	(DJ)	John Lennon On Ronnie Hawkins	1970	20.00	100.00
Cotillion PR-104/5	(DJ)	John Lennon On Ronnie Hawkins	1970	15.00	75.00
Cotillion PRO-104/5	(DJ)	John Lennon On Ronnie Hawkins	1970	10.00	50.00
Quaye/Trident 3419		Rock 'N' Roll Radio Spot	1975	100.00	400.00
		—12" Singles—			
Geffen PRO-919	(DJ)	(Just Like) Starting Over / (B-side by Yoko Ono)	1980	12.00	60.00
Geffen PRO-1079	(DJ)	Happy X-mas (War Is Over) / (B-side by Yoko Ono)	1982	8.00	40.00
Polydor PRO-250	(DJ)	Nobody Told Me / Nobody Told Me (Red label on opaque black vinyl.)	1983	8.00	40.00
Polydor PRO-250	(DJ)	Nobody Told Me / Nobody Told Me (Red label on transluscent purple vinyl; light will shine through.)	1983	10.00	50.00
Capitol SPRO-9929	(DJ)	Happy X-mas (War Is Over) / Listen, The Snow Is Falling (White vinyl)	1986	7.00	35.00
Capitol SPRO-9917	(DJ)	Rock And Roll People / Rock And Roll People	1986	7.00	35.00
Capitol SPRO-9894	(DJ)	Happy X-mas (War Is Over) / Happy X-Mas (War Is Over) (Included a numbered picture cover.)	1986	30.00	150.00
Capitol SPRO-9585	(DJ)	Imagine / Come Together	1986	8.00	40.00

LENNY & THE CHIMES

Vee Jay 605		Two Times Two / Only Forever	1964	3.00	15.00

LEO & THE PROPHETS

Totem 105		Tilt-A-Whirl / The Parking Meter	196?	3.00	15.00

LEONARD, BOBBY, & THE EXPLORERS
Features Bob Bogle of The Ventures.

Unity 2114		Project Venus / Rockin' Ship	196?	6.00	30.00

LETTERMEN, THE

Moonglow 5138		Lady Of Spain / Standin'	1960	5.00	25.00

LEVON & THE HAWKS
Levon & The Hawks later recorded as The Band. Refer to The Canadian Squires; Ronnie Hawkins.

Atco 6383	(DJ)	The Stones I Throw / He Don't Love You	1965	4.00	20.00
Atco 6383		The Stones I Throw / He Don't Love You	1965	6.00	30.00

Label & Catalog #		A-Side/B-Side	Year	VG	NM
Atco 6625	(DJ)	Go Go, Lisa Jane / He Don't Love You	1968	4.00	20.00
Atco 6625		Go Go, Lisa Jane / He Don't Love You	1968	6.00	30.00

LEWIS, DAVE

Seafair 105		Candido / Untwistin'	1962	.80	4.00
Jerden 711		David's Mood, Part 2 / David's Mood, Part 3	1963	.80	4.00
A&M 724		David's Mood / David's Mood, Part 2	1964	.80	4.00
A&M 735		Lip Service / Little Green Things	1964	.80	4.00
A&M 749		The Swim Thing / Mr. Clyde	1964	.80	4.00
A&M 756		Honky Tonk / Honky Tonk, Part 2	1964	.80	4.00
Northgate 1001		Barney's Tune / How Deep Is The Ocean?	196?	.80	4.00
Panorama 51		Searchin' / When My Dreamboat Comes Home	1967	.80	4.00
Panorama 52		Hold On, I'm Coming / Untitled	1967	.80	4.00
Piccadilly 235		Mmm-Mmm-Mmm / Hold On, I'm Coming	1967	.80	4.00
Panorama 1003		Hi Heel Sneakers / Jack Daniels Green	1968	.80	4.00
A&M 1068		Lip Service /	1969	.80	4.00

LEWIS, DONNA

Decca 31554		Surfer Boy Blue / Call Him Back	1963	4.00	20.00

LEWIS, GARY, & THE PLAYBOYS

Liberty 55756		This Diamond Ring / Hard To Find	1965	1.20	6.00
Liberty 55756		This Diamond Ring / Tijuana Wedding	1965	1.00	5.00
Liberty 55778		Count Me In / Little Miss Go Go	1965	1.00	5.00
Liberty 65-227		Doin' The Flake / This Diamond Rong / Little Miss Go Go	1965	2.00	10.00
Liberty 65-227	(PS)	Doin' The Flake / This Diamond Rong / Little Miss Go Go	1965	3.00	15.00
		(Mail order item available for 35¢ a Kellogg's Corn Flakes box top.)			
Liberty 55809		Save Your Heart For Me / Without A Word Of Warning	1965	1.00	5.00
Liberty 55818		Everybody Loves A Clown / Time Stands Still	1965	1.00	5.00
Liberty 55818	(PS)	Everybody Loves A Clown / Time Stands Still	1965	1.00	5.00
Liberty 55846		She's Just My Style / I Won't Make That Mistake Again	1965	1.00	5.00
Liberty 55846	(PS)	She's Just My Style / I Won't Make That Mistake Again	1965	1.00	5.00
Liberty 55865		Sure Gonna Miss Her / I Don't Wanna Say Goodnight	1966	.80	4.00
Liberty 55865	(PS)	Sure Gonna Miss Her / I Don't Wanna Say Goodnight	1966	.80	4.00
Liberty 55880		Green Grass / I Can Read Between The Lines	1966	.80	4.00
Liberty 55880	(PS)	Green Grass / I Can Read Between The Lines	1966	.80	4.00
Liberty 55898		My Heart's Symphony / Tina	1966	.80	4.00
Liberty 55898	(PS)	My Heart's Symphony / Tina	1966	.80	4.00
Liberty 55914		(You Don't Have To) Paint Me A Picture / Looking For The Stars	1966	.80	4.00
Liberty 55914	(PS)	(You Don't Have To) Paint Me A Picture / Looking For The Stars	1966	.80	4.00
Liberty 55933		Where Will The Words Come From? / May The Best Man Win	1966	.80	4.00
Liberty (No number)	(DJ)	Way Way Out / Way Way Out	1967	———	———
		(Promo for the film of the same name. Rare. No established value.)			
Liberty 55949		The Loser (With A Broken Heart) / Ice Melts In The Sun	1967	.80	4.00
Liberty 55949	(PS)	The Loser (With A Broken Heart) / Ice Melts In The Sun	1967	.80	4.00
Liberty 55971		Girls In Love / Let's Be More Than Friends	1967	.80	4.00
Liberty 55985		Jill / New In Town	1967	.80	4.00
Liberty 56011		Happiness / Has She Got The Nicest Eyes	1967	.80	4.00
Liberty 56037		Sealed With A Kiss / Sara Jane	1968	.80	4.00
Liberty 56075		Main Street / C. C. Rider	1968	.80	4.00
Liberty 56093		Everyday I Have To Cry / Mister Memory	1969	1.00	5.00
Liberty 56093		Rhythm Of The Rain / Mister Memory	1969	.80	4.00
Liberty 56121		Hayride / Gary's Groove	1969	.80	4.00
Liberty 56144		I Saw Elvis Presley Last Night / Something Is Wrong	1970	1.60	8.00
Liberty 56158		Great Balls Of Fire / I'm On The Right Road Now	1970	1.00	5.00

LEWIS, GARY

Epic 50068	(DJ)	One Good Woman / Ooh, Baby	1975	.80	4.00
Epic 50068		One Good Woman / Ooh, Baby	1975	1.60	8.00

LEWIS, JERRY LEE

Sun 259		Crazy Arms / End Of The Road	1956	15.00	75.00
		(First pressings credit "Jerry Lee Lewis.")			
Sun 259		Crazy Arms / End Of The Road	1956	10.00	50.00
		(Second pressings credit "Jerry Lee Lewis and His Pumping Piano.")			
Sun 267		Whole Lotta Shakin Goin' On / It'll Be Me	1957	3.00	15.00
Sun 281		Great Balls Of Fire / You Win Again	1957	3.00	15.00
Sun 281	(PS)	Great Balls Of Fire / You Win Again	1957	4.00	20.00
Sun 288		Breathless / Down The Line	1958	3.00	15.00
Sun 296		High School Confidential / Fools Like Me	1958	3.00	15.00
Sun 296	(PS)	High School Confidential / Fools Like Me	1958	4.00	20.00
Sun 301		Lewis Boogie / (B-side by George & Louis)	1958	3.00	15.00
Sun 303		Break Up / I'll Make It All Up To You	1958	2.00	10.00
Sun 312		I'll Sail My Ship Alone / It Hurt Me So	1958	2.00	10.00
Sun 317		Lovin' Up A Storm / Big Blon' Baby	1959	2.00	10.00

Label & Catalog #	A-Side/B-Side	Year	VG	NM
Sun 324	Let's Talk About Us / The Ballad Of Billy Joe	1959	2.00	10.00
Sun 330	Little Queenie / I Could Never Be Ashamed Of You	1959	2.00	10.00
Sun 337	Baby, Baby, Bye Bye / Old Black Joe	1960	1.60	8.00
Sun 344	Hang Up My Rock 'N' Roll Shoes / John Henry	1960	1.60	8.00
Sun 352	Love Made A Fool Of Me / When I Get Paid	1960	1.60	8.00
Sun 356	What'd I Say / Livin' Lovin' Wreck	1961	1.60	8.00
Sun 364	It Won't Happen With Me / Cold, Cold Heart	1961	1.60	8.00
Sun 367	Save The Last Dance For Me / As Long As I Live	1961	1.60	8.00
Sun 371	Money / Bonnie B	1961	1.60	8.00
Sun 374	I've Been Twistin' / Ramblin' Rose	1962	1.60	8.00
Sun 379	Sweet Little Sixteen / How's My Ex Treating You?	1962	1.60	8.00
Sun 382	Good Golly, Miss Molly / I Can't Trust Me (In Your Arms Anymore)	1962	1.60	8.00
Sun 384	Teenage Letter / Seasons Of My Heart	1963	1.60	8.00
Sun 396	Carry Me Back To Old Virginia / I Know What It Means	1965	1.60	8.00
Smash 1857	Hit The Road, Jack / Pen And Paper	1964	2.00	10.00
Smash 1886	I'm On Fire / Bread And Butter Man	1964	6.00	30.00
Smash 1906	She Was My Baby, He Was My Friend / The Home He Said He Built For Me	1964	2.00	10.00
Smash 1930	High Heel Sneakers / You Went Back On Your Word	1964	2.00	10.00
Smash 1969	I Believe In You / Baby, Hold Me Close	1965	2.00	10.00
Smash 1992	This Must Be The Place	1965	3.00	15.00
	Rockin' Pneumonia And The Boogie Woogie Flu / This Must Be The Place	1965	2.00	10.00
Smash 2006	The Green, Green Grass Of Home / You've Got What It Takes	1965	1.60	8.00
Smash 2027	Sticks And Stones / What A Heck Of A Mess	1966	1.60	8.00
Smash 2053	Memphis Beat / If I Had It To Do All Over	1966	1.60	8.00
Smash 2103	Holding On / It's A Hangup, Baby	1967	1.60	8.00
Smash 2122	Turn On Your Lovelight / Shotgun Man	1967	1.60	8.00
Smash 2246	Another Time, Another Place / I'm Walking The Floor Over You	1968	.80	4.00
Smash 2164	What Made Milwaukee Famous / All The Good Is Gone	1968	.80	4.00
Smash 2186	She Still Comes Around / Slipping Around	1968	.80	4.00
Smash 2202	To Make Love Sweeter For You / Let's Talk About Us	1968	.80	4.00
Smash 2220	Don't Let Me Cross Over / We Live In Two Different Worlds	1969	.80	4.00
Smash 2224	One Has My name / I Can't Stop Loving You	1969	.80	4.00
Smash 2244	She Even Woke Me Up To Say Goodbye / Echoes	1969	.80	4.00
Smash 2254	Roll Over Beethoven / Secret Places	1969	.80	4.00
Smash 2257	Once More With Feeling / You Went Out Of Your Way	1970	.80	4.00
Sun Inter. 1101	Invitation To Your Party / I Could Never Be Ashamed Of You	1969	.60	3.00
Sun Inter. 1107	Frankie And Johnny / One Minute Past Eternity	1969	.60	3.00
Sun Inter. 1115	Good Night, Irene / I Can't Seem To Say Goodbye	1969	.60	3.00
Sun Inter. 1119	Big Legged Woman / Waiting For A Train	1969	.60	3.00
Sun Inter. 1125	Matchbox / Love On Broadway	1969	.60	3.00
Sun Inter. 1128	Your Loving Ways / I Can't Trust Me In Your Arms Anymore	1969	.60	3.00
Sun Inter. 1130	Good Rockin' Tonight / I Can't Trust Me In Your Arms Anymore	1969	.60	3.00
Sun Inter. 1138	Matchbox / Am I To Be The One	197?	.60	3.00
Sun Inter. 1139	Save The Last Dance For Me / Am I To Be The One?	197?	.60	3.00
Sun Inter. 1141	Cold Cold Heart / Hello, Josephine	197?	.60	3.00
Mercury 73099	There Must Be More To Love Than This / Home Away From Home	1970	.60	3.00
Mercury 73155	I Can't Have A Merry Christmas, Mary / In Loving Memories	1971	.60	3.00
Mercury 73192	Touching Home / Woman, Woman	1971	.60	3.00
Mercury 73227	Foolish Kind Of Man / When He Walks On You	1971	.60	3.00
Mercury 73248	Me And Bobby McGee / Would You Take Another Chance On Me?	1971	.60	3.00
Mercury 73273	Chantilly Lace / Think About It, Darlin'	1972	.60	3.00
Mercury 73296	Lonely Weekends / Turn On Your Love Light	1972	.60	3.00
Mercury 73303	Handwriting On The Wall / Me And Jesus	1972	.60	3.00
Mercury 73328	No Honky Tonks In Heaven / Who's Gonna Play This Old Piano?	1972	.60	3.00
Mercury 73361	Mercy Of A Letter / No More Hanging On	1973	.60	3.00
Mercury 73374	Drinking Wine Spo-Dee O' Dee / Rock & Roll Medley	1973	.60	3.00
Mercury 73402	Jack Daniels / No Headstone On My Grave	1973	.60	3.00
Mercury 73423	I Think I Need To Pray / Sometimes A Memory Ain't Enough	1973	.60	3.00
Mercury 73452	I've Fallen To The Bottom / I'm Left, You're Right, She's Gone	1973	.60	3.00
Mercury 73462	Just A Little Bit / Meat Man	1974	.60	3.00
Mercury 73491	Tell Tale Signs / Cold, Cold Morning Light	1974	.60	3.00
Mercury 73618	He Can't Fill My Shoes / Tomorrow's Taking Baby Away	1974	.60	3.00
Mercury 73661	I Can Still Hear The Music In The Restroom / Remember Me?	1975	.60	3.00
Mercury 73685	Boogie Woogie Country Man / I'm Still Jealous Of You	1975	.60	3.00
Mercury 73729	Damn Good Country Song / When I Take My Vacation In Heaven	1975	.60	3.00

Label & Catalog #		A-Side/B-Side	Year	VG	NM
Mercury 73763		Don't Boogie Woogie / That Kind Of Fool	1976	.60	3.00
Mercury 73822		Jerry Lee's Rock & Roll Revival Show /			
		Let's Put It Back Together Again	1976	.60	3.00
Mercury 73872		Closest Thing To You / You Belong To Me	1977	.60	3.00
Elektra 46030		I Wish I Was Eighteen Again / Rockin' My Life Away	1979	.40	2.00
Elektra 46067		Rita May / Who Will The Next Fool Be?	1979	.40	2.00
Elektra 46591		When Two Worlds Collide / Good News Travels Fast	1980	.40	2.00
Elektra 46642		Honky Tonk Stuff / Rockin' Jerry Lee	1980	.40	2.00
Elektra 47026		Folsom Prison Blues / Over The Rainbow	1981	.40	2.00
Elektra 47095		Thirty-Nine And Holding / Change Places With Me	1981	.40	2.00
Elektra 69992		I'd Do It All Again / Who Will Buy The Wine?	1982	.40	2.00
		—Extended Play Albums—			
Sun 107		Jerry Lee Lewis	1958	12.00	60.00
Sun 108		Jerry Lee Lewis	1958	12.00	60.00
Sun 109		Jerry Lee Lewis	1958	12.00	60.00
Sun 110		Jerry Lee Lewis	1959	12.00	60.00
Smash SEP-2	(DJ)	Jerry Lee Lewis	196?	8.00	40.00
Smash DJS-28	(DJ)	Open End Interview With Jerry Lee Lewis	196?	7.00	35.00
Sun Inter. 108	(33)	Golden Cream Of Country (Jukebox EP)	1969	5.00	25.00
Sun Inter. 114	(33)	A Taste Of Country (Jukebox EP)	1969	5.00	25.00

LEWIS, SAMMY-WILLIE JOHNSON COMBO
Sun 218		So Long, Baby / I Feel So Worried	1955	8.00	40.00

LEWIS, WALLY
Tally 117		Kathleen / Donna	1958	4.00	20.00
Dot 15705		Kathleen / Donna	1958	3.00	15.00
Dot 15763		White Bobby Sox / I'm With You	1959	3.00	15.00
Liberty 55178		That's The Way It Goes / Every Day	1959	2.00	10.00
Liberty 55196		Sally Green / Arms Of Jo-Ann	1959	2.00	10.00
Liberty 55211		My Baby / Lover Boy	1959	2.00	10.00
Liberty 55370		Streets Of Berlin / Walking In The Footsteps Of A Fool	1961	1.00	5.00

LEWIS & CLARKE [THE LEWIS & CLARKE EXPEDITION]
Chartmaker 402		Expedition West / For Your Freedom Tonight	1966	1.25	6.00
Colgems 1006		Blue Revelations / I Feel Good (I Feel Bad)	1967	1.00	5.00
Colgems 1006	(PS)	Blue Revelations / I Feel Good (I Feel Bad)	1967	2.00	10.00
Colgems 1011		Destination Unknown / Freedom Bird	1968	1.00	5.00
Colgems 1011	(PS)	Destination Unknown / Freedom Bird	1968	2.00	10.00

LIBERTY PARTY, THE
Jerden 787		Weep On / Get Yourself Home	1966	2.00	10.00

LIFEGUARDS, THE
The Lifeguards is a pseudonym for members of Bill Haley's Comets. Refer to The Kingsmen; The Merri-Men.
ABC-Paramount 10021	(DJ)	Everybody Out Of The Pool / Teenage Tango	1959	5.00	25.00
ABC-Paramount 10021		Everybody Out Of The Pool / Teenage Tango	1959	10.00	50.00
Casa Blanca 5535		Everybody Out Of The Pool / Teenage Tango	1959	6.00	30.00
DR 69		Everybody Out Of The Pool / Teenage Tango	1965	2.00	10.00

LIFEGUARDS, THE
The Lifeguards feature Steve Barri and Phil Sloan.
Catch 104		State Beach /	1964	7.00	35.00
Reprise 0277		Swimtime U.S.A. / Swim Party	1964	5.00	25.00

LIGHT, BURT
Crossroad 3005		A Ticket To Heaven / Just Call Me Lonesome	196?	2.00	10.00

LIGHTFOOT, GORDON [GORD LIGHTFOOT]
Chateau 142		Daisy-Doo / I'm The One	196?	4.00	20.00
ABC-Paramount 10352		(Remember Me) I'm The One / Daisy-Doo	1962	3.00	15.00
ABC-Paramount 10373		It's Too Late, He Wins / Negotiations	1962	3.00	15.00
United Artists 929		Just Like Tom Thumb's Blues / Ribbon Of Darkness	1965	.80	4.00
United Artists 50055		For Lovin' Me / Spin, Spin	1966	.80	4.00
United Artists 50114		I'll Be Alright / Go Go Round	1967	.80	4.00
United Artists 50152		Peaceful Waters / The Way I Feel	1967	.80	4.00
United Artists 50281		Black Day In July / Pussywillows, Cat-Tails	1968	.80	4.00
United Artists 50447		Bitter Green / Does Your Mother Know?	1968	.80	4.00
Reprise 0926		Me And Bobby McGhee / The Pony Man	1970	.60	3.00
Reprise 0974		If You Could Read My Mind / Poor Little Allison	1970	.60	3.00
Reprise 1020		Talking In Your Sleep / Nous Vivons Ensemble	1971	.60	3.00
Reprise 1035		Summer Side Of Life / Love And Maple Syrup	1971	.60	3.00
Reprise 1088		Beautiful / Don Quixote	1972	.60	3.00
Reprise 1128		You Are What I Am / The Same Old Obsession	1973	.60	3.00
Reprise 1145		Can't Depend On You / It's Worth Believin'	1973	.60	3.00
Reprise 1194		Sundown / Too Late For Partyin'	1974	.60	3.00
Reprise 1309		Carefree Highway / Seven Island Suite	1974	.60	3.00
Reprise 1328		Rainy Day People / Cherokee Bend	1975	.60	3.00

Label & Catalog #		A-Side/B-Side	Year	VG	NM
Reprise 1369		The Wreck Of The Edmund Fitzgerald /			
		The House You Live In	1976	.60	3.00
Reprise 1380		Race Among The Ruins / Protocol	1977	.60	3.00
Warner Bros. 5621		For Lovin' Me / I'm Not Sayin'	197?	.40	2.00
Warner Bros. 8518		The Circle In Small / Sweet Genevieve	197?	.40	2.00
Warner Bros. 8579		Daylight Katy / Hangdog Hotel Room	197?	.40	2.00
Warner Bros. 8644		Dreamland / Songs The Minstrel Sang	197?	.40	2.00
Warner Bros. 49230		Dream Street Rose / Make Way For The Lady	197?	.40	2.00

LINCOLNS, THE

Dot 16958		We Got Some / Pop Kat	1966	2.00	10.00
Ripcord 0001		Listen / Girl	1967	3.00	15.00
Ripcord 0003		Humpty Dumpty / Painted Picture	1968	2.00	10.00
Tripp 1000		Smile Baby Smile / Come Along And Dream	1969	2.00	10.00
Tripp 1002		Summer Winds / In The Back Of My Mind	1969	2.00	10.00
Topaz 1303		I Don't Understand / In The Back Of My Mind	196?	2.00	10.00

LINDSAY, MARK
Mark Lindsay also recorded with Paul Revere & The Raiders and The Unknowns.

Columbia 44875		First Hymn From Grand Terrace / Old Man At The Fair	1969	.60	3.00
Columbia 45037		Arizona / Man From Houston	1969	.60	3.00
Columbia 45125		Miss America / Small Town Woman	1970	.60	3.00
Columbia 45180		Silver Bird / So Hard To Leave You	1970	.60	3.00
Columbia 45229		And The Grass Won't Pay No Mind			
		Funny How Little Men Care	1970	.40	2.00
Columbia 45286		Problem Child / Bookends	1971	.40	2.00
Columbia 45386		Been Too Long On The Road / All I Really See Is You	1971	.40	2.00
Columbia 45462		Are You Old Enough? / Don't You Know?	1971	.40	2.00
Columbia 45506		Something Big / Pretty, Pretty	1972	.40	2.00
Columbia 45895		California / Someone's Been Hiding	1973	.40	2.00
Columbia 10014		Photograph / Song For A Friend	1975	.40	2.00
Columbia 10081		Mamacita / Song For A Friend	1975	.40	2.00
Columbia CBS-1	(DJ)	Green Lights And Blue Skies / (B-side by Artie Butler)	1975	.60	3.00
Greedy 106AF		Sing Your Own Song / Sing Your Own Song	1976	.60	3.00
Busch '76 TS75-942	(DJ)	Sing Your Own Song (One sided)	1976	3.00	15.00
		(Promo for beer; Lindsay's name does not appear on the label.)			
Elka 310		Sing Your Own Song / Sing Your Own Song	1976	1.60	8.00
Warner Bros. 8359		Sing Me High (Sing Me Low) / Flips-Eyed	1977	.40	2.00
Warner Bros. 8479		Little Ladies Of The Night / Flips-Eyed	1977	.40	2.00

LISTEN
Listen features Robert Plant, later of Led Zeppelin.

Columbia 43967	(DJ)	You Better Run / Everybody's Gonna Say	1967	12.00	60.00
Columbia 43967		You Better Run / Everybody's Gonna Say	1967	20.00	100.00

LITTLE ALFRED

Lyric 1016		Walking Down The Aisle Of Love /			
		(B-side by Cookie & The Cupcakes)	1964	2.00	10.00

LITTLE BIG HORN

Burdette 4		Rebel Rouser / Theme For Mr. Nobody	196?	1.00	5.00

LITTLE BILL & THE BLUENOTES

Dolton 4		I Love An Angel / Bye Bye Bye	1959	2.00	10.00

LITTLE BILL (WITH THE BLUENOTES)

Topaz 1302		Sweet Cucumber / Why Was I Ever Born?	196?	3.00	15.00
Topaz 1305		Louie, Louie / Boy Next Door	196?	4.00	20.00
Bolo 725		Little Angel / Next Time You See Me	196?	3.00	15.00

LITTLE BILLY & THE ESSENTIALS: *Refer to BILLY & THE ESSENTIALS*

LITTLE BUTCHIE [SAUNDERS] & THE VELLS

Angletone 535		Over The Rainbow / Sometimes, Little Girl	195?	7.00	35.00

LITTLE CAL

Golden Crest 533		Young School Girl / (B-side by The Mad Plaids)	196?	5.00	25.00

LITTLE CURTIS & THE BLUES

Vanco 219		Soul Desire / Please Keep Me	196?	3.00	15.00

LITTLE DOUG (SAHM)

Sarg 113		Rollin' Rollin' / A Real American Joe	196?	6.00	30.00

LITTLE FEAT
Formed by Roy Estrada and Lowell George, members have included Richie Hayward and Bill Payne, all ex-Mothers.

Warner Bros. 7431		Hamburger Midnight / Strawberry Flats	1970	.80	4.00
Warner Bros. 8054		Oh, Atlanta / Down The Road	1975	.60	3.00

Label & Catalog #		A-Side / B-Side	Year	VG	NM
Warner Bros. 8174		Long Distance Love / Romance Dance	1976	.60	3.00
Warner Bros. 8420		Time Loves A Hero / Sailin' Shoes	1977	.60	3.00
Warner Bros. 8566		Willin' / Oh, Atlanta	1978	.60	3.00

LITTLE JOE & THE MUSTANGS

Challenge 59273		South Swell / Peach Seeds	1964	4.00	20.00

LITTLE JOHN & THE MONKS

Jerden 775		Needles And Pins / Black Winds	1965	2.00	10.00
Tork		Woman Take A Trip / All Them Lies	196?	2.00	10.00

LITTLE JUNIOR'S BLUE FLAMES

Sun 187		Feelin' Good / Fussin' And Fightin' Blues	1953	30.00	150.00
Sun 192		Mystery Train / Love My Baby	1953	20.00	100.00

LITTLE MILTON (MILTON CAMPBELL)

Sun 194		Beggin' My Baby / Somebody Told Me	1953	20.00	100.00
Sun 200		If You Love Me / Alone And Blue	1954	100.00	400.00
Sun 220		Lookin' For My Baby / Homesick For My Baby	1955	150.00	500.00

LITTLE PATTIE & THE STATESMEN

World Hits 150		He's My Blonde-Headed Stompie Wompie Real Gone Surfer Boy / Stompin' At Maroubra	196?	6.00	30.00

LITTLE RICHARD (PENNIMAN)

The self-ordained King of Rock 'N Roll, Little Richard's early R&B sides for Specialty display a sense of wreckless abandon that is the envy of many a rocker. His work as a vocal stylist and a writer have influenced rockers from Elvis to Paul McCartney to today's punks. Refer to The Beach Boys; Canned Heat; The Deuces Of Rhythm; The Upsetters.

Label & Catalog #		A-Side / B-Side	Year	VG	NM
RCA Victor 47-4392	(DJ)	Taxi Blues / Every Hour	1951	50.00	200.00
RCA Victor 47-4392		Taxi Blues / Every Hour	1951	75.00	300.00
RCA Victor 47-4582	(DJ)	Get Rich Quick / Thinkin' About My Mother	1952	75.00	300.00
RCA Victor 47-4582		Get Rich Quick / Thinkin' About My Mother	1952	100.00	400.00
RCA Victor 47-4772	(DJ)	Ain't Nothin' Happenin' / Why Did You Leave Me?	1952	75.00	300.00
RCA Victor 47-4772		Ain't Nothin' Happenin' / Why Did You Leave Me?	1952	100.00	400.00
RCA Victor 47-5025	(DJ)	Please Have Mercy On Me / I Brought It All On Myself	1952	75.00	300.00
RCA Victor 47-5025		Please Have Mercy On Me / I Brought It All On Myself	1952	100.00	400.00
Peacock 1658		Directly From My Heart To You / Little Richard's Boogie	1953	15.00	75.00
Peacock 1673		Maybe I'm Right / I Love My Baby	1954	6.00	30.00
Specialty 561		Tutti Frutti / I'm Just A Lonely Guy	1955	4.00	20.00
Specialty 572		Long Tall Sally / Slippin' And Slidin'	1956	4.00	20.00
Specialty 579		Rip It Up / Ready Teddy	1956	4.00	20.00
Specialty 584		She's Got It / Heebie Jeebies	1956	4.00	20.00
Specialty 591		The Girl Can't Help It / All Around The World	1956	4.00	20.00
Specialty 598		Lucille / Send Me Some Lovin'	1957	4.00	20.00
Specialty 606		Jenny, Jenny / Miss Ann	1957	4.00	20.00
Specialty 606	(PS)	Jenny, Jenny / Miss Ann	1957	10.00	50.00
Specialty 611		Keep A Knockin' / Can't Believe You Wanna Leave	1957	4.00	20.00
Specialty 611	(PS)	Keep A Knockin' / Can't Believe You Wanna Leave	1957	10.00	50.00
Modern 1018		Holy Mackeral / Baby, Don't You Want A Man Like Me?	1958	2.00	10.00
Modern 1018	(PS)	Holy Mackeral / Baby, Don't You Want A Man Like Me?	1958	6.00	30.00
Modern 1022		Directly From My Heart / I'm Back	1958	2.00	10.00
Specialty 624		Good Golly, Miss Molly / Hey, Hey, Hey	1958	3.00	15.00
Specialty 624	(PS)	Good Golly, Miss Molly / Hey, Hey, Hey	1958	8.00	40.00
Specialty 633		Oh! My Soul / True Fine Mama	1958	3.00	15.00
Specialty 633	(PS)	Oh! My Soul / True Fine Mama	1958	8.00	40.00
Specialty 645		Baby Face / I'll Never Let You Go	1958	3.00	15.00
Specialty 652		She Knows How To Rock / Early One Morning	1958	3.00	15.00
Specialty 660		By The Light Of The Silvery Moon / Wonderin'	1959	3.00	15.00
Specialty 664		Kansas City / Lonesome And Blue	1959	3.00	15.00
Specialty 670		Shake A Hand / All Night Long	1960	3.00	15.00
Specialty 680		Whole Lotta Shakin' Goin' On / Maybe I'm Right	1960	3.00	15.00
Specialty 681		I Got It / Baby	1960	3.00	15.00
Mercury 71965		He Got What He Wanted / Why Don't You Change Your Ways?	1962	1.60	8.00
Mercury 71884		Joy, Joy, Joy / He's Not Just A Soldier	1962	1.60	8.00
Specialty 686		Directly From My Heart To You / The Most I Can Offer	1964	2.00	10.00
Specialty 692		Bama Lama Loo / Annie's Back	1964	2.00	10.00
Specialty 697		Keep A Knockin' / Bamma Lama Loo	1964	2.00	10.00
Vee Jay 665		Without Love / Dance What You Wanna	1965	2.00	10.00
Vee Jay 698		I Don't Know What You've Got, But It's Got Me / I Don't Know What You've Got, But It's Got Me, Part 2	1965	1.60	8.00
OKeh 7251		Poor Dog / Well	1967	1.60	8.00
OKeh 7251	(PS)	Poor Dog / Well	1967	3.00	15.00
Reprise 0907		Freedom Blues / Dew Drop Inn	1970	1.20	6.00
Reprise 0942		Greenwood Mississippi / I Saw Her Standing There	1970	1.20	6.00

— *Extended Play Albums* —

RCA Camden 416		Little Richard	1955	50.00	200.00
RCA Camden 446		Little Richard Rocks	1956	30.00	150.00

Label & Catalog #	A-Side/B-Side	Year	VG	NM
Specialty 400	Here's Little Richard	1957	15.00	75.00
Specialty 401	Here's Little Richard	1957	15.00	75.00
Specialty 402	Here's Little Richard	1957	15.00	75.00
Specialty 403	Little Richard	1958	10.00	50.00
Specialty 404	Little Richard	1958	10.00	50.00
Specialty 405	Little Richard	1958	10.00	50.00

LITTLE WHEELS, THE
The Little Wheels feature Ray Hildebrand and Jill Jackson, who recorded as Paul and Paula.

Dot 16676	Four Wheeled, Ball-Bearing Surfing Board / The Bump	1964	4.00	20.00

LIVE FIVE, THE

Panorama 31	Shake A Tail Feather / Yes, You're Mine	1966	2.00	10.00
Jerden 797	Shake A Tail Feather / Yes, You're Mine	1966	1.20	6.00
Panorama 46	Hunose / Let's Go, Let's Go, Let's Go	1966	2.00	10.00
Piccadilly 233	Move Over And Let Me Fly / Been Nice Knowin' You, Baby	1967	2.00	10.00
Piccadilly 248	Hunose / Take The Good And The Bad	1967	1.20	6.00
Piccadilly 236	I Must Move / I Must Move	1967	1.00	5.00

LIVE WIRES, THE

Ref 110	Bona Vista Twist / Kick Off	196?	7.00	35.00

LIVELY ONES, THE

Del-Fi 4184	Guitarget / Crying Guitar	1962	5.00	25.00
Del-Fi 4196	Surf Rider / Surfer's Lament	1963	3.00	15.00
Del-Fi 4205	Surfer Boogie / Ric-A-Tac	1963	3.00	15.00
Del-Fi 4210	High Tide / Goofy Foot	1963	3.00	15.00
Del-Fi 4217	Telstar Surf / Surf City	1963	3.00	15.00
Smash 1880	Night And Day / Hey, Scrounge	1964	3.00	15.00

LIVELY SET, THE

Decca 31678	Pamona Drags / Turbine Montage	1964	6.00	30.00

LIVERPOOL FIVE, THE

RCA Victor 47-8578	Everything's Alright / That's What I Want	1965	1.00	5.00
RCA Victor 47-8660	Too Far Out / If You Gotta Go	1965	1.00	5.00
RCA Victor 47-8725	I Just Can't Believe It / Heart	1965	1.00	5.00
RCA Victor 47-8816	Sister Love / She's Mine	1966	1.00	5.00
RCA Victor 47-8906	What A Crazy World / New Directions	1966	1.00	5.00
RCA Victor 47-8968	Anyway That You Want Me / The Snake	1966	1.00	5.00
RCA Victor 47-9158	Cloudy / She's Got Plenty Of Love	1967	1.00	5.00
Piccadilly 255	Good Golly, Miss Molly /	1969	1.00	5.00

LIVING END, THE

Bolo 757	Skyride / Jumpin' At The Lion's Gate	196?	2.00	10.00

LLOYD, CHARLES

A&M 1415	TM / Seagull	1973	1.00	5.00
	("TM" features Al Jardine, Mike Love, and Carl Wilson.)			

LLOYD, JACKIE

Hero 342	Come And Get Me / Warm Love	195?	15.00	75.00

LOAD OF MISCHIEF

Sun 407	Back In My Arms Again / I'm A Lover	1967	7.00	35.00

LOLLIPOP SHOPPE, THE

Uni 55050		You Must Be A Witch / Don't Close The Door	1968	2.00	10.00
Uni 55050	(PS)	You Must Be A Witch / Don't Close The Door	1968	5.00	25.00
Shamley 44005		Someone I Know / Through My Window	1969	2.00	10.00

LOMAX, JACKIE

Apple 1802		Sour Milk Sea / The Eagle Laughs At You	1968	4.00	20.00
Apple 1807		New Day / Thumbin' A Ride	1969	10.00	50.00
Apple 1819		How The Web Was Woven / Fall Inside Your Eyes	1970	2.00	10.00
Apple 1819	(PS)	How The Web Was Woven / Fall Inside Your Eyes	1970	3.00	15.00
Apple 1834		Sour Milk Sea / Fall Inside Your Eyes	1971	2.00	10.00

LONDON TAXI, THE

Piccadilly 239	Feelin' Down / Last Step	196?	3.00	15.00

LONELY ONES, THE

TB-2277/78	(EP)	Stub's Pub (33)	196?	10.00	50.00

LONG, HUEY

Fidelity 4054	How To Tell My Heart / Waiting For A Letter	1961	2.00	10.00
Fidelity 4055	Elvis Stole My Gal / Ballad Of John Glenn	1961	10.00	50.00

Label & Catalog #		A-Side/B-Side	Year	VG	NM

LONNIE & THE LEGENDS

| Rev 1005/6 | | Crazy Penguin / Penguin Walk | 195? | 7.00 | 35.00 |

LOOKINLAND, MIKE
Mike Lookinland was a member of The Brady Bunch.

| Capitol 3914 | | Love Doesn't Care Who's In It / Gum Drop | 197? | 1.60 | 8.00 |
| Capitol 3914 | (PS) | Love Doesn't Care Who's In It / Gum Drop | 197? | 3.00 | 15.00 |

LOOSE GRAVEL

Kelly 26945		Frisco Band / Waiting In Line	196?	2.00	10.00
		(First pressings have plain blank labels.)			
Kelly 26945	(PS)	Frisco Band / Waiting In Line	196?	2.00	10.00

LOPEZ, TRINI
Trini Lopez also recorded with The Big Beats.

Volk 101		The Right To Rock /	1958	3.00	15.00
King 5173		Nola / Rosalia	1959	2.00	10.00
King 5187		Since I Don't Have You / Rock On	1959	2.00	10.00
King 5198		Here Comes Sally / Love Me Tonight	1959	2.00	10.00
King 5234		I'm Grateful / Don't Let Your Sweet Love Die	1959	2.00	10.00
King 5284		Nobody Listens To Our Teenage Problems / Nobody Loves Me	1960	2.00	10.00
King 5304		Chain Of Loves / Sweet Thing	1960	2.00	10.00
King 5324		Jeanie Marie / Schemer	1960	2.00	10.00
King 5344		The Search Goes On / It Hurts To Be In Love	1960	2.00	10.00
King 5418		Then You Know / Don't Treat Me That Way	1961	2.00	10.00
King 5487		You Broke The Only Heart / One Heart, One Life, One Love	1961	2.00	10.00
DRA 7008		Rosita / Only In My Dreams	1961	1.60	8.00
King 5801		Jeanie Marie / Love Me Tonight	1963	1.60	8.00
King 5820		Don't Go / It Seems	1963	1.60	8.00
Reprise 20168		A-Me-Ri-Ca / Let It Be Known	1963	.60	3.00
Reprise 20190		La Bamba / La Bamba, Part 2	1963	.60	3.00
Reprise 20198		If I Had A Hammer / Unchain My Heart	1963	.80	4.00
Reprise 20218		If I Had A Hammer / La Bamba (Italian)	1963	.80	4.00
Reprise 20223		This Land Is Your Land / Celito Lindo	1963	.60	3.00
Reprise 20224		Bye Bye Blackbird / Medley	1963	.60	3.00
Reprise 20234		This Land Is Your Land / La Bamba (German)	1963	.60	3.00
Reprise 20236		Kansas City / Lonesome Traveler	1963	.80	4.00
Reprise 0239		Granada / La Bamba	1963	.60	3.00
Reprise 0260		Jailer, Bring Me Water / You Can't Say Goodbye	1963	.80	4.00
Reprise 0276		What Have I Got Of My Own? / Ya Ya	1964	.80	4.00
Reprise 0300		Michael / San Fransisco De Assissi	1964	.80	4.00
Reprise 0328		Sad Tomorrows / I've Lost My Love For You	1964	.60	3.00
United Modern 106		Sinner, No Saint / If	1964	1.50	8.00
King 5824		The Club For Broken Hearts / Nobody Loves Me	1964	1.00	5.00
King 5849		(Won't You Be) My Queen For A Day / Yes, You Do	1964	1.00	5.00
King 6000		Nobody Listens, Nobody Cares / Jeanie Marie	1965	1.00	5.00
King 6021		Chain Of Loves / The Search Goes On	1966	1.00	5.00
Reprise 0336		Lemon Tree / Pretty Eyes	1965	.80	4.00
Reprise 0376		Are You Sincere? / You'll Be Sorry	1965	.60	3.00
Reprise 0405		Sinner Man / Double Trouble	1965	.60	3.00
Reprise 0421		My Felicidad / Regressa A Mi	1965	.60	3.00
Reprise 0435		Made In Paris / Pretty Little Girl	1965	.60	3.00
Reprise 0455		I'm Comin' Home, Cindy / The 32nd Of May	1966	.60	3.00
Reprise 0480		La Bamba / Trini's Tune	1966	.60	3.00
Reprise 0508		Hall Of Fame / Pancho Lopez	1966	.60	3.00
Reprise 0536		Your Ever Changing Mind / Takin' The Back Roads	1966	.60	3.00
Reprise 0547		Gonna Get Along Without Ya Now / Love Letters	1967	.60	3.00
Reprise 0574		Up To Now / In The Land Of Plenty	1967	.60	3.00
Reprise 0596		The Bramble Bush / The Ballad Of The Dirty Dozen	1967	.60	3.00
Reprise 0618		I Wanna Be Free / Together	1967	.60	3.00
Reprise 0648		Let's Take A Walk / It's A Great Life	1967	.60	3.00
Reprise 0659		Sally Was A Good Girl / It's A Great Life	1967	.60	3.00
Reprise 0687		Mental Journey / Good Old Morning Dew	1967	.60	3.00
Reprise 0700		If I Had A Hammer / Lemon Tree	1968	.60	3.00
Reprise 0725		La Bamba / Kansas City	1968	.60	3.00
Reprise 0770		Malaguena Salierosa / Something Tells Me	1968	.60	3.00
Reprise 0801	(DJ)	El Nino Del Tambor / Nocho De Paz-Let There Be Peace	1968	.60	3.00
Reprise 0814		Come A Little Bit Closer / My Baby Loves Sad Songs	1968	.60	3.00
Reprise 0825		Don't Let The Sun Catch You Crying / My Baby Loves Sad Songs	1969	.60	3.00
Reprise 0879		Games People Play / Love Story	1969	.60	3.00
Reprise 0912		Five O' Clock World / You Make My Day	1970	.60	3.00
Reprise 0933		Su-Kal-De-Don / Mexican Medicine Man	1970	.60	3.00
Reprise 0947		Time To Get It Together / Mexican Medicine Man	1970	.60	3.00
Reprise 0975		Let's Think About Living / There Was A Crooked Man	1970	.60	3.00
Capitol 3195		Some Kind Of Summer / Poor Old Billy	1971	.60	3.00
Capitol 312		Ruby Mountain / Y Volvere	1972	.60	3.00

Label & Catalog #		A-Side/B-Side	Year	VG	NM
Griffin 504		Butterfly / Don't Burn Your Bridge Behind You	1973	.60	3.00
Griffin 508		We Got To Make It Together / Bring Back The Sunshine	1973	.60	3.00
Private Stock 024		Sweet Life / Somethin' 'Bout You Baby I Like	1975	.60	3.00
Private Stock 035	(DJ)	Seco Sulto Y Tontos / Seco Sulto Y Tontos	1975	.60	3.00
		(Stock copies of P.S. 035 may not exist.)			
Roulette 7214		Helplessly / Beautiful People	1977	.60	3.00
		—12" Singles—			
Roulette 7214		Helplessly / Trini's Medley	1977	1.00	5.00
		—Extended Play Albums—			
King 483		The Teenage Idol	1959	15.00	75.00
Reprise 40054		Trini Lopez At PJ's	1963	5.00	25.00
		—Special/Promotional Releases—			
Reprise S-195	(33)	Bye Bye Blackbird / A-Me-Ri-Ca	1963	1.00	5.00
Reprise S-196	(33)	If I Had A Hammer / Unchain My Heart	1963	1.00	5.00
Reprise S-197	(33)	This Land Is Your Land / Granada	1963	1.00	5.00
Reprise S-198	(33)	Celito Lindo / La Bamba	1963	1.00	5.00
Reprise S-199	(33)	What'd I Say / Medley	1963	1.00	5.00
Reprise 6125	(33)	The Latin Album (Jukebox EP)	1968	2.00	10.00
Reprise 6147	(33)	The Folk Album (Jukebox EP)	1968	2.00	10.00
Reprise 6171	(33)	The Rhythm Album (Jukebox EP)	1968	2.00	10.00
Reprise 6215	(33)	The Second Latin Album (Jukebox EP)	1968	2.00	10.00
Reprise 6255	(33)	Now! (Jukebox EP)	1968	2.00	10.00
Reprise 6285	(33)	It's A Great Life (Jukebox EP)	1968	2.00	10.00
Reprise 6300	(33)	Welcome To Trini Country (Jukebox EP)	1968	2.00	10.00

LORD, BRIAN, & THE MIDNIGHTERS
The Midnighters feature Frank Zappa and Ray Collins, later of The Mothers Of Invention.

Vigah 001		The Big Surfer / Not Another One	1963	40.00	200.00
Capitol 4981		The Big Surfer / Not Another One	1963	20.00	100.00

LORD, DICK

Atco 6331		Like Ringo / The Name On The Wall	1964	2.00	10.00

LORD & THE FLIES

U.S.A. 857		Come What May / Echoes	1966	1.20	6.00

LORD DENT & THE INVADERS
Lord Dent is a pseudonym for Clayton Watson.

Shelley 1001		Wolf Call / The Greaser	196?	2.00	10.00
Shelley 1001	(PS)	Wolf Call / The Greaser	196?	3.00	15.00

LORD KALVERT & THE RESERVES

Quest 304		Procrastinator / You Are My Sunshine	196?	2.00	10.00

LORD SITAR
Originally released amidst the rumor that the Lord here was, in fact, Beatle George honing his sitar skills.

Capitol 5972		Black Is Black / Have You Seen Your Mother, Baby, Standing In The Shadows	1968	2.00	10.00

LORDS OF LONDON, THE

Decca 32196		Corn Flakes And Ice Cream / Time Waits For No One	1967	2.00	10.00
MGM 13919		Candy Rainbow / Within Your Mind	1968	1.50	8.00

LOREN, DONNA

Challenge 9173		I'm In Love With The Ticket Taker At The Bijou Movie / I'm Gonna Be Alright	1962	2.00	10.00
Challenge 9190		If You Love Me / On The Good Ship Lollipop	1963	2.00	10.00
Challenge 9203		Dream World / I'm The One Who Loves You	1963	2.00	10.00
Challenge 59213		I'm Gonna Be Alright / Johnny's Got Something	1963	2.00	10.00
Challenge 59222		I Can't Make My Heart Say Goodbye / Danny	1963	2.00	10.00
Challenge 59237	(DJ)	Muscle Bustle / How Can I Face The World	1963	5.00	25.00
Challenge 59237		Muscle Bustle / How Can I Face The World	1963	10.00	50.00
		("Muscle Bustle" features the original instrumental track produced by Brian Wilson for the film "Muscle Beach Party.")			
Capitol 5250		Blowing Out The Candles / Just A Little Girl	1964	1.20	6.00
Capitol 5337		Ten Good Reasons / 90 Day Guarantee	1964	1.20	6.00
Capitol 5409		New Love / So, Do The Zonk	1965	1.20	6.00
Capitol 5548		Call Me / Smokey Joe's	1965	1.20	6.00
Capitol 5659		I Believe / Play, Little Music Box, Play	1966	1.20	6.00
Reprise 0586		Let's Pretend / Once Before I Die	1967	1.20	6.00
Reprise 0634		As Long As I'm Holding You / It's Such A Shame	1967	1.20	6.00

LOREN, FRANKIE

Mercury 71444		Soon The School Year Will Be Over / Hey, Little Girl	1959	3.00	15.00

LOREN, SHIRLEY

Jerden 919		One Night / You Get To Me	1970	1.00	5.00

Label & Catalog #	A-Side/B-Side	Year	VG	NM
LORNETTES, THE				
Gallo 110	His Way With The Girls /			
	Down The Block And Up To Heaven	196?	3.00	15.00
LOS BRAVOS				
Refer to the Various Artists section.				
Press 60002	Black Is Black / I Want A Name	1966	1.20	6.00
Press 60003	Going Nowhere / Brand New Baby	1966	1.00	5.00
Press 60004	You'll Never Get The Chance Again / I'm All Ears	1967	1.00	5.00
Parrot 3020	Bring A Little Lovin' / Make It Last	1968	1.00	5.00
Parrot 3023	Dirty Street / Two People In Me	1968	1.00	5.00
LOS MOSQUITOS				
Canyon State 114	Wipe Out / Flame Out	1963	10.00	50.00
LOSERS, THE				
Parley 711	Snake Eyes / Balboa Party	1963	7.00	35.00
LOST				
Capitol 5519	Maybe More Than You / Back Door Blues	1965	3.00	15.00
Capitol 5708	Mean Motorcycle / Violet Gown	1965	3.00	15.00
Capitol 5725	No Reason Why / Violet Gown	1966	3.00	15.00
LOST & FOUND				
International Arts. 120	Forever Lasting Plastic / Everybody's Here	1967	3.00	15.00
International Arts. 125	Professor Black / When Will You Come Through?	1967	3.00	15.00
LOST CHILDREN, THE				
Topaz 1309	My Reason / Everything	196?	2.00	10.00
LOST SOULS, THE				
Liberty 56024	Artificial Rose / Sad Little Girl	1968	2.00	10.00
LOTHAR & THE HAND PEOPLE				
Capitol 5874	L-O-V-E / Rose Colored Glasses	1967	1.60	8.00
Capitol 5945	Every Single Word / Comic Strip	1967	1.60	8.00
Capitol 2008	Have Mercy / Let The Boy Pretend	1967	1.60	8.00
Capitol 376	Machines / Milkweed Love	1969	1.60	8.00
Capitol 556	Midnight Ranger / Yes, I Love You	1969	1.60	8.00
LOUDERMILK, JOHN D.				
John Loudermilk also recorded as Johnny Dee and Ebe Sneezer & The Epidemics.				
Columbia 41165	Yearbook / Susie's House	1958	3.00	15.00
Columbia 41209	Lover's Lane / Yo Yo	1958	3.00	15.00
Columbia 41247	Goin' Away To School / This Cold War With You	1958	3.00	15.00
RCA Victor 47-7938	Language Of Love / Darling Jane	1961	2.00	10.00
RCA Victor 47-7993	Thou Shalt Not Steal / Mister Jones	1962	2.00	10.00
RCA Victor 47-8054	Callin' Doctor Casey / Oh, How Sad	1962	2.00	10.00
RCA Victor 47-8101	Angela Jones / Road Hog	1962	2.00	10.00
RCA Victor 47-8101 (PS)	Angela Jones / Road Hog	1962	3.00	15.00
RCA Victor 47-8154	Guitar Player / Bad News	1963	2.00	10.00
RCA Victor 47-8308	Blue Train (Of The Heartbreak Line) / Rhythm And Blues	1964	2.00	10.00
RCA Victor 47-8389	Th' Wife / Nothin' To Gain	1964	2.00	10.00
LOUNGERS, THE				
Beachwood 4422	Cathy's Clown / Girls	1964	2.00	10.00
LOVE				
The original Love was Don Conka, John Echols, Ken Forssi, Arthur Lee, Bryan Maclean and Snoopy Pfisterer with Michael Stuart joining in 1967. By the time the group had joined Blue Thumb, Love was Lee with hired hands.				
LSD 1009	Do The Marlin, Baby / House Of The Rising Sun	1964	100.00	400.00
Elektra 45603	My Little Red Book / A Message To Pretty	1966	1.20	6.00
Elektra 45605	7 And 7 Is / #14	1967	1.00	5.00
Elektra 45608	Orange Skies / Stephanie Knows	1967	1.20	6.00
Elektra 45608	Orange Skies / She Comes In Colors	1967	1.00	5.00
Elektra 45613 (DJ)	Que Vida! / Hey Joe	1967	5.00	25.00
Elektra 45613	Que Vida! / Hey Joe	1967	10.00	50.00
Elektra 45629	Alone Again Or / A House Is Not A Motel	1968	1.00	5.00
Elektra 45633	Your Mind And Me Belong Together / Laughing Stock	1968	1.00	5.00
Elektra 45700	Alone Again Or / A House Is Not A Motel	1970	1.00	5.00
Blue Thumb 106	Stand Out / I'll Pray For You	1970	.80	4.00
Blue Thumb 116	Keep On Shining / The Everlasting First	1970	.80	4.00
RSO 502	Time Is Like A River / With A Little Energy	1974	.60	3.00
RSO 506	You Said You Would / Good Old Fashioned Dream	1975	.60	3.00
LOVE, BILLY, & THE LOVERS				
Dragon 4403	Legend Of Love / Hold Me Close	195?	10.00	50.00

Label & Catalog #	A-Side/B-Side	Year	VG	NM

LOVE, DARLENE
Darlene Love was produced by Phil Spector. Refer to The Crystals.

Philles 111	(Today I Met) The Boy I'm Gonna Marry /			
	My Heart Beat A Little Bit Faster	1963	4.00	20.00
Philles 111	(Today I Met) The Boy I'm Gonna Marry /			
	Playing For Keeps	1963	3.00	15.00
Philles 114	Wait Till My Bobby Gets Home / Take It From Me	1963	3.00	15.00
Philles 117	A Fine, Fine Boy / Nino And Sonny	1963	3.00	15.00
Philles 119	Christmas (Baby, Please Come Home) /			
	Harry And Milt Meet Hal B.	1963	5.00	25.00
Philles 123	(He's) A Quiet Guy / Stumble And Fall	1964	12.00	60.00
Philles 125	Christmas (Baby, Please Come Home) / X-Mas Blues	1964	75.00	300.00
Philles 125X	Christmas (Baby, Please Come Home) / Winter Wonderland	1965	3.00	15.00
Reprise 534	Too Late To Say You're Sorry / If	1966	1.20	6.00
Warner/Spector 0401	Christmas (Baby, Please Come Home) /			
	Wait Till My Bobby Gets Home	1974	1.20	6.00
Warner/Spector 0410	Lord, If You're A Woman / Stumble And Fall	1976	1.20	6.00

LOVE, FRANKIE

LaRosa 101	First Star / Save Her Love For Me	196?	2.00	10.00

LOVE, HONEY, & THE LOVE NOTES

Cameo 380	We Belong Together / Mary Ann	1965	2.00	10.00

LOVE, MIKE

Boardwalk NB7-11-128	Looking Back With Love / One Good Reason	1981	.60	3.00

LOVE, MIKE, & DEAN TORRENCE
Refer to The Beach Boys; Celebration; Jan & Dean.

Hitbound 101	(DJ)	Da Doo Ron Ron / Baby Talk	1982	2.00	10.00
Hitbound 102		Jingle Bells / (B-side by Paul Revere & The Raiders)	1983	2.00	10.00
Hitbound 102	(PS)	Jingle Bells / (B-side by Paul Revere & The Raiders)	1983	3.00	15.00

LOVE AFFAIR, THE

Date 1591	Everlasting Love / Gone Are The Songs Of Yesterday	1968	.80	4.00
Date 1608	Someone Like Me / Rainbow Valley	1968	.80	4.00
Date 1627	I'm Happy / A Day Without Love	1968	.80	4.00
Date 1646	Let Me Know / One Road	1969	.80	4.00
Date 1652	Bringing Back The Good Times / Another Day	1969	.80	4.00

LOVE EXCHANGE, THE

Uptown 775	Swallow The Sun / Meadow Memories	196?	3.00	15.00

LOVE NOTES, THE

Wilshire 200	Our Songs Of Love / Nancy	1963	3.00	15.00
Wilshire 203	Gloria / Mathematics Of Love	1963	10.00	50.00

LOVE POTION, THE

Kapp 979	This Love / Moby Binks	1969	2.00	10.00
	("Moby Binks" is the same track as July Four's "Mr. Miff")			

LOVE SCULPTURE
Love Sculpture features Dave Edmunds.

Parrot 335	Sabre Dance / I Think Of Love	1968	3.00	15.00
Parrot 342	In The Land Of The Few / Farandole	1970	2.00	10.00

LOVE SOCIETY, THE

Scepter 12236	Tobacco Road / Drops Of Rain	1968	2.00	10.00

LOVERS, THE

Casino 103	Let's / Big Axe	1958	5.00	25.00

LOVERS, THE

Agon 1011	Caravans Of Lonely Men / In My Tenement	196?	4.00	20.00

LOVERS, THE

Lamp 2005	Darling, It's Wonderful / Got A Whole Lot Of Lovin' To Do	1957	3.00	15.00
Lamp 2013	I Wanna Be Loved / Let's Elope	1957	5.00	25.00

LOVERS, THE

Philips 40353	Someone / Do This For Me	1966	2.00	10.00

LOVIN' SPOONFUL, THE
The Spoonful was formed by The Mugwumps' John Sebastian and Zalman Yanovsky with Steve Boone and Joe Butler. In 1967, Zal was replaced by Jerry Yester of The Modern Folk Quartet. The last three singles are Boone with hired extras.

Kama Sutra 201	Do You Believe In Magic? / On The Road Again	1965	1.25	6.00
Kama Sutra 205	You Didn't Have To Be So Nice / My Gal	1965	1.25	6.00
	—Original Kama Sutra singles above have an orange spiral in the center of the label.—			

Label & Catalog #		A-Side/B-Side	Year	VG	NM
Kama Sutra 201		Do You Believe In Magic? / On The Road Again	1965	1.00	5.00
Kama Sutra 205		You Didn't Have To Be So Nice / My Gal	1965	1.00	5.00
Kama Sutra 205	(PS)	You Didn't Have To Be So Nice / My Gal	1965	3.00	15.00
Kama Sutra 208		Daydream / Night Owl Blues	1966	1.00	5.00
Kama Sutra 208	(PS)	Daydream / Night Owl Blues	1966	2.00	10.00
Kama Sutra 209		Did You Ever Have To Make Up Your Mind? /	1966	1.00	5.00
		I Didn't Want To Have To Do It			
Kama Sutra 209	(PS)	Did You Ever Have To Make Up Your Mind? /			
		I Didn't Want To Have To Do It	1966	2.00	10.00
Kama Sutra 211		Summer In The City / Butchie's Tune	1966	1.00	5.00
Kama Sutra 211	(PS)	Summer In The City / Butchie's Tune	1966	2.00	10.00
Kama Sutra 216		Rain On The Roof / Pow!	1966	1.00	5.00
Kama Sutra 216	(PS)	Rain On The Roof / Pow!	1966	2.00	10.00
Kama Sutra 219		Nashville Cats / Full Measure	1966	1.00	5.00
Kama Sutra 219	(PS)	Nashville Cats / Full Measure	1966	2.00	10.00
Kama Sutra 220		Darling Be Home Soon / Darling Companion	1967	1.00	5.00
Kama Sutra 220	(PS)	Darling Be Home Soon / Darling Companion	1967	2.00	10.00
Kama Sutra 225		Six O' Clock / You're A Big Boy Now	1967	.80	4.00
Kama Sutra 225	(PS)	Six O' Clock / You're A Big Boy Now	1967	2.00	10.00
Kama Sutra 231		You're A Big Boy Now / Lonely	1967	.80	4.00
Kama Sutra 239		She Is Still A Mystery / Only Pretty, What A Pity	1967	.80	4.00
Kama Sutra 239	(PS)	She Is Still A Mystery / Only Pretty, What A Pity	1967	2.00	10.00
Kama Sutra 241		Money / Close Your Eyes	1968	.80	4.00
Kama Sutra 250		Never Going Back / Forever	1968	.80	4.00
Kama Sutra 251		Run With You / Revelation	1968	.80	4.00
Kama Sutra 255		Me About You / Amazing Air	1969	.80	4.00
Kama Sutra 608	(DJ)	Daydream / Daydream	196?	1.00	5.00

LOVEJAYS, THE

Label & Catalog #		A-Side/B-Side	Year	VG	NM
Red Bird 003		Payin' (For The Wrong I've Done) / It's Mighty Nice	1964	2.00	10.00

LOVELESS, BOBBY

Label & Catalog #		A-Side/B-Side	Year	VG	NM
Michelle 932		Night Owl / You Are Doing Me Wrong	196?	1.20	6.00

LOVELITES, THE

Label & Catalog #		A-Side/B-Side	Year	VG	NM
Phi-Dan 5008		Malady / (When I Get) Scared	196?	4.00	20.00

LOWE, VIRGINIA

Label & Catalog #		A-Side/B-Side	Year	VG	NM
Melba 107		I'm In Love With Elvis Presley / Empty Feeling	1956	5.00	25.00

LOYE, JR., BOBBY

Label & Catalog #		A-Side/B-Side	Year	VG	NM
Ember 1111		I Just Stand Here / One Of The Lonely Ones	1961	3.00	15.00
Laurie 3222		I'm Startin' Tonight / Another Mr. Blue	1963	4.00	20.00
Wilshire 202		Loving Tree / Another Mr. Blue	1963	8.00	40.00

LUCIA & JOHNNY

Label & Catalog #		A-Side/B-Side	Year	VG	NM
Jet 165		No More / Marriage Talk	1960	3.00	15.00
Roulette 4278		No More / Marriage Talk	1960	2.00	10.00

LUCKY STARS, THE

Label & Catalog #		A-Side/B-Side	Year	VG	NM
Guyden 2097		No Surfin' City Sweetheart / The Strut	1963	5.00	25.00

LUGEE & THE LIONS
Lugee is Lou Christie.

Label & Catalog #		A-Side/B-Side	Year	VG	NM
Robbee 112		The Jury / Little Did I Know	196?	6.00	30.00

LUKE, ROBIN

Label & Catalog #		A-Side/B-Side	Year	VG	NM
International 206		Susie Darlin' / Living's Loving You	1957	10.00	50.00
International 206	(PS)	Susie Darlin' / Living's Loving You	1957	10.00	50.00
International 208		My Girl / Chicka Chicka Honey	1957	6.00	30.00
International 210		You Can't Stop Me From Dreamin' / Strollin' Blues	1957	6.00	30.00
International 212		Five Minutes More / Won't You Please Be Mine?	1958	6.00	30.00
Dot 15781		Susie Darlin' / Living's Loving You	1958	2.00	10.00
Dot 15839		My Girl / Chicka Chicka Honey	1958	2.00	10.00
Dot 15899		You Can't Stop Me From Dreamin' / Strollin' Blues	1959	2.00	10.00
Dot 15959		Five Minutes More / Who's Gonna Hold Your Hand?	1959	2.00	10.00
Dot 16001		Make Me A Dreamer / Walkin' In The Moonlight	1959	2.00	10.00
Dot 16040		Bad Boy / School Bus Love Affair	1960	2.00	10.00
Dot 16096		Everlovin' / Well Oh, Well Oh	1960	2.00	10.00
Dot 16096	(PS)	Everlovin' / Well Oh, Well Oh	1960	7.00	35.00
Dot 16229		Part Of A Fool / Poor Little Rich Boy	1961	2.00	10.00
Dot 16366		Foggin' Up The Windows / Wound Time	1964	2.00	10.00
		—Extended Play Albums—			
Dot 1092		Susie Darlin'	1958	50.00	200.00

LULU (& THE LOVERS)

Label & Catalog #		A-Side/B-Side	Year	VG	NM
Parrot 9678		Shout / Forget Me, Baby	1964	2.00	10.00
Parrot 9714		Here Comes The Night / I'll Come Running	1964	2.00	10.00

Label & Catalog #		A-Side/B-Side	Year	VG	NM
Parrot 9778		Leave A Little Love / He Don't Want Your Love Anymore	1965	2.00	10.00
Parrot 9791		Try To Understand / Not In This Whole World	1965	2.00	10.00
Parrot 40021		Shout / When He Touches Me	1967	1.60	8.00
Epic 10187		Dreary Nights And Days / The Boat That I Row	1967	1.00	5.00
Epic 10187		To Sir With Love / The Boat That I Row	1967	1.20	6.00
Epic 10210		Dreary Nights And Days / Let's Pretend	1967	1.00	5.00
Epic 10260/65	(DJ)	Best Of Both Worlds / (B-side by Dave Clark Five)	1967	3.00	15.00
Epic 10260		Best Of Both Worlds / Love Loves To Love Love	1967	1.00	5.00
Epic 10260	(PS)	Best Of Both Worlds / Love Loves To Love Love	1967	2.00	10.00
Epic 10302		Me, The Peaceful Heart / Look Out	1968	1.00	5.00
Epic 10302	(PS)	Me, The Peaceful Heart / Look Out	1968	2.00	10.00
Epic 10346		Sad Memories / Boy	1968	.60	3.00
Epic 10367		Morning Dew / You And I	1968	.60	3.00
Epic 10403		Without Him / This Time	1968	.60	3.00
Epic 10420		I'm A Tiger / Rattler	1968	.60	3.00
Atco 6722		Oh Me, Oh My / Sweep Around Your Own Back Door	1969	.60	3.00
Atco 6749		Hum A Song (From Your Heart) / Where's Eddie?	1970	.60	3.00
Atco 6761		After The Feeling Is Gone / Good Day Sunshine	1970	.60	3.00
Atco 6885		It Takes A Real Man (To Bring The Woman Out Of Me) / You Ain't Wrong, You Just Ain't Right	1972	.60	3.00
Chelsea 0121		Make Believe World / Help Me Help You	1973	.80	4.00
Chelsea 3001	(DJ)	The Man Who Sold The World / The Man Who Sold The World	1973	3.00	15.00
Chelsea 3001		The Man Who Sold The World / Watch That Man (Produced by David Bowie.)	1973	6.00	30.00
Chelsea 3009	(DJ)	Man With A Golden Gun / Man With A Golden Gun	1974	2.00	10.00
Chelsea 3009		Man With A Golden Gun /	1974	4.00	20.00
Chelsea 3011	(DJ)	Take Your Mama For A Ride / Take Your Mama For A Ride	1974	1.00	5.00
Chelsea 3011		Take Your Mama For A Ride /	1974	2.00	10.00
Chelsea 3019	(DJ)	Boy Meets Girl / Boy Meets Girl	1975	1.00	5.00
Chelsea 3019		Boy Meets Girl /	1975	2.00	10.00
Chelsea 3038	(DJ)	Heaven And Earth And The Stars / Heaven And Earth And The Stars	1976	3.00	15.00
Chelsea 3038		Heaven And Earth And The Stars / (Produced by David Bowie.)	1976	6.00	30.00
		— Extended Play Albums —			
Epic 5-26339	(DJ)	To Sir With Love (Jukebox EP)	1967	3.00	15.00

LUMAN, BOB

Label & Catalog #		A-Side/B-Side	Year	VG	NM
Imperial 8311		Red Cadillac And A Black Moustache / All Night Cleanup (Maroon label)	1957	10.00	50.00
Imperial 8311		Red Cadillac And A Black Moustache / All Night Cleanup (Black label)	195?	6.00	30.00
Imperial 8313		Red Hot / Whenever You're Ready (Maroon label)	1957	15.00	75.00
Imperial 8313		Red Hot / Whenever You're Ready (Black label)	195?	10.00	50.00
Imperial 8315		Make Up Your Mind, Baby / Your Love (Maroon label)	1957	8.00	40.00
Imperial 8315		Make Up Your Mind, Baby / Your Love (Black label)	195?	4.00	20.00
Capitol 3972		Try Me / I Know My Baby Cares	1958	3.00	15.00
Capitol 4059		Precious / Svengali	1958	3.00	15.00
Warner Bros. 5081		My Baby Walks All Over Me / Classics Of '59	1959	3.00	15.00
Warner Bros. 5105		Buttercup / Dreamy Doll	1960	3.00	15.00
Warner Bros. 5172		Let's Think About Living / You've Got Everything	1960	3.00	15.00
Warner Bros. 5172	(PS)	Let's Think About Living / You've Got Everything	1960	8.00	40.00
Warner Bros. 5184		Oh, Lonesome Me / Why Bye, Bye	1961	3.00	15.00
Warner Bros. 5184	(PS)	Oh, Lonesome Me / Why Bye, Bye	1961	6.00	30.00
Warner Bros. 5204		The Great Showman / Pig Latin Song	1961	3.00	15.00
Warner Bros. 5204	(PS)	The Great Showman / Pig Latin Song	1961	6.00	30.00
Warner Bros. 5233		You've Turned Down The Light / Private Eye	1961	3.00	15.00
Warner Bros. 5233	(PS)	You've Turned Down The Light / Private Eye	1961	5.00	25.00
Warner Bros. 5255		Louisiana Man / Rocks Of Reno	1961	3.00	15.00
Warner Bros. 5272		Big River Rose / Belonging To You	1962	3.00	15.00
Warner Bros. 5299		Hey Joe / Fool	1962	3.00	15.00
Warner Bros. 5321		You're Everything / Envy	1963	3.00	15.00
		— Extended Play Albums —			
Warner Bros. 1396		Let's Think About Living	1960	50.00	200.00
Warner Bros. 5506	(DJ)	Bob Luman	1960	25.00	125.00

LUND, ALAN, & THE DIPLOMATS

Label & Catalog #		A-Side/B-Side	Year	VG	NM
MTW 1		Sieglinde /	196?	2.00	10.00

LUPE

Lupe is a pseudonym for George Tomsco of The Fireballs.

Label & Catalog #		A-Side/B-Side	Year	VG	NM
MGM 13422		Letter To Albert / Grasshopper	1965	2.00	10.00

LURCH

Lurch is the character played by Ted Cassidy in "The Addams Family" television series.

Label & Catalog #		A-Side/B-Side	Year	VG	NM
Capitol 5503		The Lurch / Wesley	1965	5.00	25.00
Capitol 5503	(PS)	The Lurch / Wesley	1965	10.00	50.00

Label & Catalog #	A-Side/B-Side	Year	VG	NM
LUREX, LARRY				
Larry Lurex later recorded as Freddie Mercury with Queen.				
Anthem 104	I Can Hear Music / Goin' Back	197?	10.00	50.00
LUV'D ONES, THE				
Dunwich 117	Walking The Dog / I'm Leaving You	1966	1.20	6.00
Dunwich 130	Stand Tall / Come Back	1966	1.20	6.00
Dunwich 136	Dance Kid, Dance / I'm Leaving You	1966	1.20	6.00
LY-DELLS, THE				
The Ly-Dells were Jackie Butler, Chuck Hatfield, Billie Schied and Gary Young.				
Master 111	Genie Of The Lamp / Teenage Tears	196?	50.00	200.00
Master 251	Wizard Of Love / Let This Night Last	1961	30.00	150.00
	(First pressing labels have block print.)			
Master 251	Wizard Of Love / Let This Night Last	1962	4.00	20.00
	(Second pressings labels have script print.)			
SCA 18001	Book Of Songs / Hear That Train	1962	4.00	20.00
Roulette 4493	Karen / Doing The Wiggle Wobble	1963	3.00	15.00
Southern Sound 122	Three Little Monkeys / Playing Hide And Seek	1965	15.00	75.00
LYDELLS, THE				
Pam 103	There Goes The Boy / Talking To Myself	1959	6.00	30.00
Parkway 897	There Goes The Boy / Talking To Myself	1964	3.00	15.00
LYME & CYBELLE				
Lyme is Warren Zevon.				
White Whale 228	Follow Me / Like The Seasons	1966	1.20	6.00
White Whale 232	If You Got To Go, Go Now / I'll Go On	1966	1.20	6.00
White Whale 245	Song #7 / Write If You Get Work	1967	1.20	6.00
LYN & THE INVADERS				
Fenton 2040	Secretly / The Boy Is Gone	1967	2.00	10.00
LYNAM, IKE, & THE LITTLE PEOPLE				
Emanon 101	Message To Pretty / I Need You	196?	2.00	10.00
LYNDON, FRANK				
Uptown 785	Don't Go Away / Lisa	196?	4.00	20.00
Sabina 520	Earth Angel / Don't Look At Me	1965	5.00	25.00
Bang 531	Earth Angel / Don't Look At Me	1965	3.00	15.00
Laurie 3322	Santa's Jet / Sing Along With Santa's Jet	1965	4.00	20.00
Jab 1004	Tonight We Wail / Cry Cry Cry	196?	4.00	20.00
	(Jab 1004 features The Regents.)			
LYNN, DEBBIE, & THE RECORDING BAND				
Flight-7 1001	Fujiyama Mama / Geisha Girl	196?	5.00	25.00
LYNN, DONNA				
Capitol 5087	Ronnie / That's Me	1963	2.00	10.00
Capitol 5127	My Boyfriend Got A Beatle Haircut / The Winter Weekend	1964	3.00	15.00
Capitol 5156	Java (Java Jones) / Things I Feel	1964	2.00	10.00
LYONS GROUP, JAMIE				
Jamie Ltyons originally recorded with The Music Explosion.				
Laurie 3409	Little Black Egg / Stay By My Side	1967	1.00	5.00
Laurie 3422	Soul Struttin' / Flowers To Sunshine	1968	.80	4.00
Laurie 3427	Gonna Have A Good Time / Heart Full O' Soul	1968	.80	4.00
Laurie 3465	Stoney / Rhapsody In F Major	1969	.80	4.00
LYRICS, THE				
GNP/Crescendo 381	So Glad / My Son	1966	2.00	10.00
GNP/Crescendo 393	Wait / Mr. Man	1967	2.00	10.00
LYTE, THE				
Bolo 761	It's Gonna Work Out Fine / I Don't Believe You	1968	1.20	6.00
LYTLE, JOHNNY				
Tuba 2004	The Loop / Hot Sauce	1966	1.00	5.00

M.

M.P.D. LIMITED					
LTD 400		Wendy (Don't Go) / Little Boy Sad	1965	2.00	10.00
MAC, JOHNNY					
Studio 108		Emotional Storm / Save Me	196?	2.00	10.00
MACH, LEON					
Lavender 1554		You Hurt Me So / It's You I Love	1960	10.00	50.00
MACK, BILL					
Starday 231		Kitty Cat / Fat Woman	1956	15.00	75.00
Starday 252		Cat Just Got In Town / Sweet Dreams, Baby	1956	10.00	50.00
MACK, LONNIE					
Fraternity 906		Memphis / Down In The Dumps	1963	2.00	10.00
Fraternity 912		Wham! / Suzie Q	1963	2.00	10.00
Fraternity 918		Baby, What's Wrong? / Where There's A Will	1963	2.00	10.00
Fraternity 920		Lonnie On The Move / Say Something Nice To Me	1964	2.00	10.00
Fraternity 925		I've Had It / Nashville	1964	2.00	10.00
Fraternity 942		Coastin' / Crying Over You	1965	2.00	10.00
Fraternity 946		Tonky-Go-Go / When I'm Alone	1964	2.00	10.00
Fraternity 951		Honky Tonk '65 / Chicken Pickin'	1965	2.00	10.00
MAD ENGLISHMEN & THE FURYS, THE					
Vee Six 1023		Beatle Mania / Janice	1964	3.00	15.00
MAD HATTERS, THE					
Fontana 1582		I'll Come Running / Hello, Girl	1967	2.00	10.00
MAD LADS, THE					
Mark-Fi 1934		Why? / Hey, Man	196?	6.00	30.00
Stax 160		Surf Jerk / Sidewalk Surf	1964	4.00	20.00
MAD MARTIANS, THE					
Satellite 33617		Outer Space Looters / Outer Space Looters, No. 2	1957	5.00	25.00
MAD MIKE & THE MANIACS					
Hunch 345		Quarter To Four / The Hunch	1961	3.00	15.00
MAD MILO					
Combo 131		Elvis On Trial / A Date With Elvis	1957	6.00	30.00
Million 20018		Elvis For Christmas / (B-side by Roy Tan)	1957	5.00	25.00
MAD PLAIDS, THE					
Golden Crest 533		Rare Blood / (B-side by Little Cal)	196?	5.00	25.00
MAD RIVER					
Wee 10021	(EP)	Mad River	1968	20.00	100.00
Capitol 2310		High All The Time / Gazelle	1968	2.00	10.00
Capitol 2559		Copper Plates / Harley Magnum	1969	2.00	10.00
MADARA, JOHNNY					
Prep 110		Lovesick / Be My Girl	1957	4.00	20.00
Bamboo 511		A Story Untold / Vacation Time	1961	3.00	15.00
Landa 687		Heavenly / Save It	1962	3.00	15.00
MADDY BROTHERS, THE					
Celestial 109		Rockin' Party / Hey, Little Girlie	195?	8.00	40.00
Ra-Ra 900		My Crazy Old Heart / Mixed Up	195?	2.00	10.00
MADISON, RONNIE					
Storm 987		Linda / Here I Stand	195?	4.00	20.00
Coral 61812		True Love Gone / Lovely Night	1957	4.00	20.00
MADISON STREET					
Madison Street is a pseudonym for Randy & The Rainbows.					
Millenium 605		Mr. Minstrel Man / King Of Love	197?	1.00	5.00
Millenium 621		Simple Love Song / We're Falling In Love	197?	1.00	5.00

Label & Catalog #		A-Side/B-Side	Year	VG	NM
MADISONS, THE					
Lawn 240		Can You Imagine It? / The Wind And The Rain	1964	7.00	35.00
MGM 13312		Cheryl Anne / Looking For True Love	1965	5.00	25.00
MADISONS, THE					
Jomada 601		Only A Fool / Stagger	1965	3.00	15.00
MADDIN, JIMMY					
American Int. 542		Don't Stop Now / Tongue Tied	196?	3.00	15.00
MADLADS, THE					
Volt 127		Don't Have To Shop Around / Tear Maker	1965	2.00	10.00
MADMAN JONES					
Cameo 146		Jess' One Mo' Time / Oh, Henry	1958	3.00	15.00
MADMEN OF NOTE, THE					
Ra-O 104		Club 21 / Peppermint Pink	196?	2.00	10.00
MADNESS, BERNIE					
Bang 529		Bikini Beach / Pleasant Memories	1966	4.00	20.00
MADONNA					
Sides marked with an asterisk are instrumentals. For additional listings refer to Jellybean; Nick Kamen.					
Sire 29841	(DJ)	Everybody / Everybody	1982	1.00	5.00
Sire 29841		Everybody / Everybody*	1982	2.00	10.00
Sire PRO-2023	(DJ)	Physical Attraction / Physical Attraction	1983	3.00	15.00
Sire 29715	(DJ)	Burning Up / Burning Up	1983	1.00	5.00
Sire 29715		Burning Up / Burning Up	1983	2.00	10.00
Sire 29478	(DJ)	Holiday / Holiday	1983	1.00	5.00
Sire 29478		Holiday / Holiday	1983	2.00	10.00
Sire 29354		Borderline / Think Of Me	1984	.80	4.00
Sire 29354	(PS)	Borderline / Think Of Me (Poster sleeve)	1984	5.00	25.00
Sire 29210		Like A Virgin / Stay	1984	.60	3.00
Sire 29210	(PS)	Like A Virgin / Stay	1984	.80	4.00
Sire 29177		Lucky Star / I Know It	1984	.60	3.00
Sire 29083		Material Girl / Pretender	1985	.60	3.00
Sire 29083	(PS)	Material Girl / Pretender	1985	.60	3.00
Geffen 29051		Crazy For You / (B-side by Berlin)	1985	.60	3.00
Geffen 29051	(PS)	Crazy For You / (B-side by Berlin)	1985	.60	3.00
Sire 29051		Angel (Two versions)	1985	.60	3.00
Sire 29051	(PS)	Angel	1985	.60	3.00
Sire 28919		Dress You Up / Shoo-Bee-Doo	1985	.60	3.00
Sire 28919	(PS)	Dress You Up / Shoo-Bee-Doo	1985	6.00	30.00
Sire 28717		Live To Tell / Live To Tell*	1986	.60	3.00
Sire 28717	(PS)	Live To Tell / Live To Tell*	1986	.60	3.00
Sire 28660		Papa Don't Preach / Pretender	1986	.60	3.00
Sire 28660	(PS)	Papa Don't Preach / Pretender	1986	.60	3.00
Sire 28591	(DJ)	True Blue / True Blue (Blue vinyl)	1986	1.60	8.00
Sire 28591		True Blue / Ain't No Big Deal	1986	.60	3.00
Sire 28591		True Blue / Ain't No Big Deal (Blue vinyl)	1986	.80	4.00
Sire 28591	(PS)	True Blue / Ain't No Big Deal	1986	.60	3.00
Sire 28508		Open Your Heart / White Heat	1986	.60	3.00
Sire 28508	(PS)	Open Your Heart / White Heat	1986	.60	3.00
Sire 28425		La Isle Bonita / La Isle Bonita*	1987	.60	3.00
Sire 28425	(PS)	La Isle Bonita / La Isle Bonita*	1987	.60	3.00
Sire 28341		Who's That Girl? / White Heat	1987	.40	2.00
Sire 28341	(PS)	Who's That Girl? / White Heat	1987	.40	2.00
Sire 28224		Causing A Commotion / Jimmy, Jimmy	1987	.40	2.00
Sire 28224	(PS)	Causing A Commotion / Jimmy, Jimmy	1987	.40	2.00
Sire 27539		Like A Prayer / Act Of Contrition	1989	.40	2.00
Sire 27539	(PS)	Like A Prayer / Act Of Contrition	1989	.40	2.00
Sire 22948		Express Yourself / The Look Of Love	1989	.40	2.00
Sire 22948	(PS)	Express Yourself / The Look Of Love	1989	.40	2.00
Sire 22883		Cherish / Supernatural	1989	.40	2.00
Sire 22883	(PS)	Cherish / Supernatural	1989	.40	2.00
Sire 22723		Oh Father / Pray For Spanish Eyes	1989	.40	2.00
Sire 19986		Keep It Together / Keep It Together*	1989	.40	2.00
Sire 19986	(PS)	Keep It Together / Keep It Together*	1989	.40	2.00
Sire 19863		Vogue (Two versions)	1990	.40	2.00
Sire 19789		Hanky Panky / More	1990	.40	2.00
Sire 19485		Justify My Love / Express Yourself 1990	1990	.40	2.00
Sire 19490		Rescue Me (Two versions)	1991	.40	2.00
		— 12" Singles—			
Sire 29899		Everybody (Two versions. PC)	1982	1.00	5.00
Sire 29715		Burning Up (Remix) / Physical Attraction (PC)	1983	1.00	5.00
Sire 20212		Borderline (Remix) / Lucky Star (Remix. PC)	1984	.60	3.00
Sire 20239		Like A Virgin (Remix) / Stay (PC)	1984	.60	3.00

Unquestionably the single most successful pop diva of the past few decades, Madonna's most collectible commercial release is this attractive fold-open picture sleeve for *Borderline*.

Label & Catalog #		A-Side/B-Side	Year	VG	NM
Sire 20304		Material Girl (Remix) / Pretender (PC)	1985	.60	3.00
Sire 20335		Angel (Two versions. PC)	1985	.60	3.00
Sire 20369		Dress You Up / Shoo-Bee-Doo (PC)	1985	.60	3.00
Sire 28717		Live To Tell / Live To Tell / Live To Tell (PC)	1986	.60	3.00
Sire 28660		Papa Don't Preach (Remix) / Pretender (PC)	1986	.60	3.00
Sire 20533		True Blue (Three versions) / Ain't No Big Deal (PC)	1986	.60	3.00
Sire 20597		Open Your Heart / Open Your Heart / White Heat (PC)	1986	.60	3.00
Sire 20633		La Isle Bonita / La Isle Bonita (Remix. PC)	1987	.60	3.00
Sire 20212		Who's That Girl? (Remix) / White Heat (PC)	1987	.60	3.00
Sire 20762		Causing A Commotion (Three versions) / Jimmy Jimmy (PC)	1987	.60	3.00
Sire 21170		Like A Prayer (Five versions) / Act Of Contrtion (PC)	1989	.60	3.00
Sire 21225		Express Yourself (Three versions) / The Look Of Love (PC)	1989	.60	3.00
Sire 21427		Keep It Together (Four versions. PC)	1989	.60	3.00
Sire 21513		Vogue (Four versions. PC)	1990	.60	3.00
Sire 21577		Hanky panky / Hanky Panky / More (PC)	1990	.60	3.00
Sire 21820		Justify My Love (Three versions) / Express Yourself (PC)	1990	.60	3.00
Sire 21813		Rescue Me (Four versions. PC)	1991	.60	3.00
		—Promotional 12" Singles—			
Sire PRO-A-20??	(DJ)	Everybody (Two versions)	1982	8.00	40.00
Sire PRO-A-20??	(DJ)	Burning Up (Remix) / Physical Attraction	1983	8.00	40.00
Sire PRO-A-2069	(DJ)	Holiday / Lucky Star (PC)	1983	6.00	30.00
Sire PRO-A-2120	(DJ)	Borderline (Two versions. PC)	1984	6.00	30.00
Sire PRO-A-2172	(DJ)	Like A Virgin / Like A Virgin (PC)	1984	5.00	25.00
Sire PRO-A-2223	(DJ)	Like A Virgin (Remix) / Like A Virgin (Remix. PC)	1984	5.00	25.00
Sire PRO-A-????	(DJ)	Material Girl / Material Girl (PC)	1985	4.00	20.00
Sire PRO-A-2292	(DJ)	Angel / Into The Grove	1985	3.00	15.00
Sire PRO-A-2353	(DJ)	Dress You Up / Dress You Up / Shoo-Bee-Doo	1985	3.00	15.00
Sire PRO-A-2470	(DJ)	Live To Tell / Live To Tell (TC)	1986	3.00	15.00
Sire PRO-A-2517	(DJ)	Papa Don't Preach (Two versions. PC)	1986	3.00	15.00
Sire PRO-A-2905	(DJ)	Where's The Party? (Two versions) / Spotlight (PC)	1989	3.00	15.00
Sire PRO-A-2906	(DJ)	Into The Grove / Into The Grove / Everybody (PC)	1989	3.00	15.00
Sire PRO-A-2907	(DJ)	Holiday / Holiday / Over And Over / Over And Over (PC)	1987	3.00	15.00
Sire PRO-A-3472	(DJ)	Like A Prayer(Six versions. PC)	1989	3.00	15.00
Sire PRO-A-3791	(DJ)	Keep It Together (Four versions. PC)	1989	3.00	15.00
Sire PRO-A-4582	(DJ)	Justify My Love (Two versions)	1991	2.00	10.00
Sire PRO-A-4613	(DJ)	Justify My Love (Four versions)	1991	2.00	10.00
Sire PRO-A-4710	(DJ)	Rescue Me (PC. Two discs with eight versions)	1991	3.00	15.00

MADURI, CARL

Cameo 202		Miss Teenage America / What A Night	1961	2.00	10.00

MAESTRO, JOHNNY

The Coed sides feature The Crests, the Buddah sides, The Brooklyn Bridge. Refer to Johnny Masters.

Coed 545		Model Girl / We've Got To Tell Him	1961	3.00	15.00
Coed 549		What A Surprise! / The Warning Voice	1961	3.00	15.00
Coed 552		Mr. Happiness / Test Of Love	1961	3.00	15.00
Coed 557		The Way You Look Tonight / I.O.U.	1961	3.00	15.00
Coed 562		Besame Baby / It Must Be Love	1961	20.00	100.00
United Artists 474		Before I Loved Her / Fifty Million Heartbeats	1962	3.00	15.00
Cameo 256		I'll Be There / Over The Weekend	1963	2.00	10.00
Cameo 305		Lean On Me / (It's Harder To) Make Up My Mind	1964	2.00	10.00
Apt 25075		She's All Mine Alone / Phone Booth On The Highway	1965	4.00	20.00
Buddah 201		Never Knew This Kind Of Hurt Before / Then Rain Came	1971	1.20	6.00
Buddah 236		Yours Until Tomorrow / Man In A Band	1972	1.20	6.00
Buddah 289	(DJ)	Snow / Snow	1972	1.20	6.00
		(Stock copies of Buddah 289 may not exist.)			

MAGIC

Monster 0001		I Think I Love You / That's How Strong My Love Is	196?	2.00	10.00

MAGIC BOTTLE, THE

Tripp 1003		Baby, Let Me Go / That's A No No	196?	2.00	10.00

MAGIC CHRISTIANS, THE

The Magic Christians feature Trevor Burton of The Move.

Commonwealth 3006		Come And Get It / Nats	1970	2.00	10.00

MAGIC FERN, THE

Jerden 813		Maggie / I Wonder Why	1966	1.00	5.00
Piccadilly 235		Maggie / I Wonder Why	1967	.80	4.00
Piccadilly 240		Nellie / Cloudy Day	1967	.80	4.00

MAGIC LANTERN, THE

Charisma 100		Country Woman /	1972	1.20	6.00

MAGIC LANTERNS, THE

Epic 10062		Excuse Me, Baby / Greedy Girl	1966	1.00	5.00
Epic 10111		Knight In Rusty Armour / Simple Things	1966	1.00	5.00

Label & Catalog #		A-Side/B-Side	Year	VG	NM
Atlantic 2560		Shame, Shame / Baby, I Got To Go	1968	.80	4.00
Atlantic 2600		Give Me Love / Biding My Time	1969	.80	4.00
Atlantic 2626		Bossa Nova 1940-Hello, You Lovers /			
		Melt All Your Troubles Away	1969	.80	4.00
Atlantic 2715		One Night Stand / Frisco Annie	1970	.80	4.00
Big Tree 109		One Night Stand / Frisco Annie	1971	.60	3.00
Big Tree 113	(DJ)	Let The Sun Shine In / Let The Sun Shine In	1971	.60	3.00
		(Stock copies of B.T. 113 may not exist.)			

MAGIC MUSHROOMS, THE

Label & Catalog #	A-Side/B-Side	Year	VG	NM
A&M 815	It's-A-Happening / Never More	1966	3.00	15.00
Warner Bros. 5846	Cry Baby / I'm Gone	1966	4.00	20.00
Philips 40483	Look In My Face / Never Let Go	1967	3.00	15.00

MAGIC RINGS, THE

Label & Catalog #	A-Side/B-Side	Year	VG	NM
Music Factory 404	Little Mary Sunshine / Do I Love You?	1968	1.00	5.00

MAGIC TOUCH, THE
The Magic Touch originally recorded as Vito & The Salutations.

Label & Catalog #	A-Side/B-Side	Year	VG	NM
Roulette 7143	Baby, You Belong To Me / Lost And Lonely Boy	1973	2.00	10.00

MAGICIANS, THE

Label & Catalog #		A-Side/B-Side	Year	VG	NM
Columbia 43435		An Invitation To Cry / Rain Don't Fall On Me No More	1965	4.00	20.00
Columbia 43435	(PS)	An Invitation To Cry / Rain Don't Fall On Me No More	1965	10.00	50.00
Columbia 43608		Angel On The Corner / About My Love	1965	2.00	10.00
Columbia 43725		And I'll Tell The World / I'd Like To Know	1965	2.00	10.00

MAGICS, THE

Label & Catalog #	A-Side/B-Side	Year	VG	NM
Debra 1003	Chapel Bells / She Can't Stop Dancing	1963	10.00	50.00

MAGISTRATES, THE

Label & Catalog #	A-Side/B-Side	Year	VG	NM
MGM 13946	Girl / (B-side by The Dovells)	1968	1.00	5.00
MGM 13980	After The Fox / Tear Down The Walls	1968	1.00	5.00

MAGNETICS, THE

Label & Catalog #	A-Side/B-Side	Year	VG	NM
Allrite 620	Where Are You? / The Train	195?	6.00	30.00

MAGNETS, THE

Label & Catalog #	A-Side/B-Side	Year	VG	NM
Groove 0058	You Just Say The Word / Surprise	1955	8.00	40.00
RCA Victor 47-7391	When The School Bells Ring / Don't Tarry, Little Mary	1958	3.00	15.00

MAGNETS, THE

Label & Catalog #	A-Side/B-Side	Year	VG	NM
London 10036	Drag Race / Joker	1963	2.00	10.00

MAGNIFICENT FOUR, THE

Label & Catalog #	A-Side/B-Side	Year	VG	NM
Whale 506	The Closer You Are / Uncle Sam	1963	7.00	35.00
Blast 210	The Closer You Are / Uncle Sam	1963	4.00	20.00

MAGNIFICENT MEN, THE

Label & Catalog #	A-Side/B-Side	Year	VG	NM
Capitol 5732	I've Got News / Maybe, Maybe, Baby	1966	.80	4.00
Capitol 5812	Much Much More Of Your Love / Stormy Weather	1967	.80	4.00
Capitol 5905	I Could Be So Happy / You Changed My Life	1967	.80	4.00
Capitol 5976	Sweet Soul Medley / Sweet Soul Medley (Part 2)	1967	.80	4.00
Capitol 2062	Babe, I'm Crazy About You / Forever Together	1967	.60	3.00
Capitol 2134	By The Time I Get To Phoenix / Tired Of Pushing	1968	.60	3.00
Capitol 2202	Almost Persuaded / I Found What I Wanted In You	1968	.60	3.00
Capitol 2319	Save The Country / So Much Love Waiting	1968	.60	3.00
Mercury 72988	Holly Go Softly / Open Up And Get Richer	1969	.60	3.00
Mercury 73028	Lay Lady Lay / What Ever It Takes	1970	.60	3.00

MAGNIFICENT VII, THE

Label & Catalog #	A-Side/B-Side	Year	VG	NM
Dimension 1050	Show Me / Boogidy	1965	2.00	10.00

MAHAFFAY, CHUCK

Label & Catalog #	A-Side/B-Side	Year	VG	NM
Panorama 35	Waltz For The N.Y. Mets / Take Me To The Ballgame	1966	2.00	10.00
Panorama 53	Soy Sauce / Like Young	1967	.80	4.00

MAHOGANY RUSH

Label & Catalog #	A-Side/B-Side	Year	VG	NM
20th Century Fox 2111	Child Of The Novelty / A New Rock And Roll	1974	.80	4.00
20th Century Fox 2166	Buddy / A New Rock And Roll	1975	.80	4.00
Columbia 11077	All Along The Watchtower / Down, Down, Down	1979	.60	3.00

MAJESTICS, THE

Label & Catalog #	A-Side/B-Side	Year	VG	NM
20th Century 171	The Lone Stranger / Sweet One	1959	3.00	15.00
Jordan 1057	Searching For A New Love / Angel Of Love	1961	6.00	30.00
Jordan 1057	Searching For A New Love / Angel Of Love (Yellow vinyl)	1961	75.00	300.00
Nu-Tone 123	Searching For A New Love / Angel Of Love	1961	5.00	25.00
Pixie 6901	Searching For A New Love / Angel Of Love	1961	3.00	15.00

Label & Catalog #		A-Side/B-Side	Year	VG	NM
Linda 111		Strange World / Everything Is Gonna Be Alright	1963	2.00	10.00
Linda 121		Girl Of My Dreams / It Hurts Me	1965	2.00	10.00
MAJESTICS, THE					
Sam 112		Jaguar / Blue Feeling	196?	7.00	35.00
Sam 117		Big Noise From Makaha / Riptide	196?	10.00	50.00
Sam 123		X-L3 / My Little Baby	196?	9.00	45.00
		(Sam 123 was also released credited to The Phantoms.)			
Dunes 2014		Boss Walk / Boss Walk, Part 2	1962	6.00	30.00
MAJIC SHIP, THE					
Crazy Horse 130		It's Over / Hummin'	1966	2.00	10.00
Crazy Horse 132		Night Time Music / To Love Somebody	1966	2.00	10.00
B.T. Puppy 548		Night Time Music / Green Plant	1966	2.00	10.00
MAJORETTES, THE					
Troy 1000		White Levis / Please Come Back	1962	2.00	10.00
Troy 1000	(PS)	White Levis / Please Come Back	1962	3.00	15.00
Troy 1004		Let's Do The Kangaroo / Dance With Me	1962	2.00	10.00
MALLORY, LEE					
Lee Mallory later recorded with Millenium.					
Valiant 751		That's The Way It's Gonna Be / Many Are The Times	1965	3.00	15.00
MAMAS & THE PAPAS, THE					
Former Journeymen John and Michelle Phillips with former Mugwumps Cass Elliot and Denny Doherty.					
Dunhill 4018	(DJ)	Go Where You Wanna Go / Somebody Groovy	1965	3.00	15.00
		(Stock copies of Dunhill 4018 may not exist.)			
Dunhill 4020	(DJ)	California Dreamin' / Somebody Groovy	1966	2.00	10.00
Dunhill 4020	(PS)	California Dreamin' / Somebody Groovy (DJ)	1966	10.00	50.00
Dunhill 4020		California Dreamin' / Somebody Groovy	1966	1.00	5.00
Dunhill 4026		Monday, Monday / Got A Feeling	1966	1.00	5.00
Dunhill 4031		I Saw Her Again / Even If I Could	1966	1.00	5.00
Dunhill 4050		Look Through My Window / Once Was A Time I Thought	1966	.80	4.00
Dunhill 4057		Words Of Love / Dancin' In The Street	1966	.80	4.00
Dunhill 4077		Dedicated To The One I Love / Free Advice	1967	.80	4.00
Dunhill 4083	(DJ)	Creeque Alley *(One sided)*	1967	2.00	10.00
Dunhill 4083	(PS)	Creeque Alley (DJ)	1967	3.00	15.00
Dunhill 4083		Creeque Alley / Did You Ever Want To Cry?	1967	.80	4.00
Dunhill 4099		Twelve Thirty / Straight Shooter	1967	.80	4.00
Dunhill 4107		Glad To Be Unhappy / Hey, Girl	1967	.80	4.00
Dunhill 4113		Dancing Bear / John's Music Box	1967	.80	4.00
Dunhill 4113	(PS)	Dancing Bear / John's Music Box	1967	.80	4.00
Dunhill 4125		Safe In My Garden / Too Late	1968	.80	4.00
Dunhill 4150		For The Love Of Ivy / Strange Young Girls	1968	.80	4.00
Dunhill 4171		Do You Wanna Dance? / My Girl	1968	.80	4.00
Dunhill 4301		Step Out / Shooting Star	1972	.80	4.00
		— *Extended Play Albums* —			
Dunhill 50006	(33)	If You Can Believe Your Eyes And Ears *(Jukebox EP)*	1968	4.00	20.00
Dunhill 50010	(33)	Mamas & Papas *(Jukebox EP)*	1968	4.00	20.00
Dunhill 50014	(33)	The Mamas & The Papas Deliver *(Jukebox EP)*	1968	4.00	20.00
ABC 50106	(33)	People Like Us *(Jukebox EP)*	1973	2.00	10.00
MAMA CASS [CASS ELLIOT]					
Cass Elliot originally recorded with The Mugwumps and The Mamas & The Papas.					
Dunhill 4145		Dream A Little Dream Of Me / Midnight Voyage	1968	.60	3.00
Dunhill 4166		California Earthquake / Talkin' To Your Toothbrush	1968	.60	3.00
Dunhill 4184		Move In A Little Closer, Baby / All For Me	1969	.60	3.00
Dunhill 4195		It's Getting Better / Who's To Blame?	1969	.60	3.00
Dunhill 4214		Make Your Own Kind Of Music / Lady Love	1969	.60	3.00
Dunhill 4225		New World Coming / Blow Me A Kiss	1969	.60	3.00
Dunhill 4226		Something To Make You Happy / Next To You	1970	.60	3.00
Dunhill 4244		I Can Dream, Can't I? / A Song That Never Comes	1970	.60	3.00
Dunhill 4253		The Good Times Are Coming / Welcome To The World	1970	.60	3.00
Dunhill 4253	(PS)	The Good Times Are Coming / Welcome To The World	1970	1.20	6.00
Dunhill 4264		Don't Let The Good Life Pass You By / A Song That Never Comes	1970	.60	3.00
RCA Victor 74-0644		Baby, I'm Yours / Cherries Jubilee	1972	.60	3.00
RCA Victor 74-0764		Disney Girls / Break Another Heart	1972	.80	4.00
RCA Victor 74-0957		Listen To The World / I Think A Lot About You	1973	.60	3.00
MAMA CASS & DAVE MASON					
Dunhill 4253		Good Times Are Coming / Welcome To The World	1970	.60	3.00
Dunhill 4271		Too Much Truth, Too Much Love / Walk To The Point	1971	.60	3.00

Label & Catalog #		A-Side/B-Side	Year	VG	NM
MAN					
Columbia 44953		Girl Of The North Country / Riverhead Jail	1969	1.00	5.00
MANCHESTERS, THE					
The Manchesters feature David Gates.					
Vee Jay 700		Dragon Fly / I Don't Come From England	1965	2.00	10.00
MANDERINS, THE					
Band Box 236		Let The Bells Ring / Going Away	195?	5.00	25.00
MANDRAKES, THE					
Nolta 349		Summer's End / Turmoil	196?	2.00	10.00
MANFRED MANN					
The original Manfred Mann consisted of Mike Hugg, Paul Jones, Manfred Mann, Tom McGuiness, and Mike Vickers.					
Other members have included Jack Bruce, Klaus Voorman and Mike D'Abo.					
Prestige 312		5-4-3-2-1 / Without You	1964	2.00	10.00
Ascot 2157		Do Wah Diddy Diddy / What You Gonna Do?	1964	1.60	8.00
Ascot 2165		Sha La La / John Hardy	1964	1.60	8.00
Ascot 2165	(PS)	Sha La La / John Hardy	1964	3.00	15.00
Ascot 2170		Come Tomorrow / What Did I Do Wrong?	1965	1.20	6.00
Ascot 2170	(PS)	Come Tomorrow / What Did I Do Wrong?	1965	3.00	15.00
Ascot 2184		My Little Red Book / What Am I Doing Wrong?	1965	1.20	6.00
Ascot 2194		If You Gotta Go, Go Now / One In The Middle	1966	1.20	6.00
Ascot 2210		She Needs Company / Hi Lili, Hi Lo	1966	1.00	5.00
Ascot 2241		My Little Red Book / I Can't Believe What You Say	1966	1.00	5.00
United Artists 55040		Pretty Flamingo / You're Standing By	1966	1.00	5.00
United Artists 55066		When Will I Be Loved? / Do You Have To Do That?	1966	1.00	5.00
Mercury 72607		Just Like A Woman / I Wanna Be Rich	1967	1.00	5.00
Mercury 72607	(PS)	Just Like A Woman / I Wanna Be Rich	1967	3.00	15.00
Mercury 72629		Semi-Detached Suburban Mr. Jones / Each And Every Day	1967	1.00	5.00
Mercury 72675		Ha Ha, Said The Clown / Feeling So Good	1967	1.00	5.00
Mercury 72770		Mighty Quinn (Quinn The Eskimo) / By Request-Edwin Garvey *(Black label)*	1968	1.00	5.00
Mercury 72770		Mighty Quinn (Quinn The Eskimo) / By Request-Edwin Garvey *(Red label)*	1968	.80	4.00
Mercury 72770		Quinn The Eskimo / By Request-Edwin Garvey	1968	1.00	5.00
Mercury 72822		My Name Is Jack / There Is A Man	1968	.80	4.00
Mercury 72822	(PS)	My Name Is Jack / There Is A Man	1968	2.00	10.00
Mercury 72879		Fox On The Run / Too Many People	1968	.80	4.00
Mercury 72921		Ragamuffin Man / A B-Side	1969	.80	4.00
		—Extended Play Albums—			
United Artists 10030	(DJ)	Manfred Mann *(Issued without a cover)*	1964	4.00	20.00
MANFRED MANN'S EARTH BAND					
Although this features Manfred Mann, it is a completely different band than the one above.					
Polydor 14097		Please, Mrs. Henry / Prayer	1971	.40	2.00
Polydor 14113		Living Without You / Tribute	1972	.40	2.00
Polydor 14130		I'm Up And I'm Leaving / Part Time Band	1972	.40	2.00
Polydor 14164		It's All Over Now, Baby Blue / Ashes	1972	.40	2.00
Polydor 14173		Mardi Gras Day / Sad Joy	1973	.40	2.00
Polydor 14191		Get Your Rocks Off / Wind	1973	.40	2.00
Polydor 14205		Joybringer / Cloudy Eyes	1973	.40	2.00
Polydor 14225		Father Of Night / Solar Fire Two	1974	.40	2.00
Warner Bros. 8176		Spirit In The Night / Questions	1976	.40	2.00
Warner Bros. 8252		Blinded By The Light / Starbird No. 2	1976	.40	2.00
Warner Bros. 8252	(PS)	Blinded By The Light / Starbird No. 2	1976	.60	3.00
Warner Bros. 8574		California / Bouillabaisse	1978	.40	2.00
Warner Bros. 8620		Davy's On The Road Again / Bouillabaisse	1978	.40	2.00
Warner Bros. 8850		You Angel, You / Bells of The Earth	1979	.40	2.00
MANHATTANS, THE					
Colpix 115		Big Wheel Express / Powder Blue	1959	4.00	20.00
MANIN BROTHERS, THE					
Apt 25033		Hot Rod Susie / Uhm De Ahde	1959	3.00	15.00
MANIS, GEORGE					
Gizmo 66347		High School Love / Oriental Rock	1961	2.00	10.00
MANN, BARRY					
JDS 5002		A Love To Last A Lifetime / All The Things You Are	1959	6.00	30.00
ABC-Paramount 10143		Counting Teardrops / War Paint	1960	3.00	15.00
ABC-Paramount 10180		Happy Birthday, Broken Heart / The Millionaire	1961	4.00	20.00
ABC-Paramount 10237		Who Put The Bomp (In The Bomp, Bomp, Bomp) / Love, True Love	1961	3.00	15.00
ABC-Paramount 10263		Little Miss U.S.A. / Find Another Fool	1961	3.00	15.00
ABC-Paramount 10356		Hey Baby, I'm Dancin' / Like I Don't Love You	1962	4.00	20.00

Label & Catalog #	A-Side/B-Side	Year	VG	NM
ABC-Paramount 10380	Bless You / Teenage Has-Been	1962	4.00	20.00
Colpix 691	Johnny Surfboard / Graduation Time	1963	4.00	20.00
Red Bird 015	Talk To Me, Baby / Amy	1964	2.00	10.00
Capitol 5695	Angelica / Looking At Tomorrow	1966	1.20	6.00
Capitol 5894	Where Do I Go From Here? / She Is Today	1967	1.20	6.00
Capitol 2082	Young Electric Psychedelic Hippy Flippy / Take Your Love	1968	2.00	10.00
Scepter 12281	Feelings / Let Me Stay With You	1970	.60	3.00
New Design 1000	Carry Me Home / Sundown	1972	.80	4.00
New Design 1005	Don't Give Up On Me / When You Get Right Down To It	1972	.80	4.00
New Design 1006	Lay It All Out / On Broadway	1972	.80	4.00
New Design 1006	Too Many Mondays / On Broadway	1972	.80	4.00
RCA Victor PB-10104	Nobody But You / Woman Woman Woman	1975	.80	4.00
RCA Victor PB-10230	Nothing Good Comes Easy / Woman Woman Woman	1975	.80	4.00
RCA Victor PB-10319	I'm A Survivor / It Don't Seem Right	1975	.80	4.00
Arista 0194	The Princess And The Punk / Jennifer	1976	.40	2.00
Warner Bros. 8752	Almost Gone / For No Reason At All	1979	.40	2.00
Warner Bros. 8752 (PS)	Almost Gone / For No Reason At All	1979	.60	3.00
United Artists 1021	The Best That I Know How / Lettin' Good Times Get Away	1978	.40	2.00
Casablanca 2287	Brown-Eyed Woman / In My Own Way	197?	.60	3.00

MANN, BOBBY
Booby Mann also recorded as Bobby Bloom.

Kama Sutra 210	Heart Of Town / Make The Radio A Little Louder	1966	2.00	10.00

MANN, CARL

Jaxon 502	Gonna Rock And Roll Tonight / Rockin' Love	1957	——	——
	(Rare. Estimated near mint value $750-1,500.)			
Phillips Inter. 3539	Mona Lisa / Foolish Love	1959	3.00	15.00
Phillips Inter. 3546	Pretend / Rockin' Love	1959	3.00	15.00
Phillips Inter. 3550	Some Enchanted Evening / I Can't Forget	1960	3.00	15.00
Phillips Inter. 3555	South Of The Border / I'm Comin' Home	1960	3.00	15.00
Phillips Inter. 3564	Born To Be Bad / The Wayward Wind	1960	3.00	15.00
Phillips Inter. 3569	I Ain't Got No Home / If I Could Change You	1960	3.00	15.00
Phillips Inter. 3579	When I Grow Too Old To Dream / Mountain Dew	1960	2.00	10.00

MANN, GLORIA

Sound 109	Earth Angel / I Love You, Yes I Do	1955	3.00	15.00
Sound 126	Teenage Prayer / Gypsy Lady	1955	4.00	20.00
Decca 29832	Why Do Fools Fall In Love? / Partners For Life	1956	3.00	15.00

MANN, JOHNNY

Tiara 6118	Too Young To Cry / Wouldn't Be Going Steady	195?	6.00	30.00

MANN, TOMMY

Flippin' 311	Too Good To Be True / That's For Me To Know	1962	2.00	10.00
Atlantic 2149	Too Good To Be True / That's For Me To Know	1962	1.60	8.00

MANNING, LINDA

Bulletin 1000	Our World Of Rock And Roll / Sweeter Than Sweet	1961	2.00	10.00

MANONE, WINGY
Dixieland stalwart Manone's version of '50s rock 'n roll!

Decca 30211	Party Doll / Real Gone	1957	3.00	15.00

MANSHIP, JIMMY & JUDY

Blue Hen 118	Teenage Sweetie / Blue, Blue Love	1959	3.00	15.00

MANUEL & THE RENEGADES

Piper 7000	Surf Walk / Woody Wagon	1963	5.00	25.00
Piper 7001	Rev-Up / Trans-Miss-Yen	1963	5.00	25.00

MANZAREK, RAY
Ray Manzarek originally recorded with The Doors.

Mercury 73477	Solar Boat / The Moorish Idol	1973	.60	3.00
Mercury 73601	Downbound Train / Choose Up And Choose Off	1974	.60	3.00
Mercury 73664	The Whole Thing Started With Rock And Roll And Now			
	It's Out Of Control / Art Deco Fandango	1974	.60	3.00

MAR-KAYS, THE

Delta 106	Nightcap / Sack O' Woe	196?	2.00	10.00

MAR-KETS, THE [THE MARKETTS; THE MARKETTES; THE NEW MARKETTS]
The Union, Arvee and Liberty credit the group as The Mar-Kets; Warner and Mercury as The Marketts or The Markettes. The Seminole, Farr and Calliope sides credit The New Marketts.

Union 501	Surfer's Start / Stomp	1961	4.00	20.00
Union 504	Balboa Blue / Stompede	1962	4.00	20.00
Union 507	Stompin' Room Only / Canadian Sunset	1962	4.00	20.00
Liberty 55401	Surfer's Start / Stomp	1962	2.50	15.00

Label & Catalog #		A-Side/B-Side	Year	VG	NM
Liberty 55443		Balboa Blue / Stompede	1962	2.50	15.00
Liberty 55506		Stompin' Room Only / Canadian Sunset	1962	2.50	15.00
Arvee 5063		Beach Bum / Sweet Potatoes	1962	3.00	15.00
Warner Bros. 5365		Woody Wagon / Cobra	1963	2.00	10.00
Warner Bros. 5391		Outer Limits / Bella Dalena	1963	2.50	15.00
Warner Bros. 5391		Out Of Limits / Bella Dalena	1963	2.00	10.00
Warner Bros. 5423		Vanishing Point / Borealis	1964	1.20	6.00
Warner Bros. 5468		Look For A Star / Come See, Come Ska	1964	1.20	6.00
Warner Bros. 5641		Miami Blues / Napoleon's Gold	1964	1.60	8.00
Warner Bros. 5670		Ready, Steady, Go / Lady In The Cage	1965	1.20	6.00
Warner Bros. 5696		Batman / Richie's Theme	1966	1.60	8.00
Warner Bros. 5814		Theme From The Avengers / Touch	1966	1.50	15.00
Warner Bros. 5874		Tarzan / Stirring Up Some Soul	1966	1.20	6.00
World Pacific 77874		Sunshine Girl / Sun Power	1968	1.20	6.00
World Pacific 77899		California Summer / Groovin' Time	1969	1.20	6.00
Uni 55173		They Call The Wind Maria / Undefeated	1969	.80	4.00
Mercury 73433		Mystery Movie Theme / Sister Condy	1973	.60	3.00
Seminde 501		Song From M.A.S.H. / Song From M.A.S.H.	1976	.80	4.00
Farr 007		Song From M.A.S.H. / Song From M.A.S.H.	1976	.60	3.00
Farr 019		The Whistle / Song From M.A.S.H.	1977	.60	3.00
Farr 021		Looking For Mr. Goodbar / Black	1977	.60	3.00
		(Farr 021 credits Danny Welton & The New Marketts.)			
Calliope 8003		Mary Hartman / Mary Hartman	1977	.60	3.00
Calliope 8009		City Nights / Soul Coaxing	1977	.60	3.00

MAR-VELS, THE

In 102		Surfing At Makaha / Endless Nights	196?	10.00	50.00

MARA, TOMMY

Felsted 8532		What Makes You So Lonely? / Where The Blue Of The Night	1958	3.00	15.00
Felsted 8561		With Someone Like You / Yancy Derringer	1958	3.00	15.00

MARAUDERS, THE

Hawk 4002		Stomp Watch / Sand Flea	196?	8.00	40.00

MARAUDERS, THE

Skyview 001		Since I Met You / I Don't Know How	196?	3.00	15.00

MARAUDERS, THE

Laurie 3356		Out Of Sight, Out Of Mind / Jugband Music	1966	2.00	10.00

MARBLES, THE

Cotillion 44029		Walls Fall Down / Love You	1969	.80	4.00
Cotillion 44036		I Can't See Nobody / Little Boy	1969	.80	4.00
Cotillion 44046		Little Laughing Girl / Breaking Up Is Hard To Do	1970	.80	4.00

MARCEL, PETE

Futura 104		Sloppy Twist A Fish / Sloppy Twist A Fish (Part 2)	1961	1.20	6.00

MARCELL, SONNY, & THE COLLEGIANS

Mayhams 212		My College Girl / My College Girl, Part 2	196?	7.00	35.00
Mayhams 214/15		Surfin' On A Swingin' Soiree / You're My Surfer Girl Forever	196?	7.00	35.00
		("Surfin' On A Swingin' Soiree" was also released as "Surfing Is A Sight To See" credited to The Biscayne Bay Surfers.)			

MARCH, (LITTLE) PEGGY

RCA Victor 47-8107		Little Me / Pagan Love Song	1962	2.00	10.00
RCA Victor 47-8139		I Will Follow Him / Wind-Up Doll	1963	2.00	10.00
RCA Victor 47-8189		I Wish I Were A Princess / My Teenage Castle	1963	2.00	10.00
RCA Victor 47-8189	(PS)	I Wish I Were A Princess / My Teenage Castle	1963	4.00	20.00
RCA Victor 47-8221		Hello Heartache, Goodbye Love / Boy Crazy	1963	1.20	6.00
RCA Victor 47-8221	(PS)	Hello Heartache, Goodbye Love / Boy Crazy	1963	4.00	20.00
RCA Victor 47-8267		The Impossible Happened / Waterfall	1963	1.20	6.00
RCA Victor 47-8302		(I'm Watching) Every Little Move You Make / After You	1964	1.20	6.00
RCA Victor 47-8357		Leave Me Alone / Takin' The Long Way Home	1964	1.20	6.00
RCA Victor 47-8418		Oh My, What A Guy / Only You Could Do That To My Heart	1964	1.20	6.00
RCA Victor 47-8460		Watch What You Do With My Baby / Can't Stop Thinking About Him	1965	1.00	5.00
RCA Victor 47-8534		Why Can't He Be You? / Losin' My Touch	1965	1.00	5.00
RCA Victor 47-8605		Let Her Go / Your Girl	1965	1.00	5.00
RCA Victor 47-8710		Heaven For Lovers / He Couldn't Care Less	1966	1.00	5.00
RCA Victor 47-8840	(DJ)	Sechs Tage Lang / Ein Boy Wie Du	1966	2.00	10.00
RCA Victor 47-8877		Old Fashioned Wedding / Play A Simple Melody	1966	1.00	5.00
RCA Victor 47-8903		Running Scared / He's Back Again	1966	1.00	5.00
RCA Victor 47-9033		Fool Fool Fool (Look In The Mirror) / Try To See It My Way	1966	1.00	5.00
RCA Victor 47-9143		How Can I Tell Him? / January First	1967	1.00	5.00
RCA Victor 47-9223		Your Good Girl's Gonna Go Bad / Mama Dear, Papa Dear	1967	1.00	5.00
RCA Victor 47-9283		Foolin' Around / This Heart Wasn't Made To Kick Around	1967	1.00	5.00

Label & Catalog #		A-Side/B-Side	Year	VG	NM
RCA Victor 47-9359		Let Me Down Hard / Have A Good Time	1967	1.00	5.00
RCA Victor 47-9494		If You Loved Me / Thinking Through My Tears	1968	1.00	5.00
RCA Victor 47-9566		Roses On The Sea / Time And Time Again	1968	1.00	5.00
RCA Victor 47-9627		I've Been Here Before / Aren't You Glad?	1968	1.00	5.00
RCA Victor 47-9718		Try To See It My Way / Purple Hat	1969	1.00	5.00
RCA Victor 74-0136		Boom Ban-A-Ban / Lilac Skies	1971	.80	4.00
Olde World 1105		Average People / Isn't This The Way We Are?	197?	.60	3.00
		—Extended Play Albums—			
RCA Victor EPA-4376		I Wish I Were A Princess	1963	10.00	50.00

MARCO, NICK, & THE VENETIANS
| Dwain 813 | | Little Boy Lost / Would It Hurt You? | 195? | 8.00 | 40.00 |

MARCUS, JONATHAN
| MGM 13580 | | What About Me? / Mad About You, Baby | 1966 | 1.60 | 8.00 |

MARCUS HOOK ROLL BAND
The Marcus Roll Band features Harry Vanda and George Young, formerly of The Easybeats.
| Capitol 3505 | | Natural Man / Boogalooing Is For Wooing | 1973 | 2.00 | 10.00 |
| EMI 3560 | | Louisiana Lady / Hoochie Coochie Har Kau | 1973 | 1.00 | 5.00 |

MARCY JO
Robbee 110		Ronnie / My First Mistake	1961	2.00	10.00
Robbee 115		What I Did This Summer / Since Gary Went In The Navy	1961	2.00	10.00
		(Robbee 110 and 115 feature Lou Christie on back-up vocals.)			

MARCY JO & EDDIE RAMBEAU
Robbee 117		Take A Word / Jumping Jack	1962	2.00	10.00
Swan 4136		Those Golden Oldies / When You Wore A Tulip	1963	3.00	15.00
Swan 4145		The Car Hop And The Hard Top / Love's Melody	1963	2.00	10.00

MARDIN, ARIF
| Atlantic 2658 | | Glass Onion / Sympathy For The Devil | 1972 | .80 | 4.00 |

MARENO, LEE (WITH THE REGENTS)
| New Art 103 | | Goddess Of Love / He's Gone | 1961 | 25.00 | 125.00 |
| Scepter 1222 | | Goddess Of Love / He's Gone | 1961 | 5.00 | 25.00 |

MARESCA, ERNIE
Ernie Maresca also recorded as Artie Chicago and with Foreign Intrigue and The Hubcaps.
Seville 107		I Don't Know Why / Lonesome Blues	1962	2.00	10.00
Seville 117		Shout! Shout! (Knock Yourself Out) / Crying Like A Baby	1962	2.00	10.00
Seville 119		Down On The Beach / Mary Jane	1962	3.00	15.00
Seville 119	(PS)	Down On The Beach / Mary Jane	1962	4.00	20.00
Seville 122		Something To Shout About / How Many Times?	1962	2.00	10.00
Seville 125		Lorelei / The Love Express	1963	7.00	35.00
Seville 138		It's Their World / I Can't Dance	1963	2.00	10.00
Rust 5076		The Beetle Dance / The Theme From "Lilly, Lilly"	1964	2.00	10.00
Laurie 3345		The Good Life / A Bum Can't Cry	1966	.80	4.00
Laurie 3371		My Shadow And Me / My Son	1967	.80	4.00
Laurie 3447		The Night My Papa Died / What Is A Marine?	1968	.80	4.00
Laurie 3496		People Get Jealous / Blind Date	1969	.80	4.00
Laurie 3519		The Spirit Of Woodstock / Web Of Love	1970	.80	4.00
		—Extended Play Albums—			
Seville SSP-1	(DJ)	Shout! Shout! (Paper sleeve)	1962	12.00	60.00

MARESCA, ERNIE, & THE DEL SATINS
| Seville 129 | | Please Be Fair / The Rovin' Kind | 1963 | 4.00 | 20.00 |

MARESCO, TONY, & THE DYNAMICS
Tony & The Dynamics later recorded as Anthony & The Sophomores.
| Herald 569 | | Betty My Own / Forever Love | 1962 | 75.00 | 300.00 |

MARGLOWS, THE: Refer to ANDY & THE MARGLOWS

MARGO, MARGO, MEDRESS & SIEGEL
Mitch Margo, Phil Margo, Hank Medress and Jay Siegel of The Tokens.
| Warner Bros. 7183 | | Mister Snail / Needles Of Evergreen | 1968 | 1.00 | 5.00 |

MARIDIAN
| Mercury 73076 | | San Francisco Woman / San Francisco Woman | 1969 | 1.20 | 6.00 |

MARIE & REX
| Carlton 502 | | I Can't Sit Down / Miracles | 1959 | 3.00 | 15.00 |

MARIE & THE DECCORS
| Cub 9115 | | Queen Of Fools / I'm The One | 1962 | 4.00 | 20.00 |

Label & Catalog #	A-Side/B-Side	Year	VG	NM
MARIO & THE FLIPS				
Decca 31252	Twistin' Train / You Made Me Love You	1962	3.00	15.00
MARION & HERBIE				
Ultra-Sonic 1717	Goin' Steady By The Numbers / School Days	1960	2.00	10.00
MARK				
Mark Gutkowski of The 1910 Fruitgum Company.				
Super-K 103	Good N' Plenty / It Could Set You Back A Month	1969	1.00	5.00
Team 521	Goodnight / Good Morning	1969	1.00	5.00
MARK & THE ESCORTS				
GNP/Crescendo 350	Get Your Baby / Tuff Stuff	1965	2.00	10.00
GNP/Crescendo 358	Dance With Me / Silly Putty	1965	2.00	10.00
MARK FOUR, THE				
Pacific Challenger 1002	Just My Dream / Swingin' Hangout	196?	2.00	10.00
Pacific Challenger 1004	Go Away Now / Forget It, Baby	196?	2.00	10.00
MARK FOUR, THE				
Iris 100	Death Freight / Patino Push	196?	2.00	10.00
MARK III, THE				
Century Custom 19930	Unchained Melody / Far Away	196?	1.20	6.00
MARK III, THE				
BRB 100	Valerie / The Man	1961	3.00	15.00
ABC-Paramount 10280	Valerie / The Man	1961	2.00	10.00
MARK IV, THE				
Cosmic 704	(Make With) The Shake / 45 R.P.M.	1958	3.00	15.00
Mercury 71403	I Got A Wife / Ah-Ooo-Gah	1959	3.00	15.00
Mercury 71445	Move Over, Rover / Dante's Inferno	1959	3.00	15.00
Columbia 43911	Better Than That / Hollow Woman	195?	2.00	10.00
MARK V, THE				
Bolo 746	Ooh Poo Pah Doo / Get On Back	1963	2.00	10.00
Jani 1258	It's Your Heart / 48 Lbs. Of Bad Luck	1965	2.00	10.00
Jani 1265	Maggie's Farm / Who Made Lonely	1965	2.00	10.00
NWI 2700	Search Your Mind / Determination	1966	2.00	10.00
MARKAYS, THE: *Refer to* DOUG SAHM				
MARKETTS/MARKETTES, THE: *Refer to* THE MAR-KETS				
MARKS, DAVID: *Refer to* DAVE & THE MARKSMEN				
MARKSMEN, THE				
The Marksmen feature Don Dixon, a.k.a. Don Wilson, of The Ventures.				
Blue Horizon 6051	For Your Love / Cry Of The Wild Goose	1960	20.00	100.00
Blue Horizon 6052	Night Run / Scratch	1960	20.00	100.00
MARKSMEN, THE: *Refer to* DAVE & THE MARKSMEN				
MARLINS, THE				
Scotty 818	Let Down / Saw Mill Run	1964	7.00	35.00
Cameo 333	Everybody Do The Swim / Everybody Do The Swim (Part 2)	1964	2.00	10.00
MARLO, MICKI				
ABC-Paramount 9762	Little By Little / It All Started	1957	3.00	15.00
MARMALADE				
Epic 10284	Man In A Shop / Cry	1968	.80	4.00
Epic 10340	Lovin' Things / Hey Joe	1968	.80	4.00
Epic 10493	Baby, Make It Soon / Time Is On My Side	1969	.80	4.00
London 20058	Reflections Of My Life / Rollin' My Thing	1970	.80	4.00
London 20059	Rainbow / The Ballad Of Cherry Flavor	1970	.60	3.00
London 20066	My Little One / Is Your Life Your Own?	1970	.60	3.00
London 20068	Lonely Man / Cousin Norman	1971	.60	3.00
London 20072	Just One Woman / Radancer	1971	.60	3.00
EMI 3676	Wishing Well / Engine Driver	1973	.60	3.00
Ariola American 7619	Fallin' Apart At The Seams / Fly Fly Fly	1976	.40	2.00
Ariola American 7631	Walking A Tightrope / My Everything	1976	.40	2.00
MAROONS, THE				
Queen 24102	Don't Leave Me, Baby, Don't / Someday I'll Be The One	1962	5.00	25.00

Label & Catalog #	A-Side/B-Side	Year	VG	NM
MARQUIS				
Earl 1004	The Drifter / Love	196?	2.00	10.00
MAROONS, THE				
Queen 24012	Don't Leave Me, Baby, Don't / Someday I'll Be The One	1962	4.00	20.00
MARRELL'S MARAUDERS				
Fan Jr. 1003	The Marauder / I Wanna Do It	196?	7.00	35.00
MARREN, HOWARD				
Fargo 1006	The Phantom Strikes Again /			
	I'm Getting To Be A Big Boy, Now	1958	4.00	20.00
MARSDEN, GERRY				
Refer to Gerry & The Pacemakers.				
Columbia 444309	Gilbert Green / Please Let Them Be	1967	1.20	6.00
MARSH, RICHIE [DICK MARSH]				
Rich Marsh later recorded as Sky Saxon with The Seeds.				
Rosco 412	There's Only One Girl / What Chance Have I?	1960	3.00	15.00
Shepherd 2203	They Say Darling / I Swear That It's True	1961	4.00	20.00
Acama 125	Baby Baby Baby / Half Angel	1961	3.00	15.00
Ava 122	Crying Inside My Heart / Goodbye	1963	3.00	15.00
MARSHANS, THE				
Etiquette 8	It's Almost Tomorrow / I Remember	196?	2.00	10.00
MARSHMALLOW HIGHWAY, THE				
Kapp 904	I Don't Wanna Live This Way / Loving You	1968	1.00	5.00
MARSHMALLOW WAY				
Marshmallow Way features Billy Carl. Refer to Billy & The Essentials.				
United Artists 50545	C'mon, Kitty Kitty / Michigan Mints	1969	2.00	10.00
United Artists 50611	Music Music / Good Day	1969	2.00	10.00
MARSHMELLOWS, THE				
Veep 1212	When I Look At My Love / I Don't Even Know His Name	1964	3.00	15.00
MARTELLS, THE [THE MARTELS]				
Nasco 6026	Where Did My Woman Go? / Teacher, Don't Keep Me In	1959	5.00	25.00
Bella 20	Rockin' Santa Claus / I Love My Baby	1959	5.00	25.00
Bella 45	Va Va Voom / Forgotten Spring	1961	8.00	40.00
Cessna 477	Va Va Voom / Forgotten Spring	1961	5.00	25.00
MARTIN, ANGELA				
Atco 6327	Dip Da Dip / Take Me To The Fair	1965	1.60	8.00
MARTIN, ASTON, & THE MOON DISCS				
Del Rio 2301	Fallout / Moonbeat	1961	7.00	35.00
MARTIN, BUZZ				
Ripcord 018	About That Welfare Cadillac / Cummin's Prison	196?	2.00	10.00
MARTIN, DANNY				
Riot 431	Rockin' Memphis Mama / Pool Cue	1957	6.00	30.00
MARTIN, DEREK				
Roulette 4631	You Better Go / You Know	1965	1.20	6.00
MARTIN, DEWEY, & MEDICINE BALL				
Dewey Martin also recorded with The Buffalo Springfield and Sir Raleigh & The Coupons.				
Uni 55245	Indian Child / I Do Believe	1970	1.00	5.00
RCA Victor 74-0489	Caress Me, Pretty Music / There Must Be A Reason	1971	.80	4.00
MARTIN, DINO, JR.				
Refer to Dino, Desi & Billy.				
Reprise 1129	Sitting In Limbo / Sitting In Limbo	1972	.80	4.00
MARTIN, GEORGE				
George Martin was, among other engagements, The Beatles' producer from 1962-1970.				
United Artists 745	And I Love Her / Ringo's Theme	1964	3.00	15.00
United Artists 745 (PS)	And I Love Her / Ringo's Theme	1964	25.00	125.00
	(The sleeve features photos of The Beatles.)			
United Artists 750	A Hard Day's Night / I Should Have Known Better	1964	15.00	75.00
United Artists 750 (PS)	A Hard Day's Night / I Should Have Known Better	1964	250.00	750.00
	(The sleeve features a photo of The Beatles.)			
United Artists 831	All Quiet On The Mersey Front / Cast Your Fate To The Wind	1965	2.00	10.00
United Artists 50148	Love In The Open Air / Bahama Sound	1966	4.00	20.00

Label & Catalog #		A-Side/B-Side	Year	VG	NM
MARTIN, JANIS					
RCA Victor 47-6491		Will You, Willyum? / Drug Store Rock And Roll	1956	6.00	30.00
RCA Victor 47-6560		Ooby Dooby / One More Year To Go	1956	8.00	40.00
RCA Victor 47-6652		My Boy Elvis / Little Bit	1956	8.00	40.00
RCA Victor 47-6744		Barefoot Baby / Let's Elope, Baby	1957	4.00	20.00
RCA Victor 47-6832		Love Me To Pieces / Two Long Years	1957	4.00	20.00
RCA Victor 47-6983		Love And Kisses / I'll Never Be Free	1956	4.00	20.00
RCA Victor 47-7104		All Right, Baby / Billy Boy, Billy Boy	1958	5.00	25.00
RCA Victor 47-7318		Bang Bang / Please Be My Love	1957	6.00	30.00
Palette 5058		Hard Times Ahead /			
		Here Today And Gone Tomorrow, Love	1959	3.00	15.00
Palette 5071		Teen Street / Cry, Guitar	1959	3.00	15.00
		—Extended Play Albums—			
RCA Victor EPA-4093		Just Squeeze Me	1956	40.00	200.00
MARTIN, JIMMY					
Decca 30703		Rock Hearts / I'll Never Take No For An Answer	1958	3.00	15.00
MARTIN, KENNY LEE					
Decca 30754		The Rock Keeps On Rollin' / The Shape I'm In	1959	3.00	15.00
MARTIN, MANDI					
Columbia 43254		Don't Let Him Get Away From You / This Is Goodbye Forever	1965	1.00	5.00
MARTIN, RICCI					
Both the Capitol and the Epic sides were produced by Carl Wilson.					
Capitol P-4164	(DJ)	Stop, Look Around / Stop, Look Around	1975	1.00	5.00
Capitol 4164		Stop, Look Around / I Had A Dream	1975	2.00	10.00
Epic 50263	(DJ)	Stop, Look Around / Stop, Look Around	1976	.60	3.00
Epic 50263		Stop, Look Around / I Had A Dream	1976	1.20	6.00
Epic 50441	(DJ)	Moonbeams / Moonbeams	1977	.60	3.00
Epic 50441		Moonbeams / Precious Love	1977	1.20	6.00
MARTIN, STEVE					
Steve Martin also recorded with The Left Banke and Montage					
Buddah 219		Two By Two / Love Songs In The Night	1971	.80	4.00
MARTIN SIX, AL					
Bell 605		Baby Beatle Walk / Prego	1965	2.00	10.00
MARTINE, LAYNG, JR.					
General Inter. 351		Pick All The Flowers That You Can / Surabian Lament	1966	1.20	6.00
Date 1511		Crazy Daisy / Love Comes And Goes	1966	1.60	8.00
MARTY					
Novelty 101		Marty On Planet Mars / Marty On Planet Mars, Part 2	1956	5.00	25.00
DiVenus 103		Since You're Mine / Dear Mom And Dad	196?	2.00	10.00
MARTY & THE MELLOW YELLOW BUNCH					
Megaphone 101		Two Bananas In Love / Two Bananas In Love, (Part 2)	1967	2.00	10.00
MARTY & THE MONKS					
Associated Arts. 3065		Mrs. Schwartz, You've Got An Ugly Daughter /	1965	2.00	10.00
MARTY & THE SYMBOLS					
Graphic Arts 1000		You're The One / (B-side by Mr. Bassman)	1963	10.00	50.00
MARVELIERS, THE					
Joany 4439		The Spider / Little Girl	196?	7.00	35.00
MARVELOWS, THE					
ABC-Paramount 10586		I Deserve To Cry / How Do You Tell A Heartache Goodbye?	1964	2.00	10.00
ABC-Paramount 10613		A Friend / Hey Hey, Baby	1964	2.00	10.00
ABC-Paramount 10629		I Do / My Heart	1965	2.00	10.00
ABC-Paramount 10708		The Shim Sham / Your Little Sister	1965	2.00	10.00
ABC-Paramount 10756		Do It / I've Got My Eyes On You	1966	2.00	10.00
ABC-Paramount 10820		Fade Away / You've Been Going With Sally	1966	2.00	10.00
MARVELLS, THE					
Winn 1916		For Sentimental Reasons / Come Back	1961	50.00	200.00
MARVELS, THE					
Laurie 3016		So Young, So Sweet / I Shed So Many Tears	1958	6.00	30.00
MARVELS, THE: Refer to NEIL SEDAKA					
MARVELS FIVE, THE					
Uptown 722		Don't Play That Song (You Lied) / Forgive Me	1966	2.00	10.00

Label & Catalog #	A-Side/B-Side	Year	VG	NM
MARX, THE				
Dahlia 1002	One Minute More / You Are My Love	195?	50.00	200.00
MARX, MELINDA				
Vee Jay 657	The East Side Of Town / How I Wish You Came	1964	1.20	6.00
MASCOTS, THE				
Mermaid 107	Bluebirds Over The Mountain / Timberlands	1961	5.00	25.00
Blast 206	Once Upon A Love / Hey, Little Angel (Red label)	1962	4.00	20.00
Blast 206	Once Upon A Love / Hey, Little Angel (White label)	196?	2.00	10.00
MASHMAKAN				
Jamie 1418	Dance A Little Step / One Night Stand	1969	1.00	5.00
Epic 10634	As The Years Go By / Days When We Are Free	1970	.80	4.00
MASKED DEMONS, THE				
RRE 1016	Hi Surfin' / Way Out	1963	7.00	35.00
MASKED MARAUDERS, THE				
The infamous Marauders is actually a pseudonym for The Cleanliness & Godliness Skiffle Band.				
Diety/Reprise 0870 (DJ)	Cow Pie / I Can't Get No Nookie	1969	3.00	15.00
	(With insert containing the group's "history.")			
MASON, BONNIE JO				
Bonnie Jo later recorded as Cher. Possibly produced by Phil Spector.				
Annette 1000 (DJ)	Ringo, I Love You / Beatles Blues	1964	40.00	200.00
Annette 1000	Ringo, I Love You / Beatles Blues	1964	100.00	400.00
MASON, JERRY				
Vanco 211	My Love Is Only Yours / Little Old Winedrinker	1968	2.00	10.00
MASON PROFFIT				
Happy Tiger 552	Sweet Lady Love / Two Hangmen	1970	2.00	10.00
Ampex 11048	Hope / Jewel	1971	.80	4.00
MASS MEDIA				
Seneca 1	Hey Hey, Momma / Don't Take It Lightly	1971	2.00	10.00
MASSI, NICK				
Nick Massi also recorded with or as Alex Alda; The Four Seasons; The Hollywood Playboys; Nick & The Nitelites; and The Victorians.				
One Way 244	The Ballad Of Mr. Nixon / Little Pony	197?	1.00	5.00
MASTERS, THE				
Bingo 1008	A Lovely Way To Spend An Evening / Dore's Blues	1960	15.00	75.00
End 1100	A Man Is Not Supposed To Cry / Look Out	1961	3.00	15.00
LeSage 713/4	I'm Searching / Crying My Heart Out	196?	4.00	20.00
MASTERS, THE				
Emmy 10082	Breaktime / 16 Tons	1962	25.00	125.00
	("Breaktime" co-written by Frank Zappa.)			
MASTERS, THE: *Refer to* RICK & THE MASTERS				
MASTERS, JOHNNY				
Johnny Masters is a pseudonym for Johnny Maestro.				
Coed 527	Say It Isn't So / The Great Physician (Red label)	1960	3.00	15.00
MASTERS, SAMMY				
Four Star 1695	Pink Cadillac / Some Like It Hot	1956	10.00	50.00
Lode 108	Rockin' Red Wing / Lonely Weekend	1960	4.00	20.00
Lode 109	Charlotte (In The Pink Corvette) / Golden Slippers	1960	3.00	15.00
Warner Bros. 5102	Rockin' Red Wing / Lonely Weekend	1960	2.00	10.00
Dot 16123	Charlotte (In The Pink Corvette) / Golden Slippers	1960	2.00	10.00
MATADORS, THE				
Jamie 1226	Listen / So Near	1962	4.00	20.00
Keith 6502	If You Left Me Today /	1963	3.00	15.00
Keith 6504	You'd Be Crying, Too / My Foolish Heart	1963	4.00	20.00
MATADORS, THE				
The Matadors were produced by Jan Berry.				
Colpix 698	Ace Of Hearts / Perfidia	1963	3.00	15.00
Colpix 718	I've Gotta Drive / La Corrida	1964	4.00	20.00
	("I've Gotta Drive" is a Jan & Dean track with a new spoken intro.)			
Colpix 741	C'mon, Let Yourself Go / C'mon, Let Yourself Go, Part 2	1964	3.00	15.00

Label & Catalog #	A-Side/B-Side	Year	VG	NM
MATHEWS, DINO				
Dot 16365	The Girl That I Love / Lenore	1962	6.00	30.00
MATHEWS, RONNIE				
Dayhill 2004	Lonesome Teenager / The Week Is Over	195?	4.00	20.00
MATHEWS, SHIRLEY				
Tamarac 602	Big Town Boy / Count On That	1963	5.00	25.00
Atlantic 2210	Big Town Boy / Count On That	1963	3.00	15.00
Atlantic 2224	Private Property / Wise Guys	1964	2.00	10.00
Amy 910	Is He Really Mine? / He Makes Me Feel So Pretty	1964	2.00	10.00
Amy 921	Stop The Clock / If I Had To Do It Again	1965	2.00	10.00
MATHEWS BROTHERS, THE				
ABC-Paramount 10473	Stupid / Mora Mora	1963	4.00	20.00
MATHIS, BOBBY, & THE SEVILLES				
Sioux 51860	Girl In The Drugstore / Going To The City	195?	10.00	50.00
MATTHEWS' SOUTHERN COMFORT				
Decca 32774	Woodstock / Ballad Of Obray Ramsey	1971	.60	3.00
Decca 32845	Mare, Take Me Home / The Brand New Tennessee Waltz	1971	.60	3.00
Decca 32874	Tell Me Why / To Love	1971	.60	3.00
MATHIS, DEAN & MARC [THE MATHIS BROTHERS]				
The Mathis Brothers also recorded with The Newbeats.				
Bullseye 1025	Tell Him No / Change Of Heart	1959	3.00	15.00
Bullseye 1026	Cry / The Beginning Of Love	1959	3.00	15.00
Check Mate 1008	Boogie Woogie Twist / Boogie Woogie Twist, Part 2	1961	2.00	10.00
	(The Bullseye and Checkmate singles credit Dean & Marc.)			
May 135	Pins And Needles / Somebody's Smiling	1963	2.00	10.00
Hickory 1227	With Tears In My Eyes / Kissin' Games	1963	1.00	5.00
Hickory 1249	There Oughta Be A Law / When I Stop Dreaming	1963	1.00	5.00
Hickory 1294	Just A Step Away / A Fallen Star	1965	1.00	5.00
Hickory 1353	In The Middle Of The Night / You'll Never Really Know	1966	1.00	5.00
Hickory 1414	With Tears In My Eyes / When I Stop Dreaming	1963	1.00	5.00
	(Hickory 1414 credits The Mathis Brothers.)			
MAUDS, THE				
Dunwich 160	Hold On / C'mon And Move	1967	2.00	10.00
Mercury 72694	Hold On / C'mon And Move	1967	1.20	6.00
Mercury 72720	You Made Me Feel So Bad / When Something Is Wrong	1967	1.20	6.00
Mercury 72832	Soul Drippin' / Forever Gone	1968	1.20	6.00
Mercury 72877	Only Love Can Save You Now / Sergeant Sunshine	1969	1.20	6.00
Mercury 72919	Satisfy My Hunger / Brother Chickee	1969	1.20	6.00
RCA Victor 74-0377	A Man Without A Dream / Forget It, I've Got It	1970	1.00	5.00
MAV-RICKS, THE				
Mav-Rick 1	What Kind Of Girls? / You're Ruining My Business	195?	5.00	25.00
MAVRICKS, THE				
Capitol 4507	Angel With A Heartache / Sugar Babe	1961	2.00	10.00
Capitol 4560	Going To The River / Just To Hear Old Cotton Sing	1961	2.00	10.00
MAXIMILLIAN				
Maximillian was Del Shannon's organist on his Big Top sides.				
Big Top 3095	The Twistin' Ghost / The Breeze-Theme From Peter Gunn	1961	4.00	20.00
MAXWELL, BOBBY, & THE EXPLOITS				
Fargo 1009/10	You're Laughing At Me / Stay With Me	1959	10.00	50.00
MAXWELL, DIANE				
Challenge 59039	Date Bait / Jimmy Kiss And Run	1959	2.00	10.00
MAXWELL, LEN				
20th Century Fox 551	Merry Monster Christmas / Sounds Of Christmas	1964	2.00	10.00
MAYALL, JOHN				
Immediate 502	Telephone Blues / I'm Your Witch Doctor	1966	.80	4.00
London 20016	Key To Love / Parchman Farm	1966	.80	4.00
London 20024	All Your Love / Hideaway	1967	.80	4.00
	(London 20024 features Eric Clapton.)			
London 20039	Broken Wings / Sonny Boy Blow	1968	.60	3.00
London 20042	Living Alone / Walking On Sunset	1968	.60	3.00
Polydor 14004	Don't Waste My Time / Don't Pick A Flower	1969	.60	3.00
Polydor 14051	Nature's Disappearing / Moving On	1970	.60	3.00
Polydor 14253	Let Me Give / Gasoline Blues	1974	.40	2.00

Label & Catalog #		A-Side/B-Side	Year	VG	NM

MC-5, THE
The Motor City Five are Mike Davis, Wayne Kramer, Fred Smith, Dennis Thompson and Rob Tyner.

Label & Catalog #		A-Side/B-Side	Year	VG	NM
AMG 1000	(DJ)	I Can Only Give You Everything /			
		I Can Only Give You Everything	1966	8.00	40.00
AMG 1001		I Can Only Give You Everything / One Of The Guys	1965	10.00	50.00
		(Yellow label)			
AMG 1001		I Can Only Give You Everything / One Of The Guys	1966	8.00	40.00
		(Black label)			
A-Square 333		Looking At You / Borderline	1967	8.00	40.00
A-Square 333	(PS)	Looking At You / Borderline	1967	15.00	75.00
Elektra 45648		Kick Out The Jams / Motor City Is Burning	1969	5.00	25.00
Elektra MC5-1	(DJ)	Kick Out The Jams / Motor City Is Burning	1969	6.00	30.00
Atlantic 2678		Tonight / Looking At You	1969	3.00	15.00
Atlantic 2724		The American Ruse / Shakin' Street	1970	3.00	15.00

McBRIDE, BARBARA, & THE CHESSMEN
Refer to The Chessmen.

Label & Catalog #		A-Side/B-Side	Year	VG	NM
Mari 451		The Only Reason / (B-side by Woody Carr)	196?	2.00	10.00

McCARTNEY, PAUL [PAUL McCARTNEY & WINGS]
Regardless of the fact that the labels may credit Paul McCartney, Paul McCartney & Wings, Paul & Linda McCartney, or simply Wings, these are all Paul's creations. Refer to The Beatles; The Country Hams; John Foster & Sons; Denny Laine; The Mystery Tour; Suzy & The Red Stripes; Fradkin & Unger Thornton.

Label & Catalog #		A-Side/B-Side	Year	VG	NM
Apple P-6193	(DJ)	Another Day / Oh Woman, Oh Why	1971	10.00	50.00
Apple 1829		Another Day / Oh Woman, Oh Why (Star label)	1971	1.20	6.00
Apple 1829		Another Day / Oh Woman, Oh Why (Starless label)	1971	1.00	5.00
Apple P-1837	(DJ)	Uncle Albert-Admiral Halsy / Too Many People	1971	10.00	50.00
Apple 1837		Uncle Albert-Admiral Halsy / Too Many People	1971	1.00	5.00
		(B-side label is a sliced apple.)			
Apple 1837		Uncle Albert-Admiral Halsy / Too Many People	1971	2.00	10.00
		(B-side label is an unsliced apple.)			
Apple 1847		Give Ireland Back To The Irish /			
		Give Ireland Back To The Irish	1972	1.00	5.00
Apple 1847	(PS)	Give Ireland Back To The Irish	1972	5.00	25.00
Apple 1851	(DJ)	Mary Had A Little Lamb / Little Woman Love	1972	60.00	250.00
Apple 1851		Mary Had A Little Lamb / Little Woman Love	1972	1.00	5.00
Apple 1851	(PS)	Mary Had A Little Lamb	1972	4.00	20.00
		(Sleeve does not list the b-side, "Little Woman Love.")			
Apple 1851	(PS)	Mary Had A Little Lamb / Little Woman Love	1972	7.00	35.00
		(Sleeve lists the b-side, "Little Woman Love.")			
Apple 1857		Hi, Hi, Hi / C-Moon (Red label)	1972	1.00	5.00
Apple 1861	(DJ)	My Love / My Love	1973	50.00	200.00
Apple 1861		My Love / The Mess	1973	1.00	5.00
Apple 1863		Live And Let Die / I Lie Around (Apple label)	1973	1.00	5.00
Apple PRO-6786	(DJ)	Helen Wheels / Helen Wheels	1973	5.00	25.00
Apple PRO-6787	(DJ)	Country Dreamer / Country Dreamer	1973	75.00	300.00
Apple 1869		Helen Wheels / Country Dreamer	1973	1.00	5.00
Apple P-1871	(DJ)	Jet / Jet	1974	8.00	40.00
Apple 1871		Jet (4:08) / Mamunia	1974	2.00	10.00
Apple 1871		Jet (2:49) / Mamunia	1974	6.00	30.00
Apple 1871		Jet / Let Me Roll It	1974	1.00	5.00
Apple P-1873	(DJ)	Band On The Run (5:09) / Band On The Run (3:50)	1974	8.00	40.00
Apple P-1873	(DJ)	Band On The Run (3:50) / Band On The Run (3:50)	1974	20.00	100.00
Apple 1873		Band On The Run / Nineteen Hundred & Eighty-Five	1974	1.00	5.00
Apple P-1875		Sally G / Sally G	1974	15.00	75.00
Apple P-1875	(DJ)	Junior's Farm / Junior's Farm	1974	8.00	40.00
Apple 1875		Junior's Farm / Sally G	1974	1.00	5.00
Apple 1875		Junior's Farm / Sally G	1974	10.00	50.00
		(Label has an "All Rights Reserved" claim.)			
Marimax CPS-4202	(DJ)	Paul McCartney & Wings Rock Show Radio Spots	1975	75.00	300.00
Capitol 4091	(DJ)	Listen To What The Man Said /	1975		
		Listen To What The Man Said	1975	5.00	25.00
Capitol 4091		Listen To What The Man Said / Love In Song	1975	.40	2.00
Capitol 4091	(PS)	Listen To What The Man Said / Love In Song	1975	1.20	6.00
Capitol 4145	(DJ)	Letting Go / Letting Go	1975	5.00	25.00
Capitol 4145		Letting Go / You Gave Me The Answer	1975	.60	3.00
Capitol 4175	(DJ)	Venus And Mars Rock Show / Venus And Mars Rock Show	1975	5.00	25.00
Capitol 4175		Venus And Mars Rock Show / Magneto And Titanium Man	1975	.60	3.00
Capitol P-4256	(DJ)	Silly Love Songs / Silly Love Songs	1976	5.00	25.00
Capitol 4256		Silly Love Songs / Cook Of The House (Black label)	1976	.80	4.00
Capitol 4256		Silly Love Songs / Cook Of The House (Photo label)	1976	.80	4.00
Capitol 4293		Let 'Em In / Let 'Em In	1975	4.00	20.00
Capitol 4293		Let 'Em In / Beware My Love (Photo label)	1976	.60	3.00
Capitol 4293		Let 'Em In / Beware My Love (Black label)	1977	.40	2.00
Capitol 8570/71	(DJ)	Maybe I'm Amazed / Maybe I'm Amazed	1977	5.00	25.00
Capitol 4385		Maybe I'm Amazed / Soily	1977	1.20	6.00

Label & Catalog #		A-Side/B-Side	Year	VG	NM
Capitol 8746/47	(DJ)	Mull Of Kintyre / Girls School	1977	5.00	25.00
Capitol 4504		Mull Of Kintyre / Girls School	1977	.60	3.00
Capitol 4504	(PS)	Mull Of Kintyre / Girls School	1977	3.00	15.00
Capitol 8812	(DJ)	With A Little Luck / With A Little Luck	1978	5.00	25.00
Capitol 4559		With A Little Luck / Backwards Traveller-Cuff Link	1978	.60	3.00
Capitol P-4594	(DJ)	I've Had Enough / I've Had Enough	1978	4.00	20.00
Capitol P-4594		I've Had Enough Insert	1978	1.00	5.00
Capitol 4594		I've Had Enough / Deliver Your Children	1978	.60	3.00
Capitol P-4625	(DJ)	London Town / London Town	1978	4.00	20.00
Capitol 4625		London Town / I'm Carrying	1978	.40	2.00
Columbia 10939	(DJ)	Goodnight Tonight / Goodnight Tonight	1979	3.00	15.00
Columbia 10939		Goodnight Tonight / Daytime, Nighttime Suffering	1979	.60	3.00
Columbia 11020	(DJ)	Getting Closer / Getting Closer	1979	3.00	15.00
Columbia 11020		Getting Closer / Spin It On	1979	.80	4.00
Columbia 11020	(PS)	Getting Closer / Spin It On	1979	6.00	30.00
Columbia 11070	(DJ)	Arrow Through Me / Arrow Through Me	1979	3.00	15.00
Columbia 11070		Arrow Through Me / Old Siam, Sir	1979	.80	4.00
Columbia 11162	(DJ)	Wonderful Christmastime / Wonderful Christmastime	1979	3.00	15.00
Columbia 11162		Wonderful Christmastime / Rudolph The Red Nosed Reindeer	1979	1.00	5.00
Columbia 11162	(PS)	Wonderful Christmastime / Rudolph The Red Nosed Reindeer (Mono)	1979	2.00	10.00
Columbia 38-04127		Wonderful Christmastime / Rudolph The Red Nosed Reindeer (Stereo)	1979	4.00	20.00
Columbia AE7-1204	(DJ)	Coming Up (One sided bonus from "McCartney II" album)	1980	1.00	5.00
Columbia 11263	(DJ)	Coming Up / Coming Up	1980	3.00	15.00
Columbia 11263		Coming Up / Coming Up-Lunch Box Odd Sox	1980	.40	2.00
Columbia 11263	(PS)	Coming Up / Coming Up-Lunch Box Odd Sox	1980	.80	4.00
Columbia 11335	(DJ)	Waterfalls / Waterfalls	1980	2.00	10.00
Columbia 11335		Waterfalls / Check My Machine	1980	.80	4.00
Columbia 11335	(PS)	Waterfalls / Check My Machine	1980	4.00	20.00
Columbia 18-03018	(DJ)	Take It Away / Take It Away	1982	1.20	6.00
Columbia 18-03018	(PS)	Take It Away / Take It Away	1982	1.20	6.00
Columbia 18-03018		Take It Away / I'll Give You A Ring	1982	.40	2.00
Columbia 18-03018	(PS)	Take It Away / I'll Give You A Ring	1982	.40	2.00
Columbia 38-02325	(DJ)	Tug Of War / Tug Of War	1982	2.00	10.00
Columbia 38-02325		Tug Of War / Get It	1982	.80	4.00
Columbia 33407		My Love / Maybe I'm Amazed (Red label)	1982	1.20	6.00
Columbia 33407		My Love / Maybe I'm Amazed (Grey label)	198?	5.00	25.00
Columbia 38-04296	(DJ)	So Bad / So Bad	1983	2.00	10.00
Columbia 38-04296	(PS)	So Bad / So Bad	1983	2.00	10.00
Columbia 38-04296		So Bad / Pipes Of Peace	1983	.40	2.00
Columbia 38-04296	(PS)	So Bad / Pipes Of Peace	1983	.80	4.00
Columbia 38-04581	(DJ)	No More Lonely Nights / No More Lonely Nights	1984	2.00	10.00
Columbia 38-04581	(PS)	No More Lonely Nights / No More Lonely Nights (DJ)	1984	2.00	10.00
Columbia 38-04581		No More Lonely Nights / No More Lonely Nights (Playout Version)	1984	.40	2.00
Columbia 38-04581		No More Lonely Nights / No More Lonely Nights (Dance Mix)	1984	6.00	30.00
Columbia 38-04581	(PS)	No More Lonely Nights / No More Lonely Nights	1984	.40	2.00
Capitol PRO-9552	(DJ)	Spies Like Us / Spies Like Us	1985	2.00	10.00
Capitol B-5537		Spies Like Us / My Carnival	1985	.60	3.00
Capitol PRO-9765/6	(DJ)	Press (Long) / Press (Short)	1986	5.00	25.00
Capitol P-5597	(DJ)	Press / Press	1986	2.00	10.00
Capitol P-5597		Press / It's Not True	1986	.40	2.00
Capitol PB-5597	(PS)	Press / It's Not True	1986	.40	2.00
Capitol PB-5636	(DJ)	Stranglehold / Stranglehold	1986	2.00	10.00
Capitol B-5636		Stranglehold / Angry	1986	.60	3.00
Capitol B-5636	(PS)	Stranglehold / Angry	1986	.60	3.00
Capitol PB-5672		Only Love Remains / Only Love Remains	1987	2.00	10.00
Capitol B-5672		Only Love Remains / Tough On A Tightrope	1987	.60	3.00
Capitol B-5672	(PS)	Only Love Remains / Tough On A Tightrope	1987	.60	3.00
Capitol 7PRO-79700	(DJ)	This One / This One	1989	50.00	250.00

— 12" Singles —

Label & Catalog #		A-Side/B-Side	Year	VG	NM
Capitol 8574	(DJ)	Maybe I'm Amazed / Maybe I'm Amazed	1977	15.00	75.00
Columbia 10940	(DJ)	Goodnight Tonight (Two versions)	1979	5.00	25.00
Columbia 10940		Goodnight Tonight / Daytime, Nighttime Suffering (PC)	1979	3.00	15.00
Columbia 10940		Goodnight Tonight / Daytime, Nighttime Suffering	1979	8.00	40.00
Columbia AS-775	(DJ)	Coming Up (Two versions. White label)	1980	12.00	60.00
Columbia AS-775	(DJ)	Coming Up (Two versions. Red label)	1980	15.00	75.00
Columbia 18-03019		Take It Away / I'll Give You A Ring / Dress Me Up As A Robber (PC)	1982	2.00	10.00
Columbia AS-1940	(DJ)	No More Lonely Nights (Two versions)	1984	4.00	20.00
Columbia 8-C8-39927		No More Lonely Nights / Silly Love Songs (Picture disc issued in a clear plastic cover.)	1984	3.00	15.00
Columbia 44-05077	(DJ)	No More Lonely Nights (Two versions). Red label. PC)	1984	2.00	10.00
Columbia 44-05077		No More Lonely Nights (Two versions) / Silly Love Songs (PC)	1984	6.00	30.00

Label & Catalog #		A-Side/B-Side	Year	VG	NM
Hot Tracks SA-3-8		No More Lonely Nights	1984	30.00	150.00
Capitol PRO-9556	(DJ)	Spies Like Us (Two versions)	1985	5.00	25.00
Capitol V-15212		Spies Like Us (Three versions) / My Carnival (PC)	1985	2.00	10.00
Capitol SPRO-9763	(DJ)	Press (Two versions)	1986	4.00	20.00
Capitol V-15235		Press (Two versions) / It's Not True / Hanglide (PC)	1986	2.00	10.00
Capitol SPRO-9797	(DJ)	Angry (Two versions)	1986	4.00	20.00
Capitol B-5636	(DJ)	Stranglehold / Angry	1986	6.00	30.00
Capitol SPRO-9928	(DJ)	Pretty Little Head (Two versions)	1986	5.00	25.00
Capitol V-15499		Ou Est Le Soleil	1989	25.00	125.00
Disconet Vol. 11 #9		Ou Est Le Soleil (Three versions. PC)	1989	2.00	10.00

McCARTNEY, PAUL, & MICHAEL JACKSON

Label & Catalog #		A-Side/B-Side	Year	VG	NM
Epic 34-03288	(DJ)	The Girl Is Mine / The Girl Is Mine (Edited)	1982	5.00	25.00
Epic 34-03288	(DJ)	The Girl Is Mine / The Girl Is Mine	1982	2.50	12.00
Epic 34-03288	(PS)	The Girl Is Mine / The Girl Is Mine	1982	1.20	6.00
Epic 34-03288		The Girl Is Mine / Can't Get Outta The Rain	1982	.60	3.00
Epic ENR-03372		The Girl Is Mine (One sided)	1982	2.00	10.00
Epic 34-03288	(PS)	The Girl Is Mine / Can't Get Outta The Rain	1982	.80	4.00
Columbia 38-04168	(DJ)	Say Say Say / Say Say Say	1983	2.00	10.00
Columbia 38-04168	(PS)	Say Say Say / Say Say Say	1983	1.20	6.00
Columbia 38-04168		Say Say Say / Ode To A Koala Bear	1983	.40	2.00
Columbia 38-04168	(PS)	Say Say Say / Ode To A Koala Bear	1983	.40	2.00
		— 12" Singles—			
Columbia AS-1758	(DJ)	Say Say Say(Two versions)	1983	2.00	10.00
Columbia 44-04169	(DJ)	Say Say Say (Two versions) / Ode To A Koala Bear (PC)	1983	4.00	20.00
Columbia 44-04169		Say Say Say (Two versions) / Ode To A Koala Bear (PC)	1983	1.20	6.00

McCARTNEY, PAUL, & STEVIE WONDER

Label & Catalog #		A-Side/B-Side	Year	VG	NM
Columbia 02860	(DJ)	Ebony & Ivory / Ebony & Ivory	1982	4.00	20.00
Columbia 02860		Ebony & Ivory / Rainclouds	1982	4.00	20.00
Columbia 02860	(DJ)	Ebony And Ivory / Ebony And Ivory	1982	2.00	10.00
Columbia 02860	(PS)	Ebony And Ivory / Ebony And Ivory	1982	2.00	10.00
Columbia 02860		Ebony And Ivory / Ebony And Ivory	1982	.40	2.00
Columbia 02860	(PS)	Ebony And Ivory / Ebony And Ivory	1982	.80	4.00
		— 12" Singles—			
Columbia 02878		Ebony & Ivory (Two versions) / Rainclouds (PC)	1982	2.00	10.00

McCORMICK, GAYLE
Gayle McCormick originally recorded with Smith.

Label & Catalog #	A-Side/B-Side	Year	VG	NM
Dunhill 4281	Gonna Be Alright Now / Save Me	1971	.40	2.00
Dunhill 4288	It's A Crying Shame / If Only You Believe	1971	.40	2.00
Dunhill 4298	You Really Got A Hold On Me / C' La Vie	1972	.40	2.00
Decca 33030	Near You / Take Me Back	1972	.40	2.00
MCA 40007	Sweet Feelings (That Old Time Feeling) / Take Me Back	1973	.40	2.00
Shady-Brook 45017	Coming In Out Of The Rain / Simon Said	197?	2.00	10.00

McCORMICK, MAUREEN
Maureen McCormick was a member of The Brady Bunch.

Label & Catalog #	A-Side/B-Side	Year	VG	NM
Paramount 0246	Little Bird / Just A Singin' Alone	197?	1.60	8.00
Paramount 0292	Love's In The Roses / Harmonize	197?	1.60	8.00

McCOY, PATTY, & THE RENEGADES

Label & Catalog #	A-Side/B-Side	Year	VG	NM
Counsel 116	Goodbye / Stranger	196?	2.50	12.00
Counsel 119	I Love Him So /	196?	3.00	15.00

McCOY BOYS, THE

Label & Catalog #	A-Side/B-Side	Year	VG	NM
Verve 10208	Reprieve Of Love / Our Man In Havana	1960	2.00	10.00

McCOYS, THE

Label & Catalog #	A-Side/B-Side	Year	VG	NM
RCA Victor 47-7204	Our Love Goes On And On / Daddy's Geisha Girl	1958	3.00	15.00
RCA Victor 47-7354	Full Grown Cat / Throwing Kisses	1958	4.00	20.00

McCOYS, THE
The McCoys feature Rick Zehringer, who later recorded as Rick Derringer.

Label & Catalog #	A-Side/B-Side	Year	VG	NM
Bang 506	Hang On Sloopy / I Can't Explain It	1965	1.60	8.00
Bang 511	Fever / Sorrow	1965	1.20	6.00
Bang 516	Up And Down / If I Tell You A Lie	1966	1.00	5.00
Bang 522	Come On, Let's Go / Little People	1966	1.00	5.00
Bang 527	(You Make Me Feel) So Good / Runaway	1966	1.00	5.00
Bang 532	Don't Worry Mother, Your Son's Heart Is Pure / Ko-Ko	1966	2.00	10.00
Bang 538	I Got To Go Back (And Watch That Little Girl Dance) / Dynamite	1967	1.00	5.00
Bang 543	Beat The Clock / Like You Do To Me	1967	1.00	5.00
Bang 549	Say Those Magic Words / I Wonder If She Remembers Me	1967	1.00	5.00
Mercury 72843	Jesse Brady / Resurrection	1968	.80	4.00
Mercury 72917	Only Human / Love Don't Stop	1968	.80	4.00

Label & Catalog #		A-Side/B-Side	Year	VG	NM
McCREA, JODY					
Canjo 106		Chicken Surfer / Looney Gooney Bird	1964	7.00	35.00
McDONALD, JOE: *Refer to* COUNTRY JOE (McDONALD)					
McDONALD, SKEETS					
Capitol 3461		You Oughta See Grandma Rock / Heart Brake Mama	1958	10.00	50.00
McFADDEN, BOB					
Bob McFadden is a pseudonym for Rod McKuen.					
Coral 62209		Dracula Cha Cha / The Transylvania Polka	195?	3.00	15.00
McFADDEN, BOB & DOR					
Brunswick 55120		Frankie And Igor At A Rock And Roll Party /			
		Children Cross The Bridge	1959	4.00	20.00
Brunswick 55140		The Mummy / The Beat Generation	1959	4.00	20.00
Brunswick 55140	(PS)	The Mummy / The Beat Generation	1959	6.00	30.00
McFARLAND, GARY					
Jazz interpretations from the Fab's first flick.					
Verve 1342		A Hard Day's Night / And I Love Her	1964	1.20	6.00
McGEE, JERRY					
Jerry McGee also recorded with The Ventures.					
Pacemaker 236		Twilight Zone / I Wonder	196?	6.00	30.00
Reprise 20057		Walkin' / Blues Train	1962	3.00	15.00
Reprise 20098		Solitude / Jam Up	1963	3.00	15.00
Reprise 20156		On The Rebound / Unknown Soldier	1963	3.00	15.00
A&M 771		Moonlight Surfin' / Cajun Guitar	1965	3.00	15.00
McGILL, JERRY & THE TOP COATS					
Sun 326		I Wanna Make Sweet Love / Love Struck	1959	4.00	20.00
McGUINN, ROGER (& THUNDERBYRD)					
Roger McGuinn also recorded with The Byrds.					
Columbia 45931		Draggin' / Time Cube	1973	.40	2.00
Columbia 10019		Same Old Sound / Gate Of Horn	1974	.40	2.00
Columbia 10044		Peace On You / Without You	1975	.40	2.00
Columbia 10181		Somebody Loves You / Easy Does It	1975	.40	2.00
Columbia 10201		Lover Of The Bayou / Easy Does It	1976	.40	2.00
Columbia 10385		Take Me Away / Friend	1976	.40	2.00
Columbia 10543		American Girl / I'm Not Lonely Anymore	1977	.40	2.00
Columbia SP-284	(DJ)	The World Turns All Around Her /			
		He Was A Friend Of Mine	197?	1.00	5.00
McGUINN, CLARK & HILLMAN					
Roger McGuinn, Gene Clark, and Chris Hillman, former Byrds all.					
Capitol 4693		Don't You Write Her Off / Sad Boy	1979	.30	1.50
Capitol 4739		Surrender To Me / Little Mama	1979	.30	1.50
Capitol 4763		Backstage Pass / Bye, Bye Baby	1979	.30	1.50
Capitol 4821		One More Chance / Street Talk	1979	.30	1.50
Capitol 4855		City / Deeper In	1979	.30	1.50
McGUINN & HILLMAN					
Capitol 4952		Making Movies / Turn Your Radio On	1980	.30	1.50
Capitol 4973		King For A Night / Love Me Tonight	1980	.30	1.50
McGUINNESS-FLINT					
Capitol 3014		When I'm Dead And Gone / Lazy Afternoon	1970	.60	3.00
Capitol 3139		Rock On / Malt And Barley Blues	1971	.60	3.00
Capitol 3186		Happy Birthday, Ruby Baby / Friends Of Mine	1971	.60	3.00
McGUIRE, BARRY					
Dunhill 4009		Eve Of Destruction / What's Exactly The Matter With You?	1965	1.60	8.00
Dunhill 4014		Child Of Our Times / Upon A Painted Ocean	1965	1.20	6.00
Dunhill 4014	(PS)	Child Of Our Times / Upon A Painted Ocean	1965	2.00	10.00
Dunhill 4019		Don't You Wonder Where It's At? / This Precious Time	1966	.80	4.00
Dunhill 4028		Cloudy Summer Afternoon (Raindrops) /			
		I'd Have To Be Outta My Mind	1966	1.00	5.00
Dunhill 4048		There's Nothing Else On My Mind /			
		Why Not Stop And Dig It?	1966	.80	4.00
Dunhill 4098		Masters Of War / Stop Now And Dig It While You Can	1967	.80	4.00
Dunhill 4116		Inner Manipulations / Lollipop Train	1968	.80	4.00
Dunhill 4124		Grasshopper Song / Top O' The Hill	1968	1.20	6.00
Dunhill 4124	(PS)	Grasshopper Song / Top O' The Hill	1968	1.20	6.00
		—Extended Play Albums—			
Dunhill DS-50005		This Precious Time (Jukebox EP)	1967	4.00	20.00

Label & Catalog #	A-Side/B-Side	Year	VG	NM
McKEE, RON, & THE RIVIERES				
Lincoln 710	Jailhouse Rock / Summertime Fun	1964	2.00	10.00
McKENZIE, SCOTT				
Scott McKenzie was formerly a member of The Journeymen.				
Capitol 5348	Look In Your Eyes / There Stands The Glass	1965	1.00	5.00
Capitol 5500	Wipe The Tears (From Your Face) / There Stands The Glass	1967	1.00	5.00
Capitol 5961	All I Want Is You / Look In Your Eyes	1967	1.00	5.00
Epic 10124	No No No No No / I Want To Be Alone	1967	.80	4.00
Ode 103	San Francisco (Be Sure To Wear Some Flowers In Your Hair) / What's The Difference?	1967	1.00	5.00
Ode 105	Like An Old Time Movie / What's The Difference, Chapter 2	1967	.80	4.00
Ode 107	Holy Man / What's The Difference, Chapter 2	1968	.80	4.00
Ode 66012	Going Home Again / Take A Moment	1970	.80	4.00
McKUEN, ROD				
Refer to Bob & Dor McFadden.				
Spiral 1407	Oliver Twist / Celebrity Twist	1962	2.00	10.00
Jubilee 5420	Oliver Twist Meets The Duke Of Oil / Steel Men	1962	2.00	10.00
McLAIN, TOMMY				
Jin 197	Sweet Dreams / I Need You So	1966	2.00	10.00
MSL 197	Sweet Dreams / I Need You So	1966	1.00	5.00
MSL 209	I Can't Take It No More / Think It Over	1966	1.00	5.00
McLEAN, PHIL				
Versatile 107	Small Sad Sam / Chicken	1961	2.00	10.00
McNATTI, DON				
Wasp 101	Diary Of Heartaches / Foggy River	196?	1.00	5.00
McVOY, CARL				
Phillips Inter. 3526	Tootsie / You Are My Sunshine	1958	3.00	15.00
ME & DEM GUYS				
Dearborn 500	Black Cloud / Don't You Just Know It	1966	3.00	15.00
Palmer 5007	Black Cloud / Come On, Little Sweetheart	1966	2.00	10.00
ME & THEM				
U.S. Songs 601	Everything I Do Is Wrong / Show You Mean It To Me	196?	2.00	10.00
MEADOWS, LARRY				
Stratolite 969	Phyllis / We're Through	195?	7.00	35.00
MEANS, KEITH, & THE KNIGHTERS				
Rena 3001	Sham-Bam / Sham-Bam (Part 2)	1961	2.00	10.00
MEANTIME				
Meantime features Ellie Greenwich.				
Atco 6524	Friday Kind Of Monday / Right Back	1967	2.00	10.00
MEDALLIONS, THE [MEDALIONS]				
Sultan 1004	Love That Girl / Carachi	1959	4.00	20.00
Card 1	Love Letters / Since You've Gone Away (Card 1 credits The Medalions.)	1960	4.00	20.00
Singular 1002	A Broken Heart / Lolo Baby	196?	3.00	15.00
MEDICINE HEAD				
Polydor 15083	Rising Son / Be My Flyer	1970	.80	4.00
Elektra 45741	(And The) Pictures In The Sky / Natural Sight	1971	.80	4.00
MEDLEY, BILL				
Bill also recorded with The Clouds; The Paramours; and The Righteous Brothers, where his first "solo" single is listed..				
MGM 13931	I Can't Make It Alone / One Day Girl	1968	.80	4.00
MGM 13959	Brown-Eyed Woman / Let The Good Times Roll	1968	.80	4.00
MGM 1400	Peace, Brother, Peace / Winter Won't Come This Year	1968	.80	4.00
MGM 14025	Something's So Wrong / This Is A Love Song	1969	.60	3.00
MGM 14081	Someone Is Standing Outside / Reaching Back	1969	.60	3.00
MGM 14099	Let Me Love Again / Eve	1969	.60	3.00
MGM 14119	Hold On, I'm Comin' / Makin' My Way	1969	.60	3.00
MGM 14145	Nobody Knows / Something's So Wrong	1970	.60	3.00
MGM 14179	Gone / What Have You Got To Love?	1970	.60	3.00
MGM 14202	Gone / Wasn't It Easy?	1970	.60	3.00
A&M 1311	We've Only Just Begun / A Song For You	1971	.80	4.00
A&M 1336	Hung On You / Help Me Make It Through The Night	1971	.60	3.00
A&M 1350	Freedom For The Stallion / Damn Good Friend	1972	.80	4.00
A&M 1371	Missing You Too Long / Simple Man	1972	.60	3.00
A&M 1434	It's Not Easy / Put A Little Love Away	1972	.60	3.00

Label & Catalog #		A-Side/B-Side	Year	VG	NM
United Artists 1256		Lay A Little Lovin' On Me / Wasn't That You Last Night?	197?	.60	3.00
United Artists 1270		Statue Of A Fool / Wasn't That You Last Night?	197?	.60	3.00
United Artists 1349		Hello, Rock And Roll / Still A Fool	197?	.60	3.00
Liberty 1402		Don't Know Much / Woman	1981	.60	3.00
Liberty 1412		Stay The Night / Grandma & Grandpa	1981	.60	3.00
Planet 13317		Right Here And Now /	1982	.60	3.00

MEDLIN, JOE

Mercury 71415		I Kneel At Your Throne / Out Of Sight, Out Of Mind	1959	2.00	10.00

MEEP MEEP & THE ROADRUNNERS

Boomerang 651		Justine / A-Flat Blues	196?	2.00	10.00

MEGATONS, THE

Dodge 808		Shimmy Shimmy Walk / Shimmy Shimmy Walk, Part 2	1962	2.00	10.00
Checker 1002		Shimmy Shimmy Walk / Shimmy Shimmy Walk, Part 2	1962	1.20	6.00

MELANIE (SAFKA)

Label & Catalog #		A-Side/B-Side	Year	VG	NM
Columbia 44349		My Beautiful People / God's Only Daughter	1967	1.20	6.00
Columbia 44349	(PS)	My Beautiful People / God's Only Daughter	1967	3.00	15.00
Columbia 44524		Why Didn't My Mother Tell Me / Garden In	1967	1.20	6.00
Columbia 44524	(PS)	Why Didn't My Mother Tell Me / Garden In	1967	3.00	15.00
Buddah 167		Lay Down (Candles In The Rain) / Candles In The Rain	1970	.60	3.00
Buddah 167	(PS)	Lay Down (Candles In The Rain) / Candles In The Rain	1970	.60	3.00
Buddah 186		Peace Will Come (According To Plan) / Stop! (I Don't Wanna Hear It Anymore)	1970	.60	3.00
Buddah 186	(PS)	Peace Will Come (According To Plan) / Stop! (I Don't Wanna Hear It Anymore)	1970	.60	3.00
Buddah 186-1	(DJ)	Stop! (I Don't Wanna Hear It Anymore) / Stop! (I Don't Wanna Hear It Anymore)	1970	.60	3.00
Buddah 202		Ruby Tuesday / Merry Christmas	1970	.60	3.00
Buddah 224		The Good Book / We Don't Know Where We're Going	1971	.40	2.00
Buddah 268		The Nickel Song / What Have They Done To My Song Ma?	1972	.40	2.00
Buddah 268	(PS)	The Nickel Song / What Have They Done To My Song Ma?	1972	.60	3.00
Buddah 304		I'm Back In Town / Johnny Boy	1972?	.40	2.00
Buddah		Melanie Picture Sleeve	196?	.80	4.00
		(Non-titled, omnibus sleeve for use with any of the Buddah singles.)			
Stork	(DJ)	Timothy Scott Bogart (One sided)	1970	2.00	10.00
		(Melanie sings "Christopher Robin" for label executive's son.)			
Neighborhood 4201		Brand New Key / Some Say (I Got The Devil)	1971	.60	3.00
Neighborhood 4202		Ring The Living Bell / Railroad	1972	.60	3.00
Neighborhood 4202	(PS)	Ring The Living Bell / Railroad	1972	.60	3.00
Neighborhood 4204		Some Say I'll Be A Farmer / Steppin'	1972	.40	2.00
Neighborhood 4207	(DJ)	Together Alone / Center Of The Circle	1972	1.00	5.00
		(Original promos of 4207 are technically defective.)			
Neighborhood 4207	(DJ)	Together Alone / Center Of The Circle	1972	1.00	5.00
		(Later promos of 4207 are technically correct and identical to commercial version.)			
Neighborhood 4207	(PS)	Together Alone / Center Of The Circle (Promo)	1972	1.00	5.00
		(Promo sleeve accompanying reissue promo single reads "This is the new pressing-please destroy the previous copy.)			
Neighborhood 4207		Together Alone / Center Of The Circle	1972	.40	2.00
Neighborhood 4207	(PS)	Together Alone / Center Of The Circle	1972	.60	3.00
Neighborhood 4210		Bitter Bad / Do You Believe?	1973	.40	2.00
Neighborhood 4210	(PS)	Bitter Bad / Do You Believe?	1973	.60	3.00
Neighborhood 4212		Seeds / Some Say (I Got The Devil)	1973	.40	2.00
Neighborhood 4212	(PS)	Seeds / Some Say (I Got The Devil)	1973	.60	3.00
Neighborhood 4213		Will You Love Me Tomorrow? / Here I Am	1973	.40	2.00
Neighborhood 4213	(PS)	Will You Love Me Tomorrow? / Here I Am	1973	.60	3.00
Neighborhood 4214		Love To Lose Again / Pine And Lose	1974	.40	2.00
Neighborhood 4214	(PS)	Love To Lose Again / Pine And Lose	1974	.60	3.00
Neighborhood 10000		You're Not A Bad Ghost, Just An Old Song / Eyes Of Man	1975	.40	2.00
Neighborhood 10001		Sweet Misery / Record Machine	1975	.40	2.00
Gordian 1947	(DJ)	Rag Doll / Rag Doll	197?	1.00	5.00
Atlantic 3380		Cyclone / If I Needed You	1977	.40	2.00
Midsong Int. 40858		I'd Rather Leave While I'm In Love / Record People	1978	.40	2.00
Midsong Int. 40903		Knock On Wood / Record People	1978	.40	2.00
Tomato 10007		Morning After Love / Holding Out	1978	.40	2.00
Portrait 51001		One More Try / Apathy	1981	.40	2.00
		—Extended Play Albums—			
Buddah SP-2	(33)	I'm Back In Town (Jukebox EP)	197?	2.00	10.00

MELCHER, TERRY

Refer to Bruce & Terry; California; Terry Day; The Osmond Brothers; The Rogues.

RCA-Equinox NB-10587	(DJ)	Fire In A Rainstorm / So Right Tonight	1976	1.00	5.00
RCA-Equinox NB-10587		Fire In A Rainstorm / So Right Tonight	1976	2.00	10.00
		(Features Bruce Johnston.)			

Melanie Safka remains a very minor footnote in pop music annals, but an enjoyable note. As recent appearances show, she has retained her effervescent outlook on life and, while the pipes are a little ragged around the edges, she sings with the same enthusiasm and infectiousness of her best hits.

Label & Catalog #	A-Side/B-Side	Year	VG	NM

MELCHER, TERRY, & BRUCE JOHNSTON
| RCA-Equinox NB-10238 *(DJ)* | Take It To Mexico / Rebecca | 1975 | 1.00 | 5.00 |
| RCA-Equinox NB-10238 | Take It To Mexico / Rebecca | 1975 | 2.00 | 10.00 |

MELLO-HARPS, THE
| Casino 104 | Gumma Gumma / No Good | 1958 | 6.00 | 30.00 |

MELO-GENTS, THE
| Warner Bros. 5056 | Baby, Be Mine / Get Off My Back | 1959 | 8.00 | 40.00 |

MELLODEERS, THE
| Shelley 127 | The Letter / Nairna, Nairna | 1961 | 3.00 | 15.00 |
| Shelley 161 | Born To Be Mine / Three Deuces And Twin Pipes | 1962 | 8.00 | 40.00 |

MELLOKINGS, THE [THE MELLO-KINGS]
Herald 502	Tonite Tonite / Do, Baby, Do	1957	40.00	200.00
	(First pressings credit The Mellokings on a yellow label with script print.)			
Herald 502	Tonite Tonite / Do, Baby, Do	1957	8.00	40.00
	(Second pressings credit The Mellotones on a yellow label with script print.)			
Herald 502	Tonite Tonite / Do, Baby, Do	1962	5.00	25.00
	(Third pressings credit The Mellokings on a yellow label with block print.)			
Herald 507	Chapel On The Hill / Sassafras	1957	10.00	50.00
Herald 511	Baby, Tell Me Why, Why, Why / The Only Girl	1957	6.00	30.00
Herald 518	Valerie / She's Real Cool	1957	6.00	30.00
	— Original Herald singles above have yellow labels with script print.—			
Herald 536	Running To You / Chip Chip	1959	5.00	25.00
Herald 548	Our Love Is Beautiful / Dear Mr. Jock	1960	5.00	25.00
	—Original Herald singles above have multi-color labels.—			
Herald 554	Kid Stuff / I Promise	1960	5.00	25.00
Herald 561	Penny / Till There Were None	1961	5.00	25.00
Herald 567	Love At First Sight / She's Real Cool	1961	5.00	25.00
Lescay 3009	But You Lied / Walk Softly	1962	6.00	30.00
	(Lescay 3009 credited to The Mello-Kings.)			

MELLOS, THE: *Refer to* TERRY & THE MELLOS

MELLOTONES, THE: *Refer to* THE MELLOKINGS

MELO GENTS, THE
| Warner Bros. 5056 | Baby, Be Mine / Git Off My Back | 1959 | 3.00 | 15.00 |

MELODEARS, THE
| Gone 5033 | Summer Romance / Charock | 1958 | 3.00 | 15.00 |
| Gone 5040 | It's Love Because / They Don't Say | 1958 | 3.00 | 15.00 |

MELODEERS, THE
| Studio 9908 | Wishing Is For Fools / Rudolph The Red Nosed Reindeer | 1960 | 2.00 | 10.00 |
| Studio 9908 *(PS)* | Wishing Is For Fools / Rudolph The Red Nosed Reindeer | 1960 | 3.00 | 15.00 |

MELODEERS, THE: *Refer to* TONY THOMAS & THE MELODEERS

MELODY CHASERS, THE
| Hickman 1 | You've Got A Heart Of Stone / Boat Of Love | 196? | 2.00 | 10.00 |

MELODY MAKERS, THE
| Hollis 1001 | Let's Make Love Worthwhile / | 195? | 40.00 | 100.00 |

MELTON, LEVY, & THE DEY BROTHERS
Mercury 72860	S. O. S. / S. O. S.	1968	.80	4.00
Mercury 73008	Them Changes / Spot On The Wall	1969	.80	4.00
Mercury 73205	Wholesale Love / Wholesale Love	1969	.80	4.00
Mercury 73170	I Still Love You Anyway / Runaway Child	1969	.80	4.00

MEMBERS, THE
| Label 101 | Jenny Jenny / | 196? | 2.00 | 10.00 |

MEMORIES, THE
Way-Lin 101	Love Bells / I Promise	195?	100.00	400.00
	(First pressing labels have normal print.)			
Way-Lin 101	Love Bells / I Promise	195?	50.00	200.00
	(Second pressing labels have lop-sided print.)			

MENAGERIE, THE
| Vision 1003 | Telephone Song / Love The Thing | 196? | 1.20 | 6.00 |

MENG, JIMMY
| Jay Em 1000 | True And Faithful / Don't Be Blue | 1961 | 3.00 | 15.00 |
| Liberty 55346 | True And Faithful / Don't Be Blue | 1961 | 2.00 | 10.00 |

Label & Catalog #	A-Side/B-Side	Year	VG	NM
MERCER, WALLY				
Dot 1099	Rock Around The Clock / Don't Wait Till Tomorrow	1952	20.00	100.00
MERCER, WILL				
Sun 329	You're Just My Kind / Ballad Of St. Marks	1959	3.00	15.00
MERCY				
Sundi 6811	Love (Can Make You Happy) / Fire Ball	1969	.80	3.00
Warner Bros. 7297	Forever / The Morning's Come	1969	.40	2.00
Warner Bros. 7331	Hello, Baby / Heard You Went Away	1969	.40	2.00
MERCY BOYS, THE				
Panorama 24	Mercy, Mercy / Lost And Found	1965	1.20	6.00
Panorama 45	Long, Tall Shorty / This Girl	1966	1.20	6.00
Merrilin 5300	Spoonful / Gimme Gimme	1967	1.20	6.00
MERLIN, JACK				
Dot 16332	Girl Of My Dreams / I Beat The Blues	1962	4.00	20.00
MERRI-MEN, THE				
The Merri-Men is a pseudonym for members of Bill Haley's Comets. Refer to The Kingsmen; The Lifeguards.				
Apt 25051	Big Daddy / St. Louis Blues	1961	3.00	15.00
MERRIT, JERRY, & THE CROWNS				
Lavender 1670	Kansas City Twist / Walkin'	1961	2.00	10.00
Lavender 1676	Bass Fever / Lost	1961	2.00	10.00
Fury 100	Liverpool Town / Remember That Day	1966	2.00	10.00
American 3366	Liverpool Town / Remember That Day	1966	1.20	6.00
Tell International 370	Buffalo Grass / Every Man Needs An Island	196?	1.00	5.00
MERRY ELVES, THE (MILTON, SLEEPY & RINGO)				
Argus 250	Rock And Roll Around The Christmas Tree / I Love Christmas	1964	3.00	15.00
MERRY GO ROUND				
Piccadilly 254	Land Of Odin / Got-Ta Got-Ta	1968	2.00	10.00
MERRY-GO-ROUND, THE				
The Merry-Go-Round features Emitt Rhodes.				
A&M 834	Live / Time Will Show You The Wiser	1967	1.60	8.00
A&M 857	We're In Love / Gonna Fight The War	1967	1.00	5.00
A&M 863	You're A Very Lovely Woman / Where Have You Been All My Life?	1967	1.60	8.00
A&M 899	Come Ride, Come Ride / She Laughed Loud	1967	1.00	5.00
A&M 920	Gonna Leave You Alone / Listen, Listen	1967	1.00	5.00
MERSEY LADS, THE				
MGM 13481	Whatcha' Gonna Do, Baby? / Johnny No Love	1966	2.00	10.00
MERSEY SOUNDS, THE				
Montel 966	Get On Your Honda And Ride / Honda Holiday	1966	2.00	10.00
MERSEYBEATS, THE				
Fontana 1882	Mister Moonlight / I Think Of You	1964	2.00	10.00
Fontana 1905	Don't Turn Around / Really Mystified	1964	2.00	10.00
Fontana 1950	See Me Back / Last Night	1964	2.00	10.00
Fontana 1513	Don't Let It Happen To Us / It Would Take A Long Time	1965	2.00	10.00
Fontana 1532	I Love You, Yes I Do / See Me Back	1965	2.00	10.00
MERSEYBOYS, THE				
Panorama 24	Mercy, Mercy / Lost And Found	1964	2.00	10.00
MERSEYS, THE				
Mercury 72582	Sorrow / Some Other Day	1966	2.00	10.00
MESSENGERS, THE				
Soul 35037	Window Shopping / California Soul	1967	.80	4.00
Rare Earth 5032	That's The Way A Woman Is / In The Jungle	1971	.80	4.00
MESSINA, JIM, & THE DRAGSTERS				
Jim Messina also recorded with The Jesters and The Buffalo Springfield.				
Ultima 705	Drag Bike Boogie / A-Rab	1964	5.00	25.00
Feature 101	Panther Pounce / Tiger Tail	1964	4.00	20.00
Audio Fidelity 98	The Breeze And I / Strange Man	1964	5.00	25.00
Viv 1000	Side Track / Sherrie	1965	3.00	15.00
METIS, FRANK				
Mayflower 20	The Wiggle / Sweet Perfume	1959	2.00	10.00

Label & Catalog #	A-Side/B-Side	Year	VG	NM
METROS, THE				
Just 1502	Lookin' / All Of My Life	195?	30.00	150.00
MICHAEL, HARLAN				
Burdette 116	Colors Of Love / For The Likes Of You And Me	196?	2.00	10.00
Era 3173	Day Sleeper / Tell Me	196?	2.00	10.00
MICHAEL, J., & THE BUSHMAN				
Corby 207	I Need Love / Little John's Revenge	196?	2.00	10.00
MICHAEL & THE CONTINENTALS				
Audio Fidelity 139	Rain In My Eyes / Little School Girl	1965	4.00	20.00
MICHAEL & THE MESSENGERS				
U.S.A. 866	In The Midnight Hour / Hard, Hard Year	1967	1.00	5.00
U.S.A. 874	Romeo And Juliet / Life (Don't Mean A Thing)	1967	1.00	5.00
U.S.A. 889	Run And Hide / She Was The Girl	1967	1.00	5.00
U.S.A. 897	Gotta Take It Easy / I Need Her Here	1968	1.00	5.00
MICHAELS, DANNY, & THE REBEL PLAYBOYS				
Chambers 200	Give The Ball To Calhoun / Chavez Ravine	1964	7.00	35.00
MICHEL, TIFFANY				
MGM 13624	Come Closer / Dixie	1966	2.00	10.00
MICKEY & BONNIE				
Jerden 717	Boys Will Be Boys / We Fell In Love	1963	1.00	5.00
Jerden 723	Ma, He's Making Eyes At Me / Test Of Love	1963	.80	4.00
MID-AMERICANS, THE				
Teardrop 3103	Lonely Surfer / Lucille	196?	6.00	30.00
Pablo 7014	Lonely Surfer / (B-side by Bonnie & The Treasures)	196?	6.00	30.00
MIDNIGHT ANGELS, THE				
Apex 77073	I'm Sufferin' / In The Moonlight	196?	2.00	10.00
MIDNIGHT SONS, THE				
KG 100	Draft Time Blues /	1966	3.00	15.00
MIGHTY ACCENTS, THE				
Rodala 69	Sabre Stomp / I Don't Want To	196?	2.00	10.00
MIGHTY AVENGERS, THE				
Press 9746	When Blue Turns To Grey / I'm Lost Without You	1965	2.00	10.00
MIKE & LULU				
Top Rank 2036	Baby Talk / Baby's Lullabye	1960	2.00	10.00
MIKE & THE RAVENS				
Empire 1	I've Taken All I Can / Mr. Heartbreak	196?	3.00	15.00
MIKE & THE UTOPIANS				
Cee Jay 574	I Wish / Erlene	195?	35.00	175.00
Cee Jay 574	I Found A Penny / Erlene	195?	15.00	75.00
	("I Found A Penny" is the same song as "I Wish.")			
MIKE, JOHN & BILL				
Features Michael Nesmith.				
Omnibus 239	How Can You Kiss Me?/ Just A Little Love	1963	5.00	25.00
MIKKELSON, DON, & THE BIRDS				
Deck 600	Chapel Of Love / Where I Came In	196?	6.00	30.00
MILAM, GEORGE, & BUZZ ELLIOT				
Lavender 2003	Preacher And The Girl / Let The Sad Times Roll On	196?	1.20	6.00
MILES, GARY				
Liberty 55261	Look For A Star / Afraid Of Love	1960	3.00	15.00
Liberty 55261 (PS)	Look For A Star / Afraid Of Love	1960	6.00	30.00
	—Extended Play Albums—			
Liberty LSX-1005	Look For A Star	1960	8.00	40.00
MILES, GARY, & THE STATUES				
Refer to The Statues.				
Liberty 55279	Dream Girl / Wishing Well	1960	3.00	15.00

Label & Catalog #	A-Side/B-Side	Year	VG	NM
MILES, LENNY				
Scepter 1212	Don't Believe Him, Donna / Invisible	1961	2.00	10.00
Scepter 1218	In Between Tears / I Know Love	1961	2.00	10.00
MILES EXPRESS, BUDDY				
Mercury 72903	'69 Freedom Special / Miss Lady	1968	.60	3.00
Mercury 72945	Memphis Train / My Chant	1969	.40	2.00
Mercury 73008	Them Changes /	1970	.40	2.00
Mercury 73086	Down By The River / Heart's Delight	1970	.40	2.00
Mercury 73119	Dreams / Your Feeling Is Mine	1970	.40	2.00
Mercury 73159	We Got To Live Together / We Got To Live Together, Part 2	1970	.40	2.00
Mercury 73205	Wholesale Love / That's The Way Life Is	1971	.40	2.00
MILK				
Milk features Johnny Cymbal.				
Buddah 80	Angela Jones / Ochiltree	1968	1.20	6.00
MILKY WAY, THE				
Capitol 2453	Sunshine Daffodils / Your Love Comes Shinin' Through	1969	1.00	5.00
MILKY WAYS, THE				
Liberty 55255	Teenage Island / My Love	1960	3.00	15.00
MILLENIUM				
Millennium, a Gary Usher creation, features Curt Boetcher and Lee Mallory.				
Columbia 44546	It's You / I Just Want To Be Your Friend	1968	1.00	5.00
Columbia 44546 (PS)	It's You / I Just Want To Be Your Friend	1968	3.00	15.00
Columbia 44607	5 A.M. / Prelude	1968	1.00	5.00
Columbia 44674	To Claudia On Thursday / There Is Nothing More To Say	1968	1.00	5.00
MILLER, CLINT				
ABC-Paramount 9878	Bertha Lou / Doggone It, Baby, I'm In Love	1958	4.00	20.00
ABC-Paramount 9979	A Lover's Prayer / No, Never My Love	1958	3.00	15.00
MILLER, HAL, & THE RAYS				
Topix 6003	An Angel Cried / Hope Faith And Dreams	1961	4.00	20.00
	("An Angel Cried" features The Four Seasons.)			
MILLER, MIKE, & JACK CASEY				
Cameo 137	Don't Mess Up My Hair / I Need You	1957	3.00	15.00
MILLER, STEVE [THE STEVE MILLER BAND]				
The original Steve Miller [Blues] Band (1967-69) consisted of James Cooke, Tim Davis, Steve Miller, Jim Peterman, Lonnie Turner and Ben Sidran, who replaced Peterman and Scaggs in 1968. Refer to The Goldberg-Miller Blues Band.				
Capitol 2156	Sittin' In Circles / Roll With It	1967	1.20	6.00
Capitol 2156 (PS)	Sittin' In Circles / Roll With It	1967	4.00	20.00
Capitol 2287	Living In The U.S.A. / Quicksilver Girl	1968	1.20	6.00
Capitol 2447	Sittin' In Circles / Roll With It	1969	1.00	5.00
Capitol 2520	My Dark Hour / Song For Our Ancestors	1969	1.00	5.00
Capitol 2638	Don't Let Nobody Turn You Around / Little Girl	1969	1.00	5.00
Capitol 2878	Going To The Country / Never Kill Another Man	1970	.80	4.00
Capitol 2945	Midnight Tango / Going To Mexico	1970	.80	4.00
Capitol 3228	Rock Love / Let Me Serve You	1971	.80	4.00
Capitol 3344	Fandango / Love's Riddle	1972	.80	4.00
Capitol 3732	The Joker / Something To Believe In	1973	.40	2.00
Capitol 3837	Your Cash Ain't Nothin' But Trash / Evil	1974	.40	2.00
Capitol 3884	Living In The U.S.A. / Kow Kow Calculator	1974	.40	2.00
Capitol 4260	Take The Money And Run / Sweet Maree	1976	.40	2.00
Capitol 4323	Rock 'N Me / Living In The U.S.A.	1976	.40	2.00
Capitol 4372	Fly Like An Eagle / Lovin' Cup	1976	.40	2.00
Capitol 4424	Jet Airliner / Babes In The Wood	1977	.40	2.00
Capitol 4466	Jungle Love / Wish Upon A Star	1977	.40	2.00
Capitol 4496	Swingtown / Winter Song	1977	.40	2.00
Capitol 5068	Heart Like A Wheel / True Fine Love	1981	.20	1.00
Capitol 5068 (PS)	Heart Like A Wheel / True Fine Love	1981	.20	1.00
Capitol 5126	Abracadabra / Give It Up	1982	.20	1.00
Capitol 5126 (PS)	Abracadabra / Give It Up	1982	.20	1.00
MILLER, WALTER				
United Artists 104	Everybody's Got A Baby But Me / Say You'll Be True	1959	10.00	50.00
MILLER SISTERS, THE				
Herald 455	Hippity Ha / Until You're Mine	1955	10.00	50.00
Flip 504	I Knew You Would / Someday You Will Pay	1955	30.00	150.00
Sun 504	I Knew You Would / Someday You Will Pay	1955	25.00	125.00
Sun 230	There's No Right Way To Do Me Wrong / You Can Tell Me	1956	10.00	50.00
Sun 255	Ten Cats Down / Finders Keepers	1956	10.00	50.00
Ember 1004	Guess Who? / How Am I To Know?	1956	5.00	25.00

Label & Catalog #		A-Side/B-Side	Year	VG	NM
Acme 111		The Flip Skip / Let's Start Anew	1957	5.00	25.00
Acme 717		Crazy Billboard Song / You Made Me A Promise	1957	5.00	25.00
Acme 721		The Flip Skip / Let's Start Anew	195?	3.00	15.00
Onyx 507		My own / Sugar Candy	1957	5.00	25.00
Miller 1140		Oh Lover / Remember That?	1960	3.00	15.00
Miller 1141		Pony Dance / Give Me Some Old Fashioned Love	1960	3.00	15.00
Glodis 1003		You Got To Reap What You Sow / Pop Your Finger	1961	3.00	15.00
Hull 718		Do You Wanna Go? / Please Don't Leave	1961	3.00	15.00
Hull 736		Just Wait And See / (B-side by Leo Price)	1962	3.00	15.00
Hull 750		Don't You Forget / Roll Back The Rug	1962	3.00	15.00
		(Hull 750 credits Jeannie & The Miller Sisters.)			
Hull 752		Hully Gully Reel / I Cried All Night	1962	3.00	15.00
Riverside 4535		Dance Close / Tell Him	1962	3.00	15.00
Roulette 4491		Baby Your Baby / Silly Girl	1963	2.00	10.00
Stardust 3001		Cooncha / Feel Good	1964	1.00	5.00
Yorktown 75		Looking Over My Life / Si Senor	1965	1.00	5.00
GMC 10006		I'm Telling It Like It Is /	1967	1.00	5.00
		Until You Come Home I'll Walk Alone			

MILLET, LOU

Label & Catalog #		A-Side/B-Side	Year	VG	NM
Ace 506		Just You And Me / Whisper Of Doubt	1955	30.00	150.00
Ace 510		My Inlaws Made An Outlaw Out Of Me / Humming Bird	1955	10.00	50.00
Republic 7130		Slip Slippin' In / Shorty The Barber	1956	15.00	75.00

MILLINGTON
Millington features Jean and June Millington, formerly Fanny.

Label & Catalog #		A-Side/B-Side	Year	VG	NM
United Artists 1045		Love Brought Us Together / Young And In Love	1977	.80	4.00
United Artists 1143	(DJ)	Ladies On The Stage / Ladies On The Stage	1978	.80	4.00
		(Stock copies of U.A. 1143 may not exist.)			

MILLIONAIRES, THE

Label & Catalog #		A-Side/B-Side	Year	VG	NM
Bunny 506		Cherry Baby / I Thought About You	1965	3.00	15.00
Big Bunny 508		Breakdown / The Party	1966	3.00	15.00
Philips 40435		A Rather Hip Thing / I'd Rather Do It Myself	1967	1.00	5.00
Philips 40477		If I Had You, Babe / Never For Me	1967	1.00	5.00
Specialty 694		And The Rains Came / Coffee And Donuts	1969	1.00	5.00
Specialty 719		Love Is Strange / It Ain't No Achievement	1971	.60	3.00

MILLS, GARY

Label & Catalog #		A-Side/B-Side	Year	VG	NM
Imperial 5674		Look For A Star / Look For A Star (Part 2)	1960	3.00	15.00

MILLS, HAYLEY

Label & Catalog #		A-Side/B-Side	Year	VG	NM
Buena Vista 385		Let's Get Together / Cobbler, Cobbler	1961	1.20	6.00
Buena Vista 385	(PS)	Let's Get Together / Cobbler, Cobbler	1961	3.00	15.00
Buena Vista 395		Johnny Jingo / Jeepers, Creepers	1962	1.20	6.00
Buena Vista 395	(PS)	Johnny Jingo / Jeepers, Creepers	1962	3.00	15.00
Buena Vista 401		Side By Side / Ding Dong Ding	1962	1.20	6.00
Buena Vista 401	(PS)	Side By Side / Ding Dong Ding	1962	3.00	15.00
Buena Vista 408		Castaway / Sweet River	1962	1.20	6.00
Buena Vista 408	(PS)	Castaway / Sweet River	1962	3.00	15.00
Buena Vista 409		Enjoy It / Let's Climb	1962	1.20	6.00
Buena Vista 409	(PS)	Enjoy It / Let's Climb	1962	3.00	15.00
		— Extended Play Albums—			
Disneyland DBR-93		Pollyanna	1960	5.00	25.00
Alco Wrap AL-701		Walt Disney's Summer Magic (With Burl Ives)	196?	3.00	15.00

MILLS, HAYLEY, & EDDIE HODGES

Label & Catalog #		A-Side/B-Side	Year	VG	NM
Buena Vista 420		Flitterin' / Beautiful Beaulah	1963	1.20	6.00

MINDBENDERS, THE
The Mindbenders feature Graham Gouldman and Eric Stewart. Refer to Wayne Fontana; Hot Legs; 10CC.

Label & Catalog #		A-Side/B-Side	Year	VG	NM
Fontana 1541		A Groovy Kind Of Love / Love Is Good	1966	1.00	5.00
Fontana 1555		Ashes To Ashes / You Don't Know About Love	1966	1.00	5.00
Fontana 1571		I Want Her, She Wants Me / Morning After	1966	1.00	5.00
Fontana 1595		It's Getting Harder All The Time / Off And Running	1967	1.00	5.00
Fontana 1620		Blessed Are The Lonely / Yellow Brick Road	1967	1.00	5.00

MIND ORCHESTRA, THE

Label & Catalog #		A-Side/B-Side	Year	VG	NM
Celestial 101		The Pan American / I Wake Up Dreaming	196?	2.00	10.00

MINERAL WATER

Label & Catalog #		A-Side/B-Side	Year	VG	NM
Family Farm 1		Free And Easy / Leaving The City	1972	.60	3.00

MINEO, SAL

Label & Catalog #		A-Side/B-Side	Year	VG	NM
Epic 9216		Start Movin' (In My Direction) / Love Affair	1957	2.00	10.00
Epic 9216	(PS)	Start Movin' (In My Direction) / Love Affair	1957	3.00	15.00
Epic 9227		Lasting Love / You Shouldn't Do That	1957	2.00	10.00
Epic 9227	(PS)	Lasting Love / You Shouldn't Do That	1957	3.00	15.00

Another cute face turned pop star with the assistance of both Walt Disney and a very willing media, Ms. Mills hailed from a notable line of thespians, recently achieving a comparable standing among her stage peers.

Label & Catalog #		A-Side/B-Side	Year	VG	NM
Epic 9246		Party Time / The Words That I Whisper	1957	2.00	10.00
Epic 9246	(PS)	Party Time / The Words That I Whisper	1957	3.00	15.00
Epic 9260		Little Pigeon / Cuttin' In	1958	2.00	10.00
Epic 9260	(PS)	Little Pigeon / Cuttin' In	1958	3.00	15.00
Epic 9327		Make Believe Baby / Young As We Are	1958	2.00	10.00
Epic 9327	(PS)	Make Believe Baby / Young As We Are	1958	3.00	15.00
Epic 9345		I'll Never Be Myself Again / Words That I Whisper	1958	2.00	10.00

—Extended Play Albums—

Label & Catalog #	A-Side/B-Side	Year	VG	NM
Epic 7187	Sal Mineo	1957	10.00	50.00
Epic 7194	Sal	1957	10.00	50.00
Epic 7195	Sal (Volume 2)	1957	10.00	50.00
Epic 7204	Souvenirs Of Summertime	1957	10.00	50.00
Epic 27283/4	Sal Sings	1957	10.00	50.00

MINETS, THE

Label & Catalog #	A-Side/B-Side	Year	VG	NM
Rock-It 200054	Secret Of Love / Together	196?	3.00	15.00

MINETS OF ENGLAND, THE

Label & Catalog #	A-Side/B-Side	Year	VG	NM
DCP 1129	Wake Up / My Love Is Yours	1965	2.00	10.00

MINI MAX

Label & Catalog #	A-Side/B-Side	Year	VG	NM
Soul Star	Hang On Sloopy / Mohair Sam	196?	2.00	10.00

MINIATURE MEN, THE

Label & Catalog #	A-Side/B-Side	Year	VG	NM
Dolton 52	Soupy's Theme / Miniature Blues	1962	2.00	10.00
Dolton 57	Baby Elephant Walk / Bool-Ya-Base	1962	2.00	10.00

MINOR CHORDS, THE
The Minor Chords also recorded with Sunny Elmo.

Label & Catalog #	A-Side/B-Side	Year	VG	NM
Flick 006	Don't Let Me Down / I'm Falling In Love With You	1959	8.00	40.00

MINT TATTOO, THE

Label & Catalog #	A-Side/B-Side	Year	VG	NM
Dot 17242	I'm Talking About You / Mark Of The Beast	1969	1.20	6.00

MINTS, THE

Label & Catalog #	A-Side/B-Side	Year	VG	NM
Lin 5001	Alone / Busy Body Rock	1957	5.00	25.00
Lin 5007	Night Air / (B-side by Ken Copeland)	1957	6.00	30.00
Imperial 5432	Night Air / (B-side by Ken Copeland)	1957	3.00	15.00

MINTZ, JUNIOR
Junior Mintz is a pseudonym for Frank Zappa & The Mothers.

Label & Catalog #		A-Side/B-Side	Year	VG	NM
Straight/Reprise 1027	(DJ)	Tears Began To Fall / Tears Began To Fall	1971	8.00	40.00
		(Stock copies of Reprise 1027 may not exist.)			

MINUTE MEN, THE

Label & Catalog #	A-Side/B-Side	Year	VG	NM
MGM 13132	Over The Top / Chile Nights	196?	2.00	10.00

MINUTE-MEN, THE

Label & Catalog #	A-Side/B-Side	Year	VG	NM
Capitol 4458	Yankee Diddle / Blue Pearl	1961	2.00	10.00
Rust 5103	Smokin' In The Boy's Room / Rollin' In Money	1964	2.00	10.00

MINUTE MEN, THE

Label & Catalog #	A-Side/B-Side	Year	VG	NM
Argo 5469	Please Keep The Beatles In England / My Love Is Gone	1964	3.00	15.00

MINUTEMEN, THE

Label & Catalog #	A-Side/B-Side	Year	VG	NM
Keltone Int. 1003	Thinking Of You / Remember	196?	2.00	10.00

MIRANDA, BOB
Bob Miranda is a member of The Happenings.

Label & Catalog #	A-Side/B-Side	Year	VG	NM
Jubilee 5709	Everybody Is A Star / Evergreen	1971	.80	4.00

MISFITS, THE

Label & Catalog #	A-Side/B-Side	Year	VG	NM
Aries (No number)	Midnight Star / I Don't Know	196?	15.00	75.00
Hush 105	Give Me Your Heart / My Mother-In-Law	1961	3.00	15.00
Sound Stage 2538	Skiing Time / It's Up To You	196?	3.00	152.00

MISFITS, THE

Label & Catalog #	A-Side/B-Side	Year	VG	NM
Joey 117	Naughty Rooster / Chicago Confidential	1961	2.00	10.00

MISFITS, THE
The Misfits feature Glenn Danzig.

Label & Catalog #		A-Side/B-Side	Year	VG	NM
Blank 101/2		Cough Cool / She	1977	30.00	150.00
Blank 101/2	(PS)	Cough Cool / She	1977	30.00	150.00
Plan-9 1001		Bullet / We Are 138 / Attitude / Hollywood Babylon	1978	10.00	50.00
Plan-9 1001		Bullet / We Are 138 / Attitude / Hollywood Babylon	1978	15.00	75.00
		(Red vinyl)			
Plan-9 1001	(PS)	Bullet (Fold-open sleeve)	1978	15.00	75.00

Label & Catalog #		A-Side/B-Side	Year	VG	NM
Plan-9 1009		Horror Business / Teenagers From Mars / Children In Heat	1979	15.00	75.00
Plan-9 1009		Horror Business / Teenagers From Mars / Children In Heat (Yellow vinyl)	1979	10.00	50.00
Plan-9 1009	(PS)	Horror Business / Teenagers From Mars / Children In Heat	1979	15.00	75.00
Plan-9 1011		Night Of The Living Dead / Where Eagles Dare / Rat Fink	1979	10.00	50.00
Plan-9 1011	(PS)	Night Of The Living Dead / Where Eagles Dare / Rat Fink	1979	10.00	50.00
Plan-9 1017		Halloween I / Halloween II	1981	10.00	50.00
Plan-9 1017		Halloween I / Halloween II (Gold vinyl)	1981	15.00	75.00
Plan-9 1017	(PS)	Halloween I / Halloween II	1981	10.00	50.00
		—Extended Play Albums—			
Plan-9 1013		Three Hits From Hell (Grey label)	1981	25.00	125.00
Plan-9 1013		Three Hits From Hell (Orange label)	1981	20.00	100.00
Plan-9 1013		Three Hits From Hell (White vinyl)	1981	30.00	150.00
Plan-9 1019		Evilive	1982	30.00	150.00
MISSILES, THE					
Novel 200		Space Ship / We Belong Together	1960	3.00	15.00
MISTAKES, THE					
Lo-Fi 2312		Chapel Bells / I Got Fired	195?	8.00	40.00
Lo-Fi 2312		Chapel Bells / I Got Fired (Red vinyl)	195?	2.00	10.00
MR. BASSMAN					
Graphic Arts 1000		Rip Van Winkle / (B-side by Marty & The Symbols)	1963	10.00	50.00
MR. CLEAN					
Original Sound 40		Mr. Clean / Jessie Lee (Both sides written, produced and guitar by Frank Zappa.)	1964	25.00	125.00
MR. CLEAN & THE CLEANERS					
Audio 118		Poison Ivy / Think	196?	2.00	10.00
Camelot 136		Karate / Karate, Part 2	196?	2.00	10.00
MR. GASSER & THE WEIRDOS					
Refer to the Various Artists EP section.					
Capitol PRO-2644	(DJ)	Doin' The Surfink / Finksville, U.S.A. (Capitol PRO-2644 was issued in a special "pocket" on the cover of 'The Superstocks.' "Surf Route 101" album.)	1964	3.00	15.00
Capitol PRO-2663	(EP)	Ratfink High (DJ)	1964	6.00	30.00
MR. LEE & THE EL CAMINOS					
Refer to The El Caminos.					
Tolta 355		Portland Jive / I Love You	196?	1.00	5.00
MR. LUCKY & THE GAMBLERS					
Kasino 1001		New Orleans / Searching	1965	2.00	10.00
United Inter. 1001		New Orleans / Searching	1965	2.00	10.00
United Inter. 4404		I Told You Once Before / Koko Joe	1966	2.00	10.00
Jerden 799		I Told You Once Before / Take A Look At Me	1966	2.00	10.00
Panorama 37		I Told You Once Before / Take A Look At Me	1966	2.00	10.00
Dot 16930		I Told You Once Before / Take A Look At Me	1966	1.20	6.00
Panorama 52		You Don't Need Me / Alice Designs	1967	2.00	10.00
MR. MILLER					
Swan 4256		Mrs. Brown, You've Got A Lovely Daughter / I'm Henry VIII	1965	1.60	8.00
MR. 12 STRING GUITAR					
Mr. 12 String Guitar is a pseudonym for Glen Campbell.					
World Pacific 77803		All I Really Want To Do / Mr. 12 String Guitar	1964	1.00	5.00
MISTICS, THE					
Capri 631		Memories / Without Love	196?	4.00	20.00
MITCHELL, DUKE					
Crystalette 743		The Lion / Strike ("The Lion" was originally released as "Boomerang" credited to The Spinners.)	1960	4.00	20.00
MITCHELL, JONI					
Reprise 0906		Big Yellow Taxi / Woodstock	1970	.60	3.00
Reprise 1029	(DJ)	Carey / Carey	1971	.80	4.00
Reprise 1049		California / Cause Of You	1971	.60	3.00
Reprise 1154		Both Sides Now / Chelsea Morning	1972	.60	3.00
Asylum 11010		You Turn Me On, I'm A Radio / Urge For Going	1972	.30	1.50
Asylum 11029		Raised On Robbery / Court And Spark	1973	.30	1.50
Asylum 11034		Help Me / Just Like This Train	1974	.30	1.50
Asylum 11041		Free Man In Paris / People's Parties	1974	.30	1.50
Asylum 45221		Big Yellow Taxi / Rainy Night House	1974	.30	1.50
Asylum 45244		Jericho / Carey	1975	.30	1.50

Label & Catalog #		A-Side/B-Side	Year	VG	NM
Asylum 45298		In France They Kiss On Main Street / The Boho Dance	1976	.30	1.50
Asylum 45377		Coyote / Blue Motel Room	1977	.30	1.50
Asylum 45467		Jericho / Dreamland	1978	.30	1.50
Asylum 46506		The Dry Cleaner From Des Moines /			
		God Must Be A Boogie Man	1979	.30	1.50
Asylum 47038		Why Do Fools Fall In Love / Black Crow	1980	.30	1.50
Geffen 29757		Underneath The Streetlight / Underneath The Streetlight	1982	.30	1.50
Geffen 29849		(You're So Square) Baby I Don't Care / Love	1982	.30	1.50
Geffen 29849	(PS)	(You're So Square) Baby I Don't Care / Love	1982	.30	1.50
Geffen 28840		Good Friends / Smokin' (Empty, Try Another)	1985	.30	1.50
Geffen 28840	(PS)	Good Friends / Smokin' (Empty, Try Another)	1985	.30	1.50
Geffen 28675		Shiny Toys / The Three Great Stimulants	1985	.30	1.50
Geffen 28675	(PS)	Shiny Toys / The Three Great Stimulants	1985	.30	1.50
Geffen 27887		My Secret Place / Lakota	1988	.30	1.50
Geffen 27887	(PS)	My Secret Place / Lakota	1988	.30	1.50

MITCHELL, LEE

Phillips Inter. 3530		The Frog / A Little Bird Told Me	1959	3.00	15.00
Sharp 0862		Rootie Tootie Baby / Who's That Big Man?	1959	50.00	200.00

MITCHELL, MARLON

Vena 100		Ice Cold Baby / Bermuda Shorts	195?	25.00	125.00

MITCHELL, TONY

Canadian American 143		Candle In The Wind / Write Me A Letter	1963	2.00	10.00
Canadian American 157		Candle In The Wind / A Million Drums	1963	2.00	10.00
Canadian American 162		Ponchinello / Write Me A Letter	1964	2.00	10.00

MITCHELL TRIO, CHAD [MITCHELL TRIO]
Many of the Mercury sides feature John Denver.

Colpix 133		Vaya Con Dios / Sally Ann	1960	1.20	6.00
May 116		Ballad Of Herbie Spear / Sally Ann	1962	1.20	6.00
Kapp 439		Lizzie Borden / Super Skier	1962	1.20	6.00
Kapp 457		The John Birch Society / Golden Vanity	1962	1.20	6.00
Kapp 510		Blowing In The Wind / Adios Mi Corazon	1962	1.20	6.00
Amy 054		What's That Gotta Do With Me? / The Bus Song	1963	1.20	6.00
Mercury 72197		Bonny Streets Of Five-10 / Marvelous Toy	1963	1.20	6.00
Mercury 72234		Tell Old Billy / Tarrier's Song	1963	1.20	6.00
Mercury 72257		Barry's Boys / What Did You Learn In School Today?	1964	1.20	6.00
Mercury 72340		I Can't Help But Wonder / Stewball And Griselda	1964	1.20	6.00
Mercury 72400		My Name Is Morgan / You Were On My Mind	1965	1.20	6.00
Mercury 72518		Violets Of Dawn / That's The Way It's Gonna Be	1965	1.20	6.00
Mercury 72544		Violets Of Dawn /			
		Your Friendly Liberal, Neighborhood Ku Klux Klan	1966	1.20	6.00
Mercury 72591		Dark Shadows And Empty Hallways / Stay With Me	1966	1.20	6.00

MITLO SISTERS, THE

Klik 8405		Let Me Tell You / Lonely Sea	196?	5.00	25.00

MIXTURES, THE

Linda 104		Rainbow Stomp / Rainbow Stomp (Part 2)	1962	2.00	10.00
Linda 106		Jawbone / It's Gonna Work Out Fine	1962	2.00	10.00
Linda 108		Canadian Sunset / Olive Oyl	1963	2.00	10.00
Linda 109		Tiki / Poochum	1963	2.00	10.00
Linda 113		Chinese Checkers / Dig These Blues	1964	2.00	10.00
Linda 115		Sen-Sa-Shun / Last Minute	1964	2.00	10.00

MIZELL, HANK

Eko 506		Jungle Rock / Then I'm In Yours Arms	1958	125.00	500.00
King 5236		Jungle Rock / Then I'm In Yours Arms	1959	40.00	200.00
Amazon		Jungle Rock / Then I'm In Yours Arms	1963	5.00	25.00

MOBY GRAPE
Moby Grape is Peter Lewis, Jerry Miller, Bob Mosley, Alexander "Skip" Spence and Don Stephenson. Spence left in 1968; by 1970 Mosley was gone. Refer to Blackburn & Snow; The Cordells; Jefferson Airplane; The San Diego Misfits; and the Various Artists EP section

Columbia 44170		Fall On You / Changes	1967	2.00	10.00
Columbia 44170	(PS)	Fall On You / Changes	1967	8.00	40.00
Columbia 44171		Sitting By The Window / Indifference	1967	2.00	10.00
Columbia 44171	(PS)	Sitting By The Window / Indifference	1967	8.00	40.00
Columbia 44172		8:05 / Mister Blues	1967	2.00	10.00
Columbia 44172	(PS)	8:05 / Mister Blues	1967	8.00	40.00
Columbia 44173		Omaha / Someday	1967	2.00	10.00
Columbia 44173	(PS)	Omaha / Someday	1967	8.00	40.00
Columbia 44174		Hey Grandma / Come In The Morning	1967	2.00	10.00
Columbia 44174	(PS)	Hey Grandma / Come In The Morning	1967	8.00	40.00
Columbia 44567		Can't Be So Bad / Bitter Wind	1968	1.00	5.00
Columbia 44789		Trucking Man / If You Can't Learn From My Mistakes	1968	1.00	5.00

Label & Catalog #	A-Side / B-Side	Year	VG	NM
Columbia 44885	It's A Beautiful Day Today / Ooh Mama Ooh	1969	1.00	5.00
Reprise 1040	Gypsy Wedding / Apocalypse	1971	.60	3.00
Reprise 1055	Goin' Down To Texas / About Time	1971	.60	3.00
Reprise 1096	Gypsy Wedding / Gone Fishin'	1972	.60	3.00

MOCKERS, THE

Monte Vista	Maladena / Children Of The Sun	1965	7.00	35.00

MOCKINGBIRDS, THE
The Mockingbirds feature Graham Gouldman and Kevin Godley, later of 10CC.

ABC-Paramount 10653	That's How (It's Gonna Stay) / I Never Should've Kissed You	1965	3.00	15.00

MOD ROCKERS, THE

Dot 16907	Stop And Smell The Roses / Lover's Lane	1966	2.00	10.00

MODERN FOLK QUARTET, THE
The original MFQ were Jerry Yester, later of The Lovin' Spoonful, Henry Diltz, Chip Douglas and Cyrus Faryar.

Warner Bros. 5387	Road To Freedom / It Was A Very Good Year	1963	.80	4.00
Warner Bros. 5459	Draft Dodger / Jim The Singing Cockroach	1965	.80	4.00
Warner Bros. 5481	The Love Of A Clown / If All You Think	1965	.80	4.00
Warner Bros. 5623	Every Minute Of The Day / That's Alright With Me	1966	.80	4.00
Dunhill 4025	Night Time Girl / Life Time	1966	1.00	5.00
Dunhill 4137	I Had A Dream Last Night / Don't You Wonder	1968	1.00	5.00

MODERN LOVERS, THE: *Refer to* JONATHAN RICHMAN (& THE MODERN LOVERS)

MODINE, JERRY

Mercury 72066	Blue Denim / Stranger To Me	1962	2.00	10.00

MOGULS, THE

Tork 1095	Another Day / Round Randy	196?	2.00	10.00
Panorama 27	Try Me / Ski Bum	1966	4.00	20.00
Century 20449	Avalanche / Ghost Slalome	196?	5.00	25.00

MOHAWKS, THE

Val-ue 211	Bewitched (Bothered And Bewildered) / I Got A Girl	1960	4.00	20.00

MOHAWKS, THE

Colpix 117	Night Run / Moccasin Walk	1959	5.00	25.00

MOJO MEN, THE [MOJO]

Tide 2000	Surfin' Fat Man / Paula	1964	8.00	40.00
Autumn 11	Off The Hook / Mama's Little Baby	1965	2.00	10.00
Autumn 19	Dance With Me / Loneliest Boy In Town	1965	2.00	10.00
Autumn 27	She's My Baby / Fire In My Heart	1965	3.00	15.00
Reprise 0486	She's My Baby / Do The Hanky Panky	1965	4.00	20.00
Reprise 0539	Sit Down, I Think I Love You / Don't Leave Me Crying Like Before	1966	1.60	8.00
Reprise 0580	Me About You / When You're In Love	1967	1.60	8.00
Reprise 0617	What Ever Happened To Happy? / Make You At Home	1967	1.60	8.00
Reprise 0661	New York City / Not Too Old To Start Crying	1968	1.60	8.00
Reprise 0689	Should I Cry? / You To Me	1968	1.60	8.00
Reprise 0759	Don't Be Cruel / Let It Be Him	1968	1.60	8.00
	(Reprise 0689 and 0759 are credited to Mojo.)			
GRT 5	I Can't Let Go / Flower Of Love	196?	2.00	10.00
GRT 8	Candle To Burn / Make You At Home	196?	2.00	10.00
GRT 16	Everyday Love / There Goes My Mind	196?	2.00	10.00

MOLES, GENE, & THE SOFTWINDS

Garpax 44176	Kaha Huna / Maria	1963	3.00	15.00
Challenge 59249	Burning Rubber / Twin Pipes	1964	3.00	15.00
	(Re-issued on Flame as "Batmobile" / "Batust" credited to The Bats.)			

MOLITTERI, PAT

Teen 414	Say That You Love Me / The U.S.A.	1961	6.00	30.00

MOLLEN, RONNIE

King 5365	Rockin' Up / Fat Mama	195?	30.00	150.00

MOMENTS, THE

Era 3099	Walk Right In / Walk Right In	1963	1.20	6.00
Era 3104	Homework / Big Round Wheel	1963	1.20	6.00
Era 3114	Surfin' Train / Mamu Zey	1963	2.00	10.00

MONARCHS, THE

Sound Stage-7 2502	Till I Hear It From You / This Old Heart	1964	3.00	15.00
Sound Stage-7 2504	Climb Every Mountain / Take Me Home	1965	2.00	10.00
Sound Stage-7 2516	Look Homeward, Angel / What Made You Change Your Mind	1965	2.00	10.00

Label & Catalog #		A-Side/B-Side	Year	VG	NM
MONARCHS IV, THE					
Erwin 1069		Surge / Weekend	196?	6.00	30.00
MONARCS, THE					
Zone 1067		Friday Night / El-Bandito	1963	3.00	15.00
MONARCS, THE					
Yucca 172		Forever Lost / Cuckoo	196?	7.00	35.00
MONDO, JOE					
EPI 1003		Last Summer Love / Doin' The Thing	196?	3.00	15.00
MONIQUES, THE					
Centaur 104		Halo / Don't Throw Stones	196?	3.00	15.00
Centaur 105		All The Way Now / Rock, Pretty Baby	196?	3.00	15.00
Benn-X 55		Goin' Down To birdland / Hey Girl	1962	2.00	10.00

MONKEES, THE
The Monkees are Mickey Dolenz, Davey Jones, Michael Nesmith and Peter Tork. Refer to Dolenz, Jones & Tork; Dolenz, Jones, Boyce & Hart.

Label & Catalog #		A-Side/B-Side	Year	VG	NM
Colgems 1001	(DJ)	Last Train To Clarksville / Take A Giant Step	1966	6.00	30.00
Colgems 1001		Last Train To Clarksville / Take A Giant Step	1966	2.00	10.00
Colgems 1001	(PS)	Last Train To Clarksville / Take A Giant Step	1966	4.00	20.00
		(Black & white sleeve with no mention of the Monkees fan club.)			
Colgems 1001	(PS)	Last Train To Clarksville / Take A Giant Step	1966	4.00	20.00
		(Full-color sleeve reads "Write The Monkees" on the bottom.)			
Colgems 101	(DJ)	Davy Jones—My Favorite Monkee / She Hangs Out	1967	50.00	200.00
Colgems 1002	(DJ)	I'm A Believer / (I'm Not Your) Stepping Stone	1966	6.00	30.00
Colgems 1002		I'm A Believer / (I'm Not Your) Stepping Stone	1966	2.00	10.00
Colgems 1002	(PS)	I'm A Believer / (I'm Not Your) Stepping Stone	1966	4.00	20.00
Colgems 1004	(DJ)	A Little Bit Me, A Little Bit You / The Girl I Knew Somewhere	1967	6.00	30.00
Colgems 1004		A Little Bit Me, A Little Bit You / The Girl I Knew Somewhere	1967	2.00	10.00
Colgems 1007	(DJ)	Pleasant Valley Sunday / Words	1967	6.00	30.00
Colgems 1007		Pleasant Valley Sunday / Words	1967	2.00	10.00
Colgems 1007	(PS)	Pleasant Valley Sunday / Words	1967	4.00	20.00
Colgems 1012	(DJ)	Daydream Believer / Goin' Down	1967	6.00	30.00
Colgems 1012		Daydream Believer / Goin' Down	1967	2.00	10.00
Colgems 1012	(PS)	Daydream Believer / Goin' Down	1967	4.00	20.00
Colgems 1019	(DJ)	Valleri / Tapioca Tundra	1968	6.00	30.00
Colgems 1019		Valleri / Tapioca Tundra	1968	2.00	10.00
Colgems 1023	(DJ)	D.W. Washburn / It's Nice To Be With You	1968	4.00	20.00
Colgems 1023		D.W. Washburn / It's Nice To Be With You	1968	1.00	5.00
Colgems 1023	(PS)	D.W. Washburn / It's Nice To Be With You	1968	4.00	20.00
Colgems 1031	(DJ)	Porpoise Song / As We Go Along	1968	4.00	20.00
Colgems 1031		Porpoise Song / As We Go Along	1968	1.00	5.00
Colgems 1031	(PS)	Porpoise Song / As We Go Along	1968	3.00	15.00
Colgems 5000	(DJ)	Teardrop City / A Man Without A Dream	1969	4.00	20.00
Colgems 5000		Teardrop City / A Man Without A Dream	1969	1.00	5.00
Colgems 5000	(PS)	Teardrop City / A Man Without A Dream	1969	5.00	25.00
Colgems 5004	(DJ)	Listen To The Band / Someday Man	1969	4.00	20.00
Colgems 5004		Listen To The Band / Someday Man	1969	1.00	5.00
Colgems 5004	(PS)	Listen To The Band / Someday Man	1969	5.00	25.00
Colgems 5004	(PS)	Someday Man / Listen To The Band	1969	4.00	20.00
		(There are two picture sleeves to Colgems 5004: the first lists "Listen To The Band as the a-side; the other, "Someday Man.")			
Colgems 5005	(DJ)	Good Clean Fun / Mommy And Daddy	1969	3.00	15.00
Colgems 5005		Good Clean Fun / Mommy And Daddy	1969	1.20	6.00
Colgems 5005	(PS)	Good Clean Fun / Mommy And Daddy	1969	5.00	25.00
Colgems 5011	(DJ)	Oh My, My / I Love You Better	1970	3.00	15.00
Colgems 5011		Oh My, My / I Love You Better	1970	1.20	6.00
Colgems 5011	(PS)	Oh My, My / I Love You Better	1970	6.00	30.00
Arista 0201		Daydream Believer / Theme From The Monkees	1976	1.60	8.00
		—Extended Play Albums—			
Colgems CGLP-101	(33)	The Monkees (Jukebox EP)	1967	30.00	150.00
Colgems CGLP-102	(33)	More Of The Monkees (Jukebox EP)	1967	30.00	150.00
MONORAYS, THE					
Tammy 1005		Guardian Angel / Five Minutes To Love	1959	50.00	200.00
Red Rocket 476		Guardian Angel / Five Minutes To Love	1959	4.00	20.00

MONTAGE
Montage features Steve Martin, formerly of The Left Banke.

Label & Catalog #	A-Side/B-Side	Year	VG	NM
Laurie 3438	I Shall Call Her Mary / An Audience With Miss Priscilla Gray	1968	.80	4.00
Laurie 3453	Wake Up, Jimmy / Tinsel And Ivy	1968	.80	4.00

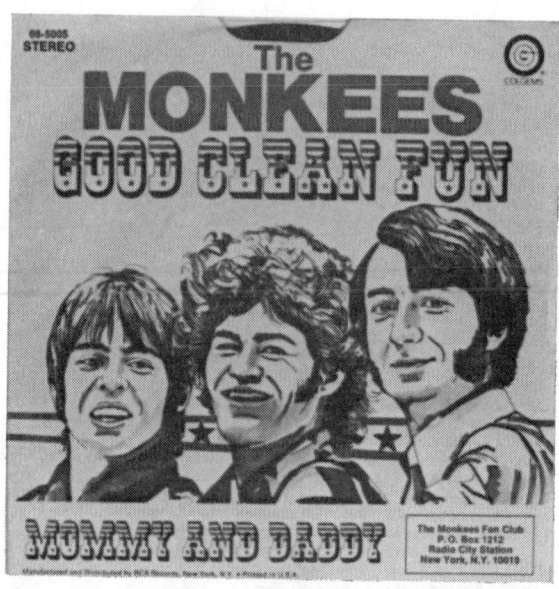

First they were four, then they were three (and, eventually, they were two plus Boyce and Hart). The Monkees offer a perplexing problem for those who hold absurd standards for the entertainment industry: If it's a sham when four white faces front an assembly line-up of studio talents (writers, arrangers and musicians) for Colgems and call themselves a "group" (what else should they have tagged themselves), then why is it not a sham when four black faces front an assembly line-up of writers, arrangers and musicians for Motown and call themselves a group?

Label & Catalog #	A-Side/B-Side	Year	VG	NM
MONTANAS, THE				
Warner Bros. 5871	Goodbye, Little Girl / That's When Happiness Began	1966	1.20	6.00
Warner Bros. 7021	Ciao, Baby / Anyone There?	1967	1.20	6.00
Warner Bros. 7208	Ciao, Baby / Anyone There?	1968	1.00	5.00
Independence 79	Take My Hand / Top Hat	1968	1.00	5.00
Independence 83	You've Got To Be Loved / Difference Of Opinion	1968	1.00	5.00
Independence 87	I'm Gonna Change / A Step In The Right Direction	1968	1.00	5.00
Independence 89	Run To Me / You're Making A Big Mistake	1968	1.00	5.00
MONTCLAIRS, THE				
Audicon 111	Goodnight, Well It's Time To Go / Broken Promise	1960	4.00	20.00
MONTCLAIRS, THE				
United Inter. 1007	Lisa / Tap Tap Daisy	196?	5.00	25.00
MONTE, LOU				
RCA Victor 47-6704	Elvis Presley For President / If I Was A Millionaire	1956	7.00	35.00
MONTE, VINNIE				
Josie 793	Your Cute Little Ways / Without Your Love	1956	5.00	25.00
Fargo 1000	Naughty, Naughty Boy / I Wrote A Poem	1958	3.00	15.00
Jubilee 5419	The Year May Be Over (But The Heartaches Are Just Beginning) / One Of The Guys	1962	2.00	10.00
RCA Victor 47-8611	I Walk Alone / I Don't Have The Heart To Tell Her	1965	2.00	10.00
TCF 7	Hey, Look At The Winter Snow / What's The Matter?	196?	5.00	25.00
MONTELLS, THE				
Golden Crest 582	A Rang A Lang Lang / Soldier Boy, I'm Sorry	196?	3.00	15.00
Golden Crest 585	Gee, Baby / My Prince Will Come	196?	3.00	15.00
MONTERAYS, THE				
Dee-Jay 1013	Turtle / Party	196?	7.00	35.00
MONTERAYS, THE				
Sure Star 5000	Deep Within My Heart / Plush 'Em Up	1964	1.20	6.00
Ultima 704	Deep Within My Heart / Plush 'Em Up	1964	1.20	6.00
MONTEREYS, THE				
Planet 57	Blast Off / You Never Cared	196?	7.00	35.00
MONTEREYS, THE				
East West 124	I'll Love You Again / The American Teens	1958	5.00	25.00
Arwin 130	Goodbye, My Love / It Hurts Me So	1959	7.00	35.00
Impala 213	Without A Girl / So Deep	195?	25.00	125.00
Blast 219	Face In The Crowd / Step Right Up	1963	100.00	400.00
GNP/Crescendo 314	For Sentimental Reasons / I Still Love You	1964	4.00	20.00
MONTEZ, CHRIS				
Refer to Chris & Kathy.				
Monogram 500	All You Had To Do (Was Tell Me) / Love Me	1962	1.60	8.00
Monogram 505	Let's Dance / You're The One	1962	3.00	15.00
Monogram 507	Some Kinda Fun / Tell Me	1962	1.60	8.00
Monogram 508	Rockin' Blues / (Let's Do) The Limbo	1962	2.40	12.00
Monogram 513	My Baby Loves To Dance / In An English Towne	1963	1.60	8.00
Monogram 517	All You Had To Do (Was Tell Me) / Love Me	1963	1.60	8.00
A&M 780	Call Me / Go Ahead On	1965	.80	4.00
A&M 796	The More I See You / You, I Love You	1966	.80	4.00
A&M 810	There Will Never Be Another You / You Can Hurt The One You Love	1966	.60	3.00
A&M 822	Time After Time / Keep Talkin'	1966	.60	3.00
A&M 855	Foolin' Around	1967	.60	3.00
A&M 855	Twiggy / Just Friends	1967	.60	3.00
A&M 906	Once In A While / The Face I Love	1968	.60	3.00
A&M 958	Our Love Is Here To Stay / Nothing To Hide	1968	.60	3.00
Paramount 0109	The End Of The Line / We Can Make The One You Love A Whole Lot Brighter	1973	.50	2.50
MONTGOMERY, CHRISTOPHER				
Dolton	Giants Of Bombora / My Paradise	1963	6.00	30.00
MONTGOMERYS, THE				
Amy 883	Promise Of Love / Gotta Make A Hit Record	195?	50.00	200.00
MONZELS, THE				
Prism 1898	Sharkskin / Don't Be Mad	196?	8.00	40.00
MOOD MAKERS, THE				
Bambi 800	Dolores / Dream A Dream	195?	15.00	75.00

Label & Catalog #	A-Side/B-Side	Year	VG	NM

MOODY & THE DELTAS

Label & Catalog #	A-Side/B-Side	Year	VG	NM
Daisy 504	Monkey Climb / Come, Clap Your Hands	1963	2.00	10.00

MOODY BLUES, THE

The original Moodys were Graeme Edge, Denny Laine, Mike Pinder, Ray Thomas, and Clint Warwick. Justin Hayward and John Lodge replaced Laine and Warwick in 1967.

Label & Catalog #	A-Side/B-Side	Year	VG	NM
London 9726	Go Now! / Lose Your Money (First pressings have white label with dark blue bars.)	1965	3.00	15.00
London 9726	Go Now! / Lose Your Money (Second pressings have blue and white swirl label.)	1965	2.00	10.00
London 9764	From The Bottom Of My Heart (I Love You) / And My Baby's Gone	1965	1.00	5.00
London 9799	Ev'ry Day / You Don't	1965	1.00	5.00
London 9810	Stop! / Bye Bye Bird	1966	1.00	5.00
London 20030	Fly Me High / I Really Haven't Got The Time	1966	1.00	5.00
London 1005	Boulevard De la Madelaine / This Is My House (But Nobody Calls)	1967	1.00	5.00
Deram 85023	Nights In White Satin / Cities	1968	1.00	5.00
Deram 85028	Tuesday Afternoon (Forever Afternoon) / Another Morning	1968	1.00	5.00
Deram 85033	Ride My See Saw / Voices In The Sky	1968	1.00	5.00
Deram 85044	Never Comes The Day / So Deep Within	1969	1.00	5.00
Threshold 67001	Out And In / Watching And Waiting	1970	.60	3.00
Threshold 67004	Question / Candle Of Life	1970	.60	3.00
Threshold 67006	The Story In Your Eyes / Melancholy Me	1971	.60	3.00
Threshold 67006 (PS)	The Story In Your Eyes / Melancholy Me	1971	.60	3.00
Threshold 67009	Isn't Life Strange? / After You Came	1972	.60	3.00
Threshold 67012	I'm Just A Singer (In A Rock And Roll Band) / For My Lady	1973	.60	3.00
London 270	Steppin' In A Slide Zone / I'll Be Level With You	1978	.40	2.00
London 273	Driftwood / I'm Your Man	1978	.40	2.00
Threshold 601	Gemini Dream / Painted Smile	1981	.40	2.00
Threshold 602	The Voice / 22,000 Days	1981	.40	2.00
Threshold 603	Talking Out Of Turn / Veteran Cosmic Rocker	1981	.40	2.00
Threshold 604	Sittin' At The Wheel / Going Nowhere	1983	.40	2.00
Threshold 605	Blue World / Sorry	1983	.40	2.00
Threshold 606	Running Water / Under My Feet	1983	.40	2.00

MOON, KEITH

Keith Moon was a member of The Who.

Label & Catalog #	A-Side/B-Side	Year	VG	NM
Track 40433	In My Life / Crazy Like A Fox	1975	3.00	15.00
Track 40316	Don't Worry, Baby / Teenage Idol	1975	3.00	15.00
Track 40387	Solid Gold / Move Over, Mrs. L	1975	3.00	15.00

MOON, THE

The Moon features David Marks, formerly of The Beach Boys.

Label & Catalog #	A-Side/B-Side	Year	VG	NM
Imperial 66285	Mothers And Fathers / Someday Girl	1968	3.00	15.00
Imperial 66330	Faces / John Automation	1968	3.00	15.00
Imperial 66415	Not To Know / Pirates	1969	3.00	15.00

MOON BEAMS, THE

Label & Catalog #	A-Side/B-Side	Year	VG	NM
Grate 100	Don't Go Away / A Lover's Plea	195?	25.00	125.00

MOON RAKERS, THE

Label & Catalog #	A-Side/B-Side	Year	VG	NM
Tower 180	I'm All Right / Come On, Let's Move	1965	2.00	10.00
Tower 239	Baby, Please Don't Go / I Don't Believe	1966	2.00	10.00

MOON STARS BAND, THE

Label & Catalog #	A-Side/B-Side	Year	VG	NM
Good Sound 108	Hot Footsie / Hot Footsie (Part 2)	1962	2.00	10.00

MOON SURFERS, THE

Label & Catalog #	A-Side/B-Side	Year	VG	NM
Genius 2101	Surfin' On The Moon / Born To Wonder	196?	8.00	40.00

MOONGOONERS, THE

The Moongooners feature Scott Engel and John Maus a.k.a. John Stewart.

Label & Catalog #	A-Side/B-Side	Year	VG	NM
Candix 335	Moongoon Stomp / The Long Trip	1962	7.00	35.00
Essar 1007	Moongoon Twist / Willie And The Hand Jive	1962	6.00	30.00
Donna 1373	Moongoon Twist / Willie And The Hand Jive	1962	5.00	25.00

MOONSHINE

Label & Catalog #	A-Side/B-Side	Year	VG	NM
United Artists 50658	Whistling In The Wind / Out A Hand	1970	1.00	5.00

MOORE, LARRY

Label & Catalog #	A-Side/B-Side	Year	VG	NM
Original Sound 30	Hooray For Weekends / Two Young Lovers	1963	6.00	30.00

MOORE, BERNIE

Label & Catalog #	A-Side/B-Side	Year	VG	NM
Burdette 1911	I'll Never Begin To Forget / 45 R.P.M.S	1966	1.60	8.00

Label & Catalog #	A-Side/B-Side	Year	VG	NM
MOORE, CECIL				
Sarg 206	Diamond Back / Rise And Shine	1964	2.00	10.00
Atco 6309	Diamond Back / Rise And Shine	1964	1.20	6.00
Sarg 211	Duck Walk / Stormy	1964	2.00	10.00
MOORE, HARV				
American Arts 20	Interview Of The Fab Four / I Feel So Fine	1964	10.00	50.00
MOORE, MATTHEW (MATTHEW MOORE + FOUR)				
White Whale 223	Codyne / You've Never Loved Before	1965	6.00	30.00
Capitol 5820	Come On / White Silk Glove	1967	3.00	15.00
	(White Whale 223 and Capitol 5820 feature David Marks.)			
Caribou/Shelter 9025	Savannah / Moon Dew	1978	.80	4.00
MOORE, STEVE				
Scott 002	Forty Days / Pledging My Love	196?	1.00	5.00
MOORPARK INTERSECTION, THE				
Capitol 2115	I Think I'll Just Go And Find Me A Flower / Yesterday Holds On	1968	2.00	10.00
MORAN				
Epic 10987	The Beatles Thing / The Lady Loves Me	1971	1.00	5.00
MORE, CHUCK, & THE ALL-STARS				
Bop City 100	Return To Me, Love / The Flip Side	196?	2.00	10.00
MORE BEAUTIFUL DAZE				
Alpha 618	City Jungle / City Jungle, Part 2	1968	2.00	10.00
MORGAN				
Laurie 1013	High School Steady / Oh, Hey There, You	1960	3.00	15.00
MORGUS & THE THREE GHOULS				
Morgus is a pseudonym for Frankie Ford.				
Vin 1013	Morgus The Magnificent / The Lonely Boys	1959	5.00	25.00
MORNING RAIN				
Buddah 247	Take Your Time / Most Peculiar	1971	1.60	8.00
MORNING REIGN, THE				
"S" 3	Please Stop / Say It Once Again	196?	2.00	10.00
Garland 2007	Any Way That You Want Me / Reach Out, I'll Be There	1967	2.00	10.00
Garland 2012	But It's Alright / Everybody	1968	2.00	10.00
MORNINGSIDE DRIVE & FRIENDS				
Laurie 3615	Na-Na-Na / Lazy Love	196?	2.00	10.00
MORRA, TONY				
Du-Well 1005	Looking For My Baby / I Can't Believe	1959	7.00	35.00
Arcade 152	My Baby Scares Me / Claire	1959	6.00	30.00
MORRIE, TINY				
Hurricane 1937	The Beetle And The Spider / Let's Talk It Over	1964	2.00	10.00
MORRILL, KENT				
Kent Morrill also recorded with The Wailers.				
Etiquette 5	This Pain In My Heart / I Had A Dream	1963	3.00	15.00
Congress 6016	The Wind Calls The Wild To It's Own / I Cannot Live Without Her	196?	2.00	10.00
BRC 103	Still The Sun Rose / Red, Black And Blue	1971	2.00	10.00
MORRISON, VAN				
Van Morrison originally recorded with Them.				
Bang 545	Brown-Eyed Girl / Goodbye, Baby	1967	1.20	6.00
Bang 552	Ro Ro Rosey / Chick-A-Boom	1967	1.00	5.00
Bang 585	Spanish Rose / Midnight Special	1968	1.00	5.00
	—Original Bang singles above have red & white labels.—			
Hip Pocket 16	Brown-Eyed Girl / Midnight Special	1968	2.00	10.00
	(4" flexidisc issued with a picture envelope.)			
Warner Bros. 7383	Come Running / Crazy Love	1970	.60	3.00
Warner Bros. 7434	Domino / Sweet Jannie	1970	.60	3.00
Warner Bros. 7462	Blue Money / Sweet Thing	1971	.60	3.00
Warner Bros. 7488	Call Me Up In Dreamland / Street Choir	1971	.60	3.00
Warner Bros. 7518	Wild Night / When That Evening Sun Goes Down	1971	.60	3.00
Warner Bros. 7543	Tupelo Honey / Starting A New Life	1972	.60	3.00
Warner Bros. 7573	Like A Cannonball / Old, Old Woodstock	1972	.60	3.00
Warner Bros. 7616	Jackie Wilson Said / You've Got The Power	1972	.60	3.00

Label & Catalog #		A-Side/B-Side	Year	VG	NM
Warner Bros. 7638		Redwood Tree / St. Dominic's Preview	1972	.60	3.00
Warner Bros. 7665		Gypsy / St. Dominic's Preview	1973	.60	3.00
Warner Bros. 7706		Warm Love / I'll Be There	1973	.60	3.00
Warner Bros. 7744		Green / Wild Children	1973	.60	3.00
Warner Bros. 7786		Gloria /	1973	.60	3.00
Warner Bros. 7797		Ain't Nothin' You Can Do / Wild Children	1974	.60	3.00
Warner Bros. 8029		Bulbs / Cul De Sac	1974	.60	3.00
Warner Bros. 8411		Joyous Sound / Mechanical Bliss	1977	.60	3.00
Warner Bros. 8450		Moondance / A Cold Wind In August	1977	.60	3.00
Warner Bros. 8660		Wavelength / Checkin' It Out	1978	.40	3.00
Warner Bros. 8743		Natalia / Lifetimes	1979	.40	3.00
Warner Bros. 8805		Kingdom Hall / Checkin' It Out	1979	.40	3.00
Warner Bros. 49086		Bright Side Of The Road / Rolling Hills	1979	.40	3.00
Warner Bros. 49162		You Make Me Feel So Real / Full Scale Force	1980	.40	3.00
Warner Bros. 50031		Cleaning Windows / Scandinavia	1982	.40	3.00
		— 12" Singles —			
Warner Bros.	(DJ)	Wavelength / Wavelength	1978	.80	4.00
Warner Bros.	(DJ)	Natalia / Natalia	1979	.80	4.00
Warner Bros.	(DJ)	Kingdom Hall / Kingdom Hall	1979	.80	4.00
Warner Bros.	(DJ)	Bright Side Of The Road / Bright Side Of The Road	1979	.80	4.00
Warner Bros.	(DJ)	Haunts Of Ancient Peace / Summertime In England	1980	.80	4.00

MORTIMER

Label & Catalog #		A-Side/B-Side	Year	VG	NM
Philips 40524		Dedicated Music Man / To Understand Someone	1968	1.00	5.00
Philips 40524	(PS)	Dedicated Music Man / To Understand Someone	1968	2.00	10.00

MOSE'S LAKE

Label & Catalog #	A-Side/B-Side	Year	VG	NM
Together 113	Oobleck / Moses	1969	1.20	6.00

MOSS, GENE

Label & Catalog #		A-Side/B-Side	Year	VG	NM
RCA Victor 47-8438		I Want To Bite Your Hand / Ghoul Days	1964	2.00	10.00
RCA Victor 47-8438	(PS)	I Want To Bite Your Hand / Ghoul Days	1964	2.00	10.00

MOSS, ROY

Label & Catalog #	A-Side/B-Side	Year	VG	NM
Fascination 1002	Wiggle Walkin' Baby /	195?	25.00	125.00
Mercury 70770	You're My Big Baby, Now /	1956	20.00	100.00
Mercury 70858	Corinne, Corinna /	1956	15.00	75.00

MOTHER EARTH

Mother Earth features Tracy Nelson.

Label & Catalog #	A-Side/B-Side	Year	VG	NM
United Artists 50303	Revolution / Stranger In My Own Home Town	1968	1.00	5.00
Mercury 72878	Down So Low / Good Night Grebe	1968	.80	4.00
Mercury 72943	I Wanna Be Your Mama Again / Wait, Wait, Wait	1969	.80	4.00
Mercury 73116	Satisfied / Andy's Song	1969	.80	4.00
Reprise 1019	Temptation Took Control Of Me And I Fell / Soul Of Sadness	1970	.80	4.00
Reprise 1041	Bring Me Home / I'll Be Long Gone	1971	.80	4.00

MOTHERLODE

Label & Catalog #	A-Side/B-Side	Year	VG	NM
Buddah 131	When I Die / Hard Life	1969	.80	4.00
Buddah 144	Memories Of A Broken Promise / What Does It Take?	1969	.60	3.00

MOTHERS OF INVENTION, THE [THE MOTHERS]: *Refer to FRANK ZAPPA*

MOTIFS, THE

Label & Catalog #	A-Side/B-Side	Year	VG	NM
Baton 23112	She's My Girl / My Babe	196?	2.00	10.00

MOTIONS, THE

Label & Catalog #	A-Side/B-Side	Year	VG	NM
Mercury 72297	Beatle Drums / Long Hair	1964	4.00	20.00
Mercury 72368	Land Beyond The Moon / I Can Dance	1964	4.00	20.00

MOTIVATIONS, THE

Label & Catalog #	A-Side/B-Side	Year	VG	NM
Pride 301	Motivate / The Birds	1963	5.00	25.00

MOTLEY, FRANK

Label & Catalog #	A-Side/B-Side	Year	VG	NM
DC 0415	Everybody Wants A Flat Top / Space Age	195?	4.00	20.00

MOTLEY CRUE

Label & Catalog #		A-Side/B-Side	Year	VG	NM
Leather MC-001		Stick To Your Guns / Toast Of The Town	1981	10.00	50.00
Leather MC-001	(PS)	Stick To Your Guns / Toast Of The Town	1981	10.00	50.00
		(Leather 001 was given out at the group's early concerts.)			
Elektra 69		Live Wire / Take Me To The Top / Merry-Go-Round	1982	1.00	5.00
Elektra 69	(PS)	Live Wire / Take Me To The Top / Merry-Go-Round	1982	1.00	5.00
Elektra 69756		Looks That Kill / Piece Of Your Action	1984	.80	4.00
Elektra 69756	(PS)	Looks That Kill / Piece Of Your Action	1984	.80	4.00
Elektra 69732		Too Young To Fall In Love / Take Me To The Top	1984	.80	4.00
Elektra 69732	(PS)	Too Young To Fall In Love / Take Me To The Top	1984	.80	4.00
Elektra 69625		Smokin' In The Boys Room / Use It Or Lose It	1985	.80	4.00
Elektra 69625	(PS)	Smokin' In The Boys Room / Use It Or Lose It	1985	.80	4.00

Label & Catalog #		A-Side/B-Side	Year	VG	NM
Elektra 68591		Home Sweet Home / Red Hot	1985	.80	4.00
Elektra 68591	(PS)	Home Sweet Home / Red Hot	1985	.80	4.00
Elektra 69449		Wild Side / Five Years Dead	1987	.60	3.00
Elektra 69449	(PS)	Wild Side / Five Years Dead	1987	.60	3.00
Elektra 69429		You're All I Need / All In The Name Of	1987	.60	3.00
Elektra 69429	(PS)	You're All I Need / All In The Name Of	1987	.60	3.00
Elektra 69248		Kickstart My Heart / She Goes Down	1989	.60	3.00
Elektra 69248	(PS)	Kickstart My Heart / She Goes Down	1989	.60	3.00
Elektra 65964		Girls, Girls, Girls / Wild Side	1989	.60	3.00
Elektra 65964	(PS)	Girls, Girls, Girls / Wild Side	1989	.60	3.00
Elektra 65		Dr. Feelgood / Sticky Sweet	1989	.60	3.00
Elektra 65	(PS)	Dr. Feelgood / Sticky Sweet	1989	.60	3.00
Elektra 64985		Without You / Slice Of Your Pie	1990	.60	3.00
Elektra 64985	(PS)	Without You / Slice Of Your Pie	1990	.60	3.00
		— 12" Singles—			
Elektra		Helter Skelter (Picture disc)	1984	2.00	10.00

MOTLEYS, THE

| Valiant 739 | | My Race Is Run / You | 1966 | 2.00 | 10.00 |

MOTORS, THE
The Motors feature Bram Tchaikovsky.

Virgin 9515		Dancing The Night Away / Whiskey And Wine	1977	.60	3.00
Virgin 9517		Cold Love /	1977	.60	3.00
Virgin 9519		Airport / Mama Rock 'N' Roller	1978	.60	3.00
Virgin 9520		Forget About You / Breathless	1978	.60	3.00
Virgin 9521		Today / The Hustler	1978	.60	3.00
Virgin 67007		Love And Loneliness / Time For Makeup	1980	.30	1.50
Virgin 67007	(PS)	Love And Loneliness / Time For Makeup	1980	.30	1.50

MOTT THE HOOPLE [MOTT]

Atlantic 2749		Rock And Roll Queen / Backsliding Fearlessly	1970	.80	4.00
Columbia 45673		All The Young Dudes / One Of The Boys	1972	.60	3.00
Columbia 45673	(PS)	All The Young Dudes / One Of The Boys	1972	1.00	5.00
		(Produced by David Bowie.)			
Columbia 45754		One Of The Boys / Sucker	1972	.60	3.00
Columbia 45784		Sweet Jane / Jerkin' Crocus	1973	.60	3.00
Columbia 45882		Honaloochie Boogie / Rose	1973	.60	3.00
Columbia 45920		All The Way From Memphis / I Wish I Was Your Mother	1973	.40	2.00
Columbia 46035		The Golden Age Of Rock 'N' Roll / Rest In Peace	1974	.40	2.00
Columbia 46076		Roll Away The Stone / Looking Glass	1974	.40	2.00
Columbia 10091		All The Young Dudes / Rose	1975	.40	2.00

MOUNT RUSHMORE

| Dot 17158 | | Stone Free / She's So Good To Me | 1968 | 1.00 | 5.00 |

MOUNTAIN

Windfall 532		Mississippi Queen / The Laird	1970	.60	3.00
Windfall 533		For Yasgur's Farm / To My Friend	1970	.40	2.00
Windfall 534		Tired Angels / The Animal Trainer And The Toad	1971	.40	2.00

MOURNING REIGN

Link 1		Satisfaction Guaranteed / Our Fate	196?	6.00	30.00
Link 1	(PS)	Satisfaction Guaranteed / Our Fate	196?	15.00	75.00
Link 2		Evil Hearted You / Get Out Of My Life, Woman	196?	2.00	10.00
Contour 601		Evil Hearted You / Get Out Of My Life, Woman	196?	2.00	10.00

MOUSE & THE TRAPS
Mouse & The Traps also recorded as Positively 13 O' Clock.

Fraternity 956		A Public Execution / All For You	1965	3.00	15.00
Fraternity 971		Would You Believe? / Like I Know You Do	1966	3.00	15.00
Fraternity 1005	(PS)	Sometimes You Just Can't Win (Promo)	1966	15.00	75.00
Fraternity 1005		Sometimes You Just Can't Win / Beg, Borrow And Steal	1966	3.00	15.00
Capitol 2460		Mouse / Streets Of A Dusty Town	1969	2.00	10.00

MOUTH & MacNEIL

Philips 40715		How Do You Do? / Land Of Milk And Honey	1972	.60	3.00
Philips 40717		Hey, You Love / Why Did You, Why?	1972	.40	2.00
Philips 40721		Hello-A / Sing A Long	1972	.40	2.00
Philips 40721	(PS)	Hello-A / Sing A Long	1972	.40	2.00

MOVE, THE
The original Move was Bev Began, Trevor Burton, Chris Kefford, Carl Wayne and Roy Wood. In 1968 Kefford and Burton were replaced by Rick Price with Wayne replaced by Jeff Lynne in 1970. The last Move recordings were, in effect, the first Electric Light Orchestra sessions. Refer to The Idle Race; The Magic Christians.

Deram 7504		Night Of Fear / The Disturbance	1967	2.00	10.00
Deram 7506		I Can Hear The Grass Grow /			
		Wave The Flag And Stop The Train	1967	2.00	10.00

Label & Catalog #	A-Side/B-Side	Year	VG	NM
A&M 884	Flowers In The Rain / Lemon Tree (Here We Go 'Round)	1968	1.00	5.00
A&M 914	Fire Brigade / Walk Upon The Water	1968	2.00	10.00
A&M 966	Yellow Rainbow / Something	1968	.80	4.00
A&M 1020	Blackberry Way / Something	1969	.80	4.00
A&M 1119	Curly / This Time Tomorrow	1969	.80	4.00
A&M 1197	Brontosaurus / Lightning Never Strikes Twice	1969	.80	4.00
Capitol 3126	Tonight / Don't Mess Me Up	1970	2.00	10.00
MGM 14332 (DJ)	Chinatown / Down On The Bay	1972	2.00	10.00
MGM 14332	Chinatown / Down On The Bay	1972	4.00	20.00
United Artists 50876	Chinatown / Down On The Bay	1972	.80	4.00
United Artists 50928	Do Ya / California Man	1972	.80	4.00
United Artists 202	Tonight / My Marge	1972	.80	4.00

MOVING SIDEWALKS, THE
The Moving Sidewalks feature Billy Gibbons, later of ZZ Top.

Label & Catalog #	A-Side/B-Side	Year	VG	NM
Wand 1156	99th Floor / What Are You Going To Do?	1967	4.00	20.00
Tantara 3101	99th Floor / What Are You Going To Do?	1969	4.00	20.00
Tantara 3108	I Want To Hold Your Hand / Joe Blues	1969	4.00	20.00

MU

Label & Catalog #	A-Side/B-Side	Year	VG	NM
Mantra 101	Ballad Of Brother Lew / Nobody Wants To Shine	196?	2.00	10.00
Mu 103	On Our Way To Hana / Too Naked For Demetrius	196?	2.00	10.00

MUDCRUTCH
Mudcrutch features Tom Petty.

Label & Catalog #	A-Side/B-Side	Year	VG	NM
Pepper 9449	Up In Mississippi / Cause Is Understood	1971	100.00	400.00
	(Privately pressed. All but a handful are believed to have been destroyed.)			
Shelter 40357 (DJ)	Depot Street / Wild Eyes	1975	4.00	20.00
Shelter 40357	Depot Street / Wild Eyes	1975	6.00	30.00

MUGWUMPS, THE
The Mugwumps are Denny Doherty and Cass Elliot, later of The Mamas & The Papas; John Sebastian and Zal Yanovsky, founders of The Lovin' Spoonful; and James Hendricks.

Label & Catalog #	A-Side/B-Side	Year	VG	NM
Warner Bros. 5471	I'll Remember Tonight / I Don't Wanna Know	1964	2.00	10.00
Warner Bros. 7018	Here It Is Another Day / Searchin'	1967	1.20	6.00

MUGWUMPS, THE

Label & Catalog #	A-Side/B-Side	Year	VG	NM
Sidewalk 900	Jug Band Music / Bald Headed Woman	1966	2.00	10.00
Sidewalk 909	My Gal / Season Of The Witch	1967	2.00	10.00

MULBERRY FRUIT BAND, THE
The Mulberry Fruit Band features Pete Anders and Vinnie Poncia.

Label & Catalog #	A-Side/B-Side	Year	VG	NM
Buddah 1	Yes, We Have No Bananas / The Audition	1967	2.00	10.00

MUNGO JERRY

Label & Catalog #	A-Side/B-Side	Year	VG	NM
Janus 125	In The Summertime / Mighty Man	1970	.60	3.00
Janus 128	Johnny B. Badde / My Friend	1970	.60	3.00
Bell 123	Lady Rose / Little Louis	1971	.50	2.50
Bell 383	Alright, Alright, Alright /	1973	.50	2.50
Bell 451	Long Legged Woman Dressed In Black /	1974	.50	2.50

MURALS, THE

Label & Catalog #	A-Side/B-Side	Year	VG	NM
Climax 110	See You In September / Ambush	1959	8.00	40.00

MURCY, T.R.

Label & Catalog #	A-Side/B-Side	Year	VG	NM
Capitol 2394	Time And The Rain / T.R. Murcy	1969	2.00	10.00
Capitol 2603	40 Miles To L.A. / Just Listen	1969	2.00	10.00

MURE, BILLY

Label & Catalog #	A-Side/B-Side	Year	VG	NM
Cosmic 1001	Haunted Guitar / (B-side by Syd Lawrence)	1956	2.00	10.00

MURE, SAL

Label & Catalog #	A-Side/B-Side	Year	VG	NM
United Artists 153	Desire / Morse Code	1959	2.00	10.00

MURMAIDS, THE

Label & Catalog #	A-Side/B-Side	Year	VG	NM
Chattahoochee 628	Popsicles And Icicles / Blue Dress	1963	4.00	20.00
Chattahoochee 628	Popsicles And Icicles / Huntington Flats	1963	3.00	15.00
Chattahoochee 636	Heartbreak Ahead / He's Good To Me	1964	2.00	10.00
Chattahoochee 641	Wild And Wonderful / Bull Talk	1964	2.00	10.00
Chattahoochee 711	Go Away / Little Boys	1967	2.00	10.00
Liberty 56078	Paper Sun / Song Through Perception	1968	2.00	10.00

MURPHY, JIMMY

Label & Catalog #	A-Side/B-Side	Year	VG	NM
Columbia 21486	Here Kitty Kitty / I'm Looking For A Mustard Patch	1956	10.00	50.00
Columbia 21534	Sixteen Tons Of Rock And Roll / My Gal Dottie	1956	15.00	75.00
Columbia 21569	Baboon Boogie / Grandpaw's Cat	1956	8.00	40.00

Label & Catalog #	A-Side/B-Side	Year	VG	NM
MURPHY, JIMMY, & THE ACCENTS				
Rev 3508	I'm Gone, Mama / Plum Crazy	1957	5.00	25.00
MURRAY, JACK				
Laurie 3199	Surfin' With Me / What Do You Think Of Me, Baby?	1963	3.00	15.00
MURRAY, RAY, & THE DYNAMICS				
Arbo 222	With All My Love / Baby, What You Want Me To Do	195?	20.00	100.00
MURRAY THE K				
Red Bird 045	It's What's Happening, Baby / Sins Of A Family	1965	2.00	10.00
MUS-TWANGS, THE				
Nero 61	Marie / Roch Lomond	1961	5.00	25.00
Smash 1700	Marie / Roch Lomond	1961	3.00	15.00
MUSHROOMS, THE				
Hideout 1121	Such A Lovely Child / Burned	196?	5.00	25.00
MUSIC CITY FIVE, THE				
Giant 9026	Surfer Girl /	196?	7.00	35.00
MUSIC EMPORIUM, THE				
Sentinel 501	Nam Myo Ho Renge Kyo / Times Like This	196?	5.00	25.00
MUSIC EXPLOSION, THE				
The Music Explosion features Jamie Lyons.				
Attack 1404	Little Black Egg / Stay By My Side	1966	4.00	20.00
Laurie 3380	I See The Light / Little Bit O' Soul	1967	2.00	10.00
	(First pressings list "I See The Light" as the a-side.)			
Laurie 3380	Little Bit O' Soul / I See The Light	1967	1.00	5.00
Laurie 3400	Sunshine Games / Can't Stop Now	1967	.80	4.00
Laurie 3414	Hearts And Flowers / We Gotta Go Home	1967	.80	4.00
Laurie 3429	Road Runner / What You Want?	1967	.80	4.00
Laurie 3440	Where Are We Going? / Flash	1968	.80	4.00
Laurie 3454	Yes, Sir / Dazzling	1968	.80	4.00
Laurie 3466	Jack In The Box / Rewind	1968	.80	4.00
Laurie 3479	What's Your Name? / Call Me Anything	1969	.80	4.00
Laurie 3500	Little Black Egg / Stay By My Side	1969	1.25	6.00
MUSIC MACHINE, THE [SEAN BONNIWELL'S MUSIC MACHINE]				
The Music Machine features Sean Bonniwell.				
Original Sound 61	Talk Talk / Come On In	1966	2.00	10.00
Original Sound 67	The People In Me / Masculine Intuition	1967	1.00	5.00
Original Sound 71	Double Yellow Line / Absolutely Positively	1967	1.00	5.00
Original Sound 75	The Eagle Never Hunts The Fly / I've Loved You	1967	1.00	5.00
Original Sound 82	Hey Joe / Wrong	1967	1.00	5.00
Original Sound	Music Machine Picture Sleeve	1967	2.00	10.00
	(Omnibus sleeve with neither titles nor a catalogue number.)			
Warner Bros. 7093	Bottom Of The Soul / Astrologically Incompatible	1968	1.00	5.00
Warner Bros. 7093 (PS)	Bottom Of The Soul / Astrologically Incompatible	1968	3.00	15.00
Warner Bros. 7199	You'll Love Me Again / To The Light	1968	1.00	5.00
Bell 764	Advise And Consent / Mother Nature, Father Earth	1969	1.00	5.00
MUSIC PRISM, THE				
NWI 2705	Feeling Better Today / It's Getting Late	196?	2.00	10.00
MUSIL COMBO, JIM				
Jay Emm 423	Grunion Run / North Beach	1963	2.00	10.00
MUSIQUE & THE LYRICS				
Valiant 740	My Love And Life /	1966	4.00	20.00
MUSSIES, THE				
Fenton 2508	Louie, Go Home / 12 O' Clock July	196?	3.00	15.00
MUSTANGS, THE				
Vest	Over The Rainbow / Look	196?	25.00	125.00
MUSTANGS, THE				
Keetch 6002	Baby, Let Me Take You Home / Davie Was A Bad Boy	196?	2.00	10.00
Providence 401	Dartell Stomp / Lazy Love	1963	2.00	10.00
Providence 407	Topsy '65 / Rumpus	1964	2.00	10.00
Sure Shot 5004	First Love / A Change	1964	2.00	10.00
MYDDLE CLASS, THE				
Tomorrow 7501	Gates Of Eden / Free As The Wind	1965	2.00	10.00
Tomorrow 7503	I Happen To Love You / Don't Let Me Sleep Too Long	1965	2.00	10.00

Long ignored by collectors, generic house sleeves like this for the Original Sound label, are taking on a life of their own, fetching up to $5 in mint condition from completists. The single here, the Music Machine's *Talk Talk,* is the group's sole claim to fame and one of the better singles from 1966, a year known for great hits.

Label & Catalog #	A-Side/B-Side	Year	VG	NM
Buddah 150	I Happen To Love You / Don't Let Me Sleep Too Long	1965	1.60	8.00
Tomorrow 912	Don't Look Back / Wind Chime Laughter	1966	2.00	10.00

MYERS, DAVE, & THE SURFTONES

Impact 20	Moment Of Truth / Frog Walk	1962	7.00	35.00
Impact 27	Church Key / Passion	1962	7.00	35.00
Wickwire 13008	Gear / Let The Good Times Roll	1964	8.00	40.00

MYRON & THE VAN DELLS

Flo-Rue 531	Heartaches / Crazy Little Mama	195?	4.00	20.00

MYSTERIANS, THE

Jox 40	Is It A Lie? / Why Should I Love You?	196?	10.00	50.00

MYSTERIONS, THE

BRS 1011	Jerico Rock / Bite	1960	2.00	10.00
Warwick 521	Amnesia / Transylvania	1960	2.00	10.00

MYSTERY TOUR, THE

MGM 14097	The Ballad Of Paul / The Ballad Of Paul	1969	5.00	25.00
	(Deals with the "Paul McCartney is dead" rumors of '69.)			

MYSTERY TREND, THE

Verve 10499	Johnny Was A Good Boy / A House On The Hill	1967	3.00	15.00

MYSTICS, THE

The Mystics also recorded with Scott Garrett; Rusty Lane; and Don Press.

Laurie 3028		Hushabye / Adam And Eve	1959	3.00	15.00
Laurie 3028	(S)	Hushabye / Adam And Eve	1959	15.00	75.00
Laurie 3038		Don't Take The Stars / So Tenderly	1959	3.00	15.00
Laurie 3047		All Through The Night / To Think Again Of You	1960	4.00	20.00
Laurie 3058		Blue Star / White Cliffs Of Dover	1960	3.00	15.00
Laurie 3086		Star Crossed Lovers / Goodbye Me Blues	1961	4.00	20.00
Laurie 3104		Sunday Kind Of Love / Darling, I Know How	1961	5.00	25.00
Nolta 353		Fox / Dan	196?	1.00	5.00
Nolta		Hushabye /	196?	1.00	5.00

Common Record Collecting Abbreviations Used For Singles In Advertising

COH .... cut-out hole	RPM ....revolutions per minute
C-33 .... compact 33⅓ rpm single or EP	2ND PR... second pressing
CVR.. cover	SLT WRP ....slight warp
DJ .... disc jockey or promotional copy	SLV ....sleeve
EP ....45 rpm extended play album	SM SPLT... seam split
FLEXI ....flexible plastic disc	SOL.. sticker on the label
IMP... import	SR........................ slight ring-wear on the front cover
LBL ....label	ST...stereo
NAP ....(does) not affect play	STKR..sticker
OL...on label	TOC .... tape on the cover
ORG...original	TOL... tape on the label
PLN CVR....... plain paper jacket (no picture or titles)	TS..taped seams
PROMO ....promotional copy	WLP.. white label promo
PS... picture sleeve	WOL .... writing on the label
RE .... reissue	XOL .... an "x" is written on the label
REPRO ....reproduction or counterfeit	

N.

NAN & JAN
Debby 069   Beatle Bug / Believe It Or Not   1964   3.00   15.00

NAPOLEAN XIV
Napolean XIV is a pseudonym for Jerry Samuels.

Warner Bros. 5831	They're Coming To Take Me Away, Ha Haaa / Aaah-Ah, Yawa Em Ekat Ot Gnimoc Er'yeht	1966	1.60	8.00
Warner Bros. 5853	Doin' The Napolean / I'm In Love With My Little Red Tricycle	1966	1.20	6.00
Warner Bros. 7726	They're Coming To Take Me Away, Ha Haaa / Aaah-Ah, Yawa Em Ekat Ot Gnimoc Er'yeht	1973	.60	3.00

NARDONE, JOE, & THE ALL STARS [JOE NARDONE'S ALL STARS]
Features Joe "Gallery Of Sound" Nardone.

Madison 124	Ten Swingin' Indians / Caravan	1959	3.00	15.00
Red Bird 070	Shake A Hand / Ride Your Pony	1967	2.00	10.00

NARTICALS, THE
Polo 210   Castaway /   196?   2.00   10.00

NASEY, RON CAMERON
Rendezvous 137   The Panic / The Stop   1960   3.00   15.00

NASH, GRAHAM
Graham Nash also recorded with The Hollies; Crosby, Stills & Nash; and Neil Young & Graham Nash.

Atlantic 2804	Chicago / Simple Man	1971	.40	2.00
Atlantic 2827	Military Madness / Sleep Song	1971	.40	2.00
Atlantic 2840	Used To Be A King / Wounded Bird	1971	.40	2.00
Atlantic 2990	Prison Song / Hey You (Looking At The Moon)	197?	.40	2.00
Capitol 4812	In The 80's / TV Guide	198?	.30	1.50
Capitol 4849	Out On The Island / Helicoptor Song	198?	.30	1.50
Capitol 4879	Earth And Sky / Magical Child	198?	.30	1.50

NASHVILLE TEENS, THE

London 9689	Tobacco Road / I Like It Like That	1964	2.00	10.00
London 9712	T.N.T. / Goggle Eye	1964	1.20	6.00
London 9736	Find My Way Back Home / Devil-In-Law	1965	1.20	6.00
MGM 13357	Little Bird / Whatcha Gonna Do?	1965	1.20	6.00
MGM 13406	I Know How It Feels To Be Loved / Soon Forgotten	1965	1.20	6.00
MGM 13483	The Hard Way / Upside Down	1966	1.20	6.00
MGM 13678	That's My Woman / Words	1967	1.20	6.00
United Artists 50880	Ella James / Tennessee	1971	1.00	5.00

NATIONAL BANK OF SOUND, THE
Sea West 103   Me And My Friends / God Save America   196?   2.00   10.00

NATURAL GAS

Private Stock 100	The Right Time / Dark Cloud	1976	.60	3.00
Private Stock 116	Once Again, A Love Song /	1976	.60	3.00

NATURALS, THE

Red Top 113	Blue Moon / How Strange	1958	5.00	25.00
Hunt 325	Blue Moon / How Strange	1959	3.00	15.00

NATURALS, THE: *Refer to* THE FOUR NATURALS

NATURE BOY & FRIENDS
Bertram Inter. 255   Surfer John / John John   1964   8.00   40.00

NAVARROS, THE
Corby 204   Moses / Ikie   196?   2.00   10.00

NAVIGATORS, THE
Monument 934   Space Coup / The Westerner   1966   1.20   6.00

NAYLOR, JERRY
Jerry Naylor also recorded with The Crickets.

Skyla 1118	Stop Your Crying / You're Thirteen	1962	2.00	10.00
Skyla 1123	Judee Malone / I'm Tired	1962	2.00	10.00
Columbia 45106	But For Love / Angeline	1970	1.00	5.00

Whether playing as the house band for San Sousci Park or opening for such as-yet-unknown acts as Neil Diamond, Joe Nardone's All Stars typified a great many regional bands, except that they made it onto two national labels. Their first was on Madison but their best is this fairly obscure Red Bird release. Rumors of an album cut "live" from the same period have Gallery of Sound habitues in a constant state of expectation...

Label & Catalog #		A-Side/B-Side	Year	VG	NM
NAZY, RON CAMERON					
Trey 3013		The Great Debate / The Great Debate	1960	2.00	10.00
NAZZ, THE					
The Nazz later recorded as The Alice Cooper Group.					
Very 001		Lay Down And Die, Goodbye /			
		Wonder Who's Loving Her Now?	1967	330.00	1,000.00
NAZZ, THE					
This Nazz was Thom Mooney, Todd Rundgren, Stewkey and Carson Van Osten.					
SGC 001	(DJ)	Hello, It's Me *(One sided)*	1968	6.00	30.00
SGC 001	(DJ)	Hello, It's Me / Hello, It's Me	1968	3.00	15.00
SGC 001	(DJ)	Hello, It's Me / Open My Eyes	1968	4.00	20.00
SGC 001		Hello, It's Me / Open My Eyes	1968	3.00	15.00
		(First pressings have yellow labels with lines.)			
SGC 001		Hello, It's Me / Open My Eyes	1968	2.00	10.00
		(Second pressings yellow labels without lines.)			
SGC 001		Hello, It's Me / Open My Eyes	1969	1.20	6.00
		(Third pressings have green & yellow labels.)			
SGC 001	(PS)	Hello, It's Me / Open My Eyes	1968	4.00	20.00
SGC 006	(DJ)	Not Wrong Long / Under The Ice	1969	4.00	20.00
SGC 006		Not Wrong Long / Under The Ice	1969	2.00	10.00
		(First pressings yellow labels without lines.)			
SGC 006		Not Wrong Long / Under The Ice	1969	1.20	6.00
		(Second pressings have green & yellow labels.)			
SGC 006	(PS)	Not Wrong Long / Under The Ice	1969	4.00	20.00
SGC 009		Some People / Magic Me	1970	2.00	10.00
SGC 009		Kicks / Magic Me	1970	5.00	25.00
NEAL, JERRY					
Dot 15810		Scratchin' / I Hate Rabbits	1958	8.00	40.00
		("Scratchin'" features Eddie Cochran on guitar.)			
NEAL & THE NEWCOMBERS					
Hall Way 1206		Reeling And Rocking / Rocking Pneumonia	1964	3.00	15.00
NED & NELDA					
Ned & Nelda are Frank Zappa and Ray Collins, soon to be Mothers.					
Vigah 002		Hey, Nelda / Surf Along	1963	25.00	125.00
NEE, BERNIE					
Columbia 40906		Hey, Janey / Hey Liley, Liley Lo	1957	3.00	15.00
Columbia 41090		Lend Me Your Comb / Medal Of Honor	1957	3.00	15.00
NEGLIGEES, THE					
Lancer 3333		No Chemise '65 /	1965	2.00	10.00
NEIGHB'RHOOD CHILDR'N, THE [NEIGHBERHOOD]					
Acta 813		Maintain / Just No Way	1976	1.20	6.00
		(Acta 813 credits Neighborhood.)			
Acta 823		Please Leave Me / Happy Child	1968	1.00	5.00
Acta 828		I Want Action / Behold The Lilies	1968	1.00	5.00
Dot 17238		On Our Way / Woman Think	1969	1.00	5.00
N.A.M.A. 2014		Dancing In The Street /	196?	1.00	5.00
NEIL, FRED					
Elektra 45008		I Know You Rider / *(B-side by Vince Martin)*	1965	1.00	5.00
Capitol 5786		Dolphins / Babi-Da	1966	.80	4.00
Capitol 2047		The Dolphins / I've Got A Secret	1967	.80	4.00
Capitol 2091		Felicity / Please Send Me Someone To Love	1968	.80	4.00
Capitol 2256		Everybody's Talkin' / That's The Bag I'm In	1968	.80	4.00
Capitol 2604		Badi-Da / Everybody's Talkin'	1969	.60	3.00
NEIL & JACK					
Neil Diamond and Jack Parker.					
Duel 508		You Are My Love At Last / What Will I Do?	1960	75.00	300.00
Duel 517		I'm Afraid / Till You Find Love	1961	75.00	300.00
NELSON, RICKY [RICK NELSON]					
Verve 10047		A Teenager's Romance / I'm Walkin'	1957	5.00	25.00
Verve 10070		You're My One And Only Love / *(B-side by Barney Kessel)*	1957	4.00	20.00
Imperial 5463		Be-Bop Baby / Have I Told You Lately That I Love You?	1957	4.00	20.00
		(Maroon label.)			
Imperial 5463		Be-Bop Baby / Have I Told You Lately That I Love You?	1957	3.00	15.00
		(Black label.)			
Imperial 5463	(PS)	Be-Bop Baby / Have I Told You Lately That I Love You?	1957	6.00	30.00
Imperial 5483		Stood Up / Waitin' In School	1957	3.00	15.00
Imperial 5483	(PS)	Stood Up / Waitin' In School	1957	5.00	25.00

Label & Catalog #		A-Side/B-Side	Year	VG	NM
Imperial 5503		Believe What You Say / My Bucket's Got A Hole In It	1958	3.00	15.00
Imperial 5503	(PS)	Believe What You Say / My Bucket's Got A Hole In It	1958	5.00	25.00
Imperial 5528		Poor Little Fool / Don't Leave Me This Way	1958	3.00	15.00
Imperial 5545		Lonesome Town / I Got A Feeling	1958	3.00	15.00
Imperial 5545	(PS)	Lonesome Town / I Got A Feeling	1958	5.00	25.00
Imperial 5565		Never Be Anyone Else But You / It's Late	1959	3.00	15.00
Imperial 5565	(PS)	Never Be Anyone Else But You / It's Late	1959	6.00	30.00
Imperial 5595		Sweeter Than You / Just A Little Too Much	1959	3.00	15.00
Imperial 5595	(PS)	Sweeter Than You / Just A Little Too Much	1959	5.00	25.00
Imperial 5614		I Wanna Be Loved / Mighty Good	1959	3.00	15.00
Imperial 5614	(PS)	I Wanna Be Loved / Mighty Good	1959	5.00	25.00
Imperial 5663		Young Emotions / Right By My Side	1960	3.00	15.00
Imperial 5663	(PS)	Young Emotions / Right By My Side	1960	5.00	25.00
Imperial 5685		I'm Not Afraid / Yes Sir, That's My Baby	1960	3.00	15.00
Imperial 5685	(PS)	I'm Not Afraid / Yes Sir, That's My Baby	1960	5.00	25.00
Imperial 5707		You Are The Only One / Milk Cow Blues	1960	3.00	15.00
Imperial 5707	(PS)	You Are The Only One / Milk Cow Blues	1960	5.00	25.00
Imperial 5741	(DJ)	Travelin' Man / Hello, Mary Lou (Red vinyl)	1961	——	——
		(Rare. Estimated near mint value $250-500.)			
Imperial 5741		Travelin' Man / Hello, Mary Lou	1961	3.00	15.00
Imperial 5741	(PS)	Travelin' Man / Hello, Mary Lou	1961	4.00	20.00
Imperial 5770		A Wonder Like You / Everlovin'	1961	3.00	15.00
Imperial 5770	(PS)	A Wonder Like You / Everlovin'	1961	4.00	20.00
Imperial 5805		(It's A) Young World / Summertime	1962	3.00	15.00
Imperial 5805	(PS)	(It's A) Young World / Summertime	1962	4.00	20.00
Imperial 5864		Teen Age Idol / I've Got My Eyes On You	1962	3.00	15.00
Imperial 5864	(PS)	Teen Age Idol / I've Got My Eyes On You	1962	4.00	20.00
Imperial 5901		It's Up To You / I Need You	1962	3.00	15.00
Imperial 5901	(PS)	It's Up To You / I Need You	1962	4.00	20.00
Imperial 5910		That's All / I'm In Love Again	1963	3.00	15.00
Imperial 5935		Old Enough To Love / If You Can't Rock Me	1963	2.00	10.00
Imperial 5935	(PS)	Old Enough To Love / If You Can't Rock Me	1963	4.00	20.00
Imperial 5958		A Long Vacation / Mad, Mad World	1963	2.00	10.00
Imperial 5985		Time After Time / There's Not A Minute	1963	2.00	10.00
Imperial 66004		Today's Teardrops / Thank You, Darling	1964	2.00	10.00
Imperial 66004	(PS)	Today's Teardrops / Thank You, Darling	1964	4.00	20.00
Imperial 66017		Congratulations / One Minute Too Late	1964	2.00	10.00
Imperial 66039		Lucky Star / Everybody But Me	1964	2.00	10.00
Decca 31475		You Don't Love Me Anymore / I Got A Woman	1963	2.00	10.00
Decca 31475	(PS)	You Don't Love Me Anymore / I Got A Woman	1963	4.00	20.00
Decca 31495		String Along / Gypsy Woman	1963	2.00	10.00
Decca 31495	(PS)	String Along / Gypsy Woman	1963	4.00	20.00
Decca 31533		Fools Rush In / Down Home	1963	2.00	10.00
Decca 31533	(PS)	Fools Rush In / Down Home	1963	4.00	20.00
Decca 31574		For You / That's All She Wrote	1963	2.00	10.00
Decca 31574	(PS)	For You / That's All She Wrote	1963	4.00	20.00
Decca 31612		The Very Thought Of You / I Wonder	1964	1.50	8.00
Decca 31612	(PS)	The Very Thought Of You / I Wonder	1964	4.00	20.00
Decca 31656		There's Nothing I Can Say / Lonely Corner	1964	1.25	6.00
Decca 31656	(PS)	There's Nothing I Can Say / Lonely Corner	1964	4.00	20.00
Decca 31703		A Happy Guy / Don't Breathe A Word	1964	1.25	6.00
Decca 31703	(PS)	A Happy Guy / Don't Breathe A Word	1964	4.00	20.00
Decca 31756		Mean Old World / When The Chips Are Down	1965	1.25	6.00
Decca 31756	(PS)	Mean Old World / When The Chips Are Down	1965	4.00	20.00
Decca 31800		Yesterday's Love / Come Out Dancin'	1965	1.25	6.00
Decca 31800	(PS)	Yesterday's Love / Come Out Dancin'	1965	4.00	20.00
Decca 31845		Love And Kisses / Say You Love Me	1965	1.25	6.00
Decca 31845	(PS)	Love And Kisses / Say You Love Me	1965	4.00	20.00
Decca 31900		Your Kind Of Lovin' / Fire-Breathin' Dragon	1965	1.25	6.00
Decca 31956		Louisiana Man / You Just Can't Quit	1966	1.25	6.00
Decca 31956	(PS)	Louisiana Man / You Just Can't Quit	1966	4.00	20.00
Decca 32026		Things You Gave Me / Alone	1966	1.25	6.00
Decca 32026	(PS)	Things You Gave Me / Alone	1966	4.00	20.00
Decca 32055		Take A Broken Heart / They Don't Give Medals	1966	1.25	6.00
Decca 32120		I'm Called Lonely / Take A City Bride	1967	1.25	6.00
Decca 32120	(PS)	I'm Called Lonely / Take A City Bride	1967	4.00	20.00
Decca 32176		Suzanne On A Sunday Morning / Moonshine	1967	1.00	5.00
Decca 32222		Dream Weaver / Baby Close Its Eyes	1967	1.00	5.00
Decca 32284		Promenade In Green / Don't Blame It On Your Wife	1968	1.00	5.00
Decca 32298		Don't Make Promises / Barefoot Boy	1968	1.00	5.00
Decca 32550		She Belongs To Me / Promises	1969	1.00	5.00
Decca 32635		Easy To Be Free / Come On In	1970	.80	4.00
Decca 32635	(PS)	Easy To Be Free / Come On In	1970	3.00	15.00
Decca 32676		If You Gotta Go, Go Now / I Shall Be Released	1970	.80	4.00
Decca 32711		We Got Such A Long Way To Go / Look At Mary	1970	.80	4.00
Decca 32739		How Long? / Down Along The Bayou Country	1971	.80	4.00
Decca 32779		Life / California	1971	.80	4.00
Decca 32860		Sing Me A Song / Thank You, Lord	1971	.80	4.00

Label & Catalog #		A-Side/B-Side	Year	VG	NM
Decca 32906		Love Minus Zero-No Limit / Gypsy Pilot	1972	.80	4.00
Decca 32980		Garden Party / So Long Mama	1972	.60	3.00
MCA 40001		Palace Guard / A Flower Opens Gently	1973	.80	4.00
MCA 40130		Evil Woman Child / Lifestream	1973	.80	4.00
MCA 40187		Windfall / Legacy	1974	.80	4.00
MCA 40214		One Night Stand / Lifestream	1974	.80	4.00
MCA 40392		Louisiana Belle / Try (To Fall In Love)	1975	.80	4.00
MCA 40458		Rock And Roll Lady / Fade Away	1975	.80	4.00
Epic 50458		It's Another Day / You Can't Dance	1977	.80	4.00
Epic 50501		Gimme A Little Sign / Something You Can't Buy	1978	.80	4.00
Epic 50674		Dream Lover / That Ain't The Way Love's Supposed To Be	1979	.60	3.00
Capitol 4974		It Hasn't Happened Yet / Call It What You Want	1981	.60	3.00
Capitol 4988		Believe What You Say / The Loser, Babe, Is You	1981	.60	3.00
Capitol 5178		Give 'Em My Number / No Fair Falling In Love	1982	.60	3.00
MCA 52781		You Know What I Mean / Don't Leave Me This Way	1986	.60	3.00
MCA 52781	(PS)	You Know What I Mean / Don't Leave Me This Way	1986	.60	3.00
Epic 06066		Dream Lover / Rave On	1986	.60	3.00
Epic 06066	(PS)	Dream Lover / Rave On	1986	.60	3.00
		—Extended Play Albums—			
Verve 5048		Ricky	1957	4.00	200.00
Imperial 153	(DJ)	Ricky (Volume 1)	1957	30.00	150.00
Imperial 153		Ricky (Volume 1)	1957	12.00	60.00
Imperial 154	(DJ)	Ricky (Volume 2)	1957	30.00	150.00
Imperial 154		Ricky (Volume 2)	1957	12.00	60.00
Imperial 155	(DJ)	Ricky (Volume 3)	1957	30.00	150.00
Imperial 155		Ricky (Volume 3)	1957	12.00	60.00
Imperial 156	(DJ)	Ricky Nelson (Volume 1)	1958	30.00	150.00
Imperial 156		Ricky Nelson (Volume 1)	1958	12.00	60.00
Imperial 157	(DJ)	Ricky Nelson (Volume 2)	1958	30.00	150.00
Imperial 157		Ricky Nelson (Volume 2)	1958	12.00	60.00
Imperial 158	(DJ)	Ricky Nelson (Volume 3)	1958	30.00	150.00
Imperial 158		Ricky Nelson (Volume 3)	1958	12.00	60.00
Imperial 159	(DJ)	Ricky Sings Again (Volume 1)	1959	30.00	150.00
Imperial 159		Ricky Sings Again (Volume 1)	1959	12.00	60.00
Imperial 160	(DJ)	Ricky Sings Again (Volume 2)	1959	30.00	150.00
Imperial 160		Ricky Sings Again (Volume 2)	1959	12.00	60.00
Imperial 161	(DJ)	Ricky Sings Again (Volume 3)	1959	30.00	150.00
Imperial 161		Ricky Sings Again (Volume 3)	1959	12.00	60.00
Imperial 162	(DJ)	Songs By Ricky (Volume 1)	1959	30.00	150.00
Imperial 162		Songs By Ricky (Volume 1)	1959	12.00	60.00
Imperial 163	(DJ)	Songs By Ricky (Volume 2)	1959	30.00	150.00
Imperial 163		Songs By Ricky (Volume 2)	1959	12.00	60.00
Imperial 164	(DJ)	Songs By Ricky (Volume 3)	1959	30.00	150.00
Imperial 164		Songs By Ricky (Volume 3)	1959	12.00	60.00
Imperial 165	(DJ)	Ricky Sings Spirituals	1959	35.00	175.00
Imperial 165		Ricky Sings Spirituals	1959	25.00	125.00
Decca ED-4419	(33)	For Your Sweet Love (Jukebox EP)	1967	15.00	75.00
Decca ED-4660	(33)	Best Always (Jukebox EP)	1967	15.00	75.00

NELSON, SANDY
Sandy Nelson also recorded with The Gamblers and The Renegades.

Label & Catalog #		A-Side/B-Side	Year	VG	NM
Original Sound 5		Teen Beat / Big Jump	1959	3.00	15.00
		("Teen Beat" features Bruce Johnston.)			
Imperial 5630		Drum Party / Big Noise From Winnetka	1960	1.00	5.00
Imperial 5648		Party Time / The Wiggle	1960	1.00	5.00
Imperial 5672		Bouncy / Lost Dreams	1961	1.00	5.00
Imperial 5708		Cool Operator / Jive Talk	1961	1.00	5.00
Imperial 5745		Big Noise From The Jungle / Get With It	1961	1.00	5.00
Imperial 5775		Let There Be Drums / Quite A Beat	1961	1.20	6.00
Imperial 5809		Drums Are My Beat / The Birth Of The Beat	1962	1.20	6.00
Imperial 5829		Drummin' Up A Storm / Drum Stomp	1962	1.00	5.00
Imperial 5860		All Night Long / Rompin' And Stompin'	1962	1.00	5.00
Imperial 5870		And Then There Were Drums / Live It Up	1962	1.00	5.00
Imperial 5884		Teenage House Party / Day Train	1962	1.00	5.00
Imperial 5904		Let The Four Winds Blow / Be Bop Baby	1963	1.00	5.00
Imperial 5932		Ooh Poo Pah Doo / Feel So Good	1963	1.00	5.00
Imperial 5940		You Name It / Alexes	1963	1.00	5.00
Imperial 5965		Here We Go Again / Just Bull	1963	1.00	5.00
Imperial 5988		Caravan / Sandy	1964	1.00	5.00
Imperial 66019		Drum Shack / Kitty's Theme	1964	.80	4.00
Imperial 66034		Castle Rock / You Don't Say	1964	.80	4.00
Imperial 66060		Teen Beat '65 / Kitty's Theme	1964	.80	4.00
Imperial 66093		Reach For A Star / Chop Chop	1964	.80	4.00
Imperial 66107		Let There Be Drums '66 / Land Of 1,000 Drums	1965	.80	4.00
Imperial 66127		Casbah / Drums A Go Go	1965	1.20	6.00
Imperial 66146		A Lover's Concerto / Treat Her Right	1965	.80	4.00
Imperial 66193		Charge / Sock It To 'em, J.B.	1966	.80	4.00
Imperial 66209		Pipeline / Let's Go Trippin'	1966	1.20	6.00

Label & Catalog #		A-Side/B-Side	Year	VG	NM
Imperial 66246		The Drums Go On / Lawdy, Miss Clawdy	1966	.80	4.00
Imperial 66253		Peter Gunn / You Got The Hummin'	1966	.80	4.00
Imperial 66284		Midnight Magic / Alligator Boogaloo	1966	.80	4.00
Imperial 66350		Rebirth Of The Beat / The Lion In Winter	1969	.80	4.00
Imperial 66375		Manhattan Spiritual / The Stripper	1969	.80	4.00
Imperial 66402		Let There Be Drums And Brass / Leap Frog	1969	.80	4.00
United Artists 383		Dance With The Devil / Sunshine Of My Life	1974	.80	4.00
Veebitronics VT2A		Hunk Of Drums / Witch Hunt	1984	.80	4.00
		—Extended Play Albums—			
Imperial 2287	(33)	Drums A Go Go (Jukebox EP)	1966	3.00	15.00
Imperial 2298	(33)	Boss Beat (Jukebox EP)	1966	3.00	15.00

NELSON, TRACY
Tracy Nelson originally recorded with Mother Earth.

Atlantic 3235		It Takes A Lot To Laugh, It Takes A Train To Cry / Lean On Me	1975	.40	2.00
MCA 40479		Sweet Soul Music / Nothing I Can't Handle	1975	.40	2.00

NELSON GROUP, TERI

Kama Sutra 245		Sweet Talkin' Willie / Backside	1968	1.00	5.00

NEON PHILHARMONIC

Warner Bros. 7261		Morning Girl / Brilliant Colors	1969	1.00	5.00
Warner Bros. 7311		No One Is Going To Hurt You / You Lied	1969	.80	4.00
Warner Bros. 7355		Clouds / Snow	1969	.80	4.00
Warner Bros. 7380		Heighdy-Ho, Princess / Don't Know The Way Around Soul	1970	.80	4.00
Warner Bros. 7419		Flowers For Your Pillow / To Be Continued	1971	.80	4.00
Warner Bros. 7457		Something To Believe In / A Little Love	1971	.80	4.00
Warner Bros. 7497		I Got A Feelin' In My Bones / Keep The Faith With Me	1971	.80	4.00
TRX 5039		Annie Poor / Love Will Find A Way	1972	.80	4.00

NEONS, THE

Gone 5090		Angel Face / Golden Dreams	1960	5.00	25.00
Tetra 4444		Angel Face / Kiss Me Quickly	1956	8.00	40.00
Tetra 4449		Road To Romance / My Chickadee	1957	8.00	40.00
Challenge 9147		Magic Moment / Fat Girls	1961	10.00	50.00
Vintage 1016		Golden Dreams / Honey Bun	1974	.60	3.00

NEPTUNES, THE

Warner Bros. 5453		Shame Girl / I've Got Plans	1964	4.00	20.00
		(Produced by Gary Usher.)			

NERVES, THE
The Nerves feature Peter Case , later of The Plimsouls.

Nerves 4501	(EP)	The Nerves (White back cover)	1976	4.00	20.00
Nerves 4501	(EP)	The Nerves (Black back cover)	1976	3.00	15.00

NERVOUS NORVOUS
Nervous Norvous originally recorded with The Four Jokers.

Dot 15470		Transfusion / Dig (Maroon label)	1956	5.00	25.00
Dot 15470		Transfusion / Dig (Black label)	195?	3.00	15.00
Dot 15485		Ape Call / Wild Dog Of Kentucky (Maroon label)	1956	4.00	20.00
Dot 15500		The Fang / The Bullfrog Hop (Maroon label)	1956	4.00	20.00
Embee 117		I Like Girls / Stoneage Woo	1959	4.00	20.00
Big Ben 101		Pure Gold / Let's Worship God Each Sunday	195?	3.00	15.00

NERVOUS SYSTEM, THE

Jambee 1002		Make Love, Not War / Bones	196?	2.00	10.00

NESMITH, MIKE (& THE FIRST/SECOND NATIONAL BAND)
Refer to The Corvettes; Michael Blessing; Mike, John & Bill; The Monkees; Wichita Train Whistle.

Edan 1001		Just A Little Love / Curson Terrace	197?	20.00	100.00
RCA Victor 47-9853		Little Red Rider / Rose City Chimes	1970	2.00	10.00
RCA Victor 74-0368		Joanne / One Rose	1970	1.20	6.00
RCA Victor 74-0399		Silver Moon / Lady Of The Valley	1970	1.20	6.00
RCA Victor 74-0453		Nevada Fighter / Here I Am	1971	1.20	6.00
RCA Victor 74-0453	(PS)	Nevada Fighter / Here I Am	1971	3.00	15.00
RCA Victor SPS-45-263	(DJ)	Texas Morning / Tumbling Tumbleweeds	1971	2.00	10.00
RCA Victor 74-0491		Texas Morning / Tumbling Tumbleweeds	1971	1.20	6.00
RCA Victor 74-0540		Propinquity / Only Bound	1972	1.20	6.00
RCA Victor 74-0629		Mama Rocker / Lazy Lady	1972	1.20	6.00
RCA Victor 74-0804		Roll With The Flow / Keep On	1973	1.20	6.00
Pacific Arts 6373		Rio / Life, The Unsuspecting Captive	1976	.80	4.00
Pacific Arts 6398		Navajo Trail / Love's First Kiss	1976	.80	4.00
Pacific Arts 101		Roll With The Flow / I've Just Begun To Care	1978	.80	4.00
Pacific Arts 104		Rio / Casablanca Moonlight	1979	.80	4.00
Pacific Arts 104	(PS)	Rio / Casablanca Moonlight	1979	2.00	10.00
Pacific Arts 106		Magic (This Night Is Magic) / Dance	1979	.80	4.00

Label & Catalog #		A-Side/B-Side	Year	VG	NM
Pacific Arts 108		Cruisin' / Horse Race	1979	.80	4.00
		— 12" Singles—			
Pacific Arts 108		Cruisin' / Cruisin'	1979	3.00	15.00

NEUMAN, ALFRED E., & THE FURSHLUGGINER FIVE

ABC-Para. 10013		What, Me Worry? / Portzebie	1959	5.00	25.00

NEVEGANS, THE

X-P-A-N-D-E-D 101		Russian Roulette / One-Armed Bandit	1963	5.00	25.00

NEW ARRIVALS, THE

Macy's 104		Let's Get With It / Just Outside My Window	196?	2.00	10.00
Southbay 102		Take Me For What I Am / You Know You're Gonna Be Mine	196?	2.00	10.00
Southbay 103		Scratch Your Name / Just Outside My Window	196?	2.00	10.00
Southbay 104		Let's Get With It / Just Outside My Window	196?	2.00	10.00

NEW BREED, THE

New Breed 13635		Don't Jive / Unlock Your Mind	1966	2.00	10.00
World United 001		Want Ad Reader / One More For The Good Guys	1966	2.00	10.00
HBR 508		Want Ad Reader / One More For The Good Guys	1966	1.00	5.00
World United 003		Fine With Me / The Sound Of The Music	1966	2.00	10.00
Mercury 72556		Leave Me Be / I've Been Wrong Before	1966	1.00	5.00
Diplomacy 22		Green Eyed Woman / I'm In Love	196?	1.00	5.00

NEW CHRISTY MINSTRELS, THE
Formed by Randy Sparks, members have included Gene Clark, John Denver, Barry McGuire and Kenny Rogers.

Columbia 42592		This Land Is Your Land / Don't Cry, Suzanne	1962	.80	4.00
Columbia 42592	(PS)	This Land Is Your Land / Don't Cry, Suzanne	1962	.80	4.00
Columbia 42673		Denver / Liza Lee	1963	.80	4.00
Columbia 42805	(DJ)	Green, Green / The Banjo (Green vinyl)	1963	3.00	15.00
Columbia 42805		Green, Green / The Banjo	1963	.80	4.00
Columbia 42887		Saturday Night / The Wheeler Dealers	1963	.60	3.00
Columbia 43000		Today / Miss Katy Cruel	1964	.60	3.00
Columbia 43092		Silly Ol' Summertime / The Far Side Of The Hill	1964	.60	3.00
Columbia 43215		Chim, Chim, Cheree /			
		They Gotta Quit Kickin' My Dog Around	1965	.60	3.00
Columbia 43822		Beautiful, Beautiful World / A Corner In The Sun	1966	.60	3.00
Columbia 43961		It Should Have Been You / Sleep Comes Easy	1966	.60	3.00

NEW COLONY SIX, THE
The New Colony Six features Ronnie Rice.

Centaur 1201		I Confess / Dawn Is Breaking	1966	1.60	8.00
Centaur 1202		I Lie Awake / At The River's Edge	1966	1.60	8.00
Centaur 1203		Sunshine / Cadillac	1966	1.60	8.00
Centaur 1204		Power Of Love / (Ballad Of The) Wingbat Marmaduke	1966	1.60	8.00
Centaur 1205		Love You So Much / Let Me Love You	1967	1.60	8.00
Centaur 1206		You're Gonna Be Mine / Woman	1967	1.60	8.00
Centaur 1207		I'm Just Waiting / Hello, Lonely	1967	1.60	8.00
Mercury 72737		Treat Her Groovy / Rap-A-Tap	1967	.80	4.00
Mercury 72737	(PS)	Treat Her Groovy / Rap-A-Tap	1967	1.60	8.00
Mercury 72775		I Will Always Think About You / Hold Me With Your Eyes	1968	.80	4.00
Mercury 72817		Can't You See Me Cry? /			
		Summertime's Another Name For Love	1968	.80	4.00
Mercury 72817	(PS)	Can't You See Me Cry? /			
		Summertime's Another Name For Love	1968	1.60	8.00
Mercury 72858		Things I'd Like To Say / Come And Give Your Love To Me	1968	.80	4.00
Mercury 72920		I Could Never Lie To You / Just Feel Worse	1969	.80	4.00
Mercury 72961		I Want You To Know / Free	1969	.80	4.00
Mercury 73004		Barbara, I Love You / Prairie Grey	1970	.80	4.00
Mercury 73063		People And Me / Ride The Wicked World	1970	.80	4.00
Mercury 73093		Close Your Eyes, Little Girl / Love, That's The Best I Can Do	1970	.80	4.00
Sunlight 1001		Roll On / If You Could See	1971	.80	4.00
Sunlight 1004		Long Time To Be Alone / Never Be Lonely	1971	.80	4.00
Sunlight 1005		Come On Down / Someone, Sometime	1972	.80	4.00
MCA 40215		Long Time To Be Alone / Never Be Lonely	1974	.80	4.00
MCA 40288		I Really Don't Want To Go / Run	1974	.80	4.00
Twilight 1004		Never Be Lonely / Long Time To Be Alone	197?	.80	4.00

NEW DAWN, THE
New Dawn originally recorded as The Countdowns.

Garland 2020		Why Did You Go / Tears	196?	2.00	10.00
Mainstream 052		If I Can't have Your Love / Loser	196?	1.00	5.00

NEW DAY

Ket 4457		Night After Day / Ada Lane	196?	1.00	5.00

NEW ERA, THE

Great Lakes 2532		We Ain't Got Time / Won't You Please Be My Friend	196?	2.00	10.00

Label & Catalog #		A-Side/B-Side	Year	VG	NM
NEW ESTABLISHMENT, THE					
Colgems 5006		Sunday's Gonna Come On Tuesday / Baby, The Rain Must Fall	1969	1.20	6.00
NEW HAPPINESS, THE					
Columbia 43851		Winchester Cathedral / I'm Gonna Spoil You, Baby	1966	1.20	6.00
Columbia 44612		Ode To Larsen Whipsdale / Dear Chester	1968	1.20	6.00
NEW HARLEQUINS, THE					
Pacific Challenger 124		Zelda Klotz /	196?	8.00	40.00
NEW HOLLYWOOD ARGYLES, THE: *Refer to* THE HOLLYWOOD ARGYLES.					
NEW HOPE, THE					
Jamie 1381		Won't Find Better (Than Me) / They Call It Love	1969	1.00	5.00
Jamie 1385		Rain / Let's Get Lost On A Country Road	1970	1.00	5.00
Jamie 1388		Look Away / Money Game	1970	1.00	5.00
NEW MARKETTS, THE: *Refer to* THE MAR-KETS					
NEW ORDER					
Qwest 28421		Bizarre Love Triangle / Everly Little Counts	1986	1.20	6.00
Qwest 27979		Blue Monday 1988 / Touched By The Hand Of God	1988	.80	4.00
		— 12" Singles—			
Rough Trade 10	(DJ)	Blue Monday / The Beach	1983	2.00	10.00
Qwest PRO-2644	(DJ)	Way Of Life / Way Of Life	1986	1.60	8.00
Factory 73R		Blue Monday 1988 / Beach Buggy	1988	1.25	6.00
NEW PHOENIX					
World Pacific 77884		Give To Me Your Love / Thanks	1968	1.20	6.00
NEW RIDERS OF THE PURPLE SAGE, THE					
Columbia 45469		Louisiana Lady / Last Lonely Eagle	1971	.40	2.00
Columbia 45526		I Don't Know You / Garden Of Eden	1972	.40	2.00
Columbia 45607		I Don't Need No Doctor / Runnin' Back To You	1972	.40	2.00
Columbia 45682		Rainbow / Dim Lights, Thick Smoke	1972	.40	2.00
Columbia 45763		Groupie / She's No Angel	1972	.40	2.00
Columbia 45976		Panama Red / Cement, Clay And Grass	1973	.40	2.00
MCA 40564		Don't Put Her Down / Fifteen Days Under The Hood	1976	.40	2.00
MCA 40591		Dead Flowers / She's Looking Better Every Beer	1976	.40	2.00
MCA 40686		Love Has Strange Ways /	1977	.40	2.00
MCA 40715		(Just) Another Night In Reno /	1977	.40	2.00
NEW SOCIETY, THE					
RCA Victor 47-8807		Do Not Ask For Love / Buttermilk	1966	1.20	6.00
RCA Victor 47-8958		Dawn Of Sorrow / We Have So Little Time	1966	1.20	6.00
NEW THINGS, THE					
Accent 1228		Dumbo / I Want You Back	196?	8.00	40.00
NEW TRADITION, THE					
United Arts. 50608		Streets In The City / I'm Happy Again	1969	1.20	6.00
NEW TWEEDY BROTHERS, THE					
Dot 16910		Good Time Car / Terms Of You Love Me	1966	4.00	20.00
NEW VENTURES, THE: *Refer to* THE VENTURES					
NEW WING, THE					
The New Wing is a pseudonym for The Sons Of Adam.					
Pentacle 104		Brown Eyed Woman / I Need Love	196?	6.00	30.00
NEW WORLD, THE					
RAK 4505		Tom Tom Turnaround / Lay Me Down	1972	.80	4.00
RAK 4514		Living Next Door To Alice / Something To Say	1973	.80	4.00
NEW YORK DOLLS, THE					
Mercury 73414		Trash / Bad Girl	1973	3.00	15.00
Mercury 73414	(PS)	Trash / Bad Girl	1973	10.00	50.00
Mercury 73478		Stranded In The Jungle / Who Are The Mystery Girls?	1974	3.00	15.00
NEW YORK ROCK (& ROLL) ENSEMBLE, THE					
Atco 6467		Biji / Biji Rock	1967	1.00	5.00
Atco 6501		Kiss Her Once / Suddenly	1967	1.00	5.00
Atco 6584		Pick Up In The Morning / Thing To Do	1968	1.00	5.00
Atco 6671		The Brandenburg / Wait Until Tomorrow	1969	1.00	5.00
Columbia 45242		Running Down The Highway / Law And Order	1970	.80	4.00
Columbia 45288		Beside You / The King Is Dead	1970	.80	4.00
Columbia 45367		Fields Of Joy / Ride, Ride My lady	1971	.80	4.00

Label & Catalog #		A-Side/B-Side	Year	VG	NM
NEW YORK ROCK EXCHANGE, THE					
United Artists 50326		Hey, Baby / Harmonica Man	1968	1.00	5.00
NEW YORK THRUWAY, THE					
MGM 14071		Daphne / Jack B. Nimble	1969	1.20	6.00
NEW YORKERS, THE					
Santana 6602		Things Are Changing / (B-side by The Fury Four)	196?	2.00	10.00
Scepter 12190		When I'm Gone / You're Not My Girl	1967	1.00	5.00
Scepter 12199		Mr. Kirby / Seeds Of Spring	1967	1.00	5.00
Scepter 12207		Show Me The Way To Love / Again	1967	1.00	5.00
Jerden 906		Ice Cream World / Adrianne	1968	1.00	5.00
Jerden 908		Michael Clover / Land Of Ur	1969	1.00	5.00
Decca 32569		I Guess The Lord Must Be In New York City / Do Wah Diddy	1969	1.00	5.00
NEWBEATS, THE					
The Newbeats are Larry Henley with Dean and Marc Mathis.					
Hickory 1269		Bread And Butter / Tough Little Buggy	1964	2.00	10.00
Hickory 1282	(DJ)	Everything's Alright / Pink Dally Rue *(Yellow vinyl)*	1964	2.00	10.00
Hickory 1282	(DJ)	Everything's Alright / Pink Dally Rue *(Black vinyl)*	1964	3.00	15.00
Hickory 1282		Everything's Alright / Pink Dally Rue	1964	1.60	8.00
Hickory 1290		Break Away (From That Boy) / Hey-O, Daddy-O	1965	1.60	8.00
Hickory 1305		The Birds Are For The Bees / Better Watch Your Step	1965	1.60	8.00
Hickory 1320		I Can't Hear You No More / Little Child	1965	1.20	6.00
Hickory 1332		Run, Baby, Run (Back Into My Arms) / Mean Wooly Willie	1965	1.20	6.00
Hickory 1366		Shake Hands (And Come Out Crying) / Too Sweet To Be Forgotten	1966	1.00	5.00
Hickory 1387		Crying My Heart Out / Short On Love	1966	1.00	5.00
Hickory 1408		Bird Dog / Evil Eva	1966	1.00	5.00
Hickory 1422		My Yesterday Love / Patent On Love	1966	1.20	6.00
Hickory 1436		So Fine / Top Secret	1967	1.20	6.00
Hickory 1467		It's Really Goodbye / Hide The Moon	1967	1.20	6.00
Hickory 1485		You And Me And Happiness / Don't Turn Loose	1967	1.20	6.00
Hickory 1496		Bad Dreams / The Swinger	1968	1.20	6.00
Hickory 1510		Michelle De Ann / I've Been A Long Time Loving You	1968	1.20	6.00
Hickory 1522		The Girls And The Boys / Ain't That Loving You, Baby	1969	2.00	10.00
Hickory 1539		Thou Shalt Not Steal / Great Balls Of Fire	1969	1.20	6.00
Hickory 1552		Groovin' (Out On Life) / Bread And Butter	1969	1.20	6.00
Hickory 1562		Laura (What's He Got That I Ain't Got?) / Break Away From That Boy	1970	1.20	6.00
Hickory 1569		She Won't Hang Her Love (Out On The Line) / I'm A Teardrop	1970	1.20	6.00
Hickory 1600	(DJ)	Run, Baby, Run (Back Into My Arms) / Am I Not My Brother's Keeper?	1971	2.00	10.00
Hickory 1624	(DJ)	Remember Love / Oh, Pretty Woman	1972	2.00	10.00
Hickory 1637	(DJ)	Love Gets Sweeter / Everything's Alright	1972	2.00	10.00
		(Stock copies of Hickory 1600, 1624 and 1637 may not exist.)			
Buddah 390	(DJ)	The Way You Do The Things You Do / The Way You Do The Things You Do	197?	1.00	5.00
		(Stock copies of Buddah 390 may not exist.)			
Playboy 6013		I Know (You Don't Want Me No More) / I Believe I'm In Love With You	1974	1.20	6.00
		—Extended Play Albums—			
Hickory 120-005	(33)	Bread And Butter *(Jukebox EP)*	1967	6.00	30.00
NEWCOMERS, THE					
NWI 2697		A Time For Love / Mr. Sun	196?	2.00	10.00
NEWELL, SKIP, & THE MUSTANGS					
Trend 4107		Road Runner / Little Bit Of Nothing	196?	7.00	35.00
NEWLOOK, THE					
TRX 5011		East Of The Dawn (In The Year Of Our Love) / What Did You Take Me For?	1968	1.00	5.00
NEWMAN, RANDY					
Dot 16411		Golden Gridiron Boy / Country Boy	1962	6.00	30.00
		(Produced by Pat Boone and Jimmie Haskell!)			
Reprise 0284	(DJ)	I Think It's Going To Rain Today / The Beehive State	1968	2.00	10.00
		(10" 78 rpm single.)			
Reprise 0771	(DJ)	Last Night I Had A Dream / Old Man On The Farm	1968	——	——
		(In the quotable words of contributor Steve Braitman, "Last Night I Had A Dream" is a "radically different version than the LP, a completely freaked out acid casualty big rock band version." Estimated near mint value $25-75. Stock copies may not exist.)			
Reprise 1102		Sail Away / Political Science	1970	.60	3.00
Reprise 1387		Louisiana 1927 / Marie	1974	.60	3.00
Warner Bros. 8492		Short People / Old Man On The Farm	1977	.40	2.00

Label & Catalog #		A-Side/B-Side	Year	VG	NM
Warner Bros. 8550		Baltimore / You Can't Fool The Fat Man	1978	.40	2.00
Warner Bros. 8630		Raider In The Rain / Sigmund Freud's Impersonation			
		Of Albert Einstein In America	1978	.40	2.00
Warner Bros. 49088		It's Money That I Love / Ghosts	1979	.40	2.00
Warner Bros. 49149		The Story Of A Rock And Roll Band / Half A Man	1979	.40	2.00

NEWPORT NOMADS, THE

Prince 6304		Blue Mallard / Harem Belles	1962	8.00	40.00

NEWPORTERS, THE
The Newporters feature Scott Engel and John Maus a.k.a. John Stewart.

Scotchtown 500		Adventures In Paradise / Loose Board	1963	10.00	50.00

NEWPORTS, THE

Contour 301		Chicky Chop Chop / Hurry, Arthur Murray	196?	3.00	15.00
Guyden 2067		If I Could Tonight / A Fellow Needs A Girl	1962	2.00	10.00
Guyden 2116		Tears / Disillusioned Love	1964	4.00	20.00

NEWPORTS, THE

Parrot 40008		Listen (To Your Big Brother) / Party Night	1966	2.00	10.00

NEWTON BROTHERS, THE
Features Wayne Newton.

Capitol 4236		The Real Thing / I Spy	1959	10.00	50.00

NEWTON-JOHN, OLIVIA
Olivia Newton-John originally recorded with Toomorrow.

Uni 55281		If Not For You / The Bigger Clown	1971	1.00	5.00
Uni 55304		Banks Of The Ohio / It's So Hard To Say Goodbye	1971	1.00	5.00
Uni 55317		What Is Life? / I'm A Small And Lonely Light	1972	1.00	5.00
Uni 55348		Just A Little Too Much / My Old Man's Got A Gun	1972	1.00	5.00
MCA 40043	(DJ)	Take Me Home, Country Roads /	1973	3.00	15.00
		(Stock copies of MCA 40043 may not exist.)			
MCA 40101		Let Me Be There / Maybe Then I'll Think Of You	1973	.40	2.00
MCA 40209		If You Love Me (Let Me Know) / Brotherly Love	1974	.40	2.00
MCA 40280		I Honestly Love You / Home Ain't Home Anymore	1974	.40	2.00
MCA 40349		Have You Never Been Mellow? / Water Under The Bridge	1975	.40	2.00
MCA 40418		Please Mr. Please / And In The Morning	1975	.40	2.00
MCA 40418	(PS)	Please Mr. Please / And In The Morning	1975	.40	2.00
MCA 40459		Something Better To Do / He's My Rock	1975	.40	2.00
MCA 40459	(PS)	Something Better To Do / He's My Rock	1975	.40	2.00
MCA 40495		Let It Shine / He Ain't Heavy, He's My Brother	1975	.40	2.00
MCA 40525		Come On Over / Small Talk And Pride	1976	.40	2.00
MCA 40600		Don't Stop Believin' / Greensleeves	1976	.40	2.00
MCA 40600	(PS)	Don't Stop Believin' / Greensleeves	1976	.40	2.00
MCA 40642		Every Face Tells A Story / Hold The Key	1976	.40	2.00
MCA 40670		Sam / I'll Bet You A Kangaroo	1977	.40	2.00
MCA 40737		Making A Good Thing Better / I Think I'll Say Goodbye	1977	.40	2.00
MCA 40811		I Honestly Love You / Don't Cry For Me, Argentian	1977	.40	2.00
MCA 40811	(PS)	I Honestly Love You / Don't Cry For Me, Argentian	1977	.40	2.00
RSO 903		Hopelessly Devoted To You / (Instrumental b-side)	1978	.40	2.00
MCA 40975		A Little More Love / Borrowed Time	1978	.40	2.00
MCA 40975	(PS)	A Little More Love / Borrowed Time	1978	.40	2.00
MCA 41009		Deeper Than The Night / Please Don't Keep Me Waiting	1979	.40	2.00
MCA 41074		Totally Hot / Dancin' 'Round And 'Round	1979	.40	2.00
MCA 41074	(PS)	Totally Hot / Dancin' 'Round And 'Round	1979	.40	2.00
MCA 41247		Magic / Fool Country	1980	.40	2.00
MCA 41247	(PS)	Magic / Fool Country	1980	.40	2.00
MCA 51182		Physical / The Promise (The Dolphin Song)	1981	.40	2.00
MCA 51182	(PS)	Physical / The Promise (The Dolphin Song)	1981	.40	2.00
MCA 5200		Make A Move On Me /	1982	.40	2.00

NEWTON-JOHN, OLIVIA / THE ELECTRIC LIGHT ORCHESTRA

MCA 41285		Xanadu / Whenever I'm Away From You	1980	.30	1.50
MCA 2315	(DJ)	Xanadu / Whenever I'm Away From You (10" picture disc)	1980	150.00	600.00

NEWTON-JOHN, OLIVIA, & ANDY GIBB

RSO 1026		I Can't Help It / (B-side by Andy Gibb)	1980	.30	1.50
Polydor PRO-104	(DJ)	Rest Your Love On Me / Rest Your Love On Me	1979	3.00	15.00

NEWTON-JOHN, OLIVIA, & CLIFF RICHARD

MCA 51007		Suddenly / You Made Me Love You	1980	.30	1.50
MCA 51007	(PS)	Suddenly / You Made Me Love You	1980	.30	1.50

NEWTON-JOHN, OLIVIA, & JOHN TRAVOLTA

RSO 891		You're The One That I Want / Alone At A Drive-In Movie	1978	.30	1.50
RSO 891	(PS)	You're The One That I Want / Alone At A Drive-In Movie	1978	.30	1.50
RSO 906		Summer Nights / Rock 'N' Roll Party Queen	1978	.30	1.50

Label & Catalog #	A-Side/B-Side	Year	VG	NM
NEWTON, JOHNNY, & THE TAGS				
Bell 114	Sorry, Sorry (I Ran All The Way Home) / A Teenager In Love	1959	4.00	20.00
NEXT EXIT				
Spirit 0004	Soulful Child / Know	196?	1.20	6.00
NEXT EXIT, THE				
The Next Exit is a pseudonym for The Tokens.				
Warner Bros. 7220	I'm The Only One / Break Away	1968	1.00	5.00
NIC NACKS, THE				
Ovation 6201	Jolene / Since You Came	1963	2.00	10.00
NICK & THE NACKS				
Barry 108	The Night / That Old Black Magic	195?	50.00	200.00
NICKIE & THE NITELITES				
Nickie is Nick Massi.				
Brunswick 55155	I'm Lonely / Tell Me You Care	1959	25.00	125.00
NICKS & BUCKINGHAM: *Refer to* BUCKINGHAM NICKS				
NICKY & THE NOBLES				
End 1021	Schoolhouse Rock / A Way To Tell Her	1958	6.00	30.00
Gone 5039	School Day Crush / School Bells *(Black label)*	1959	6.00	30.00
Gone 5039	School Day Crush / School Bells *(Color label)*	1960	3.00	15.00
End 1098	School Day Crush / School Bells	1961	3.00	15.00
NIGHT HAWKS, THE				
Stars 550	You're My Baby /	196?	4.00	20.00
NIGHT OWLS, THE				
Bethlehem 3087	Bells Ring / Let's Go Again	1964	3.00	15.00
NIGHT PEOPLE, THE				
Seafair 103	Istanbul / Zazerac	1960	1.20	6.00
Seafair 103 (PS)	Istanbul / Zazerac	1960	2.00	10.00
Outlaw 2	The Troubled Streets / Lonely Before Dawn	196?	2.00	10.00
Berma 1311	So Deep / Nothing	1961	2.00	10.00
NIGHT RAIDERS, THE				
Profile 4007	Cotton Pickin' / Hidi Hidi Hidi	196?	3.00	15.00
NIGHT WALKERS, THE				
Detroit 2648	Sticks And Stones / Give Me Love	196?	3.00	15.00
NIGHTCAPS, THE				
Vandan 7491	Wine, Wine, Wine / Nightcap Rock	1960	3.00	15.00
Vandan 4280	Next Time You See Me /	1966	2.00	10.00
Vandan 4733	Wine, Wine, Wine / Walking The Dog	1966	2.00	10.00
NIGHTCRAWLERS, THE				
The Nightcrawlers originally recorded as Conlan & The Crawlers.				
Lee 1012	Little Black Egg / If I Were You	1966	10.00	50.00
Kapp 709	Little Black Egg / If I Were You	1966	3.00	15.00
Kapp 746	Basket Of Flowers / Washboard	1966	3.00	15.00
Kapp 826 (Can)	Today I'm Happy / My Butterfly	1967	6.00	30.00
Marlien 194	Basket Of Flowers / Washboard	196?	3.00	15.00
NIGHTRANES, THE				
Cucu 0444	Rockin' Abe / Hangover	1960	2.00	10.00
NIKITA THE K				
Warner Bros. 7005	Go Go Radio Moscow / The Spoiler	1967	2.00	10.00
NILSSON [HARRY NILSSON]				
Harry Nilsson originally recorded as Bo-Pete.				
Spindletop 923	Donna, I Understand / Wig Job	1963	2.00	10.00
Tower 103	Sixteen Tons / I'm Gonna Lose My Mind	1964	1.00	5.00
Tower 136	You Can't Take Your Love Away From Me / Born In Grenada	1966	1.00	5.00
Tower 244	She's Yours / Growin' up	1966	1.00	5.00
Tower 518	Good Times / Growin' Up	1969	1.00	5.00
RCA Victor 47-9206	Without Her / Freckles	1967	.80	4.00
RCA Victor 47-9298	You Can't Do That / Ten Little Indians	1967	.80	4.00
RCA Victor 47-9462	One / Sister Marie	1968	.80	4.00
RCA Victor 47-9544	Everybody's Talkin' / Don't Leave Me	1968	.80	4.00
RCA Victor 47-9675	Rainmaker / I Will Take You There	1968	.80	4.00

Label & Catalog #		A-Side/B-Side	Year	VG	NM
RCA Victor 74-0161		Everybody's Talkin' / Rainmaker	1969	.80	4.00
RCA Victor 74-0207		Marchin' Down Broadway / Maybe	1969	.80	4.00
RCA Victor 74-0261		I Guess The Lord Must Be In New York City / Maybe	1969	.80	4.00
RCA Victor 74-0310		Waiting / I'll Be Home	1970	.80	4.00
RCA Victor 74-0362		Down To The Valley / Buy My Album	1970	.80	4.00
RCA Victor 74-0336		Caroline / Yellow Man	1970	.80	4.00
RCA Victor SP-248	(DJ)	Me And My Arrow / The Town-Me And My Arrow	1971	1.20	6.00
RCA Victor 74-0443		Me And My Arrow / Are You Sleeping?	1971	.60	3.00
RCA Victor 74-0524		Without Her / Good Old Desk	1971	.60	3.00
RCA Victor 74-0604		Without You / Gotta Get Up	1971	.60	3.00
RCA Victor 74-0673		Jump Into The Fire / The Moonbeam Song	1972	.60	3.00
RCA Victor 74-0718		Coconut / Down	1972	.60	3.00
RCA Victor 74-0788		Spaceman / Turn On Your Radio	1972	.60	3.00
RCA Victor 74-0855		Remember (Christmas) / The Lottery Song	1972	.60	3.00
RCA Victor 74-0039		As Time Goes By / Lullabye In Ragtime	1973	.80	4.00
RCA Victor 74-0246		Daybreak / Dawn	1974	.60	3.00
RCA Victor 74-0246	(PS)	Daybreak / Dawn	1974	.60	3.00
RCA Victor PB-10001		Many Rivers To Cross / Don't Forget Me	1974	1.00	5.00
RCA Victor PB-10078		Subterranean Homesick Blues / Mucho Mungo-Mt. Elga	1974	1.00	5.00
		(RCA 10001 and 10078 feature John Lennon.)			
RCA Victor PB-10139		Don't Forget Me / Loop De Loop	1975	.60	3.00
RCA Victor PB-10183		Kojak Columbo / Turn Out The Light	1975	.60	3.00
RCA Victor PB-10183	(PS)	Kojak Columbo / Turn Out The Light	1975	.60	3.00
RCA Victor PB-10634		Sail Away / Moonshine Shadow	1976	.60	3.00
RCA Victor PB-10759		Just One Look-Baby, I'm Yours / That Is All	1977	.60	3.00
RCA Victor PB-11059		Who Done It? / Perfect day	1977	.60	3.00
RCA Victor PB-11193		Ain't It Kinda Wonderful? / I'm Bringing A Red, Red Rose	1978	.80	4.00
		— Extended Play Albums—			
RCA Victor SP-248	(DJ)	The Point	1971	5.00	25.00

NIMBLE, JACK B., & THE QUICKS

Label & Catalog #	A-Side/B-Side	Year	VG	NM
Del Rio 2305	Nut Rocker / Never On Sunday	1962	3.00	15.00
Dot 16319	Nut Rocker / Never On Sunday	1962	2.00	10.00

1910 FRUITGUM COMPANY, THE
The 1910 Fruitgum Co. features Mark Gutkowski, who also recorded as Mark and J.C.W. Ratfink.

Label & Catalog #	A-Side/B-Side	Year	VG	NM
Buddah 24	Simon Says / Reflections From The Looking Glass	1967	.60	4.00
Buddah 39	May I Take A Giant Step (Into Your Heart) /			
	(Poor Old) Mr. Jensen	1968	.80	4.00
Buddah 54	1, 2, 3 Red Light / Sticky, Sticky	1968	.80	4.00
Buddah 71	Goody, Goody Gumdrops / Candy Kisses	1968	.80	4.00
Buddah 91	Indian Giver / Pow Wow	1969	.80	4.00
Buddah 114	Special Delivery / No Good Annie	1969	.80	4.00
Buddah 130	The Train / Eternal Light	1969	.80	4.00
Buddah 146	When We Get Married / Baby Bret	1969	.80	4.00
Super-K 15	Go Away / The Track	1970	1.20	6.00
Attack 10293	Lawdy, Lawdy / The Clock	1970	2.00	10.00

1929 DEPRESSION, THE
The 1929 Depression originally recorded as The Regents.

Label & Catalog #	A-Side/B-Side	Year	VG	NM
Providence 422	Child Of Clay / You've Been Cheatin' On Me, Baby	196?	3.00	15.00

NINO & THE EBB TIDES
The Ebb-Tides also recorded with Lenny Coleman; Frankie Nolan; and Danny Winchell.

Label & Catalog #	A-Side/B-Side	Year	VG	NM
Acme 720	Darling, I'll Love You Only / Franny Franny	1957	50.00	200.00
Recorte 405	Puppy Love / You Make Me Want To Rock And Roll	1958	6.00	30.00
Recorte 408	The Real Meaning Of Christmas / Purple Shadows	1958	50.00	200.00
Recorte 409	I'm Confessin' / Tell The World I Do	1959	8.00	40.00
Recorte 413	I Love Girls / Don't Look Around	195?	15.00	75.00
Marco 105	Little Miss Blue / Someday	1961	6.00	30.00
Mr. Peacock 102	A Happy Girl / Wished I Was Home	1961	5.00	25.00
Mr. Peacock 117	Stamps, Baby, Stamps / Lovin' Time	1962	4.00	20.00
Madison 162	Those Oldies But Goodies (Remind Me Of You) /			
	Don't Run Away	1962	5.00	25.00
Madison 166	Jukebox Saturday Night / (Someday) I'll Fall In Love	1962	2.50	12.00
Mr. Peeke 123	Tonight / Nursery Rhymes	1963	5.00	25.00
Mala 480	Automatic Reaction / Linda Lou Garrett	1964	2.00	10.00

NIPTONES, THE

Label & Catalog #	A-Side/B-Side	Year	VG	NM
Lorraine 1001	Angle / It's Gonna Be Too Late	1965	3.00	15.00

NITE-NIKS, THE

Label & Catalog #	A-Side/B-Side	Year	VG	NM
Lawn 207	Horn Shakin' / Shawnee	1963	5.00	25.00

NITE SOUNDS, THE

Label & Catalog #	A-Side/B-Side	Year	VG	NM
Seafair 112	Get Clean / On Broadway	1962	1.00	5.00

Label & Catalog #		A-Side/B-Side	Year	VG	NM
NITE WALKERS, THE					
Russell 43107		High Class / You've Got Me	196?	2.00	10.00
NITEBEATS, THE					
Tide 1088		Scrambled Eggs / I Think It's Love	1963	2.00	10.00
NITEWALKERS, THE					
Nite 115/6		Corner Of The World / Money	196?	7.00	35.00
NITTY GRITTY DIRT BAND, THE [THE DIRT BAND]					
United Artists 830 through 1330 lists the group as The Dirt Band.					
Liberty 55948		Buy For Me The Rain / Candy Man	1967	1.00	5.00
Liberty 56982		Truly Right / The Teddy Bear's Picnic	1967	1.00	5.00
Liberty 56982	(PS)	Truly Right / The Teddy Bear's Picnic	1967	3.00	15.00
Liberty 56045		These Days / Collegiana	1968	1.00	5.00
Liberty 56134		Some Of Shelly's Blues / Yukon Railroad	1969	1.00	5.00
Liberty 56197		Rave On / The Cure	1970	1.00	5.00
Liberty 56159		Mr. Bojangles / Uncle Charlie	1970	1.00	5.00
United Artists 50769		House On Pooh Corner / Travelin' Mood	1971	.60	3.00
United Artists 50769	(PS)	House On Pooh Corner / Travelin' Mood	1971	1.00	5.00
United Artists 50817		Some Of Shelly's Blues / The Cure	1971	.60	3.00
United Artists 50849		I Saw The Light / The Precious Jewel	1971	.60	3.00
United Artists 50890		Jambalaya (On The Bayou) / Hoping To Say	1972	.60	3.00
United Artists 50890	(PS)	Jambalaya (On The Bayou) / Hoping To Say	1972	1.00	5.00
United Artists 50921		Baltimore / Fish Song	1972	.60	3.00
United Artists 177		Will The Circle Be Unbroken? / Honky Tonkin'	1973	.30	1.50
United Artists 263		Cosmic Cowboy / Fish Song	1973	.30	1.50
United Artists 544		The Battle Of New Orleans / Mountain Whipporwill	1974	.30	1.50
United Artists 544	(PS)	The Battle Of New Orleans / Mountain Whipporwill	1974	.60	3.00
United Artists 655		(All I Have To Do Is) Dream / Raleigh-Durham Reel	1975	.30	1.50
United Artists 741		Mother Of Love / The Moon Just Turned Blue	1975	.30	1.50
United Artists 830		Cosmic Cowboy / Stars And Stripes Forever	1976	.30	1.50
United Artists 936		Buy For Me The Rain / Mother Earth (Provides For Me)	1977	.30	1.50
United Artists 1228		In For The Night / Wild Nights	1978	.30	1.50
United Artists 1268		For A Little While / On The Loose	1979	.30	1.50
United Artists 1312		In Her Eyes / Jas' Moon	1979	.30	1.50
United Artists 1330		An American Dream / Take Me Back	1979	.30	1.50
		— Extended Play Albums —			
United Artists SP-69	(DJ)	All The Good Times *(Double EP with booklet)*	1971	6.00	30.00
NITZSCHE, JACK					
Reprise 0202		The Lonely Surfer / Song For A Summer Night	1963	3.00	15.00
Reprise 0202	(PS)	The Lonely Surfer / Song For A Summer Night	1963	7.00	35.00
NO DEPOSIT NO RETURN					
Philips 40451		I've Got My Needs / Your Love Is My Love	1967	1.00	5.00
NO NAMES, THE					
Guyden 2114		Love / Jam	1964	7.00	35.00
NOAH'S DOVE					
Piccadilly 255		Noah's Dove / Camels And Dragons	1967	2.00	10.00
NOBELLS, THE					
Mar 101		Searchin' For My Love / Crying Over You	1962	15.00	75.00
NOBLE, BEVERLY					
Sparrow 100		Why Must I Cry? / You Cheated	196?	3.00	15.00
NOBLEMEN, THE					
U.S.A. 1213		Thunder Wagon / Dragon Walk	1963	3.00	15.00
Bee 1826		Tiddlewinks / Vibration	1963	6.00	30.00
Profile 4012		Dirty Robber /	196?	4.00	20.00
NOBLES, THE					
Tee Gee 101		Oops, Oh Lawdy / Stop Crying	195?	7.00	35.00
		(Tee Gee 101 was also released credited to The Timbers.)			
Klik 305		Poor Rock And Roll / Ting A Ling	1958	7.00	35.00
Times Square 1		Poor Rock And Roll / Ting A Ling *(Blue vinyl)*	1962	4.00	20.00
Times Square 1		Poor Rock And Roll / Ting A Ling *(Green vinyl)*	1962	3.00	15.00
Times Square 12		Crime Doesn't Pay / Darkness	1963	2.00	10.00
NOBLES, THE					
Selbon 1005		Black Widow / Jaguar	1963	5.00	25.00
NOBLES, THE					
Vee Jay 520		Body Surf / Mary Ann	1963	5.00	25.00

Label & Catalog #	A-Side/B-Side	Year	VG	NM
NOBLES, THE				
U.S.A. 788	Marlene / That Special One	1965	3.00	15.00
NOBLETONES, THE				
C&M 182	Cha-Lyp-So Baby / Who Cares About Love?	1958	8.00	40.00
C&M 182	I Love You / I'm Really Too Young	1958	10.00	50.00
C&M 188/9	I'm Crying / Mambo Boogie	1968	8.00	40.00
Times Square 17	I Love You / I'm Really Too Young	1963	2.00	10.00
Times Square 18	Calypso Baby / Who Cares About Love?	1963	2.00	10.00
NODAENS, THE				
Gold 1001	Beach Girl / Gypsy	196?	7.00	35.00
NOEL, SID				
Aladdin 331	Flying Saucer / Flying Saucer (Part 2)	1956	6.00	30.00
NOISES 'N' SOUNDS				
Piccadilly 222	Yum Yum Eat 'Em Up / How Much Lovin'	1966	2.00	10.00
NOLAN, (MISS) FRANKIE				
Features Frankie Valli.				
ABC-Paramount 10231	I Still Care / I Wish It Were Summer All Year Round	1961	6.00	30.00
NOLAN, (MISS) FRANKIE, & THE EBB TIDES				
Refer to Nino & The Ebb Tides.				
Madison 151	A Week From Sunday / Say No More	1961	6.00	30.00
NOLAND, TERRY				
Brunswick 55010	Hypnotized / Ten Little Women	1957	8.00	40.00
Brunswick 55036	Patty Baby / Don't Do Me This Way	1957	3.00	15.00
Brunswick 55054	Puppy Love / Look At Me	1958	3.00	15.00
Brunswick 55069	Everyone But Me / Crazy Dream	1958	3.00	15.00
Brunswick 55092	There Was A Fungus Among Us / Sugar Drop	1958	6.00	30.00
Brunswick 55122	Guess I'm Gonna Fall / Teenage Teardrops	1959	3.00	15.00
Apt 25065	Long Gone Baby / There Goes A Girl	1960	3.00	15.00
NOMADS, THE				
Rust 5028	Bounty Hunter / Desert Tramp	1961	2.00	10.00
ABC-Paramount 10191	I'm Popeye The Sailor Man / On The Atchison, Topeka And The Santa Fe	1961	2.00	10.00
Genie 7817	Popeye The Sailor / Santa Fe Rock	1961	2.00	10.00
Pharos 101	San Francisco Bay Blues / Oh, Jennie	196?	2.00	10.00
NOMADS, THE				
Prelude 1112	Last Summer Day / Icky Poo	196?	7.00	35.00
NOONE, PETER				
Peter Noone originally recorded as Herman of Herman's Hermits.				
Philips 40730	Getting Over You / All Sing Together	1971	.80	4.00
Casablanca 0016	Meet Me On The Corner Down At Joe's Cafe / On The Pony Express	1974	.60	3.00
Casablanca 0017	Meet Me On The Corner Down At Joe's Cafe / On The Pony Express	1974	.60	3.00
Casablanca 802	Meet Me On The Corner Down At Joe's Cafe / (Blame It On) The Pony Express	1974	.60	3.00
Casablanca 824	Something Old, Something New / Something Old, Something New (Stock copies of Casablanca 824 may not exist.)	1975	.60	3.00
NORMAN, GENE, & THE ROCKIN' ROCKETS				
Snag 101	Snaggle Tooth Ann / Long Gone Night Train	1958	250.00	750.00
NORMAN, JIMMY, & THE HOLLYWOOD TEENERS				
Fun 101	A Boy And A Girl / Bride	1960	2.00	10.00
Fun 102	My Thanks / Para Siempre	1960	2.00	10.00
NORMAN, LARRY				
Larry Norman originally recorded with People and The Files.				
Capitol 2766	Sweet, Sweet Song Of Salvation / Walking Backwards Down The Stairs	1970	4.00	20.00
Verve 10718	I've Got To Learn To Live Without You / Reader's Digest	1972	4.00	20.00
Verve 10720	I've Got To Learn To Live Without You / The Outlaw	1972	4.00	20.00
MGM 14351	Righteous Rocker, Holy Rocker / Peace, Polution, Revolution	1972	3.00	15.00
MGM 14676	It's The Same Old Story / Christmas Time	1973	3.00	15.00
MGM 14703	Nightmare / Baroquen Spirits	1974	3.00	15.00

Label & Catalog #		A-Side/B-Side	Year	VG	NM
NORRELL, JERRY					
Hamilton 50022		Comic Book Hop / The Freshman	1959	6.00	30.00
Brunswick 55148		Comic Book Hop / The Freshman	1959	4.00	20.00
Legend 124		What Is Surfing All About? / (B-side by Morty Jay)	1963	2.50	12.00
NORSEMEN, THE					
M&M		Home On A Cloud / Can't You Fall In Love	196?	3.00	15.00
NORTH ATLANTIC INVASION FORCE, THE					
Congressional 999		Blue And Green Gown / Fire, Wind And Rain	1968	2.00	10.00
Mr. G 808		Black In White / The Orange Patch	1968	2.00	10.00
NOTHERN LIGHTS, THE					
The Northern Lights feature Bjorn Ulvaeus, later of Abba.					
United Artists 991		No Time / Time To Move Along	1966	3.00	15.00
NORTONES, THE					
Warner Bros. 5065		Susie Jones / That's The Way The Cookie Crumbles	1959	2.00	10.00
Warner Bros. 5115		Boy / Smile, Just Smile	1959	2.00	10.00
Warner Bros. 5115	(PS)	Boy / Smile, Just Smile	1959	2.00	10.00
Stack 502		I'm Gonna Find You /	1960	2.00	10.00
NOTABLES, THE					
Big Top 3141		Surfside / Lisa Maree	1963	6.00	30.00
		(Re-issued on Capitol credited to Digger Revell.)			
NOTATIONS, THE					
Wonder 100		What A Night For Love / Chapel Doors	195?	40.00	200.00
NOTATIONS, THE					
Beverly 1555		Miserlou / Everything's All Right	196?	10.00	50.00
NOTATIONS, THE					
Camelot 101		Ram Charger / Tapered Drawers	196?	2.00	10.00
NOTATIONS, THE					
Sue 5		You Should Know / Eleven O' Clock	1969	1.60	8.00
NOTE TORIALS, THE					
Sunbeam 119		My Valerie / Loved And Lost	1959	40.00	200.00
NOTES FROM THE UNDERGROUND					
Changes 601	(EP)	Notes From The Underground	1968	10.00	50.00
Vanguard 35073		Down In The Basement / I Wish I Was A Punk	1969	2.00	10.00
NOVA-TONES, THE					
Rosco 417		Walk On The Surfside / Lost Love	196?	7.00	35.00
NOVAS, THE					
Parrott 45005	(DJ)	The Crusher / Take 7	1964	8.00	40.00
Parrott 45005		The Crusher / Take 7	1964	12.00	60.00
NRBQ [NEW RHYTHM & BLUES QUINTET]					

NRBQ [NEW RHYTHM & BLUES QUINTET]
Original members of NRBQ were Terry Adams, Steve Ferguson, Frank Gadler, Joey Spampinato and Tom Staley with Al Anderson joing in 1971. Ferguson and Gadler were replaced by Donn Adams, Tom Ardolino and Keith Spring in 1974. Refer to Baxter; The Dickens.

Label & Catalog #		A-Side/B-Side	Year	VG	NM
Columbia 44865		Stomp / I Don't Know Myself	1969	1.20	6.00
Columbia 44937		C'mon Everybody / Rocket #9	1969	1.20	6.00
Columbia 45019		Down In My Heart / Sure To Fall In Love With You	1969	1.20	6.00
Columbia 45107		All Mama's Children / Step Aside	1970	1.20	6.00
		(Columbia 45107 features Carl Perkins.)			
Kama Sutra 544		Howard Johnson's Got His Mojo Workin' / Do You Feel It?	1972	1.20	6.00
Kama Sutra 549		Magnet / Only You	1973	1.20	6.00
Kama Sutra 575		C'mon If You're Comin' / RC Cola And A Moon Pie	1973	1.20	6.00
Kama Sutra 586		Get That Gasoline Blues / Mona	1974	1.20	6.00
Select-O-Hit 822		Sourpuss / Rumors	1974	1.00	5.00
Button 037		Froggy Went A Courtin' / Bless Your Beautiful Hide	1975	1.00	5.00
Red Rooster 1001		Ridin' In My Car / Do The Bump	1977	.80	4.00
Red Rooster 1002		Tapdancin' Bats / I Got A Rocket In My Pocket	1977	.80	4.00
Red Rooster 1002	(PS)	Tapdancin' Bats / I Got A Rocket In My Pocket	1977	.80	4.00
Mercury 73991		I Love Her, She Loves Me / Green Light	1978	1.00	5.00
Rounder 4521		Hot Biscuits And Sweet Marie / She Don't Look Good	1979	.80	4.00
Rounder 4522		Get That Gasoline Blues / Wacky Tobacky	1979	.80	4.00
Rounder 4531		Me And The Boys / People	1980	.80	4.00
Rounder 4531	(PS)	Me And The Boys / People	1980	.80	4.00
Rounder 4525		Christmas Wish / Jolly Old St. Nicholas	1980	.80	4.00
Rounder 4525	(PS)	Christmas Wish / Jolly Old St. Nicholas	1980	.80	4.00

Label & Catalog #		A-Side/B-Side	Year	VG	NM
Rounder 4539		Never Take The Place Of You / Captain Lou Albano For Tiddlywinks	1980	1.00	5.00
Rounder 1010		Captain Lou! / Boardin' House Pie	1982	.80	4.00
Rounder 1010	(PS)	Captain Lou! / Boardin' House Pie	1982	.80	4.00
Bearsville 29588		Rain At The Drive-In / Smackeroo	1983	.80	4.00
Rounder 4556		Things To You / I Can't Stop Loving You Now (Both sides feature Skeeter Davis.)	1985	.80	4.00
Virgin 99161		Wild Weekend / The Love Is True	1989	.60	3.00
Virgin 99130		If I Don't Have You / Fireworks	1990	.60	3.00
		— Extended Play Albums —			
Red Rooster EP-1		Merry Christmas From NRBQ	1978	2.00	10.00
Red Rooster EP-2		NRBQ In Person	1982	2.00	10.00

NU-DIMENSIONS, THE

Label & Catalog #		A-Side/B-Side	Year	VG	NM
Burdette 1		The Other Side / Look Thru Any Window	1967	2.00	10.00

NUGGETS, THE: Refer to DEAN MARTIN

NUMBERS, THE

Label & Catalog #		A-Side/B-Side	Year	VG	NM
Bonneville 101		My Pillow / Big Red	1962	50.00	200.00
Dore 641	(DJ)	My Pillow / Big Red	1962	10.00	50.00

NUTTY NED & MARVIN

Label & Catalog #		A-Side/B-Side	Year	VG	NM
Arch 1812		The Big Trial / Comin' Down The Track	196?	3.00	15.00

NUTTY SQUIRRELS, THE

The Nutty Squirrels were a couple of beatnik rodents with their own cartoon show in the '50s. The [jazz] music was provided by Don Elliot's band featuring Cannonball Adderley, Bobby Jaspar, Hal McKusick, Sam Most, Romeo Penque and Sol Schlinger with Sacha Burland's vocals.

Label & Catalog #		A-Side/B-Side	Year	VG	NM
Hanover 4540		Uh! Oh! / Uh! Oh! (Part 2)	1959	3.00	15.00
Hanover 4540	(PS)	Uh! Oh! / Uh! Oh! (Part 2)	1959	5.00	25.00
Hanover 4551		Eager Beaver / Zowee	1960	3.00	15.00
Columbia 41818		Please Don't Take Our Tree For Christmas / Nutty Noel	1960	3.00	15.00
Columbia 41818	(PS)	Please Don't Take Our Tree For Christmas / Nutty Noel	1960	4.00	20.00
RCA Victor 47-8287		Hello Again / Bluesette	1963	2.00	10.00
		— Extended Play Albums —			
Hanover DP-301		Salt Peanuts (Paper sleeve)	1959	6.00	30.00

NYLONS, THE

The Nylons also recorded as The Rumblers.

Label & Catalog #		A-Side/B-Side	Year	VG	NM
Downey 109		Maid-N-Japan / Gospel Truth	1963	3.00	15.00

NYLONS, THE

Label & Catalog #		A-Side/B-Side	Year	VG	NM
CBS 323		Some People (Song For Sheenan) / Mirage	196?	3.00	15.00

NYRO, LAURA

Label & Catalog #		A-Side/B-Side	Year	VG	NM
Verve/Folkways 5024		Stoney End / Wedding Bell Blues	1966	1.00	5.00
Verve/Folkways 5038		Goodbye Joe / Billie's Blues	1967	1.00	5.00
Verve/Folkways 5051		And When I Die / Flim Flam Man	1967	Unreleased?	
Columbia 44531	(PS)	Eli's Comin' / Sweet Blindness (Promo)	1968	3.00	15.00
Columbia 44531		Eli's Comin' / Sweet Blindness	1968	.60	3.00
Columbia 44592		Save The Country / Timer	1968	.60	3.00
Columbia 45041		Time And Love / Man Who Sends Me Home	1969	.60	3.00
Columbia 45230		Up On The Roof / Captain St. Lucifer	1970	.60	3.00
Columbia 45298		When I Was A Freeport & You Were The Main Drag / Been On A Train	1970	.60	3.00
Columbia 45537		It's Gonna Take A Miracle / Desiree	1972	.50	2.50
Columbia 45791		Wedding Bell Blues / Hands Off The Man (Flim Flam Man)	1973	.50	2.50

O'DELL, KENNY

Mar-Kay 3696	Old Time Lovin' / Take Another Look	196?	1.00	5.00
Vegas 718	Beautiful People / Flower Girl	1967	.80	4.00
Vegas 722	Springfield Plane / I'm Gonna Take It	1968	.80	4.00
Vegas 724	Happy With You / I Couldn't Love You	1968	.80	4.00

O'HENRY, LENNY

ABC-Paramount 10222	Cheated Heart / Billy The Continental Kid	1961	3.00	15.00
ABC-Paramount 10272	Goin' To A Party / The Touch Of You	1961	3.00	15.00
Atco 6312	Sweet Young Love / Savin' All My Love	1965	2.00	10.00
Atco 6525	Saturday Angel / Across The Street	1967	2.00	10.00

O'KEEFE, DANNY

Jerden 806	That Old Sweet Song / Don't Wake Me In The Morning	1966	.80	4.00
Piccadilly 228	That Old Sweet Song / Don't Wake Me In The Morning	196?	.60	3.00
Piccadilly 237	Today One Day Later / Good Time Charlie's Got The Blues	196?	.60	3.00

O'MALLEY, KEITH

Go-Gee 289	Turned Out / I Won't Be Far Behind	196?	2.00	10.00

O'NEILL, JIM

Del-Fi 4141	Face On The Penny / Happy Town	1960	2.00	10.00

O'RYAN, JACK, & AL TERCEK

Nocturne 8	Political Circus / Political Circus (Part 2)	1956	7.00	35.00

O'SULLIVAN, GILBERT

Mam 3602		Nothing Rhymed / Everybody Knows	1971	.40	2.00
Mam 3607		Underneath The Blanket Go /	1971	.40	2.00
Mam 3613		I Don't Know What To Do / We Will	1972	.40	2.00
Mam 3617		No Matter How I Try / If I Don't Get You Back	1972	.60	3.00
Mam 3619		Alone Again (Naturally) / Save It	1972	.60	3.00
Mam 3626		Clair / Ooh-Wakka-Doo	1972	.40	2.00
Mam 3626	(PS)	Clair / Ooh-Wakka-Doo	1972	.40	2.00
Mam 3628		Out Of The Question / Everybody Knows	1973	.40	2.00
Mam 3629		Get Down / A Very Extraordinary Sort Of Girl	1973	.40	2.00
Mam 3631		Out Of The Question / Everybody Knows	1973	.40	2.00
		(Mam 3631 credits Big Jim Sullivan.)			
Mam 3633		Ooh Baby / Good Company	1973	.40	2.00
Mam 3636		Happiness Is Me And You / Breakfast, Dinner And Tea	1974	.40	2.00
Mam 3641		A Woman's Place / Too Bad	1974	.40	2.00
Mam 3642		You Are You / To Cut A Long Story Short	1974	.40	2.00
Mam 3643		Marriage Machine / Tell Me Why	1974	.40	2.00
Mam 3644		I Don't Love You But I Think I Like You / That's A Fact	1974	.40	2.00
Mam 3645		Christmas Song / Just As You Are	1974	.40	2.00

O. K.'S, THE

Summer 290	Sugar Bowl Blues / Don't Leave Me Now	1957	4.00	20.00

OBERLE, SCOTT

Atco 6293	Cupid's Poison Dart / You're My Dream Girl	1964	2.00	10.00

OCHS, PHIL

A&M 881		Flower Lady / Cross My Heart	1967	1.20	6.00
A&M 891	(DJ)	Outside Of A Small Circle Of Friends (Censored version) / Outside Of A Small Circle Of Friends	1967	3.00	15.00
A&M 891		Outside Of A Small Circle Of Friends / Miranda	1967	1.20	6.00
A&M 932		The Harder They Fall / The War Is Over	1967	1.20	6.00
A&M 1070		The World Began In Eden And Ended In Los Angeles / My Life	1969	1.20	6.00
A&M 1180		One Way Ticket Home / My Kingdom For A Car	1970	2.00	10.00
A&M 1376		Kansas City Bomber / Gas Station Woman	1972	2.00	10.00
A&M 1509		Here's To The State Of Richard Nixon / Power And Glory	1974	2.00	10.00

OCTAVES, THE

Val 1001	You're Too Young / Mombo Carolyn	195?	5.00	25.00

OCTOBER, JOHNNY

First 106	First Time / You're My Girl	195?	3.00	15.00
Capitol 4267	Growin' Prettier / Young And In Love	1959	3.00	15.00

Label & Catalog #	A-Side/B-Side	Year	VG	NM
OCTOBER COUNTRY				
Epic 10252	October Country / Baby, What I Mean	1968	.80	4.00
Epic 10320	My Girl Friend Is A Witch / I Just Don't Know	1969	.80	4.00
OCTOBERS, THE				
Chairman 4402	Stop It, Little Girl / I Should'a Listened To Mama	1963	2.00	10.00
ODDIS, RAY				
VIP 25012	Happy Ghoultide / Ray The Newspaper Boy	1965	4.00	20.00
ODDS & ENDS				
Southbay 102	You Don't Love Me / Be Happy, Baby	196?	1.20	6.00
ODDS & ENDS				
Today 1003	Yesterday My Love / Love Makes The World Go Round	196?	2.00	10.00
OFF-BEATS, THE				
Tower 205	You Tell Me / Mary	1965	2.00	10.00
OFF KEYS, THE				
The Off-Keys also recorded with Jerry Evans.				
Rowe 003	Our Wedding Day / Singing Bells	1962	10.00	50.00
Technichord 1001	Our Wedding Day / Singing Bells	1962	4.00	20.00
OFFBEATS, THE [CRAIG CAHILL & THE OFFBEAT]				
Merritt 0001	Landslide / Mr. Machine	1963	7.00	35.00
Merritt 0002	Grind / Some Are Lonely	1963	7.00	35.00
Merritt 0003	Surfin' Elephant / Pipe City	1964	15.00	75.00
	(Merritt 0003 credited to Craig Cahill & The Offbeats.)			
OHIO EXPRESS, THE [OHIO LTD.]				
The Ohio Express originally recorded as The Rare Breed..				
Cameo 483	Beg, Borrow And Steal / Maybe	1967	2.00	10.00
Cameo 2001	Try It / Soul Struttin' (Pink & white label)	1967	2.00	10.00
Cameo 2001	Try It / Soul Struttin' (Yellow & orange label)	1967	1.60	8.00
Buddah 28	Yummy Yummy Yummy / Zig Zag	1968	.80	4.00
Buddah 56	Down At Lulu's / She's Not Comin' Home	1968	.80	4.00
Buddah 70	Chewy Chewy / Firebird	1968	.80	4.00
Buddah 92	Sweeter Than Sugar / Bitter Lemon	1969	.60	3.00
Buddah 102	Mercy / Roll It Up	1969	.60	3.00
Buddah 117	Pinch Me / Peanuts	1969	.60	3.00
Buddah 129	Sausalito / Make Love Not War	1969	.80	4.00
	("Sausalito" features Graham Gouldman on vocals.)			
Buddah 147	Cowboy Convention / The Race	1969	.80	4.00
Buddah 160	Love Equals Love / Peanuts	1969	.80	4.00
Buddah 178	Cowboy Convention / The Race (That Took Place)	1969	1.00	5.00
Buddah 178 (PS)	Cowboy Convention / The Race (That Took Place)	1969	2.00	10.00
Super-K 14	Hot Dog / Ooh La La	1969	2.00	10.00
Buddah 386 (DJ)	Wham Bam / Slow And Steady	1972	3.00	15.00
	(Buddah 386 credits Ohio LTD. Stock copies may not exist)			
OLENN, JOHNNY				
Antler 1105	Born Reckless / You Loveable You	1959	5.00	25.00
Antler 4009	My Sweetie Pie / Smile	1959	5.00	25.00
OLIVER, O. JAY, & THE CRACKERJACKS				
Coed 500	Real Love And Affection / Good Gravy	1958	3.00	15.00
OLIVER & THE TWISTERS				
Colpix 615	The Locomotion Twist / The Mother Goose Twist	1961	2.00	10.00
OMEGAS				
Decca 31008	When You Touch me / Froze	1960	3.00	15.00
Decca 31094	So How Come (No One Loves You)? / Study Hall	1960	3.00	15.00
Decca 31138	Falling In Love / No One Will Ever Know	1961	3.00	15.00
Groove 4-4	Midnight Run / I Wanna Go Home	1961	3.00	15.00
ONION				
Epic 10529	Hello / Been A Long Time	1969	1.20	6.00
ONO, YOKO				
Many of Yoko Ono's tracks were issued as the flips to hubby John's, thus promos and picture sleeves are listed in Lennon's section.				
Apple 1809	Remember Love / (B-side by John Lennon)	1969	1.00	5.00
Apple 1813	Don't Worry, Kyoko (Mummy's Only Looking			
	For A Hand In The Snow) / (B-side by John Lennon)	1969	.80	4.00
Apple 1818	Who Has Seen The Wind? / (B-side by John Lennon)	1970	1.60	8.00
	(Apple label reads "Mfd. by Capitol Records" below the apple.)			

Label & Catalog #		A-Side/B-Side	Year	VG	NM
Apple 1818		**Who Has Seen The Wind?** / *(B-side by John Lennon)*	1970	1.00	5.00
		(Apple label reads "Mfd. by Apple Records Inc" below the apple.)			
Apple 1827		**Why?** / *(B-side by John Lennon) (Star label)*	1970	2.00	10.00
Apple 1827		**Why?** / *(B-side by John Lennon) (Starless label)*	1970	1.00	5.00
Apple 1830		**Touch Me** / *(B-side by John Lennon) (Star label)*	1971	1.25	6.00
Apple 1830		**Touch Me** / *(B-side by John Lennon)*	1971	1.00	5.00
Apple OYB-1/GM-1	*(DJ)*	**Open Your Box** / **Greenfield Morning**	1972	——	——
		(Rare. Estimated near mint value $500-1,000.)			
Apple 1839		**Mrs. Lennon** / **Midsummer New York**	1972	1.20	6.00
Apple S-45X-47663	*(DJ)*	**Listen, The Snow Is Falling** / *(B-side by John Lennon)*	1971	150.00	600.00
Apple 1842		**Listen, The Snow Is Falling** / *(B-side by John Lennon)*	1971	2.00	10.00
		(Photo label on green vinyl.)			
Apple 1842		**Listen, The Snow Is Falling** / *(B-side by John Lennon)*	1971	1.60	8.00
		(Apple label on green vinyl.)			
Apple P-1853	*(DJ)*	**Now Or Never** / **Move On Fast**	1972	6.00	30.00
Apple 1853		**Now Or Never** / **Move On Fast**	1972	1.20	6.00
Apple 1853	*(PS)*	**Now Or Never** / **Move On Fast**	1972	3.00	15.00
Apple 1859		**Death Of Samantha** / **Yang Yang**	1972	1.20	6.00
Apple P-1867	*(DJ)*	**Woman Power** / **Men, Men, Men**	1973	6.00	30.00
Apple 1867		**Woman Power** / **Men, Men, Men**	1973	1.20	6.00
		(Apple 1857 features Elephant's Memory.)			
Geffen 49604		**Kiss, Kiss, Kiss** / *(B-side by John Lennon)*	1980	.40	2.00
Geffen 49644		**Beautiful Boy** / *(B-side by John Lennon)*	1981	.40	2.00
Geffen 49695		**Yes, I'm Your Angel** / *(B-side by John Lennon)*	1981	.40	2.00
Geffen 29855		**Beautiful Boy** / *(B-side by John Lennon)*	1982	.40	2.00
Polydor 821-107-7		**Sleepless Night** / *(B-side by John Lennon)*	1984	.40	2.00
Polydor 821-204-7		**Your Hands** / *(B-side by John Lennon)*	1984	.60	3.00
Polydor 817-254-7		**O' Sanity** / *(B-side by John Lennon)*	1985	.40	2.00
		(Label reads "Mfg. by Polygram.")			
Polydor 817-254-7		**O' Sanity** / *(B-side by John Lennon)*	1985	3.00	15.00
		(Label reads "Mfg. by Polydor.")			
		— Special/Promotional Releases —			
Americom 435		**Remember Love** / *(B-side by John Lennon) (4" flexti-disc)*	1969	330.00	1,000.00
Evatone Aspen 7		**Radio Play** *(Flexi-disc)*	1969	75.00	300.00
		— 12" Singles —			
Geffen PRO-919	*(DJ)*	**Kiss, Kiss, Kiss** / *(B-side by John Lennon)*	1980	12.00	60.00
Geffen PRO-1079	*(DJ)*	**Beautiful Boy** / *(B-side by John Lennon)*	1982	8.00	40.00
Capitol SPRO-9929	*(DJ)*	**Listen, The Snow Is Falling** / *(B-side by John Lennon)*	1986	7.00	35.00
		(White vinyl)			

ONYX
| Burdette 6 | | **It's All Put On** / **You've Got To Be With Me** | 1968 | .80 | 4.00 |
| Great Northwest 708 | | **Evasive Action** / **I Could Really Make You Happy** | 196? | .80 | 4.00 |

OPALS, THE
| Laurie 3288 | | **No, No, Never Again** / **Just Like A Little Bitty Baby** | 1965 | 2.00 | 10.00 |

OPPOSITE SIX, THE
| South Shore 721 | | **Continental Surf** / **Church Key, Part 68** | 196? | 7.00 | 35.00 |
| South Shore 720 | | **Down The Tubes** / **Ooh-Poo-Poh-Doo** | 196? | 7.00 | 35.00 |

OPPOSITES, THE
The Opposites feature Ernest Bringas and Phillip Stewart, who later recorded as The Rip Chords.
| Columbia 42641 | | **Karen** / **Ding Dong** | 1962 | 3.00 | 15.00 |

OPUS ONE
| Mustang 3017 | | **Back Seat '38** / **Dodge In My Mind** | 1965 | 8.00 | 40.00 |

ORANGE COLORED SKY
Uni 55088		**Orange Colored Sky** / **The Shadow Of Summer**	1968	2.00	10.00
Uni 55156		**Sweet Poatato** / **The Sun And I**	1968	2.00	10.00
MGM 14578		**Morning Light** / **Who Are You Fooling?**	1973	1.00	5.00

ORBISON, DON, & THE BASICS
| Lavender 2002 | | **Time** / **Oh Lonely Me** | 196? | 1.00 | 5.00 |

ORBISON, ROY
Roy Orbison also recorded with Ken Cook; Weldon Rogers; The Traveling Wilburys; the Various Artists EPs section.
JeWel 101		**Ooby Dooby** / **Trying To Get To You**	1956	——	——
		(Jewel 101 credits The Teen Kings. Estimated near mint value $1,500-3,000.)			
Sun 242		**Ooby Dooby** / **Go! Go! Go!**	1956	15.00	75.00
Sun 251		**You're My Baby** / **Rockhouse**	1956	5.00	25.00
		(Sun 242 and 251 credited to Roy Orbison & The Teen Kings.)			
Sun 265		**Sweet And Easy To Love** / **Devil Doll**	1956	7.00	35.00
		(Sun 265 credited to Roy Orbison & The Roses.)			
Sun 284		**Chicken Hearted** / **I Like Love**	1958	4.00	20.00
Sun 353		**Sweet And Easy To Love** / **Devil Doll**	1961	20.00	100.00
		(Although a reissue of 265, Sun 353 is rare and a must for completists.)			

Label & Catalog #		A-Side/B-Side	Year	VG	NM
RCA Victor 47-7381		Seems To Me / Sweet And Innocent	1958	6.00	30.00
RCA Victor 47-7447		Almost Eighteen / Jolie	1959	6.00	30.00
Monument 409		Paper Boy / With The Bug	1959	8.00	40.00
Monument 412		Up Town / Pretty One	1959	6.00	30.00
Monument 421		Only The Lonely / Here Comes That Song Again	1960	3.00	15.00
Monument 425		Blue Angel / Today's Teardrops	1960	2.00	10.00
Monument 433		I'm Hurtin' / I Can't Stop Loving You	1960	2.00	10.00
Monument 433	(PS)	I'm Hurtin' / I Can't Stop Loving You	1960	5.00	25.00
Monument 438		Running Scared / Love Hurts	1961	3.00	15.00
Monument 438	(PS)	Running Scared / Love Hurts	1961	4.00	20.00
Monument 447		Crying / Candy Man	1961	3.00	15.00
Monument 447	(PS)	Crying / Candy Man	1961	4.00	20.00
Monument 456		Dream Baby / The Actress	1962	3.00	15.00
Monument 456	(PS)	Dream Baby / The Actress	1962	4.00	20.00
Monument 461		The Crowd / Mama	1962	3.00	15.00
Monument 461	(PS)	The Crowd / Mama	1962	4.00	20.00
Monument 467		Leah / Working For The Man	1962	3.00	15.00
Monument 467	(PS)	Leah / Working For The Man	1962	5.00	25.00
Monument 806		In Dreams / Shahdaroba	1963	2.00	10.00
Monument 806	(PS)	In Dreams / Shahdaroba	1963	4.00	20.00
Monument 815		Falling / Distant Drums	1963	2.00	10.00
Monument 815	(PS)	Falling / Distant Drums	1963	4.00	20.00
Monument 824		Mean Woman Blues / Blue Bayou	1963	2.00	10.00
Monument 830		Pretty Paper / Beautiful Dreamer	1963	2.00	10.00
Monument 837		It's Over / Indian Wedding	1964	2.00	10.00
Monument 837	(PS)	It's Over / Indian Wedding	1964	4.00	20.00
Monument 851		Oh, Pretty Woman / Ye Te Amo, Maria	1964	2.00	10.00
Monument 873		Goodnight / Only With You	1965	2.00	10.00
Monument 891		(Say) You're My Girl / Sleepy Hollow	1965	2.00	10.00
Monument 906		Let The Good Times Roll / Distant Drums	1965	3.00	15.00
Monument 939		Lana / Our Summer Song	1966	3.00	15.00
		—Monument Reissues—			
Monument 503		Paper Boy / With The Bug	1966	4.00	20.00
Monument 505		Up Town / Pretty One	1966	3.00	15.00
Monument 508		Only The Lonely / Here Comes That Song Again	1966	2.00	10.00
Monument 509		Blue Angel / Today's Teardrops	1966	2.00	10.00
Monument 510		I'm Hurtin' / I Can't Stop Loving You	1966	2.00	10.00
Monument 514		Running Scared / Love Hurts	1966	2.00	10.00
Monument 517		Crying / Candy Man	1966	2.00	10.00
Monument 519		Dream Baby / The Actress	1966	2.00	10.00
Monument 520		The Crowd / Mama	1966	2.00	10.00
Monument 521		Leah / Working For The Man	1966	2.00	10.00
Monument 526		In Dreams / Shahdaroba	1966	2.00	10.00
Monument 527		Falling / Distant Drums	1966	2.00	10.00
Monument 530		Mean Woman Blues / Blue Bayou	1966	2.00	10.00
Monument 531		Pretty Paper / Beautiful Dreamer	1966	2.00	10.00
Monument 533		It's Over / Indian Wedding	1966	2.00	10.00
Monument 534		Oh, Pretty Woman / Ye Te Amo, Maria	1966	2.00	10.00
		—Extended Play Albums—			
Monument	(DJ)	In Dreams, Volume 1 (Paper sleeve)	1962	10.00	50.00
Monument	(DJ)	In Dreams, Volume 2 (Paper sleeve)	1962	10.00	50.00
Monument	(33)	Roy Orbison's Greatest Hits (Jukebox EP)	1967	8.00	40.00
Monument	(33)	More Of Roy Orbison's Greatest Hits (Jukebox EP)	1967	8.00	40.00
Monument	(33)	The Very Best Of Roy Orbison (Jukebox EP)	1967	8.00	40.00
		—Post Monument Recordings—			
MGM 11386		Ride Away / Wondering	1965	1.20	6.00
MGM 11386	(PS)	Ride Away / Wondering	1965	3.00	15.00
MGM 13410		Crawling Back / If You Can't Say Something Nice	1965	1.20	6.00
MGM 13410	(PS)	Crawling Back / If You Can't Say Something Nice	1965	3.00	15.00
MGM 13446		Breaking Up Is Breaking My Heart / Wait	1965	1.20	6.00
MGM 13446	(PS)	Breaking Up Is Breaking My Heart / Wait	1965	3.00	15.00
MGM 13498		Twinkle Toes / Where Is Tomorrow?	1966	1.20	6.00
MGM 13498	(PS)	Twinkle Toes / Where Is Tomorrow?	1966	2.00	10.00
MGM 13549		Too Soon To Know / You'll Never Be Sixteen Again	1966	1.20	6.00
MGM 13549	(PS)	Too Soon To Know / You'll Never Be Sixteen Again	1966	3.00	15.00
MGM 13634		Communication Breakdown / Going Back To Gloria	1966	1.20	6.00
MGM 13685		So Good / Memories	1967	1.20	6.00
MGM CS 9-5	(DJ)	MGM Celebrity Scene: Roy Orbison	1967	15.00	75.00
		(Boxed set of five stereo singles, MGM 13756-13760, with a cue sheet, bio and jukebox title strips; the price is for the complete set. The five promo singles are priced separately below.)			
MGM 13756	(DJ)	Ride Away / Crawling Back	1967	2.00	10.00
MGM 13757	(DJ)	Breaking Up Is Breaking My Heart / Too Soon To Know	1967	2.00	10.00
MGM 13758	(DJ)	Twinkle Toes / Communication Breakdown	1967	2.00	10.00
MGM 13759	(DJ)	Sweet Dreams / Going Back To Gloria	1967	2.00	10.00
MGM 13760	(DJ)	There Won't Be Many Coming Home / You'll Never Be Sixteen Again	1967	2.00	10.00

Label & Catalog #		A-Side/B-Side	Year	VG	NM
MGM 13764		Cry Softly, Lonely One / Pistolero	1967	1.20	6.00
MGM 13764	(PS)	Cry Softly, Lonely One / Pistolero	1967	3.00	15.00
MGM 13817		She / Here Comes The Rain, Baby	1967	1.60	8.00
MGM 13889		Born To Be Loved By You / Shy Away	1968	1.60	8.00
MGM 13950		Walk On / Flowers	1968	1.60	8.00
MGM 13991		Heartache / Sugar Man	1968	1.60	8.00
MGM 14039		Southbound Jericho Park (Way) / My Friend	1969	1.60	8.00
MGM 14079		Penny Arcade / Tennessee Owns My Heart	1969	1.60	8.00
MGM 14105		She Cheats On Me / How Do You Start Over?	1969	1.60	8.00
MGM 14121		So Young / If I Had A Woman Like You	1970	1.60	8.00
MGM 14293		(Love Me Like You Did) Last Night / Close Again	1970	1.60	8.00
MGM 14258		Changes / God Love You	1971	1.60	8.00
MGM 11443		Harlem Woman / Remember The Good	1971	1.60	8.00
MGM 11443		If Only For A While / Remember The Good	1971	1.60	8.00
MGM 14441		Memphis, Tennessee / I Can Read Between The Lines	1972	1.60	8.00
MGM 14552		Blue Rain (Coming Down) / Sooner Or Later	1973	1.60	8.00
MGM 14626		I Wanna Live / You Lay So Easy On My Mind	1973	1.60	8.00
Mercury 73610		Sweet Mama Blue / Heartache	1974	.80	4.00
Mercury 73652		Hung Up On You / Spanish Nights (And You)	1975	.80	4.00
Mercury 73705		It's Lonely / Still	1975	.80	4.00
Monument 8690		Belinda / No Chain At All	1976	.80	4.00
Monument 200		(I'm A) Southern Man / Born To Love Me	1976	.80	4.00
Monument 215		Drifting Away / Under Suspicion	1976	.80	4.00
Asylum 46058		Easy Way Out / Tears	1979	.60	3.00
Asylum 46541		Poor Baby / Lay It Down	1979	.60	3.00
Virgin 99434		In Dreams / Leah	1987	.40	2.00
Virgin 99434	(PS)	In Dreams / Leah	1987	.80	4.00
Virgin 99388		Crying / Falling	1987	.40	2.00
Virgin 99388	(PS)	Crying / Falling	1987	.40	2.00
		("Crying" is a duet with K.D. Laing.)			
Virgin 99245		You Got It / The Only One	1989	.40	2.00
Virgin 99245	(PS)	You Got It / The Only One	1989	.40	2.00
		—12" Singles—			
Virgin 99245		You Got It / The Only One	1989	1.00	5.00

ORBISON, ROY, & EMMYLOU HARRIS

| Warners 49262 | | That Lovin' You Feeling Again / (B-side by Craig Hundley.) | 1980 | .40 | 2.00 |

ORBIT ROCKERS, THE

| Willamette 106 | | Dynamic / Windfall | 1960 | 3.00 | 15.00 |
| Willamette 107 | | Rock It / In The Area | 1960 | 3.00 | 15.00 |

ORBITS, THE

| Flair-X 5000 | | Message Of Love / I Really Do | 1956 | 7.00 | 35.00 |

ORCHIDS, THE

Roulette 4412		Good Time Stomp / Pony Walk	1962	2.00	10.00
Columbia 42913		That Boy Is Messin' Up My Mind / Harlem Tango	1963	4.00	20.00
Columbia 43066		Tell Me A Story / From Bad To Worse	1964	4.00	20.00
Columbia 43175		Christmas Is The Time To Be With Your Baby / It Doesn't Matter	1964	4.00	20.00
Roulette 4633		Good Good Time / Love Is What You Make Of It	1965	2.00	10.00

ORIENTALS, THE

| Kayo 927 | | Please Come Back Home / | 195? | 6.00 | 30.00 |

ORIENTS, THE

| Laurie 3232 | | Queen Of The Angels / Shouldn't I? | 1964 | 4.00 | 20.00 |

ORIGINAL CASTE, THE

T.A. 186		One Tin Soldier / Live For Tomorrow	1969	2.00	10.00
T.A. 186	(PS)	One Tin Soldier / Live For Tomorrow	1969	2.00	10.00
T.A. 192		Mr. Monday / Highway	1970	2.00	10.00

ORIGINAL CASUALS, THE [THE CASUALS]

Back Beat 503		So Tough / I Love My Darling	1958	4.00	20.00
		(First pressings credit The Casuals.)			
Back Beat 503		So Tough / I Love My Darling	1958	3.00	15.00
		(Second pressings credit The Original Casuals.)			
Back Beat 510		Judy / Don't Pass Me By	1958	3.00	15.00
Back Beat 514		Three Kisses Past Midnight / It's Been A Long Time	1958	3.00	15.00
		—Back Beat singles above have multi-color labels.—			
		—Extended Play Albums—			
Back Beat 40		The Original Casuals	1958	75.00	300.00

ORIGINAL HUSTLERS, THE

| LaBelle 64121 | | Cueball / Barefoot | 1964 | 7.00 | 35.00 |

Label & Catalog #	A-Side/B-Side		Year	VG	NM

ORIGINAL SURFARIS, THE: *Refer to* **THE SURFARIS**

ORIGINAL PYRAMIDS, THE: *Refer to* **THE PYRAMIDS**

ORION
Orion is a pseudonym for Jimmy Ellis.

Sun 1142	Ebony Eyes / Honey		1979	.80	4.00
Sun 1147	Washing Machine / Before The Next Teardrop Falls		1979	.80	4.00
Sun 1148	Remember Bethlehem / Silent Night		1980	.60	3.00
Sun 1151	Break-Up / Be Bop A Lula		1980	.60	3.00
Sun 1152	A Stranger In My Place / It Ain't No Mystery		1980	.60	3.00
Sun 1153	Texas Tea / Faded Love		1980	.60	3.00
Sun 1156	Am I That Easy To Forget? / Crazy Arms		1981	.60	3.00
Sun 1159	Rockabilly Rebel / Memphis Sun		1981	.60	3.00
Sun 1162	Crazy Little Thing Called Love / Matchbox		1981	.60	3.00
Sun 1165	Born / If I Can't Have You		1981	.60	3.00
Sun 1170	Some You Win / Ain't No Good		1981	.60	3.00
Sun 1172	Feelings / Baby, Please Say Yes		1982	.60	3.00
Sun 1177	Listen To Daddy / Remember Bethlehem		1982	.60	3.00
Sun 1175	Morning Noon And Night / Honky Tonk Heaven		1983	.60	3.00
Kristal 2292	I'm Saving Up My Pennies / Starting Over		1985	.60	3.00

ORLANDO, TONY
Refer to The Bottom Line; Bertell Dache; Billy Shields; Wind.

Milo 101	Ding Dong / You And Only You		1959	15.00	75.00
Epic 9441	Halfway To Paradise / Lonely Tomorrows		1961	2.00	10.00
Epic 9441	Halfway To Paradise / Lonely Tomorrows	(PS)	1961	3.00	15.00
Epic 9452	Bless You / Am I The Guy?		1961	2.00	10.00
Epic 9452	Bless You / Am I The Guy?	(PS)	1961	3.00	15.00
Epic 9476	Happy Times (Are Here To Stay) / Lonely Am I		1961	1.00	5.00
Epic 9476	Happy Times (Are Here To Stay) / Lonely Am I	(PS)	1961	3.00	15.00
Epic 9491	My Baby's A Stranger / Talkin' About You		1962	1.00	5.00
Epic 9491	My Baby's A Stranger / Talkin' About You	(PS)	1962	3.00	15.00
Epic 9502	I'd Never Find Another You / Love On Your Lips		1962	1.00	5.00
Epic 9519	At The Edge Of Tears / Chills		1962	1.00	5.00
Epic 9519	At The Edge Of Tears / Chills	(PS)	1962	3.00	15.00
Epic 9562	Loneliest / Beautiful Dreamer		1962	1.00	5.00
Epic 9570	Shirley / Joanie		1963	1.00	5.00
Epic 9622	I'll Be There / What Am I Gonna Do?		1963	1.00	5.00
Epic 9668	She Doesn't Know It / Tell Me, What Can I Do?		1964	1.00	5.00
Epic 9715	To Wait For Love / Accept It		1964	1.00	5.00
Atco 6376	Think Before You Act / She Loves Me For What I Am		1965	1.00	5.00
Cameo 471	Sweet, Sweet / Manuelito		1967	1.00	5.00
Casablanca 967	I Got Rhythm/Fascinating Rhythm / They're Playing Our Song/Sweet Melody		197?	.40	2.00
Casablanca 991	High Steppin' / Sweets For My Sweet		197?	.40	2.00
Casablanca 2249	Pullin' Together / She Always Knew		197?	.40	2.00

ORLANDO, TONY, & DAWN [DAWN]
Dawn was Orlando with Telma Hopkins and Joyce Vincent-Wilson.

Bell 903	Candida / Look At	1970	.60	3.00
Bell 938	Knock Three Times / Home	1970	.60	3.00
Bell 970	I Play And Sing / Get Out From Where We Are	1971	.50	2.50
Bell 45107	Summer Sand / Sweet Soft Sounds Of Love	1971	.50	2.50
Bell 141	What Are You Doing Sunday? / The Sweet Soft Sound Of Love	1971	.50	2.50
Bell 45175	Runaway-Happy Together / Don't Act Like A Baby	1972	.50	2.50
Bell 45225	Vaya Con Dios / I Can't Believe How Much I Love You	1972	.50	2.50
Bell 45285	You're A Lady / In The Park	1972	.50	2.50
Bell 45318	Tie A Yellow Ribbon 'Round The Old Oak Tree / I Can't Believe How Much I Love You	1973	.60	3.00
Bell 45374	Say, Has Anybody Seen My Sweet Gypsy Rose? / Love Is Kindlin'	1973	.60	3.00
	(Bell 903-45374 credits Dawn.)			
Bell 45424	Who's In The Strawberry Patch With Sally? / Ukelele Man	1973	.50	2.50
Bell 45450	It Only Hurts When I Try To Smile / Sweet Summer Days	1974	.50	2.50
Bell 45601	Steppin' Out (Gonna Boogie Tonight) / She Can't Hold A Candle To You	1974	.50	2.50
Bell 45620	Look In My Eyes, Pretty Woman / My Love Has No Pride	1974	.50	2.50
Elektra 45240	He Don't Love You (Like I Love You) / Pick It Up	1975	.60	3.00
Elektra 45260	Mornin,' Beautiful / Dance, Rosie, Dance	1975	.40	2.00
Elektra 45275	You're All I Need To Get By / Know You Like A Book	1975	.40	2.00
Arista 0105	Gimme A Good Old Mammy Song / Little Heads In Bunkbeds	1975	.40	2.00
Arista 01156	Skybird / That's The Way A Wallflower Grows	1975	.40	2.00
Arista 0301	Tie A Yellow Ribbon 'Round The Old Oak Tree / Say, Has Anybody Seen My Sweet Gypsy Rose?	1976	.40	2.00
Elektra 45302	Cupid / You're Growin' On Me	1976	.40	2.00
Elektra 45387	Sing / Sweet On Candy	1977	.40	2.00

Label & Catalog #	A-Side/B-Side	Year	VG	NM
Elektra 45432	You're All I Need To Gey By / You're Growin' On Me	1977	.40	2.00
Elektra 45501	Bring It On Home To Me / Don't Let Go	1977	.40	2.00
Elektra 45542	I Count The Tears / A Lover's Question	1978	.40	2.00

ORPHANS, THE

Epic 10288	There's No Flowers In My Garden / One Spoken Word	1968	2.00	10.00
Epic 10348	This Is The Time / Deserted	1968	2.00	10.00

ORPHENS, THE

Red Bird 041	My Life / Music Minus Orphens	1965	2.00	10.00

ORPHEUS

Red 041	My Life / Music Minus Orpheus	1965	2.00	10.00
MGM 13882	Can't Find The Time / Lesley's World	1968	1.00	5.00
MGM 13947	I've Never Seen Love Like This / Congress Alley	1968	.80	4.00
MGM 14022	Brown Arms In Houston / I Can't Make The Sun Rise	1969	.80	4.00
MGM 14022 (PS)	Brown Arms In Houston / I Can't Make The Sun Rise	1969	2.00	10.00

ORRISON, BOB

Liberty 55237	Sarah Lee / Florecita	1960	2.00	10.00

ORSI, PHIL, & THE LITTLE KINGS

Lucky 1009	Come On Everybody / Oh, My Darling	1963	15.00	75.00
U.S.A. 841	Stay / Who Ever He May Be	1966	3.00	15.00
U.S.A. 847	Sorry, I Ran All The Way Home / Who Ever He May Be	1966	3.00	15.00

OSBORN, BILL

Camelot 126	I'll Wait For You / Give Me Back My Soul	196?	1.00	5.00

OSBORNE, BILL, JR.

Abel 229	Road To Happiness / Stars Are Falling (In My Heart)	196?	1.00	5.00
RPR 1717	Visions / If I Were Birds	196?	1.00	5.00

OSBORNE, KELL

Brunswick 55068	Hey, Ruby / Don't Give Me Heartaches	1958	6.00	30.00
Trey 3006	Bells Of St. Mary's / That's Alright, Baby	1960	3.00	15.00
	(Produced by Phil Spector.)			

OSBORNE, KELL, & THE CHICKS

Class 302	Do You Mind? / Little Chick-A-Dee	1962	2.00	10.00

OSHINS, MILT

Pelvis 169	All About Elvis / All About Elvis, Part 2	1956	8.00	40.00

OSMOND BROTHERS, THE
The Osmond Brothers feature Donny Osmond.

MGM 13162	Be My Little Baby Bumble Bee / I Wouldn't Trade The Silver In My Mother's Hair	1963	2.00	10.00
MGM 13174	The Travels Of Jamie McPheeters / Aura Lee	1963	2.00	10.00
MGM 13281	Mister Sandman / My Mom	1964	3.00	15.00
MGM 13281 (PS)	Mister Sandman / My Mom	1964	5.00	25.00
	("Mister Sandman" was produced by Terry Melcher in a surf-vocal style.)			
Uni 55015	I Can't Stop / Flower Music	1967	1.00	5.00
Barnaby 2002	Mary Elizabeth / Speak Like A Child	1968	1.00	5.00
Barnaby 2004	I've Got Loving On My Mind / Mollie A	1968	1.00	5.00

OTHER HALF, THE
The Other Half features Randy Holden, formerly of Fender IV.

GNP/Crescendo 378	Mr. Pharmacist / I've Come So Far	1967	4.00	20.00
Acta 801	Wonderful Day / Flight Of The Dragon Lady	1967	1.20	6.00
Acta 806	I Need You / No Doubt About It	1967	1.20	6.00
Acta 819	What Can I Do For You? / Bad Day	1968	1.20	6.00
Acta 825	Morning Fire / Oz Leek Eaves Drops	1968	1.20	6.00

OTHER SIDE, THE

Brent 7061	Walking Down The Road / Streetcar	1964	2.00	10.00

OTHER TWO, THE

Jerden 777	Don't Lock Me In / Look Around	1965	1.20	6.00
Panorama 40	When I Sleep / Don't Say No	1966	1.20	6.00

OTHERS, THE

Fontana 1944	Oh, Yeah! / I'm Taking Her Home	1964	4.00	20.00

OUR GANG
Our Gang features Gary Zekley.

Br'er Bird 001	Summertime, Summertime / Theme From Leon's Garage	1966	50.00	200.00

Label & Catalog #		A-Side/B-Side	Year	VG	NM
OUTCASTS, THE					
Vette 425		Surfer's Paradise / Undertow	1963	7.00	35.00
OUTCASTS, THE					
Cameo 477		Today's The Day / I Didn't have To Love Her Anymore	1967	2.00	10.00
OUTCASTS, THE					
The Outcasts later recorded as The Union Gap.					
Karate 531		I Can't Get Through To You / I Found Out About You	196?	3.00	15.00
OUTLAWS, THE					
Dot 16512		Hold Up / Somethin' Else	1963	4.00	20.00
OUTRAGE					
Kama Sutra 252		Be My Baby / The City	1968	2.00	10.00
Kama Sutra 259		The Letter / The Letter	1969	2.00	10.00
OUTSIDERS, THE					
The Outsiders originally recorded as The Starfires.					
Karate 505		The Guy With The Long Liverpool Hair / Outsider	1964	4.00	20.00
Ellen 503		Rickity-Boom-Bal-Aye / The Bird Rattle	196?	3.00	15.00
Capitol 5573		Time Won't Let Me / Was It Really Real?	1966	1.60	8.00
Capitol 5646		Girl In Love / What Makes You So Bad?	1966	1.60	8.00
Capitol 5646	(PS)	Girl In Love / What Makes You So Bad?	1966	3.00	15.00
Capitol 5701		Respectable / Lost In My World	1966	1.60	8.00
Capitol 5759		Help Me, Girl / You Gotta Look	1966	1.20	6.00
Capitol 5759	(PS)	Help Me, Girl / You Gotta Look	1966	3.00	15.00
Capitol 5843		I'll Give You Time / I'm Not Tryin' To Hurt You	1967	1.20	6.00
Capitol 5843	(PS)	I'll Give You Time / I'm Not Tryin' To Hurt You	1967	3.00	15.00
Capitol 5892		I Just Can't See You Anymore / Gotta Leave Us Alone	1967	1.20	6.00
Capitol 5955		And Now You Want My Sympathy / I'll See You In The Summertime	1967	1.20	6.00
Capitol 5955	(PS)	And Now You Want My Sympathy / I'll See You In The Summertime	1967	3.00	15.00
Capitol 2055		Little Bit Of Lovin' / I Will Love You	1967	1.20	6.00
Capitol 2216		Oh, How It Hurts / We Ain't Gonna Make It	1968	1.20	6.00
Bell 904		Changes / Lost In My World	1970	1.20	6.00
Kapp 2104		Tinker Tailor / You're Not So Pretty	1970	1.20	6.00
OVATIONS, THE					
Andie 5017		Whole Wide World / My Lullabye	1960	4.00	20.00
Barry 101		The Day We Fell In Love / My Lullabye	1961	6.00	30.00
Epic 9470		Oh, What A Day / Real True Love	1961	6.00	30.00
OVATIONS, THE					
Josie 916		Remembering / Who Needs Love?	1964	3.00	15.00
OVATIONS, THE					
Hawk 153		Runaround / I Still Love You	195?	75.00	300.00
OVERLANDERS, THE					
Hickory 1258		Yesterday's Gone / Over The Rainbow	1964	1.25	6.00
Hickory 1275		Don't It Make You Feel Good? / Movin'	1964	1.25	6.00
Hickory 1295		Leaves Are Falling / January	1965	1.25	6.00
Hickory 1362		Michelle / Cradle Of Love	1965	1.25	6.00
Hickory 1384		My Life / Girl From Indiana	1966	1.25	6.00
OVERTONES, THE					
Ajax 173		You're The Only Girl /	196?	3.00	15.00
OWEN, MACK					
Sun 336		Walkin' And Talkin' / Somebody Just Like You	1960	2.00	10.00
OWENS, DONNIE					
Guyden 2001		Need You / If I'm Wrong	1958	3.00	15.00
Guyden 2006		Tomorrow / Out Of My Heart	1959	3.00	15.00
Guyden 2013		Between Midnight And Dawn / Ask Me Anything	1959	3.00	15.00
Trey 124		Stormy / What A Dream	1960	2.00	10.00
ARA 1966		My World / A Soldier's Last Letter	1966	1.20	6.00
OXFORD CIRCLE, THE					
World United 2		Mind Destruction / Foolish Woman	196?	10.00	50.00

P.

P. K. LIMITED

Colgems 5104	Shades Of Grey / My Imagination	1970	1.00	5.00

P. S. C. P.

Vanco 232	A Small Cloud In Your Way / Linda	196?	2.00	10.00

P-NUT BUTTER

Tower 265	What Am I Doing Here With You? / Still In Love With You	1966	2.00	10.00

P-NUT GALLERY, THE

Buddah 239	Do You Know What Time It Is? / Lanny's Tune	1971	1.00	5.00

PACE-SETTERS, THE

Ava 161	Head's Up / Mustang	1964	8.00	40.00
Aurora 1971	Setting The Pace / Ooh Poo Pah Doo	196?	7.00	35.00

PACERS, THE

Guyden 2064	How Sweet / No Wonder	1961	100.00	400.00

PACERS, THE

Coral 62398	Sassy Sue / You Got Me Bugged	1963	2.00	10.00

PACETTES, THE

Regina 306	Don't Read The Letter / You Don't Know, Baby	1963	3.00	15.00

PACIFIC GAS & ELECTRIC [PG&E]

Power 1701	Wade In The Water / Live Love	1969	2.00	10.00
Columbia 45158	Are You Ready? / Stagolee	1970	.80	4.00
Columbia 45221	Father, Come On Home / Elvira	1970	.80	4.00
Columbia 45519	Thank God For You, Baby / See The Monkey Run	1972	.60	3.00
Columbia 45621	(Love Is Like A) Heat Wave / We Did What We Could	1972	.60	3.00

PACK, THE: *Refer to* TERRY KNIGHT & THE PACK

PACKERS, THE

Pure Soul Music 1107	Hole In The Wall / Go 'Head On	1965	1.00	5.00

PAGE, MAYETTA

Etiquette 13	You're So Fine / Don't Worry About Me	1964	2.00	10.00

PAGE, ROCKY

Rendezvous 1349	Yes, I'm Lonesome Tonight / Standing On A Mountain Top	1961	3.00	15.00

PAGE-BOYS, THE

Whirl 126	Twist Enos, Twist / I Got The Blues Again	196?	2.00	10.00

PAGEANTS, THE: *Refer to* TONY DEE

PAGE BOYS, THE

Camelot 114	Our Love / Things Are Going To Break Up	196?	2.00	10.00

PAGENTS, THE

Ike 631	Enchanted Surf / Big Daddy	1963	5.00	25.00
Era 3119	Enchanted Surf / Big Daddy	1963	5.00	25.00
Era 3134	Pa-Cha / Sad And Lonely	1964	4.00	20.00

PAIGE, JOEY

Warner Bros. 5377	Surfer From Tennessee / Such Wonderful Dreams	1963	5.00	25.00

PALACE GUARD, THE
The Palace Guard features Emitt Rhodes. Refer to Don Grady.

Orange Empire 331	All Night Long / Playgirl	1965	2.00	10.00
Orange Empire 332	A Girl You Can Depend On / If You Need Me	1965	2.00	10.00
Orange Empire 400	Falling Sugar / Oh, Blue	1966	2.00	10.00
Verve 10410	Falling Sugar / Oh, Blue	1966	2.00	10.00
Parkway 111	Saturday's Child / Party Lights	1966	2.00	10.00

PALISADES, THE

Calico 113	Close Your Eyes / I Can't Quit	1960	4.00	20.00
Leader 806	Dear Joan / The Shrine	1960	2.00	10.00
Dore 609	Hometown Girl / Oh, My Love	1961	2.00	10.00

Label & Catalog #	A-Side/B-Side	Year	VG	NM
Medieval 205	This Is The Nite / Relic Rock	1962	3.00	15.00
Chairman 4401	Make The Night A Little Longer / It's Heaven Being With You	1963	5.00	25.00
	(Chairman 4401 features Carole King.)			
PALS, THE				
Turf 1000	My Baby Likes To Rock / Summer Is Here	1958	8.00	40.00
Guyden 2019	My Baby Likes To Rock / Summer Is Here	1959	4.00	20.00
PAN				
Pan features Ron Elliott, formerly of The Beau Brummels.				
Columbia 45806	Lady Honey / Long Way Home	1973	.40	2.00
Columbia 45870	More Than My Guitar / Long Way Home	1973	.40	2.00
PANDA				
General 2512	Little Louie / Lonely Lady	196?	2.00	10.00
PANDORAS, THE				
Liberty 55945	About My Baby / New Day	1967	1.20	6.00
Liberty 55999	Games / Don't Bother	1967	1.20	6.00
PANICKS, THE				
Kyra 1001	Bad Doreen /	196?	7.00	35.00
PANICS, THE				
The Panics also recorded with Sonny Richards.				
Chancellor 1109	Bony Maronie / Panicsville	1962	3.00	15.00
Philips 40230	The Kangaroo / It Ain't What You Got	1964	2.00	10.00
PANICS, THE				
Hickman 1/2	Panic / Blues After Hours	196?	1.20	6.00
PAPA DOO RUN RUN				
RCA/Equinox 10404 (DJ)	Be True To Your School / Disney Girls	1975	1.00	5.00
RCA/Equinox 10404	Be True To Your School / Disney Girls	1975	2.00	10.00
	(Features Bruce Johnston.)			
PAPER DOLLS, THE				
MGM 13766	'Cause I Love You / You're The Boy I Want To Marry	1967	2.00	10.00
PAPER DOLLS, THE				
Warner Bros. 7191	Something Here In My Heart / All The Time In The World	1968	2.00	10.00
PAPER TRAIN, THE				
Capitol 2464	Brother / Time Waits For No One	1969	1.20	6.00
PAPPAS, PETER				
RuVal 4503	Sound Of Angels / The Dive	196?	2.00	10.00
PARAGONS, THE				
Century Custom 19317	Surf Drums / (B-side by The Samohi Serenaders)	196?	8.00	40.00
PARAKEETS, THE				
Jubilee 5407	Shangri-La / Come Back	1961	4.00	20.00
PARALLELS, THE				
Twilight 405	Surf-A-Nova / Da Doity	1963	7.00	35.00
	(Also released on Twilight 405 credited to The Tri-Tones.)			
PARAMOUNTS, THE				
Carlton 524	Girl Friend / Trying	1960	3.00	15.00
Dot 16175	Why Do You Have To Go? / Congratulations	1960	5.00	25.00
Dot 16201	When You Dance / You're Seventeen	1960	6.00	30.00
PARAMOUNTS, THE				
Laurie 3201	Just To Be With You / One More For The Road	1963	5.00	25.00
PARAMOUNTS, THE				
Centaur 103	Where's Carolyn Tonight? / When I Dream	196?	6.00	30.00
Fleetwood 1014	I Know You'll Be My Love / Christopher Columbus	196?	5.00	25.00
PARAMOUNTS, THE				
The Paramounts later recorded as Procol Harum.				
Liverpool Sound 903	I Feel Good All Over / Poison Ivy	1964	10.00	50.00
PARAMOURS, THE				
The Paramours are Bobby Hatfield and Bill Medley, who later recorded as The Righteous Brothers.				
Smash 1701	That's The Way We Love / Prison Break	1961	4.00	20.00

Label & Catalog #		A-Side/B-Side	Year	VG	NM
Smash 1718		Cutie Cutie / Miss Social Climber	1961	4.00	20.00
Moonglow 214		That's All I Want Tonight / There She Goes	1962	4.00	20.00
Moonglow 214		That's All I Want Tonight / There She Goes (Red vinyl)	1962	8.00	40.00

PARIS SISTERS, THE
The Paris Sisters also recorded with Gary Crosby.

Label & Catalog #		A-Side/B-Side	Year	VG	NM
Decca 29372		Ooh La La / Who's Arms Are You Missing?	195?	3.00	15.00
Decca 29448		Blueberry Pie / Baby, Honey, Baby	195?	3.00	15.00
Decca 29744		Lover Boy / Oh Yes, You Do	195?	3.00	15.00
Decca 29891		I Love You, Dear / Mistaken	195?	3.00	15.00
Decca 29970		Daughter, Daughter! / So Much-So Very Much	195?	3.00	15.00
Decca 30554		Don't Tell Anybody / Mind Reader	1958	3.00	15.00
Imperial 5465		Old Enough To Cry / Tell Me More	1959	3.00	15.00
Imperial 5487		My Original Love / Someday	1959	3.00	15.00
Gregmark 2		Be My Boy / I'll Be Crying Tomorrow	1961	4.00	20.00
Gregmark 6		I Love How You Love Me / All Through The Night	1961	4.00	20.00
Gregmark 10		He Knows I Love Him Too Much / A Lonely Girl's Prayer	1962	4.00	20.00
Gregmark 12		Let Me Be The One / What Am I To Do?	1962	4.00	20.00
Gregmark 13		Yes, I Love You / Once Upon A While Ago	1962	4.00	20.00
		(Gregmark 2, 6, 10, 12 and 13 were produced by Phil Spector.)			
MGM 13236		Dream Lover / Lonely Girl	1964	3.00	15.00
MGM 13236	(PS)	Dream Lover / Lonely Girl	1964	5.00	25.00
Mercury 72320		Once Upon A Time / When I Fall In Love	1964	2.00	10.00
Mercury 72468		Always Waitin' / Why Do I Take It From You?	1965	2.00	10.00
Reprise 0440		Sincerely / Too Good To Be True	1966	2.00	10.00
Reprise 0472		You / I'm Me	1966	2.00	10.00
Reprise 0511		My Good Friend / It's My Party	1966	2.00	10.00
Reprise 0548		Some Of Your Lovin' / Long After Tonight Is All Over	1967	2.00	10.00
Capitol 2081		Golden Days / Greener days	1968	1.00	5.00
Crescendo 410		Stand Naked, Clown / The Ugliest Girl In Town	1968	.80	4.00

PARISIANS, THE

Label & Catalog #	A-Side/B-Side	Year	VG	NM
Pova 1004	Why? / On The Sunny Side Of The Street	1962	3.00	15.00

PARKAYS, THE

Label & Catalog #	A-Side/B-Side	Year	VG	NM
ABC-Paramount 10242	Late Date / Get It	1961	2.00	10.00

PARKER, BOBBY

Label & Catalog #	A-Side/B-Side	Year	VG	NM
V-Tone 223	Watch Your Step / Steal Your Heart Away	1961	2.00	10.00

PARKER, GIGI, & THE LOVELIES

Label & Catalog #	A-Side/B-Side	Year	VG	NM
MGM 13225	Beatles, Please Come Back / In This Room	1964	3.00	15.00

PARKER, GRAHAM, & THE RUMOR

Label & Catalog #		A-Side/B-Side	Year	VG	NM
Mercury 73834		Soul Shoes / You've Got To Be Kidding	1976	.80	4.00
Mercury 73876		Heat Treatment / Back Door Love	1976	.80	4.00
Mercury 73970		The Heat In Harlem / Stick To Me	1977	.80	4.00
Mercury 74000		Hold Back The Night / (Let Me Get) Sweet On You	1977	.80	4.00
Arista 0420		Local Girls / I Want You Back	1979	.80	4.00
Arista 0420	(PS)	Local Girls / I Want You Back	1979	.80	4.00

PARKER, RICHARD

Label & Catalog #	A-Side/B-Side	Year	VG	NM
Philips 40133	Monkey All Over / Welcome To Paradise	1963	2.00	10.00

PARKS, VAN DYKE
Van Dyke Parks also recorded as George Washington Brown.

Label & Catalog #	A-Side/B-Side	Year	VG	NM
MGM 13441	Do What You Wanta / Number Nine	1966	2.00	10.00
MGM 13570	Come To The Sunshine / Further Along	1967	2.00	10.00
Warner Bros. 7409	On The Rolling Sea When Jesus Speaks To Me / The Eagle And Me	1970	2.00	10.00
Warner Bros. 7609	Occapello / Ode To Tobago	1972	1.00	5.00

PARKTOWNS, THE

Label & Catalog #	A-Side/B-Side	Year	VG	NM
Thor 3258	You Hurt Me Inside / Stop, Look And Listen	196?	7.00	35.00

PARLETTES, THE

Label & Catalog #	A-Side/B-Side	Year	VG	NM
Jubilee 5467	Tonight I Met An Angel / Because We're Very Young	1963	3.00	15.00

PARLIAMENTS, THE

Label & Catalog #	A-Side/B-Side	Year	VG	NM
Symbol 917	I'll Get You Yet / You're Cute	1963	5.00	25.00

PARRISH & GURVITZ

Label & Catalog #	A-Side/B-Side	Year	VG	NM
Decca 32967	Janine / I've Got Time	1972	.80	4.00

PARSONS, BILL
Whether intentional or not, this is a pseudonym for country singer Bobby Bare.

Label & Catalog #	A-Side/B-Side	Year	VG	NM
Fraternity 835	The All-American Boy / Rubber Dolly	1958	4.00	20.00
Fraternity 838	Educated Rock And Roll / The Carefree Wanderer	1958	3.00	15.00

Label & Catalog #		A-Side/B-Side	Year	VG	NM
Fraternity 838		Educated Rock And Roll / The Carefree Wanderer	1958	3.00	15.00

PARSONS, GRAM
Gram Parsons also recorded with The International Submarine Band; The Byrds; and The Flying Burrito Brothers.

Reprise 1139		She / That's All I Took	1973	.80	4.00
Reprise PRO-557	(DJ)	Cry One More Time / Streets Of Baltimore	1973	2.00	10.00
Reprise 1192		Love Hurts / In My Hour Of Darkness	1974	.80	4.00
Warner Bros. 50013		The Return Of The Grievous Angel / Hearts On Fire	1981	.40	2.00
Sierra 105		Love Hurts / The New Soft Shoe	1983	.80	4.00
		—Extended Play Albums—			
Sierra 104		The Big Finish	1982	2.00	10.00

PARTRIDGE FAMILY, THE
The Partridge Family features David Cassidy and Shirley Jones.

Tiger Beat		Welcome To Our Club (Cardboard picture disc)	197?	6.00	30.00
Bell 910		I Think I Love You / Somebody Wants To Love You	1970	.80	5.00
Bell 910	(PS)	I Think I Love You / Somebody Wants To Love You	1970	2.00	10.00
Bell 963		Doesn't Somebody Want To Be Wanted? /			
		You Are Always On My Mind	1971	.80	5.00
Bell 963	(PS)	Doesn't Somebody Want To Be Wanted? /			
		You Are Always On My Mind	1971	2.00	10.00
Bell 996		I'll Meet You Halfway / Morning Rider On The Road	1971	.80	4.00
Bell 130		I Woke Up In Love This Morning / Twenty-Four Hours A Day	1971	.80	4.00
Bell 160		It's One Of Those Nights (Yes Love) / One Night Stand	1971	.80	4.00
Bell 200		Am I Losing You? / If You Ever Go	1972	.80	4.00
Bell 235		Breaking Up Is Hard To Do / I'm Here, You're Here	1972	.80	4.00
Bell 301		Looking Through The Eyes Of Love / Storybook Love	1972	.80	4.00
Bell 336		A Friend And A Lover / Something's Wrong	1973	.80	4.00
Bell 414	(DJ)	Lookin' For A Good Time / Lookin' For A Good Time	1973	1.00	5.00
		(Stock copies of Bell 414 may not exist.)			

PARTY FAVORS, THE
The Party Favors are Dorene Lapone and Vinnie "Winnie Esposito" Mossucco.

R.S.V.P. 1109		You're Not The Marrying Kind / Changed Disposition	1965	3.00	15.00

PASS, TONY

Atco 6421		Spring Fever / True, True Love	1966	1.00	5.00

PASSECALLO, DAVE, & THE FOUR ESCORTS

Bi Mi 102		By The Fire / Baby, Where Are You?	195?	10.00	50.00

PASSIONS, THE
The Passions also recorded with Rocky Hart and Johnny Saber.

Capitol 3963		My Aching Heart / Jackie Brown	1958	4.00	20.00
Dore 505		Tango Of Love / Nervous About Love	1958	4.00	20.00
Audicon 102		Just To Be With You / Oh, Melancholy Me	1959	4.00	20.00
Audicon 105		I Only Want You / This Is My Love	1960	4.00	20.00
		—Original Audicon singles above have red labels.—			
Audicon 102		Just To Be With You / Oh, Melancholy Me	196?	3.00	15.00
Audicon 105		I Only Want You / This Is My Love	196?	3.00	15.00
Audicon 106		Gloria / Jungle Drums	1960	4.00	20.00
Audicon 108		Beautiful Dreamer / One Look Is All It Took	1960	3.00	15.00
Audicon 112		Made For Lovers / Don't Love Me Anymore	1961	4.00	20.00
		—Audicon singles above have orange & black labels.—			
Jubilee 5406		Lonely Road / One Look	1961	3.00	15.00
Octavia 8005		Aphrodite / I've Gotta Know	1962	50.00	200.00
ABC-Paramount 10436		The Bully / The Empty Seat	1963	3.00	15.00
Diamond 146		Sixteen Candles / The Third Floor	1963	3.00	15.00
Diamond 146		Sixteen Candles / The Third Floor (Grey vinyl)	1963	6.00	30.00
GSF 6880		A Toast / A One Night Affair	196?	2.00	10.00
Fantastic 79		Too Many Memories / The Reason	196?	2.00	10.00

PASSIONS, THE

Topaz 1317		It Ain't Fair / I'm So Afraid	196?	2.00	10.00

PASTEL SIX, THE
The Pastel Six also recorded with Sonny Patterson.

Zenith 101		Cinnamon Cinder (It's A Very Nice Dance) / Bandido	1962	3.00	15.00
Zenith 105		A Sing-A-Long Song / The Strange Ghost	1962	3.00	15.00
Downey 101		Twitchin' / Open House At The Center	1963	4.00	20.00
Downey 101		Twitchin' / Wino Stomp	1963	4.00	20.00
Downey 102		Brahm's Nightmare / Open House	1963	3.00	15.00

PASTELS, THE

Josie 833		Swingin' Sam / (B-side by The Debs)	1958	3.00	15.00

PASTELS, THE

Ark 298		Jungle Run / K-Nif	196?	7.00	35.00

Label & Catalog #		A-Side/B-Side	Year	VG	NM
PASTELS, THE					
Century 22103		Why Don't You Love Me / What Can I Say?	1964	4.00	20.00
Century 22698		Circuit Breaker / Don't Know	196?	4.00	20.00
PAT & THE CALIFORNIANS					
Downey 122		Bad / Be Billy	1964	5.00	25.00
PAT & THE SATELLITES					
Atco 6131		Jupiter-C / Oh! Oh! Darlin'	1959	3.00	15.00
PAT & THE WILDCATS					
Crusader 100		The Gigler / Green Tomatoes	1964	1.20	6.00
PATE, JOHNNY					
Gig 225		Stay In The Know / Don't Worry About Me	1956	3.00	15.00
PATENTS, THE					
Hart-Van 0127		Blue Surf / Jumpin' In	1963	8.00	40.00
PATEY BROTHERS, THE					
Ron Mar 1004		Hey, Doll Baby / Jeannie	1959	4.00	20.00
PATIENCE & PRUDENCE					
Liberty 55022		Tonight You Belong To Me / A Smile And A Ribbon	1956	4.00	20.00
Liberty 55040		Gonna Get Along Without Ya Now / The Money Tree	1956	4.00	20.00
Liberty 55084		You Tattle Tale / Very Nice Is Bali Bali	1957	3.00	15.00
Liberty 55084	(PS)	You Tattle Tale / Very Nice Is Bali Bali	1957	6.00	30.00
Chattahoochee 665		Tonight You Belong To Me / How Can I Tell Him?	1965	1.25	6.00
PATTERSON, MIKE, & THE FUGITIVES					
Imperial 66083		Jerky / Cookin' Beans	1964	2.00	10.00
PATTERSON, SONNY, & THE PASTEL SIX					
Vault 903		Troubles / Gone So Long	1963	2.00	10.00
PATTON, JIMMY					
Sage 261		Yah! I'm Movin' /	1958	35.00	175.00
Sims 117		Okies In The Pokie / Lonely Heart	1959	40.00	200.00
PATTY & THE EMBLEMS					
Herald 590		Mixed-Up, Shook-Up Girl / Ordinary Guy	1964	2.00	10.00
Herald 593		The Sound Music Makes /			
		You Took Advantage Of A Good Thing	1964	2.00	10.00
Herald 595		And We Danced / You Can't Get Away From Me	1964	2.00	10.00
PATTY CAKES, THE					
Tuff 378		I Understand Them / I Understand Them	1964	2.00	10.00
PAUL, DENNIS					
Kapp 815		Peggy Sue / (B-side by Wes Dakus)	1967	2.00	10.00
PAUL					
Paul is a pseudonym for Ray Hildebrand. Refer to Jill & Ray; Paul & Paula.					
Josie 935		Happines Across The Street / Last One	196?	1.60	8.00
Charay 48		Hey You, Walk With Me / Happy Music	1966	1.60	8.00
Dot 16936		Hey You, Walk With Me / Happy Music	1966	1.20	6.00
Tower 304		Paper Clown / Patsy	1967	1.60	8.00
PAUL & PAULA					
Ray Hildebrand and Jill Jackson, who also recorded as Jill & Ray.					
LeCam 99		Beginning Of Love / All I Want Is You	1963	3.00	15.00
Philips 40084		Hey, Paula / Bobby Is The One	1963	2.00	10.00
Philips 40096		Young Lovers / Ba-Hey-Be	1963	2.00	10.00
Philips 40096	(PS)	Young Lovers / Ba-Hey-Be	1963	3.00	15.00
Philips 40114		First Quarrel / School Is Through	1963	1.60	8.00
Philips 40114	(PS)	First Quarrel / School Is Through	1963	3.00	15.00
Philips 40130		Something Old, Something New / Flipped Over You	1963	1.60	8.00
Philips 40142		First Day Back At School / A Perfect Pair	1964	1.60	8.00
Philips 40158		Holiday For Teens / Holiday Hootenanny	1964	1.60	8.00
Philips 40168		Crazy Little Things / We'll Never Break Up For Good	1964	1.60	8.00
Philips 40174		It's All Over, Paula / Snow Girl	1964	1.60	8.00
Philips 40209		Darlin' / The Young Years	1964	1.20	6.00
Philips 40234		No Other Baby / Too Dark To See	1964	1.20	6.00
Philips 40234	(PS)	No Other Baby / Too Dark To See	1964	3.00	15.00
Philips 40268		True Love / Any Way You Want Me	1965	1.20	6.00
Philips 40296		Dear Paul / All The Love	1965	1.20	6.00
Philips 40352		All I Want Is You / The Beginning Of Love	1965	1.20	6.00
Uni 55052		All These Things / The Wedding	1968	.80	4.00

Label & Catalog #	A-Side/B-Side	Year	VG	NM
PAUL & THE VICTORS				
Corby 216	The Trip / (B-side by Kim Fowley)	1965	5.00	25.00
PAULA, MARLENA				
Regent 7506	I Wanna Spend Christmas With Elvis /			
	Once More It's Christmas	1956	7.00	35.00
PAULSON, BUTCH				
Virgelle 708	Man From Mars / My Own Brother	195?	8.00	40.00
Virgelle 718	Candy Lou / Today Was Blue Tomorrow	195?	2.00	10.00
PAXTON, GARY				

Gary Paxton also recorded with or as The Captivations; Gary & Clyde; The Hollywood Argyles; The Pledges; The Road Runners; Robbins & Paxton; and Skip & Flip.

Garpax 44172	We're Going Back Together / It Had To Be You	1962	3.00	15.00
Felsted 8691	Kansas City / Sweet Senorita From Santa Fe	1963	3.00	15.00
Liberty 55407	Teenage Crush / It's So Funny	1963	3.00	15.00
Liberty 55485	Alley Oop Was A Two-Dab Man / Stop Twistin', Baby	1963	3.00	15.00
Liberty 55584	Spooky Movies / Spooky Movies, Part 2	1963	3.00	15.00
Garpax 44177	How To Be A Fool (In Six Easy Lessons) / The Scavenger	1964	3.00	15.00
Garpax 44180	Your Past Is Back Again /			
	Dual Hump Camel Named Robert E. Lee	1964	2.00	10.00
Capitol 5467	My Heart Won't Let My Lips Say Goodbye /			
	It's My Way (Of Loving You)	1965	2.00	10.00
Capitol 5675	Mother-In-Law / Miles And Cities	1966	2.00	10.00
Capitol 5707	Goin' Through The Motions / You Got To Do The Best	1966	2.00	10.00
Capitol 5975	Mother In Law / Miles And Cities	1966	2.00	10.00
MGM 14306	Carin' For Karen / Out On A Limb	197?	.80	4.00
MGM 14362	Parchman Farm / Rocky Tot	197?	.80	4.00
RCA Victor PB-10449	Freedom Lives In A Country Song /			
	Too Far Gone (To Care What You Done To Me)	1976	.80	4.00

PAYMARKS, THE: *Refer to* THE RAYMARKS

PAYNE, TOMMY				
Felsted 8531	I Go Ape / Trouble And Pain	1958	4.00	20.00
XYZ 601	Shy Boy / Fire Engine Red Bandana	1959	3.00	15.00
XYZ 603	My Steady Girl / Cruisin' Around	1959	4.00	20.00
PEANUT BUTTER CONSPIRACY, THE				
Vault 933	Time Is After You / Floating Dream	1966	2.00	10.00
Challenge 500	Back In L.A. / Have A Little Faith	1967	1.20	6.00
Columbia 43985	It's A Happening Thing / Twice As Life	1967	1.00	5.00
Columbia 44063	Dark On You Now / Then Came Love	1967	1.00	5.00
Columbia 44356	Turn On A Friend (To The Good Life) / Captain Sandwich	1967	1.00	5.00
	(Columbia sides were produced by Gary Usher.)			
PEBBLES & BAMM BAMM				

Pebbles Flintstone and Bamm Bamm Rubble. Refer to Fred Flintstone.

HBR 449		Open Up Your Heart / The Lord Is Counting On You	1965	3.00	15.00
HBR 449	(PS)	Open Up Your Heart / The Lord Is Counting On You	1965	6.00	30.00
HBR 484		Daddy / The World Is Full Of Joys			
		(For Little Girls And Boys)	1965	3.00	15.00

PEDICIN, MIKE				
RCA Victor 47-6369	Hotter Than A Pistol / Large, Large House	1956	3.00	15.00
Cameo 125	Shake A Hand / The Dickie Doo	1957	3.00	15.00
PEDRICK, BOBBY, JR.				

Refer to Bobby & The Consoles.

Shell 722	Come Out, Come Out / School Crush	1958	4.00	20.00
Big Top 3004	White Bucks And Saddle Shoes / Stranded	1958	3.00	15.00
Big Top 3008	Pajama Party / Betty Blue Eyes	1959	2.00	10.00
Big Top 3024	Summer Nights / My Private Joy	1960	2.00	10.00
Duel 504	I'm Scared / That Girl Is You	1962	3.00	15.00
Duel 516	Dining And Dancing / Two Ton Tessie	1962	3.00	15.00
Duel 525	If Mary Only Knew / If I Had My Life To Live Over	1963	3.00	15.00
MGM 13384	Don't Try To Change My Ways / Teach Myself How To Cry	1965	2.00	10.00
Verve 10402	Karine / Maybe	1966	8.00	40.00
PEEK, PAUL				
NRC 001	The Rock Around / Sweet Skinny Jenny	1958	6.00	30.00
NRC 008	I'm Not Your Fool Anymore / Oldsmo William	1958	5.00	25.00
NRC 033	Waikiki Beach / Gee, But I Miss That Girl	1959	3.00	15.00
NRC 048	Hurtin' Inside / Walkin' The Floor Over You	1960	3.00	15.00
NRC 059	I'm A Happy Man / Where There's A Will	1960	3.00	15.00
Fairlane 702	Brother-In-Law / Through The Teenage Years	1961	2.00	10.00

Label & Catalog #	A-Side/B-Side	Year	VG	NM
Columbia 43527	Pin The Tail On The Donkey / Rockin' Pneumonia And The Boogie Woogie Flu	1966	2.00	10.00
Columbia 43771	The Shadow Knows / I'm Moving Uptown	1966	2.00	10.00
1-2-3 1714	Sweet Lorraine / Out Went The Lights Of My World	1969	1.00	5.00

PEELS, THE

Karate 522	Juanita Banana / Fun	1966	2.00	10.00

PEEPS, THE

Philips 40315	Got Plenty Of Love / Now Is The Time	1965	2.00	10.00

PEMBROKE LTD.

Debutone 779	Love's So Easy Now / Sleepyjohn	1967	2.00	10.00

PENDARVIS, TRACY (& THE SWAMPERS)

Sun 335	A Thousand Guitars / Is It Too Late?	1960	2.00	10.00
Sun 345	Is It Me? / Southbound Line	1960	3.00	15.00
Sun 359	Bell Of The Swanee / Eternally	1961	2.00	10.00

PENDELTONS, THE
The Pendeltons feature Gary Usher and Richie Burns of The Hondells.

Dot 16511 (DJ)	Board Party / Barefoot Adventure	1963	12.00	60.00
Dot 16511	Board Party / Barefoot Adventure	1963	25.00	125.00
Rendezvous 194	The Waddle / Itchy Bon Mass	1963	8.00	40.00

PENDULUM
Pendulum is a pseudonym for The Alessi Brothers.

Kama Sutra 253	Silly Sally Sunday / I Do You	1969	1.00	5.00
Kama Sutra 257	Now I'll Cry / Dead Dog	1969	1.00	5.00

PENETRATIONS, THE

Icon 1002	Bring 'Em In / Fackin' Out	196?	7.00	35.00
Icon 1002	Bring 'Em In / Fackin' Out (Blue vinyl)	196?	15.00	75.00

PENGUINS, THE
The Penguins are one of the seminal R&B doo-wop groups of the '50s. Their sole entry in this book is included for collectors Zappa, who wrote "Memories Of El Monte."

Original Sound 27	Memories Of El Monte / Be Mine	1962	10.00	50.00

PENN, LITTLE LAMBSIE

Atco 6082	I Wanna Spend Christmas With Elvis / Painted Lips & Pig-Tails	1956	5.00	25.00

PENN, WILLIAM, & THE QUAKERS

Melron 5013	California Sun / No More Love	1966	3.00	15.00
Melron 5024	Philly / Santa Needs Ear Muffs On His Nose	1966	1.50	8.00
Melron 5024	Sweet Caroline / Santa Needs Ear Muffs On His Nose	1966	1.50	8.00

PENN, WILLIAM, & THE QUAKERS

Duane 104	Coming Up My Way / Care Free	196?	3.00	15.00
Twilight 410	Ghost Of The Monks / Goodbye, My Love	196?	3.00	15.00
Hush 230	Little Girl / Somebody's Dum Dum	196?	5.00	25.00

PENN FYVE, WILLIAM

Thunderbird 502	Blow My Mind / Swami	196?	6.00	30.00

PENNA, D.R., & THE MISSISSIPPI JOOK BAND

P&M 39	Pledging My Love / Mystery Train	195?	3.00	15.00

PENNER, DICK

Sun 282	Your Honey Love / Cindy Lou	1957	6.00	30.00

PENNSYLVANIA PLAYERS, THE
The Pennsylvania Players is a pseudonym for Dickie Goodman.

Oron 101	Washington Uptight / The Cat	1967	3.00	15.00

PENNY, JOE

Federal 12322	Bip A Little, Bop A Lot / Mercy, Mercy, Mercy	195?	3.00	150.00

PENNY, PAUL

Jam 108	Change In Plans / True Fine Mama	196?	1.00	5.00

PENNY ARCADE, THE

United Artists 50221	Francine / Me And My Piano (U.A. 50221 features Pete Anders and Vinnie Poncia.)	1968	2.00	10.00
Smash 2190	Tears In My Heart / The Bubble Gum Tree	1968	1.00	5.00

Label & Catalog #	A-Side/B-Side	Year	VG	NM
PENTAGONS, THE				
Specialty 644	Silly Dilly / It's Spring Again	1958	4.00	20.00
Fleetwood Inter. 100	To Be Loved (Forever) / Down At The Beach	1961	25.00	125.00
Donna 1337	To Be Loved (Forever) / Down At The Beach	1961	4.00	20.00
Donna 1344	I Like The Way You Look (At Me) / For A Love That Is Mine	1961	3.00	15.00
Jamie 1201	I Wonder / She's Mine	1961	2.00	10.00
Jamie 1210	I'm In Love / Until Then	1962	2.00	10.00
Sutter 100	Forever Yours / Gonna Wait For You	196?	3.00	15.00
PENTANGLE				
Reprise 0784	Let No Man Steal Your Thyme / Way behind The Sun	1968	1.00	5.00
Reprise 0843	I Saw An Angel / Once I Had A Sweetheart	1969	1.00	5.00
PEOPLE				
The Capitol sides feature Larry Norman.				
Capitol 5920	Riding High / Organ Grinder	1967	2.00	10.00
Capitol 2078	I Love You / Somebody Tell Me My Name	1968	2.00	10.00
Capitol 2251	Ashes Of Me / Apple Cider	1968	2.00	10.00
Capitol 2449	Ulla / Turnin' Me In	1969	2.00	10.00
Paramount 0005	Love Will Take Us Higher And Higher / Livin' It Up	1969	1.20	6.00
Paramount 0011	Sunshine Lady / Crosstown Bus	1969	1.20	6.00
Paramount 0019	For What It's Worth / Maple Street	1970	1.20	6.00
Paramount 0028	One Chain Don't Make No Prison / Keep It Alive	1970	1.20	6.00
Polydor 14087	Chant For Peace / I Don't Carry No Guns	1971	1.20	6.00
PEPE & THE ASTROS				
Swami 553/4	Judy, My Love / Now, Ain't That A Shame	195?	7.00	35.00
PEPPER POTS, THE				
Panlin 7320	Ruby Duby Du / Leather Jacket Cowboy	1960	2.00	10.00
PEPPERMINT, DANNY, & THE JUMPING JACKS				
Carlton 565	The Peppermint Twist / Somebody Else Is Taking My Place	1961	3.00	15.00
PEPPERMINT RAINBOW, THE				
Decca 32316	Pink Lemonade / Walking In Different Circles	1968	1.00	5.00
Decca 32410	Will You Be Staying After Sunday? / And I'll Be There	1968	1.00	5.00
Decca 32498	Don't Wake Me Up In The Morning, Michael / Rosemary	1969	1.00	5.00
Decca 32498 (PS)	Don't Wake Me Up In The Morning, Michael / Rosemary	1969	2.00	10.00
Decca 34667 (DJ)	You're The Sound Of Love / You're The Sound Of Love	197?	1.00	5.00
	(Stock copies of Decca 34667 may not exist.)			
PEPPERMINT TROLLEY COMPANY, THE				
Valiant 752	Lollipop Train / Bored To Tears	196?	2.00	10.00
Acta 809	It's A Lazy Summer Day / Blue Eyes	1968	1.00	5.00
Acta 813	Beautiful Sun / I've Got To Be Going	1968	1.00	5.00
Acta 815	Baby, You Come Rolling Across My Mind /			
	9 O' Clock Business Man	1968	1.00	5.00
Acta 829	Trust / I Remember Long Ago	1968	1.00	5.00
Acta 835	New York City / Spinnin' Whirlin' Round	1968	1.00	5.00
PEPPERMINTS, THE				
House Of Beauty 1	Teen Age Idol / Believe Me	1959	7.00	35.00
PEPPERMINTS, THE				
R.S.V.P. 1112	Peppermint Jerk / We All Warned You	1965	1.20	6.00
PEPS, THE: *Refer to* **THE FABULOUS PEPS**				
PERCELLS, THE				
ABC-Paramount 10401	What Are Boys Made Of? / Cheek To Cheek	1963	2.00	10.00
ABC-Paramount 10449	Look At That Guy / Boy Friends	1963	2.00	10.00
ABC-Paramount 10476	My Guy / Hully Gully Guitar	1963	2.00	10.00
ABC-Paramount 10516	I Stand Alone / The Greatest	1963	2.00	10.00
PERFECT STRANGERS, THE				
Capitol 5607	Take A Chance / I Will Always Wait For You	1966	2.00	10.00
PERFECTIONS, THE				
SVR 1005	Am I Gonna Lose You? / I Love You, My Love	196?	5.00	25.00
PERFIDIANS, THE				
Husky 1	La Paz / Whiplash	1962	7.00	35.00
Husky 1	La Paz / Whiplash *(Red vinyl)*	1962	15.00	75.00
PERIDOTS, THE				
Deauville 100	Hully Gully All Night Long / It's The Bomp	1961	2.00	10.00

Label & Catalog #		A-Side/B-Side	Year	VG	NM
PERISCOPES, THE					
WDR 2274		Beavershot / I'm Happy To Be	1965	7.00	35.00
PERKINS, CARL					
Carl Perkins also recorded with NRBQ.					
Flip 501		Movie Magg / Turn Around	1955	150.00	500.00
Sun 224		Gone, Gone, Gone / Let The Juke Box Keep On Playing	1955	15.00	75.00
Sun 234		Blue Suede Shoes / Honey Don't	1956	5.00	25.00
Sun 243		Boppin' The Blues / All Mama's Children	1956	4.00	20.00
Sun 249		Dixie Fried / I'm Sorry I'm Not Sorry	1956	3.00	15.00
Sun 261		Matchbox / Your True Love	1956	3.00	15.00
Sun 274		Forever Yours / That's Right	1957	3.00	15.00
Sun 287		Glad All Over / Lend Me Your Comb	1958	3.00	15.00
Columbia 41131		Pink Pedal Pushers / Jive After Five	1958	3.00	15.00
Columbia 41131	(PS)	Pink Pedal Pushers / Jive After Five	1958	15.00	75.00
Columbia 41207		Levi Jacket / Pop, Let Me Have The Car	1958	3.00	15.00
Columbia 41296		Y-O-U / This Life I Lead	1959	3.00	15.00
Columbia 41379		Pointed Toe Shoes / Highway Of Love	1959	3.00	15.00
Columbia 41449		One Ticket To Loneliness /			
		I Don't See Me In Your Arms Anymore	1959	3.00	15.00
Columbia 41651		L-O-V-E-V-I-L-L-E / Too Much For A Man To Understand	1960	3.00	15.00
Columbia 41825		Just For You / Honey, 'Cause I Love You	1961	3.00	15.00
Columbia 42061		Any Way The Wind Blows / The Unhappy Girls	1961	3.00	15.00
Columbia 42405		Hollywood City / The Fool I Used To Be	1962	3.00	15.00
Columbia 42405	(PS)	Hollywood City / The Fool I Used To Be	1962	10.00	50.00
Columbia 42514		Sister Twister / Hambone	1962	3.00	15.00
Columbia 42514	(PS)	Sister Twister / Hambone	1962	25.00	125.00
Columbia 42753		Forget Me Next Time Around / I Just Got Back From There	1963	3.00	15.00
Decca 31548		Help Me Find My Baby / For A Little While	1963	1.60	8.00
Decca 31591		After Sundown / I Wouldn't Have You	1964	1.60	8.00
Decca 31709		Let My Baby Be / The Monkeyshine	1964	1.60	8.00
Decca 31786		One Of These Days / Mama Of My Song	1965	1.60	8.00
Dollie 505		Country Boy's Dream / If I Could Come Back	1967	1.20	6.00
Dollie 508		Shine, Shine, Shine / Almost Love	1967	1.20	6.00
Dollie 512		Without You / You Can Take The Boy Out Of The Country	1968	1.20	6.00
Dollie 514		Back To Tennessee / My Old Home Town	1968	1.20	6.00
Columbia 44723		Restless / 1143	1969	1.00	5.00
Columbia 44883		For Your Love / Four Letter Word	1969	1.00	5.00
Columbia 45253		What Every Little Boy Ought To Know / Just As Long	1970	1.00	5.00
Columbia 45347		Me Without You / Red Headed Woman	1971	.80	4.00
Columbia 45466		Cotton Top / About All I Can Give You Is Love	1972	.80	4.00
Columbia 45582		Take Me Back To Memphis / High On Love	1972	.80	4.00
Columbia 45694		Someday / The Trip	1972	.80	4.00
Mercury 73393		Help Me Dream /You Tore My Heaven All To Hell	1973	.40	2.00
Mercury 73425		(Let's Get) Dixie Fried / One More Loser Goin' Home	1973	.40	2.00
Mercury 73489		Ruby, Don't Take Your Love To Town / Sing My Song	1973	.40	2.00
Mercury 73653		You'll Always Be A Lady To Me / Low Class	1974	.40	2.00
Mercury 73690		The E.P. Express / Big Bad Blues	1975	.40	2.00
Suede 102		Rock-A-Billy Fever / Till You Get Through With Me	197?	.60	3.00
Music Hill 1007		Born To Boogie / Take Me Back			
MMI 1013		Don't Get Off Gettin' It On / We Did It In '54	197?	.60	3.00
MMI 1016		Don't Get Off Gettin' It On / Georgia Court Room	197?	.60	3.00
MMI 1019		Standing In The Need Of Love / Georgia Court Room	197?	.60	3.00
Jet 5054		Blue Suede Shoes / Rock On Around The World	197?	.60	3.00
		—*Extended Play Albums*—			
Sun 115		Carl Perkins	1957	100.00	400.00
Columbia 12341		Whole Lotta Shakin'	1958	150.00	500.00
PERKINS, DAL					
Challenge 59288		If You Were Mine / Money Greases The Wheel	1965	.80	4.00
Challenge 59318		Second Choice / Standing In Your Shadow	1965	.80	4.00
Columbia 44204		Here's To The Girls / One Day A Week	1967	1.00	5.00
Columbia 44343		Helpless / Woman In The Darkness	1967	1.00	5.00
		(Columbia sides were produced by Gary Usher.)			
PERKINS, REGGIE					
Ray Note 9		Date Bait Baby / High School Caesar	1959	6.00	30.00
PERMANENTS, THE					
Chairman 4405		Let Me Be, Baby / Oh Dear, What Can The Matter Be?	1963	3.00	15.00
PERPETUAL MOTION WORKSHOP, THE					
Rally 66506		Infiltrate Your Mind / Won't Come Down	196?	8.00	40.00
PERRY, FRANK					
Belle 251		Santa's Caught On The Freeway / Young And Innocent	1959	2.00	10.00

Label & Catalog #		A-Side/B-Side	Year	VG	NM
PERRY, JIM, & THE HESITATIONS					
Bandbox 310		Surfside Twist / Surfside Twist, Part 2	196?	8.00	40.00
PERRY, JO-ANN					
Glad 1006		Yes, I'm Lonesome Tonight /			
		When You're In Doubt, Do Without	1961	3.00	15.00
PERSIANS, THE					
RTO 100		Sunday Kind Of Love / When We Get Married	1962	2.00	10.00
RSVP 114		Tears Of Love / Dance Now	1962	5.00	25.00
Goldisc 1		Vault Of Memories / Teardrops Are Falling	1963	6.00	30.00
Goldisc 17		(When You Said) Let's Get Married / At The Party	1963	4.00	20.00
Music World 102		(When You Said) Let's Get Married / At The Party	1963	3.00	15.00
Pageant 601		Get A Hold Of Yourself / Steady Kind	1963	3.00	15.00
PERSONALITIES, THE					
Safari 1002		Yours To Command / Woe Woe, Baby	1957	30.00	150.00
		(First pressing labels features a giraffe logo.)			
Safari 1002		Yours To Command / Woe Woe, Baby	1957	8.00	40.00
		(Second pressing labels lack the giraffe logo.)			
PERSUADERS, THE					
The Persuaders feature Chuck Rio of The Champs.					
Saturn 404		Surfing Strip / Hanging Ten	1963	7.00	35.00
Saturn 405		Caught In The Soup / Gremmie Bread	1963	7.00	35.00
PERSUADERS, THE					
Bum Bum 701		Miseriou / World Of Wonder	196?	7.00	35.00
PERSUADERS, THE: *Refer to* THE HOLLYWOOD PERSUADERS					
PERSUASIONS, THE					
Tower 197		Big Brother / Deep Down Love	1966	2.00	10.00
PETE & VINNIE					
Pete Anders and Vinnie Poncia.					
Big Top 3155		Hand Clappin' Time / Hand Clappin' Time (Part 2)	1963	4.00	20.00
PETER & GORDON					
Peter Asher and Gordon Waller.					
Capitol 5175		A World Without Love / If I Were You	1964	1.20	6.00
Capitol 5211		Nobody I Know / You Don't Have To Tell Me	1964	1.20	6.00
Capitol 5211	(PS)	Nobody I Know / You Don't Have To Tell Me	1964	2.00	10.00
Capitol 5272		I Don't Want To See You Again / I Would Buy You Presents	1964	1.20	6.00
Capitol 5272	(PS)	I Don't Want To See You Again / I Would Buy You Presents	1964	2.00	10.00
Capitol 5335		I Go To Pieces / Love Me, Baby	1965	1.20	6.00
Capitol 5335	(PS)	I Go To Pieces / Love Me, Baby	1965	2.00	10.00
Capitol 5406		True Love Ways / If You Wish	1965	1.20	6.00
Capitol 5406	(PS)	True Love Ways / If You Wish	1965	2.00	10.00
Capitol 5461		To Know You Is To Love You / I Told You So	1965	1.20	6.00
Capitol 5461	(PS)	To Know You Is To Love You / I Told You So	1965	2.00	10.00
Capitol 5532		Don't Pity Me / Crying In The Rain	1965	1.20	6.00
Capitol 5579		Woman / Wrong From The Start	1966	1.20	6.00
Capitol C.P. 51	(DJ)	Wrong From The Start / (B-side by The Lettermen)	1966	1.20	6.00
Capitol 5650		There's No Living Without Your Loving /			
		Stranger With A Black Dove	1966	1.20	6.00
Capitol 5650	(PS)	There's No Living Without Your Loving /			
		Stranger With A Black Dove	1966	2.00	10.00
Capitol 5684		To Show I Love You / Start Trying Someone Else	1966	1.20	6.00
Capitol 5684	(PS)	To Show I Love You / Start Trying Someone Else	1966	2.00	10.00
Capitol 5740		Lady Godiva / You've Had Better Days	1966	1.20	6.00
Capitol 5808		Knight In Rusty Armor / Flower Lady	1966	1.20	6.00
Capitol 5808	(PS)	Knight In Rusty Armor / Flower Lady	1966	2.00	10.00
Capitol 5864		Sunday For Tea / Hurtin' Is Lovin'	1967	1.00	5.00
Capitol 5864	(PS)	Sunday For Tea / Hurtin' Is Lovin'	1967	2.00	10.00
Capitol 5919		The Jokers / Red, Cream And Velvet	1967	1.00	5.00
Capitol 2071		Never Ever / Greener Days	1967	1.00	5.00
Capitol 2214		Sippin' My Wine / You've Had Better Days	1968	1.00	5.00
Capitol 2544		I Can Remember / Hard Times, Rainy Day	1968	1.00	5.00
Capitol PRO-4587		Sippin' My Wine / You've Had Better Days	196?	1.60	8.00
		— Extended Play Albums —			
Capitol PRO-2681	(DJ)	Interview / Nobody I Know	1964	10.00	50.00
PETER, PAUL & MARY [PETER YARROW, PAUL STOOKEY & MARY TRAVERS]					
Warner Bros. 5274		Lemon Tree / Early In The Morning	1962	1.00	5.00
Warner Bros. 5296		If I Had A Hammer / Gone The Rainbow	1962	1.00	5.00
Warner Bros. 5325		Big Boat / Tiny Sparrow	1962	1.00	5.00
Warner Bros. 5325	(PS)	Big Boat / Tiny Sparrow	1962	2.00	10.00

Label & Catalog #		A-Side/B-Side	Year	VG	NM
Warner Bros. 5334		Settle Down (Goin' Down That Highway) / 500 Miles	1963	1.00	5.00
Warner Bros. 5348		Puff (The Magic Dragon) / Pretty Mary	1963	1.00	5.00
Warner Bros. 5368		Blowin' In The Wind / Flora	1963	1.00	5.00
Warner Bros. 5385		Don't Think Twice, It's Alright / Autumn To May	1963	1.00	5.00
Warner Bros. 5399		Stewball / The Cruel War	1963	1.00	5.00
Warner Bros. 5402		A' Soalin' / Hush-A-Bye	1963	.80	4.00
Warner Bros. 5402	(PS)	A' Soalin' / Hush-A-Bye	1963	2.00	10.00
Warner Bros. 5418		Tell It On The Mountain / Old Coat	1964	.80	4.00
Warner Bros. 5442		Oh, Rock My Soul / Oh, Rock My Soul (Part 2)	1964	.80	4.00
Warner Bros. 5496		For Lovin' Me / Monday Morning	1965	.80	4.00
Warner Bros. 5625		When The Ship Comes In / The Times They Are A Changing	1965	.80	4.00
Warner Bros. 5659		Early Morning Rain / The Rising Of The Moon	1965	.80	4.00
Warner Bros. 5809		The Cruel War / Mon Vrai Destin	1966	.80	4.00
Warner Bros. 5849		The Other Side Of This Life / Sometime Lovin'	1966	.80	4.00
Warner Bros. 5883		For Baby (For Bobby) / Hurry Sundown	1966	.80	4.00
Warner Bros. 7067		I Dig Rock And Roll Music / Great Mandala (Wheel Of Life)	1967	.80	4.00
Warner Bros. 7092		Too Much Of Nothing / House Song	1967	.80	4.00
Warner Bros. 7232		Yesterday's Tomorrow / Love City (Postcard To Duluth)	1968	.80	4.00
(No label)	(DJ)	Eugene McCarthy For President (If You Love Your Country)	1968	5.00	25.00
		(This plain white label single contains a song with speeches for the only anti-war candidate in recent American history.)			
Warner Bros. 7279		Day Is Done / Make Believe Town	1969	.80	4.00
Warner Bros. 7340		Leaving On A Jet Plane / The House Song	1969	.80	4.00
Warner Bros. 7359		The Marvelous Toy / Christmas Dinner	1969	.80	4.00
Warner Bros. 8684		Like The First Time / Best Of Friends	1978	.60	3.00
Warner Bros. 8728		Forever Young / Best Of Friends	1978	.60	3.00

PETER G. & PATTY

Label & Catalog #		A-Side/B-Side	Year	VG	NM
Shirley 105		The Whisper / Peter Good, Private Eye	196?	3.00	15.00

PETERSEN, PAUL
Paul Peterson also recorded with Shelly Fabares.

Label & Catalog #		A-Side/B-Side	Year	VG	NM
Colpix 620		She Can't Find Her Keys / Very Unlikely	1962	2.00	10.00
Colpix 632		Keep Your Love Locked (Deep In Your Heart) / Everything To Anyone You Love	1962	2.00	10.00
Colpix 632	(PS)	Keep Your Love Locked (Deep In Your Heart) / Everything To Anyone You Love	1962	4.00	20.00
Colpix 649		Lollipops And Roses / Please, Mr. Sun	1962	2.00	10.00
Colpix 663		My Dad / Little Boy Sad	1962	2.00	10.00
Colpix 663	(PS)	My Dad / Little Boy Sad	1962	4.00	20.00
Colpix 676		Amy / Goody Goody	1963	2.00	10.00
Colpix 697		Girls In The Summertime / Mama, Your Little Boy Fell	1963	2.00	10.00
Colpix 707		The Cheer Leader / Polka Dots And Moonbeams	1963	2.00	10.00
Colpix 720		She Rides With Me / Poorest Boy In Town	1964	12.00	60.00
		("She Rides With Me" was produced by Brian Wilson and features The Honeys.)			
Colpix 730		Hey There, Beautiful / Where Is She?	1964	2.00	10.00
Colpix 763		Little Dreamer / Happy	1964	2.00	10.00
Colpix 785		The Ring / You Don't Need Money	1965	2.00	10.00
Motown 1108		Don't Let It Happen To Us / Chained	1968	.80	4.00
Motown 1129		Your Love's Got Me Burning Alive / Little Bit For Sandy	1968	.80	4.00

PETERSON, EARL

Label & Catalog #		A-Side/B-Side	Year	VG	NM
Sun 197		Boogies Blues / In The Dark	1954	75.00	300.00

PETERSON, RAY

Label & Catalog #		A-Side/B-Side	Year	VG	NM
RCA Victor 47-7098		Fever / We're Old Enough To Cry	1957	3.00	15.00
RCA Victor 47-7165		Let's Try Romance / Shirley Purly	1958	3.00	15.00
RCA Victor 47-7255		Suddenly / Tail Light	1958	3.00	15.00
RCA Victor 47-7303		My Blue-Eyed Baby / Patricia	1958	3.00	15.00
RCA Victor 47-7336		Dream Way / I'll Always Want You Near	1958	3.00	15.00
RCA Victor 47-7404		Richer Than I / Love Is A Woman	1958	3.00	15.00
RCA Victor 47-7513		The Wonder Of You / I'm Gone	1959	3.00	15.00
RCA Victor 47-7578		My Blue Angel / Come And Get It	1959	3.00	15.00
RCA Victor 47-7635		Goodnight My Love (Pleasant Dreams) / What Do You Want To Make Those Eyes At Me For?	1959	3.00	15.00
RCA Victor 47-7635	(PS)	Goodnight My Love (Pleasant Dreams) / What Do You Want To Make Those Eyes At Me For?	1959	5.00	25.00
RCA Victor 47-7703		Answer Me, My Love / What Do You Want To Make Those Eyes At Me For?	1960	3.00	15.00
RCA Victor 47-7745		Tell Laura I Love Her / Wedding Day	1960	3.00	15.00
RCA Victor 61-7745	(S)	Tell Laura I Love Her / Wedding Day	1960	6.00	30.00
RCA Victor 47-7779		Teenage Heartache / I'll Always Want You Near	1960	3.00	15.00
RCA Victor 47-7845		My Blue Angel / I'm Tired	1960	3.00	15.00
Dunes 2002		Corrina Corrina / Be My Girl	1960	4.00	20.00
Dunes 2002	(PS)	Corrina Corrina / Be My Girl	1960	5.00	25.00
		("Corrina Corrina" was produced by Phil Spector.)			
Dunes 2004		Sweet Little Kathy / You Didn't Care	1961	2.00	10.00
Dunes 2006		Missing You / You Thrill Me	1961	2.00	10.00

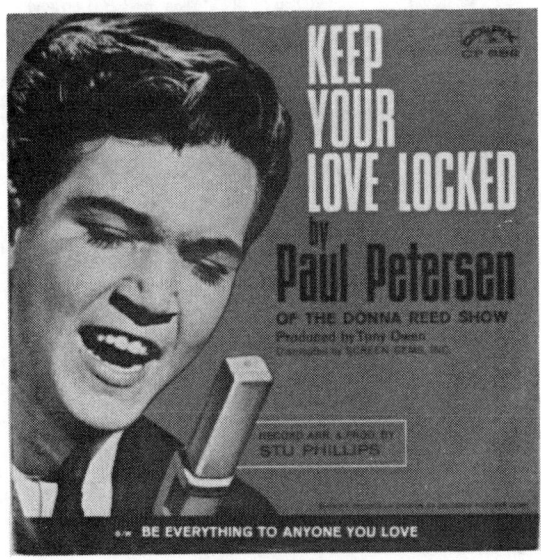

Paul Petersen, known to America as Shelly Fabares' kid brother on TV's Donna Reed Show, was also pushed as a pop singer. The sleeve on top shows him in the Elvis/Ricky mold so popular with up-and-coming celebrities while the single on the bottom fetches big bucks due to the production of Brian Wilson.

Label & Catalog #		A-Side/B-Side	Year	VG	NM
Dunes 2009		I Could Have Loved You So Well / Why Don't You Write Me?	1961	3.00	15.00
		("I Could Have Loved You So Well" was produced by Phil Spector.)			
Dunes 2013		You Know Me Much Too Well / You Didn't Care	1962	2.00	10.00
Dunes 2018		If Only Tomorrow / You Didn't Care	1962	2.00	10.00
Dunes 2019		Is It Wrong? / Slowly	1962	2.00	10.00
Dunes 2022		I'm Not Jimmy / A Love To Remember	1962	2.00	10.00
Dunes 2024		Where Are You? / Deep Are The Roots	1963	2.00	10.00
Dunes 2025		Give Us Your Blessing / Without Love	1963	2.00	10.00
Dunes 2027		Be My Girl / I Forgot What It Was Like	1963	2.00	10.00
Dunes 2030		Sweet Little Kathy / Promises You Made Are Broken	1963	2.00	10.00
RCA Victor 47-8333		The Wonder Of You / I'm Gone	1964	2.00	10.00
MGM 13269		If You Were Here / Oh, No!	1964	1.00	5.00
MGM 13269	(PS)	If You Were Here / Oh, No!	1964	2.00	10.00
MGM 13299		Across The Street / When I Stop Dreaming	1964	1.00	5.00
MGM 13330		Unchained Melody / That's All	1965	1.00	5.00
MGM 13336		A House Without Windows / I Wish I Could Say No To You	1965	1.00	5.00
MGM 13388		I'm Only Human / One Lonesome Rose	1965	1.00	5.00
MGM 13436		Everybody / Love Hurts	1965	1.00	5.00
MGM 13508		I'm Gonna Change Everything / Amanda	1966	1.00	5.00
MGM 13564		Whole World Goin' Crazy / Just One Smile	1966	1.00	5.00
Reprise 0811		Together / Love Rules The World	1969	1.00	5.00
Uni 55249		Oklahoma City Blues / Love The Understanding Way	1970	.80	4.00
Uni 55268		Tell Laura I Love Her / To Wait For Love	1970	.80	4.00
Uni 55275		Forever / Changes	1971	.80	4.00
Decca 32861		There's A Better Way / Stamp Out Loneliness	197?	.80	4.00
		—Extended Play Albums—			
RCA Victor EPA-4367		Tell Laura I Love Her	1960	30.00	150.00

PETERSON, RON, & THE ACCENTS
Refer to The Accents.

Jerden 728	Sticky / Linda Lou	196?	1.20	6.00

PETITE TEENS, THE

Brunswick 55119	My Singing Idol-Poor Little Fool / We're In Our Teens	1959	3.00	15.00

PETITES, THE

Spinning 6005	Sweety Pie / Who Kicked The Light Plug Out Of The Socket	1958	4.00	20.00
Columbia 41662	Get Your Daddy's Car Tonight / Sun Showers	1960	2.00	10.00
Elmor 304	Beating Of My Heart / Nobody But You	1962	2.00	10.00
Ascot 2166	I'm Gonna Love Him /			
	Is Thirteen Too Young To Fall In Love?	1964	2.00	10.00

PETRICOIN, BARRY, & THE BELAIRS

Al-Stan 103	Pretty Little Angel / Come Back To Sorrento	195?	10.00	50.00

PETRIFIED FOREST, THE

Fontana 1596	So Mystifying / She's The Only Thing That Keeps Me Going	1967	3.00	15.00

PETTICOATS, THE

Challenge 9211	Surfin' Sally / Why Does Billy Play In Your Yard?	1963	5.00	25.00

PETTY, TOM, & THE HEARTBREAKERS
The Heartbreakers are Ron Blair, Mike Campbell, Stan Lynch and Benmont Tench. Blair was replaced by Howie Epstein in 1982. Refer to Mudcrutch; The Traveling Wilburys.

Shelter 62006		Breakdown / The Wild One, Forever	1976	.80	4.00
Shelter 62007		American Girl / Luna	1977	.60	3.00
Shelter 62008		Breakdown / Fooled Again	1977	.60	3.00
Shelter/ABC 62010		I Need To Know / No Second Thoughts	1978	.60	3.00
Shelter/ABC 62011		Listen To Her Heart / I Don't Know What To Say To You	1978	.80	4.00
Shelter/ABC 62011	(PS)	Listen To Her Heart / I Don't Know What To Say To You	1978	.80	4.00
Backstreet 41138		Don't Do Me Like That / Casa Dega	1979	.60	3.00
Backstreet 41138	(PS)	Don't Do Me Like That / Casa Dega	1979	.60	3.00
Backstreet 41169		Refugee / It's Rainin' Again	1980	.60	3.00
Backstreet 41169	(PS)	Refugee / It's Rainin' Again	1980	.60	3.00
Backstreet 41227		Here Comes My Girl / Louisiana Rain	1980	.60	3.00
Backstreet 41227	(PS)	Here Comes My Girl / Louisiana Rain	1980	.60	3.00
Backstreet 51100		The Waiting / Nightwatchman	1981	.60	3.00
Backstreet 51100	(PS)	The Waiting / Nightwatchman	1981	.60	3.00
Backstreet 51136		A Woman In Love (It's Not Me) / Gator On The Lawn	1981	.60	3.00
Backstreet 51136	(PS)	A Woman In Love (It's Not Me) / Gator On The Lawn	1981	.60	3.00
Backstreet 52114		You Got Lucky / Between Two Worlds	1982	.60	3.00
Backstreet 52114	(PS)	You Got Lucky / Between Two Worlds	1982	.60	3.00
Backstreet 52181		Change Of Heart / Heartbreakers' Beach Party (Red vinyl)	1983	1.00	5.00
		(Issued in a clear plastic sleeve.)			
Backstreet 52181		Change Of Heart / Heartbreakers' Beach Party	1983	.40	2.00
Backstreet 52181	(PS)	Change Of Heart / Heartbreakers' Beach Party	1983	.40	2.00
MCA 52496		Don't Come Around Here No More / Trailer	1985	.40	2.00
MCA 52496	(PS)	Don't Come Around Here No More / Trailer	1985	.40	2.00

Label & Catalog #		A-Side/B-Side	Year	VG	NM
MCA 52605		Make It Better / Cracking Up	1985	.40	2.00
MCA 52605	(PS)	Make It Better / Cracking Up	1985	.40	2.00
MCA 52658		Rebels / Southern Accents	1985	.40	2.00
MCA 52658	(PS)	Rebels / Southern Accents	1985	.40	2.00
MCA 52772		Needles And Pins / Spike (Live)	1985	.40	2.00
MCA 52772	(PS)	Needles And Pins / Spike (Live)	1985	.40	2.00
MCA 53065		Jammin' Me / Make That Connection	1987	.40	2.00
MCA 53065	(PS)	Jammin' Me / Make That Connection	1987	.40	2.00
MCA 53153		All Mixed Up / Let Me Up (I've Had Enough)	1987	.40	2.00
MCA 53153	(PS)	All Mixed Up / Let Me Up (I've Had Enough)	1987	.40	2.00
MCA 53369		I Won't Back Down / The Apartment Song	1989	.40	2.00
MCA 53682		Runnin' Down A Dream / Alright For Now	1989	.40	2.00
MCA 53748		Free Fallin' / Down The Line	1989	.40	2.00
MCA 53781		A Face In The Crowd / A Mind With A Heart Of Its Own	1990	.40	2.00
MCA 53833		Yer So Bad / Love Is A Long Road	1990	.40	2.00
MCA 54124		Learning To Fly / Too Good To Be True	1991	.40	2.00
		— 12" Singles —			
Shelter SPDJ-37	(DJ)	Listen To Her Heart / Listen To Her Heart (PC)	1978	1.20	6.00
MCA 4574		Make It Better / Make It Better (PC)	1985	.80	4.00

PETTY TRIO, NORMAN

Columbia 41039	(DJ)	Moondreams / Toy Boy	1957	10.00	50.00
Columbia 41039		Moondreams / Toy Boy	1957	20.00	100.00
		("Moondreams" features Buddy on guitar.)			

PEWTER, JIM

Jim Pewter also recorded as Deviny James; The Pewter Pals.

Circus 100		Tarzan / Sick Man	1961	4.00	20.00
MGM 14446		Ebony / Linda Lu	1972	1.60	8.00
		(Features Davie Allan, Jerry Allison and Sonny Curtis.)			
MGM 14658		Little Miss Riding Hood, Surfer Queen Of Hollywood / Bop-A-Rock (Features Davie Allan on guitar)	1973	1.60	8.00
RCA Victor 74-0186		Father Kline / Sunday Morning Light	1972	.80	4.00

PEWTER PALS, THE

Manhattan 807		Childhood / Shame, Shame On Jane	1967	1.20	6.00

PEYTON, DORIE

Ohio 101		Ringo Boy / In The Spring Of The Year	1964	4.00	20.00
Margo 105		Ringo Boy / Unforgettable	1964	4.00	20.00

PH FACTOR (JUGBAND), THE

Piccadilly 241		Minglewood Blues / Barefoot John	1967	2.00	10.00

PHAETONS, THE

The Phaetons feature Dean Torrence.

Sahara 103		The Beatle Walk / (B-side by The Premiers)	1964	7.00	35.00

PHANTOM, THE

Rumors abound as to the identity of this "Phantom" and his risque rockabilly rave-up. Hints include the label and the song's production company, Algoon Agooc.

Dot 16056		Love Me / Whisper Your Love	1960	30.00	150.00
Dot 16056	(PS)	Love Me / Whisper Your Love	1960	75.00	300.00

PHANTOM'S DIVINE COMEDY, THE

Hideout 1080		Calm Before The Storm / Black Magic, White Magic	1973	3.00	15.00

PHANTOM FIVE, THE

Skull		Graveyard / Cool It	196?	8.00	40.00

PHANTOMS, THE

Original Sound 11		Night Theme / Night Beat	1960	2.00	10.00

PHANTOMS, THE

Ford 137		The Cruel Sea / I Want You	196?	7.00	35.00

PHANTOMS, THE

Sam 123		X-L3 / My Little Baby	196?	10.00	50.00
		(Also released on Sam credited to The Majestics.)			

PHANTOMS, THE

Ridon 859		Story Of A Rich Man / Our Great Society	196?	1.20	6.00
Graves 1104		Hallucinogenic Odyssey /	196?	2.00	10.00

PHAROAS, THE

Donna 1327		Tender Touch / Heads Up, High Hopes Over You	1963	7.00	35.00

Label & Catalog #	A-Side/B-Side	Year	VG	NM
PHAROS, THE				
Del-Fi 4208	Rhythm Surfer / Pintor	1963	8.00	40.00
PHEASANTS, THE				
Throne 802	Out Of The Mist / Hot Biscuits	196?	3.00	15.00
PHIL & DEL				
Linda 105	My Girl / Don't Play With Love	1962	2.00	10.00
PHIL & THE FLAKES				
Fink 1010	Blower Scooped / Chrome Reverse Wheels	196?	8.00	40.00
PHILADELPHIANS, THE				
Campus 101	Dear / The Love That I Lost	1962	3.00	15.00
Campus 103	Coming Home To You / Church Bells	1962	3.00	15.00
Cameo 216	The Vow / I Missed Her	1962	3.00	15.00
PHILIPS, TERRY				
V.A. 351	Hands Of A Fool / My Foolish Way	196?	15.00	75.00
PHILLIPS, JOHN				
John Phillips originally recorded with The Journeymen and The Mamas & The Papas.				
Dunhill 4236	Mississippi / April Anne	1970	.60	3.00
PHILLIPS, MICHELLE				
Michelle Phillips originally recorded with The Mamas & The Papas.				
A&M 1824	No Love Today / Aloha Louie	1975	.60	3.00
A&M 1824 (PS)	No Love Today / Aloha Louie	1975	.80	4.00
PHILLIPS, PHIL (& THE TWILIGHTS)				
Khoury's 11	Sea Of Love / Juella	1959	25.00	125.00
Mercury 71465	Sea Of Love / Juella	1959	3.00	15.00
Mercury 51531	Take This Heart / Verdie Mae	1959	3.00	15.00
Mercury 71611	What Will I Tell My Heart? / Your True Love Once More	1960	3.00	15.00
Mercury 71657	Nobody Knows And Nobody Cares / Come Back, My Darling	1960	3.00	15.00
PHILLIPS, WALT, & BARRY YOUNG				
Deltone 5023	Surfin' Annie / Teasin' Baby	196?	6.00	30.00
PICARDY				
Dunhill 4140	In The Name Of You / 5:30 Plane	1968	1.00	5.00
PICKETT, BOBBY "BORIS" (& THE CRYPT-KICKERS)				
Garpax 44167	Monster Mash / Monster Mash Party	1962	4.00	20.00
Garpax 44167 (PS)	Monster Mash / Monster Mash Party	1962	6.00	30.00
Garpax 724	I'm Down To My Last Heartbreak / I Can't Stop	1962	3.00	15.00
Garpax 44171	Monster's Holiday / Monster Motion	1962	5.00	25.00
Garpax 44171 (PS)	Monster's Holiday / Monster Motion	1962	5.00	25.00
Garpax 44175	The Humpty Dumpty / Graduation Day	1963	3.00	15.00
Garpax 44175 (PS)	The Humpty Dumpty / Graduation Day	1963	5.00	25.00
Capitol 5063	Simon The Sensible Surfer / Simon Says "So What?"	1963	3.00	15.00
RCA Victor 47-8312	Smoke, Smoke, Smoke / Gotta Leave This Town	1964	2.00	10.00
RCA Victor 47-8459	Monster Swim / The Werewolf Watusi	1964	2.00	10.00
White Whale 363 (DJ)	Monster Man Jam / Monster Man Jam	1970	4.00	20.00
	(Stock copies of W.W. 363 may not exist.)			
Parrot 348	Monster Mash / Monster Mash Party	1970	1.00	5.00
Parrot 366	Monster Holiday / Monster Minuet	1970	1.00	5.00
Metromedia 089	Me And My Mummy / It's Not The Same Without You	1973	1.00	5.00
PICKETT, BOBBY, & PETER FERRARA				
Polydor 14361	King Kong / Disco Kong	1976	.80	4.00
Pizzeria 1	Stardrek / Mangy Old Sidewinder	1977	2.00	10.00
	(First pressings were autographed by both Pickett and Ferrara on the label.)			
PICKETTYWITCH				
Janus 118	That Same Old Feeling / Maybe We've Loved Too Long	1970	.80	4.00
PICONE, VITO [VITO]				
Vito Picone also recorded with The Elegants.				
Admiral 302	Still Waters Run Deep / Bolt Of Lightning	1963	6.00	30.00
Admiral 103	Songs From The Moulin Rouge / I Like To Run	1963	4.00	20.00
I.P.G. 1016	Path In The Wilderness / Get On The Right Track	1963	3.00	15.00
PICTURES, THE: *Refer ot C.L. & THE PICTURES*				
PIERCE, ALAN				
Challenge 59093	Swampwater / The Growl	1960	2.00	10.00

Label & Catalog #	A-Side/B-Side	Year	VG	NM
PIERMEN, THE				
Jesse 1000	Piermen Stomp / Nancy	1962	5.00	25.00
PIERSON, CAN, & THE EKHOES				
LeMans 007	I Heard Those Bells / Six Pretty Girls	196?	5.00	25.00
PILTDOWN FIVE, THE				
Parliament 102	'32 Ford / The Tick	196?	10.00	50.00
PILTDOWN MEN, THE				
Capitol 4414	Brontosaurus Stomp / McDonald's Cave	1960	3.00	15.00
Capitol 4460	Bubbles In The Tar / Piltdown Rides Again	1960	3.00	15.00
Capitol 4501	Goodnight, Mrs. Flintstone / The Great Imposter	1961	3.00	15.00
Capitol 4703	Big Lizard / A Pretty Girl Is Like A Melody	1961	3.00	15.00
Capitol 4851	Fossil Rock / Gargantua	1961	3.00	15.00
Capitol 4875	Night Surfin' / Tequila Bossanova	1962	3.00	15.00
PIN-UPS, THE				
Stork 1	Kenny / Lookin' For Boys	1964	3.00	15.00
PINA, JOHNNY				
Dimension 1030	Goodbye To Hillside High / Why Must You Love Him Instead Of Me?	1964	2.00	10.00
PINAFORES, THE				
Capitol 4818	I Don't Care What Anyone Says / It Only Happens In The Movies	1962	2.00	10.00
PINARD, HENRY, & THE THREE D'S				
Lowell 212	My Fraternity Dance / Summertime Sweetheart	195?	3.00	15.00

PINK FLOYD
Original members were Syd Barrett, Nick Mason, Roger Waters and Richard Wright. David Gilmour joined in 1968; shortly after, Barrett left this world's stage.

Label & Catalog #		A-Side/B-Side	Year	VG	NM
Tower 333	(DJ)	Arnold Layne / Candy And A Currant Bun	1967	10.00	50.00
Tower 333	(PS)	Arnold Layne / Candy And A Currant Bun	1967	250.00	750.00
Tower 333		Arnold Layne / Candy And A Currant Bun	1967	20.00	100.00
Tower 356	(DJ)	See Emily Play / Scarecrow	1967	8.00	40.00
Tower 356	(PS)	See Emily Play / Scarecrow *(Promo picture sleeve)*	1967	200.00	600.00
Tower 356	(PS)	See Emily Play / Scarecrow *(Promo title sleeve)*	1967	100.00	400.00
Tower 356		See Emily Play / Scarecrow	1967	16.00	80.00
Tower 378	(DJ)	The Gnome / Flaming	1968	15.00	75.00
Tower 378		The Gnome / Flaming	1968	30.00	150.00
Tower 426	(DJ)	Julia Dream / It Would Be So Nice	1968	15.00	75.00
Tower 426		Julia Dream / It Would Be So Nice	1968	30.00	150.00
Tower 440	(DJ)	Let There Be More Light / Remember A Day	1968	15.00	75.00
Tower 440		Let There Be More Light / Remember A Day	1968	30.00	150.00
Capitol P-3240	(DJ)	One Of These Days / Fearless	1971	2.00	10.00
Capitol 3240		One Of These Days / Fearless	1971	4.00	20.00
Capitol P-3391	(DJ)	Free Four / Stay	1972	2.00	10.00
Capitol 3391		Free Four / Stay	1972	4.00	20.00
Harvest 3609		Money / Any Colour You Like	1973	3.00	15.00
Harvest 3832		Time / Us And Them	1974	3.00	15.00
Columbia 10248		Welcome To The Machine / Have A Cigar	1975	2.00	10.00
Columbia 11187		Another Brick In The Wall (Part 2) / One Of My Turns	1979	.60	3.00
Columbia 11187	(PS)	Another Brick In The Wall (Part 2) / One Of My Turns	1979	1.00	5.00
Columbia 11265		Run Like Hell / Don't Leave Me Now	1979	.60	3.00
Columbia 11311		Comfortably Numb / Hey You	1979	.60	3.00
Columbia AE7-1653	(DJ)	Not Now John (Obscured Version) / Not Now John (Obscured Version)	1983	1.00	5.00
Columbia AE7-1653	(PS)	Not Now John (Obscured Version) / Not Now John (Obscured Version)	1983	1.00	5.00
Columbia 03142		When The Tigers Broke Free / Bring The Boys Back Home	1982	.40	2.00
Columbia 03142	(PS)	When The Tigers Broke Free / Bring The Boys Back Home	1982	.40	2.00
Columbia 07363		Learning To Fly / Terminal Frost	1987	.40	2.00
Columbia 07363	(PS)	Learning To Fly / Terminal Frost	1987	.40	2.00
Columbia 07660		On The Turning Away / Run Like Hell (Live)	1987	.40	2.00
Columbia 07660	(PS)	On The Turning Away / Run Like Hell (Live)	1987	.40	2.00
		— Extended Play Albums —			
Harvest SPRO-	(33)	Dark Side Of The Moon *(Paper sleeve)*	1973	50.00	200.00

Label & Catalog #	A-Side/B-Side	Year	VG	NM
PINKERTON'S ASSORTED COLOURS				
Parrot 9820	Mirror, Mirror / She Don't Care	1965	1.00	5.00
PIPKIN, JIM, & THE BOSS FIVE				
Camelot 128	Mr.C.C. / I'm Just A Lonely Guy	196?	1.00	5.00

Label & Catalog #		A-Side / B-Side	Year	VG	NM
PIPKINS, THE					
Capitol 2819		Gimme Dat Ding / To Love You	1970	.80	4.00
Capitol 2874		Sugar 'N Spice / Yakety Yak	1970	.80	4.00
PIT MEN, THE					
Pit 402		Surf Bored / Cruisin' Along The Highway	196?	7.00	35.00
PITCH PIKES, THE					
Mercury 71099		Zing Zing / Never Never Land	1957	4.00	20.00
PITNEY, GENE					
Gene Pitney also recorded as Billy Bryan and Jamie & Jane.					
Festival 25002		Please Come Back / I'll Find You	1960	4.00	20.00
Musicor 1002		(I Wanna) Love My Life Away / I Laughed So Hard I Cried	1961	2.00	10.00
Musicor 1002	(PS)	(I Wanna) Love My Life Away / I Laughed So Hard I Cried	1961	3.00	15.00
Musicor 1006		Louisiana Mama / Take Me Tonight	1961	2.00	10.00
Musicor 1006	(PS)	Louisiana Mama / Take Me Tonight	1961	3.00	15.00
Musicor 1009		Town Without Pity / Air-Mail Special Delivery	1961	1.20	6.00
Musicor 1011		Every Breath I Take / Mr. Moon, Mr. Cupid And I *(Produced by Phil Spector)*	1961	2.00	10.00
Musicor 1011	(PS)	Every Breath I Take / Mr. Moon, Mr. Cupid And I	1961	2.00	10.00
Musicor 1020		(The Man Who Shot) Liberty Valance / Take It Like A Man	1962	1.20	6.00
Musicor 1022		Only Love Can Break A Heart / If I Didn't Have A Dime	1962	1.20	6.00
Musicor 1026		Half Heaven-Half Heartache / Tower Tall	1962	1.20	6.00
Musicor 1028		Mecca / Teardrop By Teardrop	1963	1.20	6.00
Musicor 1028	(PS)	Mecca / Teardrop By Teardrop	1963	1.20	6.00
Musicor 1032		True Love Never Runs Smooth / Donna Means Heartbreak	1963	1.20	6.00
Musicor 1034		Twenty Four Hours From Tulsa / Lonely Night Dreams	1963	1.20	6.00
Musicor 1034	(PS)	Twenty Four Hours From Tulsa / Lonely Night Dreams	1963	1.20	6.00
Musicor 1036		That Girl Belongs To Yesterday / Who Needs It?	1964	2.00	10.00
Musicor 1036	(PS)	That Girl Belongs To Yesterday / Who Needs It?	1964	2.00	10.00
Musicor 1038		Yesterday's Hero / Cornflower Blue	1964	1.20	6.00
Musicor 1039		I'm Gonna Find Myself A Girl / Lips Are Redder	1964	*Unreleased?*	
Musicor 1040		It Hurts To Be In Love / Hawaii	1964	1.20	6.00
Musicor 1040	(PS)	It Hurts To Be In Love / Hawaii	1964	1.20	6.00
Musicor 1045		I'm Gonna Be Strong / Aladdin's Lamp	1964	1.20	6.00
Musicor 1045		I'm Gonna Be Strong / E Se Domani	1964	1.20	6.00
Musicor 1045	(PS)	I'm Gonna Be Strong / E Se Domani	1964	1.20	6.00
Musicor 1065		Amici Miei / I Tuoi Anni Piu Belli	1965	*Unreleased?*	
Musicor 1070		I Must Be Seeing Things / Marianne	1965	1.00	5.00
Musicor 1070	(PS)	I Must Be Seeing Things / Marianne	1965	1.00	5.00
Musicor 1093		Last Chance To Turn Around / Save Your Love	1965	1.00	5.00
Musicor 1103		Looking Through The Eyes Of Love / There's No Livin' Without Your Lovin'	1965	1.00	5.00
Musicor 1130		Princess In Rags / Amore Mio	1965	1.00	5.00
Musicor 1150		Jojos Muertas / Me Voy Para El Campo	1966	*Unreleased?*	
Musicor 1155		Nessuno Mi Puo Guidicare / Lei Mi Aspetta	1966	2.00	10.00
Musicor 1171		Backstage / Blue Color	1966	1.00	5.00
Musicor 1171	(PS)	Backstage / Blue Color	1966	1.00	5.00
Musicor 1200		(In The) Cold Light Of Day / The Boss' Daughter	1966	1.00	5.00
Musicor 1200	(PS)	(In The) Cold Light Of Day / The Boss' Daughter	1966	1.00	5.00
Musicor 1219		Just One Smile / Innamorato	1966	1.00	5.00
Musicor 1233		I'm Gonna Listen To Me / For Me, This Is Happy	1967	1.00	5.00
Musicor 1234		Don't Mean To Be A Preacher / Animal Crackers	1967	1.00	5.00
Musicor 1235		Flower Girl / Animal Crackers	1967	1.00	5.00
Musicor 1245		Where Did The Magic Go? / Tremblin'	1967	1.00	5.00
Musicor 1252		Something's Gotten Hold Of My Heart / Building Up My Dream World	1968	1.00	5.00
Musicor 1299		The More I Saw Of Her / Won't Take Long	1968	1.00	5.00
Musicor 1306		She's A Heartbreaker / Conquistador	1968	1.00	5.00
Musicor 1308		Lonely Drifter / Somewhere In The Country	1969	*Unreleased?*	
Musicor 1331		Billy, You're My Kind Of Woman / She Believes In Me	1969	*Unreleased?*	
Musicor 1331		Billy, You're My Kind Of Woman / Hate	1969	.60	3.00
Musicor 1331	(PS)	Billy, You're My Kind Of Woman / Hate	1969	1.00	5.00
Musicor 1348		Baby, You're My Kind Of Woman / Lonely Drifter	1969	.60	3.00
Musicor 1358		Maria Elena / The French Horn	1969	*Unreleased?*	
Musicor 1361		California / Playing Games For Love	1969	.60	3.00
Musicor 1384		She Lets Her Hair Down / I Remember	1969	.60	3.00
Musicor 1394		All Young Women / I Remember	1970	.60	3.00
Musicor 1405		Think Of Us / A Street Called Hop	1970	.60	3.00
Musicor 1419		Billy, You're My Friend / Shady Lady	1970	.60	3.00
Musicor 1439		Higher And Higher / Beautiful Sounds	1970	.60	3.00
Musicor 1453		I Just Can't Help Myself / Beautiful Sounds	1971	.60	3.00
Musicor 1474		Shady Lady / Run, Run, Roadrunner	1972	.60	3.00
Epic 50332		Dedication (This Song I Want To Dedicate To You) / Sandman	1977	.60	3.00
Epic 50461		It's Over Medley / Walkin' In The Sun	1977	.60	3.00

Label & Catalog #	A-Side/B-Side	Year	VG	NM
PITNEY, GENE, & GEORGE JONES				
Musicor 1066	I've Got Five Dollars And It's Saturday Night / Wreck On The Highway	1965	1.20	6.00
Musicor 1071	I've Got A New Heartache / My Shoes Keep Walking Back To You	1965	Unreleased?	
Musicor 1097	I'm A Fool To Care / Louisiana Man	1965	1.20	6.00
Musicor 1097 (PS)	I'm A Fool To Care / Louisiana Man	1965	1.20	6.00
Musicor 1115	Your Old Standby / Big Job	1965	1.20	6.00
Musicor 1165	That's All It Took / Y' All Come	1966	1.20	6.00
PITNEY, GENE, & MELBA MONTGOMERY				
Musicor 1135	Baby, Ain't That Fine / Everybody Knows But You And Me	1965	1.00	5.00
Musicor 1173	Being Together / King And Queen	1966	1.00	5.00
PITTMAN, BARBARA				
Sun 253	I Need A Man / No Matter Who's To Blame	1956	15.00	75.00
Phillips Inter. 3518	Two Young Fools In Love / I'm Getting Better All The Time	1958	5.00	25.00
Phillips Inter. 3527	Everlasting Love / Cold, Cold Heart	1959	3.00	15.00
PITTS, CLYDE				
Toppa 1018	Shakin' Like A Leaf / Just Remember	196?	2.00	10.00
PIXIES, THE				
AMC 102	Cry Like A Baby / Just A Little Tear	1962	5.00	25.00
Don-Dee 102	Cry Like A Baby / Just A Little Tear	1963	3.00	15.00
PIXIES, THE				
Autumn 12	Geisha Girl / He's Got You	1965	2.00	10.00
PIXIES THREE, THE				
Mercury 72130	Birthday Party / Our Love	1963	3.00	15.00
Mercury 72208	Cold, Cold Winter / 442 Glenwood Avenue	1963	3.00	15.00
Mercury 72208 (PS)	Cold, Cold Winter / 442 Glenwood Avenue	1963	4.00	20.00
Mercury 72250	Gee / After The Party	1964	3.00	15.00
Mercury 72288	It's Summertime, U.S.A. / The Hootch	1964	3.00	15.00
Mercury 72331	Orphan Boy / Love Walked In	1965	3.00	15.00
Mercury 72357	Love Me, Love Me / Your Way	1965	3.00	15.00
PIZANI, FRANK: *Refer to* THE HIGHLIGHTS				
PLAGUES, THE				
Fenton 2070	I've Been Through It Before / Tears From My Eyes	195?	15.00	75.00
Quarantined 2020	Why Can't You Be True? / Through This World	195?	8.00	40.00
Quarantined 41369	That'll Never Do / Badlands	195?	8.00	40.00
PLAIDS, THE				
Liberty 55167	Hungry For Your Love / Chit-Chat	1958	4.00	20.00
Nasco 6011	My Pretty Baby / Till The End Of The Dance	1958	4.00	20.00
Era 3002	Around The Corner / He Stole Fio	1963	4.00	20.00
PLAIN BROWN WRAPPER, THE				
Monster 0002	Junior Saw It Happen / Real Person	196?	2.00	10.00
Spirit 0010	Stretch Out Your Hand / Stretch Out Your Hand (Part 2)	196?	2.00	10.00
PLANETS, THE				
Roulette 4551	You Are My Sunshine / Mr. Moon	1964	3.00	15.00
PLANT LIFE				
Date 1572	Flower Girl / Say It Over Again	1967	1.00	5.00
PLATT, EDDIE				
Gone 5031	Cha-Hua-Hua / Vodka	1958	2.50	12.00
ABC-Paramount 9899	Tequila / Popcorn	1958	2.50	12.00
PLAYBOYS, THE				
Tetra 447	One Question / So Good	1956	5.00	25.00
Mercury 71288	Why Do I Love You, Why Do I Care? / Don't Do Me Wrong	1957	4.00	20.00
Martinique 101	Over The Weekend / Double Talk	1958	4.00	20.00
Cameo 142	Over The Weekend / Double Talk	1958	2.00	10.00
Martinique 400	Please Forgive Me / Sing Along	1959	2.00	10.00
Imperial 5586	Craisy Daisy / Sweet Talk	1959	3.00	15.00
ABC-Paramount 10070	Memories / You're All I See	1959	4.00	20.00
PLAYBOYS, THE				
Chancellor 1074	Boston Hop / (B-side by The Cousins)	1961	2.00	10.00
Chancellor 1106	Duck Walk / If I Had My Way	1962	2.00	10.00

Label & Catalog #		A-Side/B-Side	Year	VG	NM

PLAYBOYS, THE
Cotton 1008 — Careful With My Heart / Girl Of My Dreams — 1962 — 5.00 — 25.00

PLAYBOYS, THE
Catalina 1069 — Shortenin' Bread / Cheater Stomp — 196? — 7.00 — 35.00

PLAYBOYS, THE
Seville 135 — When I Meet A Girl Like You / I Have Love — 1963 — 3.00 — 15.00

PLAYBOYS, THE: *Refer to* THE FOUR PLAYBOYS; JOHN FRED & THE PLAYBOYS

PLAYBOYS OF EDINBURGH, THE
"1,2,3" 1722 — Let's Get Back To Rock 'N' Roll / Homemade Cookin' — 1966 — 3.00 — 15.00

Columbia 43716 — Look At Me / News Sure Travels Fast — 1966 — 2.00 — 10.00
Columbia 43933 — Dream World / One Way Ticket — 1966 — 2.00 — 10.00
Columbia 44093 — Mickey's Monkey / Sanford Ringleton I Of Abernathy — 1967 — 2.00 — 10.00

PLAYERS, THE
Artemis 101 — Memories Of A High School Bride / The Rebel — 196? — 3.00 — 15.00

PLEASE, BOBBY, & THE PLEASES
Jamie 1118 — The Monster / The Switch — 1959 — 3.00 — 15.00
Era 3044 — Your Driver's License, Please / Heartache Street — 1961 — 2.00 — 10.00

PLEASURE FAIR, THE
Uni 55016 — Morning Glory Days / Fade In, Fade Out — 1967 — 1.20 — 6.00
Uni 55078 — I'm Gonna Havta Let You Go / Today — 1968 — 1.20 — 6.00

PLEASURE SEEKERS, THE
The Pleasure Seekers feature Susie Quatro.
Hideout 1006 — Never Thought You'd Leave Me / What A Way To Go — 1967 — 20.00 — 100.00
Mercury 72800 — Good Kind Of Hurt / Light Of Love — 1968 — 5.00 — 25.00

PLEASURES, THE
RSVP 1113 — Let's Have A Beach Party / Don't You Know? — 196? — 7.00 — 35.00

PLEDGES, THE
The Pledges are Clyde Battin and Gary Paxton.
Revere 3517 — Bermuda / Betty Jean — 1957 — 5.00 — 25.00

PLIMSOULS, THE
The Plimsouls feature Peter Case., originally with The Nerves.
Planet 47923 — (DJ) — Now / Now — 1981 — .60 — 3.00
Planet 47923 — — Now / When You Find Out — 1981 — 2.00 — 10.00
Planet 47930 — (DJ) — Zero Hour / Zero Hour — 1981 — .60 — 3.00
Planet 47930 — — Zero Hour / Hush Hush-Dizzy Miss Lizzie — 1981 — 2.00 — 10.00
Shaky City 134 — — A Million Miles Away / I'll Get Lucky — 1982 — .80 — 4.00
Shaky City 134 — (PS) — A Million Miles Away / I'll Get Lucky — 1982 — 1.25 — 6.00
Geffen 29600 — (DJ) — A Million Miles Away / A Million Miles Away — 1983 — .60 — 3.00
Geffen 29600 — — A Million Miles Away / Play The Breaks — 1983 — .60 — 3.00
Geffen 29496 — (DJ) — Oldest Story In The World / Oldest Story In The World — 1984 — .80 — 4.00
Geffen 29496 — — Oldest Story In The World / Hobo — 1984 — 1.00 — 5.00
— *12" Singles* —
Geffen PRO- — (DJ) — A Million Miles Away / A Million Miles Away — 1983 — 1.00 — 5.00

PLUM RUN, THE
Avco Embassy 4511 — My Boy, Lollipop / Little Miss Inside — 1969 — 1.00 — 5.00

PLUMMER, DAVE, & THE PLUNGERS
Maybrook 320 — Surfin' Monster / King Of The Road — 196? — 7.00 — 35.00

PLUNDERERS, THE
Roulette 4665 — Batman / Boss — 1966 — 3.00 — 15.00

PLURALS, THE
Wanger 186/7 — Miss Annie / Donna, My Dear — 1958 — 4.00 — 20.00
Bergen 186/7 — Miss Annie / Donna, My Dear — 1958 — 3.00 — 15.00
Wanger 188 — Goodnight / I'm Sold (Label has small print) — 1959 — 3.00 — 15.00

PLUSHTONES, THE
Plush 601 — Raindrops / Penny Loafers — 1960 — 10.00 — 50.00

PLYMOUTH ROCKERS, THE
Warner Bros. 5475 — Brown Eyed Handsome Man / Around And Around — 1964 — 2.00 — 10.00
Valiant 729 — Roll Over, Stephen Foster / Girl From The North Country — 1965 — 3.00 — 15.00
Valiant 737 — Don't Say Why / Walk A Lonely Mile — 1966 — 3.00 — 15.00

Label & Catalog #	A-Side / B-Side	Year	VG	NM
POINDEXTER, DOUG, & THE STARLITE WRANGLERS				
Sun 202	My Kind Of Carryin' On / Now She Cares No More For Me	1954	——	——
	(Rare. Estimated near mint value $500-1,000.)			
POLARAS, THE				
Pharos 100	Breaker / Cricket	1963	7.00	35.00
PONDEROSAS, THE				
Co & Ce 236	Everybody's Surfing / The High Country	1966	5.00	25.00
PONI-TAILS, THE				
Marc 1001	Can I Be Sure? / Still In Your Teens	1957	3.00	15.00
Point 8	Your Wild Heart / Que La Bozena	1957	3.00	15.00
ABC-Paramount 9846	It's Just My Luck To Be Fifteen / Wild Eyes And Tender Lips	1958	3.00	15.00
ABC-Paramount 9934	Born Too Late / Come On, Joey, Dance With Me	1958	4.00	20.00
ABC-Paramount 9969	Seven Minutes In Heaven / Close Friends	1958	3.00	15.00
ABC-Paramount 9995	Father Time / Early To Bed	1959	3.00	15.00
ABC-Paramount 10027	Moody / Oo-Pah Polka	1959	3.00	15.00
ABC-Paramount 10047	I'll Be Seeing You / I'll Keep Tryin'	1959	3.00	15.00
ABC-Paramount 10077	Before We Say Goodnight / Come Be My Love	1960	3.00	15.00
ABC-Paramount 10114	Who, When And Why? / Oh, My, You!	1960	3.00	15.00
POOH & THE HEFFALUMPHS				
Laurie 3281	Lady Godiva / Rooty Toot	1966	1.00	5.00
POOLE, BRIAN, & THE TREMELOES				
Refer to The Tremeloes.				
London 9600	Keep On Dancing / Blue	1963	2.00	10.00
London 9625	Do You Love Me? / Why Can't You Love Me?	1963	3.00	15.00
Monument 840	I Can Dance / Candy Man	1964	1.60	8.00
Monument 846	Someone Someone / (Meet Me) Where We Used To Meet	1964	1.60	8.00
Monument 882	After A While / Don't Cry	1965	1.60	8.00
Date 1539	Everything I Touch Turns To Tears / I Need Her Tonight	1966	1.60	8.00
Audio Fidelity 121	Good Lovin' / Could It Be You?	196?	1.60	8.00
POP, IGGY				
Iggy originally recorded with The Stooges and, later, with David Bowie.				
Siamese 001	I Got A Right / Gimme Some Skin	1977	2.00	10.00
Siamese 9213	I Got A Right / Gimme Some Skin	1978	.80	4.00
Siamese 9213 (PS)	I Got A Right / Gimme Some Skin	1978	.80	4.00
	(Produced by David Bowie.)			
POP TOPS, THE				
Calla 154	Voice Of A Dying Man / Oh, Lord, Why, Lord?	1968	.80	4.00
POP UPS, THE				
HBR 459	Candy Rock / Lurking	1966	1.00	5.00
POPPIES, THE				
Epic 9893	Lullabye Of Love / I Wonder Why	1966	1.20	6.00
Epic 10019	He's Got Real Love / He's Ready	1966	1.20	6.00
Epic 10059	Do It With Soul / He Means So Much To Me	1966	1.20	6.00
Epic 10086	My Love And I / There's Pain In My Heart	1966	1.20	6.00
POPPY FAMILY, THE				
London 129	Which Way Are You Goin,' Billy? / Endless Sleep	1970	.60	3.00
London 139	That's Where I Went Wrong / Shadows On My Wall	1970	.60	3.00
London 148	Where Evil Grows / I Was Wondering	1971	.60	3.00
London 164	No Good To Cry / I'll See You There	1971	.60	3.00
London 172	Good Friends / Tryin'	1972	.60	3.00
POPSICLES, THE				
Knight 2002	Thumb Print / This Is The End	196?	2.00	10.00
GNP/Crescendo 336	I Don't Want To Be Your Baby Anymore / Baby, I Miss You	1965	1.20	6.00
PORTRAITS, THE				
Tri-Disc 109	Three Blind Mice / We're Gonna Party	1963	3.00	15.00
PORTRAITS, THE				
Sidewalk 928	A Million To One / Let's Tell The World	1967	3.00	15.00
Sidewalk 935	Runaround Girl / Over The Rainbow	1968	3.00	15.00
POSITIVELY 13 O'CLOCK				
Positively 13 O' Clock is a pseudonym for Mouse & The Traps.				
HBR 500	Psychotic Reaction / 13 O' Clock Theme For Psychotics	1966	7.00	35.00
POSSESSIONS, THE				
Britton 1003	No More Love / You And Your Lies	1964	4.00	20.00

Label & Catalog #	A-Side/B-Side	Year	VG	NM
Britton 1003	No More Love / You And Your Lies *(Blue vinyl)*	1964	8.00	40.00
Parkway 930	No More Love / You And Your Lies	1964	3.00	15.00
POSSUM				
Highland 10	The Cockroach That Ate Cincinnati / Chula Vista	1966	2.00	10.00
POVERTY FIVE, THE				
Thumbs Down 1002	Cry Cry Cry / Sorrow	196?	2.50	12.00
POWDER PUFFS, THE				
Imperial 66014	My Boyfriend's Woody / My Boyfriend's Woody, Part 2	1964	5.00	25.00
Imperial 66014	My Boyfriend's Woody / Woody Wagon	1964	5.00	25.00
POWELL, SANDY				
Herald 557	Pistol Packin' Mama / Bon Bon	1961	15.00	75.00
POWER				
MGM 13815	Children Ask (If He Is Dead) / She Is The Color Of	1967	3.00	15.00
POWER, DUFFY				
Veep 1204	Where Am I? / I Don't Care	1964	1.00	5.00
Epic 10650	Hellhound / Hummingbird	1970	.80	4.00
POWERS, JOEY				
Amy 892	Midnight Mary / Where Do You Want The World Delivered	1963	2.00	10.00
Amy 898	Billy, Old Buddy / In The Morning, Gloria	1963	2.00	10.00
Amy 903	You Comb Her Hair / Love Is A Reason	1964	2.00	10.00
Amy 914	Tears Keep Falling / Where Did The Summer Go?	1964	2.00	10.00
POWERS, JOHNNY				
Fortune 199	Honey, Let's Go (To A Rock And Roll Show) / Your Love	1955	35.00	175.00
Fox 916	Rock Rock / Long Blonde Hair, Red Rose Lips	1957	125.00	500.00
Sun 327	With Your Love, With Your Kiss / Be Mine, All Mine	1959	8.00	40.00
Tridex 103	A Teenager's Prayer / A Young Boy's Heart	1960	3.00	15.00
POWERS, TINA				
Parkway 847	Making Up Is Fun To Do / Back To School	1962	2.00	10.00
POWERS, WAYNE				
Phillips Inter. 3523	My Love Song / Point Of View	1958	5.00	25.00
PRANCERS, THE				
Guaranteed 204	Rudolph The Red Nosed Reindeer / Short Short'nin'	1959	3.00	15.00
PRECISIONS, THE				
D-Town 1055	Mexican Love Song / You're Sweet	1965	2.00	10.00
Drew 1001	Lover's Plea / Such Misery	1966	2.00	10.00
Drew 1002	What I Want / Why, Girl?	1967	2.00	10.00
Drew 1003	Is This Love? / You'll Soon Be Gone	1967	2.00	10.00
Drew 1004	Instant Heartbreak / Dream Girl	1968	2.00	10.00
Drew 1005	Never Let Her Go / A Place	1968	2.00	10.00
Atco 6643	Don't Double / Into My Life	1969	1.00	5.00
Atco 6669	New York City / You're The Best That Ever Did It	1969	1.00	5.00
PRELUDES, THE				
Pik 231	Starlight / Don't You Know Love?	1961	3.00	15.00
PRELUDES FIVE THE				
Pik 231	Starlight / Don't You Know Love?	1961	3.00	15.00
PREMEERS, THE				
Herald 577	Diary Of Our Love / Gee, Oh Gee	1962	4.00	20.00
PREMIERE, RONNIE, & THE ROYAL LANCERS				
Sara 1020	You May Not Be An Angel / So Loved Am I	195?	20.00	100.00
PREMIERES, THE				
Nu-Phi 429	Firewater / Younger Than You	196?	2.00	10.00
PREMIERS, THE				
Mink 021	I Think I Love You / Tonight	1959	4.00	20.00
Parkway 807	I Think I Love You / Tonight	1961	3.00	15.00
PREMIERS, THE				
The Premiers feature Roger Koob.				
Alert 706	Jolene / Oh, Theresa	1959	7.00	35.00
Fury 1029	Pigtails, Eyes Are Blue / I Pray	1960	4.00	20.00
Rust 5032	Falling Star / She Gives Me Fever	1960	8.00	40.00

Label & Catalog #		A-Side/B-Side	Year	VG	NM
PREMIERS, THE					
Sahara 103		**Frantic** / (B-side by The Phaetons)	1964	7.00	35.00
PREMIERS, THE					
Faro 615		**Farmer John** / **Duffy's Blues**	1964	4.00	20.00
Warner Bros. 5443		**Farmer John** / **Duffy's Blues**	1964	2.00	10.00
Warner Bros. 5464		**Annie Oakley** / **Blues For Arlene**	1964	2.00	10.00
Faro 621		**Little Ways** / **Get Your Baby**	1964	2.00	10.00
Faro 624		**Come On And Dream** / **Get On This Plane**	1964	2.00	10.00
Faro 627		**Ring Around My Rosie** / **Ring Around My Rosie, Part 2**	1964	2.00	10.00
PREMIERS, THE					
Scepter 12298		**I Won't Stand In Your Way** / **Lonely Weatherman**	1970	.60	3.00
PREPS, THE					
Coast Recorders		**Moon Racers** / **It Ain't Green Cheese On The Moon, Baby**	195?	10.00	50.00

PRESLEY, ELVIS (WITH THE JORDANAIRES)

Elvis' first five singles, released on tiny Sun records, stand as the pivotal moment—the Rosetta Stones—in the transformation of exclusively black rhythm 'n blues into the two-toned rock 'n roll. Enough praise cannot be heaped on the other men who made these records possible: Bill Black, bass, Scotty Moore, guitar, and D.J. Fontana, who joined on drums in 1955. And, of course, producer extraordinaire Sam Phillips...

Throughout his career, Elvis recorded with the best musicians available, especially when he cut studio material in Nashville. Such stalwarts as Chet Atkins, Floyd Cramer and Boots Randolph worked with The King. Regardless of the names on paper, most of Elvis' sides were cut with him actively directing from the studio; thus, Elvis functioned as his own producer from the time he left Sun. Notable exceptions are the majestic sides he cut in 1969 in Chip Moman's American Sound Studios in Memphis (9741-9791). Finally, The Jordanaires, whether credited or not, appeared on 47-6604 and virtually every side from 47-6643 through 1968's releases.

Some copies of 47-6357 through 7035 issued with the silver line were also issued completely lacking the Nipper logo on top; these are worth approximately $200 each. Beginning with 47-8243, picture sleeves were generally issued with two variations, usually advertising a new Elvis album on a strip at the bottom of the sleeve. First pressings were often worded "Coming Soon!" followed by the information. Later pressings read "Ask For" followed by the data. The later sleeves were pressed in much smaller quantities and are generally worth 20-50% more than the listed first pressings.

Label & Catalog #		A-Side/B-Side	Year	VG	NM
Sun 209		**That's All Right** / **Blue Moon Of Kentucky**	1954	——	——
		(Rare. Estimated near mint value $600-1,000.)			
Sun 210		**Good Rockin' Tonight** / **I Don't Care If The Sun Don't Shine**	1954	——	——
		(Rare. Estimated near mint value $600-1,000.)			
Sun 215		**Milkcow Blues Boogie** / **You're A Heartbreaker**	1955	——	——
		(Rare. Estimated near mint value $750-1,500.)			
Sun 217		**Baby, Let's Play House** / **I'm Left, You're Right, She's Gone**	1955	150.00	600.00
Sun 223		**Mystery Train** / **I Forgot To Remember To Forget**	1955	90.00	350.00
RCA Victor 47-6357	(DJ)	**Mystery Train** / **I Forgot To Remember To Forget**	1955	90.00	300.00
RCA Victor 47-6357		**Mystery Train** / **I Forgot To Remember To Forget** (Lines label)	1955	20.00	100.00
RCA Victor 47-6380		**That's All Right** / **Blue Moon Of Kentucky**	1955	10.00	50.00
RCA Victor 47-6380		**That's All Right** / **Blue Moon Of Kentucky** (Lines label)	1955	20.00	100.00
RCA Victor 47-6381		**Good Rockin' Tonight** / **I Don't Care If The Sun Don't Shine**	1955	10.00	50.00
RCA Victor 47-6381		**Good Rockin' Tonight** / **I Don't Care If The Sun Don't Shine** (Lines label)	1955	20.00	100.00
RCA Victor 47-6382		**Milkcow Blues Boogie** / **You're A Heartbreaker**	1955	10.00	50.00
RCA Victor 47-6382		**Milkcow Blues Boogie** / **You're A Heartbreaker** (Lines label)	1955	20.00	100.00
RCA Victor 47-6383		**Baby, Let's Play House** / **I'm Left, You're Right, She's Gone**	1955	10.00	50.00
RCA Victor 47-6383		**Baby, Let's Play House** / **I'm Left, You're Right, She's Gone** (Lines label)	1955	20.00	100.00
RCA Victor 47-6420		**Heartbreak Hotel** / **I Was The One**	1956	5.00	25.00
RCA Victor 47-6420		**Heartbreak Hotel** / **I Was The One** (Lines label)	1956	8.00	40.00
RCA Victor 47-6540		**I Want You, I Need You, I Love You** / **My Baby Left Me**	1956	4.00	20.00
RCA Victor 47-6540		**I Want You, I Need You, I Love You** / **My Baby Left Me** (Lines label)	1956	6.00	30.00
RCA Victor 47-6604		**Hound Dog** / **Don't Be Cruel**	1956	5.00	25.00
RCA Victor 47-6604		**Hound Dog** / **Don't Be Cruel** (Lines label)	1956	7.00	35.00
RCA Victor 47-6604	(PS)	**Hound Dog** / **Don't Be Cruel**	1956	15.00	75.00
RCA Victor 47-6604	(PS)	**Don't Be Cruel** / **Hound Dog**	1956	25.00	125.00
RCA Victor 47-6636		**Blue Suede Shoes** / **Tutti Frutti**	1956	18.00	90.00
RCA Victor 47-6636		**Blue Suede Shoes** / **Tutti Frutti** (Lines label)	1956	25.00	125.00
RCA Victor 47-6637		**I Got A Woman** / **I'm Counting On You**	1956	7.00	35.00
RCA Victor 47-6637		**I Got A Woman** / **I'm Counting On You** (Lines label)	1956	10.00	50.00
RCA Victor 47-6638		**I'll Never Let You Go (Little Darlin')** / **I'm Gonna Sit Right Down And Cry**	1956	7.00	35.00
RCA Victor 47-6638		**I'll Never Let You Go (Little Darlin')** / **I'm Gonna Sit Right Down And Cry** (Lines label)	1956	10.00	50.00
RCA Victor 47-6639		**Tryin' To Get To You** / **I Love You Because**	1956	7.00	35.00
RCA Victor 47-6639		**Tryin' To Get To You** / **I Love You Because** (Lines label)	1956	10.00	50.00
RCA Victor 47-6640		**Blue Moon** / **Just Because**	1956	6.00	30.00
RCA Victor 47-6640		**Blue Moon** / **Just Because** (Lines label)	1956	10.00	50.00

Label & Catalog #		A-Side/B-Side	Year	VG	NM
RCA Victor 47-6641		Money Honey / One Sided Love Affair	1956	7.00	35.00
RCA Victor 47-6641		Money Honey / One Sided Love Affair (Lines label)	1956	10.00	50.00
RCA Victor 47-6642		Shake, Rattle And Roll / Lawdy, Miss Clawdy	1956	5.00	25.00
RCA Victor 47-6642		Shake, Rattle And Roll / Lawdy, Miss Clawdy (Lines label)	1956	8.00	40.00
RCA Victor 47-6643		Love Me Tender / Anyway You Want Me	1956	4.00	20.00
RCA Victor 47-6643		Love Me Tender / Anyway You Want Me (Lines label)	1956	6.00	30.00
RCA Victor 47-6643	(PS)	Love Me Tender / Anyway You Want Me (Black & white PS)	1956	30.00	150.00
RCA Victor 47-6643	(PS)	Love Me Tender / Anyway You Want Me (Green PS)	1956	12.00	60.00
RCA Victor 47-6643	(PS)	Love Me Tender / Anyway You Want Me (Pink PS)	1956	6.00	30.00
RCA Victor 47-6800		Too Much / Playing For Keeps	1957	5.00	25.00
RCA Victor 47-6800		Too Much / Playing For Keeps (Lines label)	1957	8.00	40.00
RCA Victor 47-6800	(PS)	Too Much / Playing For Keeps	1957	7.00	35.00
RCA Victor 47-6870		All Shook Up / That's When Your Heartaches Begin	1957	5.00	25.00
RCA Victor 47-6870		All Shook Up / That's When Your Heartaches Begi (Lines label)	1957	8.00	40.00
RCA Victor 47-6870	(PS)	All Shook Up / That's When Your Heartaches Begin	1957	8.00	40.00
RCA Victor 47-7000		Teddy Bear / Loving You	1957	5.00	25.00
RCA Victor 47-7000		Teddy Bear / Loving You (Lines label)	1957	8.00	40.00
RCA Victor 47-7000	(PS)	Teddy Bear / Loving You	1957	10.00	50.00
RCA Victor 47-7035		Jailhouse Rock / Treat Me Nice	1957	5.00	25.00
RCA Victor 47-7035		Jailhouse Rock / Treat Me Nice (Lines label)	1957	10.00	50.00
RCA Victor 47-7035	(PS)	Jailhouse Rock / Treat Me Nice	1957	10.00	50.00
RCA Victor 47-7150		Don't / I Beg Of You	1958	3.00	15.00
RCA Victor 47-7150	(PS)	Don't / I Beg Of You	1958	8.00	40.00
RCA Victor 47-7240		Wear My Ring Around Your Neck / Doncha Think It's Time?	1958	3.00	15.00
RCA Victor 47-7240	(PS)	Wear My Ring Around Your Neck / Doncha Think It's Time?	1958	8.00	40.00
RCA Victor 47-7280		Hard Headed Woman / Don't Ask Me Why	1958	3.00	15.00
RCA Victor 47-7280	(PS)	Hard Headed Woman / Don't Ask Me Why	1958	8.00	40.00
RCA Victor 47-7410		One Night / I Got Stung	1958	3.00	15.00
RCA Victor 47-7410	(PS)	One Night / I Got Stung	1958	8.00	40.00
RCA Victor 47-7506		A Fool Such As I / I Need Your Love Tonight	1959	3.00	15.00
RCA Victor 47-7506	(PS)	A Fool Such As I / I Need Your Love Tonight (The back advertises the "Elvis Sails" EP. Rare. Estimated near mint value $500-1,000.)	1959	——	——
RCA Victor 47-7506	(PS)	A Fool Such As I / I Need Your Love Tonight (The back advertises Elvis' Gold Standard catalog.)	1959	8.00	40.00
RCA Victor 47-7600		A Big Hunk O' Love / My Wish Came True	1959	3.00	15.00
RCA Victor 47-7600	(PS)	A Big Hunk O' Love / My Wish Came True	1959	6.00	30.00
RCA Victor 47-7740		Stuck On You / Fame And Fortune	1960	3.00	15.00
RCA Victor 47-7740	(PS)	Stuck On You / Fame And Fortune	1960	7.00	35.00
RCA Victor 61-7740	(S)	Stuck On You / Fame And Fortune	1960	75.00	300.00
RCA Victor 47-7777		It's Now Or Never / A Mess Of Blues	1960	3.00	15.00
RCA Victor 47-7777	(PS)	It's Now Or Never / A Mess Of Blues	1960	7.00	35.00
RCA Victor 61-7777	(S)	It's Now Or Never / A Mess Of Blues	1960	90.00	350.00
RCA Victor 47-7810		Are You Lonesome Tonight? / I Gotta Know	1960	2.00	10.00
RCA Victor 47-7810	(PS)	Are You Lonesome Tonight? / I Gotta Know	1960	7.00	35.00
RCA Victor 61-7810	(S)	Are You Lonesome Tonight? / I Gotta Know	1960	90.00	350.00
RCA Victor 37-7850	(33)	Surrender / Lonely Man	1961	90.00	350.00
RCA Victor 37-7850	(PS)	Surrender / Lonely Man (Rare. Estimated near mint value $500-1,000.)	1961	——	——
RCA Victor 47-7850		Surrender / Lonely Man	1961	2.00	10.00
RCA Victor 47-7850	(PS)	Surrender / Lonely Man	1961	6.00	30.00
RCA Victor 61-7850	(S)	Surrender / Lonely Man	1961	100.00	400.00
RCA Victor 68-7850	(S)	Surrender / Lonely Man (Compact-33 stereo single) (Rare. Estimated near mint value $1,500-2,000.)	1961	——	——
RCA Victor 37-7880	(33)	I Feel So Bad / Wild In The Country	1961	90.00	350.00
RCA Victor 37-7880	(PS)	I Feel So Bad / Wild In The Country (Rare. Estimated near mint value $500-1,000.)	1961	——	——
RCA Victor 47-7880		I Feel So Bad / Wild In The Country	1961	2.00	10.00
RCA Victor 47-7880	(PS)	I Feel So Bad / Wild In The Country	1961	5.00	25.00
RCA Victor 37-7908	(33)	(Marie's The Name) His Latest Flame / Little Sister	1961	90.00	350.00
RCA Victor 37-7908	(PS)	(Marie's The Name) His Latest Flame / Little Sister (Rare. Estimated near mint value $500-1,000.)	1961	——	——
RCA Victor 47-7908		(Marie's The Name) His Latest Flame / Little Sister	1961	2.00	10.00
RCA Victor 47-7908	(PS)	(Marie's The Name) His Latest Flame / Little Sister	1961	5.00	25.00
RCA Victor 37-7968	(33)	Can't Help Falling In Love / Rock-A-Hula Baby (Rare. Estimated near mint value $500-1,000.)	1961	——	——
RCA Victor 37-7968	(PS)	Can't Help Falling In Love / Rock-A-Hula Baby (Rare. Estimated near mint value $1,000-1,500.)	1961	——	——
RCA Victor 37-7968		Can't Help Falling In Love / Rock-A-Hula Baby	1961	2.00	10.00
RCA Victor 47-7968	(PS)	Can't Help Falling In Love / Rock-A-Hula Baby	1961	5.00	25.00
RCA Victor 37-7992	(33)	Good Luck Charm / Anything That's Part Of You (Rare. Estimated near mint value $500-1,000.)	1962	——	——
RCA Victor 37-7992	(PS)	Good Luck Charm / Anything That's Part Of You (Rare. Estimated near mint value $1,200-2,000.)	1962	——	——
RCA Victor 47-7992		Good Luck Charm / Anything That's Part Of You	1962	2.00	10.00
RCA Victor 47-7992	(PS)	Good Luck Charm / Anything That's Part Of You	1962	4.00	20.00

When RCA Victor announced their Gold Standard Series of reissues in 1959, they essentially moved Elvis' entire catalog in and let the series run. While first pressings on the classic glossy black label with Nipper directly on top are the most collectible, the rarest is the handful of titles issued briefly in 1969 on the then current orange label. While *Blue Christmas* and *Kiss Me Quick* appear to be the most common, they are easy $35 sales in collectible condition; the others have been known to sell between $50-100!

Label & Catalog #		A-Side/B-Side	Year	VG	NM
RCA Victor 47-8041		She's Not You / Just Tell Her Jim Said Hello	1962	2.40	12.00
RCA Victor 47-8041	(PS)	She's Not You / Just Tell Her Jim Said Hello	1962	5.00	25.00
RCA Victor 47-8100		Return To Sender / Where Do You Come From?	1962	2.00	10.00
RCA Victor 47-8100	(PS)	Return To Sender / Where Do You Come From?	1962	5.00	25.00
RCA Victor 47-8134		One Broken Heart For Sale / They Remind Me Too Much Of You	1963	2.00	10.00
RCA Victor 47-8134	(PS)	One Broken Heart For Sale / They Remind Me Too Much Of You	1963	5.00	25.00
RCA Victor 47-8188		(You're The) Devil In Disguise / Please Don't Drag That String Around	1963	1.60	8.00
RCA Victor 47-8188	(PS)	(You're The) Devil In Disguise / Please Don't Drag That String Around	1963	3.00	15.00
RCA Victor 47-8243		Bossa Nova Baby / Witchcraft	1963	2.00	10.00
RCA Victor 47-8243	(PS)	Bossa Nova Baby / Witchcraft	1963	4.00	20.00
RCA Victor 47-8307		Kissin' Cousins / It Hurts Me	1964	2.00	10.00
RCA Victor 47-8307	(PS)	Kissin' Cousins / It Hurts Me	1964	4.00	20.00
RCA Victor 47-8360	(DJ)	Viva Las Vegas / What'd I Say	1964	8.00	40.00
RCA Victor 47-8360		Viva Las Vegas / What'd I Say	1964	2.00	10.00
RCA Victor 47-8360	(PS)	Viva Las Vegas / What'd I Say	1964	5.00	25.00
RCA Victor 47-8400	(DJ)	Such A Night / Never Ending	1964	——	——
		(Rare. Estimated near mint value $500-1,000.)			
RCA Victor 47-8400		Such A Night / Never Ending	1964	2.00	10.00
RCA Victor 47-8400	(PS)	Such A Night / Never Ending	1964	5.00	25.00
RCA Victor 47-8440	(DJ)	Ain't That Loving You, Baby / Ask Me	1964	6.00	30.00
RCA Victor 47-8440		Ain't That Loving You, Baby / Ask Me	1964	1.60	8.00
RCA Victor 47-8440	(PS)	Ain't That Loving You, Baby / Ask Me	1964	3.00	15.00
RCA Victor 47-8500	(DJ)	Do The Clam / You'll Be Gone	1965	6.00	30.00
RCA Victor 47-8500		Do The Clam / You'll Be Gone	1965	1.60	8.00
RCA Victor 47-8500	(PS)	Do The Clam / You'll Be Gone	1965	4.00	20.00
RCA Victor 47-8585	(DJ)	(It's Such An) Easy Question / It Feels So Right	1965	6.00	30.00
RCA Victor 47-8585		(It's Such An) Easy Question / It Feels So Right	1965	1.60	8.00
RCA Victor 47-8585	(PS)	(It's Such An) Easy Question / It Feels So Right	1965	3.00	15.00
RCA Victor 47-8657	(DJ)	I'm Your's / (It's A) Long Lonely Highway	1965	6.00	30.00
RCA Victor 47-8657		I'm Your's / (It's A) Long Lonely Highway	1965	1.60	8.00
RCA Victor 47-8657	(PS)	I'm Your's / (It's A) Long Lonely Highway	1965	5.00	25.00
RCA Victor 47-8740	(DJ)	Tell Me Why / Blue River	1965	6.00	30.00
RCA Victor 47-8740		Tell Me Why / Blue River	1965	1.60	8.00
RCA Victor 47-8740	(PS)	Tell Me Why / Blue River	1965	4.00	20.00
RCA Victor 47-8780	(DJ)	Frankie And Johnny / Please Don't Stop Loving Me	1966	6.00	30.00
RCA Victor 47-8780		Frankie And Johnny / Please Don't Stop Loving Me	1966	1.60	8.00
RCA Victor 47-8780	(PS)	Frankie And Johnny / Please Don't Stop Loving Me	1966	4.00	20.00
RCA Victor 47-8870	(DJ)	Love Letters / Come What May	1966	6.00	30.00
RCA Victor 47-8870		Love Letters / Come What May	1966	1.60	8.00
RCA Victor 47-8870	(PS)	Love Letters / Come What May	1966	3.00	15.00
RCA Victor 47-8941	(DJ)	Spinout / All That I Am	1966	6.00	30.00
RCA Victor 47-8941		Spinout / All That I Am	1966	1.60	8.00
RCA Victor 47-8941	(PS)	Spinout / All That I Am	1966	4.00	20.00
RCA Victor 47-8950	(DJ)	If Every Day Was Like Christmas / How Would You Like To Be?	1966	8.00	40.00
RCA Victor 47-8950		If Every Day Was Like Christmas / How Would You Like To Be?	1966	3.00	15.00
RCA Victor 47-8950	(PS)	If Every Day Was Like Christmas / How Would You Like To Be?	1966	15.00	75.00
RCA Victor 47-9056	(DJ)	Indescribably Blue / Fools Fall In Love	1967	6.00	30.00
RCA Victor 47-9056		Indescribably Blue / Fools Fall In Love	1967	1.60	8.00
RCA Victor 47-9056	(PS)	Indescribably Blue / Fools Fall In Love	1967	4.00	20.00
RCA Victor 47-9115	(DJ)	Long Legged Girl / That's Someone You Never Forget	1967	6.00	30.00
RCA Victor 47-9115		Long Legged Girl / That's Someone You Never Forget	1967	1.60	8.00
RCA Victor 47-9115	(PS)	Long Legged Girl / That's Someone You Never Forget	1967	4.00	20.00
RCA Victor 47-9287	(DJ)	There's Always Me / Judy	1967	7.00	35.00
RCA Victor 47-9287		There's Always Me / Judy	1967	3.00	15.00
RCA Victor 47-9287	(PS)	There's Always Me / Judy	1967	8.00	40.00
RCA Victor 47-9341	(DJ)	Big Boss Man / You Don't Know Me	1967	6.00	30.00
RCA Victor 47-9341		Big Boss Man / You Don't Know Me	1967	1.60	8.00
RCA Victor 47-9341	(PS)	Big Boss Man / You Don't Know Me	1967	4.00	20.00
RCA Victor 47-9425	(DJ)	Guitar Man / High Heel Sneakers	1968	5.00	25.00
RCA Victor 47-9425		Guitar Man / High Heel Sneakers	1968	1.60	8.00
RCA Victor 47-9425	(PS)	Guitar Man / High Heel Sneakers	1968	3.00	15.00
RCA Victor 47-9465	(DJ)	Stay Away / U.S. Male	1968	5.00	25.00
RCA Victor 47-9465		Stay Away / U.S. Male	1968	1.60	8.00
RCA Victor 47-9465	(PS)	Stay Away / U.S. Male	1968	3.00	15.00
RCA Victor 47-9547	(DJ)	Let Yourself Go / Your Time Hasn't Come Yet, Baby	1968	5.00	25.00
RCA Victor 47-9547		Let Yourself Go / Your Time Hasn't Come Yet, Baby	1968	1.60	8.00
RCA Victor 47-9547	(PS)	Let Yourself Go / Your Time Hasn't Come Yet, Baby	1968	4.00	20.00
RCA Victor 47-9600	(DJ)	We Call On Him / You'll Never Walk Alone	1968	6.00	30.00
RCA Victor 47-9600		We Call On Him / You'll Never Walk Alone	1968	3.00	15.00
RCA Victor 47-9600	(PS)	We Call On Him / You'll Never Walk Alone	1968	20.00	100.00

Label & Catalog #		A-Side/B-Side	Year	VG	NM
RCA Victor 47-9610	(DJ)	A Little Less Conversation / Almost In Love	1968	5.00	25.00
RCA Victor 47-9610		A Little Less Conversation / Almost In Love	1968	1.60	8.00
RCA Victor 47-9610	(PS)	A Little Less Conversation / Almost In Love	1968	4.00	20.00
RCA Victor 47-9670	(DJ)	If I Can Dream / Edge Of Reality	1968	4.00	20.00
RCA Victor 47-9670		If I Can Dream / Edge Of Reality	1968	2.00	10.00
RCA Victor 47-9670	(PS)	If I Can Dream / Edge Of Reality	1968	4.00	20.00
		(Sleeve advertises Elvis' NBC-TV Special.)			
RCA Victor 47-9670	(PS)	If I Can Dream / Edge Of Reality	1968	3.00	15.00
RCA Victor 47-9731	(DJ)	Memories / Charro	1969	4.00	20.00
RCA Victor 47-9731		Memories / Charro	1969	1.00	5.00
RCA Victor 47-9731	(PS)	Memories / Charro	1969	4.00	20.00
RCA Victor 47-9741	(DJ)	In The Ghetto / Any Day Now	1969	4.00	20.00
RCA Victor 47-9741		In The Ghetto / Any Day Now	1969	1.00	5.00
RCA Victor 47-9741	(PS)	In The Ghetto / Any Day Now	1969	2.00	10.00
RCA Victor 47-9747	(DJ)	Clean Up Your Own Backyard / The Fair's Moving On	1969	4.00	20.00
RCA Victor 47-9747		Clean Up Your Own Backyard / The Fair's Moving On	1969	1.00	5.00
RCA Victor 47-9747	(PS)	Clean Up Your Own Backyard / The Fair's Moving On	1969	4.00	20.00
RCA Victor 74-0130	(DJ)	How Great Thou Art / His Hand In Mine	1969	8.00	40.00
RCA Victor 74-0130		How Great Thou Art / His Hand In Mine	1969	5.00	25.00
RCA Victor 74-0130	(PS)	How Great Thou Art / His Hand In Mine	1969	25.00	125.00
RCA Victor 47-9764	(DJ)	Suspicious Minds / You'll Think Of Me	1969	4.00	20.00
RCA Victor 47-9764		Suspicious Minds / You'll Think Of Me	1969	1.00	5.00
RCA Victor 47-9764	(PS)	Suspicious Minds / You'll Think Of Me	1969	2.40	12.00
RCA Victor 47-9768	(DJ)	Don't Cry, Daddy / Rubberneckin'	1969	4.00	20.00
RCA Victor 47-9768		Don't Cry, Daddy / Rubberneckin'	1969	1.00	5.00
RCA Victor 47-9768	(PS)	Don't Cry, Daddy / Rubberneckin'	1969	2.00	10.00
RCA Victor 47-9791	(DJ)	Kentucky Rain / My Little Friend	1970	4.00	20.00
RCA Victor 47-9791		Kentucky Rain / My Little Friend	1970	1.00	5.00
RCA Victor 47-9791	(PS)	Kentucky Rain / My Little Friend	1970	2.00	10.00
RCA Victor 47-9835	(DJ)	The Wonder Of You / Mama Liked The Roses	1970	4.00	20.00
RCA Victor 47-9835		The Wonder Of You / Mama Liked The Roses	1970	1.00	5.00
RCA Victor 47-9835	(PS)	The Wonder Of You / Mama Liked The Roses	1970	2.00	10.00
RCA Victor 47-9873	(DJ)	I've Lost You / The Next Step Is Love	1970	3.00	15.00
RCA Victor 47-9873		I've Lost You / The Next Step Is Love	1970	.80	4.00
RCA Victor 47-9873	(PS)	I've Lost You / The Next Step Is Love	1970	2.00	10.00
RCA Victor 47-9916	(DJ)	You Don't Have To Say You Love Me / Patch It Up	1970	3.00	15.00
RCA Victor 47-9916		You Don't Have To Say You Love Me / Patch It Up	1970	.80	4.00
RCA Victor 47-9916	(PS)	You Don't Have To Say You Love Me / Patch It Up	1970	3.00	15.00
RCA Victor 47-9960	(DJ)	I Really Don't Want To Know / There Goes My Everything	1970	3.00	15.00
RCA Victor 47-9960		I Really Don't Want To Know / There Goes My Everything	1970	.80	4.00
RCA Victor 47-9960	(PS)	I Really Don't Want To Know / There Goes My Everything	1970	2.00	10.00
RCA Victor 47-9980	(DJ)	Where Did They Go, Lord? / Rags To Riches	1971	3.00	15.00
RCA Victor 47-9980		Where Did They Go, Lord? / Rags To Riches	1971	.80	4.00
RCA Victor 47-9980	(PS)	Where Did They Go, Lord? / Rags To Riches	1971	3.00	15.00
RCA Victor 47-9985	(DJ)	Life / Only Believe	1971	3.00	15.00
RCA Victor 47-9985		Life / Only Believe	1971	.80	4.00
RCA Victor 47-9985	(PS)	Life / Only Believe	1971	3.00	15.00
RCA Victor 47-9998	(DJ)	I'm Leavin' / Heart Of Rome	1971	3.00	15.00
RCA Victor 47-9998		I'm Leavin' / Heart Of Rome	1971	.80	4.00
RCA Victor 47-9998	(PS)	I'm Leavin' / Heart Of Rome	1971	3.00	15.00
RCA Victor 48-1017	(DJ)	It's Only Love / The Sound Of Your Cry	1971	3.00	15.00
RCA Victor 48-1017		It's Only Love / The Sound Of Your Cry	1971	.80	4.00
RCA Victor 48-1017	(PS)	It's Only Love / The Sound Of Your Cry	1971	3.00	15.00
RCA Victor 74-0572	(DJ)	Merry Christmas, Baby / O, Come All Ye Faithful	1971	5.00	25.00
RCA Victor 74-0572		Merry Christmas, Baby / O, Come All Ye Faithful	1971	2.00	10.00
RCA Victor 74-0572	(PS)	Merry Christmas, Baby / O, Come All Ye Faithful	1971	7.00	35.00
RCA Victor 74-0619	(DJ)	Until It's Time For You To Go / We Can Make The Morning	1972	3.00	15.00
RCA Victor 74-0619		Until It's Time For You To Go / We Can Make The Morning	1972	.80	4.00
RCA Victor 74-0619	(PS)	Until It's Time For You To Go / We Can Make The Morning	1972	3.00	15.00
RCA Victor 74-0651	(DJ)	The Bosom Of Abraham / He Touched Me	1972	8.00	40.00
RCA Victor 74-0651		The Bosom Of Abraham / He Touched Me	1972	3.00	15.00
RCA Victor 74-0651	(PS)	The Bosom Of Abraham / He Touched Me	1972	15.00	75.00
RCA Victor 74-0672	(DJ)	An American Trilogy / The First Time Ever I Saw Your Face	1972	5.00	25.00
RCA Victor 74-0672		An American Trilogy / The First Time Ever I Saw Your Face	1972	3.00	15.00
RCA Victor 74-0672	(PS)	An American Trilogy / The First Time Ever I Saw Your Face	1972	10.00	50.00
RCA Victor 74-0769	(DJ)	Burning Love / It's A Matter Of Time	1972	3.00	15.00
RCA Victor 74-0769		Burning Love / It's A Matter Of Time (Orange label)	1972	.80	4.00
RCA Victor 74-0769		Burning Love / It's A Matter Of Time (Grey label)	1972	25.00	125.00
RCA Victor 74-0769	(PS)	Burning Love / It's A Matter Of Time	1972	2.40	12.00
RCA Victor 74-0815	(DJ)	Separate Ways / Always On My Mind	1972	3.00	15.00
RCA Victor 74-0815		Separate Ways / Always On My Mind	1972	.80	4.00
RCA Victor 74-0815	(PS)	Separate Ways / Always On My Mind	1972	2.40	12.00
RCA Victor 74-0910	(DJ)	Steamroller Blues / Fool	1973	3.00	15.00
RCA Victor 74-0910		Steamroller Blues / Fool	1973	.80	4.00
RCA Victor 74-0910	(PS)	Steamroller Blues / Fool	1973	2.00	10.00
RCA Victor DJAO-0088	(DJ)	Raised On Rock / For Ol' Times Sake	1973	3.00	15.00
RCA Victor APBO-0088		Raised On Rock / For Ol' Times Sake	1973	.80	4.00
RCA Victor APBO-0088	(PS)	Raised On Rock / For Ol' Times Sake	1973	4.00	20.00

Label & Catalog #		A-Side/B-Side	Year	VG	NM
RCA Victor DJBO-0196	(DJ)	I've Got A Thing About You Baby / Take Good Care Of Her	1974	3.00	15.00
RCA Victor APBO-0196		I've Got A Thing About You Baby / Take Good Care Of Her	1974	.80	4.00
RCA Victor APBO-0196	(PS)	I've Got A Thing About You Baby / Take Good Care Of Her	1974	1.00	5.00
RCA Victor DJBO-0280	(DJ)	If You Talk In Your Sleep / Help Me	1974	3.00	15.00
RCA Victor APBO-0280		If You Talk In Your Sleep / Help Me	1974	.80	4.00
RCA Victor APBO-0280	(PS)	If You Talk In Your Sleep / Help Me	1974	3.00	15.00
RCA Victor JA-10074	(DJ)	Promised Land / It's Midnight	1974	2.40	12.00
RCA Victor PB-10074		Promised Land / It's Midnight (Orange label)	1974	2.00	10.00
RCA Victor PB-10074		Promised Land / It's Midnight (Grey label)	1974	2.00	10.00
RCA Victor PB-10074		Promised Land / It's Midnight (Brown label)	1974	5.00	25.00
RCA Victor PB-10074	(PS)	Promised Land / It's Midnight	1974	3.00	15.00
RCA Victor JH-10191	(DJ)	My Boy / My Boy	1975	3.00	15.00
RCA Victor PB-10191		My Boy / Thinking About You (Orange label)	1975	.80	4.00
RCA Victor PB-10191		My Boy / Thinking About You (Brown label)	1975	.80	4.00
RCA Victor PB-10191	(PS)	My Boy / Thinking About You	1975	3.00	15.00
RCA Victor JH-10278	(DJ)	T-R-O-U-B-L-E / T-R-O-U-B-L-E	1975	3.00	15.00
RCA Victor PB-10278	(DJ)	T-R-O-U-B-L-E / Mr. Songman (Orange label)	1975	1.00	5.00
RCA Victor PB-10278		T-R-O-U-B-L-E / Mr. Songman (Brown label)	1975	2.00	10.00
RCA Victor PB-10278	(PS)	T-R-O-U-B-L-E / Mr. Songman	1975	3.00	15.00
RCA Victor JB-10401	(DJ)	Bringin' It Back / Pieces Of My Life	1975	2.00	10.00
RCA Victor PB-10401		Bringin' It Back / Pieces Of My Life (Orange label)	1975	12.00	60.00
RCA Victor PB-10401		Bringin' It Back / Pieces Of My Life (Brown label)	1975	.80	4.00
RCA Victor PB-10401	(PS)	Bringin' It Back / Pieces Of My Life	1975	2.00	10.00
RCA Victor JB-10601	(DJ)	For The Heart / Hurt	1976	2.40	12.00
RCA Victor PB-10601		For The Heart / Hurt (Brown label)	1976	.80	4.00
RCA Victor PB-10601		For The Heart / Hurt (Black label)	1976	15.00	75.00
RCA Victor PB-10601	(PS)	For The Heart / Hurt	1976	2.40	12.00
RCA Victor JB-10857	(DJ)	Moody Blue / She Thinks I Still Care	1976	2.40	12.00
RCA Victor PB-10857		Moody Blue / She Thinks I Still Care	1976	.40	2.00
RCA Victor PB-10857	(PS)	Moody Blue / She Thinks I Still Care	1976	2.00	10.00
RCA Victor JB-10998	(DJ)	Way Down / Pledging My Love (White label)	1977	30.00	150.00
RCA Victor JB-10998	(DJ)	Way Down / Pledging My Love (Cream label)	1977	3.00	15.00
RCA Victor PB-10998		Way Down / Pledging My Love	1977	.40	2.00
RCA Victor PB-10998	(PS)	Way Down / Pledging My Love	1977	2.00	10.00
RCA Victor JH-11165	(DJ)	My Way / America	1977	2.40	12.00
RCA Victor PB-11165		My Way / America	1977	.40	2.00
RCA Victor PB-11165	(PS)	My Way / America	1977	.80	4.00
RCA Victor PB-11165		My Way / America The Beautiful	1977	3.00	15.00
RCA Victor PB-11165	(PS)	My Way / America The Beautiful	1977	10.00	50.00
RCA Victor JB-11212	(DJ)	Unchained Melody / Softly, As I Leave You	1978	2.00	10.00
RCA Victor PB-11212		Unchained Melody / Softly, As I Leave You	1978	.40	2.00
RCA Victor PB-11212	(PS)	Unchained Melody / Softly, As I Leave You	1978	1.60	8.00
RCA Victor JB-11679	(DJ)	There's A Honky Tonk Angel / I Got A Feeling In My Body	1979	2.40	12.00
RCA Victor PB-11679		There's A Honky Tonk Angel / I Got A Feeling In My Body	1979	.40	2.00
RCA Victor PB-11679	(PS)	There's A Honky Tonk Angel / I Got A Feeling In My Body	1979	2.00	10.00
RCA Victor PB-12158	(DJ)	Guitar Man / Faded Love (Red vinyl)	1981	40.00	200.00
RCA Victor PB-12158	(DJ)	Guitar Man / Faded Love	1981	2.00	10.00
RCA Victor PB-12158		Guitar Man / Faded Love	1981	.40	2.00
RCA Victor PB-12158	(PS)	Guitar Man / Faded Love	1981	.40	2.00
RCA Victor PB-12205	(DJ)	Lovin' Arms / You Asked Me To (Green vinyl)	1981	50.00	250.00
RCA Victor PB-12205	(DJ)	Lovin' Arms / You Asked Me To	1981	2.40	12.00
RCA Victor PB-12205		Lovin' Arms / You Asked Me To	1981	.40	2.00
RCA Victor JB-13058	(DJ)	There Goes My Everything / You'll Never Walk Alone	1982	2.00	10.00
RCA Victor PB-13058		There Goes My Everything / You'll Never Walk Alone	1982	.40	2.00
RCA Victor PB-13058	(PS)	There Goes My Everything / You'll Never Walk Alone	1982	.80	4.00
RCA Victor PB-13351	(DJ)	The Elvis Medley / Always On My Mind (Gold vinyl)	1982	40.00	200.00
RCA Victor PB-13351	(DJ)	The Elvis Medley / Always On My Mind	1982	2.00	10.00
RCA Victor PB-13351		The Elvis Medley / Always On My Mind	1982	.40	2.00
RCA Victor PB-13351	(PS)	The Elvis Medley / Always On My Mind	1982	.40	2.00
RCA Victor PB-13500	(DJ)	I Was The One / Wear My Ring Around Your Neck (Gold vinyl)	1983	20.00	100.00
RCA Victor PB-13500	(DJ)	I Was The One / Wear My Ring Around Your Neck	1983	2.00	10.00
RCA Victor PB-13500		I Was The One / Wear My Ring Around Your Neck	1983	.40	2.00
RCA Victor PB-13500	(PS)	I Was The One / Wear My Ring Around Your Neck	1983	.60	3.00
RCA Victor PB-13547	(DJ)	Little Sister / Paralyzed (Blue vinyl)	1983	25.00	125.00
RCA Victor PB-13547	(DJ)	Little Sister / Paralyzed	1983	2.00	10.00
RCA Victor PB-13547		Little Sister / Paralyzed	1983	.40	2.00
RCA Victor PB-13547	(PS)	Little Sister / Paralyzed	1983	4.00	20.00
RCA 8760	(DJ)	Heartbreak Hotel / Heartbreak Hotel	1988	2.00	10.00
		(The a-side is by Elvis; the b-side is by David Keith.)			
RCA 8760	(DJ)	Heartbreak Hotel / Heartbreak Hotel	1988	1.00	5.00
		(While this is technically not an Elvis record—both sides are by David Keith— it carries the same catalog number as the Elvis disc and is by an actor playing Elvis in a movie...)			
RCA 8760	(DJ)	Heartbreak Hotel / Heartbreak Hotel	1988	10.00	50.00
		(Promotional sleeve features "The Infamous Butch Waugh As Elvis.")			
RCA 8760		Heartbreak Hotel / Heartbreak Hotel	1988	.40	2.00
RCA 8760	(PS)	Heartbreak Hotel / Heartbreak Hotel	1988	.40	2.00

Label & Catalog #		A-Side/B-Side	Year	VG	NM
		—Special/Promotional Releases—			
RCA Victor	(PS)	**This Is His Life**	1956	——	——
		(This is a black & white sleeve featuring a cartoon biography of Elvis. The sleeve bears no catalog number or titles but all known copies were found with 47-6540. Rare. Estimated near mint value $1,000-1,500.)			
RCA Victor CR-15		**Old Shep** *(One sided)*	1956	——	——
		(Rare. Estimated near mint value $1,000-1,500.)			
RCA Victor 0808		**Blue Christmas / Blue Christmas**	1957	——	——
		(Rare. Estimated near mint value $1,000-1,500.)			
RCA Victor SP-45-76		**Don't / Wear My Ring Around Your Neck**	1960	250.00	750.00
RCA Victor SP-45-76	(PS)	**Don't / Wear My Ring Around Your Neck**	1960	——	——
		(Rare. Estimated near mint value $1,200-1,600.)			
RCA Victor SP-45-118		**King Of The Whole Wide World / Home Is Where The Heart Is**	1960	30.00	150.00
RCA Victor SP-45-118	(PS)	**King Of The Whole Wide World / Home Is Where The Heart Is**	1960	75.00	300.00
RCA Victor SP-45-139	(DJ)	**Roustabout / One Track Heart**	1964	75.00	300.00
RCA Victor SP-45-162	(DJ)	**How Great Thou Art / So High**	1967	25.00	125.00
RCA Victor SP-45-162	(PS)	**How Great Thou Art / So High**	1967	40.00	200.00
RCA Victor JH-10951	(DJ)	**Let Me Be There / Let Me Be There**	1974	40.00	200.00
RCA Victor PB-10857		**Moody Blue / She Thinks I Still Care** *(Solid colored vinyl)*	1976	——	——
		(Rare. Estimated near mint value $900-1,200.)			
RCA Victor PB-10857		**Moody Blue / She Thinks I Still Care** *(Two colored vinyl)*	1976	——	——
		(Rare. Estimated near mint value $1,000-1,500.)			
RCA Victor JH-13302	(DJ)	**The Impossible Dream / An American Trilogy**	1982	10.00	50.00
RCA Victor JH-13302	(PS)	**The Impossible Dream / An American Trilogy**	1982	10.00	50.00

—RCA Gold Standard Series—

Elvis' Gold Standard singles have gone through several label changes; identifying originals can be difficult. This series started in 1959 with a black label with Nipper on top (447-0600 through 0720 were first issued this way). In 1965 Nipper was moved to the left side of the label (447-9643 through 0658). In the early '70s the label was changed to a flat red (447-0659 through 0685). Following Elvis' death in 1977, almost his entire catalog was reissued on the "new" black label with Nipper in the upper right; most of these are rather common. Note: In 1969 approximately two dozen titles were reissued in minute print runs on the then current orange labels. These are amongst the rarest of all Elvis records! Near mint copies have an estimated value of $50-75 each.

Label & Catalog #		A-Side/B-Side	Year	VG	NM
		—1959-1964: Black label with Nipper on top.—			
RCA Victor 447-0600		**Mystery Train / I Forgot To Remember To Forget**	1959	4.00	20.00
RCA Victor 447-0601		**That's All Right / Blue Moon Of Kentucky**	1959	4.00	20.00
RCA Victor 447-0602		**Good Rockin' Tonight / I Don't Care If The Sun Don't Shine**	1959	4.00	20.00
RCA Victor 447-0603		**Milkcow Blues Boogie / You're A Heartbreaker**	1959	4.00	20.00
RCA Victor 447-0604		**Baby, Let's Play House / I'm Left, You're Right, She's Gone**	1959	4.00	20.00
RCA Victor 447-0605		**Heartbreak Hotel / I Was The One**	1959	3.00	15.00
RCA Victor 447-0607		**I Want You, I Need You, I Love You / My Baby Left Me**	1959	3.00	15.00
RCA Victor 447-0608		**Hound Dog / Don't Be Cruel**	1959	3.00	15.00
RCA Victor 447-0609		**Blue Suede Shoes / Tutti Frutti**	1959	5.00	25.00
RCA Victor 447-0610		**I Got A Woman / I'm Counting On You**	1959	4.00	20.00
RCA Victor 447-0611		**I'll Never Let You Go (Little Darlin') / I'm Gonna Sit Right Down And Cry (Over You)**	1959	4.00	20.00
RCA Victor 447-0612		**Tryin' To Get To You / I Love You Because**	1959	4.00	20.00
RCA Victor 447-0613		**Blue Moon / Just Because**	1959	3.00	15.00
RCA Victor 447-0614		**Money Honey / One Sided Love Affair**	1959	4.00	20.00
RCA Victor 447-0615		**Shake, Rattle And Roll / Lawdy, Miss Clawdy**	1959	3.00	15.00
RCA Victor 447-0616		**Love Me Tender / Anyway You Want Me**	1959	3.00	15.00
RCA Victor 447-0617		**Too Much / Playing For Keeps**	1959	3.00	15.00
RCA Victor 447-0618		**All Shook Up / That's When Your Heartaches Begin**	1959	3.00	15.00
RCA Victor 447-0619		**Jailhouse Rock / Treat Me Nice**	1960	3.00	15.00
RCA Victor 447-0620		**Teddy Bear / Loving You**	1960	3.00	15.00
RCA Victor 447-0621		**Don't / I Beg Of You**	1960	3.00	15.00
RCA Victor 447-0622		**Wear My Ring Around Your Neck / Doncha Think It's Time?**	1960	3.00	15.00
RCA Victor 447-0623		**Hard Headed Woman / Don't Ask Me Why**	1960	3.00	15.00
RCA Victor 447-0624		**One Night / I Got Stung**	1960	3.00	15.00
RCA Victor 447-0625		**A Fool Such As I / I Need Your Love Tonight**	1960	3.00	15.00
RCA Victor 447-0626		**A Big Hunk O' Love / My Wish Came True**	1962	3.00	15.00
RCA Victor 447-0627		**Stuck On You / Fame And Fortune**	1962	2.00	10.00
RCA Victor 447-0628		**It's Now Or Never / A Mess Of Blues**	1962	2.40	12.00
RCA Victor 447-0629		**Are You Lonesome Tonight? / I Gotta Know**	1962	2.00	10.00
RCA Victor 447-0630		**Surrender / Lonely Man**	1962	4.00	20.00
RCA Victor 447-0631		**I Feel So Bad / Wild In The Country**	1962	2.40	12.00
RCA Victor 447-0634		**(Marie's The Name) His Latest Flame / Little Sister**	1962	2.40	12.00
RCA Victor 447-0635		**Can't Help Falling In Love / Rock-A-Hula Baby**	1962	2.00	10.00
RCA Victor 447-0636		**Good Luck Charm / Anything That's Part Of You**	1962	2.40	12.00
RCA Victor 447-0637		**She's Not You / Just Tell Her Jim Said Hello**	1963	2.40	12.00
RCA Victor 447-0638		**Return To Sender / Where Do You Come From?**	1963	2.40	12.00
RCA Victor 447-0639	(DJ)	**Kiss Me Quick / Suspicion**	1964	6.00	30.00
RCA Victor 447-0639		**Kiss Me Quick / Suspicion**	1964	2.00	10.00
RCA Victor 447-0639	(PS)	**Kiss Me Quick / Suspicion**	1964	7.00	35.00

Label & Catalog #		A-Side/B-Side	Year	VG	NM
RCA Victor 447-0640		One Broken Heart For Sale /			
		They Remind Me Too Much Of You	1964	4.00	20.00
RCA Victor 447-0641		(You're The) Devil In Disguise /			
		Please Don't Drag That String Around	1964	4.00	20.00
RCA Victor 447-0642		Bossa Nova Baby / Witchcraft	1964	4.00	20.00
RCA Victor 447-0644		Kissin' Cousins / It Hurts Me	1964	5.00	25.00
RCA Victor 447-0645		Such A Night / Never Ending	1964	5.00	25.00
RCA Victor 447-0646		Viva Las Vegas / What'd I Say	1964	5.00	25.00
RCA Victor 447-0720	(DJ)	Blue Christmas / Wooden Heart	1964	10.00	50.00
RCA Victor 447-0720		Blue Christmas / Wooden Heart	1964	3.00	15.00
RCA Victor 447-0720	(PS)	Blue Christmas / Wooden Heart	1964	10.00	50.00

—1964: In conjunction with RCA's "Elvis Summer Special," five titles were reissued on promotional white labels and sent out to radio stations with a picture sleeve. These sleeves were also sent out with commercial copies of the single.—

RCA Victor 447-0601	(DJ)	That's All Right / Blue Moon Of Kentucky	1964	15.00	75.00
RCA Victor 447-0601	(PS)	That's All Right / Blue Moon Of Kentucky	1964	35.00	175.00
RCA Victor 447-0602	(DJ)	Good Rockin' Tonight / I Don't Care If The Sun Don't Shine	1964	15.00	75.00
RCA Victor 447-0602	(PS)	Good Rockin' Tonight / I Don't Care If The Sun Don't Shine	1964	35.00	175.00
RCA Victor 447-0605	(DJ)	Heartbreak Hotel / I Was The One	1964	15.00	75.00
RCA Victor 447-0605	(PS)	Heartbreak Hotel / I Was The One	1964	35.00	175.00
RCA Victor 447-0607	(DJ)	Hound Dog / Don't Be Cruel	1964	15.00	75.00
RCA Victor 447-0607	(PS)	Hound Dog / Don't Be Cruel	1964	35.00	175.00
RCA Victor 447-0618	(DJ)	All Shook Up / That's When Your Heartaches Begin	1964	15.00	75.00
RCA Victor 447-0618	(PS)	All Shook Up / That's When Your Heartaches Begin	1964	35.00	175.00

—1965-1969: Black label with Nipper on the left. With the exception of 447-0720, all of the Gold Standards were repressed on this second black label, although many were out of print shortly thereafter. These pressings—not listed below—are worth approximately $8-12 each—

RCA Victor 447-0643	(DJ)	Crying In The Chapel / I Believe In The Man In The Sky	1965	8.00	40.00
RCA Victor 447-0643		Crying In The Chapel / I Believe In The Man In The Sky	1965	1.60	8.00
RCA Victor 447-0643	(PS)	Crying In The Chapel / I Believe In The Man In The Sky	1965	6.00	15.00
RCA Victor 447-0647	(DJ)	Blue Christmas / Santa Claus Is Back In Town	1965	8.00	40.00
RCA Victor 447-0647		Blue Christmas / Santa Claus Is Back In Town	1965	2.40	12.00
RCA Victor 447-0647	(PS)	Blue Christmas / Santa Claus Is Back In Town	1965	8.00	40.00
RCA Victor 447-0648		Do The Clam / You'll Be Gone	1965	2.00	10.00
RCA Victor 447-0649		Ain't That Loving You, Baby / Ask Me	1965	1.60	8.00
RCA Victor 447-0650	(DJ)	Puppet On A String / Wooden Heart	1965	6.00	30.00
RCA Victor 447-0650		Puppet On A String / Wooden Heart	1965	2.00	10.00
RCA Victor 447-0650	(PS)	Puppet On A String / Wooden Heart	1965	5.00	25.00
RCA Victor 447-0651	(DJ)	Joshua Fit The Battle / Known Only To Him	1966	10.00	50.00
RCA Victor 447-0651		Joshua Fit The Battle / Known Only To Him	1966	4.00	20.00
RCA Victor 447-0651	(PS)	Joshua Fit The Battle / Known Only To Him	1966	30.00	150.00
RCA Victor 447-0652	(DJ)	Milky White Way / Swing Down Sweet Chariot	1966	10.00	50.00
RCA Victor 447-0652		Milky White Way / Swing Down Sweet Chariot	1966	4.00	20.00
RCA Victor 447-0652	(PS)	Milky White Way / Swing Down Sweet Chariot	1966	20.00	100.00
RCA Victor 447-0653		(It's Such An) Easy Question / It Feels So Right	1966	2.00	10.00
RCA Victor 447-0654		I'm Your's / (It's A) Long Lonely Highway	1966	1.60	8.00
RCA Victor 447-0655		Tell Me Why / Blue River	1968	1.60	8.00
RCA Victor 447-0656		Frankie And Johnny / Please Don't Stop Loving Me	1968	1.60	8.00
RCA Victor 447-0657		Love Letters / Come What May	1968	1.60	8.00
RCA Victor 447-0658		Spinout / All That I Am	1968	1.60	8.00

—1970-1975: Many of the Gold Standards were repressed on a new red label. These pressings—not listed below—are worth approximately $6-10 each.—

RCA Victor 447-0659		Indescribably Blue / Fools Fall In Love	1970	2.00	10.00
RCA Victor 447-0660		Long Legged Girl / That's Someone You Never Forget	1970	5.00	25.00
RCA Victor 447-0661		There's Always Me / Judy	1970	3.00	15.00
RCA Victor 447-0662		Big Boss Man / You Don't Know Me	1970	1.60	8.00
RCA Victor 447-0663		Guitar Man / High Heel Sneakers	1970	1.00	5.00
RCA Victor 447-0664		Stay Away / U.S. Male	1970	1.60	8.00
RCA Victor 447-0666		Let Yourself Go / Your Time Hasn't Come Yet, Baby	1970	2.00	10.00
RCA Victor 447-0665		We Call On Him / You'll Never Walk Alone	1970	4.00	20.00
RCA Victor 447-0667		A Little Less Conversation / Almost In Love	1970	1.60	8.00
RCA Victor 447-0668		If I Can Dream / Edge Of Reality	1970	1.60	8.00
RCA Victor 447-0669		Memories / Charro	1970	1.00	5.00
RCA Victor 447-0671		In The Ghetto / Any Day Now	1970	1.00	5.00
RCA Victor 447-0672		Clean Up Your Own Backyard / The Fair's Moving On	1970	1.00	5.00
RCA Victor 447-0670		How Great Thou Art / His Hand In Mine	1970	4.00	20.00
RCA Victor 447-0673		Suspicious Minds / You'll Think Of Me	1970	.80	4.00
RCA Victor 447-0674		Don't Cry, Daddy / Rubberneckin'	1970	1.00	5.00
RCA Victor 447-0675		Kentucky Rain / My Little Friend	1971	1.00	5.00
RCA Victor 447-0676		The Wonder Of You / Mama Liked The Roses	1971	1.00	5.00
RCA Victor 447-0677		I've Lost You / The Next Step Is Love	1971	1.00	5.00
RCA Victor 447-0678		You Don't Have To Say You Love Me / Patch It Up	1972	1.00	5.00
RCA Victor 447-0679		I Really Don't Want To Know / There Goes My Everything	1972	.80	4.00
RCA Victor 447-0680		Where Did They Go, Lord? / Rags To Riches	1972	1.60	8.00
RCA Victor 447-0681		If Every Day Was Like Christmas / How Would You Like To Be	1972	1.60	8.00
RCA Victor 447-0682		Life / Only Believe	1972	1.60	8.00

Label & Catalog #		A-Side/B-Side	Year	VG	NM
RCA Victor 447-0683		I'm Leavin' / Heart Of Rome	1972	.80	4.00
RCA Victor 447-0684		It's Only Love / The Sound Of Your Cry	1972	1.25	6.00
RCA Victor 447-0685		An American Trilogy / The First Time Ever I Saw Your Face	1973	1.00	5.00

—Extended Play Albums—

From 1956 through 1964, Elvis' EPs appeared on black labels with Nipper on top. Some copies (EPA 747-4054) with the horizontal silver line were also issued completely lacking the Nipper logo on top; these are worth approximately $200 each. Several titles were pressed on RCA's classical maroon label in 1960; these are quite rare and regularly undervalued.

With few exceptions, from 1965 through 1968, the EPs were reissued on a black label with Nipper on the left. In 1969, almost all of the previous titles were repressed with an orange label. One can only guess as to why these were pressed up in 1969, when there was virtually no market for EPs in the U.S. The reissues on both the black label with Nipper on the left and the orange labels are considerably rarer—and slightly more valuable than the originals to completists.

Label & Catalog #		A-Side/B-Side	Year	VG	NM
RCA Victor EPA-747	(PS)	Elvis Presley	1956	330.00	1,000.00
		(White paper sleeve reads "Blue Suede Shoes By Elvis Presley.")			
RCA Victor EPA-747		Elvis Presley	1956	20.00	100.00
RCA Victor EPA-747		Elvis Presley (Line label)	1956	25.00	125.00
RCA Victor EPB-1254		Elvis Presley	1956	50.00	250.00
RCA Victor EPB-1254		Elvis Presley (Line label)	1956	75.00	300.00
RCA Victor EPA-821		Heartbreak Hotel	1956	15.00	75.00
RCA Victor EPA-821		Heartbreak Hotel (Line label)	1956	18.00	90.00
RCA Victor EPA-830		Elvis Presley	1956	15.00	75.00
RCA Victor EPA-830		Elvis Presley (Line label)	1956	18.00	90.00
RCA Victor EPA-940		The Real Elvis	1956	15.00	75.00
RCA Victor EPA-940		The Real Elvis (Line label)	1956	20.00	100.00
RCA Victor EPA-965		Any Way You Want Me	1956	15.00	75.00
RCA Victor EPA-965		Any Way You Want Me (Line label)	1956	18.00	90.00
RCA Victor EPA-4006		Love Me Tender	1956	5.00	25.00
RCA Victor EPA-4006		Love Me Tender (Line label)	1956	7.00	35.00
RCA Victor EPA-992		Elvis (Volume 1)	1956	5.00	25.00
RCA Victor EPA-992		Elvis (Volume 1) (Line label)	1956	6.00	30.00
RCA Victor EPA-993		Elvis (Volume 2)	1956	7.00	35.00
RCA Victor EPA-993		Elvis (Volume 2) (Line label)	1956	10.00	50.00
RCA Victor EPA-994		Strictly Elvis (Elvis, Volume 3)	1956	10.00	50.00
RCA Victor EPA-994		Strictly Elvis (Elvis, Volume 3) (Line label)	1956	15.00	75.00
RCA Victor EPA-1515		Loving You, Volume 1	1957	10.00	50.00
RCA Victor EPA-1515		Loving You, Volume 1 (Line label)	1957	12.00	60.00
RCA Victor EPA-1515		Loving You, Volume 2	1957	10.00	50.00
RCA Victor EPA-1515		Loving You, Volume 2 (Line label)	1957	12.00	60.00
RCA Victor EPA-4041		Just For You	1957	12.00	60.00
RCA Victor EPA-4041		Just For You (Line label)	1957	15.00	75.00
RCA Victor EPA-4054		Peace In The Valley	1957	8.00	40.00
RCA Victor EPA-4054		Peace In The Valley (Line label)	1957	10.00	50.00
RCA Victor EPA-4108		Elvis Sings Christmas Songs	1957	6.00	30.00
RCA Victor EPA-4114		Jailhouse Rock	1957	6.00	30.00
RCA Victor EPA-4319		King Creole (Volume 1)	1958	10.00	50.00
RCA Victor EPA-4321		King Creole, Volume 2	1958	10.00	50.00
RCA Victor EPA-4325		Elvis Sails	1958	25.00	125.00
RCA Victor EPA-4340		Christmas With Elvis	1958	30.00	150.00
RCA Victor EPA-5088		A Touch Of Gold, Volume 1	1959	18.00	90.00
RCA Victor EPA-5088		A Touch Of Gold, Volume 1 (Maroon label)	1960	75.00	300.00
RCA Victor EPA-5101		A Touch Of Gold, Volume 2	1959	25.00	125.00
RCA Victor EPA-5101		A Touch Of Gold, Volume 2 (Maroon label)	1960	100.00	400.00
RCA Victor EPA-5120		The Real Elvis	1959	15.00	75.00
RCA Victor EPA-5120		The Real Elvis (Maroon label)	1960	100.00	400.00
RCA Victor EPA-5121		Peace In The Valley	1959	10.00	50.00
RCA Victor EPA-5121		Peace In The Valley (Maroon label)	1960	100.00	400.00
RCA Victor EPA-5122		King Creole (Volume 1)	1959	10.00	50.00
RCA Victor EPA-5122		King Creole (Volume 1) (Maroon label)	1960	100.00	400.00
RCA Victor EPA-5141		A Touch Of Gold, Volume 3	1960	25.00	125.00
RCA Victor EPA-5141		A Touch Of Gold, Volume 3 (Maroon label)	1960	100.00	400.00
RCA Victor LPC-128		Elvis By Request (Flaming Star)	1961	15.00	75.00
RCA Victor EPA-4368		Follow That Dream	1962	6.00	30.00
RCA Victor EPA-4371		Kid Galahad	1962	5.00	25.00
RCA Victor EPA-4382		Viva Las Vegas	1964	8.00	40.00
RCA Victor EPA-5157		Elvis Sails	1964	12.00	60.00
RCA Victor EPA-4383		Tickle Me	1965	8.00	40.00
RCA Victor EPA-4387		Easy Come, Easy Go	1969	10.00	50.00

—Special/Promotional Releases—

Label & Catalog #		A-Side/B-Side	Year	VG	NM
RCA Victor EPB-1254		Elvis Presley	1956	——	——
		(Black label EP issued in a green paper sleeve that reads "the most talked about new personality in the last ten years of recorded music." Rare. Estimated near mint value $2,000-3,000.)			
RCA Victor SPD-22		Elvis Presley	1956	——	——
		(Double-EP. Rare. Estimated near mint value $500-750.)			

Label & Catalog #		A-Side/B-Side	Year	VG	NM
RCA Victor SPD-23		**Elvis Presley**	1956	—	—
		(Triple-EP. Rare. Estimated near mint value $3,000-5,000.)			
RCA Victor DJ-7		**Elvis Presley / Jean Chapel**	1956	50.00	250.00
RCA Victor 8705		**TV Guide Presents Elvis Presley** *(Blue label)*	1956	—	—
		(Triple-EP. Rare. Estimated near mint value $900-1,200.)			
RCA Victor 8705		**TV Guide Presents Elvis Presley** *(White label)*	1956	—	—
		(Rare. Estimated near mint value $1,200-1,500.)			
RCA Victor SPA-7-37		**Perfect For Parties**	1956	35.00	175.00
		(Promotional black label with a horizontal silver line.)			
RCA Victor SPA-7-37		**Perfect For Parties**	1956	50.00	250.00
		(Promotional black label without the horizontal silver line.)			
RCA Victor EPA-992		**Elvis (Volume 1) / Jaye P. Morgan**	1956	—	—
		(Double-EP contains one Elvis record and one by Ms. Morgan.			
		Rare. Estimated near mint value $2,000-3,000.)			
RCA Victor DJ-56		**Elvis Presley / Dinah Shore**	1957	50.00	250.00

PRESTON, BILLY
Billy Preston also recorded with The Beatles.

Label & Catalog #		A-Side/B-Side	Year	VG	NM
Apple 1808	(DJ)	**That's The Way God Planned It /**			
		That's The Way God Planned It	1969	10.00	50.00
Apple 1808		**That's The Way God Planned It / What About You**	1969	2.00	10.00
Apple 1808	(PS)	**That's The Way God Planned It / What About You**	1969	4.00	20.00
Americom 433		**That's The Way God Planned It / What About You**	1969	125.00	500.00
		(4" flexidisc)			
Apple 1814		**Everything's All Right / I Want To Thank You**	1969	2.00	10.00
Apple 1817		**All That I've Got / As I Get Older**	1970	2.00	10.00
Apple 1817	(PS)	**All That I've Got / As I Get Older**	1970	2.50	12.00
Apple 1826		**My Sweet Lord / Little Girl**	1970	2.00	10.00

PRESTON, JOHNNY

Label & Catalog #		A-Side/B-Side	Year	VG	NM
Mercury 71474		**Running Bear / My Heart Knows**	1959	3.00	15.00
Mercury 71528		**Cradle Of Love / City Of Tears**	1960	2.00	10.00
Mercury 10027	(S)	**Cradle Of Love / City Of Tears**	1960	4.00	20.00
Mercury 71651		**Feel So Fine / I'm Starting To Go Steady**	1960	2.00	10.00
Mercury 71691		**Up In The Air / Charming Billy**	1960	2.00	10.00
Mercury 71728		**(I Want A) Rock And Roll Guitar / New Baby For Christmas**	1960	2.00	10.00
Mercury 71761		**Leave My Kitten Alone / Token Of Love**	1961	2.00	10.00
Mercury 71803		**I Feel Good / Willy Walk**	1961	2.00	10.00
Mercury 71865		**She Once Belonged To Me / Let Them Talk**	1961	2.00	10.00
Mercury 71903		**Free Me / Kissin' Tree**	1961	2.00	10.00
Mercury 71903	(PS)	**Free Me / Kissin' Tree**	1961	3.00	15.00
Mercury 71951		**Broken Hearts Anonymous / Let's Leave It That Way**	1962	2.00	10.00
Mercury 72049		**Big Boss Man / The Day After Forever**	1962	2.00	10.00
Imperial 5924		**This Little Bitty Bear / The Day The World Stood Still**	1963	2.00	10.00
Hallway 1201		**All Around The World / Just Plain Hurt**	1964	2.00	10.00
Hallway 1204		**Willie And The Hand Jive / I've Got My Eyes On You**	1965	2.00	10.00
TCF Hall 101		**Running Bear '65 / Dedicated To The One I Love**	1965	1.20	6.00
TCF Hall 120		**Good, Good Lovin' / I'm Asking Forgiveness**	1965	1.20	6.00
ABC 11085		**There's Only One Like You / I'm Only Human**	1968	1.00	5.00
ABC 11187		**I've Just Been Wastin' My Time / Kick The Can**	1968	1.00	5.00
		— Extended Play Albums —			
Mercury 3397		**Running Bear**	1959	30.00	150.00

PRESTON, MIKE

Label & Catalog #	A-Side/B-Side	Year	VG	NM
London 1834	**A House, A Car And A Wedding Ring / My Lucky Love**	1958	3.00	15.00

PRETENDERS, THE

Label & Catalog #	A-Side/B-Side	Year	VG	NM
Power-Martin 1001	**Smile / I'm So Happy** *(Black label)*	1961	15.00	75.00
Power-Martin 1001	**Smile / I'm So Happy**	197?	1.00	5.00
Power-Martin 1005	**Could This Be Magic?** / *(B-side by The Earls)*	1976	.80	4.00
Power-Martin 1006/7	**A Very Precious Love / Could This Be Magic?**	197?	1.00	5.00

PRETTY THINGS, THE

Label & Catalog #	A-Side/B-Side	Year	VG	NM
Fontana 1916	**Rosalyn / Big Boss Man**	1964	2.00	10.00
Fontana 1941	**Don't Bring Me Down / We'll Be Together**	1964	2.00	10.00
Fontana 1508	**Honey, I Need / I Can Never Say**	1965	2.00	10.00
Fontana 1518	**Cry To Me / I Can Never Say**	1965	2.00	10.00
Fontana 1518	**Judgement Day / Cry To Me**	1965	2.00	10.00
Fontana 1540	**Midnight To Six Man / Can't Stand The Pain**	1965	2.00	10.00
Fontana 1550	**Progress / Come See Me**	1966	2.00	10.00
Fontana 1550	**Judgement Day / Come See Me**	1966	2.00	10.00
Laurie 3458	**Talkin' About The Good Times / Walking Thru My Dreams**	1968	4.00	20.00
Rare Earth 5005	**Private Sorrow / Balloon Burning**	1968	3.00	15.00
Swan Song 70104	**Joey / Come Home, Momma**	1975	1.00	5.00
Swan Song 70107	**Isn't It Rock 'N' Roll? / Remember That Boy**	1975	1.00	5.00

Label & Catalog #		A-Side/B-Side	Year	VG	NM
PRICE, ALAN					
Refer to The Animals; Fame & Price.					
Parrot 3001		I Put A Spell On You / Lechy-Da	1966	1.00	5.00
Parrot 3007		Hi-Lili, Hi-Lo / Take Me Home	1966	1.00	5.00
Parrot 3008		Willow Weep For Me / Yours Until Tomorrow	1966	.80	4.00
Parrot 3009		Simon Smith / Tickle Me	1966	.80	4.00
Parrot 30-013		The House That Jack Built / Who Cares?	1966	.80	4.00
Parrot 300-14		Shame / Don't Do That Again	1966	.80	4.00
Parrot 3019		Not Born To Follow / To Ramona	1966	1.00	5.00
Cotillion 44044		Falling In Love / Sly Sadie	1969	.60	3.00
Warner Bros. 7717		O Lucky Man / Poor People	1972	.80	4.00
Abkco 4025		House Of The Rising Sun / Bring It On Home To Me	1973	.80	4.00
Abkco 4026		We've Gotta Get Out Of This Place / It's My Life	1973	.80	4.00
Jet 1119		I Wanna Dance / Just For You	1977	.60	3.00
Jet 1119	(PS)	I Wanna Dance / Just For You	1977	.60	3.00
Jet 5056		This Is Your Lucky Day (The Girl Won't Get Under) /			
		Mama, Don't Go Home	1979	.60	3.00
Epic 04319		I Don't Feel No Pain /	1982	.40	2.00
PRICE, LEO, & HIS BAND					
Up-Down 712		Quick Down / Hey Now, Baby	195?	7.00	35.00
PRICE, RONNIE, & THE VELVETS					
Carousel 1001		White Bucks / Look At Me	195?	4.00	20.00
PRIDE & JOY					
Acta 817		That's The Way It Is / We Got A Long Way To Go	1967	3.00	15.00
Dunwich 152		Girl / If You're Ready	1967	3.00	15.00
PRIMITIVES, THE					
The Primitives feature Lou Reed.					
Pickwick 1001		The Ostrich / Sneaky Pete	1964	40.00	200.00
PRINCE					
Warner Bros. 8619	(DJ)	Soft And Wet / Soft And Wet	1978	3.00	15.00
Warner Bros. 8619		Soft And Wet / So Blue	1978	6.00	30.00
Warner Bros. 8713	(DJ)	Just As Long As We're Together /			
		Just As Long As We're Together	1978	3.00	15.00
Warner Bros. 8713		Just As Long As We're Together / In Love	1978	6.00	30.00
Warner Bros. 49050	(DJ)	I Wanna Be Your Lover / I Wanna Be Your Lover	1979	3.00	15.00
Warner Bros. 49050		I Wanna Be Your Lover / My Love Is Forever	1979	6.00	30.00
Warner Bros. 49178	(DJ)	Why You Wanna Treat Me So Bad? /			
		Why You Wanna Treat Me So Bad?	1980	3.00	15.00
Warner Bros. 49178		Why You Wanna Treat Me So Bad? / Baby	1980	5.00	25.00
Warner Bros. 49178	(PS)	Why You Wanna Treat Me So Bad? / Baby	1980	10.00	50.00
Warner Bros. 49226	(DJ)	Still Waiting / Still Waiting	1980	3.00	15.00
Warner Bros. 49226		Still Waiting / Bambi	1980	5.00	25.00
Warner Bros. 49559	(DJ)	Uptown / Uptown	1980	2.00	10.00
Warner Bros. 49559		Uptown / Crazy You	1980	3.00	15.00
Warner Bros. 49559	(PS)	Uptown / Crazy You	1980	3.00	15.00
Warner Bros. 49638	(DJ)	Dirty Mind / Dirty Mind	1980	2.00	10.00
Warner Bros. 49638		Dirty Mind / When We're Dancing Close & Slow	1980	4.00	20.00
Warner Bros. 49808	(DJ)	Controversy / Controversy	1981	2.00	10.00
Warner Bros. 49808		Controversy / When You Were Mine	1981	3.00	15.00
Warner Bros. 50002	(DJ)	Let's Work / Let's Work	1982	2.00	10.00
Warner Bros. 50002		Let's Work / Ronnie Talk To Russia	1982	4.00	20.00
Warner Bros. 29942	(DJ)	Do Me, Baby / Do Me, Baby	1982	2.00	10.00
Warner Bros. 29942		Do Me, Baby / Private Joy	1982	3.00	15.00
Warner Bros. 29883	(DJ)	1999 / 1999	1982	1.00	5.00
Warner Bros. 29883		1999 / How Come U Don't Call Me Anymore?	1982	1.00	5.00
Warner Bros. 29883	(PS)	1999 / How Come U Don't Call Me Anymore?	1982	2.00	10.00
Warner Bros. 29746		Little Red Corvette / All The Critics Love U In New York	1983	.80	4.00
Warner Bros. 29746	(PS)	Little Red Corvette / All The Critics Love U In New York	1983	.80	4.00
Warner Bros. 20129		Little Red Corvette / 1999 (Picture disc)	1983	3.00	15.00
Warner Bros. 29503		Delirious / Horny Toad	1983	2.00	10.00
Warner Bros. 29503	(PS)	Delirious / Horny Toad	1983	3.00	15.00
Warner Bros. 29548		Let's Pretend We're Married / Irresistible Bitch	1983	.80	4.00
Warner Bros. 29548	(PS)	Let's Pretend We're Married / Irresistible Bitch	1983	.80	4.00
Warner Bros. 29286		When Doves Cry / 17 Days (Purple vinyl)	1984	2.00	10.00
Warner Bros. 29286		When Doves Cry / 17 Days	1984	.60	3.00
Warner Bros. 29286	(PS)	When Doves Cry / 17 Days	1984	.60	3.00
Warner Bros. 29216		Let's Go Crazy / Erotic City	1984	.60	3.00
Warner Bros. 29216	(PS)	Let's Go Crazy / Erotic City	1984	.60	3.00
Warner Bros. 29174		Purple Rain / God (Purple vinyl)	1984	.60	3.00
Warner Bros. 29174		Purple Rain / God	1984	2.00	10.00
Warner Bros. 29174	(PS)	Purple Rain / God	1984	.60	3.00
Warner Bros. 29121		I Would Die 4 U / Another Lonely Christmas	1984	.60	3.00
Warner Bros. 29121	(PS)	I Would Die 4 U / Another Lonely Christmas	1984	.60	3.00

Label & Catalog #		A-Side/B-Side	Year	VG	NM
Warner Bros. 29079		Take Me With U / Baby, I'm A Star	1985	.60	3.00
Warner Bros. 29079	(PS)	Take Me With U / Baby, I'm A Star	1985	3.00	15.00
Warner Bros. 29052		Paisley Park / She's Always In My Hair	1985	Unreleased	
Warner Bros. 29052	(PS)	Paisley Park / She's Always In My Hair	1985	40.00	200.00
Warner Bros. 28972		Raspberry Beret / She's Always In My Hair	1985	.60	3.00
Warner Bros. 28972	(PS)	Raspberry Beret / She's Always In My Hair	1985	.60	3.00
Warner Bros. 28998		Pop Life / Hello	1985	.60	3.00
Warner Bros. 28998	(PS)	Pop Life / Hello	1985	.60	3.00
Warner Bros. 28999		America / Girl	1985	.60	3.00
Warner Bros. 28999	(PS)	America / Girl	1985	.60	3.00
Warner Bros. 28751		Kiss / Love Or Money	1986	.60	3.00
Warner Bros. 28751	(PS)	Kiss / Love Or Money	1986	.60	3.00
Warner Bros. 28711		Mountains / Alexis de Paris	1986	.60	3.00
Warner Bros. 28711	(PS)	Mountains / Alexis de Paris	1986	.60	3.00
Warner Bros. 28620		Anotherloverholenyohead / Girls And Boys	1986	.60	3.00
Warner Bros. 28620	(PS)	Anotherloverholenyohead / Girls And Boys	1986	.60	3.00
Warner Bros. 28399		Sign 'O The Times / La La La He Hee Hee	1987	.60	3.00
Warner Bros. 28399	(PS)	Sign 'O The Times / La La La He Hee Hee	1987	.60	3.00
Warner Bros. 28334		If I Was Your Girlfriend / Shockadelica	1987	.60	3.00
Warner Bros. 28334	(PS)	If I Was Your Girlfriend / Shockadelica	1987	.60	3.00
Warner Bros. 28289		U Got The Look / Housequake	1987	.60	3.00
Warner Bros. 28289	(PS)	U Got The Look / Housequake	1987	.60	3.00
Warner Bros. 28288		I Could Never Take The Place Of Your Man / Hot Thing	1987	.60	3.00
Warner Bros. 28288	(PS)	I Could Never Take The Place Of Your Man / Hot Thing	1987	.60	3.00
Warner Bros. 27900		Alphabet St. / Alphabet St.	1988	.60	3.00
Warner Bros. 27900	(PS)	Alphabet St. / Alphabet St.	1988	.60	3.00
Warner Bros. 27806		Glam Slam / Escape	1988	.60	3.00
Warner Bros. 27806	(PS)	Glam Slam / Escape	1988	.60	3.00
Warner Bros. 27745		I Wish You Heaven / Scarlett Pussy	1988	.60	3.00
Warner Bros. 27745	(PS)	I Wish You Heaven / Scarlett Pussy	1988	.60	3.00
Warner Bros. 22924		Batdance / 200 Balloons	1989	.60	3.00
Warner Bros. 22924	(PS)	Batdance / 200 Balloons	1989	.60	3.00
Warner Bros. 22814		Party Man / Feel You Up	1989	.60	3.00
Warner Bros. 22814	(PS)	Party Man / Feel You Up	1989	.60	3.00
Warner Bros. 22757		Arms Of Orion / I Love U In Me	1989	.60	3.00
Warner Bros. 22757	(PS)	Arms Of Orion / I Love U In Me	1989	.60	3.00
Warner Bros. 22824		Scandalous / When 2 R In Love	1989	.60	3.00
Warner Bros. 19751		Thieves In The Temple / Thieves In The Temple, Part 2	1990	.40	2.00
Warner Bros. 19525		New Power Generation / New Power Generation, Part 2	1990	.40	2.00
Warner Bros. 19225		Gett Off / Horny Pony	1991	.40	2.00
Warner Bros. 19175		Cream / Horny Pony	1991	.40	2.00
Warner Bros. 19090		Insatiable / I Love You In Me	1991	.40	2.00
Warner Bros. 19083		Diamonds & Pearls / Excerpts From Diamonds & Pearls	1991	.40	2.00
Warner Bros. 19020		Money Don't Matter 2 Night / Call The Law	1992	.40	2.00
		— 12" Singles—			
Warner Bros. 50028		Let's Work / Gotta Stop (Messin' Around) (PC)	1982	15.00	75.00
Warner Bros. 20120		Little Red Corvette / 1999 (PC)	1983	1.00	5.00
Warner Bros. 20170		Let's Pretend We're Married / Irresistible Bitch (PC)	1983	1.00	5.00
Warner Bros. 20228		When Doves Cry / 17 Days (PC)	1984	1.00	5.00
Warner Bros. 20246		Let's Go Crazy / Erotic City (PC)	1984	1.00	5.00
Warner Bros. 20267		Purple Rain / God (Purple vinyl with PC)	1984	1.00	15.00
Warner Bros. 20267		Purple Rain / God (Black vinyl with PC)	1984	1.00	5.00
Warner Bros. 20291		I Would Die 4 U / Another Lonely Christmas (PC)	1984	1.00	15.00
		(First pressings do not have a UPC bar code printed on the picture cover.)			
Warner Bros. 20291		I Would Die 4 U / Another Lonely Christmas (PC)	1984	.60	3.00
Warner Bros. 20355		Raspberry Beret / She's Always In My Hair (PC)	1985	.60	3.00
Warner Bros. 20357		Pop Life / Hello (PC)	1985	.60	3.00
Warner Bros. 20389		America / Girl (PC)	1985	.60	3.00
Warner Bros. 20442		Kiss / Love Or Money (PC)	1986	.60	3.00
Warner Bros. 20465		Mountains / Alexa de Paris (PC)	1986	.60	3.00
Warner Bros. 20466		Anotherloverholenyohead / Girls And Boys (PC)	1986	.60	3.00
Warner Bros. 20648		Sign 'O The Times / La La La He Hee Hee (PC)	1987	.60	3.00
Warner Bros. 20697		If I Was Your Girlfriend / Shockadelica (PC)	1987	.60	3.00
Warner Bros. 20727		U Got The Look / Housequake (PC)	1987	.60	3.00
Warner Bros. 20728		I Could Never Take The Place Of Your Man / Hot Thing (PC)	1987	.60	3.00
Warner Bros. 20930		Alphabet St. / This Is Not Music This Is A Trip	1988	.60	3.00
Warner Bros. 21005		Glam Slam / Escape (Free Yo Mind From This Rat Race)	1988	.60	3.00
Warner Bros. 21074		I Wish You Heaven / Scarlett Pussy (PC)	1988	.60	3.00
Warner Bros. 21257		Batdance / 200 Balloons (PC)	1989	.60	3.00
Warner Bros. 21370		Party Man / Feel You Up (PC)	1989	.60	3.00
Warner Bros. 21422		Scandalous Sex Suite / When 2 R In Love (PC)	1989	.60	3.00
Warner Bros. 21598		Theives In The Temple (3 versions) (PC)	1990	.60	3.00
Warner Bros. 21783		New Power Generation (Funky Weapon Remix)	1990	.60	3.00
Warner Bros. 40138		Get Off (3 versions) / Violet The Organ Grinder / Gangster Glam / Clockin' The Jizz (PC)	1991	.60	3.00
Warner Bros. 40197		Cream (2 versions) / +7 (PC)	1991	.60	3.00
Warner Bros. 40220		Money Doesn't Matter 2 Night (2 versions) / +10 (PC)	1992	.60	3.00

Prince is the single most collectible artist of the past two decades, easily blowing the two former contenders, Messrs. Bowie and Springsteen, outta the running. Many of his truly rare pieces have skyrocketed in value (given their age) and will remain reliable investments for as long as the man remains an active force in pop music.

Label & Catalog #	A-Side/B-Side	Year	VG	NM
	—Promotional 12" Singles—			
Warner Bros. PRO-A-741	**Soft & Wet / Just As Long As We're Together**	1978	20.00	100.00
Warner Bros. PRO-A-832	**I Wanna Be Your Lover** (2 versions. TC)	1970	20.00	100.00
Warner Bros. PRO-A-848	**Why You Wanna Treat Me So Bad / Bambi**	1979	20.00	100.00
Warner Bros. PRO-A-870	**Still Waiting / Why You Wanna Treat Me So Bad / Sexy Dancer**	1979	12.00	60.00
Warner Bros. PRO-A-904	**Uptown** (2 versions)	1980	12.00	60.00
Warner Bros. PRO-A-915	**Head / Sister / Party Up** (One sided)	1980	12.00	60.00
Warner Bros. PRO-A-916	**When You Were Mine / Gotta Broken Heart Again / Uptown**	1980	12.00	60.00
Warner Bros. PRO-A-929	**Dirty Mind** (2 versions)	1980	12.00	60.00
Warner Bros. PRO-A-937	**Gotta Stop Messin' About / Party Up / When You Were Mine / Uptown**	1981	12.00	60.00
Warner Bros. PRO-A-938	**Gotta Stop Messin' About / Party Up / When You Were Mine**	1981	25.00	125.00
Warner Bros. PRO-A-980	**Controversy** (2 versions (TC)	1981	12.00	60.00
Warner Bros. PRO-A-1004	**Let's Work** (2 versions. TC)	1981	12.00	60.00
Warner Bros. PRO-A-1035	**Do Me Baby / Private Joy** (TC)	1981	12.00	60.00
Warner Bros. PRO-A-1070	**1999** (2 versions. TC)	1982	5.00	25.00
Warner Bros. PRO-A-1082	**Let's Pretend We're Married / D.M.S.R. / Automatic** (TC)	1982	6.00	30.00
Warner Bros. PRO-A-2001	**Little Red Corvette** (2 versions (TC)	1982	5.00	25.00
Warner Bros. PRO-A-2042	**1999 / Free / Automatic** (TC)	1982	5.00	25.00
Warner Bros. PRO-A-2080	**Delirious** (2 versions. TC)	1982	4.00	20.00
Warner Bros. PRO-A-2139	**When Doves Cry** (2 versions. PC)	1984	4.00	20.00
Warner Bros. PRO-A-2173	**Let's Go Crazy** (2 versions. TC)	1984	4.00	20.00
Warner Bros. PRO-A-2182	**Let's Go Crazy** (2 versions. TC)	1984	4.00	20.00
Warner Bros. PRO-A-2233	**I Would Die For You** (2 versions. TC)	1984	3.00	15.00
Warner Bros. PRO-A-2263	**Take Me With You** (2 versions. TC)	1984	3.00	15.00
Warner Bros. PRO-A-2192	**Purple Rain** (2 versions. Purple vinyl. TC)	1984	6.00	30.00
Warner Bros. PRO-A-2313	**Raspberry Beret** (2 versions. TC)	1985	1.60	8.00
Warner Bros. PRO-A-2331	**Pop Life** (2 versions. TC)	1985	1.60	8.00
Warner Bros. PRO-A-2300	**America** ((2 versions. TC)	1985	1.60	8.00
Warner Bros. PRO-A-2476	**Mountains** (2 versions)	1986	1.60	8.00
Warner Bros. PRO-A-2448	**Kiss** (Edited version) / **Kiss** (Edited version)	1986	1.00	5.00
Warner Bros. PRO-A-2458	**Kiss** (Extended version) / **Kiss** (Extended version)	1986	1.60	8.00
Warner Bros. PRO-A-2687	**Sign Of The Times** (2 versions)	1987	1.60	8.00
Warner Bros. PRO-A-2758	**If I Was Your Girlfriend** (2 versions)	1987	1.60	8.00
Warner Bros. PRO-A-2771	**You Got The Look** (2 versions)	1987	1.60	8.00
Warner Bros. PRO-A-2770	**I Could Never Take The Place Of Your Man** (2 versions)	1987	1.60	8.00
Warner Bros. PRO-A-2927	**Hot Thing** (2 versions)	1987	1.60	8.00
Warner Bros. PRO-A-3283	**I Wish You Heaven** (2 versions)	1988	1.00	5.00
Warner Bros. PRO-A-3702	**Batdance** (4 versions)	1989	1.60	8.00
Warner Bros. PRO-A-3705	**Party Man** (2 versions)	1989	1.00	5.00
Warner Bros. PRO-A-3704	**Scandalous** (2 versions)	1989	1.00	5.00
Warner Bros. PRO-A-4345	**Thieves In The Temple** (2 versions. PC)	1990	1.60	8.00
Warner Bros. PRO-A-4515	**New Power Generation** (2 versions)	1990	1.00	5.00
Warner Bros. PRO-A-4578	**New Power Generation** (Funky weapon remix) / **New Power Generation** (Funky weapon remix)	1990	1.60	8.00
Warner Bros. PRO-A-4977	**Gett Off** (Six versions)	1991	3.00	15.00
Paisley Park JUN-7	**Gett Off** (One sided 10" minute version. TC)	1991	100.00	400.00
Warner Bros. PRO-A-5141	**Insatiable** (2 versions. PC)	1991	1.60	8.00
Warner Bros. PRO-A-5148	**Diamonds & Pearls** (2 versions)	1991	1.00	5.00
Warner Bros. PRO-A-5298	**Money Don't Matter 2 Night** (2 versions)(PC)	1992	1.60	8.00
Warner Bros. PRO-A-5302	**Willing & Able** (2 versions)	1992	1.00	5.00

PRINCE, ROD

Label & Catalog #	A-Side/B-Side	Year	VG	NM
Comet 2140	**Rainbow Of Love / My Star All Alone**	195?	5.00	25.00

PRINCE & THE PAUPERS

Label & Catalog #	A-Side/B-Side	Year	VG	NM
Clarity 115	**Don't Wake Up / No Shame To Hide**	196?	2.00	10.00
Clarity	**Exit /**	196?	4.00	20.00

PRINCE CHARLES

Label & Catalog #	A-Side/B-Side	Year	VG	NM
Class 301	**Twistin' At The Pool / Good Luck Charm**	1962	2.00	10.00

PRINCE CHARLES & THE CRUSADERS

Label & Catalog #	A-Side/B-Side	Year	VG	NM
Garland 2001	**The Lights Of Town / Mr. Love**	196?	.80	4.00

PRINCE LA LA

Label & Catalog #	A-Side/B-Side	Year	VG	NM
AFO 301	**She Put The Hurt On Me / Don't You Know, Little Girl**	1961	3.00	15.00
AFO 303	**Gettin' Married Soon / Come Back To Me**	1961	3.00	15.00

PRISONAIRES, THE

Label & Catalog #	A-Side/B-Side	Year	VG	NM
Sun 186	**Just Walkin' In The Rain / Baby, Please**	1953	40.00	200.00
Sun 189	**My God Is Real / Softly And Tenderly**	1953	40.00	200.00
Sun 191	**A Prisoner's Prayer / I Know**	1953	30.00	150.00
Sun 207	**There Is Love In You / What'll You Do Next?**	1954	——	——
	(Rare. Estimated near mint value $10,000-15,000.)			

Label & Catalog #		A-Side/B-Side	Year	VG	NM
PROBY, P. J.					
Surfside 714		You Got Me Crying / I Need Love	196?	4.00	20.00
London 9688		Hold Me / The Tip Of My Fingers	1964	2.00	10.00
London 9705		Together / Sweet And Tender Romance	1964	2.00	10.00
Liberty 55367		Try To Forget Her / There Stands The One	1964	1.60	8.00
Liberty 55505		The Other Side Of Town / Watch Me Walk Away	1964	1.60	8.00
Liberty 55588		I Can't Take It Like You Can / So Do I	1964	1.60	8.00
Liberty 55757		Somewhere / Just Like Me	1965	1.60	8.00
Liberty 55777		I Apologize / Rockin' Pneumonia	1965	1.60	8.00
Liberty 55791		Mission Bell / Stagger Lee	1965	1.60	8.00
Liberty 55806		That Means A Lot / Let The Water Run Down	1965	1.60	8.00
Liberty 55850		Maria / Good Things Are Coming My Way	1966	1.60	8.00
Liberty 55850	(PS)	Maria / Good Things Are Coming My Way	1966	4.00	20.00
Liberty 55875		My Prayer / Wicked Woman	1966	1.60	8.00
Liberty 55915		I Can't Make It Alone / If I Ruled The World	1967	2.00	10.00
Liberty 55915	(PS)	I Can't Make It Alone / If I Ruled The World	1967	4.00	20.00
Liberty 55936		Niki Hokey / Good Things Are Coming My Way	1967	2.00	10.00
Liberty 55974		Work With Me, Annie / You Can't Come Home Again (If You Leave Me Now)	1967	1.60	8.00
Liberty 55989		Just Holding On / Butterfly High	1967	1.60	8.00
Liberty 56031		It's Your Turn Today / I Apologize, Baby	1968	1.60	8.00
Liberty 56051		What's Wrong With My World? / Turn Her Away	1968	1.60	8.00
PROCOL HARUM					

Gary Brooker, Matthew Fisher, Bobby Harrison, Dave Knights and Ray Royer with lyricist Keith Reid recorded the first single. Royer and Harrison were replaced by Robin Trower and B.J. Wilson. In 1970 Fisher and Knights left, Chris Copping joined. Brooker, Copping, Trower and Wilson had originally recorded as The Paramounts.

Label & Catalog #		A-Side/B-Side	Year	VG	NM
Deram 7507		A Whiter Shade Of Pale / Lime St. Blues	1967	2.00	10.00
A&M 885		Homburg / Good Captain Clack	1967	1.00	5.00
A&M 927		In The Wee Small Hours Of Sixpence / Quite Rightly So	1968	1.00	5.00
A&M 1069		A Salty Dog / Long Gone Geek	1969	.80	4.00
A&M 1111		Boredom / The Devil Came From Kansas	1969	1.00	5.00
A&M 1218		Whiskey Train / About To Die	1970	.80	4.00
A&M 1264		Broken Barricades / Power Failure	1971	.80	4.00
A&M 1287		Simple Sister / Song For A Dreamer	1971	.80	4.00
A&M 1347		Conquistador / A Salty Dog	1972	.60	3.00
A&M 1347	(PS)	Conquistador / A Salty Dog	1972	.60	3.00
A&M 1389		A Whiter Shade Of Pale / Lime Street Blues	1973	.60	3.00
A&M 1389	(PS)	A Whiter Shade Of Pale / Lime Street Blues	1973	.60	3.00
A&M PRO-562	(DJ)	Fires Of London / Souvenir Of London	197?	1.00	5.00
Chrysalis 2011		Bringing Home The Bacon / Toujours L' Amour	1973	.60	3.00
Chrysalis 2013		Grand Hotel / Fire (Which Burnt Brightly)	1973	.60	3.00
Chrysalis 2013	(PS)	Grand Hotel / Fire (Which Burnt Brightly)	1973	.60	3.00
Chrysalis 2032		Nothing But The Truth / Drunk Again	1974	.60	3.00
Chrysalis 2109		Pandora's Box / The Piper's Tune	1977	.60	3.00
Warner Bros. 2115		Wizard Man / Something Magic	1977	.60	3.00
		— Extended Play Albums —			
A&M X2	(DJ)	Procol Harum	1969	5.00	25.00
PRODIGALS, THE					
Acadain 1000		I Need You / You Better Move On	196?	3.00	15.00
PROFESSOR BUG					
Beetle 1600		Beatlemania / Beatlemania, Part 2	1964	3.00	15.00
PROFESSOR MORRISON'S LOLLIPOP					
White Whale 275		You Got The Love / Gypsy Lady	1968	1.00	5.00
White Whale 288		Angela / Duba Duba Do	1969	1.00	5.00
White Whale 293		You Take It / Ooh-Poo-Pah-Susie	1969	1.00	5.00
PROFILES, THE					
Gait 1444		Right By Her Side / Never	195?	35.00	175.00
PROFITS, THE					
Sire 353		Wind / Vagabond	196?	2.00	10.00
PROFITT, RANDY, & THE BEACHCOMBERS					
Bett-Coe 103		Check That Baby Out One Time / Young Love In Spring	196?	10.00	50.00
PROGRESSIVES, THE					
Dot 16514		Hot Cinders / Man Of Mystery	1963	5.00	25.00
PROMISES, THE					
Ascot 2201		I Don't Want To Talk About It / Try It Again	1966	2.00	10.00
PROPHETS, THE					
Jairick 201		Little Miss Dreamer /	195?	10.00	50.00

Label & Catalog #		A-Side/B-Side	Year	VG	NM
PROPHETS, THE: *Refer to RONNIE DIO*					
PROVIDENCE					
Threshold 67013		Fantasy Fugue / Fantasy Fugue	197?	1.00	5.00
PSYCHOS, THE					
Fernwood 126		Mack The Knife / Tragedy	1960	2.00	10.00
PUCKETT, GARY, & THE UNION GAP					
The Union Gap originally recorded as The Outcasts. Refer to the Kerry Chater; the Various Artists EP section.					
Columbia 44297		Woman, Woman / Don't Make Promises	1967	1.00	5.00
Columbia 44297	(PS)	Woman, Woman / Don't Make Promises	1967	2.00	10.00
		(Columbia 44297 credits The Union Gap Featuring Gary Puckett.)			
Columbia 44450		Young Girl / I'm Losing You	1968	.80	4.00
Columbia 44450	(PS)	Young Girl / I'm Losing You	1968	1.20	6.00
Columbia 44547		Lady Willpower / Daylight Stranger	1968	.80	4.00
Columbia 44547	(PS)	Lady Willpower / Daylight Stranger	1968	1.20	6.00
Columbia 44644		Over You / If The Day Would Come	1968	.80	4.00
Columbia 44644	(PS)	Over You / If The Day Would Come	1968	1.20	6.00
Columbia 44788		Don't Give In To Him / Could I?	1969	.60	3.00
Columbia 44967		This Girl Is A Woman Now / His Other Woman	1969	.60	3.00
Columbia 45097		Let's Give Adam And Eve Another Chance / The Beggar	1970	.60	3.00
Columbia 45097	(PS)	Let's Give Adam And Eve Another Chance / The Beggar	1970	1.20	6.00
Columbia 45249		I Just Don't Know What To Do With Myself / All That Matters	1970	.60	3.00
Columbia 45303		Keep The Customer Satisfied / No One Really Knows	1971	.60	3.00
Columbia 45358		Life Has Its Little Ups And Downs / Shimmering Eyes	1971	.60	3.00
Columbia 45438		Gentle Woman / Hello, Morning	1971	.60	3.00
Columbia 45509		I Can't Hold On / Hello, Morning	1972	.60	3.00
Columbia 45678		Leavin' In The Morning / Bless The Child	1972	.60	3.00
PUDDING					
Press 5010		Magic Bus / It's Too Late	1968	1.20	6.00
PUFF, RAY, & THE CHECKMATES					
Lin 5034		Beatles Manias / Took A Liking To You	1964	3.00	15.00
PUFFS, THE					
Dore 757		Moon Out There / I Only Cry Once A Day Now	1968	1.20	6.00
PULLEN, DWIGHT					
Carlton 455	(DJ)	Sunglasses After Dark / Teenage Bug	1961	15.00	75.00
Carlton 455		Sunglasses After Dark / Teenage Bug	1961	30.00	150.00
PULLINS, LEROY					
Kapp 758		I'm A Nut / Knee Deep	1966	1.00	5.00
Kapp 775		Taterville Women's Auxiliary Sewing Circle / Tickled Pink	1966	1.00	5.00
PULSE					
Atco 6530		Can Can Girl / Burritt Bradley	1967	1.00	5.00
PUPPET, POLLY					
Challenge 9126		The Puppeteer / Puppet Serenade	1961	2.00	10.00
PURPLE GANG, THE					
Jerden 794		Answer The Phone / I Know Where I Am	1966	2.00	10.00
PUSSYCATS, THE					
Keyman 6000		Anniversary Of Love / Mickey Mouse March	196?	15.00	75.00
PYRAMIDS, THE [THE ORIGINAL PYRAMIDS]					
Shell 711		Ankle Bracelet / Hot Dog Dooly Wah *(Grey label)*	1959	4.00	40.00
Shell 711		Ankle Bracelet / Hot Dog Dooly Wah *(Red & white label)*	196?	4.00	20.00
RCA Victor 47-7556		Long, Long Time / Oh No You Won't	1959	3.00	15.00
Cub 9112		Cryin' / I'm The Playboy	1962	3.00	15.00
Vee Jay 489		What Is Love? / Shakin' Fit	1962	3.00	15.00
Shell 304		Ankle Bracelet / Hot Dog Dooly Wah	196?	2.00	10.00
		(Shell 304 credits the Original Pyramids.)			
PYRAMIDS, THE					
Best 101		Pyramid's Stomp / Paul	1962	5.00	25.00
Best 102		Penetration / Here Comes Marsha	1962	3.00	15.00
Best 102	(PS)	Penetration / Here Comes Marsha	1962	6.00	30.00
Best 13001		Pyramid's Stomp / Paul	1964	4.00	20.00
Best 13002		Penetration / Here Comes Marsha	1964	3.00	15.00
Best 13002		Penetration / Here Comes Marsha	1964	2.00	10.00
		(Later pressings read "Dist. by London.")			
Cedwicke 13005		Midnight Run / Custom Caravan	1964	8.00	40.00
Cedwicke 13006		Contact / Pressure	1964	8.00	40.00

QUADS, THE
Vault 907	Surfin' Hearse / Little Queenie	1963	6.00	30.00

QUAKER CITY BOYS, THE
Swan 4023	Teasin' / Woncha Come Out Tonight?	1959	2.00	10.00
Swan 4026	Everywhere You Go / Love Me Tonight	1959	2.00	10.00
Swan 4045	Goodbye 50's, Hello 60's / You Call Everybody	1959	2.00	10.00

QUARTER NOTES, THE
Dot 15685	Like, You Bug Me / Please Come Home	1957	3.00	15.00
Wizz 715	Record Hop Blues / Suki-Yaki-Rocki	1959	3.00	15.00
Guyden 2083	Pretty Pretty Eyes / I Don't Want To Go Home	1963	4.00	20.00
Boom 018	I've Been Loved / Hey, Little Girl	196?	3.00	15.00

QUATRO, SUZI [SUSIE QUATRO]
Suzi Quatro originally recorded with The Pleasure Seekers.
Rak 4512	Rolling Stone / Brain Confusion	1972	2.00	10.00
Bell 45401	48 Crash / Little Bitch Blue	1974	1.00	5.00
Bell 45477	All Shook Up / Glycerine Queen	1974	.60	3.00
Bell 45609	Devil Gate Drive / In The Morning	1974	.80	4.00
Bell 45615	Keep A Knockin' / Cat's Eye	1974	1.00	5.00
Big Tree 16053	Can The Can / Don't Mess Around	1976	.60	3.00
Arista 0106	Your Mama Won't Like Me / Peter, Peter	197?	.80	4.00
RSO 917	Stumblin' In / A Stranger To Paradise	1979	.60	3.00
RSO 1001	I've Never Been In Love / Space Cadets	1979	.60	3.00
RSO 1014	She's In Love With You / Starlight Lady	1979	.60	3.00
Dreamland 104	Rock Hard / State Of Mind	1980	.60	3.00
Dreamland 104	(PS) Rock Hard / State Of Mind	1980	.60	3.00

QUEEN
Queen, who originally recorded as Smile, features John Deacon, Brian May, Roger Meadows-Taylor and Freddie Mercury, who originally recorded as Larry Lurex.
Elektra 45226	Killer Queen / Flick Of The Wrist	1975	.80	4.00
Elektra 45268	Keep Yourself Alive / Lily Of The Valley-God Save The Queen	1975	.80	4.00
Elektra 45297	Bohemian Rhapsody / I'm In Love With My Car	1975	.80	4.00
Elektra 45318	You're My Best Friend / '39	1976	.60	3.00
Elektra 45362	Somebody To Love / White Man	1976	.60	3.00
Elektra 45385	Tie Your Mother Down / Drowse	1977	.60	3.00
Elektra 45412	Long Away / You And I	1977	.60	3.00
Elektra 45441	We Are The Champions / We Will Rock You	1977	.40	2.00
Elektra 45441	(PS) We Are The Champions / We Will Rock You	1977	.60	3.00
Elektra 45478	It's Late / Sheer Heart Attack	1978	.40	2.00
Elektra 45478	(PS) It's Late / Sheer Heart Attack	1978	.60	3.00
Elektra 45541	Bicycle Race / Fat Bottomed Girls	1978	.40	2.00
Elektra 45541	(PS) Bicycle Race / Fat Bottomed Girls	1978	1.00	5.00
Elektra 45891	Seven Seas Of Rhye / See What A Fool I've Been	1979	2.00	10.00
Elektra 46008	Don't Stop Me Now / More Of That Jazz	1979	.40	2.00
Elektra 46039	Jealousy / Fun It	1979	.40	2.00
Elektra 46532	We Will Rock You / Let Me Entertain You	1979	.40	2.00
Elektra 46579	Crazy Little Thing Called Love / Spread Your Wings	1979	.40	2.00
Elektra 46652	Play The Game / A Human Body	1980	.40	2.00
Elektra 46652	(PS) Play The Game / A Human Body	1980	.60	3.00
Elektra 47031	Another One Bites The Dust / Don't Try Suicide	198?	.40	2.00
Elektra 47086	Rock It (Prime Jive) / Need Your Lovin' Tonight	198?	.40	2.00
Elektra 47092	Flash's Theme A/K/A Flash / Football Fight	1980	.40	2.00
Elektra 47092	(PS) Flash's Theme A/K/A Flash / Football Fight	1980	.60	3.00
Elektra 47452	Body Language / His Life Is Real (Song For Lennon)	1982	.40	2.00
Elektra 47452	(PS) Body Language / His Life Is Real (Song For Lennon)	1982	.60	3.00
Elektra 69981	Calling All Girls / Put Out The Fire	1982	.40	2.00
Elektra 69981	(PS) Calling All Girls / Put Out The Fire	1982	.60	3.00

QUEEN & DAVID BOWIE
EMI 47235	Under Pressure / Soul Brother	1981	.40	2.00
EMI 47235	(PS) Under Pressure / Soul Brother	1981	.40	2.00

? & THE MYSTERIANS
Mysterians were Robert Baldarrama, Larry Borjas, Frank Lugo, Robert Martinez, Frank Rodriguez and Edward Serrat. Members also recorded as The Fun Sons and The Semi-Colons.
Pa-Go-Go 102	96 Tears / Midnight Hour	1965	100.00	400.00
Cameo 428	96 Tears / Midnight Hour	1966	3.00	15.00
Cameo 441	I Need Somebody / "8" Teen	1966	2.00	10.00

Fat Bottom Girls remains one of the truly outrageous picture sleeves from the past twenty years (or more). The recent death of front man Freddie Mercury from AIDS has given many a rock fan a pause to reconsider exactly what this group of flamboyant glam-rockers was really all about...

Label & Catalog #	A-Side/B-Side	Year	VG	NM
Cameo 467	Can't Get Enough Of You, Baby / Smokes	1967	2.00	10.00
Cameo 479	Girl (You Captivate Me) / Got To	1967	2.00	10.00
Cameo 496	Do Something To Me / Love Me, Baby	1967	2.00	10.00
Capitol 2162	Make You Mine / I Love You, Baby	1968	3.00	15.00
Chicory 410	Talk Is Cheap / She Goes To Church On Sunday	1968	6.00	30.00
Tangerine 989X	Ain't It A Shame? /			
	Turn Around, Baby (Don't Ever Look Back)	196?	2.00	10.00
Super-K 102	Hang In / Sha La La	1969	2.00	10.00
Luv 159	Funky Lady / Hot N' Groovin'	1975	2.00	10.00
Abkco 4020	96 Tears / Can't Get Enough Of You, Baby	1983	1.60	8.00
Abkco 4033	I Need Somebody / Girl (You Captivate Me)	1983	2.00	10.00

QUESTS, THE

Tangerine	Shadows In The Night / I'm Tempted	196?	20.00	100.00
Fenton	Shadows In The Night / I'm Tempted	196?	8.00	40.00
Fenton 2032	Scream Loud / Psychic	196?	4.00	20.00

QUICK, THE
The Quick features Eric Carmen.

Epic 10516	Ain't Nothing Gonna Stop Me / Southern Comfort	1969	5.00	25.00

QUICKLY, TOMMY

Liberty 55732	You Might As Well Forget Him / It's As Simple As That	1964	2.00	10.00
Liberty 55753	Wild Side Of Life / Forget The other Guy	1964	2.00	10.00

QUICKSILVER MESSENGER SERVICE, THE [QUICKSILVER]
Original members of QMS were John Cippolina, David Freiberg (both of whom left in 1970), Gary Duncan and Greg Elmore, who were joined by Dino Valenti (a member before recording who spent the group's halcyon years in jail for possession) in 1970. Other members include Nicky Hopkins, 1969-70, and Mark Naftalin, 1970-71. Refer to The Brogues; Copperhead.

Capitol 2194	Pride Of Man / Dino's Song	1968	1.25	6.00
Capitol 2320	Stand By Me / Bears	1969	1.25	6.00
Capitol 2557	Who Do You Love? / Which Do You Love?	1969	1.25	6.00
Capitol 2670	Holy Moly / Words Can't Say	1969	1.25	6.00
Capitol 2800	Shady Grove / Three Or Four Feet from Home	1970	.80	4.00
Capitol 2920	Fresh Air / Free Way Flyer	1970	.80	4.00
Capitol 3046	What About Me? / Good Old Rock And Roll	1971	.80	4.00
Capitol 3233	Hope / I Found Love	1971	.80	4.00
Capitol 3349	Doin' Time In The U.S.A. / Changes	1972	.80	4.00
Capitol 4206	Gypsy Lights / Witch's Moon	1976	.80	4.00

QUINN, CAROLE

MGM 13265	What's So Sweet About Sweet Sixteen? / Good Boy, Bad Boy	1964	2.00	10.00
MGM 13326	I'll Do It For You / Little Things	1964	2.00	10.00

QUINTEROS, EDDIE

Brent 7009	Come Dance With Me / Vivian	1960	5.00	25.00
Brent 7012	Lookin' For My Baby / Please Don't Go	1960	6.00	30.00
Brent 7014	Lindy Lou / Slow Down, Sandy	1960	8.00	40.00

QUOTATIONS, THE

Verve 10245	Imagination / Ala Men Sy	1961	4.00	20.00
Verve 10252	This Love Of Mine / We'll Reach Heaven Together	1961	6.00	30.00
Verve 10261	See You In September / Summertime Goodbyes	1962	10.00	50.00
DeVenus 107	It Can Happen To You / I Don't Have To Worry	196?	2.00	10.00

R.

R.E.M.

Hib-Tone		Radio Free Europe / Sitting Still	1982	15.00	75.00
Hib-Tone	(PS)	Radio Free Europe / Sitting Still	1982	15.00	75.00
I.R.S. 9916		Radio Free Europe / There She Goes Again	1983	3.00	15.00
I.R.S. 9916	(PS)	Radio Free Europe / There She Goes Again	1983	3.00	15.00
I.R.S. 9927		S. Central Rain (I'm Sorry) / King Of The Road	1984	1.00	5.00
I.R.S. 9927	(PS)	S. Central Rain (I'm Sorry) / King Of The Road	1984	1.00	5.00
I.R.S. 9931		(Don't Go Back To) Rockville / Catapult (Live)	1984	1.00	5.00
I.R.S. 9931	(PS)	(Don't Go Back To) Rockville / Catapult (Live)	1984	1.00	5.00
I.R.S. 52642		Can't Get There From Here / Bandwagon	1985	.80	4.00
I.R.S. 52642	(PS)	Can't Get There From Here / Bandwagon	1985	.80	4.00
I.R.S. 52678		Driver 8 / Crazy	1985	.80	4.00
I.R.S. 52678	(PS)	Driver 8 / Crazy	1985	.80	4.00
I.R.S. 52883		Fall On Me / Rotary Ten	1986	.80	4.00
I.R.S. 52883	(PS)	Fall On Me / Rotary Ten	1986	.80	4.00
I.R.S. 52971		Superman / White Tornado	1986	.80	4.00
I.R.S. 52971	(PS)	Superman / White Tornado	1986	.80	4.00
I.R.S. 53171		The One I Love / Maps And Legends	1987	.80	4.00
I.R.S. 53171	(PS)	The One I Love / Maps And Legends	1987	.80	4.00
I.R.S. 53220		It's The End Of The World As We Know It / Last Date	1987	.80	4.00
I.R.S. 53220	(PS)	It's The End Of The World As We Know It / Last Date	1987	.80	4.00
Warner Bros. 27640		Pop Song 89 / Pop Song 89 (Acoustic)	1988	.40	2.00
Warner Bros. 27640	(PS)	Pop Song 89 / Pop Song 89 (Acoustic)	1988	.40	2.00
Warner Bros. 27688		Stand / Memphis Train Blues	1988	.40	2.00
Warner Bros. 27688	(PS)	Stand / Memphis Train Blues	1988	.40	2.00
Warner Bros. 22780		Single Action Green	1989	4.00	20.00
		(Boxed set of four 45s with PSs and poster.)			
Warner Bros. 22791		Get Up / Fun Time	1989	.40	2.00
Warner Bros. 22791	(PS)	Get Up / Fun Time	1989	.40	2.00
Warner Bros. 922 934		Orange Crush / Ghost Riders	1989	.40	2.00
Warner Bros. 922 934	(PS)	Orange Crush / Ghost Riders	1989	.40	2.00
		—Special/Promotional Releases—			
Evatone		Femme Fatale *(One sided flexidisc)*	198?	3.00	15.00
Evatone	(PS)	Femme Fatale	198?	5.00	25.00
Fan Club U23518		Parade Of The Wooden Soldiers / See No Evil *(Green vinyl)*	1988	15.00	75.00
Fan Club U23518	(PS)	Parade Of The Wooden Soldiers / See No Evil	1988	15.00	75.00
Fan Club		Good King Wenceslas / Academy Fight Song	1989	10.00	50.00
Fan Club	(PS)	Good King Wenceslas / Academy Fight Song	1989	10.00	50.00
Fan Club		Ghost Reindeer In The Sky / Summertime	1990	10.00	50.00
Fan Club	(PS)	Ghost Reindeer In The Sky / Summertime	1990	10.00	50.00

R.P.M.'S, THE

Port 70032		Street Scene / Love Me	1963	2.00	10.00
Mala 508		Memphis Beat / You Can Love Me	1965	2.00	10.00

R.T.'S, THE

Merrilyn 5304		Once Upon A Time / Soul Searchin'	196?	2.00	10.00

RABON, MICHAEL, & THE FIVE AMERICANS: *Refer to* THE FIVE AMERICANS

RACERS, THE

RSVP 1115		Skate Board / It's Happening	196?	7.00	35.00

RACHEL & THE REVOLVERS

Dot 16392	(DJ)	The Revo-Lution / Number One	1962	60.00	250.00
Dot 16392		The Revo-Lution / Number One	1962	125.00	400.00
		(Produced by Brian Wilson.)			

RADER, QUANTRELL

RCA Victor 47-8317		I Lose More Girls That Way / The Special Way	1964	1.60	8.00

RADHA KRISHNA TEMPLE, The

Apple P-1810	(DJ)	Hare Krishna Mantra / Prayer To The Spiritual Master	1969	4.00	20.00
Apple 1810		Hare Krishna Mantra / Prayer To The Spiritual Master	1969	1.20	6.00
Apple P-1821	(DJ)	Govinda / Govinda Jai Jai	1970	4.00	20.00
Apple 1821		Govinda / Govinda Jai Jai	1970	1.20	6.00
Apple 1821	(PS)	Govinda / Govinda Jai Jai	1970	2.00	10.00

RAE, DONNY, & THE DEFIANTS

Arlen 521		Beatle Mania / Hold On	1964	3.00	15.00

R.E.M. combines a flashing potpourri of '60s influences — notably the Byrds jingle jangle guitar sound — with a reasonably hip and contemporarily aware attitude to produce some of the best white pop/rock of recent memory. Along the way they have become the single most collectible major group in the hobby.

Label & Catalog #	A-Side/B-Side	Year	VG	NM
RAG DOLLS, THE				
Parkway 921	Society Girl / Ragen	1964	2.00	10.00
Mala 493	Dusty / Hey, Hoagy	1965	2.00	10.00
Mala 499	Baby's Gone / We Almost Made It	1965	2.00	10.00
Mala 506	Put A Ring On My Finger / Little Girl Tears	1965	3.00	15.00
RAGAMUFFINS, THE				
The Ragamuffins feature Gary Zekley.				
Tollie 9027	The Fun We had / Don't Be Gone Long	1964	5.00	25.00
RAGING STORMS, THE				
Trans Atlas 691	Down At The Corner / So Hard To Take	1962	2.00	10.00
Warwick 677	Hound Dog / Dribble Twist	1962	2.00	10.00
RAIDERS, THE				
Atco 6125	The Castle Of Love / Raiders From Outer Space	1958	10.00	50.00
Brunswick 55090	Walking Through The Jungle / My Steady Girl	1958	4.00	20.00
RAIDERS, THE				
Spring-Dale 102	Raider's Rhythm /	196?	7.00	35.00
RAIDERS, THE				
Van	Stick Shifty / Skipping Around	1963	5.00	25.00
Vee Jay 504	Stick Shifty / Skipping Around	1963	3.00	15.00
RAIDERS, THE: *Refer to* PAUL REVERE & THE RAIDERS				
RAIN				
A.P.I. 336	Outta My Life / E.S.P.	196?	6.00	30.00
London	Outta My Life / E.S.P.	196?	3.00	15.00
RAINBO				
Roulette 7030	C'mon, Teach Me To Live /			
	John, You Went Too Far This Time	1968	2.00	10.00
RAINBOW, LITTLE MARY				
Piccadilly 321	You Must Be The One / Graveyard Shift	1967	2.00	10.00
RAINBOWS, THE				
Dave 908	Only A Picture / I Know	1963	7.00	35.00
Dave 909	It Wouldn't Be Right /	1963	7.00	35.00
Gramo 5508	Till Tomorrow / Mama, Take Your Daughter Back	196?	3.00	15.00
RAINBOWS, THE				
Dot 16612	My Ringo / He's Hooked On J's	1964	3.00	15.00
RAINBOWS, THE				
Epic 9900	Ju Ju Hand / Bala Bala	1966	2.00	10.00
RAINBOWS, THE: *Refer to* RANDY & THE RAINBOWS				
RAINDROPS, THE				
Corsair 104	Love Is Like A Mountain / Maybe	1960	15.00	75.00
Dore 561	Love Is Like A Mountain / Maybe	1960	5.00	25.00
RAINDROPS, THE				
Imperial 5785	I Remember In The Still Of The Night /			
	The Sweetheart Song	1961	5.00	25.00
RAINDROPS, THE				
The Raindrops feature Jeff Barry and Ellie Greenwich.				
Jubilee 5444	What A Guy / It's So Wonderful	1963	3.00	15.00
Jubilee 5455	The Kind Of Boy You Can't Forget /			
	Even Though You Can't Dance	1963	3.00	15.00
Jubilee 5466	That Boy John / Hanky Panky	1963	3.00	15.00
Jubilee 5469	Book Of Love / I Won't Cry	1964	3.00	15.00
Jubilee 5475	Let's Get Together / You Got What I Want	1964	3.00	15.00
Jubilee 5487	One More Tear / Another Boy Like Mine	1964	3.00	15.00
Jubilee 5497	Don't Let Go / My Mama Don't Like Him	1964	3.00	15.00
RAINEY, MA				
Big Memphis Ma Rainey is a pseudonym for Lillian Glover.				
Sun 184	Call Me Anything But Call Me / Baby No, No, No	1953	——	——
	(Rare. Estimated near mint value $2,500-5,000.)			
RAINING LOVE, THE				
Garland 2021	Come And Gone / Why	196?	2.00	10.00

Label & Catalog #		A-Side/B-Side	Year	VG	NM
RAINMAKERS, THE					
Discotheque 875		Don't Be Afraid / I Won't Turn Away Now	196?	4.00	20.00
Phalanx 1029		Tell Her No / You're Not The Only One	196?	4.00	20.00
RAINY DAYS, THE					
Panik 7542		Turn On Your Lovelight / Go On And Cry	196?	2.00	10.00
RAINY DAZE					
Chickory 404		That Acapulco Gold / In My Mind Lives A Forest	1967	3.00	15.00
Uni 55002		That Acapulco Gold / In My Mind Lives A Forest	1967	2.00	10.00
Uni 55011		Discount City / Good Morning, Mr. Smith	1967	2.00	10.00
Uni 55026		Blood Of Oblivion / Stop Sign	1967	2.00	10.00
White Whale 279		My Door Is Always Open / Make Me Laugh	1968	3.00	15.00
RALLY PACKS, THE					
The Rally Packs are Steve Barri and Phil Sloan.					
Imperial 66036	(DJ)	Move Out, Little Mustang / Bucket Seats	1964	6.00	30.00
Imperial 66036		Move Out, Little Mustang / Bucket Seats	1964	12.00	60.00
		("Move Out, Little Mustang" was written by Brian Wilson with vocal backing by Jan & Dean.)			
RAMADAS, THE					
Philips 40097		Teenage Dream / My Angel Eyes	1963	2.00	10.00
Philips 40117		Summer Steady / Lonely Tears	1963	2.00	10.00
RAMBEAU, EDDIE					
DynoVoice 204		Concrete And Clay / Don't Believe Him	1965	1.20	6.00
DynoVoice 207		I Just Need Your Love / My Name Is Mud	1965	1.20	6.00
DynoVoice 211		Yesterday's Newspaper / The Train	1965	1.20	6.00
DynoVoice 225		Clock / If I Were You	1966	1.20	6.00
RAMBLERS, THE					
Addit 1257		Rambling / Devil Train	1960	3.00	15.00
Almont 311		Barbara (I Loved You) / Father Sebastian	1964	3.00	15.00
Almont 315		Surfin' Santa / Silly Little Boy	1964	7.00	35.00
Sidewinder 101		Ticonderoga / Mozart Stomp	1964	6.00	30.00
RAMBLETTES, THE					
Kapp 104		Girls Cry Faster Than Boys / I Can't Go Through It Again	1964	3.00	15.00
Decca 31752		Thinking Of You / Back Street	1965	3.00	15.00
RAMISTELLA, JOHNNY, & THE SPADES					
Johnny Ramistella later recorded as Johnny Rivers.					
Suede		Hey, Little Girl /	1957	10.00	50.00
RAMONES, THE					
The Ramones are Dee Dee, Joey, Johnny and Tommy, who left in 1977, replaced by Marky.					
Sire 725	(DJ)	Blitzkreig Bop / Blitzkreig Bop *(White label)*	1976	4.00	20.00
Sire 725	(DJ)	Blitzkreig Bop / Havana Affair *(White label)*	1976	5.00	25.00
Sire 725		Blitzkreig Bop / Havana Affair	1976	6.00	30.00
Sire 734	(DJ)	I Wanna Be Your Boyfriend / California Sun (Live) / I Don't Wanna Walk Around With You (Live)	1976	1.20	6.00
Sire 734		I Wanna Be Your Boyfriend / California Sun (Live) / I Don't Wanna Walk Around With You (Live)	1976	2.00	10.00
Sire 734	(PS)	I Wanna Be Your Boyfriend / California Sun (Live) / I Don't Wanna Walk Around With You (Live)	1976	3.00	15.00
Sire 738	(DJ)	Swallow My Pride / Pinhead	1976	1.20	6.00
Sire 738		Swallow My Pride / Pinhead	1976	2.00	10.00
Sire 738	(PS)	Swallow My Pride / Pinhead	1976	3.00	15.00
Sire 746	(DJ)	Sheena Is A Punk Rocker / I Don't Care	1977	1.20	6.00
Sire 746		Sheena Is A Punk Rocker / I Don't Care	1977	2.00	10.00
Sire 746	(PS)	Sheena Is A Punk Rocker / I Don't Care	1977	3.00	15.00
Sire 1006		Sheena Is A Punk Rocker / I Don't Care	1977	1.20	6.00
Sire 1006	(PS)	Sheena Is A Punk Rocker / I Don't Care	1977	3.00	15.00
Sire 1008		Rockaway Beach / Locket Love	1977	1.20	6.00
Sire 1008	(PS)	Rockaway Beach / Locket Love	1977	3.00	15.00
Sire 1017		Do You Wanna Dance? / Baby Sitter	1978	1.20	6.00
Sire 1017	(PS)	Do You Wanna Dance? / Baby Sitter	1978	3.00	15.00
Sire 1025		Don't Come Close / I Don't Want You	1978	1.60	8.00
Sire 1025	(PS)	Don't Come Close / I Don't Want You	1978	3.00	15.00
Sire 1045		Needles And Pins / I Wanted Everything	1979	1.20	6.00
Sire 1051		Rock 'N' Roll High School / Do You Wanna Dance? (Live)	1979	1.20	6.00
Sire 1051	(PS)	Rock 'N' Roll High School / Do You Wanna Dance? (Live)	1979	1.60	8.00
		(Sire 1045 and 1051 produced by Phil Spector.)			
Sire 49182		Baby I Love You / High Risk Insurance	1980	1.20	6.00
Sire 49261		Do You Remember Rock 'N Roll Radio? / Let's Go	1980	1.20	6.00
RSO 1055		I Wanna Be Sedated / Return Of Jackie And Judy	1980	1.20	6.00
Sire 49812		We Want The Airwaves / All's Quiet On The Western Front	1981	1.00	5.00

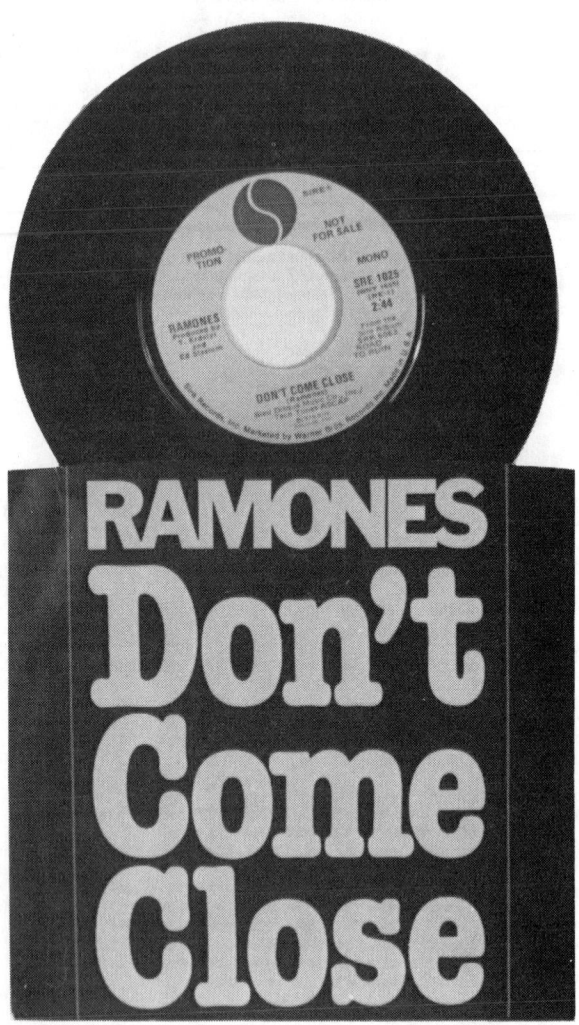

The Ramones as collectible artists continue to grow steadily. Early singles and sleeves are rather rare — especially the first few commercial releases — and are sure sellers in shops and shows around the country.

Label & Catalog #		A-Side/B-Side	Year	VG	NM
Sire 29606		Time Has Come Today / Psycho Therapy	1983	1.00	5.00
Sire 29107		Howling At The Moon (Sha La La) / Warthog	1984	1.00	5.00
Sire 28599		Something To Believe In / Animal Boy	1986	1.00	5.00
Sire 27663		I Wanna Be Sedated / Sedated Mega-Mix	1988	1.00	5.00
Sire 22911		Pet Sematary / Sheena Is A Punk Rocker	1988	.60	3.00
Sire 22911	(PS)	Pet Sematary / Sheena Is A Punk Rocker	1988	1.00	5.00
Sire 27663		I Wanna Be Sedated / Ramones On 45 Mega-Mix	1988	1.00	5.00
		—Special/Promotional Releases—			
New World Pictures	(DJ)	Rock 'N' Roll High School (Radio spots)	1979	10.00	50.00
		—12" Singles—			
Sire PRO-2816	(DJ)	I Wanna Live / I Wanna Live	1987	2.00	10.00
Sire PRO-3193	(DJ)	I Wanna Be Sedated / Ramones On 45 Mega-Mix (PC)	1988	2.00	10.00
Sire 22911		Pet Sematary / Sheena Is A Punk Rocker / Life Goes On	1988	2.00	10.00
RAMPAGES, THE					
Wedge 1011		Alligator Stomp / My Dear Heart	1964	3.00	15.00
RAMRODS, THE					
Amy 813		(Ghost) Riders In The Sky / Zigzag	1960	3.00	15.00
Amy 817		Take Me Back To My Boots And Saddles /			
		Loch Lomond Rock	1961	2.00	10.00
Amy 846		Boing / War Cry	1962	2.00	10.00
Queen 240145		Slee-Zee / Slouchee	1962	2.00	10.00
RAMRODS, THE					
R&H 1001		Moonlight Surf / Night Ride	196?	7.00	35.00
RAMRODS, THE: *Refer to* THE ROCKIN' RAMRODS					
RAN-DELLS, THE					
Chairman 4403		Martian Hop / Forgive Me, Darling (I Have Lied)	1963	2.00	10.00
Chairman 4403	(PS)	Martian Hop / Forgive Me, Darling (I Have Lied)	1963	6.00	30.00
Chairman 4407		Sound Of The Sun / Come On And Love Me, Too	1964	2.00	10.00
RSVP 1104		Beyond The Stars / Wintertime	1964	2.00	10.00
RANCHEROS, THE					
Lonnie 5005		Linda's Tune / Little Linda	1963	7.00	35.00
Dot 16572		Linda's Tune / Little Linda	1963	5.00	25.00
RAND, BOBBY					
Dot 15580		Don't Make My Poor Heart Weep / Talking To Myself	1957	3.00	15.00
RANDAL, PAUL					
Roulette 4352		I'm Lonesome For You / What Is A Grandmother?	1961	2.00	10.00
RANDAZZO, TEDDY, & THE DAZZLERS					
ABC-Paramount 10350		Dance To The Locomotion / Cotton Fields	1962	1.00	5.00
RANDELL, BUDDY					
Uni 55209		Be My Baby / Randi, Randi	1970	1.00	5.00
RANDELL, DENNY					
Jamie 1241		Lonely Melody / Limbo Lou	1962	3.00	15.00
Cameo 255		Hey, Chickie Baby / There's Gonna Be A Showdown	1963	2.00	10.00
Ascot 2137		I'm Back, Baby / Blues For A Four String Guitar	1963	3.00	15.00
RANDLE, DELL					
Shakari 101		Introducing The Beatles To Money Land /			
		The Monkey And The Beatles	1964	3.00	15.00
RANDOLPH, DEAN					
Chancellor 1122		How About That? / Come With Me	1963	2.00	10.00
Chancellor 1138		Girl In The White Convertible / False Love	1963	2.00	10.00
RANDY & RALPH					
United Artists 146		Don't Leave Me Lonely Tonight / Hungry	1958	3.00	15.00
RANDY & THE RADIANTS					
Sun 395		Peek-A-Boo / Mountain High	1965	3.00	15.00
Sun 398		My Ways Of Thinking / Truth From My Eyes	1966	3.00	15.00
RANDY & THE RAINBOWS					
The Rainbows also recorded as The Dialtones; Madison Street; and Triangle.					
Rust 5059		Denise / Come Back (Blue label)	1963	5.00	25.00
Rust 5059		Denise / Come Back (White label)	1963	3.00	15.00
Rust 5073		Why Do Kids Grow Up? / She's My Angel	1963	3.00	15.00
Rust 5080		Happy Teenager / Dry Your Eyes	1964	3.00	15.00
Rust 5091		Little Star / Sharin'	1964	3.00	15.00

Label & Catalog #		A-Side/B-Side	Year	VG	NM
Rust 5101		Joyride / Little Hot Rod Susie	1964	3.00	15.00
Mike 4001		I'll Forget Her Tomorrow / Lovely Lies	1966	3.00	15.00
Mike 4004		Quarter The Three / He's A Fugitive	1966	3.00	15.00
Mike 4008		Bonnie's Part Of Town / Can It Be?	1966	3.00	15.00
B.T. Puppy 535		I'll Be Seeing You / Oh, To Get Away	1967	2.00	10.00
Crystal Ball 106		Angel Face / I Wonder Why	197?	.60	3.00

RANDY & THE ROCKETS

Viking 1000		Genevieve / If You Really Care	1959	3.00	15.00
Jin 161		Let's Do The Cajun Twist / Rocket's Twist	1962	2.00	10.00

RANGERS, THE

FTP 404		Riders In The Sky / Four On The Floor	1961	3.00	15.00
Challenge 59239		Justine / Reputation	1964	2.00	10.00
Challenge 9196		Mogul Monster / Snow Skiing	1964	2.00	10.00

RANGLIN, ERNEST

Studio 1		Surfing / Surfing, Part 2	196?	7.00	35.00

RANK, KEN

Fenton 2194		Twin City Saucer / Ken's Thing	196?	5.00	25.00

RARE BREED, THE
The Rare Breed later recorded as The Ohio Express.

Attack 1401		Beg, Borrow And Steal / Jeri's Theme	1966	5.00	25.00
Attack 1403		Come And Take A Ride In My Boat / Take Me To This World Of Yours	1966	3.00	15.00

RARE EARTH

Verve 10622		Stop! Where Did Our Love Go? / Mother's Oats	1968	1.20	6.00
Rare Earth 5012		Get Ready / Magic Key	1970	1.00	5.00
Rare Earth 5017		(I Know) I'm Losing You / When Joanie Smiles	1970	1.00	5.00
Rare Earth 5021		Born To Wander / Here Comes The Night	1970	1.00	5.00
Rare Earth 5031		I Just Want To Celebrate / The Seed	1971	1.00	5.00
Rare Earth 5031	(PS)	I Just Want To Celebrate / The Seed	1971	1.20	6.00
Rare Earth 5038		Hey, Big Brother / Under God's Light	1971	.60	3.00
Rare Earth 5043		What'd I Say? / Nice To Be With You	1972	.60	3.00
Rare Earth 5048		Good Time Sally / Love Shines Down	1972	.60	3.00
Rare Earth 5052		We're Gonna Have A Good Time / Would You Like To Come Along?	1973	.60	3.00
Rare Earth 5057		Chained / Fresh From The Can	1973	.60	3.00
Rare Earth 5058		It Makes You Happy / Boogie With Me, Children	1975	.60	3.00
Rare Earth 5060		Midnight Lady / Walking Schtick	1976	.60	3.00
Prodigal 0640		Warm Ride / Would You Like To Come Along?	1978	.60	3.00
Prodigal 0643		I Can Feel My Love Rising / S.O.S. (Stop Her On Sight)	1978	.60	3.00

RASBERRY PIRATES, THE

Atco 6624		Looky, Looky, My Cookie's Gone / Good Morning, Baby	1968	1.20	6.00

RASCALS, THE [THE YOUNG RASCALS]
The Rascals are Eddie Brigati, Felix Cavaliere, Gene Cornish and Dino Danelli. Refer to Gene Cornish & The Unbeatables;
Felix & The Escorts; Bulldog; Fotomaker.

Atlantic 2312		I Ain't Gonna Eat Out My Heart Anymore / Slow Down	1965	2.00	10.00
Atlantic 2321		Good Lovin' / Mustang Sally	1966	1.00	5.00
Atlantic 2338		You Better Run / Love Is A Beautiful Thing	1966	1.00	5.00
Atlantic 2338	(PS)	You Better Run / Love Is A Beautiful Thing	1966	3.00	15.00
Atlantic 2353		Come On Up / What Is The Reason?	1966	1.00	5.00
Atlantic 2377		I've Been Lonely Too Long / If You Knew	1967	1.00	5.00
Atlantic 2377	(PS)	I've Been Lonely Too Long / If You Knew	1967	3.00	15.00
Atlantic 2401		Groovin' / Sueno	1967	1.00	5.00
Atlantic 2401	(PS)	Groovin' / Sueno	1967	3.00	15.00
Atlantic 2424		A Girl Like You / It's Love	1967	1.00	5.00
Atlantic 2424	(PS)	A Girl Like You / It's Love	1967	3.00	15.00
Atlantic 2428		Groovin' (Italian) / Groovin' (Spanish)	1967	2.00	10.00
Atlantic 2438		How Can I Be Sure? / I'm So Happy	1967	1.00	5.00
Atlantic 2463		It's Wonderful / Of Course	1967	1.00	5.00
		(Atlantic 2312-2463 credit The Young Rascals.)			
Atlantic 2493		It's A Beautiful Morning / Rainy Day	1968	.80	4.00
Atlantic 2493	(PS)	It's A Beautiful Morning / Rainy Day	1968	3.00	15.00
Atlantic 2537		People Gotta Be Free / My World	1968	.80	4.00
Atlantic 2537	(PS)	People Gotta Be Free / My World	1968	1.60	8.00
Atlantic 2534		See / Away Away	1969	.80	4.00
Atlantic 2534	(PS)	See / Away Away	1969	1.60	8.00
Atlantic 2584		A Ray Of Hope / Any Dance'll Do	1969	.80	4.00
Atlantic 2584	(PS)	A Ray Of Hope / Any Dance'll Do	1969	1.60	8.00
Atlantic 2599		Heaven / Baby, I'm Blue	1969	.80	4.00
Atlantic 2664		Carry Me Back / Real Thing	1969	.80	4.00
Atlantic 2664	(PS)	Carry Me Back / Real Thing	1969	1.60	8.00

Label & Catalog #		A-Side/B-Side	Year	VG	NM
Atlantic 2695		Hold On / I Believe	1970	.80	4.00
Atlantic 2695	(PS)	Hold On / I Believe	1970	1.60	8.00
Atlantic 2743		Glory Glory / You Don't Know	1970	.80	4.00
Atlantic 2743	(PS)	Glory Glory / You Don't Know	1970	1.60	8.00
Atlantic 2773		Right On / Almost Home	1970	.80	4.00
Columbia 45400		Love Me / Happy Song	1971	.60	3.00
Columbia 45491		Lucky Day / Love Letter	1971	.60	3.00
Columbia 45568		Brother Tree / Saga Of New York	1971	.60	3.00
Columbia 45600		Echoes / Hummin' Song	1972	.60	3.00
Columbia 45649		Jungle Walk / Saga Of New York	1972	1.00	5.00

RASPBERRIES, THE
Members include Jim Bonfanti, Wally Bryson, Eric Carmen and Dave Smalley. Bonfanti and Smalley left in 1973, replaced by Mike McBride and Scott McCarl. Refer to The Choir.

Capitol 3280		Don't Want To Say Goodbye / Rock And Roll Mama	1972	1.60	8.00
Capitol 3280	(PS)	Don't Want To Say Goodbye / Rock And Roll Mama	1972	5.00	25.00
Capitol 3348		Go All The Way / With You In My Life	1972	.80	4.00
Capitol 3473		I Wanna Be With You / Goin' Nowhere	1972	.80	4.00
Capitol 3546		Let's Pretend / Every Way I Can	1973	.80	4.00
Capitol 3546	(PS)	Let's Pretend / Every Way I Can	1973	2.00	10.00
Capitol 3610		Tonight / Hard To Get Over A Heartbreak	1973	.80	4.00
Capitol 3765		I'm A Rocker / Money Down	1973	.80	4.00
Capitol 3826		Ecstasy / Don't Wanna Say Goodbye	1974	.80	4.00
Capitol 3885		Drivin' Around / Might As Well	1974	.80	4.00
Capitol 3946		Overnight Sensation (Hit Record) / Hands On You	1974	.80	4.00
Capitol 4001		Cruisin' Music / The Party's Over	1974	.80	4.00

RAT PACK, THE

DCP 1145		I Can Do The Mouse, Now / Crazy, Crazy Love	1965	3.00	15.00

RATFINK, J.C.W.
J.C.W. Ratfink features Mark Gutkowski, formerly of The 1910 Fruitgum Company.

Buddah 40		Pop Goes The Weasel / Magic Windmill	1968	2.00	10.00

RATIONALS, THE

A-Square 101		Look What You're Doin' / Gave My Name	1966	4.00	20.00
A-Square 103		Little Girls Cry / Feelin' Lost	1966	3.00	15.00
A-Square 104		Respect / Leavin' Here	1966	3.00	15.00
A-Square 107		I Need You / Out In The Streets	1966	3.00	15.00
Cameo 437		Respect / Feelin' Lost	1966	2.00	10.00
Cameo 455		Hold On, Baby / Sing	1966	2.00	10.00
Crewe 340		Handbags And Gladrags / Guitar Army	1969	2.00	10.00
Capitol 2124		I Need You / Out In The Streets	1969	1.25	6.00

RATTLES, THE

Mercury 72403		Shame Shame Shame / Someone Who Is Just Like You	1965	2.00	10.00
Mercury 72554		Sha La La La Lee / Dance	1966	2.00	10.00
Probe 480		The Witch / Geraldine	1970	2.00	10.00
London 1047		Devil's On The Loose / I Know You Don't Know	1971	1.00	5.00

RAVELLES, THE

Mobie 3430		Psychedelic Movement / She's Forever On My Mind	1968	4.00	20.00
Mobie		Get Ready /	1968	2.00	10.00

RAVEN

Rust 5123		Now She's Gone / Calamity Jane	1963	2.00	10.00

RAVEN

Columbia 44988		Feelin' Good / Green Mountain Dream	1969	1.00	5.00
Columbia 45163		Children At Our Feet / Here Comes A Truck	1970	1.00	5.00

RAVENAIRS, THE

Algonquin 718		Together Forever / A Night To Remember	195?	10.00	50.00

RAVENSCROFT, THURL

Aardell 105		Dr. Geek / I'll Pay As I Go	196?	2.00	10.00

RAVONS, THE

Davis 464		Teen-Age Idol / I'm A Fugitive	1959	2.00	10.00
Arrow 734		Teenage Hop / Wrapped, Tangled And Tied	195?	2.00	10.00

RAY, ALDER

Liberty 55175		'Cause I Love Him / A Little Love (Will Go A Long Way)	1964	5.00	25.00

RAY, ANITA, & THE NATURE BOYS

Dream 1300		The Elvis Presley Blues / Frankie's Song	1956	7.00	35.00

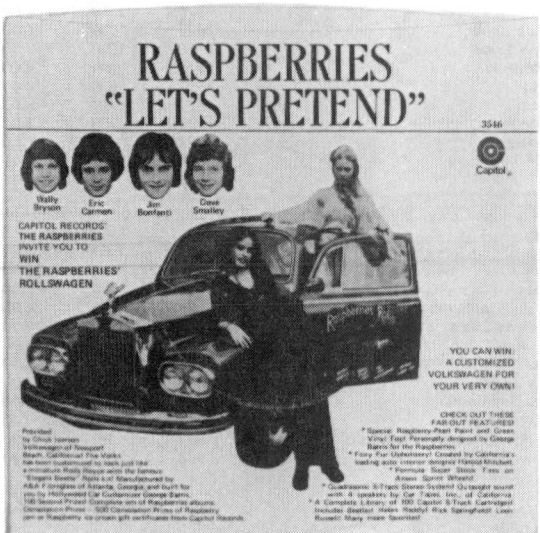

Credited with starting the "power pop" trend, Eric Carmen's Raspberries were very much in the mold of Badfinger, constructing pop music with classic guitar lines and soaring vocals. Capitol's plan to break the group included this gimmick sleeve, which serves as part of a contest to win a custom car.

Label & Catalog #		A-Side/B-Side	Year	VG	NM
RAY, DIANE					
Mercury 72117		Please Don't Talk To The Lifeguard /			
		That's All I Want From You	1963	2.00	10.00
Mercury 72117	(PS)	Please Don't Talk To The Lifeguard /			
		That's All I Want From You	1963	5.00	25.00
Mercury 72195		Where Is The Boy? / My Summer Love	1963	2.00	10.00
Mercury 72195	(PS)	Where Is The Boy? / My Summer Love	1963	5.00	25.00
Mercury 72223		Snow Man / Just So Bobby Can See	1963	2.00	10.00
Mercury 72223	(PS)	Snow Man / Just So Bobby Can See	1963	4.00	20.00
RAY, RITCHIE					
Imperial 5981		The Twirl / Come Back To Me	1963	2.00	10.00
RAY & THE DARCHAES					
Refer to The Darchaes.					
Buzzy 202		Darling Forever / There Will Always Be	196?	20.00	100.00
Aljon 1249		Carol / Little Girl So Fine	1962	7.00	35.00
RAY-VONS, THE					
Laurie 3248		Judy / Regina	1964	3.00	15.00
RAYE, CAL					
Super 101		You're My Lovin' Baby / My Tears Start To Fall	196?	2.00	10.00
RAYE, PATSY, & THE BEATNIKS					
Roulette 4208		Beatnik's Wish / Beatnik's Blues	1959	3.00	15.00
RAYMARKS, THE					
Panorama 6		Work Song / Backfire	1964	2.00	10.00
Jerden 752		Dollar Bill / Louise	1965	2.00	10.00
Jerden 752		Dollar Bill / Louise	1965	3.00	15.00
		(Label mis-print credits The Paymarks.)			
Jerden 774		I Believed / Dr. Feelgood	1965	2.00	10.00
RAYMEN, THE					
The Raymen feature Link Wray.					
Diamond 186		Baby (What Cha Want Me To Do?) /			
		Walkin' Down The Street	1965	2.00	10.00
RAYMOND, LEE					
World Pacific 77894		Ever On My Mind / Would You Like	196?	2.00	10.00
RAYS, THE					
The Rays feature Frankie Valli. Refer to Hal Miller.					
Perri 1004		Are You Happy Now? / Bright Brown Eyes	1962	7.00	35.00
RAZOR'S EDGE, THE					
Pow 101		Let's Call It A Day, Girl / Avril	1966	2.00	10.00
Pow 415		Don't Let Me Catch You In His Arms / Night And Day	1966	2.00	10.00
RE' VELLS, THE					
Roman Press 201		Let It Please Be You / Love Walked In	195?	20.00	100.00
REACTIONS, THE					
Mutual 509		That Girl / Our Wonderful Life	195?	5.00	25.00
Cool Sound 701		Just A Little Love / Let Me Hang Around You	195?	6.00	30.00
READYMEN, THE					
Bangar 655		Surfer's Blues / Shortenin' Bread	196?	7.00	35.00
REAL ORIGINAL BEATLES, THE					
Dot 16655		The Beatles Story / The Beatles Story (Part 2)	1964	4.00	20.00
REASONS, THE					
United Artists 961		Window Shopping / Then Came Heartbreak	1965	2.00	10.00
United Artists 50005		Baby Baby / My Kinda Guy	1966	2.00	10.00
United Artists 50005	(PS)	Baby Baby / My Kinda Guy	1966	2.00	10.00
REBEL ROUSERS, THE					
Memphis 107		Night Surfin' / Thunder	1964	3.00	15.00
REBELS, THE [THE BUFFALO REBELS; THE ROCKIN' REBELS]					
The Rebels originally recorded as The Hot Toddys.					
Mar-Lee 94		Wild Weekend / Wild Weekend Cha Cha	1960	10.00	50.00
Mar-Lee 95		Buffalo Blues / Donkey Walk	1961	3.00	15.00
Mar-Lee 96		Theme From Rebel / Any Way You Want Me	1961	3.00	15.00
		(Mar-Lee 95 and 96 credit The Buffalo Rebels.)			
Swan 4125		Wild Weekend / Wild Weekend Cha Cha	1962	3.00	15.00

Label & Catalog #	A-Side/B-Side	Year	VG	NM
Swan 4140	Rockin' Crickets / Hully Gully Rock	1963	3.00	15.00
Swan 4150	Another Wild Weekend / Happy Popcorn	1963	3.00	15.00
Swan 4161	Monday Morning / Flibbity Jibbit	1963	3.00	15.00
Stork 3	Burn Baby, Burn / Bongo Blue Beat	1964	4.00	20.00
	(Swan and Stork singles credit The Rockin' Rebels.)			

REBBENACK, MAC
Mac Rebbenack also recorded as Dr. John.

Ace 611	Good Times / Sahara	1961	5.00	25.00
Rex 1008	Storm Warning / Foolish Little Girl	196?	5.00	25.00

REBOUNDS, THE
The Rebounds later recorded as The Stampeders.

Tower 288	(I'm Not Your) Stepping Stone / Since I Fell For You	1966	3.00	15.00

RECALLS, THE

Arrow 2002	No Reason /	196?	3.00	15.00
Arrow 2003	Nobody's Guy /	196?	5.00	25.00

RED RIVER DAVE

Marathon 101	A Tribute To Elvis' Mother /	1958	6.00	30.00

REDELL, TEDDY

Vaden 112	Pipeliner / I Want To Hold You	1960	7.00	35.00
Hi 2024	Pipeliner / I Want To Hold You	1960	3.00	15.00
Atco 6162	Judy / Can't You See?	1960	3.00	15.00

REDJACKS, THE

Oklahoma 5005	Big Brown Eyes / To Make You Mine	1958	6.00	30.00
Apt 25006	Big Brown Eyes / To Make You Mine	1958	4.00	20.00

REDWING

Fantasy 57	California Blues / Dark Thursday	1971	.80	4.00
Fantasy 670	Bonnie Bones / I'm Your Lover Man	1971	.80	4.00
Fantasy 682	Soul Theft / Reaching Out	1972	.80	4.00
Fantasy 730	Foxfire / Early Morning Sunrise	1972	.80	4.00

REDWOODS, THE
The Redwoods feature Jeff Barry.

Epic 9347	Shake Shake Sherry / The Memory Lingers On	1962	6.00	30.00
Epic 9473	Never Take It Away / Unemployment Insurance	1962	5.00	25.00
Epic 9505	Where You Used To Be / Please, Mr. Scientist	1962	8.00	40.00

REED, CHUCK

Choctaw 101	Just Plain Hurt / Talkin' No Trash	1962	2.00	10.00
Hit 101	Just Plain Hurt / Talkin' No Trash	1962	2.00	10.00

REED, DENNY

MCI 1024	A Teenager Feels It, Too / Hat Water	1960	4.00	20.00
Trey 3007	A Teenager Feels It, Too / Hat Water	1960	2.00	10.00
Trey 3014	Little Lonely Bluebird / No One Cares	1961	2.00	10.00

REED, LARRY, & THE SHADO'S

Arlen 515	Little Miss Surfer / Bread And Butter	1963	6.00	30.00

REED, LOU
Lou Reed originally recorded with The Jades; The Primitives; and The Velvet Underground.

RCA Victor 74-0784	Walk And Talk It /	1972	.60	3.00
RCA Victor 74-0887	Walk On The Wild Side / Perfect Day	1973	.80	4.00
RCA Victor 74-0964	Satellite Of Love / Walk And Talk It	1973	.80	4.00
	(RCA 0887 and 0964 were produced by David Bowie.)			
RCA Victor APBO-0054	Vicious / Good Night Ladies	1973	.60	3.00
RCA Victor APBO-0172	Lady Day / How Do You Think It Feels	1974	.60	3.00
RCA Victor APBO-0238	Sweet Jane / Lady Day	1974	.60	3.00
RCA Victor PB-10053	Vicious /	1974	.60	3.00
RCA Victor PB-10081	Sally Can't Dance / Ennui	1974	.60	3.00
RCA Victor PB-10573	Charley's Girl / Nowhere At All	1976	.60	3.00
RCA Victor PB-10648	Crazy Feeling / Nowhere At All	1976	.60	3.00
Arista 0215	I Believe In Love / Senselessly Cruel	1976	.60	3.00
Arista 0431	City Lights / I Want To Boogie With You	1979	.40	2.00
Arista 0535	Growin' Up In Public / The Power Of Positive Drinking	1980	.40	2.00

REED, TOMMY, & THE RUNAWAYS

Token 103	Swamp Rider / Durango	196?	7.00	35.00

REEKERS, THE

Ry-Jac 13	Grindin' / Don't Call Me Flyface	196?	7.00	35.00

Label & Catalog #	A-Side/B-Side	Year	VG	NM
REFLECTIONS, THE				
Gaity 6017	Have A Good Time / Treasure Of Love	196?	5.00	25.00
REFLECTIONS, THE				
Tigre 602	In The Still Of The Night / Tic Toc	196?	6.00	30.00
Cross Roads 401	I Really Must Know / Tomorrow	1961	7.00	35.00
Cross Roads 402	Because Of You / Rocket To The Moon	1961	8.00	40.00
REFLECTIONS, THE				
Golden World 9	(Just Like) Romeo And Juliet /			
	Can't You Tell By The Look In My Eyes?	1964	2.00	10.00
Golden World 12	Like Columbus Did / Lonely Girl	1964	1.20	6.00
Golden World 15	Talkin' 'Bout My Girl / Oowee Wow	1964	1.20	6.00
Golden World 16	Don't Do That To Me / A Henpecked Guy	1964	1.20	6.00
Golden World 19	You're My Baby / Shabby Little Hut	1964	1.20	6.00
Golden World 20	Poor Man's Son / Comin' At You	1965	1.20	6.00
Golden World 22	Wheelin' And Dealin' / Deborah Ann	1965	1.20	6.00
Golden World 24	Out Of The Picture / June Bride	1965	1.20	6.00
Golden World 29	The Girl In The Candy Store / Your Kind Of Love	1966	1.20	6.00
ABC 10794	Like Adam And Eve / Vito's House	1966	1.00	5.00
ABC 10822	You're Gonna Find Out You Need Me / Long Cigarette	1966	1.00	5.00
REGAL, MIKE				
Kapp 506	Too Young / It's True What They Say About Barbara	1963	3.00	15.00
REGALS, THE				
Lavender 1452	See You In The Morning / Yes My Love	196?	6.00	30.00
Last Chance 109	See You In The Morning / Yes My Love	196?	2.00	10.00
REGALS, THE				
United Artists 380	Icy Fingers / Tiger Tears	196?	5.00	25.00
REGAN, TEX, & JIM MYERS				
Fortune 211	Pretty Baby, Rock / J&D Hop	1960	2.00	10.00
REGAN, TOMMY (& THE TIDES)				
Colpix 725	Never Stop Loving You / This Time I'm Losing You	1964	15.00	75.00
World Artists 1049	I Adore You / Nine To Five	1965	3.00	15.00
REGENTS, THE				
The Regents feature Chuck Fassert and Guy Villari. Refer to Cardboard Zeppelin; Jimmy Curtis; The Desires; Chuck Harper; Frank Lyndon; Lee Mareno; The 1929 Depression; The Runarounds.				
Cousins 1002	Barbara-Ann / I'm So Lonely	1961	75.00	300.00
Gee 1065	Barbara-Ann / I'm So Lonely	1961	4.00	20.00
Gee 1071	Runaround / Laura, My Darling	1961	4.00	20.00
Gee 1073	Don't Be A Fool / Liar	1961	4.00	20.00
Gee 1075	Lonesome Boy / Oh, Baby	1961	4.00	20.00
REGENTS, THE				
Blue Cat 110	Me And You / Playmates	1965	2.00	10.00
REGENTS, THE				
Peoria 0008	Summertime Blues /	196?	3.00	15.00
REGENTS, THE				
Kayo 101	(That's What I Call) A Real Good Time / No Hard Feelings?	196?	4.00	20.00
REID, MATHEW				
Topix 6006	Cry Myself To Sleep / Lollipops Went Out Of Style	1961	5.00	25.00
ABC-Paramount 10259	Jane / Why Start?	1961	5.00	25.00
ABC-Paramount 10305	Through My Tears / The Tarzan Twist	1962	5.00	25.00
Scepter 1238	Faded Roses / Tomorrow	196?	5.00	25.00
REJOICE				
Dunhill 4158	Golden Gate Park / Sonora	1968	1.00	5.00
Dunhill 4176	Quick Draw Man / November Snow	1968	1.00	5.00
RELATIONS, THE				
Davy Jones 664	Back To The Beach / Too Proud To Let You Know	196?	7.00	35.00
Davy Jones 664 (PS)	Back To The Beach / Too Proud To Let You Know	196?	7.00	35.00
Demand 501	Back To The Beach / Too Proud To Let You Know	196?	1.00	5.00
RELATIONS, THE				
Kape 504	Smile / Until We Two Are One	1963	2.00	10.00
Kape 703	Too Proud To Let You Know / What Did I Do Wrong?	196?	1.00	5.00
RELATIVES, THE				
Burdette 102	I Can't Belive You're Gone / Quesera Machine	196?	2.00	10.00

Label & Catalog #		A-Side/B-Side	Year	VG	NM
RELF, KEITH					
Keith Relf originally recorded with The Yardbirds. and Armaggedon.					
Epic 10044	(DJ)	**Mr. Zero / Mr. Zero** (Red vinyl)	1966	25.00	125.00
Epic 10044	(DJ)	**Mr. Zero / Knowing**	1966	5.00	25.00
Epic 10044		**Mr. Zero / Knowing**	1966	7.00	35.00
Epic 10110	(DJ)	**Shapes In My Mind / Blue Sands**	1967	5.00	25.00
Epic 10110		**Shapes In My Mind / Blue Sands**	1967	7.00	35.00
Epic 10110	(PS)	**Shapes In My Mind / Blue Sands**	1967	20.00	100.00
REMAINS, THE					
The Reamins are Bill Briggs, Vern Miller, N.D. Smart and Barry Tashian.					
Epic 9783		**Why Do I Cry? / My Babe**	1965	8.00	40.00
Epic 9842		**I Can't Get Away / But I Ain't Got You**	1965	8.00	40.00
Epic 10001	(DJ)	**Diddy Wah Diddy / Diddy Wah Diddy** (Red vinyl)	1966	20.00	100.00
Epic 10001	(PS)	**To Be Seen And Heard** (Promotional title sleeve)	1965	20.00	100.00
Epic 10001		**Diddy Wah Diddy / Once Before**	1966	10.00	50.00
Epic 10060		**Don't Look Back / Me About You**	1966	8.00	40.00
RENAY, DIANE					
20th Century Fox 456		**Navy Blue / Unbelievable Guy**	1964	3.00	15.00
20th Century Fox 477		**Kiss Me, Sailor / Soft Spoken Guy**	1964	2.00	10.00
20th Century Fox 514		**Waitin' For Joey / Growin' Up Too Fast**	1964	2.00	10.00
20th Century Fox 533		**Present From Eddie / It's In Your Tears**	1964	2.00	10.00
MGM 13296		**Billy Blue Eyes / Watch Out, Sally**	1964	2.00	10.00
MGM 13335		**I Had A Dream / Troublemaker**	1964	3.00	15.00
RENDELLS, THE					
Carmax 101		**Hot Licks / Oh, It Hurts**	1963	4.00	20.00
RENDEZVOUS, THE					
Reprise 20089		**Congratulations, Baby / Faithfully**	1962	6.00	30.00
Rust 5041		**It Breaks My Heart / Take A Break**	1963	3.00	15.00
RENDEZVOUS STOMPERS, THE					
Dore 626		**Gremmies Unite / Rock Me Gently**	1962	6.00	30.00
RENE & RAY					
Donna 160		**Queen Of My Heart / Do What You Feel**	1962	2.00	10.00
RENEGADES, THE					
The Renegades feature Kim Fowley, Bruce Johnston and Sandy Nelson.					
American Inter. 537		**Charge / Geronimo**	1959	6.00	30.00
RENEGADES, THE					
GNP/Crescendo 193		**Surfin' Tragedy / Exotic**	1963	3.00	15.00
RENEGADES, THE					
Citation 5005		**Istanbul / Come On Out**	1963	6.00	30.00
RENEGADES, THE					
Garland 2036		**I'm A Loner / Travelin' Through This Countryside**	196?	2.00	10.00
RENO, AL					
Kapp 432		**Cheryl / Congratulations**	1961	8.00	40.00
RENO, NICK					
Ges 100		**I Had A Dream / My Darling**	196?	7.00	35.00
RENOLDS, MIKE, & THE INFANTS OF SOUL					
Frog Death 3		**When Will I Find Her? / It's Judy**	1966	5.00	25.00
RENOVATIONS, THE					
Angel Town 101		**Thanks To Him / As We Danced**	196?	2.00	10.00
RENOWNS, THE					
Everest 19396		**My Mind's Made Up / Wild One**	1961	5.00	25.00
REPARATA & THE DELRONS [REPARATA]					
Laurie 3252		**Your Big Mistake / Leave Us Alone**	1964	7.00	35.00
		(*Laurie 3252 credits The Delrons.*)			
World Artists 1036		**Whenever A Teenager Cries / He's My Guy**	1965	2.00	10.00
World Artists 1051		**Tommy / Mama Don't Allow**	1965	1.20	6.00
World Artists 1062		**The Boy I Love / I Found My Place**	1965	1.20	6.00
World Artists 1075		**He's The Greatest / Summer Thoughts**	1966	1.20	6.00
RCA Victor 45-8420		**I'm Nobody's Baby Now / Loneliest Girl In Town**	1966	1.20	6.00
RCA Victor 45-8721		**I Can Tell / Take A Look Around You**	1965	1.20	6.00
RCA Victor 45-8921		**Mama's Little Girl / He Don't Want You**	1966	1.20	6.00

Label & Catalog #	A-Side/B-Side	Year	VG	NM
RCA Victor 45-9123	The Kind Of Trouble I Love / Boys And Girls	1967	1.20	6.00
RCA Victor 45-9185	I Can Hear The Rain / Always Waitin'	1967	1.20	6.00
Mala 573	I Believe / It's Waiting There For You	1967	1.00	5.00
Mala 589	Captain Of Your Ship / Toom Toom (Is A Little Boy)	1968	1.00	5.00
Mala 12000	Saturday Night Didn't happen / Panic	1968	1.00	5.00
Mala 12016	Weather Forecast / You Can't Change A Young Boy's Mind	1968	1.00	5.00
Mala 12026	Heaven Only Knows / Summer Laughter	1968	1.00	5.00
Kapp 989	I've Got An Awful Lot Of Losing To Do / (That's What Sends Men To The) Bowery	1969	1.00	5.00
Kapp 2010	We're Gonna Hold The Night / San Juan	1969	1.00	5.00
Kapp 2050	Walking In The Rain / I've Got An Awful Lot Of Losing To Do	1969	1.00	5.00
Laurie 3589	Octopus's Garden / Your Life Is Gone	1972	.80	4.00
	(Label only credits Reparata.)			
Big Tree 114	There's So Little Time / Just You	197?	.80	4.00
Polydor 14271	Shoes / A Song For All	1975	.60	3.00
	(Polydor 14271 credits Reparata.)			

RESIDENTS, THE
Refer to Schwump.

Ralph RR1272	Santa Dog	1972	125.00	500.00
	(Two singles issued in a numbered, hand-colored picture sleeve. The two discs are worth $100; the sleeve, $400.)			
Ralph RR0776	Satisfaction / Loser=Weed	1976	40.00	200.00
	(Issued in a numbered, hand-colored picture sleeve.)			
Ralph RR0577	The Residents Play The Beatles	1977	40.00	200.00
	(A montage of Beatles recordings. Issued in a numbered, hand-colored picture sleeve.)			
Ralph RR7803	Satisfaction / Loser=Weed (Yellow vinyl)	1976	.40	2.00
Ralph RR7803 (PS)	Satisfaction / Loser=Weed	1976	.40	2.00
Ralph RR7812	Santa Dog '78 / Santa Dog	1978	5.00	25.00
Ralph RR7812 (PS)	Santa Dog '78 / Santa Dog	1978	5.00	25.00
Ralph RZ8422	The White Single	1983	2.00	10.00
	—12" Singles—			
Ralph RZ8006	Diskomo / Goosebump (PC)	1980	2.00	10.00
	—Extended Play Albums—			
Ralph RR0377	Babyfingers	197?	30.00	150.00
W.E.I.R.D. 1	Babyfingers (Fan club reissue)	1981	3.00	15.00
Ralph RR1177	Duck Stab (Coated stock cover)	1978	10.00	50.00
Ralph RR1177	Duck Stab (Matte stock cover)	1978	2.00	10.00
Ralph RZ8252	Intermission	1982	3.00	15.00

RESNICK, ARTIE

White Whale 294	Balloon Man / Here We Go	1969	1.00	5.00

RESONICS, THE

Lucky Token 108	I'm Really In Love / Think Right	195?	10.00	50.00

RESTIVO, JOHNNY

RCA Victor 47-7559	The Shape I'm In / Ya Ya	1959	2.00	10.00
RCA Victor 61-7559 (S)	The Shape I'm In / Ya Ya	1959	6.00	30.00
RCA Victor 47-7601	I Like Girls / Dear Someone	196?	2.00	10.00
20th Century Fox 279	Doctor Love / The Magic Age Is Seventeen	1961	2.00	10.00

REV-LONS, THE

Garpax 44168	Give Me One More Chance / Boy Trouble	1962	3.00	15.00

REVALONS, THE

Pet 802	Dreams Are For Fools / This Is The Moment	1958	8.00	40.00

REVELIERS, THE

G-Clef 702	Hangin' Five / Patch	196?	7.00	35.00

REVELL, DIGGER (& THE DENVERMEN)

Capitol 4934	Surfside / Lisa Maree	1963	3.00	15.00
	(Also issued on Big Top credited to The Note-Ables.)			

REVELLES, THE

Freeport 1005	One More Day / You Love Me No More	196?	2.00	10.00

REVELS, THE

Vee Jay 306	Shombalor / Lonely One	1959	5.00	25.00

REVELS, THE

Norgolde 103	Dead Man's Stroll / Talking To My Heart	1959	25.00	125.00
Norgolde 103	Midnight Stroll / Talking To My Heart	1959	3.00	15.00
Norgolde 104	Tweedley Dee / Foo Man Choo	1959	4.00	20.00
Palette 5074	I Met My Lost Love / Oh, How I Love You	1961	3.00	15.00

Label & Catalog #		A-Side/B-Side	Year	VG	NM

REVELS, THE

Label & Catalog #		A-Side/B-Side	Year	VG	NM
CT-1		Church Key / Vesuvius	1961	15.00	75.00
Impact 1		Church Key / Vesuvius	1961	4.00	20.00
Impact 1		Church Key / Vesuvius (Yellow vinyl)	1961	8.00	40.00
Impact 3		Intoxica / Tequila	1961	4.00	20.00
Impact 3		Intoxica / Tequila (Yellow vinyl)	1961	8.00	40.00
Impact 7		Commanche / Rampage	1962	4.00	20.00
Impact 7		Commanche / Rampage (Yellow vinyl)	1962	8.00	40.00
Impact 13		Party Time / Soft Hop	1963	4.00	20.00
Impact 13		Party Time / Soft Hop (Yellow vinyl)	1963	8.00	40.00
Impact 22		The Monkey Bird / Revellion	1964	4.00	20.00
Impact 22		The Monkey Bird / Revellion (Yellow vinyl)	1964	8.00	40.00
Impact 22		Conga Twist / Revellion	1964	4.00	20.00
Impact 22		Conga Twist / Revellion (Yellow vinyl)	1964	8.00	40.00
Downey 123		Intoxica / Commanche	1964	5.00	25.00
Westco 3/4		It's Party Time / Soft Hop	1963	5.00	25.00
Lynn 1302		Six Pack / Good Grief	1964	6.00	30.00
Swingin' 620		Six Pack / Good Grief	1964	6.00	30.00

REVENUERS, THE

Label & Catalog #		A-Side/B-Side	Year	VG	NM
Sin A-Way 302		Moving On / Night Dream	196?	2.00	10.00

REVERE, PAUL, & THE RAIDERS (THE RAIDERS)

The Raiders are centered around Revere and Mark Lindsay. The Gardena group included Bill Hibbard, Jerry Labrum, Richard White and Robert White. Sande sides featured Mike Smith, Steve West and Dick Walker. The 1964-67 Columbia records featured Smith, Drake Levin and Doc Holliday, replaced in 1964 by Phil Volk and Jim Valley, 1966-67. Later members were Freddie Weller, Joe Correro, Charlie Coe and Keith Allison. Refer to The Unknowns; The Volk Brothers.

Label & Catalog #		A-Side/B-Side	Year	VG	NM
Apex 106		Beatnick Sticks / Orbit (The Spy)	1960	20.00	100.00
Gardena 106		Beatnick Sticks / Orbit (The Spy)	1960	4.00	20.00
Gardena 115		Paul Revere's Ride / Unfinished Fifth	1961	4.00	20.00
Gardena 116		Like, Long Hair / Sharon	1961	3.00	15.00
Gardena 118		Like, Charleston / Midnite Ride	1961	4.00	20.00
Gardena 124		All Night Long / Groovey	1962	5.00	25.00
Gardena 127		Like, Bluegrass / Leatherneck	1962	5.00	25.00
Gardena 131		Shake It Up (Part 1) / Shake It Up (Part 2)	1962	5.00	25.00
Gardena 137		Tall Cool One / Road Runner	1962	5.00	25.00
Jerden 807		So Fine / Blues Stay Away	1963	3.00	15.00
Sande 101		Louie, Louie / Night Train	1963	—	—
		(Rare. Estimated near mint value $50-150.)			
Columbia 42814		Louie, Louie / Night Train	1963	2.00	10.00
Columbia 43008		Louie, Go Home / Have Love, Will Travel	1964	2.00	10.00
Columbia 43114		Over You / Swim	1964	1.60	8.00
Columbia 43273		Ooh Poo Pah Doo / Sometimes	1965	1.60	8.00
Columbia 43375	(DJ)	Steppin' Out / Steppin' Out (Red vinyl)	1965	7.00	35.00
Columbia 43375		Steppin' Out / Blue Fox	1965	1.20	6.00
Columbia 43461	(DJ)	Just Like Me / Just Like Me (Red vinyl)	1965	7.00	35.00
Columbia 43461		Just Like Me / B. F. D. R. F. Blues	1965	1.20	6.00
Columbia 43556	(DJ)	Kicks / Kicks (Red vinyl)	1966	7.00	35.00
Columbia 43556		Kicks / Shake It Up	1966	1.20	6.00
Columbia 43678	(DJ)	Hungry / Hungry (Red vinyl)	1966	7.00	35.00
Columbia 43678		Hungry / There She Goes	1966	1.20	6.00
Columbia 43678	(PS)	Hungry / There She Goes	1966	2.00	10.00
Columbia 43810	(DJ)	The Great Airplane Strike / The Great Airplane Strike (Red vinyl)	1966	8.00	40.00
Columbia 43810		The Great Airplane Strike / In My Community	1966	1.20	6.00
Columbia 43810	(PS)	The Great Airplane Strike / In My Community	1966	2.00	10.00
Columbia 43907	(DJ)	Good Thing / Good Thing (Red vinyl)	1966	7.00	35.00
Columbia 43907		Good Thing / Undecided Man	1966	1.00	5.00
Columbia 43907	(PS)	Good Thing / Undecided Man	1966	2.00	10.00
Columbia 44018		Ups And Downs / Leslie	1967	1.00	5.00
Columbia 44018	(PS)	Ups And Downs / Leslie	1967	2.00	10.00
Columbia 44094		Him Or Me-What's It Gonna Be? / Legend Of Paul Revere	1967	1.00	5.00
Columbia 44094	(PS)	Him Or Me-What's It Gonna Be? / Legend Of Paul Revere	1967	2.00	10.00
Columbia 44207		I Had A Dream / Upon You Leaving	1967	.80	4.00
Columbia 44207	(PS)	I Had A Dream / Upon You Leaving	1967	1.20	6.00
Columbia 44335		Peace Of Mind / Do Unto Others	1967	.80	4.00
Columbia 44335	(PS)	Peace Of Mind / Do Unto Others	1967	1.00	5.00
Columbia 44444		Too Much Talk / Happening '68	1968	1.00	5.00
Columbia 44444	(PS)	Too Much Talk / Happening '68	1968	1.20	6.00
Columbia 44553		Don't Take It So Hard / Observation From Flight 285	1968	.80	4.00
Columbia 44553	(PS)	Don't Take It So Hard / Observation From Flight 285	1968	1.20	6.00
Columbia 44655		Cinderella Sunshine / Theme From "It's Happening"	1968	.80	4.00
Columbia 44655		Cinderella Sunshine / Theme From "What's Happening"	1968	1.20	6.00
		(Misprint erroneously lists TV show as "What's Happening.")			
Columbia 44744		Mr. Sun, Mr. Moon / Without You	1969	.80	4.00
Columbia 44744	(PS)	Mr. Sun, Mr. Moon / Without You	1969	1.20	6.00
Columbia 44854		Let Me / I Don't Know	1969	.80	4.00
Columbia 44970		We Gotta All Get Together / Frankfort Side Street	1969	.80	4.00

Label & Catalog #		A-Side / B-Side	Year	VG	NM
Columbia 45082		Just Seventeen / Sorceress With Blue Eyes	1970	.80	4.00
Columbia 45150		Gone Movin' On / Interlude (To Be Forgotten)	1970	.80	4.00
Columbia 45332		Indian Reservation (The Lament Of The Cherokee Reservation Indian) / Terry's Tune	1971	.80	4.00
Columbia 45453		Birds Of A Feather / The Turkey	1971	.80	4.00
Columbia 45535		Country Wine / It's So Hard Getting Up Today	1972	.80	4.00
Columbia 45601		Powder Blue Mercedes Queen / Golden Girls Sometimes	1972	.80	4.00
Columbia 45688		Song Seller / Simple Song	1972	.80	4.00
Columbia 45759		Love Music / Goodbye #9	1973	.80	4.00
Columbia 45898		All Over You / Seaboard Line Boogie	1973	.80	4.00
Columbia 10126		Gonna Have A Good Time / Your Love	1975	1.00	5.00
		(Columbia 45082-10126 credits The Raiders.)			
20th Century 2281		The British Are Coming / (B-side by Susie Allanson)	1976	.80	4.00
Drive 6248		Ain't Nothing Wrong / You're Really Saying Something	1976	.60	3.00
Raider America Fan Club		Kicks (Live) /	1982	2.00	10.00
Hitbound 102		Jingle Bells / (B-side by Mike Love & Dean Torrence)	1983	1.00	5.00
Hitbound 102	(PS)	Jingle Bells / (B-side by Mike Love & Dean Torrence)	1983	2.00	10.00
		—Special/Promotional Releases—			
Columbia CSP-262		SS 396 / Corvair Baby	1965	3.00	15.00
Columbia CSM-466		SS 396 / (B-side by the Cyrkle)	1967	2.00	10.00
Columbia CSM-466	(PS)	SS 396 / Camaro	1967	3.00	15.00
Jerden JRL-7004	(33)	In The Beginning (Jukebox EP)	1967	5.00	25.00
Teen Scoop		Paul Revere Interviews The Raiders	1967	10.00	50.00
		(Cardboard picture disc from Teen Scoop magazine.)			
Columbia 9665	(33)	Something Happening (Jukebox EP)	1968	4.00	20.00
What's It All About 112		Country Wine / Interview With Mark Lindsay/Freddy Weller	1972	4.00	20.00

REVERES, THE

Jubilee 5463		Beyond The Sea / The Show Must Go On	1963	5.00	25.00
Valiant 6041		Big T / Me And My Spider	1964	10.00	50.00
		(Bruce Johnston provides vocals on both sides of Valiant 6041.)			

REVLONS, THE

Rae Cox 105		This Restless Heart / I Promise Love	1961	3.00	15.00
Capitol 4739		Dry Your Eyes / She'll Come To Me	1962	3.00	15.00
Times Square 15		Ride Away / Betty	1963	2.00	10.00

REY, LITTLE BOBBY

Original Sound 08		Rockin' "J" Bells / Corrido De Auld	1959	2.00	10.00

REY, RANER

Jerden 781		Whiplash / Rovin' Young Man	196?	1.00	5.00

REYNOLDS, ALLEN

RCA 47-8190		Here Comes Raggedy Ann / She Really Lied	1963	2.00	10.00

REYNOLDS, JODY

Demon 1507		Endless Sleep / Tight Capris	1958	4.00	20.00
Demon 1509		Fire Of Love / Daisy Mae	1958	3.00	15.00
Demon 1511		Closin' In / Elope With Me	1958	3.00	15.00
Demon 1515		Golden Idol / Beaulah Lee	1959	5.00	25.00
Demon 1519		Please Remember / The Storm	1959	3.00	15.00
Demon 1523		I Wanna Be With You Tonight / The Whipping Post	1959	3.00	15.00
Demon 1524		Stone Cold / (The Girl With The) Raven Hair	1959	3.00	15.00

REYNOLDS, JODY, & THE STORMS

Refer to The Storms.

Indigo 127		Thunder / Tarantula	1961	7.00	35.00

REYNOLDS, JOEY

The Four Seasons sing the theme song for Reynolds' WIBG and WXYX shows.

Wibbage WIBO		Joey Reynolds' Theme / Rat Fink Fink	1965	20.00	100.00
WXYZ 121003		Joey Reynolds' Theme / Rats In The Room	1965	20.00	100.00

RHINOCEROUS

Rhinocerous features Billy Mundi. Refer to Earth Opera; The Mothers Of Invention.

Elektra 45640		You're My Girl (I Don't Want To Discuss It) / I Will Serenade You	1968	1.00	5.00
Elektra 45647		Apricot Brandy / When You Say You're Sorry	1969	1.00	5.00

RHODES, EMITT

Emitt Rhodes originally recorded with The Palace Guard and The Merry-Go-Round.

Dunhill 4267		Fresh As A Daisy / You Take The Dark Out Of The Night	1971	1.00	5.00
Dunhill 4280		With My Face On The Floor / Lullabye	1971	.80	4.00
Dunhill 4295		Really Wanted You / Love Will Stone You	1971	.80	4.00
Dunhill 4315	(DJ)	Tame The Lion / Golden Child Of God	1971	1.00	5.00
Dunhill 4315	(PS)	Tame The Lion / Golden Child Of God	1971	1.00	5.00
		(Stock copies of Dunhill 4315 may not exist.)			

Label & Catalog #	A-Side/B-Side	Year	VG	NM
RHODES, SLIM				
Sun 216	Don't Believe / Uncertain Love	1955	10.00	50.00
Sun 225	The House Of Sin / Are You Ashamed Of Me?	1955	50.00	200.00
Sun 238	Gonna Romp And Stomp / Bad Girl	1956	15.00	75.00
Sun 256	Do What I Do / Take And Give	1956	5.00	25.00
RHYTHM ACES, THE				
Roulette 4268	Mohawk Rock / It'll Do	1960	3.00	15.00
Roulette 4426	Raunchy Twist / Mocking Bird Twist	1962	2.00	10.00
RHYTHM KINGS, THE				
Challenge 9178	Bordertown / The Soul	1962	5.00	25.00
GNP/Crescendo 196	Exotic / Blue Soul	196?	4.00	20.00
RHYTHM ROCKERS, THE				
Sun 248	Juke Box, Help Me Find My Baby / Fiddle Bop	1956	8.00	40.00
RHYTHM ROCKERS, THE				
Satin 921	We Belong Together / Oh, Boy	1960	10.00	50.00
Satin 921 (PS)	We Belong Together / Oh, Boy	1960	20.00	100.00
Wiped Out 1001	Foot Cruising / Get It On	1962	8.00	40.00
Wipe Out 1001	Foot Cruising / Get It On	1962	6.00	30.00
Challenge 9196	Rendezvous Stomp / The Slide	1963	5.00	25.00
Moonglow 202	Pachuko Hop / Stranger	196?	4.00	20.00
RHYTHM ROCKERS, THE				
Fenton 944	Surf Around / Three Strikes	196?	7.00	35.00
RHYTHM STARS, THE				
Clock 1007	Oh, Moon / Lynn	1959	8.00	40.00
RHYTHM SURFERS, THE				
Daytone 6301	Big City Surfer / 502	1963	7.00	35.00
RHYTHMERES, THE				
Brunswick 55083	Elaine / Bow Legged Baby	1958	7.00	35.00
RHYTHMETTES, THE				
Coral 62186	High School Lovers / Snow Queen	1960	3.00	15.00
RIA & THE REASONS				
Amy 888	Memories Linger On / Sorry I Lied (Opaque blue vinyl)	1964	25.00	100.00
RIBBONS, THE				
Marsh 35	After Last Night / This Is Our Melody	1963	2.00	10.00
Marsh 202	Ain't Gonna Kiss You / My Baby Said	1963	3.00	15.00
Parkway 912	They Played A Sad Song / Melodie A'mour	1964	2.00	10.00
RIC-A-SHAYS, THE				
Lola 002	Groovy / Turn On	196?	3.00	15.00
RICE, RONNIE				
Ronnie Rice also recorded with The New Colony Six.				
I.R.C. 6910	Over The Mountain / T.N.T.	196?	2.00	10.00
I.R.C. 6917	Come Back, Little Girl / Who's The New Girl?	196?	2.00	10.00
I.R.C. 6931	Tell Her / I Want You, I Need You	196?	2.00	10.00
RICE, RONNIE, & THE GENTS				
Quill 106	Warm Baby / La-Do-Da-Da	196?	3.00	15.00
RICE, RONNIE, & THE SILVERTONES				
Limelight 3029	She's Not Yours / I Want You To Be My Girl	1964	2.00	10.00
RICE, TONY, & THE OVERTONES				
Action 100	My Darling Y-O-U / I Thank You, Baby	1961	6.00	30.00
Rae Cox 106	Little School Girl / Blue Bird Of Happiness	1961	3.00	15.00
RICH, CHARLIE				
Charlie Rich also recorded as Bobby Sheridan.				
Phillips Inter. 3532	Whirlwind / Philadelphia Baby	1959	4.00	20.00
Phillips Inter. 3542	Big Man / Rebound	1959	3.00	15.00
Phillips Inter. 3552	Lonely Weekends / Everything I Do Is Wrong	1960	3.00	15.00
Phillips Inter. 3560	Gonna Be Waiting / School Days	1960	2.00	10.00
Phillips Inter. 3562	Stay / On My Knees	1960	2.00	10.00
Phillips Inter. 3566	Who Will The Next Fool Be? / Caught In The Middle	1961	2.00	10.00
Phillips Inter. 3572	Just A Little Sweet / It's Too Late	1961	2.00	10.00
Phillips Inter. 3576	Easy Money / Midnite Blues	1962	2.00	10.00
Phillips Inter. 3582	Sittin' And Thinkin' / Finally Found Out	1963	2.00	10.00

Label & Catalog #		A-Side/B-Side	Year	VG	NM
Phillips Inter. 3584		There's Another Place I Can't Go / I Need Your Love	1963	2.00	10.00
Groove 0020		She Loved Everybody But Me / The Grass Is Always Greener	1963	1.60	8.00
Groove 0020	(PS)	She Loved Everybody But Me / The Grass Is Always Greener	1963	5.00	25.00
Groove 0035		The Ways Of A Woman In Love / Mountain Dew	1964	1.60	8.00
Smash 1993		Mohair Sam / I Washed	1965	1.00	5.00
Smash 2012		The Dance Of Love / I Can't Go On	1965	1.00	5.00
Smash 2022		Something Just Came Over Me / Hawg Jaw	1966	1.00	5.00
Smash 2038		Tears Ago / No Home	1966	1.00	5.00

RICH & THE RAYS

Richly 101		My Heart / The Way You Look Tonight *(Red vinyl)*	195?	20.00	100.00
Richly 101		My Heart / The Way You Look Tonight *(Multi-color vinyl)*	195?	50.00	200.00

RICHARD, CLIFF, & THE DRIFTERS
The Drifters changed their name to The Shadows in 1959 to avoid confusion with the American R&B group.

Capitol 4096		Move It / High Class Baby	1959	6.00	30.00
Capitol 4154		Livin,' Lovin' Doll / Steady With You	1959	6.00	30.00
ABC-Paramount 10042		Living Doll / Apron Strings	1959	4.00	20.00
ABC-Paramount 10066		Travelin' Light / Dynamite	1959	3.00	15.00
ABC-Paramount 10093		A Voice In The Wilderness / Don't Be Mad At Me	1960	2.00	10.00
ABC-Paramount 10109		Fall In Love With You / Choppin' 'N' Changin'	1960	3.00	15.00
ABC-Paramount 10136		Please Don't Tease / Where Is My Heart?	1960	2.00	10.00
ABC-Paramount 10175		Catch Me, I'm Falling / "D" In Love	1961	2.00	10.00
ABC-Paramount 10195		Theme For A Dream / Mumblin' Mosie	1961	7.00	35.00
Big Top 31-1		The Young Ones / We Say Yeah	1962	3.00	15.00
Dot 16399		It's Wonderful To Be Young / Got A Funny Feeling	1962	3.00	15.00

RICHARD, CLIFF, & THE SHADOWS
Refer to The Shadows.

Epic 9597		Lucky Lips / The Next Time	1963	2.00	10.00
Epic 9597	(PS)	Lucky Lips / The Next Time	1963	3.00	15.00
Epic 9633		It's All In The Game / I'm Looking Out Of The Window	1963	2.00	10.00
Epic 9633	(PS)	It's All In The Game / I'm Looking Out Of The Window	1963	3.00	15.00
Epic 9670		I'm The Only One / I Only Have Eyes For You	1964	2.00	10.00
Epic 9670	(PS)	I'm The Only One / I Only Have Eyes For You	1964	3.00	15.00
Epic 9691		Bachelor Boy / True, True Lovin'	1964	2.00	10.00
Epic 9737		I Don't Wanna Love You / Look In My Eyes, Maria	1964	1.60	8.00
Epic 9757		The Minute You're Gone / Again	1965	1.60	8.00
Epic 9810		I Could Easily Fall / On My Word	1965	1.60	8.00
Epic 9839		The Twelfth Of Never / Paradise Lost	1965	1.60	8.00
Epic 9867		Wind Me Up / The Eye Of The Needle	1965	1.60	8.00
Epic 10018		Blue Turns To Grey / I'll Walk Alone	1966	1.60	8.00
Epic 10018	(PS)	Blue Turns To Grey / I'll Walk Alone	1966	3.00	15.00
Epic 10070		Visions / Quando, Quando, Quando	1966	1.60	8.00
Epic 10101		Time Drags By / La La La Song	1967	1.60	8.00
Epic 10101	(PS)	Time Drags By / La La La Song	1967	3.00	15.00
Epic 10178		Heartbeat / It's All Over	1968	1.60	8.00
		— Extended Play Albums—			
Epic 26089	(33)	I'm In The Mood For Love *(Jukebox EP)*	1967	4.00	20.00

RICHARD, CLIFF

Uni 55061		All My Love / Our Story Book	1968	.80	4.00
Uni 55069		Congratulations / High 'N' Dry	1968	.80	4.00
Uni 55145		The Day I Met Marie / Sweet Little Jesus Boy	1969	.80	4.00
Light 601		Two A Penny / I'll Love You Forever Today	196?	.80	4.00
Warner Bros. 7734		Throw Down The Line / Reflections	1969	.80	4.00
Monument 1211		You Never Can Tell / Goodbye Sam, Hello Samantha	1972	.80	4.00
Monument 1229		I Ain't Got Time Anymore / Monday Comes Too Soon	1972	.80	4.00
Sire 703		Living In Harmony / Jesus	1973	.80	4.00
Sire 707		Power To All Our Friends / Come Back, Billie Jo	1973	.80	4.00
Rocket 40531		Miss You Nights / Love Enough	1976	.60	3.00
Rocket 40574		Devil Woman / Love On (Shine On)	1976	.60	3.00
Rocket 40652		I Can't Ask For Anymore Than You / Junior Cowboy	1976	.60	3.00
Rocket 40724		Don't Turn The Light On / Nothing Left For Me To Say	1977	.60	3.00
Rocket 40771		Try A Smile / You've Got Me Wondering	1977	.60	3.00

RICHARD, SCOTT CASE

A-Square 301		I'm So Glad / Who Is That Girl?	196?	5.00	25.00

RICHARD & THE YOUNG LIONS

Philips 40381		Open Up Your Door / Once Upon Your Smile	1966	1.60	8.00
Philips 40381	(PS)	Open Up Your Door / Once Upon Your Smile	1966	5.00	25.00
Philips 40414		Lost And Found / Nasty	1966	2.00	10.00

RICHARDS, CAL

Vitose 100		Let Him Get His Own Girl / Small Town Girl	196?	3.00	15.00

Label & Catalog #		A-Side/B-Side	Year	VG	NM
RICHARDS, KEITH					
Keith Richards is a member of The Rolling Stones.					
Rolling Stones 316		Before They Make Me Run / Before They Make Me Run	1978	4.00	20.00
Rolling Stones 316	(PS)	Before They Make Me Run / Before They Make Me Run	1978	6.00	30.00
		(Counterfeits of this sleeve exist without the pupils in Keith's eyes.)			
Rolling Stones 19311	(DJ)	Run Rudolph, Run / Run Rudolph, Run	1978	2.00	10.00
Rolling Stones 19311		Run Rudolph, Run / The Harder They Come	1978	3.00	15.00
RICHARDS, MARTY					
Music Makers 102		Evaline / I'll Speak Now	196?	2.00	10.00
RICHARDS, SONNY, & THE PANICS					
Refer to The Panics.					
Chancellor 1127		Skinny Minnie Olive Oil / The Voodoo Walk	1962	2.00	10.00
RICHARDS, TONY, & THE TWILIGHTS					
Colpix 178		Please Believe Me / Paper Boy	1960	20.00	100.00
RICHARDSON, JAPE					
Jape Richardson also recorded as The Big Bopper.					
Mercury 71219	(DJ)	Beggar To A King / Crazy Blues	1957	6.00	30.00
Mercury 71219		Beggar To A King / Crazy Blues	1957	8.00	40.00
Mercury 71312	(DJ)	Teenage Moon / Monkey Song	1958	6.00	30.00
Mercury 71312		Teenage Moon / Monkey Song	1958	8.00	40.00
RICHARDSON, RUDI					
Sun 271		Fool's Hall Of Fame / Why Should I Cry?	1957	3.00	15.00
RICHIE & THE HALLMARKS					
Amy 877		Whoever You Are / Joanie, Don't You Cry	1963	4.00	20.00
RICHIE & THE REBELS					
Barclay 13348		Rebel Rock / With Love That's True	196?	6.00	30.00
RICHIE & THE SAXONS					
Tip 1020		Bottom Of The Barrel / Easy Now	196?	7.00	35.00
RICHIE & THE ROYALS					
Rello 1		And When I'm Near You / Goody Goody	1961	6.00	30.00
Rello 3		Be My Girl / We're Strollin'	1962	25.00	125.00
RICHIE'S RENEGADES					
Polaris 65		Baby, It's Me /	196?	4.00	20.00
RICHMAN, JONATHAN (& THE MODERN LOVERS)					
Refer to the Various Artists EP section.					
Beserkley 5701		Roadrunner / (B-side by Earthquake:)	1975	1.00	5.00
Beserkley 5701	(PS)	Roadrunner / (B-side by Earthquake:)	1975	2.00	10.00
Beserkely 5743		New England / Here Come The Martians	1976	1.00	5.00
Beserkely 5743	(PS)	New England / Here Come The Martians	1976	1.00	5.00
RICHY, PAUL					
Sun 338		Legend Of The Big Steeple / Broken Hearted Willie	1960	2.00	10.00
RICK & EDDY					
Hit-Teen 877		Jeannie (With The Light Brown Hair) / I Never Loved	196?	2.00	10.00
RICK & THE KEENS					
Austin 303		Peanuts / I'll Be Home	1961	15.00	75.00
Le Cam 721		Peanuts / I'll Be Home	1961	5.00	25.00
Smash 1705		Peanuts / I'll Be Home	1961	3.00	15.00
Smash 1722		Maybe / Popcorn	1961	3.00	15.00
Jamie 1219		Your Turn To Cry / Tender Years	1962	3.00	15.00
Le Cam 113		Darla / Someone New	1964	6.00	30.00
Tollie 9016		Darla / Someone New	1964	4.00	20.00
RICK & THE LEGENDS					
United Artists 50093		I Wonder Why / Love Me Like I Know You Can	1963	2.00	10.00
RICK & THE MASTERS					
Haral 778		Bewitched, Bothered And Bewildered / A Kissin' Friend	1962	10.00	50.00
Taba 101		Flame Of Love / Here Comes Nancy	1962	25.00	125.00
Cameo 226		Flame Of Love / Here Comes Nancy	1962	4.00	20.00
Cameo 247		Let It Please Be You / I Don't Want Your Love	1963	4.00	20.00
RICK & THE RANDELLS					
ABC-Paramount 10055		Let It Be You / Honey Doll	1959	7.00	35.00

For some, Jonathan Richman has developed a reputation as a primitive genius in a sort of idiot savant manner. For most, he remains an acquired taste.

Label & Catalog #		A-Side/B-Side	Year	VG	NM
RICK & THE RAVENS					
Posae 101		Rampage / Big Bucket T	196?	15.00	75.00
RICK & THE RAVENS					
The Ravens feature Ray Manzarek, later of The Doors.					
Aura 4511		Soul Train / (B-side by Ray Daniels)	1965	10.00	50.00
RICK & THE RICK-A-SHAYS					
Reprise 20226		The Drag / Running Bear	1963	2.00	10.00
RICK & THE RIDERS					
Sonic 76234		I Know That I Love You / What Can I Do?	196?	3.00	15.00
RICKY & THE SAINTS					
Seven Teen 101		When The Saints Twist / My Special Angel	1962	2.00	10.00
RICKY & THE VACELS					
Refer to The Vacels.					
Fargo 1050		His Girl / Don't Want Your Love No More	1960	5.00	25.00
Fargo 1050		His Girl / Don't Want Your Love No More *(Blue vinyl)*	1960	15.00	75.00
Express 711		Lorraine / Bubble Gum	196?	5.00	25.00
RICO & THE RAVENS					
Rally 1601		Don't You Know / In My Heart	1965	8.00	40.00
Autumn 6		Don't You Know / In My Heart	1965	3.00	15.00
RIDDELL FOUR, DON					
General 723		Girl Of My Best Friend / Don't Be Cruel	1961	3.00	15.00
RIDDLES, THE					
Mercury 72669		Sweets For My Sweet / It's One Thing To Say	1967	2.00	10.00
RIELS, THE					
Laurie 3237		Let Him Go / Paul	1964	2.00	10.00
RIFFS, THE					
Sunny 22		Little Girl / Why Are The Nights So Cold?	195?	25.00	125.00
Old Town 1179		Tell Tale Friends / Why Are The Nights So Cold?	1965	8.00	40.00
Jamie 1296		Tell Her / I Been Thinkin'	1965	2.00	10.00
RIGHTEOUS BROTHERS, THE					
The Righteous Brothers are Bobby Hatfield and Bill Medley, who originally recorded as The Paramours. Jimmy Walker of The Knickerbockers replaced Medley in 1968. Sides below may be credited solely to Hatfield or Medley.					
Moonglow 215	(DJ)	Little Latin Lupe Lu / Little Latin Lupe Lu (Red vinyl)	1963	6.00	30.00
Moonglow 215		Little Latin Lupe Lu / I'm So Lonely	1963	1.60	8.00
Moonglow 220		I Need A Girl / Hot Tamale	1963	1.20	6.00
Moonglow 221		Gotta Tell You How I Feel / If You're Lying, You'll Be Crying	1963	1.20	6.00
Moonglow 223		My Babe / Fee-Fi-Fiddly-I-Oh	1963	1.20	6.00
Moonglow 224		Ko Ko Joe / B Flat Blues	1963	1.20	6.00
Moonglow 231		Try To Find Another Man / I Still Love You	1964	1.20	6.00
Moonglow 234		Bring Your Love To Me / If You're Lying, You'll Be Crying	1964	1.20	6.00
Moonglow 235		This Little Girl Of Mine / If You're Lying, You'll Be Crying	1965	1.20	6.00
Moonglow 238		Fannie Mae / Bring Your Love To Me	1965	1.20	6.00
Moonglow 239		You Can Have Her / Love Or Magic?	1965	1.20	6.00
Moonglow 242		Justine / In That Great Gettin' Up Morning	1965	1.20	6.00
Moonglow 243		For Your Love / Gotta Tell You How I Feel	1965	1.20	6.00
Moonglow 244		Georgia On My Mind / My Tears Will Go Away	1965	1.20	6.00
Moonglow 245		I Need A Girl / Bring Your Love To Me	1965	1.20	6.00
Philles 124		You've Lost That Lovin' Feelin' / There's A Woman	1964	1.50	8.00
		("You've Lost That Lovin' Feelin' " was produced by Phil Spector.)			
Philles 127		Just Once In My Life / The Blues	1965	2.00	10.00
Philles 127	(PS)	Just Once In My Life / The Blues	1965	3.00	15.00
		("Just Once In My Life" was produced by Phil Spector.)			
Philles 129		Hung On You / Unchained Melody	1965	2.00	10.00
Philles 130		Ebb Tide / (I Love You) For Sentimental Reasons	1965	2.00	10.00
Philles 130	(PS)	Ebb Tide / (I Love You) For Sentimental Reasons	1965	3.00	15.00
Philles 132		The White Cliffs Of Dover / She's Mine, All Mine	1966	3.00	15.00
Philles 132	(PS)	The White Cliffs Of Dover / She's Mine, All Mine	1966	3.00	15.00
		(Philles 129, 130 and 132 were produced by Phil Spector.)			
Verve 10383		(You're My) Soul And Inspiration / B Side Blues	1966	1.20	6.00
Verve 10383	(PS)	(You're My) Soul And Inspiration / B Side Blues	1966	2.00	10.00
Verve 10403		Rat Race / Green Onions	1966	1.00	5.00
Verve 10406		He / He Will Break Your Heart	1966	1.00	5.00
Verve 10406	(PS)	He / He Will Break Your Heart	1966	1.00	5.00
Verve 10430		Go Ahead And Cry / Things Didn't Go Your Way	1966	1.00	5.00
Verve 10449		On This Side Of Goodbye / A Man Without A Dream	1966	1.00	5.00
Verve 10479		Along Came Jones / Jimmy's Blues	1967	.80	4.00
Verve 10507		Melancholy Music Man / Don't Give Up On Me	1967	.80	4.00

After moving from Moonglow Records to Philles, the brother righteous, Bill Medley and Bobby Hatfield, saw half of their material produced by Phil Spector, including such brilliant singles as *You've Lost That Lovin' Feeling* and *Just Once In My Life*. They signed a lucrative deal with MGM/Verve in 1966 and, under the control of Medley (who had produced the bulk of their LPs) created at least one more masterful single in a Spectorian vein, *(You're My) Soul and Inspiration* before settling into a more predictable groove.

Label & Catalog #		A-Side/B-Side	Year	VG	NM
Verve CS8-5	(DJ)	The Righteous Brothers	1967	10.00	50.00
		(Boxed set of five stereo singles, Verve 10520-10524, with a cue sheet, bio and jukebox title strips. The price is for the complete set. The five promo singles are priced separately below.)			
Verve 10520	(DJ)	(You're My) Soul And Inspiration / Go Ahead And Cry	1967	1.20	6.00
Verve 10521	(DJ)	He Will Break Your Heart / Hold On, I'm Coming	1967	1.20	6.00
Verve 10522	(DJ)	I Believe / Melancholy Music	1967	1.20	6.00
Verve 10523	(DJ)	I (Who Have Nothing) / Island In The Sun	1967	1.20	6.00
Verve 10524	(DJ)	Something You Got / My Girl	1967	1.20	6.00
Verve 10551		Stranded In The Middle Of No Place / Been So Nice	1967	.80	4.00
Verve 10551	(PS)	Stranded In The Middle Of No Place / Been So Nice	1967	.80	4.00
Verve 10569		That Lucky Old Sun / My Darling Clementine	1967	.80	4.00
Verve 10577		Here I Am / So Many Lonely Nights Ahead	1968	.80	4.00
Verve 10637		Let The Good Times Roll / You've Lost That Lovin' Feeling	1968	.80	4.00
Verve 10648		And The Party Goes On / Woman, Man Needs Ya	1968	.80	4.00
Verve 10649		Good 'Nuff / Po Folks	1968	.80	4.00
Haven 7002		Rock And Roll Heaven / I Just Wanna Be Me	1974	.60	3.00
Haven 7004		Give It To The People / Love Is Not A Dirty Word	1974	.60	3.00
Haven 7006		Dream On / Doctor Rock And Roll	1974	.60	3.00
Haven 7011		High Blood Pressure / Never Say I Love You	1975	.60	3.00
Haven 7014		Young Blood / Substitute	1975	.60	3.00
Haven 800		Hold On (To What You've Got) / Let Me Make The Music	1975	.60	3.00
		— Extended Play Albums —			
Moonglow 1004	(33)	The Righteous Brothers' Greatest Hits (Jukebox EP)	1967	4.00	20.00

RILEY, ALLAN

Label & Catalog #		A-Side/B-Side	Year	VG	NM
Prospect 701		The True Story Of Tom Dooley / Ballad Of Ma Dooley	1965	2.00	10.00

RILEY, BILLY (& HIS LITTLE GREEN MEN)

Label & Catalog #		A-Side/B-Side	Year	VG	NM
Sun 245		Trouble Bound / Rock With Me, Baby	1956	10.00	50.00
Sun 260		Flyin' Saucers Rock And Roll / I Want You, Baby	1957	7.00	35.00
Sun 277		Red Hot / Pearly Lee	1957	4.00	20.00
Sun 289		Wouldn't You Know / Baby, Please Don't Go	1958	8.00	40.00
Sun 313		Down By The Riverside / No Name Girl	1958	3.00	15.00
Sun 322		Got The Water Boiling / One More Time	1959	8.00	40.00

RILEY, BOB

Label & Catalog #		A-Side/B-Side	Year	VG	NM
Tibor 4500		Weekend Vacation / Memories Of Home	196?	2.00	10.00

RINCON SURFSIDE BAND, THE
The Rincon Surfside Band are Steve Barri and P.F. Sloan.

Label & Catalog #		A-Side/B-Side	Year	VG	NM
Dunhill D-1	(EP)	The Rincon Surfside Band (Paper sleeve)	1963	12.00	60.00

RINGO, RON

Label & Catalog #		A-Side/B-Side	Year	VG	NM
Juggy 701		Ringo's Jerk / Queen Of The Jerk	1964	3.00	15.00

RINKY DINKS, THE: *Refer to BOBBY DARIN*

RINKY DINKS, THE

Label & Catalog #		A-Side/B-Side	Year	VG	NM
Enjoy 1010		Hot Potato / Hot Potato, Part 2	1963	2.00	10.00

RIO, BOBBY (& THE REVELLES)

Label & Catalog #		A-Side/B-Side	Year	VG	NM
Lenox 5569		Don Diddley / I Got You	1963	3.00	15.00
ABC-Paramount 10656		Boy Meets Girl / Don't Break My Heart And Run Away	1965	2.00	10.00

RIO, CHUCK (& THE ORIGINALS)
Chuck Rio also recorded as Danny Flores with The Champs. Refer to The Persuaders.

Label & Catalog #		A-Side/B-Side	Year	VG	NM
Challenge 59019		Bad Boy / Denise	1958	4.00	20.00
Jackpot 48016		Margarita / C' Est La Vie	1959	3.00	15.00
Flair 103		Big Boy / You Don't Have To Be A Baby To Cry	1962	6.00	30.00

RIO, CHUCK, & THE INDIVIDUALS

Label & Catalog #		A-Side/B-Side	Year	VG	NM
Tequila 103		Cell Block #9 / If You Were The Only Girl In The World	196?	5.00	25.00

RIO, CHUCK, & THE KRESHENDOS
The Kreshendos also recorded as The Creshendoes and The Cruchendoes.

Label & Catalog #		A-Side/B-Side	Year	VG	NM
Saturn 402		Kreshendo Stomp / Rock-A-Nova	1962	7.00	35.00

RIO, JERRY, & THE STOMPMEN

Label & Catalog #		A-Side/B-Side	Year	VG	NM
PNR-1		Doin' The Empire Stomp / Doin' The Empire Stomp, Pt. 2	1962	7.00	35.00

RIOS, AUGIE (& THE NOTATIONS)

Label & Catalog #		A-Side/B-Side	Year	VG	NM
Shelley 181		I've Got A Girl / There's A Girl Down The Way	195?	8.00	40.00
Shelley 192		Teach Me To-Night / Linda Lou	195?	3.00	15.00
Metro 20010		Donde Esta Santa Claus / Ol' Fatso	1958	3.00	15.00
Metro 20016		Hop, Skip And Jump / Run Rattler, Run	1959	3.00	15.00
MGM 13292		Donde Esta Santa Claus / Ol' Fatso	1964	1.20	6.00

Label & Catalog #		A-Side/B-Side	Year	VG	NM
RIOT SQUAD, THE					
Roulette 4621		I Wanna Talk About My Baby / Gonna Make You Mine	1965	2.00	10.00
Reprise 0457		Cry, Cry, Cry / How Is It Done?	1966	2.00	10.00
HBR 485		I Take It That We're Through? / Working Man	1967	3.00	15.00
RIP CHORDS, THE					
The Rip Chords are Ernest Bringas and Phil Stewart, late of The Opposites, with Bruce Johnston and Terry Melcher.					
Columbia 42687	(DJ)	Here I Stand / Here I Stand (Green vinyl)	1963	8.00	40.00
Columbia 42687	(PS)	Here I Stand (Promo picture sleeve)	1963	8.00	40.00
Columbia 42687		Here I Stand / Karen	1963	2.00	10.00
Columbia 42812	(DJ)	Gone / Gone (Blue vinyl)	1963	8.00	40.00
Columbia 42812	(PS)	Gone (Promo picture sleeve)	1963	8.00	40.00
Columbia 42812		Gone / She Thinks I Still Care	1963	2.00	10.00
Columbia 42921	(DJ)	Hey, Little Cobra / Hey, Little Cobra (Yellow vinyl)	1963	8.00	40.00
Columbia 42921		Hey, Little Cobra / The Queen	1963	1.60	8.00
Columbia 43035	(DJ)	Three Window Coupe / Three Window Coupe (Red vinyl)	1964	8.00	40.00
Columbia 43035		Three Window Coupe / Hot Rod U.S.A.	1964	2.00	10.00
Columbia 43093		One Piece Topless Bathing Suit / Wah-Wahini	1964	3.00	15.00
Columbia 43221	(DJ)	Don't Be Scared / Bunny Hill	1965	2.00	10.00
Columbia 43221		Don't Be Scared / Bunny Hill	1965	4.00	20.00
RIP TIDES, THE					
Challenge 59058		Machine Gun / Deep Blue	1959	3.00	15.00
Challenge 9062		Hanky Panky / Let's Run Away	1961	3.00	15.00
RIP TIDES, THE					
Sidewalk 904		Sally Ann / April	1966	3.00	15.00
RIS-KAYS, THE					
Hi-G Lo-C 3109		Topless Bathing Suit / Salt Crackers	1964	2.00	10.00
RISING SONS, THE					
Columbia 43534		Candy Man / The Devil's Got My Woman	1966	5.00	25.00
RISING SUNS, THE					
Amy 931		Talk To Me, Baby / Try To Be A Man	1965	2.00	10.00
RITUALS, THE					
The Rituals feature Arnie Ginsberg, who originally recorded as Jan & Arnie.					
Arwin 120		Girl In Zanzibar / Guitarro	1963	6.00	30.00
Arwin 127		This Is Paradise / Gone	1964	6.00	30.00
Arwin 128		Surfer's Rule / Gone	1964	6.00	30.00
RIVALS, THE					
Darryl 722		I Must See You Again / Rigelty Tick	196?	3.00	15.00
RIVERA, SCARLET					
Warner Bros. 8587		Scarlet Fever / Morning Glories	1978	.80	4.00
RIVERS, JOHNNY					
Johnny Rivers originally recorded as Johnny Ramistella.					
Gone 5026		Baby, Come Back / Long, Long Walk (Black label)	1958	5.00	25.00
Guyden 2003		You're The One / Hole In The Ground	1959	4.00	20.00
Cub 9047		Every Day / Darling, Talk To Me	1959	4.00	20.00
Cub 9058		Answer Me, My Love / The Customary Thing	1960	4.00	20.00
Dee Dee 239		Your First And Last Love / The White Cliffs Of Dover	1960	4.00	20.00
Era 3037		Call Me / Andersonville	1961	3.00	15.00
Chancellor 1070		Knock Three Times / I Get So Doggone Lonesome	1961	3.00	15.00
Chancellor 1108		To Be Loved / Too Good To Last	1962	3.00	15.00
Capitol 4850		Long Black Veil / This Could Be The One	1962	2.00	10.00
Capitol 4913		If You Want It I've Got It / My Heart Is In Your Hands	1963	2.00	10.00
Capitol 5232		Long Black Veil / Don't Look Now	1964	2.00	10.00
Guyden 2110		You're The One / Hole In The Ground	1964	3.00	15.00
Roulette 4565		Baby, Come Back / Long, Long Walk	1964	3.00	15.00
MGM 13266		Answer Me, My Love / The Customary Thing	1964	2.00	10.00
Coral 62425		That's My Babe / Your First And Last Love	1964	2.00	10.00
United Artists 741		Knock Three Times / Oh, What A Kiss	1964	1.60	8.00
United Artists 769		To Be Loved / Dream Doll	1964	1.60	8.00
Imperial 66032		Memphis / It Wouldn't Happen With Me	1964	1.20	6.00
Imperial 66056		Maybellene / Walk Myself On Home	1964	1.20	6.00
Imperial 66056	(PS)	Maybellene / Walk Myself On Home	1964	2.00	10.00
Imperial 66075		Mountain Of Love / Moody River	1964	1.20	6.00
Imperial 66087		Midnight Special / Cupid	1965	1.20	6.00
Imperial 66112		Seventh Son / Un-Square Dance	1965	1.20	6.00
Imperial 66112	(PS)	Seventh Son / Un-Square Dance	1965	2.00	10.00
Imperial 66133		Where Have All The Flowers Gone? / Love Me While You Can	1965	1.20	6.00
Imperial 66144		Under Your Spell Again / Long Time Man	1965	1.20	6.00
Imperial 66144	(PS)	Under Your Spell Again / Long Time Man	1965	2.00	10.00

Label & Catalog #		A-Side/B-Side	Year	VG	NM
Imperial 66159		Secret Agent Man / You Dig	1966	1.20	6.00
Imperial 66159	(PS)	Secret Agent Man / You Dig	1966	2.00	10.00
Imperial 66175		(I Washed My Hands In) Muddy Water / Roogalator	1966	1.20	6.00
Imperial 66205		Poor Side Of Town / A Man Can Cry	1966	1.20	6.00
Imperial 66205	(PS)	Poor Side Of Town / A Man Can Cry	1966	2.00	10.00
Rowe AMI	(DJ)	Play Me (Red vinyl)	1966	3.00	15.00
		(Rivers plugs Rowe's juke boxes.)			
Imperial 66227		Baby, I Need Your Lovin' / Gettin' Ready For Tomorrow	1967	1.20	6.00
Imperial 66227	(PS)	Baby, I Need Your Lovin' / Gettin' Ready For Tomorrow	1967	2.00	10.00
Imperial 66244		The Tracks Of My Tears / Rewind Medley	1967	1.20	6.00
Imperial 66244	(PS)	The Tracks Of My Tears / Rewind Medley	1967	2.00	10.00
Imperial 66267		Summer Rain / Memory Of The Coming Good	1967	1.20	6.00
Imperial 66286		Look To Your Soul / Something Strange	1968	1.00	5.00
Imperial 66286	(PS)	Look To Your Soul / Something Strange	1968	1.00	5.00
Imperial 66335		Right Relations / A Better Life	1968	1.60	8.00
Imperial 66335	(PS)	Right Relations / A Better Life	1968	1.00	5.00
Imperial 66360		These Are Not My People / Going Back To Big Sur	1969	1.00	5.00
Imperial 66386		Muddy River / Resurrection	1969	1.00	5.00
Imperial 66386	(PS)	Muddy River / Resurrection	1969	1.60	8.00
Imperial 66418		One Woman / Ode To John Lee	1969	1.00	5.00
Imperial 66448		Into The Mystic / Jesus Was A Soul Man	1970	1.00	5.00
Imperial 66453		Fire And Rain / Apple Tree	1970	1.00	5.00
United Artists 50778		Sea Cruise / Our Lady Of The Well	1971	.60	3.00
United Artists 50778	(PS)	Sea Cruise / Our Lady Of The Well	1971	1.00	5.00
United Artists 50822		Think His Name / Permanent Change	1971	.60	3.00
United Artists 50948		Come Home, America / On The Borderline	1972	.60	3.00
United Artists 50960		Rockin' Pneumonia-Boogie Woogie Flu / Come Home, America	1972	.60	3.00
United Artists 198		Blue Suede Shoes / Stories To A Child	1973	.60	3.00
United Artists 226		Searchin'-So Fine / New York City Dues	1973	.60	3.00
United Artists 310		I'll Feel A Whole Lot Better / Over The Line	1973	.60	3.00
Atlantic 3011		Sittin' In Limbo / Artists And Poets	1974	.60	3.00
Atlantic 3028		Six Days On The Road / Artists And Poets	1974	.60	3.00
Atlantic 3230		Get It Up For Love / John Lee Hooker '74	1974	.60	3.00
Epic 50121	(PS)	Help Me, Rhonda (Promo picture sleeve)	1975	1.60	8.00
Epic 50121		Help Me, Rhonda / New Lovers And Old Friends	1975	.80	4.00
		("Help Me, Rhonda" features Brian Wilson's backing vocal.)			
Epic 50150		Can I Change My Mind? / John Lee Hooker	1975	.60	3.00
Epic 50208		Outside Help / Welcome Home	1976	.60	3.00
Epic 50248	(DJ)	Linda Lu / Outside Help	1976	.60	3.00
Epic 50248		Linda Lu / Outside Help	1976	1.20	6.00
Soul City 007		Ashes And Sand / Outside Help	1977	.60	3.00
Soul City 008	(DJ)	Swayin' To The Music (Slow Dancin') / Outside Help	1977	.60	3.00
Soul City 008		Swayin' To The Music (Slow Dancin') / Outside Help	1977	1.20	6.00
Big Tree 16094		Swayin' To The Music (Slow Dancin') / Outside Help	1977	.60	3.00
Big Tree 16106		Curious Mind (Um, Um, Um, Um, Um, Um) / Ashes And Sand	1977	.60	3.00
Soul City 010		Little White Lie / Be My Baby	1980	1.00	5.00
RSO 1030		Romance / Don't Need No Other Know	1980	.60	3.00
RSO 1045		The Price / China	1980	.60	3.00
Soul City 014		The Price / RSVP	1982	1.00	5.00
MCA 52502		Heartbreak Love / Why Can't We Communicate?	1984	.60	3.00
		—12" Singles—			
Soul City 007		Secret Agent Man-Seventh Son / You Know What I Mean (PC)	1983	2.00	10.00
		—Extended Play Albums—			
Imperial 2264	(33)	At The Whiskey A Go Go (Jukebox EP)	1967	3.00	15.00
Imperial 2274	(33)	Here We A Go Go Again (Jukebox EP)	1967	3.00	15.00
Imperial 2293	(33)	Rocks The Folks (Jukebox EP)	1967	3.00	15.00
Imperial JRC-1	(DJ)	Realization (Radio spot)	1968	4.00	20.00
Imperial JRC-372	(DJ)	Srecial Interview With Johnny Rivers	1968	6.00	30.00
		(Issued with a script but without a cover.)			
United Artists SP-77	(DJ)	Voter Registration Spot	1972	3.00	15.00
What's It All About 148	(DJ)	What's It All About? Interview	1972	2.00	10.00

RIVIERAS, THE

Label & Catalog #	A-Side/B-Side	Year	VG	NM
Riviera 1401	California Sun / H. P. Goose Step	1964	3.00	15.00
Riviera 1402	Little Donna / Let's Have A Party	1964	3.00	15.00
Riviera 1403	Battle Line / Rockin' Robin	1964	3.00	15.00
Riviera 1405	Rip It Up / Whole Lotta Shakin'	1964	3.00	15.00
Riviera 1406	Let's Go To Hawaii / Lakeview Lane	1965	3.00	15.00

RIVIARES, THE

Label & Catalog #	A-Side/B-Side	Year	VG	NM
Aden 101	The Bug / Mocolotion	196?	5.00	25.00

ROACHES, THE

Label & Catalog #	A-Side/B-Side	Year	VG	NM
Crossway 447	Beatlemania Blues / Angel Of Angels	1964	3.00	15.00

Label & Catalog #		A-Side/B-Side	Year	VG	NM
ROAD					
Kama Sutra 256		She's Not There / A Bummer	1969	1.00	5.00
Kama Sutra 531		If I Ever Needed A Woman / Alone	1971	1.00	5.00
ROAD RUNNERS, THE					
Felsted 8692		Quasimoto / Road Runnah	1963	6.00	30.00
ROAD RUNNERS, THE					
Challenge 9197		Dead Man / Pretty Girls	1963	3.00	15.00
ROAD RUNNERS, THE					
Miramar 116		I'll Make It Up To You / Take Me	1965	3.00	15.00
Morocco 001		Tell Her You Love Her / Goodbye	1966	4.00	20.00
ROAD RUNNERS, THE (& GARY PAXTON)					
London 5208	(DJ)	Cute Little Colt / Super Torque 427	1964	5.00	25.00
		("Cute Little Colt" features Gary Usher on lead vocal. Stock copies may not exist.)			
ROADSTERS, THE					
Donna 1390		Mag Rims / Candymatic	1963	7.00	35.00
20th Century Fox 486		Drag / Joy Ride	1964	3.00	15.00
ROBB, DEE					
Dee Robb also recorded with The Robbs.					
Argo 5439		The Prom / Bye Bye, Baby	1963	3.00	15.00
Score 1006		He's Got The Whole World In His Hands / Say That Thing	1964	3.00	15.00
ROBBINS, EDDIE					
Power 214		A Girl Like You / Dear Parents	1958	20.00	100.00
Dot		A Girl Like You / Dear Parents	1958	10.00	50.00
David 1001		Janice / It Was Fun	195?	5.00	25.00

ROBBINS, MARTY

One of country/western's most popular singers, Marty Robbins' early sides were rock 'n roll/rockabilly. When these met with no success, he modified his sound to a more accessible pop/country and scored twenty-two chart hits between 1957 and 1963. As his sound became more country, he lost his teenage audience, although he enjoyed an extraordinarily successful stay with Columbia till his death in 1982.

Label & Catalog #		A-Side/B-Side	Year	VG	NM
Columbia 21351		That's All Right / Gossip	1954	6.00	30.00
Columbia 21446		Maybellene / This Broken Heart Of Mine	1955	6.00	30.00
Columbia 21461		Pretty Mama / Don't Let Me Hang Around	1955	6.00	30.00
Columbia 21477		Tennessee Toddy / Mean Mama Blues	1955	6.00	30.00
Columbia 21545		Singing The Blues / I Can't Quit	1956	5.00	25.00
Columbia 40679		Long Tall Sally / Mr. Teardrop	1956	6.00	30.00
Columbia 40706		Respectfully, Miss Brooks / You Don't Owe Me A Thing	1956	6.00	30.00
Columbia 40815		Knee Deep In The Blues / The Same Two Lips	1956	4.00	20.00
Columbia 40864		A White Sport Coat (& A Pink Carnation) / Grown Up Tears	1957	3.00	15.00
Columbia 40864	(PS)	A White Sport Coat (& A Pink Carnation) / Grown Up Tears	1957	4.00	20.00
Columbia 41013		The Story Of My Life / Once-A-Week Date	1957	3.00	15.00
Columbia 41013	(PS)	The Story Of My Life / Once-A-Week Date	1957	4.00	20.00
Columbia 41143		Just Married / Stairway Of Love	1958	3.00	15.00
Columbia 41208		She Was Only Seventeen (He Was One Year More) / Sittin' In A Tree House	1958	3.00	15.00
Columbia 41208	(PS)	She Was Only Seventeen (He Was One Year More) / Sittin' In A Tree House	1958	4.00	20.00
Columbia 41325		The Hanging Tree / The Blues, Country Style	1959	3.00	15.00
Columbia 41325	(PS)	The Hanging Tree / The Blues, Country Style	1959	4.00	20.00
Columbia 41408		Cap And Gown / Last Night About This Time	1959	3.00	15.00
Columbia 41511		El Paso / Running Gun	1960	2.00	10.00
Columbia 41511	(PS)	El Paso / Running Gun	1960	3.00	15.00
Columbia 41589		Big Iron / Saddle Tramp	1960	2.00	10.00
Columbia 41589	(PS)	Big Iron / Saddle Tramp	1960	3.00	15.00
Columbia 41686		Is There Any Chance? / I Told My Heart	1960	2.00	10.00
Columbia 41771		Five Brothers / Ride, Cowboy, Ride	1960	2.00	10.00
Columbia 41809		Ballad Of The Alamo / A Time And A Place	1960	2.00	10.00
Columbia 41809	(PS)	Ballad Of The Alamo / A Time And A Place	1960	3.00	15.00
Columbia 41922		Don't Worry / Like All The Other Times	1961	2.00	10.00
Columbia 41922	(PS)	Don't Worry / Like All The Other Times	1961	3.00	15.00
Columbia 42008		Jimmy Martinez / Ghost Train	1961	2.00	10.00
Columbia 42008	(PS)	Jimmy Martinez / Ghost Train	1961	3.00	15.00
Columbia 42065		It's Your World / You Told Me So	1961	2.00	10.00
Columbia 42065	(PS)	It's Your World / You Told Me So	1961	3.00	15.00
Columbia 42246		I Told The Brook / Sometimes I'm Tempted	1961	2.00	10.00
Columbia 42246	(PS)	I Told The Brook / Sometimes I'm Tempted	1961	3.00	15.00
Columbia 42375		Love Can't Wait / Too Far Gone	1962	2.00	10.00
Columbia 42375	(PS)	Love Can't Wait / Too Far Gone	1962	3.00	15.00
Columbia 42486		Devil Woman / April Fool's Day	1962	2.00	10.00
Columbia 42486	(PS)	Devil Woman / April Fool's Day	1962	3.00	15.00

Label & Catalog #		A-Side/B-Side	Year	VG	NM
Columbia 42614		Ruby Ann / Won't You Forgive?	1962	2.00	10.00
Columbia 42614	(PS)	Ruby Ann / Won't You Forgive?	1962	3.00	15.00
Columbia 42672		Hawaii's Calling Me / Ka-Lu-A	1962	3.00	15.00
Columbia 42701		Cigarettes And Coffee Blues / Teenager's Dad	1963	1.60	8.00
Columbia 42701	(PS)	Cigarettes And Coffee Blues / Teenager's Dad	1963	3.00	15.00
Columbia 42781		No Sign Of Loneliness Here / I'm Not Ready Yet	1963	1.60	8.00
Columbia 42781	(PS)	No Sign Of Loneliness Here / I'm Not Ready Yet	1963	3.00	15.00
Columbia 42831		Not So Long Ago / I Hope You Learn A Lot	1963	1.60	8.00
Columbia 42890		Begging To You / Over High Mountain	1963	1.60	8.00

ROBBINS, MEL

Argo 5340	Save It / To Know You	195?	10.00	50.00

ROBBINS & PAXTON
Features Gary Paxton.

Rori 704	Teen Angel / Strange Rain	1962	3.00	15.00

ROBBS, THE
The Robbs feature Dee Robb.

Mercury 72579		Race With The Wind / In A Funny Sort Of Way	1966	1.20	6.00
Mercury 72616		Next Time You See Me / I Don't Feel Alone	1966	1.20	6.00
Mercury 72641		Bittersweet / End Of The Week	1966	1.20	6.00
Mercury 72641	(PS)	Bittersweet / End Of The Week	1966	2.00	10.00
Mercury 72678		Rapid Transit / Cynthia Loves	1967	1.20	6.00
Mercury 72730		Girls, Girls / Violets Of Dawn	1967	1.20	6.00
Atlantic 2578		Changin' Winds / A Good Time Song	1968	1.00	5.00
Dunhill 4233		Last Of The Wine / Written In The Dust	1970	1.00	5.00
ABC 11270		I'll Never Get Enough / It All Comes Back	1971	1.00	5.00

ROBBY & THE ROBINS

Todd 1089	Surfer's Life / She Cried	1963	7.00	35.00

ROBERTS, BUDDY, & THE HI LITERS

Bonanza 689/90	Ding Dong / Black And Blue	196?	5.00	25.00

ROBERTS, DENNIS

Sims 1	Muleskinner Blues / Blue Carnation	196?	2.00	10.00
Jerden 733	Strange And Lonely World / Muddy River	1964	.80	4.00
Jerden 748	Touch Me / Prison Bound	1965	.80	4.00

ROBERTS, JACK

Jerden 718	Don't Be Fooled / A Dream Will Have To Do	1963	.80	4.00

ROBERTS, LANCE

Sun 348	The Good Guy Always Wins / The Time Is Right	1960	2.00	10.00

ROBERTS, ROCKIN' ROBIN

Etiquette 1	Louie Louie / Maryann	1961	3.00	15.00
	(Roberts is backed by The Wailers.)			
Reprise 0321	You'd Better Come Home /	196?	2.00	10.00
Etiquette 26	You Weren't Using Your Head / You Don't Love Me	1966	4.00	20.00

ROBERTS, STAN

Deb-Lyn 102	Dream Time / Hold On, Baby	196?	2.00	10.00

ROBERTS, WAYNE (WITH THE CONCORDS)

20th Century Fox 644	Little Girl / One Piece Bathing Suit	1965	3.00	15.00

ROBERTSON, DON

Jerden 103	Rock-O-Letto / Bongo Train	1960	.80	4.00
Capitol 3391	The Happy Whistler / You're Free To Go	196?	.80	4.00

ROBERTSON, DOUG, & THE GOOD GUYS

Jerden 729	Greenfields / Sweets For My Sweet	1964	1.60	8.00
Jerden 729	Quiet Riot / Sweets For My Sweet	196?	1.60	8.00
Jerden 739	Desiree / Driving Home	1964	1.60	8.00
Jerden 767	Runaround Sue / Gloria	196?	1.60	8.00
Jerden 703	Love You So / Desiree	196?	1.60	8.00

ROBERTSON, JESSE, WITH LEON SMITH

Willamette 113	I'm Walking Alone / Love Falls In Funny Places	196?	2.00	10.00

ROBIN: *Refer to* **ROBIN WARD**

ROBIN, CHERI, & THE STINGRAYS

Rivers 1002	Don't Cry / My Phone	196?	.80	4.00
Rivers 1008	Please Stay Away / The Dance	196?	.80	4.00

Label & Catalog #	A-Side/B-Side	Year	VG	NM
ROBIN, DON				
Jerden 738	Big Dan / My Home Town	196?	.80	4.00
ROBIN, TINA				
Coral 61935	Everyday / Believe Me	1957	3.00	15.00
Coral 61977	No School Tomorrow / Sugar Blues	1958	3.00	15.00
Coral 62015	A Little Bird Told Me / We've All Gotta Live In This House	1958	3.00	15.00
Coral 62121	Too Young / River Of Tears	1959	3.00	15.00
Mercury 71852	Play It Again / Nothing Is Impossible	1961	2.00	10.00
ROBIN & THE THREE HOODS				
Hollywood 1110	I Wanna Do It / That's Tuff	196?	3.00	15.00
ROBINS, THE				
Sweet Taffy 400	Johnny / Doing The Popeye	196?	3.00	15.00
ROBINS, THE				
Musicor 1050	Lucy Watusi / Cry Over You	1964	1.20	6.00
ROBINS, THE				
Knight 2001	A Quarter To Twelve / Pretty Little Dolly	1965	2.00	10.00
Ardent 106	Batman / Batarang	1966	3.00	15.00
ROBINSON, FLOYD				
RCA Victor 45-7529	Makin' Love / My Girl	1959	2.00	10.00
RCA Victor 47-7637	Tonight You Belong To Me / Let It Be Me	1959	2.00	10.00
United Artists 986	Sidewalk Surf Board / Motorcycle Man	1966	4.00	20.00
	—Extended Play Albums—			
RCA Victor EPA-4350	Makin' Love	1959	8.00	40.00
ROBINSON, STAN				
Monument 402	Boom-A-Dip-Dip / My Heart Beats	1959	2.00	10.00
ROBISON, CHRIS (WITH THE ROCKAWAYS)				
Buddah 406	I'm Gonna Stay With My Baby Tonight / Jimmy Row	1974	1.00	5.00
ROCHELL & THE CANDLES				
Challenge 9158	Each Night / Turn Her Down	1963	2.00	10.00
Challenge 9191	Let's Run Away And Get Married /			
	Annie's Not An Orphan Anymore	1963	3.00	15.00
	("Let's Run Away And Get Married " was written by Gary Usher.)			
ROCK, JIMMY				
Todd 1024	The Drag / We Two	1959	3.00	15.00
ROCK-A-TEENS, THE				
Doran 3515	Woo-Hoo / Untrue	1959	25.00	125.00
Roulette 4192	Woo-Hoo / Untrue	1959	3.00	15.00
Roulette 4217	Twangy / Doggone It, Baby	1959	4.00	20.00
ROCK & ROLL DOUBLE BUBBLE TRADING CARD CO. OF PHILADELPHIA, THE				
Buddah 78	Bubble Gum Music / On A Summer Night	1968	1.00	5.00
ROCK BROTHERS, THE				
King 4851	Dungaree Doll / Livin' It Up	1955	4.00	20.00
King 4882	I Gotta Get Back / Oh, Didn't I Ramble?	1955	3.00	15.00
ROCK COLLECTION, THE				
Piccadilly 243	A Sunny Day / Get Ready	1967	.80	4.00
ROCK GARDEN, THE				
B.T. Puppy 536	Joy Of Giving / Sweet Pajamas	1968	1.00	5.00
ROCK-N-SOULS, THE				
Rich Tone 2369/70	Not Like You / Got No Love	196?	2.00	10.00
ROCKAWAYS, THE				
The Rockaways also recorded with Chris Robison.				
Red Bird 005	Top Down Time / Don't Cry (Tomorrow's Tears Tonight)	1964	3.00	15.00
ROCKBUSTERS, THE				
Cadence 1371	Tough Chick / Chico	1959	3.00	15.00
ROCKET, ROBIN				
Lode 107	Changing Schools / You Hold The Key	1960	2.00	10.00
ROCKETEERS, THE				
Val-ue 102	Rippin' And Rockin' / Downtown	1960	3.00	15.00

Label & Catalog #	A-Side/B-Side	Year	VG	NM
ROCKETS, THE				
Columbia 41512	Gibraltar Rock / Walkin' Home	1959	3.00	15.00
ROCKETS, THE				
The Rockets feature Ralph Molina, Billy Talbot, and Danny Whitten, later of Crazy Horse.				
White Whale 270	Hole In My Pocket / Let Me Go	1967	2.00	10.00
ROCKETS, THE				
The Rockets originally recorded as The Detroit Wheels with Mitch Ryder.				
Tortoise 11207	She's A Pretty One / I've Got To Move	1978	1.00	5.00
RSO 926	Can't Sleep / Something Ain't Right	1979	.80	4.00
RSO 935	Oh, Well / Love Me Once Again	1979	.80	4.00
ROCKIN' BERRIES, THE				
Reprise 0321	You'd Better Come Home / I Didn't Mean To Hurt You	1964	2.00	10.00
Reprise 0329	He's In Town / Flashback	1964	1.60	8.00
Reprise 0355	What In The World's Come Over You? / You Don't Know What To Do	1965	1.60	8.00
Reprise 0377	Poor Man's Son / Follow Me	1965	1.60	8.00
Reprise 0400	You're My Girl / Brother Bill (Last Clean Shirt)	1965	1.60	8.00
Reprise 0442	Doesn't Time Fly? / The Water Is Over My Head	1966	1.60	8.00
ROCKIN' CHAIRS, THE				
The Rockin' Chairs also recorded with Lenny Dean.				
Recorte 402	A Kiss Is A Kiss / Rockin' Chair Boogie	196?	8.00	40.00
Recorte 404	Come On, Baby / Please, Mary Lou	196?	5.00	25.00
ROCKIN' FOO				
Hobbit 42001	Rochester River /	1969	2.00	10.00
ROCKIN' G'S, THE				
Town 1967	Cyclone / Lani-Town	1960	2.00	10.00
ROCKIN' R'S, THE				
Tempus 7541	Crazy Baby / The Beat	1959	5.00	25.00
Tempus 1507	Nameless / Heat	1959	4.00	20.00
Tempus 1515	Mustang / I'm Still In Love With You	1960	4.00	20.00
Vee Jay 334	Mustang / I'm Still In Love With You	1960	2.00	10.00
Vee Jay 346	Hum Bug / Mix	1960	3.00	15.00
Stephany 1842	Walkin' You To School / Bewitched (Bothered And Bewildered)	1960	3.00	15.00
ROCKIN' RAMRODS, THE [THE RAMRODS]				
Plymouth 2961	I Wanna Be Your Man / I'll Be On My Way	1964	4.00	20.00
Bon Bon 1315	She Lied / The Girl Can't Help It	1964	7.00	35.00
Southern Sound 205	Wild About You / Cry In My Room	1965	6.00	30.00
Claridge 301	Don't Fool With Fu Manchu / Tears	1965	3.00	15.00
Claridge 317	Play It / Got My Mojo Workin'	1966	3.00	15.00
Plymouth 2963	Bright Lit Blue Skies / Mister Wind	1966	4.00	20.00
Plymouth 2965	Flowers In My Mind / Mary, Mary	1966	6.00	30.00
(The Plymouth singles credit The Ramrods.)				
ROCKIN' REBELS, THE: *Refer to* **THE REBELS**				
ROCKIN' RONALD & THE REBELS				
The price here is based on the assumption that this is Ronnie Hawkins & The Hawks, an assertion Hawkins denies.				
End 1043	Kansas City / Cuttin' It Out	1959	5.00	25.00
ROCKIN' SAINTS, THE				
Decca 30990	Alright, Baby / The Saints Rock	1959	5.00	25.00
Decca 31144	Cheatin' On My Baby / Half And Half	1960	12.00	60.00
ROCKIN' STOCKINGS, THE				
Sun 350	Yulesville U.S.A. / Rockin' Old Lang Syne	1960	2.00	10.00
Sun 1960	Yulesville U.S.A. / Rockin' Old Lang Syne	197?	1.00	5.00
ROCKIN' VICKERS, THE				
Columbia 43818	Dandy / I Don't Need Your Kind	1966	3.00	15.00
ROCKY & HIS FRIENDS				
Also recorded as Rocky & The Riddlers.				
Tower 178	Riot City / You're Not Wrong	196?	3.00	15.00
ROCKY & THE BORDER GUARDS				
Rocky & The Border Guards is a pseudonym for Kim Fowley with The Sir Douglas Quintet.				
Epic 10901	Michoacan / Gulf Of Mexico	1972	2.00	10.00

Label & Catalog #		A-Side/B-Side	Year	VG	NM
ROCKY & THE RIDDLERS					
Also recorded as Rocky & His Friends.					
Panorama 28		Batman / Flash And Crash	1966	3.00	15.00
ROCKY FELLERS, THE					
Donna 1383		The Beachcomber Song / Don't Sit Down	1963	2.00	10.00
Scepter 1245		Santa Santa / Great Big World	1962	3.00	15.00
Scepter 1246		Killer Joe / Lonely Teardrops	1963	3.00	15.00
Scepter 1254		Like The Big Guys Do / Great Big World	1963	2.00	10.00
Scepter 1254	(PS)	Like The Big Guys Do / Great Big World	1963	4.00	20.00
Scepter 1258		Ching-A-Ling Baby / Hey, Little Donkey	1963	2.00	10.00
Scepter 1263		She Makes Me Wanna Dance / Bye Bye, Baby	1963	2.00	10.00
Warner Bros. 5440		Tiger (Everybody Wants To Be A) / Jeannie Memsah	1964	1.60	8.00
Warner Bros. 5469		Nina / Better Let Her Go	1965	1.60	8.00
Warner Bros. 5497		Don't Throw My Toys Away / The Man With The Blue Guitar	1965	1.60	8.00
Warner Bros. 5613		Rented Tuxedo / Two Steps Downstairs In The Basement	1965	1.60	8.00
RODGERS, JIMMIE					
Roulette 4015		Honeycomb / Their Hearts Were Full Of Spring	1957	3.00	15.00
Roulette 4031		Kisses Sweeter Than Wine / Better Loved You'll Never Be	1957	3.00	15.00
Roulette 4045		Oh-Oh, I'm Falling In Love Again / The Long Hot Summer	1958	3.00	15.00
Roulette 4070		Secretly / Make Me A Miracle	1958	3.00	15.00
Roulette 4070	(PS)	Secretly / Make Me A Miracle	1958	4.00	20.00
Roulette 4090		Are You Really Mine? / The Wizard	1958	3.00	15.00
Roulette 4090	(PS)	Are You Really Mine? / The Wizard	1958	4.00	20.00
Roulette 4116		Bimbombey / You Understand Me	1958	2.00	10.00
Roulette 4129		I'm Never Gonna Tell / Because They're Young	1959	2.00	10.00
Roulette 4129		Froggy Went A-Courtin' / Because They're Young	1959	2.00	10.00
Roulette 8007	(S)	Froggy Went A-Courtin' / Because You're Young	1959	5.00	25.00
Roulette 4158		Ring-A-Ling-A-Lario / Wonderful You	1959	2.00	10.00
Roulette 4158	(PS)	Ring-A-Ling-A-Lario / Wonderful You	1959	3.00	15.00
Roulette 4158	(S)	Ring-A-Ling-A-Lario / Wonderful You	1959	5.00	25.00
Roulette 4191		Tucumcari / The Night You Became Seventeen	1959	2.00	10.00
Roulette 4205		It's Christmas Once Again / Wistful Willie	1959	2.00	10.00
Roulette 4218		T.L.C. (Tender Loving Care) / Waltzing Matilda	1960	2.00	10.00
Roulette 4218	(S)	T.L.C. (Tender Loving Care) / Waltzing Matilda	1960	4.00	20.00
Roulette 4234		Just A Closer Walk With Thee / Joshua Fit The Battle Of Jericho	1960	1.60	8.00
Roulette 4260		The Wreck Of The John B / A Little Girl In Boston	1960	1.60	8.00
Roulette 4293		Woman From Liberia / Come Along, Julie	1961	1.60	8.00
Roulette 4293	(PS)	Woman From Liberia / Come Along, Julie	1961	2.00	10.00
Roulette 4318		When Love Is Young / The Little Shepherd From Kingdom Come	1961	1.60	8.00
Roulette 4349		Everytime My Heart Sings / I'm On My Way	1961	1.60	8.00
Roulette 4371		I'm Goin' Home / John Brown's Body	1961	1.60	8.00
Roulette 4384		A Little Dog Cried / English Country Garden	1961	1.20	6.00
Roulette 4439		You Are Everything To Me / Wanderin' Eyes	1962	1.20	6.00
Roulette SSR-8010	(S)	St. James Infirmary / Just A Wearyin' For You	196?	5.00	25.00
Dot 16378		No One Will Ever Know / Because	1962	1.00	5.00
Dot 16378	(PS)	No One Will Ever Know / Because	1962	1.20	6.00
Dot 16407		Rainbow At Midnight / Rhumba Boogie	1962	1.00	5.00
Dot 16428		I'll Never Stand In Your Way / Afraid	1963	1.00	5.00
Dot 16428	(PS)	I'll Never Stand In Your Way / Afraid	1963	1.20	6.00
Dot 16450		Face In The Crowd / Lonely Tears	1963	1.00	5.00
Dot 16467		(I Don't Know Why) I Just Do / Load 'Em Up (And Keep On Steppin')	1963	1.00	5.00
Dot 16490		Poor Little Raggedy Ann / I'm Gonna Be The Winner	1963	1.00	5.00
Dot 16527		Two-Ten, Six-Eighteen (Doesn't Anybody Know My Name?) / The Banana Boat Song	1963	1.00	5.00
Dot 16561		Together / Mama Was A Cotton Picker	1964	1.00	5.00
Dot 16595		The World I Used To Know / I Forgot More Than You'll Ever Know	1964	1.00	5.00
Dot 16653		Water Boy / Some Place Green	1964	1.00	5.00
Dot 16673		Two Tickets / I Forgot More Than You'll Ever Know	1965	.80	4.00
Dot 16694		(All My Friends Are Gonna Be) Strangers / Bon Soire, Mademoiselle	1965	.80	4.00
Dot 16749		Little Schoolgirl / Are You Going My Way (Little Beachcomber)	1965	.80	4.00
Dot 16781		Bye Bye Love / Hollow Words	1965	.80	4.00
Dot 16795		The Chipmunk Song / In The Snow	1965	.80	4.00
Dot 16826		A Fallen Star / Brother, Where Are You?	1966	.80	4.00
Dot 16861	(DJ)	It's Over / It's Over (Blue vinyl)	1966	4.00	20.00
Dot 16861		It's Over / Anita, You're Dreaming	1966	.80	4.00
Dot 16916		Morning Means Tomorrow / New Ideas	1966	.80	4.00
Dot 16973		Love Me, Please Love Me / Wonderful You	1966	.80	4.00
Dot 17040		Time / Yours And Mine	1965	.80	4.00
A&M 842		I'll Say Goodbye / Shadows	1967	.60	3.00
A&M 871		Child Of Clay / Turn Around	1967	.80	4.00

Label & Catalog #		A-Side/B-Side	Year	VG	NM
A&M 898		What A Strange Town / If I Were The Man	1968	.60	3.00
A&M 902		I Believed It All / You Pass Me By	1968	.60	3.00
A&M 930		How Do You Say Goodbye? / I Wanna Be Free	1968	.60	3.00
A&M 976		Today / The Lovers	1968	.60	3.00
A&M 1055		Windmills Of Your Mind / L.A. Breakdown (And Take Me In)	1969	.60	3.00
A&M 1120		Me About You / Father Paul	1969	.60	3.00
A&M 1152		Tomorrow, My Friend / Cycles	1969	.60	3.00
Scrimshaw 1313		Dancing On The Moon / Just A Little Time	1977	.80	4.00
Scrimshaw 1314		Everytime I Sing A Love Song / Just A Little Time	1978	.80	4.00
Scrimshaw 1316		When Our Love Began (Cowboys And Indians) /	1978	.80	4.00
Scrimshaw 1318		Secretly / Shoveling Coal Missouri	1978	.80	4.00
Scrimshaw 1319/20		Easy To Love / Easy	1979	.80	4.00
		— Extended Play Albums—			
Roulette 1-103		Jimmie Rodgers (Volume 1)	196?	8.00	40.00
Roulette 2-103		Jimmie Rodgers (Volume 2)	196?	8.00	40.00
Roulette 3-103		Jimmie Rodgers (Volume 3)	196?	8.00	40.00
Roulette 1-315		Jimmie Rodgers Sings Folk Songs (Volume 1)	1963	6.00	30.00
Roulette 2-315		Jimmie Rodgers Sings Folk Songs (Volume 2)	1963	6.00	30.00
Roulette 3-315		Jimmie Rodgers Sings Folk Songs (Volume 3)	1963	6.00	30.00

RODNEY & THE BLAZERS

Label & Catalog #		A-Side/B-Side	Year	VG	NM
Kampus 100		Teenage Cinderella / Summertime	1960	5.00	25.00
Dore 588		Snow White / Tell Me, Baby	1961	3.00	15.00

RODNEY & THE BRUNETTES
Rodney Bingenheimer with Diane Rovell and Marilyn Wilson of Spring. "Little G.T.O." features Blondie.

Label & Catalog #		A-Side/B-Side	Year	VG	NM
Bomp 127		Little G.T.O. / Holocaust On Sunset Boulevard	1980	.60	3.00
Bomp 127	(PS)	Little G.T.O. / Holocaust On Sunset Boulevard	1980	.60	3.00

ROE, TOMMY

Label & Catalog #		A-Side/B-Side	Year	VG	NM
Mark-IV 1001		Caveman / I Gotta Girl	1960	10.00	50.00
Trumpet 001		Caveman / I Gotta Girl	1960	25.00	125.00
		(Contrary to previous publications, Tommy Roe asserts that Mark-IV 1001 was his first release although Trumpet 001 remains his rarest.)			
Mark-IV 1018		I Gotta Girl / Pretty Girl	1960	8.00	40.00
Mark-IV 1018	(PS)	I Gotta Girl / Pretty Girl	1960	20.00	100.00
Judd 1018		Caveman / I Gotta Girl	1960	8.00	40.00
		(Features The Flamingos and The Satins.)			
Judd 1022		Sheila / Pretty Girl	1962	10.00	50.00
ABC-Paramount 10329		Sheila / Save Your Kisses	1962	3.00	15.00
ABC-Paramount 10362		Susie Darlin' / Piddle De Pat	1962	2.00	10.00
ABC-Paramount 10362	(PS)	Susie Darlin' / Piddle De Pat	1962	3.00	15.00
ABC-Paramount 10379		Town Crier / Rainbow	1963	1.20	6.00
ABC-Paramount 10379	(PS)	Town Crier / Rainbow	1963	5.00	25.00
ABC-Paramount 10389		Don't Cry, Donna / Gonna Take A Chance	1963	1.20	6.00
ABC-Paramount 10423		The Folk Singer / Count On Me	1963	1.20	6.00
ABC-Paramount 10454		Kiss And Run / What Makes The Blues?	1963	1.20	6.00
ABC-Paramount 10478		Everybody / Sorry I'm Late, Lisa	1963	2.00	10.00
ABC-Paramount 10515		Come On / There Will Be Better Years	1964	1.20	6.00
ABC-Paramount 10543		Carol / Be A Good Little Girl	1964	2.00	10.00
ABC-Paramount 10555		Dance With Me, Henry / Water Skiing Weekend	1964	3.00	15.00
ABC-Paramount 10579		Oh, So Right / I Think I Love You	1964	2.00	10.00
		(Features The Roemans.)			
ABC-Paramount 10604		Party Girl / Oh, How Could I Love You?	1964	1.20	6.00
ABC-Paramount 10623		Diane From Manchester / Love Me, Love Me	1965	2.00	10.00
		(Features The Roemans.)			
ABC-Paramount 10665		Fourteen Pair Of Shoes / Combo Music	1965	1.20	6.00
ABC-Paramount 10696		I'm A Rambler / Gun Fighter	1965	4.00	20.00
ABC-Paramount 10706		I Keep Remembering / Wish You Didn't Have To Go	1965	1.20	6.00
ABC-Paramount 10738		Every Time A Bluebird Cries / Doesn't Anybody Know My Name?	1965	1.20	6.00
ABC-Paramount 10738	(PS)	Every Time A Bluebird Cries / Doesn't Anybody Know My Name?	1965	1.20	6.00
ABC-Paramount 10762		Sweet Pea / Much More Love	1965	2.00	10.00
ABC 10762		Sweet Pea / Much More Love	1966	3.00	15.00
ABC 10852		Hooray For Hazel / Need Your Love	1966	1.00	5.00
ABC 10888		It's Now Winter's Day / Kick Me, Charlie	1966	1.00	5.00
ABC 10888	(PS)	It's Now Winter's Day / Kick Me, Charlie	1966	2.00	10.00
ABC 10908		Sing Along With Me / Nighttime	1967	.60	3.00
ABC 10933		Moon Talk / Sweet Sounds	1967	.60	3.00
ABC 10945		Little Miss Sunshine / The You I Need	1967	.60	3.00
ABC 10989		Paisly Dream / Melancholy Mood	1967	.60	3.00
ABC 11039		Soft Words / Dottie, I Like It	1968	.60	3.00
ABC 11140		Gotta Keep Rolling Along / It's Gonna Hurt Me	1968	.60	3.00
ABC 11164		Dizzy / The You I Need	1969	.60	3.00
ABC 11211		Heather Honey / Money Is My Pay	1969	.60	3.00
ABC 11229		Jack And Jill / Tip Toe Tina	1969	.60	3.00

Label & Catalog #		A-Side/B-Side	Year	VG	NM
ABC 11247		Jam Up And Jelly Tight / Moontalk	1969	.60	3.00
ABC 11247	(PS)	Jam Up And Jelly Tight / Moontalk	1969	1.00	5.00
ABC 11258		Stir It Up And Serve It / Fire Fly	1970	.60	3.00
ABC 11266		Pearl / A Dollar's Worth Of Pennies	1970	.60	3.00
ABC 11273		We Can Make Music / Gotta Keep Rolling Along	1970	.60	3.00
ABC 11273	(PS)	We Can Make Music / Gotta Keep Rolling Along	1970	1.00	5.00
ABC 11281		Brush A Little Sunshine / King Of Fools	1971	.60	3.00
ABC 11287		Little Miss Goodie Two Shoes / Traffic Jam	1971	.60	3.00
ABC 11293		Pistol Legged Woman / King Of Fools	1971	.60	3.00
ABC 11307		Stagger Lee / Back Streets And Alleys	1971	.60	3.00
MGM/South 7001		Mean Little Woman / Rosalie	1972	.60	3.00
MGM/South 7008		Chewing On Sugar Cane / Sarah, My Love	1972	.60	3.00
MGM/South 7013		Working Class Hero / Sun In My Eyes	1973	.60	3.00
MGM/South 7025		Memphis Me / Silver Eyes	1973	.80	4.00
Monument 8644		Glitter And Gleam / Bad News	1972	.60	3.00
Monument 8662		Snowing Me Under / Rita And Her Band	1974	.60	3.00
Monument 8684		Slow Dancing / Burn On, Love Light	1976	.60	3.00
Monument 8705		Energy / Everybody	1976	.80	4.00
Monument 205		Early In The Morning / Bad News	1976	.80	4.00
Monument 2287		Your Love Will See Me Through / Working Class Hero	1977	.80	4.00
Warner/Curb 8660		Dreamin' Again / Love The Way You Love To Love Me	1978	.60	3.00
Warner/Curb 8720		Just Look At Me / Love The Way You Love Me Up	1978	.60	3.00
Warner/Curb 8800		Just Look At Me / Massachusetts	1979	.60	3.00
Warner Bros. 49085		You Better Move On / Just Look At Me	1979	.60	3.00
Warner Bros. 49235		Charlie, I Love Your Wife / There's No Sun On Sunset Blvd.	1980	.60	3.00
BGO 1003		She Do Run Run /	1982	2.00	10.00
Awesome 104		First Things First /	1984	2.00	10.00
Awesome 108		Sittin' In A Mood /	1984	2.00	10.00

ROEMANS, THE
Refer to Tommy Roe.

ABC-Paramount 10583		Give Me A Chance / Your Friend	1964	3.00	15.00
ABC-Paramount 10671		Miserlou / Don't	1965	3.00	15.00
ABC-Paramount 10723		Universal Soldier / Lost Little Girl	1965	3.00	15.00
ABC-Paramount 10757		Listen To Me / You Make Me Feel Good	1965	3.00	15.00
ABC-Paramount 10814		Love (That's All I Want) / When The Sun Shines In The Morning	1966	2.00	10.00
ABC 10871		Pleasing You Pleases Me / All The Good Things	1966	2.00	10.00

ROFFLER, CHRISTINA

Topaz 1330		Kissing Yodal, The / Lili Marlene	196?	2.00	10.00

ROGER & THE TRAVELERS

Ember 1079		You're Daddy's Little Girl / Just Gotta Be That Way	1962	10.00	50.00

ROGERS, KENNY
Kenny Rogers also recorded with The New Christy Minstrels and The First Edition.

Carlton 454		That Crazy Feeling / We'll Always Have Each Other	1958	8.00	40.00
Carlton 468		I've Got A Lot To Learn / For You Alone	1958	8.00	40.00
Ken-Lee 102		Jole Blon / Lonely	195?	5.00	25.00
Mercury 72545		Here's That Rainy Day / Take Life In Stride	1966	5.00	25.00

ROGERS, MILT

Dot 16296		Let's Go Trippin' / Lonely Road To Damascus	1961	3.00	15.00

ROGERS, ROD

Film City 3024		Move Along Surfing Girl /	196?	7.00	35.00

ROGERS, TIMMIE "OH YEAH!"

Cameo 116		Back To School Again / I've Got A Dog Who Loves Me	1957	3.00	15.00
Cameo 131		Take Me To Your Leader / Fla-Ga-La-Pa	1958	3.00	15.00

ROGERS, WELDON

JeWel 103		Everybody Wants You / This Song Just For You	1956	250.00	750.00
Imperial 5451	(DJ)	So Long, Good Luck And Goodbye / Trying To Get To You	1957	15.00	75.00
Imperial 5451		So Long, Good Luck And Goodbye / Trying To Get To You	1957	20.00	100.00
		(Roy Orbison plays guitar on one or both sides of Imperial 5451.)			

ROGUES, THE

Counsel 122		Pete's Body Shop / (B-side by The Crayons)	1963	6.00	30.00

ROGUES, THE

Bing 4900		Barracuda / Jezebel	1964	10.00	50.00

ROGUES, THE
The Rogues are Bruce Johnston and Terry Melcher.

Columbia 43190	(DJ)	Everyday / Rogue's Reef	1964	2.00	10.00
Columbia 43190		Everyday / Rogue's Reef	1964	4.00	20.00

Label & Catalog #		A-Side/B-Side	Year	VG	NM
Columbia 43253	(DJ)	C'mon, Let's Go / Rogue's Reef, Part 2	1965	3.00	15.00
Columbia 43253		C'mon, Let's Go / Rogue's Reef, Part 2	1965	5.00	25.00

ROGUES, THE

Wasp 102		The Sound / Love Is A Beautiful Thing	196?	3.00	15.00

ROKES, THE

RCA Victor 47-9199		Let's Live For Today / I'll Change My Papers	1967	2.00	10.00

ROLLERS, THE

Liberty 55303		Bonneville / Got My Eye On You	1961	2.00	10.00
Liberty 55320		The Continental Walk / I Want You So	1961	2.00	10.00
Liberty 55357		Bounce / Teenager's Walk	1961	2.00	10.00

ROLLERS, THE: Refer to THE BAY CITY ROLLERS

ROLLING STONES, THE

Original recording members were Mick Jagger, Brian Jones, Keith Richards, Charlie Watts, Bill Wyman and unofficial member Ian Stewart. Jones left in 1969 and was replaced by Mick Taylor, who left in 1975. Ron Wood officially joined in '76. Refer to The Faces; Marianne Faithful; Peter Tosh.

London 9641	(DJ)	I Wanna Be Your Man / Stoned	1964	125.00	500.00
London 9641		I Wanna Be Your Man / Stoned	1964	—	—
		(Rare. Estimated near mint value $1,500-3,000.)			
London 9657	(DJ)	Not Fade Away / I Wanna Be Your Man	1964	15.00	75.00
London 9657		Not Fade Away / I Wanna Be Your Man	1964	3.00	15.00
London 9657	(PS)	Not Fade Away / I Wanna Be Your Man	1964	25.00	125.00
London 9682	(DJ)	Tell Me / I Just Want To Make Love To You	1964	6.00	30.00
London 9682		Tell Me / I Just Want To Make Love To You	1964	3.00	15.00
London 9682	(PS)	Tell Me / I Just Want To Make Love To You	1964	15.00	75.00
London 9687	(DJ)	It's All Over, Now / Good Times, Bad Times	1964	6.00	30.00
London 9687		It's All Over, Now / Good Times, Bad Times	1964	3.00	15.00
London 9687	(PS)	It's All Over, Now / Good Times, Bad Times	1964	15.00	75.00
London 9708	(DJ)	Time Is On My Side / Congratulations	1964	6.00	30.00
London 9708		Time Is On My Side / Congratulations	1964	3.00	15.00
London 9708	(PS)	Time Is On My Side / Congratulations	1964	8.00	40.00
London 9725	(DJ)	Heart Of Stone / What A Shame	1964	6.00	30.00
London 9725		Heart Of Stone / What A Shame	1964	3.00	15.00
London 9725	(PS)	Heart Of Stone / What A Shame	1964	100.00	400.00
London 9741	(DJ)	The Last Time / Play With Fire	1965	6.00	30.00
London 9741		The Last Time / Play With Fire	1965	3.00	15.00
London 9741	(PS)	The Last Time / Play With Fire	1965	8.00	40.00
		— London 9641-9741 originally issued on white labels with blue print.—			
London 9657		Not Fade Away / I Wanna Be Your Man	1965	1.60	8.00
London 9682		Tell Me / I Just Want To Make Love To You	1965	1.60	8.00
London 9687		It's All Over, Now / Good Times, Bad Times	1965	1.60	8.00
London 9708		Time Is On My Side / Congratulations	1965	1.60	8.00
London 9725		Heart Of Stone / What A Shame	1965	1.60	8.00
London 9741		The Last Time / Play With Fire	1965	1.60	8.00
London 9766	(DJ)	(I Can't Get No) Satisfaction / The Under Assistant West Coast Promo Man	1965	5.00	25.00
London 9766		(I Can't Get No) Satisfaction / The Under Assistant West Coast Promo Man	1965	1.60	8.00
London 9766	(PS)	(I Can't Get No) Satisfaction / The Under Assistant West Coast Promo Man	1965	20.00	100.00
London 9792	(DJ)	Get Off Of My Cloud / I'm Free	1965	5.00	25.00
London 9792		Get Off Of My Cloud / I'm Free	1965	1.60	8.00
London 9792	(PS)	Get Off Of My Cloud / I'm Free	1965	4.00	20.00
London 9808	(DJ)	As Tears Go By / Gotta Get Away	1965	5.00	25.00
London 9808		As Tears Go By / Gotta Get Away	1965	1.60	8.00
London 9808	(PS)	As Tears Go By / Gotta Get Away	1965	4.00	20.00
London 9823	(DJ)	19th Nervous Breakdown / Sad Day	1966	5.00	25.00
London 9823		19th Nervous Breakdown / Sad Day	1966	1.60	8.00
London 9823	(PS)	19th Nervous Breakdown / Sad Day	1966	6.00	30.00
London 901	(DJ)	Paint It Black / Stupid Girl	1966	5.00	25.00
London 901		Paint It Black / Stupid Girl	1966	1.60	8.00
London 901	(PS)	Paint It Black / Stupid Girl	1966	4.00	20.00
London 902	(DJ)	Mother's Little Helper / Lady Jane	1966	5.00	25.00
London 902		Mother's Little Helper / Lady Jane	1966	1.60	8.00
London 902	(PS)	Mother's Little Helper / Lady Jane	1966	4.00	20.00
London 903	(DJ)	Have You Seen Your Mother, Baby, Standing In The Shadows / Who's Driving Your Plane?	1966	5.00	25.00
London 903		Have You Seen Your Mother, Baby, Standing In The Shadows / Who's Driving Your Plane?	1966	1.60	8.00
London 903	(PS)	Have You Seen Your Mother, Baby, Standing In The Shadows / Who's Driving Your Plane?	1966	5.00	25.00
London 904	(DJ)	Ruby Tuesday / Let's Spend The Night Together	1967	5.00	25.00
London 904		Ruby Tuesday / Let's Spend The Night Together	1967	1.60	8.00
London 904	(PS)	Ruby Tuesday / Let's Spend The Night Together	1967	3.00	15.00

While this sleeve has the Stones decked out in full psychedelic regalia, the single itself represented the group's turn from the forays of conspicuous consciousness expansion and return to a grittier sound. The sleeve is a very clever affair, although it was used to even better effect on a Decca UK compilation titled *No Stone Unturned*...

Label & Catalog #		A-Side/B-Side	Year	VG	NM
London 905	(DJ)	We Love You / Dandelion	1967	5.00	25.00
London 905		We Love You / Dandelion	1967	2.00	10.00
London 905	(PS)	We Love You / Dandelion	1967	30.00	150.00
London 906	(DJ)	She's A Rainbow / 2,000 Light Years From Home	1967	5.00	25.00
London 906		She's A Rainbow / 2,000 Light Years From Home	1967	2.00	10.00
London 906	(PS)	She's A Rainbow / 2,000 Light Years From Home	1967	5.00	25.00
London 907	(DJ)	In Another Land / The Lantern	1967	6.00	30.00
London 907		In Another Land / The Lantern	1967	3.00	15.00
London 907	(PS)	In Another Land / The Lantern	1967	8.00	40.00
		("In Another Land" is credited to Bill Wyman.)			
London 908	(DJ)	Jumpin' Jack Flash / Child Of The Moon	1968	5.00	25.00
London 908		Jumpin' Jack Flash / Child Of The Moon	1968	1.60	8.00
London 908	(PS)	Jumpin' Jack Flash / Child Of The Moon	1968	3.00	15.00
London 909	(DJ)	Street Fighting Man / No Expectations	1968	5.00	25.00
London 909		Street Fighting Man / No Expectations	1968	1.60	8.00
London 909	(PS)	Street Fighting Man / No Expectations	1968	—	—
		(Probably the rarest collectible picture sleeve in the world. Estimated near mint value $3,000-5,000.)			
London 910	(DJ)	Honky Tonk Women / You Can't Always Get What You Want	1969	3.00	15.00
London 910		Honky Tonk Women / You Can't Always Get What You Want	1969	1.00	5.00
		—London singles above have blue swirl labels; the promos have orange swirl labels.—			
London 910	(PS)	Honky Tonk Women / You Can't Always Get What You Want	1969	2.00	10.00
		—Special/Promotional Releases—			
London	(33)	12 X 5 (Jukebox EP)	1967	60.00	250.00
London	(33)	The Rolling Stones, Now! (Jukebox EP)	1967	60.00	250.00
London	(33)	Out Of Our Heads (Jukebox EP)	1967	60.00	250.00
London	(33)	Their Satanic Majesties Request (Jukebox EP)	1967	75.00	300.00
		—Abkco Records—			
ABKCO 4701	(DJ)	I Don't Know Why / I Don't Know Why	1975	3.00	15.00
ABKCO 4701		I Don't Know Why / Try A Little Harder	1975	2.00	10.00
		(A-side label erroneously credits the writers as Jagger, Richards, Taylor.)			
ABKCO 4701		I Don't Know Why / Try A Little Harder	1975	1.00	5.00
		(A-side label correctly credits the writers as Wonder, Riser, Hunter, Hardaway.)			
ABKCO 4702	(DJ)	Out Of Time / Jiving Sister Fanny	1975	3.00	15.00
ABKCO 4702		Out Of Time / Jiving Sister Fanny	1975	1.25	6.00

—Rolling Stones Records—

Rolling Stones singles through "She Was Hot" (99788) were manufactured and distributed by Atlantic. With the release of "Harlem Shuffle," the label was manufactured and distributed by Columbia and bears their catalogue numbering.

Label & Catalog #		A-Side/B-Side	Year	VG	NM
Roll. Stones 19100	(DJ)	Brown Sugar / Brown Sugar	1971	5.00	25.00
Roll. Stones 19100		Brown Sugar / Bitch	1971	1.00	5.00
Roll. Stones 19101	(DJ)	Wild Horses / Wild Horses	1971	4.00	20.00
Roll. Stones 19101		Wild Horses / Sway	1971	.80	4.00
Roll. Stones 19103	(DJ)	Tumbling Dice / Tumbling Dice	1972	4.00	20.00
Roll. Stones 19103		Tumbling Dice / Sweet Black Angel	1972	.80	4.00
Roll. Stones 19104	(DJ)	Happy / All Down The Line	1972	3.00	15.00
Roll. Stones 19104		Happy / All Down The Line	1972	.80	4.00
Roll. Stones 19104	(DJ)	Doo Doo Doo Doo Doo (Heartbreaker) / Dancing With Mr. D	1974	3.00	15.00
Roll. Stones 19104		Doo Doo Doo Doo Doo (Heartbreaker) / Dancing With Mr. D	1974	.80	4.00
Roll. Stones 19105	(DJ)	Angie / Angie	1973	4.00	20.00
Roll. Stones 19105		Angie / Silver Train	1973	.80	4.00
Roll. Stones 19301	(DJ)	It's Only Rock 'N Roll / Through The Lonely Nights	1974	3.00	15.00
Roll. Stones 19301		It's Only Rock 'N Roll / Through The Lonely Nights	1974	.80	4.00
Roll. Stones 19302	(DJ)	Ain't Too Proud To Beg / Ain't Too Proud To Beg	1974	3.00	15.00
Roll. Stones 19302		Ain't Too Proud To Beg / Dance Little Sister	1974	.80	4.00
Roll. Stones 228	(DJ)	Time Waits For No One / Time Waits For No One	1976	5.00	25.00
Roll. Stones 228	(PS)	Time Waits For No One / Time Waits For No One	1976	6.00	30.00
Roll. Stones 19304	(DJ)	Fool To Cry / Fool To Cry	1976	3.00	15.00
Roll. Stones 19304	(DJ)	Hot Stuff / Hot Stuff	1976	3.00	15.00
Roll. Stones 19304		Fool To Cry / Hot Stuff	1976	.60	3.00
Roll. Stones 19307	(DJ)	Miss You / Far Away Eyes	1978	2.00	10.00
Roll. Stones 19307	(DJ)	Far Away Eyes / Far Away Eyes	1978	30.00	150.00
Roll. Stones 19307		Miss You / Far Away Eyes	1978	.60	3.00
Roll. Stones 19307	(PS)	Miss You / Far Away Eyes	1978	.60	3.00
Roll. Stones 19309	(DJ)	Beast Of Burden / Beast Of Burden	1978	2.00	10.00
Roll. Stones 19309		Beast Of Burden / When The Whip Comes Down	1978	.60	3.00
Roll. Stones 19309	(PS)	Beast Of Burden / When The Whip Comes Down	1978	150.00	500.00
Roll. Stones 19310	(DJ)	Shattered / Shattered	1978	2.00	10.00
Roll. Stones 19310		Shattered / Everything Is Turning To Gold	1978	.60	3.00
Roll. Stones 19310	(PS)	Shattered / Everything Is Turning To Gold	1978	.60	3.00
Roll. Stones 20001	(DJ)	Emotional Rescue / Down In The Hole	1980	2.00	10.00
Roll. Stones 20001		Emotional Rescue / Down In The Hole	1980	.60	3.00
Roll. Stones 20001	(PS)	Emotional Rescue / Down In The Hole	1980	.60	3.00
Roll. Stones 21001	(DJ)	She's So Cold / She's So Cold	1980	2.00	10.00
Roll. Stones 21001		She's So Cold / Send It To Me	1980	.40	2.00
Roll. Stones 21001	(PS)	She's So Cold / Send It To Me	1980	.60	3.00

This nifty promotional item was pulled from the Stones' monster *Some Girls* album and issued with a burnoosed Keith sleeve that has led many to mistake this as a Richards' solo item (including the first edition of this book). As the label makes clear, this is very much a part of the Rolling Stones' catalog.

Label & Catalog #		A-Side / B-Side	Year	VG	NM
Roll. Stones 21003	(DJ)	Start Me Up / Start Me Up	1981	2.00	10.00
Roll. Stones 21003		Start Me Up / No Use Crying	1981	.40	2.00
Roll. Stones 21003	(PS)	Start Me Up / No Use Crying	1981	.60	3.00
Roll. Stones 21004	(DJ)	Waiting On A Friend / Waiting On A Friend	1981	2.00	10.00
Roll. Stones 21004		Waiting On A Friend / Little T&A	1981	.40	2.00
Roll. Stones 21004	(PS)	Waiting On A Friend / Little T&A	1981	.60	3.00
Roll. Stones 21300	(DJ)	Hang Fire / Hang Fire	1981	2.00	10.00
Roll. Stones 21300		Hang Fire / Neighbours	1981	.40	2.00
Roll. Stones 21301	(DJ)	Going To A Go Go / Going To A Go Go	1981	2.00	10.00
Roll. Stones 21301		Going To A Go Go / Beast Of Burden	1981	.40	2.00
Roll. Stones 21301	(PS)	Going To A Go Go / Beast Of Burden	1981	.60	3.00
Roll. Stones 99978	(DJ)	Time Is On My Side / Time Is On My Side	1982	1.00	5.00
Roll. Stones 99978		Time Is On My Side / Twenty Flight Rock	1982	.40	2.00
Roll. Stones 99978	(PS)	Time Is On My Side / Twenty Flight Rock	1982	.60	3.00
Roll. Stones 99813	(DJ)	Undercover Of The Night / Undercover Of The Night	1983	1.00	5.00
Roll. Stones 99813		Undercover Of The Night / All The Way Down	1983	.40	2.00
Roll. Stones 99813	(PS)	Undercover Of The Night / All The Way Down	1983	.40	2.00
Roll. Stones 99788	(DJ)	She Was Hot / Think I'm Going Mad	1983	1.00	5.00
Roll. Stones 99788		She Was Hot / Think I'm Going Mad	1983	.40	2.00
Roll. Stones 99788	(PS)	She Was Hot / Think I'm Going Mad	1983	.40	2.00
Roll. Stones 05802	(DJ)	Harlem Shuffle / Harlem Shuffle	1986	1.00	5.00
Roll. Stones 05802		Harlem Shuffle / Had It With You	1986	.40	2.00
Roll. Stones 05802	(PS)	Harlem Shuffle / Had It With You	1986	.40	2.00
Roll. Stones 05906	(DJ)	One Hit (To The Body) / One Hit (To The Body)	1986	1.00	5.00
Roll. Stones 05906		One Hit (To The Body) / Fight	1986	.40	2.00
Roll. Stones 05906	(PS)	One Hit (To The Body) / Fight	1986	.40	2.00
		—Special/Promotionanl Releases—			
Roll. Stones	(33)	Exile On Main Street (Jukebox EP)	1976	20.00	100.00
Roll. Stones	(33)	Goat's Head Soup (Jukebox EP)	1976	20.00	100.00
Roll. Stones PR-287	(33)	Love You Live (Paper sleeve)	1976	15.00	75.00
Rolling Stones PR-316		Before They Make Me Run / Before They Make Me Run	1978	4.00	20.00
Rolling Stones PR-316	(PS)	Before They Make Me Run / Before They Make Me Run	1978	6.00	30.00
W.I.A.A. 1790		What's It All About Interview	1980	10.00	50.00
		—12" Singles—			
Roll. Stones PR-70	(DJ)	Hot Stuff / Crazy Mama	1976	15.00	75.00
		(Originals have an attractive black and blue "splash" vinyl; reproductions have the black spotted through the blue vinyl.)			
Roll. Stones PR-119	(DJ)	Miss You / Miss You	1978	3.00	15.00
Roll. Stones 4609		Miss You / Far Away Eyes	1978	1.20	6.00
Atlantic DSKO-174	(DJ)	Miss You / Hot Stuff	1978	6.00	30.00
Roll. Stones 4616		Miss You / Hot Stuff	1978	4.00	20.00
Roll. Stones PR-253	(DJ)	If I Was A Dancer (Dance, Part 2) / Dance	1980	3.00	15.00
Roll. Stones PR-367	(DJ)	Emotional Rescue / Down In The Hole	1980	4.00	20.00
Roll. Stones PR-397	(DJ)	Start Me Up / Start Me Up	1981	4.00	20.00
Roll. Stones 685	(DJ)	Undercover Of The Night / Undercover Of The Night (White label promo.)	1983	5.00	25.00
Roll. Stones 685	(DJ)	Undercover Of The Night / Undercover Of The Night (Yellow label promo.)	1983	2.00	10.00
Roll. Stones 69780		Undercover Of The Night / Feel On Baby (PC)	1983	1.26	6.00
Roll. Stones PR-692	(DJ)	Too Much Blood / Too Much Blood	1984	2.00	10.00
Roll. Stones 96902		Too Much Blood / Too Much Blood	1984	.80	4.00
Roll. Stones 05365	(DJ)	Harlem Shuffle / Had It With You (PC)	1986	1.00	5.00
Roll. Stones 05365		Harlem Shuffle / Had It With You (PC)	1986	.60	3.00

ROLLINS, DEBBIE

Ascot 2150		My Johnny Doesn't Come Around / Who Cares What People Say?	1964	1.25	6.00
Ascot 2159		Don't Let It Get You / Meet Me Tonight	1964	1.25	6.00

ROMAN, RON

Daani 101		Love Of My Life / Tell Me ("Love Of My Life" was co-written by Frank Zappa.)	1963	25.00	125.00

ROMAN NUMERALS, THE

Columbia 44314		Matchstick In A Whirlpool / The Come On	1967	1.00	5.00
Columbia 44314	(PS)	Matchstick In A Whirlpool / The Come On	1967	1.00	5.00

ROMANCERS, THE

Celebrity 701		No Greater Love / You'll Never Know	1961	7.00	35.00
Beacon 701		No Greater Love / You'll Never Know	1961	7.00	35.00
Selma 1501		Let's Do The Swim /	196?	2.00	10.00
Linda 117		Don't Let Her Go / I Did The Wrong Thing	1964	3.00	15.00

ROME & PARIS

Roulette 4681		Because Of You / Why Oh, Why?	1966	2.00	10.00

ROMEO, AL

Laurie 3177		Moonlight Becomes You / Hot Fudge Sunday	1963	2.00	10.00

Label & Catalog #	A-Side/B-Side		Year	VG	NM
ROMEOS, THE					
Amy 840	The Tiger's Awake / Hitch Hikin'		1962	2.00	10.00
ROMEOS, THE					
Mark II 101	Precious Memories / Juicy Lucy		1967	2.00	10.00
ROMERO, CHAN					
Del-Fi 4119	The Hippy Hippy Shake / If I Had A Way		1959	6.00	30.00
Del-Fi 4126	My Little Ruby / I Don't Care Now		1959	4.00	20.00
Challenge 59285	Funny Things / It's Not Fair		196?	2.00	10.00
Philips 40391	Humpy Bumpy / Man Can't Dog A Woman		196?	2.00	10.00
RON & JOE & THE CREW					
Strand 25001	Riot In Cell Block #9 / Ain't Love Grand?		1959	3.00	15.00
RON-DELS, THE					
Smash 1986	If You Really Want Me To, I'll Go / Walk About		1965	2.00	10.00
RONALD & RUBY					
RCA Victor 47-7174	Lollipop / Fickle Baby		1958	2.00	10.00
RONDELLS, THE					
Amy 825	Back Beat #1 / Shades Of Green		1961	3.00	15.00
Amy 830	My Prayer / Satan's Theme		1961	3.00	15.00
Amy 839	Caldonia / 110 Pounds Of Drums		1962	3.00	15.00
Amy 857	Meet Us A The Peppermint Lounge / Cover Charge		1962	3.00	15.00
RONDELLS, THE					
Shalimar 104	Matilda / Tina		1963	3.00	15.00
Dot 16598	On The Run / Far Horizon		1964	3.00	15.00
Dot 17323	Matilda / Tina		1969	2.00	10.00
RONETTES, THE					
The Ronettes—Estelle Bennett, Nedra Talley and Veronica Bennett a.k.a. Ronnie Spector—were produced by Phil Spector on Philles. Refer to Joey Dee; Ronnie & The Relatives.					
May 114	Silhouettes / You Bet I Would		1962	10.00	50.00
May 138	Good Girls / Memories		1962	10.00	50.00
Colpix 646	I'm Gonna Quit While I'm Ahead / I'm On The Wagon		1962	6.00	30.00
Philles 116	Be My Baby / Tedesco And Pitman		1963	4.00	20.00
Philles 118	Baby, I Love You / Miss Joan And Mr. Sam		1963	4.00	20.00
Dimension 1046	He Did It / Recipe For Love		1964	10.00	50.00
Philles 120	(The Best Part Of) Breakin' Up / Big Red		1964	4.00	20.00
Philles 121	Do I Love You? / Bebe And Susu		1964	4.00	20.00
Philles 123	Walkin' In The Rain / How Does It Feel?		1964	4.00	20.00
Philles 123	Walkin' In The Rain / How Does It Feel?	(PS)	1964	10.00	50.00
	—Original Philles singles above have blue labels.—				
Philles 126	Born To Be Together / Blues For Baby		1965	3.00	15.00
Philles 126	Born To Be Together / Blues For Baby	(PS)	1965	10.00	50.00
Philles 128	Is This What I Get For Loving You? / Oh, I Love You		1965	3.00	15.00
Philles 128	Is This What I Get For Loving You? / Oh, I Love You	(PS)	1965	15.00	75.00
Philles 133	I Can Hear Music / When I Saw You		1966	3.00	15.00
A&M 1040	You Came, You Saw, You Conquered / Oh, I Love You		1969	3.00	15.00
Buddah 384	Lover, Lover / Go Out And Get It	(DJ)	1973	1.00	5.00
Buddah 384	Lover, Lover / Go Out And Get It		1973	2.00	10.00
Buddah 408	I Wish I Never Saw The Sunshine /	(DJ)			
	I Wonder What He's Doing		1974	1.00	5.00
Buddah 408	I Wish I Never Saw The Sunshine /				
	I Wonder What He's Doing		1974	2.00	10.00
RONNIE & JOEY					
Little Star 106	Frozen Dinners / I Want		1961	2.00	10.00
RONNIE & THE CRAYONS					
Domain 1402	Am I In Love? / Birchard's Bread		1964	2.00	10.00
RONNIE & THE DEL-AIRES					
Coral 62404	The Drag / My Funny Valentine		1964	6.00	30.00
RONNIE & THE DIRT RIDERS					
Ronnie is Ron Dante.					
RCA Victor PB-10651	Yellow Van / Love Will Never Hurt You		1976	1.20	6.00
RONNIE & THE MANHATTANS					
Enjoy 2008	Come On Back / Long Time No See		1963	3.00	15.00
RONNIE & THE POMONA CASUALS					
The Pomona Casuals reputedly feature Arthur Lee.					
Donna 1400	Swinging At The Rainbow / Casual Blues		1964	3.00	15.00

Label & Catalog #		A-Side/B-Side	Year	VG	NM
Donna 1402		I Wanna Do The Jerk / Out Of The Blue	1965	3.00	15.00
RONNIE & THE PREMIERS					
Highland 1014		Sharon / Cha Cha Rock	1961	5.00	25.00
RONNIE & THE RELATIVES					
Ronnie & The Relatives later recorded as The Ronettes.					
Colpix 481		Sweet Sixteen / I Want A Boy	1961	10.00	50.00
May 111		I'm Gonna Quit While I'm Ahead / My Guiding Angel	1962	10.00	50.00
RONNIE & THE SCHOOLMATES					
Coed 605		Don't, Don't, Don't (Drop Out) / Just Born (To Be Your Baby)	1965	2.00	10.00
RONNY & THE DAYTONAS					
The Daytonas feature Buzz Cason and John "Buck" Wilkins. Refer to John Buck & His Blazers; Buzz & Bucky.					
Mala 481		G. T. O. / Hot Rod Baby	1964	2.00	10.00
Mala 490		California Bound / Hey, Little Girl	1964	2.00	10.00
Mala 492		Bucket "T" / Little Rail Job	1965	2.00	10.00
Mala 497		Little Scrambler / Teenage Years	1965	2.00	10.00
Mala 503		Beach Boy / No Wheels	1965	3.00	15.00
Mala 513		Sandy / Sandy	1965	2.00	10.00
Mala 525		Goodbye Baby / Somebody To Love Me	1966	2.00	10.00
Mala 531		Antique '32 Studebaker Dictator Coupe /			
		Then The Rains Came	1966	2.00	10.00
Mala 542		I'll Think Of Summer / Little Scrambler	1966	2.00	10.00
RCA Victor 47-8896		Dianne, Dianne / All American Girl	1966	1.60	8.00
RCA Victor 47-8896	(PS)	Dianne, Dianne / All American Girl	1966	4.00	20.00
RCA Victor 47-9022		Winter Weather / Young	1966	1.60	8.00
RCA Victor 47-9107		Walk With The Sun / Last Letter	1967	1.60	8.00
RCA Victor 47-9253		Brave New World / Hold Onto Your Heart	1967	1.60	8.00
RCA Victor 47-9435		Alfie / The Girls And The Boys	1968	1.60	8.00
Show Biz 21207	(DJ)	4-Cast She'll Love Me Again *(One sided)*	1968	4.00	20.00
RONSTADT, LINDA, & THE STONE PONEYS					
Sidewalk 937	(DJ)	So Fine / Everybody Has Their Own Ideas	1966	20.00	100.00
Sidewalk 937		So Fine / Everybody Has Their Own Ideas	1966	40.00	200.00
Capitol 5838		All The Beautiful Things / Sweet Summer Blue And Gold	1967	2.00	10.00
Capitol 5910		Evergreen / One For All	1967	2.00	10.00
Capitol 2004		Different Drum / I've Got To Know	1967	1.20	6.00
Capitol 2110		Up To My Neck In High Muddy Water / Carnival Bear	1968	1.20	6.00
Capitol 2110	(PS)	Up To My Neck In High Muddy Water / Carnival Bear	1968	4.00	20.00
Capitol 2195		Some Of Shelly's Blues / Hobo (Morning Glory)	1968	1.60	8.00
RONSTADT, LINDA					
Refer to Christmas Spirit.					
Capitol 2438		Dolphins / Long Way Around	1969	1.60	8.00
Capitol 2767		Will You Love Me Tomorrow? Lovesick Blues	1970	1.00	5.00
Capitol 2846		Long, Long Time / Nobody's	1970	1.00	5.00
Capitol 3021		(She's A) Very Lovely Woman / Long Way Around	1971	1.20	6.00
Capitol 3210		I Fall to Pieces / Can It Be True?	1972	1.00	5.00
Capitol 3273		Rock Me On The Water / Crazy Arms	1972	1.00	5.00
Capitol 3990		You're No Good / When Will I Be Loved?	1974	.60	3.00
Capitol 4050		When Will I Be Loved? / It Doesn't Matter Anymore	1975	.60	3.00
Asylum 11026		Love Has No Pride / I Can Almost See It	1973	.60	3.00
Asylum 11032		Silver Threads And Golden Needles / Don't Cry For Now	1974	.60	3.00
Asylum 45271		Silver Blue / Love Is A Rose	1975	.40	2.00
Asylum 45282		Heat Wave / Love Is A Rose	1975	.40	2.00
Asylum 45295		Tracks Of My Tears / The Sweetest Gift	1976	.40	2.00
Asylum 45340		That'll Be The Day / Try Me Again	1976	.40	2.00
Asylum 45361		Someone To Lay Down Beside Me / Crazy	1976	.40	2.00
Asylum 45402		Lose Again / La Siento Mi Vida	1977	.40	2.00
Asylum 45431		Blue Bayou / Old Paint	1977	.40	2.00
Asylum 45438		It's So Easy / La Siento Mi Vida	1977	.40	2.00
Asylum 45462		Poor, Poor Pitiful Me / Simple Man, Simple Dreams	1978	.40	2.00
Asylum 45464		Lago Azul / La Siento Mi Vida	1978	.40	2.00
Asylum 45479		Tumbling Dice / I Will Never Marry	1978	.40	2.00
Asylum 45519		Back In The U.S.A. / White Rhythm And Blues	1978	.40	2.00
Asylum 45519	(PS)	Back In The U.S.A. / White Rhythm And Blues	1978	.60	3.00
Asylum 45546		Ooh Baby Baby / Blowin' Away	1978	.40	2.00
Asylum 46011		Just One Look / Love Me Tender	1979	.40	2.00
Asylum 46034		Alison / Mohammed's Radio	1979	.60	3.00
Asylum 46602		How Do I Make You? / Rambler Gambler	1980	.40	2.00
Asylum 46602	(PS)	How Do I Make You? / Rambler Gambler	1980	.60	3.00
Asylum 46624		Hurt So Bad / Justine	1980	.40	2.00
Asylum 46654		I Can't Let Go / Look Out For My Love	1980	.40	2.00
Asylum 69948		Get Closer / Sometimes You Just Can't Win	1982	.40	2.00
Asylum 69948	(PS)	Get Closer / Sometimes You Just Can't Win	1982	.40	2.00

Label & Catalog #		A-Side/B-Side	Year	VG	NM
Asylum 69853		I Knew You When / Talk To Me Of Mendocino	1982	.40	2.00
Asylum 69853	(PS)	I Knew You When / Talk To Me Of Mendocino	1982	.40	2.00
Asylum 69780		What's New? / Crazy He Calls Me	1983	.40	2.00
Asylum 69383		Easy For You To Say / Mr. Radio	1986	.40	2.00
		—Special/Promotional Releases—			
Asylum	(DJ)	Spun Gold Hits Kit	1980	6.00	30.00
		(Box of four Spun Gold reissues—45073, 45081, 45089, and 45092—and her latest single, Asylum 46602.)			

ROOKS, THE
| Etiquette 14 | | I'll Be The One / Believe In You | 1965 | 3.00 | 15.00 |
| Mustang 3008 | | Bound To Lose / Gimme A Break | 1965 | 3.00 | 15.00 |

ROOKS, WAYNE
| Capitol 4772 | | Where Does The Clown Go? / Chi Chico Teek | 1962 | 1.20 | 6.00 |
| Capitol 4866 | | Fraternity Pin / Postcard From Paris | 1963 | 1.20 | 6.00 |

ROOMATES, THE [THE ROOMMATES]
Refer to Cathy Jean & The Roomates.
Promo 2211		I Want A Little Girl / Making Believe	1960	3.00	15.00
Valmor 008		Glory Of Love / Never Knew	1961	3.00	15.00
Valmor 013		My Foolish Heart / My Kisses For Your Thoughts	1962	3.00	15.00
Cameo 233		Sunday Kind Of Love / A Lovely Way To Spend An Evening	1962	3.00	15.00
Philips 40105		Answer Me, My Love / Gee	1963	4.00	20.00
Philips 40153		The Nearness Of You / Please Don't Cheat On Me	1963	3.00	15.00
Philips 40161		The Nearness Of You / Please Don't Cheat On Me	1964	3.00	15.00
Canadian American 166		My Heart / Just For Tonight	1964	4.00	20.00

ROOSTERS, THE
Shar-Dee 704		Fun House / Chicken Hop	1959	4.00	20.00
Felsted 8642		Fun House / Chicken Hop	1962	2.00	10.00
Epic 9487		Pretty Girl / Let's Try Again	1962	2.00	10.00

ROOSTERS, THE
| Progressive Sounds 1151 | | One Of These Days / You Gotta Run | 196? | 7.00 | 35.00 |

ROSE, C. G.
C. G. Rose is a pseudonym for Ron Dante.
| Mercury 72789 | | Sayonara Baby / Man Of The Family | 1968 | 1.00 | 5.00 |

ROSE, TIM
Columbia 43563		I'm Bringing It Home / Mother, Father, Where Are You?	1966	.60	3.00
Columbia 43648		Hey, Joe / King Lonely The Blue	1966	.60	3.00
Columbia 43722		I Gotta Do Things My Way / Where Was I?	1966	.60	3.00
Columbia 43958		I'm Gonna Be Strong / I Got A Loneliness	1967	.60	3.00
Columbia 44031		Morning Dew / You're Slipping Away From Me	1967	.60	3.00
Columbia 44387		Long Time Man / Come Away, Melinda	1967	.60	3.00

ROSE GARDEN, THE
| Atco 6510 | | Next Plane To London / Flower Town | 1967 | 1.00 | 5.00 |
| Atco 6564 | | Here Today / If My World Falls Through | 1968 | .80 | 4.00 |

ROSE MARIE
| Mercury 71144 | | Chenaluna Rock And Roll / Two Dollars, Please | 1957 | 2.00 | 10.00 |

ROSELLA, CARMELA
| Nancy 1004 | | Oh, It Was Elvis! / Where? | 1961 | 5.00 | 25.00 |

ROSS, STAN
| Reprise 20119 | | Drowning In The Surf / Ahab The Arab | 1962 | 4.00 | 20.00 |
| Del-Fi 4200 | | 50 Mile Hike / 50 Mile Hike, Part 2 | 1963 | 3.00 | 15.00 |

ROSSI, FRANKIE, & THE DREAMS
| Mark 7001 | | Dream Boy / Around The Corner | 195? | 4.00 | 20.00 |

ROSSI, KENNY
| Gee 1050 | | But I Do / Watch Your P's And Q's | 1961 | 2.00 | 10.00 |

ROSSINI, TONY (& THE CHIPPERS)
Sun 349		I Gotta Know Where I Stand / Is It Too Late?	1960	2.00	10.00
Sun 366		Darlena / Well, I Ask Ya	1961	2.00	10.00
Sun 378		(Meet Me) After School / Just Around The Corner	1962	2.00	10.00
Sun 380		You Make It Sound So Easy / New Girl In Town	1962	2.00	10.00
Sun 387		Moved To Kansas City / Nobody	1964	2.00	10.00

ROTATIONS, THE
| Original Sound 41 | | Heavies / The Cruncher | 1964 | 15.00 | 75.00 |
| | | (Produced by Frank Zappa.) | | | |

Label & Catalog #		A-Side/B-Side	Year	VG	NM
ROTATIONS, THE					
MY 0263		I Can See A Light / One Way Road	196?	2.00	10.00
ROTATORS, THE					
Felsted 8632		Double Exposure / Double Exposure (Part 2)	1961	2.00	10.00
ROTH, LINDA					
Intrastate 42		Teenage Diary / Right As Rain	1959	2.00	10.00
ROTTEN KIDS, THE					
Mercury 72558		Let's Stomp / Twelve Months Later	1966	1.20	6.00
ROUBIAN, BOB					
Capitol 3373		Blue Suede Shoes / Candy Coated Kisses	1956	3.00	15.00
Prep 101		Rocket To The Moon / It's Only A Paper Moon	1957	3.00	15.00
Prep 109		Cracker Stacker / Man, What A Past	1957	3.00	15.00
ROULETTES, THE					
Champ 102		I See A Star / Come On, Baby	1959	6.00	30.00
ROULETTES, THE					
Angle 1001		Surfer's Charge / Archibald The II	1963	7.00	35.00
ROULETTES, THE					
United Artists 718		Can You Go? / Soon You'll Be Leaving Me	1964	2.00	10.00
United Artists 990		Junk / Long Cigarette	1966	2.00	10.00
ROUTERS, THE					
Warner Bros. 5283		Let's Go / Mashy	1962	2.00	10.00
Warner Bros. 5332		Half Time / Make It Snappy	1963	1.20	6.00
Warner Bros. 5349		Sting Ray / Snap Happy	1963	2.00	10.00
ROVIN' FLAMES, THE					
Fuller 2627		Gloria / J. J. J. P.	1965	5.00	25.00
ROVIN' KIND, THE					
Dunwich 146		My Generation / Girl	1967	3.00	15.00
Dunwich 154		She / Didn't Wanta Have To Do It	1967	3.00	15.00
ROWLAND, STEVE, & THE RING LEADERS					
Cross Country 1818		Out-Ridin' / Here Kum The Karts	196?	2.00	10.00
Cross Country 1818	(PS)	Out-Ridin' / Here Kum The Karts	196?	4.00	20.00
ROXY & THE DAYCHORDS					
Don-el 46		I'm So In Love / Mary Lou	195?	25.00	125.00
ROY, BOBBY, & THE CHORD-A-ROYS					
JDS 5001		Little Girl Lost / Girls Were Made For Boys	195?	5.00	25.00
ROYAL, BILLY JOE					
Fairlane 21009		Never In A Hundred Years / We Haven't A Moment To Lose	1961	3.00	15.00
Fairlane 21013		Dark Glasses / Perhaps	1962	3.00	15.00
All Wood 401		If It Wasn't For A Woman / Wait For Me, Baby	1962	3.00	15.00
Tollie 9011		Mama Didn't Raise No Fools / Get Behind Me, Devil	1963	2.00	10.00
Tollie 9011	(PS)	Mama Didn't Raise No Fools / Get Behind Me, Devil (DJ)	1963	3.00	15.00
Players 1		I'm Specialized / Really You	196?	3.00	15.00
Columbia 43305		Down In The Boondocks / Oh, What A Night	1965	1.20	6.00
Columbia 43465		I've Got To Be Somebody / You Make Me Feel Like A Man	1965	1.00	5.00
Atlantic 2328		Never In A Hundred Years / We Haven't A Moment To Lose	1966	1.00	5.00
Columbia 43622		Heart's Desire / Deep Inside Me	1966	1.00	5.00
Columbia 43740		Should I Come Back? / Campfire Girls	1966	1.00	5.00
Columbia 43883		Yo Yo / We Tried	1966	1.00	5.00
Columbia 43990		I Knew You When / Steal Away	1967	1.00	5.00
Columbia 44033		Wisdom Of A Fool / Everything Turned Blue	1967	1.00	5.00
Columbia 44277		Hush / Watching From The Bandstand	1967	1.00	5.00
Columbia 44574		Storybook Children / Just Between You And Me	1968	1.00	5.00
Columbia 44902		Cherry Hill Park / Helping Hand	1969	1.00	5.00
Columbia 45220		Every Night / Burning A Hole	1970	.80	4.00
Columbia 45289		Tulsa / Pick Up The Pieces	1971	.80	4.00
Columbia 45557		The Family / Later	1971	.80	4.00
Columbia 45620		Child Of Our Time / Natchez Trace	1972	.80	4.00
MGM/South 7011		This Magic Moment / Mountain Woman	1973	.80	4.00
MGM/South 7018		This Magic Moment / Mountain Woman	1973	.80	4.00
MGM/South 7022		This Magic Moment / Mountain Woman	1973	.80	4.00
MGM/South 7032		Start Again / Sugar Blue	1973	.80	4.00
Scepter 12419		All Night Rain / Time Don't Pass By Here	1976	.60	3.00
Private Stock 45192		Under The Boardwalk / Precious Time	1978	.80	4.00

Label & Catalog #	A-Side/B-Side	Year	VG	NM
ROYAL COACHMEN, THE				
Challenge 59251	Loophole / Repeating	1964	5.00	25.00
Ge Ge 102	Tidal Wave / Tremor	196?	7.00	35.00
ROYAL DEBS, THE				
Tifco 826	I Do / Jerry	1961	3.00	15.00
ROYAL DRIFTERS, THE				
Teen 506	Little Linda /	196?	6.00	30.00
Teen 508	To Each His Own /	196?	6.00	30.00
ROYAL FLAIRS, THE				
Marine 502	One Pine Box / Suicide	196?	8.00	40.00
ROYAL GUARDSMEN, THE				
The Royal Guardsmen feature Barry Winslow.				
Laurie 3359	Baby, Let's Wait / Leaving Me	1966	2.00	10.00
Laurie 3366	Snoopy Vs. The Red Baron / I Needed You	1966	1.00	5.00
Laurie 3379	Return Of The Red Baron / Sweetmeats Slide	1967	1.00	5.00
Laurie 3391	Airplane Song / Om	1967	1.00	5.00
Laurie 3397	So Right (To Be In Love) / Wednesday	1967	1.00	5.00
Laurie 3416	Snoopy's Christmas / It Kinda Looks Like Christmas	1968	1.00	5.00
Laurie 3416 (PS)	Snoopy's Christmas / It Kinda Looks Like Christmas	1968	3.00	15.00
Laurie 3428	I'm Not Gonna Stay / I Say Love	1968	1.00	5.00
Laurie 3451	Snoopy For President / Down Behind The Lines	1968	1.00	5.00
Laurie 3461	Baby, Let's Wait / Biplane "Evermore"	1968	1.00	5.00
Laurie 3461	Baby, Let's Wait / So Right (To Be In Love)	1968	1.00	5.00
Laurie 3494	Mother, Where's Your Daughter? / Magic Window	1969	1.20	6.00
ROYAL JACKS, THE				
20th Century Fox 100	I'm In Love Again / The Big Ring	1958	4.00	20.00
Studio 9903	Night After Night / Who, What, Where, When And Why?	1959	6.00	30.00
Amy 865	Tam-O-Shanter / Anticipation	1962	2.00	10.00
ROYAL KINGS, THE				
Forlin 502	Peter Peter / Keep It To Yourself	195?	7.00	35.00
ROYAL KNIGHTS, THE				
Fireball 104	Knight-Mare / Forever Little Girl	195?	7.00	35.00
ROYAL LANCERS, THE				
The Royal Lancers feature Paul Stefen.				
Citation 5004	Angel In My Eyes / Baby, I Don't Care	1963	3.00	15.00
ROYAL PLAYBOYS, THE				
Dodo 101	Goodbye, Bo /	196?	2.00	10.00
ROYAL ROCKERS, THE				
Bee 1112	Swinging Mambo / Jet 11	1959	3.00	15.00
ROYAL TEENS, THE				
The Royal Teens feature Bob Gaudio, later of The Four Seasons and Turner Disentri.				
Power 113	Sittin' With My Baby / Mad Gas	1957	6.00	30.00
Power 215	Short Shorts / Planet Rock	1957	15.00	75.00
ABC-Paramount 9882	Short Shorts / Planet Rock	1958	4.00	20.00
ABC-Paramount 9918	Big Name Button / Sham Rock	1958	3.00	15.00
ABC-Paramount 9945	Harvey's Got A Girl Friend / Hangin' Round	1958	3.00	15.00
ABC-Paramount 9955	My Kind Of Dream / Open The Door	1958	3.00	15.00
Mighty 111	Leotards / Royal Blues	1958	3.00	15.00
Mighty 112	Cave Man / Wounded Heart	1959	4.00	20.00
Mighty 200	My Memories Of You / Little Trixie	1960	3.00	15.00
Capitol 4261	Believe Me / Little Cricket	1959	3.00	15.00
Capitol 4335	The Moon's Not Meant For Lovers / Was It A Dream?	1969	3.00	15.00
Capitol 4402	It's The Talk Of The Town / With You	1960	3.00	15.00
All New 1415	Short Short Twist / Royal Twist	1962	2.00	10.00
Jubilee 5418	Short Short Twist / Royal Twist	1961	3.00	15.00
Blue Jay 101	I'll Love You Till The End Of Time / I'll Love You Till The End Of Time, Part 2	1965	2.00	10.00
Swan 4200	I'll Love You Till The End Of Time / I'll Love You Till The End Of Time, Part 2	1965	3.00	15.00
TCF 117	Bad Girl / Do The Montoona	1965	2.00	10.00
Astra 1012	Sittin' With My Baby / Mad Gas	196?	2.00	10.00
Musicor 1398	Hey Jude / Smile A Little Smile For Me	1969	1.00	5.00
ROYAL TONES, THE				
Titanic 5014	Surfer's Junction / Black Lightnin'	196?	8.00	40.00

Label & Catalog #		A-Side/B-Side	Year	VG	NM
ROYAL VIKINGS, THE					
Metropolis 7001		Surfin' Mary / Baby Blues	196?	7.00	35.00
ROYALE MONARCHS, THE					
Dell 101		Sombrero Stomp / Whole Lotta Shakin' Goin' On	1962	7.00	35.00
Dell Star 102		Surf's Up / My Babe	1962	7.00	35.00
ROYALITES, THE					
Mojak 5265		Wiggle Waggle / Harlem Nocturne	196?	7.00	35.00
ROYALS, THE					
Vagabond 444		Christmas Party / White Christmas	1962	6.00	30.00
Vagabond 444		Christmas Party / White Christmas (Red vinyl)	1962	15.00	75.00
Vagabond 134		Surfin' Lagoon / Wild Safari	1963	6.00	30.00
ROYALS, THE					
Penguin		Thunder Wagon / Teen Beat	196?	3.00	15.00
RUBEN & THE JETS: *Refer to* FRANK ZAPPA & THE MOTHERS OF INVENTION					
RUBEN & THE JETS					
This is a different group of Jets, produced by Frank Zappa.					
Mercury 73381		If I Could Be Your Love Again / Wedding Bells	1972	1.00	5.00
RUBIES, THE					
Empress 103		He Was An Angel / He's Mine	196?	6.00	30.00
Vee Jay 596	(PS)	Spanish Boy (Promo picture sleeve)	1965	6.00	30.00
Vee Jay 596		Spanish Boy / Deeper	1965	2.00	10.00
RUBINOOS, THE					
Beserkley 5741		I Think We're Alone Now / As Long As I'm With You	1977	.60	3.00
Beserkley 5741	(PS)	I Think We're Alone Now / As Long As I'm With You	1977	.60	3.00
Beserkley 5750		Hold Me / Lightning Love Affair	1977	.60	3.00
Beserkley 5810		Nothing A Little Love Won't Cure / Leave My Heart Alone	1977	.60	3.00
Beserkley 5810	(PS)	Nothing A Little Love Won't Cure / Leave My Heart Alone	1977	.60	3.00
Beserkley 46518		I Wanna Be Your Boyfriend / Lightning Love Affair	1979	.60	3.00
RUBY					
Ruby features Tom Fogerty.					
PBR 507		Life Is But A Dream /	1977	.80	4.00
RUDOLPH, RANDY					
Preview 1507		Little Surfer Teen / Pardon Me For Falling In Love	196?	7.00	35.00
RUE-TEENS, THE					
Louis 6805		Lucky Boy / I Don't Cry Over Girls	196?	2.00	10.00
Old Timer 612		Happy Teenager / Come A Little Bit Closer	196?	2.00	10.00
RUFF, RAY					
Lin 5034		Beatlemania / I Took A Liking To You	1964	3.00	15.00
RUFF, RAY, & THE CHECKMATES					
Bolo 741		Pledge Of Love / A Fool Again	196?	2.00	10.00
RUFF & REDDY					
Cavalier 876		Henry Goes To The Moon / Henry Goes To The Moon, Part 2	1956	2.00	10.00
RUGBYS, THE					
Top Dog 2315		Walking In The Streets Tonight / Endlessly	196?	2.00	10.00
Smash 1997		Till The Day I Die / James Is The Name	1965	1.20	6.00
Amazon 1	(DJ)	You, I / You, I (Blue vinyl)	1969	2.00	10.00
Amazon 1		You, I / Stay With Me	1969	1.00	5.00
Amazon 4		Windeghal The Warlock / The Light	1969	1.00	5.00
Amazon 6		Rockin' All Over /	1970	.80	4.00
RUMBLERS, THE					
The Rumblers, featuring Adrian Lloyd of Adrian & The Sunsets, also recorded as The Nylons.					
Highland 1026		Intersection / Stomping Theme	1962	8.00	40.00
Downey 103		Boss / I Don't Need You No More	1962	4.00	20.00
Downey 106		Boss Strikes Back / Sorry	1963	4.00	20.00
Downey 107		Angry Sea (Waimea) / Bugged	1963	4.00	20.00
Downey 114		Hi Octane / Night Scene	1963	4.00	20.00
Downey 111		It's A Gass / Tootenanny	1963	4.00	20.00
Dot 16421		Boss / I Don't Need You No More	1963	2.00	10.00
Dot 16455		Boss Strikes Back / Sorry	1963	2.00	10.00
Dot 16480		Angry Sea (Waimea) / Bugged	1963	2.00	10.00
Dot 16521		It's A Gass / Tootenanny	1963	2.00	10.00

Label & Catalog #		A-Side/B-Side	Year	VG	NM
Downey 127		Soulful Jerk / Hey-Did-A-Da-Da	1964	4.00	20.00
Downey 133		Boss Soul / Till Always	1965	4.00	20.00
RUMBLES LTD.					
Dad's 103		The Wildest Christmas / Santa Claus Is Coming To Town	1966	2.00	10.00
Mercury 72690		It'll Be Alright / Out Of Harmony	1967	1.00	5.00
Mercury 72723		Jezebel / Music In Me	1967	1.00	5.00
Mercury 72815		99% Sure / Everyday Kind Of Love	1968	1.00	5.00
GNP/Crescendo 430		Try A Little Harder / California My Way	1968	1.00	5.00
Sire 4110		Push Push / First To Know	1969	1.00	5.00
RUMORS, THE					
Gemcor 5002		Hold Me Now / Without Her	196?	6.00	30.00
RUN-A-BOUTS, THE					
Kay-Gee		Hi Hat / Wildfire	196?	3.00	15.00
RUNABOUTS, THE					
Vox		The Chase / I Need Time	1965	7.00	35.00
RUNABOUTS, THE					
Gama 699		Surfer's Fright / Walkin' Dream	196?	8.00	40.00
RUNABOUTS, THE					
Hi Jinx 9661		Swampwater / Freeloader	196?	7.00	35.00
RUNAROUNDS, THE					
Pio 107		Lovers Lane / The Nearest Thing To Heaven	1961	3.00	15.00
RUNAROUNDS, THE [THE RUN-A-ROUNDS]					
The Runarounds feature Guy Vitari and Chuck Fassert of The Regents.					
Tarheel 65		Let The Talk / Are You Looking For A Sweetheart?	1963	4.00	20.00
KC 116		Hooray For Love / Unbelievable *(Brown vinyl)*	1963	6.00	30.00
KC 116		Hooray For Love / Unbelievable	1963	3.00	15.00
Cousins 1004		Mashed Potato Mary / I'm All Alone	196?	4.00	20.00
Felsted 8704		Carrie (You're An Angel) / Send Her Back	1964	6.00	30.00
Capitol 5644		Perfect Woman / You're A Drag	1966	5.00	25.00
RUNAWAYS, THE					
Teensound 1924		Teenage Style / Kangaroo Hop	196?	4.00	20.00
RUNAWAYS, THE					
The Runaways feature Cherie and Marie Currie and Joan Jett.					
Mercury 73819		Cherry Bomb / Black Mail	1976	2.00	10.00
Mercury 738890		Heartbeat / Neon Angels On The Road To Ruin	1977	2.00	10.00
RUNDGREN, TODD [RUNT]					
Todd Rundgren also recorded with Shaun Cassidy; Nazz; and Utopia.					
Ampex 31001		We Gotta Get You A Woman / Baby, Let's Swing Medley	1970	1.20	6.00
Bearsville 31002		Be Nice To Me / Broke Down And Busted	1971	1.00	5.00
Bearsville 31004		A Long Time, A Long Way Ago / Parole	1971	1.00	5.00
		(Ampex 31001 and Bearsville 31002 and 31004 credit Runt.)			
Bearsville 0003	(DJ)	I Saw The Light / Marlene *(Blue vinyl)*	1972	3.00	15.00
Bearsville 0003		I Saw The Light / Marlene *(Blue vinyl)*	1972	2.00	10.00
Bearsville 0003		I Saw The Light / Marlene *(Black vinyl)*	1972	3.00	15.00
Bearsville 0007		Couldn't I Just Tell You? / Wolfman Jack	1972	.80	4.00
Bearsville 0009		Hello, It's Me / Cold Morning Light	1973	1.00	5.00
Bearsville PRO-562	(DJ)	Just One Victory / International Feel-Never Never Land	1973	3.00	15.00
Bearsville 0015		Sometimes I Don't Know What To Feel / Does Anybody Love You?	1973	.80	4.00
Bearsville 0020		A Dream Goes On Forever / Heavy Metal Kids	1974	.80	4.00
Bearsville 0301		Breathless / Wolfman Jack	1974	.80	4.00
Bearsville 0304		Real Man / Prana	1975	.60	3.00
Bearsville 0309		Good Vibrations / When I Pray	1976	.60	3.00
Bearsville 0310		Love Of The Common Man / Black And White	1976	.60	3.00
Bearsville 0324		Can We Still Be Friends? / Determination	1978	.60	3.00
Bearsville 0324		Can We Still Be Friends? / Out Of Control	1978	.80	4.00
Bearsville 0330		You Cried Wolf / Onomatopoeia	1978	.60	3.00
Bearsville 0335		It Wouldn't Have Made Any Difference /	1979	.60	3.00
Bearsville 49696		Time Heals / Tiny Demons	1981	.60	3.00
Bearsville 49771		Compassion /	1981	.60	3.00
Bearsville 29759		Hideaway /	1982	.60	3.00
Bearsville 29686		Bang The Drum All Day / Chant	1982	.60	3.00
Warner Bros. 28821		Something To Fall Back On / Lockjaw	1985	.60	3.00
Warner Bros. 22868		Parallel Lines / I Love My Life	1989	.60	3.00
Warner Bros. 22868	(PS)	Parallel Lines / I Love My Life	1989	1.00	5.00

Label & Catalog #		A-Side/B-Side	Year	VG	NM
RUSH					
Ducal		Life In The In City / Summer For Bonnie Jean	196?	1.00	5.00
RUSH					
Moon 001	(Can)	Not Fade Away / You Can't Fight It	1973	75.00	300.00
Mercury 406	(DJ)	Finding My Way / Finding My Way	1974	7.00	35.00
Mercury 73681		Fly By Night / Anthem	1975	.80	4.00
Mercury 73737		Bastille Day / Lakeside Park	1976	.60	3.00
Mercury 73803		Lessons / The Twilight Zone	1976	.60	3.00
Mercury 73873		Fly By Night-In The Mood / Something For Nothing	1976	.60	3.00
Mercury 73912		Making Memories / The Temples Of Syrinx	1977	.60	3.00
Mercury 73958		Closer To The Heart / Madrigal	1977	.60	3.00
Mercury 73990		Fly By Night / Anthem	1978	.60	3.00
Mercury 74051		The Trees / Circumstances	1979	.60	3.00
Mercury 76109		Tom Sawyer / Witch Hunt	1981	.60	3.00
Mercury 76109	(PS)	Tom Sawyer / Witch Hunt	1981	1.00	5.00
Mercury 76179		New World Man / Vital Signs (Live)	1982	.40	2.00
Mercury 76179	(PS)	New World Man / Vital Signs (Live)	1982	.40	2.00
Mercury 884 191		The Big Money / Red Sector A (Live)	1985	.40	2.00
Mercury 884 191	(PS)	The Big Money / Red Sector A (Live)	1985	.40	2.00
Mercury 888 891		Time Stand Still / High Water	1987	.40	2.00
Mercury 888 891	(PS)	Time Stand Still / High Water	1987	.40	2.00
RUSH, MERRILEE (& THE TURNABOUTS)					
Ruro 0411		Party Song / It's Alright	196?	1.20	6.00
Merrilinn 5301		Tell Me The Truth / Lovers Never Say Goodbye	196?	1.00	5.00
Merrilinn 4306		See Me I'm Smiling / How's The Weather In Your Street	196?	1.00	5.00
Bell 705		Angel Of The Morning / Reap What You Sow	1968	1.00	5.00
Bell 738		That Kind Of Woman / Sunshine And Roses	1968	.80	4.00
AGP 107		Reach Out / Love Street	1968	.80	4.00
AGP 112		Everyday Livin' Days / Your Lovin Eyes Are Blind	1969	.80	4.00
AGP 121		Sign On For The Good Times / Robin McCarver	1969	.80	4.00
AGP 126		Angel On My Shoulder / It's Worth It All	1969	.80	4.00
RUSS & THE STING RAYS					
Coral 102		Do The Surf / I'm Cryin'	196?	6.00	30.00
RUSSELL, LEE					
Roulette 4049		Honky Tonk Woman / Rainbow At Midnight	1958	3.00	15.00
RUSSELL, LEON					
Refer to The Asylum Choir; Dave & Lee.					
Shelter 301		Hummingbird / Roll Away The Stone	1970	1.00	5.00
Shelter 7325		Tight Rope / This Masquerade	1972	.60	3.00
Shelter 7328		Slipping Into Christmas / Christmas In Chicago	1972	.60	3.00
Shelter 7337		Queen Of The Roller Derby / Roll Away The Stone	1973	.30	1.50
Shelter 40210		If I Were A Carpenter / Wild Horses	1974	.30	1.50
Shelter 40210	(PS)	If I Were A Carpenter / Wild Horses	1974	.60	3.00
Shelter 40277		Time For Love / Leaving Whippoorwill	1975	.30	1.50
Shelter 40378		Lady Blue / Laying Right Here In Heaven	1975	.30	1.50
Shelter 40483		Back To The Island / Little Hideaway	1976	.30	1.50
Paradise 8208		Rainbow In Your Eyes / Love's Supposed To Be That Way	1976	.30	1.50
Paradise 8274		Satisfy You / Windsong	1976	.30	1.50
Paradise 8369		Love Crazy / Say You Will	1977	.30	1.50
Paradise 8438		Easy Love / Hold On To This Feeling	1977	.30	1.50
		(Paradise 8208-8438 credit Leon & Mary Russell.)			
Paradise 8667		Elvis And Marilyn / Anita Bryant	1978	.30	1.50
Paradise 8667	(PS)	Elvis And Marilyn / Anita Bryant	1978	.40	2.00
Paradise 8719		From Maine To Mexico / Midnight Lover	1978	.30	1.50
RUSSO BROTHERS, THE					
Era 3011		Velvet Eyes / There's More	1960	2.00	10.00
RUSTIX					
Cadet 5628		When I Get Home / Leaving Here	1968	1.00	5.00
RUSTY & DUSTY					
Caprice 0061		Goodbye Twelve, Hello Teens / Boys Will Be Boys	1960	2.00	10.00
RUTLES, THE					
Warner Bros. 8560		Doubleback Alley / I Must Be In Love	1978	2.00	10.00
RYAN, BARRY					
MGM 14010		Eloise / Love, I Almost Found You	1968	.80	4.00
Prise 1032		Can't Let You Go / L.A. Woman	1971	.80	4.00
RYAN, JAMIE					
Columbia 44045		The Worst Of The Hurt Is Over / 21 Inches Of Heaven	1967	1.00	5.00

Label & Catalog #		A-Side/B-Side	Year	VG	NM
RYAN, PAUL & BARRY					
MGM 13422		Don't Bring Me No Heartaches / To Remind Me	1965	1.00	5.00
MGM 13911		Pictures Of Today / Madrigal	1968	1.00	5.00
RYAN, PETER					
Aardvark 101		If We Try / I Can Hear The Music	196?	3.00	15.00
RYDELL, BOBBY					
Venise 201		Fatty Fatty / Happy Happy	1958	5.00	25.00
Veko 731		Fatty Fatty / Dream Age	1958	3.00	15.00
Cameo 160		Please Don't Be Mad / Makin' Time	1959	3.00	15.00
Cameo 164		All I Want Is You / For You, For You	1959	3.00	15.00
Cameo 167		Kissin' Time / You'll Never Tame Me	1959	3.00	15.00
Cameo 167	(PS)	Kissin' Time / You'll Never Tame Me	1959	4.00	20.00
Cameo 169		We Got Love / I Dig Girls	1959	3.00	15.00
Cameo 169	(PS)	We Got Love / I Dig Girls	1959	4.00	20.00
Cameo 171		Wild One / Itty Bitty Girl	1960	3.00	15.00
Cameo 171	(PS)	Wild One / Itty Bitty Girl	1960	4.00	20.00
Cameo 175		Swingin' School / Ding A Ling	1960	3.00	15.00
		—Original Cameo singles above have orange labels.—			
Cameo 160		Please Don't Be Mad / Makin' Time	1961	1.60	8.00
Cameo 164		All I Want Is You / For You, For You	1961	1.60	8.00
Cameo 167		Kissin' Time / You'll Never Tame Me	1961	1.60	8.00
Cameo 169		We Got Love / I Dig Girls	1961	1.60	8.00
Cameo 171		Wild One / Itty Bitty Girl	1961	1.60	8.00
Cameo 175		Swingin' School / Ding A Ling	1961	1.60	8.00
Cameo 179		Volare / I'll Do It Again	1960	1.60	8.00
Cameo 179	(PS)	Volare / I'll Do It Again	1960	3.00	15.00
Cameo 182		Sway / Groovy Tonight	1960	1.60	8.00
Cameo 182	(PS)	Sway / Groovy Tonight	1960	2.00	10.00
Cameo 186		Good Time Baby / Cherie	1961	1.60	8.00
Cameo 186	(PS)	Good Time Baby / Cherie	1961	2.00	10.00
Cameo 190		That Old Black Magic / Don't Be Afraid	1961	1.60	8.00
Cameo 190	(PS)	That Old Black Magic / Don't Be Afraid	1961	2.00	10.00
Cameo 192		The Fish / The Third House	1961	1.60	8.00
Cameo 192	(PS)	The Fish / The Third House	1961	2.00	10.00
Cameo 201		I Wanna Thank You / The Door To Paradise	1961	1.60	8.00
Cameo 201	(PS)	I Wanna Thank You / The Door To Paradise	1961	2.00	10.00
Cameo 209		I've Got Bonnie / Lose Her	1962	1.00	5.00
Cameo 209	(PS)	I've Got Bonnie / Lose Her	1962	2.00	10.00
Cameo 217		I'll Never Dance Again / Gee, It's Wonderful	1962	1.00	5.00
Cameo 217	(PS)	I'll Never Dance Again / Gee, It's Wonderful	1962	2.00	10.00
Cameo 228		The Cha-Cha-Cha / The Best Man Cried	1962	1.00	5.00
Cameo 228	(PS)	The Cha-Cha-Cha / The Best Man Cried	1962	2.00	10.00
Cameo 242		Butterfly Baby / Love Is Blind	1963	1.00	5.00
Cameo 242	(PS)	Butterfly Baby / Love Is Blind	1963	2.00	10.00
Cameo 252		Wildwood Days / Will You Be My Baby?	1963	1.00	5.00
Cameo 252	(PS)	Wildwood Days / Will You Be My Baby?	1963	2.00	10.00
Cameo 265		Little Queenie / The Woodpecker Song	1963	1.00	5.00
Cameo 265	(PS)	Little Queenie / The Woodpecker Song	1963	2.00	10.00
Cameo 272		Let's Make Love Tonight / Childhood Sweetheart	1963	1.00	5.00
Cameo 272	(PS)	Let's Make Love Tonight / Childhood Sweetheart	1963	2.00	10.00
Cameo 280		Forget Him / Love, Love, Go Away	1963	1.00	5.00
Cameo 280	(PS)	Forget Him / Love, Love, Go Away	1963	2.00	10.00
Cameo 309		Make Me Forget / Little Girl, I've Had A Busy Day	1964	1.00	5.00
Cameo 309	(PS)	Make Me Forget / Little Girl, I've Had A Busy Day	1964	2.00	10.00
Cameo 320		A World Without Love / Our Faded Love	1964	1.00	5.00
Cameo 320	(PS)	A World Without Love / Our Faded Love	1964	2.00	10.00
Cameo 361		Ciao, Ciao, Bambino / Voice De La Notte	1964	.80	4.00
Cameo	(DJ)	Steel Pier (One sided)	196?	2.00	10.00
		—Cameo singles above have red & black labels.—			
Capitol 5305		I Just Can't Say Goodbye / Two Is The Loneliest Number	1964	.80	4.00
Capitol 5305	(PS)	I Just Can't Say Goodbye / Two Is The Loneliest Number	1964	2.00	10.00
Capitol 5352		Diana / Stranger In The World	1965	.80	4.00
Capitol 5436		Sideshow / The Joker	1965	.80	4.00
Capitol 5513		It Takes Two / When I See That Girl Of Mine	1965	.80	4.00
Capitol 5556		Roses In The Snow / The Word For Today	1965	.80	4.00
Capitol 5696		She Was The Girl / Not You	1966	.80	4.00
Capitol 5780		You Gotta Enjoy Joy / Open For Business As Usual	1966	.80	4.00
Reprise 0656		The Lovin' Things / It's Getting Better	1968	.80	4.00
Reprise 0684		The River Is Wide / Absence Makes The Heart Grow Fonder	1968	.80	4.00
Reprise 0751		Every Little Bit Hurts / Time And Changes	1968	.80	4.00
RCA Victor 47-9892		Chapel On The Hill / It Must Be Love	1970	.80	4.00
Perception 519		California Sunshine / Honey Buns	197?	.60	3.00
Perception 552		Everything Seemed Better (When I Was Younger) / Sunday Son	197?	.60	3.00
Pickwick Int. 6515		Sway / Sway (Disco)	197?	.60	3.00
Pickwick Int. 6521		Give Me Your Answer / You're Not The Only Girl For Me	197?	.60	3.00

Label & Catalog #		A-Side/B-Side	Year	VG	NM
Pickwick Int. 6531		The Single Scene / It's Getting Better	197?	.80	3.00
		— Extended Play Albums—			
Capitol 2281		Somebody Loves You	1965	3.00	15.00
RYDELL, BOBBY, & CHUBBY CHECKER					
Cameo 12E	(DJ)	Your Hits And Mine / (One sided)	1961	5.00	25.00
Cameo 205		Jingle Bell Rock / Jingle Bell Imitations	1961	2.00	10.00
Cameo 205	(PS)	Jingle Bell Rock / Jingle Bell Imitations	1961	3.00	15.00
Cameo 214		Swingin' Together / Teach Me To Twist	1962	2.00	10.00
Cameo 214	(PS)	Swingin' Together / Teach Me To Twist	1962	3.00	15.00
RYDER, MITCH, & THE DETROIT WHEELS					
Refer to Billy & The Rivieras; Detroit; The Detroit Wheels.					
New Voice 801		I Need Help / I Hope	1965	1.20	6.00
New Voice 806		Jenny Take A Ride! / Baby Jane	1965	1.20	6.00
New Voice 808		Little Latin Lupe Lu / I Hope	1966	1.20	6.00
New Voice 811		Break Out / I Need Help	1966	1.20	6.00
New Voice 814		Takin' All I Can Get / You Get Your Kicks	1966	1.20	6.00
New Voice 817		Devil With A Blue Dress On-Good Golly Miss Molly /			
		I Had It Twice	1966	1.20	6.00
New Voice 820		Sock It To Me, Baby! / I Never Had It Better	1967	5.00	25.00
		(Original pressings contain lyrics that sound like			
		"Every time you kiss me, feels like a fuck!")			
New Voice 820		Sock It To Me, Baby! / I Never Had It Better	1967	1.20	6.00
		(Later pressings were overdubbed so that the lyrics			
		sound like "Every time you kiss me, feels like a punch!")			
New Voice 820	(PS)	Sock It To Me, Baby! / I Never Had It Better	1967	2.00	10.00
New Voice 822		Too Many Fish In The Sea-Three Little Fishes /			
		One Grain Of Sand	1967	1.20	6.00
New Voice 822	(PS)	Too Many Fish In The Sea-Three Little Fishes /			
		One Grain Of Sand	1967	2.00	10.00
RYDER, MITCH					
New Voice 824		Joy / I'd Rather Go To Jail	1967	.60	3.00
New Voice 826		You Are My Sunshine / Wild Child	1967	.60	3.00
New Voice 828		Come See About Me / Face In The Crowd	1967	.60	3.00
New Voice 830		Ruby Baby / You Get Your Kicks	1967	.60	3.00
DynoVoice 901		What Now My Love / Blessing In Disguise	1967	.60	3.00
DynoVoice 905		(You've Got) Personality-Chantilly Lace /			
		I Make A Fool Of Myself	1968	.60	3.00
DynoVoice 916		The Lights Of Night / I Need Your Loving	1968	.60	3.00
DynoVoice 934		Ring Your Bell / Baby, I Need Your Lovin'	1968	.60	3.00
Avco Embassy 4550	(DJ)	Jenny Take A Ride / I Never Had It Better	1969	2.00	10.00
Dot 17290		Sugar Bee (We Three) / I Believe (There Must Be Someone)	1969	.60	3.00
Dot 17325		It's Been A Long, Long, Long Time / Direct Me	1969	.60	3.00
		— 12" Singles—			
Seeds & Stems 1011		Rock And Soul / Soul Kitchen	1979	1.00	5.00
Personal 49820		Like A Rolling Stone / Can Do	1985	1.00	5.00

When the Motor City's Billy Lee & The Rivieras opened for the Dave Clark Five in 1965, their future was made when producer Bob Crewe signed them to his New Voice label. Recording as Mitch Ryder & The Detroit Wheels, they enjoyed a run of chart hits with the Detroit Wheels in 1966-67 (seven sides reached the national surveys). He specialized in breakneck, all-stops-out versions of older r&b material, including his last real success, a medley of the Marvelettes' *Too Many Fish In The Sea* and *Three Little Fishes*.

SA-SHAYS, THE

Alfi 1	Boo Hoo Hoo / You Got Love	1961	3.00	15.00
Zen 101	Boo Hoo Hoo / You Got Love	1961	2.00	10.00

SABER, JOHNNY, & THE PASSIONS
Refer to The Passions.

Adonis 103	Wish It Could Be Me / Dolly In A Toy Shop	195?	30.00	150.00

SACCO
Sacco is a pseudonym for Lou Christie.

Lifesong 1175		Theme From "People" / Theme From "People," Part 2	1978	.80	4.00
Lifesong 1176	(12")	Theme From "People" / Theme From "People," Part 2	1978	1.20	6.00

SADDLEMEN, THE: *Refer to* LOU GRAHAM; BILL HALEY

SAFARIS, THE
The Safaris originally recorded as The Enchanters.

Eldo 101	Image Of A Girl / Four Steps To Love	1960	4.00	20.00
Eldo 105	The Girl With The Story In Her Eyes / Summer Nights	1960	5.00	25.00
Eldo 110	In The Still Of The Night / Shadows	1961	4.00	20.00
Eldo 113	Soldier Of Fortune / Garden Of Love	1961	3.00	15.00

SAFARIS, THE

Valiant 6036	Lonely Surf Guitar / Kick Out	1963	5.00	25.00

SAGITTARIUS
Sagittarius features Curt Boetcher, Glen Campbell and Gary Usher, who produced.

Columbia 44163	My World Fell Down / Libra	1967	2.00	10.00
	(A-side features Bruce Johnston.)			
Columbia 44289	Virgo / Hotel Indiscreet	1967	2.00	10.00
Columbia 44398	Another Time / Pisces	1967	2.00	10.00
Columbia 44503	You Know I've Found A Way / Truth Is Not Real	1967	2.00	10.00
Columbia 44613	I'm Not Living Here / Keeper Of The Games	1968	2.00	10.00
Together 105	In My Room / Navajo Girl	1969	2.00	10.00
Together 122	I Can Still See Your Face /			
	I Guess The Lord Must Be In New York City	1969	2.00	10.00

SAHARAS, THE

Fenton 2016	I'm Free / The Mornin'	196?	6.00	30.00

SAHM, DOUG
Doug Sahm also recorded as Wayne Douglas; Him; Little Doug. and with The Sir Douglas Quintet.

Warrior 507		Crazy Daisy / If I Ever Need You	1958	7.00	35.00
Satin 100		Crazy Daisy / I Can't Believe You Wanna Leave	1959	7.00	35.00
Harlem 107		Why, Why, Why? / If You Ever Need Me	1960	4.00	20.00
Harlem 108	(DJ)	Baby, Tell Me / Sapphire *(Gold vinyl)*	1960	20.00	100.00
Harlem 108		Baby, Tell Me / Sapphire	1960	5.00	25.00
Harlem 113		Slowdown / More And More	1960	8.00	40.00
Swingin' 625		Why, Oh, Why? / If You Ever Need Me	1960	5.00	25.00
Cobra 116		Just A Moment / Sapphire	1961	10.00	50.00
Renner 212	(DJ)	Makes No Difference / Big Hat *(Red vinyl)*	1961	15.00	75.00
Renner 212		Makes No Difference / Big Hat	1961	7.00	35.00
Renner 215	(DJ)	Baby, What's On Your Mind / Crazy, Crazy Feeling *(Red vinyl)*	1961	15.00	75.00
Renner 215		Baby, What's On Your Mind / Crazy, Crazy Feeling	1961	7.00	35.00
Renner 226		Just Because / Two Hearts In Love	1962	5.00	25.00
Renner 232		Cry / Little Angel	1963	7.00	35.00
Renner 240		Lucky Me / A Year Ago Today	1963	10.00	50.00
Renner 247		Mr. Kool / Bill Beatty	1964	10.00	50.00
Personality 260		Baby, What's On Your Mind / Crazy, Crazy Feeling	1964	4.00	20.00
Soft 1031		Cry / Down The Pike	1964	4.00	20.00
Atlantic 2946		(Is Anybody Going To) San Antone? / Don't Turn Around	1973	.80	4.00
Warner Bros. 7819		Groover's Paradise /			
		Girls Today (Don't Like To Sleep Alone)	1974	.80	4.00
		(Warner Bros. 7819 credits Doug Sahm & The Tex Mex Trip,			
		which includes former CCR members Stu Cook and Doug Clifford.)			
Dot 17656		I Love The Way You Love / Cowboy Peyton Place	1976	.80	4.00
Dot 17674		Cryin' Inside / Sometimes	1976	1.00	5.00
		(Dot 17656 and 17654 credit Doug Sahm & The Texas			
		Tornados, another incarnation of the Sir Douglas Quintet.)			

Label & Catalog #		A-Side/B-Side	Year	VG	NM
SAHM, DOUG, & AUGIE MEYER					
Teardrop 3479		Who Were You Thinking Of? / Velma From Selma	1982	.80	4.00
Teardrop 3480		Love Taker / Life In The City	1982	.80	4.00
Teardrop 3481		I'm Not A Fool Anymore / Don't Fight It	1982	.80	4.00
Teardrop 3482		I'm Not A Fool Anymore / Don't Fight It	1983	.80	4.00
Teardrop 3482	(PS)	I'm Not A Fool Anymore / Don't Fight It	1983	1.00	5.00
SAIGON SAUCERS, THE					
Wade 101		Howdy Doody, Doctor Death / Not My Fault	196?	3.00	15.00
SAINT, BILLY					
Seafair 101		Polly Ann / Midnight Freeze	1960	1.00	5.00
Dot 16169		Polly Ann / Midnight Freeze	1960	1.00	5.00
Seafair 106		Tanganyika / Who Walks In The Garden?	196?	1.00	5.00
Dore 656		Tear Down The Wall / Baby Doll	196?	1.00	5.00
Jerden 716		Oh, Jennie / How She's Gone	1963	1.00	5.00
A&M 720		Oh, Jennie / How She's Gone	1963	1.00	5.00
Jerden 724		Just Another Kind Of Love / Watching Over You	1965	1.00	5.00
SAINT, CATHY					
Daisy 501		Big Bad World / Mr. Heartbreak	1964	3.00	15.00
ST. JOHN, DICK					
Refer to Dick & Dee Dee.; Sandy & Dick.					
Pom Pom 4156		Sha-Ta / Gonna Stick By You	1961	4.00	20.00
Liberty 55380		Sha-Ta / Gonna Stick By You	1961	2.00	10.00
Rona 1001		Hey, Little Gal / Boogie Man (I Ain't Afraid Of You)	1961	2.00	10.00
Philips 40256		Believe Me, Baby / Love's A Funny Little Game	1965	1.20	6.00
Philips 40325		You Know What I Mean? / Swanee River	1965	1.20	6.00
Dot 17080		Childhood / Lady Of The Burning Green Jade	1968	1.00	5.00
Dot 17140		Brand New Season / Leaving On A Jet Plane	1968	1.00	5.00
ST. JOHN & THE CARDINALS					
Shurfine 010		Rampage / The Rise	196?	5.00	25.00
ST. LOUIS UNION, THE					
Parrot 9812		Girl / Respect	1966	2.00	10.00
ST. PETERS, CRISPIAN					
Jamie 1309		At This Moment / No No No	1966	1.00	5.00
Jamie 1310		You Were On My Mind / What I'm Gonna Be	1966	1.00	5.00
Jamie 1320		The Pied Piper / Sweet Dawn, My True Love	1966	1.20	6.00
Jamie 1324		Changes / My Little Brown Eyes	1966	1.00	5.00
Jamie 1328		But She's Untrue / Your Ever Changin' Mind	1967	1.00	5.00
Jamie 1344		Free Spirits / I'm Always Crying	1967	1.00	5.00
ST. ROMAIN, KIRBY					
Inette 103		Summer's Comin' / Walk On	1963	1.60	8.00
SAL & THE CONTINENTALS					
Four Four One 34		I'm Goin' Away / The Tomahawk	196?	7.00	35.00
SAL & THE WATCHERS					
Pio 106		Spooky / The Watchers	196?	3.00	15.00
SALAS BROTHERS, THE					
Faro 614		Darling (Please Bring Your Love) / Leaving You	1964	2.00	10.00
Faro 619		The Return Of Farmer John / Love Is Strange	1964	2.00	10.00
SALEMS, THE					
EPK 9480		Maria / Ol' Man River	196?	2.00	10.00
SALES, SOUPY					
Reprise 20041		Hippy's Cha Cha Hips / White Fang	1962	3.00	15.00
Reprise 20064		Soupy's Theme / Because Of Black Tooth	1962	3.00	15.00
Reprise 20108		My Baby's Got A Crush On Frankenstein / Doggone Doggie	1963	3.00	15.00
Reprise 20189		And That's A Shame / Hilly Billy Ding Dong Choo Choo	1963	3.00	15.00
Reprise 20244		Santa Claus Is Surfin' To Town / Santa Claus Is Comin' To Town	1963	3.00	15.00
Reprise 0368		Soupy Sez / Pie In The Face	1964	3.00	15.00
Reprise 0368	(PS)	Soupy Sez / Pie In The Face	1964	4.00	20.00
Wonderland 00342		Bingity Bangity Bus / Bingity Bangity Bus, Part 2	196?	1.00	5.00
Wonderland 00342	(PS)	Bingity Bangity Bus / Bingity Bangity Bus, Part 2	196?	2.00	10.00
Golden 00187		Sally Sidney / Sally Sidney, Pt. 2	196?	1.00	5.00
Golden 00187	(PS)	Sally Sidney / Sally Sidney, Pt. 2	196?	1.00	5.00
Capitol 5752		Spanish Flea / That Wasn't No Girl	1966	2.00	10.00
Capitol 5752	(PS)	Spanish Flea / That Wasn't No Girl	1966	4.00	20.00
Capitol 5766		Use Your Noggin' / The Backwards Alphabet	1966	2.00	10.00

Label & Catalog #		A-Side/B-Side	Year	VG	NM
ABC-Paramount 10646		The Mouse / Pachalafaka	1965	1.20	6.00
ABC-Paramount 10681		Speedy Gonzales / Hey, Pearl	1965	1.20	6.00
ABC-Paramount 10747		I'm A Bird Watching Man / Where The Blue Folks Go	1965	1.20	6.00
Brunswick 55472		Break Your Back / Tom Jones	196?	1.00	5.00
Motown 1141		Muck-Arty-Park / Green Grow The Lilacs	197?	1.00	5.00
Wizdom 1978		It's My Ego /	1978	.80	4.00

SALESMEN, THE
| NY Skyline 507 | | Soupy's Mouse / Don't Go Steady With Freddy | 1965 | 2.00 | 10.00 |

SALISBURY, SANDY
Sandy Salisbury was produced by Gary Usher.
| Together 102 | | Do Unto Others / | 1969 | 2.00 | 10.00 |
| Together 139 | | On And On She Goes / Goody Goodbye | 1969 | 2.00 | 10.00 |

SALLES, JESSIE, & THE CRYPT-KICKERS
| Garpax 44169 | | The Jog / (B-side by Gary Paxton) | 1962 | 2.00 | 10.00 |

SALLY & THE ROSES
| Columbia 42895 | | Chicken Back / Usher Boy | 1963 | 4.00 | 20.00 |

SALMA, DOUG, & THE HIGHLANDERS
| Philips 40131 | | Scavenger / Highland Fling | 1963 | 2.00 | 10.00 |

SALTWATER TAFFY
| Metromedia 220 | | Summertime Girl / Spend The Sunshine | 1971 | 1.00 | 5.00 |

SALUTATIONS, THE: *Refer to* VITO & THE SALUTATIONS

SALVIN, DICK
| Graveyard 3000 | | Dr. Finkenstein's Castle / | 196? | 3.00 | 15.00 |

SALVO, SAMMY
| RCA Victor 47-7097 | | Oh, Julie / Say Yeah | 1957 | 3.00 | 15.00 |
| RCA Victor 47-7516 | | Wolf Boy / My Perfect Love | 1959 | 3.00 | 15.00 |

SAM & THE WESTSIDERS
| Integrity 692 | | Let's Go Surfing / Why, Little Girl? | 1964 | 7.00 | 35.00 |

SAM THE SHAM & THE PHARAOHS [THE SAM THE SHAM REVUE[
Sam The Sham is Sam Samudio. Refer to The Shamettes.
Tupelo 2982		Betty And Dupree / Manchild	1963	8.00	40.00
Dingo 1		Haunted House / How Does A Cheating Woman Feel?	1964	40.00	200.00
"XL" 905		The Signifying Monkey / Juimonos	1964	6.00	30.00
"XL" 906		Wooly Bully / Ain't Gonna Move	1965	20.00	100.00
MGM 13322		Wooly Bully / Ain't Gonna Move	1965	1.60	8.00
MGM 13364		Ju Ju Hand / Big City Lights	1965	1.60	8.00
MGM 13364	(PS)	Ju Ju Hand / Big City Lights	1965	3.00	15.00
MGM 13397		Ring Dang Doo / Don't Try It	1965	1.60	8.00
MGM 13397	(PS)	Ring Dang Doo / Don't Try It	1965	3.00	15.00
MGM 13452		Red Hot / A Long, Long Way	1966	1.60	8.00
MGM 13506		Lil' Red Riding Hood / Love Me Like Before	1966	1.60	8.00
MGM 13581		The Hair On My Chinny Chin Chin / The Out Crowd	1966	1.60	8.00
MGM 13581	(PS)	The Hair On My Chinny Chin Chin / The Out Crowd	1966	3.00	15.00
MGM 13649		How Do You Catch A Girl? / The Love You Left Behind	1966	1.20	6.00
MGM 13649	(PS)	How Do You Catch A Girl? / The Love You Left Behind	1966	3.00	15.00
MGM 13713		Oh That's Good, No That's Bad / Take What You Can Get	1967	1.20	6.00
MGM 13747		Black Sheep / My Day's Gonna Come	1967	1.20	6.00
MGM 13803		Banned In Boston / Money's My Problem	1967	1.20	6.00
MGM 13863		Yakety Yak / Let Your Love Light Shine	1967	1.20	6.00
		(MGM 13803 and 13863 credited to The Sam The Sham Revue.)			
MGM 13920		Old MacDonald Has A Boogaloo Farm / I Never Had No One	1968	1.20	6.00
MGM 13972		I Couldn't Spell !!@! / The Down Home Spirit	1968	2.00	10.00
MGM 14021	(DJ)	Wooly Bully / Ain't Gonna Move	1970	2.00	10.00
MGM 14642	(DJ)	Fate / Oh, Lo	1973	2.00	10.00
		(Stock copies of MGM 14021 and 14642 may not exist.)			
Fretone 048		Wookie / Wookie, Part 2	1977	.80	4.00
Fretone 049		Baby, You Got It / Ain't No Lie	1978	.80	4.00
Samara 1		Running With The Rabbits / I've Got The Victory	1985	1.00	5.00

SAMMY & THE DEL-LANDS
| Stop 101 | | Little Darling / Sleep Walk | 196? | 4.00 | 20.00 |

SAMMY & THE FIVE NOTES
| Lucky Four 1019 | | Doodle Bug Twist / The Lion Is Awake | 196? | 7.00 | 35.00 |

SAMMY & THE TEASERS
| Airport 101 | | As I Remember You / Penny In A Wishing Well | 195? | 10.00 | 50.00 |

Label & Catalog #	A-Side/B-Side	Year	VG	NM
SAMOHI SERENADERS, THE				
Century Custom 19317	Sunday Morning / (B-side by The Paragons)	196?	8.00	40.00
SAMUDIO, SAM				
Sam Samudio also recorded as Sam The Sham.				
Atlantic 2767	Key To The Highway / Me And Bobby McGhee	1970	.80	4.00
SAMUELS, JERRY				
Jerry Samuels also recorded as Napolean XIV.				
J.E.P. 1175	Who Are You To Tell Me Not To Smoke Marijuana? /	196?	3.00	15.00
	I Owe A Lot To Iowa Pot			
SAN DIEGO MISFITS, THE				
The Misfits feature Bob Mosley, later of Moby Grape.				
Troy 227	The Uncle Willie / Big Bad Wolf	196?	3.00	15.00
Imperial 66054	This Little Piggie / Lost Love	196?	3.00	15.00
SAN FRANCISCO EARTHQUAKE, THE				
Smash 2117	I Feel Loved / That Same Old Fat Man	1967	1.60	8.00
Smash 2157	Fairy Tales Can Come True / Su Su	1968	1.60	8.00
Smash 2179	March Of The Jingle Jangle People / Bring Me Back	1968	1.60	8.00
Smash 2218	The Day Lorraine Came Home / Everybody Laughed	1969	1.60	8.00
SANDABS, THE				
Bamboo 522	Beach Ball / Crab Louie	1962	3.00	15.00
SANDALS, THE [THE SANDELLS]				
Aura 4501	Wild As The Sea / School's Out	1963	4.00	20.00
World Pacific 405	Out Front / Scrambler	1964	4.00	20.00
	(Aura and W.P. 405 credit The Sandells.)			
World Pacific 415	Endless Summer / 6-Pac (Instrumental Version)	1964	4.00	20.00
	(Reportedly, a vocal version of "6-Pac" exists on some copies of W.P. 415.)			
World Pacific 77840	Endless Summer / 6-Pac	1965	2.00	10.00
World Pacific 77852	Tell Us, Dylan / Why Should I Cry?	1965	2.00	10.00
World Pacific 77867	Cloudy / House Of Painted Glass	1966	2.00	10.00
SANDERS, ARLEN, & THE PACIFICS				
Faro 616	Hopped Up Mustang / A Letter To Paul	1964	7.00	35.00
SANDERS, BOBBY				
Refer to Bobby & The Velvets; The Extremes.				
Kaybo 618	I'm On My Way / It Was You	1961	6.00	30.00
Pick-A-Hit 100	Lover / The Way I Feel	196?	2.00	10.00
SANDERS, GARY				
Warner Bros. 5676	Ain't No Beatle / Ain't I Good To You?	1964	3.00	15.00
SANDI & THE ACCENTS: *Refer to* THE ACCENTS				
SANDI & THE SPADES				
Three Rivers 112	A Million Pieces / Lonely One	196?	4.00	20.00
SANDI & THE STYLERS				
Rachel 101	Sandi's Eddie's Girl / Mixed Up Mommy	196?	4.00	20.00
SANDOVAL, JIM, & THE GAUCHOS: *Refer to* JIM DOVAL				
SANDPAPERS, THE				
Charger 114	Ain't Gonna Kiss Ya / My Baby Said	1965	1.20	6.00
SANDS, EVIE				
ABC-Paramount 10458	Roll / My Dog	1964	1.60	8.00
Blue Cat 118	Take Me For A Little While / Run Home To Your Mama	1965	1.60	8.00
Blue Cat 22	I Can't Let Go / You've Got Me Uptight	1965	1.60	8.00
Cameo 413	Picture Me Gone / It Makes Me Laugh	1966	1.00	5.00
Cameo 436	The Love Of A Boy / We Know Better	1966	1.00	5.00
Cameo 475	Angel Of The Morning / Dear John	1967	1.20	6.00
Cameo 2002	Billy Sunshine / It Makes Me Laugh	1968	1.00	5.00
A&M 1090	Anyway You Want Me / I'll Never Be Alone	1969	.80	4.00
A&M 1157	Crazy Annie / Maybe Tomorrow	1970	.80	4.00
A&M 1175	But You Know I Love You / Maybe Tomorrow	1970	.80	4.00
A&M 1192	Take Me For A Little While / It's This I Am, I Find	1970	.80	4.00
Haven 7010	You Brought The Woman Out Of Me /	1975	.60	3.00
	Early Morning Sunshine			
Haven 7013	I Love Makin' Love To You / One Thing On Your Mind	1975	.60	3.00
Haven 7020	Yesterday Can't Hurt Me / (Am I) Crazy 'Cause I Believe	1975	.60	3.00

Label & Catalog #		A-Side/B-Side	Year	VG	NM
SANDS, JODIE					
Teen 109		Love Me Always / Everybody Needs Somebody	1955	5.00	25.00
Bernlo 1003		Love Me Always / Everybody Needs Somebody	1957	3.00	15.00
Chancellor 1003		With All My Heart / More Than Only Friends	1957	2.00	10.00
Chancellor 1005		If You're Not Completely Satisfied / Sayonara	1959	2.00	10.00
Chancellor 1023		Someday / Always In My Heart	1958	2.00	10.00
Thor 101		Hold Me / What Does It Matter?	1959	2.00	10.00
SANDS, TOMMY					
Tommy Sands also recorded with Annette.					
Capitol 3639		Teen-Age Crush / Hep Dee Hootie	1957	3.00	15.00
Capitol 3690		Ring-A-Ding-A-Ding / My Love Song	1967	3.00	15.00
Capitol 3723		Goin' Steady / Ring My Phone	1957	3.00	15.00
Capitol 3743		Let Me Be Loved / Fantastically Foolish	1958	3.00	15.00
Capitol 3810		A Swingin' Romance / Man, Like Wow	1958	3.00	15.00
Capitol 3867		Sing Boy, Sing / Crazy 'Cause I Love You	1958	3.00	15.00
Capitol 3953		Teenage Doll / Hawaiian Rock	1958	3.00	15.00
Capitol 3985		After The Senior Prom / Big Date	1958	2.00	10.00
Capitol 3985	(PS)	After The Senior Prom / Big Date	1958	4.00	20.00
Capitol 4036		Blue Ribbon Baby / I Love You Because	1958	2.00	10.00
Capitol 4082		The Worryin' Kind / Bigger Than Texas	1958	2.00	10.00
Capitol 4259		I'll Be Seeing You / That's The Way I Am	1959	2.00	10.00
Capitol 4259	(PS)	I'll Be Seeing You / That's The Way I Am	1959	4.00	20.00
		—Capitol singles above have purple labels with the Capitol logo on top.—			
Capitol 4316		You Hold The Future / I Gotta Have You	1959	2.00	10.00
Capitol 4321		Bring Me Your Love / Sinner Man	1959	2.00	10.00
Capitol 4366		That's Love / Crossroads	1960	2.00	10.00
Capitol 4407		The Old Oaken Bucket / These Are The Things You Are	1960	2.00	10.00
Capitol 4470		Doctor Heartache / On And On	1960	2.00	10.00
		—Capitol singles above have purple labels with the Capitol logo on the left.—			
ABC-Paramount 10466		Young Man's Fancy / Connie	1963	1.00	5.00
		—Extended Play Albums—			
Capitol 1-848		Steady Date With Tommy Sands (Volume 1)	1957	10.00	50.00
Capitol 2-848		Steady Date With Tommy Sands (Volume 2)	1957	10.00	50.00
Capitol 3-848		Steady Date With Tommy Sands (Volume 3)	1957	10.00	50.00
Capitol 851		Teenage Crush	1957	10.00	50.00
Capitol 1-929		Sing Boy, Sing (Volume 1)	1958	8.00	40.00
Capitol 2-929		Sing Boy, Sing (Volume 2)	1958	8.00	40.00
Capitol 3-929		Sing Boy, Sing (Volume 3)	1958	8.00	40.00
Capitol 1123		This Thing Called Love	1959	8.00	40.00
SANDS OF TIME, THE					
The Sands of Time is a pseudonym for The Tokens.					
Kirshner 4263		Tribute To The Beach Boys / Banjis, Cincinnati	1976	2.00	10.00
SANDY & DICK					
Features Dick St. John.					
Congress 6015		Groove With What You Got / Sing Along With "Groove With What You Got"	1970	1.60	8.00
Congress 6021		Sweet, Sweet Lovin' / Quick Like A Bunny	1970	1.60	8.00
SANDY & THE CUPIDS					
Charter 2		Rebel / I Don't Know Him	195?	2.00	10.00
Charter CR-1017		Then He Starts To Cry / I've Got Better Things To Do	195?	2.00	10.00
SANDY, FRANK, & THE JACKALS					
MGM 12678		Let's Go Rock 'N' Roll / Midnight Stomp	1958	5.00	25.00
SANTA'S LITTLE HELPER					
Jerden 110		Is There A Santa Claus? / Santa Claus Square Dance	196?	2.00	10.00
SANTANA					
Columbia 45010		Jin-Go-Lo-Ba / Persuasion	1969	.80	4.00
Columbia 45069		Evil Ways / Waiting	1970	.80	4.00
Columbia 45270		Black Magic Woman / Hope You're Feeling Better	1970	.80	4.00
Columbia 45270	(PS)	Black Magic Woman / Hope You're Feeling Better	1970	.80	4.00
Columbia 45330		Oyo Como Va / Samba Pa' Ti	1971	.60	3.00
Columbia 45330	(PS)	Oyo Como Va / Samba Pa' Ti	1971	.60	3.00
Columbia 45552		No One To Depend On / Taboo	1972	.60	3.00
Columbia 45552	(PS)	No One To Depend On / Taboo	1972	.60	3.00
Columbia 45666		Evil Ways / Them Changes	1972	.60	3.00
Columbia 45772		Everybody's Everything / Guajira	1973	.60	3.00
Columbia 45999		Samba De Sausalito / When I Look Into Your Eyes	1974	.60	3.00
Columbia 46067		Incident At Neshabur / Samba Pa' Ti	1974	.60	3.00
Columbia 10073		Flor De Canela / Mirage	1974	.60	3.00
Columbia 10088		Give And Take / Life Is Anew	1975	.60	3.00
Columbia 10336		Let It Shine / Tell Me, Are You Tired?	1976	.60	3.00
Columbia 10353		Dance, Sister, Dance / Let Me	1976	.60	3.00

Label & Catalog #		A-Side/B-Side	Year	VG	NM
Columbia 10421		Europa (Earth's Cry, Heaven's Smile) / Take Me With You	1976	.60	3.00
Columbia 10481		Let The Children Play / Carnival	1977	.60	3.00
Columbia 10524		Give Me Love / Revelations	1977	.60	3.00
Columbia 10616		She's Not Here / Zulu	1977	.60	3.00
Columbia 10677		Black Magic Woman / I'll Be Waiting	1978	.60	3.00
Columbia 10839		Well, All Right / Wham!	1978	.60	3.00
Columbia 10873		Stormy / Move On	1978	.60	3.00
Columbia 10938		One Chain (Don't Make No Prison) / Life Is A Lady-Holiday	1979	.60	3.00
Columbia 11114		You Know That I Love You / Aqua Marine	1979	.60	3.00
SANTO & JOHNNY					
Canadian Am. 103		Sleep Walk / All Night Diner	1959	3.00	15.00
Canadian Am. 107		Tear Drop / The Long Way Home	1959	2.00	10.00
Canadian Am. 111		Caravan / Summertime	1960	2.00	10.00
Canadian Am. 115		The Breeze And I / Lazy Day	1960	2.00	10.00
Canadian Am. 118		Love Lost / Annie	1960	2.00	10.00
Canadian Am. 118	(PS)	Love Lost / Annie	1960	4.00	20.00
Canadian Am. 120		Twistin' Bells / Bullseye	1960	2.00	10.00
Canadian Am. 120	(PS)	Twistin' Bells / Bullseye	1960	4.00	20.00
Canadian Am. 124		Hop Scotch / Sea Bells	1961	2.00	10.00
Canadian Am. 128		Theme From "Come September" / The Long Walk Home	1961	1.60	8.00
Canadian Am. 131		Birmingham / The Mouse	1961	1.60	8.00
Canadian Am. 132		Twistin' Bells / (B-side by Linda Scott)	1961	3.00	15.00
Canadian Am. 137		Spanish Harlem / Stage To Cimarron	1962	1.60	8.00
Canadian Am. 141		Step Aside / Three Caballeros	1962	1.60	8.00
Canadian Am. 144		Miserlou / Tokyo Twilight	1962	1.60	8.00
Canadian Am. 148		Manhattan / Twistin' Bells	1962	1.60	8.00
Canadian Am. 151		On Your Mark / Manhattan	1963	1.60	8.00
Canadian Am. 155		Manhattan Spiritual / The Wandering Sea	1963	1.60	8.00
Canadian Am. 164		I'll Remember (In The Still Of The Night) / Song For Rosemary	1964	1.20	6.00
Canadian Am. 164	(PS)	I'll Remember (In The Still Of The Night) / Song For Rosemary	1964	4.00	20.00
Canadian Am. 167		A Thousand Miles Away / Road Block	1964	1.20	6.00
Canadian Am. 167	(PS)	A Thousand Miles Away / Road Block	1964	4.00	20.00
Canadian Am. 174		Sugar Stroll / Rattler	1964	1.20	6.00
Canadian Am. 177		A Hard Day's Night / And I Love Her	1964	2.00	10.00
Canadian Am. 182		Goldfinger / Sleep Walk	1964	1.20	6.00
Canadian Am. 189		Brazilian Summer / Mucho Tempo	1964	1.20	6.00
Canadian Am. 194		Watermelon man / Return To Naples	1964	1.20	6.00
Canadian Am. 204		Come With Me / The Young World	1964	1.20	6.00
United Artists 970		Thunderball / Mister Kiss Kiss Bang Bang	1966	.80	4.00
Imperial 269		See You In September / Live For Life	1968	.80	4.00
Imperial 66292		Sleep Walk '68 / It Must Be Him	1968	.80	4.00
Pause 703		Come Back, Soldier / Flamingo	196?	.80	4.00
SANTOS, LARRY (& THE TUNES)					
Baton 265		Three Little Lovers / We Belong Together	1959	3.00	15.00
Atlantic 2250		Someday (When I'm Gone) / True (Atlantic 2250 features The Four Seasons.)	1964	4.00	20.00
SANTS, THE					
Formatt 118		High Tide / Leaving You, Baby	1966	5.00	25.00
SAPPHIRES, THE					
RCA Victor 47-7357		Everyone Knows / So Glad	1958	4.00	20.00
Ravin' 100		So Much In Love / Sh-Boom	196?	4.00	20.00
Swan 4143		Your True Love / Where Is Johnny Now?	1963	3.00	15.00
Swan 4162		Who Do You Love? / Oh, So Soon	1964	3.00	15.00
Swan 4177		I've Got Mine / You Better Get Yours / I Found Out Too Late	1964	3.00	15.00
Swan 4148		Gotta Be More Than Friends / Song From Moulin Rouge	1964	3.00	15.00
ABC-Paramount 10559		Hearts Are Made To Be Broken / Let's Break Up For A While	1964	3.00	15.00
ABC-Paramount 10590		Thank You For Loving Me / Our Love Is Everywhere	1964	3.00	15.00
ABC-Paramount 10639		Gotta Have Your Love / Gee, I'm Sorry, Baby	1965	3.00	15.00
ABC-Paramount 10693		How Could I Say Goodbye? / Evil One	1965	3.00	15.00
ABC-Paramount 10753		You'll Never Stop Me From Loving You / Gonna Be A Big Thing	1965	3.00	15.00
SARDO, FRANKIE [FRANK SARDO]					
Refer to Frankie & Johnny.					
Lido 602		The Girl I'm Gonna Dream About / Kiss And Make Up	1958	3.00	15.00
Rayna 5005		Ring Of Love / She Taught Me How To Cry	1958	3.00	15.00
Studio 9910		Just You Watch Me / I'm Sittin' At Home	1959	10.00	50.00
20th Century Fox 208		When The Bells Stop Ringing / I Know Why And So Do You	1959	2.50	12.00
20th Century Fox 208	(PS)	When The Bells Stop Ringing / I Know Why And So Do You	1959	5.00	25.00
20th Century Fox 221		Dream Lover / Bonnie, Bonnie	1959	5.00	25.00

Label & Catalog #	A-Side/B-Side	Year	VG	NM
ABC-Paramount 9963	Class Room / Fake Out	1959	3.00	15.00
ABC-Paramount 10003	Oh, Linda / No Love Like Mine	1959	3.00	15.00
Newtown 5005	Mr. Make Believe / Mean Mistreater	1960	5.00	25.00
MGM 12621	May I? / My Story Of Love	1960	4.00	20.00

SARDO, JOHNNY
Refer to Frankie & Johnny.

Chock Full-O-Hits 104	(Hip Hop) Take A Ride With Me / Hollywood Sign	195?	7.00	35.00
Warner Bros. 5044	Late, Late, Late To School / New Kid In Town	1959	4.00	20.00

SARSTEDT, PETER

World Pacific 77911	Where Do You Go To, My Lovely / I Am A Cathedral	1969	.80	4.00
World Pacific 77919	Frozen Orange Juice / Aretusa Loser	1969	.80	4.00
World Pacific 77919 (PS)	Frozen Orange Juice / Aretusa Loser	1969	2.00	10.00
Sire 1028	Beirut / Hollywood Sign	1978	.80	3.00

SATAN & THE DISCIPLES
Satan is a pseudonym for Freddy Fender.

Goldband 1188	Mummie's Curse / Cat's Meow	196?	2.00	10.00

SATANS, THE

Manhattan 801	Making Deals / Lines And Squares	1966	3.00	15.00

SATANS FOUR, THE

B.T. Puppy 515	Oh, Kathy / Can't Find The Girl On My Mind	1966	3.00	15.00

SATELLITES, THE

ABC-Paramount 10038	Linda Jean / Rockateen	1959	7.00	35.00

SATELLITES, THE

Parrot 313	Bodacious / El San Juan	1962	4.00	20.00

SATISFACTIONS, THE

Imperial 66170	Daddy, You Just Gotta Let Him In / Bring It All Down	1966	2.00	10.00

SATURDAY, PATTY

Swan 4022	Love Is A Beautiful Thing / Ladies Choice	1959	3.00	15.00

SATURDAY KNIGHTS, THE

Swan 4075	Ticonderoga / Tiger Lily	1961	3.00	15.00

SATURDAY'S CHILDREN

Dunwich 139	You Don't Know Better / Born On Saturday	1966	3.00	15.00
Dunwich 144	The Christmas Song / Deck Five	1967	3.00	15.00
Dunwich 156	Leave That Baby Alone / I Hardly Know Her	1967	3.00	15.00

SAUNDERS, LITTLE BUTCHIE, & HIS BUDDIES
Refer to Little Butchie & The Vells.

Herald 485	Lindy Lou / Rock And Roll Indian Dance	1956	6.00	30.00
Herald 491	Great Big Heart / I Wanna Holler	1956	5.00	25.00

SAVAGE, LEE

Merri 101	Riders In The Sky / Teenage World	1960	2.00	10.00

SAVAGE RESURRECTION

Mercury 72778	Thing In "E" / Fox Is Sick	1968	1.20	6.00
Mercury 72778 (PS)	Thing In "E" / Fox Is Sick	1968	3.00	15.00

SAVAGE ROSE

Gregar 0104	Sunday Morning / Speak Softly	196?	1.20	6.00
Gregar 0104 (PS)	Sunday Morning / Speak Softly	196?	2.00	10.00

SAVONICS, THE

M.T.A. 145	I Had A Girl / Soul Groove	1968	2.00	10.00

SAVOY, RONNIE

MGM 12950	And The Heavens Cried / Big Chain	1960	2.00	10.00

SAVOY BROWN

Parrot 40037	Grits Ain't Groceries / She's Got A Ring	1969	1.00	5.00
Parrot 40042	I'm Tired / Stay With Me, Baby	1969	1.00	5.00
Parrot 40046	A Hard Way To Go / The Incredible Gnome Meets Jaxman	1970	1.00	5.00
Parrot 40066	Tell Mama / Rock And Roll On The Radio	1971	1.00	5.00
Parrot 40075	Coming Down Your Way / I Can't Find You	1972	1.00	5.00
London 206	Everybody Loves A Drinking Man / Ride On, Babe	1974	.80	4.00
London 234	Walkin' And Talkin' / Stranger Blues	1975	.80	4.00
London 362	Lost And Lonely Child / If I Could See An End	1976	.80	4.00

Label & Catalog #		A-Side/B-Side	Year	VG	NM
SAWBUCK					
Fillmore 7007		There Will Be Love / Bible Burning	196?	1.20	6.00
SAWYER, TOMMY, & THE TWAINS					
Diamond 112		How Deep Is The Ocean? / 15th Row Down	1962	2.00	10.00
SAXON, SKY					
Sky Saxon is a pseudonym of Ritchie Marsh. Refer to The Seeds; Sky Sunlight & The New Seeds.					
Conquest 777		They Say / Go Ahead And Cry	196?	5.00	25.00
SAXTONS, THE					
Regina 305		The Beatle Dance / Sittin' On Top Of The World	1964	3.00	15.00
SCAFFOLD					
Bell	(DJ)	Charity Bubbles / Charity Bubbles	1968	6.00	30.00
Bell 701		Thank U Very Much / Ide B The First	1968	1.00	5.00
Bell 724		Do You Remember? / Carry On, Krow	1968	1.00	5.00
Bell 747		Lily The Pink / Buttons Of Your Mind	1968	1.00	5.00
Warner Bros. 8001		Liverpool Lou / Ten Years After On Strawberry Jam	1974	.80	4.00
SCALLYWAGS, THE					
Sola 5		Surfin' Mickey / The Big Wave	196?	7.00	35.00
SCANDLIN, BILLY, & THE EMBERS					
Viking 1002		You'll Always Have Someone / I Keep On Walking	196?	3.00	15.00
SCARLETS, THE					
Prince 1207		Stampede / Park Avenue	1959	7.00	35.00
Dot 16004		Stampede / Park Avenue	1959	5.00	25.00
SCAVENGERS, THE					
Mobile Fidelity 1005		The Angels Listened In / My Love Waits For Me	1963	4.00	20.00
SCAVENGERS, THE					
Stars of Hollywood 1210		Shot Gun / Cream Puff	1963	7.00	35.00
Stars of Hollywood 1211		Shot Gun / Zip Code	1963	7.00	35.00
Stars of Hollywood 1212		Devil's Reef / Little Annie	1963	7.00	35.00
Fenton 987		Oasis / Curfew	1964	7.00	35.00
SCAVENGERS, THE					
Suemei 4552		Bogus / Ghost Riders '65	1965	3.00	15.00
SCENE, THE					
B.T. Puppy 533		Scenes From Another World / You're In A Bad Way	1967	2.00	10.00
SCHICKEL, STEVE					
Mercury 70999		Leave My Sideburns Be / Cry Baby Boogie	1956	5.00	25.00
SCHILLING, JOHNNY, & THE SHERWOODS					
C&A 507		King Of The World / Marcelle	195?	15.00	75.00
SCHOLARS, THE					
Imperial 5449		Beloved / I Didn't Want To Do It	1957	3.00	15.00
Imperial 5459		Eternally Yours / Kan-Gu-Wa	1957	3.00	15.00
SCHOOL BELLES, THE					
Crest 1104		Don't Believe Him / Valley High	1962	2.00	10.00
SCHWUMP					
Ralph RRX0776		Aphids In The Wall / You're A Martian-Home	1976	20.00	100.00
		(Issued in a hand-colored picture sleeve, numbered #1-200.)			
SCOTT, BILLY					
Cameo 121		You're The Greatest / That's Why I Was Born	1957	3.00	15.00
Cameo 143		A Million Boys / The Town Of Never Worry	1958	3.00	15.00
Everest 19315		Carole / Stairways To The Stars	1959	5.00	25.00
SCOTT, JACK					
ABC-Paramount 9818	(DJ)	Baby, She's Gone / You Can Bet Your Bottom Dollar	1957	12.00	60.00
ABC-Paramount 9818		Baby, She's Gone / You Can Bet Your Bottom Dollar	1957	15.00	75.00
ABC-Paramount 9860	(DJ)	Two Timin' Woman / I Need Your Love	1957	12.00	60.00
ABC-Paramount 9860		Two Timin' Woman / I Need Your Love	1957	15.00	75.00
Carlton 462		My True Love / Leroy	1958	3.00	15.00
Carlton 483		With Your Love / Geraldine	1958	3.00	15.00
Carlton 483	(PS)	With Your Love / Geraldine	1958	7.00	35.00
Carlton 493		Goodbye, Baby / Save My Soul	1958	3.00	15.00
Carlton 493	(PS)	Goodbye, Baby / Save My Soul	1958	7.00	35.00
Carlton 504		I Never Felt Like This / Bella	1959	3.00	15.00

Label & Catalog #		A-Side/B-Side	Year	VG	NM
Carlton 514		The Way I Walk / Midgie	1959	3.00	15.00
Carlton 519		There Comes A Time / Baby Marie	1959	3.00	15.00
Guaranteed 209		What Am I Living For? / Indiana Waltz	1960	4.00	20.00
Guaranteed 211		Go Wild, Little Sadies / No One Will Ever Know	1960	5.00	25.00
Top Rank 2028		What In The World's Come Over You? / Baby Baby	1960	2.00	10.00
Top Rank 2041		Burning Bridges / Oh, Little One	1960	2.00	10.00
Top Rank 2041	(PS)	Burning Bridges / Oh, Little One	1960	3.00	15.00
Top Rank 2055		It Only Happened Yesterday / Cool Water	1960	7.00	35.00
Top Rank 2075		Patsy / Old Time Religion	1960	2.00	10.00
Top Rank 2093		Is There Something On Your Mind? / Found A Woman	1960	2.00	10.00
Top Rank 2093	(PS)	Is There Something On Your Mind? / Found A Woman	1960	8.00	40.00
Capitol 4554		A Little Feeling (Called Love) / Now That	1961	2.00	10.00
Capitol 4554	(PS)	A Little Feeling (Called Love) / Now That	1961	6.00	30.00
Capitol 4597		My Dreams Come True / Strange Desire	1961	2.00	10.00
Capitol 4597	(PS)	My Dreams Come True / Strange Desire	1961	6.00	30.00
Capitol 4637		Steps 1 And 2 / One Of These Days	1961	2.00	10.00
Capitol 4637	(PS)	Steps 1 And 2 / One Of These Days	1961	6.00	30.00
Capitol 4689		Cry, Cry, Cry / Grizzly Bear	1962	3.00	15.00
Capitol 4689	(PS)	Cry, Cry, Cry / Grizzly Bear	1962	6.00	30.00
Capitol 4738		The Part Where I Cry / You Only See What You Want To See	1962	2.00	10.00
Capitol 4738	(PS)	The Part Where I Cry / You Only See What You Want To See	1962	6.00	30.00
Capitol 4796		Sad Story / I Can't Hold Your Letters (In My Arms)	1962	2.00	10.00
Capitol 4855		If Only / Green, Green Valley	1963	2.00	10.00
Capitol 4903		Strangers / Laugh And The World Laughs With You	1963	3.00	15.00
Capitol 4955		All I See Is Blue / Me-O, My-O	1963	3.00	15.00
Groove 0027		There's Trouble Brewing / Jingle Bell Slide	1963	3.00	15.00
Groove 0031		I Knew You First / Blue Skies	1964	2.00	10.00
Groove 0037		Wiggle On Out / What A Wonderful Night Out	1964	4.00	20.00
Groove 0042		Thou Shalt Not Steal / I Prayed For An Angel	1964	2.00	10.00
Groove 0049		Tall Tales / Flakey John	1964	3.00	15.00
RCA Victor 47-8505		I Don't Believe In Tea Leaves / Separation's Now Granted	1965	2.00	10.00
RCA Victor 47-8685		Looking For Linda / I Hope, I Think, I Wish	1965	2.00	10.00
RCA Victor 47-8724		Don't Hush The Laughter / Let's Learn To Live And Love Again	1965	2.00	10.00
ABC-Paramount 10843		Before The Bird Flies / Insane	1966	3.00	15.00
ABC-Paramount 10843		Before The Bird Flies / Insane	1966	3.00	15.00
Jubilee 5606		My Special Angel / I Keep Changing My Mind	1967	4.00	20.00
GRT 35		Billy Jack / Mary Marry Me	1970	1.00	5.00
Dot 17475		May You Never Be Alone / Face To The Wall	1973	.80	4.00
Dot 17504		You're Just Getting Better / Walk Through My Mind	1974	.80	4.00
Ponie 4104-30		Spirit Of '76 / Spirit Of '76	1976	.80	4.00
Ponie 5121-15		Baby, She's Gone / Two Timin' Woman	197?	.80	4.00
Ponie 6063-20		Leroy / Go Wild, Little Sadie	197?	.80	4.00
Ponie 6083-20		Country Witch / Blues, Stay Away From Me / Stones	197?	.80	4.00
Ponie 7021-10		Geraldine / Midgie	197?	.80	4.00
Ponie 7021-11		Jingle Bell Slide / Trouble's Brewing	197?	.80	4.00
Ponie 7021-12		Flakey John / Wiggle On Out	197?	.80	4.00
		—Extended Play Albums—			
Carlton 1070		Presenting Jack Scott (Volume 1)	1958	50.00	200.00
Carlton 1071		Presenting Jack Scott (Volume 2)	1958	50.00	200.00
Carlton 1072		Jack Scott Sings	1958	50.00	200.00
Carlton 1073		Starring Jack Scott	1958	50.00	200.00
Top Rank 1001		What In The World's Come Over You?	1960	50.00	200.00

SCOTT, JOEL

Philles 101	Here I Stand / You're My Only Love	1962	5.00	25.00

SCOTT, KAREN

Karicraft 103	There's A Goldmine In The Sky / Morningtown Ride	196?	.80	4.00
Karicraft 109	Blue Eyes Crying In The Rain / Tell Me Honey	196?	.80	4.00

SCOTT, LINDA

Canadian Am. 123	I Told Every Little Star / Three Guesses	1961	3.00	15.00
Canadian Am. 127	Don't Bet Money, Honey / Starlight, Starbright	1961	3.00	15.00
Canadian Am. 129	I Don't Know Why / It's All Because	1961	3.00	15.00
Canadian Am. 132	Christmas Day / (B-side by Santo & Johnny)	1961	3.00	15.00
Canadian Am. 133	Count Every Star / Land Of Stars	1962	3.00	15.00
Canadian Am. 134	Bermuda / Lonely For You	1962	3.00	15.00
Congress 101	Yesiree / Town Crier	1962	2.00	10.00
Congress 103	Never In A Million Years / Through The Summer	1962	2.00	10.00
Congress 106	I Left My Heart In The Balcony / Lopsided Love Affair	1962	2.00	10.00
Congress 108	Loneliest Girl In Town / I'm So Afraid Of Losing You	1963	2.00	10.00
Congress 110	Ain't That Fun / Sit Right Down And Write Myself A Letter	1963	2.00	10.00
Congress 200	Let's Fall In Love / I Know You Know It	1963	3.00	15.00
Congress 204	Who's Been Sleeping In My Bed? / My Heart	1964	3.00	15.00
Congress 206	Let's Fall In Love / I Know You Know It	1964	3.00	15.00
Congress 209	Everybody Stopped / I Envy You	1964	2.00	10.00
Kapp 610	This Is My Prayer / That Old Feeling	1964	1.60	8.00

Label & Catalog #	A-Side/B-Side	Year	VG	NM
Kapp 641	If I Love Again / Patch It Up	1965	1.60	8.00
Kapp 677	I'll See You In My Dreams / Don't Lose Your Head	1965	1.60	8.00
Kapp 713	You Baby / I Can't Get Through To You	1965	1.60	8.00
Kapp 762	Take A Walk, Bobby / Toys	1965	1.60	8.00
RCA Victor 47-9424	They Don't Know You / Three Miles High	1968	1.60	8.00

SCOTT, NEAL (& THE CONCORDS)

Portrait 102	Bobby / I Haven't Found It With Another	1961	2.00	10.00
Herald 581	One Piece Bathing Suit / Little Girl	1963	4.00	20.00
Comet 2151	Tomboy / Run To Me	196?	3.00	15.00
Cameo 476	Let Me Think It Over / I Don't Stand A Ghost Of A Chance	1967	1.20	6.00

SCOTT, RODNEY

Cannon 225	Granny Went Rockin' / Bitter Tears	195?	50.00	200.00
Mr. Peeke 119	You're So Square / He'll Be There	1962	10.00	50.00

SCOTT, SHERRE (& HER MELODY ROCKERS)

Sherree Heart 1479	Easy Payments / Go Away, Shadow (Red vinyl)	195?	15.00	75.00
Rocket 1036	Fascinating Baby / You And I	195?	20.00	100.00
Robbins 101	Whole Lot Of Shakin' Goin' On / Unhappy Birthday	195?	10.00	50.00
Robbins 101 (PS)	Whole Lot Of Shakin' Goin' On / Unhappy Birthday	195?	20.00	100.00

SCOTT, WALTER

Musicland 014	It's Been A Long Time / Proud	196?	3.00	15.00
Musicland 111	Just You Wait / Silly Girl	196?	3.00	15.00
White Whale 259	Just You Wait / Silly Girl	196?	2.00	10.00
Vanessa 131	There'll Always Be A Love Song /	196?	2.00	10.00

SCOTT BROTHERS, THE

Ribbon 6905	Stolen Angel / Keep Laughin'	1959	3.00	15.00
Ribbon 6911	Lost Love / Only Then	1959	3.00	15.00
Skyline 501	Celebrity Party / Do You Want My Love?	1959	4.00	20.00
Skyline 502	Part Of You / Kingdom Of Love	1960	5.00	25.00
FTP 409	Cindy, Oh Cindy / Mama's Little Baby	1961	4.00	20.00
FTP 415	Lonely Bluebird / Kingdom Of Love	1961	4.00	20.00
FTP 418	On Again, Off Again / Sometimes I Wonder	1961	4.00	20.00
Fabor 117	Yuggi Guggi / Our Tune	1963	2.00	10.00
Comet 2153	A Letter From My Baby / Welcome Home	1963	3.00	15.00
Smash 2139	My Day Has Come / Got To Get A Groove	1967	1.00	5.00

SCOTSMEN, THE

Panorama 22	Sorry, Charlie / Tuff Enough	196?	2.00	10.00

SCOTSMEN, THE

Scotty 1051	Beer Bust Blues / Scotch Mist	196?	2.00	10.00

SCRAMBLERS, THE

Del-Fi 4237	The Beetle Walk / Beetle Blues	1964	2.00	10.00
Arvee 6502	Super Surfer U.S.A. / Go, Gilerra, Go	1965	4.00	20.00

SCREWBALLS, THE

Columbia 42209	Just Because / The Screwball March	1961	2.00	10.00

SCUBA CLOWNS, THE

Challenge 9204	Scuba Dive / Concentration	1963	4.00	20.00

SEA SHELLS, THE

Goliath 1357	Love Those Beach Boys / Close To Jimmy	1964	7.00	35.00
Jubilee 5587	Hit The Surf / Barefoot In The Sand	196?	4.00	20.00

SEAGRAMS, THE

RIK 5017	Unknown / Offbeat	196?	5.00	25.00

SEALS, JIMMY

Jimmy Seals originally recorded with The Champs.

Challenge 9153	Wish For You, Want For You, Wait For You / Runaway Heart	1962	3.00	15.00
Challenge 9200	Lady Heartbreak / Grounded	1964	3.00	15.00
Challenge 59270	Everybody's Doin' The Jerk / Wa-Hoo	1964	2.00	10.00

SEAN & THE BRANDYWINES

Decca 31910	Cod'ine / She Ain't No Good	1966	2.00	10.00
	(Produced by Gary Usher.)			

SEARCHERS, THE

Liberty 55646	Sugar And Spice / Saints And Sinners	1963	3.00	15.00
Liberty 55689	Sugar And Spice / Saints And Sinners	1964	2.00	10.00
Kapp 27	Love Potion #9 / Hi-Heel Sneakers	1964	1.60	8.00
Kapp 49	Bumble Bee / A Tear Fell	1964	1.60	8.00

Label & Catalog #		A-Side/B-Side	Year	VG	NM
Kapp 577		Needles And Pins / Saturday Night Out	1964	1.60	8.00
Kapp 577	(PS)	Needles And Pins (Promo picture sleeve)	1964	7.00	35.00
Kapp 577	(PS)	Needles And Pins / Saturday Night Out	1964	3.00	15.00
Kapp 584		Ain't That Just Like Me / Ain't Gonna Kiss You	1964	1.60	8.00
Kapp 584	(PS)	Ain't That Just Like Me (Promo picture sleeve)	1964	7.00	35.00
Kapp 593		Don't Throw Your Love Away / I Pretend I'm With You	1964	1.60	8.00
Kapp 609		Some Day We're Gonna Love Again / No One Else Could Love Me	1964	1.60	8.00
Kapp 609	(PS)	Some Day We're Gonna Love Again / No One Else Could Love Me	1964	3.00	15.00
Kapp 618		When You Walk In The Room / I'll Be Missing You	1964	1.60	8.00
Mercury 72172		Sweets For My Sweets / It's All Been A Dream	1965	2.00	10.00
Mercury 72390		Ain't That Just Like Me / I Can Tell	1965	2.00	10.00
Kapp 644		What Have They Done To The Rain? /The Feeling Inside	1965	1.60	8.00
Kapp 658		Goodbye, My Lover, Goodbye / Till I Meet You	1965	1.60	8.00
Kapp 686		He's Got No Love / So Far Away	1965	1.60	8.00
Kapp 706		Don't Know Why / You Can't Lie To A Liar	1965	1.60	8.00
Kapp 729		Take Me For What I'm Worth / Too Many Miles	1966	1.60	8.00
Kapp 783		Have You Ever Loved Somebody? / It's Just The Way	1966	1.60	8.00
Kapp 811		Lovers / Popcorn Double Feature	1966	1.60	8.00
Sire 49175		It's Too Late / Don't hang On	1979	.60	3.00
		—Extended Play Albums—			
Kapp KS-3409	(33)	This Is Us (Jukebox EP)	1964	8.00	40.00

SEARS, BUZZ, & THE KORDS

NWI 2765		Dream World Of My Mind /	1970	.80	4.00
NWI 2793		Worked Hard All My Life / Don't Mess With My Baby	1971	.80	4.00

SEATRAIN

A&M 994		Let The Duchess Know / As I Lay Losing	1968	1.00	5.00
A&M 1106		Caroline, Caroline / Suite For Almond	1968	1.00	5.00
Warner Bros. 562	(DJ)	Pack Of Fools / Abbeville Fair	1970	1.00	5.00
Capitol 3067		Thirteen Questions / Oh, My Love	1971	.60	3.00
Capitol 3140		Song Of Job / Waiting For Elisa	1971	.60	3.00
Capitol 3275		Grammercy / How Sweet Thy Song	1971	.60	3.00
Capitol 3421		I'm Willing / Broken Morning	1972	.60	3.00

SEBASTIAN

Mr. Maestro 801		Too Young / Darlin,' I Do	196?	6.00	30.00

SEBASTIAN

Decca 32655		Elaine / Now That It's Over	1970	1.00	5.00

SEBASTIAN, JOHN

John Sebastian originally recorded with The Mugwumps and The Lovin' Spoonful.

Kama Sutra 254		She's A Lady / The Room Nobody Lives In	1969	1.00	5.00
Kama Sutra 254	(PS)	She's A Lady / The Room Nobody Lives In	1969	2.00	10.00
MGM 14122		Rainbows All Over Your Blues / You're A Big Boy Now	1970	.80	4.00
Reprise 0902		Magical Connection / Fa-Fana-Fa	1970	.60	3.00
Reprise 0918		What She Thinks About / Red-Eye Express	1970	.60	3.00
Reprise 1026		I Don't Want Nobody Else / Sweet Muse	1971	.60	3.00
Reprise 1050		Well, Well, Well / We'll See	1971	.60	3.00
Reprise 1074		Give Us A Break / Music For People Who Don't Speak English	1972	.60	3.00
Reprise 1349		Welcome Back, Kotter / Warm Baby	1976	.80	4.00
Reprise 1349		Welcome Back / Warm Baby	1976	.60	3.00
Reprise 1355		Hideaway / One Step Forward, Two Steps Back	1976	.60	3.00

SECOND COMING, THE

Steady 001		I Feel Free / She Has Funny Cars	1970	5.00	25.00

SECOND COMING, THE

Mercury 73184		747 / Take Me Home	1970	1.00	5.00

SECRET AGENT & THE VICE SQUAD

Jerden 784		Things Happen / I Saw Sloopy	1965	2.00	10.00

SECRETS, THE: *Refer to* THE FIVE SECRETS

SECRETS, THE

Swan 4097		Twin Exhaust / Hot Toddy	1962	2.00	10.00

SECRETS, THE

Philips 40146		The Boy Next Door / Learnin' To Forget	1963	2.00	10.00
Philips 40173		Hey, Big Boy / The Other Side Of Town	1964	2.00	10.00
Philips 40173	(PS)	Hey, Big Boy / The Other Side Of Town	1964	4.00	20.00
Philips 40196		Here He Comes Now / Oh, Donnie	1964	2.00	10.00
Philips 40222		He's The Boy / He Doesn't Want You	1964	2.00	10.00

Label & Catalog #		A-Side/B-Side	Year	VG	NM
DCP 1139		Shy Guy / No Matter What You Do To Me	1965	1.60	8.00
Omen 15		Here I Am / I Feel A Thrill Coming On	1966	2.00	10.00

SEDAKA, NEIL
Neil Sedaka also recorded with The Tokens.

Label & Catalog #		A-Side/B-Side	Year	VG	NM
Legion 133		Ring-A-Rockin' / Fly, Don't Fly On Me	1958	15.00	75.00
Guyden 2004		Ring-A-Rockin' / Fly, Don't Fly On Me	1958	8.00	40.00
Decca 30520		Laura Lee / Snowtime	1958	8.00	40.00
RCA Victor 47-7408		The Diary / No Vacancy	1958	2.00	10.00
RCA Victor 47-7473		I Go Ape / Moon Of Gold	1959	2.00	10.00
RCA Victor 47-7530		You Gotta Learn Your Rhythm And Blues /			
		Crying My Heart Out For You	1959	2.00	10.00
RCA Victor 47-7595		Oh, Carol! / One Way Ticket	1959	2.00	10.00
RCA Victor 61-7595	(S)	Oh, Carol! / One Way Ticket	1959	6.00	30.00
RCA Victor 47-7709		Stairway To Heaven / Forty Winks Away	1960	2.00	10.00
RCA Victor 61-7709	(S)	Stairway To Heaven / Forty Winks Away	1960	6.00	30.00
RCA Victor 47-7781		You Mean Everything To Me / Run, Sampson, Run	1960	2.00	10.00
RCA Victor 47-7781	(PS)	You Mean Everything To Me / Run, Sampson, Run	1960	3.00	15.00
RCA Victor 61-7781	(S)	You Mean Everything To Me / Run, Sampson, Run	1960	6.00	30.00
RCA Victor 37-7829	(33)	Calendar Girl / The Same Old Fool	1960	6.00	30.00
RCA Victor 47-7829		Calendar Girl / The Same Old Fool	1960	2.00	10.00
RCA Victor 47-7829	(PS)	Calendar Girl / The Same Old Fool	1960	3.00	15.00
RCA Victor 61-7829	(S)	Calendar Girl / The Same Old Fool	1960	6.00	30.00
RCA Victor 37-7874	(33)	Little Devil / I Must Be Dreaming	1961	6.00	30.00
RCA Victor 47-7874		Little Devil / I Must Be Dreaming	1961	2.00	10.00
RCA Victor 47-7874	(PS)	Little Devil / I Must Be Dreaming	1961	3.00	15.00
RCA Victor 37-7922	(33)	Sweet Little You / I Found My World In You	1961	6.00	30.00
RCA Victor 47-7922		Sweet Little You / I Found My World In You	1961	2.00	10.00
RCA Victor 47-7922	(PS)	Sweet Little You / I Found My World In You	1961	3.00	15.00
RCA Victor 37-7957	(33)	Happy Birthday, Sweet Sixteen / Don't Lead Me On	1961	6.00	30.00
RCA Victor 47-7957		Happy Birthday, Sweet Sixteen / Don't Lead Me On	1961	2.00	10.00
RCA Victor 37-8007	(33)	King Of Clowns / Walk With Me	1962	6.00	30.00
RCA Victor 47-8007		King Of Clowns / Walk With Me	1962	2.00	10.00
RCA Victor 47-8007	(PS)	King Of Clowns / Walk With Me	1962	3.00	15.00
RCA Victor 47-8046		Breaking Up Is Hard To Do / As Long As I Live	1962	2.00	10.00
RCA Victor 47-8046	(PS)	Breaking Up Is Hard To Do / As Long As I Live	1962	3.00	15.00
RCA Victor 47-8086		Next Door To An Angel / I Belong To You	1962	2.00	10.00
RCA Victor 47-8086	(PS)	Next Door To An Angel / I Belong To You	1962	3.00	15.00
Pyramid 623		Oh, Delilah / Neil's Twist	1962	4.00	20.00
RCA Victor 47-8137		Alice In Wonderland / Circulate	1963	2.00	10.00
RCA Victor 47-8137	(PS)	Alice In Wonderland / Circulate	1963	3.00	15.00
RCA Victor 47-8169		Let's Go Steady Again / Waiting For Never	1963	2.00	10.00
RCA Victor 47-8169	(PS)	Let's Go Steady Again / Waiting For Never	1963	3.00	15.00
RCA Victor 47-8209		The Dreamer / Look Inside Your Heart	1963	1.60	8.00
RCA Victor 47-8209	(PS)	The Dreamer / Look Inside Your Heart	1963	3.00	15.00
RCA Victor 47-8254		Bad Girl / Wait 'Til You See My Baby	1963	1.60	8.00
RCA Victor 47-8341		The Closest Thing To Heaven / Without A Song	1964	1.20	6.00
RCA Victor 47-8341	(PS)	The Closest Thing To Heaven / Without A Song	1964	3.00	15.00
RCA Victor 47-8382		Sunny / She'll Never Be You	1964	1.20	6.00
RCA Victor 47-8453		I Hope He Breaks Your Heart / Too Late	1964	1.20	6.00
RCA Victor 47-8511		Let The People Talk / In The Chapel With You	1965	1.20	6.00
RCA Victor 47-8511	(PS)	Let The People Talk / In The Chapel With You	1965	3.00	15.00
RCA Victor 47-8637		The World Through A Tear / High On A Mountain	1965	1.20	6.00
RCA Victor 47-8637	(PS)	The World Through A Tear / High On A Mountain	1965	3.00	15.00
RCA Victor 47-8737		The Answer To My Prayer / Blue Boy	1966	1.20	6.00
RCA Victor 47-8844		The Answer Lies Within / Grown Up Games	1966	2.00	10.00
RCA Victor 47-9004		We Can Make It If We Try / Too Late	1966	1.20	6.00
SGC 005		Star Crossed Lovers / We Had Good Thing Goin'	1969	1.20	6.00
SGC 008		Rainy Jane / Jeannine	1970	1.20	6.00
Kirshner 5017		I'm A Song (Sing Me) / Silent Movies	1972	1.00	5.00
Kirshner 5020		Superbird / Rosemary Blue	1972	1.00	5.00
Kirshner 5024		Anywhere You're Gonna Be (Leba's Song /			
		Beautiful You	1972	1.00	5.00
MGM 14564		Standing On The Inside / Let Daddy Alone	1973	.60	3.00
MGM 14661		Alone In New York In The Rain / Suspicions	1973	.60	3.00
Rocket 40313		Laughter In The Rain / Endlessly	1974	.60	3.00
Rocket 40370		The Immigrant / Hey, Mr. Sunshine	1975	.60	3.00
Rocket 40426		That's When The Music Takes Me /			
		Standing On The Inside	1975	.60	3.00
Rocket 40460		Bad Blood / Your Favorite Entertainer	1975	.60	3.00
		("Bad Blood" features Elton John.)			
Rocket 40500		Breaking Up Is Hard To Do / Nana's Song	1975	.60	3.00
Rocket 40543		Love In The Shadows /			
		(Baby) Don't Let It Mess Your Mind	1976	.60	3.00
Rocket 40582		Steppin' Out / I Let You Walk Away	1976	.60	3.00
		("Steppin' Out" features Elton John.)			
Rocket 40614		You Gotta Make Your Own Sunshine / Perfect Strangers	1976	.60	3.00
Elektra 45406		Amarillo / The Leaving Game	1977	.60	3.00

Label & Catalog #		A-Side/B-Side	Year	VG	NM
Elektra 45421		Alone At Last / Sleazy Love	1977	.60	3.00
Elektra 45525		All You Need Is The Music / Candy Kisses	1978	.60	3.00
Elektra 46017		Sad, Sad Story / Tillie The Twiller	1978	.60	3.00
Elektra 46115		Should Have Never Let You Go / You're So Good For Me	1979	.60	3.00
Elektra 47017		Letting Go / It's Good To Be Alive Again	1979	.60	3.00
		—Extended Play Albums—			
RCA Victor EPA-4334		I Go Ape	1959	15.00	75.00
RCA Victor EPA-4353		Oh! Carol	1959	15.00	75.00
RCA Victor LPC-135		Little Devil (& His Other Hits)	1961	10.00	50.00
RCA Victor LPC-105		Neil's Best	1961	10.00	50.00

SEEDS, THE
The Seeds are Rick Andridge, Daryl Hooper, Jan Savage and Sky Saxon a.k.a. Ritch Marsh.

Label & Catalog #		A-Side/B-Side	Year	VG	NM
GNP/Crescendo 354		I Can't Seem To Make You Mine / Daisy Mae	1966	3.00	15.00
GNP/Crescendo 354		I Can't Seem To Make You Mine / I Tell Myself	1966	1.00	5.00
GNP/Crescendo 354	(PS)	I Can't Seem To Make You Mine / I Tell Myself	1966	3.00	15.00
GNP/Crescendo 370		The Other Place / Try To Understand	1966	3.00	15.00
GNP/Crescendo 364		You're Pushin' Too Hard / Try To Understand	1966	3.00	15.00
GNP/Crescendo 372		Pushin' Too Hard / Try To Understand	1966	1.00	5.00
GNP/Crescendo 383		Mr. Farmer / No Escape	1967	1.00	5.00
GNP/Crescendo 383	(PS)	Mr. Farmer / Up In Her Room	1967	4.00	20.00
GNP/Crescendo 394		A Thousand Shadows / March Of The Flower Children	1967	1.00	5.00
GNP/Crescendo 394	(PS)	A Thousand Shadows / March Of The Flower Children	1967	3.00	15.00
GNP/Crescendo 398		The Wind Blows Your Hair / Six Dreams	1968	1.00	5.00
GNP/Crescendo 408		900 Million People Daily / (Making Love) Satisfy You	1968	1.00	5.00
GNP/Crescendo 408	(PS)	900 Million People Daily / (Making Love) Satisfy You	1968	3.00	15.00
GNP/Crescendo 422		Fallin' Off The Edge Of The World / Wild Blood	1969	1.25	6.00
MGM 14163	(DJ)	Bad Part Of Town / Wish Me Up	1969	4.00	20.00
MGM 14190	(DJ)	Did He Die? / Love Is A Summer Basket	1969	4.00	20.00
		(Stock copies of MGM 14163 and 14190 may not exist.)			

SEGER, BOB (& THE SILVER BULLET BAND)
Bob Seger originally recorded with The Beach Bums and Doug Brown & The Omens. Note: Cameo 438-494 credited to Bob Seger & The Last Heard. Capitol 2143-2748 credited to The Bob Seger System.

Label & Catalog #		A-Side/B-Side	Year	VG	NM
Hideout 1013		East Side Story / East Side Sound	1966	7.00	35.00
Hideout 1014		Persecution Smith / Chain Smokin'	1966	7.00	35.00
Cameo 438		East Side Story / East Side Sound	1966	4.00	20.00
Cameo 444		Sock It To Me, Santa / Florida Time	1966	5.00	25.00
Cameo 465		Persecution Smith / Chain Smokin'	1966	4.00	20.00
Cameo 473		Vagrant Winter / Very Few	1967	4.00	20.00
Cameo 494		Heavy Music / Heavy Music, Part 2	1967	1.20	6.00
Capitol 2143		2 + 2 = What? / Death Row	1968	2.00	10.00
Capitol 2297		Ramblin Gamblin' Man / Tales Of Lucy Blue	1968	1.00	5.00
Capitol 2480		Ivory / The Lost Song (Love Needs To Be Loved)	1969	1.20	6.00
Capitol 2576		Noah / Lennie Johnson	1969	1.20	6.00
Capitol 2640		Lonely Man / Innervenus Eyes	1970	1.20	6.00
Capitol 2748		Lucifer / Big River	1970	1.20	6.00
Capitol 3187		Lookin' Back / Highway Child	1971	1.20	6.00
Reprise 1117		Turn On Your Love Light / Who Do You Love?	1972	1.60	8.00
Reprise 1143		Rosalie / Neon Sky	1973	1.60	8.00
Palladium 1079		If I Were A Carpenter / Jesse James	1972	1.20	6.00
Palladium 1143		Rosalie / Neon Sky	1972	1.20	6.00
Palladium 1171		Need Ya / Seen A Lot Of Floors	1973	1.60	8.00
Palladium 1205		Get Out Of Denver / Long Song Comin'	1974	1.20	6.00
Palladium 1316		This Old House / U.M.C.	1975	2.00	10.00
Abkco 4016		Persecution Smith / Chain Smokin'	1975	.80	4.00
Abkco 4017		Heavy Music / Heavy Music, Part 2	1975	.80	4.00
Capitol 4062		Beautiful Loser / Fine Memory	1975	.40	2.00
Capitol 4116		Katmandu / Black Night	1975	.40	2.00
Capitol 4183		Nutbush City Limits / Travelin' Man	1975	.40	2.00
Capitol 4269		Nutbush City Limits / Lookin' Back	1976	.40	2.00
Capitol 4300		Beautiful Loser / Travelin' Man	1976	.40	2.00
Capitol 4369		Night Moves / Ship Of Fools	1976	.40	2.00
Capitol 4422		Mainstreet / Jody Girl	1977	.40	2.00
Capitol 4449		Rock And Roll Never Forgets	1977	.40	2.00
Capitol 4581		Still The Same / Feel Like A Number	1978	.40	2.00
Capitol 4618		Hollywood Nights / Brave Strangers	1978	.40	2.00
Capitol 4653	(DJ)	We've Got Tonight / Ain't Got No Money (Silver vinyl)	1978	1.00	5.00
Capitol 4653		We've Got Tonight / Ain't Got No Money	1978	.40	2.00
Capitol 4653	(PS)	We've Got Tonight / Ain't Got No Money	1978	.40	2.00
Capitol 4702		Old Time Rock And Roll / Sunspot Baby	1979	.40	2.00
Capitol 4702	(PS)	Old Time Rock And Roll / Sunspot Baby	1979	.40	2.00
Capitol 4836		Fire Lake / Long Twin Silver Line	1980	.40	2.00
Capitol 4836	(PS)	Fire Lake / Long Twin Silver Line	1980	.40	2.00
Capitol 4863		Against The Wind / No Man's Land	1980	.40	2.00
Capitol 4863	(PS)	Against The Wind / No Man's Land	1980	.30	1.50
Capitol 4904		You'll Accompany Me / Betty Lou's Gettin' Out Tonight	1980	.30	1.50
Capitol 4904	(PS)	You'll Accompany Me / Betty Lou's Gettin' Out Tonight	1980	.30	1.50

Label & Catalog #		A-Side/B-Side	Year	VG	NM
Capitol 4951		Her Strut / Horizontal Bop	1980	.30	1.50
Capitol 5042		Trying To Live My Life Without You / Brave Strangers	1981	.30	1.50
Capitol 5042	(PS)	Trying To Live My Life Without You / Brave Strangers	1981	.30	1.50
Capitol 5077		Feel Like A Number / Hollywood Nights	1981	.30	1.50
Capitol 5077	(PS)	Feel Like A Number / Hollywood Nights	1981	.30	1.50
Capitol 5187		Shame On The Moon /	1982	.30	1.50
Capitol 5187	(PS)	Shame On The Moon /	1982	.30	1.50
Capitol 5213		Even Now /	1983	.30	1.50
Capitol 5213	(PS)	Even Now /	1983	.30	1.50
Capitol 5276		Old Time Rock & Roll /	1983	.30	1.50
Capitol 5276	(PS)	Old Time Rock & Roll /	1983	.30	1.50
Capitol 5325		Roll Me Away /	1983	.30	1.50
Capitol 5325	(PS)	Roll Me Away /	1983	.30	1.50
Capitol 5413		Understanding /	1984	.30	1.50
Capitol 5413	(PS)	Understanding /	1984	.30	1.50
Capitol 5532		American Storm / Fortunate Son	1986	.30	1.50
Capitol 5532	(PS)	American Storm / Fortunate Son	1986	.30	1.50
Capitol 5592		Like A Rock / Livin' Inside My Heart	1986	.30	1.50
Capitol 5592	(PS)	Like A Rock / Livin' Inside My Heart	1986	.30	1.50
Capitol 5623		It's You /	1986	.30	1.50
Capitol 5623	(PS)	It's You /	1986	.30	1.50

SELECTIONS, THE

Label & Catalog #		A-Side/B-Side	Year	VG	NM
Antone 101		Guardian Angel / Soft And Sweet	195?	50.00	200.00
Mona Lee 121		Guardian Angel / Soft And Sweet	195?	10.00	50.00

SELF, MACK

Label & Catalog #	A-Side/B-Side	Year	VG	NM
Sun 273	Easy To Love / Every Day	1957	3.00	15.00

SELF, RONNIE

Label & Catalog #	A-Side/B-Side	Year	VG	NM
ABC-Paramount 9714	Pretty Bad Blues / Three Hearts Later	1956	10.00	50.00
ABC-Paramount 9768	Sweet Love / Alone	1956	10.00	50.00
Columbia 40989	Ain't I'm A Dog / Rocky Road Blues	1957	6.00	30.00
Columbia 41101	Bop-A-Lena / I Ain't Goin' Nowhere	1958	5.00	25.00
Columbia 41166	Big Blon' Baby / Date Bait	1958	5.00	25.00
Columbia 41241	You're So Right For Me / Petrified	1958	5.00	25.00
Decca 30958	This Must Be The Place / Big Town	1959	3.00	15.00
Decca 31131	I've Been There / So High	1960	3.00	15.00
Decca 31351	Some Things You Can't Change / Instant Man	1960	3.00	15.00
Decca 31431	Oh Me, Oh My / Past, Present And Future	1962	3.00	15.00
Kapp 546	Bless My Broken Heart / Houdine	1963	2.00	10.00
	—Extended Play Albums—			
Columbia 2149	Ain't I'm A Dog	1958	75.00	300.00

SELLERS, PETER, & THE HOLLIES

Label & Catalog #		A-Side/B-Side	Year	VG	NM
United Artists 50079		After The Fox / Fox Trot	1965	1.60	8.00
United Artists 50079	(PS)	After The Fox / Fox Trot	1965	3.00	15.00

SEMI-COLONS, THE
The Semi-Colons is a pseudonym for ? & The Mysterians.

Label & Catalog #	A-Side/B-Side	Year	VG	NM
Cameo 468	Beachcomber / Set Aside	1967	5.00	25.00

SENA, TOMMY

Label & Catalog #	A-Side/B-Side	Year	VG	NM
Valmont 905	The Wobble / Onions Remind Me Of You	195?	10.00	50.00

SENATOR BOBBY / SENATOR McKINLEY

Label & Catalog #	A-Side/B-Side	Year	VG	NM
Parkway 127	Wild Thing / Wild Thing	1966	1.60	8.00
Parkway 137	Mellow Yellow / White Christmas-3:00 Weather Report	1967	1.20	6.00
RCA Victor 47-9522	Sock It To Me, Baby / Sock It To Me, Bobby	1968	1.20	6.00

SENIORS, THE

Label & Catalog #	A-Side/B-Side	Year	VG	NM
ABC-Paramount 10736	No Surfin' 'Round Here / Cindy	1966	4.00	20.00

SENTINALS, THE

Label & Catalog #	A-Side/B-Side	Year	VG	NM
Admiral 900	Roughshod / Copy Cat Walk	1961	7.00	35.00

SENTINALS, THE [THE SENTINAL SIX]
The Sentinals feature Kenny Hinkle a.k.a. Kenny Hill.

Label & Catalog #	A-Side/B-Side	Year	VG	NM
WCEB 23	Latin'ia / Tor-chula	1962	8.00	40.00
Westco 1/2	Latin'ia / Tor-chula	1962	5.00	25.00
Point 5101	Blue Booze / Bony Moroney	1962	7.00	35.00
Era 3082	Latin'ia / Tor-chula	1962	5.00	25.00
Era 3097	Latin Soul / Christmas Eve	1962	5.00	25.00
Era 3117	Infinity / Encinada	1963	6.00	30.00
	(Era 3117 credits The Sentinal Six.)			
Westco 12	I've Been Blue / Hit The Road	1964	5.00	25.00
Westco 14	Tell Me / Hit The Road	1964	5.00	25.00

Label & Catalog #		A-Side/B-Side	Year	VG	NM
SEQUINS, THE					
Cameo 161		To Be Young / The Mountains	1959	5.00	25.00
SERATT, HOWARD					
Sun 198		Troublesome Waters / I Must Be Saved	1954	——	——
		(Rare. Estimated near mint value $500-1,000.)			
SERENDIPITY SINGERS, THE					
Philips 40236		Autumn Wind / Same Old Reason	1964	.60	3.00
Philips 40236	(PS)	Autumn Wind / Same Old Reason	1964	.60	3.00
Philips 40246		Little Brown Jug / High North Star	1964	.60	3.00
Philips 40246	(PS)	Little Brown Jug / High North Star	1964	.60	3.00
Philips 40273		My Heart Keeps Following You / Rider	1965	.60	3.00
Philips 40292		Run, Run Chicken Run / We Belong Together	1965	.60	3.00
Philips 40309		Bells Of Rhymney / Oh, Brother	1965	.60	3.00
Philips 40331		When Peaches Grow On Lilac Trees / Plastic	1965	.60	3.00
Philips 40356		Phoenix Love Theme (Sinza Fina) / If You Come Back In Summer	1966	.60	3.00
Philips 40356	(PS)	Phoenix Love Theme (Sinza Fina) / If You Come Back In Summer	1966	.60	3.00
Philips 40410		Autumn Bound / Born Free	1966	.60	3.00
SESSIONS, LITTLE RONNIE					
Pike 5908		Keep A Knockin' / Lot On My Mind	1961	3.00	15.00
SESSIONS, THE					
Kedlen 2005		Lonesome Surf / Fannie Mae	196?	7.00	35.00
SETTLE, MIKE					
Uni 55309		Saturdays Only / The Nights Of Your Life	1971	.80	4.00
Uni 55333		If You Really Love Me /	1971	.80	4.00
SEVENTEENS, THE					
Golden Crest 503		Steady Guy / Bug Out	196?	5.00	25.00
SEVENTH COURT, THE					
Prophonics 2027		One Eyed Witch / Shake	196?	3.00	15.00
SEVENTH DAWN, THE					
GSR 2425		Don't Worry Me / Wings Of Flight	196?	2.00	10.00
SEVILLE, DAVID					
David Seville— a pseudonym for Ross Bagdasarian— also was the mastermind behind The Chipmunks and Alfi & Harry.					
Liberty 55041		Armen's Theme / Carousel In Rome	1956	3.00	15.00
Liberty 55079		Gotta Get To Your House / Camel Rock	1957	3.00	15.00
Liberty 55079	(PS)	Gotta Get To Your House / Camel Rock	1957	4.00	20.00
Liberty 55132		Witch Doctor / Don't Whistle At Me	1958	3.00	15.00
Liberty 55140		The Bird On My Head / Hey There, Moon	1958	2.00	10.00
Liberty 55153		Little Brass Band / Take Five	1958	2.00	10.00
Liberty 55193		Judy / Maria From Madrid	1959	2.00	10.00
Liberty 55314		Freddy, Freddy / Oh Judge, Your Honor, Dear Sir, Sweet Heart	1961	2.00	10.00
SEX PISTOLS, THE					
The Sex Pistols were Paul Cook, Steve Jones, Glen Matlock and Johnny Rotten.					
Warner Bros. 8516		Pretty Vacant / Sub-mission	1978	2.00	10.00
Warner Bros. 8516	(PS)	Pretty Vacant / Sub-mission	1978	3.00	25.00
SHA NA NA					
Kama Sutra 507		Pay Day / Rock And Roll Is Here To Stay	1970	.60	3.00
Kama Sutra 522		Only One Song / Yakety Yak	1971	.60	3.00
Kama Sutra 528		Top Forty / Wonder Why	1971	.60	3.00
Kama Sutra 592		Maybe I'm Old Fashioned / Strong All Night	1972	.60	3.00
Kama Sutra 592	(PS)	Maybe I'm Old Fashioned / Strong All Night	1972	.60	3.00
Kama Sutra 602		Just Like Romeo And Juliet / Circles Of Love	1973	.60	3.00
SHADES, THE					
Scottie 1309		Splashin' / Strollin' After Dark	1959	2.00	10.00
SHADOWS, THE					
Del-Fi 4109		Under The Stars Of Love / Jungle Fever	1958	5.00	25.00
SHADOWS, THE					
The Shadows also recorded with Cliff Richard.					
ABC-Paramount 10073		Saturday Dance / Lonesome Fella	1960	3.00	15.00
Atlantic 2111		The Frightened City / F.B.I.	1961	2.00	10.00
Atlantic 2177		Dance On / The Rumble	1962	2.00	10.00
Atlantic 2135		Kon-Tiki / Man Of Mystery	1962	2.00	10.00

Label & Catalog #		A-Side/B-Side	Year	VG	NM
Atlantic 2146		Stars Fell On Stockton / Wonderful Land	1962	2.00	10.00
Atlantic 2166		Guitar Tango / What A Lovely Tune	1962	2.00	10.00
Atlantic 2235		Theme For Young Lovers / The Rise And Fall Of Flingel Blunt	1964	2.00	10.00
Atlantic 2257		Rhythm And Greens / The Miracle	1964	2.00	10.00
Epic 9793		Mary Anne / Chu Chi	1965	2.00	10.00
Epic 9826		Stingray / Alice In Wonderland	1965	2.00	10.00
Epic 9848		Don't Make My Baby Blue / My Grandfather's Clock	1965	2.00	10.00

SHADOWS FOUR, THE

Fleetwood 4553		Heart Of Wood /	196?	7.00	35.00

SHADOWS OF KNIGHT, THE

A later version of the Shadows functioned as the "house band" for Buddah, recording the instrumental tracks for the bubblegum productions of Kasenetz-Katz on the Buddah label.

Dunwich 116		Gloria / Spaniard At My Door	1966	4.00	20.00
		(First pressings have a yellow label that makes no mention of Atco Records.)			
Dunwich 116		Gloria / Spaniard At My Door	1966	3.00	15.00
		(Second pressings have a yellow label that read "Distributed by Atco Records.")			
Dunwich 116		Gloria / Spaniard At My Door	1966	2.00	10.00
		(Third pressings have a pink label.)			
Dunwich 122		Oh Yeah / Light Bulb Blues	1966	2.00	10.00
Dunwich 122	(PS)	Oh Yeah / Light Bulb Blues	1966	6.00	30.00
Dunwich 128		Bad Little Woman / Gospel Zone	1966	2.00	10.00
Dunwich 128	(PS)	Bad Little Woman / Gospel Zone	1966	8.00	40.00
Dunwich 141		I'm Gonna Make You Mine / I'll Make You Sorry	1966	5.00	25.00
Dunwich 151		The Behemoth / Willie Jean	1967	4.00	15.00
Dunwich 167		Someone Like Me / Three For Love	1967	4.00	20.00
Auravision	(33)	Potato Chip *(One sided cardboard picture disc)*	1967	15.00	75.00
Team 520		Shake / From Way Out To Way In	1968	2.00	10.00
Atco 6634		Gloria '69 / Spaniard At My Door	1969	3.00	15.00
Atco 6676		I Am The Hunter / Warwick Court Affair	1969	3.00	15.00
Super-K 8		Yaurus / My Fire Department Needs A Fireman	1969	2.00	10.00
Super-K 10		Run, Run, Billy Porter / My Fire Department Needs A Fireman	1969	2.00	10.00
Atlantic 13138		Gloria / Dark Side	197?	.60	3.00

SHAG, THE

Jo-Jo 101		Crying / You're A Loser	196?	3.00	15.00
Palmer 5010		The Way I Care / Ring Around The Rose	1966	2.00	10.00
Capitol 5995		Stop And Listen / Melissa	1968	3.00	15.00

SHAGGY BOYS, THE

Red Bird 074		In The Morning / Stop The Clock	1966	2.00	10.00
United Artists 50100		You And Me / Joy In The Morning	1966	1.60	8.00
United Artists 50135		Behind Those Stained Glass Windows / That's The Only Way	1967	1.60	8.00

SHAGS, THE

Kayden 407		As Long As I Have You / Tell Me	1967	3.00	15.00
Kayden 408		Breathe In My Ear / Easy Street	1967	3.00	15.00
Cameo 470		As Long As I Have You / Tell Me	1967	2.00	10.00
Laurie 3353		I Call Your Name / Hideaway	1967	2.00	10.00
Sammy 102		'Cause Of You / By My Side	196?	2.00	10.00

SHAKERS, THE

Normal 1372		Just Like A Baby / Go Go Girl	196?	2.00	10.00

SHAKERS, THE

Audio Fidelity 119		Ticket To Ride / Break It All	1966	2.00	10.00
ABC 10960		One Wonderful Moment / Love, Love, Love	1967	2.00	10.00

SHALONS, THE

Ronnie 203		Angel / True Love Came My Way	196?	3.00	15.00

SHAMETTES, THE

The Shamettes are part of The Sam The Sham Revue.

MGM 13618		Hey There, Big Bad Wolf / I'd Rather Have You	1966	1.20	6.00
MGM 13798		You're Welcome Back / He'll Come Back	1967	1.20	6.00

SHANES, THE

Capitol 5963		Chris Craft #9 / Time	1967	1.00	5.00

SHANGRI-LAS, THE [THE SHANGRA-LAS]

The Shangri-Las, originally The Bon-Bons, are sisters Marge and Mary Ann Ganser and Betty and Mary Weiss.

Smash 1866		Simon Says / Simon Speaks	1963	8.00	40.00
		(Smash 1866 credits The Shangra-Las.)			
Spokane 4006		Wishing Well / Hate To Say I Told You So	1964	6.00	30.00
Scepter 1291		Wishing Well / Hate To Say I Told You So	1965	3.00	15.00
Red Bird 008		Remember (Walkin' In The Sand) / It's Easier To Cry	1964	3.00	15.00

After reaching the top 10 on most national charts with a cover of Van Morrison and Them's *Gloria*, Chicago's Shadows Of Knight bounced back into the top 40 with *Oh Yeah*, their last real chance for a really big hit.

Label & Catalog #		A-Side/B-Side	Year	VG	NM
Red Bird 014		Leader Of The Pack / What Is Love?	1964	3.00	15.00
Red Bird 018		Give Him A Great Big Kiss / Twist And Shout	1964	3.00	15.00
Red Bird 019		Maybe / Shout	1964	3.00	15.00
Red Bird 025		Out In The Streets / The Boy	1965	3.00	15.00
Red Bird 030		Give Us Your Blessings / Only Heaven Knows	1965	3.00	15.00
Red Bird 036		Right Now And Not Later / Train From Kansas City	1965	3.00	15.00
Red Bird 043		I Can Never Go Home Anymore / Sophisticated Boom Boom	1965	4.00	20.00
Red Bird 043		I Can Never Go Home Anymore / Bulldog	1965	3.00	15.00
Red Bird 048		Long Live Our Love / Sophisticated Boom Boom	1966	3.00	15.00
Red Bird 053		He Cried / Dressed In Black	1966	3.00	15.00
Red Bird 068		Past, Present And Future / Love You More Than Yesterday	1966	3.00	15.00
Mercury 72645		I'll Never Learn / Sweet Sound Of Summer	1966	2.00	10.00
Mercury 72670		Take The Time / Footsteps On The Roof	1967	2.00	10.00

SHANNON, DEL
Refer to Maximilian.

Label & Catalog #		A-Side/B-Side	Year	VG	NM
Big Top 3067		Runaway / Jody	1961	3.00	15.00
Big Top 3075		Hats Off To Larry / Don't Gild The Lily, Lily	1961	3.00	15.00
Big Top 3083		So Long Baby / The Answer To Everything	1961	3.00	15.00
Big Top 3091		Hey! Little Girl / I Won't Care Anymore	1961	3.00	15.00
Big Top 3098		Ginny In The Mirror / I Won't Be There	1962	3.00	15.00
Big Top 3112		Cry Myself To Sleep / I'm Gonna Move On	1962	3.00	15.00
Big Top 3117		The Swiss Maid / You Never Talked About Me	1962	3.00	15.00
Big Top 3131		Little Town Flirt / The Wamboo	1962	3.00	15.00
Big Top 3143		Two Kinds Of Teardrops / Kelly	1963	3.00	15.00
Big Top 3152		From Me To You / Two Silhouettes	1963	6.00	30.00
		(Big To 3152 is the first American cover of a Lennon-McCartney song.)			
Ber-Lee 501		Sue's Gotta Be Mine / Now She's Gone	1963	2.00	10.00
Ber-Lee 502		That's The Way Love Is / Time Of The Day	1964	2.00	10.00
Amy 897		Mary Jane / Stains On My Letter	1964	3.00	15.00
Amy 905		Handy Man / Give Her Lots Of Love	1964	1.60	8.00
Amy 911		Do You Want To Dance? / This Is All I Have To Give	1964	1.60	8.00
Amy 915		Keep Searchin' (We'll Follow The Sun) / Broken Promises	1964	1.60	8.00
Amy 919		Stranger In Town / Over You	1965	1.60	8.00
Amy 925		Break Up / Why Don't You Tell Him?	1965	1.60	8.00
Amy 937		She Still Remembers Tony / Move It Over	1965	2.00	10.00
Amy 947		I Can't Believe My Ears / I Wish I Wasn't Me Tonight	1965	2.00	10.00
Liberty 55886		The Big Hurt / I Got It Bad	1966	1.20	6.00
Liberty 55889		For A Little While / Hey, Little Star	1966	1.20	6.00
Liberty 55894		Show Me / Never Thought I Could	1966	1.20	6.00
Liberty 55904		Under My Thumb / She Was Mine	1966	3.00	15.00
Liberty 55939		She / What Makes You Run?	1967	1.20	6.00
Liberty 55961		Led Along / I Can't Be True	1967	1.20	6.00
Liberty 55993		Runaway / He Cheated	1967	1.20	6.00
Liberty 56018		Thinkin' It Over / Runnin' On Back	1968	1.20	6.00
Liberty 56018	(PS)	Thinkin' It Over / Runnin' On Back	1968	3.00	15.00
Liberty 56036		Gemini / Magical Music Box	1968	1.20	6.00
Liberty 56070		Raindrops / You Don't Love Me	1968	1.20	6.00
Dunhill 4193		Comin' Back To Me / Sweet Mary Lou	1969	1.60	8.00
Dunhill 4224		Sister Isabelle / Colorado Rain	1969	1.60	8.00
Island 021	(DJ)	Tell Her No / Tell Her No	1975	1.00	5.00
Island 021	(DJ)	Restless / Restless	1975	1.00	5.00
Island 021		Tell Her No / Restless	1975	2.00	10.00
Island 038	(DJ)	Cry Baby Cry / Cry Baby Cry	1975	1.00	5.00
Island 038		Cry Baby Cry / In My Arms Again	1975	2.00	10.00
Network 479511		Sea Of Love / Midnight Train	1981	.60	3.00
Network 4795??		To Love Someone	1981	.60	3.00
Warner Bros. 28853		Stranger On The Run /	1985	.60	3.00

SHANNON, JACKIE (& THE CAJUNS)
Jackie Shannon is a pseudonym for Jackie DeShannon.

Label & Catalog #		A-Side/B-Side	Year	VG	NM
P.J. 101		Trouble / Lies	1959	8.00	40.00
Sage 290		Just Another Lie / Cajun Blues	1959	6.00	30.00
Sand 330		Trouble / Lies	1959	6.00	30.00
Fraternity 836		Just Another Lie / Cajun Blues	1959	4.00	20.00
Dot 15928		Just Another Lie / Cajun Blues	1959	3.00	15.00
Dot 15980		Trouble / Lies	1959	3.00	15.00

SHANNON, PAT

Label & Catalog #	A-Side/B-Side	Year	VG	NM
Decca 30905	Snake And The Bookworm / Summertime's Coming	1959	2.00	10.00
Warner Bros. 7210	She Sleeps Alone / Candy Apples And Cotton Candy	1968	1.00	5.00
Uni 55191	Back To Dreamin' Again / Moody	1969	.80	4.00

SHARELL, JERRY

Label & Catalog #	A-Side/B-Side	Year	VG	NM
Alanna 560	Everybody Knows / That's My Business	1959	4.00	20.00

SHARING, THE

Label & Catalog #	A-Side/B-Side	Year	VG	NM
General 6706	Wanton Girl / Superfine Woman	196?	1.00	5.00

Label & Catalog #	A-Side/B-Side	Year	VG	NM
SHARKS, THE				
Sapien 1003	Big Surf / Spookareno	1963	3.00	15.00
SHARMETTES, THE				
King 5648	Answer Me / My Dream	1962	2.00	10.00
King 5656	Wonderful Love / I Gotta Tell It	1962	2.00	10.00
King 5686	Tell Me / I Want To Be Loved	1962	2.00	10.00
SHARON MARIE				
Produced by Brian Wilson with "Run-Around Lover" and "Thinkin' 'Bout You, Baby" featuring The Honeys.				
Capitol 5064	Run-Around Lover / Summertime	1963	30.00	150.00
Capitol 5195	Thinkin' 'Bout You, Baby / Story Of My Life	1964	30.00	150.00
SHARPE, RAY				
Jamie 1128	Monkeys Uncle / Linda Lu	1959	3.00	15.00
Jamie 1128	Red Sails In The Sunset / Linda Lu	1959	3.00	15.00
Jamie 1138	T.A. Blues / Long John	1959	2.00	10.00
Jamie 1149	Bermuda / Gonna Let It Go This Time	1960	2.00	10.00
Jamie 1155	Red Sails In The Sunset / For You My Love	1960	2.00	10.00
Jamie 1164	Kewpie Doll / Givin' Up	1960	2.00	10.00
Gregmark 14	Linda Lu / The Bus Song	1962	2.00	10.00
SHARPE & KERLIN				
Cape 1999	The Big Goof / (B-side by The Blast)	196?	4.00	20.00
SHARPEES, THE				
One-Derful 4835	Do The 45 / Make Up Your Mind	1965	2.00	10.00
One-Derful 4839	Tired Of Being Lonely / Just To Please You	1965	2.00	10.00
One-Derful 4843	I've Got A Secret / Make Up Your Mind	1966	2.00	10.00
One-Derful 4845	The Sock / My Girl Jean	1966	2.00	10.00
SHARPS, THE				
Star-Hi 10460	If Love Is What You Want / Double Clutch	196?	4.00	20.00
SHATTOES, THE				
Studio City 1010	Surf Fever / Do You Love Me?	196?	8.00	40.00
SHAW, JOHNNY, & THE JAYWALKERS				
Jubilee 5511	Wild Surfer's Call / Fanny Jones	1965	7.00	35.00
SHAW, SANDI				
Reprise 0320	(There's) Always Something There To Remind Me / Don't You Know?	1964	1.20	6.00
Reprise 0342	Girl, Don't Come / I'd Be Far Better Off Without You	1965	1.20	6.00
Reprise 0375	Long Live Love / I've Heard About Him	1965	1.20	6.00
Reprise 0394	I'll Stop At Nothing / Stop Feeling Sorry For Yourself	1965	1.00	5.00
Reprise 0427	How Can You Tell? / If You Ever Need Me	1965	1.00	5.00
Reprise 0449	Tomorrow / Hurting You	1966	1.00	5.00
Reprise 0488	Nothing Comes Easy / Stop Before You Start	1866	1.00	5.00
RCA Victor 74-0118	Monsieur Dupont / Voice In The Crowd	1969	.80	4.00
RCA Victor 74-0370	Love Is For The Two Of Us / Wight Is Wight	1969	.80	4.00
SHAYNE, CHARITY				
Autumn 22	Isn't It, Babe? / Then You Try	1965	2.00	10.00
SHEAN & JENKYNS				
GNP/Crescendo 197	Goofy Footer Ho-Dad / Do The Commercial	1963	5.00	25.00
SHEEP, THE				
The Sheep are Bob Feldman and Jerry Goldstein. Refer to Bob & Jerry; The Strangeloves.				
Boom 60000	Hide And Seek / Twelve Months Later	1965	2.00	10.00
Boom 60007	Dynamite / I Feel Good	1965	2.00	10.00
SHELBY, ERNIE				
Capitol 4879	Tonight You Belong To Me / That I'm In Love With You	1962	1.60	8.00
SHELTON, COLE				
Wasp 125	Little Tina Marie / I'm A Son Of A Gun	196?	.80	4.00
SHELTON, GARY				
Mercury 71310	Kissin' At The Drive-In / Yours Till I Die	1958	5.00	25.00
Mark 145	Goodbye, Little Darlin,' Goodbye / Stop The World	1960	25.00	125.00
SHENANDOAH TRIO, THE				
Nefi 113	Surfin' Man / The River And I	1963	7.00	35.00
SHEPHERD, JOHNNY				
Tilden 3001	How Blue My Heart / Boom Boom Boomerang	196?	3.00	15.00

Label & Catalog #		A-Side/B-Side	Year	VG	NM
SHEPHERD, RED, & THE FLOCK					
Philips 40398		She's A Grabber / I Can't Hold On	1966	2.00	10.00
Philips 40398	(PS)	She's A Grabber / I Can't Hold On	1966	3.00	15.00
SHEPPARD, BUDDY, & THE HOLIDAYS					
The Holidays is a pseudonym for The Belmonts.					
Sabina 506		Brahms Lullabye / (Time To Dream) My Love Is Real	1962	8.00	40.00
Sabina 510		Now It's All Over / That Back Sound	1963	10.00	50.00
SHEPPARD, NEIL					
Almont 314		You Can't Go Far Without A Guitar (Unless You're Ringo Starr) / Betty Is The Girl For You	1964	6.00	30.00
SHEPPARD, ZEKE					
President 831		Snow Surfin' / What Does Too Young Mean?	196?	7.00	35.00
SHEPPHERD SISTERS, THE [THE SHEPPARD SISTERS]					
Capitol 2706		Rock And Roll Cha Cha / Gone With The Wind	1954	4.00	20.00
Mercury 71244		Gettin' Ready For Freddy / The Best Thing There Is	1957	3.00	15.00
		(Mercury 71244 credits The Sheppard Sisters.)			
Melba 101		Rock And Roll Cha Cha / Gone With The Wind	1957	3.00	15.00
Melba 108		Remember That Crazy Rock 'N' Roll Tune? / I Walked Beside The Sea	1957	3.00	15.00
Lance 125		Alone / Congratulations To Someone	1957	4.00	20.00
Warwick 511		Here Comes Heaven Again / I Think It's Time	1959	2.00	10.00
MGM 12766		Heart And Soul / (It's No) Sin	1959	2.00	10.00
Atlantic 2176		Don't Mention My Name / What Makes Little Girls Cry?	1963	1.20	6.00
Atlantic 2195		Talk Is Cheap / (Take A Look At My Guy) The Greatest Lover	1963	1.20	6.00
York 50002		Alone / Alone	1965	1.20	6.00
SHERIDAN, BOBBY					
Bobby Sheridan is a pseudonym for Charlie Rich.					
Sun 354		Red Man / Sad News	1960	4.00	20.00
SHERIDAN, MIKE, & THE NIGHTRIDERS					
Liverpool Sound 902		Please, Mr. Postman / In Love	1964	25.00	125.00
SHERIDAN, TONY, & THE BEAT BROTHERS: *Refer to* THE BEATLES					
SHERMAN, BOBBY					
Starcrest 100		Judy, You'll Never Know / Telegram	196?	3.00	15.00
Dot 16566		I Want To Hear It From Her / Nobody's Sweetheart	1964	2.00	10.00
Decca 31672		You Make Me Happy / Man Overboard	1964	2.00	10.00
Decca 31741		It Hurts Me / Give Me Your Word	1965	2.00	10.00
Decca 31741	(PS)	It Hurts Me / Give Me Your Word	1965	7.00	35.00
Decca 31779		Hey, Little Girl / Well, All Right	1965	2.00	10.00
		(The Decca singles were produced by Gary Usher.)			
Parkway 967		Anything Your Little Heart Desires / Goody Galum-Shus	1965	1.20	6.00
Parkway 967	(PS)	Anything Your Little Heart Desires / Goody Galum-Shus	1965	3.00	15.00
Cameo 403	(DJ)	Happiness Is (One sided)	1965	4.00	20.00
Cameo 403		Happiness Is / Can't Get Used To Losing You	1965	1.60	8.00
Condor 1002		I'll Never Tell You / Telegram	196?	1.60	8.00
Epic 10181		Cold Girl / Think Of Rain	1967	1.00	5.00
Epic 10181	(PS)	Cold Girl / Think Of Rain	1967	2.00	10.00
Metromedia 121		Little Woman / One Too Many Mornings	1969	.40	2.00
Metromedia 121	(PS)	Little Woman / One Too Many Mornings	1969	.60	3.00
Metromedia 150		La La La (If I Had You) / Time	1969	.40	2.00
Metromedia 150	(PS)	La La La (If I Had You) / Time	1969	.60	3.00
Metromedia 177		Easy Come, Easy Go / Sounds Along The Way	1970	.40	2.00
Metromedia 177	(PS)	Easy Come, Easy Go / Sounds Along The Way	1970	.60	3.00
Metromedia 188		Hey, Mister Sun / Two Blinds Minds	1970	.40	2.00
Metromedia 188	(PS)	Hey, Mister Sun / Two Blinds Minds	1970	.60	3.00
Metromedia 194		Julie, Do Ya Love Me? / Spend Some Time Lovin' Me	1970	.40	2.00
Metromedia 194	(PS)	Julie, Do Ya Love Me? / Spend Some Time Lovin' Me	1970	.60	3.00
Metromedia 204		Goin' Home (Sing A Song Of Christmas Cheer) / Love's What You're Gettin' For Christmas	1971	.40	2.00
Metromedia 204	(PS)	Goin' Home (Sing A Song Of Christmas Cheer) / Love's What You're Gettin' For Christmas	1971	.60	3.00
Metromedia 206		Cried Like A Baby / Is Anybody There?	1971	.40	2.00
Metromedia 206	(PS)	Cried Like A Baby / Is Anybody There?	1971	.60	3.00
Metromedia 217		The Drum / Free Now To Roam	1971	.40	2.00
Metromedia 217	(PS)	The Drum / Free Now To Roam	1971	.60	3.00
Metromedia 222		Waiting At The Bus Stop / Runaway	1971	.40	2.00
Metromedia 222	(PS)	Waiting At The Bus Stop / Runaway	1971	.60	3.00
Metromedia 227		Going Together / Jennifer	1971	.40	2.00
Metromedia 227	(PS)	Going Together / Jennifer	1971	.60	3.00
Metromedia 240		Together Again / Picture A Little Girl	1972	.40	2.00
Metromedia 240	(PS)	Together Again / Picture A Little Girl	1972	.60	3.00

Label & Catalog #		A-Side/B-Side	Year	VG	NM
Metromedia 249		I Don't Believe In Magic / Just A Little While Longer	1972	.40	2.00
Metromedia 249	(PS)	I Don't Believe In Magic / Just A Little While Longer	1972	.60	3.00
Metromedia 0100		Early In The Morning / Unborn Melody	1972	.40	2.00
Janus 254		Our Last Song Together / Sunshine Rose	197?	.40	2.00
Janus 1700		Our Last Song Together / Sunshine Rose	197?	.40	2.00

SHERRILL, BILLY

ABC-Paramount 10465		Drag Race / Tipsy	1963	2.00	10.00

SHERRYS, THE [THE SHERRY SISTERS]
The Guyden, Mercury and Roberts discs credit The Sherrys.

Guyden 2068		Pop Pop Pop Pie / Your Hand In Mine	1962	2.00	10.00
Guyden 2077		Slop Time / Let's Stomp Again	1963	2.00	10.00
Guyden 2084		Saturday Night / I've Got No One	1963	2.00	10.00
Guyden 2098		That Boy Of Mine / Monk Monk Monkey	1963	2.00	10.00
OKeh 7169		Stay Away From Bobby / Dancing With Tears In My Eyes	1963	2.00	10.00
Mercury 72256		No No Baby / That Guy Of Mine	1964	2.00	10.00
Epic 9693		Sailor Boy / He's Just Another Guy	1964	1.60	8.00
Epic 9784		Not Tonight / Only Time Will Tell	1965	1.60	8.00
Epic 9888		No More Tonights / Two Flights Up	1966	1.60	8.00
Roberts 701		Slow Jerk / Confusion	196?	1.60	8.00
Jamie 1399		I've Got A Whole Lot Of Music In My Soul / I've Got A Whole Lot Of Music In My Soul	1972	.60	3.00
Jamie 1408		If You Have The Love / And Then I Think Of You	1972	.60	3.00

SHERWOODS, THE
The Sherwoods is a pseudonym for The Concords.

Herald 597		Cold And Frosty Morning / You Started It	1963	4.00	20.00

SHERWOODS, THE
The Sherwoods were produced by Bobby Fuller.

Exeter 121		Just As I Love Her / You Hold My Letters	1964	7.00	35.00
Exeter 123		Tickler / Back Out	1964	7.00	35.00
Eastwood 121		Just As I Love Her / You Hold My Letters	1964	5.00	25.00

SHEVELLES, THE

World Artists 1023		Like I Love You / Ooh Poo Pah Doo	1964	2.00	10.00
World Artists 1025		I Could Conquer The World / How Would You Like Me To Love You?	1964	2.00	10.00

SHIEKS, THE

Trine 1101		Baghdad Rock / Baghdad Rock (Part 2)	1959	7.00	35.00
MGM 12876		Baghdad Rock / Baghdad Rock (Part 2)	1959	3.00	15.00

SHIELDS, BILLY
Billy Shields is a pseudonym for Tony Orlando.

Harbour 304		I Was A Boy / Moments From Now	195?	4.00	20.00

SHIELDS, ED, & THE SOPHISTICATES

Kon Tiki 1244		Drinkin' Wine / Cute	196?	2.00	10.00

SHILLINGS, THE

Fontana 1543		Just For You, Baby / Laugh	1966	3.00	15.00

SHILLINGS, THE

Fantasy 594		It Was My Mistake / Not The Least Bit True	1967	2.00	10.00

SHIN-DIGGERS, THE

ABC-Paramount 10612		Shindig / Station Break	1964	1.60	8.00

SHINDIGS, THE
The Shindigs feature Bobby and Randy Fuller.

Mustang 3003		Thunder Reef / (B-side by Bobby Fuller Four)	1965	5.00	25.00

SHINDOGS, THE
The Shindogs feature Bonnie and Delaney Bramlett.

Warner Bros. 5665		Someone, Someone / Why?	1965	2.00	10.00
Viva 601		Who Do You Think You Are? / Yes, I'm Coming Home	1966	2.00	10.00

SHIRTS, THE

Capitol 4750		Can't Cry Anymore / I'm In Love Again	1979	.80	4.00

SHIVA'S HEAD BAND

Ignite 681		Kaleidoscopic / Song For Peace	1967	5.00	25.00
Armadillo 811		Country Boy / Such A Joy	1971	2.00	10.00
Armadillo 811	(PS)	Country Boy / Such A Joy	1971	6.00	30.00
Armadillo 3		Take Me To The Mountains /	1971	2.00	10.00
Armadillo 6		Don't Blame Me / Extension	1976	2.00	10.00

Label & Catalog #		A-Side/B-Side	Year	VG	NM
SHOCKING BLUE, THE					
Colossus 108		Venus / Hot Sand	1969	1.00	5.00
Colossus 108	(PS)	Venus / Hot Sand	1969	2.00	10.00
Colossus 111		Mighty Joe / I'm A Woman	1971	1.00	5.00
Colossus 111	(PS)	Mighty Joe / I'm A Woman	1971	2.00	10.00
Colossus 116		Long And Lonesome Road / Ackaragh	1970	1.00	5.00
Colossus 123		Never Marry A Railroad Man / Never Marry	1971	1.00	5.00
Colossus 141		Bool Weevil / Long And Lonesome Road	1971	1.00	5.00
MGM 14481		When I Was A Girl / Eve And The Apple	1972	.60	3.00
MGM 14543		Inkpot / Oh, Lord	1973	.60	3.00
SHOES, THE					
Bomp 116		Tomorrow Night / Okay	1978	1.20	6.00
Bomp 116	(PS)	Tomorrow Night / Okay	1978	3.00	15.00
Elektra 46498		I Don't Miss You / I Don't Miss You	1979	.60	3.00
Elektra 46498	(PS)	I Don't Miss You / I Don't Miss You	1979	.60	3.00
Elektra 46557		Too Late / Now Or Never	1979	.60	3.00
Elektra 46557	(PS)	Too Late / Now Or Never	1979	1.20	6.00
Elektra 47130	(DJ)	Karen / Karen	1979	.60	3.00
		(Stock copies of Elektra 47130 may not exist.)			
SHOESTRING					
20th Century Fox 6706		Candy Andy / Sloop-De-Hoop-Twine	196?	1.20	6.00
SHOESTRING ORCHESTRA, THE					
Burdette 701		I Ain't Gonna Cheat On You /	196?	2.00	10.00
SHONDELL, TROY [TROY SHUNDELL]					
Gaye 2010		This Time / I Catch Myself Crying	1961	6.00	30.00
		(Gaye 2010 credits Troy Shundell.)			
Goldcrest 161		This Time / Girl After Girl	1961	4.00	20.00
Goldcrest 161		This Time / Girl After Girl	1961	2.00	10.00
Goldcrest 161-A		This Time / Girl After Girl	1961	2.00	10.00
Liberty 55353		This Time / Girl After Girl	1961	2.00	10.00
Liberty 55398		Tears From An Angel / Island In The Sky	1961	2.00	10.00
Liberty 55445		Na-Ne-No / Just Because	1962	3.00	15.00
		(A-side produced by Phil Spector.)			
Everest 2015		Gone / Some People Never Learn	1963	2.00	10.00
Ric 174		Just A Dream / Just Like Me	1965	1.60	8.00
TRX 5015		Let's Go All The Way / Let Me Love You	1969	1.60	8.00
TRX 5019		Something's Wrong In Indiana / A Rose And A Baby Ruth	1969	1.60	8.00
SHONDELLS, THE: *Refer to* **TOMMY JAMES & THE SHONDELLS**					
SHORR, MICKEY, & THE CUT-UPS					
Tuba 11636		Dr. Ben Casey / Roaring '20's Rag	1962	2.00	10.00
SHORT CUTS, THE					
Carlton 513		Don't Say He's Gone / I'll Hide My Love	1959	3.00	15.00
SHOTGUN EXPRESS					
Shotgun Express features Rod Stewart.					
Uptown 747		I Could Feel The Whole World Turn 'Round / Curtains	1966	6.00	30.00
SHU-SHU & THE SPACE JOCKEYS					
King Of Music 11081		Visit To Planet Earth / Visit To Planet Earth (Part 2)	196?	3.00	15.00
SHUE, DUANE					
Rivers 1009		Forest Ranger / Spanish Cavalier	196?	.80	4.00
SHUE, DUANE, & BILLY WILEY					
Rivers 1004		His Last Day / Brave American President	196?	.80	4.00
SHUNDELL, TROY: *Refer to* **TROY SHONDELL**					
SHUTDOWNS, THE					
Karsong 101		Straightaway /	1963	7.00	35.00
Dimension 1016		Beach Buggy / Four In The Floor	1963	5.00	25.00
SICKNICKS, THE					
Amy 824		Presidential Press Conference / Presidential Press Conference, Part 2	1961	2.00	10.00
Amy 824	(PS)	Presidential Press Conference	1961	3.00	15.00
Amy 831		Wadja Say, Mr. K? / Wadja Say, Mr. K? (Part 2)	1961	2.00	10.00
SIDEKICKS, THE					
RCA Victor 47-8864		Suspicions / Up On The Roof	1966	1.20	6.00
RCA Victor 47-8969		Fifi The Flea / Not Now	1966	1.20	6.00

Label & Catalog #	A-Side/B-Side	Year	VG	NM
SIDEWALK SURFERS, THE				
Surf 101	Skateboarding / Shoot The Curb	1964	10.00	50.00
	(These two tracks are the instrumental tracks—with new vocals— from "Skateboarding, Part 1" and "Walk On The Wet Side" from Jan & Dean's "Ride The Wild Surf" album.)			
SIDEWALK SURFERS, THE				
The Sidewalk Surfers feature Bruce Johnston.				
Jubilee 5496 (DJ)	Skate Board / Fun Last Summer	1965	5.00	25.00
Jubilee 5496	Skate Board / Fun Last Summer	1965	10.00	50.00
SIDEWINDERS, THE				
Imperial 5572	Sidewinder / Gulley Washer	1959	5.00	25.00
SIDRAN, BEN				
Capitol 3178	Poor Girl / Feel Your Groove	1971	.80	4.00
Blue Thumb 236	Space Cowboy / Think Twice	1973	.60	3.00
Blue Thumb 250	Hey Hey, Baby /	1974	.60	3.00
SILBERMAN, BENEDICT				
Palette 5037	The Chipmunk Song / Lovers Of Paris	1959	3.00	15.00
SILKIE, THE				
Fontana 1525	You've Got To Hide Your Love Away / City Winds	1965	1.60	8.00
Fontana 1536	Leave Me To Cry / Keys To My Soul	1966	1.20	6.00
Fontana 1551	Born To Be With You / I'm So Sorry	1966	1.20	6.00
SILLY SAVAGES, THE				
Dore 772	Are You Old Enough To Love? / Moon Dog	1966	1.20	6.00
SILVA-TONES, THE				
Monarch 5281	That's All I Want From You / Roses Are Blooming	1957	8.00	40.00
SILVER FLEET, THE				
Uni 55271	Look Out, World / Come On, Plane	1968	4.00	20.00
SILVER METERE, THE				
National General 001	Superstar / Now They've Found Me	1969	1.20	6.00
National General 001	Superstar / Now They've Found Me	1969	1.00	5.00
National General 010	Ballad Of A Well-Known Gun / Compromising Situation	1969	1.00	5.00
SILVERTONES, THE				
Joey 302	Thinking Of You / Canadian Sunset	195?	10.00	50.00
SILVERTONES, THE				
Goliath 1355	Bathsheba / Get It	1964	7.00	35.00
Valiant 6045	Bathsheba / Get It	1964	3.00	15.00
Sweet 16	Seven Piece Bathing Suit / Wait For My Gal	1964	7.00	35.00
SILVERTONES, THE: *Refer to* RONNIE RICE				
SIMMONS, GENE				
Sun 299	Drinkin' Wine / I Done Told You	1958	16.00	80.00
SIMMONS, GENE				
Gene Simmons is a member of Kiss.				
Casablanca 951	Radioactive / See You In Your Dreams	1979	1.00	5.00
SIMMONS, MORRIS "JUMPIN'" GENE				
Sandy 1027	The Waiting Game / Shenandoah Waltz	1960	3.00	15.00
	(Sandy 1027 credits Morris Gene Simmons.)			
Hi 2034	Teddy Bear / Your True Love	1962	1.00	5.00
Hi 2050	Caldonia / Be Her Number One	1962	1.00	5.00
Hi 2076	Haunted House / Hey, Hey, Little Girl	1964	1.00	5.00
Hi 2080	The Dodo / The Jump	1964	1.00	5.00
Hi 2086	Skinny Minny / I'm A Ramblin' Man	1964	1.00	5.00
Hi 2102	Batman / Bossy Boss	1967	1.60	8.00
Mala 12012	I'm Just A Loser / Lila (Don't Worry)	1968	.80	4.00
Epic 10601	Magnolia Street / She's There When I Come Home	1970	.80	4.00
SIMMS, JOHNNY				
Alite 101	Talk To Me / This Is The Moment	196?	3.00	15.00
SIMON & GARFUNKEL				
Paul Simon and Art Garfunkel originally recorded as Tom & Jerry.				
Columbia 43396 (DJ)	The Sounds Of Silence / The Sounds Of Silence (Red vinyl)	1965	6.00	30.00
Columbia 43396	The Sounds Of Silence / We've Got A Groovy Thing Goin'	1965	1.60	8.00

Label & Catalog #		A-Side/B-Side	Year	VG	NM
Columbia 43511	(DJ)	Homeward Bound / Homeward Bound (Red vinyl)	1966	6.00	30.00
Columbia 43511		Homeward Bound / Leaves That Are Green	1966	1.00	5.00
Columbia 43617	(DJ)	I Am A Rock / I Am A Rock (Red vinyl)	1966	6.00	30.00
Columbia 43617		I Am A Rock / Flowers Never Bend With The Rainfall	1966	1.00	5.00
Columbia 43728		Dangling Conversation / Big Bright Green, Pleasure Machine	1966	1.00	5.00
Columbia 43728	(PS)	Dangling Conversation / Big Bright Green, Pleasure Machine	1966	1.25	6.00
Columbia 43873		A Hazy Shade Of Winter / For Emily, Wherever I May Find Her	1966	1.00	5.00
Columbia 44046		At The Zoo / 59th Street Bridge Song (Feeling Groovy)	1967	1.00	5.00
Columbia 44046	(PS)	At The Zoo / 59th Street Bridge Song (Feeling Groovy)	1967	5.00	25.00
Columbia 44232		Fakin' It / You Don't Know Where Your Interest Lies	1967	1.00	5.00
Columbia 44465		Scarborough Fair-Canticle / April, Come She Will	1967	1.00	5.00
Columbia 44511		Mrs. Robinson / Old Friends-Bookends	1968	1.00	5.00
Columbia 44785		The Boxer / Baby Driver	1969	1.00	5.00
Columbia 44785	(PS)	The Boxer / Baby Driver	1969	1.00	5.00
Columbia 45079		Bridge Over Troubled Water / Keep The Customer Satisfied	1970	.80	4.00
Columbia 45079	(PS)	Bridge Over Troubled Water / Keep The Customer Satisfied	1970	.80	4.00
Columbia 45133		Cecilia / The Only Living Boy In New York City	1970	.80	4.00
Columbia 45133	(PS)	Cecilia / The Only Living Boy In New York City	1970	.80	4.00
Columbia 45237		El Condor Pasa / Why Don't You Write Me?	1970	.80	4.00
Columbia 45663		America / For Emily, Wherever I May Find Her	1972	.60	3.00
Columbia 10230		My Little Town / Rag Doll-You're Kind	1975	.60	3.00
Columbia 10230	(PS)	My Little Town / Rag Doll-You're Kind	1975	.80	4.00
		— Extended Play Albums—			
Columbia 9529	(33)	Bookends (Jukebox EP)	1968	3.00	15.00
Columbia 9914	(33)	Bridge Over Troubled Waters (Jukebox EP)	1970	3.00	15.00

SIMON, PAUL
Refer to Gregory Harrison; Paul Kane; Jerry Landis; True Taylor; Tico & The Triumphs; Dana Valery.

Label & Catalog #		A-Side/B-Side	Year	VG	NM
Columbia 45547		Mother And Child Reunion / Paranoia Blues	1972	.60	3.00
Columbia 45585		Me And Julio Down By The Schoolyard / Congratulations	1972	.60	3.00
Columbia 45638		Duncan / Run That Body Down	1972	.60	3.00
Columbia 45859		Kodachrome / Tenderness	1973	.60	3.00
Columbia AE7-1105	(DJ)	American Tune / American Tune	1973	.80	4.00
Columbia AE7-1105	(PS)	American Tune / American Tune	1973	2.00	10.00
Columbia 45900		American Tune / One Man's Ceiling Is Another Man's Floor	1973	.60	3.00
Columbia 45900	(PS)	American Tune / One Man's Ceiling Is Another Man's Floor	1973	.60	3.00
Columbia 45907		Loves Me Like A Rock / Learn How To Fall	1973	.60	3.00
Columbia 10197		Gone At Last / Take Me To The Mardis Gras	1975	.60	3.00
Columbia 10270		Fifty Ways To Leave Your Lover / Some Folk's Lives Roll Easy	1975	.60	3.00
Columbia 10332		Still Crazy After All These Years / I Do It For Your Love	1976	.60	3.00
Columbia 10630		Slip Slidin' Away / Something So Right	1977	.60	3.00
Columbia 10711		Stranded In A Limousine / Have A Good Time	1977	.60	3.00
Warner Bros. 49511		Late In The Evening / How The Heart Approaches What It Yearns	1978	.40	2.00
Warner Bros. 49601		One-Trick Pony / Long, Long Day	1978	.40	2.00
Warner Bros. 49675		Oh, Marion / God Bless The Absentee	1979	.40	2.00

SIMON SISTERS, THE
Carly and Lucy Simon.

Label & Catalog #		A-Side/B-Side	Year	VG	NM
Kapp 586		Winkin,' Blinkin' And Nod / So Glad I'm Here	1964	2.00	10.00
Kapp 624		Cuddle Bug / No One To Talk My Troubles To	1964	2.00	10.00

SINATRA, NANCY [NANCY SINATRA & LEE HAZLEWOOD]
Some sides may be credited to Nancy & Lee or to Nancy & Frank..

Label & Catalog #		A-Side/B-Side	Year	VG	NM
Reprise 20017	(DJ)	Cuff Links And A Tie Clip / Not Just Your Friend	1961	1.00	5.00
Reprise 20017		Cuff Links And A Tie Clip / Not Just Your Friend	1961	2.00	10.00
Reprise 20045	(DJ)	To Know Him Is To Love Him / Like I Do	1962	1.00	5.00
Reprise 20045		To Know Him Is To Love Him / Like I Do	1962	2.00	10.00
Reprise 20097	(DJ)	June, July And August / Think Of Me	1962	1.00	5.00
Reprise 20097		June, July And August / Think Of Me	1962	2.00	10.00
Reprise 20127	(DJ)	You Can Have Any Boy / Tonight You Belong To Me	1963	1.00	5.00
Reprise 20127		You Can Have Any Boy / Tonight You Belong To Me	1963	2.00	10.00
Reprise 20144	(DJ)	I See The Moon / Put Your Head On My Shoulder	1963	1.00	5.00
Reprise 20144		I See The Moon / Put Your Head On My Shoulder	1963	2.00	10.00
Reprise 20188	(DJ)	The Cruel War / One Way	1963	1.00	5.00
Reprise 20188		The Cruel War / One Way	1963	2.00	10.00
Reprise 20238	(DJ)	Thanks To You / Tammy	1964	1.00	5.00
Reprise 20238		Thanks To You / Tammy	1964	2.00	10.00
Reprise 20263	(DJ)	Where Do The Lonely Go? / Just Think About The Good Times	1964	1.00	5.00
Reprise 20263		Where Do The Lonely Go? / Just Think About The Good Times	1964	2.00	10.00
Reprise 0292	(DJ)	This Love Of Mine / There Goes The Bride	1964	1.00	5.00
Reprise 0292		This Love Of Mine / There Goes The Bride	1964	2.00	10.00
Reprise 0307		Tell Her / Here's To The Losers	1964	1.00	5.00
Reprise 0307		Tell Her / When Somebody Loves You	1964	1.00	5.00
Reprise 0335		True Love / Answer To Everything	1965	1.00	5.00

Label & Catalog #		A-Side/B-Side	Year	VG	NM
Reprise 0407		So Long, Babe / If He'd Love Me	1965	1.20	6.00
Reprise 0432		These Boots Are Made For Walkin' / The City Never Sleeps At Night	1965	1.20	6.00
Reprise 0461		How Does That Grab You, Darlin'? / The Last Of The Secret Agents	1966	1.20	6.00
Reprise 0491		Friday's Child / Hutchinson Jail	1966	1.00	5.00
Reprise 0514		In Our Time / Leave My Dog Alone	1966	1.00	5.00
Reprise 0527		Sugar Town / Summer Wine	1966	1.00	5.00
Reprise 0559		Love Eyes / Coastin'	1967	1.00	5.00
Reprise 0561		Somethin' Stupid / (B-side by Frank Sinatra)	1967	1.00	5.00
Reprise 0595		You Only Live Twice / Jackson	1967	1.00	5.00
Reprise 0620		Lightning's Girl / Until It's Time For You To Go	1967	1.00	5.00
Reprise 0620	(PS)	Lightning's Girl / Until It's Time For You To Go	1967	2.00	10.00
Reprise 0629		Lady Bird / Sand	1967	1.00	5.00
Reprise 0636		Tony Rome / This Town	1967	1.00	5.00
Reprise 0651		Some Velvet Morning / Oh, Lonesome Me	1968	1.00	5.00
Reprise 0670		100 Years / See The Little Children	1968	1.00	5.00
Reprise 0756		Happy / Nice 'N' Easy	1968	1.00	5.00
Reprise 0789		Good Time Girl / Old Devil Moon	1968	1.00	5.00
Reprise 0813		God Knows I Love You / Just Being Plain Old Me	1969	1.00	5.00
Reprise 0821		Here We Go Again / Memories	1969	1.00	5.00
Reprise 0851		Drummer Man / Home	1969	1.00	5.00
Reprise 0890		Love Them All (The Boys In The Band) / Home	1970	.80	4.00
Reprise 0932		Hello L.A., Bye Bye Birmingham / White Tattoo	1970	.80	4.00
Reprise 0960		How Are Things In California? / I'm Not A Girl Anymore	1970	.80	4.00
Reprise 0968		How Are Things In California? / I'm Not A Girl Anymore	1970	.60	3.00
Reprise 0980		Feelin' Kinda Sunday / Kids	1970	.60	3.00
Reprise 0991		Is Anybody Goin' To San Antone? / Hook And Ladder	1971	.80	4.00
Reprise 0991	(PS)	Is Anybody Goin' To San Antone? / Hook And Ladder	1971	2.00	10.00
Reprise 1011		Life's A Trippy Thing / (B-side by Frank Sinatra)	1971	.60	3.00
Reprise 1021		Did You Ever? / Back On The Road	1971	.80	4.00
Reprise 1034		Glory Road / Is Anybody Goin' To San Antone?	1971	.60	3.00
RCA Victor 74-0614		Paris Summer / Down From Dover	1971	.80	4.00
RCA Victor 74-0864		It's The Love (That Keeps It All Together) / Kind Of A Woman	1972	.80	4.00
RCA Victor 447-0922		These Boots Are Made For Walkin' / How Does That Grab You, Darlin'?	197?	.60	3.00
RCA Victor APBO-0029		Sugar Me / Ain't No Sunshine	1973	.60	3.00
Private Stock 022		Annabel Of Mobile /	1975	.60	3.00
Private Stock 075		Kinky Love / She Played The Piano And He Beat The Drum	1976	.60	3.00
Private Stock 108		Indian Summer / Dolly And Hawkeye	1977	.60	3.00
Private Stock 158		A Gentle Man Like You / It's For My Dad	1977	.60	3.00
Elektra 46659		Let's Keep It That Way / One Jump Ahead Of The Strom	1980	.60	3.00
		—Extended Play Albums—			
Reprise 6202	(33)	Boots (Jukebox EP)	1968	4.00	20.00
Reprise 6207	(33)	How Does That Grab You Darlin' (Jukebox EP)	1968	3.00	15.00
Reprise 6221	(33)	Nancy In London (Jukebox EP)	1968	3.00	15.00
Reprise 6239	(33)	Sugar (Jukebox EP)	1968	3.00	15.00
Reprise 6251	(33)	Country My Way (Jukebox EP)	1968	3.00	15.00
Reprise 6277	(33)	Movin' With Nancy (Jukebox EP)	1968	3.00	15.00

SINBAD, PAUL

Hype 104		Since I Met You /	196?	2.00	10.00

SINCERES, THE

Sigma 1003		Darling / Do You Remember?	1960	75.00	300.00
Jordan 117		You're Too Young / Forbidden Love	1960	50.00	200.00
Richie 545		Please Don't Cheat On Me / If You Should Leave Me	1961	3.00	15.00
Epic 9583		Our Winter Love / Kookie Ookie	1963	3.00	15.00
Columbia 43110		Sincerely / Snap Your Fingers	1964	3.00	15.00
Taurus 377		The Magic Of Love / Tell Her	1966	6.00	30.00

SINGING JOES, THE

Madison 126		Someone Loves You, Joe / The Empty Mailbox	1960	2.00	10.00

SINNERS, THE

Mercury 72388		You Don't Love Me / I Like The Look Of You ("You Don't Love Me" features Davie Allan on guitar.)	1965	6.00	30.00

SIR ARTHUR

Tower 216		Louie Louie / Walk Right In	196?	.80	4.00

SIR DOUGLAS QUINTET, THE [THE SIR DOUGLAS BAND]
Doug Sahm's Quintet featuring Augie Meyer. Refer to The Devons; Don Goldie; Rocky & The Border Kings.

Pacemaker 260		Sugar Bee / Blue Norther	1964	3.00	15.00
Tribe 8308		She's About A Mover / We'll Take Our Last Walk Tonight	1965	1.60	8.00
Tribe 8310		The Tracker / Blue Norther	1965	1.60	8.00
Tribe 8312		The Story Of John Hardy / In Time	1965	1.60	8.00

Label & Catalog #		A-Side/B-Side	Year	VG	NM
Tribe 8314		The Rains Came / Bacon Fat	1966	1.60	8.00
Tribe 8317		Quarter To Three / She's Gotta Be Boss	1966	1.60	8.00
Tribe 8318		Beginning Of The End / Love Don't Treat Me Fair	1966	1.60	8.00
Tribe 8321		She Digs My Love / When I Sing The Blues	1966	1.60	8.00
Smash 2169		Are Inlaws Really Outlaws? / Sell A Song	1968	1.00	5.00
Smash 2191		Mendocino / I Wanna Be Your Mama Again	1969	1.00	5.00
Smash 2222		Lawd, I'm Just A Country Boy In This Great Big Freaky City / And It Didn't Even Bring Me Down	1960	1.00	5.00
Smash 2233		Dynamite Woman / Too Many Docile Minds	1969	1.00	5.00
Smash 2253		At The Crossroads / Texas Me	1969	1.00	5.00
Smash 2259		Nuevo Laredo / I Don't Want To Go Home	1970	1.00	5.00
Philips 40676		What About Tomorrow? / A Nice Song	1971	1.00	5.00
Philips 40676	(PS)	What About Tomorrow? / A Nice Song	1971	2.00	10.00
Philips 40687	(DJ)	Catch The Man On The Rise / Pretty Flower	1971	2.00	10.00
		(Stock copies of Philips 40687 may not exist.)			
Philips 40708		Me And My Destiny / Wasted Days And Wasted Nights	1972	1.20	6.00
Mercury 73257		Michoacan / West Side Blues	1972	1.20	6.00
Atlantic 2965		Nitty Gritty / I'm Just Tired Of Gettin' Burned	1973	1.00	5.00
Atlantic 2985		Texas Tornado / Blue Horizon	1973	.80	4.00
		(Atlantic 2965 and 2985 credit The Sir Douglas Band.)			
Crazy Cajun 2004		If You Really Want Me To I'll Go / Hot Tomato Man	1974	1.00	5.00
Casablanca 0828		Roll With The Punches / I'm Not That Kat Anymore	1975	5.00	25.00
Texas Record 108		Henrietta / Country Groove	1976	2.00	10.00
Chrysalis 102779		Sheila Tequila / Down On The Border	1981	.80	4.00
Chrysalis 102779	(PS)	Sheila Tequila / Down On The Border	1981	.80	4.00
		—Extended Play Albums—			
Chrysalis 2404		Sheila Tequila	1981	2.00	10.00

SIR FROG & THE TOADS

Downey 131		Mustang / The Frog	1965	4.00	20.00

SIR JOE & THE MAIDENS

Lenox 5563		Jivin' Jean / Pen Pal	1963	2.00	10.00

SIR RALEIGH & THE COUPONS
Sir Raleigh is a pseudonym for Dewey Martin.

Jerden 757		White Cliffs Of Dover / Somethin' Or Other	1965	1.00	5.00
Jerden 764		While I Wait / Somethin' Or Other	1965	1.00	5.00
Jerden 760		Tomorrow's Gonna Be Another Day / Whitcome Street	1965	1.25	6.00

SIR WALTER RALEIGH
Walter Raleigh is a pseudonym for Dewey Martin..

Tower 156		Tell Her Tonight / If You Need Me	1965	1.60	8.00
Tower 220		I Don't Want To Cry / Always	1966	1.60	8.00

SIRES, THE

Graves 1094		Come To Me Baby / Don't Look Now	1966	2.00	10.00

SIRS, THE

Amerco 103		Off In A Daydream / Help Me	1965	1.20	6.00
Amerco 103	(PS)	Off In A Daydream / Help Me	1965	2.00	10.00
Amerco 106		I'm In Love / Drop Me A Line	1966	1.20	6.00

SISK, SHIRLEY

Sun 365		I Forgot To Remember To Forget / Other Side	1961	2.00	10.00

SITES, BETTY

GRC 112		I Feel A Tear / Whole Lotta Women	196?	2.00	10.00

SITES, LINDA & BETTY

Jerden 715		No Letter Today / Miss You At Midnight	196?	.60	3.00

SIX O' CLOCK NEWS, THE

Ridon 858		Diffusion Of Mary / Bridge At Frisco	1968	2.00	10.00

SIX THE HARD WAY
Six The Hard Way features Chuck Girard of The Hondells.

Warner Bros. 7052		Come Home (Little Girl) / Sunrise	1967	2.00	10.00
Capitol 2508		Come Home (Little Girl) / Guess Who	1969	2.00	10.00

SIXPENCE
Sixpence later recorded as The Strawberry Alarm Clock.

Impact 1025		You're The Love / What To Do	1967	5.00	25.00
Brent 7062		Imitation Situation / Please Come Home	1967	4.00	20.00

SKARLETTONES, THE

Ember 1053		Do You Remember? / Will You Dream?	1959	20.00	100.00

Label & Catalog #	A-Side/B-Side	Year	VG	NM
SKEENE, DANNY, & THE RICQUETTES				
Valex 106	Over The Rainbow / Seven Days	195?	15.00	75.00
SKEL, BOBBY				
Soft 826	Kiss And Run / Say It Now	1964	1.25	6.00
SKELTON, EDDIE				
Starday 294	My Heart Gets Lonely / Let Me Be With You Forever	1957	15.00	75.00
Dixie 2011	Keep It Swinging / Without You	1958	——	——
	(Rare. Estimated near mint value $500-1,000.)			
SKIDMORE, BILL				
Crest 1040	Date Bait / I'm Out Of My Mind	1960	2.00	10.00
SKIP				
Bolo 712/3	Come On Here To Me / Searching For Linda	196?	4.00	20.00
SKIP & FLIP				
Clyde "Skip" Battin and Gary "Flip" Paxton, who also recorded as Gary & Clyde.				
Brent 7002	It Was I / Lunch Hour	1959	3.00	15.00
Brent 7005	Fancy Nancy / It Could Be	1959	2.00	10.00
Brent 7010	Cherry Pie / Cryin' Over You	1960	2.00	10.00
Brent 7013	Teenage Honeymoon / Hully Gully Cha Cha Cha	1960	2.00	10.00
Brent 7017	Willow Tree / Green Door	1961	2.00	10.00
Time 1031	Betty Jean / Doubt	1960	2.00	10.00
California 2325	Tossin' And Turnin' / Everyday I Have To Cry	1963	2.00	10.00
SKIP & THE HUSTLERS				
Invicta 9001	Dance Of The Sand Flea / In The Soup	196?	8.00	40.00
SKIPPY & THE HI-LITES				
Streamlite 1027	Waiting To Take You Home / Old Man River	195?	10.00	50.00
SKUNKS, THE				
U.S.A. 865	Elvira / The Journey	1967	1.60	8.00
Teen Town 103	I Recommend Her / I Need No One	1968	1.60	8.00
Teen Town 106	Small Town Girl / You Better Hold On To Me	1968	1.60	8.00
Teen Town 110	Doing Nothing / Listen To The News Today	1969	1.60	8.00
White Whale	Doing Nothing / Listen To The News Today	1969	1.00	5.00
World Pacific 77889	I Recommend Her / I Need No One	1969	.80	4.00
SKY				
RCA Victor 74-0419	Goodie Two Shoes / Make It In Time	1971	.60	3.00
RCA Victor 74-0611	Let It Lie Low / Taking The Long Way Home	1972	.60	3.00
SKYLARKS, THE				
Admiral 500	I'll Surf Around The World / How Many Times?	1963	7.00	35.00
SKYLINE DRIVE				
Revue 11043	Tonight Could Be The Night-Little Darlin' / Make It To Spain	196?	1.20	6.00
SKYLINERS, THE				
The Skyliners feature Jimmy Beaumont.				
Calico 103/4	Since I Don't Have You / One Night, One Night	1959	4.00	20.00
Calico 106	This I Swear / Tomorrow	1959	4.00	20.00
Calico 109	It Happened Today / Lonely Way	1959	4.00	20.00
Calico 114	How Much? / Lorraine From Spain	1960	4.00	20.00
Calico 117	Pennies From Heaven / I'll Be Seeing You	1960	4.00	20.00
Calico 120	Believe Me / Happy Time	1960	3.00	15.00
Colpix 188	The Door Is Still Open / I'll Close My Eyes	1960	7.00	35.00
Colpix 607	The End Of The Story / Baion Rhythms	1961	5.00	25.00
Colpix 613	Close Your Eyes / Our Love Will Last	1961	8.00	40.00
Cameo 215	Everyone But You / Three Coins In The Fountain	1960	5.00	25.00
Viscount 104	Comes Love / Tell Me	1962	3.00	15.00
Atco 6270	Since I Fell For You / I'd Die	1963	5.00	25.00
Original Sound 35	Since I Don't Have You / One Night, One Night	196?	2.00	10.00
Original Sound 36	Pennies From Heaven / I'll Be Seeing You	196?	2.00	10.00
Original Sound 37	This I Swear / It Happened Today	196?	2.00	10.00
Jubilee 5506	The Loser / Everything Is Fine	1965	2.00	10.00
Jubilee 5512	Get Yourself A Baby / Who Do You Love?	1966	2.00	10.00
Jubilee 5520	Don't Hurt Me, Baby / I Run To You	1966	3.00	15.00
Tortoise Inter. 11343	Oh, How Happy / We've Got Love On Our Side	1978	1.50	8.00
SKYLITERS, THE				
Scotte 2667	Call It A Night / Wild Cherry	1963	7.00	35.00
Scotte 2666	Tidal Wave / Schroeder Walk	1963	7.00	35.00

Label & Catalog #		A-Side/B-Side	Year	VG	NM

SLADE: *Refer to* **THE IN-BE-TWEENS**

SLADES, THE

Domino 500		You Cheated / The Waddle	1959	8.00	40.00
Domino 800		You Gambled / No Time	1959	3.00	15.00
Domino 901		Just You / It's Better To Love	1959	3.00	15.00
Domino 906		It's Tour Turn / Take my Heart	1959	3.00	15.00
Domino 1000		You Must Try / Summertime	1959	3.00	15.00
Liberty 55118		You Mean Everything To Me / Baby	1959	3.00	15.00
		(Label misprint credits "The Spades.")			
Liberty 55118		You Mean Everything To Me / Baby	1959	4.00	20.00

SLED, BOB, & THE TOBOGGANS
Bob Sled is reputedly one Bruce Johnston.

| Cameo 400 | (DJ) | Here We Go (The Surfer Boys Are Going Skiing) / Sea & Ski | 1966 | 5.00 | 25.00 |
| Cameo 400 | | Here We Go (The Surfer Boys Are Going Skiing) / Sea & Ski | 1966 | 10.00 | 50.00 |

SLLEDNATS, THE: *Refer to* **THE STANDELLS**

SLOAN, P.F. [PHIL SLOAN]
Phil Sloan also recorded as or with—usually paired with Steve Barri—The Fantastic Baggys; The Grass Roots; The Imaginations; The Inner Circles; Jan & Dean; The Lifeguards; The Rally Packs; The Rincoln Surfside Band; The Street Cleaners; and Willie & The Wheels.

Mart 802		She's My Girl / If You Believe In Me	196?	4.00	20.00
Dunhill 4007		The Sins Of A Family / This Mornin'	1965	2.00	10.00
Dunhill 4016		Halloween Mary / I'd Have To Be Out Of My Mind	1965	2.00	10.00
Dunhill 4016	(PS)	Halloween Mary (Promo picture sleeve)	1965	3.00	15.00
Dunhill 4024	(DJ)	From A Distance / Patterns, Seg. 4	1966	2.00	10.00
Dunhill 4024		From A Distance / Patterns, Seg. 4	1966	3.00	15.00
Dunhill 4054		I Found A Girl / A Melody For You	1966	2.00	10.00
Dunhill 4060	(DJ)	Karma / I Can't Help But Wonder	1967	2.00	10.00
Dunhill 4060		Karma / I Can't Help But Wonder	1967	3.00	15.00
Dunhill 4064	(DJ)	Sunflower, Sunflower / The Man Behind The Red Balloon	1967	2.00	10.00
Dunhill 4064		Sunflower, Sunflower / The Man Behind The Red Balloon	1967	3.00	15.00
Dunhill 4064	(PS)	Sunflower, Sunflower / The Man Behind The Red Balloon	1967	4.00	20.00
Atco 6663	(DJ)	New Design / Star Gazin'	1968	2.00	10.00
Atco 6663		New Design / Star Gazin'	1968	3.00	15.00
Mums	(DJ)	Let Me Be / Springtime	1972	2.00	10.00
Mums		Let Me Be / Springtime	1972	4.00	20.00
		—Extended Play Albums—			
Atco 268	(33)	Measure Of Pleasure (Jukebox EP)	1968	6.00	30.00

SLOOPYS, THE

| Sidewalk 918 | | Wait, Johnny, For Me / Gonna Give You Back Your Diamond Ring | 1968 | 2.00 | 10.00 |

SMACK

| Garland 2015 | | Suzie Q / Hit The Road, Jack | 196? | 1.00 | 5.00 |

SMALL FACES, THE [THE FACES]
Original members include Kenny Jones, Ronnie Lane, Steve Marriott and Jimmy Winston, who was replaced by Ian McLagen in 1965; Marriott left in '68. In 1969, Rod Stewart and Ron Wood joined and the group became The Faces. Warner Bros. 8066 and 8102 credit Rod Stewart & The Faces. Refer to Jeff Beck; The Who.

Press 9794		Whatcha Gonna Do About It / What's The Matter Baby '66	1966	5.00	25.00
Press 9826		Sha-La-La-La-Lee / Grow Your Own	1966	3.00	15.00
RCA Victor 47-8949		All Or Nothing / Understanding	1966	4.00	20.00
RCA Victor 47-8949	(PS)	All Or Nothing / Understanding	1966	10.00	50.00
RCA Victor 47-9055		My Mind's Eye / I Can't Dance With You	1966	4.00	20.00
Immediate 501		Itchykoo Park / I'm Only Dreaming	1967	2.00	10.00
Immediate 1902		Here Comes The Nice / Talk To You	1967	2.00	10.00
Immediate 5003		Tin Soldier / I Feel Much Better	1968	2.00	10.00
Immediate 5003	(PS)	Tin Soldier / I Feel Much Better	1968	5.00	25.00
Immediate 5007		Rollin' Over / Lazy Sunday	1968	2.00	10.00
Immediate 5009		Universal / Donkey Rides	1968	2.50	12.00
Immediate 5012		Mad John / The Journey	1968	2.50	12.00
Immediate 5014		Afterglow Of Your Love / Wham Bam, Thank You, Ma'am	1968	3.00	15.00
Press 5007		Hey Girl / Almost Grown	1968	4.00	20.00
Warner Bros. 7442	(PS)	Had Me A Real Good Time / Had Me A Real Good Time, Part 2 (Promo)	1970	2.00	10.00
Warner Bros. 7442		Had Me A Real Good Time / Had Me A Real Good Time, Part 2	1970	.80	4.00
Warner Bros. 7483		Maybe I'm Amazed / Oh Lord, I'm Browned Off	1971	.60	3.00
Warner Bros. 7545		Stay With Me / You're So Rude	1971	.60	3.00
Warner Bros. 7681	(PS)	Cindy Incidentally (Promo picture sleeve)	1973	2.00	10.00
Warner Bros. 7681		Cindy Incidentally / Skewiff (Mend The Fuse)	1973	.60	3.00
Warner Bros. 7681	(PS)	Cindy Incidentally / Skewiff (Mend The Fuse)	1973	.60	3.00
Warner Bros. 7711		Ooh-La-La / Borstal Boys	1973	.60	3.00

Label & Catalog #		A-Side/B-Side	Year	VG	NM
Warner Bros. 8066		You Can Make Me Dance, Sing Or Anything / As Long As You Tell Him	1974	.60	3.00
Warner Bros. 8102		You Can Make Me Dance, Sing Or Anything / As Long As You Tell Him	1975	.60	3.00
SMART TONES, THE					
Herald 529		Ginny / Bob-O-Link	1958	20.00	100.00
SMILE					
Smile later recorded as Queen.					
Mercury 72977	(DJ)	Earth / Step On Me (Stock copies of Mercury 72977 may not exist.)	1968	40.00	200.00
SMITH					
Smith features Gayle McCormick.					
Dunhill 4206		Baby, It's You / I Don't Believe (I Believe)	1969	.80	4.00
Dunhill 4206	(PS)	Baby, It's You / I Don't Believe (I Believe)	1969	1.00	5.00
Dunhill 4228		Take A Look Around / Mojalesky Ridge	1970	.60	3.00
Dunhill 4238		What Am I Gonna Do? / Born In Boston	1970	.60	3.00
Dunhill 4246		Goin' Back To Me / Minus Plus	1970	.60	3.00
SMITH, ARLENE					
Spectorious 150		Good Girls / Everything	196?	20.00	100.00
Big Top 3073		Love, Love, Love / He Knows I Love Him Too Much	1962	2.00	10.00
SMITH, BOB					
Bob Smith also recorded as The Thorndike Pickledish (Pacifist Choir).					
Yonah 2003		Poetry Readings In The Bathroom / The Interview With Mrs. Malooka	1963	4.00	20.00
SMITH, BOBBIE, & THE DREAM GIRLS					
Refer to The Dream Girls.					
Big Top 3085		Mr. Fine / Wanted	1961	3.00	15.00
Big Top 3100		Duchess Of Earl / Mine, All Mine	1962	4.00	20.00
Big Top 3111		Here Comes Baby / I Get A Feeling, My Love	1962	3.00	15.00
Big Top 3129		Your Lovey Dovey Ways / Now He's Gone	1962	3.00	15.00
SMITH, DALE, & THE GOOD SISTERS					
Bolo 726		When Christmas Bells Are Ringing / Christmas Glory	196?	.60	3.00
SMITH, HURRICANE					
Capitol 3383		Oh Babe, What Would You Say? / Getting To Know You	1972	.80	4.00
Capitol 3455		Who Was It? / Take Suki Home	1973	.60	3.00
EMI 3809		Beautiful Day, Beautiful Night / Sam	1974	.60	3.00
SMITH, JENNIE					
RCA Victor PJ-340	(DJ)	We'll Be Together / He's My Guy	1957	3.00	15.00
RCA Victor PJ-340	(PS)	We'll Be Together / He's My Guy	1957	6.00	30.00
Canadian American 150		(I Won't) Go Away, Little Boy / Let It Be Me	1963	1.60	8.00
SMITH, LENDON, & THE JESTERS					
Meteor 5030		Lost Love / Women	1956	15.00	75.00
SMITH, LEON, & THE BASICS					
Refer to Jackie Johnson; Jesse Robertson.					
Willamette 101		Little Ford / Once I Had A Heart	1959	7.00	35.00
Willamette 105		Honey Honey / That's The Way	196?	3.00	15.00
Willamette 109		Flip, Flop And Fly / Sweet Love	196?	3.00	15.00
Epic 9326		Little 40 Ford / Cry All The Time	196?	6.00	30.00
Lavender 1851		Basic Surf / Jailer Bring Me Water	196?	6.00	30.00
SMITH, MACK ALLEN					
Ace 3011		King Of Rock And Roll / Lonely Street	1975	2.00	10.00
SMITH, MELVIN					
Cameo 135		Open The Door, Richard / Zaki Sue	1958	2.00	10.00
Smash 1775		Ugly George / Nobody's Fault	1962	2.00	10.00
SMITH, PATTI					
Mer 601		Hey, Joe / Piss Factory	1974	20.00	100.00
Arista 0171		Gloria / My Generation	1976	1.00	5.00
Arista 0171	(PS)	Gloria / My Generation	1976	2.00	10.00
Sire 1009		Hey, Joe / Piss Factory	1977	2.00	10.00
Sire 1009	(PS)	Hey, Joe / Piss Factory	1977	3.00	15.00
Arista 0318		Because The Night / God Speed	1978	.40	2.00
Arista 0318	(PS)	Because The Night / God Speed	1978	.40	2.00
Arista 0427		Frederick / Frederick	1979	.40	2.00
Arista 0427	(PS)	Frederick / Frederick	1979	.40	2.00

Label & Catalog #		A-Side/B-Side	Year	VG	NM
Arista 0453		So You Want To Be A Rock 'N' Roll Star / 5-4-3-2-1	1979	.40	2.00
Arista 0453	(PS)	So You Want To Be A Rock 'N' Roll Star / 5-4-3-2-1	1979	.40	2.00

SMITH, RAY

Heart 250		Gone Baby, Gone /	1958	----	----
		(Rare. Estimated near mint value $500-1,000.)			
Sun 298		Right Behind You, Baby / So Young	1958	3.00	15.00
Sun 308		Why, Why, Why? / You Made A Hit	1958	3.00	15.00
Sun 319		Rockin' Bandit / Sail Away	1959	3.00	15.00
Sun 372		Travelin' Salesman / I Won't Miss You (Til You're Gone)	1962	3.00	15.00
Sun 375		Candy Doll / Hey, Boss Man	1962	3.00	15.00
Judd 1016		Rockin' Little Angel / That's All Right	1960	3.00	15.00
Judd 1017		Put Your Arms Around Me, Honey / Maria Elena	1960	3.00	15.00
Judd 1019		One Wonderful Love / Makes Me Feel Good	1960	3.00	15.00
Judd 1021		Blonde Hair, Blues Eyes / You Don't Want Me	1961	3.00	15.00
Smash 1787		Room 503 / Those Four Precious Years	1962	2.00	10.00
Zirkon 1055		Turn On The Moonlight / After This Night Is Through	1962	2.00	10.00
Infinity 003		Turn On The Moonlight / After This Night Is Through	1962	2.00	10.00
Infinity 007		Let Yourself Go / Johnny The Hummer	1962	2.00	10.00
Toppa 1071		Almost Alone / A Place Within My Heart	1962	3.00	15.00
Tollie 9029		Did We Have A Party? / Here Comes My Baby Back Again	1962	3.00	15.00
Warner Bros. 5371		Turn Over A New Leaf / I'm Snowed	1963	2.00	10.00
Vee Jay 579		Robbin' The Cradle / Rockin' Robin	1964	3.00	15.00
Celebrity Circle 6901		I Walk The Line / Fool Number One	1964	2.00	10.00
Nu-Tone 1182		Deep In My Heart / She's Mine	1964	3.00	15.00
Diamond 193		Everybody's Goin' Somewhere / Au Go Go	1965	2.00	10.00
BC 351		I Guess I Better Move Along / Four Seasons Of My Life	196?	2.00	10.00
BC 4100		Walk On By / Did He Hurt You All That Bad?	196?	2.00	10.00
BC 7130		Let The Four Winds Blow / I'm In Love Again	196?	3.00	15.00

SMITH, RONNIE

Imperial 5679		I Hear You Knocking / I Started Out Walkin'	1960	5.00	25.00

SMITH, SHELBY

Rebel 728		Rockin' Mama / Since My Baby Said Goodbye	1962	50.00	250.00

SMITH, SNUFFY, & THE HOOTIN' HOLLER TWISTERS

Tempwood 1035		Snuffy Twister / Buffalo Twister	1962	2.00	10.00

SMITH, SUSAN

Dynamic Sound 502		A Letter From Susan / Will You Love Me When I'm Old?	1960	2.00	10.00
		(Produced by Buchanan & Goodman.)			

SMITH, VERDELLE

Capitol 5567		In My Room / Walk Tall	1966	1.00	5.00
Capitol 5632		Tar And Cement / Piece Of The Sky	1966	1.00	5.00

SMITH, WARREN

Sun 239		Rock 'N' Roll Ruby / I'd Rather Be Safe Than Sorry	1956	6.00	30.00
Sun 250		Ubangi Stomp / Black Jack David	1956	4.00	20.00
Sun 268		So Long, I'm Gone / Miss Froggie	1957	4.00	20.00
Sun 286		I've Got Love If You Want It / I Fell In Love	1958	3.00	15.00
Sun 314		Sweet, Sweet Girl / Goodbye, Mr. Love	1959	4.00	20.00
Liberty 55248		Cave In / I Don't Believe I'll Fall In Love Today	1959	2.00	10.00
Liberty 55302		A Whole Lot Of Nothin' / Odds And Ends (Bits And Pieces)	1961	2.00	10.00
Liberty 55336		Old Lonesome Feeling / Call Of The Wild	1961	2.00	10.00
Liberty 55361		Why, Baby, Why? / Why I'm Walking	1961	2.00	10.00
Liberty 55409		Bad News Gets Around / Five Minutes Of The Latest Blues	1962	2.00	10.00
Liberty 55475		Book Of Broken Hearts / 160 Pounds Of Hurt	1963	2.00	10.00

SMITHEREENS, THE

Enigma 75002		Behind The Wall Of Sleep / Blood And Roses	1987	.80	4.00
Enigma 75003		In A Lonely Room / Blood And Roses	1987	.80	4.00
Capitol 44150		Only A Memory / The Sneeker	1988	.80	4.00
Capitol 44174	(PS)	House We Used To Live In / Only A Memory	1988	2.00	10.00
		(Unreleased single; the sleeve was used for foreign releases.)			
Capitol PRO-79842	(DJ)	A Girl Like You / A Girl Like You	1989	.60	3.00
		—12" Singles—			
Enigma EPRO-5	(DJ)	Blood And Roses / Blood And Roses	1986	1.60	8.00
Enigma EPRO-14	(DJ)	Behind The Wall Of Sleep / Behind The Wall Of Sleep	1986	1.60	8.00
Enigma EPRO-21	(DJ)	Behind The Wall Of Sleep / White Castle Blues / Behind The Wall Of Sleep	1986	1.60	8.00
Enigma EPRO-22	(DJ)	In A Lonely Place / In A Lonely Place	1986	1.60	8.00
Enigma EPRO-26	(DJ)	Time And Time Again / Time And Time Again	1986	1.60	8.00
Enigma 75501		In A Lonely Place / Behind The Wall Of Sleep / Beauty And Sadness	1987	1.20	6.00
Enigma 1T		In A Lonely Place / Blood And Roses / Beauty And Sadness / Mr. Eliminator	1987	1.20	6.00

Label & Catalog #		A-Side/B-Side	Year	VG	NM
Capitol SPRO-79270	(DJ)	Only A Memory / Only A Memory	1988	1.20	6.00
Capitol SPRO-79335	(DJ)	House We Used To Live In / House We Used To Live In	1988	1.20	6.00
		— Extended Play Albums—			
d-tone 150		Girls About Town	1980	2.00	10.00
Little Ricky 103		Beauty And Sadness (12")	1983	6.00	30.00
Enigma 73220		Beauty And Sadness (12")	1988	1.20	6.00
SMITHS, THE					
Columbia 44494		Now I Taste The Tears / I Can't Stop	1968	2.00	10.00
SMOKE RING					
Buddah 77		No, Not Much / How Did You Get To Be So Wonderful?	1969	.80	4.00
SMOKEY JO					
Refer to Bill Taylor.					
Flip 228		The Signifying Monkey / Listen To Me, Baby	1955	75.00	300.00
Sun 228		The Signifying Monkey / Listen To Me, Baby	1956	50.00	200.00
Sun 393		The Signifying Monkey / Listen To Me, Baby	1964	25.00	125.00
SMOKESTACK					
Daisy 101		There's A World Between Us / Take A Look	196?	2.00	10.00
Dakar 4503		There's A World Between Us / Take A Look	196?	1.20	6.00
SMOKESTACK LIGHTNIN'					
White Whale 243		Crossroads Blues / Nadine	1967	2.00	10.00
White Whale 256		Look What You've Done / Got A Good Love	1967	2.00	10.00
Bell 755		Light In My Window / Long Stemmed Eyes	1968	1.00	5.00
Bell 777		Something's Got A Hold On Me / I Idolize You	1969	1.00	5.00
Bell 836		Baby, Don't Get Crazy / The Blue Albino Shuffle	1969	1.00	5.00
Bell 861		Hello L.A., Bye Bye Birmingham / Well, Tuesday	1970	1.00	5.00
SNAKEFINGER [SNAKEFINGER'S VESTAL VIRGINS]					
Ralph 7805		The Spot / Smelly Tongues (Blue vinyl)	1976	.60	3.00
Ralph 7805	(PS)	The Spot / Smelly Tongues	1976	.60	3.00
Ralph 7907		Kill The Great Raven / What Wilbur?	1979	.60	3.00
Ralph 7907	(PS)	Kill The Great Raven / What Wilbur?	1979	.60	3.00
Ralph 8005		The Model / Talkin' In The Town	1980	.60	3.00
Ralph 8005	(PS)	The Model / Talkin' In The Town	1980	.60	3.00
Ralph 8051		Man In The Dark Sedan / Womb To Worm	1980	.60	3.00
Ralph 8051	(PS)	Man In The Dark Sedan / Womb To Worm	1980	.60	3.00
Ralph 8715		There's No Justice In Life / Move	1987	.60	3.00
Ralph 8715	(PS)	There's No Justice In Life / Move	1987	.60	3.00
Undergrowth 1303		I Gave Myself To You / (This Is Nota) Disco Song	198?	2.00	10.00
Undergrowth 1303	(PS)	I Gave Myself To You / (This Is Nota) Disco Song	198?	2.00	10.00
SNEED, BRADY & GRADY					
Dolton 38		Little Bitty Heart / Leavin' It All Up To You	1961	2.00	10.00
SNEED, LESLIE					
Cascade 103		Oh Baby Doll / (B-side By Don Earl & The Sneeds)	196?	2.00	10.00
SNEED FAMILY, THE					
Cascade 101		Date With An Angel / Stand Clear	196?	1.00	5.00
SNEEKERS, THE					
Columbia 43438		Soul Sneaker / Sneaker Talk	1965	2.00	10.00
Columbia 43438	(PS)	Soul Sneaker / Sneaker Talk	1965	4.00	20.00
SNEEZER, EBE, & THE EPIDEMICS					
Ebe Sneezer is a pseudonym for John D. Loudermilk.					
Colonial 436		That's All I've Got / Asiatic Flu	1957	3.00	15.00
SNIDER, LEN, & THE JOKERS					
All Boy 8507		Everyone Knows / I'll Be Coming Home Tonight	196?	2.00	10.00
SNO-FLAKES, THE					
Hi-Note 183		Joey The Snowy Snowflake / Jingle Bells	196?	2.00	10.00
SNOW, EDDIE					
Sun 226		Ain't That Right? / Bring Your Love Back Home	1955	20.00	100.00
SNOW MEN, THE					
The Snow Men later recorded as The Sunrays.					
Challenge 59227		Ski Storm / Ski Storm, Part 2	1963	5.00	25.00
SNOWMEN, THE					
The Snowmen is a pseudonym for The Concords.					
Dot 16540		Cold And Frosty Morning / You Started It	1963	4.00	20.00

Label & Catalog #	A-Side/B-Side	Year	VG	NM
SOCIETY GIRLS, THE				
Vee Jay 524	S.P.C.L.G. (Society For The Prevention Of Cruelty To Little Girls) / You Better Stay Home	1963	2.00	10.00
SOCIETY'S CHILDREN				
Atco 6538	White Christmas / I'll Let You Know	1967	2.00	10.00
Atco 6597	Live For Today / I'll Let You Know	1968	2.00	10.00
Atco 6618	A Tribute To The Four Seasons / Golden Child	1968	3.00	15.00
SOFTWINDS, THE				
Hac 105	Cross My Heart / Oh, Baby	1961	4.00	20.00
SOLOMON, ED				
Diamond 160	Beatle Flying Saucer / Whistling Drifter	1964	3.00	15.00
SOMETHING WILD				
Psychedelic 1691	Trippin' Out / She's Kinda Weird	1966	8.00	40.00
SOMMERS, RONNY				
Ronny Sommers is a pseudonym for Sonny Bono.				
Swami 1001	Don't Shake My Tree / (Mama) Come Get Your Baby Boy	1961	2.00	10.00
SONG				
MGM 14151	Like We Were Before / Sugar Lady	1970	.80	4.00
SONICS, THE				
The Sonics also recorded with Jim Brady.				
Etiquette 11	The Witch / Keep A Knockin'	1964	3.00	15.00
Etiquette 16	Boss Hoss / The Hustler	1965	5.00	25.00
Etiquette 18	Shot Down / Don't Be Afraid Of The Dark	1965	3.00	15.00
Etiquette 22	Don't Believe In Christmas / (B-side by The Wailers)	1966	6.00	30.00
Etiquette 23	Louie Louie / Cinderella	1966	3.00	15.00
Jerden 809	Love Lights / You Got Your Head On Backwards	1966	2.00	10.00
Jerden 810	The Witch / Like No Other Man	1966	2.00	10.00
Jerden 811	Psycho / Maintaining My Cool	1966	2.00	10.00
Uni 55039	Anyway The Way The Wind Blows / Lost Love	1967	4.00	20.00
Piccadilly 244	Anyway The Way The Wind Blows / Lost Love	1967	3.00	15.00
	("Anyway The Way The Wind Blows" is a Frank Zappa composition.)			
Burdette 106	Dirty Old Man / Bama Lama Bama Loo	1975	1.00	5.00
Great Northwest 702	The Witch / Bama Lama Bama Loo	1979	.80	4.00
SONNY [SONNY BONO]				
Salvatore Bono, who also recorded as Don Christy; Don & Dewey; and Ronny Sommers.				
Highland 160	I'll Change / Try It Out On Me	196?	5.00	25.00
Vee Jay 710	Midnight Run / Ride The Wild Quetzel	1965	3.00	15.00
Specialty 733	Comin' Down The Chimney / One Little Answer	1965	4.00	20.00
Atco 6369	Laugh At Me / Gip Pony	1965	1.00	5.00
Atco 6386	The Revolution Kind / Georgia And John Quetzal	1966	1.00	5.00
Atco 6531	My Best Friend's Girl Is Out Of Sight / Pammie's On A Bummer	1967	1.20	6.00
MCA 40139	Laugh At Me / Rub Your Nose	197?	.60	3.00
MCA 40271	Classified 1A / Our Last Show	197?	.60	3.00
SONNY & CHER				
Salvatore Bono and Cherilyn LaPier, who originally recorded as Caesar & Cleo. Refer to Hale & The Hushabyes.				
Vault 916	The Letter / Spring Fever	1963	3.00	15.00
Vault 916 (PS)	The Letter / Spring Fever	1963	8.00	40.00
Reprise 0309	Baby Don't Go / Walkin' The Quetzal	1964	3.00	15.00
Reprise 0392	Baby Don't Go / Walkin' The Quetzal	1965	2.00	10.00
Reprise 0392	Baby Don't Go / Love Is Strange	1965	1.20	6.00
Atco 6345	Just You / Sing C'est La Vie	1965	1.00	5.00
Atco 6359	I Got You, Babe / It's Gonna Rain	1965	1.00	5.00
Atco 6381	But You're Mine / Hello	1965	1.00	5.00
Atco 6395	What Now My Love / I Look For You	1966	1.00	5.00
Atco 6420	Have I Stayed Too Long? / Leave Me Be	1966	1.00	5.00
Atco 6440	Little Man / Monday	1966	1.00	5.00
Atco 6449	Living For You / Love Don't Come	1966	1.00	5.00
Atco 6461	The Beat Goes On / Love Don't Come	1967	1.00	5.00
Atco 6480	A Beautiful Story / Podunk	1967	1.00	5.00
Atco 6486	Plastic Man / It's The Little Things	1967	1.00	5.00
Atco 6507	It's The Little Things / Don't talk To Strangers	1967	1.00	5.00
Atco 6541	Good Combination / You And Me	1967	1.00	5.00
Atco 6555	I Would Marry You Today / Circus	1968	1.00	5.00
Atco 6605	You Gotta Have A Thing Of Your Own / I Got You, Babe	1968	1.00	5.00
Atco 6683	You're A Friend Of Mine / I Would Marry You Today	1968	1.00	5.00
Atco 6758	Get It Together / Hold Me Tighter	1968	1.00	5.00
Kapp 2141	Real People / Somebody	1971	.40	2.00
Kapp 2151	All I Ever Need Is You / I Got You, Babe	1971	.40	2.00

Label & Catalog #		A-Side/B-Side	Year	VG	NM
Kapp 2163		A Cowboy's Work Is Never Done / Somebody	1972	.40	2.00
Kapp 2176		When You Say Love / Crystal Clear Muddy Water	1972	.40	2.00
Warner Bros. 8341		You're Not Right For Me / Wrong Number	197?	.40	2.00
MCA 40026		Mama Was A Rock And Roll Singer, Papa Used To Write All Her Songs /	1973	.40	2.00
MCA 40083		The Greatest Show On Earth / You Know Darn Well	1973	.40	2.00
		—Extended Play Albums—			
Reprise 0392	(33)	Baby Don't Go (Jukebox EP)	1967	7.00	35.00

SONNY & JOYCE

| Ember 1034 | | Mister Froggie / You Keep Doggin' Me | 1958 | 5.00 | 25.00 |

SONS OF ADAM

Sons of Adam slso recorded as The New Wing.

Alamo		Baby Show The World / Feathered Fish	196?	7.00	35.00
Alamo		Take My Hand / Tomorrow's Gonna Be Another Day	196?	6.00	30.00
Pentacle 101		The Thinking Animal / My Petite	196?	5.00	25.00
Decca 31887		Take My Hand / Tomorrow's Gonna Be Another Day	1965	3.00	15.00
Decca 31995		You're A Better Man Than I / Saturday's Son	1966	3.00	15.00
		(The Decca sides were produced by Gary Usher.)			

SONS OF CHAMPLIN, THE

Verve 10500		Sing Me A Rainbow / Fat City	1967	2.00	10.00
Capitol 4668	(DJ)	Jesus Is Coming / Jesus Is Coming (Part 2)	1968	2.00	10.00
Capitol 4668	(PS)	Jesus Is Coming / Jesus Is Coming (Part 2)	1968	8.00	40.00
		(Compact-33 give-away mail-order promoting their first Capitol album.)			
Capitol 2437		Black And Blue Rainbow / 1982-A	1969	1.00	5.00
Capitol 2534		Freedom / Hello, Sunlight	1969	1.00	5.00
Capitol 2663		It's Time / Why Do People Run?	1969	1.00	5.00
Columbia 45872		Welcome To The Dance / Swim	1973	.80	4.00
Goldmine 101		Lookout / Lookout	1976	.80	4.00
Ariola America 7606		Lookout / Lookout	1976	.40	2.00
Ariola America 7626		Hold On / Still In Love With You	1976	.40	2.00
Ariola America 7633		Imagination's Sake / You	1976	.40	2.00
Ariola America 7653		Here Is Where Your Love Belongs / Follow Your Heart	1976	.40	2.00
Ariola America 7664		Saved By The Grace Of Your Love / West End	1977	.40	2.00

SOOTZ, MANNY

| Pirate 841 | | Cape Canaveral / Cape Canaveral (Part 2) | 1957 | 4.00 | 20.00 |

SOPHISTICATES, THE

| Viva 61 | | When Elvis Comes Marching Home / Woody's Place | 1960 | 7.00 | 35.00 |

SOPHISTICATES, THE

The Sophisticates also recorded with Ed Shields.

| Souvenir 1005 | | Flamingo / Caravan | 196? | 1.00 | 5.00 |

SOPWITH CAMEL, THE

Kama Sutra 217		Hello, Hello / Treadin'	1966	2.00	10.00
Kama Sutra 224		Postcard From Jamaica / Little Orphan Annie	1967	2.00	10.00
Kama Sutra 224	(PS)	Postcard From Jamaica / Little Orphan Annie	1967	4.00	20.00
Kama Sutra 236		Saga Of The Lowdown Let Down / The Great Morpheum	1967	2.00	10.00
Kama Sutra 236	(PS)	Saga Of The Lowdown Let Down / The Great Morpheum	1967	5.00	25.00

SORENSON BROTHERS, THE

| Marlinda 7507/8 | | They've Landed / Stowaway | 196? | 7.00 | 35.00 |

SOUL, DAVID

MGM 13510		I Will Warm Your Heart / Covered Man	1966	.80	4.00
MGM 13589		Was I Ever So Young? / Before	1966	.80	4.00
MGM 13842		No One's Gonna Cry / Quiet Kind Of Hate	1967	.80	4.00
Private Stock 45129		Don't Give Up On Us / Black Bean Soup	1977	.40	2.00
Private Stock 45150		Going In With My Eyes Open / Topanga	1977	.40	2.00
Private Stock 45163		Silver Lady / Rider	1977	.40	2.00

SOUL POTION, THE

| Sunburst 524 | | Circle Full Of Love / Soul Baby | 196? | 4.00 | 20.00 |

SOUL SURFERS, THE

| Challenge 59246 | | Cannonball / (B-side by Jerry Wallace) | 1964 | 3.00 | 15.00 |
| Challenge 59267 | | Home From Camp / (B-side by The Delicates) | 1964 | 3.00 | 15.00 |

SOUL SURVIVORS, THE

| Dot 16793 | | Can't Stand To Be In Love With You / Look At Me | 1966 | 4.00 | 20.00 |
| Dot 16830 | | Snow Man / Hung Up On Losing | 1966 | 1.50 | 8.00 |

SOUL SURVIVORS, THE

| Decca 32080 | | Devil With A Blue Dress On / Shakin' With Linda | 1967 | 3.00 | 15.00 |

Label & Catalog #	A-Side/B-Side	Year	VG	NM
Crimson 1010	Expressway To Your Heart / Hey Gyp	1967	2.00	10.00
Crimson 1012	Explosion In Your Soul / Dathon's Theme	1967	1.60	8.00
Crimson 1016	Impossible Mission / Poor Man's Dream	1968	1.60	8.00
Atco 6627	Turn Out The Fire / Go Out Walking	1968	1.20	6.00
Atco 6650	Tell Daddy / Mama Soul	1968	1.20	6.00
Atco 6735	Still Got My Head / Tempting 'Bout To get Me	1969	1.20	6.00
SOUND COMPANY, THE				
Garland 2023	Searchin' For The Green Grass / Hey Baby	196?	2.00	10.00
SOUND FARM LTD., THE				
AMH 169	Little Witch / Sunshine In Your Smile	196?	3.00	15.00
SOUND MACHINE, THE				
Canterbury 511	Gotta Ease My Mind / Spanish Flash	1967	2.00	10.00
SOUND TRIP				
Piece 1011	Someday / Skies Above	196?	2.00	10.00
SOUND VENDOR				
Liquid Stereo 25	In Paradise / Mr. Sun	196?	2.00	10.00
Ridon 857	It's Snowing / She Knows	196?	2.00	10.00
SOUNDS OF HARLEY, THE				
MGM 14248	The Hard Ride / Victorville Blues	1971	5.00	25.00
	("The Hard Ride " features Davie Allan on lead guitar.)			
SOUR TONES, THE				
Terri Ann 100	Desafinado (Completely Out Of Tune) / Sour Georgia Brown	1962	2.00	10.00
SOUTH, JOE				
NRC 5000	The Purple People Eater Meets The Witch Doctor / My Fondest Memories	1958	3.00	15.00
NRC 5001	One Fool To Another / Texas Ain't The Biggest Anymore	1958	3.00	15.00
NRC 5002	I'm Snowed / It's Only You	1958	5.00	25.00
Fairlane 21006	You're The Reason / Jukebox	1961	2.00	10.00
Fairlane 21010	I'm Sorry For You / The Masquerade	1961	2.00	10.00
Fairlane 21015	Slippin' Around / Just To Be With You Again	1961	2.00	10.00
Allwood 402	Just Remember You're Mine / Silly Me	1962	2.00	10.00
MGM 13145	Same Old Song / Standing Invitation	1963	2.00	10.00
MGM 13196	Concrete Jungle / Last One To Know	1963	2.00	10.00
MGM 13276	Naughty Claudie / Little Queenie	1964	2.00	10.00
Apt 25084	I've Got To Be Somebody / Deep Inside Me	1965	2.00	10.00
Columbia 43893	Backfield In Motion / I'll Come Back To You	1967	.80	4.00
Columbia 44218	Fool In Love / Great Day	1967	.80	4.00
Capitol 2060	Birds Of A Feather / It Got Away	1967	.80	4.00
Capitol 2169	How Can I Unlove You? / She's Almost You	1968	.80	4.00
Capitol 2248	Games People Play / Mirror Of Your Mind	1968	.80	4.00
Capitol 2284	Don't Throw Your Love To The Wind / Redneck	1968	.80	4.00
A&M 922	Yo Yo / Naughty Claudie	1968	1.00	5.00
Capitol 2491	Leanin' On You / Don't You Be Ashamed	1969	.80	4.00
Capitol 2532	Birds Of A Feather / These Are Not My People	1969	.80	4.00
Capitol 2592	Don't It Make You Want To Go Home? / Heart's Desire	1969	.80	4.00
Capitol 2704	Walk A Mile In My Shoes / Shelter	1970	.80	4.00
Capitol 2755	Children / Clock Up On The Wall	1970	.60	3.00
Capitol 2916	Why Does A Man Do What He Has To Do? / Be A Believer	1970	.80	4.00
Capitol 3204	Fool Me / Devil May Care	1971	.60	3.00
Capitol 3497	I'm A Star / Misunderstanding	1972	.60	3.00
Capitol 3554	Save Your Best / Real Thing	1973	.60	3.00
Capitol 3717	It Hurts Me, Too / Riverdog	1973	.60	3.00
SOUTH, JOE, & THE DELLS				
Starday 8022	Freight Train Boogie / Blues Stay Away From Me	1971	1.00	5.00
SOUTHBOUND FREEWAY				
Roulette 4739	Psychedelic Used Car Lot / Southbound Freeway	1967	3.00	15.00
SOUTHERN COMFORT				
Cotillion 44043	Don't Take Your Sweet Love Away / Milk And Honey	1969	.80	4.00
Capitol 3133	I Sure Like Your Smile / Return To Frog City	1971	.60	3.00
Capitol 3271	River Woman / Cosmic Jig	1972	.60	3.00
SOUTHERN, JOHNNY				
Liberty 55482	In The Middle Of A Lonely, Lonely Night / I Will Get By	1962	2.00	10.00
SOUTHWEST F.O.B.				
GPC 1945	Smell Of Incense / Green Skies	1968	2.00	10.00
Hip 8002	Smell Of Incense / Green Skies	1968	1.60	8.00

Label & Catalog #		A-Side/B-Side	Year	VG	NM
Hip 8009		All One Big Game / Nadine	1968	1.20	6.00
Hip 8022		Feelin' Groovy / Beggar Man	1969	1.20	6.00
SOUVENIRS, THE					
Inferno 2001		I Could Have Danced All Night / It's Too Bad	195?	10.00	50.00
SPACE MAN & THE SATELLITES					
Chess 1789		Man In Orbit / Blast Off	1961	2.00	10.00
SPACEMEN, THE					
Alton 254		The Clouds / The Lonely Jet Pilot	1959	2.00	10.00
Felsted 8578		Blast Off / Jersey Bounce	1959	3.00	15.00
Jubilee 53689		Round Up / Cinderella's Parade	1959	2.00	10.00
Markey 100		Venus Twist / Orbital Twist	1962	2.00	10.00
SPADES, THE: *Refer to* THE SLADES					
SPADES, THE					
The Spades later recorded as The Thirteenth Floor Elevators.					
Zero 10002		You're Gonna Miss Me / We Sell Soul	1966	75.00	300.00
SPAIN, DICK, WITH THE ROGUE VALLEY BOYS					
Oasis 1001		Straw Broom Boogie / Candy Heart	195?	8.00	40.00
SPAK, EMIL (WITH THE ENCORES)					
WGW 3004		Hold Up / Stuck Up	195?	7.00	35.00
SPANDELLS, THE					
Dimension 1041		Say No, Girl / The Boy Next Door	1965	2.00	10.00
SPANKY & OUR GANG					
Mercury 72679		Sunday Will Never Be The Same / Distance	1967	.80	4.00
Mercury 72714		Making Every Minute Count / If You Could Only Be Me	1967	.80	4.00
Mercury 72714	(PS)	Making Every Minute Count / If You Could Only Be Me	1967	1.00	5.00
Mercury 72732		Lazy Day / Byrd Avenue	1967	.80	4.00
Mercury 72732	(PS)	Lazy Day / Byrd Avenue	1967	1.00	5.00
Mercury 72765		Sunday Morning / Echoes	1967	.80	4.00
Mercury 72765	(PS)	Sunday Morning / Echoes	1967	1.00	5.00
Mercury 72795		Like To Get To Know You / Three Ways From Tomorrow	1968	.80	4.00
Mercury 72795	(PS)	Like To Get To Know You / Three Ways From Tomorrow	1968	1.00	5.00
Mercury 72831		Give A Damn / Swinging Gate	1968	.80	4.00
Mercury 72831	(PS)	Give A Damn / Swinging Gate	1968	1.00	5.00
Mercury 72871		Yesterday's Rain / Without Rhyme Or Reason	1968	.80	4.00
Mercury 72871	(PS)	Yesterday's Rain / Without Rhyme Or Reason	1968	1.00	5.00
Mercury 72890		Anything You Choose / Mecca Flats Blues	1969	.80	4.00
Mercury 72926		And She's Mine / Leopard Skin Phones	1969	.80	4.00
Mercury 72982		Everybody's Talkin' /	1969	.80	4.00
		—Extended Play Albums—			
Mercury MEP-90	(DJ)	Spanky & Our Gang Radio Special	1969	5.00	25.00
SPARKLES, THE					
Hickory 1443		No Friend Of Mine / First Forget (What Has Made You Blue)	1967	4.00	20.00
Hickory 1474		I Want To Be Free / Hipsville 29 B.C.	1967	3.00	15.00
SPARKLETONES, THE: *Refer to* JOE BENNETT					
SPARKS					
Bearsville 006		Wonder Girl / (No More) Mr. Nice Guys	1972	1.00	5.00
Island 001		This Town Ain't Big Enough For Both Of Us / Barbecutie	1974	.60	3.00
Island 009		Talent Is An Asset / Lost And Found	1974	.60	3.00
Island 009	(PS)	Talent Is An Asset / Lost And Found	1974	.80	4.00
Island 023		Achoo / Something For The Girl With Everything	1974	.60	3.00
Island 023	(PS)	Achoo / Something For The Girl With Everything	1974	.80	4.00
Island 043		Looks, Looks, Looks /			
		Wedding Of Jacqueline Kennedy To Russell Mael	1975	3.00	15.00
Island 8282		Hold Your Hand / England	1976	.60	3.00
Columbia 10579	(DJ)	Over The Summer / Forever Young	1978	.60	3.00
Columbia 10579		Over The Summer / Forever Young	1978	3.00	15.00
Elektra 46045		Tryouts For The Human Race / The #1 Song In Heaven	1979	.50	2.50
Atlantic 4030		I Predict / Moustache	1982	.50	2.50
Atlantic 4030	(PS)	I Predict / Moustache	1982	.50	2.50
Atlantic 4065		Eaten By The Monster Of Love / Mickey Mouse	1982	.50	2.50
Atlantic 89866		Cool Places / Sports	1983	.50	2.50
Atlantic 89866	(PS)	Cool Places / Sports	1983	.50	2.50
Atlantic 89797		All You Ever Think About Is Sex /			
		I Wished I Looked A Little Better	1983	.50	2.50
Atlantic 89797	(PS)	All You Ever Think About Is Sex /			
		I Wished I Looked A Little Better	1983	.50	2.50

Label & Catalog #		A-Side/B-Side	Year	VG	NM
Atlantic 89645		With All My Might / Sparks In The Dark	1984	.50	2.50
Atlantic 89645	(PS)	With All My Might / Sparks In The Dark	1984	.50	2.50
Atlantic 89616		Pretending To Be Drunk / Kiss Me Quick	1984	.50	2.50
Curb 52879		Music You Can Dance To / Shopping Mall Of Love	1986	.50	2.50

SPARROW, THE
Sparrow later recorded as Steppenwolf.

Columbia 43755	(PS)	Tomorrow's Ship (Promo picture sleeve)	1966	5.00	25.00
Columbia 43755		Tomorrow's Ship / Isn't It Strange?	1966	3.00	15.00
Columbia 43960		Green Bottle Lover / Down Goes Your Love Life	1967	3.00	15.00

SPARTANS, THE

| Web 1 | | Can You Waddle? / Can You Waddle? (Part 2) | 1962 | 2.00 | 10.00 |

SPARTANS, THE

| Princess 53 | | Mr. Moto / Chieflado | 1965 | 8.00 | 40.00 |
| | | *(Princess 53 was also released credited to The Challengers.)* | | | |

SPATS, THE

Enith 1268		Gator Tails And Monkey Ribs / The Roach	1964	3.00	15.00
ABC-Paramount 10585		Gator Tails And Monkey Ribs / The Roach	1964	2.00	10.00
ABC-Paramount 10600		There's A Party In The Pad Down Below / She Kissed Me Last Night	1964	2.00	10.00
ABC-Paramount 10640		Gotta Tell Ya All About It, Baby / Billy, The Blue Grasshopper	1965	2.00	10.00
ABC-Paramount 10711		Go Go Yamaha / Have You Seen Me Crying?	1965	4.00	20.00
ABC-Paramount 10790		Scoobee Doo / She Done Moved	1966	2.00	10.00

SPEARMINTS, THE

| Autumn 7 | | Jo-Ann / Little One | 1965 | 2.00 | 10.00 |

SPEARS, THE: *Refer to FRANKIE ERVIN*

SPECTOR, PHIL
Phil Spector's studio works place him at the pinnacle of creative producers and a direct influence on many '60s studio wizzes, notably Brian Wilson. The work he has done with various artists are collected for his production involvement; the list here is partial, as it does not include several R&B singers: The Alley Cats; The Blackwells; The Blossoms; Bobb B. Soxx & The Blue Jeans; Bonnie & The Treasures; The Castle Kings; Sonny Charles & The Checkmates; Cher; Cher & Nilsson; The Crystals; Derek & The Dominos; Dion; Steve Douglas; Jean Du Shon; The Ducanes; Connie Francis; Phil Harvey; Harvey & Doc; Karen Lake; Curtis Lee; Darlene Love; Kell Osborne; The Paris Sisters; Ray Peterson; Gene Pitney; The Righteous Brothers; The Ronettes; Arlene Smith; Bobby Sheen; Troy Shondell; The Spectors Three; The Teddy Bears; Gene Toone; Ike & Tina Turner.

SPECTOR, RONNIE
Ronnie also recorded as Veronica and with Ronnie & The Relative a.k.a. The Ronettes..

Apple P-1832	(DJ)	Try Some, Buy Some / Tandoori Chicken	1971	4.00	20.00
Apple 1832		Try Some, Buy Some / Tandoori Chicken	1971	1.60	8.00
Apple 1832	(PS)	Try Some, Buy Some / Tandoori Chicken	1971	2.00	10.00
Tom Cat 10380	(DJ)	You'd Be Good For Me / Something Tells Me (Blue vinyl)	197?	3.00	15.00
Tom Cat 10380		You'd Be Good For Me / Something Tells Me	197?	1.00	5.00
Warner/Spector 0409		When I Saw You / Paradise	1976	2.00	10.00
Cleve. Int. 50374		Say Goodbye To Hollywood / Baby Please Don't Go	1977	1.25	6.00
Cleve. Int. 50374	(PS)	Say Goodbye To Hollywood / Baby Please Don't Go	1977	3.00	15.00
Alston 3738		It's A Heartache / I Wanna Come Over	1978	.80	4.00
Polish 202		Darlin' / Tonight	197?	1.00	5.00

SPECTORS THREE, THE
The Spectors Three feature Phil Spector.

Trey 3001		I Really Do / I Know Why	1959	3.00	15.00
Trey 3001	(PS)	I Really Do / I Know Why	1959	5.00	25.00
Trey 3005		My Heart Stood Still / Mr. Robin	1960	4.00	20.00

SPEEDY & THE REVERBS

| Reverb 51 | | 100 Proof / Gas Chamber | 196? | 7.00 | 35.00 |

SPEIDELS, THE

| Crosley 201 | | Dear Joan / No | 196? | 5.00 | 25.00 |

SPEKTRUMS, THE

| Impact 5 | | Sundown / The Santa Maria | 1961 | 2.00 | 10.00 |

SPELLBINDERS, THE

Columbia 43384		For You / Stone In Love	1965	1.20	6.00
Columbia 43522		Chain Reaction / Little On The Blue Side	1966	1.20	6.00
Columbia 43611		Long Lost Love / We're Acting Like Lovers	1966	1.20	6.00
Columbia 43830		Help Me / Danny Boy	1966	1.20	6.00

Label & Catalog #		A-Side/B-Side	Year	VG	NM
SPENCER & SPENCER					
Argo 5331		Russian Bandstand / Brass Wail	1959	3.00	15.00
Gone 5053		Stagger Lawrence / Stroganoff Cha Cha	1959	3.00	15.00
SPI-DELLS, THE					
Little Town 574		Never Ever / Gee, But I Wish	196?	6.00	30.00
SPICE OF LIFE, THE					
Poppy 503		Dedications / The Spice Of Life	1968	1.20	6.00
SPIDERS, THE					
The Spiders feature Vince Furnier a.k.a. Alice Cooper.					
Mascot 112		Why Don't You Love Me? / Hitch Hike	1965	——	——
		(Rare. Estimated near mint value $1,000-2,000.)			
Santa Cruz 003		Don't Blow Your Mind / No Price Tag	1966	——	——
		(Rare. Estimated near mint value $500-1,000.)			
SPIDERS FROM MARS, THE					
David Bowie's Ziggy Stardust band.					
Pye 71063		(I Don't Want To Do No) Limbo / (I Don't Want To Do No) Limbo	1976	1.00	5.00
		(Stock copies of Pye 71063 may not exist.)			
SPIEDELS, THE					
Crosley 201		Dear Joan / No	195?	4.00	20.00
SPINAL TAP					
Enigma 1143		Christmas With The Devil / Christmas With The Devil *(Scratch Mix)*	1984	1.00	5.00
Enigma 1143	(PS)	Christmas With The Devil	1984	1.00	5.00
Enigma 1144		Christmas With The Devil *(Picture disc)*	1984	3.00	15.00
SPINDLE					
Piccadilly 252		Little Lies / Til The End Of Time	1968	1.00	5.00
Jerden 911		Because I Love You / That's The Time	1969	1.00	5.00
SPINNERS, THE					
Crystalette 736		Boomerang / Slave Chain	1960	5.00	25.00
		(Re-issued as "Surf Stomp" / "Surfin' Fever" credited to The Crestriders. "Boomerang" was reissued as "The Lion" credited to Duke Mitchell.)			
Lawson 324		Surfing Monkey / Beetel Mania	196?	7.00	35.00
SPIRAL STAIRCASE, THE					
The Staircase was produced by Gary Usher.					
Columbia 44442		Baby What I Mean / Makin' My Mind Up	1968	.80	4.00
Columbia 44566		I'll Run / Inside, Outside, Upside Down	1968	.80	4.00
Columbia 44741		More Than Yesterday / Broken Hearted Man	1969	.80	4.00
Columbia 44924		No One For Me To Turn To / Sweet Little Thing	1969	.60	3.00
Columbia 45048		She's Ready / Judas To The Love We Knew	1970	.60	3.00
SPIRALS, THE					
Smash 1719		Please Be My Love / Forever And A Day	1961	20.00	100.00
SPIRIT					
The original group through 1971 was Mark Andes, Randy California, Ed Cassidy, Jay Ferguson and John Locke.					
Ode 108		Mechanical World / Uncle Jack	1967	1.60	8.00
Ode 115		I Got A Line On You / She Smiles	1968	1.60	8.00
Ode 122		Dark Eyed Woman / New Dope In Town	1970	1.20	6.00
Ode 128		1984 / Sweet Stella Baby	1970	1.20	6.00
Epic 10648		Animal Zoo / Red Light, Roll On	1970	1.00	6.00
Epic 10685		Nature's Way / Soldier	1970	*Unreleased?*	
Epic 10701		Mr. Skin / Nature's Way	1973	.80	4.00
Epic 10849		Cadillac Cowboys / Darkness	1972	.80	4.00
Epic 10849	(PS)	Cadillac Cowboys / Darkness	1972	2.00	10.00
Mercury 73697		America The Beautiful / Lady Of The Lakes	1975	.80	4.00
Mercury 73722		Holy Man / Looking Into Darkness	1975	.80	4.00
Mercury 73837		Atomic Boogie / Farther Along	1976	.80	4.00
SPIRITS OF BLUE LIGHTNING					
Lavender 2009		Love Muscle / Well Baby	196?	2.00	10.00
SPLINTER					
Dark Horse 10002		Costafine Town / Elly-May	1974	.60	3.00
Dark Horse 10003		China Light / Haven't Got Time	1975	.60	3.00
Dark Horse 10007		Which Way Will I Get Home? / What Is It	1976	.60	3.00
Dark Horse 10010		After Five Years / Half Way There	1976	.60	3.00
Dark Horse 8439		Round And Round / I'll Bend For You	1977	.60	3.00
Dark Horse 8523		Motions Of Love / I Need Your Love	1977	.60	3.00

Label & Catalog #		A-Side/B-Side	Year	VG	NM
SPOELSTRA, MARK					
Fantasy 664		Workin' With A Woman / Tonight's For Lovin'	1971	1.00	5.00
SPOKESMEN, THE					
Refer to the Various Artists EP section.					
Decca 31844		The Dawn Of Correction / For You, Babe	1965	1.60	8.00
Decca 31874		Have Courage, Be Careful / It Ain't Fair	1965	.80	4.00
Decca 31895		Better Days Are Yet To Come / Michelle	1966	.80	4.00
Decca 31949		Today's The Day / Enchante	1966	.80	4.00
Decca 32049		I Love How You Love Me / Beautiful Girl	1966	.80	4.00
Winchester 1001		Mary Jane / Flash Back	1967	2.00	10.00
SPONGY & THE DOLLS					
Bridgeview 7001		It Looks Like Love / Really, Really, Really Love	195?	50.00	200.00
SPONTANEOUS COMBUSTION					
Harvest 3558		Chessboard / Rainy Day	1972	.80	4.00
SPOTLIGHTS, THE					
Smash 2020		Batman And Robin / Dayflower	1966	3.00	15.00
SPRING [AMERICAN SPRING]					
Spring—Diane Rovell and Marilyn Wilson, formerly of The Honeys—was produced by Brian Wilson, Stephen Desper and					
David Sandler. Refer to Jan & Dean; Rodney & The Brunettes.					
United Artists 50848	(DJ)	Now That Everything's Been Said / Awake	1971	4.00	20.00
United Artists 50848		Now That Everything's Been Said / Awake	1971	6.00	30.00
United Artists 50907	(DJ)	Good Time / Sweet Mountain	1972	10.00	50.00
United Artists 50907		Good Time / Sweet Mountain	1972	15.00	75.00
Columbia 45834	(DJ)	Shyin' Away / Fallin' In Love	1973	3.00	15.00
Columbia 45834		Shyin' Away / Fallin' In Love	1973	4.00	20.00
Columbia 45834	(PS)	Shyin' Away / Fallin' In Love	1973	3.00	15.00
		(Columbia 45834 is credited to American Spring.)			
SPRINGERS, THE					
Way Out 2699		I Know My Baby Loves Me So / I Know Why	196?	3.00	15.00
SPRINGFIELD, DUSTY					
Dusty Springfield originally recorded with The Springfields.					
Philips 40162		I Only Want To Be With You / Once Upon A Time	1964	1.60	8.00
Philips 40180		Stay Awhile / Something Special	1964	1.60	8.00
Philips 40180	(PS)	Stay Awhile / Something Special	1964	3.00	15.00
Philips 40207		Wishin' And Hopin' / Do Re Me (Forget About The Do And Think About Me)	1964	1.60	8.00
Philips 40229		All Cried Out / I Wish I Never Loved You	1964	1.60	8.00
Philips 40229	(PS)	All Cried Out / I Wish I Never Loved You	1964	3.00	15.00
Philips 40245		Guess Who? / Live It Up	1964	1.60	8.00
Philips 40245	(PS)	Guess Who? / Live It Up	1964	3.00	15.00
Philips 40270		Losing You / Here She Comes	1965	1.60	8.00
Philips 40270	(PS)	Losing You / Here She Comes	1965	3.00	15.00
Philips 40303		In The Middle Of Nowhere / Baby, Don't You Know?	1965	1.00	5.00
Philips 40303	(PS)	In The Middle Of Nowhere / Baby, Don't You Know?	1965	3.00	15.00
Philips 40319		Some Of Your Lovin' / I Just Don't Know What To Do With Myself	1965	1.20	6.00
Philips 40319	(PS)	Some Of Your Lovin' / I Just Don't Know What To Do With Myself	1965	3.00	15.00
Philips 40371		You Don't Have To Say You Love Me / Little By Little	1966	1.20	6.00
Philips 40371	(PS)	You Don't Have To Say You Love Me / Little By Little	1966	3.00	15.00
Philips 40396		All I See Is You / I'm Gonna Leave You	1965	1.20	6.00
Philips 40396	(PS)	All I See Is You / I'm Gonna Leave You	1965	3.00	15.00
Philips 40439		I'll Try Anything / Corrupt Ones	1967	1.20	6.00
Philips 40439	(PS)	I'll Try Anything / Corrupt Ones	1967	3.00	15.00
Philips 40465		The Look Of Love / Give Me Time (L' Amore So Ne Va)	1967	1.20	6.00
Philips 40498		What's It Gonna Be? / Small Town Girl	1967	1.20	6.00
Philips 40498	(PS)	What's It Gonna Be? / Small Town Girl	1967	3.00	15.00
Philips 40553		I Close My Eyes And Count To ten / La Bamba	1967	1.20	6.00
Atlantic 2580		Son Of A Preacher Man / Just A Little Lovin' (Early In The Mornin')	1968	1.00	5.00
Atlantic 2580	(PS)	Son Of A Preacher Man / Just A Little Lovin' (Early In The Mornin')	1968	3.00	15.00
Atlantic 2606		Don't Forget About Me / Breakfast In Bed	1969	1.00	5.00
Atlantic 2623		The Windmills Of Your Mind / I Don't Want To Hear It Anymore	1969	1.00	5.00
Atlantic 2647		Willie And Laura Mae Jones / That Old Sweet Roll (Hi-De-Ho)	1969	.80	4.00
Atlantic 2673		So Much Love / The Land Of Make Believe	1969	.80	4.00
Atlantic 2685		A Brand New Me / Bad Case Of The Blues	1969	.80	4.00
Atlantic 2705		Silly, Silly Fool / Joe	1970	.80	4.00
Atlantic 2729		I Wanna Be A Free Girl / Let Me In Your Way	1970	.80	4.00

Label & Catalog #		A-Side/B-Side	Year	VG	NM
Atlantic 2739		Lost / Never Love Again	1970	.80	4.00
Atlantic 2771		What Good Is I Love You? / What Do You Do When Love Dies?	1971	.80	4.00
Atlantic 2825		Haunted / Nothing Is Forever	1971	.80	4.00
Atlantic 2841		Someone Who Cared / I Believe In You	1972	.80	4.00
Dunhill 4341		Who Gets Your Love? / Of All The Things	1973	1.00	5.00
Dunhill 4344		Learn To Say Goodbye / Mama's Little Girl	1973	1.00	5.00
Dunhill 4357		Learn To Say Goodbye / Mama's Little Girl	1973	1.00	5.00
Dunhill 4357	(PS)	Learn To Say Goodbye / Mama's Little Girl	1973	2.00	10.00
United Artists 1006		Let Me Love You Once Before I Go / I'm Your Child	1977	.80	4.00
United Artists 1205		Sandra / Checkmate	1977	.80	4.00
United Artists 1225		Give Me The Night / Checkmate	1978	.80	4.00
United Artists 1255		Living Without Your Love / Get Yourself To Love	1979	.80	4.00
20th Century 2457		I Wish That Love Would Last / It Goes Like It Goes	197?	.80	4.00

SPRINGFIELD RIFLE, THE

Label & Catalog #	A-Side/B-Side	Year	VG	NM
Jerden 812	Stop And Take A Look Around / 100 Or Two	1966	1.00	5.00
Jerden 815	All She Said / It Ain't Happened	1966	1.00	5.00
ABC 10878	The Bears / There Is Life On Mars	1966	1.00	5.00
Tower 455	I Love Her / That's I Really Need	1967	1.00	5.00
Jerden 901	I'll Be Standing There / Will You Love Me Tomorrow	1968	1.00	5.00
Jerden 902	Left Of Nowhere / I Must Go For A Walk	1968	1.00	5.00
Jerden 900	What Kind Of Day / Big Fat Mama	1968	1.00	5.00
Jerden 905	That's All I Really Need / I Love Her	1968	1.00	5.00
Burdette 455	That's All I Really Need / I Love Her	1968	1.00	5.00
Burdette 475	He Will Break Your Heart / My Girl	1968	1.00	5.00
Burdette 577	Angelene / Start At The Bottom	1969	1.00	5.00
Jerden 925	That's The Way It Is / What We Will Be	1971	.80	4.00
Jerden 926	Keep On Loading / If You Live	1971	.80	4.00

SPRINGFIELDS, THE
Dusty and Tom Springfield.

Label & Catalog #	A-Side/B-Side	Year	VG	NM
Philips 40038	Silver Thread And Golden Needles / Aunt Rhody	1962	2.00	10.00
Philips 40072	Dear Hearts And Gentle People / Gotta Travel On	1962	1.60	8.00
Philips 40099	Foggy Mountain Top / Island Of Dreams	1963	1.60	8.00
Philips 40121	Say I Won't Be There / Little Boat	1963	1.60	8.00
Philips 40162	Little By Little / Waf-Woof	1963	1.60	8.00

SPRINGSTEEN, BRUCE (& THE E STREET BAND)
Refer to the Various Artists EP section.

Label & Catalog #		A-Side/B-Side	Year	VG	NM
Columbia 45805	(DJ)	Blinded By The Light / Blinded By The Light	1972	10.00	50.00
Columbia 45805		Blinded By The Light / The Angel	1972	100.00	400.00
Columbia 45805	(PS)	Blinded By The Light / The Angel	1972	50.00	250.00
Columbia 45864	(DJ)	Spirit In The Night / Spirit In The Night	1973	8.00	40.00
Columbia 45864		Spirit In The Night / For You	1973	330.00	1,000.00
Columbia AE7-1088	(DJ)	Spirit In The Night / Growin' Up / Rosalita (Come Out Tonight) (33)	1974	75.00	300.00
Columbia 10209	(DJ)	Born To Run / Born To Run	1975	6.00	30.00
Columbia 10209		Born To Run / Meeting Across The River	1975	2.00	10.00
Columbia 10274	(DJ)	Tenth Avenue Freeze-Out / Tenth Avenue Freeze-Out	1976	6.00	30.00
Columbia 10274		Tenth Avenue Freeze-Out / She's The One	1976	2.00	10.00
Columbia 33323		Born To Run / Spirit In The Night (Red label)	1976	.80	4.00
Columbia 33323		Born To Run / Spirit In The Night (Grey label)	198?	.60	3.00
Columbia 10763	(DJ)	Prove It All Night / Prove It All Night	1978	4.00	20.00
Columbia 10763		Prove It All Night / Factory	1978	1.20	6.00
Columbia 10801	(DJ)	Badlands / Badlands	1978	3.00	15.00
Columbia 10801		Badlands / Streets Of Fire	1978	1.20	6.00
Columbia 11391	(DJ)	Hungry Heart / Hungry Heart	1980	3.00	15.00
Columbia 11391		Hungry Heart / Held Up Without A Gun	1980	.60	3.00
Columbia 11391	(PS)	Hungry Heart / Held Up Without A Gun	1980	1.20	6.00
Columbia 11431	(DJ)	Fade Away / Fade Away	1981	2.00	10.00
Columbia 11431		Fade Away / To Be True	1981	3.00	15.00
		(First pressings erroneously titles the b-side "To Be True.")			
Columbia 11431		Fade Away / Be True	1981	.60	3.00
Columbia 11431	(PS)	Fade Away / Be True	1981	1.20	6.00
Columbia AE7-1332	(DJ)	Santa Claus Is Coming To Town / Santa Claus Is Coming To Town	1981	3.00	15.00
Columbia AE7-1332	(PS)	Santa Claus Is Coming To Town / Santa Claus Is Coming To Town (DJ)	1981	3.00	15.00
Columbia 03243		Hungry Heart / Fade Away (Red label)	1983	.80	4.00
Columbia 03243		Hungry Heart / Fade Away (Grey label)	198?	.60	3.00
Columbia 04463	(DJ)	Dancing In The Dark / Dancing In The Dark	1984	2.00	10.00
Columbia 04463	(PS)	Dancing In The Dark / Dancing In The Dark	1984	2.00	10.00
Columbia 04463		Dancing In The Dark / Pink Cadillac	1984	.60	3.00
Columbia 04463	(PS)	Dancing In The Dark / Pink Cadillac	1984	.60	3.00
Columbia 04561	(DJ)	Cover Me / Cover Me	1984	1.60	8.00
Columbia 04561	(PS)	Cover Me / Cover Me	1984	1.60	8.00
Columbia 04561		Cover Me / Jersey Girl	1984	1.00	5.00
		(First pressings have spoken intro to the b-side.)			

Label & Catalog #		A-Side/B-Side	Year	VG	NM
Columbia 04561		**Cover Me / Jersey Girl**	*1984*	.60	**3.00**
Columbia 04561	(PS)	**Cover Me / Jersey Girl**	*1984*	.60	**3.00**
Columbia 04680	(DJ)	**Born In The U.S.A. / Born In The U.S.A.**	*1984*	1.60	**8.00**
Columbia 04680	(PS)	**Born In The U.S.A. / Born In The U.S.A.**	*1984*	1.60	**8.00**
Columbia 04680		**Born In The U.S.A. / Shut Out The Light**	*1984*	.60	**3.00**
Columbia 04680	(PS)	**Born In The U.S.A. / Shut Out The Light**	*1984*	.60	**3.00**
Columbia 04772	(DJ)	**I'm On Fire / I'm On Fire**	*1985*	1.60	**8.00**
Columbia 04772	(PS)	**I'm On Fire / I'm On Fire**	*1985*	1.60	**8.00**
Columbia 04772		**I'm On Fire / Johnny Bye Bye**	*1985*	.60	**3.00**
Columbia 04772	(PS)	**I'm On Fire / Johnny Bye Bye**	*1985*	.60	**3.00**
Columbia 04924	(DJ)	**Glory Days / Glory Days**	*1985*	1.60	**8.00**
Columbia 04924	(PS)	**Glory Days / Glory Days**	*1985*	1.60	**8.00**
Columbia 04924		**Glory Days / Stand On It**	*1985*	.60	**3.00**
Columbia 04924	(PS)	**Glory Days / Stand On It**	*1985*	.60	**3.00**
Columbia 05603	(DJ)	**I'm Goin' Down / I'm Goin' Down**	*1985*	1.60	**8.00**
Columbia 05603	(PS)	**I'm Goin' Down / I'm Goin' Down**	*1985*	1.60	**8.00**
Columbia 05603		**I'm Goin' Down / Janey, Don't You Lose Heart**	*1985*	.60	**3.00**
Columbia 05603	(PS)	**I'm Goin' Down / Janey, Don't You Lose Heart**	*1985*	.60	**3.00**
Columbia 05728	(DJ)	**My Hometown / My Hometown**	*1985*	1.60	**8.00**
Columbia 05728	(PS)	**My Hometown / My Hometown**	*1985*	1.60	**8.00**
Columbia 05728		**My Hometown / Santa Claus Is Coming To Town**	*1985*	.60	**3.00**
Columbia 05728	(PS)	**My Hometown / Santa Claus Is Coming To Town**	*1985*	.60	**3.00**
		—*12" Singles*—			
Asylum 11442	(DJ)	**Medley / (B-side by Jackson Browne) (33 1/3 rpm)**	*1979*	40.00	**200.00**
Asylum 11442	(DJ)	**Medley / (B-side by Jackson Browne) (45 rpm)**	*1979*	10.00	**50.00**
Columbia AS-928	(DJ)	**Fade Away / Be True / Held Up Without A Gun**	*1981*	10.00	**50.00**
Columbia AS-1329	(DJ)	**Santa Claus Is Coming To Town / Santa Claus Is Coming To Town**	*1981*	8.00	**40.00**
Columbia AS-1862	(DJ)	**Dancing In The Dark / Dancing In The Dark (PC)**	*1984*	5.00	**25.00**
Columbia 05028		**Dancing In The Dark / Dancing In The Dark / Dancing In The Dark (PC)**	*1984*	1.00	**5.00**
Columbia 05087		**Cover Me / Cover Me / Cover Me (PC)**	*1984*	1.00	**5.00**
Columbia AS-1959	(DJ)	**Born In The U.S.A. / Born In The U.S.A.**	*1984*	3.00	**15.00**
Columbia 05147		**Born In The U.S.A. / Born In The U.S.A. / Born In The U.S.A. (PC)**	*1984*	1.00	**5.00**
Columbia AS-2007	(DJ)	**I'm On Fire / I'm On Fire (PC)**	*1985*	3.00	**15.00**
Columbia CAS-2082	(DJ)	**Glory Days / Glory Days (PC)**	*1985*	3.00	**15.00**
Columbia CAS-2147	(DJ)	**I'm Goin' Down / I'm Goin' Down (PC)**	*1985*	3.00	**15.00**
Columbia CAS-2233	(DJ)	**My Hometown / My Hometown (PC)**	*1985*	3.00	**15.00**
SPROUTS, THE					
Spangle 2002		**Goodbye, She's Gone / Teen Billy Baby**	*1957*	6.00	**30.00**
RCA Victor 47-7080		**Goodbye, She's Gone / Teen Billy Baby**	*1957*	3.00	**15.00**
SPUD, BUD, & THE SPROUTS					
E.M. 1001		**The Mash / Slow Jam**	*1962*	2.00	**10.00**
SPYDELLS, THE					
MZ 103		**No More Teasing / Wanted Dead Or Alive**	*196?*	3.00	**15.00**
Addit 1220		**Big McGoon / We're In Love**	*1960*	3.00	**15.00**
Assault 1860		**Change Your Mind / Peace Of Mind**	*196?*	2.00	**10.00**
SQUARES, THE					
Roulette 4598		**The Out Crowd / Melvin's Theme**	*1965*	2.00	**10.00**
SQUIRES, THE					
Chan 102		**Movin' Out / Our Theme**	*1961*	4.00	**20.00**
MGM 13044		**Movin' Out / Our Theme**	*1961*	2.00	**10.00**
SQUIRES, THE					
The Squires feature Neil Young.					
"V" 109		**The Sultan / Aurora**	*1961*	75.00	**300.00**
SQUIRES, THE					
Gee 1082		**So Many Tears Ago / Don't Accuse Me**	*1962*	4.00	**20.00**
Herald 580		**Why Should I Suffer? / Walkin'**	*1963*	3.00	**15.00**
SQUIRES, THE					
Congress 223		**Joyce / Can't Believe You've Grown Up**	*1964*	10.00	**50.00**
SQUIRES, THE					
Starlite 1/2		**Movin' On / Night Road**	*1964*	7.00	**35.00**
SQUIRES, THE					
Atco 2115		**Go Ahead / Goin' All The Way**	*1966*	8.00	**40.00**
SQUIRES, THE					
Northwester 2605		**Don't You Just Know It / Big Boy Pete**	*196?*	3.00	**15.00**

Label & Catalog #	A-Side/B-Side	Year	VG	NM
STACCATOS, THE				
Kandy Kane 1004	Moon Dawg / Something On Your Mind	196?	8.00	40.00
STACCATOS, THE				
The Staccatos later recorded as The Five Man Electrical Band.				
Tower 277	Let's Run Away / Face To Face	1966	2.00	10.00
Tower 322	Half Past Midnight / Weather Man	1966	2.00	10.00
Capitol 5979	Catch The Love Parade / Whisper Words	1967	1.60	8.00
Capitol 2126	Walker Street / She Fancies Herself A Lady	1968	1.60	8.00
Capitol 2260	Didn't Know The Time / We Go Together Well	1968	1.60	8.00
STACY, CLYDE				
Candlelight 1015	Hoy Hoy / So Young	1957	6.00	30.00
Candlelight 1018	Dream Boy / A Broken Heart	1957	4.00	20.00
Argyle 101	So Young / Hoy Hoy	1958	4.00	20.00
G&H 101	Baby Shame / Nobody's Darlin'	1958	4.00	20.00
Bullseye 1004	Baby Shame / Nobody's Darlin'	1958	2.00	10.00
STAFFORD, TERRY				
Crusader 101	Suspicion / Judy	1964	2.00	10.00
Crusader 105	I'll Touch A Star / Playing With Fire	1964	1.20	6.00
Crusader 109	Follow The Rainbow / Are You A Fool Like Me?	1964	1.20	6.00
Crusader 110	A Little Bit Better / Hoping	1964	1.20	6.00
Sidewalk 914	The Joke's On Me / A Step Or Two Behind	1965	2.00	10.00
MGM 14232	Mean Woman Blues / Candy Man	1971	1.00	5.00
STAGG, TOMMY				
Bambi 802	Memories Of Love / Four In Love	195?	10.00	50.00
STAINED GLASS				
RCA Victor 47-8889	If I Needed Someone / How Do You Expect Me?	1966	2.00	10.00
RCA Victor 47-8952	Vanity Fair / My Buddy Sin	1966	1.60	8.00
RCA Victor 47-9166	We Got A Long Way To Go / Corduroy Joy	1967	1.60	8.00
RCA Victor 47-9354	A Scene In Between / Mediocre Me	1967	1.60	8.00
Capitol 2372	Fahrenheit / Twiddle My Thumbs	1968	1.00	5.00
Capitol 2521	Gettin' On's Gettin' Rough / The Necromancer	1969	1.00	5.00
STAIRWAY TO THE STARS				
Brite-Star 728	Dry Run / Cry	196?	7.00	35.00
STAMPEDERS, THE				
MGM 13970	Be A Woman / I Don't Believe	1968	2.00	10.00
Polydor 14060	Carry Me / I Didn't Love You Anyhow	1969	2.00	10.00
Bell 120	Sweet City Woman / Gator Road	1971	.80	4.00
Bell 154	Devil You / Giant In The Streets	1971	.60	3.00
Bell 188	Monday Morning Choo-Choo / Then Came The White Man	1972	.80	4.00
Bell 226	Wild Eyes / Carryin' On	1972	.80	4.00
Bell 331	Oh, My Lady / No Destination	1972	.80	4.00
Capitol 3868	Me And My Stone / Goodbye, Goodbye	1973	.60	3.00
Capitol 3964	Ramona / Running Out Of Time	1974	.60	3.00
Quality 501	Hard Lovin' Woman / Hit The Road, Jack	1976	.60	3.00
Quality 505	Sweet Love Bandit / Let It Begin	1976	.60	3.00
STAN & MIKE				
Topaz 31692	Call Of The Wind / Baby Me	196?	.80	4.00
STANDARDS, THE				
Debro 3178	Tears Bring Heartaches / No No No	1963	50.00	200.00
Roulette 4487	Tears Bring Heartaches / No No No	1963	3.00	15.00
Magna 1314	Hello, Love / My Heart Belongs To Only You	1963	4.00	20.00
Magna 1315	It Isn't Fair / Everybody Knows	1963	3.00	15.00
Chess 1869	Hello, Love / My Heart Belongs To Only You	1963	2.00	10.00
Glenden 1315	It Isn't Fair / Everybody Knows	1964	2.00	10.00
Amos 134	When You Wish Upon A Star / When You Wish Upon A Star	1969	1.00	5.00
STANDELLS, THE [THE SLLEDNATS]				
The Standells feature Dick Dodd and Larry Tamblyn.				
Liberty 55680	Peppermint Beatles / The Shake	1964	4.00	20.00
Liberty 55722	I'll Go Crazy / Help Yourself	1964	3.00	15.00
Liberty 55743	Linda Lou / So Fine	1964	3.00	15.00
Linda 112	You'll Be Mine Someday / Girl In My Heart	1965	5.00	25.00
	(Linda 112 credits Larry Tamblyn & The Standells.)			
Vee Jay 643	The Boy Next Door / B. J. Quezal	1965	3.00	15.00
Vee Jay 643 (PS)	The Boy Next Door / B. J. Quezal	1965	8.00	40.00
Vee Jay 679	Don't Say Goodbye / Big Boss Man	1965	3.00	15.00
MGM 13350 (DJ)	Someday You'll Cry / Zebra In The Kitchen	1965	3.00	15.00
MGM 13350	Someday You'll Cry / Zebra In The Kitchen	1965	5.00	25.00
Sunset 61000	Ooh Poo Pah Doo / Help Yourself	1966	4.00	20.00

Label & Catalog #		A-Side/B-Side	Year	VG	NM
Tower 185		Dirty Water / Rori	1966	2.00	40.00
Tower 185		Dirty Water / Rori	1966	2.00	10.00
Tower 257	(DJ)	Sometimes Good Guys Don't Wear White /			
		Why Did You Hurt Me?	1966	2.00	40.00
Tower 257		Sometimes Good Guys Don't Wear White /			
		Why Did You Hurt Me?	1966	2.00	10.00
Tower 282	(DJ)	Why Pick On Me? / Mr. Nobody	1966	2.00	40.00
Tower 282		Why Pick On Me? / Mr. Nobody	1966	2.00	10.00
Tower 310	(DJ)	Try It / Poor Shell Of A Man	1967	2.00	40.00
Tower 310		Try It / Poor Shell Of A Man	1967	2.00	10.00
Tower 310	(PS)	Try It / Poor Shell Of A Man	1967	4.00	20.00
Tower 312	(DJ)	Don't Tell Me What To Do / When I Was A Cowboy	1967	4.00	50.00
Tower 312		Don't Tell Me What To Do / When I Was A Cowboy	1967	4.00	20.00
		(Label credits The Sllednats, which is Standells spelled backwards.)			
Tower 314	(DJ)	Riot On Sunset Strip / Black Hearted Woman	1967	2.00	30.00
Tower 314		Riot On Sunset Strip / Black Hearted Woman	1967	2.00	10.00
Tower 314	(PS)	Riot On Sunset Strip / Black Hearted Woman	1967	4.00	20.00
Tower 348	(DJ)	Can't Help But Love You / Ninety-Nine-And-A-Half	1967	2.00	30.00
Tower 348		Can't Help But Love You / Ninety-Nine-And-A-Half	1967	2.00	10.00
Tower 348	(PS)	Can't Help But Love You / Ninety-Nine-And-A-Half	1967	5.00	25.00
Tower 398	(DJ)	Animal Girl / Soul Drippin'	1968	2.00	30.00
Tower 398		Animal Girl / Soul Drippin'	1968	2.00	10.00

STANLEY, PAUL
Paul Stanley is a member of Kiss.

Casablanca 940		Hold Me, Touch Me / Goodbye	1978	1.20	6.00

STANLEY, RAY

Zephyr 011		Market Place / Pushin'	1956	6.00	30.00
Zephyr 012		My Lovin' Baby / Love Charms	1956	6.00	30.00
		(Zephyr 011 and 012 feature Eddie Cochran on guitar.)			

STAR FIRES, THE

Laurie 3332		You Done Me Wrong / Like Socks And Shoes	1966	4.00	20.00

STAR STEPPERS, THE

Amy 801		The First Signs Of Love / You're Gone	1960	5.00	25.00

STAR TONES, THE

Band Box 354		The Chase / Harlem Nocturne	196?	8.00	40.00

STAR TREKS, THE

Veep 1254		Gonna Need Magic / Dreamin'	1967	2.00	10.00

STARDRIFTS, THE

Goldisc 3		She's Gone / An Eye For An Eye	196?	5.00	25.00

STARDUSTERS, THE

Jo-Ray-Me		Percussion Twist / Rockin' Boat	1962	7.00	35.00

STARDUSTERS, THE

Julian 113		Get Away, Girl / Miss You, Darling	196?	2.00	10.00

STARFIRES, THE

Haral 777		Each Night At Night / What Good Is Money?	195?	20.00	100.00
Duel 518		Fools Fall In Love / Under The Stars	195?	10.00	50.00
Decca 30730		I Have Someone / Three Roses	1958	7.00	35.00
Decca 30916		Love Is Here To Stay / Tomorrow	1959	7.00	35.00
D&H 200		These Foolish Things / Let's Do The Pony	196?	2.00	10.00

STARFIRES, THE

Apt 25030		Camel Walk / Fender Bender	1959	4.00	20.00
Triumph 61		Fink / Work Out Fine	196?	2.00	10.00

STARFIRES, THE

Sonic 7163		Hand Full Of Blood / Re-Entry	196?	5.00	25.00

STARFIRES, THE

Round 1016		Space Needle / The Jordan Stomp	1962	7.00	35.00
Round 1016	(PS)	Space Needle / The Jordan Stomp	1962	7.00	35.00

STARFIRES, THE
The Starfires later recorded as The Outsiders.

Pama 117		Chartreuse Caboose / Billy's Blues	196?	5.00	25.00

STARFIRES, THE: *Refer to* RAL DONNER

Label & Catalog #		A-Side / B-Side	Year	VG	NM
STARLETS, THE					
Siana 717		**Ringo / All Dressed Up**	1964	3.00	15.00
STARLETS, THE					
The Starlets later recorded as The Angels.					
Astro 202/3		**Where Is My Love Tonight? / P.S. I Love You**	1960	3.00	15.00
Astro 204		**Romeo And Juliet / Listen For A Lonely Tambourine**	1960	3.00	15.00
STARLETS, THE					
The Starlets also recorded with Jenny Lee.					
Pam 1003		**Better Tell Him No / You Are The One**	1961	3.00	15.00
Pam 1004		**My Last Cry / Money Honey**	1961	3.00	15.00
Tower 115		**Multiply By Three / You Won't Even Know Her Name**	1965	2.00	10.00
Tower 144		**You Don't Love Me / I've Had It**	1965	3.00	15.00
		("You Don't Love Me" features Davie Allan on guitar.)			
Chess 1997		**My Baby's Real / Loving You Is Something New**	1967	1.60	8.00
Chess 2038		**I Wanna Be Good To You / Watered Down**	1968	1.60	8.00
STARLIGHTERS, THE					
End 1031		**It's Twelve O' Clock / The Birdland**	1958	125.00	500.00
End 1049		**I Cried / You're The One To Blame**	1959	15.00	75.00
End 1072		**A Story Of Love / Let's Take A Stroll**	1960	15.00	75.00
STARLINERS, THE					
No-Nee 101		**Gatz / Spider**	196?	7.00	35.00
STARLITERS, THE: *Refer to* JOEY DEE					
STARR, ANDY					
MGM 12263		**Rockin' Rollin' Stone / I Wanna Go South**	1956	20.00	100.00
MGM 12315		**She's A Goin,' Jessie / Old Deacon Jones**	1956	16.00	80.00
MGM 12364		**Round And Round / Give Me A Woman**	1957	30.00	150.00
MGM 12421		**No Room For Your Kind / One More Time**	1957	20.00	100.00
STARR, RINGO					
Ringo Starr originally recorded with The Beatles.					
Apple 2969		**Beaucoups Of Blues / Coochy Coochy** *(Star label)*	1970	3.00	15.00
		(Original pressings have the Capitol logo on the bottom of the label.)			
Apple 2969		**Beaucoups Of Blues / Coochy Coochy** *(Star label)*	1970	5.00	25.00
Apple 2969		**Beaucoups Of Blues / Coochy Coochy** *(Starless label)*	1970	2.00	10.00
		(Second pressings-with and without the star—have Apple Records on the bottom of the label.)			
Apple 2969	(PS)	**Beaucoups Of Blues / Coochy Coochy**	1970	6.00	30.00
		(Sleeve erroneously lists "1826" as the catalogue number.)			
Apple 2969	(PS)	**Beaucoups Of Blues / Coochy Coochy**	1970	7.00	35.00
		(Sleeve correctly lists "2969" as the catalogue number.)			
Apple 1831		**It Don't Come Easy / Early 1970** *(Star label)*	1971	2.00	10.00
Apple 1831		**It Don't Come Easy / Early 1970**	1971	1.020	6.00
Apple 1831	(PS)	**It Don't Come Easy / Early 1970**	1971	4.00	20.00
Apple 1849	(DJ)	**Back Off Boogaloo / Blindman**	1972	25.00	125.00
Apple 1849		**Back Off Boogaloo / Blindman** *(Green label)*	1972	1.20	6.00
Apple 1849		**Back Off Boogaloo / Blindman** *(Blue label)*	1972	10.00	50.00
Apple 1849	(PS)	**Back Off Boogaloo / Blindman**	1972	3.00	15.00
		(Sleeve is non-glossy black on both sides.)			
Apple 1849	(PS)	**Back Off Boogaloo / Blindman**	1972	5.00	25.00
		(Sleeve is glossy black on both sides.)			
Apple 1849	(PS)	**Back Off Boogaloo / Blindman**	1972	4.00	20.00
		(Sleeve is glossy grey on the front and glossy black on the back.)			
Apple P-1865	(DJ)	**Photograph / Photograph**	1973	6.00	30.00
Apple 1865		**Photograph / Down And Out**	1973	1.20	6.00
Apple 1865	(PS)	**Photograph / Down And Out**	1973	3.00	15.00
Apple P-1870	(DJ)	**You're Sixteen / You're Sixteen**	1973	6.00	30.00
Apple 1870		**You're Sixteen / Devil Woman** *(Photo label)*	1973	1.20	6.00
Apple 1870		**You're Sixteen / Devil Woman** *(Apple label)*	1973	2.00	10.00
Apple 1870	(PS)	**You're Sixteen/ Devil Woman**	1973	3.00	15.00
Apple P-1872	(DJ)	**Oh My My / Oh My My**	1974	6.00	30.00
Apple 1872		**Oh My My / Step Lightly** *(Photo label)*	1974	1.20	6.00
Apple 1872		**Oh My My / Step Lightly** *(Apple label)*	1974	1.25	6.00
Apple P-1876	(DJ)	**Only You / Only You**	1974	6.00	30.00
Apple 1876		**Only You / Call Me** *(Photo label)*	1974	1.20	6.00
Apple 1876		**Only You / Call Me** *(Apple label)*	1974	2.00	10.00
Apple 1876	(PS)	**Only You / Call Me**	1974	2.00	10.00
Apple P-1880	(DJ)	**No No Song / Snookeroo** *(Mono)*	1975	6.00	30.00
Apple P-1880	(DJ)	**No No Song / Snookeroo** *(Stereo)*	1975	6.00	30.00
Apple 1880		**No No Song / Snookeroo**	1975	1.20	6.00
Apple 1882	(DJ)	**It's All Down To Goodnight Vienna / It's All Down To Goodnight Vienna**	1975	6.00	30.00
Apple P-1882	(DJ)	**Oo-Wee / Oo-Wee**	1975	8.00	40.00

Label & Catalog #		A-Side/B-Side	Year	VG	NM
Apple 1882		It's All Down To Goodnight Vienna / Oo-Wee	1975	1.20	6.00
Apple 1882	(PS)	It's All Down To Goodnight Vienna / Oo-Wee	1975	2.00	10.00
Atlantic 3361	(DJ)	Dose Of Rock 'N' Roll / Dose Of Rock 'N' Roll (White label)	1976	8.00	40.00
Atlantic 3361	(DJ)	Dose Of Rock 'N' Roll / Dose Of Rock 'N' Roll (Red & blue label)	1976	3.00	15.00
Atlantic 3361		Dose Of Rock 'N' Roll / Cryin'	1976	2.00	10.00
Atlantic 3371	(DJ)	Hey, Baby / Hey, Baby (White label)	1976	8.00	40.00
Atlantic 3371	(DJ)	Hey, Baby / Hey, Baby (Red & blue label)	1976	3.00	15.00
Atlantic 3371		Hey, Baby / Lady Gaye	1976	2.00	10.00
Atlantic 3412	(DJ)	Drowning In The Sea Of Love / Drowning In The Sea Of Love	1977	3.00	15.00
Atlantic 3412		Drowning In The Sea Of Love / Just A Dream	1977	10.00	50.00
Atlantic 3429	(DJ)	Wings / Wings (White label)	1977	8.00	40.00
Atlantic 3429	(DJ)	Wings / Wings (Red & blue label)	1977	3.00	15.00
Atlantic 3429		Wings / Just A Dream	1977	4.00	20.00
Portrait 70015	(DJ)	Lipstick Traces / Lipstick Traces	1978	3.00	15.00
Portrait 70015		Lipstick Traces / Old Time Relovin'	1978	2.00	10.00
Portrait 70018	(DJ)	Heart On My Sleeve / Heart On My Sleeve	1979	3.00	15.00
Portrait 70018		Heart On My Sleeve / Who Needs A Heart	1979	2.00	10.00
Boardwalk 130	(DJ)	Wrack My Brain / Wrack My Brain	1981	2.50	12.00
Boardwalk 130		Wrack My Brain / Drumming Is My Madness	1981	.60	3.00
Boardwalk 130	(PS)	Wrack My Brain / Drumming Is My Madness	1981	1.20	6.00
Boardwalk 134	(DJ)	Private Property / Private Property	1982	2.50	12.00
Boardwalk 134		Private Property / Stop And Smell The Roses	1982	2.00	10.00
		— 12" Singles—			
Atlantic DSKO-93	(DJ)	Drowning In The Sea Of Love / Drowning In The Sea Of Love	1977	6.00	30.00

STARR, RUBY

Capitol 4301		Maybe I'm Amazed / Who's Who	1976	.60	3.00

STARR, SALLY

Arcade 157		Rocky, The Rockin' Rabbit / Sing A Song Of Happiness	1960	3.00	15.00

STARSHIP
Starship features Mickey Dolenz.

Lion 132	(DJ)	Johnny B. Goode / It's Amazing To Me	1972	2.00	10.00
Lion 132		Johnny B. Goode / It's Amazing To Me	1972	5.00	25.00

STATENS, THE

Mark-X 8011		Summertime Is Time For Love / That Certain Kind	1961	10.00	50.00

STATESMEN, THE

Bradley 200		Rampage / Forever	196?	1.20	6.00

STATICS, THE

Mantis 102		Shanghaied / Soft-Touch	1961	7.00	35.00

STATICS, THE
The Statics feature Tiny Tony.

Bregg 1000		Buster Brown / Buster Brown, Part 2	196?	3.00	15.00
Camelot 110		The Girl Can't Help It / Harlem Shuffle	196?	3.00	15.00
Camelot 115		Tell Me The Truth / Rinky Dink	196?	3.00	15.00

STATUES, THE
The Statues also recorded with Gary Miles.

Liberty 55245		Blue Velvet / Keep The Hall Light Burning	1960	4.00	20.00
Liberty 55292		White Christmas / Jeanie With The Light Brown Hair	1960	4.00	20.00
Liberty 55363		The Commandments Of Love / Love At First Sight	1961	4.00	20.00

STATUS QUO

Cadet Concept 7001		Pictures Of Matchstick Men / Gentleman Joe's Sidewalk Cafe	1968	1.60	8.00
Cadet Concept 7006		Ice In The Sun / When My Mind Is Not Live	1968	1.20	6.00
Cadet Concept 7010		Spicks And Specks / Technicolor Dreams	1969	1.20	6.00
Janus 127		Down The Dustpipe / Face Without A Soul	1970	1.20	6.00
Janus 141		In My Chair / Gerdundula	1970	1.20	6.00
Bell 417	(DJ)	Good Thinking / Good Thinking	1973	1.00	5.00
Bell 417	(DJ)	Gerdundula / Gerdundula	1973	1.00	5.00
		(Stock copies of Bell 417 may not exist.)			
A&M 1425		Don't Waste My Time / All The Reasons	1973	.80	4.00
A&M 1445		Paper Plane / All The Reasons	1973	.80	4.00
A&M 1510		Caroline / Softer Ride	1974	.80	4.00
Pye 65000		Tune To The Music / Good Thinking	1975	.80	4.00
Pye 65017		Mean Girl / Everything	1975	.80	4.00
Capitol 4039		Nightride / Down Down	1975	.60	3.00
Capitol 4125		Bye Bye Johnny / Down Down	1975	.60	3.00
Capitol 4407		Wild Side Of Life / All Through The Night	1977	.60	3.00

Label & Catalog #		A-Side/B-Side	Year	VG	NM
STEAM					
Fontana 1667		Na Na Hey Hey (Kiss Him Goodbye) /			
		It's The Magic In You, Girl	1969	1.00	5.00
Mercury 73020		I've Gotta Make You Love Me / One Good Woman	1970	.80	4.00
Mercury 73053		What I'm Saying Is True /	1970	.80	4.00
Mercury 73117		Do Unto Others / Don't Stop Loving Me	1970	.80	4.00
Mercury 30160		Na Na Hey Hey (Kiss Him Goodbye) / Don't Stop Lovin' Me	1972	.60	3.00
Mercury 30160	(PS)	Na Na Hey Hey (Kiss Him Goodbye) / Don't Stop Lovin' Me	1972	1.20	6.00
STEELE, TRACY					
Delaware 1705		A Letter To Paul / Your Ring	196?	2.00	10.00
STEELEYE SPAN					
Chrysalis 2008		Gaudette / Royal Forester	1972	.80	4.00
Chrysalis 2102		Gaudette / Royal Forester	1974	.60	3.00
Chrysalis 2262		Rag Doll / Hunting The Wren	1978	.60	3.00
STEELY DAN					
Steely Dan features Walter Becker and Donald Fagen.					
ABC 11323		Dallas / Sail The Waterway	1972	.60	3.00
ABC 11338		Do It Again / Fire In The Hole	1972	.60	3.00
ABC 11352		Reeling In The Years / Only A Fool Would Say That	1973	.60	3.00
ABC 11382		Show Biz Kids / Razor Boys	1973	.60	3.00
ABC 11396		My Old School / Pearl Of The Quarter	1973	.60	3.00
ABC 11439		Rikki Don't Lose That Number /			
		Any Major Dude Will Tell You	1974	.60	3.00
ABC 12033		Pretzel Logic / Through With Buzz	1974	.60	3.00
ABC 12101		Black Friday / Throw Back The Little Ones	1975	.60	3.00
ABC 12128		Bad Sneakers / Chain Lightning	1975	.60	3.00
ABC 12195		Kid Charlemegne / Green Earrings	1976	.60	3.00
ABC 12222		The Fez / Sign In, Stranger	1977	.60	3.00
ABC 12320		Peg / I Got The News	1977	.60	3.00
ABC 12355		Deacon Blues / Home At Last	1978	.60	3.00
ABC 12404		Josie / Black Cow	1978	.60	3.00
MCA 40894		FM (No Static At All) / FM (No Static At All) Reprise	1978	.60	3.00
STEFAN & THE WILD BOYS					
Artists Of America 116		Dying In St. Louis	196?	2.00	10.00
STEFFEN, PAUL, & THE APOLLOS					
Refer to The Royal Lancers.					
Citation 5008		You / Cry Angel, Cry	196?	3.00	15.00
STEIN, FRANK N., & THE TOMBSTONES					
Marco 003		Mess Around / Graveyard Giggle	1962	8.00	40.00
STEIN, FRANKIE, & THE GHOULS					
Power 338		Weerdo The Wolf / Goon River	1964	3.00	15.00
Power 338	(PS)	Weerdo The Wolf / Goon River	1964	5.00	25.00
STEPPENWOLF					
Steppenwolf, featuring John Kay, originally recorded as The Sparrow.					
Dunhill 4109		A Girl I Know / The Ostrich	1968	1.20	6.00
Dunhill 4123		Sookie Sookie / Take What You Need	1968	1.20	6.00
Dunhill 4138		Born To Be Wild / Everybody's Next One	1968	1.20	6.00
Dunhill 4160		Magic Carpet Ride / Sookie Sookie	1968	1.20	6.00
Dunhill 4182		Rock Me / Jupiter Child	1969	1.00	5.00
Dunhill 4192		It's Never Too Late / Happy Birthday	1969	1.00	5.00
Dunhill 4205		Move Over / Power Play	1969	1.00	5.00
Dunhill 4221		Monster / Berry Rides Again	1969	1.00	5.00
Dunhill 4234		Hey Lawdy Mama / Twisted	1970	1.00	5.00
Dunhill 4248		Screaming Night Hog / Corrina Corrina	1970	1.00	5.00
Dunhill 4248		Screaming Night Hog / Spiritual Fantasy	1970	.80	4.00
Dunhill 4261		Who Needs Ya? / Earschplitten Loudenboomer	1970	.80	4.00
Dunhill 4269		Snow Blind Friend / Hippo Stomp	1971	.80	4.00
Dunhill 4283		Ride With Me / Black Pit	1971	.80	4.00
Dunhill 4283		Ride With Me / For Madmen Only	1971	.80	4.00
Dunhill 4283	(PS)	Ride With Me / For Madmen Only	1971	1.20	6.00
Dunhill 4292		For Ladies Only / Sparkle Eyes	1971	.80	4.00
ABC 11436	(PS)	Born To Be Wild / The Pusher	1973	.80	4.00
		(Special picture sleeve included with this back-to-back-hits reissue.)			
Mums 6031		Straight Shootin' Woman / Just Don't Be Slow	1974	.80	4.00
Mums 6031	(PS)	Straight Shootin' Woman / Just Don't Be Slow	1974	1.20	6.00
Mums 6034		Get Into The Wind / Morning Blue	1974	.80	4.00
Mums 6036		A Fool's Fantasy / Smokey Factory Blues	1975	.80	4.00
Mums 6040		Caroline (Are You Ready For The Outlaw World?) /			
		Angeldrawers	1975	.80	4.00

Label & Catalog #		A-Side/B-Side	Year	VG	NM
STEPPING STONES, THE					
Diplomacy 15		Little Girl Of Mine /	196?	3.00	15.00
Diplomacy 21		So Tough / Pills	196?	3.00	15.00
Philips 40108		The Nearness Of You /	1963	2.00	10.00
		I Got The Job Through The New York Times			
STEREOS, THE					
Mink 22 was reissued credited to The Tams. The Stereos later recorded as The Hippies.					
Mink 22		Memory Lane / Teenage Kids	1959	5.00	25.00
STERN, NINA					
Jerden 759		Take It From Me / Please Come Back To Me	196?	.80	4.00
STEVE & THE EMPERORS					
Best 103		The Breeze And I / Great Balls Of Fire	1962	8.00	40.00
STEVENS, APRIL [APRIL]					
Prior to turning to teen pop music—usually teamed with Nino Tempo—Ms. Stevens recorded big band for RCA and King.					
Imperial 5626		Teach Me, Tiger / That Warm Afternoon	1959	2.00	10.00
Imperial 5666		In Other Words / Johnny	1960	1.60	8.00
Imperial 5761		Love Kitten / You And You Only	1961	1.60	8.00
Contract 429		Love Kitten / You And You Only	1961	1.60	8.00
Imperial 5907		Fly Me To The Moon / That's My Name	1963	1.60	8.00
Imperial 5930		Hello Stranger / For A Little While	1963	1.60	8.00
King 5826		How Could Red Riding Hood? / Soft Warm Lips	1964	1.60	8.00
Atco 6346		Teach Me Tiger (1965) / Morning Til Midnight	1965	1.60	8.00
Atco 361121	(DJ)	America's Weather Girl	1965	2.00	10.00
Verve 10661		Story Of Love / Story Of Love, Part 2	1971	1.60	8.00
A&M 1528		Wake Up And Love Me / Gotta Leave You, Baby	1974	.60	3.00
		(A&M 1528 credits April.)			
A&M 1636		(Won't You) Marry Me Again / Gotta Leave You, Baby	1975	.60	3.00
STEVENS, CAT					
Deram 5872		I Love My Dog / Portobello Road	1966	1.00	5.00
Deram 7501		I Love My Dog / Portobello Road	1967	1.00	5.00
Deram 7505		Matthew And Son / Granny	1967	1.00	5.00
Deram 7518		Kitty / Blackness Of Night	1967	1.00	5.00
Deram 85006		I'm Gonna Get Me A Gun / School Is Out	1967	1.00	5.00
Deram 85015		Bad Night / Laughing Apple	1967	1.00	5.00
Deram 85079		Kitty / Where Are You?	1971	.60	3.00
A&M 1211		Lady D' Arbanville / Fill My Eyes	1970	.60	3.00
A&M 1231		Wild World / Miles From Nowhere	1971	.60	3.00
A&M 1265		Moon Shadow / I Think I See The Light	1971	.60	3.00
A&M 1265	(PS)	Moon Shadow / I Think I See The Light	1971	.80	4.00
A&M 1291		Peace Train / Where Do The Children Play?	1971	.60	3.00
A&M 1291	(PS)	Peace Train / Where Do The Children Play?	1971	.80	4.00
A&M 1335		Morning Has Broken / I Want To Live In A Wigwam	1972	.60	3.00
A&M 1335	(PS)	Morning Has Broken / I Want To Live In A Wigwam	1972	.80	4.00
A&M 1396		Sitting / Crab Dance	1972	.60	3.00
A&M 1396	(PS)	Sitting / Crab Dance	1972	.80	4.00
A&M 1418		The Hurt / Silent Sunlight	1973	.60	3.00
A&M 1418	(PS)	The Hurt / Silent Sunlight	1973	.80	4.00
A&M 1503		Oh, Very Young / 100 Dreams	1974	.60	3.00
A&M 1503	(PS)	Oh, Very Young / 100 Dreams	1974	.80	4.00
A&M 1602		Another Saturday Night / Home In The Sky	1974	.60	3.00
A&M 1602	(PS)	Another Saturday Night / Home In The Sky	1974	.80	4.00
A&M 1645		Ready / I Think I See The Light	1974	.40	2.00
A&M 1700		Two Fine People / A Bad Penny	1975	.40	2.00
A&M 1785		Banapple Gas / Ghost Town	1976	.40	2.00
A&M 1924		(I Never Wanted) To Be A Star /	1977	.40	2.00
		Land O' Freelove And Goodbye			
A&M 1948		(Remember The Days Of The) Old Schoolyard /	1977	.50	2.50
		Land O' Free Love And Goodbye			
A&M 1948	(PS)	(Remember The Days Of The) Old Schoolyard /	1977	.50	2.50
		Land O' Free Love And Goodbye			
A&M 1971		Was Dog A Doughnut? / Sweet Jamaica	1977	.40	2.00
A&M 2109		Bad Brakes / Nascimento	1978	.40	2.00
A&M 2126		Randy / Nascimento	1978	.40	2.00
		—12" Singles—			
A&M 8440	(DJ)	Was Dog A Doughnut? / Sweet Jamaica	1977	.80	4.00
STEVENS, DEBBIE					
Apt 25027		If You Can't Rock Me / What Will My Heart Tell?	1959	4.00	20.00
STEVENS, DODIE					
Crystalette 724		Pink Shoe Laces / Coming Of Age	1959	4.00	20.00
Crystalette 724	(PS)	Pink Shoe Laces / Coming Of Age	1959	8.00	40.00
Crystalette 728		Yes-Sir-Ee / The Five Pennies	1959	3.00	15.00

Label & Catalog #	A-Side/B-Side	Year	VG	NM
Dot 15975	Miss Lonely Hearts / Poor Butterfly	1959	3.00	15.00
Dot 16002	Mairzy Doats / Steady Eddy	1959	3.00	15.00
Dot 16067	Candy Store Blues / Amigo's Guitar	1960	2.00	10.00
Dot 16103	No / A-Tisket, A-Tasket	1960	2.00	10.00
Dot 16139	Am I Too Young? / So, Let's Dance	1960	2.00	10.00
Dot 16166	Merry Christmas, Baby / Merry Christmas, Baby	1960	3.00	15.00
Dot 16167	Yes, I'm Lonesome Tonight / Too Young	1961	3.00	15.00
Dot 16200	I Fall To Pieces / Turn Around	1961	2.00	10.00
Dot 16259	Let Me Tell You About Johnny / You Are The Only One	1961	2.00	10.00
Dot 16279	Trade Winds, Trade Winds / In Between Years	1961	2.00	10.00
Dot 16339	Dancing On My Ceiling / I Cried	1962	2.00	10.00
Imperial 5930	For A Little While / Hello, Stranger	1963	2.00	10.00

STEVENS, MARK, & THE CHARMERS

Allison 821	Come Back To My Heart / Magic Rose	195?	10.00	50.00

STEVENS, NEIL, & THE TEMPTATIONS

Goldisc 3019	Ballad Of Love / Tonight My Heart She Is Crying	1961	4.00	20.00

STEVENS, RANDY

Loma 301	Sweet Hop / All My Love	1959	2.00	10.00

STEVENS, RAY

Ray Stevens also recorded as The Henhouse Five.

Label & Catalog #	A-Side/B-Side	Year	VG	NM
Trumpet 14400	Sergeant Preston Of The Yukon	1957	3.00	15.00
Prep 102	Part Of The Time / That's What She Means To Me	1957	3.00	15.00
Prep 108	Rang Tang Ding Dong / Silver Bracelet	1957	3.00	15.00
Prep 122	Five More Steps / Tingle	1957	3.00	15.00
Capitol 3967	Chickie Chickie Wah Wah / Crying Goodbye	1958	3.00	15.00
Capitol 4030	Cat Pants / Love Goes On Forever	1958	4.00	20.00
Capitol 4101	The Clown / School	1959	2.50	12.00
NRC 031	High School Yearbook / Truly True	1959	3.00	15.00
NRC 042	My Heart Cries For You / What Would I Do Without You?	1960	3.00	15.00
NRC 057	Sergeant Preston Of The Yukon / Who Do You Love?	1960	3.00	15.00
NRC 063	Happy Blue Year / White Christmas	1960	3.00	15.00
Mercury 71843	Jeremiah Peabody's Poly Unsaturated Quick Dissolving Fast Acting Pleasant Tasting Green And Purple Pills / Teen Years	1961	1.6	8.00
Mercury 71843 (PS)	Jeremiah Peabody's Poly Unsaturated Quick Dissolving Fast Acting Pleasant Tasting Green And Purple Pills / Teen Years	1961	3.00	15.00
Mercury 71888	Scratch My Back / When You Wish Upon A Star	1961	1.60	8.00
Mercury 71888 (PS)	Scratch My Back / When You Wish Upon A Star	1961	3.00	15.00
Mercury 71966	Ahab The Arab / It's Been So Long	1962	1.60	8.00
Mercury 71966 (PS)	Ahab The Arab / It's Been So Long	1962	4.00	20.00
Mercury 72039	Further More / Saturday Night At The Movies	1962	1.60	8.00
Mercury 72058	Santa Claus Is Watching You / Loved And Lost	1962	1.60	8.00
Mercury 72058 (PS)	Santa Claus Is Watching You / Loved And Lost	1962	3.00	15.00
Mercury 72098	Funny man / Just One Of Life's Little Tragedies	1963	1.60	8.00
Mercury 72125	Harry The Hairy Ape / Little Stone Statue	1963	1.60	8.00
Mercury 72125 (PS)	Harry The Hairy Ape / Little Stone Statue	1963	3.00	15.00
Mercury 72189	Speed Ball / It's Party Time	1963	1.60	8.00
Mercury 72255	Butch Barbarian / Don't Say Anything	1963	1.60	8.00
Mercury 72255 (PS)	Butch Barbarian / Don't Say Anything	1963	5.00	25.00
Mercury 72307	Bubble Gum The Bubble Dancer / Laughing Over My Grave	1964	1.60	8.00
Mercury 72307 (PS)	Bubble Gum The Bubble Dancer / Laughing Over My Grave	1964	3.00	15.00
Mercury 72382	Rockin' Teenage Mummies / It Only Hurts When I Love	1965	2.00	10.00
Mercury 72430	Mr. Baker The Undertaker / The Old English Surfer	1965	2.00	10.00
Mercury 72816	Funny Man / Just One Of Life's Little Tragedies	1965	2.00	10.00
Monument 911	A-B-C / Party People	1966	1.00	5.00
Monument 927	Make A Few Memories / Devil May Care	1966	1.00	5.00
Monument 946	Freddie Feelgood (And His Funky Little Five Piece Band) / There's One In Every Crowd	1966	1.00	5.00
Monument 1001	Mary My Secretary / Answer Me, My Love	1967	.80	4.00
Monument 1048	Unwind / For He's A Jolly Good Fellow	1968	.80	4.00
Monument 1083	Mr. Businessman / Face The Music	1968	.80	4.00
Monument 1099	The Great Escape / Isn't It Lonely Together	1968	.80	4.00
Monument 1131	Guitarzan / Bagpipes, That's My Bag	1969	.80	4.00
Monument 1150	Along Came Jones / Yakety Yak	1969	.80	4.00
Monument 1163	Sunday Mornin' Comin' Down / The Minority	1969	.60	3.00
Monument 1171	Have A Little Talk With Myself / The Little Woman	1970	.60	3.00
Monument 1187	The Fool On The Hill / I'll Be Your Baby Tonight	1970	.60	3.00
Barnaby 2011	Everything Is Beautiful / A Brighter Day	1970	.60	3.00
Barnaby 2016	America, Communicate With Me / Monkey See, Monkey Do	1970	.60	3.00
Barnaby 2021	Sunset Strip / Islands	1970	.60	3.00
Barnaby 2024	Bridget The Midget / Night People	1970	.60	3.00
Barnaby 2024 (PS)	Bridget The Midget / Night People	1970	1.00	5.00
Barnaby 2029	A Mama And A Papa / Melt	1971	.60	3.00

Label & Catalog #		A-Side/B-Side	Year	VG	NM
Barnaby 2039		All My Trials / Have A Little Talk With Myself	1971	.60	3.00
Barnaby 2048		Turn Your Radio On / Loving You On Paper	1971	.60	3.00
Barnaby 2058		Love Lifted / Glory Special	1972	.60	3.00
Barnaby 2058		Love Lifted / Monkey See, Monkey Do	1972	.60	3.00
Barnaby 2065		Losing Streak / Inside	1972	.60	3.00
Barnaby 5020		Golden Age / Nashville	1973	.60	3.00
Barnaby 5028		Float / Love Me Longer	1973	.60	3.00
Barnaby 600		The Streak / You've Got The Music Inside	1974	.60	3.00
Barnaby 604		The Moonlight Special / Just So Proud To Be Here	1974	.60	3.00
Barnaby 610		Everybody Needs A Rainbow / Inside	1974	.60	3.00
Barnaby 614		Misty / Sunshine	1975	.60	3.00
Barnaby 616		Indian Love Call / Piece Of Paradise	1975	.60	3.00
Barnaby 618		Young Love / Deep Purple	1976	.60	3.00
Barnaby 619		Lady Of Spain / Mockingbird Hill	1976	.60	3.00
Warner Bros. 8198		You Are So Beautiful / One Man Band	1976	.40	2.00
Warner Bros. 8237		Honky Tonk Waltz / Om	1977	.40	2.00
Warner Bros. 8318		Get Crazy With Me / Dixie Hummingbird	1977	.40	2.00
Warner Bros. 8393		Feel The Music / Dixie Hummingbird	1977	.40	2.00
Warner Bros. 8603		With A Smile / Be Your Own Best Friend	1978	.40	2.00
Warner Bros. 8785		I Need Your Help, Barry Manilow / Daydream Romance	1979	.40	2.00
Warner Bros. 8785	(PS)	I Need Your Help, Barry Manilow / Daydream Romance	1979	.40	2.00
Warner Bros. 8848		The Feeling's Not Right Again / Get Crazy With Me	1979	.40	2.00

STEVENS, SCOTT

ABC-Paramount 10054		I Like Girls And Girls Like Me / I Found A Girl	1959	3.00	15.00

STEVENS, SCOTT, & THE CAVALIERS

Apt 25004		Play By The Rules Of Love / Dance Dance Dance	1958	4.00	20.00

STEVENS, TARI

Fairmont 1001		False Alarm / A Bad Boy	1966	1.20	6.00

STEVENS, TRACY

Lord Bingo 106		Surfin' At Ami's / My Golden One	1963	7.00	35.00

STEWART, JIM, & THE SIRS

Uni 55090		Sixteen Candles / Wow	1968	1.60	8.00

STEWART, JOHN, & SCOTT ENGEL

John & Scott also recorded as The Dalton Brothers and 2/3 of The Walker Brothers.

Tower 218		I Only Came To Dance With You / Greens	1966	1.20	6.00

STEWART, JOHNNY

Johny Stewart later recorded with The Kingston Trio.

Vita 169		Rockin' Anna / Lorraine	1958	40.00	200.00

STEWART, JUDY, & HER BEATLE BUDDIES

Diplomat 0101		Who Can I Believe? / I'll Take You Back Again	1964	3.00	15.00

STEWART, MARIO, & HIS FOUR GUITARS

Souvenir 102		Riptide / Surfer's Serenade	196?	7.00	35.00
Souvenir 102	(PS)	Riptide / Surfer's Serenade	196?	7.00	35.00
Souvenir 102		Rip Tide / Sky Surfin'	196?	7.00	35.00

STEWART, MARLOW

VP 201		Earthquake / (B-side by The Illusions)	1964	7.00	35.00

STEWART, ROD

Rod Stewart also recorded with The Jeff Beck Group; The Small Faces; Python Lee Jackson; and Shotgun Express.

Press 9722		Good Morning, Little Schoolgirl / I'm Gonna Move To The Outskirts Of Town	196?	6.00	30.00
Mercury 73009		Handbags And Gladrags / An Old Raincoat Won't Let You Down	1969	1.20	6.00
Mercury 73031		Handbags And Gladrags / Man Of Constant Sorrow	1969	.80	4.00
Mercury 73095		It's All Over Now /	1970	.80	4.00
Mercury 73115		Only A Hobo /	1970	.80	4.00
Mercury 73156		Cut Across, Shorty / Gasoline Alley	1970	.60	3.00
Mercury 73175		Lady Day / My Way Of Giving	1970	.60	3.00
Mercury 73196		Country Comfort / Gasoline Alley	1971	.60	3.00
Mercury 73224		Maggie May / Reason To Believe	1971	.60	3.00
Mercury 73244		(I Know) I'm Losing You / Mandolin Wind	1971	.60	3.00
Mercury 73330		You Wear It Well / True Blue	1972	.60	3.00
Mercury 73330	(PS)	You Wear It Well / True Blue	1972	3.00	15.00
Mercury 73344		Angel / Lost Paraguayos	1972	.60	3.00
Mercury 73412		Twisting The Night Away / True Blue-Lady Day	1973	.60	3.00
Mercury 73412	(PS)	Twisting The Night Away / True Blue-Lady Day	1973	1.20	6.00
Mercury 73426		Oh! No, Not My Baby / Jodie	1973	.60	3.00
Mercury 73426	(PS)	Oh! No, Not My Baby / Jodie	1973	.60	3.00

Label & Catalog #		A-Side/B-Side	Year	VG	NM
Mercury 73636		Mine For Me / Farewell	1974	.60	3.00
Mercury 73660		Sailing / Let Me Be Your Car	1975	.60	3.00
Mercury 73802		What's Made Milwaukee Famous /			
		Every Picture Tells A Story	1975	.60	3.00
Warner Bros. 8146		Sailing / All In The Name Of Rock N' Roll	1975	.40	2.00
Warner Bros. 8170		This Old Heart Of Mine / Still Love You	1976	.40	2.00
Warner Bros. 8262		Tonight's The Night (Gonna Be Alright) / Fool For You	1976	.40	2.00
Warner Bros. 8321		The First Cut Is The Deepest / Rosie	1977	Unreleased	
Warner Bros. 8321		The First Cut Is The Deepest / The Ball Trap	1977	.40	2.00
Warner Bros. 8396		The Killing Of Georgie / Rosie	1977	.30	1.50
Warner Bros. 8475		You're In My Heart (The Final Acclaim) / You Got A Nerve	1977	.30	1.50
Warner Bros. 8535		Hot Legs / You're Insane	1978	.30	1.50
Warner Bros. 8535	(PS)	Hot Legs / You're Insane	1978	.30	1.50
Warner Bros. 8568		I Was Only Joking / Born Loose	1978	.30	1.50
Warner Bros. 8568	(PS)	I Was Only Joking / Born Loose	1978	.30	1.50
Warner Bros. 8724		Do Ya Think I'm Sexy? / Scarred & Scared	1978	.30	1.50
Warner Bros. 8724	(PS)	Do Ya Think I'm Sexy? / Scarred & Scared	1978	.30	1.50
Warner Bros. 8810		Ain't Love A Bitch / Last Summer	1979	.30	1.50
Warner Bros. 8810	(PS)	Ain't Love A Bitch / Last Summer	1979	.30	1.50
Warner Bros. 49138		I Don't Want To Talk About It / The Best Days Of My Life	1979	.30	1.50
Warner Bros. 49617		Passion / Better Off Dead	1980	.20	1.00
Warner Bros. 49686		Somebody Special / She Won't Dance With Me	1981	.20	1.00
Warner Bros. 49843		Young Turks / Sonny	1981	.20	1.00
Warner Bros. 49886		Tonight I'm Yours / Tora, Tora, Tora	1981	.20	1.00
Warner Bros. 50051		How Long / Jealous	1982	.20	1.00
Warner Bros. 29874		Guess I'll Always Love You / Rock My Plimsoul	1982	.20	1.00
Warner Bros. 29608		Baby Jane / Ready Now	1983	.20	1.00
Warner Bros. 29564		What Am I Gonna Do? / Dancing Alone	1983	.20	1.00
Warner Bros. 29526		Infatuation / She Won't Dance	1984	.20	1.00
Warner Bros. 29215		Some Guys Have All The Luck /	1984	.20	1.00
Warner Bros. 29122		Alright Now /	1984	.20	1.00
Warner Bros. 29668		Love Touch / Heart Is On The Line	1986	.20	1.00
Warner Bros. 28631		Another Heartache /	1986	.20	1.00
Warner Bros. 28625		Every Beat Of My Heart /	1986	.20	1.00
Geffen 28303		Twistin' The Night Away /	1987	.20	1.00
Warner Bros. 27927		Lost In Love / Almost Illegal	1988	.20	1.00
Warner Bros. 27796		Forever Young / Days Of Rage	1988	.20	1.00
Warner Bros. 27729		My Heart Can't Tell You No / Wild Horses	1989	.20	1.00
Warner Bros. 27657		Crazy About Her / / Dynamite	1989	.20	1.00
Warner Bros. 22685		Downtown Train / Killing Of Georgie, Parts 1 & 2	1989	.20	1.00
Warner Bros. 19983		This Old Heart Of Mine / You're In My Heart	1990	.20	1.00
Warner Bros. 19366		Rhythm Of My Heart / Moment Of Glory	1990	.20	1.00
Warner Bros. 19322		The Motown Song / Sweet Soul Music	1990	.20	1.00
Warner Bros. 19274		Broken Arrow / The Wild Horse	1990	.20	1.00

STEWART, TY, & THE JOKERS
Amy 828		Young Girl / Here I Am	1962	5.00	25.00

STICKS & THE STONES, THE
Coral 62524		Try / Live To Be Free	1968	2.00	10.00

STILLS, STEPHEN (& MANASSAS)
Steve Stills also recorded with The Buffalo Springfield; Mike Bloomfield; and Crosby, Stills & Nash.
Atlantic 2778		Love The One You're With / To A Flame	1970	.60	3.00
Atlantic 2790		Sit Yourself Down / We Are Not Helpless	1971	.60	3.00
Atlantic 2806		Change Partners / Relaxing Town	1971	.60	3.00
Atlantic 2820		Mariane / Nothing To Do	1971	.60	3.00
Atlantic 2876		It Doesn't Matter / Rock & Roll Crazy Medley	1972	.60	3.00
Atlantic 2888		Rock & Roll Crazies / Colorado	1972	.60	3.00
Atlantic 2917		Down The Road / Guaguanco De Vero	1972	.60	3.00
Atlantic 2959		Isn't It About Time? / So Many Times	1973	.60	3.00
Columbia 10179		Turn Back The Pages / Shuffle Just As Bad	1975	.40	2.00
Columbia 10369		Buyin' Time / Soldier	1976	.40	2.00
Columbia 10804		Can't Get No Booty / Lowdown	1978	.40	2.00
Columbia 10872		Thoroughfare Gap / Lowdown	1978	.40	2.00

STILLS-YOUNG BAND, THE
Steve Stills and Neil Young.
Reprise 1365		Long May You Run / 12-8 Blues (All The Same)	1976	.60	3.00
Reprise 1378		Midnight On The Bay / Black Coral	1976	.60	3.00

STINGLEY, ROY
Jerden 801		11:45 / Long Live The Queen	196?	.80	4.00

STINGRAYS OF SPRINGFIELD, ILLINOIS
Ray 877		Mad Surfer / Surfer's Walk	196?	8.00	40.00

Label & Catalog #		A-Side/B-Side	Year	VG	NM
STINIT, DANE					
Sun 402		Don't Knock What You Don't Understand /			
		Always On The Go	1966	2.00	10.00
Sun 405		Sweet Country Girl / That Muddy Old River	1967	2.00	10.00
STITES, GARY					
Carlton 508		Lonely For You / Shine That Ring	1959	3.00	15.00
Carlton 516		A Girl Like You / Hey, Little Girl	1959	3.00	15.00
Carlton 521		Starry Eyed / Without Your Love	1959	3.00	15.00
Carlton 525		Don't Wanna Say Goodbye / Lawdy, Miss Clawdy	1960	3.00	15.00
Madison 138		Young Love / Little Tiger	1960	3.00	15.00
Madison 155		Honey Girl / Little Lonely One	1961	3.00	15.00
STOKES, SIMON T.					
Simon Stokes also recorded with The Flower Children.					
HBR 487		Big City Blues / Truth Is Stranger Than Fiction	1966	3.00	15.00
STOKES, SIMON, & THE NIGHTHAWKS					
Elektra 45670		Voo Doo Woman / Voo Doo Woman (Part 2)	1970	1.60	8.00
MGM 14189		Ballad Of Little Fauss And Big Halsy / Where Are You Going?	197?	1.00	5.00
Casablanca 0007		Captain Howdy /			
		I Fell For Her, She Fell For Him And He Fell For Me	1974	.60	3.00
Casablanca 0007	(PS)	Captain Howdy /			
		I Fell For Her, She Fell For Him And He Fell For Me	1974	.60	3.00
Apache 71554	(DJ)	Chucky / Chucky	1988	.60	3.00
STOMPERS, THE					
Souvenir 1003		Blue Moon Of Kentucky / I Miss You So	196?	20.00	100.00
STOMPERS, THE					
Landa 684		Quarter To Four Stomp / Foolish One	1961	2.00	10.00
Landa 684		Surf Stompin' / Foolish One	1961	2.00	10.00
Gone 5120		Stompin' 'Round The Christmas Tree /			
		Stompin' 'Round The Christmas Tree (Part 2)	1961	3.00	15.00
Mercury 72111		Frump / Blacksmith Blues	1963	3.00	15.00
STONE, JEFF					
Freedom 44002		My Baby / (B-side by The Four Dots)	1958	7.00	35.00
STONE, JOHN					
Jerden 104		My Blue Heaven / On What It Seemed To Be	196?	.80	4.00
Jerden 708		Choice / Treasure Of Love	196?	.80	4.00
STONE CRUSHERS, THE					
RCA Victor 47-7309		Crawfish / Tadpole Wiggle	1958	4.00	20.00
STONE PONEYS, THE: *Refer to* **LINDA RONSTADT & THE STONE PONEYS**					
STONEGROUND					
Stoneground features Sal Valentino, formerly of The Beau Brummels.					
Warner Bros. 7452		Total Destruction / Queen Street Blues	1971	.80	4.00
Warner Bros. 7469		Looking For You / Added Attraction (Come And See Me)	1971	.80	4.00
Warner Bros. 7535		You Must Be One Of Us / Corrina	1972	.80	4.00
Flat Out 002		Way Back /	1976	.80	4.00
Warner/Curb 8676		Prove It / Lead Me Down	1978	.60	3.00
STONES, THE					
Solly 928		She Said Yeah / Watch Me	1966	5.00	25.00
		(Re-issued on Solly credited to The Tracers.)			
STOOGES, THE					
The Stooges feature Iggy Pop.					
Elektra 45664	(DJ)	I Wanna Be Your Dog / I Wanna Be Your Dog, Part 2	1969	3.00	15.00
Elektra 45664		I Wanna Be Your Dog / I Wanna Be Your Dog, Part 2	1969	6.00	30.00
Elektra 45695	(DJ)	Down On The Street / I Feel Alright	1970	3.00	15.00
Elektra 45695		Down On The Street / I Feel Alright	1970	6.00	30.00
Columbia 45877	(DJ)	Search And Destroy / Penetration	1971	5.00	25.00
Columbia 45877		Search And Destroy / Penetration	1971	10.00	50.00
STOP					
Garland 2010		Cathy's Clown / Hip Girl	196?	.80	4.00
STOP, DICKIE					
B.E.A.T. 1007		Class Cutter / Ruth Ann	1959	2.00	10.00
STOREY SISTERS, THE					
The Storey Sisters originally recorded as The Twinkles.					
Baton 255		Which Way Did My Heart Go? / Cha Cha Boom	1958	3.00	15.00

Label & Catalog #		A-Side/B-Side	Year	VG	NM
Cameo 126		Bad Motorcycle / Sweet Daddy	1958	3.00	15.00
Mercury 71457		Lost Love / Lover, How I Miss You	1959	3.00	15.00

STORIES
Stories features Michael Brown , formerly of The Left Banke

Label & Catalog #		A-Side/B-Side	Year	VG	NM
Kama Sutra 545	(PS)	I'm Coming Home (Promo picture sleeve)	1972	1.00	5.00
Kama Sutra 545		I'm Coming Home / You Told Me	1972	.60	3.00
Kama Sutra 558		Top Of The City / Step Back	1972	.60	3.00
Kama Sutra 566		Darling / Take Cover	1973	.60	3.00
Kama Sutra 574		Love's In Motion / Changes Have Begun	1973	.60	3.00
Kama Sutra 577		Brother Louie / What Comes After?	1973	.60	3.00
Kama Sutra 584		Mammy Blue / Traveling Underground	1973	.60	3.00
Kama Sutra 588		If It Feels Good, Do It / Circles	1973	.60	3.00
Kama Sutra 594		Another Love / Love Is In Motion	1973	.60	3.00

STORM, ROY, & THE HURRICANES

Label & Catalog #	A-Side/B-Side	Year	VG	NM
Columbia 43018	I Can Tell / (B-side by Faron's Flamingos)	1964	2.00	10.00

STORM, TOM, & THE PEPS
Refer to The Peps.

Label & Catalog #	A-Side/B-Side	Year	VG	NM
Ge Ge 501	I Love You / That's The Way Love Is	1965	3.00	15.00

STORM, WARREN

Label & Catalog #	A-Side/B-Side	Year	VG	NM
Nasco 6015	The Prisoner Song / Mama, Mama, Mama	1958	3.00	15.00
Nasco 6025	Trouble Troubles / My Moments Of Sorrow	1959	3.00	15.00
Nasco 6028	So Long, So Long #1 / I've Got My Heart In My Hand	1959	3.00	15.00
Nasco 6031	I'm A Little Boy / Birmingham Jail	1959	3.00	15.00
Top Rank 2086	No, No #2 / Bohawk Georgia Grind	1960	3.00	15.00
Dot 16272	Gotta Go Back To School / I Can't Love You	1961	2.00	10.00
Dot 16344	Take These Chains From My Heart / It's Hard But It's Fair	1962	2.00	10.00
Atco 6577	Rock Down In My Shoe / Nobody Would Know	1964	1.60	8.00

STORMS, THE

Label & Catalog #	A-Side/B-Side	Year	VG	NM
Sundown 114	Thunder / Tarantula	1959	4.00	20.00

STORYTELLERS, THE

Label & Catalog #	A-Side/B-Side	Year	VG	NM
Stack 500	You Played Me For A Fool / Hey, Baby	1959	50.00	200.00

STORYTELLERS, THE

Label & Catalog #	A-Side/B-Side	Year	VG	NM
Columbia 42930	Engagement Party / The Blue Grass Of Kentucky	1963	2.00	10.00

STORYTELLERS, THE
The Storytellers feature Steve Barri.

Label & Catalog #	A-Side/B-Side	Year	VG	NM
Ramarca 501	When Two People / Time Will Tell	1963	6.00	30.00
Dimension 1014	When Two People / Time Will Tell	1963	4.00	20.00
Capitol 5042	I Don't Want An Angel / Down In The Valley	1963	4.00	20.00

STRANGE BROTHERS SHOW, THE

Label & Catalog #	A-Side/B-Side	Year	VG	NM
Sire 4120	Shakey Jakes / Right On	196?	2.00	10.00

STRANGELOVES, THE
The Strangeloves are Bob Feldman and Jerry Goldstein, who also recorded as Bob & Jerry and The Sheep.

Label & Catalog #	A-Side/B-Side	Year	VG	NM
Swan 4192	I'm On Fire / Love, Love (That's All I Want From You)	1964	3.00	15.00
Bang 501	I Want Candy / It's About My Baby	1965	2.00	10.00
Bang 508	Cara-Lin / (Roll On) Mississippi	1965	1.60	8.00
Bang 514	Night Time / Rhythm Of Love	1966	1.60	8.00
Bang 524	Hand Jive / I Gotta Dance	1966	1.60	8.00
Bang 544	Quarter To Three / Just The Way You Are	1966	1.60	8.00
Sire 4102	Honey Do / I Wanna Do It	196?	1.00	5.00

STRANGERS, THE

Label & Catalog #	A-Side/B-Side	Year	VG	NM
Titan 1701	Rockin' Rebel / The Caterpillar Crawl	1959	4.00	20.00
Titan 1702	Hill Stomp / A Lost Soul	1959	3.00	15.00
Titan 1704	Boogie Man / Young Maggie	1960	3.00	15.00
Titan 1711	Dance Of The Ants / Navaho	1960	3.00	15.00

STRANGERS, THE
The Strangers also recorded with Bill Velline.

Label & Catalog #	A-Side/B-Side	Year	VG	NM
Cuca 1172	Runaway / John Henry	1960	25.00	125.00

STRANGERS, THE

Label & Catalog #	A-Side/B-Side	Year	VG	NM
Choice 5	Bart Maverick / Bret Maverick	1960	2.00	10.00

STRANGERS, THE

Label & Catalog #	A-Side/B-Side	Year	VG	NM
Warner Bros. 5438	Night Winds / These Are The Things I Love	1964	2.00	10.00

STRANGERS, THE

Label & Catalog #	A-Side/B-Side	Year	VG	NM
Christy 107	Crab Louie / We're In Love, We're In Love, We're In Love	196?	2.00	10.00

Label & Catalog #		A-Side/B-Side	Year	VG	NM
STRASSMAN, MARCIA					
Uni 55006		The Flower Children / Out Of The Picture	1967	2.00	10.00
Uni 55023		Groovy World Of Jack And Jill / The Flower Shop	1967	2.00	10.00
Uni 55023	(PS)	Groovy World Of Jack And Jill / The Flower Shop	1967	3.00	15.00
Uni 55056		Self-Analysis / Star Gazer	1967	2.00	10.00
STRAT-O-JACS, THE					
Parrot 45003		Sunset Surfer / Hot Toddy	1964	2.00	10.00
STRAWBERRY ALARM CLOCK					
The Strawberry Alarm Clock originally recorded as Sixpence.					
All American 373		Incense And Peppermints / Birdman Of Alkatrash	1967	15.00	75.00
Uni 55018		Incense And Peppermints / Birdman Of Alkatrash	1967	1.60	8.00
Uni 55046		Tomorrow / Birds In My Tree	1967	1.20	6.00
Uni 55055		Sit With The Guru / Pretty Song From "Psych-Out"	1968	1.20	6.00
Uni 55076		Barefoot In Baltimore / Angry Young Man	1968	1.20	6.00
Uni 55093		Sea Shell / Paxton's Back Street Carnival	1968	1.20	6.00
Uni 55113		Stand By / Miss Attraction	1969	1.20	6.00
Uni 55125		Good Morning Starshine / Me And The Township	1969	1.20	6.00
Uni 55158		Desiree / Changes	1969	1.20	6.00
Uni 55185		Starting Out The Day / Small Package	1969	1.20	6.00
Uni 55190		I Climbed The Mountain / Three	1970	1.20	6.00
Uni 55218		California Day / Three	1970	1.20	6.00
Uni 55241		Girl From The City / Three	1970	1.20	6.00
STRAWBS, THE					
A&M 944		Oh, How She Changed / Or Am I Dreaming?	1968	1.00	5.00
A&M 998		Poor Jimmy Wilson / The Man Who Called Himself Jesus	1968	1.00	5.00
A&M 1364		Benedictus / Heavy Disguise	1972	.80	4.00
A&M 1687		Lemon Pie / Where Do You Go (When You Need A Hole To Crawl In?)	1974	.80	4.00
A&M 1747		Little Sleepy / Golden Salamander	1975	.80	4.00
Oyster 702		I Only Want My Love To Grow In You / (Wasting My Time) Thinking Of You	1976	.60	3.00
Oyster 704		So Close And Yet So Far Away /	1977	.60	3.00
Oyster 705		Burning For Me / Heartbreaker	1977	.60	3.00
Arista 0327		I Don't Want To Talk About It / Words Of Wisdom	1978	.60	3.00
STREAMERS, THE					
Dot 16648		Slipstream / Blue Mountain	196?	5.00	25.00
		("Slipstream" features Davie Allan on guitar.)			
STREET CLEANERS, THE					
The Street Cleaners are Steve Barri and Phil Sloan.					
Amy 916		Garbage City / That's Good, That's Trash	1964	6.00	30.00
STREET PEOPLE, THE					
Musicor 1365		Jennifer Tomkins / All Night Long	1969	.80	4.00
Musicor 1401		Thank You, Girl / The World Doesn't Matter Anymore	1970	.80	4.00
Musicor 1412		I Remember / I Wonder What Happened To Sally?	1970	.80	4.00
STRENGTH, BILL					
Sun 346		I Guess I'd Better Go / Senorita	1960	3.00	15.00
STRICKLAND, JOHNNY					
Roulette 4119		She's Mine / You've Got What It Takes	1959	10.00	50.00
Roulette 4147		I've Heard That Line Before / Don't Leave Me Lonely	1959	3.00	15.00
STRIKES, THE					
Lin 5006		Baby, I'm Sorry / If You Can't Rock Me	1957	8.00	40.00
Imperial 5433		Baby, I'm Sorry / If You Can't Rock Me	1957	3.00	15.00
Imperial 5446		I Don't Want To Cry Over You / Rockin'	1957	3.00	15.00
STROLLS, THE					
Sky Rocket		Madisonville / Madisonville (Part 2)	1960	2.00	10.00
STUART, CHAD					
Refer to Chad & Jeremy; California Music.					
Sidewalk 944		Good Morning Sunrise / Paxton's Song	1966	1.00	5.00
Sidewalk 944	(PS)	Good Morning Sunrise / Paxton's Song	1966	2.00	10.00
STUART, CHAD & JILL					
Columbia 43467		The Cruel War / I Can't Talk To You	1966	1.00	5.00
Columbia 43467	(PS)	The Cruel War / I Can't Talk To You	1966	1.60	8.00
STUART CHORUS, GLEN					
Abel 235		Drip Drop / Ruby Baby	196?	3.00	15.00

Label & Catalog #	A-Side/B-Side	Year	VG	NM
STYLE KINGS, THE				
Sotoplay 0011	Kissing Behind The Moon /	195?	7.00	35.00
STYLES, THE				
Serene 1501	Scarlet Angel / Gotta Go, Go, Go	196?	25.00	125.00
Josie 920	I Love You For Sentimental Reasons /			
	School Bells To Chapel Bells	1964	15.00	75.00
STYX, THE				
The Styx also recorded as Butch Engel & The Styx.				
Onyx 2200	Hey, I'm Lost / Puppetmaster	1966	3.00	15.00
STYX				
Wooden Nickel 0106	Best Thing / What Has Come Between Us?	1972	1.00	5.00
Wooden Nickel 0111	I'm Gonna Make You Feel It / Quick Is The Beat Of My Heart	1973	1.00	5.00
Wooden Nickel 0116	Lady / You Better Ask	1973	1.00	5.00
Wooden Nickel 10102	Lady / Children Of The Land	1974	.80	4.00
Wooden Nickel 10272	You Need Love / You Better Ask	1975	.80	4.00
Wooden Nickel 10329	Havin' A Ball / Best Thing	1975	.80	4.00
Wooden Nickel 11205	Winner Take All / Best Thing	1978	.60	3.00
SUADES, THE				
Spinning 6011	Everybody's Trying To Be My Baby / Wrong Yo Yo	1961	7.00	35.00
SUB ZERO BAND, THE				
Lavender 2017	Angel Baby / Flapjack	196?	2.00	10.00
SUBURBANS, THE				
Port 70011	Alphabet Of Love / Sweet Diane Cha Cha	196?	6.00	30.00
SUDDENS, THE				
Sudden 103	Childish Ways / Garden Of Love	1961	20.00	100.00
SUDELS, THE				
American Arts 12	Pow Wow / Suzuki	1964	7.00	35.00
SUGAR				
Sugar features Ginger Blake, formerly of The Honeys.				
Carousel 30059	Dynamite / A Million To One	1972	1.60	8.00
Rocky Road 30063	Dancing In The Street / Dancing In The Street	1973	1.60	8.00
SUGAR BEATS, THE				
A&M 795	First Love / Begin-Give In	1966	1.60	8.00
SUGAR BUNS, THE				
Warner Bros. 5046	Pajama Party / Nails And Snails	1959	2.00	10.00
SUGAR CANES, THE				
King 5157	Poor Boy / Sioux Rock	1958	2.00	10.00
SUGARLOAF [JERRY CORBETTA & SUGARLOAF]				
Liberty 56183	Green-Eyed Lady / West Of Tomorrow	1970	.80	4.00
Liberty 56281	Tongue In Cheek / Woman	1971	.60	3.00
Liberty 56281 (PS)	Tongue In Cheek / Woman	1971	1.20	6.00
United Artists 50784	Mother Nature's Wine / Back Door Man-Chest Fever	1971	.60	3.00
Brut 805	Round And Round / Colorado Jones	1973	.60	3.00
Brut 815	I Got A Song / Myra Myra	1973	.60	3.00
Brut 815 (PS)	I Got A Song / Myra Myra	1973	1.20	6.00
Claridge 402	Don't Call Us, We'll Call You / Texas Two Lane	1974	.60	3.00
Claridge 405	Stars In My Eyes / Myra Myra	1975	.60	3.00
Claridge 408	Boogie Man / I Got A Song	1975	.60	3.00
Claridge 415	Have A Good Time / You Set My Dreams To Music	1976	.60	3.00
Claridge 422	Last Dance, Take A Chance / Satisfaction Guaranteed	1976	.60	3.00
SUGGS, BRAD				
Phillips Int. 3571	Elephant Walk / Like Catchin' Up	1959	4.00	20.00
SULLIVAN, NIKI				
Niki Sullivan also recorded with The Crickets; The Hollyhawks.				
Dot 15751	It's All Over / Three Steps To Heaven	1958	15.00	75.00
Joli 073	My Lost Dream / Doin' The Dive	195?	10.00	50.00
Joli 075	It Really Doesn't Matter / You Better Get A Move On	195?	15.00	75.00
SULTANS, THE				
Tilt 782	It'll Be Easy / You Got Me Goin' (Yellow label)	1961	15.00	75.00
Tilt 782	It'll Be Easy / You Got Me Goin' (Black label)	196?	4.00	20.00
Guyden 2079	Christina / Someone You Can Trust	1963	3.00	15.00
Ascot 2228	Gloria / I Wanna Know	1964	4.00	20.00

Label & Catalog #	A-Side/B-Side	Year	VG	NM
Jam 107	Mary, Mary / How Far Does A Friendship Go?	196?	3.00	15.00
SUMMER, FALL, WINTER, SPRING				
United Artists 50112	For A Moment / Please Don't Forget Tonight	1967	2.00	10.00
SUMMERS, BOB				
Crusader 107	Honda Hawk / Organization	1964	2.00	10.00
SUMMERS, BOBBY				
Capitol 4143	Parade Rock / Pad	1959	2.00	10.00
Capitol 4404	Back Beat / Comin' Round The Mountain	1960	2.00	10.00
Uni 1900	Jingle Jangle Jingle / Teeter Totter	1961	2.00	10.00
SUMMERS, GENE				
Jan 100	School Of Rock 'N Roll / Straight Skirt	196?	8.00	40.00
Jan 102	Gotta Lotta That / Nervous	196?	8.00	40.00
Mercury 72606	Green-Eyed Monster / The Clown	1966	3.00	15.00
SUMMERS, LITTLE DAVEY				
Vim 101	Calling All Cars / Good Ship Love	1963	2.00	10.00
Dore 684	Gonna Climb That Big Ole Hill / Doin' The Davey Drag	1963	2.00	10.00
SUMMITS, THE				
Harmon 1017	He's An Angel / Hanky Panky	1963	6.00	30.00
Rust 5072	He's An Angel / Hanky Panky	1963	3.00	15.00
SUN-RAYS, THE				
Sun 293	The Lonely Hours / Love Is A Stranger	1958	3.00	15.00
SUNDANCERS, THE				
Break Out 111	Devil Surf /	196?	7.00	35.00
SUNDAY FUNNIES, THE				
Hideout 1070	Heavy Music /	1965	10.00	50.00
Mercury 72571	Wonder Woman / She's Not At All Like You	1966	1.60	8.00
SUNDAY MORNING				
NWI 2757	Lay Back Day / Sunday Morning	1970	.60	3.00
SUNDIALS, THE				
Guyden 2065	Chapel Of Love / Whether To Resist	1962	30.00	150.00
SUNDOWN PLAYBOYS, The				
Apple 1852	Saturday Night Special / Valse De Soleil Coucher	1972	2.00	10.00
SUNGLOWS, THE [SUNNY & THE SUNGLOWS]				
Refer to Sunny & The Sunliners.				
Sunglow 104	Golly Gee / Touring	1962	2.00	10.00
OKeh 7143	Golly Gee / Touring	1962	1.60	8.00
Tear Drop 3014	Talk To Me / Every Week, Every Month, Every Year	1963	1.60	8.00
	(Tear Drop 3014 credits Sunny & The Sunglows.)			
Tear Drop 3022	Rags To Riches / Not Even Judgement Day	1963	1.60	8.00
Tear Drop 3034	It's Too Late / You Gave Me A True Tune	1964	1.60	8.00
Tear Drop 3040	You Send Me / His Greatest Creation	1964	1.60	8.00
Disco Grande 1021	Peanuts (La Cacahuta) / Happy Hippo	1965	2.00	10.00
Sunglow 107	Peanuts (La Cacahuta) / Happy Hippo	1965	1.60	8.00
Sunglow 110	Talk To Me / Every Week, Every Month, Every Year	1965	1.60	8.00
Sunglow 111	Rags To Riches / Not Even Judgement Day	1965	1.60	8.00
SUNLIGHT, SKY, & THE NEW SEEDS				
Sky Sunlight is a pseudonym of Ritch Marsh a.k.a. Sky Saxon of The Seeds.				
Expression 777	Beautiful Stars / Universal Stars	1977	2.00	10.00
SUNNY & THE HORIZONS				
Luxor 1013	Nature's Creation / Because They Tell Me	195?	50.00	200.00
SUNNY & THE SUNLINERS				
Tear Drop 3027	Out Of Sight, Out Of Mind / No One Else Will Do	1964	1.60	8.00
SUNNY BOYS, THE				
Mr. Maestro 805	For The Rest Of My Life / My Friend Sam	196?	5.00	25.00
Mr. Maestro 806	Chapel Bells / My Friend Sam	196?	4.00	20.00
Take Three 201	For The Rest Of My Life / Chapel Bells	196?	4.00	20.00
SUNRAYS, THE				
The Sunrays feature Rick Henn and were produced by Murry Wilson. Refer to Joy; The Snowmen.				
Tower 101	Car Party / Outta Gas	1964	4.00	20.00
Tower 148	I Live For The Sun / Bye, Baby, Bye	1965	1.60	8.00

Label & Catalog #		A-Side/B-Side	Year	VG	NM
Tower 191		Andrea / You Don't Phase Me	1965	1.60	8.00
Tower 224		Still / When You're Not Me	1966	1.60	8.00
Tower 256		Don't Take Yourself So Seriously / I Look Baby, I Can't See	1966	1.60	8.00
Tower 256	(PS)	Don't Take Yourself So Seriously / I Look Baby, I Can't See	1966	5.00	25.00
Tower 290		Just 'Round The River Bend / Hi, How Are You?	1966	3.00	15.00
Tower 340		Loaded With Love / Time	1966	2.00	10.00
Tower 340	(PS)	Loaded With Love / Time	1966	7.00	35.00

SUNS, THE

Times Square 32		That's My Baby / (B-side by The Camelots)	197?	1.60	8.00
Times Square 32		That's My Baby / (B-side by The Camelots) (Colored vinyl)	197?	3.00	15.00

SUNSETS, THE

Petal 1040		Lydia / Only You, Only Me	1963	3.00	15.00

SUNSETS, THE
The Sunsets were produced by Gary Usher.

Challenge 9186	(DJ)	C. C. Cinder / The Chug-A-Lug	1963	4.00	20.00
Challenge 9186		C. C. Cinder / The Chug-A-Lug	1963	8.00	40.00
Challenge 9198	(DJ)	Playmate Of The Year / Lonely Surfer Boy	1963	4.00	20.00
Challenge 9198		Playmate Of The Year / Lonely Surfer Boy	1963	8.00	40.00
Challenge 9208	(DJ)	My Little Surfin' Woodie / My Little Beach Bunny	1963	5.00	25.00
Challenge 9208		My Little Surfin' Woodie / My Little Beach Bunny	1963	10.00	50.00

SUNSHINE

Capitol 3051		I Just Can't Help You / Is There Anybody Else?	1971	1.00	5.00

SUNSHINE COMPANY, THE

Imperial 66247		Happy / Blue May	1967	.80	4.00
Imperial 66260		Back On The Street Again / A Year Of Janie's Time	1967	.80	4.00
Imperial 66280		Look, Here Comes The Sun / It's Sunday	1968	.80	4.00
Imperial 66324		Love Poem / Willie Jean	1968	.80	4.00

SUNSHINEWARD, THE
The Sunshineward is a pseudonym for The Astronauts.

RCA Victor 47-9227		Sally Go Round The Roses / Pay The Price	1967	2.00	10.00

SUNSHYNE

PN 500		Dance Like An Animal / Mighty Rough Road	196?	2.00	10.00

SUPER K GENERATION, THE

Laurie 3413		Heart Full O' Soul / Heart Full O' Soul (Part 2)	1967	1.00	5.00

SUPER-PHONICS, THE

Lindy 102		Teenage Partner /	196?	10.00	50.00

SUPER STOCKS, THE
The Super Stocks were a studio creation of Gary Usher. Refer to the Various Artists EP section.

Capitol 5153		Thunder Road / Wheel Stands	1964	5.00	25.00
Capitol PRO-2642	(DJ)	Midnight Run / Santa Barbara	1964	5.00	25.00
		(Capitol PRO-2642 was issued in a special "pocket" on the cover of the "Surfink" album.)			

SUPERBS, THE

Melmar 121		My Love For You / Beans	1961	4.00	20.00
Dore 704		The Story Book Of Love / Better Get Your Own, Buddy	1964	3.00	15.00
Dore 715		Baby, Baby All The Time / Raindrops, Memories And Tears	1964	3.00	15.00
Dore 722		My Heart Isn't In It / Sad, Sad Day	1964	4.00	20.00
Dore 727		The Big Hurt / I Was Blind	1965	3.00	15.00
Dore 731		Baby's Gone Away / Twine And Slide	1965	3.00	15.00
Dore 733		The Girl In The Bikini / I'm Beginning To Understand Them	1965	4.00	20.00
Dore 736		It Hurts So Much / Born When You Kissed Me	1965	3.00	15.00
Dore 748		Goddess Of Love / He Broke A Young Girl's Heart	1965	3.00	15.00
Dore 755		It's A Million Miles To Paradise / He Broke A Young Girl's Heart	1966	2.00	10.00
Dore 782		He Broke A Young Girl's Heart / I Wanna Do It With You, Baby	1967	1.00	5.00

SUPERTONES, THE

Everest 19325		Slippin' And Stoppin' / Slippin' And Stoppin' (Part 2)	1960	2.00	10.00

SUPREMES, THE

E.O.E.O.C.		Things Are Changing / Things Are Changing	1965	50.00	200.00
E.O.E.O.C.	(PS)	Things Are Changing / Things Are Changing	1965	50.00	200.00
		(Manufactured for the Equal Opportunity Employment Opportunities Campaign using a Phil Spector production of Brian Wilson's "Don't Hurt My Little Sister" with Brian on piano. The same backing track was used on performances by The Blossoms and Jay & The Americans. Note: The Supremes extensive catalog of soul singles are not included in this edition.)			

Label & Catalog #		A-Side/B-Side	Year	VG	NM
SURF, ADAM, & THE PEBBLE BEACH BAND					
Paladin 3		Blue Surf / Fun Fun Fun	196?	6.00	30.00
SURF BOYS, THE					
Karate 526		Da Doo Ron Ron / Hurt	1966	5.00	25.00
Scepter 12180		I Told Santa Claus I Want You / Stuck In The Chimney	1966	5.00	25.00
SURF BREAKERS, THE					
Mercury 72174		Hang Ten / Ridin' In Number Nine	1963	7.00	35.00
SURF BUNNIES, THE					
Goliath 1352		Surf Bunny Beach / Our Surfer Boys	1963	10.00	50.00
Goliath 1353		Surf City High / Met The Boy I Adore	1963	10.00	50.00
Dot 16523		Surf Bunny Beach / Our Surfer Boys	1963	6.00	30.00
SURF SIDERS, THE					
Astro 101		Chug-A-Lug Charlie / I Want To Love You My Way	196?	6.00	30.00
SURFMEN, THE					
Titan 1723		Paradise Cove / The Ghost Hop	1962	6.00	30.00
		(First pressings make no mention of Era Records.)			
Titan 1723		Paradise Cove / The Ghost Hop	1962	4.00	20.00
		(Second pressing labels read "Distributed by Era.")			
Titan 1727		Malibu Run / El Toro	1962	5.00	25.00
Titan 1729		The Breakers / The Casanova	1963	5.00	25.00
SURF RIDERS, THE					
Brass 172		Island In The Sun / Fennerio	196?	7.00	35.00
Cloister 6202		Surf Fair / Surfboard	1962	7.00	35.00
Cloister 6202	(PS)	Surf Fair / Surfboard	1962	8.00	40.00
SURF STOMPERS, THE: *Refer to* BRUCE JOHNSTON					
SURF TEENS, THE					
Westco 9		Moonshine / Moment Of Truth	1963	7.00	35.00

SURFARIS, THE [THE ORIGINAL SURFARIS]
The Surfaris originally recorded as The Customs. The first five singles are credited to The Surfaris. After legal action, they changed their name to The Original Surfaris, which they are listed as on the Surfari and Regano singles.

Northridge 1001		Moment Of Truth / (B-side by The Biscaynes)	1963	7.00	35.00
Reprise 2047		Moment Of Truth / (B-side by The Biscaynes)	1963	5.00	25.00
Del-Fi 4219		Surfari / Bombora	1963	15.00	75.00
Chancellor 1143		Midnight Surf / Psych-Out	1963	7.00	35.00
Felsted 8688		Torchula / Psych-Out	1964	7.00	35.00
Surfari 301		Gum Dipped Slicks / High Time	1964	15.00	75.00
Regano 1062		Surfin' '63 / Boss Beat	1964	10.00	50.00
		(Originally issued as "Hi Hat" / "Steppin' Out" credited to The Customs.)			

SURFARIS, THE
The original Surfaris were Bob Berryhill, Pat Connolly, Jim Fuller, Jim Pash and Ron Wilson. The Decca sides feature a Gary Usher studio group with only Wilson allowed to participate as lead singer. Refer to the Various Artists EP section.

DFS 11/2		Wipe Out / Surfer Joe	1962	—	—
		(Rare. Estimated near mint value $500-1,000.)			
Princess 53		Wipe Out / Surfer Joe (Long versions)	1962	25.00	125.00
Princess 53		Wipe Out / Surfer Joe (Short versions)	1962	15.00	75.00
Dot 16479		Wipe Out / Surfer Joe	1963	3.00	15.00
Universal	(DJ)	Wipe Out / Wiggle Wobble	1963	10.00	50.00
Decca 31538		Point Panic / Waikiki Run	1963	3.00	15.00
Decca 31561		Surfer's Christmas List / Santa's Speed Shop	1963	6.00	30.00
Decca 31581		I Wanna Take A Trip To The Islands / Scattershield	1963	4.00	20.00
		(Although uncredited, "I Wanna Take A Trip To The Islands" features The Honeys.)			
Decca 31605		Murphy The Surfie / Go Go Go For Louie's Place	1964	3.00	15.00
Decca 31641		Boss Barracuda / Dune Buggy	1964	3.00	15.00
Decca 31682		Karen / Hot Rod High	1964	3.00	15.00
Decca 31731	(DJ)	Black Denim / Beat '65	1965	3.00	15.00
Decca 31731		Black Denim / Beat '65	1965	6.00	30.00
Decca 31784	(DJ)	Something Else / Theme For The Battle Maiden	1965	2.00	10.00
Decca 31784		Something Else / Theme For The Battle Maiden	1965	4.00	20.00
Decca 31835	(DJ)	Don't Hurt My Little Sister / Catch A Ride With Me	1965	3.00	15.00
Decca 31835		Don't Hurt My Little Sister / Catch A Ride With Me	1965	6.00	30.00
Decca 31954	(DJ)	Hey Joe, Where Are You Going? / So Get Out	1966	2.00	10.00
Decca 31954		Hey Joe, Where Are You Going? / So Get Out	1966	4.00	20.00
		(Decca 31731-31954 produced by Gary Usher.)			
Decca 32003		Wipe Out / I'm A Hog For You	1965	2.00	10.00
Dot 16757		Surfer Joe / (B-side by the Challengers)	1965	7.00	35.00
Dot 16757		Surfer Joe / You Can't Sit Down	1965	7.00	35.00
		(The b-side lists the artist as The Surfaris, although it is actually the Challengers.)			
Dot 16966		Chicago Green / Show Biz	1966	2.00	10.00

Label & Catalog #		A-Side/B-Side	Year	VG	NM
Dot 16966		Chicago Green / Show Biz	1966	2.00	10.00
Dot 144	(DJ)	Wipe Out / Wipe Out (Red vinyl)	1966	30.00	150.00
		(While "Wipe Out" is listed on both sides, "Surfer Joe" plays on both sides.)			
Dot 144	(DJ)	Wipe Out / Surfer Joe (Red vinyl)	1966	30.00	150.00
Dot 144		Wipe Out / Surfer Joe	1966	2.00	10.00
Dot 17008		Search / Shake	1967	2.00	10.00
MCA 60005		Wipe Out / I'm A Hog For You, Baby	1973	1.00	5.00
MCA 2703		Wipe Out / Surfer Joe	1978	1.00	5.00
Koinkidink 101		Punk Line / Scattershield	1982	1.00	5.00
Koinkidink 101	(PS)	Punk Line / Scattershield	1982	2.00	10.00
		—Extended Play Albums—			
Decca 2765		Wipe Out	1963	20.00	100.00
Decca 34292	(33)	Hit City '65 (Jukebox EP)	1968	8.00	40.00
Decca 34293	(33)	It Ain't Me Babe (Jukebox EP)	1968	8.00	40.00

SURFER GIRLS, THE

Columbia 4-43001		Draggin' Wagon / One Boy Tells Another	1964	5.00	25.00

SURFERS, THE

DRA 318		Stompin' At The Surfside / Widgit	1962	7.00	35.00

SURFETTES, THE
The Surfettes feature Carol Connors.

Mustang 3001		Sammy The Sidewalk Surfer / Blue Surf	1964	10.00	50.00

SURFSIDE FOUR, THE

Astra 101		Chug-A-Lug Charlie / I Want To Love You	1964	7.00	35.00

SURFSIDE SIX, THE

Palisades 20		South Bay / Redondo Rock	1962	8.00	40.00

SURFSIDERS, THE

Astro 101		Chug-A-Lug Charlie / I Want To Love You	1964	7.00	35.00

SURPRISE

Kare 102		Denise / Blue Moon	196?	3.00	15.00

SURPRISE PACKAGE, THE

Columbia 44294		The Other Me / The Merry-Go-Round Is Slowin' You Down	1967	1.00	5.00
Columbia 43922		Out Of My Mind / Everything Fine	1966	1.00	5.00
Columbia 44460		I'll Run / East Side, West Side	1968	1.00	5.00
LHI 10		Free Up / Free Up, Part 2	1967	1.20	6.00
LHI 15		New Way Home / MacArthur Park	1968	1.20	6.00

SURVIVORS, THE
Written, arranged, produced and performed by Brian Wilson with Bob Norberg. Refer to Bob & Bobby; Bob & Sherri.

Capitol 5102		Pamela Jean / After The Game	1964	100.00	400.00

SUSIE & THE FOUR TRUMPETS

United Artists 471		Starry Eyes / Blue Little Girl	1962	4.00	20.00

SUSIE & THE NIGHT OWLS

Bolo 733		Take That Monorail Ride / Medley	196?	1.00	5.00

SUTCH, SCREAMING LORD

Cameo 341		She's Fallen In Love With The Monster Man / Bye, Bye Baby	1965	2.00	10.00

SUZY & THE RED STRIPES
Suzy & The Red Stripes is a pseudonym for Linda McCartney with Wings.

Epic 8-50403	(DJ)	Seaside Woman / Seaside Woman (Orange & white label)	1977	20.00	100.00
Epic 8-50403	(DJ)	Seaside Woman / Seaside Woman (White label)	1977	15.00	75.00
Epic 8-50403	(DJ)	Seaside Woman / Seaside Woman (Red vinyl)	1977	5.00	25.00
Epic 8-50403		Seaside Woman / B-Side To Seaside	1977	2.00	10.00
		—12" Singles—			
Epic ASF-361	(DJ)	Seaside Woman / B-Side To Seaside	1977	6.00	30.00

SWAGS, THE

West Wind 1003		Rockin' Matilda / Blowing The Blues	196?	3.00	15.00
West Wind 1003	(PS)	Rockin' Matilda / Blowing The Blues	196?	5.00	25.00
Del-Fie 4143		Rockin' Matilda / Blowing The Blues	196?	2.50	12.00

SWAMP RATS, THE

St. Clair 711		It's Not Easy / No Friend Of Mine	1966	8.00	40.00
St. Clair 2222		Psycho / Here, There And Everywhere	1966	15.00	75.00
St. Clair 69		Louie Louie / Hey, Joe	1966	8.00	40.00
Co&Ce 245		In The Midnight Hour / It's Not Easy	1967	4.00	20.00

Long believed to be a pseudonym for the Beach Boys (*Pamela Jean* supposedly an outtake from the *Shut Down, Vol. 2* album), the Survivors was actually head Beach Boy Brian Wilson along with several friends (including former roomie Bob Norberg of Bob & Sherri fame) and studio cats doing a powerhouse remake of *Car Crazy Cutie*. A very rare record indeed.

Label & Catalog #		A-Side/B-Side	Year	VG	NM
SWAMPSEEDS, THE					
Epic 10281		Can I Carry Your Balloon? / Coney Island Parade	1968	2.00	10.00
Epic 10371		If You Could Love Me / Love Is On The Way	1968	1.00	5.00
Epic 10445		Plastic Man / Can I Help You?	1969	1.00	5.00
SWAN, MARY					
Swan 4028		Prisoner Of Love / My Girl Friend, Betty	1959	2.00	10.00
SWANS, THE					
Dot 16210		Why Must I Cry? / Just A Little Bit More	1961	5.00	25.00
SWANS, THE					
Swan 4151		He's Mine / You Better Be A Good Girl Now	1963	6.00	30.00
Cameo 302		The Boy With The Beatle Hair / Please Hurry Home	1964	8.00	40.00
SWANSON, BOBBY					
Igloo 1003		Rockin' Little Eskimo / Ballad Of An Angel	1959	100.00	400.00
Donna 1326		Tom And Suzie / China Doll	1969	3.00	15.00
SWEATHOG					
Columbia 45492		Hallelujah / Still On The Road	1971	.80	4.00
SWEET					
Bell 106	(DJ)	Funny, Funny / Funny, Funny	1971	1.00	5.00
		(Stock copies of Bell 106 may not exist.)			
Bell 126		Co-Co / Burn It Down	1971	1.00	5.00
Bell 184		Poppa Joe / Jeannie	1972	1.00	5.00
Bell 251		Little Willy / Man From Mecca	1973	1.00	5.00
Bell 361		Blockbuster / Need A Lot Of Lovin'	1973	1.00	5.00
Bell 408		New York Connection / Wigwam Bam	1973	1.00	5.00
Capitol 4055		Ballroom Blitz / Restless	1975	.80	4.00
Capitol 4157		Fox On The Run / Turn On The Flame	1975	.80	4.00
Capitol 4220		Action / Medussa	1976	.80	4.00
Capitol 4549		Love Is Like Oxygen / Cover Girl	1977	.80	4.00
Capitol 4454		Funk It Up (David's Song) / Stairway To The Stars	1977	.80	4.00
Capitol 4610		California Nights / A Girl Like You	1978	.80	4.00
Capitol 4730		Mother Earth / Why Don't You	1979	.80	4.00
Capitol 4908		Waters Edge / Sixties Man	1980	.80	4.00
SWEET LINDA DEVINE					
Columbia 44954		Good Day Sunshine / Same Time, Same Place	1969	2.00	10.00
SWEET ROLLE					
Lionel 3204		Squares And Triangles / Little Sister	196?	2.00	10.00
SWEET SICK TEENS, THE					
RCA Victor 47-7940		The Pretzel / Agnes, The Teenage Russian Spy	1962	5.00	25.00
RCA Victor 37-7940	(33)	The Pretzel / Agnes, The Teenage Russian Spy	1962	8.00	40.00
SWEET SMOKE					
Jan-Gi 101		Mary Jane Is To Love / Morning Dew	196?	4.00	20.00
Bell		Mary Jane Is To Love / Morning Dew	196?	2.00	10.00
SWEET SOULS, THE					
The Sweet Souls feature Johnny Fortune.					
R.P.R. 112		I Want To Make It With You / Your Baby	1966	2.00	10.00
SWEET THURSDAY					
Great Western 5023		Dealer / Jenny	1972	.80	4.00
SWIFT, ALLEN					
Leader 815		Are You Lonesome Tonight? / Look Out Below	1961	2.00	10.00
SWIFT, BASIL, & THE SEEGRAMS					
Basil Swift features Danny Hutton on all backing vocals, although speculation of Brian Wilson involvement persists.					
Mercury 72386	(DJ)	Farmer's Daughter / Shambles	1965	15.00	75.00
Mercury 72386		Farmer's Daughter / Shambles	1965	30.00	150.00
SWINGIN' MEDALLIONS, THE					
Four Sale 002		Double Shot (Of My Baby's Love) / Here It Comes Again	1966	6.00	30.00
Smash 2033		Double Shot (Of My Baby's Love) / Here It Comes Again	1966	2.00	10.00
Smash 2050		She Drives Me Out Of My Mind / You Gotta Have Faith	1966	1.20	6.00
Smash 2107		Turn On The Music / Summer's Hot This Time Of Year	1967	1.20	6.00
Smash 2129		Where Can I Go To Get Some Soul? / Bow And Arrow	1967	1.20	6.00
SWINGIN' ROCKS, THE					
Esta 1001		Satellite Rock / Satellite Rock (Part 2)	1959	3.00	15.00

Label & Catalog #	A-Side/B-Side	Year	VG	NM

SWINGING BLUE JEANS, THE
Swingin' Blue Jeans members include Les Braid, Ralph Ellis, Ray Ennis, Norm Kuhlke and Terry Sylvester.

Imperial 66021	Hippy Hippy Shake / Now I Must Go	1964	2.00	10.00
Imperial 66030	Good Golly, Miss Molly / Shaking Feeling	1964	1.60	8.00
Imperial 66049	You're No Good / Shake, Rattle And Roll	1964	1.60	8.00
Imperial 66059	Promise You'll Tell Her / Tutti Frutti	1964	1.60	8.00
Imperial 66090	It Isn't There / One Of These Days	1964	1.60	8.00
Imperial 66154	Don't Make Me Over / What Can I Do Today?	1965	1.60	8.00
Imperial 66225	Rumors, Gossip, Words Untrue / Now The Summer's Gone	1965	1.60	8.00
Imperial 66255	Something's Coming Along / Trembling	1965	1.60	8.00

SWISHER, DEBRA

Boom 60001	You're So Good To Me / Thank You And Good Night	1966	2.00	10.00

SYLVESTER, TERRY
Terry Sylvester also recorded with The Swingin' Blue Jeans and The Hollies..

Epic 2002		Pick Up The Pieces / For The Peace Of All Mankind	1974	.50	2.50
Epic 2002	(PS)	Pick Up The Pieces / For The Peace Of All Mankind	1974	.50	2.50
Epic 50532		Realistic Situation / Silver And Gold	1978	.50	2.50

SYMBOLS, THE

Laurie 3401	Bye Bye, Baby / The Things You Do To Me	1967	4.00	20.00
Laurie 3435	Again / The Best Part Of Breaking Up	1968	2.00	10.00

SYMPHONICS, THE

Tru-Lite 116	Our Love Will Grow / Way Down Low	1963	5.00	25.00
Enrica 1002	Come On, Honey / A Blessing To You	1964	3.00	15.00
Brunswick 55313	No More / She's Just A Sad Girl	1967	1.00	5.00
ABC 11068	Boy / It's Gonna Be Real Hard	1968	1.00	5.00

SYNDICATE OF SOUND, THE

Scarlet 503	Tell The World / Prepare For Love	1965	6.00	30.00
Del Fi 4304	Tell The World / Prepare For Love	1965	4.00	20.00
Hush 228	Little Girl / You	1966	10.00	50.00
Bell 640	Little Girl / You	1966	2.00	10.00
Bell 646	Rumors / The Upper Hand	1966	2.00	10.00
Bell 655	Good Time Music / Keep It Up	1966	2.00	10.00
Bell 666	Mary / That Kind Of Man	1967	2.00	10.00
Capitol 2426	Change The World / You're Looking Fine	1969	1.60	8.00
Buddah 156	Brown Paper Bag / Reverb Beat	1969	1.60	8.00
Buddah 183	The First To Love You / Mexico	1969	1.60	8.00

T.

T-BIRDS, THE

Gone 5141		Wild Stomp / Soft Smoke	1963	3.00	15.00

T-BONES, THE

Liberty 55677		Draggin' / Rail Vette	1964	1.60	8.00
Liberty 55814		Pearlin' / That's Where It's At	1964	1.00	5.00
Liberty 55836		No Matter What Shape (Your Stomach's In) / Feelin' Fine	1965	1.00	5.00
Liberty 55867		Slippin' And Chippin' / Moment Of Softness	1966	.80	4.00
Liberty 55885		Underwater / Wherever You Look	1966	.80	4.00
Liberty 55906		Fare Thee Well / Let's Go Get Stoned	1966	.80	4.00
Liberty 55925		Walkin' My Cat Named Dog / Balboa Blue	1966	.80	4.00
Liberty 55951		Tee Hee Hee / The Proper Thing To Do	1967	.80	4.00
Liberty 55963		The Beat Goes On / Bonesville	1967	.80	4.00

T. C. ATLANTIC

B-Sharp 272		Mona / My Babe (Pink & yellow label)	196?	6.00	30.00
B-Sharp 272		Mona / My Babe (Pink & black label)	196?	4.00	20.00
Candy Floss 101		Twenty Years Ago / I'm So Glad	1969	6.00	30.00
Turtle 1103		Faces / Baby, Please Don't Go	1969	10.00	50.00
Turtle 1105		Shake / Spanish Harlem	1969	5.00	25.00
Parrot 330		Twenty Years Ago / I'm So Glad	1969	3.00	15.00
Parrot 338		Faces / Love Is Just	1970	3.00	15.00
Aesops 6044		Once Upon A Melody / I Love You So, Little Girl	196?	5.00	25.00

T. I. M. E.

Liberty 56020		Take Me Along / Make It Alright	1968	2.00	10.00
Liberty 56020	(PS)	Take Me Along / Make It Alright	1968	3.00	15.00
Liberty 56060		Trip Into Sunshine / What Would Life Be Without It?	1968	2.00	10.00

T. R. & THE YARDMEN

Hideout 1005		I Tried / Movin' up	196?	3.00	15.00

T-REX [TYRANNOSAURUS REX]
A&M 995, Blue Thumb 6115 and 7121 credit Tyrannosaurus Rex. T-Rex features Marc Bolan.

A&M 995		Child Star / Debora	1968	1.20	6.00
Blue Thumb 6115	(DJ)	Ride A White Swan / Is It Love	1970	2.00	10.00
		(Bonus single from the album "A Beard Of Stars.")			
Blue Thumb 7121		Ride A White Swan / Summertime Blues	1971	1.00	5.00
Blue Thumb 212		By The Light Of The Magical Moon / Find A Little Wood	1972	.80	4.00
Reprise 1006		Hot Love / One Inch Rock	1971	1.00	5.00
Reprise 1032		Bang A Gong (Get It On) / Raw Ramp	1971	.80	4.00
Reprise 1056		Jeepster / Rip Off	1971	.60	3.00
Reprise 1078		Telegram Sam / Cadillac	1972	.60	3.00
Reprise 1095		Metal Guru / Lady	1973	.80	4.00
Reprise 1161		The Groover / Born To Boogie	1974	.80	4.00
Reprise 1170		Hot Love / Rip Off	1974	.60	3.00
Casablanca 810		Precious Star /	1975	.60	3.00

TABBYS, THE

Time 1008		My Darling / Yes, I Do (Blue label)	1959	7.00	35.00
Time 1008		My Darling / Yes, I Do (Red label)	196?	4.00	20.00

TABS, THE

Nasco 6016		Still Love You, Baby / Will We Meet Again?	1958	5.00	25.00
Dot 15887		First Star / Avenue Of Tears	1959	5.00	25.00
Noble 719		Never Forget / Rock And Roll Holiday	1959	25.00	125.00
Noble 720		Oops! /	1959	50.00	200.00
Gardena 110		Never Forget / Rock And Roll Holiday	1960	5.00	25.00
Vee Jay 418		Dance All By Myself / Dance Party	1961	3.00	15.00
Vee Jay 446		Mash Dem Taters / But You're My Baby	1962	3.00	15.00
Wand 130		Two Stupid Feet / The Wallop	1963	1.60	8.00
Wand 139		Take My Love Along With You / I'm With You	1963	1.60	8.00

TAGES, THE
The Tages feature Peter Frampton.

Verve 10626		Halcyon Days / I Read You Like An Open Book	1968	2.00	10.00

TAKEOFFS, THE

Ford 142		Knock Down The Door / Take Three Plus One	196?	2.00	10.00

Label & Catalog #		A-Side/B-Side	Year	VG	NM
TALENTS, THE Twink 1215		Three Little Fishes / My Favorite Things	196?	2.00	10.00
TALISMEN, THE Dot 16068		Surfin' Man / Jailbreak	1960	5.00	25.00
TALISMEN, THE Hideout 1221		Taxman / Vintage N.S.U.	196?	4.00	20.00
TALISMEN, THE Julian 105 Julian 109		She Was Good / (B-side by Debbie & Gaylis) I Know A Girl / I'll Take A Walk	1966 1966	9.00 4.00	45.00 20.00
TALLYSMEN, THE Tully		Little By Little / You Don't Care About Me	1966	15.00	75.00
TAMBLYN, LARRY *Larry Tamblyn also recorded with The Standells.* Faro 601 Faro 603 Faro 612		Patty Ann / Dearest The Lie / My Bridge To You This Is The Night / Destiny	1965 1965 1965	2.00 2.00 2.00	10.00 10.00 10.00
TAMERLANES, THE: *Refer to* BARRY & THE TAMERLANES					
TAMS, THE Mink 22		Memory Lane / Teeenage Kids *(Mink 22 wasa originally released credited to The Stereos.)*	1959	4.00	20.00
TAMMYS, THE United Artists 632 United Artists 678 Veep 1210		Take Back Your Ring / Part Of Growing Up Egyptian Shumba / What's So Sweet About Sweet Sixteen? *(U.A. 678 was produced by Lou Christie.)* Gypsy / Hold Back The Light Of Dawn	1964 1964 1966	3.00 4.00 2.00	15.00 20.00 10.00
TAN, ROY Tan 3002 Dot 15551		Isabella / I Don't Like It Isabella / I Don't Like It	1957 1957	6.00 4.00	30.00 20.00
TANDI & THE TEAMATES Ember 1068		Week-End Lover / Trampoline Queen	1960	2.00	10.00
TANDY, SHARON Atco 6518		Hold On Stay With Me	196?	2.00	10.00
TANGENTS, THE Fresh 1 United Artists 201		Send Me Something / I Can't Live Alone The Wiggle / The Waddle	1960 1960	5.00 2.00	25.00 10.00
TANGENTS, THE Impression III		Hey Joe / Stand By Me	1966	3.00	15.00
TANGERINE DREAM Virgin PR-214 Virgin ZS8 9516 Virgin ZS8 9516 Virgin ZS8 9516 Virgin ZS8 9516	(DJ) (DJ) (DJ) (DJ) (DJ)	Mysterious Semblance At The Strand Of Nightmares / Phaedra Cherokee Lane / Moonlight Desert Dream / Moonlight Coldwater Canyon-Part II / Moonlight-Part II Moonlight-Part II (Mono) / Moonlight-Part II (Stereo) *(While four different promos for Virgin 9516 exist, apparently no stock copies do.)*	1974 1977 1977 1977 1977	2.00 2.00 2.00 2.00 2.00	10.00 10.00 10.00 10.00 10.00
MCA 40740 MCA 40740 Evatone 104833-1	(DJ)	Betrayal / Betrayal Betrayal [Sorceror's Theme] / Grind House Of The Rising Sun (One sided flexi) *(Issued with Reflex magazine.)* — 12" Singles —	1977 1977 1989	1.50 1.50 1.00	8.00 8.00 5.00
Elektra 5 E-521-ASP Elektra AS-11499 Relativity 80382 Relativity EMC 8044 Relativity 88561-8120	(DJ) (DJ) (EP) (EP) (EP)	Beach Theme / Burning Bar Dr. Destructo / Diamond Diary Street Hawk Street Hawk Dolphin Dance	1980 1981 1985 1985 1986	2.00 1.60 1.20 1.20 2.00	10.00 8.00 6.00 6.00 10.00
TANGIERS, THE Strand 25039		Ping Pong / Don't Stop The Music	1960	7.00	35.00
TANNO, MARC Whale 501		Dear Abby / Angel	1961	4.00	20.00

Label & Catalog #	A-Side/B-Side	Year	VG	NM
TARANTULAS, THE				
Atlantic 2102	Tarantula / Black Widow	1961	4.00	20.00
TARRYTONS, THE				
Exclusive 2270	Rough Surfin' / Mansion On The Hill	1963	7.00	35.00
Dot 16537	Rough Surfin' / Mansion On The Hill	1963	4.00	20.00
TARTANS, THE				
Impact 1010	I Need You / Nothing But Love	196?	3.00	15.00
TASSELS, THE				
Madison 117	To A Toy Soldier / The Boy For Me	1959	4.00	20.00
Madison 121	My Guy And I / To A Young Lover	1959	3.00	15.00
Amy 949	To A Toy Soldier / The Boy For Me	1966	2.00	10.00
TASMANIANS, THE				
Power 4933	I Can't Explain This Feeling / If I Don't	1966	3.00	15.00
TATTLETALES, THE				
Warner Bros. 5066	Double Trouble / Magic Wand	1959	2.00	10.00
TAURUS				
Taurus features Johnny Cymbal.				
Tower 487	Hey, Jane / Bless You	1969	3.00	15.00
TAYLOR, AUSTIN				
Laurie 3067	Push Push / Heart That's True	1960	2.00	10.00
TAYLOR, BILL, & THE CLEFS				
Fame 502	Little Jewel / Study Hall Romance	195?	75.00	300.00
TAYLOR, BILL, & SMOKEY JO (CLYDE LEOPPARD'S SNEARLY RANCH BOYS)				
Refer to Smokey Jo.				
Flip 502	Split Personality / Lonely Sweetheart	1955	330.00	1,000.00
TAYLOR, BILLY				
Citation 5002	Income Taxes And You / Lullabye To Carolyn	195?	3.00	15.00
Felco 101	Wombie Zombie / I'm Young	1959	2.00	10.00
TAYLOR, BOB				
Fathom 101	I'd Take You Back / Losing You	196?	2.00	10.00
TAYLOR, BOBBY				
Hour 102	Seven Steps To Heaven / Ubangi Stomp	196?	4.00	20.00
TAYLOR, CHIP				
Mala 476	Angel Of The Morning / Swear To God, Your Honor	1966	2.00	10.00
TAYLOR, FELICE				
Mustang 3024	It May Be Winter Outside / Winter Again	1967	.80	4.00
Mustang 3026	I'm Under The Influence Of Love / Love Theme	1967	.80	4.00
TAYLOR, JAMES				
Apple P-1805 (DJ)	Carolina On My Mind / Something's Wrong	1970	6.00	30.00
Apple 1805	Carolina On My Mind / Something's Wrong	1970	2.00	10.00
Apple 1805	Carolina On My Mind / Taking It In	1970	100.00	400.00
TAYLOR, MEL				
Mel Taylor is a member of The Ventures.				
Toppa 1054	That's It / Drum Fever	196?	6.00	30.00
Rendezvous 187	Big Bad Pogo / Drumstick	196?	4.00	20.00
Warner Bros. 5839	Spanish Armada / Bang Bang Rhythm	1966	2.00	10.00
Warner Bros. 5960	Young Man, Old Man / I've Got My Love To Keep Me Warm	1967	2.00	10.00
TAYLOR, MICK				
Mick Taylor also recorded with The Rolling Stones.				
Columbia 11065	Leather Jacket / Slow Blues	1979	1.00	5.00
TAYLOR, R. DEAN				
Mala 444	It's A Long Way To St. Louis / I'll Remember	1964	5.00	25.00
Rare Earth 5013	Indiana Wants Me / Love's Your Name	1970	.80	4.00
Rare Earth 5023	Ain't It A Sad Thing? / Back Street	1971	.80	4.00
Rare Earth 5023 (PS)	Ain't It A Sad Thing? / Back Street	1971	.80	4.00
Rare Earth 5026	Gotta See Jane / Back Street	1971	1.20	6.00
Rare Earth 5041	Taos, New Mexico / Shadow	1972	.80	4.00

Label & Catalog #	A-Side/B-Side	Year	VG	NM
TAYLOR, TRUE				
True Taylor is a pseudonym for Paul Simon.				
Big 614	True Or False / Teenage Fool	1958	15.00	75.00
TAYLOR, VERNON				
Sun 310	Breeze / Today Is Blue Day	1958	3.00	15.00
Sun 325	Mystery Train / Sweet And Easy To Love	1959	5.00	25.00
TAYLOR BROTHERS, THE				
United 98	Your Last Chance / Slow Down	196?	3.00	15.00
TEA COMPANY, THE				
Smash 2176	Come And Have Some Tea With Me / Flowers	196?	2.00	10.00
TEACHERS, THE				
PTA 101	Love Walked In / Sound Of Music	196?	2.00	10.00
TEAMATES, THE				
LeMans 006	Calendar Of Love / I Say Goodbye	196?	3.00	15.00
Philips 40029	We've Believed In Love / Once There Was A Time	1962	3.00	15.00
TEARDROPS, THE				
Dot 15669	Bridge Of Love / Jellyfish	1957	3.00	15.00
Rendezvous 102	Catch Me, I'm Falling Again / Sugar Baby	1958	3.00	15.00
TEARS, THE				
Scorpio 409	Weatherman / Read All About It	1967	2.00	10.00
Onyx 2201	Rat Race / People Through My Glasses	1967	5.00	25.00
TECHNIQUES, THE				
Stars 551	Hey! Little Girl / In A Round About Way	1957	8.00	40.00
Roulette 4030	Hey! Little Girl / In A Round About Way	1957	3.00	15.00
Roulette 4048	Let Her Go / Marindy	1958	2.00	10.00
Roulette 4097	Moon Tan / The Wisest Man In Town	1958	2.00	10.00
TEDDY & HIS PATCHES				
Chance 101	Suzy Creamcheese / From Day To Day	1967	20.00	100.00
Chance 668	Suzy Creamcheese / It Ain't Nothin'	1967	20.00	100.00
Chance 669	Haight Ashbury / It Ain't Nothin'	1967	20.00	100.00
TEDDY & THE CONTINENTALS				
Richie 445	Do You? / Tighten Up	195?	8.00	40.00
Richie 453	Crying Over You / Crossfire With My Baby	195?	7.00	35.00
Richie 1001	Ev'rybody Pony / Tick Tick Tock	1961	4.00	20.00
Rago 201	Tick Tick Tock / (B-side by The Teen Kings)	1962	5.00	25.00
TEDDY & THE PANDAS				
Timbri 101	The Lovelight / Day In The City	1966	2.00	10.00
Coristine 574	Once Upon A Time / Out The Window	1966	2.00	10.00
Musicor 1190	We Can't Go On This Way / Smokey Fire	1966	2.00	10.00
Musicor 1212	Searchin' For The Good Times / Sunnyside Up	1966	2.00	10.00
Tower 433	Childhood Friends / 68 Days Til September	1968	2.00	10.00
TEDDY & THE TWILIGHTS				
Swan 4102	Woman Is A Man's Best Friend / Goodbye To Love	1962	3.00	15.00
Swan 4115	Running Around Town / You Gotta Be Alone To Cry	1962	3.00	15.00
Swan 4126	I'm Just Your Clown / Bimini Bimbo	1962	3.00	15.00
TEDDY BEARS, THE				
The Teddy Bears feature Phil Spector and Annette Kleinbard, who also recorded as Annette Bard and Carol Connors.				
Dore 503	To Know Him Is To Love Him /			
	Don't You Worry, My Little Pet	1958	4.00	20.00
Dore 520	Wonderful, Loveable You / Till You'll Be Mine	1959	3.00	15.00
Imperial 5562	I Don't Need You Anymore / Oh, Why?	1959	3.00	15.00
Imperial 5581	If You Only Knew / You Said Goodbye	1959	3.00	15.00
Imperial 5594	Don't Go Away / Seven Lonely Days	1959	3.00	15.00
TEDDY BOYS, THE				
MGM 13575	Jezebel / It's You	1967	2.00	10.00
Cameo 448	Mona / Good Morning Blues	1967	2.00	10.00
TEE SET, THE				
Colossus 107	Ma Belle Amie / Angels Coming In The Holy Night	1970	.80	4.00
Colossus 107 (PS)	Ma Belle Amie / Angels Coming In The Holy Night	1970	1.00	5.00
Colossus 114	If You Do Believe In Love / Charmaine	1970	.60	3.00
Colossus 139	She Likes Weeds /	1971	.60	3.00

Label & Catalog #	A-Side/B-Side	Year	VG	NM
TEEGARDEN & VAN WINKLE				
Westbound 170	God, Love And Rock And Roll / Work Me Tomorrow	1970	.60	3.00
Westbound 170 (PS)	God, Love And Rock And Roll / Work Me Tomorrow	1970	.60	3.00
Westbound 171	Everything Is Going To Be Alright / You Do	1970	.60	3.00
Westbound 187	I Need You / Stoned On The Love For Jesus	1971	.60	3.00
TEEN, SANDRA				
Impact 4	Angel Baby / Stranger In Love	1960	2.00	10.00
TEEN ANGELS, THE				
Sun 388	Ain't Gonna Let You (Break My Heart) / Tell Me, My Love	1964	4.00	20.00
TEEN BEATS, THE				
Original Sound 07	Slop Beat / California Boogie	1960	4.00	20.00
Original Sound 16	Night Surfing / Clair De Lune Rock	1961	5.00	25.00
Original Sound 46	Big Bad Boss Beat / Down Below	1964	4.00	20.00
Original Sound 49	Swimmin' / Swimmin,' Part 2	1964	4.00	20.00
Teenbeat	Surf Bound / Mr. Moto	1963	10.00	50.00
TEEN BUGS, THE				
Blue River 208	Yes, You Can Hold My hand / Teenitis	1964	4.00	20.00
TEEN FIVE, THE				
Times Square	'Til The End Of Time / (B-side by The Gents)	1964	3.00	15.00
Times Square	Darling, I Love You / (B-side by The Gents)	1964	2.00	10.00
TEEN KINGS, THE				
Rago 201	Wild Christening Party / (B-side by Teddy & The Continentals)	1962	5.00	25.00
TEEN-KINGS, THE				
Bee 1115	That's A Teen-Age Love / Tell Me If You Know	1959	330.00	1,000.00
Willett 118	Don't Just Stand There / My Greatest Wish	1959	25.00	125.00
TEEN KINGS, THE				
Drift	She's Gone / Hurry To Me	195?	20.00	100.00
TEEN KINGS, THE: _Refer to_ ROY ORBISON				
TEEN NOTES, THE				
Deb 121	Loco In The Coco / My Precious Jewel	1960	2.00	10.00
TEEN ROCKERS, THE				
Deltone 5015	Rinky Dink Blues / Rinky Dink Blues, Part 2	1960	2.00	10.00
TEEN TONES, THE				
Wynne 107	Faded Love / Gypsy Boogie	1959	5.00	25.00
Tri Disc 102	I'm So Happy / Shoutin' Twist	1961	5.00	25.00
Decca 30895	Yes, You May / Don't Call Me, Baby, I'll Call You	196?	1.00	5.00
TEEN TONES, THE				
T&T 2488	Long Cold Winter Ahead / Do You Wanna Dance?	1965	2.00	10.00
TEENBEATS, THE				
Myri 407	Nightspot / Only The Stars	1961	3.00	15.00
TEENETTES, THE				
Sandy 250	Bye Bye, Baby / Let Me Be The One	1963	3.00	15.00
TEENOS, THE				
Dub 2839	Love Only One / Alrighty	1958	4.00	20.00
TEENTONES, THE				
Dandy Dan 2	Darling, I Love You / My Sweet	1959	15.00	75.00
TEIG, DAVE				
Signature 12042	Splish Splash / Tutti Frutti	1960	2.00	10.00
TELEVISION				
Television features Richard Hell and Tom Verlaine.				
Ork 81975	Little Johnny Jewel / Little Johnny Jewel (Part 2)	1975	6.00	30.00
Elektra 45516	Ain't That Nothin' / Glory	1978	2.00	10.00
TELLERS, THE				
Fire 1038	Tears Fell From My Eyes / I Wanna Run To You	1960	5.00	25.00

Label & Catalog #	A-Side/B-Side	Year	VG	NM
TELSTARS, THE				
Teen 510	Continental Mash / Stomp Happy	1962	7.00	35.00
Imperial 5905	Continental Mash / Stomp Happy	1962	2.00	10.00
Teen 513	Pow Wow / Lovina	1963	6.00	30.00
Teen 516	Topless / Spaghetti Strap	1964	6.00	30.00
TEMPESTS, THE				
Willamette 103	Never Let Go-Go / Falling Like The Rain	196?	4.00	20.00
Scott	All Of Your Heart / Miguel The Organ Grinder	196?	2.00	10.00
Panorama 30	Our Lovin' Eyes / All Of Your Heart	1966	1.60	8.00
TEMPESTS, THE				
Smash 2126	What You Gonna Do? / Can't Get You Out Of My Mind	1967	1.25	6.00
TEMPO, NINO				
RCA Victor 47-7424	Fifteen Girls Friends / Loonie 'Bout Junie	1959	2.00	10.00
RCA Victor 47-7647	Ring-A-Ling / When You Were Sweet Sixteen	1960	2.00	10.00
RCA Victor 47-7694	Jack The Ripper / (B-side by Pete Rugolo)	1960	2.00	10.00
United Artists 256	Lipstick On Your Lips / What Is Love To A Teenager?	1960	2.00	10.00
Tower 369	Boys Town / Boys Town (Sing Along)	1967	1.00	5.00
A&M 1461	Sister James / Claire De Lune	1973	.60	3.00
A&M 1499	Hawkeye / Roll It	1974	.60	3.00
A&M 1532	Come See Me 'Round Midnight / High On The Music	1974	.60	3.00
A&M 1625	Don't Stop Now / Gettin' Off	1974	.60	3.00
Epic 50294	I Want To Spend My Life With You / For The Good Times	1977	.50	2.50
	— 12" Singles—			
A&M 12015	Young Stuff / Young Stuff	197?	.80	4.00
TEMPO, NINO, & APRIL STEVENS				
Ms. Stevens also recorded as a solo artist.				
United Artists 272	High School Sweetheart / Ooeah (That's What You Do To Me)	1961	1.60	8.00
Atco 6224	Sweet And Lovely / True Love	1962	1.60	8.00
Atco 6248	Paradise / Indian Love Call	1962	1.60	8.00
Atco 6263	Baby Weemus / Together We'll Always Be	1963	1.60	8.00
Atco 6273	Deep Purple / I've Been Carrying A Torch For You For So Long That I Burned A Great Big Hole In My Heart	1963	2.00	10.00
Atco 6281	Whispering / Tweedle Dee	1963	2.00	10.00
Atco 6286	Stardust / Stardust, Part 2	1964	1.60	8.00
Atco 62945	I'm Confessin' (That I Love You) / Tea For Two	1964	1.60	8.00
Atco 6306	I Surrender, Dear / Who?	1964	1.60	8.00
Atco 6314	Ooh La La / Melancholy Baby	1964	1.60	8.00
Atco 6325	Honeywell Rose / Our Love	1965	1.60	8.00
Atco 6337	These Arms Of Mine / Coldest Night Of The Year	1965	1.60	8.00
Atco 6350	Swing Me / Tomorrow Is Soon A Memory	1965	1.60	8.00
Atco 6360	Think Of Me / I'm Sweet On You	1965	1.60	8.00
Atco 6375	I Love How You Love Me / Tears Of Sorrow	1965	1.60	8.00
Atco 6391	Hey, Baby / The Poison Of Your Kisses	1965	1.60	8.00
Atco 6410	Bye Bye Blues / King Kong	1966	1.60	8.00
White Whale 236	All Strung Out / I Can't Go On Living Without You	1966	1.25	6.00
White Whale 241	Habit Of Loving You, Baby / You'll Be Needing Me, Baby	1966	1.00	5.00
White Whale 246	Wings Of Love / My Old Flame	1967	1.00	5.00
White Whale 252	I Can't Go On Living Without You / Little Child	1967	1.25	6.00
White Whale 268	Let It Be Me / Wings Of Love	1968	1.00	5.00
White Whale 271	Ooh Poo Pa Do / Let It Be Me	1968	1.00	5.00
MGM 13825	Falling In Love Again / Wanting You	1968	.80	4.00
Bell 823	Sea Of Love/Dock Of The Bay / Twilight Time	1969	.80	4.00
Atlantic 2738	Lonesome Holy Roller / Keep The Customer Satisfied	1970	.80	4.00
MGM 14266	How About Me? / Making Love To Rainbow Clouds	1971	.80	4.00
Atco 6897	She's My Baby / Tomorrow Is Soon A Memory	1972	.80	4.00
Marina 507	You're Losing Me / Darling, You Were All That I Had	1972	.80	4.00
A&M 1394	Hoochy-Coochy-Wing Dang Do / Love Story	1972	.60	3.00
A&M 1443	Put It Where You Want It / I Can't Get Over You, Baby	1973	.60	3.00
A&M 1674	You Turn Me On / Never Had A Lover	1975	.60	3.00
Niagara 1635	What Kind Of Fool Am I? / You And You Only	1975	.60	3.00
Chelsea 3052	What Kind Of Fool Am I? / You And You Only	1976	.60	3.00
Horn 3	I Never Loved Anyone Like I Love You / I Wonder Who's Kissing Her Now	1980	.40	2.00
TEMPOS, THE				
Kapp 178	Kingdom Of Love / That's What You Do To Me	1957	3.00	15.00
Kapp 199	The Prettiest Girl In School / Never You Mind	1957	3.00	15.00
Kapp 213	I Got A Job / Strollin' With My Baby	1958	3.00	15.00
Climax 102	See You In September / Bless You, My Love	1959	3.00	15.00
Climax 105	Crossroads Of Love / Whatever Happens	1959	3.00	15.00
Paris 550	Look Homeward, Angel / Under Ten Flags	1959	3.00	15.00

Label & Catalog #	A-Side/B-Side	Year	VG	NM
TEMPOS, THE				
Hi-Q 100	It's Tough / Sham Rock	1959	8.00	40.00
TEMPOS, THE				
U.S.A. 810	Why Don't You Write Me? / A Thief In The Night	1965	3.00	15.00
Ascot 2167	When You Loved Me / My Barbara Ann	1965	3.00	15.00
Ascot 2173	I Wish It Were Summer / My Barbara Ann	1965	3.00	15.00
TEMPTATIONS, THE				
Savoy 1532	Mad At Love / Mister Juke Box	1958	4.00	20.00
Savoy 1550	I Love You, This I Know / Don't You Know	1958	4.00	20.00
King 5118	Standing Alone / Roach's Rock	1958	75.00	300.00
TEMPTATIONS, THE [THE FOUR TEMPTATIONS]				
The Temptations originally recorded with Neil Stevens.				
ABC-Paramount 9920	Rock And Roll Baby / Cathy	1958	3.00	15.00
	(ABC 9920 credits The Four Temptations.)			
Goldisc 3001	Barbara / Someday (Black label)	1960	3.00	15.00
Goldisc 3007	Fickle Little Girl / Letter Of Devotion	1960	3.00	15.00
TEMPTATIONS, THE				
P&L 1001	Blue Surf / Egyptian Surf	1963	10.00	50.00
TEMPTONES, THE				
Arctic 130	Girl, I Love You / Goodbye	196?	8.00	40.00
Arctic 136	Say Those Words Of Love /			
	This Could Be The Start Of Something Good	1967	8.00	40.00
10CC				
10CC is Graham Gouldman, Eric Stewart, Lol Creme and Kevin Godley, both of whom left in 1976; Paul Burgess, Rick Fenn, Tony O' Malley and Stuart Tosh joined. Refer to Crazy Elephant; Hotlegs; The Mindbenders; The Mockingbirds.				
UK 49005	Donna / Hot Sun Rock	1972	.80	4.00
UK 49015	Rubber Bullets / Waterfall	1973	.80	4.00
UK 49019	Headline Hustler / Speed Kills	1973	.80	4.00
UK 4923	The Wall Street Shuffle / Gismo My Way	1974	.80	4.00
Mercury 73678	I'm Not In Love / Channel Swimmer	1975	.60	3.00
Mercury 73678 (PS)	I'm Not In Love / Channel Swimmer	1975	1.25	6.00
Mercury 73725	Art For Art's Sake / Get It While You Can	1975	.60	3.00
Mercury 73725 (PS)	Art For Art's Sake / Get It While You Can	1975	1.25	6.00
Mercury 73779	I'm Mandy, Fly Me / How Dare You	1976	.60	3.00
Mercury 73805	Life Is A Minestrone / Lazy Ways	1976	.60	3.00
Mercury 73875	The Things We Do For Love / Hot To Trot	1977	.60	3.00
Mercury 73917	People In Love / Don't Squeeze Me Like Toothpaste	1977	.60	3.00
Mercury 73980	The Wall Street Shuffle / You've Got A Cold	1977	.60	3.00
Polydor 14511	Dreadlock Holiday / Nothing Can Move Me	1978	.60	3.00
Polydor 14528	For You And I / Take These Chains	1978	.60	3.00
TEN WHEEL DRIVE				
Polydor 14037	Stay With Me / Morning's Much Better	1971	.60	3.00
TEN YEARS AFTER				
Deram 85027	Portable People / The Sounds	1968	1.00	5.00
Deram 85035	I'm Going Home / Hear Me Calling	1968	1.00	5.00
Deram 7529	Love Like A Man / If You Should Love Me	1970	.80	4.00
Columbia 45457	I'd Love To Change The World / Let The Sky Fall	1971	.80	4.00
Columbia 45530	Baby, Won't You Let Me Rock 'N' Roll You? /			
	Once There Was A Time	1972	.80	4.00
Columbia 45736	Choo Choo Mama / You Can't Win Them All	1972	.80	4.00
Columbia 45787	Tomorrow I'll Be Out Of Town / Convention Prevention	1972	.80	4.00
Columbia 45915	I'm Going Home / You Give Me Loving	1973	.80	4.00
Columbia 46061	It's Getting Harder / I Wanted To Boogie	1973	.80	4.00
TENNANT, JIMMY				
Amp 790	Heartbreak Avenue / You're The Beat Within My Heart	1959	3.00	15.00
Warwick 533	Salute / The Big Retreat	1960	3.00	15.00
TEO, ROY				
Nasco 6027	Mama Doll / Please, My Love	1959	3.00	15.00
TERMITES, THE				
See 1825	Carrie Lou / Give Me Your Heart	196?	2.00	10.00
TERRACE TONES, THE				
Apt 25016	Words Of Wisdom / The Ride Of Paul Revere	1958	10.00	50.00
TERRI, DARLENE				
Pocono 802	My Best Friend, Barbara / Snow Man	1964	2.00	10.00
Columbia 43042	Ringo Ringo / A Real Live Boy	1964	2.00	10.00

Label & Catalog #	A-Side/B-Side	Year	VG	NM
TERRI & THE KITTENS Imperial 5728	Wedding Bells / You Cheated	1961	3.00	15.00
TERRI & THE VELVETEENS Kerwood 711	You've Broken My Heart / Bells Of Love	196?	7.00	35.00
TERRI-TONES, THE Cortland 105	The Sinner / Go	1962	6.00	30.00
TERRY, MARLENE Maria 102	Whoever You Are / There's A Boy	196?	4.00	20.00
TERRY & JERRY Class 226	People Are Doing It Everyday / Mama Julie	1958	3.00	15.00
TERRY & THE CHAIN GANG United Artists 50199	Keep Your Cool / Stop Stopping Me	1967	1.00	5.00
TERRY & THE MELLOS *Features Terry Cortn.* Rider 108	Truly, I Love You Truly / Why Did You Do It?	195?	5.00	25.00
TERRY & THE TAGS Sylvester 100	Rampage / The Twomp	1962	6.00	30.00
TERRY & THE TUNISIANS Seville 131	The Street / Tom-Tom	1963	3.00	15.00
TERRY & THE TYRANTS Kent 399	Yea, Yea, Yea, Yea / Weep No More	1964	3.00	15.00
TERRYTONES, THE *The Terrytones also recorded with Claire Charles and Gayle Fortune.* Wye 1010	Three Steps To The Phone / I Beg Your Pardon	1961	6.00	30.00
TEX & THE CHEX Newtown 5010 20th Century Fox 411	Watching Willie Wobble / Be On The Lookout For My Girl Beach Party / Now	196? 1963	3.00 6.00	15.00 30.00
TEXANS, THE *The Texans are Dorsey and Johnny Burnette.* Jox 001 Infinity 001 Vee Jay 658	Rockin' Johnny Home / Old Reb Green Grass Of Texas / Bloody River Green Grass Of Texas / Bloody River	196? 1961 1961	5.00 4.00 3.00	25.00 20.00 15.00
THARP, CHUCK, & THE FIREBALLS: *Refer to* THE FIREBALLS				
THAXTON, LLOYD Capitol 4982 Decca 31689	Image Of A Surfer / My Name Is Lloyd Thaxton *("Image Of A Surfer" was p produced by Gary Usher.)* Chug-A-Lug / Tennessee Ska	1963 1964	5.00 2.00	25.00 10.00
THEE MIDNIGHTERS Chattahoochee 511 Chattahoochee 666 Chattahoochee 675 Chattahoochee 684 Chattahoochee 693 Chattahoochee 694 Chattahoochee 695 Chattahoochee 706 Whittier 500 Whittier 501 Whittier 501 (PS) Whittier 503 Whittier 504 Whittier 504 Whittier 507 Whittier 508 Whittier 509 Whittier 511 Whittier 512 Whittier 674 Whittier 694 Whittier 201 Uni 55170	You're Gonna Make Me Cry / Make Ends Meet Land Of 1,000 Dances / Land Of 1,000 Dances (Part 2) Sad Girl / Heat Wave Whittier Boulevard / Evil Love Empty Heart / I Need Somebody It's Not Unusual / That's All Brother, Where Are You? / Heat Wave I Found A Peanut / Are You Angry? Love, Special Delivery / Don't Go Away The Midnight Feeling / It'll Never Be Over For Me The Midnight Feeling / It'll Never Be Over For Me Dragon Fly / The Big Ranch Walking Song / Never Knew I Had It So Bad Everybody Needs Somebody / Never Knew I Had It So Bad Looking Out A Window / Jump, Jive And Harmonize Chile Con Soul / The Despedida Dreaming Casually / Breakfast On The Grass Make Ends Meet / You're Gonna Make Me Cry The Ballad Of Cesar Chavez / The Ballad Of Cesar Chavez *(English and Spanish versions.)* Sad Girl / Heat Wave It's Not Unusual / It's Not Unusual That's All / To Be With You She Only Wants What She Can't Get / I've Come Alive	1965 1965 1965 1965 1965 1966 1966 1966 1966 1966 1966 1966 1966 1967 1967 1967 1967 1968 1968 1968 1969 196? 1969	10.00 2.00 2.00 2.00 3.00 2.00 2.00 3.00 2.00 2.00 4.00 2.00 3.00 4.00 4.00 2.00 2.00 2.00 2.00 2.00 2.00 2.00 1.60	50.00 10.00 10.00 10.00 15.00 10.00 10.00 15.00 10.00 10.00 20.00 10.00 15.00 20.00 20.00 10.00 10.00 10.00 10.00 10.00 10.00 10.00 8.00

Label & Catalog #	A-Side/B-Side	Year	VG	NM

THEM
The Parrot sides feature Van Morrison as lead singer. Them also recorded as The Belfast Gypsies.

Label & Catalog #	A-Side/B-Side	Year	VG	NM
Parrot 9702	Don't Start Crying Now / One, Two Brown Eyes	1964	3.00	15.00
Parrot 9727	Gloria / Baby, Please Don't Go	1965	2.00	10.00
Parrot 9749	Here Comes The Night / All For Myself	1965	2.00	10.00
Parrot 9784	Gonna Dress In Black / (It Won't Hurt) Half As Much	1965	2.00	10.00
Parrot 9796	Mystic Eyes / If You And I Could Be As Two	1965	2.00	10.00
Parrot 9819	Bring 'Em On In / Call My Name	1966	2.00	10.00
Parrot 3003	Richard Corey / Don't You Know	1966	2.00	10.00
Parrot 3006	I Can Only Give You Everything / Don't Start Crying Now	1966	2.00	10.00
Ruff 1088	Walking In The Queen's Garden / I Happen To Love You	1967	2.00	10.00
Tower 384	Walking In The Queen's Garden / I Happen To Love You	1967	2.00	10.00
Tower 384 (PS)	Walking In The Queen's Garden / I Happen To Love You	1967	4.00	20.00
Tower 407	But It's Alright / Square Room	1968	2.00	10.00
Tower 461	We've All Agreed To Help / Waltz Of The Flies	1969	2.00	10.00
Tower 493	Corinna / Dark Are The Shadows	1969	2.00	10.00
Happy Tiger 525	Lonely Weekends / I Am Waiting	1969	2.00	10.00
Parrot 365	Gloria / Bring 'Em On In	1969	1.00	5.00

THEM FEATURING HIM

Label & Catalog #	A-Side/B-Side	Year	VG	NM
HEG 501	Shattered Dreams / I'm Sorry Now	196?	4.00	20.00

THEMES, THE

Label & Catalog #	A-Side/B-Side	Year	VG	NM
Stork 001	There's No Moon Tonight / Marnie	196?	4.00	20.00

THIN LIZZY

Label & Catalog #	A-Side/B-Side	Year	VG	NM
London 20076	Whiskey In The Jar / Black Boys On The Corner	1972	1.00	5.00
London DJ-475 (DJ)	Rocky / Rocky	1973	1.50	8.00
London 20082	The Rocket / Little Darling	1974	1.00	5.00
Vertigo 202	Showdown / Nightlife	1974	.80	4.00
Vertigo 205	Wild One / Freedom Song	1975	.80	4.00
Mercury 73786	The Boys Are Back In Town / Jailbreak	1976	.80	4.00
Mercury 73841	Cowboy Song / Angel From The Coast	1976	.80	4.00
Mercury 73867	Rocky / Half Caste	1976	.80	4.00
Mercury 73882	Johnny The Fox Meets Jimmy The Weed / Old Flame	1977	.80	4.00
Mercury 73892	Don't Believe A Word / Boogie Woogie Dance	1977	.80	4.00
Mercury 73945	Dancing In The Moonlight / Bad Reputation	1977	.80	4.00
Warner Bros. 8648	Cowboy Song / Johnny The Fox Meets Jimmy The Weed	1978	.80	4.00
Warner Bros. 49019	Do Anything You Want To / S&M	1979	.80	4.00

THINGS TO COME

Label & Catalog #	A-Side/B-Side	Year	VG	NM
Dunwich 124	I'm Not Talkin' / 'Til The End	1966	10.00	50.00
Warner Bros. 7164	Come Alive / Dancer	1966	2.50	12.00

THIRD BOOTH, THE

Label & Catalog #	A-Side/B-Side	Year	VG	NM
Independence 86	I Need Love / Mysteries	1968	4.00	20.00

THIRD RAIL, THE

Label & Catalog #	A-Side/B-Side	Year	VG	NM
Cameo 445	The Subway Train That Came To Life / Train Rush Hour Stomp	1966	3.00	15.00
Epic 10191	Run, Run, Run / No Return	1967	1.60	8.00
Epic 10240	Invisible Man / Boppa Down Down	1967	1.00	5.00
Epic 10285	It's Time To Say Goodbye / Overdose Of Love	1968	1.00	5.00
Epic 10323	Shapes Of Things To Come / She Ain't No Choir Girl	1968	1.00	5.00
Epic 10457	Begging Me To Stay / Ballad Of General Humpty	1969	1.00	5.00

THIRD STONE, THE

Label & Catalog #	A-Side/B-Side	Year	VG	NM
Garland 2017	True Justice / Take It As It Comes	1969	2.00	10.00

13TH COMMITTEE, THE

Label & Catalog #	A-Side/B-Side	Year	VG	NM
Manhattan 810	Sha La La / You Really Got A Hold On Me ("Sha La La" features Davie Allan on guitar.)	1967	3.00	15.00

THIRTEENTH FLOOR ELEVATORS, THE
The Thirteenth Floor Elevators originally recorded as The Spades. Features Roky Erickson.

Label & Catalog #	A-Side/B-Side	Year	VG	NM
HBR 492	You're Gonna Miss Me / Tried To Hide	1966	20.00	100.00
Contact 5269	You're Gonna Miss Me / Tried To Hide	1966	15.00	75.00
International Arts. 107	You're Gonna Miss Me / Tried To Hide (Blue label)	1966	4.00	20.00
International Arts. 107	You're Gonna Miss Me / Tried To Hide	1966	3.00	15.00
International Arts. 111	Reverberation (Doubt) / Fire Engine	1966	3.00	15.00
International Arts. 113	I've Got Levitation / Before You Accuse Me	1967	3.00	15.00
International Arts. 121	She Lives (In A Time Of Her Own) / Baby Blue	1967	3.00	15.00
International Arts. 122	Slip Inside This House / Splash	1967	3.00	15.00
International Arts. 126	May The Circle Remain Unbroken / I'm Gonna Love You, Too	1967	3.00	15.00
International Arts. 130	Livin' On / Scarlet And Gold	1968	7.00	35.00

—International Artists singles above have yellow & green labels.—

Label & Catalog #	A-Side/B-Side	Year	VG	NM
THIRTEENTH STORY, THE				
NWI 2708	I See The Light / Come A Runnin'	1966	2.00	10.00
13TH POWER, THE				
Sidewalk 927	I See A Change Is Gonna Come / Captain Hassle	1967	3.00	15.00
31ST OF FEBRUARY, THE				
Vanguard 35066	Sandcastles / Pick A Gripe	1968	2.00	10.00
THOMAS, B. J.				
Bragg 1013	Billy And Sue / Never Tell	1964	3.00	15.00
Warner Bros. 5491	Billy And Sue / Never Tell	1964	2.00	10.00
Hickory 1395	Billy And Sue / Never Tell	196?	1.00	5.00
Valerie 226	I Got A Feeling / Hey, Judy	196?	2.00	10.00
Pacemaker 227	I'm So Lonesome I Could Cry / Candy Baby	1964	1.60	8.00
Pacemaker 231	Mama / Wendy	1964	1.00	5.00
Pacemaker 234	Bring Back The Time / I Don't Have A Mind Of My Own	1965	1.00	5.00
Pacemaker 239	Tomorrow Never Comes / Your Tears Left Me Cold	1965	1.00	5.00
Pacemaker 247	My Home Town / Plain Jane	1965	1.00	5.00
Pacemaker 253	Baby Cried / I'm Not A Fool Anymore	1965	1.00	5.00
Pacemaker 256	I Can't Help It (If I'm Still In Love With You) / Baby Cried	1965	1.00	5.00
Pacemaker 259	Pretty Country Girl / Houston Town	1965	1.00	5.00
Scepter 12129	I'm So Lonesome I Could Cry / Candy Baby	1965	1.00	5.00
	(Scepter 12129 credits B.J. Thomas & The Triumphs.)			
Scepter 12139	Mama / Wendy	1966	.80	4.00
Scepter 12154	Bring Back The Time / I Don't Have A Mind Of My Own	1966	.80	4.00
Scepter 12165	Tomorrow Never Comes / Your Tears Leave Me Cold	1966	.80	4.00
Scepter 12179	My Home Town / Plain Jane	1966	.80	4.00
Scepter 12194	I Can't Help It (If I'm Still In Love With You) / Baby Cried	1967	1.00	5.00
Scepter 12200	Just The Wisdom Of A Fool / Treasure Of Love	1968	.80	4.00
Scepter 12201	Wisdom Of A Fool / Human	1968	.80	4.00
Scepter 12205	The Girl Can't Help It / Walkin' Back	1968	.80	4.00
Scepter 12219	Eyes Of A New York Woman / I May Never Get To Heaven	1968	.80	4.00
Scepter 12230	Hooked On A Feeling / I've Been Down This Road Before	1968	.80	4.00
Scepter 12244	It's Only Love / You Don't Love Me Anymore	1969	.80	4.00
Scepter 12255	Pass The Apple, Eve / Fairy Tale Of Time	1969	.60	3.00
Scepter 12259	Skip A Rope / You Don't Love Me Anymore	1969	.60	3.00
Scepter 12265	Raindrops Keep Falling On My Head / Never Had It So Good	1969	.80	4.00
Scepter 12277	Everybody's Out Of Town / Living Again	1970	.80	4.00
Scepter 12283	I Just Can't Help Believin' / Send My Picture To Scranton, PA	1970	.60	3.00
Scepter 12299	Most Of All / The Mask	1970	.60	3.00
Scepter 12307	No Love At All / Have A Heart	1971	.60	3.00
Scepter 12320	Life / Mighty Clouds Of Joy	1971	.60	3.00
Scepter 12335	Long Ago Tomorrow / Burnin' A Hole In My Head	1971	.60	3.00
Scepter 12344	Rock And Roll Lullabye / Are We Losing Touch?	1972	.60	3.00
Scepter 12354	That's What Friends Are For / I Get Enthused	1972	.60	3.00
Scepter 12364	Happier Than The Morning Sun / We Have Got To Get Our Ship Together	1972	.60	3.00
Scepter 12379	Roads / Sweet Cherry Wine	1973	.60	3.00
THOMAS, CLIFF				
Phillips Inter. 3521	Treat Me Right / I'm On The Way Home	1959	3.00	15.00
Phillips Inter. 3531	Sorry I Lied / Leave It To Me	1959	3.00	15.00
THOMAS, GENE				
Refer to Gene & Debbie.				
Venus 1439	Sometime / Every Night	1961	3.00	15.00
Venus 1441	Lamp Of Love / Two Lips	1961	3.00	15.00
Venus 1444	Down The Road /	1961	4.00	20.00
United Artists 338	Sometime / Every Night	1961	1.60	8.00
United Artists 418	That's What You Are To Me / Mysteries Of Love	1962	1.60	8.00
United Artists 501	It's Make Believe / So Wrong	1962	1.60	8.00
United Artists 583	Peace Of Mind / The Puppet	1963	1.60	8.00
United Artists 640	Baby's Gone / Stand By Love	1963	1.60	8.00
United Artists 725	Last Song / Bobby And The Boys	1964	1.60	8.00
THOMAS, JAMO				
Thomas 303	I Spy / Snake Hip Mama	1966	2.00	10.00
THOMAS, JUDY				
Tollie 9021	Don't Feel Like The Lone Ranger / Golden Records	1964	3.00	15.00

Label & Catalog #	A-Side/B-Side	Year	VG	NM
THOMAS, RAY				
Ray Thomas is a member of The Moody Blues.				
Threshold 67020	Love Is The Key / High Above My Head	1975	.80	4.00
Threshold 67023	One Night Stand / Carousel	1976	.80	4.00
THOMAS, TONY, & THE MELODEERS				
Capri 777	Say You Care / Sometimes I'm Happy	196?	4.00	20.00
THOMAS, VIC (WITH THE FOUR-EVERS)				
Philips 40183	Napoleon Bonaparte / Marianne	1964	15.00	75.00
Philips 40228	Village Of Love / Down The Stream To The River	1964	15.00	75.00
THOMAS, RUFUS, JR.				
Sun 181	Bearcat (The Answer To Hound Dog) / Walkin' In The Rain	1953	30.00	150.00
Sun 181	Bearcat / Walkin' In The Rain	1953	15.00	75.00
Sun 188	Tiger Man (King Of The Jungle) / Save That Money	1953	40.00	200.00
THOMAS, TRACY, & THE TRU-SONICS				
Refer to The Tru-Sonics.				
Bolo 729	Twist Around The Puget Sound / Hard To Hold	196?	.80	4.00
THOMAS GROUP, THE				
Dunhill 4027	Penny Arcade / Ordinary Girl	1966	1.60	8.00
Dunhill 4030	Don't Start Me Talkin' 'Bout My Baby / Autumn	1966	1.25	6.00
THOMPSON, HAYDEN				
Profile 4015	What Cha' Gonna Do? /	195?	10.00	50.00
Philips Inter. 3517	Love My Baby / One Broken Heart	1957	6.00	30.00
THOMPSON, LORETTA				
Skoop 1050	Buddy-Big Bopper-Ritchie / Square From Nowhere	1959	10.00	50.00
THOMPSON, DON, & THE YELLOW JACKET				
Maverick 618	Don't Let Me Go / Kathy	195?	5.00	25.00
THOMPSON, SUE				
Hickory 1153	Sad Movies (Make Me Cry) / Nine Little Teardrops	1961	3.00	15.00
Hickory 1159	Norman / Never Love Again	1961	3.00	15.00
Hickory 1166	Two Of A Kind / It Has To Be	1962	2.00	10.00
Hickory 1174	Have A Good Time / If The Boy Only Knew	1962	2.00	10.00
Hickory 1183	James (Hold The Ladder Steady) / My Hero	1962	2.00	10.00
Hickory 1196	Willie Can / Too Much In Love	1962	2.00	10.00
Hickory 1204	What's Wrong, Bill? / I Need A Harbor	1963	2.00	10.00
Hickory 1204 (PS)	What's Wrong, Bill? / I Need A Harbor	1963	3.00	15.00
Hickory 1217	True Confessions / Suzie	1963	2.00	10.00
Hickory 1217 (PS)	True Confessions / Suzie	1963	3.00	15.00
Hickory 1284	Paper Tiger / Mama Didn't Cry At My Wedding	1964	2.00	10.00
THORINSHIELD				
Philips 40492	Life Is A Dream / The Best Of It	1967	1.00	5.00
Philips 40492 (PS)	Life Is A Dream / The Best Of It	1967	2.00	10.00
Philips 40521	Lonely Mountain Again / Family Of Man	1968	1.00	5.00
THORNDIKE PICKLEDISH (PACIFIST CHOIR), THE				
Thorndike Pickledish is Bob Smith.				
MTA 114	The Ballad Of Walter Wart / It's Warts On The Flip Side That Counts	1966	1.60	8.00
MTA 126	Lonely Bull (Frog) / What Now, My Love	1966	1.20	6.00
Lo Fi 1	Lenny Frog / D.J. At The End Of The World	1967	1.20	6.00
Lo Fi 1A	Sleepy Stonewall's Brotherhood Boogie / Except Robert O. Smut	1968	1.00	5.00
Piccadilly 247	The Imperial Grand Mother / S.F. Bound Paranoia	1967	1.00	5.00
	— Extended Play Albums —			
Piccadilly 247	The Thorndike Pickledish Pacifist Choir	197?	2.00	10.00
THORNTON, FRADKIN & UNGER				
ESP-Disk 63019	God Bless California / Sometimes (Features Paul McCartney.)	1972	3.00	15.00
THORNTON, LES				
Do-Well 1009	What's Holding Up Her Bikini? / Candy B.	1961	2.00	10.00
THORPE, BILLY, & THE AZTECS				
Refer to The Aztecs.				
GNP/Crescendo 340	Over The Rainbow / That I Love	1965	2.00	10.00
GNP/Crescendo 359	Twilight Time / My Girl Josephine	1965	2.00	10.00

Label & Catalog #		A-Side/B-Side	Year	VG	NM
THOSE FIVE GUYS					
Quill 103		You-Eff-Oh / (You-Eff-Oh Part 2)	196?	3.00	15.00
THOUGHTS, THE					
Planet 118		All Night Stand / Memory Of Your Love	196?	4.00	20.00
THREE BLOND MICE, THE					
Atco 6324		Ringo Bells / The Twelve Days Of Christmas	1964	5.00	25.00
THREE CHIMES, THE					
Crossway 444		Tears And Pain / Show Me The Way	196?	3.00	15.00
THREE D'S, THE					
The Three D's also recorded with Henry Pinard.					
Pilgrim 719		Tell Me That You Love Me / Broken Dreams	1956	4.00	20.00
Paris 503		Little Billy Boy / Let Me Know	1957	3.00	15.00
Paris 508		Birth Of An Angel / Never Let You Go	1957	3.00	15.00
Paris 511		Crazy Little Woman / Baby Doll	1958	3.00	15.00
Paris 514		I Never See My Baby Alone / Jumpin' Jack	1958	3.00	15.00
Brunswick 55152		The Happiest Boy And Girl / Nothin' To Wear	1959	3.00	15.00
Square 502		Squeeze / Graveyard Cha Cha	195?	6.00	30.00
THREE DEES, THE					
Dean 521		Broken Hearted / I Love You So	196?	3.00	15.00
THREE DOG NIGHT					
Three Dog Night features Danny Hutton and Cory Wells, formerly of The Enemys, and Chuck Negron..					
Dunhill 4168		Nobody / It's For You	1968	1.00	5.00
Dunhill 4168	(PS)	Nobody (Promo picture sleeve)	1968	6.00	30.00
Dunhill 4177		Try A Little Tenderness / Bet No One Ever Hurt This Bad	1969	.80	4.00
Dunhill 4191		One / Chest Fever	1969	.80	4.00
Dunhill 4203		Easy To Be Hard / Dreaming Isn't Good For You	1969	.80	4.00
Dunhill 4215		Eli's Coming / Circle For A Landing	1969	.80	4.00
Dunhill 4229		Celebrate / Feeling Alright	1970	.80	4.00
Dunhill 4239		Mama Told Me Not To Come / Rock And Roll Widow	1970	.60	3.00
Dunhill 4239	(PS)	Mama Told Me Not To Come / Rock And Roll Widow	1970	1.00	5.00
Dunhill 4250		Out In The Country / Good Time Living	1970	.60	3.00
Dunhill 4262		One Man Band / It Ain't Easy	1970	.60	3.00
Dunhill 4272		Joy To The World / I Can Hear You Calling	1971	.60	3.00
Dunhill 4282		Liar / Can't Get Enough Of It	1971	.60	3.00
Dunhill 4294		An Old Fashioned Love Song / Jam	1971	.60	3.00
Dunhill 4299		Never Been To Spain / Peace Of Mind	1971	.60	3.00
Dunhill 4306		The Family Of Man / Going In Circles	1972	.60	3.00
Dunhill 4317		Black And White / Freedom For The Stallion	1972	.60	3.00
Dunhill 4331		Pieces Of April / The Writings On The Wall	1972	.60	3.00
Dunhill 4352		Shambala / Our B Side	1973	.60	3.00
Dunhill 4370		Let Me Serenade You / Storybook Feeling	1973	.60	3.00
Dunhill 4382		The Show Must Go On / On The Way Back Home	1973	.60	3.00
Dunhill 15001		Sure As I'm Sittin' Here / Anytime, Babe	1974	.60	3.00
Dunhill 15010		The Show Must Go On / On The Way Back Home	1974	1.00	5.00
Dunhill 15013		Play Something Sweet (Brickyard Blues) / I'd Be So Happy	1974	.60	3.00
ABC 12114		Til The World Ends / Ye Te Quiero Hablar	1975	.60	3.00
ABC 12192		Everybody Is A Masterpiece / Drive On, Ride On	1975	.60	3.00
Passport 7921		It's A Jungle Out There / Somebody's Gonna Get Hurt		.60	3.00
THREE FRIENDS, THE					
Lido 500		Blanche / Baby, I'll Cry (Grey label)	1956	5.00	25.00
Lido 500		Blanche / Baby, I'll Cry (Blue label)	195?	3.00	15.00
Lido 502		I'm Only A Boy / Jinx	1957	4.00	20.00
Lido 504		Now That You've Gone / Chinese Tea Room	1957	4.00	20.00
Brunswick 55032		Chinese Tea Room / Jinx	1957	3.00	15.00
Cal Gold 169		Walkin' Shoes / Blue Ribbon Baby	1959	2.00	10.00
Imperial 5763		Dedicated (To The Songs I Love) / Happy As A Man Can Be	1961	2.00	10.00
Imperial 5773		Go On To School / You're A Square	1961	2.00	10.00
THREE G'S, THE					
Columbia 41175		Let's Go Steady For The Summer / Wild Man	1958	2.00	10.00
Columbia 41256		I'd Wait Forever / Sweet Thing	1958	2.00	10.00
Columbia 41292		These Are The Little Things / Wonder	1958	2.00	10.00
Columbia 41383		Oh, Suzette! / When It's Summer Again	1959	2.00	10.00
Columbia 41513		Barbara / Don't Cry, Katy	1959	2.00	10.00
Columbia 41584		Take That Step / Eeny-Meeny-Miny-Moe	1960	2.00	10.00
Columbia 41678		Let's Go Steady For The Summer / Love Call	1960	2.00	10.00
Columbia 41868		She's Mine / Take My Love	1960	2.00	10.00
Columbia 41955		Blueberry Hill / Foolish Tears	1961	2.00	10.00

THREE GRACES, THE: *Refer to* **THE WAILERS**

Label & Catalog #	A-Side/B-Side	Year	VG	NM
THREE PENNIES, THE				
Golden Crest 1312	I Was A Fool (Just A Fool) / I've Got Bells On My Heart	196?	2.00	10.00
THREE REASONS, THE				
JRE 223	Beach Time / Cruel, Cruel, Cruel	196?	7.00	35.00
THREE WISHES, THE				
Dolton 72	Guiding Light / It's All Said And Done	1963	2.00	10.00
THREETEENS, THE				
Rev 3516	Dear 53310761 / Doowaddie	1958	7.00	35.00
Rev 3522	For The Love Of Mike / X Plus Y Equals 2	1959	3.00	15.00
Todd 1021	For The Love Of Mike / X Plus Y Equals 2	1959	2.00	10.00
THRILLS, THE				
Capitol 5631	No One / What Can Go Wrong?	1966	1.60	8.00
Capitol 5719	Bring It On Home To Me / Here's A Heart	1966	1.60	8.00
Capitol 5871	Show The World Where It's At / Underneath My Make-Up	1967	1.60	8.00
THUMB, TOM, & THE CASUALS				
Bolo 753	Movin' On / The Shuffle Thing	196?	3.00	15.00
Panorama 21	I Should Know / I Don't Want Much	1965	2.00	10.00
Panorama 36	The Draft / Irresistible You	1966	2.00	10.00
THUNDER & ROSES				
United Artists 50536	Country Life / I Love A Woman	1969	.80	4.00
THUNDER BOLTS, THE				
Rondack 7546	Thunder Head / Blending	196?	7.00	35.00
THUNDER HEADS, THE				
Cartwheel 100	Thunder Head / Unemployment	1966	7.00	35.00
THUNDERBIRDS, THE				
Ermine 54	Simmering / Summertime	196?	6.00	30.00
THUNDERBIRDS, THE				
Delaware 1710	Your Ma Said You Cried (In Your Sleep Last Night) / Before It's Too Late	1965	2.00	10.00
THUNDERBOLTS, THE				
Dot 16496	Lost Planet / March Of The Spacemen	1964	2.00	10.00
THUNDERCLAP NEWMAN				
Track 2656	Something In The Air / Wilhelmina	1969	1.00	5.00
Track 218	Accidents / I See It All	1970	.80	4.00
Track 2769	Something In The Air / Wilhelmina	1972	.60	3.00
Track 60132	Something In The Air / Hollywood #1	1975	.60	3.00
THUNDERGRIN				
Epic 10215	Women In The Streets / Mr. Simms	1967	1.00	5.00
THUNDERNOTES, THE				
Donna 1343	Thunder Rhythm / Pay Day	1961	6.00	30.00
THUNDERTONES, THE				
Dot 16137	Jungle Fever / Hot Ice	1960	2.00	10.00
THURSDAY'S CHILDREN				
International Arts. 110	Air Conditioned Man / Dominoes	1966	25.00	125.00
International Arts. 115	Help, Murder, Police / You Can Forget About That	1967	25.00	125.00
THYME				
A-Square 201	Shame, Shame / Somehow	196?	4.00	20.00
A-Square 202	Time Of The Season / I Found A Love	196?	4.00	20.00
Bang 546	Love To Love / Very Last Day	1967	2.00	10.00
TICKLERS, THE				
Mustang 3007	Millie The Ghoul / Don't Tickle My Feet	1965	2.00	10.00
TICO & THE TRIUMPHS				
Tico is a pseudonym for Paul Simon.				
Madison 169	Motorcycle / I Don't Believe Them	1961	15.00	75.00
Amy 835	Motorcycle / I Don't Believe Them	1962	12.00	60.00
Amy 845	Express Train / Wildflower	1962	12.00	60.00
Amy 860	Cry, Little Boy, Cry / Get Up And Do The Wonder	1962	12.00	60.00
Amy 876	Cards Of Love / Noise	1963	20.00	100.00

Label & Catalog #		A-Side/B-Side	Year	VG	NM
TIDAL WAVE Buddah 46		Sinbad The Sailor / Searching For Love	1968	1.00	5.00
TIDAL WAVES, THE Strafford 6503 Tide 0020		You Name It / So I Guess Booma Shooma Rock / The Clock	196? 1961	3.00 3.00	15.00 15.00
TIDAL WAVES, THE SVR 1007 HBR 482 HBR 501 HBR 515		Farmer John / She Left Me Alone Farmer John / She Left Me Alone I Don't Need Love / Big Boy Pete Action! / Hot Stuff	1966 1966 1966 1967	4.00 2.00 2.00 3.00	20.00 10.00 10.00 15.00
TIDES, THE Dore 529 Dore 579 Dore 611 Dore 611 Dore 618 Mercury 71990 Mercury 72045		Rock Me Gently / Stoned Say You're Mine / Follow Me Ring A Ding Ding / Dear Mr. President Ring A Ding Ding / Chicken Spaceman Limbo Rock / Midnight Limbo Banana Boat Song / Patricia	1959 1961 1961 1961 1962 1962	3.00 4.00 6.00 3.00 2.00 2.00	15.00 20.00 30.00 15.00 10.00 10.00
TIFFANY SYSTEM, THE Minaret 128		Wayward One / Let's Get Together	1966	2.00	10.00
TIFFANYS, THE Swan 4104		The Pleasure Of Love / Atlanta	1962	4.00	20.00
TIFFANYS, THE RKO 120		He's Good For Me / It's Got To Be A Great Song	196?	2.00	10.00
TIGERS, THE Colpix 773 Colpix 773 Colpix 773	 (PS)	GeeTO Tiger / The Prowl GeeTO Tiger / The Prowl GeeTO Tiger / Sounds Of The GTO	1965 1965 1965	4.00 15.00 4.00	20.00 75.00 20.00
TIJUANA BRATS, THE RCA 47-9666		Yakety Brats / Karate Chop	1968	1.00	5.00
TIKIS, THE Dial 4048		Somebody's Son / Little Miss Lovelight	1966	3.00	15.00
TIKIS & THE FABULONS, THE *Refer to The Fabulons.* Rex Panorama 13 Tower 181		Do Wa Diddy / La La La La Take A Look / For Your Love Take A Look / Cherry Pie	196? 1965 1965	3.00 2.00 2.00	15.00 10.00 10.00
TILLOTSON, JOHNNY *Johnny Tillotson also recorded with Genevieve.* Cadence 1353 Cadence 1365 Cadence 1372 Cadence 1377 Cadence 1377 Cadence 1384 Cadence 1391 Cadence 1391 Cadence 1404 Cadence 1409 Cadence 1418 Cadence 1424 Cadence 1432 Cadence 1434 Cadence 1437 Cadence 1441 MGM 13181 MGM 13181 MGM 13193 MGM 13193 MGM 13232 MGM 13232 MGM 13255 MGM 13255 MGM 13284 MGM 13284 MGM 13316 MGM 13316	 (PS) (PS) (PS) (PS) (PS) (PS) (PS) (PS)	 Dreamy Eyes / Well, I'm Your Man True, True Happiness / Love Is Blind Why Do I Love You So? / Never Let Me Go Earth Angel / Pledging My Love Earth Angel / Pledging My Love Poetry In Motion / Princess, Princess Jimmy's Girl / His True Love Said Goodbye Jimmy's Girl / His True Love Said Goodbye Without You / Cutie Pie Dreamy Eyes / Well I'm Your Man It Keeps Right On A-Hurtin' / She Gave Sweet Love To Me Send Me The Pillow That You Dream On / What'll I Do? I Can't Help It (If I'm Still In Love With You) / I'm So Lonesome I Could Cry Out Of My Mind / Empty Feeling You Never Can Stop Me Loving You / Judy Judy Judy Funny How Time Slips Away / Good Year For Girls Talk Back, Trembling Lips / Another You Talk Back, Trembling Lips / Another You Worried Guy / Please Don't Go Away Worried Guy / Please Don't Go Away I Rise, I Fall / I'm Watching My Watch I Rise, I Fall / I'm Watching My Watch Worry / Sufferin' From A Heartache Worry / Sufferin' From A Heartache She Understands Me / Tomorrow She Understands Me / Tomorrow Angel / Little Boy Angel / Little Boy	1958 1959 1960 1960 1960 1960 1961 1961 1961 1961 1962 1962 1962 1963 1963 1963 1963 1963 1964 1964 1964 1964 1964 1964 1964 1964 1965 1965	3.00 2.50 2.50 2.50 3.00 2.50 1.60 3.00 1.60 1.60 1.60 1.20 1.20 1.20 1.20 1.20 3.00 1.20 3.00 1.20 3.00 1.20 3.00 1.20 3.00 1.20 3.00	15.00 15.00 15.00 15.00 15.00 15.00 8.00 15.00 8.00 8.00 8.00 6.00 6.00 6.00 6.00 6.00 15.00 6.00 15.00 6.00 15.00 6.00 15.00 6.00 15.00 6.00 15.00

Label & Catalog #		A-Side/B-Side	Year	VG	NM
MGM 13344		Then I'll Count Again / One's Yours, One's Mine	1965	1.20	6.00
MGM 13344	(PS)	Then I'll Count Again / One's Yours, One's Mine	1965	3.00	15.00
MGM 13376		Heartaches By The Number / Your Mem'ry Comes Along	1965	1.20	6.00
MGM 13376	(PS)	Heartaches By The Number / Your Mem'ry Comes Along	1965	3.00	15.00
MGM 13408		Our World / (Wait Till You See) My Gidget	1965	1.20	6.00
MGM 13445		I Never Loved You Anyway / Hello, Enemy	1966	1.20	6.00
MGM 13445	(PS)	I Never Loved You Anyway / Hello, Enemy	1966	2.00	10.00
MGM 13499		Me, Myself And I / Country Boy, Country Girl	1966	1.20	6.00
MGM 13519		No Love At All / What Am I Gonna Do?	1966	1.20	6.00
MGM 13598		Open Up Your Heart / Baby's Gone	1966	1.20	6.00
MGM 13598		Open Up Your Heart / More Than Before	1966	1.20	6.00
MGM 13633		Christmas Country Style / Christmas Is The Best Of All	1966	1.20	6.00
MGM 13684		Strange Things Happen / Tommy Jones	1967	1.00	5.00
MGM 13738		Don't Tell Me It's Raining / Takin' It Easy	1967	1.00	5.00
MGM 13829		Counting My Teardrops / You're The Reason	1967	1.00	5.00
MGM 13888		It Keeps Right On A-Hurtin' / I Can Spot A Cheater	1968	1.00	5.00
MGM 13924		I Haven't Begun To Love You Yet / I Can Spot A Cheater	1968	1.00	5.00
MGM 13977		A Letter To Emily / Your Mem'ry Comes Along	1968	1.00	5.00
Amos 117		Tears On My Pillow / Remember When?	1969	.80	4.00
Amos 125		What Am I Living For? / Joy To The World	1969	.80	4.00
Amos 128		Raining In My Heart / Today I Started Loving You Again	1969	.80	4.00
Amos 136		Susan / Love Waits For Me	1969	.80	4.00
Amos 146		I Don't Believe In If Anymore /	1970	.80	4.00
Buddah 232		Apple Bend / Star Spangled Bus	1971	.60	3.00
Buddah 256		Welfare Hero / The Flower Kissed The Shoes That Jesus Wore	1971	.60	3.00
Buddah 279		Make Believe / The Flower Kissed The Shoes That Jesus Wore	1971	.60	3.00
Buddah 311		Your Love's Been A Long Time Comin' / Apple Bend	1973	.80	4.00
Columbia 45842		If You Won't Be My Lady / Sunshine Of My Life	1973	.60	3.00
Columbia 45984		I Love How She Needs Me / So Much Of My Life	1973	.60	3.00
Columbia 46065		Till I Can't take It Anymore / Sunday Kind Of Woman	1974	.60	3.00
Columbia 10125		Big Ole Jean / Mississippi Lady	1974	.60	3.00
Columbia 10199		Right Here In Your Arms / Willow County Request Time	1974	.60	3.00
United Artists 860		Summertime Lovin' / It Could've Been Nashville	1977	.60	3.00
United Artists 986		Toy Hearts / Just An Ordinary Man	1977	.60	3.00

—Extended Play Albums—

Cadence 114		Johnny Tillotson	195?	8.00	40.00
Cadence LLP-331	(33)	This Is Johnny Tillotson (Jukebox EP)	1968	4.00	20.00
Cadence LLP-332	(33)	Words And Music By Johnny Tillotson(Jukebox EP)	1968	4.00	20.00

TIM & TONEY

Panorama 51		Forgotten Bells / Anna Marie	196?	2.00	10.00

TIM TAM & THE TURN-ONS

Palmer 5002		Wait A Minute / Ophelia	1966	5.00	25.00
Palmer 5003		Cheryl Ann / Seal It With A Kiss	1966	5.00	25.00
Palmer 5006		Kimberly / I Leave You In Tears	1966	5.00	25.00
Palmer 5014		Don't Say Hi / Don't Say Hi	1967	3.00	15.00

TIMBERS, THE

Tee Gee 101		Oops, Oh Lawdy / Stop Crying	195?	7.00	35.00

(Tee Gee 101 was also released credited to The Nobles.)

TIME MACHINE, THE

New Sound		All Or Nothing /	1967	3.00	15.00

TIME STOPPERS, THE

HBR 516		I Need Love / Fickle Frog	1967	3.00	15.00

TIMETONES, THE [THE TIME TONES]

Atco 6201		Pretty Pretty Girl / I've Got A Feeling	1961	4.00	20.00

(Atco 6201 credits The Time Tones.)

Times Square 421		My Love / Here In My Heart	1961	3.00	15.00
Times Square 421		My Love / In My Heart	1961	2.00	10.00
Times Square 26		Sunday Kind Of Love / Angels In The Sky	1964	2.00	10.00
Times Square 34		Get A Hold Of Yourself / The House Where Lovers Dream	1964	2.00	10.00

TIMEBOX

Deram 85031		Beggin' / A Woman That's Waiting	1968	1.00	5.00

TIMERS, THE

The Timers feature Brian Wilson and Chuck Girard and was produced by Wilson and Gary Usher.

Reprise 231	(DJ)	No-Go Showboat / Competition Coupe	1963	8.00	40.00
Reprise 231		No-Go Showboat / Competition Coupe	1963	16.00	80.00

TIMON

Threshold 67003		And Now She Says She Is Young / I'm Just A Travelling Man	1970	.80	4.00

Label & Catalog #	A-Side/B-Side	Year	VG	NM
TIN TIN				
Atco 6794	Toast And Marmalade For Tea / Manhattan Woman	1971	.80	4.00
Atco 6821	Is That The Way? / Swans On The Canal	1971	.60	3.00
TINKERS, THE				
Stop 106	You're Just Like All The Rest / Love Lights	197?	2.00	10.00
Stop 107	You're Making Me Sad / Love Lights	197?	2.00	10.00
TINO & THE REVLONS				
Mark 154	Story Of Our Love / Black Bermudas And Knee Socks	195?	6.00	30.00
Pip 4000	Wedding Bells Will Ring / Heidi	196?	4.00	20.00
Dearborn 525	Little Girl, Little Girl / Rave On	196?	2.00	10.00
Dearborn 530	Little Mary Memphis / I'm Coming Home	196?	2.00	10.00
TINY TIP & THE TIP TOPS				
Chess 1822	Matrimony / Say It	1962	3.00	15.00
TINY TONY & THE STATICS				
Refer to The Statics.				
Bolo 734	Hey, Mrs. Jones / I Wanna Hold Your Hand	1962	2.00	10.00
TITANS, THE				
Specialty 614	Sweet Peach / Free And Easy	1957	3.00	15.00
Specialty 617	Just A Little Lovin' / When The Sun Has Begun To Shine	1958	3.00	15.00
Specialty 625	Can It Be? / Don't You Just Know It?	1958	4.00	20.00
Specialty 632	Arlene / Love Is A Wonderful Thing	1958	4.00	20.00
Class 244	No Time / Tottin' Tutor	1959	4.00	20.00
TITANS, THE				
Soma 1402	Summer Place / Tchaikovsky Rides Again	1963	3.00	15.00
Bangar 00611	Surfer's Lullabye / Motivation	1964	3.00	15.00
TITANS, THE				
Nolta 351	Marquette / A-Rab	196?	2.00	10.00
TITONES, THE				
Scepter 1206	Symbol Of Love / The Movies *(White label)*	1959	6.00	30.00
Scepter 1206	Symbol Of Love / The Movies *(Red label)*	196?	3.00	15.00
Wand 105	My Movie Queen / Symbol Of Love	1960	2.00	10.00
TOADS, THE				
Brent 7050	Backaruda / *(B-side by The Golden Boys)*	1963	3.00	15.00
TOADS, THE				
The Toads feature Chuck Girard and were produced by Gary Usher.				
Decca 31847	Leaving It All Behind / Babe, While The Wind Blows Goodbye	1965	3.00	15.00
TOBY & RAY				
Blue Moon 411	Bom Do Wa / Just Waiting For You	1959	3.00	15.00
TODAY & TOMORROW				
Noose 812	Dooley Swings / Dooley Swings, Part 2	1959	8.00	40.00
TODD, NICK				
Dot 15643	Plaything / The Honey Song	1957	2.00	10.00
Dot 15675	I Do / At The Hop	1957	2.00	10.00
Dot 15893	Little Rosey Red / Red Roses For A Blue Lady	1959	2.00	10.00
TODDS, THE				
Todd 1064	May We Always / Tennessee	1962	2.00	10.00
Todd 1076	Popsicle / Sugar Hill	1962	2.00	10.00
TOGGERY FIVE, THE				
Tower 119	I'm Gonna Jump / Bye Bye Bird	1966	3.00	15.00
TOKAYS, THE				
Bonnie 102	Fatty Boom Bi Laddy / Lost And Found	195?	20.00	100.00
TOKAYS, THE				
Scorpio 403	Now / Ask Me No Questions	1969	3.00	15.00
TOKENS, THE				
The Tokens are Mitch Margo, Phil Margo, Hank Medress, Jay Siegel and Joe Venneri. Refer to The Buddies; The Coeds; The Companions; Cross Country; Tom Damphier; Darrell & The Oxfords; The Four Winds; Margo, Margo, Medress & Siegel; The Next Exit; The Sands Of Time; U.S. Double Quartet.				
Melba 104	While I Dream / I Love My Baby	1956	8.00	40.00
	(Features Neil Sedaka as lead vocalist. Re-issued in the early '60s.)			
Warwick 615	Tonight I Fell In Love / I'll Always Love You	1961	3.00	15.00

Label & Catalog #		A-Side/B-Side	Year	VG	NM
RCA Victor 47-7896		When I Go To Sleep At Night / Dry Your Eyes	1961	3.00	15.00
RCA Victor 47-7896	(PS)	When I Go To Sleep At Night / Dry Your Eyes	1961	4.00	20.00
RCA Victor 47-7925		When The Summer Is Through / Sincerely	1961	3.00	15.00
RCA Victor 47-7954		The Lion Sleeps Tonight / Tine	1961	3.00	15.00
RCA Victor 47-7991		B'wana Nina / Weeping River	1962	2.00	10.00
RCA Victor 47-7991	(PS)	B'wana Nina / Weeping River	1962	3.00	15.00
RCA Victor 47-8018		The Riddle / Big Boat	1962	2.00	10.00
RCA Victor 47-8018	(PS)	The Riddle / Big Boat	1962	3.00	15.00
RCA Victor 47-8052		La Bomba / A Token Of Love	1962	2.00	10.00
RCA Victor 47-8052	(PS)	La Bomba / A Token Of Love	1962	3.00	15.00
RCA Victor 47-8089		I'll Do My Crying Tomorrow / Dream Angel, Goodnight	1962	2.00	10.00
RCA Victor 47-8089	(PS)	I'll Do My Crying Tomorrow / Dream Angel, Goodnight	1962	3.00	15.00
RCA Victor 47-8114		A Bird Flies Out Of Sight / Wishing	1963	2.00	10.00
RCA Victor 47-8114	(PS)	A Bird Flies Out Of Sight / Wishing	1963	3.00	15.00
RCA Victor 47-8148		Tonight I Met An Angel / Hindi Lullaby	1963	3.00	15.00
RCA Victor 47-8148	(PS)	Tonight I Met An Angel / Hindi Lullaby	1963	4.00	20.00
RCA Victor 47-8210		Hear The Bells / A-B-C 1-2-3	1963	2.00	10.00
RCA Victor 47-8210	(PS)	Hear The Bells / A-B-C 1-2-3	1963	3.00	15.00
RCA Victor 47-8309		Let's Go To The Drag Strip / Two Cars	1964	2.00	10.00
Laurie 3180		Please Write / I'll Always Love You	1963	2.50	12.00
B.T. Puppy 500		A Girl Named Arlene / Swing	1964	1.20	6.00
B.T. Puppy 502		He's In Town / Oh, Cathy	1964	1.60	8.00
B.T. Puppy 504		You're My Girl / Havin' Fun	1964	1.20	6.00
B.T. Puppy 505		Nobody But You / Mr. Cupid	1965	1.20	6.00
B.T. Puppy 507		Sylvie Sleepin' / A Message To The World	1965	1.20	6.00
B.T. Puppy 512		Only My Friend / Cattle Call	1965	1.20	6.00
B.T. Puppy 513		The Bells Of St. Mary's / Just One Smile	1964	1.20	6.00
B.T. Puppy 516		The Three Bells / A Message To The World	1966	1.20	6.00
B.T. Puppy 518		I Hear Trumpets Blow / Don't Cry Sing Along With The Music	1966	1.20	6.00
B.T. Puppy 519		Greatest Moments In A Girl's Life / Breezy	1966	1.20	6.00
B.T. Puppy 519	(PS)	Greatest Moments In A Girl's Life / Breezy	1966	2.00	10.00
B.T. Puppy 524		Life Is Groovy / Split	1966	1.20	6.00
B.T. Puppy 525		Green Plant / Saloogy	1967	1.20	6.00
B.T. Puppy 552		Please Say You Want Me / Get A Job	1967	1.20	6.00
Warner Bros. 5900		Portrait Of My Love / She Comes And Goes	1967	1.00	5.00
Warner Bros. 5900	(PS)	Portrait Of My Love / She Comes And Goes	1967	3.00	15.00
Warner Bros. 7056		It's A Happening World / How Nice	1967	.80	4.00
Warner Bros. 7099		Bye, Bye, Bye / Ain't That Peculiar	1967	.80	4.00
Warner Bros. 7169		Till / Poor Man	1968	.80	4.00
Warner Bros. 7202		Bathroom Wall / Animal	1968	.80	4.00
Warner Bros. 7233		Banana Boat Song / Grandfather	1968	.80	4.00
Warner Bros. 7255		The World Is Full Of Wonderful Things / Some People Sleep	1968	.80	4.00
Warner Bros. 7280		Go Away, Little Girl-Young Girl / I Want To Make Love To You	1969	.80	4.00
Warner Bros. 7323		I Could Be / End Of The World	1969	.80	4.00
Buddah 151		She Let's Her Hair Down (Early In The Morning) / Oh, To Get Away	1970	.60	3.00
Buddah 159		Don't Worry, Baby / Some People Sleep	1970	.60	3.00
Buddah 174		Both Sides Now / I Can See Me Dancing With You	1970	.80	4.00
Buddah 187		Groovin' On The Sunshine / Listen To The Words (Listen To The Music)	1970	.60	3.00
Bell 190		Throw My Head Back And Sing / You And Me	1972	.60	3.00
Atco 7009		Penny Whistle Band / The Lord Can't Do A Solo	1974	.60	3.00
Kirshner 4264		Mr. Radio Man / Everybody Tries	197?	.80	4.00
Rust 5094		Rumble In The Park / A Girl Named Arlene	197?	.80	4.00
Music Maker 110		Rumble In The Park / A Girl Named Arlene	197?	.80	4.00

TOLLIVER, MICKEY, & THE CAPITOLS

Cindy 3002		Rose-Marie / Millie	1957	50.00	50.00

TOM & JERRY

Tom & Jerry are Art Garfunkel and Paul Simon.

Big 613		Hey, Schoolgirl / Dancin' Wild	1957	10.00	50.00
King 5167		Hey, Schoolgirl / Dancin' Wild	1957	10.00	50.00
Big 616		Our Song / Two Teenagers	1958	10.00	50.00
Big 618		That's My Story / Don't Say Goodbye	1958	10.00	50.00
Big 621		Baby Talk / Two Teenagers	1958	15.00	75.00
Hunt 319		That's My Story / Don't Say Goodbye	1958	10.00	50.00
Ember 1094		I'm Lonesome / Looking At You	1959	10.00	50.00
Mercury 71930		I'll Drown In My Tears / The French Twist	1961	7.00	35.00
ABC-Paramount 10363		Surrender, Please Surrender / Fighting Mad	1962	7.00	35.00
ABC-Paramount 10788		That's My Story / Tia-Juana Blues	1966	3.00	15.00
Bell 120		Baby Talk / (B-side by Ronnie Lawrence)	1971	4.00	20.00

TOM & THE CATS

Paula 242		Summertime Blues / Walkin' Man	1967	2.00	10.00

Label & Catalog #	A-Side/B-Side	Year	VG	NM
TOMMY & THE HUSTLERS				
Fantasy 573	Diggin' Out / The Right Size (Green vinyl)	1963	8.00	40.00
Fantasy 573	Diggin' Out / The Right Size (Black vinyl)	1963	5.00	25.00
TOMMY & THE TRUE BLUE FACTS				
A&M 900	Who's Got The Right? / I'm Back	1967	2.00	10.00
TOMPALL & THE GLAZERS				
Robbins 1006	Yakety Yak / Sweet Lies	196?	2.00	10.00
TONETTES, THE				
Doe 101	Oh, What A Baby / Howie	1958	6.00	30.00
ABC-Paramount 9905	Oh, What A Baby / Howie	1958	3.00	15.00
Modern 997	Tonight You Belong To Me / Don't Fall In Love Too Soon	1956	5.00	25.00
Volt 101	Please Don't Go / No Tears	196?	2.00	10.00
Volt 104	Stolen Angel / Teardrop Sea	196?	2.00	10.00
TONGUE				
Hemisphere 101	Keep On Truckin' / Jazz On The Rag	1970	1.00	5.00
TONGUE & GROOVE				
Fontana 1640	Cherry Ball / Devil	1969	1.00	5.00
Fontana 1653	Come On In My Kitchen / Mailman's Sack	1969	1.00	5.00
TONY & JO				
Era 1075	The Freeze / Gonna Get A Little Kissin' Tonight	1958	3.00	15.00
Dore 688	The Freeze / Gonna Get A Little Kissin' Tonight	1962	3.00	15.00
Dore 619	Twist And The Freeze / Long Black Stockings	1962	3.00	15.00
TONY & THE BANDITS				
Coral 62461	It's A Bit Of Alright / (Oh No!) I Can't Lose	1965	1.20	6.00
Coral 62473	The Sun Don't Shine Now That You're Gone / I'm Goin' Away From You	1965	1.20	6.00
TONY & THE DAY DREAMS				
Features Tony Carmen.				
Planet 1008	I'll Never Tell / Why Don't You Be Nice?	1958	20.00	100.00
Planet 1054	Christmas Lullabye / Handin' Hand	1958	50.00	200.00
TONY & THE HOLIDAYS				
ABC-Paramount 10029	There Goes My Heart Again / My Love Is Real	1959	5.00	25.00
TONY & THE RAINDROPS				
Chesapeake 609	While Walking / Our Love Is Over	196?	8.00	40.00
TONY & THE TECHNIQUES				
Chex 1010	Ha Ha, He Told On You / Workout With You, Pretty Girl	1962	4.00	20.00
TONY'S TYGERS [THE TYGERS]				
Teen Town 104	Little By Little / Days And Nights	1968	2.00	10.00
Teen Town 105	Can't Believe / Still Love Her	1968	2.00	10.00
Teen Town 107	Debbie On My Mind / I'll Know	1968	2.00	10.00
A&M 921	Little By Little / Days And Nights	1968	1.00	5.00
TOOMORROW				
Toomorrow features Olivia Newton-John.				
Kirshner 5005 (DJ)	You're My Baby Now / Going Back	1971	5.00	25.00
Kirshner 5005	You're My Baby Now / Going Back	1971	15.00	75.00
TOONE, GENE, & THE BLAZERS				
Produced by Phil Spector.				
Annette 1001	You're My Baby / Jose	1964	20.00	100.00
TOPICS, THE				
The Topics also recorded with Billy Dixon & The Topics and later recorded as The Four Seasons.				
Perri 1007	The Girl In My Dreams (One sided)	1961	30.00	150.00
TOPICS, THE				
Topics 100	The Devil / Come, Little Baby	196?	1.00	5.00
TOPSIDERS, THE				
Atlantic 2215	You Can't Be Happy By Yourself / Baby Of Mine	1964	2.00	10.00
TORKAYS, THE				
Stacy 960	Karate / I Don't Like It (But What Can I Do?)	1963	2.00	10.00
TORNADOES, THE [THE HOLLYWOOD TORNADOES]				
Aertaun 100	Bustin' Surfboards / Beyond The Surf	1962	4.00	20.00

Label & Catalog #		A-Side/B-Side	Year	VG	NM
Aertaun 101		The Gremmie / The Gremmie, Part 2	1962	3.00	15.00
Aertaun 102		Moon Dawg / The Inebriated Surfer	1963	4.00	20.00
		(Aertaun 101 and 102 credited to The Hollywood Tornadoes.)			
Aertaun 103		Shootin' Beavers / Phantom Surfer	1963	4.00	20.00
Aertaun 103		Lightnin' / Phantom Surfer	1964	3.00	15.00
TORNADOES, THE					
London 9561		Telstar / Jungle Fever	1962	3.00	15.00
London 9579		Like Locomotion / Globe Trottin'	1963	2.00	10.00
London 9581		Ridin' The Wind / The Breeze And I	1963	2.00	10.00
London 9599		Life On Venus / Robot	1963	2.00	10.00
London 9614		Scales Of Justice / Ice Cream Man	1963	2.00	10.00
Tower 152		Stompin' Through The Rye / Early Bird	1965	2.00	10.00
Tower 171		Stingray / Aqua Marina	1965	3.00	15.00
TORNADOS, THE					
Cuca 1092		Scalping Party / 7-0-7	196?	7.00	35.00
TORNADOS OF KENNEWICK WASHINGTON, THE					
Century 13181	(EP)	The Tornados Of Kennewick Washington	196?	5.00	25.00
TORQUAYS, THE					
Gee Cee Cee 8163		Surfer's City / Escondido	196?	7.00	35.00
Rock-It 1004		Image Of A Girl / Stolen Moments	1965	4.00	20.00
Colpix 782		Image Of A Girl / Stolen Moments	1965	2.00	10.00
Rock-It 1005		Stoked On Her / Harmonica Man	1965	4.00	20.00
Punch 1007		Shake A Tail Feather / Temptation	196?	4.00	20.00
TORQUAYS, THE					
Gypsy 265		Busting Point / The Other Side	196?	7.00	35.00
Original Sound		Busting Point / The Other Side	196?	4.00	20.00
Aertaun 1020		Turmoil / Crying In The Chapel	196?	6.00	30.00
TORQUAYS, THE					
Original Sound 66		Harmonica Man / Our Teenage Love	1966	3.00	15.00
TORQUES, THE					
Lemco 880		Tidal Wave / Harlem Nocturne	196?	3.00	15.00
TORQUETTS, THE					
Santa Cruz 10002		(Who's Got The) Tortillas? / Any More	196?	7.00	35.00
TORQUETTS, THE					
Torquett 005/6		Feedback / Bacardi	196?	8.00	40.00
Torquett 007/8		Side Swiped / Blue Coral	196?	4.00	20.00
TOSH, PETER					
Roll. Stones 19308		(You Got To Walk And) Don't Look Back / Soon Come	1978	1.00	5.00
Roll. Stones 19308	(PS)	(You Got To Walk And) Don't Look Back / Soon Come	1978	1.00	5.00
		("Don't Look Back" features Mick Jagger.)			
Roll. Stones 20000		Buk-In-Hamm Palace / Recruiting Soldiers	1979	.60	3.00
TOUCH					
Touch features Don Galucci of Don & The Goodtimes.					
Lecasver		Blue On Green / Pick And Shovel	1969	1.00	5.00
Coliseum 2712		Miss Teach / We Feel Fine	196?	1.00	5.00
TOW-AWAY ZONE, THE					
Epic 10369		Searchin' / Shabad	1968	1.20	6.00
TOWNSHEND, PETE					
Pete Townshend is a member of The Who. Refer to Angie.					
Atco 7217		Let My Love Open The Door / And I Moved	1980	.60	3.00
Atco 7312		A Little Is Enough / Cat's In The Cupboard	1980	.60	3.00
Atco 7318		Rough Boys / Jools And Jim	1980	.60	3.00
Atco 99973		Uniforms / Slit Skirts	1982	.40	2.00
Atco 99989		Face Dances, Part 2 / Man Watching	1982	.40	2.00
Atco 99989	(PS)	Face Dances, Part 2 / Man Watching	1982	.40	2.00
Atco 99884		Bargain / Dirty Water	1983	.40	2.00
Atco 99884	(PS)	Bargain / Dirty Water	1983	.40	2.00
Atco 99590		Face The Face / Hiding Out	1985	.40	2.00
Atco 99590	(PS)	Face The Face / Hiding Out	1985	.40	2.00
Atco 99577		Give Blood / Magic Bus	1985	.40	2.00
Atco 99577	(PS)	Give Blood / Magic Bus	1985	.40	2.00
Atco 99553		Second Hand Love / White City Fighting	1985	.40	2.00

Label & Catalog #	A-Side/B-Side	Year	VG	NM
TOWNSHEND, PETE, & RONNIE LANE				
Refer to The Small Faces; The Who.				
MCA 40818	My Baby Gives It Away / April Fool	1977	.80	4.00
MCA 40878	Keep Me Turning / Nowhere To Run	1978	.80	4.00
TOWNSMEN, THE				
P.J. 1340/1	That's All I'll Ever Need / I Can't Let Go	1963	15.00	75.00
Joey 6202	Moonlight Was Made For Lovers /			
	I'm In The Mood For Love	1963	5.00	25.00
Herald 585	It Is All Over / Just A Little Bit	1963	3.00	15.00
Columbia 43207	Please Don't Say Goodbye / Gotta Get Moving	1965	1.00	5.00
TOWNSMEN, THE				
Vanity 579/80	It's Time / Little Jeannie	196?	2.00	10.00
TRACERS, THE				
Sully 928	She Said Yeah / Watch Me	1966	5.00	25.00
	(Sully 928 was originally released credited to The Stones.)			
TRACES, THE				
Laurie 3493	What Am I To Do? / Love Me Forever	1969	2.00	10.00
Laurie 3515	Runaround Sue / Nothing Matters Now	1969	2.00	10.00
TRACKERS, THE				
Whip 1001	Trackin' / Jilted Fever	196?	7.00	35.00
TRADEMARKS, THE				
Jubal 100	Baba-Ree-Ba / Baba-Ree-Ba, Part 2	1963	7.00	35.00
TRADEMARKS, THE				
Palmer 5018	If I Was Gone / I Need You	1967	3.00	15.00
TRADEWINDS, THE				
RCA Victor 47-7511	Twins / Toni	1959	2.00	10.00
RCA Victor 47-7553	Crossroads / Furry Murray	1959	2.00	10.00
TRADEWINDS, THE				
Dawn Cory 1005	Surfin' Thunder / Gotcha	196?	10.00	50.00
TRADEWINDS, THE				
The Tradewinds feature Pete Anders and Vince Poncia.				
Red Bird 020	New York's A Lonely Town / Club 17	1965	3.00	15.00
Red Bird 028	Rock And Roll Show In Town /			
	Girl From Greenwich Village	1965	2.00	10.00
Red Bird 033	Summertime Girl / The Party Starts At Nine	1965	3.00	15.00
Kama Sutra 212	Mind Excursion / Little Susan's Dreaming	1966	2.00	10.00
Kama Sutra 218	I Believe In Her / Catch Me In The Meadow	1966	1.60	8.00
Kama Sutra 234	Mind Excursion / Only When I'm Dreaming	1967	1.60	8.00
TRAFFIC				
The original group consisted of Jim Capaldi, Steve Winwood, Chris Wood and on-again off-again member Dave Mason.				
Later members included Rick Grech and Jim Gordon. Refer to Spencer Davis Group.				
United Artists 50195	Paper Sun / Giving To You	1967	1.20	6.00
United Artists 50218	Hole In My Shoe / Smiling Phases	1967	1.20	6.00
United Artists 50218 (PS)	Hole In My Shoe / Smiling Phases	1967	3.00	15.00
United Artists 50232	Here We 'Round The Mulberry Bush / Coloured Rain	1968	1.00	5.00
United Artists 50460	Feelin' Alright / Withering Tree	1968	.80	4.00
United Artists 50500	Pearly Queen / Medicated Goo	1969	.80	4.00
United Artists 50692	Empty Pages / Stranger To Myself	1970	.80	4.00
United Artists 50841	Gimme Some Lovin' / Gimme Some Lovin' (Part 2)	1971	.60	3.00
Island 1201	Rock And Roll Stew / Rock And Roll Stew (Part 2)	1972	.60	3.00
TRAGEDY, THE				
Panorama 1004	Unfaithful Love / The Entertainer	1968	.80	4.00
TRAINS, THE				
Swan 4196	The Plan / We Two	1965	2.00	10.00
Swan 4203	Fourteen And Getting Older / The Beware Song	1965	2.00	10.00
TRAITS, THE				
Universal 30494	Harlem Shuffle / Somewhere	1966	3.00	15.00
Scepter 12169	Harlem Shuffle / Somewhere	1966	1.00	5.00
Renner 221	Linda Lou / Little Mama	196?	3.00	15.00
TRAMMELL, BOBBY LEE				
Fabor 4038	Shirley Lee / I Sure Do Love You, Baby	1957	15.00	75.00
ABC-Paramount 9890	Shirley Lee / I Sure Do Love You, Baby	1958	8.00	40.00
Warrior 1554	Woe Is Me /	1959	10.00	50.00

Label & Catalog #		A-Side/B-Side	Year	VG	NM
TRAMPS, THE					
Arvee 548		Ride On / You're A Square	1959	3.00	15.00
Arvee 570		Your Love / Midnight Flyer	1959	3.00	15.00
TRAN-SISTERS, THE					
Pickwick City 1003		Let It In / Tomorrow The World Will Know	196?	2.00	10.00
TRAPEZE					
Threshold 67011		Your Love Is Alright / Coast To Coast	1972	.80	4.00
TRASH					
Apple P-1804	(DJ)	Road To Nowhere / Illusions	1969	6.00	30.00
Apple 1804		Road To Nowhere / Illusions	1969	15.00	75.00
Apple 1811		Golden Slumbers / Trash Can	1969	2.00	10.00
TRASHMEN, THE					
Garrett 4002		Surfin' Bird / King Of The Surf	1963	3.00	15.00
Garrett 4003		Bird Dance Beat / A-Bone	1964	3.00	15.00
Garrett 4005		Bad News / On The Move	1964	4.00	20.00
Garrett 4010		Peppermint Man / New Generation	1964	5.00	25.00
Garrett 4012		Whoa, Dad / Walkin' My Baby	1964	4.00	20.00
Garrett 4012	(PS)	Whoa, Dad / Walkin' My Baby	1964	20.00	100.00
Garrett 4013		Dancing With Santa / Real Live Doll	1966	3.00	15.00
Garrett 4013	(PS)	Dancing With Santa / Real Live Doll	1966	30.00	150.00
Tribe 8315		Same Lines / Hangin' On Me	1966	2.00	10.00
Metromedia 7927		Green, Green Backs Of Home / Address Enclosed	1968	2.00	10.00
Lana 136		Surfin' Bird / King Of The Surf	197?	.40	2.00
Soma 1469		Surfin' Bird / (B-side by The Castaways)	197?	.40	2.00
TRAVEL AGENCY, THE					
Viva 3438		What's A Man? /	1968	1.00	5.00
TRAVELERS, THE					
Atlas 1086		Lenora / Betty Jean	1957	10.00	50.00
TRAVELERS, THE					
Atlas 1086		Lenora / Betty Jean	1957	4.00	20.00
Andex 3-4006		Why? / Teen Age Machine Age	1958	4.00	20.00
Andex 2011		I'll Be Home For Christmas / Katie The Kangaroo	1958	4.00	20.00
Andex 4012		He's Got The Whole World In His Hands / Green Town Girl	1958	4.00	20.00
Andex 4033		I Go For You / I'll Always Be In Love With You	1959	4.00	20.00
TRAVELERS, THE					
Decca 31215		Cadwaller 00002 / Ivy On The Old School Wall	1961	8.00	40.00
Decca 31282		Oh, My Love / White Rose	1961	8.00	40.00
TRAVELERS, THE					
ABC-Paramount 10119		June, July, August And September / What A Weekend	1960	2.00	10.00
TRAVELERS, THE					
Gass 1000		Tie Me Surfer Board Down, Sports / In The Pines	1963	7.00	35.00
TRAVELERS, THE					
Don Ray 5965		Traveler / Seven Minutes Till Four	1963	7.00	35.00
Yellow Sand 2		Windy And Warm / Last Date	1963	7.00	35.00
TRAVELERS, THE					
Princess 52		Spanish Moon / She's Got The Blues	1963	3.00	15.00
Vault 911		Spanish Moon / She's Got The Blues	1963	3.00	15.00
TRAVELERS, THE: *Refer to* FRANKIE VALLEY					
TRAVELERS IV, THE					
Rox 1001		A Message For You / This Happens To Me	196?	2.00	10.00
TRAVELING WILBURYS, THE					
The Wilburys are Bob Dylan, George Harrison, Jeff Lynne, Roy Orbison and Tom Petty.					
Wilbury 277323	(DJ)	Handle With Care / Margarita	1989	2.00	10.00
Wilbury 277323		Handle With Care / Margarita	1989	.40	2.00
Wilbury 277323	(PS)	Handle With Care / Margarita	1989	.40	2.00
Wilbury 27637	(DJ)	End Of The Line / Congratulations	1989	2.00	10.00
Wilbury 27637		End Of The Line / Congratulations	1989	.40	2.00
Wilbury 27637	(PS)	End Of The Line / Congratulations	1989	2.00	10.00
TRAVIS & BOB					
Sandy 1017		Tell Him No / We're Too Young	1959	3.00	15.00
		(First pressings make no mention of Dot Records)			

Label & Catalog #		A-Side/B-Side	Year	VG	NM
Sandy 1017		Tell Him No / We're Too Young	1959	2.00	10.00
		(Second pressings read "Distributed by Dot Records.")			
Sandy 1019		Little Bitty Johnny / Teenage Vision	1959	2.00	10.00
Sandy 1024		Oh, Yeah / Lover's Rendezvous	1959	2.00	10.00
Sandy 1029		Wake Up And Cry / That's How Long	1959	2.00	10.00
Big Top 3054		Pocohantas / Day Dreams	1960	2.00	10.00

TRAYLOR, JACK, & STEELWIND

Grunt 0057		Child Of Nature / Time To Be Happy	196?	.80	4.00

TRAYNOR, JAY

Jay Traynor was the original lead singer with Jay & The Americans.

Coral 62396		I Rise, I Fall / How Sweet It Is	1965	1.00	5.00
Coral 62420		Little Sister / I've Known You All My Life	1965	1.00	5.00
ABC-Paramount 10809		Come On / Merry-Go-Round Is Slowing You Down	1966	1.00	5.00
ABC-Paramount 10845		Up And Over / Don't Let The End Begin	1966	1.00	5.00
Roaring 800		Dusty Said Goodbye / Love Got In The Way	197?	.60	3.00

TREASURES, THE

Valor 4750		Minor Chaos / Valley Of The Broken Hearts	1964	15.00	75.00
Valor 4750		Minor Chaos / Valley Of The Broken Hearts (Green vinyl)	1964	40.00	200.00
Valor 4750		Minor Chaos / Valley Of The Broken Hearts (Marble vinyl)	1964	100.00	400.00
Valor 5534		Lean Jean /	1965	15.00	75.00

TREASURES, THE: *Refer to* PETE ANDERS

TREBLE CHORDS, THE

Decca 31015		Teresa / My Little Girl	1959	15.00	75.00

TREBLE TONES, THE

Atlas 260		The Crawl / Treble Rock	1960	3.00	15.00

TREBLETONES, THE

Souvenir 1010		Guitar Movement / Little Laura	1962	3.00	15.00

TREE SWINGERS, THE

Guyden 2036		Kookie Little Paradise / Teaching The Natives To Sing	1960	2.00	10.00

TREM-LOS, THE

Nolta 350		Walkin' Along / Silly Affair	196?	1.00	5.00

TREMELOES, THE

The Tremeloes—Alan Blakely, Len Hawkes, Dave Munden and Rick Westwood—originally recorded with Brian Poole.

Epic 10075		Good Day Sunshine / What A State I'm In	1967	2.00	10.00
Epic 10139		Here Comes My Baby / Gentleman Of Pleasure	1967	1.20	6.00
Epic 10184		Silence Is Golden / Let Your Hair Hang Down	1967	1.20	6.00
Epic 10184	(PS)	Silence Is Golden / Let Your Hair Hang Down	1967	2.00	10.00
Epic 10233		Even The Bad Times Are Good / Jenny's All Right	1967	1.20	6.00
Epic 10233	(PS)	Even The Bad Times Are Good / Jenny's All Right	1967	3.00	15.00
Epic 10293		Suddenly You Love Me / Suddenly Winter	1968	1.00	5.00
Epic 10328		Helule Helule / Girl From Nowhere	1968	1.00	5.00
Epic 10376		My Little Lady / All The World To Me	1969	1.00	5.00
Epic 10437		I Shall Be Released / Miss My Baby	1969	1.20	6.00
Epic 10467		Hello World / Up, Down, All Around	1969	.80	4.00
Epic 10548		(Call Me) Number One / Instant Whip	1969	.80	4.00
Epic 10621		Breakheart Motel / By The Way	1970	2.00	10.00
Epic 10682		Me And My Life / Try Me	1970	.80	4.00
Epic 10807		Hello Buddy / My Woman	1972	.80	4.00
Epic 10996		Blue Suede Tie / Yodelay	1973	.80	4.00
DJM 1008		Hard Woman / My Friend Delaney	1974	1.00	5.00
DJM 1016	(DJ)	September, November, December / September, November, December	1974	1.00	5.00
		(Stock copies of DJM 1016 may not exist.)			

TREMELOS, THE

Rockland 102		Jaguar / Fly	196?	7.00	35.00

TREMONT, JIMMY, & THE BRONX DUKES

Street Corner 113		I Never Tell Her I Love Her / Submarine Races	1979	.80	4.00

TREMONTS, THE

The Tremonts feature Joey Dee.

Pat Riccio 101		Believe My Heart / Legend Of Love	1961	10.00	50.00
Brunswick 55217		Believe My Heart / Legend Of Love	1961	4.00	20.00

TREN-DELLS, THE [THE TREND-ELS]

Tilt 779		I'm So Young / Don't You Hear Me Calling, Baby?	1961	4.00	20.00
		(Tilt 779 credits The Trend-Els.)			

Label & Catalog #	A-Side/B-Side	Year	VG	NM
Tilt 788	Moments Like This / I Miss You So	1961	4.00	20.00
Jam 1100	Night Owl / Hully Gully Jones	1962	4.00	20.00
Capitol 4852	Night Owl / Hully Gully Jones	1962	2.00	10.00
Southtwon 22001	Everyday / I'll Be There	1964	2.00	10.00

TREN-TEENS, THE

Carnival 501	My Baby's Gone / Your Yah Yah Is Gone	196?	4.00	20.00

TREN-TONES, THE

Superb 100	This Is Love / Never Again	196?	8.00	40.00

TRENTONS, THE

Shepherd 2204	All Alone / Star Bright	1962	10.00	50.00

TREVOR, VAN

Atlantic 2175	I Want To Cry / Tuesday Girl	1962	2.00	10.00
Vivid 1004	C'mon Now, Baby / A Fling Of The Past	196?	7.00	35.00
	(Vivid 1004 features The Four Seasons.)			

TREYTONES, THE

BW 604	Blind Date / Cool Baby	1959	3.00	15.00

TRI-FIVE, THE

The Tri-Five features Carl and Dennis—maybe Brian?—Wilson and was produced by Gary Usher.

Damark 2400 (DJ)	Come And Get It / Like Chop	1962	8.00	40.00
	(Stock copies of Damark 2400 may not exist.)			

TRI-LADS, THE

Bullseye 1003	Cherry Pie / Always Be True	1959	2.50	12.00

TRI-LITES, THE

Enith 721	Will Tomorrow Be Just Another Day? / Hot Dog, Here He Comes	196?	3.00	15.00

TRI-TONES, THE

Grand 126	Blues In The Closet / Sweet And Lonely	1955	6.00	30.00

TRI-TONES, THE

Miss Julie 6501	Teardrops / Every Time I Think Of You	195?	50.00	200.00

TRI-TONES, THE

Twilight 405	Surf-A-Nova / Kiss And Run	1963	7.00	35.00
	(Twilight 405 was also released credited to The Parallels.)			

TRIANGLE

Triangle is a pseudonym for Randy & The Rainbows.

Paramount 0055	Jacqueline / Your Love Comes Shinin' Through	197?	1.00	5.00
Paramount 0123	Judge And Jury / Midnight Magic Man	197?	1.00	5.00

TRIANGLES, THE

Fifo 107	My, Oh My / Really I Do	196?	25.00	125.00

TRIBUNES, THE

Derrick 502	The Code Of Love / Now That You're Gone	196?	3.00	15.00

TRIBUTES, THE

Donna 1391	Here Comes Ringo / Ringo Dingo	1964	5.00	25.00

TRICKLES, THE

Gone 5075	When I Fall In Love / With Each Step A Tear	1960	10.00	50.00
Gone 5078	Outside The Chapel Door / With Each Step A Tear	1960	10.00	50.00

TRIDELS, THE

San-Dee 1009	Land Of Love / Image Of My Love	196?	6.00	30.00

TRIPLETS, THE

Dore 574	Gently, My Love / Bagdad Beat	1960	2.00	10.00

TRIPPERS, THE

Ruby-Doo 5	Taking Care Of Business / Charlena	1967	3.00	15.00
GNP/Crescendo 387	Taking Care Of Business / Charlena	1967	2.00	10.00

TRIPSICHORD MUSIC BOX, THE

San Fran. Sound 115	Times And Seasons / Sunday The Third	196?	3.00	15.00

TRIUMPHS, THE

Iff 151	Surfside Date / Susie In My History Class	196?	5.00	25.00

Label & Catalog #		A-Side/B-Side	Year	VG	NM
TRIUMPHS, THE					
Dante 3002		I Know It's Wrong / The Lazy Man	1962	5.00	25.00
Dante 3011		You're Mine Tonight / People Sure Act Funny	1962	5.00	25.00
TRIUMPHS, THE					
The Triumphs also recorded with B.J. Thomas.					
Pacemaker 238		Better Come Get Her / Morticia Baker	1965	5.00	25.00
TRIUMPHS, THE					
Century 13954		Out To Lunch / Eclipse	196?	2.00	10.00
TROGGS, THE					
The Troggs are Ronnie Bond, Chris Britton, Peter Staples and Reg Presley.					
Atco 6415		Wild Thing / With A Girl Like You	1966	2.00	10.00
Atco 6415		Wild Thing / I Want You	1966	2.00	10.00
Atco 6444		I Can't Control Myself / Gonna Make You Mine	1966	2.00	10.00
Fontana 1548		Wild Thing / From Home	1966	1.60	8.00
Fontana 1552		With A Girl Like You / I Want You	1966	1.20	6.00
Fontana 1557		I Can't Control Myself / Gonna Make You Mine	1966	1.20	6.00
Fontana 1576		Give It To Me / You're Lying	1967	1.20	6.00
Fontana 1585		Any Way You Want Me / 6-5-4-3-2-1	1968	1.00	5.00
Fontana 1593		Girl In Black / Night Of The Long Grass	1968	1.00	5.00
Fontana 1607		Love Is All Around / When Will The Rain Come?	1968	1.20	6.00
Fontana 1622		You Can Cry If You Want To / There's Something About You	1968	1.00	5.00
Fontana 1630		Surprise, Surprise (I Need You) / Cousin Jane	1968	1.00	5.00
Fontana 1634		Say Darlin' / Hip Hip Hooray	1969	1.00	5.00
Page One 21026		Evil Woman / Heads Or Tails	1969	.60	3.00
Page One 21030		Easy Lovin' / Give Me Something	1969	.60	3.00
Page One 21032		Lover / Come Now	1970	.60	3.00
Page One 21035		The Raver / You	1970	.60	3.00
Bell 405		Listen To The Man / Queen Of Sorrow	197?	1.20	6.00
Bell 426		Strange Movies / I'm On Fire	197?	1.20	6.00
Pye 65011		Everything's Funny / Feels Like A Woman	1972	.60	3.00
Pye 71015		Good Vibrations / Push It Up To Me	1975	.60	3.00
Pye 71035		Summertime / Jenny Come Down	1976	.60	3.00
Pye 71054		Satisfaction /	1976	.60	3.00
Private Stock 45102		Rolling Stone /	1977	.60	3.00
TROIANO, DOMINIC					
Mercury 73312		The Wear And Tear On My Mind / The Writing's On The Wall	1972	1.00	5.00
Capitol 4709		We All Need Love / Ambush	1979	.80	4.00
TROJANS, THE					
Triangle 51317		All Night Long / I Wanted You So Long	1960	10.00	50.00
TROLLEY, THE					
Piccadilly 246		Toy Shop / Breakdown	1967	2.00	10.00
TROLLS, THE					
Warrior 173		Stupid Girl / I Don't Recall	1966	3.00	15.00
Warrior 173	(PS)	Stupid Girl / I Don't Recall	1966	4.00	20.00
TROLLS, THE					
ABC 10820		Every Day And Every Night / Are You The One?	1966	1.20	6.00
ABC 10884		Laughing All The Way / Something Here Inside	1966	1.20	6.00
ABC 10916		There Was A Time / They Don't Know	1967	1.20	6.00
ABC 10952		Who Was That Boy? / Baby, What You Ain't Got	1967	1.20	6.00
U.S.A. 905		I Got To Have You / Don't Come Around	1968	1.20	6.00
TRONICS, THE					
Landa 676		Pickin' And Stompin' / Cantina	1961	2.00	10.00
Landa 680		The Big Scroungy / South American Sunset	1961	2.00	10.00
TROPHIES, THE					
Challenge 9133		Desire / Doggone It	1962	6.00	30.00
Challenge 9149		Peg O' My Heart / I Laughed So Hard I Cried	1962	4.00	20.00
Challenge 9170		Felicia / That's All I Want From You	1962	3.00	15.00
TROY, DORIS					
R&B singer Doris Troy was another Apple attempt to broaden their horizons which, unfortunately, did not succeed.					
Apple 1820		Ain't That Cute / Vaya Con Dios	1970	1.00	5.00
Apple 1824		Get Back / Jacob's Ladder	1970	1.00	5.00
TROYS, THE					
The Troys also recorded as Dicky Dell & The Bing Bongs.					
OKeh 7120		The Cling / Ding-A-Ling-A-Ling	1959	3.00	15.00

Label & Catalog #		A-Side/B-Side	Year	VG	NM
TRU-SONICS, THE					
The Tru-Sonics also recorded with Tracy Thomas.					
Bolo 724		Forgotten Love / Lover	196?	1.00	5.00
TRU-TONES, THE					
Tru		Surfin,' Here We Go / Darlin,' I'm Sorry	196?	7.00	35.00
TRUANTS, THE					
Rock-It 1003		Sunset Surf / The Truant	1963	5.00	25.00
TU-TONES, THE					
Lin 5021		Still In Love With You / Saccharin Sally	1959	6.00	30.00
TUBES, THE					
A&M 11864	(DJ)	White Punks On Dope / White Punks On Dope	1975	1.00	5.00
A&M 11864	(PS)	White Punks On Dope / White Punks On Dope	1975	2.00	10.00
A&M 1733		White Punks On Dope / White Punks On Dope, Part 2	1975	.80	4.00
A&M 1733	(PS)	White Punks On Dope / White Punks On Dope, Part 2	1975	2.00	10.00
TUESDAY CLUB, THE					
Philips 478		Only Human / A Goddess In Many Ways	1966	4.00	20.00
TUFANO & GIAMMERESE					
Ode 66033		Music Everywhere / Just A Dream Away	1973	.80	4.00
Ode 66122		Time Change / Let In The Light	1976	.80	4.00
TULLY, LEE					
Flair-X 3007		Around The World With Elwood Pretzel / Around The World With Elwood Pretzel, Part 2	1956	3.00	15.00
TU-TONES, THE					
Lin 5021		Still In Love With You / Saccharin Sally	195?	5.00	25.00
TUNE ROCKERS, THE					
United Artists 139		The Green Mosquito / Warm Up	1958	3.00	15.00
TURBO-JETS, THE					
Federal 12349		Bingo / In Reverse	1960	2.00	10.00
TURFITS, THE					
Capitol 2018		Losin' One / If It's Love You Want	1967	2.00	10.00
TURKS, THE					
P.B.D. 112		Baja / Dianne	196?	7.00	35.00
P.B.D. 113		Wipeout / Hideaway	196?	7.00	35.00
TURNBOW, JEANNE					
Ben-Ron 1393		Beatle Bug / Summertime	1964	5.00	25.00
TURNER, IKE & TINA					
Ike & Tina Turner had a long career with many R&B hits on a variety of labels; those included in this book are due to Phil Spector's involvement.					
Philles 131		River Deep-Mountain High / I'll Keep You Happy	1966	3.00	15.00
		("River Deep-Mountain High" was produced by Phil Spector.)			
Philles 135		I'll Never Need More Than This / The Cashbox Blues	1967	3.00	15.00
Philles 136		A Love Like Yours / I Idolize You	1967	3.00	15.00
		("A Love Like Yours" was produced by Phil Spector.)			
Philles 134		A Man Is A Man Is A Man / Two To Tango	1966	3.00	15.00
A&M 1118		River Deep-Mountain High / I'll Keep You Happy	1969	2.00	10.00
A&M 1170		A Love Like Yours / Save The Last Dance For Me	1969	2.00	10.00
		(Produced by Phil Spector.)			
TURNER, JESSE LEE					
Fraternity 855		Teen-Age Misery / That's My Girl	1959	3.00	15.00
Fraternity 855	(PS)	Teen-Age Misery / That's My Girl	1959	6.00	30.00
Carlton 496		The Little Space Girl / Shake, Baby, Shake	1959	3.00	15.00
Carlton 509		Baby, Please Don't Tease / Thinkin'	1959	2.00	10.00
Carlton 509	(PS)	Baby, Please Don't Tease / Thinkin'	1959	3.00	15.00
Top Rank 2064		Do I Worry? (Yes, I Do) / All Right, Be That Way	1960	3.00	15.00
Imperial 5649		The Little Space Girl's Father / Valley Of Lost Soldiers	1960	3.00	15.00
GNP-Crescendo 184		All You Gotta Do / The Voice Changing Song	1963	1.60	8.00
GNP-Crescendo 188		Ballad Of Billie Sol Estes / Shotgun Boogie	1963	1.60	8.00
TURNER, TITUS					
Glover 302		When The Sergeant Comes Marching Home /	1960	7.00	35.00

Label & Catalog #		A-Side/B-Side	Year	VG	NM
TURTLES, THE					
Original Turtles were Howard Kaylan, Don Murray, Al Nichol, Chuck Portz and Mark Volman, formerly The Crossfires,					
and later, John Barbata, Jim Pons and Jim Tucker. Refer to Christmas Spirit; The Dedications; Flo & Eddie.					
White Whale 222		It Ain't Me, Babe / Almost There	1965	1.20	6.00
White Whale 224		Let Me Be / Your Ma Said You Cried	1965	1.20	6.00
White Whale 227		You Baby / Wanderin' Kind	1966	1.20	6.00
White Whale 231		Grim Reaper Of Love / Come Back	1966	3.00	15.00
White Whale 234		Outside Chance / We'll Meet Again	1966	2.00	10.00
White Whale 237		Outside Chance / Making My Mind Up	1966	1.60	8.00
White Whale 238		Can I Get To Know You Better? / Like The Seasons	1966	1.60	8.00
White Whale 244		Happy Together / Like The Seasons	1967	1.00	5.00
White Whale 244	(PS)	Happy Together / Like The Seasons	1967	3.00	15.00
White Whale 249		She'd Rather Be With Me / Walking Song	1967	1.00	5.00
White Whale 249	(PS)	She'd Rather Be With Me / Walking Song	1967	4.00	20.00
White Whale 251		Guide For The Married Man / Think I'll Run Away	1967	5.00	25.00
		(Pulled from distribution immediately after release.)			
White Whale 254		You Know What I Mean / Rugs Of Wood And Flowers	1967	1.00	5.00
White Whale 254	(PS)	You Know What I Mean / Rugs Of Wood And Flowers	1967	2.00	10.00
White Whale 260		She's My Girl / Chicken Little Was Right	1967	1.00	5.00
White Whale 260	(PS)	She's My Girl / Chicken Little Was Right	1967	3.00	15.00
White Whale 264		Sound Asleep / Umbassa And The Dragon	1968	1.00	5.00
White Whale 264	(PS)	Sound Asleep / Umbassa And The Dragon	1968	2.00	10.00
White Whale 273		The Story Of Rock & Roll / Can't You Hear The Cows?	1968	1.20	6.00
White Whale 273	(PS)	The Story Of Rock & Roll / Can't You Hear The Cows?	1968	5.00	25.00
White Whale 276		Elenore / Surfer Dan	1968	1.00	5.00
White Whale 276	(PS)	Elenore / Surfer Dan	1968	1.60	8.00
White Whale 292		You Showed Me / Buzz Saw	1969	1.00	5.00
White Whale 292	(PS)	You Showed Me / Buzz Saw	1969	1.60	8.00
White Whale 306		House On The Hill / Come Over	1969	1.00	5.00
White Whale 308		You Don't Have To Walk In The Rain / Come Over	1969	1.00	5.00
White Whale 308	(PS)	You Don't Have To Walk In The Rain / Come Over	1969	1.60	8.00
White Whale 326		Love In The City / Bachelor Mother	1969	1.00	5.00
White Whale 326	(PS)	Love In The City / Bachelor Mother	1969	1.60	8.00
White Whale 334		Lady-O / Somewhere Friday Night	1969	1.00	5.00
		(W.W. 306, 308, 326 and 334 were produced by Raymond Douglas Davies.)			
White Whale 341		Who Would Ever Think That I Could Marry Margaret? /			
		Ain't Gonna Party No More	1970	1.60	8.00
White Whale 350		Is It Any Wonder? / Wanderin' Kind	1970	1.00	5.00
White Whale 355		Eve Of Destruction / Wanderin' Kind	1970	1.00	5.00
White Whale 364		Me About You / Think I'll Run Away	1970	1.00	5.00
TWANGY REBELS, THE					
General American 719		Rebel Rouser '65 / Lazy Rebel	1965	2.00	10.00
TWEEDS, THE					
Coral 62542		A Thing Of The Past / What's Your Name?	1967	1.20	6.00
Coral 62551		I Want Her To Know / We Got Time	1968	1.20	6.00
TWEENS, THE					
DC 0429		Seventeen Little Kisses / The Witches Crew	196?	3.00	15.00
TWENTIETH CENTURY ZOO, THE					
Vault 961		Only Thing That's Wrong / Stallion Of Fate	1967	2.00	10.00
TWICE AS MUCH					
MGM 13530		Sittin' On A Fence / Baby, I Want You	1966	2.00	10.00
MGM 13530	(PS)	Sittin' On A Fence / Baby, I Want You	1966	3.00	15.00
MGM 13600		Simplified / Step Out Of Line	1966	1.00	5.00
TWIGGS, THE					
Jerden 917		Flowers And Beads / Moon Maiden	1970	2.00	10.00
SST Inter. 800		Flowers And Beads / Moon Maiden	1970	2.00	10.00
TWIGGY					
Capitol 5903		Over And Over / When I Think Of You	1967	2.00	10.00
Capitol 5903	(PS)	Over And Over / When I Think Of You	1967	4.00	20.00
Bell 45115	(DJ)	Zoo De Zoo Song / Zoo De Zoo Song	196?	1.00	5.00
		(Stock copies of Bell 45115 may not exist.)			
TWIGS, THE					
Dot 16830		Down The Road Apiece / I Need Your Love, Babe	1966	2.00	10.00
TWILIGHTERS, THE					
Bubble 1334		My Silent Prayer / Little Bitty Bed Bug	196?	4.00	20.00
Nix 102		Hey, There / Caused By You	1961	6.00	30.00
Nic 103		Love Bandit / Back To School	1961	4.00	20.00

This sleeve makes effective use of contrasts: One side is basically a black on white collage while the flip side is reversed. Oh, and it's a great single, too...

Label & Catalog #		A-Side/B-Side	Year	VG	NM
TWILIGHTERS, THE					
Roulette 4546		My Beatle Haircut / Sweet Lips	1964	5.00	25.00
TWILIGHTERS, THE					
Vanco 204		Out Of My Mind / I Need Your Lovin'	1968	2.00	10.00
Twi-Note 1		Shiftin' / The Shift	196?	3.00	15.00
TWILIGHTS, THE					
Six Star 1001		Bohemian / Little Richard	196?	3.00	15.00
Twilight 1028		It Could Be True / Sum'pin Else	196?	3.00	15.00
TWILIGHTS, THE: *Refer to* PHIL PHILLIPS; TONY RICHARDS; TEDDY & THE TWILIGHTS					
TWINKLE					
Tollie 9040		Terry / Boy Of My Dreams	1965	2.00	10.00
Tollie 9040	(PS)	Terry / Boy Of My Dreams (Promo)	1965	5.00	25.00
Tollie 9047	(DJ)	Golden Lights / Ain't Nobody Home But Me	1965	2.00	10.00
		(Stock copies of Tollie 9047 may not exist.)			
Aurora 163		What Am I Doing Here With You? / The End Of The World	196?	1.50	8.00
TWINKLES, THE					
The Twinkles later recorded as The Storey Sisters.					
Peak 5001		Bad Motorcycle / Sweet Daddy	1958	5.00	25.00
Musicor 1031		Fairy Tales / Oh, Little Star	1963	2.00	10.00
TWINS, THE					
RCA Victor 47-7235		Jo Ann's Sister / Who Knows The Secret?	1958	2.00	10.00
RCA Victor 47-7235	(PS)	Jo Ann's Sister / Who Knows The Secret?	1958	4.00	20.00
TWISTERS, THE					
Sun-Set 501		Please Come Back / This Is The End	195?	150.00	500.00
TWISTERS, THE					
Felco 103		Count Down 1-2-3 / Speed Limit	1959	2.50	12.00
TWISTERS, THE					
Apt 25045		Pretty Little Girl Next Door / Come Go With Me	1960	4.00	20.00
Capitol 4451		Dancing Little Clown / Turn The Page	1960	2.00	10.00
Campus 125		Elvis Leaves Sorrento / Street Dance	1961	7.00	35.00
Dual 502		Peppermint Twist / Silly Chili	1961	2.00	10.00

TWITTY, CONWAY

Conway Twitty appeared to burst on the scene in 1958 with a song that was apparently first offered to Elvis, who inexplicably turned it down. "It's Only Make Believe" topped the charts; through 1960 he managed seven more Top 40 hits on MGM before changing gears and heading for the country. From the mid '60s on, Conway has enjoyed monumental success as one of America's favorite country artists, a position he holds today for MCA.

Mercury 71086		I Need Your Lovin' / Born To Sing The Blues	1957	5.00	25.00
Mercury 71148		Shake It Up / Maybe Baby	1957	4.00	20.00
Mercury 71384		Double Talk Baby / Why Can't I Get Through To You?	1957	6.00	30.00
MGM 12677		It's Only Make Believe / I'll Try	1958	4.00	20.00
MGM 50107	(S)	It's Only Make Believe / I'll Try	1958	8.00	40.00
MGM 12748		The Story Of My Love / Make Me Know You're Mine	1959	3.00	15.00
MGM 12785		Hey, Little Lucy! (Don'tcha Put No Lipstick On) /			
		When I'm Not With You	1959	3.00	15.00
MGM 12804		Mona Lisa / Heavenly	1959	3.00	15.00
MGM 12826		Danny Boy / Halfway To Heaven	1959	4.00	20.00
MGM 50130	(S)	Danny Boy / Halfway To Heaven	1959	8.00	40.00
		—Original MGM singles above have yellow labels.—			
MGM 12857		Lonely Blue Boy / Star Spangled Heaven	1959	4.00	20.00
MGM 12886		What Am I Living For? / The Hurt In My Heart	1960	3.00	15.00
MGM 12886	(PS)	What Am I Living For? / The Hurt In My Heart	1960	5.00	25.00
MGM 12911		Is A Blue Bird Blue? / She's Mine	1960	3.00	15.00
MGM 12911	(PS)	Is A Blue Bird Blue? / She's Mine	1960	5.00	25.00
MGM 12918		Tell Me One More Time / What A Dream	1960	2.00	10.00
MGM 12943		I Need You So / Teasin'	1960	2.00	10.00
MGM 12962		Whole Lot Of Shakin' Goin' On / The Flame	1960	2.00	10.00
MGM 12969		C'est Si Bon (It's So Good) / Don't You Dare Let Me Down	1960	2.00	10.00
MGM 12969	(PS)	C'est Si Bon (It's So Good) / Don't You Dare Let Me Down	1960	5.00	25.00
MGM 12998		The Next Kiss (Is The Last Goodbye) / Man Alone	1961	2.00	10.00
MGM 12998	(PS)	The Next Kiss (Is The Last Goodbye) / Man Alone	1961	5.00	25.00
MGM 13011		A Million Teardrops / I'm In A Blue, Blue Mood	1961	2.00	10.00
MGM 13034		It's Drivin' Me Wild / Sweet Sorrow	1961	2.00	10.00
MGM 13034	(PS)	It's Drivin' Me Wild / Sweet Sorrow	1961	4.00	20.00
MGM 13050		Portrait Of A Fool / Tower Of Tears	1962	2.00	10.00
MGM 13072		Comfy 'N Cozy / A Little Piece Of My Heart	1962	2.00	10.00
MGM 13089		There's Something On Your Mind / Unchained Melody	1962	2.00	10.00
MGM 13112		The Pickup / I Hope, I Think, I Wish	1962	2.00	10.00
MGM 13149		Got My Mojo Working / She Ain't No Angel	1962	2.00	10.00

Label & Catalog #	A-Side/B-Side	Year	VG	NM
MGM 14172	Lonely Blue Boy / It's Only Make Believe	1970	.60	3.00
MGM 14205	I'll Try / What Am I Living For?	1970	.60	3.00
MGM 14274	Long Black Train / What A Dream	1971	.60	3.00
MGM 14355	I Hope, I Think, I Wish / It's Too Late	1971	.60	3.00
MGM 14088	Walk On By / Hey, Miss Ruby	1972	.60	3.00
MGM 14447	Boss Man / Fever	1972	.60	3.00
MGM 14582	Danny Boy / The Pickup	1972	.60	3.00
	— Extended Play Albums—			
MGM 1623	It's Only Make Believe	1958	30.00	150.00
MGM 1640	Conway Twitty Sings (Volume 1)	1958	30.00	150.00
MGM 1641	Conway Twitty Sings (Volume 2)	1958	30.00	150.00
MGM 1642	Conway Twitty Sings (Volume 3)	1958	30.00	150.00
MGM 1678	Saturday Night With Conway Twitty (Volume 1)	1959	30.00	150.00
MGM 1679	Saturday Night With Conway Twitty (Volume 2)	1959	30.00	150.00
MGM 1680	Saturday Night With Conway Twitty (Volume 3)	1959	30.00	150.00
MGM 1701	Lonely Blue Boy	1959	30.00	150.00

TWO CHAPS, THE
The Two Chaps feature Jay Black.

Atlantic 1195	Forgive Me / No More	1959	4.00	20.00

TWO OF CLUBS, THE

Fraternity 972	Heart / My First Heartbreak	1966	1.20	6.00
Fraternity 975	Walk Tall / So Blue Is Fall	1967	1.20	6.00
Fraternity 990	Let Me Walk With You / You Love Me	1967	1.20	6.00
Fraternity 994	River Deep, Mountain High / You Love Me	1967	1.20	6.00

TWO'S COMPANY

Cross Road 7003	Come Kiss Me, Love / Twelve Gates To The City	196?	2.00	10.00

TYGERS, THE: *Refer to* **TONY'S TYGERS**

TYLER, FRANKIE
Frankie Tyler is a pseudonym for Frankie Valli.

OKeh 7103	(DJ)	I Go Ape / If You Care	1958	25.00	125.00
OKeh 7103		I Go Ape / If You Care	1958	35.00	175.00

TYLER, KIP

Challenge 1014	She Got Eyes / Shadow Street	1957	4.00	20.00
Challenge 59008	Jungle Hop / Ooh Yeah, Baby	1958	10.00	50.00
Ebb 154	She's My Witch / Rumble Rock	1958	7.00	35.00
	(Ebb 154 features Bruce Johnston.)			
Ebb 156	Oh, Linda / Kali Lou	1958	7.00	35.00
Gyro Disc 711	Surfer's Lament / Toledo	1963	7.00	35.00

TYLER, TERRY

Landa 679	A Thousand Feet Below / Answer Me	1961	2.00	10.00

TYMES CHILDREN, THE

Panorama 38	Got To Him / Take Me Back	1966	2.00	10.00

TYRANNOSAURUS REX: *Refer to* **T-REX.**

TYRELL, DANNY, & THE CLEECHAYS

Eastman 784	You're Only Seventeen / Let's Walk, Let's Talk	196?	3.00	15.00

TYRELL, STEVE

Philips 40150	Young Boy Blues / A Boy Without A Girl	1963	2.00	10.00

TYRONE & THE NU PORTS

Darrow 5-20	Feel Like A Million / On A Saturday Night	196?	4.00	20.00

TYROS, THE

Rondack 9780	Torquay / Tryin' To Get To You	196?	7.00	35.00

U.

U.S. BEATLEWIGS, THE

Orbit 531		She's So Innocent (Oh Yeah) / Finger Poppin' Girl	1964	6.00	30.00

U.S. DOUBLE QUARTET, THE
The U.S. Double Quartet is a pseudonym for The Tokens.

B.T. Puppy 524		Life Is Groovy / Split	1967	2.00	10.00
B.T. Puppy 547		Walking Along-Happy Wanderer / When I Lock My Door	1968	2.00	10.00

U2
U2 is Adam Clayton, Dave Evans, Larry Mullen and Bono Vox.

Island 49716		I Will Follow / Out Of Control (Live)	1981	2.00	10.00
Island 49716	(PS)	I Will Follow / Out Of Control (Live)	1981	8.00	40.00
Island 49716		I Will Follow / Boy-Girl	1981	1.00	5.00
Island 49716	(PS)	I Will Follow / Boy-Girl	1981	3.00	15.00
Island 99915		New Year's Day / Treasure (Whatever Happened To Pete The Chop?)	1983	1.00	5.00
Island 99789		I Will Follow (Live) / Two Hearts Beat As One	1984	.60	3.00
Island 99704		Pride (In The Name Of Love) / Boomerang II	1984	.40	2.00
Island 99704	(PS)	Pride (In The Name Of Love) / Boomerang II	1984	.60	3.00
Island 99469		With Or Without You / Luminous Times-Walk To The Water	1987	.40	2.00
Island 99469	(PS)	With Or Without You / Luminous Times-Walk To The Water	1987	.40	2.00
Island 99407		Where The Streets Have No Name / Silver And Gold	1987	.40	2.00
Island 99408		Where The Streets Have No Name / Silver And Gold-Sweetest Thing	1987	.40	2.00
Island 99408	(PS)	Where The Streets Have No Name / Silver And Gold-Sweetest Thing	1987	.40	2.00
Island 99384		In God's Country / Bullet The Blue Sky	1987	.40	2.00
Island 99385		In God's Country / Bullet The Blue Sky-Running To Stand Still	1987	.60	3.00
Island 99385	(PS)	In God's Country / Bullet The Blue Sky-Running To Stand Still	1987	.80	4.00
Island 99254		Angel Of Harlem / A Room At The Heartbreak Hotel	1988	.40	2.00
Island 99254	(PS)	Angel Of Harlem / A Room At The Heartbreak Hotel	1988	.40	2.00
Island 99250		Desire / Hallelujah Here She Comes	1988	.40	2.00
Island 99250	(PS)	Desire / Hallelujah Here She Comes	1988	.40	2.00
Island 99225		When Love Comes To Town / Dancing Barefoot	1989	.40	2.00
Island 99225	(PS)	When Love Comes To Town / Dancing Barefoot	1989	.40	2.00
Island 99199		All I Want Is You / Unchained Melody	1989	.40	2.00
Island 99199	(PS)	All I Want Is You / Unchained Melody	1989	.40	2.00
		— 12" Singles—			
Island PRO-A2-940	(DJ)	I Will Follow / (B-side by Steve Winwood)	1980	6.00	30.00
Manhattan SPRO	(DJ)	Voices Of Sun City (Interview with Bono)	1985	3.00	15.00

ULTIMATES, THE

Ultima 707		Autumn Wind / April's Theme	1964	3.00	15.00

ULTIMATES, THE

Envoy 2302		I Can Tell You Love Me, Too / Lonely Nights	196?	3.00	15.00

ULTIMATES, THE

Garland 2009		Keep On Lookin' / Black Is Black	196?	4.00	20.00

ULTIMATES, THE

Lavender 2001		My Babe / Little Girl	196?	2.00	10.00

ULTRATONES, THE

Cary 2001		Locomotion / Sister Of The Girl I Once Loved	1962	2.00	10.00
San Tana 101		Restless / Chain Reaction	196?	4.00	20.00

UNBELIEVABLE UGLIES, THE

Liberty 55935		Get Straight / Sorry	1967	2.00	10.00
Universal Audio 66367		I Ain't Gonna Eat Out My Heart Anymore / When The Saints	196?	2.00	10.00

UNCALLED FOR, THE

Dollie 509		Do Like Me / Get Out Of The Way	1967	5.00	25.00
Laurie 3394		Do Like Me / Get Out Of The Way	1967	3.00	15.00

UNCHAINED MYNDS, THE

Transaction 705		We Can't Go On This Way / Going Back To Miami	1969	4.00	20.00
Buddah 111		We Can't Go On This Way / Going Back To Miami	1969	1.60	8.00
Buddah 119		Every Day /	1969	1.60	8.00

Label & Catalog #	A-Side/B-Side	Year	VG	NM
UNCLE SOUND				
Warner Bros. 7197	Beverly Hills / I'm Gonna Ask Him	1968	1.00	5.00
UNDERBEATS, THE				
Garret 4004	Foot Stompin' / Route 66	1964	2.00	10.00
Soma 1449	Darling Lorraine / Book Of Love	1965	4.00	20.00
Soma 1458	I Can't Stand It / Shake It For Me	1965	2.00	10.00
Twin Town 706	Our Love / Jo Jo Gunne	196?	2.00	10.00
UNDERDOGS, THE				
Hideout 1001	The Man In The Glass / Judy Be Mine	196?	5.00	25.00
Hideout 1004	Don't Pretend / Little Girl	196?	5.00	25.00
Hideout 1011	Sunrise / Get Down On Your Knees	196?	5.00	25.00
Bangar 00632	Annie Do The Dog / Sweet Words Of Love	196?	5.00	25.00
VIP 25040	Love's Gone Bad / Mo Jo Hanna	1966	2.00	10.00
UNDERGROUND SUNSHINE, THE				
Intrepid 75002	Birthday / All I Want Is You	1969	1.00	5.00
Intrepid 75012	Don't Shut Me Out / Take Me, Break Me	1969	1.00	5.00
UNION GAP, THE: *Refer to* GARY PUCKETT				
UNIQUE ECHOES, THE				
Southern Sound 108	Zoom / Italian Twist	196?	10.00	50.00
UNIQUE TEENS, THE				
Hanover 4510	At The Ball / Jeannie	1958	6.00	30.00
Ivy 112	At The Ball / Jeannie	1958	4.00	20.00
Dynamic 110	Whatcha Know New? / Run Fast	195?	3.00	15.00
UNIQUES, THE				
Demand 2396	Merry Christmas, Darling / Rockin' Rudolph	1963	10.00	50.00
Demand 2396 (PS)	Merry Christmas, Darling / Rockin' Rudolph	1963	10.00	50.00
Dot 16533	Merry Christmas, Darling / Rockin' Rudolph	1963	4.00	20.00
Demand 2490	Times Change / Alright, Okay, You Win	1964	7.00	35.00
UNIQUES, THE				
Amber 2004	Ghost Riders In The Sky / Taboo	1961	7.00	35.00
United Southern 104	Renegade / Malaguena	1961	3.00	15.00
UNIQUES (FEATURING JOE STAMPLEY), THE				
Paula 219	Not Too Long Ago / Fast Way Of Living	1965	1.60	8.00
Paula 222	Too Good To Be True / Never Been In Love	1965	1.60	8.00
Paula 227	Lady's Man / Bolivar	1965	1.60	8.00
Paula 231	Strange / You Ain't Tuff	1965	1.60	8.00
Paula 238	All These Things / Tell Me What To Do	1966	1.60	8.00
Paula 245	Good Bye, So Long / Run And Hide	1966	1.60	8.00
Paula 255	Please Come Home For Christmas / Please Come Home For Christmas (Part 2)	1966	1.60	8.00
Paula 264	Groovin' Out (On Your Good, Good Lovin') / Areba	1966	1.60	8.00
Paula 275	Every Now And Then / Love Is A Precious Thing	1967	1.60	8.00
Paula 289	Go On And Leave / (B-side by University Of Utah)	1967	1.60	8.00
Paula 299	All I Took Was Love / It's All Over Now	1968	1.00	5.00
Paula 307	I Sure Feel More (Like I Do Than I Did When I Got Here) / It Hurts Me To Remember	1968	1.00	5.00
Paula 313	How Lucky Can One Man Be? / You Don't Miss Your Water	1968	1.00	5.00
Paula 320	Sha-la Love / You Know	1969	1.00	5.00
Paula 324	My babe / Toys Are Made For Children	1969	1.00	5.00
Paula 332	All These Things / You Know That I Love You	1970	1.00	5.00
Paramount 0017	Eunice / No One But You	1970	.80	4.00
Paramount 0116	Lucille / One Night With You	1971	.80	4.00
Paramount 0172	I Am A Gemini / Will You Love Me Tomorrow	1972	.80	4.00
UNIT 4 + 2				
London 9732	Sorrow And Pain / Woman From Liberia	1964	1.00	5.00
London 9751	Concrete And Clay / Wild As The Wind	1965	1.00	5.00
London 9751	Concrete And Clay / When I Fall In Love	1965	1.00	5.00
London 9761	You've Never Been In Love Like This Before / Somebody You Know	1965	1.00	5.00
London 9790	Stop Wasting Your Time / Hark	1965	1.00	5.00
London 1009	I Won't Let You Down / I Was Only Playing Games	1966	1.00	5.00
UNITED FRUIT CO., THE				
York 403	Ain't It, Babe / Yes, We Have No Bananas	196?	2.00	10.00
Laurie 3408	On The Good Ship Lollipop / Sunshine Street	1968	1.60	8.00
UNITED NATIONS, THE				
Cha-Cha 771	'Cause I Love You / In My Dreams	1967	2.00	10.00

Label & Catalog #	A-Side/B-Side	Year	VG	NM
UNITED TRAVEL SERVICE, THE				
Ridon 854	Wind And Stone / Drummer Of Your Mind	196?	1.20	6.00
Ridon	Gypsy Eyes / Echo Of You	196?	1.20	6.00
UNKNOWN, THE				
The Unknown is a pseudonym for Jimmy Fielda.				
Autograph 206	I Have Returned / Keep Talking, Baby	1960	6.00	30.00
UNKNOWNS, THE				
The Unknowns feature Steve Alaimo, Keith Allison and Mark Lindsay.				
Marlin 16008	Young Enough To Cry / Tighter	1966	3.00	15.00
Parrot 307	Young Enough To Cry / Tighter	1966	2.00	10.00
Parrot 366	Melody For An Unknown Girl / Peat's Song	1966	2.00	10.00
Shield 7101	One More Chance / You And Me	1966	2.00	10.00
UNRELATED SEGMENTS, THE				
HBR 514	Story Of My Life / It's Unfair	1966	4.00	20.00
Liberty 55992	Where You Gonna Go? / It's Gonna Rain	1967	5.00	25.00
Liberty 56052	Cry, Cry, Cry / It's Not Fair	1968	8.00	40.00
UNTAMED, THE				
Planet 117	It's Not True / Gimmie, Gimmie Some Shade	1966	4.00	20.00
UNTOUCHABLES, THE				
Wasp 105	Don't Go, I'm Beggin / Baby, Let's Wait	196?	5.00	25.00
UNTOUCHABLES, THE				
Alan K 6901	Little Mary / Funny What A Little Kiss Can Do	196?	3.00	15.00
Madison 128	Poor Boy Needs A Preacher / New Fad	1960	2.00	10.00
Madison 134	Goodnight Sweetheart, Goodnight / Vickie Lee	1960	2.00	10.00
Madison 139	Sixty Minute Man / Everybody's Laughing	1960	2.00	10.00
Madison 147	Raisin' Sugar Cane / Do Your Nest	1961	2.00	10.00
Liberty 55335	You're On Top / Lovely Dee	1961	2.00	10.00
Liberty 55423	Papa / Medicine Man	1962	2.00	10.00
UNUSUALS, THE				
Mainstream 653	I Could Go On / Summer Is Over	196?	2.00	10.00
UNUSUALS WITH KATHY MCDONALD, THE				
Panorama 23	I'm Walkin,' Babe / Babe, It's Me	1965	2.00	10.00
UPBEATS, THE				
Prep 119	Never In My Life / I Don't Know	1957	3.00	15.00
Prep 131	Will You Be Mine? / My Last Frontier	1958	3.00	15.00
Swan 4010	Just Like In The Movies / My Foolish Heart	1958	3.00	15.00
Joy 223	The Night We Both Said Goodbye /			
	Oh, What It Seemed To Be	1958	3.00	15.00
Joy 227	Keep Cool, Crazy Heart / You're The One I Care For	1959	3.00	15.00
Joy 229	Teenie Weenie Bikini / Satin Shoes	1959	3.00	15.00
Joy 233	To Me You're A Song / Unbelievable Love	1959	3.00	15.00
UPBEATS, THE: *Refer to* RAY ALLEN				
UPCHURCH, PHIL				
Boyd 329	You Can't Sit Down / You Can't Sit Down (Part 2)	1961	2.00	10.00
United Artists 329	You Can't Sit Down / You Can't Sit Down (Part 2)	1961	1.20	6.00
United Artists 385	That's Where It Is / The Hog	1961	1.20	6.00
UPFRONTS, THE				
Lummtone 103	It Took Time / Betty Lou And The Lion *(Pink label)*	1960	7.00	35.00
Lummtone 103	It Took Time / Betty Lou And The Lion *(Blue label)*	196?	4.00	20.00
Lummtone 104	Too Far To Turn Around / Married Jive	1960	6.00	30.00
Lummtone 106	When You Kiss Me / Little Girl	1961	7.00	35.00
Lummtone 107	I Stopped The Duke Of Earl / Baby, For Your Love	1961	75.00	300.00
Lummtone 107	Send Me Someone To Love Who Will Love Me? /			
	Baby, For Your Love	1962	6.00	30.00
Lummtone 108	It Took Time / Baby, For Your Love	1962	2.00	10.00
Lummtone 114	Do The Beatle / Most Of The Pretty Girls	1964	15.00	75.00
UPPER U DISTRICT SINGERS, THE				
Jerden 725	Sing Hallelujah / Green Satin	1964	.80	4.00
UPSETTERS, THE				
The Upsetters feature Little Richard				
Little Star 123	Yes, It's Me / Every Night About This Time	1962	10.00	50.00
UPSETTERS, THE				
Autumn 4	Draggin' The Main / Autumn's Here	1963	2.00	10.00

Label & Catalog #	A-Side/B-Side	Year	VG	NM

UPSTARTS, THE: *Refer to* DON DELL

UPTONES, THE

Lute 6225	I'll Be There / No More *(Black label)*	1962	6.00	30.00
Lute 6225	I'll Be There / No More *(Color label)*		4.00	20.00
Lute 6229	Be Mine / Dreamin'	1962	6.00	30.00
Magnum 714	Dreaming / Wear My Ring	1963	4.00	20.00

UPTOWN GIRLS, THE

Pickwick City 1004	Crazy Talk / Summer Story	196?	2.00	10.00

URBAN RENEWAL, THE

St. George Inter. 702271	Love Eyes / People	196?	3.00	15.00

US

Patty 1373	Promise Me / American Girl And Liverpool Boy	1964	4.00	20.00

US FOUR

Rising Sons 701	By My Side / The Alligator	196?	3.00	15.00

US GROUP, THE

Uptown 736	Little Bit Of Something / Just A Year Ago Today	196?	3.00	15.00

US KIDS, THE

Rex 2629 / 30	Check Out / I Love The Rain	1967	4.00	20.00

USHER, GARY [& THE USHERETTES]

Gary Usher was a major mover in the California scene of the early '60s as a performer and a writer, collaborating with Brian Wilson during The Beach Boys' early years. Refer to Keith Allison; Curt Boetcher; Don Brandon; The Buddies; The Byrds; Chad & Jeremy; Keith Colley; The Competitors; The Devons; The Forte Four; The Four Speeds; The Go-Gos; Keith Green; The Hondells; The Knights; The L.A. Teens; Millennium; The Neptunes; Peanut Butter Conspiracy; The Pendeltons; Dal Perkins; Rochell & The Candles; Sagittarius; Sandy Salisbury; Sean & The Brandywines; Bobby Sherman; The Sons Of Adam; The Sunsets; The Super Stocks; The Surfaris; Lloyd Thaxton; The Toads; The Wheel Men; The Wierd-Ohs; Beverly Williams; the Various Artists EP section.

Titan 1716	You're The Girl / Driven Insane	1960	25.00	125.00
Lan-cet 144	Tomorrow / Lies	196?	6.00	30.00
Dot 16158	Three Surfer Boys / Milky Way	1963	75.00	300.00
	("Three Surfer Boys" features The Honeys as The Usherettes.)			
Capitol 5128	The Beetle / Jody	1964	6.00	30.00
Capitol 5193	Sacramento / Just The Way I Feel	1964	15.00	75.00
	(Produced by Brian Wilson; "Sacramento" features The Honeys.)			
Capitol 5403	It's A Lie / Jody	1965	10.00	50.00

UTOPIA

Utopia features Todd Rundgren.

Bearsville 0317	Sunburst Finish / Communion With The Sun	1976	60	3.00
Bearsville 0321	Love Is The Answer / The Marriage Of Heaven And Hell	1977	.60	3.00
Bearsville 49180	Set Me Free / Umbrella Man	1980	1.00	5.00
Bearsville 49247	The Very Last Time / Love Alone	1980	.60	3.00
Bearsville 49545	Second Nature / You Make Me Crazy	1980	.60	3.00
Bearsville 49579	I Just Want To Touch You / Always Late	1980	.60	3.00
Bearsville 50062	One World / Special Interest	1980	1.20	6.00
Bearsville 29947	Lysistrata / Junk Rock	1982	.60	3.00
Network 69859	Feet, Don't Fail Me Now / There Goes My Inspiration	1982	60	3.00
Network 69830	Hammer In My Heart /			
	I'm Looking At You But I'm Talking To Myself	1982	60	3.00
Passport 7923	Cry Baby / Winston Smith Takes It On The Jaw	1984	60	3.00
Passport 7923 (PS)	Cry Baby / Winston Smith Takes It On The Jaw	1984	1.00	5.00
Passport 7927	Mated / Stand For Something	1985	60	3.00

UTOPIANS, THE

Imperial 5861	Dutch Treat / Ain't No Such Thing	1962	4.00	20.00
Imperial 5876	Along My Lonely Way / Hurry To Your Date	1962	75.00	300.00
Imperial 5921	Let Love Come Later / Opera Vs. The Blues	1963	3.00	15.00

UTOPIANS, THE: *Refer to* MIKE & THE UTOPIANS

V-EIGHTS, THE

Most 713	Please Come Back / Pretty Girl	1959	4.00	20.00
Vibro 4005	My Heart / Papa's Yellow Tie	1960	4.00	20.00
Vibro 4007	Let's Take A Chance / Hot Water	1961	5.00	25.00
ABC-Paramount 10201	My Heart / Papa's Yellow Tie	1961	2.00	10.00

VACELS, THE
Refer to Ricky & The Vacels.

Kama Sutra 200	You're My Baby / Hey Girl, Stop Leading Me On	1965	2.00	10.00
Kama Sutra 204	Can You Please Crawl Out Your Window? /			
	I'm Just A Poor Boy	1965	3.00	15.00

VACQUEROS, THE

Bangar 00647	Eighty Foot Wave / Birds And Bees	196?	7.00	35.00

VAGABONDS, THE

Abco 1001	Night Drag / Baby Face McCall	1964	2.00	10.00

VAGRANTS, THE
The Vagrants feature Leslie West.

Southern Sound 204	Oh, These Eyes / You're Too Young	1966	4.00	20.00
Vanguard 35038	I Can't Make A Friend / Young Blues	1966	3.00	15.00
Vanguard 35038 (PS)	I Can't Make A Friend / Young Blues	1966	15.00	75.00
Atco 6473	Respect / I Love, Love You	1967	2.00	10.00
Atco 6513	Beside The Sea / A Sunny Summer Rain	1968	2.00	10.00
Atco 6552	I Don't Need Your Loving / And When It's Over	1968	2.00	10.00

VAILON, BOBBY

Camelot 118	Surfin' Alone / Poor Little Fool	196?	3.00	15.00

VAL-AIRES, THE
The Val-Aires later recorded as The Vogues.

Coral 62177	Laurie, My Love / Which One Will It Be?	1959	6.00	30.00

VAL-CHORDS, THE

Gametime 104	Candy Store Love / You're Laughing At Me	1957	40.00	200.00
	(First pressing labels do not have a sword logo.)			
Gametime 104	Candy Store Love / You're Laughing At Me	1957	8.00	40.00
	(Second pressing labels have a sword logo.)			

VALA QUONS, THE

Laguna 102	Teardrops / Madelaine	195?	35.00	175.00
Rayco 516	Jolly Green Giant / Diddy Bop	195?	7.00	35.00

VALE, BOBBY

Lawn 209	Miss High School U.S.A. / Two Fast Guns	1963	2.00	10.00

VALENS, RITCHIE
Ritchie Valens also recorded as Arvee Allens.

Del-Fi 4106	Come On, Let's Go / Framed	1958	8.00	40.00
Del-Fi 4110	Donna / La Bamba (Green label)	1958	4.00	20.00
Del-Fi 4110	Donna / La Bamba	1958	3.00	15.00
Del-Fi 4111	Fast Freight / Big Baby Blues	1959	3.00	15.00
Del-Fi 4114	That's My Little Suzie / In A Turkish Town	1959	3.00	15.00
Del-Fi 4114 (PS)	That's My Little Suzie / In A Turkish Town	1959	15.00	75.00
Del-Fi 4117	Little Girl / We Belong Together	1959	3.00	15.00
Del-Fi 4117 (PS)	Little Girl / We Belong Together	1959	15.00	75.00
	— Original Del-Fi singles above have grey & black labels with circles.—			
Del-Fi 4106	Come On, Let's Go / Framed	1960	2.00	10.00
Del-Fi 4110	Donna / La Bamba	1960	2.00	10.00
Del-Fi 4111	Fast Freight / Big Baby Blues	1960	2.00	10.00
Del-Fi 4114	That's My Little Suzie / In A Turkish Town	1960	2.00	10.00
Del-Fi 4117	Little Girl / We Belong Together	1960	2.00	10.00
Del-Fi 4128	Stay Beside Me / Big Baby Blues	1960	3.00	15.00
Del-Fi 4133	Cry, Cry, Cry / Paddiwack Song	1960	2.00	10.00
	— Del-Fi singles above have blue labels.—			
Del-Fi 4106	Come On, Let's Go / Framed	1961	1.20	6.00
Del-Fi 4110	Donna / La Bamba	1961	1.20	6.00
Del-Fi 4111	Fast Freight / Big Baby Blues	1961	1.20	6.00
Del-Fi 4114	That's My Little Suzie / In A Turkish Town	1961	1.20	6.00

Label & Catalog #	A-Side/B-Side	Year	VG	NM
Del-Fi 4117	Little Girl / We Belong Together	1961	1.20	6.00
Del-Fi 4128	Stay Beside Me / Big Baby Blues	1961	1.20	6.00
Del-Fi 4133	Cry, Cry, Cry / Paddiwack Song	1961	1.20	6.00
	—Del-Fi singles above have black labels.—			
	—12" Singles—			
Del-Fi DF-1287	La Bamba / La Bamba / La Bamba / La Bamba	1987	1.20	6.00
	—Extended Play Albums—			
Del-Fi PR-1	Ritchie Valens	1959	50.00	200.00
Del-Fi DFEP-101	Ritchie Valens (Cardboard cover)	1959	50.00	200.00
Del-Fi DFEP-101	Ritchie Valens (Paper cover)	1959	50.00	200.00
Del-Fi DFEP-111	Ritchie Valens	1959	50.00	200.00
VALENTINE, JIMMY				
Cub 9024	Just Keep Walkin' (Ambrose) / Rockin' Hula	1959	2.00	10.00
VALENTINE, PENNY				
Liberty 55774	I Want To Kiss Ringo Goodbye /			
	Show Me The Way To Love You	1964	6.00	30.00
VALENTINE & THE LOVERS				
Donna 1345	I'm Gonna Love / One Teardrop Too Late	1962	6.00	30.00
VALENTINES, THE				
Iona 1003	The Sock / Sixteen Senoritas	196?	2.00	10.00
VALENTINO, DANNY				
MGM 12835	Stampede / Music Man	1959	3.00	15.00
MGM 12881	A Million Years / Biology	1960	2.00	10.00
VALENTINO, MARK				
Swan 4121	The Push And Kick / Walking Alone	1962	2.00	10.00
Swan 4135	Do It / Hey! You're Lookin' Good	1963	2.00	10.00
Swan 4142	Part Time Job / Jivin' At The Drive-In	1963	2.00	10.00
VALENTINO, SAL				
Sal Valentino also recorded with The Beau Brummels and Stoneground.				
Falco 306	I Wanna Twist /	196?	7.00	35.00
Warner Bros. 7268	Alligator Man / An Added Attraction	1969	1.60	8.00
Warner Bros. 7368	Silkie / Song For Rochelle	1970	1.60	8.00
VALERY, DANA				
Columbia 44004	Having You Around /			
	You Don't Know Where Your Interest Lies	1967	3.00	15.00
	(Features Paul Simon.)			
VALIANTS, THE				
Valor 101	Something / The Valor	196?	2.00	10.00
VALIANTS, THE				
KC 108	Are You Ready? / Frankie's Angel	196?	3.00	15.00
Imperial 5843	You Are Sweeter Than Wine / Love Comes In Many Ways	1962	3.00	15.00
Imperial 5915	Living In Paradise / I'm In A World Of My Own	1963	3.00	15.00
VALIANTS, THE				
Roulette 4510	Eternal Triangle / Johnny Lonely	1963	3.00	15.00
VALIDS, THE				
Amber 855	Barbara Ann / Hey Senorita	1966	2.00	10.00
Amber 855	Barbara Ann / Congratulations	1966	2.00	10.00
VALLEY, JIM "HARPO"				
Jim Valley also recorded with The Viceroys and Paul Revere & The Raiders.				
Dream	I Love A Girl /	196?	2.00	10.00
Jerden 814	There Is Love / I'm Real	1966	2.00	10.00
	(Jerden 814 features Don & The Goodtimes.)			
Dunhill 4096	Try, Try, Try / Invitation	1967	1.20	6.00
Dunhill 4096 (PS)	Try, Try, Try / Invitation	1967	2.00	10.00
Dunhill 4103	Go Go Round / Maintain	1967	1.20	6.00
VALLI				
Scepter 1233	Hurry Home To Me (Soldier Boy) / Jimmy's In A Hurry	1962	3.00	15.00

VALLE, FRANKIE, & THE ROMANS: *Refer to* FRANKIE VALLI

VALLEY, FRANKIE, & THE TRAVELLERS: *Refer to* FRANKIE VALLI

Label & Catalog #		A-Side/B-Side	Year	VG	NM

VALLI, FRANKIE

In his early career, Frankie Casteluccio used a variety of pseudonyms before settling on Frankie Valli: Cindy 3012 credits Frankie Valle & The Romans; Mercury 70381 credits Frankie Valley & The Travelers; and Decca 30994 credits Frankie Vally. Refer to Cyclone III; The Four Lovers; The Four Seasons; Ken Hartford; Frankie Nolan; The Rays; Frankie Tyler.

Label & Catalog #		A-Side/B-Side	Year	VG	NM
Corona 1234		My Mother's Eye / The Laugh's On Me	1953	—	—
		(Rare. Estimated near mint value $600-1,000.)			
Mercury 70381	(DJ)	Somebody Else Took Her Home / Forgive And Forget	1954	30.00	150.00
Mercury 70381		Somebody Else Took Her Home / Forgive And Forget	1954	50.00	250.00
		(Maroon label)			
Mercury 70381		Somebody Else Took Her Home / Forgive And Forget	1954	30.00	150.00
		(Black label)			
Cindy 3012		Real (This Is Real) / Come Si Bella	1959	40.00	200.00
Decca 30994	(DJ)	Please Take A Chance / It May Be Wrong	1959	20.00	100.00
Decca 30994		Please Take A Chance / It May Be Wrong	1959	40.00	200.00
Smash 1995		The Sun Ain't Gonna Shine (Anymore) / This Is Goodbye	1965	1.20	6.00
Smash 2015		(You're Gonna) Hurt Yourself / Night Hawk	1965	1.20	6.00
Smash 2037		You're Ready Now / Cry For Me	1966	1.20	6.00
Philips 40407		The Proud One / Ivy	1966	1.00	5.00
Philips 40407	(PS)	The Proud One / Ivy	1966	2.00	10.00
Philips 40446		Can't Take My Eyes Off Of You / The Trouble With Me	1967	1.00	5.00
Philips 40446	(PS)	Can't Take My Eyes Off Of You / The Trouble With Me	1967	3.00	15.00
Philips 40484		September Rain (Here Comes The Rain) / I Make A Fool Of Myself	1967	1.00	5.00
Philips 40484	(PS)	September Rain (Here Comes The Rain) / I Make A Fool Of Myself	1967	1.60	8.00
Philips 40510		To Give (The Reason I Live) / Watch Where You Walk	1967	2.00	10.00
Philips 40510	(PS)	To Give (The Reason I Live) / Watch Where You Walk	1967	3.00	15.00
Bob Crewe CGC1B	(DJ)	The Girl I'll Never Know (Angels Never Fly This Low) / A Face Without A Name	1969	3.00	15.00
Philips 40622		The Girl I'll Never Know (Angels Never Fly This Low) / A Face Without A Name	1969	2.00	10.00
Philips 40622	(PS)	The Girl I'll Never Know (Angels Never Fly This Low) / A Face Without A Name	1969	3.00	15.00
Philips 40661		You've Got Your Troubles / The Dream Of Kings	1969	3.00	15.00
Motown 1251		You've Got Your Troubles / Listen To Yesterday	1969	1.25	6.00
Motown 1279		Listen To Yesterday / The Scalawag Song	1970	1.00	5.00
Philips 40680		My Mother's Eyes / Circles In The Sand	1970	2.00	10.00
Philips 40688		Heartaches And Raindrops / Lay Me Down	1971	1.00	5.00
Mowest 5011		Love Isn't Here / Poor Fool	1971	1.00	5.00
Mowest 5025	(DJ)	The Night / The Night	1971	2.00	10.00
		(Stock copies of Mowest 5025 may not exist.)			
Private Stock 003		My Eyes Adored You / Watch Where You Walk	1975	.60	3.00
Private Stock 021		Swearin' To God / Why?	1975	.60	3.00
Private Stock 043		Our Day Will Come / You Can Bet (I Ain't Goin' Nowhere)	1975	.60	3.00
Private Stock 074		Fallen Angel / Carrie (I Would Marry You)	1976	.60	3.00
Private Stock 098		We're All Alone / You To Me Are Everything	1976	.60	3.00
Private Stock 109		Boomerang / Look At The World, It's Changing	1976	.60	3.00
Private Stock 141		What Good Am I Without You? / Easily	1977	.60	3.00
Private Stock 154		Second Thoughts / So She Says	1977	.60	3.00
Private Stock 169		I Need You / I'm Gonna Love You	1977	.60	3.00
Private Stock 180		I Could Have Loved You / Rainstorm	1978	.60	3.00
RSO 897		Grease / Grease	1978	1.00	5.00
RSO 897	(PS)	Grease / Grease	1978	1.00	5.00
Warner-Curb 8670		Save Me, Save Me / No Love At All	1978	.60	3.00
		—12" Singles—			
Motown PR-10	(DJ)	Just Look What You Have Done / Just Look What You Have Done	1973	2.00	10.00
Private Stock 5101		Swearin' To God / Why?	1975	1.00	5.00

VALOR, TONY

Label & Catalog #		A-Side/B-Side	Year	VG	NM
Musictone 1119		There's A Story In My Heart / So Tenderly	1963	25.00	125.00

VALRAYS, THE

Label & Catalog #		A-Side/B-Side	Year	VG	NM
Parkway 880		Get A Board / Pee Wee	1963	7.00	35.00
Parkway 904		I Ask Myself / Honky Tonk	1964	3.00	15.00

VALS, THE

Label & Catalog #		A-Side/B-Side	Year	VG	NM
Ascot 2163		Too Late / I'm Stepping Out With My Memories	1964	7.00	35.00

VAN, TRUDY, & THE REALM

Label & Catalog #		A-Side/B-Side	Year	VG	NM
VJV 301		Surf Is Up / Do The Surf	196?	7.00	35.00

VAN BECK TRIO, DOUG

Label & Catalog #		A-Side/B-Side	Year	VG	NM
Fargo 1064		Surfin' Little Girl / Working Man's Day Is Never Done	1964	7.00	35.00

VAN DELLES, THE

Label & Catalog #		A-Side/B-Side	Year	VG	NM
Bolo 731		Time After Time / I Got The Blues	1962	3.00	15.00

Label & Catalog #		A-Side/B-Side	Year	VG	NM
VAN DOREN					
Hickory 1262		Surfin' Liza / Huntington Beach	1964	3.00	15.00
VAN EATON, LON & DEREK					
Apple 1845		Sweet Music / Song Of Songs	1972	2.00	10.00
A&M 1662		Who Do You Out Do? / All You're Hungry For Is Love	1975	.80	4.00
A&M 1662	(PS)	Who Do You Out Do? / All You're Hungry For Is Love	1975	.80	4.00
VAN RONK, DAVE (& THE HUDSON DUSTERS)					
Verve/Forecast 5070		Head Inspector / Dink's Song	1967	.80	4.00
Verve/Forecast 5080		Romping Through The Swamp /			
		Clouds (From Both Sides Now)	1967	.80	4.00
VAN ZANDT, TOWNES					
Poppy 506		Waitin' Around To Die / Talking Karate Blues	1968	1.00	5.00
Poppy 510		Second Lovers /	1969	1.00	5.00
Poppy 90104		Come Tomorrow / Delta Mama Blues	197?	.80	4.00
Poppy 90108		Greensboro Woman / Stand In	197?	.80	4.00
Poppy 90113		If I Needed You / Sunshine Boy	197?	.80	4.00
Poppy 90116		Honky Tonkin' / Snow Don't Fall	197?	.80	4.00
Poppy 170		Don't Let The Sunshine Fool You / Fraulein	1971	.80	4.00
Poppy 238		Poncho And Lefty /	1972	.80	4.00
Tomato 10003		Who Do You Love? /	1978	.80	4.00
Tomato 10005		No Place To Fall / When She Don't Need Me	1978	.80	4.00
VANCE, TOMMY, & THE CHECKMATES					
Refer to The Checkmates.					
Jerden 790		Yo Yo / You Must Be The One	1966	2.00	10.00
Jerden 790		Off The Hook / You Must Be The One	1966	2.00	10.00
VANDALS, THE					
Golden Gate 0009		I Really Want To Want You / A Reason	1966	2.00	10.00
Golden Gate 0011		It's Like Now, Baby / Wet And Wild	1966	2.00	10.00
Golden Gate 0011	(PS)	It's Like Now, Baby / Wet And Wild	1966	3.00	15.00
VANGUARDS, THE					
Ivy 103		I'm Movin' / Moonlight (Thick vinyl)	1958	7.00	35.00
Ivy 103		I'm Movin' / Moonlight (Thin vinyl)	1958	4.00	20.00
Dot 15791		Baby Doll / My Friend, Mary Ann	1958	3.00	15.00
VANGUARDS, THE					
Mecca 2423		Wild / (B-side by the Du-Ettes)	196?	1.20	6.00
VANILLA FUDGE, THE					
Atco 6495		You Keep Me Hangin' On / Take Me For A Little While	1967	1.20	6.00
Atco 6590		You Keep Me Hangin' On / Come By Day, Come By Night	1967	1.00	5.00
Atco 6554		Where Is My Mind? / Look Of Love	1968	.80	4.00
Atco 6616		Take Me For A Little While / Thoughts	1968	.80	4.00
Atco 6632		Season Of The Witch / Season Of The Witch (Part 2)	1968	.80	4.00
Atco 6655		Shotgun / Good, Good Lovin'	1969	.80	4.00
Atco 6679		Some Velvet Morning / People	1969	.80	4.00
Atco 6703		I Can't Make It Alone / Need Love	1969	.80	4.00
VANITY FARE					
Brent 7067		Salt Water Babies / Peter Who?	1967	1.00	5.00
Page One 21007		I Live For The Sun / On The Other Side	1969	.80	4.00
Page One 21027		Early In The Morning / You Made Me Love You	1969	.80	4.00
Page One 21029		Hitchin' A Ride / Man Child	1970	.80	4.00
Page One 21033		(I Remember) Summer Morning /			
		Megowd (Something Tells Me)	1970	.60	3.00
20th Century Fox 2012		Rock And Roll Is Back / Making For The Sun	1973	.60	3.00
20th Century Fox 2036		Take It, Shake It, Break My Heart / Down Home	1973	.60	3.00
DJM 70024		Where Did All The Good Times Go? / Stand	1975	.60	3.00
DJM 70029		The Big Parade / Nowhere To Go	1975	.60	3.00
VANN, JOEY					
Joey Vann originally recorded with The Duprees.					
Coed 606		Try To Remember / My Love, My Love	1964	3.00	15.00
VANN, TEDDY					
Triple-X 101		Cindy / I'm Waiting	1960	3.00	15.00
Columbia 41996		Lonely Crowd / I Was Born To Love You	1961	2.00	10.00
VANN, TOMMY, & THE ECHOES					
Academy 118		Too Young / Give A Little Bit	1966	3.00	15.00
Academy 123		Is This Love? / What Can You Do With A Broken Heart?	1966	3.00	15.00

Label & Catalog #		A-Side/B-Side	Year	VG	NM
VANN, TOMMY, & THE PROFESSIONALS					
Congress 6001		I'm So Alone / Does Your Mama Know About Me?	196?	1.20	6.00
VAQUEROS, THE					
Audition 6102		Desert Wind / Echo	196?	6.00	30.00
VARE, RONNIE, & THE INSPIRATIONS					
Dell 5203		Let's Rock, Little Girl / Love Is Just For Two	1959	7.00	35.00
VAREEATIONS, THE					
Dionn 506		The Time / Ssab-brom	196?	2.00	10.00
Dionn 510		Foolish One / It's The Loving Season	196?	2.00	10.00
VAUGHAN, FRANKIE					
Epic 9273		Judy / Am I Wasting My Time On You?	1958	2.00	10.00
VAUGHT, BOB, & THE RENEGADES					
Impact 24		Church Key Twist / Bo' Gator	1963	7.00	35.00
Bamboo 520		Church Key Twist / Bo' Gator	1963	7.00	35.00
GNP/Crescendo 193		Surfin' Tragedy / Exotic	1963	5.00	25.00
VAUGHT, BOB, & THE WHEELS					
Felsted 8682		Surfin' In Paradise / Doin' The Surf	1963	7.00	35.00
VEE, BOBBY					
Soma 1110		Suzie Baby / Flyin' High	1959	8.00	40.00
Liberty 55208		Suzie Baby / Flyin' High	1959	4.00	20.00
		(Bobby's first sides credit Bobby Vee & The Shadows.)			
Liberty 55234		What Do You Want? / My Love Loves Me	1960	2.00	10.00
Liberty 55251		One Last Kiss / Laurie	1960	2.00	10.00
Liberty 55270		Devil Or Angel / Since I Met You, Baby	1960	2.00	10.00
Liberty 55270	(PS)	Devil Or Angel / Since I Met You, Baby	1960	4.00	20.00
Liberty 55287		Rubber Ball / Every Day	1960	2.00	10.00
Liberty 55287	(PS)	Rubber Ball / Every Day	1960	4.00	20.00
Liberty 55296		Stayin' In / More Than I Can Say	1961	2.00	10.00
Liberty 55296	(PS)	Stayin' In / More Than I Can Say	1961	4.00	20.00
Liberty 55325		How Many Tears / Baby Face	1961	2.00	10.00
Liberty 55325	(PS)	How Many Tears / Baby Face	1961	4.00	20.00
Liberty 3331	(33)	How Many Tears / Baby Face	1961	5.00	25.00
Liberty 55354		Take Good Care Of My Baby / Bashful Bob	1961	2.00	10.00
Liberty 55388		Run To Him / Walkin' With My Angel	1961	2.00	10.00
Liberty 55419		Please Don't Ask About Barbara / I Can't Say Goodbye	1962	2.00	10.00
Liberty 55419	(PS)	Please Don't Ask About Barbara / I Can't Say Goodbye	1962	3.00	15.00
Liberty 55451		Sharing You / In My Baby's Eyes	1962	2.00	10.00
Liberty 55479		Punish Her / Someday	1962	2.00	10.00
Liberty 55479	(PS)	Punish Her / Someday	1962	4.00	20.00
		(Liberty 55479 credits Bobby Vee & The Crickets.)			
Liberty 55517		Christmas Vacation / A Not So Merry Christmas	1962	3.00	15.00
Liberty 55521		The Night Has A Thousand Eyes / Anonymous Phone Call	1962	2.00	10.00
Liberty 55530		Charms / Bobby, Tomorrow	1963	2.00	10.00
Liberty 55530	(PS)	Charms / Bobby, Tomorrow	1963	3.00	15.00
Liberty 55581		Be True To Yourself / A Letter From Betty	1963	1.60	8.00
Liberty 55581	(PS)	Be True To Yourself / A Letter From Betty	1963	3.00	15.00
Liberty 55636		Yesterday And You (Armen's Theme) / Never Love A Robin	1963	1.20	6.00
Liberty 55654		Stranger In Your Arms / 1963	1964	1.20	6.00
Liberty 55654	(PS)	Stranger In Your Arms / 1963	1964	3.00	15.00
Liberty 55670		I'll Make You Mine / She's Sorry	1964	1.20	6.00
Liberty 55700		Hickory, Dick And Doc / I Wish You Were Mine Again	1964	1.20	6.00
Liberty 55726		Where Is She? / How To Make A Farewell	1964	1.20	6.00
Liberty 55751		(There'll Come A Day When) Ev'ry Little Bit Hurts /			
		Pretend You Don't See Her	1964	1.20	6.00
Liberty 55761		Cross My Heart / This Is The End	1965	1.20	6.00
Liberty 55790		You Won't Forget Me / Keep On Trying	1965	1.00	5.00
Liberty 55828		Run Like The Devil / Take A Look Around Me	1965	1.00	5.00
Liberty 55843		The Story Of My Life / High Coin	1966	1.00	5.00
Liberty 55854		Gone / A Girl I Used To Know	1966	1.00	5.00
Liberty 55877		Look At Me Girl / Butterfly	1966	1.00	5.00
Liberty 55877		Look At Me Girl / Save A Love	1966	.80	4.00
Liberty 55921		Here Today / Before You Go	1967	.80	4.00
Liberty 55964		Come Back When You Grow Up / Swahili Serenade	1967	.80	4.00
Liberty 55964	(S)	Come Back When You Grow Up / That's All In The Past	1967	10.00	50.00
		(Promotional compact-33 stereo single.)			
Liberty 56009		Beautiful People / I May Be Gone	1967	.80	4.00
Liberty 56014		Maybe Just Today / You're A Big Girl Now	1968	.60	3.00
Liberty 56014	(PS)	Maybe Just Today / You're A Big Girl Now	1968	.60	3.00
Liberty 56033		My Girl-My Guy / Just Keep It Up	1968	.60	3.00
Liberty 56057		Do What You Gotta Do / Thank You	1968	.60	3.00
Liberty 56080		I'm Lookin' For Someone To Love Me / Thank You	1968	.60	3.00

Label & Catalog #	A-Side/B-Side	Year	VG	NM
Liberty 56096	Jenny Came To Me / Santa Cruz	1969	.60	3.00
Liberty 56124	Let's Call It A Day, Girl / I'm Gonna Make It Up To You	1969	.60	3.00
Liberty 56149	Electric Trains And You / In And Out Of Love	1970	.60	3.00
Liberty 56178	No Obligations / Woman In My Life	1970	.60	3.00
Liberty 56208	Sweet Sweetheart / Rock 'N Roll Music And You	1970	.60	3.00
United Artists 50755	Signs / Something To Say	1971	.60	3.00
United Artists 50875	Electric Trains And You / Sweet Sweetheart	1971	.60	3.00
United Artists 199	Take Good Care Of My Baby / Every Opportunity	1972	.60	3.00
United Artists 1142	Well All Right / Something Has Come Between Us	1972	.60	3.00
Shady-Brook 013	I'm Lovin' You / Sayin' Goodbye	197?	.60	3.00
Shady-Brook 026	You're Never Gonna Find Someone Like Me (Long) / You're Never Gonna Find Someone Like Me (Short)	197?	.60	3.00
Shady-Brook 030	It's Good To Be Here / If I Needed You	197?	.60	3.00
	—Extended Play Albums—			
Liberty 1006	Devil Or Angel	1960	12.00	60.00
Liberty 1010	Bobby Vee's Hits	1960	10.00	50.00
Liberty 1013	Bobby Vee	1960	10.00	50.00
United Artists 85 (DJ)	Robert Thomas Velline Interview	1972	5.00	25.00

VEGAS, LOLLY

Label & Catalog #	A-Side/B-Side	Year	VG	NM
Audio International 101	I'm Gonna Say We're Through / It's Love	1961	2.00	10.00

VEGAS, PAT & LOLLY

Label & Catalog #	A-Side/B-Side	Year	VG	NM
Reprise 20199	Two Figures (On The Wedding Cake) / Boom Boom (Radda-Dadda-Da)	1963	2.00	10.00
Apogee 101	Don't You Remember? / The Robot Walk	1964	3.00	15.00
Mercury 72509	Walk On (Right Out Of My Life) / Let's Get It On	1965	2.00	10.00

VEJTABLES, THE

Label & Catalog #	A-Side/B-Side	Year	VG	NM
Uptown 741	Feel The Music / Shadows	196?	5.00	25.00
Autumn 15	I Still Love You / Anything	1965	2.00	10.00
Autumn 23	The Last Thing On My Mind / Mansion Of Tears	1965	2.00	10.00

VELAIRES, THE

Label & Catalog #	A-Side/B-Side	Year	VG	NM
Jamie 1198	Brazil / Roll Over, Beethoven	1961	2.00	10.00
Jamie 1198	Frankie And Johnny / Roll Over, Beethoven	1961	2.00	10.00
Jamie 1203	Dream / Sticks And Stones	1961	2.00	10.00
Jamie 1211	Ubangi Stomp / It's Almost Tomorrow	1961	2.00	10.00
Hi-Mar 9173	Yes, It was Me / I Could Have Cried	1965	1.00	5.00

VELLINE, BILL, & THE STRANGERS
The Strangers feature Robert Velline, a.k.a. Bobby Vee, on guitar. Refer to The Strangers.

Label & Catalog #	A-Side/B-Side	Year	VG	NM
Vee 1001	What'll I Do? /	1957	50.00	200.00

VELLINE, ROBERT THOMAS: *Refer to* BOBBY VEE

VELONS, THE

Label & Catalog #	A-Side/B-Side	Year	VG	NM
Blast 216	Shelly / From The Chapel	1963	20.00	100.00
BJM 6568	Why Don't You Write? / Summer Love	196?	4.00	20.00
BJM 6569	That's What Love Can Do / That's All Right	196?	4.00	20.00

VELS, THE

Label & Catalog #	A-Side/B-Side	Year	VG	NM
Amy 881	In-Laws / Do The Walk	1963	3.00	15.00

VELTONES, THE

Label & Catalog #	A-Side/B-Side	Year	VG	NM
Satellite 100	Someday / Fool In Love	1959	15.00	75.00
Satellite 100	Someday / Fool In Love	1959	4.00	20.00
Zara 901	Now / I Need You So	195?	7.00	35.00
Lost Nite 103	Now / I Need You So	196?	2.00	10.00
Vel 9178	Broken Heart /	196?	3.00	15.00

VELVATONES, THE

Label & Catalog #	A-Side/B-Side	Year	VG	NM
Meteor 5042	Real Gone Baby / Feeling Kinda Lonely	1957	5.00	25.00

VELVET, JIMMY [JIMMY VELVIT]

Label & Catalog #	A-Side/B-Side	Year	VG	NM
Velvet 201	We Belong Together / I'm Gonna Try (To Forget The One I Love)	1961	3.00	15.00
Division 102	Look At Me / Sometimes At Night	1961	3.00	15.00
Cub 9100	Look At Me / Sometimes At Night	1961	2.00	10.00
Cub 9111	Bouquet Of Flowers / When I Needed You	1962	2.00	10.00
ABC-Paramount 10528	To The Aisle / Lonely, Lonely Night	1964	2.00	10.00
Tollie 9037	Teen Angel / Mission Bell	1964	2.00	10.00
Velvet Tone 102	It's Almost Tomorrow / Young Hearts	1965	2.00	10.00
Philips 40285	It's Almost Tomorrow / Blue Eyes (Don't Run Away)	1965	1.60	8.00
Philips 40314	Young Hearts / I Won't Be Back This Year	1965	1.60	8.00

VELVET ANGELS, THE

Label & Catalog #	A-Side/B-Side	Year	VG	NM
Medieval 201	I'm In Love / Let Me Come Back	196?	2.00	10.00

Label & Catalog #		A-Side/B-Side	Year	VG	NM
VELVET KEYS, THE					
King 5090		Let's Stay After School / My Baby's Gone	1957	15.00	75.00
King 5109		The Truth About Youth / Don't Take My Picture, Take Me	1958	15.00	75.00
VELVET NIGHT, THE					
Metromedia 110		Velvet Night / I'm Sure He'll Come	1969	1.00	5.00
VELVET SATINS, THE					
General American 716		An Angel Like You / Cherry	1964	3.00	15.00
General American 720		Angel Adorable / Heading For The Rooftop	1965	8.00	40.00
General American 006		Up To The Rooftop / Nothing Can Compare To You	1965	3.00	15.00
VELVET UNDERGROUND, THE					
The Velvet Underground is John Cale, Sterling Morrison, Lou Reed and Maureen Tucker with Nico on the first two singles.					
Verve 10427	(DJ)	All Tomorrow's Parties / I'll Be Your Mirror	1966	25.00	125.00
Verve 10427	(PS)	All Tomorrow's Parties (Promo picture sleeve)	1966	—	—
		(Rare. Estimated near mint value $500-1,000.)			
Verve 10427		All Tomorrow's Parties / I'll Be Your Mirror	1966	50.00	250.00
Verve 10466	(DJ)	Sunday Morning / Femme Fatale	1966	25.00	125.00
Verve 10466		Sunday Morning / Femme Fatale	1966	50.00	250.00
Verve 10560	(DJ)	White Light, White Heat / I Heard Her Call My Name	1968	50.00	250.00
Verve 10560	(DJ)	White Light, White Heat / Here She Comes Now	1968	50.00	250.00
Verve 10560		White Light, White Heat / Here She Comes Now	1968	50.00	250.00
MGM 14057	(DJ)	What Goes On? / Jesus	1969	20.00	100.00
		(Stock copies of MGM 14057 may not exist.)			
Cotillion 44107	(DJ)	Who Loves The Sun? / Who Loves The Sun?	1971	10.00	50.00
Cotillion 44107		Who Loves The Sun? / Who Loves The Sun?	1971	20.00	100.00
		—Special/Promotional Releases—			
Aspen Magazine		Loop (Flexidisc)	1966	25.00	125.00
Index		Index	1966	25.00	125.00
		(Cardboard picture disc from Andy Warhol's book, "Index.")			
MGM VU-1	(DJ)	Velvet Underground Radio Spot	1969	75.00	300.00
MGM VU-1	(PS)	Velvet Underground Radio Spot	1969	100.00	400.00
		— 12" Singles—			
Polygram 349	(DJ)	Foggy Notion / I Can't Stand It	1985	2.00	10.00
VELVETEENS, THE					
Stark 101		Baby Baby / Teen Prayer	1961	3.00	15.00
Stark 105		I Thank You / Meant To Be	1962	3.00	15.00
Laurie 3126		I Thank You / Meant To Be	1962	2.00	10.00
Golden Artists 614		I Feel Sorry For You, Baby / Ching Bam Bah	196?	2.00	10.00
Golden Artists 614	(PS)	I Feel Sorry For You, Baby / Ching Bam Bah	196?	3.00	15.00
VELVETONES, THE					
Velvet 101		Diheny Run / Static	196?	10.00	50.00
Glenn 309		Diheny Run / Static	196?	7.00	35.00
GARP 102		Mister X /	1965	10.00	50.00
GARP 102		Mister X / (Red vinyl)	1965	25.00	125.00
VELVIT, JIMMY: *Refer to* JIMMY VELVET					
VENEERS, THE					
Princeton 102		Believe Me (My Angel) / I	1960	3.00	15.00
VENNY & MELVIN					
Laurie 3574		Dip Dip Doodle / Doodle Dip Dance	1971	1.00	5.00
VENTRILLS, THE					
Ivanhoe 5000		Confusion / Alone In The Night	1967	5.00	25.00
Parkway 141		Confusion / Alone In The Night	1967	2.00	10.00
VENTURAS, THE					
Donna 1352		High Noon Rumble / Corrido Twist	1961	5.00	25.00
VENTURAS, THE					
Drum Boy 107		Ram-Charger / Apache	1964	7.00	35.00
Drum Boy 108		Welcome Beatles / My Happiness	1964	7.00	35.00
VENTURES, THE					
The original Ventures were Bob Bogle, Nokie Edwards, Howie Johnston and Don Wilson, who also recorded as The Venture Quintet with Scott Douglas and as The Marksmen. Johnston left in 1963, replaced by Mel Taylor; Edwards was replaced by Jerry McGee, 1967-70, and Johnny Durrill joined in 1968.					
Blue Horizon 100		The Real McCoy / Cookies And Coke	1960	—	—
		(Rare. Estimated near mint value $250-500.)			
Blue Horizon 101		Walk-Don't Run / Home	1960	—	—
		(Rare. Estimated near mint value $500-750.)			
Dolton 25X		Walk-Don't Run / The McCoy	1960	4.00	20.00

Label & Catalog #		A-Side/B-Side	Year	VG	NM
Dolton 25		Walk-Don't Run / Home	1960	3.00	15.00
Dolton 28		Perfidia / No Trespassing	1960	3.00	15.00
Dolton 28	(PS)	Perfidia / No Trespassing	1960	5.00	25.00
Dolton 32		Ram-Bunk-Shush / Lonely Heart	1961	3.00	15.00
Dolton 41		Lullaby Of The Leaves / Ginchy	1961	2.00	10.00
Dolton 44		(Theme From) Silver City / Bluer Than Blue	1961	2.00	10.00
Dolton 47		Blue Moon / Lady Of Spain	1961	2.00	10.00
Dolton 50		Yellow Jacket / Genesis	1962	2.00	10.00
Dolton 55		Instant Mashed / My Bonnie	1962	2.00	10.00
Dolton 60		Lolita Ya-Ya / Lucille	1962	2.00	10.00
Dolton 67		The 2,000 Pound Bee / The 2,000 Pound Bee, Part 2	1962	2.00	10.00
Dolton 68		Skip To M' Limbo / El Cumbanchero	1963	2.00	10.00
Dolton 78		The Ninth Wave / Damaged Goods	1963	2.00	10.00
Dolton 85		The Chase / The Savage	1963	2.00	10.00
Dolton 91		Journey To The Stars / Walkin' With Pluto	1964	2.00	10.00
Dolton 94		Fugitive / Scratchin'	1964	2.00	10.00
Dolton 96		Walk-Don't Run '64 / The Cruel Sea	1964	2.00	10.00
Dolton 96	(PS)	Walk-Don't Run '64 / The Cruel Sea	1964	3.00	15.00
Dolton 300		Slaughter On Tenth Avenue / Rap City	1964	2.00	10.00
Dolton 300	(PS)	Slaughter On Tenth Avenue / Rap City	1964	3.00	15.00
Dolton 303		Diamond Head / Lonely Girl	1965	1.60	8.00
Dolton 306		Pedal Pusher / The Swingin' Creeper	1965	1.60	8.00
Dolton 308		Ten Seconds To Heaven / Bird Rocker	1965	2.00	10.00
Dolton 311		La Bamba / Gemini	1965	1.60	8.00
Dolton 312		Sleigh Ride / Snow Flakes	1965	2.00	10.00
Dolton 316		Secret Agent Man / 007-11	1966	1.60	8.00
Dolton 320		Blue Star / Comin' Home, Baby	1966	1.60	8.00
Dolton 320	(PS)	Blue Star / Comin' Home, Baby	1966	3.00	15.00
Dolton 321		Arabesque / Ginza Lights	1966	1.60	8.00
Dolton 323		Green Hornet Theme / Fuzzy And Wild	1966	1.60	8.00
Dolton 323	(PS)	Green Hornet Theme / Fuzzy And Wild	1966	3.00	15.00
Dolton 325		Wild Thing / Penetration	1966	1.60	8.00
Dolton 325	(PS)	Wild Thing / Penetration	1966	3.00	15.00
Dolton 327		Theme From "The Wild Angels" / Kickstand	1967	1.60	8.00
Liberty TV-1	(DJ)	The Horse (Album spot)	196?	3.00	15.00
Liberty 54518		Walk-Don't Run / Ram Bunk Shush	1967	1.00	5.00
Liberty 54519		Perfidia / Blue Moon	1967	1.00	5.00
Liberty 54542		Telstar / Out Of Limits	1967	1.00	5.00
Liberty 54557		Secret Agent Man / Wipe Out	1967	1.00	5.00
Liberty 54563		The Lonely Bull / Tequila	1967	1.00	5.00
Liberty 55967		Strawberry Fields Forever / Endless Dream	1967	1.20	6.00
Liberty 55977		Strawberry Fields Forever / Theme From "Endless Summer"	1967	1.20	6.00
Liberty 56007		On The Road / Mirrors And Shadows	1967	1.00	5.00
Liberty 56019		Flights Of Fantasy / Vibration	1967	1.00	5.00
Liberty 56044		Walk, Don't Run-Land Of 1,000 Dances / Too Young To Know My Mind	1968	1.00	5.00
Liberty 56068		Hawaii Five-O / Soul Breeze	1969	1.00	5.00
Liberty 56115		Theme From A Summer Place / A Summer Love	1969	1.00	5.00
Liberty 56163		Swan Lake / Expo-Seven O	1970	1.00	5.00
Liberty 56169		The Mercenary / The Wanderer	1970	1.00	5.00
Liberty 56189		Storefront Lawyers / Kern County Line	1970	1.00	5.00
Liberty 56213	(DJ)	Delilah (One sided)	1970	5.00	25.00
United Artists 50800		Indian Sun / Squaw Man	1970	1.00	5.00
United Artists 50800	(PS)	Indian Sun / Squaw Man	1970	1.00	5.00
United Artists 50851		Theme From Shaft / Tight Fit	1971	1.00	5.00
United Artists 50872		Joy / Cherries Jubilee	1971	1.00	5.00
United Artists 50903		Beethoven's Sonata / Peter And The Wolf	1972	1.00	5.00
United Artists 50925		Honky Tonk / Honky Tonk, Part 2	1972	1.00	5.00
United Artists 50989		Ram-Bunk-Shush / Last Night	1972	1.00	5.00
United Artists 207		Last Tango In Paris / Prima Vera	1973	1.00	5.00
United Artists 277		Sky Lab / Little People	1977	1.00	5.00
United Artists 333		2001 / Cisco Kid	1973	1.00	5.00
United Artists 392		Young And The Restless / Fur Elise	1974	1.00	5.00
United Artists 392	(PS)	Young And The Restless / Fur Elise	1974	1.00	5.00
United Artists 578		Airport '75 / Man With The Golden Gun	1974	1.00	5.00
United Artists 687		Superstar Revue / Superstar Revue, Part 2	1975	1.00	5.00
United Artists 784		Moonlight Serenade / Moonlight Serenade, Part 2	1976	1.00	5.00
United Artists 942		Theme From Starsky And Hutch / Theme From Charlie's Angels	1977	1.20	6.00
		(United Artists 784 and 942 credit The New Ventures.)			
United Artists 1100		Walk Don't Run '77 / Amanda's Theme	1977	1.20	6.00
TDX 501		Surfin' And Spyin' / Showdown At Newport	1981	.60	3.00
TDX 501	(PS)	Surfin' And Spyin' / Showdown At Newport	1981	.60	3.00
		— 12" Singles—			
Tridex 1245	(DJ)	Surfin' And Spyin' / Showdown At Newport	197?	4.00	20.00
Award EPV-8401		Out Of Limits / Telstar	197?	3.00	15.00
		—Extended Play Albums—			
Dolton 503		Walk-Don't Run	1960	15.00	75.00

Label & Catalog #		A-Side/B-Side	Year	VG	NM
Dolton 48014	(DJ)	The Ventures' Twist Party, Volume 2 (Jukebox EP)	1962	6.00	30.00
Dolton 48019	(DJ)	The Ventures Play Telstar, The Lonely Bull (Jukebox EP)	1963	6.00	30.00
Dolton 48031	(DJ)	Walk-Don't Run, Volume 2 (Jukebox EP)	1964	6.00	30.00
Dolton 48037	(DJ)	The Ventures A Go Go (Jukebox EP)	1965	6.00	30.00

VENUS, VIC

Buddah 118	Moonflight / Everybody's On Strike	1969	1.00	5.00

VENUS FLYTRAP, THE

Jaguar 103	Have You Ever? / The Note	196?	4.00	20.00

VERA, BILLY, & THE CONTRASTS

Rust 5051	All My Love / My Heart Cries	1962	3.00	15.00

VERA, BILLY, & JUDY CLAY

Atlantic 2445	Storybook Children / Really Together	1967	1.00	5.00
Atlantic 2480	Country Girl-City Boy / So Good	1968	.80	4.00

VERA, BILLY
Billy Vera also recorded with Blue Eyed Soul.

Atlantic 2526	With Pen In Hand / Good Morning Blues	1968	.80	4.00
Atlantic 2555	I've Been Loving You Too Long /			
	Are You Coming To My Party?	1968	.80	4.00
	Julie / Time Doesn't Matter Anymore	1968	.80	4.00
Atlantic 2586	The Bible Salesman / Are You Coming To My Party?	1969	.80	4.00
Atlantic 2628	The Bible Salesman / Are You Coming To My Party?	1969	2.00	10.00
Atlantic 2628 (PS)	Reaching For The Moon / Good Morning Blues	1969	.80	4.00
Atlantic 2654				

VERDICTS, THE

East Coast 103	My Life's Desire / The Mummy's Ball	1961	30.00	150.00

VERNON, RAY

Cameo 109	Remember You're Mine / Evil Angel	1957	6.00	30.00
Cameo 109	I'll Take Tomorrow Today / Evil Angel	195?	5.00	25.00
Cameo 115	Terry (You're Asking Too Much) / I'm Countin' On You	1958	3.00	15.00
Cameo 136	Window Shopping / I'll Be So Good To You	1958	3.00	15.00
Mark 614	It's So Easy / Two Teenage Hearts	1958	3.00	15.00

VERNON'S GIRLS

Challenge 59234	We Love The Beatles / Hey, Lover Boy	1964	5.00	25.00

VERONICA
Veronica Bennett a.k.a. Ronnie Spector of The Ronettes.

Phil Spector 1	So Young / Larry L	1964	25.00	125.00
Phil Spector 2	Why Don't They Let Us Fall In Love? / Chubby Danny D	1964	25.00	125.00

VERSAILLES, THE

Harlequin 401	Little Girl Of Mine / Teenager's Dream	196?	2.00	10.00

VERSATILES, THE

Ro-Cal 1002	Whisper In Your Ear / Lundee Lundee	1960	20.00	100.00

VERSATILES, THE

Ramco 3717	Just Pretending / Blue Feeling	1962	3.00	15.00

VERSATILES, THE

Sea Crest 6001	Moon Dawg / Lonely Boy	196?	2.00	10.00

VERTUES FOUR, THE

Sea Seven 22	Uphill, Downhill / Angel Baby	1963	7.00	35.00

VESPERS, THE
The Vespers originally recorded as The Four Epics.

Swan 4156	Mr. Cupid / When I Walk With My Angel	1964	8.00	40.00

VESTEE, RUSS

Amy 833	Teardrops / Well, All Right	1961	7.00	35.00

VESTELLES, THE

Decca 30733	Come Home / Ditta Wa Do	1958	6.00	30.00

VETTES, THE

MGM K-13186 (DJ)	Little Ford Ragtop / Happy Hodaddy	1963	3.00	15.00
MGM K-13186	Little Ford Ragtop / Happy Hodaddy	1963	6.00	30.00
	("Little Ford Ragtop" vocal by Bruce Johnston.)			

VI-COUNTS, THE

Vi-Tone 101	Wipe Out / Shootin' The Pier	196?	7.00	35.00

Label & Catalog #	A-Side/B-Side	Year	VG	NM
VI-KINGS, THE				
Del-Mann 545	Rock A Little Bit / Desert Boots	1960	4.00	20.00
VIBES, THE				
Rayna 103	You Got Me Crying / A Killer Came To Town	196?	5.00	25.00
VIBRA-SONICS, THE				
Ideal 94874	Thunder Storm / Drag Race	1964	7.00	35.00
VIBRANTS, THE [THE VIBRENTS]				
Triumph 101	Scorpion / Wild Fire	196?	7.00	35.00
Bay Towne 409	Fuel Injection / The Breeze And I	196?	7.00	35.00
VIC & THE CATALINAS				
Bar Clay 1967	Talkin' About My Girl / Hello Girl	1967	1.00	5.00
VICEROYS, THE				
Bethlehem 3045	Seagram's / Moanin'	1962	2.00	10.00
Bethlehem 3045	Sea Green / Moanin'	1962	2.00	10.00
Bethlehem 3088	Not Too Much Twist / Tears On My Pillow	1963	2.00	10.00
Bethlehem 3070	Buzz Bomb / The Fox	1963	2.00	10.00
VICEROYS, THE [THE VICEROYS FIVE]				
The Viceroys feature Jim Valley. Refer to Wink & Judy.				
E'den 9001	Don't Let Go / Down Beat Blues	1962	2.00	10.00
Bolo 736	Granny's Pad / Blues Bouquet	1962	2.00	10.00
Dot 16456	Granny's Pad / Blues Bouquet	1963	1.00	5.00
Bolo 739	Goin' Back To Granny's / Get Set	1963	1.20	6.00
Bolo 743	Dartell Stomp / Granny's Medley	1964	1.20	6.00
Bolo 749	Please Please Please / Tiger Shark	1964	1.20	6.00
Imperial 6658	Death Of An Angel / Earth Angel	1964	1.20	6.00
Bolo 750	Bacon Fat / Until	1965	1.20	6.00
Bolo 754	That Sound / Tired Of Waiting For You	1965	1.20	6.00
VICTORIANS, THE				
Arnold 571	Move In A Little Closer / Lovin'	1963	4.00	20.00
Liberty 55574	Climb Every Mountain / What Makes Little Girls Cry?	1963	3.00	15.00
Liberty 55656	You're Invited To A Party / The Monkey Stroll	1963	3.00	15.00
Liberty 55693	Happy Birthday Blues / Oh, What A Night For Love	1963	2.00	10.00
Liberty 55728	If I Loved You / Monkey Stroll	1964	2.00	10.00
VICTORIANS, THE				
The Victorians feature Nick Massi.				
Reprise 0434	Baby Toys / I Saw My Girl	1966	3.00	15.00
Bang 550	Merry-Go-Round / Wasn't The Summer Short?	1966	3.00	15.00
VICTORS, THE				
Dot 16558	Bird Walk / Peter	1963	4.00	20.00
VIDALTONES, THE				
Josie 900	Forever / Someone To Love	1961	6.00	30.00
VIDELS, THE				
The Videls feature Pete Anders and Vinnie Poncia.				
Rhody 2000	Be My Girl / A Place In My Heart	1959	10.00	50.00
Medieval 203	Be My Girl / A Place In My Heart	1959	6.00	30.00
JDS 5004	Mr. Lonely / I'll Forget You	1960	6.00	30.00
JDS 5005	Now That Summer Is Here / She's Not Coming Home	1960	4.00	20.00
Kapp 361	I'll Keep Waiting / Streets Of Love	1961	3.00	15.00
Kapp 495	A Letter From Anne / This Year's Mister New	1961	3.00	15.00
Musicnote 117	We Belong Together / It's All Over	1963	3.00	15.00
Tic Tac Toe 5005	Now That Summer Is Here / She's Not Coming Home	196?	2.00	10.00
VIKINGS, THE				
Athens 201	Sneaky Surfin' / Nicotine	196?	6.00	30.00
VIKINGS, THE: *Refer to* **ERIK & THE VIKINGS**				
VILLA, JOEY				
Chevron 500	Blanche / Mona Lisa	196?	5.00	25.00
De-Lite 501	Honest, Darling / Chloe	196?	2.00	10.00
Capitol 4484	All-American Girl / Mickey Mouse Got A Girl Friend	1961	2.00	10.00
VILLAGE VOICES, THE				
The Village Voices later recorded as The Four Seasons.				
Topix 6000	Red Lips / Too Young To Start *(Yellow & black label)*	1960	30.00	150.00
Topix 6000	Red Lips / Too Young To Start *(Yellow, black & white label)*	196?	20.00	100.00

Label & Catalog #	A-Side/B-Side	Year	VG	NM
VILLARI, GARY				
Gary Villari also recorded with The Regents and The Runarounds.				
Cousins 1004	**Mash Potato Mary / I'm All Alone**	*196?*	**3.00**	**15.00**
VINCE & THE VICTORS				
Jerden 744	**The Village '65 / Some Kind Of Drums**	*1964*	**1.00**	**5.00**
VINCE & THE WAIKIKI RUMBLERS				
Zodiac 1004	**Waikiki Rumble / Pacifica**	*1965*	**7.00**	**35.00**
VINCENT, DANNY				
Roulette 4334	**Carolyn / The Days Are Gone**	*1961*	**2.00**	**10.00**
VINCENT, GENE, & THE BLUE CAPS				
The Blue Caps were Cliff Gallup, Dickie Harrell, Jack Neal and Willie Williams, who also recorded with Wanda Jackson.				
Capitol 3450	**Be-Bop-A-Lula / Woman Love**	*1956*	**7.00**	**35.00**
	(First pressings have a purple label with a large Capitol logo on top.)			
Capitol 3450	**Be-Bop-A-Lula / Woman Love**	*1956*	**4.00**	**20.00**
Capitol 3530	**Race With The Devil / Gonna Back Up, Baby**	*1956*	**4.00**	**20.00**
Capitol 3558	**Blue Jean Bop / Who Slapped John?**	*1956*	**4.00**	**20.00**
Capitol 3617	**Crazy Legs / Important Words**	*1957*	**6.00**	**30.00**
Capitol 3678	**B-I-Bickey-Bi, Bobo-Go / Five Days, Five Days**	*1957*	**6.00**	**30.00**
Capitol 3763	**Lotta Lovin' / Wear My Ring**	*1957*	**4.00**	**20.00**
Capitol 3839	**Dance To The Bop / I Got It**	*1957*	**5.00**	**25.00**
Capitol 3874	**Walkin' Home From School / I Got A Baby**	*1958*	**5.00**	**25.00**
Capitol 3959	**Baby Blue / True To You**	*1958*	**10.00**	**50.00**
Capitol 4010	**Yes I Love You, Baby / Rocky Road Blues**	*1958*	**5.00**	**25.00**
Capitol 4051	**Git It / Little Lover**	*1958*	**5.00**	**25.00**
Capitol 4105	**Say Mama / Be Bop Boogie Boy**	*1959*	**8.00**	**40.00**
Capitol 4153	**Who's Pushin' Your Swing? / Over The Rainbow**	*1959*	**5.00**	**25.00**
Capitol 4237	**Right Now / The Night Is So Lonely**	*1959*	**10.00**	**50.00**
Capitol 4237	(PS) **Right Now / The Night Is So Lonely**	*1959*	**330.00**	**1,000.00**
	—Capitol singles above have purple labels with a small Capitol logo on top.—			
Capitol 4313	**Wild Cat / Right Here On Earth**	*1960*	**10.00**	**50.00**
Capitol 4442	**Pistol Packin' Mama / Anna-Annabelle**	*1960*	**8.00**	**40.00**
Capitol 4525	**Mister Loneliness / If You Want My Lovin'**	*1961*	**5.00**	**25.00**
Capitol 4665	**Lucky Star / Baby, Don't Believe Him**	*1961*	**5.00**	**25.00**
	—Capitol singles above have purple labels with the Capitol logo on the left.—			
Capitol 6042	**Be-Bop-A-Lula / Lotta Lovin'**	*1965*	**4.00**	**20.00**
Challenge 59337	**Bird Doggin' / Ain't That Too Much**	*1966*	**4.00**	**20.00**
Challenge 59347	**Lonely Street / I've Got My Eyes On You**	*1966*	**4.00**	**20.00**
Challenge 59365	**Born To Be A Rolling Stone / Hurtin' For You, Baby**	*1967*	**4.00**	**20.00**
Playground 100	**Story Of The Rockers / Pickin' Poppies**	*1968*	**15.00**	**75.00**
Forever 6001	**Story Of The Rockers / Pickin' Poppies**	*1969*	**10.00**	**50.00**
Kama Sutra 514	**Sunshine / Geese**	*1971*	**2.00**	**10.00**
Kama Sutra 518	**High On Life / The Day The World Turned Blue**	*1971*	**2.00**	**10.00**
	— Extended Play Albums—			
Capitol 1-764	**Bluejean Bop! (Volume 1)**	*1957*	**50.00**	**250.00**
Capitol 2-764	**Bluejean Bop! (Volume 2)**	*1957*	**50.00**	**250.00**
Capitol 3-764	**Bluejean Bop! (Volume 3)**	*1957*	**50.00**	**250.00**
Capitol PRO-438	(DJ) **Dance To The Bop** *(Issued without a cover.)*	*1957*	**75.00**	**300.00**
Capitol 1-811	**Gene Vincent & The Blue Caps (Volume 1)**	*1957*	**50.00**	**250.00**
Capitol 2-811	**Gene Vincent & The Blue Caps (Volume 2)**	*1957*	**50.00**	**250.00**
Capitol 3-811	**Gene Vincent & The Blue Caps (Volume 3)**	*1957*	**50.00**	**250.00**
Capitol 1-970	**Gene Vincent Rocks! & The Blue Caps Roll (Volume 1)**	*1958*	**50.00**	**250.00**
Capitol 2-970	**Gene Vincent Rocks! & The Blue Caps Roll (Volume 2)**	*1958*	**50.00**	**250.00**
Capitol 3-970	**Gene Vincent Rocks! & The Blue Caps Roll (Volume 3)**	*1958*	**50.00**	**250.00**
Capitol PRO-985	(DJ) **Hot Rod Gang**	*1958*	**100.00**	**400.00**
Capitol 1-1059	**A Gene Vincent Record Date (Volume 1)**	*1958*	**50.00**	**250.00**
Capitol 2-1059	**A Gene Vincent Record Date (Volume 2)**	*1958*	**50.00**	**250.00**
Capitol 3-1059	**A Gene Vincent Record Date (Volume 3)**	*1958*	**50.00**	**250.00**
VINCENT, RUDY				
End 1042	**Rockin' Crickets / Five Points**	*1959*	**2.00**	**10.00**
VINCENT, STAN				
MGM 13220	**Hi-Lili Hi-Lo / Miami**	*1964*	**1.20**	**6.00**
Marlu 7003	**Angel By Your Side / Little Teardrops**	*196?*	**3.00**	**15.00**
Gold 101	**Runnin' Scared / You're Everything I Love**	*196?*	**2.00**	**10.00**
VINE STREET BOYS, THE				
Era 3105	**Come On Over / That Certain Someone**	*1966*	**2.00**	**10.00**
VINTON, BOBBY				
Alpine 50	**You'll Never Forget / First Impression**	*1959*	**4.00**	**20.00**
Alpine 59	**The Sheik / A Freshman And A Sophomore**	*1960*	**3.00**	**15.00**
Melody 5001	**Always In My Heart / Harlem Nocturne**	*1960*	**3.00**	**15.00**
Epic 9417	**Tornado / Posin'**	*1961*	**2.00**	**10.00**

Label & Catalog #		A-Side/B-Side	Year	VG	NM
Epic 9440		Corrina, Corrina / Little Lovely One	1961	3.00	15.00
Epic 9469		Well, I Ask Ya /			
		Hip-Swinging, High-Stepping Drum Majorette	1962	2.00	10.00
Epic 9509		Roses Are Red (My Love) / You And I	1962	1.20	6.00
Epic 9509	(PS)	Roses Are Red (My Love) / You And I	1962	1.60	8.00
Epic 9532		Rain, Rain, Go Away / Over And Over	1962	1.00	5.00
Epic 9532	(PS)	Rain, Rain, Go Away / Over And Over	1962	1.60	8.00
Epic 9561		Trouble Is My Middle Name / Let's Kiss And Make Up	1962	1.00	5.00
Epic 9561	(PS)	Trouble Is My Middle Name / Let's Kiss And Make Up	1962	1.60	8.00
Diamond 121		I Love You The Way You Are / (B-side by Chuck & Johnny)	1962	2.00	10.00
Epic 9577		Over The Mountain (Across The Sea) / Faded Pictures	1963	1.00	5.00
Epic 9577	(PS)	Over The Mountain (Across The Sea) / Faded Pictures	1963	1.60	8.00
Epic 9593		Blue On Blue / Those Little Things	1963	1.20	6.00
Epic 9593	(PS)	Blue On Blue / Those Little Things	1963	1.20	6.00
Epic 9614		Blue Velvet / Is There A Place?	1963	1.20	6.00
Epic 9614	(PS)	Blue Velvet / Is There A Place?	1963	1.20	6.00
Epic 9638		There! I've Said It Again /			
		The Girl With The Bow In Her Hair	1963	1.20	6.00
Epic 9638	(PS)	There! I've Said It Again /			
		The Girl With The Bow In Her Hair	1963	1.20	6.00
Epic 9662		My Heart Belongs To Only You / Warm And Tender	1964	1.00	5.00
Epic 9662	(PS)	My Heart Belongs To Only You / Warm And Tender	1964	1.20	6.00
Epic 9687		Tell Me Why / Remembering	1964	1.00	5.00
Epic 9687	(PS)	Tell Me Why / Remembering	1964	1.20	6.00
Epic 9705	(DJ)	Clinging Vine / Imagination Is A Magic Dream (Red vinyl)	1964	3.00	15.00
Epic 9705		Clinging Vine / Imagination Is A Magic Dream	1964	1.00	5.00
Epic 9705	(PS)	Clinging Vine / Imagination Is A Magic Dream	1964	1.20	6.00
Epic 9730	(DJ)	Mr. Lonely / It's Better To Have Loved (Red vinyl)	1964	3.00	15.00
Epic 9730		Mr. Lonely / It's Better To Have Loved	1964	1.20	6.00
Epic 9730	(PS)	Mr. Lonely / It's Better To Have Loved	1964	1.20	6.00
Epic 9741		Dearest Santa / The Bell That Couldn't Jingle	1964	1.20	6.00
Epic 9741	(PS)	Dearest Santa / The Bell That Couldn't Jingle	1964	1.60	8.00
Epic 9768		Long, Lonely Nights / Satin	1965	1.20	6.00
Epic 9768	(PS)	Long, Lonely Nights / Satin	1965	1.20	6.00
Epic 9791		L-O-N-E-L-Y / Graduation Tears	1965	1.00	5.00
Epic 9791	(PS)	L-O-N-E-L-Y / Graduation Tears	1965	1.20	6.00
Epic 9814		Theme From "Harlowe" (Lonely Girl) /			
		If I Should Use Your Love	1965	1.00	5.00
Epic 9814	(PS)	Theme From "Harlowe" (Lonely Girl) /			
		If I Should Use Your Love	1965	1.20	6.00
Epic 9846		What Color (Is A Man)? / Love Or Infatuation?	1965	1.00	5.00
Epic 9869		Satin Pillows / Careless	1965	1.00	5.00
Epic 9869	(PS)	Satin Pillows / Careless	1965	1.20	6.00
Epic 9894		Tears / Go Away, Pain	1966	1.00	5.00
Epic 10014		Dum-De-Da / Blue Clarinet	1966	1.00	5.00
Epic 10014	(PS)	Dum-De-Da / Blue Clarinet	1966	1.20	6.00
Epic 10048		Petticoat White (Summer Sky Blue) / All The King's Horses	1966	1.00	5.00
Epic 10048	(PS)	Petticoat White (Summer Sky Blue) / All The King's Horses	1966	1.20	6.00
Epic 10090		Coming Home Soldier / Don't Let My Mary Go Around	1966	1.00	5.00
Epic 10090	(PS)	Coming Home Soldier / Don't Let My Mary Go Around	1966	1.20	6.00
Epic 10136		For He's A Jolly Good Fellow / Sweet Maria	1967	1.00	5.00
Epic 10136	(PS)	For He's A Jolly Good Fellow / Sweet Maria	1967	1.20	6.00
Epic 10168		Red Roses For Mom / College Town	1967	1.00	5.00
Epic 10168	(PS)	Red Roses For Mom / College Town	1967	1.20	6.00
Epic 10228		Please Love Me Forever / Miss America	1967	1.00	5.00
Epic 10228	(PS)	Please Love Me Forever / Miss America	1967	1.20	6.00
Epic 10266		Just As Much As Ever / Another Memory	1967	.60	3.00
Epic 10266	(PS)	Just As Much As Ever / Another Memory	1967	1.20	6.00
Epic 10305		Take Good Care Of My Baby / Strange Sensations	1968	.60	3.00
Epic 10305	(PS)	Take Good Care Of My Baby / Strange Sensations	1968	1.20	6.00
Epic 10350		Halfway To Paradise / (My Little) Christie	1968	.60	3.00
Epic 10350	(PS)	Halfway To Paradise / (My Little) Christie	1968	1.00	5.00
Epic 10397		I Love How You Love Me / Little Barefoot Boy	1968	.60	3.00
Epic 10397	(PS)	I Love How You Love Me / Little Barefoot Boy	1968	1.00	5.00
Epic 10461		To Know You Is To Love You / The Beat Of My Heart	1969	.60	3.00
Epic 10461	(PS)	To Know You Is To Love You / The Beat Of My Heart	1969	1.00	5.00
Epic 10485		The Days Of Sand And Shovels / So Many Lonely Girls	1969	.60	3.00
Epic 10485	(PS)	The Days Of Sand And Shovels / So Many Lonely Girls	1969	1.00	5.00
Epic 10554		For All We Know / Where Is Love?	1969	.60	3.00
Epic 10576		My Elusive Dreams / Over And Over	1970	.60	3.00
Epic 10629		No Arms Can Ever Hold You /			
		I've Got That Lovin' Feeling (Back Again)	1970	.60	3.00
Epic 10651		Why Don't They Understand? / Where Is Love?	1970	.60	3.00
Epic 10651	(PS)	Why Don't They Understand? / Where Is Love?	1970	.80	4.00
Epic 10689		Christmas Eve In My Home Town / Christmas Angel	1970	.60	3.00
Epic 10711		I'll Make You My Baby / She Loves Me	1971	.60	3.00
Epic 10736		And I Love You So / She Loves Me	1971	.60	3.00
Epic 10790		A Little Bit Of You / God Bless America	1971	.60	3.00

Label & Catalog #		A-Side/B-Side	Year	VG	NM
Epic 10822		Every Day Of My Life / You Can Do It To Me Anytime	1972	.60	3.00
Epic 10822	(PS)	Every Day Of My Life / You Can Do It To Me Anytime	1972	.80	4.00
Epic 10861		Sealed With A Kiss / All My Life	1972	.60	3.00
Epic 10861	(PS)	Sealed With A Kiss / All My Live	1972	.80	4.00
Epic 10936		But I Do / When You Love	1972	.60	3.00
Epic 10936	(PS)	But I Do / When You Love	1972	.80	4.00
Epic 10980		Hurt / I Love You The Way You Are	1972	.60	3.00
Epic 11038		Where Are Your Children? / I Can't Believe That It's All Over	1973	.60	3.00
Epic 50080		Clinging Vine / I Can't Believe That It's All Over	1973	.60	3.00
Epic 50169		Christmas Eve In My Home Town / Christmas Angel	1973	.60	3.00

VINNY & KENNY

Fire 1005	Who (Is The Girl?) / School Time	1959	2.00	10.00

VIRGOS, THE

Pioneer 6621	You're A Stranger / Humpty Dumpty	196?	3.00	15.00

VIRTUES, THE

Sure 501		Guitar Boogie Shuffle / Guitar In Orbit	1960	4.00	20.00
ABC-Paramount 10071		Blues In The Cellar / Vaya Con Dios	1960	2.00	10.00
Virnon 603		Guitar Boogie Twist / Guitar Shimmy	1960	2.00	10.00
Wynne 123		Highland Guitar / Pickin' Plankin' Boogie	1960	2.00	10.00
Hunt 324		Guitar Boogie Shuffle / Guitar In Orbit	1959	3.00	15.00
Hunt 324	(S)	Guitar Boogie Shuffle / Guitar In Orbit	1960	4.00	20.00
Hunt 327		Shufflin' Along / Flippin' In	1960	3.00	15.00
Hunt 328		Virtue's Boogie Woogie / Pickin' The Stroll	1960	3.00	15.00
Hunt 331		Blues In The Cellar / Vaya Con Dios	1961	3.00	15.00
Sure 1733		Guitar Boogie Shuffle Twist / Guitar Boogie Stomp	1962	2.00	10.00
Sure 1779		Telstar Boogie / Jersey Bounce	1962	2.00	10.00
Highland 2505		Bye Bye Blues / Happy Guitar	1962	4.00	20.00
Fayette 1626		Guitar Boogie Shuffle '65 / Moon Maid	1965	3.00	15.00
Virtue 2503		Guitar On The Wild Side / Meditation Of The Soul	1969	2.00	10.00

VISAS, THE

Timely 904	Marriage Is A Bag (And I Can't Punch My Way Out) / Night Train	1964	2.00	10.00
Dot 16591	Marriage Is A Bag (And I Can't Punch My Way Out) / Night Train	1964	1.20	6.00

VISCOUNTS, THE

Donick 100	Passion / Take Me To Your Leader	1959	3.00	15.00
Madison 123	Harlem Nocturne / Dig	1959	2.00	10.00
Madison 123	Harlem Nocturne / Dig (Blue vinyl)	1959	4.00	20.00
Madison 129	Chug-A-Lug / The Touch	1960	2.00	10.00
Madison 133	Night Train / Summertime	1960	2.00	10.00
Madison 140	Wabash Cannonball / So Slow	1960	2.00	10.00
Madison 152	This Place / Shadrach	1961	2.00	10.00
Madison 159	Little Brown Jug / Opus #1	1961	2.00	10.00
Mr. Peeke 125	Night For Love / Ballin' The Jack	1962	3.00	15.00
Amy 940	Harlem Nocturne / Dig	1965	2.00	10.00
Amy 949	Night Train / When The Saints Go Marching In	1966	2.00	10.00

VISCOUNTS, THE

A&R 1000	Weer'd / Tidewater	1964	7.00	35.00

VISCOUNTS, THE: *Refer to SAMMY HAGEN*

VISIONS, THE

Elgey 1003	Little Moon /	1960	6.00	30.00
Lost Nite 102	Teenager's Life /	1960	3.00	15.00
Big Top 3092	All Through The Night / Tell Me You're Mine	1961	4.00	20.00
Big Top 3119	Swingin' Wedding / Secret World (Of Tears)	1962	4.00	20.00
Mercury 72188	Tommy's Girl / Oh Boy, What A Girl	1963	5.00	25.00
Co-Ed 598	Down In My Heart / Tell Her Now	1965	3.00	15.00

VISIONS, THE

The Visions features Gary Zekeley under the pseudonym of Yodar Critch.

Uni 55031	How Can I Be Down? / Threshold Of Love	1967	2.00	10.00
Uni 55042	Small Town Commotion / Keepin' Your Eyes On The Sun	1967	2.00	10.00

VISITORS, THE

Tower 268	The Wild Angels / It Is Them Or Me	1966	2.00	10.00

VISTAS, THE

Rebel 77755	Surfer's Minuet / Ghost Wave	1963	10.00	50.00
Venpro 1000	Surfer's Minuet / Ghost Wave	1963	7.00	35.00

Label & Catalog #	A-Side/B-Side	Year	VG	NM
VISTAS, THE				
Tuff 990	Moon Relay / No Return	196?	7.00	35.00
VISUALS, THE				
Poplar 115	Maybe You / The Submarine Race	1962	3.00	15.00
Poplar 117	My Juanita / Boy, Girl And A Dream	1963	7.00	35.00
Poplar 121	Please Don't Be Mad At Me / Blue Enough To Cry	1963	75.00	300.00
VITA-MEN, THE				
Challenge 59327	Frog Legs / I Can't Help Myself	1965	2.00	10.00
VITALE, JO JO				
May 127	My Little Cinderella / One Million To One	1963	2.00	10.00
VITO: Refer to VITO PICONE				
VITO, SONNY				
ABC-Paramount 9958	Teenage Blues / Cameo Ring	1958	3.00	15.00
Chancellor 1112	I Remember The Night / Put 'Em Down, Joe	1962	3.00	15.00
VITO & THE ELEGANTS: Refer to THE ELEGANTS				
VITO & THE SALUTATIONS				
The Salutations later recorded as The Magic Touch.				
Kran 1202	Your Way / Hey Hey, Baby	1962	8.00	40.00
Rayna 5009	Gloria / Let's Untwist The Twist	1962	6.00	30.00
Red Boy 1001	So Wonderful / I'd Best Be Going	1962	4.00	20.00
Herald 583	Unchained Melody / Hey Hey, Baby	1963	4.00	20.00
Herald 586	Extraordinary Girl / Eenie Meenie	1963	4.00	20.00
Wells 1008	Can I Depend On You? / Liverpool Bound (Yellow vinyl)	1964	8.00	40.00
Wells 1008	Can I Depend On You? / Liverpool Bound	1964	4.00	20.00
Wells 1010	Don't Count On Me / Day-O (Banana Boat Song)	1964	4.00	20.00
Rust 5106	Can I Depend On You? / Hello, Dolly	1964	3.00	15.00
Boom 60020	I Want You To Be My Baby / Bring Back Yesterday	196?	4.00	20.00
Regina 1320	Get A Job / Girls I Know	196?	4.00	20.00
Apt 25079	Walkin' / High Noon	1965	6.00	30.00
Sandbag 103	So Wonderful / I'd Best Be Going	1968	2.00	10.00
Crystal Ball 105	So Much / Unchained Melody	197?	.60	3.00
VITRONES, THE				
Audition 6104	Linda / London Fog	196?	7.00	35.00
VOCAL-AIRES, THE				
Herald 573	These Empty Arms / Dance Dance	1962	6.00	30.00
Ronnie 200	Dream Ship /	196?	2.00	10.00
VOCAL LORDS, THE				
Able	Girl Of Mine / At Seventeen	1959	15.00	75.00
VOCAL-TEENS, THE				
Downstairs 1000	Till Then / Be A Slave	196?	2.00	10.00
VOGUES, THE				
The Vogues originally recorded as The Val-Aires.				
Dot 15798	Love's A Funny Little Game / Which Witch Doctor	1959	3.00	15.00
Dot 15859	Falling Star / Try, Baby, Try	1959	3.00	15.00
Cascade 5908	Ev'ry Day, Ev'ry Night / Now I Lay Me Down To Cry	1959	3.00	15.00
ABC-Paramount 10672	Big Man / Golden Locket	1965	2.00	10.00
Blue Star 229	You're The One / Some Words	1965	2.00	10.00
Co&Ce 229	You're The One / Some Words	1965	1.20	6.00
Co&Ce 232	Five O' Clock World / Nothing To Offer You	1965	1.20	6.00
Co&Ce 234	Magic Town / Humpty Dumpty	1966	1.20	6.00
Co&Ce 238	The Land Of Milk And Honey / True Lovers	1966	1.20	6.00
Co&Ce 240	Please, Mr. Sun / Don't Blame The Rain	1966	1.00	5.00
Co&Ce 242	That's The Tune / Midnight Dreams	1966	1.00	5.00
Co&Ce 244	Summer Afternoon / Take A Chance On Me, Baby	1967	1.00	5.00
Co&Ce 246	Lovers Of The World, Unite / Brighter Days	1967	1.00	5.00
MGM 13813	Lovers Of The World, Unite / Brighter Days	1967	.80	4.00
Reprise 0663	Just What I've Been Looking For / I've Got You On My Mind	1967	.80	4.00
Reprise 0686	Turn Around, Look At Me / Then	1968	.80	4.00
Reprise 0766	My Special Angel / I Keep It Hid	1968	.80	4.00
Reprise 0788	Till / I Will	1968	.80	4.00
Reprise 0803	No, Not Much / Woman Helping Man	1969	.80	4.00
Reprise 0820	Earth Angel / P.S. I Love You	1969	.80	4.00
Reprise 0831	Moments To Remember / Once In A While	1969	.80	4.00
Reprise 0844	Green Fields / Easy To Say	1969	.60	3.00
Reprise 0856	See That Girl / If We Only Have Love	1969	.60	3.00
Reprise 0887	God Only Knows / Moody	1969	.60	3.00

Label & Catalog #	A-Side/B-Side	Year	VG	NM
Reprise 0909	Hey, That's No way To Say Goodbye / Over The Rainbow	1970	.60	3.00
Reprise 0931	Theme (The Good Old Songs) / Come Into My Arms	1970	.60	3.00
Reprise 0969	Since I Don't Have You / I Know You As A Woman	1970	.60	3.00
Bell 991	Love Song / We're On Our Way	197?	.60	3.00
Bell 127	I'll Be With You / Take Time To Tell Her	1971	.60	3.00
Bell 158	American Family / Gotta Have You Back	1971	.60	3.00
20th Century 2041	My Prayer / I've Got To Learn To Live Without You	1972	.60	3.00
20th Century 2060	Wonderful Summer / Guess Who?	1972	.60	3.00
20th Century 20485	Prisoner Of Love / As Time Goes By	1972	.60	3.00
Astra 1029	You're The One / Goodnight My Love	1973	.60	3.00
Mainstream 5524	Need You /	1971	.60	3.00

VOLKSWAGONS, THE
| Do-Re-Mi 201 | Astronaut / Blues For My Baby | 196? | 3.00 | 15.00 |

VOLCHORDS, THE
| Regatta 2004 | Bongo Love / Peek-A-Boo Love | 195? | 4.00 | 20.00 |

VOLK, VAL, & THE MATCHED ACES
| Rocket 1050 | There'll Be A Rockin' Party Tonight / Spring Time Rock | 195? | 10.00 | 50.00 |

VOLK BROTHERS, THE
The Volk Brothers feature Phil, later of The Viceroys and Paul Revere & The Raiders.
Rivers 1003	Judy Hone / Baby, I Say Get Up	196?	3.00	15.00
Rivers 1011	The Walk / Dancing By The Old Mill Stream	196?	3.00	15.00
Clover 1003	Wash, Don't Soak / Ducks Flying Backward	196?	4.00	20.00

VOLUMES, THE
| Impact 1017 | The Trouble I've Seen / That Same Old Feeling | 196? | 3.00 | 15.00 |

VOXPOPPERS, THE
Refer to Freddie & The Voxpoppers.
Amp-3 1004	Wishing For Your Love / The Last Drag	1958	5.00	25.00
Mercury 71282	Wishing For Your Love / The Last Drag	1958	3.00	15.00
Mercury 71315	Pony Tail / Ping Pong Baby	1958	3.00	15.00
Poplar 107	A Love To Last A Lifetime / Come Back, Little Girl	1958	3.00	15.00
Versailles 200	Can't Understand It / A Blessing After All	1959	3.00	15.00

VROOMAN, LYNN
| Penguin 1010 | Hopeless Love / Let The Good Times Roll | 196? | 3.00 | 15.00 |

VULCANES, THE [THE VULCAINES]
Goliath 1348	Stomp Sign / Public Record #1	1962	7.00	35.00
Goliath 1350	Cozimotto / Last Prom	1963	8.00	40.00
	(Goliath 1350 credits The Vulcaines.)			
Capitol 5199	Moon Probe / Twilight City	1964	3.00	15.00
Capitol 5285	Liverpool / The Outrage	1964	2.00	10.00
Capitol 5423	My Heart Won't Believe It / Poison Ivy	1965	2.00	10.00

VY-DELLS, THE
| Garnet 101 | Unknown / What I'm Gonna Do | 195? | 20.00 | 100.00 |

W.

WADE, DEKE
Panorama 15 — Tall Oak Tree / Sheri — 196? — .80 — 4.00

WADE & DICK ("THE COLLEGE KIDS")
Sun 269 — Bop Bop Baby / Don't Need Your Lovin,' Baby — 1957 — 4.00 — 20.00

WADSWORTH, JERRY
Topaz 1302 — Pretty Janell / Path Of Broken Dreams — 196? — 2.00 — 10.00

WAGNER, CLIFF
Jolum 2510 — When You're Dancin' / Somethings Got A Hold On Me — 196? — 2.00 — 10.00

WAGNER, DICK, & THE FROSTS
Dick Wagner also recorded with The Bossmen; The Cherry Slush; and Frost.
Date 1577 — Bad Girl / A Rainy Day — 1967 — 2.00 — 10.00
Date 1596 — Little Girl / Sunshine — 1968 — 2.00 — 10.00

WAILERS, THE
Original members on the Golden Crest sides were Mike Burk, Richard Dangel, John Greek, Mark Marush, Kent Morrill and Buck Ormsby. Later members include Neil Anderson, Ron Gardner, Dave Roland and Denny Weaver. Refer to Rockin' Robin Roberts.
Golden Crest 518 — Tall Cool One / Road Runner — 1959 — 3.00 — 15.00
Golden Crest 526 — Dirty Robber / Mau Mau — 1959 — 3.00 — 15.00
Golden Crest 532 — Shanghai'd / Wailin' — 1960 — 3.00 — 15.00
Golden Crest 545 — Scratchin' / Lucille — 1960 — 3.00 — 15.00
— *Original Golden Crest singles above have picture labels.* —
Golden Crest 518 — Tall Cool One / Road Runner — 196? — 1.20 — 6.00
Golden Crest 526 — Dirty Robber / Mau Mau — 196? — 1.20 — 6.00
Golden Crest 532 — Shanghai'd / Wailin' — 196? — 1.20 — 6.00
Golden Crest 545 — Scratchin' / Lucille — 196? — 1.20 — 6.00
Etiquette 2 — Mashi / Velva — 1961 — 1.20 — 6.00
Etiquette 4 — Stompin' Willie / Doin The Seaside — 1962 — 1.20 — 6.00
Etiquette 6 — We're Goin' Surfin' / Shakedown — 1963 — 1.20 — 6.00
Etiquette 7 — Seattle / Partime U.S.A. — 1963 — 1.20 — 6.00
Imperial 66045 — Mashi / On The Rocks — 1964 — 1.20 — 6.00
Golden Crest 591 — Beat Guitar / Mau Mau — 1964 — 1.00 — 5.00
Golden Crest 3751 — Beat Guitar / Driftwood — 1964 — 1.60 — 8.00
Etiquette 9 — Tall Cool One / Frenzy — 1964 — 1.20 — 6.00
Etiquette 12 — Don't Take It So Hard / You Better Believe It — 1964 — 1.20 — 6.00
Etiquette 15 — Back To You / You Weren't Using Your Head — 1965 — 1.20 — 6.00
Etiquette 19 — Dirty Robber / Hang Up — 1965 — 1.20 — 6.00
Etiquette 21 — Out Of Our Tree / I Got Me — 1965 — 1.20 — 6.00
Etiquette 22 — Christmas Spirit / (B-side by The Sonics) — 1965 — 2.00 — 10.00
Etiquette 24 — It's You Alone / Tears — 1966 — 1.20 — 6.00
United Artists 66045 — Mashi / On The Rocks — 1964 — 1.20 — 6.00
United Artists 50026 — It's You Alone / Tears — 1966 — 1.00 — 5.00
United Artists 50065 — Think Kindly, Baby / End Of The Summer — 1966 — 1.00 — 5.00
United Artists 50110 — You Won't Lead Me On / Tears (Don't Have To Fall) — 1966 — 1.00 — 5.00
Viva 614 — I'm Determined / I Don't Want To Follow You — 1967 — 1.20 — 6.00
Bell 694 — You Can't Fly / Thinking Out Loud — 1968 — 1.00 — 5.00

WAILERS, THE / THE THREE GRACES
Golden Crest 88602 (EP) — The Wailers / The Three Graces *(Issued without a cover)* — 196? — 5.00 — 25.00

WAKELIN, JOHNNY
Pye 45460 — Tennessee Hero / Say Hello To Mr. Blues — 1975 — .60 — 3.00

WALE, STEVE
Lute 6007 — Boy Meets Girl / You Can't Take It With You — 1961 — 2.00 — 10.00

WALES, HOWARD, & JERRY GARCIA
Douglas 76501 — South Side Strut / Uncle Martin's — 1971 — 1.20 — 6.00

WALKER, BOOTS
Rust 5115 — They're Here / A Bum Can't Cry — 1967 — 1.00 — 5.00

WALKER, GARY
Gary Walker is a pseudonym for Gary Leeds, who also recorded with The Biscaynes and The Walker Brothers.
Date 1506 — You Don't Love Me / Get It Right — 1966 — 1.00 — 5.00

Label & Catalog #	A-Side/B-Side		Year	VG	NM
WALKER, (RHETT) HAMILTON					
Uni 55010	Graveyard Shift / You Must Be The One		1967	.80	4.00
Jerden 791	I Don't Know What It Is / It's Hurtin' Me		1966	.80	4.00
WALKER, JACKIE					
Imperial 5490	Only Teenagers Allowed / Oh, Lonesome Me		1958	3.00	15.00
WALKER, JOHN					
John Walker is a pseudonym for John Stewart, who also recorded with The Biscaynes; The Dalton Brothers; The Moongooners; and The Walker Brothers.					
Smash 2108	Annabella / You Don't Understand Me		1967	1.00	5.00
Smash 2213	Woman / A Dream		1968	1.00	5.00
Green Mount. 416	Good Days / Midnight Morning		1973	2.00	10.00
	(Features Bill Wyman.)				
WALKER, ROBERT, & THE NIGHT RIDERS					
Detroit Sound 224	Keep On Runnin' / Everything's Alright		196?	1.20	6.00
WALKER, SCOTT					
Scott Walker is a pseudonym for Scott Engel, who also recorded with The Biscaynes; The Dalton Brothers; The Moongooners; and The Walker Brothers.					
Smash 2156	I Don't Want To Hear It Anymore / You're All Around Me		1968	1.00	5.00
Smash 2228	Two Weeks Since You've Gone / Lights Of Cincinnati		1969	1.00	5.00
Philips 40713	I Still See You / My Way Home		1973	.80	4.00
WALKER, WAYNE					
ABC-Paramount 9735	All I Can Do Is Cry / It's My Way		195?	10.00	50.00
WALKER, WILMER					
Philips 40030	Stompin' Roaches / Somebody Will		1962	1.25	6.00
WALKER BROTHERS, THE					
Kay-Y 66785	Beautiful Brown Eyes / Ninety-Seven		1960	5.00	25.00
WALKER BROTHERS, THE					
The Walker Brothers are Gary Leeds, John Stewart and Scott Engel.					
Smash 1952	Pretty Girls Everywhere / Doin' The Jerk		1965	1.20	6.00
Smash 1976	Seventh Dawn / Love Her		1965	1.20	6.00
Smash 2000	Make It Easy On Yourself / But I Do		1965	1.60	8.00
Smash 2009	Make It Easy On Yourself / Doin' The Jerk		1965	1.60	8.00
Smash 2009	(PS) Make It Easy On Yourself / Doin' The Jerk		1965	4.00	20.00
Smash 2016	My Ship Is Comin' In / You're All Around Me		1966	1.60	8.00
Smash 2016	(PS) My Ship Is Comin' In / You're All Around Me		1966	4.00	20.00
Smash 2032	The Sun Ain't Gonna Shine (Anymore) / After The Lights Go Down		1966	1.60	8.00
Smash 2032	(PS) The Sun Ain't Gonna Shine (Anymore) / After The Lights Go Down		1966	4.00	20.00
Smash 2048	You Don't Have To Tell Me, Baby / The Young Man Cried		1966	1.20	6.00
Smash 2063	Another Tear Falls / Saddest Night In The World		1967	1.20	6.00
Tower 218	I Only Came To Dance With You / Greens		1966	1.60	8.00
WALLER, GORDON					
Refer to Peter & Gordon.					
Capitol 5886	Speak For Me / Little Nonie		1967	.80	4.00
Capitol 2436	Everyday / Because Of A Woman		1968	.80	4.00
WALLER, JIM, & THE DELTAS					
Refer to Jay & The Deltas.					
Trac 502	I've Been Blue / What I Want		1961	10.00	50.00
Arvee 5072	Surfin' Wild / Church Key		1962	7.00	35.00
Cambridge 124	Goodnight My Love / Give My Love A Chance		1964	4.00	20.00
WALLFLOWERS, THE					
Ridon 855	No Love Today / The Kind Of Love		196?	2.00	10.00
WALTER & FANCY					
Magic Lamp 612	Campaign Trail / (Part 2)		1964	2.00	10.00
WAMMACK, TRAVIS					
Ara 204	Scratchy / Fire Fly		1964	2.00	10.00
WANDERERS THREE, THE					
Dolton 59	Cry I Do / Toro		196?	.80	4.00
Dolton 66	My Glory Land / Turn Around		196?	.80	4.00
WANTED					
Detroit Sound 222	In The Midnight Hour / Here To Stay		1967	3.00	15.00

Label & Catalog #	A-Side/B-Side	Year	VG	NM
Detroit Sound 230	Knock On Wood / Lots More Where They Came From	1967	3.00	15.00
A&M 844	In The Midnight Hour / Hard To Stay	1967	2.00	10.00
A&M 856	Don't Worry, Baby / Big Town Girl	1967	2.00	10.00

WARD, BURT
Burt Ward was a member of Batman & Robin.

MGM 13632 (DJ)	Boy Wonder, I Love You / Orange Colored Sky	1967	15.00	75.00
MGM 13632	Boy Wonder, I Love You / Orange Colored Sky	1967	20.00	100.00
	(Arranged and conducted by Frank Zappa.)			
Soultown 12	I've Got Love For My Baby / I've Got Love For My Baby	196?	12.00	60.00

WARD, DALE
Dale Ward also recorded with The Crescendos.

Dot 16520	Letter From Sherry / Oh, Julie	1963	3.00	15.00
Dot 16590	Crying For Laura / I've Got A Girl Friend	1964	2.00	10.00
Dot 16632	I'll Never Love Again (After Loving You) /			
	Young Lovers After Midnight	1964	2.00	10.00
Dot 16672	One Last Kiss, Cherie / The Fortune	1964	2.00	10.00
Boyd 118	Big Dale Twist / Here's Your Hat	196?	2.00	10.00
Boyd 150	You Gotta Let Me Know / Shake, Rattle And Roll	196?	3.00	15.00
Boyd 152	Living On Coal / I Tried	196?	2.00	10.00

WARD, DART, & THE CUT-UPS

Rip 134	Q-T-Cute / Misery	196?	1.2	6.00

WARD, RICHARD, & THE HUSTLERS

Downey 121	The Well Of Loneliness / Topless Bathing Suit	1964	3.00	15.00

WARD, ROBIN [ROBIN]

Dot 16519	Top Forty Blues / Bluegrass Blue	1963	2.00	10.00
Song Unlimited 37	Loser's Lullabye / Lolly Too Dum	1963	1.60	8.00
Dot 16530	Wonderful Summer / Dream Boy	1963	1.20	6.00
Dot 16578	Winter's Here / Bobby	1964	1.20	6.00
Dot 16599	Johnny, Come And Get Me /			
	Where The Blue Meets The Gold	1964	1.20	6.00
Dot 16624	In His Car / Wishing	1964	1.20	6.00

WARLOCKS, THE

Washington Square 2023	Girl / Hey, Joe	196?	4.00	20.00

WARLOCKS, THE
The Warlocks feature future members of ZZ Top.

Paradise 1021	Splash / Life's A Mystery	1968	3.00	15.00
Ara 1017	If You Really Want Me To Stay / Good Time Trippin'	1968	3.00	15.00
Ara 1915	Lady Wilde / Another Year / Poor Kids	1968	3.00	15.00

WARMER, FARON

Jo-Ree 501	Cruisin' Central / The Switch	1959	5.00	25.00

WARREN, BEVERLY

B.T. Puppy 5236	He's So Fine / March	1966	2.00	10.00

WARREN FIVE, BOBBY

Jordan 119	Nite-Beat / Medicine Man	196?	7.00	35.00

WASDEN, JAYBEE

Trepur 1011	Elvis In The Army / De Castrow	1959	5.00	25.00

WASHINGTON, GEORGE, & THE CHERRY BOMBS

MGM 13450	Don't You Just Know It / Brother Ward	1966	1.20	6.00

WASHINGTON, GINO

Son Bert 3770	Gino Is A Coward / Puppet On A String	1964	3.00	15.00
Ric Tic 100	Gino Is A Coward / Puppet On A String	1964	2.00	10.00
Wand 147	Out Of This World / Come Monkey With Me	1964	1.20	6.00

WASHINGTON MERRY GO ROUND

Piccadilly 254	Land Of Odin / Got-ta Got-ta	1969	1.00	5.00

WATERPROOF CANDLE

Dunhill 4143	Veronica's Pigskin / Session Report	1968	2.00	10.00

WATERPROOF TINKERTOY

Laurie 3457	Groovy Girl / This And That	1968	2.00	10.00

WATERS, JUNIOR

MGM 13004	Rockin' That History / I'll See You In My Dreams	1961	2.00	10.00

Label & Catalog #	A-Side/B-Side	Year	VG	NM
WATSON, CLAYTON, & THE SILHOUETTES				
Clayton Watson also recorded as Lord Dent & The Invaders; The Silhouettes with Jim Barnet.				
Lavender 2454	Everybody's Boppin' / Tall Skinny Annie	1958	15.00	75.00
WATTS, NOBLE				
Baton 249	Hard Times (The Slop) / I'm Walkin' The Floor Over You	1957	3.00	15.00
Cub 9078	Frog Hop / The Beaver	1960	2.00	10.00
WAVERIDERS, THE				
Guyden 2095	Shootin' The Curl / Malibu	1963	7.00	35.00
WAYNE, ARTIE				
Liberty 55625	Where Does A Rock And Roll Singer Go? / I Hurt That Girl	1963	2.00	10.00
WAYNE, BOBBY				
LJV 101	Sally Ann / War Paint	196?	15.00	75.00
Jerden 709	The Valley / Big Train	1963	1.20	6.00
Jerden 713	Tip Toes / Bobby's Boogie #1	1963	1.20	6.00
Jerden 720	The Last Ride / TV Dream	1963	1.00	5.00
Epic 9595	Big Train / Last Valley	1963	1.00	5.00
A&M 716	Tip Toes / Bobby's Boogie #1	1963	1.00	5.00
A&M 736	Last Date / Twinkle Toes	1964	.80	4.00
Warner Bros. 5427	Half Breed / Last Ride	1964	1.00	5.00
Jerden 737	River Queen / Ballad Of A Teenage Queen	1964	1.00	5.00
Jerden 751	Wheels / Moonshine	1964	.80	4.00
Jerden 765	Big Wheels / Hobo	1965	.80	4.00
Jerden 766	Blue Tango / Honky Tonk	1965	.80	4.00
Jerden 786	The Letter / Uncle Sam's Got My Number	1966	.80	4.00
WAYNE, DENNIS				
Northwestern 2430	Teenage Boogie / Walk Walk	195?	50.00	200.00
WAYNE, SCOTTY				
Scotty Wayne is a pseudonym for Freddy Fender.				
Talent Scout 1008	Only One / I'm Gonna Leave	1960	3.00	15.00
Talent Scout 1009	Pretty Baby / Sweet Summer Day	1960	3.00	15.00
Talent Scout 1011	You Told Me You Loved Me / Roobie Doobie	1960	3.00	15.00
WAYNE, SUSAN				
Columbia 43148	Riding On A Rainbow / You Don't Do What I Say	1964	1.20	6.00
Columbia 43237	That's What I Love About You / Think Summer	1965	1.20	6.00
WAYNE, THOMAS (& THE DE LONS)				
Fernwood 106	This Time / You're The One That Done It	1959	10.00	50.00
Mercury 71454	This Time / You're The One That Done It	1959	5.00	25.00
Fernwood 109	Tragedy / Saturday Date	1959	5.00	25.00
Fernwood 111	Eternally / Scandalizing My Name	1959	5.00	25.00
Fernwood 113	Gonna Be Waitin' / Just Beyond	1959	5.00	25.00
Fernwood 120	Guilty Of Love / Poncho Villa	1959	5.00	25.00
Fernwood 122	The Girl Next Door / Because Of You	1960	5.00	25.00
Capehart 5009	No More, No More / Tragedy	1961	5.00	25.00
Santo 9053	Stop The River / Eighth Wonder Of The World	1962	5.00	25.00
WAYNE & DWAIN				
Crusader 102	Ski Surfin' Man / Sand Castles And You	196?	7.00	35.00
WAYNE & THE EXCEPTIONS				
Laurie 3376	Have Faith, Baby / Have Faith, Baby (Part 2)	1967	1.20	6.00
WE FIVE				
A&M 770	You Were On My Mind / Small World	1965	1.00	5.00
A&M 784	Let's Get Together / Cast Your Fate To The Wind	1965	.80	4.00
A&M 793	You Let A Love Burn Out / Somewhere Beyond The Sea	1966	.80	4.00
A&M 800	Somewhere / There Stands The Door	1966	.80	4.00
A&M 820	High Flying Bird / What Do I Do Now?	1966	.80	4.00
Vault 964	Never Goin' Back / Here Comes The Sun	1967	.80	4.00
Vault 969	Catch The Wind / Oh, Lonesome Me	1967	.80	4.00
Verve 10716	Rejoice / Bandstand Singer	1968	.60	3.00
A&M 1072	Walk On By / It Really Doesn't Matter	1969	.60	3.00
WE THE PEOPLE				
Challenge 59333	Mirror Of Your Mind / The Color Of Love	1966	4.00	20.00
Challenge 59340	Up And Down / About It Right	1966	4.00	20.00
Challenge 59351	You Burn Me / He Doesn't Go	1967	4.00	20.00
RCA Victor 47-9498	When I Arrive / Ain't Gonna Find Nobody	1968	4.00	20.00

Label & Catalog #	A-Side/B-Side	Year	VG	NM
WEBB, ROGER				
Swan 4188	She Loves You / Do You Want To Know A Secret?	1964	2.00	10.00
WEBB, SPIDER, & THE INSECTS				
Lugar 100	Big Noise From Winnetka / Maggie	1963	3.00	15.00
WEBBER, ROLLIE				
Wasp 113	Stealin' My World / Cotton Fields	197?	.80	4.00
Arco 725	Flash, Crash And Thunder / Look At Me Now	197?	.80	4.00
WEBS, THE				
Heart 933	Blue Skies / Lost (Cricket In My Ear)	196?	4.00	20.00
Lite 9004	Blue Skies / Lost (Cricket In My Ear)	196?	2.00	10.00
WEBSPINNERS, THE				
The Webspinners feature Ron Dante.				
Buddah 327	Theme From Spiderman / Goin' Crosstown	1972	.80	4.00
WEDLAW, FRANKIE				
Skyla 1054	Have You Got A Crush On Me? / Run, Buddy, Run	1962	2.00	10.00
WEED, GENE				
20th Century Fox 416	Poor Poor Billie / Just For Tonight	1963	2.00	10.00
WEEDS, THE				
Teenbeat 1006	It's Your Time, Girl /	1966	10.00	50.00
N.W.I. 2745	No Good News / Stop	1969	4.00	20.00
N.W.I. 2745 (PS)	No Good News / Stop	1969	6.00	30.00
WEEKENDS, THE				
Le-Mans 001	Ringo / I Want You	1964	3.00	15.00
Columbia 43597	You're #1 With Me / Canadian Sunset	1966	3.00	15.00
WEEKS, CHRISTOPHER, & FRAN STACEY				
Clan 1	My Son, The President /	196?	2.00	10.00
WEHBA, DALE				
Kings-X 3364	Russian Roulette / The Screwdriver	196?	1.20	6.00
WEIGAND, JACK				
Cameo 178	Shangri-La / Stairway To The Stars	1960	2.00	10.00
Cameo 185	Sixteen Candles / Prisoner Of Love	1960	2.00	10.00
WEIGHT				
Bertram Inter. 230	Flip, Flop And Fly / Another Side Of This Life	1969	2.00	10.00
WEIR, BOBBY				
Bobby Weir is a member of The Grateful Dead.				
Warner Bros. 2627	One More Saturday Night / Cassidy	1972	1.60	8.00
Arista 315	Bombs Away / Easy To Slip	1977	.80	4.00
Arista 336	I'll Be Doggone / Shades Of Grey	1977	.80	4.00
WEIRDOS, THE				
Lan-cet 145	E.S.P. / Shape Of Mind	1961	2.00	10.00
WELDON, DANNY				
Enith 715	Surf Dreamin' /	196?	7.00	35.00
WELLER, FREDDY				
Freddy Weller also recorded with Paul Revere & The Raiders.				
Dore 595	No One To Love / Mary, I'm Glad To See You	1961	3.00	15.00
WELLS, CORY				
Cory Wells originally recorded with The Enemys and Three Dog Night.				
A&M 2013	Starlight / I Know You're Willin', Darlin'	197?	.60	3.00
A&M 2035	Midnight Lady (Hiding In The Shadows) /			
	I Know You're Willin,' Darlin'	197?	.60	3.00
A&M 2060	Let Tomorrow Be / You Can Count On Me	197?	.60	3.00
WELLS & FARGO				
Virgelle 716	Heartaches And Honky Tonks / Lonely Side Of Town	196?	.80	4.00
Virgelle 726	That's How Things Are / Honky Tonkin'	196?	.80	4.00
WELLINGTON FIVE, THE				
Quest 302	Please Have Mercy / Summertime (Blues)	196?	1.20	6.00

WELTON, DANNY, & THE NEW MARKETTS: *Refer to* THE NEW MARKETTS

Label & Catalog #	A-Side/B-Side	Year	VG	NM
WELZ, JOEY				
Joey Welz was a member of Bill Haley's Comets.				
Bat 1001	Shore Patrol / Boppin' The Stroll	1959	5.00	25.00
WENDIGO				
Cousins 1010	Gimme Some Lovin' / Gimme Some Lovin' (Part 2)	1968	2.00	10.00
Scepter 12111	Gimme Some Lovin' / Gimme Some Lovin' (Part 2)	1968	1.25	6.00
WESLEY, GATE				
Atlantic 2319	Do The Batman / Do The Thing	1966	3.00	15.00
WEST				
Epic 10335	Just Like Tom Thumb's Blues / Baby, You Been On My Mind	1968	1.00	5.00
Epic 10387	Step By Step / Summer Flower	1968	1.00	5.00
WEST, RED				
Jaro 77031	What Must I Do? / The F.B.I. Story	1960	2.00	10.00
Dot 16268	Midnight Ride / Unforgiven	1961	3.00	15.00
Santo 9006	My Babe / Bossa Nova Momza	1963	2.00	10.00
Loma 2005	Midnight Ride / Unforgiven	1965	2.00	10.00
Sonnet 2960	Ain't Nobody Gonna Take My Place / My Thanks To You	196?	1.20	6.00
WEST COAST FIVE, THE				
Boom 1	Still In Love With You, Baby / Good Golly, Miss Molly	196?	3.00	15.00
WEST COAST POP ART EXPERIMENTAL BAND, THE				
The W.C.P.A.E.B. features Shawn Harris.				
Reprise 0552	Shifting Sands / 1906	1966	2.00	10.00
Reprise 0582	Help, I'm A Rock / Transparent Day	1967	2.00	10.00
Reprise 0776	Smell Of Incense / Unfree Child	1968	2.00	10.00
WEST SIDERS, THE				
Leopard 5004	Don't You Know? / No Tears Left For Crying	1963	8.00	40.00
WEST WINDS, THE				
Kapp 588	You're Lookin' At My Guy / Oowee, Oowee, Oowee, Oowee	1963	2.00	10.00
WESTWOODS, THE				
A&M 763	I Miss My Surfer Boy, Too / Will You Love Me?	1965	7.00	35.00
WETBACKS, THE				
Wildcat 0047	Jose Jimenez / Jose Jimenez (Part 2)	1960	2.00	10.00
WEYMOUTH, BOB				
Celestial 112	Girl Of My Dreams / If You Only Knew	196?	1.00	5.00
WHAT FOUR, THE				
Reprise 0387	Night Surf / Gemini Four	1965	6.00	30.00
WHALEY, MARGE				
Celestial 110	Marge's Monday Boogie / Wabash Blues	196?	2.00	10.00
WHEEL OF FORTUNE, THE				
Jamie 1360	All The World / Funny Looks	196?	1.20	6.00
Ridon 856	Before You Leave / Long, Long Day	196?	1.20	6.00
WHEEL MEN, THE				
The Wheel Men feature Gary Usher.				
Warner Bros. 5480 (DJ)	Hon-Da Beach / School Is A Gas	1964	7.00	35.00
Warner Bros. 5480	Hon-Da Beach / School Is A Gas	1964	12.00	60.00
WHEELER, MARY, & THE KNIGHTS				
Atom 701	A Falling Tear / I Feel In My Heart	196?	7.00	35.00
WHEELER, ONIE				
Sun 315	Jump Right Out Of This Juke Box / Tell 'Em Off	1959	4.00	20.00
WHEELERS, THE				
Cenco 107	Once I Had A Girl / Shine 'Em On	196?	8.00	40.00
WHEELS, THE				
Atco 7062	Skateboard U.S.A. / Skateboard U.S.A.	1961	5.00	25.00
WHEELS, THE				
Sidewalk 946	Wheels / Chain Fight	1967	2.00	10.00

Label & Catalog #	A-Side/B-Side	Year	VG	NM
WHIPPETS, THE				
Josie 921	Go Go Go With Ringo / I Want To Talk With You	1964	5.00	25.00
WHIPPORWHILS, THE				
Drift 1446	Baby, Let's Face It / You're In Oregon, My Friend	196?	.80	4.00
WHISPERS, THE				
Laurie 3344	Here Comes The Summer / If You Don't Care	1966	4.00	20.00
WHITCOMB, IAN				
Jerden 735	Soho / Boney Morone	1964	1.00	5.00
Jerden 747	This Sporting Life / Fizz	1965	1.00	5.00
Tower 120	This Sporting Life / Fizz	1965	1.00	5.00
Tower 134	You Turn Me On / Poor But Honest	1965	1.60	8.00
Tower 155	N-E-R-V-O-U-S / The End	1965	1.20	6.00
Tower 170	18 Whitcomb St. / Fizz	1965	1.00	5.00
Tower 189	Be My Baby / No Tears For Johnny	1966	1.00	5.00
Tower 192	High Blood Pressure / Good Hard Rock	1966	1.00	5.00
Tower 212	Lover's Prayer / Your Baby Has Gone Down The Plug Hole	1966	1.00	5.00
Tower 251	Please Don't Leave Me On The Shelf / You Won't See Me	1966	1.00	5.00
Tower 274	Where Did Robinson Cruso Go? / Poor Little Bird	1966	1.00	5.00
Tower 355	Rolling Home Georgeanne / You Really Bent Me Out Of Shape	1967	1.00	5.00
Tower 385	Sally Sails The Sky / Groovy Day	1968	1.00	5.00
United Artists 162	They Go Wild, Simply Wild Over Me / Yaaka Hula Hickey	1973	.60	3.00
WHITE, BEN, & THE DARCHAES				
Refer to The Darchaes.				
Aljon 1247/8	Jocko Sent Me / Nationwide Stamps	1962	2.00	10.00
WHITE, BOBBY				
End 1097	Our Last Goodbye / No Need To Worry	1961	3.00	15.00
WHITE, TONY JOE				
Monument 1003	Georgia Pines / Ten More Miles To Louisiana	1967	.80	4.00
Monument 1053	Watching The Trains Go By / Old Man Willis	1968	.80	4.00
Monument 1070	I Protest / Man Can Only Stand So Much Pain	1968	.80	4.00
Monument 1086	Soul Francisco / Whomp Out On You	1969	.80	4.00
Monument 1104	Polk Salad Annie / Aspen, Colorado	1969	1.00	5.00
Monument 1169	Roosevelt And Ira Lee / The Migrant	1969	.80	4.00
Monument 1193	High Sheriff / Groupy Girl	1970	.60	3.00
Monument 1206	Save Your Sugar For Me / My Friend	1970	.60	3.00
Monument 1227	Scratch My Back / Old Man Willie	1970	.60	3.00
Warner Bros. 7468	The Daddy / Voodoo Village	1971	.50	2.50
Warner Bros. 7477	I Just Walked Away / My Kind Of Woman	1971	.50	2.50
Warner Bros. 7505	I Just Walked Away / Lustful Earl And The Married Woman	1971	.50	2.50
Warner Bros. 7523	Delta Love / That On The Road Look	1971	.50	2.50
Warner Bros. 7591	Even Trolls Love Rock & Roll / If I Ever Saw A Good Thing	1972	.50	2.50
Warner Bros. 7607	I've Got A Thing About You, Baby / Gospel Singer	1972	.60	3.00
Warner Bros. 7712	Backwoods Preacher Man / Saturday Night In Oak Grove	1973	.50	2.50
Warner Bros. 7780	Love 'Tween You And Me / Sign Of The Lion	1973	.50	2.50
Warner Bros. 8042	Don't Let The Door (Hit You In The Butt) / Wishful Thinking	1974	.50	2.50
20th Century 2276	It Must Be Love / Susie-Q	1976	.40	2.00
Arista 0395	It Must Be Love /	1979	.40	2.00
Casablanca 2279	I Get Off On It / Feelin' Loose	1980	.40	2.00
Casablanca 2304	Disco Blues / Mamma Don't Let Your Cowboys Grow Up To Be Babies	1980	.40	2.00
WHITE CAPS, THE				
Blue Roll 201	Fender Vender / Hi Roll	196?	2.00	10.00
WHITE CLOUD				
Tammy Jo 2	Paper Caper /	196?	2.00	10.00
WHITE LIGHTNING				
Hexagon 6801	Of Paupers And Poets / William	1969	5.00	25.00
Atco 6660	Of Paupers And Poets / William	1969	2.00	10.00
WHITESIDE, BOBBY				
U.S.A. 775	Wendy / I'm Goin' Your Way	1964	2.00	10.00
WHITLEY, RAY				
Vee Jay 433	Yessiree Yessiree / A Love We Can Hold	1962	2.00	10.00
Vee Jay 448	Deeper In Love / It Hurts	1962	2.00	10.00
WHITNEY, TY				
20th Cen.-Fox 448	Surfin' Santa Claus / Winter Wonderland	1963	6.00	30.00

Label & Catalog #		A-Side/B-Side	Year	VG	NM

WHO, THE
The Who—Roger Daltrey, John Entwhistle, Keith Moon and Pete Townshend—originally recorded as The High Numbers.
Kenny Jones, late of The Small Faces, replaced the departed Moon in 1979.

Label & Catalog #		A-Side/B-Side	Year	VG	NM
Decca 31725		I Can't Explain / Bald Headed Woman	1965	4.00	20.00
Decca 31801		Anyway, Anywhere, Anyhow / Anytime You Want Me	1965	7.00	35.00
Decca 31877		My Generation / Out In The Street	1965	4.00	20.00
Decca 31988		The Kids Are Alright / A Legal Matter	1966	3.00	15.00
Decca 32058		I'm A Boy / In The City	1966	5.00	25.00
Atco 6409		Substitute / Waltz For A Pig	1966	6.00	30.00
Atco 6509		Substitute / Waltz For A Pig	1967	3.00	15.00
Decca 32114		Happy Jack / Whiskey Man	1967	2.00	10.00
Decca 32114	(PS)	Happy Jack / Whiskey Man	1967	4.00	20.00
Decca 32156		Pictures Of Lilly / Doctor, Doctor	1967	2.00	10.00
Decca 32206		I Can See For Miles / Mary-Anne With The Shaky Hands	1967	2.00	10.00
Decca 32288		Call Me Lightning / Dr. Jekyll & Mr. Hyde	1968	2.50	12.00
Decca 32362		Magic Bus / Someone's Coming	1968	2.00	10.00
Decca 32465		Pinball Wizard / Dogs, Part 1	1969	1.60	8.00
Decca 32465	(PS)	Pinball Wizard / Dogs, Part 1	1969	3.00	15.00
Decca 32519		I'm Free / We're Not Gonna Take It	1969	1.60	8.00
Decca 32670		The Seeker / Here For More	1970	1.60	8.00
Decca 32708		Summertime Blues / Heaven And Hell	1970	1.60	8.00
Decca 32729		See Me, Feel Me / Overture From Tommy	1970	1.60	8.00
Decca 32729	(PS)	See Me, Feel Me / Overture From Tommy	1970	3.00	15.00
Decca 32737	(DJ)	Substitute / Young Man	1970	25.00	125.00
Decca 32737	(PS)	Substitute / Young Man	1970	75.00	300.00
Decca 32856		Won't Get Fooled Again / I Don't Even Know Myself	1971	1.20	6.00
Decca 32888		Behind Blue Eyes / My Wife	1971	1.20	6.00
Decca 32983		Join Together / Baby, Don't You Do It	1972	1.20	6.00
Track 33041		The Relay / Waspman	1972	1.20	6.00
Track 60106		See Me, Feel Me / Overture From Tommy	1973	.60	3.00
Track 60110		I Can't Explain / Bald Headed Woman	1973	.60	3.00
Track 60174		Pinball Wizard / Dogs, Part 1	1973	.60	3.00
Track 40152		Love Reign O'er Me / Water	1973	.60	3.00
Track 40182		The Real Me / I'm One	1974	.60	3.00
Track 40330		Postcard / Put The Money Down	1974	.60	3.00
Polydor 15098		Listening To You / Overture From "Tommy"	1975	.60	3.00
Polydor 15098	(PS)	Listening To You / Overture From "Tommy"	1975	.60	3.00
		(From the film "Tommy" with one side Daltrey and the other Townshend.)			
MCA 40475	(PS)	Squeeze Box (Promo picture sleeve)	1975	6.00	30.00
MCA 40475		Squeeze Box / Success Story	1975	.60	3.00
MCA 40603		Slip Kid / Dreaming From The Waist	1975	.60	3.00
MCA 40978		Trick Of The Light / 905	1978	.60	3.00
MCA 40948		Who Are You? / Had Enough?	1978	.60	3.00
MCA 41053		Long Live Rock / My Wife	1979	.60	3.00
Polydor 2022		5:15 / I'm One	1979	.40	2.00
Polydor 2022	(PS)	5:15 / I'm One	1979	.60	3.00
Warner Bros. 49698		You Better You Bet / The Quiet One	1981	.40	2.00
Warner Bros. 49698	(PS)	You Better You Bet / The Quiet One	1981	.40	2.00
Warner Bros. 49743		Don't Let Go The Coat / You	1981	.40	2.00
Warner Bros. 29905		Athena / It's Your Turn	1982	.40	2.00
Warner Bros. 29905	(PS)	Athena / It's Your Turn	1982	.40	2.00
Warner Bros. 29814		Eminence Front / One At A Time	1982	.40	2.00
Warner Bros. 29731		It's Hard / Dangerous	1982	.40	2.00
		—Special/Promotional Releases—			
Decca 73279	(DJ)	See Me, Feel Me / Overture From Tommy	1969	3.00	15.00
Decca 73410-13	(DJ)	Tommy	1969	30.00	150.00
		(Boxed set of four singles on gold labels with a special insert.			
		The four singles are listed and priced separately below)			
Decca 73410	(DJ)	Amazing Journey / Acid Queen	1969	4.00	20.00
Decca 73411	(DJ)	Go To The Mirror / Tommy Can You Hear Me?	1969	4.00	20.00
Decca 73412	(DJ)	Smash The Mirror / Sensation	1969	4.00	20.00
Decca 73413	(DJ)	Sally Simpson / I'm Free	1969	4.00	20.00
MCA 545-1809	(DJ)	Had Enough? / Had Enough?	1978	3.00	15.00
MCA 41053	(DJ)	Long Live Rock Picture Disc	1979	10.00	50.00
		(The back advertises Disc.)			
MCA 41053	(DJ)	Long Live Rock Picture Disc	1979	10.00	50.00
		(The back of the disc advertises Eli's.)			
MCA 41053	(DJ)	Long Live Rock Picture Disc	1979	10.00	50.00
		(The back of the disc advertises Gibson's.)			
MCA 41053	(DJ)	Long Live Rock Picture Disc	1979	10.00	50.00
		(The back of the disc advertises Musicland.)			
MCA 41053	(DJ)	Long Live Rock Picture Disc	1979	10.00	50.00
		(The back of the disc advertises National Record Mart.)			
MCA 41053	(DJ)	Long Live Rock Picture Disc	1979	10.00	50.00
		(The back of the disc advertises NARM.)			
		—12" Singles—			
Warner Bros. PRO-938	(DJ)	You Better, You Bet / You Better, You Bet (TC)	1981	1.60	8.00
Warner Bros. PRO-1065	(DJ)	Athena / Athena (TC)	1981	1.60	8.00

After producing a run of singles in the mid to late '60s that placed them at the vanguard of British rock, The Who achieved worldwide fame (and fortune) with the release of the bloated two-fer, Tommy. From that point on, success took its toll. While The Who continued to produce, little of what made it onto vinyl captured the glory of their earlier tracks, especially their choice of singles. Released in late '75 with this nifty connect-the-dots picture sleeve (courtesy of bassist John Entwhistle), they achieved a modest top 20 hit in early '76, an achievement that would seem more and more difficult as time went on...

Label & Catalog #		A-Side/B-Side	Year	VG	NM
Warner Bros. PRO-938	(DJ)	Eminence Front / Eminence Front (TC)	1981	1.60	8.00
MCA L33-1257	(DJ)	Twist And Shout / I Can't Explain / My Generation	1984	1.20	6.00
MCA L33-17-72	(DJ)	I Don't Even Know Myself / When I Was A Boy / I'm A Boy / Bargain	1985	1.60	8.00
WHYTE BOOTS, THE					
Philips 40422		Nightmare / Let No One	1967	15.00	75.00
WICHITA TRAIN WHISTLE					
Wichita Train Whistle was produced by Michael Nesmith.					
Dot 17152		Tapioca Tundra / Don't Cry Now	196?	3.00	15.00
WICKED TRUTH, THE					
Teru 119		Take A Chance / Rock No More	196?	2.00	10.00
WIERD-OHS, THE					
The Wierd-Ohs is a pseudonym for Gary Usher and The Hondells.					
Mercury 72410		Digger / Leaky Boat	1965	4.00	20.00
WIG, THE					
Black Knight 903		Crackin' Up / Bluescene	196?	7.00	35.00
WILD-CATS, THE					
United Artists 154		Gazachstahagen / Billy's Cha Cha	1958	2.00	10.00
United Artists 154	(S)	Gazachstahagen / Billy's Cha Cha	1958	5.00	25.00
United Artists 169		King Size Guitar / Dancing Elephants	1959	2.00	10.00
WILD CHILDS, THE					
Cascade 102		I'm Leaving Town, Baby / Rockin' Heart	196?	6.00	30.00
WILD ONES, THE					
Mainline 500		Caught In The Cookie Jar / Super Fox	1965	2.00	10.00
United Artists 947		Wild Thing / Just Can't Cry Anymore	1965	1.20	6.00
United Artists 971		My Love / Lord Love A Duck	1966	1.20	6.00
United Artists 50043		Never Givin' Up / For Your Love	1966	1.20	6.00
Mala 564		Valerie / Heigh Ho	1967	1.60	8.00
WILD SIDE, THE					
Garland 2005		Valorie / Plastic People	196?	2.00	10.00
WILD THINGS, THE					
Showboat 1516		I'm Not For You / Love Comes, Love Dies	196?	5.00	25.00
WILD UNCERTAINTY					
Planet 120		A Man With Money / Broken Truth	1966	3.00	15.00
WILDCATS, THE					
Counsel 1301		The Swim / Up Stream	196?	1.20	6.00
WILDE, JIMMY					
Chelsea 1006		Crazy Eyes For You / Bonnie, Bonnie	196?	3.00	15.00
WILDE KNIGHTS, THE					
Star-Bright 3052		Just Like Me / I Don't Care	1965	4.00	20.00
Star-Bright 3051		Beaver Patrol / Tossin' And Turnin'	1965	4.00	20.00
Modern 1014		Beaver Patrol / Tossin' And Turnin'	1965	4.00	20.00
WILDFLOWER					
Mainstream 659		Wind Dream / Baby Dear	1968	2.00	10.00
United Artists 50504		Butterfly / Holly	1969	1.00	5.00
WILDING, BOBBY					
DCP 1009		Since I've Been Wearing My Hair Like A Beatle / I Want To Be A Beatle	1964	3.00	15.00
WILDWEEDS, THE					
The Wildweeds feature Al Anderson, later of NRBQ.					
Cadet 5561		No Good To Cry / Never Mind	1967	1.00	5.00
Cadet 5572		Someday Morning / Can't You See That I'm Lonely?	1967	1.00	5.00
Cadet 5586		It Was Fun / Sorrow's Anthem	1968	1.00	5.00
Cadet Concept 7004		I'm Dreaming / Happiness Is Just An Illusion	1968	1.00	5.00
Vanguard 35134		And When She Smiles / Paint And Powder Ladies	1971	1.00	5.00
Vanguard 35155		C'mon If You're Coming / Goin' Back To Indiana	1971	1.00	5.00
WILDWOOD					
Magnum 420		Plastic People / Swimming	1968	3.00	15.00
Magnum 421		Wildwood Country / Free Ride	1968	2.00	10.00

Label & Catalog #	A-Side/B-Side	Year	VG	NM
WILDWOODS, THE				
May 106	Golden Sunset / Here Comes Ed	1961	7.00	35.00
WILL-O-BEES, THE				
Date 1543	Shades Of Grey / If You're Ready	1968	.80	4.00
Date 1583	It's Not Easy / Looking Glass	1968	.80	4.00
SGC 002	Make Your Own Kind Of Music / Listen To The Music	1969	.80	4.00
SGC 004	I Can't Quit Loving You / The Ugliest Girl In Town	1969	.80	4.00
WILLANS, RICHARD, & THE FLAME TONES				
Bell 192	Oldies But Goodies / Little Sister Nell	1972	1.00	5.00
WILLIAMS, BEVERLY				
Decca 31912	Heart / He's Hurtin' Me	1966	2.00	10.00
	(Produced by Gary Usher.)			
WILLIAMS, GARY				
Panorama 4	Alaska / Rule Number One	1964	.80	4.00
Panorama 32	Step Into My Heart / The Great Northwest	1966	.80	4.00
WILLIAMS, JERRY				
Laurie 3339	Runaround Sue / The Wanderer	1966	1.60	8.00
WILLIAMS, JIM				
Sun 270	Please Don't Cry Over Me / That Depends On You	1957	3.00	15.00
WILLIAMS, LEE, & THE MOONRAYS				
King 5409	I'm So In Love / (No) I Won't Cry Anymore	1960	40.00	200.00
WILLIAMS, TOM B.				
Toptx 6009	Wishing Well / Come Back	1962	5.00	25.00
WILLIE & THE WHEELS				
Willie & The Wheels are Steve Barri and Phil Sloan.				
Dunhill 4002 (DJ)	Skateboard Craze / Do What You Want	1965	3.00	15.00
Dunhill 4002	Skateboard Craze / Do What You Want	1965	6.00	30.00
WILLIS, BILLY JACK				
MGM 11966	There's Good Rockin' Tonight / Red Mittens	1955	7.00	35.00
WILLIS, HAL				
Atlantic 1114	Bop-A-Dee, Bop-A-Doo / My Pink Cadillac	1957	40.00	200.00
WILLIS, ROD				
Chic 1010	Somebody's Been Rockin' My Baby / Old Man Mose	1959	7.00	35.00
WILLS, TOMMY				
Air Town 001	Honky Tong '66 / Night Train '66	1966	1.60	8.00
WILSON, ANDY				
Athens 700	Little Mama / Tonite Tonite	196?	4.00	20.00
WILSON, ANN, & THE DAYBREAKS				
Ann Wilson later recorded with Heart.				
Topaz 1311	Standin' Watchin' You / Wonder How I Managed	1967	15.00	75.00
Topaz 1312	Through Eyes And Glass / I'm Gonna Drink My Hurt Away	1967	15.00	75.00

WILSON, BRIAN

Brian's first "solo" single, Capitol 5610, is from Beach Boys' sessions and is listed under the group. Refer to The Beach Boys; Jan Berry; The Blossoms; Bob & Bobby; Bob & Sherri; California Music; Glen Campbell; The Castells; Celebration; Tim Curry; The Date With Soul; Jackie DeShannon; Dino, Desi & Billy; Hale & The Hushabyes; The Hondells; The Honeys; Julio Iglesias; Jan & Dean; Jay & The Americans; Kenny & The Cadets; The Laughing Gravy; Paul Petersen; Rachel & The Revolvers; The Rally Packs; The Reveres; Johnny Rivers; Sharon Marie; The Supremes; The Survivors; Spring; The Timers; Gary Usher; Ron Wilson.

Sire 28350 (DJ)	Let's Go To Heaven In My Car / Let's Go To Heaven In My Car	1987	1.00	5.00
Sire 28350	Let's Go To Heaven In My Car / Too Much Sugar	1987	2.00	10.00
Sire 28350 (PS)	Let's Go To Heaven In My Car / Too Much Sugar	1987	1.00	5.00
Sire 27814 (DJ)	Love And Mercy / Love And Mercy	1988	1.00	5.00
Sire 27814	Love And Mercy / He Couldn't Get His Poor Old Body To Move	1988	2.00	10.00
Sire 27814 (PS)	Love And Mercy / He Couldn't Get His Poor Old Body To Move	1988	.80	4.00
Sire 27787 (DJ)	Night Time / Night Time	1988	6.00	30.00
Sire 27787 (PS)	Night Time / Night Time	1988	12.00	60.00
	(Stock copies of Sire 27787 do not exist.)			
Sire 27694 (DJ)	Melt Away / Melt Away	1988	2.00	10.00

Label & Catalog #		A-Side/B-Side	Year	VG	NM
Sire 27694		Melt Away / Being With The One You Love	1988	4.00	20.00

WILSON, BRIAN, & MIKE LOVE: *Refer to THE BEACH BOYS*

WILSON, CARL
Carl Wilson originally recorded with Kenny & The Cadets and is a Beach Boy.

Caribou 01049	(DJ)	Hold Me / Hold Me	1981	.60	3.00
Caribou 01049	(DJ)	Hold Me / Hold Me (DJ Reservice)	1981	.40	2.00
Caribou 01049		Hold Me / Hurry Love	1981	.80	4.00
Caribou 02136	(DJ)	Heaven / Heaven	1981	.40	2.00
Caribou 02136		Heaven / Hurry Love	1981	1.00	5.00
Caribou 03590	(DJ)	What You Do To Me / What You Do To Me	1983	.40	2.00
Caribou 03590		What You Do To Me / Time	1983	1.00	5.00
Caribou 04020	(DJ)	Givin' You Up / Givin' You Up	1983	.40	2.00
Caribou 04020		Givin' You Up / Too Early To Tell	1983	1.00	5.00
		— 12" Singles—			
Caribou AS-931	(DJ)	Hold Me / The Right Lane	1981	1.25	6.00

WILSON, COLLEEN

Jerden 802		Rose City '66 / They'd Never Let You Darken Their Door	1966	.60	3.00

WILSON, DENNIS, & RUMBO
Rumbo is a pseudonym for Daryl Dragon, later of The Captain & Tennille.

Stateside 2184	(UK)	Sound Of Free / Lady	1970	30.00	150.00

WILSON, DENNIS
Refer to The Beach Boys; The Four Speeds; The Tri-Five, and the Various Artists EP section.

Caribou 9023	(DJ)	You And I / You And I	1977	2.00	10.00
Caribou 9023		You And I / Friday Night	1977	3.00	15.00

WILSON, DON [DON LEE WILSON]
Don Wilson also recorded with The Ventures.

Blue Horizon 6054	The Twomp / Heart On My Sleeve	1960	20.00	100.00
Unity 2117	Angel / Forever And Ever	1962	6.00	30.00
L&M 100	Seattle In The Rain / How Can I Help You, Girl?	196?	4.00	20.00
Imperial 66091	Angel / Feel So Fine	1965	3.00	15.00
Imperial 66038	Ain't That Funny / What'd I Say	1965	2.50	12.00
Liberty 55862	Angel / No Matter What Shape	1965	2.50	12.00
Liberty 55890	Sally / Don't Avoid Me	1966	2.50	12.00
Liberty 55946	Sally / Kiss Tomorrow Goodbye	1967	2.50	12.00
Liberty 55991	Hey There, Sunshine / Behind These Stained Glass Windows	1967	2.50	12.00
Tridex 101	Bad Boy / Tell Laura I Love Her	1982	2.00	10.00

WILSON, J. FRANK (& THE CAVALIERS)

LeCam 722	Last Kiss / Carla	1964	3.00	15.00
LeCam 1015	Kiss And Run / Teardrops In My Heart	1965	2.00	10.00
Tamara 761	Last Kiss / That's How Much I Love You	1964	2.50	12.00
Josie 923	Last Kiss / That's How Much I Love You	1964	2.00	10.00
Josie 924	Tears Of Happiness / (B-side by The Cavaliers)	1964	2.00	10.00
Josie 926	Hey, Little One / Speak To Me	1964	2.00	10.00
Josie 929	Six Boys / Say It Now	1965	1.20	6.00
Josie 931	Dreams Of A Fool / Open Your Eyes	1965	1.20	6.00
Josie 938	Forget Me Not / A White Sport Coat And A Pink Carnation	1965	1.20	6.00
Sully 927	Unmarked And Uncovered With Sand / Me And My Teardrops	1965	2.00	10.00
Charay 13	Last Kiss '69 / Kiss And Run	1969	.80	4.00
Charay 80	The Clown / Cool	1969	1.00	5.00

WILSON, MURRY
Father of Brian, Carl and Dennis Wilson of The Beach Boys. Refer to The Sunrays.

Capitol 2063	The Plumber's Tune / Leaves	1967	2.00	10.00

WILSON, PEANUTS

Brunswick 55039	(DJ)	Cast Iron Arm / You Got Love	1958	20.00	100.00
Brunswick 55039		Cast Iron Arm / You Got Love	1958	40.00	200.00

WILSON, PHIL

Huron 22000	Wishin' On A Rainbow / Just Me	1961	2.00	10.00

WILSON, RON
Ron Wilson was an original member of The Surfaris. Produced by Brian Wilson and Ron Wilson.

Columbia 44636	(DJ)	I'll Keep On Loving You / As Tears Go By	1968	10.00	50.00
Columbia 44636		I'll Keep On Loving You / As Tears Go By	1968	15.00	75.00

WILSON, SONNY

Sun 341	I'm Gonna Take A Walk / The Great Pretender	1960	2.00	10.00

Label & Catalog #	A-Side/B-Side	Year	VG	NM
WIMBERLY, MAGGIE SUE				
Sun 229	How Long? / Daydreams Come True	1956	8.00	40.00
WINCHELL, DANNY				
Danny Winchell is backed by Nino & The Ebbtides.				
Recorte 406	Jeannie / Beware You're Falling In Love	1959	4.00	20.00
Recorte 410	We're Gonna Have A Rockin' Party / Don't Say You're Sorry	1959	6.00	30.00
Recorte 415	Come Back, Baby / I've Chosen You	1959	5.00	25.00
WIND				
Wind features Tony Orlando.				
Life 200	Make Believe / Groovin' With Mr. Blue	1969	1.00	5.00
Life 202	Teeny Bopper / I'll Hold Out My Hand	1969	1.00	5.00
WIND, ADAM				
Cat 5621	Gotta Be Goin' / High Rain	196?	1.00	5.00
Spindle 3795	Take Some Time / Something Else	196?	1.00	5.00
WINDSORS, THE				
Wig Wag 203	Carol Ann / Keep Me From Crying	195?	30.00	150.00
WINGS: *Refer to* PAUL McCARTNEY				
WINK & JUDY (WITH THE VICEROYS FIVE)				
Seafair 109	I Still Love You So / Mary Sue	196?	.80	4.00
WINKLE PICKERS, THE				
Colpix 7986	(My Name Is) Granny Goose / I Haven't Got You	1966	2.00	10.00
WINKLEY & NUTLEY				
MK 101	Report To The Nation / Report To The Nation, Part 2	1960	2.00	10.00
WINSLOW, BARRY				
Barry Winslow originally recorded with The Royal Guardsmen.				
Laurie 3509	The Smallest Astronaut (A Race To The Moon With The Red Baron) / Quality Woman	1969	1.20	6.00
WINTERS, DAVID				
Addison 15504	Sunday Kind Of Love / Princess	196?	6.00	30.00
Rori 703	Bye Bye / Dori Anne	1962	7.00	35.00
Mercury 72537	Anti-Protest Protest Song / Hucklebuck Shoes	196?	1.00	5.00
WINTERS, RON (& THE PATRIOTS)				
Dimension 1022	Snow Girl / Motor City	1964	2.00	10.00
Dimension 1029	Back In The U.S.A. / Let Me Prove It To You	1964	2.00	10.00
Dimension 1033	Red MG / How Can You Kiss A Sports Car?	1964	4.00	20.00
WISDOMS, THE				
Gaity 169	Two Hearts Make One Love / Lost In Dreams	1959	150.00	500.00
WITCHES & WARLOCKS				
Sew City 103	Behind Locked Doors / Behind Locked Doors (Part 2)	1966	1.20	6.00
Sew City 105	What Will I Do Now? / Which Way Did He Go?	1968	1.20	6.00
Sew City 106	Nowhere To Run, Nowhere To Hide / The Wanderer	1968	1.20	6.00
WOBBLERS, THE				
King 5585	The Wobble / Blow Out	1962	2.00	10.00
WOLFE, DANNY				
Dot 15591	Pretty Blue Jean Baby / Once With You	1957	7.00	35.00
WOLFMEN, THE				
Bobbette 380	Watusi Beat / She Loves Me, She Loves Me Not	196?	1.60	8.00
WOMB, THE				
Dot 17250	Hang On / My Baby Thinks About The Good Things	1969	1.00	5.00
WOMBATS, THE: *Refer to* GARY & THE WOMBATS				
WONDER WHO?, THE				
The Wonder Who? is a pseudonym for The Four Seasons.				
Philips 40324	Don't Think Twice / Sassy	1965	1.20	6.00
Philips 40324 (PS)	Don't Think Twice / Sassy	1965	3.00	15.00
Philips 40380	On The Good Ship Lollipop / You're Nobody Till Somebody Loves You	1966	1.25	6.00
Philips 40380 (PS)	On The Good Ship Lollipop / You're Nobody Till Somebody Loves You	1966	3.00	15.00

Label & Catalog #		A-Side/B-Side	Year	VG	NM
Philips 40471		Lonesome Road / Around And Around	1966	1.25	6.00
Philips 40471	(PS)	Lonesome Road / Around And Around	1966	3.00	15.00
WONDERS, THE					
Ember 1051		I'll Write A Book / Hey Senorita	1959	4.00	20.00
Colpix 699		Say There / Marilyn	1963	3.00	15.00
WOOD, ANITA					
Sun 361		I'll Wait Forever / I Can't Show How I Feel	1961	3.00	15.00
Santo 9008		Memories Of You / Two Young Fools In Love	1961	2.00	10.00
WOOD, BILL					
Audan 119		Rock And Roll Heaven / Wicked Women Never Win	1961	2.00	10.00
WOOD, BOBBY					
Sun 369	(DJ)	Everybody's Searchin' / Human Emotions	1963	——	——
		(One of the rarest Suns. There are no known stock copies and the price for the promo is undetermined at the time of publication.)			
WOOD, EDDIE					
Ember 1064		Girl Of My Best Friend / I Need Love	1960	2.00	10.00
WOOD, RON					
Ron Wood also recorded with Jeff Beck; The Small Faces; and The Rolling Stones.					
Warner Bros. 8036		I Can Feel The Fire / Breathe On Me	1975	.80	4.00
Warner Bros. 8131		If You Don't Want My Love / I Got A Feeling	1976	.80	4.00
Columbia 11014		Seven Days / Breakin' My Heart	1979	.60	3.00
WOOD, ROY					
Roy Wood also recorded with The Move and The Electric Light Orchestra..					
United Artists 160		Ballpark Incident / The Carlsberg Special	1973	.60	3.00
United Artists 272		See My Baby Jive / Got A Crush On You	1973	.60	3.00
United Artists 394		Forever / Woodbe	1974	.60	3.00
United Artists 792		Any Old Time Will Do / Why Does Such A Pretty Girl Sing Those Sad Songs?	1976	.60	3.00
WOOD, SCOTT					
Beat 1008		Chicken Rock / Three Friends	1959	2.00	10.00
WOODS, LITTLE EDDIE					
Comet 2165		Bug Killer / Is It So Wrong?	1964	3.00	15.00
WOODY, DON					
Decca 30277		You're Barking Up The Wrong Tree / Bird-Dog	1958	20.00	100.00
WOODY WAGGERS, THE					
Daytone 6407		Sahara Hop / Three Guns	1964	7.00	35.00
WOODYS, THE					
California 304		Red River Valley / The Saints	1963	4.00	20.00
WOOL					
Columbia 45452		It's Alright / Take Me To The Pilot	1972	.60	3.00
WOOL, ED, & THE NOMADS					
RCA Victor 8940		I Need Somebody / Please, Please	1966	4.00	20.00
WOOLIES, THE					
Dunhill 4052		Who Do You Love? / Feelin' Good	1966	2.00	10.00
Dunhill 4088		Love Words / Duncan And Brandy	1967	2.00	10.00
Spirit 0003		Bring It With You When You Come / We Love You, B.B. King	197?	1.00	5.00
Spirit 0006		Two-Way Wishes / Chuck's Chunk	197?	1.00	5.00
Spirit 0007		Vandegraf's Blues / Vandegraf's Blahs	197?	1.00	5.00
Spirit 0008		Super Ball / Back For More	197?	1.00	5.00
Spirit 0009		Ride, Ride, Ride / We Love You, J.B. Lenoir	197?	1.00	5.00
Spirit 0013		Who Do You Love? / Feelin' Good	197?	1.00	5.00
Spirit 0014		The Hootchie Cootchie Man Is Back / Can't Get That Stuff	197?	1.00	5.00
WOOLY ONES, THE					
Titan 1733		Put Her Down / Slings And Arrows	1966	10.00	50.00
WORDS OF LUV					
Hickory 1462		Tomorrow Is A Long Time / I'd Have To Be Out Of My Mind	1966	1.60	8.00
WORKMAN, AL					
Wasp 130		The Whole Thing / Hornet	196?	.60	3.00

Label & Catalog #	A-Side/B-Side	Year	VG	NM
WORLD OF MILAN, THE				
Brunswick 55292	Follow The Sun / I'm Cryin' In The Rain	1966	3.00	15.00
Brunswick 55298	One Track Mind / Shades Of Blue	1966	4.00	20.00
WORLD OF OZ, THE				
Deram 85034	Jack / King Croesus	1968	1.00	5.00
WORLOCKS, THE				
NWI 2709	You Keep Me Hanging On / Banana Soul	1968	3.00	15.00
WOW WOWS, THE				
Challenge 59046	Richmond Rally / Count Down	1959	3.00	15.00
WRAY, CHUCK				
Garland 2022	Laura / Don't Be Angry	196?	2.00	10.00
WRAY, DOUG				
Epic 9322	School Girl / Goose Bumps	1959	3.00	15.00
WRAY, LINK (& HIS RAY MEN)				
Refer to The Raymen.				
Starday 552	Sick And Tired / It's Music, She Says	1956	40.00	200.00
Starday 575	Got Another Baby / Whatcha Say, Honey?	1957	40.00	200.00
Starday 608	Teenage Cutie / You're My Song	1957	40.00	200.00
	(Starday 552, 575 and 608 credit Lucky Wray.)			
Cadence 1347	Rumble / The Swag	1958	4.00	20.00
Epic 9300	Raw Hide / Dixie Doodle	1959	4.00	20.00
Epic 9321	Comanche / Lillian	1959	3.00	15.00
Epic 9343	Slinky / Rendezvous	1959	3.00	15.00
Epic 9343 (PS)	Slinky / Rendezvous	1959	8.00	40.00
Epic 9361	Golden Strings / Trail Of The Lonesome Pine	1960	3.00	15.00
Epic 9419	Ain't That Lovin' You, Baby / Mary Ann	1960	3.00	15.00
Epic 9454	Tijuana / El Toro	1961	3.00	15.00
Rumble 1000	Jack The Ripper	1961	6.00	30.00
Atlas 687	Big City Stomp / Poppin' Popeye	1962	2.00	10.00
OKeh 7166	Rumble Mambo / (B-side by Red Saunders)	1963	2.00	10.00
OKeh 7166 (PS)	Rumble Mambo / (B-side by Red Saunders)	1963	6.00	30.00
OKeh 7282	Rumble Mambo / (B-side by Red Saunders)	1967	2.00	10.00
Trans Atlas 687	Poppin' Popeye / Big City Stomp	196?	2.00	10.00
Swan 4137	Jack The Ripper / Black Widow	1963	3.00	15.00
Swan 4154	Week End / Turn Pike, U.S.A.	1963	2.00	10.00
Swan 4163	Run, Chicken, Run / Sweeper	1963	2.00	10.00
Swan 4171	The Shadow Knows / My Alberta	1964	2.00	10.00
Swan 4187	Deuces Wild / Summer Dream	1964	2.00	10.00
Swan 4201	Good Rockin' Tonight / I'll Do Anything For You	1965	2.00	10.00
Swan 4211	I'm Branded / Hang On	1965	2.00	10.00
Swan 4232	Girl From The North Country / You Hurt Me So	1965	2.00	10.00
Swan 4239	Ace Of Spades / The Fuzz	1965	3.00	15.00
Swan 4244	Batman Theme / Alone	1966	3.00	15.00
Swan 4261	Ace Of Spades / Hidden Charms	1966	3.00	15.00
Swan 4273	Let The Good Times Roll / Soul Train	1966	2.00	10.00
Swan 4284	I'll Do Anything For You / Jack The Ripper	1967	2.00	10.00
Heavy 101	Rumble '68 / Blow Your Mind	1968	2.00	10.00
Mr. G 820	Rumble '69 / Mind Blower	1969	2.00	10.00
Polydor 14084	Fire And Brimstone / Juke Box Mama	1970	1.00	5.00
Polydor 14096	Fallin' Rain / Juke Box Mama	1970	1.00	5.00
Polydor 14188	Shine The Light / Lawdy Miss Clawdy	1971	1.00	5.00
Polydor 14256	I Got To Ramble / She's That Kind Of Woman	1974	.80	4.00
WRAY, LUCKY: Refer to LINK WRAY				
WRAY BROTHERS, THE				
The Wray Brothers are Doug, Link and Vernon.				
Infinity 033	You're Sweeter Than Sugar / 99 Years To Go	1962	2.00	10.00
WRIGHT, CHARLES, & THE MALIBUS				
Titanic 5003	Latinia / Funky	196?	4.00	20.00
WRIGHT, DALE				
Fraternity 792	She's Neat / Say That You Care	1958	3.00	15.00
Fraternity 818	Please Don't Do It / Goody Goody Goodbye	1958	3.00	15.00
WRIGHT, RUBY				
Fraternity 787	Let's Light The Christmas Tree / Merry, Merry Christmas	1957	3.00	15.00
King 5192	Three Stars / I Only Have One Lifetime	1959	3.00	15.00
WRIGHT, STEVE				

Label & Catalog #		A-Side/B-Side	Year	VG	NM
Lin 5022		**Wild, Wild Woman / Love You**	1959	8.00	40.00
WRIGHT, STEVE					
Steve Wright was formerly the lead singer of The Easybeats.			1974	1.00	5.00
Atco 7016		**Hard Road / I Got You Good**			
WYLDE HEARD, THE					
Philips 40454		**Stop It, Girl / Take It On Home**	1966	2.00	10.00
Philips 40454	(PS)	**Stop It, Girl / Take It On Home**	1966	4.00	20.00
WYMAN, BILL					
Bill Wyman is a member of The Rolling Stones, where his first "solo" single is listed. Refer to The End and John Walker.					
Rolling Stones 19111		**White Lightnin' / I Wanna Get A Gun**	1974	1.00	5.00
Rolling Stones 19119		**A Quarter To Three / Soul Satisfying**	1975	1.00	5.00
Rolling Stones 19303		**Apache Woman / Soul Satisfying**	1975	1.00	5.00
A&M 2367		**(Si Si) Je Suis Un Rock Star / Rio De Janeiro**	1981	1.00	5.00
A&M 2367	(PS)	**(Si Si) Je Suis Un Rock Star / Rio De Janeiro**	1981	2.00	10.00
		— 12" Singles —			
A&M 12041	(DJ)	**(Si Si) Je Suis Un Rock Star / Rio De Janeiro** *(PC)*	1981	5.00	25.00
A&M 12041		**(Si Si) Je Suis Un Rock Star / Rio De Janeiro**	1981	2.00	10.00
WYMORE, BUDDY, & THE KNAVES					
Mitchell 101		**Surf Mad / Patty**	196?	7.00	35.00

Label & Catalog #		A-Side/B-Side	Year	VG	NM
X-TERMINATORS, THE					
Century Custom 19694		**X-Termination / Wild Hare**	196?	4.00	20.00
X-TREMES, THE					
Star Trek		**Facts Of Life / Substitute**	1966	2.00	10.00
X-25					
NWI 2693		**Cold, Cold, World / You Wouldn't Know Her**	1965	2.00	10.00
XTC					
XTC is Dave Gregory, Colin Moulding and Andy Partridge, a.k.a. The Dukes Of Stratosphear.					
Virgin PR-344	(DJ)	**Day In Day Out / Chain Of Command / Limelight**	1979	1.00	5.00
		(Included with XTC's "Drums And Wire" album.)			
Virgin 67004		**Ten Feet Tall / Helicoptor / The Somnambulist**	1980	1.00	5.00
Virgin 67004	(PS)	**Ten Feet Tall / Helicoptor / The Somnambulist**	1980	1.00	5.00
Virgin 67009		**Making Plans For Nigel /**			
		This Is Pop? / Meccanik Dancing	1980	1.00	5.00
Virgin 67009	(PS)	**Making Plans For Nigel /**			
		This Is Pop? / Meccanik Dancing	1980	1.00	5.00
RSO 300		**Generals And Majors / Living Through Another Cuba**	1981	.80	4.00
RSO 301		**Love At First Sight / Rocket From A Bottle**	1981	.80	4.00
Epic AS-1405	(DJ)	**Senses Working Overtime / Ball And Chain**	1982	.80	4.00
Epic 1402975		**Senses Working Overtime / English Roundabout**	1982	.80	4.00
Geffen 29351		**Wonderland / Jump**	1983	.60	3.00
Geffen PRO-2214	(DJ)	**All You Pretty Girls / Washaway / Red Brick Dream**	1984	.80	4.00
Geffen 28394		**Dear God / Mermaid Smiled**	1987	.60	3.00
Geffen 22953		**King For A Day / Toys**	1989	.40	2.00
Geffen 22953	(PS)	**King For A Day / Toys**	1989	.60	3.00
Geffen 27552		**The Mayor Of Simpleton / One Of The Millions**	1989	.40	2.00
Geffen 27552	(PS)	**The Mayor Of Simpleton / One Of The Millions**	1989	.60	3.00
		— 12" Singles —			
Geffen 20630		**Grass / Earn Enough For Us / Extrovert / Dear God**	1986	1.00	5.00
Geffen 21160		**The Mayor Of Simpleton / One Of The Millions / Ella Guru /**			
		Living In A Haunted Heart / The Good Things	1989	.80	4.00
		— Extended Play Albums —			
Geffen PRO-2117	(DJ)	**Great Fire**	1983	1.20	6.00

Y.

YANKEE DOLLAR, THE

Dot 17123		City Sidewalks / Sanctuary	1968	1.20	6.00
Dot 17155		Live And Let Live / Sanctuary	1968	1.20	6.00
Dot 17213		Reflections Of A Shattered Mind / Mucky Trucky River	1969	1.20	6.00

YANOVSKY, ZALMON

Zallie originally recorded with The Mugwumps and The Lovin' Spoonful.

Buddah 12		As Long As You're Here / Ereh Er'uoy As Gnol Sa	1968	.80	4.00
Buddah 12	(PS)	As Long As You're Here / Ereh Er'uoy As Gnol Sa	1968	1.20	6.00

YARDBIRDS, THE

The Original Yardbirds were Eric Clapton, Chris Dreja, Jim McCarty, Keith Relf and Paul Samwell-Smith. Clapton left after "For Your Love" and was replaced by Jeff Beck, featured on Epic 9823-10094. Samwell-Smith left in 1966 and was replaced by Jimmy Page, who led the group on their last recordings. Refer to Led Zeppelin.

Epic 9709	(DJ)	I Wish You Could / A Certain Girl	1965	8.00	40.00
Epic 9709	(DJ)	I Wish You Could (Promo picture sleeve)	1965	125.00	500.00
Epic 9709		I Wish You Could / A Certain Girl	1965	6.00	30.00
Epic 9709		I Wish You Would / A Certain Girl	1965	8.00	40.00
Epic 9790	(DJ)	For Your Love / Got To Hurry	1965	6.00	30.00
Epic 9790		For Your Love / Got To Hurry	1965	2.00	10.00
Epic 9823	(DJ)	Heart Full Of Soul / Steel Blues	1965	6.00	30.00
Epic 9823		Heart Full Of Soul / Steel Blues	1965	2.00	10.00
Epic 9823	(PS)	Heart Full Of Soul / Steel Blues	1965	8.00	40.00
Epic 9857	(DJ)	I'm A Man / Still I'm Sad	1965	6.00	30.00
Epic 9857		I'm A Man / Still I'm Sad	1965	2.00	10.00
Epic 9891	(DJ)	Shapes Of Things / I'm Not Talking	1966	6.00	30.00
Epic 9891		Shapes Of Things / I'm Not Talking	1966	2.00	10.00
Epic 10006	(DJ)	Shapes Of Things / New York City Blues	1966	5.00	25.00
Epic 10006		Shapes Of Things / New York City Blues	1966	2.00	10.00
Epic 10035	(DJ)	Over Under Sideways Down / Jeff's Boogie	1966	5.00	25.00
Epic 10035		Over Under Sideways Down / Jeff's Boogie	1966	2.00	10.00
Epic 10035	(PS)	Over Under Sideways Down / Jeff's Boogie	1966	5.00	25.00
Epic 10094	(DJ)	Happening Ten Years Time Ago / The Nazz Are Blue	1966	5.00	25.00
Epic 10094		Happening Ten Years Time Ago / The Nazz Are Blue	1966	2.00	10.00
Epic 10094	(PS)	Happening Ten Years Time Ago / The Nazz Are Blue	1966	4.00	20.00
Epic 10156	(DJ)	Little Games / Puzzles	1967	5.00	25.00
Epic 10156		Little Games / Puzzles	1967	4.00	20.00
Epic 10204	(DJ)	Ha Ha Said The Clown / Tinker, Tailor, Soldier, Sailor	1967	5.00	25.00
Epic 10204		Ha Ha Said The Clown / Tinker, Tailor, Soldier, Sailor	1967	4.00	20.00
Epic 10248	(DJ)	Ten Little Indians / Drinkin' Muddy Water	1967	5.00	25.00
Epic 10248		Ten Little Indians / Drinkin' Muddy Water	1967	4.00	20.00
Epic 10303	(DJ)	Goodnight, Sweet Josephine / Think About It	1968	12.00	60.00
Epic 10303		Goodnight, Sweet Josephine / Think About It	1968	15.00	75.00
		—Reissues—			
Epic 2247	(DJ)	I'm A Man / Shapes Of Things	196?	3.00	15.00
Epic 2247		I'm A Man / Shapes Of Things	196?	1.00	5.00

YATES, BILL (& HIS T-BIRDS)

Sun 390		Don't Step On My Dog / Stop, Wait, Listen	1964	2.00	10.00
Sun 397		Carleen / Too Late To Right My Wrong	1966	2.00	10.00
Sun 399		Big, Big World / I Dropped My M&M's	1966	2.00	10.00

YATES, LITTLE SAMMY

Genie 104		Comic Book Crazy / Dodge City Baby	1959	3.00	15.00

YELLOW BALLOON, THE

The Yellow Balloon features Don Grady and Gary Zekley.

Canterbury 508		Yellow Balloon / Noollab Wolley	1967	1.60	8.00
Canterbury 513		Good Feelin' Time / I've Got A Feelin' For Love	1967	1.60	8.00
Canterbury 516		Can't Get Enough Of Your Love / Stained Glass Window	1968	1.60	8.00

YELLOW HAIR

Pacific Avenue 457		Somewhere / Talent For Lovin'	196?	3.00	15.00

YELLOW JACKETS, THE

Smash 2180		Hi, Boy / When I First Saw Her Face	1969	1.00	5.00

YELLOW PAYGES, THE

Showplace 217		Jezebel / We Got A Love In The Makin'	1967	1.60	8.00
Uni 55072		Childhood Friends / Judge Carter	1968	.80	4.00
Uni 55089		Crowd Pleaser / You're Just What I Was Looking For Today	1968	.80	4.00

Label & Catalog #		A-Side/B-Side	Year	VG	NM
Uni 55107		Never Put Away My Love For You / The Two Of Us	1969	.80	4.00
Uni 55176		Slow Down / Frisco Annie	1969	.80	4.00
Uni 55192		Follow The Bouncing Ball / Little Woman	1970	.80	4.00
Uni 55225		Home Again / I'm A Man	1970	.80	4.00
Uni	(DJ)	Finger Poppin' Time / Moonfire	197?	1.50	8.00
YELVINGTON, MALCOLM (& THE STAR RHYTHM BOYS)					
Sun 211		Drinkin' Wine Spo-Dee-O-Dee / Just Rolling Along	1954	10.00	50.00
Sun 246		Rockin' With My Baby / It's Me, Baby	1956	15.00	75.00
YES					
Atlantic 2709		Every Little Thing / Sweetness	1970	.80	4.00
Atlantic 2819		Your Move / Clap	1971	.80	4.00
Atlantic 2854	(DJ)	Roundabout / Roundabout (Yellow vinyl)	1972	10.00	50.00
Atlantic 2854		Roundabout / Long Distance Run Around	1972	.80	4.00
Atlantic 2899		America / Total Mass Retain	1972	.80	4.00
Atlantic 2920		And You And I / And You And I (Part 2)	1972	.80	4.00
Atlantic 3140		Roundabout / Long Distance Runaround	1972	.60	3.00
Atlantic 3141		America / Your Move	1972	.60	3.00
Atlantic 3222		Soon / Sound Chaser	1975	.60	3.00
Atlantic 3416		Wondrous Stories / Awaken	1977	.80	4.00
Atlantic 3534		Release, Release / Don't Kill The Whale	1978	.60	3.00
Atlantic 3767		Into The Lens / Does It Really Happen	1980	.40	2.00
Atlantic 3801		Run Through The Light / White Car	1980	.40	2.00
Atco 99817		Owner Of A Lonely Heart / Our Song	1983	.40	2.00
Atco 99817	(PS)	Owner Of A Lonely Heart / Our Song	1983	.40	2.00
Atco 99787		Leave It / Leave It	1984	.40	2.00
Atco 99745		It Can Happen / It Can Happen (Live)	1984	.40	2.00
Atco 99745	(PS)	It Can Happen / It Can Happen (Live)	1984	.40	2.00
Atco 99449		Love Will Find A Way / Holy Lamb	1987	.40	2.00
Atco 99419		Rhythm Of Love / City Of Love (Live)	1987	.40	2.00
— 12" Singles —					
Atco PR-529	(DJ)	Owner Of A Lonely Heart / Owner Of A Lonely Heart	1983	1.00	5.00
Atco 96881	(DJ)	Owner Of A Lonely Heart / Our Song / Owner Of A Lonely Heart	1983	1.00	5.00
Atco PR-587	(DJ)	Leave It (Hello Goodbye Mix) / Leave It / Leave It	1984	1.00	5.00
Atco 96964		Leave It (Hello Goodbye Mix) / Leave It / Leave It	1984	.80	4.00
Atco PR-615	(DJ)	It Can Happen / It Can Happen (live)	1984	1.00	5.00
Atco 2088	(DJ)	Love Will Find A Way / Love Will Find A Way	1987	1.00	5.00
Atco 1133	(DJ)	Rhythm Of Love (3 versions)	1987	1.00	5.00
Atco 96722		Rhythm Of Love (3 versions)	1987	.80	4.00
YESTER, JERRY					
Jerry Yester also recorded with The Modern Folk Quartet and The Lovin' Spoonful.					
Dunhill 4042		Sound Of Summer Showers / Ashes Have Turned	1966	1.00	5.00
Dunhill 4061		I Can Live Without You / Garden Of Imagining	1966	1.00	5.00
Dunhill 4061	(PS)	I Can Live Without You / Garden Of Imagining	1966	2.00	10.00
YO-YOZ, THE					
Ikon 517		Leave Me Alone / Stay With Me	196?	2.00	10.00
YOLANADA & THE NATURALS					
Kimley 923		My Memories Of You / Jawbone	196?	2.00	10.00
YORK, DAVE, & THE BEACHCOMBERS					
Lancelot 6		I Wanna Go Surfin' / Beach Party	1962	6.00	30.00
PKM 6700		I Wanna Go Surfin' / Beach Party	1962	5.00	25.00
YORK, RUSTY					
P.J. 100		Sugaree / Red Rooster	1959	5.00	25.00
Note 10021		Sugaree / Red Rooster	1959	4.00	20.00
Chess 1730		Sugaree / Red Rooster	1959	3.00	15.00
King 5511		Love Struck / Goodnight Cincinnati, Good Morning Tennessee	1961	2.00	10.00
King 5587		Tore Up Over You / Tremblin'	1961	2.00	10.00
Gaylord 6428		Sally Was A Good Old Girl / I Might Just Walk Right Back Again	1962	2.00	10.00
YORKSHIRES, THE					
Westchester 1000		And You're Mine / Tossed Aside	196?	2.00	10.00
YOU KNOW WHO GROUP, THE					
Four Corners 113		My Love / Playboy	1963	2.00	10.00
Casual 84621		Roses Are Red, My Love / Playboy	1965	2.00	10.00
Casual 94725		Don't Play It (No More) / Run (I Wanna Be Free)	1965	2.00	10.00
International Allied 822		Hey You And The Wind And The Rain / This Day Love	196?	2.00	10.00
International Allied 822	(PS)	Hey You And The Wind And The Rain / This Day Love	196?	4.00	20.00

Label & Catalog #		A-Side / B-Side	Year	VG	NM
YOUNG, DON					
Bang 574		She Let Her Hair Down (Early In The Morning) / Movin'	1969	1.00	5.00
YOUNG, GEORGE					
Mercury 71259		Can't Stop Me / Come Back To Me	1958	15.00	75.00
Cameo 150		Nine More Miles / Sneak	1958	3.00	15.00
YOUNG, JERRY					
Callender 2276		Debra / I Can't See It From Here	1961	2.00	10.00
YOUNG, KATHY, & THE INNOCENTS					
Refer to The Innocents.					
Indigo 108		A Thousand Tears / Eddie, My Darling	1960	3.00	15.00
Indigo 115		Happy Birthday Blues / Someone To Love	1961	3.00	15.00
Indigo 121		Our Parents Talked It Over / Just As	1961	3.00	15.00
Indigo 125		Magic Is The Night / Do Du'nt Du	1961	3.00	15.00
Indigo 137		Baby, Oh Baby / The Great Pretender	1961	3.00	15.00
Indigo 146		Lonely Blue Nights / I'll Hang My Letters Out To Dry	1962	3.00	15.00
Indigo 147		Dream Awhile / Send Her Away	1962	3.00	15.00
Monogram 506		Dream Boy / I'll Love That Man	1962	3.00	15.00
Port 3025		A Thousand Tears / Eddie, My Darling	196?	1.00	5.00
YOUNG, NEIL (& CRAZY HORSE)					
Neil Young originally recorded with The Squires; The Buffalo Springfield; and Crosby, Stills & Nash.					
Reprise 0785	(DJ)	The Loner / Sugar Mountain	1968		
Reprise 0785		The Loner / Sugar Mountain	1968	4.00	20.00
Reprise 0819	(DJ)	Everybody Knows This Is Nowhere / Emperor Of Wyoming	1969	10.00	50.00
		(First pressings feature an acoustic version of "Everybody Knows This Is Nowhere," recorded for Neil's first album.)		20.00	100.00
Reprise 0819	(DJ)	Everybody Knows This Is Nowhere / Emperor Of Wyoming	1969	4.00	20.00
		(Second pressings feature the later version with Crazy Horse. There is an "RE 1" etched in the trail-off vinyl. Stock copies of Reprise 0819 may not exist.)			
Reprise 0836	(DJ)	Down By The River / The Losing End	1969		
Reprise 0836		Down By The River / The Losing End	1969	4.00	20.00
Reprise 0898	(DJ)	Oh, Lonesome Me / I've Been Waiting For You	1969	5.00	25.00
Reprise 0898		Oh, Lonesome Me / I've Been Waiting For You	1969	4.00	20.00
Reprise 0911	(DJ)	Cinnamon Girl / Sugar Mountain	1970	5.00	25.00
Reprise 0911		Cinnamon Girl / Sugar Mountain	1970	3.00	15.00
Reprise 0958	(DJ)	Only Love Can Break A Heart / Birds	1970	1.00	5.00
Reprise 0958		Only Love Can Break A Heart / Birds	1970	3.00	15.00
Reprise 0992	(DJ)	When You Dance I Can Really Love / Sugar Mountain	1970	1.00	5.00
Reprise 0992		When You Dance I Can Really Love / Sugar Mountain	1971	3.00	15.00
Reprise 1065	(DJ)	Heart Of Gold / Heart Of Gold	1971	1.00	5.00
Reprise 1065		Heart Of Gold / Sugar Mountain	1971	3.00	15.00
Reprise 1065		Heart Of Gold / Sugar Mountain	1971	1.25	6.00
		(Second pressing labels read "From The Reprise Album Harvest.")		.80	4.00
Reprise 1084	(DJ)	Old Man / The Needle And The Damage Done	1972	3.00	15.00
Reprise 1084		Old Man / The Needle And The Damage Done	1972	.80	4.00
Reprise 1184		Time Fades Away / Last Trip To Tulsa	1973	1.20	6.00
Reprise 1209	(DJ)	Walk On / Walk On (Small spindle hole)	1974	3.00	15.00
Reprise 1209	(DJ)	Walk On / Walk On (Large spindle hole)	1974	2.00	10.00
Reprise 1209		Walk On / For The Turnstiles	1974	.80	4.00
Reprise 1344		Lookin' For A Love / Sugar Mountain	1975	.80	4.00
Reprise 1350		Drive Back / Stupid Girl	1976	.80	4.00
Reprise 1390		Hey Babe / Homegrown	1977	.80	4.00
Reprise 1391		Like A Hurricane / Hold Back The Tears	1977	.80	4.00
Reprise 1393		Sugar Mountain / The Needle And The Damage Done	1977	.80	4.00
Reprise 1395		Comes A Time / Motorcycle Mama	1978	.80	4.00
Reprise 1395	(PS)	Comes A Time / Motorcycle Mama	1978	.80	4.00
Reprise 1396		Four Strong Winds / Human Highway	1979	.80	4.00
Reprise 49031		Rust Never Sleeps (Hey Hey, My My, Into The Black) / Rust Never Sleeps (Hey Hey, My My, Out Of The Blue)	1979	.80	4.00
Reprise 49031	(PS)	Rust Never Sleeps (Hey Hey, My My, Into The Black) / Rust Never Sleeps (Hey Hey, My My, Out Of The Blue)	1979	1.60	8.00
Reprise 49189		The Loner / Cinnamon Girl	1980	1.00	5.00
Reprise 49555		Hawks And Doves / Union Man	1980	.40	2.00
Reprise 49555	(PS)	Hawks And Doves / Union Man	1980	.40	2.00
Reprise 49641		Stayin' Power / Captain Kennedy	1980	.60	3.00
Reprise 49870		Southern Pacific / Motor City	1980	.60	3.00
Reprise 49895	(DJ)	Southern Pacific / Motor City (Picture disc)	1980	75.00	300.00
Reprise 49895	(DJ)	Southern Pacific / Motor City (Green vinyl)	1980	40.00	200.00
Reprise 49895	(DJ)	Southern Pacific / Motor City (Black vinyl)	1980	1.60	8.00
Reprise 49895		Southern Pacific / Motor City (Red vinyl)	1980	2.00	10.00
		(All four versions of Reprise 49895 are triangle-shaped.)			
Reprise 50014		Opera Star / Surfer Joe And Moe The Sleeze	1981	.80	4.00
Geffen 29887		Little Thing Called Love / We Are In Control	1982	.60	3.00
Geffen 29887	(PS)	Little Thing Called Love / We Are In Control	1982	.60	3.00

Label & Catalog #		A-Side / B-Side	Year	VG	NM
Geffen 29707		Mr. Soul / Mr. Soul, Part 2	1983	.80	4.00
Geffen 29574		Wonderin' / Payola Blues	1983	.80	4.00
Geffen 29574	(PS)	Wonderin' / Payola Blues	1983	.80	4.00
Geffen 29433	(DJ)	Cry, Cry, Cry / Cry, Cry, Cry	1983	.60	3.00
Geffen 29433		Cry, Cry, Cry / Payola Blues	1983	.80	4.00
Columbia 05566		Are There Any More Real Cowboys? / (B-side by Willie)	1985	1.00	5.00
		("Are There Any More Real Cowboys?" is a duet with Willie Nelson.)			
Geffen 28883		Back To The Country / Misfits	1985	.80	4.00
Geffen 28753		Old Ways / Once An Angel	1985	1.00	5.00
Geffen 28623		Weight Of The World / Pressure	1986	.60	3.00
Geffen 28623	(PS)	Weight Of The World / Pressure	1986	1.00	5.00
Geffen 28196		Mideast Vacation / Long Walk Home	1987	.60	3.00
Reprise 27908		Ten Men Workin' / I'm Goin'	1988	.60	3.00
Reprise 27908	(PS)	Ten Men Workin' / I'm Goin'	1988	1.20	6.00
Reprise 27848		This Note's For You (Live) / This Note's For You	1988	.60	3.00
Reprise 27848	(PS)	This Note's For You (Live) / This Note's For You	1988	.60	3.00
Reprise 22776	(DJ)	Rockin' In The Free World / Rockin' In The Free World (Live)	1989	2.00	10.00
Reprise 22776		Rockin' In The Free World / Rockin' In The Free World (Live)	1989	.40	2.00
Reprise 22776	(PS)	Rockin' In The Free World / Rockin' In The Free World (Live)	1989	.40	2.00
		—12" Singles—			
Backstreet 1878	(DJ)	Buffalo Stomp-Ode To Wild Bill / (B-side by Bill Murray)	1980	5.00	25.00
Reprise PRO-901	(DJ)	Hawks And Doves / Union Man (TC; blue vinyl)	1980	3.00	15.00
Reprise 1014	(DJ)	Opera Star / Surfer Joe And Moe The Sleeze (TC)	1981	2.00	10.00
Geffen 20105		Sample And Hold / Mr. Soul / Sample And Hold	1982	1.60	8.00
Geffen PRO-2373	(DJ)	Get Back To The Country / Misfits (PC)	1985	1.00	5.00
Geffen PRO-2541	(DJ)	Touch The Night / Touch The Night (PC)	1986	1.20	6.00
Geffen PRO-2528	(DJ)	Weight Of The World / Weight Of The World (TC)	1986	.80	4.00
Geffen PRO-2623	(DJ)	People On The Street / People On The Street (PC)	1986	.80	4.00
Geffen PRO-2754	(DJ)	Long Walk Home / Long Walk Home (PC)	1987	.80	4.00
Geffen PRO-2811	(DJ)	Too Lonely / Too Lonely	1987	1.00	5.00
		—Special/Promotional Releases—			
Reprise PRO-314		Neil Young (Radio spots)	1968	20.00	100.00
Reprise PRO		Everybody Knows This Is Nowhere (Radio spots)	1969	20.00	100.00
Reprise PRO-424		After The Goldrush (Radio spots)	1970	20.00	100.00
Reprise LLP-183	(33)	Harvest (Jukebox EP)	1973	3.00	15.00

YOUNG, NEIL, & GRAHAM NASH

Label & Catalog #		A-Side / B-Side	Year	VG	NM
Reprise 1099	(DJ)	War Song / The Needle And The Damage Done	1972	2.00	10.00
		(Promo issued with lyric sheet insert.)			
Reprise 1099		War Song / The Needle And The Damage Done	1972	.60	3.00

YOUNG LADS, THE

Label & Catalog #	A-Side / B-Side	Year	VG	NM
Felice 712	Night After Night / Graduation Kiss	196?	8.00	40.00

YOUNG LIONS, THE

Label & Catalog #	A-Side / B-Side	Year	VG	NM
Dot 16172	Little Girl / It Would Be	1961	7.00	35.00
Loma 2022	We Better Get Along / Live And Learn	196?	2.00	10.00

YOUNG MEN, THE

Label & Catalog #	A-Side / B-Side	Year	VG	NM
Camelot 109	Cloudy Summer Afternoon / The Flowers Cried	196?	1.00	5.00
Camelot	I Want To Be Happy / Up And Adam	196?	.80	4.00
Camelot	Lester Leans / Lester Leans, Part 2	196?	.80	4.00
Camelot 134	All Your Love / To Each His Own	196?	.80	4.00
Bolo 742	Charlie Browning / Walkin' Along	1963	.80	4.00
Panorama 1	Go And Run To Him / Come On, Let's Swim	1964	.80	4.00
Bolo 744	Rovin' Young Man / It's Luv	1964	.80	4.00
Bolo 748	(Junior's) Backfield Beat / It's Luv	1964	.80	4.00

YOUNG ONES, THE [THE YOUNGONES]

Label & Catalog #	A-Side / B-Side	Year	VG	NM
Yussels 7701	Marie / Those Precious Love Letters	196?	2.00	10.00
	(Yussels 7001 credits The Youngones.)			
Yussels 7703	No No, Don't Cry / I'm In The Mood For Love	196?	3.00	15.00
Yussels 7704	Diamonds And Pearls / Three Coins In The Fountain	196?	2.00	10.00
Times Square 28	Gloria / Just Two Kinds Of People	1964	2.00	10.00
Times Square 1204	I Only Want You / Over The Rainbow	1964	2.00	10.00

YOUNG SISTERS, THE

Label & Catalog #	A-Side / B-Side	Year	VG	NM
Mala 467	Jerry Boy / She Took His Love Away	1963	2.00	10.00
Twirl 2001	My Guy / Casanova Brown	196?	2.00	10.00

YOUNG TYRANTS, THE

Label & Catalog #	A-Side / B-Side	Year	VG	NM
In 10	I Try / She Don't Got Me Right	1966	4.00	20.00

YOUNGBLOOD, EDISON

Label & Catalog #	A-Side / B-Side	Year	VG	NM
Comet 101	Summertime Fool / Big Bad Betty	196?	3.00	15.00

Label & Catalog #		A-Side/B-Side	Year	VG	NM
YOUNGBLOODS, THE					
The Youngbloods are Jesse Colin Young, Lowell "Banana" Levinger, Joe Bauer and Jerry Corbitt, who left in 1969.					
Michael Kane joined in 1971.					
RCA Victor 47-9015		**Grizzely Bear / Tears Are Falling**	1966	1.20	6.00
RCA Victor 47-9015	(PS)	**Grizzely Bear / Tears Are Falling**	1966	5.00	25.00
RCA Victor 47-9142		**Foolin' Around (The Waltz) / Merry-Go-Round**	1967	1.20	6.00
RCA Victor 47-9222		**Euphoria / Wine Song**	1967	1.20	6.00
RCA Victor 47-9264		**Get Together / All My Dreams Blue**	1967	1.20	6.00
RCA Victor 47-9360		**I Can Tell / Fool Me**	1967	1.20	6.00
RCA Victor 47-9422		**Quicksand / Dreamer's Dream**	1968	1.00	5.00
RCA Victor 47-9752		**Get Together / Beautiful**	1969	1.00	5.00
RCA Victor 74-0129		**Darkness, Darkness / On Sir Francis Drake**	1969	1.00	5.00
Mercury 73068	(DJ)	**Sometimes / Sometimes**	1969	1.20	6.00
		(Stock copies of Mercury 73068 may not exist.)			
RCA Victor 74-0270		**Sunlight / Trillium**	1969	.80	4.00
RCA Victor 74-0360		**Darkness, Darkness / On Sir Francis Drake**	1970	.80	4.00
RCA Victor 74-0465		**Reason To Believe / Sunlight**	1971	.80	4.00
Warner/Raccoon 7639		**Dreamboat / Kind Hearted Woman**	1972	.40	2.00
Warner/Raccoon 7445		**Hippie From Olema / Misty Roses**	1970	.40	2.00
Warner/Raccoon 7499		**It's A Lovely Day / Ice Bag**	1971	.40	2.00
Warner/Raccoon 7563		**Light Shine / Will The Circle Be Unbroken?**	1972	.40	2.00
Warner/Raccoon 7660		**Kind Hearted Woman / Running Bear**	1972	.40	2.00
YUM YUMS, THE					
ABC-Paramount 10697		**Gonna Be A Big Thing / Looky Looky (What I Got)**	1965	1.00	5.00

Common Record Collecting Abbreviations Used For Singles In Advertising

COH.. cut-out hole
C-33............................ compact 33⅓ rpm single or EP
CVR.. cover
DJ .... disc jockey or promotional copy
EP ....45 rpm extended play album
FLEXI ....flexible plastic disc
IMP... import
LBL...label
NAP ....(does) not affect play
OL..on label
ORG..original
PLN CVR....... plain paper jacket (no picture or titles)
PROMO ....promotional copy
PS.. picture sleeve
RE .... reissue
REPRO...........................reproduction or counterfeit

RPM ....revolutions per minute
2ND PR.. second pressing
SLT WRP ....slight warp
SLV ....sleeve
SM SPLT.. seam split
SOL.. sticker on the label
SR..................... slight ring-wear on the front cover
ST...stereo
STKR ....sticker
TOC ....tape on the cover
TOL... tape on the label
TS...taped seams
WLP.. white label promo
WOL .... writing on the label
XOL .... an "x" is written on the label

Z.

Z, JOHNNY

Dore 667	Midnight Beach Party / Beach Bum	1963	8.00	40.00

ZACHARIAH

Black Market 101	Dog Lady / Rock 'N' Gypsies	1973	2.00	10.00

ZACHERLE, JOHN [ZACHERLEY]

Cameo 130	Dinner With Drac / Igor	1958	5.00	25.00
Cameo 130	Dinner With Drac / Dinner With Drac, Part 2	1958	5.00	25.00
Cameo 139	Lunch With Mother Goose / 82 Tombstones	1958	3.00	15.00
Cameo 145	I Was A Teenage Caveman / Dummy Doll	1958	4.00	20.00
	—Original Cameo singles above have orange labels.—			
Cameo 130	Dinner With Drac / Dinner With Drac, Part 2	1960	3.00	15.00
	(Red & black label)			
Elektra 45013	Coolest Little Monster / Ring-A-Ding Orangutang	1960	5.00	25.00
Parkway 853	Dinner With Drac / Hurry, Bury Harry	1962	4.00	20.00
Colpix 743	Monsters Have Problems, Too / Hello, Dolly	1964	5.00	25.00

ZACK, EDDIE

Columbia 21387	I'm Gonna Rock 'N Roll / Rocky Road Blues	1955	4.00	20.00

ZAGER & EVANS

Truth	In The Year 2525 (Exordium And Terminus) / Little Kids	1969	3.00	15.00
RCA Victor 74-0174	In The Year 2525 (Exordium And Terminus) / Little Kids	1969	.80	4.00
RCA Victor 74-0246	Cary Lynn Jones / Mister Turn Key	1970	.60	3.00
RCA Victor 74-0359	Crutches / Plastic Park	1970	.60	3.00
Vanguard 35125	Hydra 15,000 / I Am	1971	.60	3.00
Vanguard 35125 (PS)	Hydra 15,000 / I Am	1971	.60	3.00

ZAKARY THAKS

J-Beck 1006	I Need You / Bad Girl	196?	3.00	15.00
Thak 1001	My Door / Green Crystal Ties	196?	3.00	15.00

ZANIES, THE

Era 1080	The Blob / Do You Dig Me, Mr. Pigmy	1958	5.00	25.00
Dore 509	The Blob / Do You Dig Me, Mr. Pigmy	1958	3.00	15.00
Dore 515	The Mad Scientist / She's A Winner	1958	3.00	15.00
Dore 597	It's Love / Saxaphone Safari	1961	3.00	15.00
Dore 632	Frustration / Rockin' Chopin	1962	3.00	15.00
Dore 638	London Rock / Stalled	1962	3.00	15.00
Dore 647	Alexander's Ragtime Band / Sleepwalker	1962	3.00	15.00
Dore 655	Comin' Down The Track / Hello, Jackie	1962	3.00	15.00
Dore 658	Caught In A Ringer / Russian Roulette	1963	3.00	15.00
Dore 683	Chicken Surfer / London Rock	1963	3.00	15.00
Dore 705	Slinky / Camel Walk	1963	3.00	15.00
Dore 734	Bless 'Em All / Let's Dance At The Prom	1965	2.00	10.00
Dore 853	Will The Real Dr. Frankenstein Please Stand Up / Frankenstein's Laboratory	1971	2.00	10.00
Dore 875	Mr. President-To-Be / Do The 1-2-3	1972	1.20	6.00
Dore 889	Let Out A Scream / Let Out A Scream, Part 2	1973	1.00	5.00
Dore 900	Let Out A Scream / Los Angeles, Los Angeles	1974	1.00	5.00
Dore 920	Ole Man River / Los Angeles, Los Angeles	1974	1.00	5.00

ZAPPA, FRANK, & THE MOTHERS OF INVENTION

While the label credits the group, the records below are the work of Frank Zappa. The original Mothers (essentially 1966-69, the Verve and Bizarre singles, including one as Junior Mintz) included Jimmy Carl Black, Ray Collins, Dave Coronado, Roy Estrada and Eliot Ingber with Bunk Gardner, Billy Mundi, Don Preston and Motorhead Sherwood. Later members included George Duke, Aynsley Dunbar, Lowell George, Jim Pons, Art Tripp III, Ian Underwood and Mark Volman and Howard Kaylan, both late of The Turtles, as Flo & Eddie. Refer to Captain Beefheart; Earth Opera; Rhinocerous.

Verve 10418 (DJ)	How Could I Be Such A Fool? / Help, I'm A Rock: 3rd Movement: It Can't Happen Here	1966	10.00	50.00
Verve 10418	How Could I Be Such A Fool? / Help, I'm A Rock: 3rd Movement: It Can't Happen Here	1966	30.00	150.00
Verve 10458 (DJ)	Trouble Comin' Every Day / Who Are The Brain Police?	1966	10.00	50.00
	(Stock copies of Verve 10458 may not exist.)			
Verve 10513 (DJ)	Why Don't You Do Me Right? / Big Leg Emma	1967	10.00	50.00
Verve 10513	Why Don't You Do Me Right? / Big Leg Emma	1967	30.00	150.00
Verve 10570 (DJ)	Lonely Little Girl / Mother People	1967	10.00	50.00
	(Stock copies of Verve 10570 may not exist.)			

Label & Catalog #		A-Side/B-Side	Year	VG	NM
Verve 10632	(DJ)	Jelly Roll Gumdrop / Deseri	1968	10.00	50.00
Verve 10632		Jelly Roll Gumdrop / Deseri	1968	20.00	100.00
Verve 10632	(DJ)	Jelly Roll Gumdrop / Any Way The Wind Blows	1968	10.00	50.00
Verve 10632		Jelly Roll Gumdrop / Any Way The Wind Blows	1968	20.00	100.00
		(Verve 10632 credits Ruben & The Jets, the Mothers nom de plume from their album "Cruising With Ruben & The Jets.")			
Bizarre/Reprise 0840	(DJ)	My Guitar / Dog Breath	1969	7.00	35.00
Bizarre/Reprise 0840		My Guitar / Dog Breath	1969	10.00	50.00
Bizarre/Reprise 0889	(DJ)	Peaches En Regalia / Peaches En Regalia	1970	7.00	35.00
Bizarre/Reprise 0889		Peaches En Regalia / Little Umbrellas	1970	10.00	50.00
Bizarre/Reprise 0892	(DJ)	WPLJ / My Guitar	1970	7.00	35.00
Bizarre/Reprise 0892		WPLJ / My Guitar	1970	10.00	50.00
Bizarre/Reprise 0967	(DJ)	Tell Me You Love Me / Would You Go All The Way?	1970	7.00	35.00
Bizarre/Reprise 0967		Tell Me You Love Me / Would You Go All The Way?	1970	10.00	50.00
Bizarre/Reprise 1052	(DJ)	Tears Began To Fall / Tears Began To Fall	1971	7.00	35.00
Bizarre/Reprise 1052		Tears Began To Fall / Junior Mintz Boogie	1971	10.00	50.00
Bizarre/Reprise 1127	(DJ)	Cletus Awreetus-Awrightus / Cletus Awreetus-Awrightus	1972	5.00	25.00
Bizarre/Reprise 1127		Cletus Awreetus-Awrightus / Eat That Question	1972	7.00	35.00
United Artists 50857	(DJ)	Magic Fingers / Magic Fingers	1971	7.00	35.00
United Artists 50857		Magic Fingers / Daddy, Daddy, Daddy	1971	10.00	50.00
DiscReet 1180		I'm The Slime / Montana	1973	5.00	25.00
DiscReet 1312	(DJ)	Don't Eat The Yellow Snow / Don't Eat The Yellow Snow	1974	4.00	20.00
DiscReet 1312		Don't Eat The Yellow Snow/ Cosmic Debris	1974	5.00	25.00
Warner Bros. 8296	(DJ)	Find Her Finer / Find Her Finer	1976	4.00	20.00
Warner Bros. 8296		Find Her Finer / Zoot Allures	1976	5.00	25.00
Warner Bros. 8342	(DJ)	Disco Boy / Disco Boy	1976	4.00	20.00
Warner Bros. 8342		Disco Boy / Ms. Pinky	1976	5.00	25.00
		—Special/Promotional Releases—			
Reprise PRO-366	(33)	Hot Rats (Radio spots)	1970	50.00	250.00
Reprise PRO-	(33)	Weasels Ripped My Flesh (Radio spots)	1970	100.00	400.00
United Artists	(33)	200 Motels (Radio spots)	1971	50.00	250.00

ZAPPA, FRANK

For Zappa's various endeavors as writer, guitarist or producer, refer to Baby Ray & The Ferns; Conrad & The Hurricanes; Mr. Clean; Bob Guy; The Heartbreakers; The Hogs; The Hollywood Persuaders; Bobby Jameson; Brian Lord & The Midnighters; The Masters; Ned & Nelda; The Penguins; Ron Roman; The Rotations; Burt Ward.

Label & Catalog #		A-Side/B-Side	Year	VG	NM
Zappa Z-10		Dancin' Fool / Baby Snakes	1979	1.20	6.00
Zappa Z-10	(PS)	Dancin' Fool / Baby Snakes	1979	3.00	15.00
Zappa Z-31		Joe's Garage / Central Scrutinizer	1979	1.60	8.00
Zappa ZR-1001		I Don't Want To Get Drafted / Ancient Armaments	1980	.80	4.00
Zappa ZR-1001	(PS)	I Don't Want To Get Drafted	1980	1.00	5.00
Zappa WS7-73000	(PS)	I Don't Want To Get Drafted	1980	1.00	5.00
Bark. Pump. 02972		Valley Girl / You Are What You Is	1982	.60	3.00
Bark. Pump. 02972	(PS)	Valley Girl / You Are What You Is	1982	1.20	6.00
		—Special/Promotional Releases—			
DiscReet PRO-586	(DJ)	Uncle Remus / Cosmic Debris	1974	4.00	20.00
W.I.A.A. MA-1791	(DJ)	What's It All About? Interview	1978	10.00	50.00
Zappa MK-107	(DJ)	Joe's Garage / Central Scrutinizer	1979	2.00	10.00
Bark. Pump. AS-1328	(DJ)	Goblin Girl / Pink Napkins	1981	3.00	15.00
		—12" Singles—			
Zappa MK-83	(DJ)	Dancin' Fool / Dancin' Fool	1979	3.00	15.00
Zappa MK-83		Dancin' Fool / Dancin' Fool	1979	5.00	25.00
Zappa MK-107	(DJ)	Joe's Garage / Joe's Garage	1979	5.00	25.00
Zappa ZR-1001		I Don't Want To Get Drafted / Ancient Armaments (PC)	1980	5.00	25.00
Bark. Pump. 02616		Goblin Girl (Picture disc)	1981	2.00	10.00
Bark. Pump. AS-1485	(DJ)	Valley Girl / Valley Girl (PC)	1982	5.00	25.00
Bark. Pump. 4W9-03069		Valley Girl / You Are What You Is (PC)	1982	2.00	10.00

ZARRA, MICHAEL, & THE COMPLIMENTS

Shell 313		Angels Of Mercy / Nobody Knows	195?	8.00	40.00

ZEBRA

White Whale 305		Bring Me To My Knees / Too Hot To Handle	1969	1.00	5.00
Blue Thumb 109		Christmas Morning / Christmas Morning (Part 2)	1970	1.20	6.00

ZEBRA, THE

Philips 40535		Groovy Personality / Miss Anne (Isn't That Kind Of Nan)	1968	1.00	5.00

ZEKELEY, GARY

Gary Zekeley also recorded with The Group; Our Gang; The Ragamuffins; The Visions; and The Yellow Balloon.

Ava 151		Other Towns, Other Girls / When I Go To Sleep	196?	6.00	30.00
		("Other Towns, Other Girls" features Dean Torrence on backing vocals.)			

ZELLA, DANNY

Fox 10057		Wicked Ruby /	1959	6.00	30.00

ZELLA, DANNY, & THE LARADOS
ZEPHYRS, THE

Label & Catalog #		A-Side/B-Side	Year	VG	NM
Rotate 5006		She's Lost You / There's Something About You	1965	3.00	15.00
Amber 213		Hear Him / Pink Rhapsody	1964	2.00	10.00
Amber 214		She's Mine / Bicycle Ride	1965	2.00	10.00
Amber 215		Don't Miss The Boat / Yes, My Love	1965	2.00	10.00
ZEPPA, BEN, & THE FOUR JACKS					
Tops 278		Why Do Fools Fall In Love? /	196?	4.00	20.00
ZEPPA, BEN JOE					
Hush 1000		Young Heartaches / Ridin' Herd	196?	2.00	10.00
ZERO END, THE					
Garland 2002		Blow Your Mind / Fly Today	1967	2.00	10.00
Garland 2003		Lid To Go / Hey Joe	1967	2.00	10.00
ZEROS, THE					
Kam 005		All One Two / In The Night	1969	3.00	15.00
ZIGGY & THE ZEU REVIEW					
Zeu 5011		Come Go With Me / Little Star	196?	10.00	50.00
Zeu 5011		Da Doo Run Run / Sherry	196?	8.00	40.00
ZILL, PAT					
Sand 336		Pick Me Up On Your Way Home / La Mirada	1961	3.00	15.00
Indigo 119		Pick Me Up On Your Way Home / La Mirada	1961	2.00	10.00
ZIP, DANNY					
MGM 13254		Hey Hey, Girl / Please Listen To Me	1964	7.00	35.00
ZIP CODES, THE					
Liberty 55703		Run, Little Mustang / Fancy Filly From Detroit City	1964	3.00	15.00
ZIRCONS, THE					
Federal 12452		No Twistin' On Sunday / Mama Wants To Drive	1962	2.00	10.00
Federal 12478		Get Up And Go To School / Mr. Jones	1962	2.00	10.00
ZIRCONS, THE					
Bagdad 1007		Surfin' In The Sunset / Goin' Places	1963	10.00	50.00
ZIRCONS, THE					
Cool Sound 1030		Silver Bells / You Are My Sunshine	1964	2.00	10.00
Old Timer 603		Sincerely / Stormy Weather	1964	2.00	10.00
ZIRCONS, THE					
Mellomood 1000		Lonely Way / Your Way	196?	3.00	15.00
Heigh Ho 607		Where There's A Will / Don't Put Off For Tomorrow	196?	2.00	10.00
ZISKA, STOSH					
Stosh Ziska originally recorded with The Del-Satins.					
Avco 4542		A Little Love /	196?	3.00	15.00
ZITTS, THE					
O&W 76		Surfin' And Sleepin' / Pepluai	196?	10.00	50.00
ZODIAC					
Uni 55138		X Rated / Then Goodbye	1969	1.00	5.00
ZODIACS, The					
Cole 100		Golly Gee / T Town	1963	5.00	25.00
Cole 101		She's Mine / Lover	1963	3.00	15.00
Soma 1410		Another Little Darling / Lita	1963	2.00	10.00
Soma 1418		Anything / Little Sally Walker	1964	2.00	10.00
ZOMBIES, THE					
The Zombies are Rod Argent, Paul Atkinson, Colin Blunstone, Hugh Grundy and Chris White.					
Parrot 9695		She's Not There / You Make Me Feel So Good	1964	2.00	10.00
Parrot 9723		Tell Her No / Leave Me Be	1965	2.00	10.00
Parrot 9723	(PS)	Tell Her No / Leave Me Be	1965	5.00	25.00
Parrot 9747		She's Coming Home / I Must Move	1965	2.00	10.00
Parrot 9747	(PS)	She's Coming Home / I Must Move	1965	5.00	25.00
Parrot 9769		I Want You Back Again / Once Upon A Time	1965	2.00	10.00
Parrot 9786		I Love You / Whenever You're Ready	1965	2.00	10.00
Parrot 9797		Just Out Of Reach / Remember You	1965	2.00	10.00
Parrot 9821		Don't Go Away / Is This The Dream?	1965	2.00	10.00
Parrot 3004		How We Were Before / Indication	196?	2.00	10.00
Date 1604		Time Of The Season / I'll Call You Mine	1967	1.60	8.00
Date 1612	(PS)	Butcher's Tune / This Will Be Your Year *(Promo)*	1968	3.00	15.00
Date 1612		Butcher's Tune / This Will Be Your Year	1968	1.20	6.00

Label & Catalog #		A-Side / B-Side	Year	VG	NM
Date 1628		Time Of The Season / Friends Of Mine	1969	1.20	6.00
Date 1644		Imagine The Swan / Conversation On Floral Street	1969	1.20	6.00
Date 1648		If It Don't Work Out / Don't Cry For Me	1969	1.20	6.00
Date 1203		Time Of The Season / Imagine The Swan	197?	.40	4.00
Epic 11145		Time Of The Season / Imagine The Swan	1972	.60	3.00
ZONE					
Wildflower 1		Tornado / Ways Of Living	196?	2.00	10.00
ZOO					
PKC 1013		Gonna Miss Me / Sometimes	1966	1.20	6.00
Parkway 147		Good Day Sunshine / Where Have All The Good Times Gone?	1966	2.00	10.00
Sunburst 775		Sunset Strip / One Night Man	1968	1.20	6.00
ZORRO, JOHNNY					
Bravo 123		Road Hog / Camel Train	1959	3.00	15.00
Warner Bros. 5111		Road Hog / Coolsville	1959	2.00	10.00
Warner Bros. 5162		Call Out My Name / It's So Real	1960	2.00	10.00

ZZ TOP

ZZ Top is Frank Beard, Billy Gibbons, and Dusty Hill. Refer to American Blues; The Moving Sidewalks; The Warlocks.

Label & Catalog #		A-Side / B-Side	Year	VG	NM
Scat 500		Salt Lick / Miller's Farm	1969	8.00	40.00
London 131		Salt Lick / Miller's Farm	1970	1.00	5.00
London 138		(Somebody Else Been) Shakin' Your Tree / Neighbor, Neighbor	1970	1.00	5.00
London 179		Francene / Francene (Spanish)	1972	.80	4.00
London 203		La Grange / Just Got Paid	1974	.60	3.00
London 220		Tush / Blue Jean Blues	1975	.60	3.00
London 220	(PS)	Tush / Blue Jean Blues	1975	1.00	5.00
London 241		It's Only Love / Asleep In The Desesrt	1976	.60	3.00
London 241	(PS)	It's Only Love / Asleep In The Desesrt	1976	1.00	5.00
London 251		Arrested For Driving While Blind / It's Only Love	1977	.60	3.00
London 252		Enjoy And Get It On / El Diablo	1977	.60	3.00
Warner Bros. 49163		I Thank You / Fool For Your Stockings	1980	.40	2.00
Warner Bros. 49220		Cheap Sunglasses / Esther, Be The One	1980	.40	2.00
Warner Bros. 49782		Leila / Don't Tease Me	1981	.40	2.00
Warner Bros. 49865		Tube Snake Boogie / Heaven, Hell Or Houston	1981	.40	2.00
Warner Bros. 29693		Gimme All Your Lovin' / If I Could Only Flag Her Down	1983	.40	2.00
Warner Bros. 29576		Sharp Dressed Men / I Got The Six	1983	.40	2.00
Warner Bros. 29272		Legs / Bad Girl	1984	.40	2.00
Warner Bros. 28884		Sleeping Bag / Party On The Patio	1985	.40	2.00
Warner Bros. 28810		Can't Stop Rockin' / Stages	1986	.40	2.00
Warner Bros. 28733		Delirious / Rough Boy	1986	.40	2.00
Warner Bros. 28650		Velcro Fly / Woke Up With Wood	1986	.40	2.00
Warner Bros. 19812		Doubleback / Planet Of Women	1990	.40	2.00
		— 12" Singles—			
Warner Bros. PRO-887	(DJ)	Cheap Sunglasses / Cheap Sunglasses (Live)	1980	1.20	6.00
Warner Bros. PRO-2011	(DJ)	Gimme All Your Lovin' / Got Me Under Pressure	1983	1.20	6.00
Warner Bros. PRO-2052	(DJ)	Sharp Dressed Man / Legs	1983	1.20	6.00
Warner Bros. PRO-2094	(DJ)	Gimme All Your Lovin' / TV Dinners / Sharp Dressed Man	1983	1.20	6.00
Warner Bros. 20207		Legs (Dance mix) / Legs (Dance mix)	1984	1.00	5.00
Warner Bros. 20395		Sleeping Bag (Extended mix) / Party On The Patio	1985	1.00	5.00
Warner Bros. 20524		Velcro Fly (Extended mix) / Velcro Fly (Dub mix) / Woke Up With Wood	1986	1.00	5.00

VARIOUS ARTISTS EPS

Each EP or set of 45s contains tracks by at least two different artists. All have picture covers unless noted otherwise.

Artistic 227	(DJ)	Original Golden Hits *(Features Champs, Jan & Dean*	1967	3.00	15.00
Atlantic OP-7501		Profiles In Gold *(Features Abba.)*	1977	2.00	10.00
Beserkley		Great Ideas From Beserkley	197?	2.00	10.00
		(Features Earthquake; Greg Kihn; Jonathan Richman; The Rubinoos.)			
Capitol PRO-2537/8	(DJ)	All Together Now *(Features Kingston Trio)*	1961	2.00	10.00
Capitol PRO-2661/2	(DJ)	The Big Surfing Sounds Are On Capitol	1963	10.00	50.00
		(Features Jerry Cole; Dick Dale; Mr. Gasser; The Superstocks.)			
Capitol SPRO-2905/6	(DJ)	The Capitol Souvenir Record	1965	40.00	200.00
		(Features The Beach Boys; The Beatles; The Kingston Trio.)			
Capitol SPRO-2905/6	(PS)	The Capitol Souvenir Record	1965	75.00	300.00
Capitol 8464	(DJ)	A Surprise Gift From The Beatles, The Beach Boys			
		And The Kingston Trio! *(Flexi-disc)*	1964	150.00	500.00
Coca Cola, Vol. 1	(DJ)	Coca Cola Jingle A Go Go	1962	8.00	40.00
Coca Cola, Vol. 2	(DJ)	Coca Cola Jingle A Go Go	1962	15.00	75.00
		(Features Ray Charles; The Everly Brothers.)			
Coca Cola, Vol. 1	(DJ)	Coca Cola Jingle A Go Go *(Features The Four Seasons)*	1963	15.00	75.00
Coca Cola, Vol. 2	(DJ)	Coca Cola Jingle A Go Go	1963	8.00	40.00
Coca Cola	(DJ)	Coca Cola Jingles	1965	15.00	75.00
		(Features The Everly Brothers; The Four Seasons; Jan & Dean;			
		Roy Orbison; The Shirelles.)			
Coca Cola 2227	(DJ)	Bubble Up	1965	8.00	40.00
Coca Cola	(DJ)	Swing The Jingle	1965	15.00	75.00
		(Features The Drifters; Lesley Gore; Los Bravos; Roy Orbison.)			
Coca Cola	(DJ)	Coke *(Features Roy Orbison)*	1965	10.00	50.00
Coca Cola 105-112	(DJ)	Things Go Better With Coke	1966	4.00	20.00
Coca Cola 105-112	(PS)	Things Go Better With Coke	1966	4.00	20.00
		(Features Petula Clark; Dave Dee, Dozy, Beaky, Mick & Tich.)			
Columbia SP-223	(DJ)	5th Avenue Parade Of Stars *(Features Dave Clark Five)*	1964	2.00	10.00
Columbia SP-245	(DJ)	The Lively New Sound *(Features Dave Clark Five)*	1964	2.00	10.00
Columbia SP-319	(DJ)	Step Lively *(Features Bob Dylan; Dave Clark Five)*	1965	8.00	40.00
Columbia SP-437	(DJ)	Swingin' Party	1966	25.00	125.00
		(Box of five singles with picture sleeves includes Bob Dylan's "I Want You.")			
Columbia SP-468	(DJ)	Great Shakes Shake Out *(Features Dave Clark Five)*	1965	2.00	10.00
Columbia CSM-546	(DJ)	The Moving Crowd	196?	2.00	10.00
		(Features Byrds, Paul Revere, Simon & Garfunkel)			
Columbia CSM-566	(DJ)	Great Shakes Shake-out	1967	2.00	10.00
		(Features Buckinghams, Byrds, Paul Revere)			
Columbia SS-600	(DJ)	The Super Set	196?	2.00	10.00
		(Features Keith Allison, Gene Clark, Peanut Butter Conspiracy)			
Columbia CSM-614	(DJ)	Fresh Sound *(Features Cyrkle, Paul Revere)*	1968	2.00	10.00
Columbia CSM-678	(DJ)	Swingin' School Days	1966	2.00	10.00
		(Features The Cyrkle; Paul Revere & The Raiders.)			
Columbia SP	(DJ)	Wurlitzer Dance Music	1965	15.00	75.00
		(Ten record set intended for jukebox play. Features Bruce Johnston.)			
Columbia SP	(DJ)	Discotheque Dance Music	1965	50.00	200.00
		(Boxed set of ten jukebox EPs issued by Wurlitzer. Features Bob Dylan.)			
Columbia SP	(DJ)	The Hit Pack	1965	——	——
		(Set of three white label promo singles on colored vinyl: Bob Dylan's			
		"Subterannean Homesick Blues" on red; Barbra Streisand's "Why Did			
		I Choose You" on blue; and Andy Williams' "And Roses And Roses" on yellow.			
		Issued in an envelope with a picture of the three artists			
		Rare. Estimated near mint value $500-1,500.)			
Columbia CSM-870	(DJ)	Great Contemporary Music	1968	2.00	10.00
		(Features Moby Grape; The New Christy Minstrels; Gary Puckett.)			
Columbia AE7-1128	(DJ)	Music For Every Ear *(Features Dennis Wilson)*	1977	2.00	10.00
Columbia AS-45	(33)	Playback	1973	15.00	75.00
		(Contains "Blinded By The Light" by Bruce Springsteen.)			
Columbia AS-52	(33)	Playback	1973	20.00	100.00
		(Contains "Circus Song" by Bruce Springsteen.)			
Columbia AS-66	(33)	Playback	1973	15.00	75.00
		(Contains "Rosalita (Come Out Tonight)" by Bruce Springsteen.)			
Columbia AS-66	(33)	Playback	1973	100.00	400.00
		(White label in-house promo with a completely different label design.)			
Decca 2661		Top Teen Hits *(Features Bill Haley)*	1959	10.00	50.00
Decca-Webcor 4247	(DJ)	Eloise *(Features Bill Haley)*	1964	10.00	50.00
Decca 34441		Tunes For Teens		7.00	35.00
		(Features Brenda Lee; Len Barry; Bobbi Martin; The Spokesmen; The Surfaris.)			
Diplomat 66-2		Come Twist With Me	1962	8.00	40.00
		(Features Joey Dee & The Starlighters.)			
Dixie 530		Ballad Of A Teenage Queen *(Features Sleepy LaBeef)*	195?	25.00	125.00
Mercury MEP-53A	(DJ)	Shorties *(White label)*	1959	8.00	40.00
		(Features 60 seconds edits from Big Bopper, Del Vikings, Diamonds, Gaylords)			
Miller High Life GA-621	(DJ)	If You've Got The Time, We've Got The Beer	197?	7.00	35.00
Philles X-EP		The Philles Christmas EP *(Without sleeve)*	1963	30.00	150.00

Label & Catalog #		A-Side/B-Side	Year	VG	NM
Philles X-EP	(PS)	**The Philles Christmas EP** *(With paper title sleeve)*	1963	**125.00**	**500.00**
		(Promo includes The Ronettes; Bobb B. Soxx; Darlene Love; The Crystals.)			
Warner Bros.	(DJ)	**Warners Loves You** *(Flexi-disc)*	1969	**2.00**	**10.00**
		(Features Gary Puckett, Paul Revere)			

Another Brief Author's Bio

While I am willing to admit that there certainly seems to be an awful lot of good sounding singles released in the past decade or so, I also notice that the bulk of the ones that catch my ear don't end up on top of the charts. Rather, it seems that the best singles (my opinion) can only be heard on "alternative" radio stations, particularly those located on college campuses. Similarly, the few attempts I have made recently to do some "clubbing" usually leaves me with the not too pleasant notion that disco never really died...

A good many writers have attempted to come to grips with just why popular culture sinks into the individual's subconscious during formative years and then stays while later forms of pop culture — even plainly derivative of the original — leave the observer cold. Having been born at the end run of the baby boom generation, I spent my childhood in the '50s and have a lasting love for the rock 'n roll of that period. The more or less original "oldies" stations came of age at the same time that I spent many a summer on the beaches with a transistor radio wondering why the girls didn't like me.

I spent my teen years in the '60s and that is where the bulk of my taste lies. Of course, that the '60s also appears to be an aberration of some sort certainly occludes my judgement. Serious (i.e., "academic") interest is being paid by sociologists, etc., to just what *did* occur in Western cultures around the world during the latter half of that decade. Whatever it was (*I* think it was magic), it embraced virtually every aspect of human life, although it's the stuff we put on our turntables that is being discussed here.

While my earliest memories of rock 'n roll are the days I spent at Gramma's listening to my teenage Aunt Judy's record collection (Ricky, Fats, Little Richard, Fabian and lots of Elvis), in the summer of '65 everything changed: The loping bass, the ringing 12 string and those wondrous harmonies of "Mr. Tambourine Man" forever changed my perception of rock music. I realized that there was a potential for rock music to be something else, something *other*... "Look Through Any Window," "Eve Of Destruction," "California Dreaming," "Nowhere Man," "Like A Rolling Stone," "Paint It Black," "Sloop John B;" this was not what the previous generation of rockers had envisioned would be their legacy!

Just for the sake of argument, I'd rate "Hound Dog"/ "Don't Be Cruel" as the greatest double-sided hit of the '50s and "Strawberry Fields Forever" / "Penny Lane" as the best of the '60s, with "Eight Miles High" / "Why" right behind. Without having really done all of the homework necessary to make anything other than a guess, I'd say that the years 1954-56 and 1965-67 were the best ever for singles while '66-69 would be the LP era. The past twenty years or so seem to have reduced the stuff that sells to formulaic babble, fast-food for the ears with no fiber for the digestive tract.

Through an odd series of events, in 1985 I was interviewed for the position of editor of O'Sullivan Woodside's line of record collectors price guides; I landed the job after discussing baseball with Don Woodside for two hours after the interview was over. This led me to compile the sixth edition of their *Rock & Roll Record Albums Price Guide* (1985) and the third edition of the *Elvis Presley Record Price Guide* (1986). Aside from *Goldmine's* series of price guides, I am working on a book dealing with the phenomenon of the "concept album" of the late '60s, tentatively titled *Rubber Soul: Meaningful Rock Albums of the '60s...*

SOUND INVESTMENTS

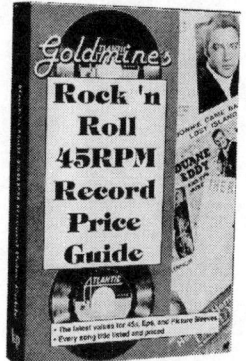

GOLDMINE'S ROCK 'n ROLL 45 RPM PRICE GUIDE

$19⁹⁵

Available Sept. 1992

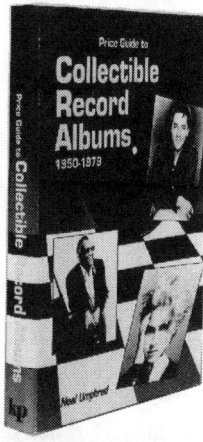

GOLDMINE'S PRICE GUIDE TO COLLECTIBLE RECORD ALBUMS

$19⁹⁵

GOLDMINE'S PRICE GUIDE TO JAZZ RECORDS 1949-1969

$19⁹⁵

Available Sept. 1992

DOO-WOP: The Forgotten Third of Rock 'n Roll

$19⁹⁵